Introduction to
PSYCHOLOGY

Edition
10

Rod Plotnik

San Diego State University

Haig Kouyoumdjian

WADSWORTH
CENGAGE Learning™

Australia • Brazil • Japan • Korea • Mexico • Singapore • Spain • United Kingdom • United States

Introduction to Psychology, 10th Edition
Rod Plotnik and Haig Kouyoumdjian

Senior Publisher: Linda Schreiber

Executive Editor: Jon-David Hague

Senior Editor, Psychology: Jaime Perkins

Development Editors: Trina McManus, Tangelique Williams-Grayer

Assistant Editor: Paige Leeds

Editorial Assistant: Audrey Espey

Media Editor: Jasmin Tokatlian

Senior Brand Manager: Elisabeth Rhoden

Market Development Manager: Chris Sosa

Senior Content Project Managers: Carol Samet, Pat Waldo

Senior Art Director: Vernon Boes

Manufacturing Planner: Karen Hunt

Rights Acquisitions Specialist: Dean Dauphinais

Production Service: diacriTech, Inc.

Text Designer: Diane Beasley

Photo Researcher: Terri Wright Design

Copy Editor: Carol Reitz

Concept Illustrator: Tim Jacobus

Cover Design: Cheryl Carrington

Cover Image: Created by Picture Mosaic.
Main image: Masterfile/royalty free. Inset images: Tim Jacobus; Shutterstock. For detailed listing of Shutterstock photographers see page iv.

Compositor: Paige Larkin, diacriTech, Inc.

For product information and technology assistance, contact us at
Cengage Learning Customer & Sales Support, 1-800-354-9706.

For permission to use material from this text or product,
submit all requests online at **www.cengage.com/permissions**.
Further permissions questions can be e-mailed to
permissionrequest@cengage.com.

Library of Congress Control Number: 2009938503

Student Edition:
ISBN-13: 978-1-133-94349-5
ISBN-10: 1-133-94349-7

Paper Edition:
ISBN-13: 978-1-133-93953-5
ISBN-10: 1-133-93953-8

Loose-leaf Edition:
ISBN-13: 978-1-133-94350-1
ISBN-10: 1-133-94350-0

Wadsworth
20 Davis Drive
Belmont, CA 94002-3098
USA

Cengage Learning is a leading provider of customized learning solutions with office locations around the globe, including Singapore, the United Kingdom, Australia, Mexico, Brazil, and Japan. Locate your local office at **www.cengage.com/global**.

Cengage Learning products are represented in Canada by Nelson Education, Ltd.

To learn more about Wadsworth visit **www.cengage.com/Wadsworth**
Purchase any of our products at your local college store or at our preferred online store **www.CengageBrain.com**.

Printed in Canada
1 2 3 4 5 6 7   17 16 15 14 13

To All Students Everywhere

We begin each revision with great enthusiasm, which usually begins to fade at the halfway point. The one sure way we have to revive our motivation is to read the many uplifting students' comments that we have received. To show you what we mean, we've included a sample of their wonderful comments, for which we are eternally grateful. (If you too would like to comment on the text, please fill out and send in the form on the last page of this text.)

The psychology book was amazing. I do not know how and where to begin, because I just loved it so much.
—**NATOSHA**, SAINT DOMINIC ACADEMY

I really liked how easy the book was to comprehend. The examples help make the definitions easy to memorize.
NATALIE, ONONADAGA COMMUNITY COLLEGE

The diagrams were easy to understand. Good pictures and real-life examples people can *relate* to. Best psychology book I've read.
—**SARAH**, ROCHESTER COMMUNITY COLLEGE

Since I consider myself a visual learner, I benefited a lot from the pictures, drawings, and graphs included throughout the book. Also the "chunking" made the material fun to learn.
—**ROXANNE**, WHARTON COUNTY JUNIOR COLLEGE

How visual it is. The many pictures helped me to remember the text better. The simple writing style, but still academic, was helpful to make it interesting. I am really glad that we read this book. It made my course!
—**JULIA**, NORWALK COMMUNITY COLLEGE

I enjoyed so much the photos, the text, the stories, the whole layout of the book—I truly learned just from reading and remembered things because of the way they were used in the book, like next to a picture or highlighted!
—**RICHELLE**, WESTERN IOWA TECH COMMUNITY COLLEGE

I was astonished at how gripping this textbook was. I actually looked forward to the reading. I really enjoyed the real-life situations that were incorporated into each module. I have decided to keep this book and do more reading than what was required during class.
—**AMANDA**, LANIER TECHNICAL COLLEGE

Your book made learning all the material really easy & very interesting. The way you explained everything made sense & kept me intrigued & wanting to learn more. No joke.
—**AVANI**, HENRY FORD COMMUNITY COLLEGE

The summary tests!! I couldn't have passed psychology with out those tests!! THANK YOU!! I'll keep this book forever!!
—**SHANNON**, GRIFFITH UNIVERSITY

I truly enjoyed the "little stories." They help me understand what we were studying. Please continue on with the Cultural Diversity sections!
—**PHARIK**, PLATT COLLEGE

This is one of the best textbooks I've read and enjoyed; you did a great job organizing and writing material in such a friendly way. I plan on keeping this book as I enjoyed it so much.
—**JANET**, IVY TECH COMMUNITY COLLEGE

The newspaper articles at the end of each chapter were so interesting, I wanted to read every single one. Thank you for putting together such a visual book and making everything seem so much more interesting.
—**TRACY**, WAYNE COMMUNITY COLLEGE

About the Cover

Our cover was created by Picture Mosaic using more than 180 photographs and 30 illustrations from our text. The cover underscores the book's visual learning philosophy and reflects our modular "parts are as great as the sum" approach. All of these small images come together to create a whole picture.

Each page throughout our 25 modules is a complete "part," meaning that each page is individually formatted to cover specific content from beginning to end. We create this format by "chunking" information on each page into small units. Also, we integrate the text on each page with interesting visuals so students have meaningful visual cues to help them learn and remember content. The "parts" of all of the pages within the modules come together to provide the learner with the whole picture.

Created by Picture Mosaic. Main image: Masterfile/royalty free. Inset images: Tim Jacobus; Shutterstock photographers: Marco Mayer, Nokhoog Buchachon, Helder Almeida, Suzanne Tucker, Serhiy Kobyakov, Greg Daniels, Javier Tuana, Luchschen, Darren Baker, Fivespots, Africa Studio, Ninell, Artsem Martysiuk, Blend Images, Blend Images, AISPIX by Image Source, Byland, Golden Pixels LLC, Oleg Znamenskiy, Testing, Gosphotodesign, Sportgraphic, Sima, Guido Vrola, Michael Woodruff, Micro10x, Lee O'Dell, Cejen, MJTH, Dariush M., Scott E Read, HomeArt, Amy Walters, Blend Images, Takayuki, Monkey Business Images, Joe Seer, Fedor Kondratenko, Kravtsov Sergey, Featureflash, Aletia, Darrin Henry, Phil Date, Regien Paassen, Antart, Evgeny Atamanenko, Aletia, Alexander Raths, Jabiru, Cynthia Kidwell, Al Mueller, Clive Chilvers, CREATISTA, Lightpoet, Hannamariah, Melinda Fawver, Monkey Business Images, Pedro Jorge Henriques Monteiro, Siart, DPS, Volodymyr Goinyk, Ilya D. Gridnev, Steve Bower, Worakit Sirijinda, Kentoh, Mike Price, Dgmata, PhotoStock10, Wavebreakmedia Ltd, Nina Vaclavova, Andy Dean Photography, Lisa F. Young, Waschnig, Daniel Korzeniewski, Blend Images, Monkey Business Images, Iriana Shiyan, TerryM, Northfoto, Dirk Ercken, Michael Rosskothen, Alicia Shields, Robert Kneschke, Iodrakon, Ssuaphotos, J.K. York, Carlos E. Santa Maria, Michal Kowalski, Featureflash, AVAVA, 1971yes, Monkey Business Images, Featureflash, Helga Esteb, Darrin Henry, Africa924, Monkey Business Images, Patricia Hofmeester, Iofoto, Richard Paul Kane, Featureflash, FuzzBones, Andresr, Auremar, Vasilchenko Nikita, Gudmundur Fylkisson, DmitriMaruta, Mayskyphoto, Holly Kuchera, Yeo2205, Ariwasabi, J. Henning Buchholz, Olly, Olly, Andrey Armyagov, William George Hagerbaumer, Darren Baker, Andrew Lever, Monkey Business Images, Featureflash, Featureflash, Helga Esteb, Featureflash, Featureflash, Anita Patterson Peppers, Neale Cousland, Helga Esteb, Pefostudio5, John Keith, Dereje, Monkey Business Images, Jan Mika, EDHAR, Melanie DeFazio, Studio 1One, Monkey Business Images, Howard Sayer, S. Bukley, Suzanne Tucker, Gladskikh Tatiana, Ilya Andriyanov, Intellistudies, S. Bukley, Masson, Featureflash, Zulufoto, Katrina Brown, Monkey Business Images, Diego Cervo, Ken Tannenbaum, Sascha Burkard, Tlorna, Monkey Business Images, Julia Zakharova, Paul Matthew Photography, CREATISTA, DEKANARYAS, Alexander Raths, Yuri Arcurs, Cjmac, Jose AS Reyes, Felix Mizioznikov, S. Bukley, Greg Epperson, Monkey Business Images, Lilya Espinosa, Tudor Catalin Gheorghe, Ilolab, Oscar C. Williams, Iofoto, Helga Esteb, Straight 8 Photography, Bikeriderlondon, Yuri Arcurs, YanLev, Nejron Photo, Greg Epperson, YanLev, Sfam Photo, Christopher Edwin Nuzzaco.

Contents

Unless otherwise noted, all images are © Cengage Learning

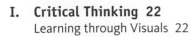

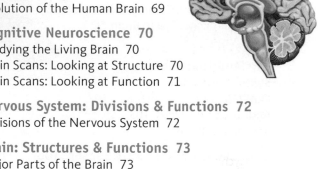

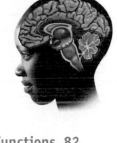

Unless otherwise noted, all images are © Cengage Learning

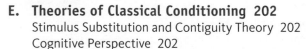

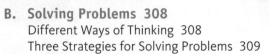
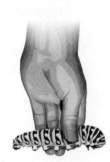

Unless otherwise noted, all images are © Cengage Learning

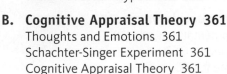
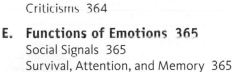
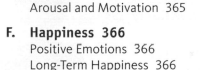

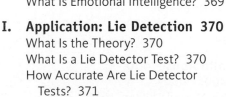
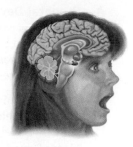

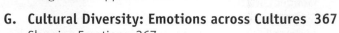

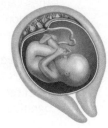

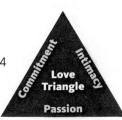

Unless otherwise noted, all images are © Cengage Learning

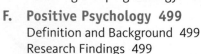
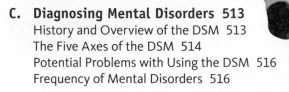

Unless otherwise noted, all images are © Cengage Learning

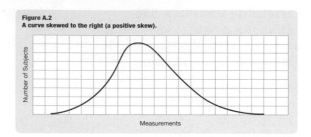

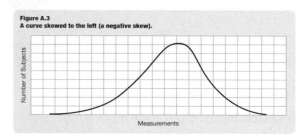

Figure A.2
A curve skewed to the right (a positive skew).

Number of Subjects

Measurements

Figure A.3
A curve skewed to the left (a negative skew).

Number of Subjects

Measurements

To the Instructor: Changes & Features

What Are the Major Content Changes?

During the past decade, new findings in the related areas of biology, genetics, and cognitive neuroscience have had a great impact on the field of psychology. Because such findings help psychologists better understand and explain behavior, we included many new and exciting discoveries not only from the field of psychology but also from the related fields of biology, genetics, and cognitive neuroscience.

In updating the 10th edition, we added nearly 750 new references, all from recent years!

Here is a sample of some of the major content changes in the 10th edition:

Module 1: Discovering Psychology
- Revised discussion of autism
- New coverage of sociocultural approach
- New coverage of biopsychosocial approach
- New coverage of neuroscience
- Updated discussion on test anxiety and passive perfectionism
- New discussion on behavioral approach to test anxiety
- New coverage of positive psychology
- Updated coverage of autism prevalence in South Korea
- Updated Cultural Diversity: Early Discrimination feature
- Updated research regarding employment opportunities for psychologists
- New discussion about test taking and recalling information
- New Critical Thinking: Learning through Visuals feature, discussing visual learning and the book's modular format

Module 2: Psychology & Science
- Completely revised organization of module, including coverage of descriptive research, correlational research, and experimental research as overarching research method types
- Thoroughly updated introduction to the six-step scientific method and descriptive research, including detailed discussion of steps, "armchair psychology," new illustrations, and advantages, and disadvantages of the descriptive research method
- New research example of survey, involving reported versus observed hand washing after use of public bathroom
- New discussion of and illustrations for naturalistic observation and its advantages and disadvantages
- New discussion and explanation of "personal beliefs" and "self-fulfilling prophecy" as disadvantages of the case study method, as well as a revised discussion of the advantages
- Updated Cultural Diversity: Use of Placebos feature with research related to medical uses of placebos, a study linking placebo relief consistent with medical relief in IBS patients, and garlic as a cure for H1N1 in China
- New discussion of correlation between kindergarten test scores and adulthood earnings as disadvantage of the correlational research method, with new illustrations
- New discussion of "population" and "sample" in discussion of how to choose participants in an experiment
- New illustrations created for the experimental research section

Module 3: Brain's Building Blocks
- Revised introduction, including updated research about Alzheimer's disease, its diagnosis, possible genetic factors, and proposed medical treatments accompanied by a new illustration and real-world example about dementia in Alzheimer's patients
- New in-depth coverage and integration of neuroscience

- Revised organization and coverage of the development and structure of the brain in Overview: Human Brain discussion, including new research about the function of glial cells, new research about the complexity of neurons and the neural network, new coverage of neurogenesis, and updated example, figure, and imagery about Alzheimer's effects on the neural activity of the brain
- New coverage and figure about the synapse in Neurons: Structure & Function discussion, including a close-up look at and description of the bulb, dendrites, and neurotransmitters
- New discussion about transplanting limbs, including the example of 54-year-old Karl Merk who received a double arm transplant from a donor
- New research on how damage to the central nervous system effects neurons, resulting in conditions like multiple sclerosis and Alzheimer's disease
- Updated coverage, organization, section titles, and figures in Neurons: Communication section, including revised figures and illustrations, new descriptions of well-known neurotransmitters and their purposes, and new discussion of neuropeptides with endorphins as an example of brain-born painkillers
- Updated Cultural Diversity: Plants & Drugs feature, including new imagery, as well as a new cultural and contemporary discussion of salvia, the popularity of its use, and its effect on the behavior of celebrity Miley Cyrus
- Updated discussion of Parkinson's disease and actor Michael J. Fox's continuing struggle with the condition
- New research about and revised discussion of stem cells, including the use of embryonic human stem cells in treatment of a patient with spinal cord injury and the up and coming engineering of induced pluripotent stem cells (iPSCs)
- Updated research on deep brain stimulation (DBS) in the treatment of patients with Parkinson's disease and coverage of newer, more effective DBS systems

Module 4: Incredible Nervous System
- New Introduction about Stu Bryant, who suffers from frontotemporal disease, including a description of his symptoms and diagnosis along with an introduction to cognitive neuroscience and discussion of how genes affect behavior
- Updated research about the genome, including new information on the number of genes found on the 23 pairs of human chromosomes, and new research about Tibetans as a recent example of human evolution in Genes & Evolution section
- Updated discussion of brain scans in Cognitive Neuroscience section, including revised MRI example, new headings for and organization of discussion, new discussion of magneto-encephalography (MEG) scan, and new discussion of and imagery for electroencephalograph (EEG), with updated Concept Review and Summary Test
- Updated discussion of the brain in Brain: Structures and Functions section, including references to new introductory example about Stu Bryant and damage to the frontal and temporal lobes
- New research example about amygdala and effect of genetic disease deterioration on experience of fear and recognition of fear in others' facial expressions
- Updated Research Focus: Sex Differences in the Brain? feature, with new conclusion discussion regarding recent research in sex differences in the brain
- New Cultural Diversity: Cultural Neuroscience feature, including introduction to the field, research methods involved in cultural neuroscience, and three diverse examples featuring studies including brain activity

differences between cultures in relation to behaviors, emotions, and thoughts with new accompanying illustration

- New Critical Thinking: Consciousness during Coma feature, including a compare-and-contrast discussion of two well-publicized cases of people in comas, Terri Schiavo and Jean-Dominique Bauby, whose conditions caused them to have different states of consciousness and mental ability along with a revised set of critical thinking questions, and new transcranial magnetic stimulation (TMS) and electroencephalograph (EEG) discussion and illustration

Module 5: Sensation
- Updated Introduction to sensation module, including revised discussion of Terry Byland, whose retina were damaged but can now see with help of a microchip and special glasses, and a new visual discussion identifying the five senses
- New discussions about visual accommodation and blind spots in the retitled Vision section, along with updated imagery throughout and updated research related to color blindness
- Retitled Audition section with revised use of key terms, like *frequency, hammer, anvil, stirrup, eardrum,* and *pinna,* and imagery, like an updated ear diagram, as well as new research about the likelihood of hearing loss in college students
- New Vestibular & Kinesthetic Senses section, including the key terms *vestibular sense* and *semicircular canals,* and a new Kinesthetic Sense discussion with updated inclusion in the Concept Review and Summary Test
- Updated Chemical Senses section, including new research about brain cells in mice and response to types of taste, new research about human sensitivity to bitterness and link to evolution, updated research on supertasters, updated olfactory cell diagram, and new research in functions of olfaction, including five real-world examples of how smells affect things like our emotions, choices for reproduction, and everyday purchases
- Updated Touch section, including revised discussion of sensory receptors and new inclusion of and research about the Merkel cell, which is sensitive to gentle, localized touch, along with updated inclusion in the Concept Review and Summary Test
- Updated Cultural Diversity: Disgust feature, including new research about how disgust can influence public hygiene behaviors and updated imagery
- Updated Research Focus: Mind over Body? feature, including new research about placebo response tracked in the brain using neuroscience
- New research example of how being in love can affect one's experience of pain and updated research in acupuncture discussion in the Pain section
- Updated Application: Artificial Senses feature, including new real-world example of Erik Weihenmayer and his ability to "see" with his tongue using an electrode-heavy tool called the BrainPort, along with new research about the prevalence of cochlear implants and their use in children and adults
- Updated Critical Thinking: What Would It Be Like Never to Feel Pain? feature, including revised description of Ashlyn Blocker's continued struggle with congenital insensitivity to pain with anhidrosis (CIPA)

Module 6: Perception
- Updated Introduction to module, including new imagery and revised examples
- Updated and retitled Thresholds section, including revised discussion of absolute threshold with examples of absolute thresholds for the human eye, ear, tongue, nose, and skin as well as a revised discussion of subliminal stimuli with new historical example of subliminal messaging in advertising
- Updated imagery in Sensation Versus Perception section
- Completely revised and retitled Perceptual Organization section, including new compare-and-contrast discussion of top-down and bottom-up processing with contextual examples, and a revised discussion of Gestalt psychology and updated Concept Review and Summary Test

- Updated imagery throughout Perceptual Constancy section
- New visual examples for linear perspective, relative size, light and shadow, atmospheric perspective, texture gradient, and motion parallax depth cues in Depth Perception discussion
- Updated Cultural Diversity: Influence on Perceptions feature, including new imagery
- Revised Research Focus: Unconscious Perceptions feature, including new discussion of research study involving unconscious imagery and visual perception and updated imagery
- Updated Concept Review and Summary Test, including new imagery and review questions
- Updated and retitled Strange Perceptions section, including new moon illusion and Ames room illusion imagery, new location for ESP: Extrasensory Perception discussion, and new strange perceptions problems discussion with description of prosopagnosia with real-world examples of the condition
- Updated imagery throughout Application: Creating Perceptions feature
- Updated Critical Thinking: Taste Shapes? Hear Colors? Smell Sounds? feature

Module 7: Sleep & Dreams
- Updated Introduction, including new imagery, revised discussion of rapid eye movement, and new discussion about REM behavior disorder and sleepwalking
- Revised Continuum of Consciousness section, including updated research about distracted driving, misconceptions about daydreaming, and new imagery
- Retitled and updated Rhythms of Consciousness section, including new research example about mice and circadian rhythms involving light exposure and weight gain along with updated imagery
- Retitled and updated Stages of Sleep section with new imagery, revised illustrations, and an updated discussion of the four stages of sleep
- Revised Research Focus: Circadian Preference feature, including new research about changes to sleep patterns across the lifespan along with new imagery
- New research about sleeping and old age, new discussion on theories about why we sleep, and research study involving rats, sleep deprivation, and consciousness
- Updated Cultural Diversity: Incidence of SAD feature, including updated information about treatment for seasonal affective disorder
- Retitled and updated Theories of Dream Interpretation section, including new definitions and descriptions of manifest content and latent content in the discussion about Freud's theory of dream interpretation, and new imagery
- Updated Application: Sleep Problems Treatments feature, including new research about cognitive-behavioral therapy and drug therapy as treatments for insomnia, updated research on narcolepsy, and suggested treatment for those who experience nightmares
- Revised Critical Thinking: Texting: How Distracting Can It Be? feature, including updated discussion regarding state and national laws about texting while driving accompanied by new information on a study discussing the frequency of near-crashes due to texting

Module 8: Hypnosis & Drugs
- Slight reorganization of drug discussions in module, including a new outline with drugs covered under their comprehensive type: stimulants, depressants, hallucinogens, and opiates
- New research in the Hypnosis section, including discussion of a case study in which eye movements support altered state theory of hypnosis imagery
- New Research Focus: Meditation & School Stress feature that discusses transcendental meditation (TM) and how it can be used to reduce school stress, including data from a recent study involving minority college students and their experience of stress with and without use of TM

- Updated Drugs: Overview section, including new research about drug abuse and cost in the United States, a revised definition of psychoactive drugs, a new discussion of physiological and psychological dependency, a revised discussion of the effect of drug addiction and dependency on dopamine levels, new research on the prevalence of drug use in young adults, and updated imagery and illustrations
- Updated Stimulants section, including new research about cocaine use in the United States, with the real-world example of Whitney Houston, whose cocaine use contributed to her death, research about long-term drug abuse and decision-making abilities, and a completely revised nicotine discussion with new research on cigarette smoking, smoking-related deaths, and the dangers of smoking on one's own and other's bodies
- Updated and newly titled Depressants section, including new definition of depressant, new real-world example of Amy Winehouse who died of alcohol poisoning, updated research on genetic risk factors for alcoholism, and new discussion about barbiturates and tranquilizers, their effects and uses, along with new imagery
- New research on alcohol abuse prevalence in the United States in the Cultural Diversity: Alcoholism Rates feature
- Revised Concept Review and Summary Test to include new concepts like transcendental meditation, physiological dependence, barbiturates, and tranquilizers
- New research on study involving the use of MDMA for patients who have developed treatment-resistant posttraumatic stress disorder (PTSD) conducted by the U.S. government in the designer drugs discussion
- A part of the Hallucinogens section, the updated marijuana discussion includes new research about illicit marijuana use, uses for medical marijuana, public interest in marijuana legalization, and a revised definition of marijuana
- Revised opiates discussion, including new definition of narcotics, revised discussion of heroin use and popularity, new research on the prevalence of heroin in drug abuse-related deaths, and new imagery
- Updated Application: Treatment for Drug Abuse feature, including new research about the prevalence of alcohol abuse and the percentage of the population that seeks treatment, the use of vaccines as treatment for substance addiction, and new imagery
- Updated Critical Thinking: Brain-Boosting Drugs: Myth or Fact? feature, including new research about caffeine consumption and its use in the U.S. military

Module 9: Classical Conditioning
- Updated Procedure: Classical Conditioning section to include definition of acquisition as a learning process involved in classical conditioning
- New Cultural Diversity: Conditioning Racial Prejudice feature, including discussions relating classical conditioning and racial prejudice, a classic 1930s research study example involving preschool children, white dolls, and black dolls, how people become prejudiced through conditioning, and how to uncondition racial prejudice through extinction with new imagery
- Updated imagery throughout module
- Updated Summary Test to include new content and imagery about new Cultural Diversity feature

Module 10: Operant & Cognitive Approaches
- Updated Operant Conditioning section, including new definition of Skinner box with new illustrations and imagery
- Updated Reinforcers section, including new definition of reinforcer with updated imagery and examples
- Revised Cognitive Learning section with new definition of latent learning, new discussion about the "aha!" moment or flash of insight experience, including four main characteristics of this experience based on research studies, along with new imagery
- Updated Research Focus: Viewing Aggression feature, including new research example about reality television shows, relational aggression, and viewer behavior

- Updated Application: Behavior Modification feature, including new use of term *intellectual impairment*, new research about the cost of treatments for those with autism, new example of contingency management as a behavior modification treatment for autism as well as a variety of conditions with examples of HIV-positive patients who took medication and people who ate more healthfully because of this form of behavior modification, as well as an updated discussion of spanking and what research says about its effectiveness
- Updated Critical Thinking: How Do You Train a Killer Whale? feature, highlighting the danger involved in this work, along with new imagery
- Updated Concept Review and Summary Test, incorporating new key terms, key concepts, and imagery

Module 11: Types of Memory
- Updated Introduction, including revised key terms, definitions, and explanations for memory, information-processing model, storage, and retrieval and new imagery
- Newly titled Three Stages of Memory section, which discusses sensory memory, short-term memory, long-term memory, memory processes, iconic memory, and echoic memory with new imagery
- Revised discussion of short-term memory and working memory as separate concepts in the Short-Term Memory: Working section, including updated imagery and new definitions
- New key terms *explicit memory* and *implicit memory* introduced in the Long-Term Memory: Storing section, including new imagery
- New Research Focus: Strengthening Episodic Memories feature, including study about memory-enhancing hormones and new discussion of memories of amnesia patients with case study of Claire Robertson, who has amnesia and uses a camera to "memorize" her daily activities
- Updated Repressed Memories section, including updated research about repressed memories and sexual abuse and a new example of therapy bringing about false traumatic memories
- Revised Cultural Diversity: Oral Versus Written feature, including a whole new section on the oral tradition and the importance of griots to community, history, and cultural identity in Africa
- Updated Application: Unusual Memories feature, including new research on the consistency of flashbulb memories associated with 9/11 attacks and new imagery
- Revised Concept Review and Summary Test, including new imagery, key terms, and key concepts

Module 12: Remembering & Forgetting
- New imagery throughout the module
- New research example about early memories and listening to music while in the womb in the forgetting curves section
- Revised discussion about interference, a new discussion about and definition of decay, revised discussion about and definition of retrieval cues, and new research example about tip-of-the-tongue phenomenon in the reasons for forgetting section
- New discussion about the complexities associated with identifying the biological bases of memory
- New Cultural Diversity: Differences in Episodic Memory feature discussing the differences in Euro-Americans and Asians in encoding episodic memories, including synopses of three studies and new imagery
- Revised title for the Research Focus feature, now Recalling Sexual History
- Updated Application: Eyewitness Testimony feature, including revised data about wrongful convictions based on DNA evidence, a new discussion of the accuracy of eyewitness testimonies in an accident involving two trains, multiple fatalities, and millions of dollars in damages, and a new discussion of the misinformation effect, with new imagery throughout
- Updated Critical Thinking: Can Bad Memories Be Erased? feature, including new research about bad memories and how it might be possible to add to, alter, or erase them

Module 13: Intelligence

- New Introduction section, including updates to information about Halle Berry and new inclusion of John Grisham, Mark Zuckerberg, and Jeremy Lin as examples of various types of intelligence, with new imagery
- Revised discussions of general intelligence theory (or *g*-factor theory), multiple intelligence theory, and triarchic theory in the Defining Intelligence section, along with updated research examples and imagery
- In the Measuring Intelligence section, new research example about brain size and intelligence (IQ scores), new discussion of the Stanford-Binet Intelligence Scale, and new examples of Quentin Tarantino and Laura Shields in the discussion of whether IQ is the same as intelligence, with updated imagery
- Revised Distribution & Use of IQ Scores section, including new introduction featuring *Glee* actress Lauren Potter, retitling of sections, new discussion of intellectual disability and replacement of term *mental retardation* throughout, and revised discussion of giftedness with updated imagery and figures
- Updated Nature-Nurture Question section, including new introductory examples of Lang Lang and Sufiah Yusof as child prodigies in music and mathematics respectively, new discussion of the interaction between nature and nurture, new discussion of heritability of intelligence, all-new discussion of neuroscience and intelligence in a study involving impoverished children and brain activity, and a new research study involving adopted children, with new imagery and illustrations
- Updated Application: Intervention Programs feature, including updated research, definitions, and imagery
- Updated Concept Review and Summary Test, incorporating new key concepts and people, new imagery

Module 14: Thought & Language

- Revised introduction, including updated imagery and introduction of the key term *cognition*
- Updated Solving Problems section, including new real-world examples of world chess champion Vladimir Kramnik and his match with computer Deep Fritz as well as a discussion about advertising created by lottery companies and the availability heuristic, new discussion of and real-world example for key term *representative heuristic,* new key term *mental set* and updated imagery throughout
- Revised Thinking Creatively section, including updated introductory information about music and fashion mogul Shawn Carter, new definition of *creativity,* and new discussion about convergent and divergent thinking and learned creativity with new imagery throughout
- New section titled Reasoning & Decision Making, including definitions of and discussions about deductive reasoning, inductive reasoning, confirmation bias, theory of linguistic relativity, and decision making, including how it relates to gambling, emotions, thoughts, and words, with new imagery throughout
- Revised Language: Basic Rules section, including updated introduction, new research about bilingualism in infants, with updated imagery and illustrations
- Revised Acquiring Language section, including updated research and discussion about language acquisition in infants with new research for each of the four stages, including discussion of receptive and productive vocabularies as well as a new study about smart baby DVD programs and environmental factors in language acquisition, with new imagery throughout
- Updated Research Focus: Dyslexia feature, including revised definition of dyslexia, new real-world example of Benjamin Bolger, and updated research and imagery throughout
- Updated Cultural Diversity: Influences on Thinking feature, with revised titles and a new illustration

- Updated Application: Do Animals Have Language? feature, including descriptions of four studies involving researchers, gorillas and chimpanzees with descriptions of primates Koko, Washoe, Nim, Kanzee, and Panzee and related research
- Updated Concept Review and Summary Test with new imagery and new key concepts and terms included
- Revised Critical Thinking article titled Does Music Improve Language Skills in Children?, and new imagery

Module 15: Motivation

- New example of Shaquille O'Neal as example of achievement in Introduction, including brief synopsis of his athletic, musical, academic, and acting careers
- Revised Theories of Motivation section, including retitled and updated sections Instinct Approach and Maslow's Hierarchy of Needs, new sections Arousal Theory and Arousal Approach, revised Reward/Pleasure Center Approach section, and new discussions of self-determination theory, the Yerkes-Dodson law, and sensation seekers, with updated imagery and illustrations throughout
- Revised Hunger section, including newly titled Obesity section with discussions of body mass index (BMI) and research related to prevalence and causes of obesity in the United States, revised Biological Hunger Factors and Psychological Hunger Factors sections, including cross-cultural research about eating habits and dangerous dieting tactics, and updated imagery throughout
- Updated Sexual Behavior section, including revised discussion of and research about the activity of the hypothalamus in males and females, new discussion about gender dysphoria with examples of Chaz/Chastity Bono juxtaposed against landmark example of John/Joan, and updated research about sexual orientation in the United States, updated discussion on male-female sex differences, including new research study involving testosterone levels in Filipino men with and without children and the study's relationship with evolutionary theory, updated research on prevalence of homosexuality in men with several older biological brothers, and updated research on the prevalence and progression of AIDS virus worldwide with updated imagery and illustrations throughout
- Updated Cultural Diversity: Genital Cutting feature, including updated research about anti-genital cutting activist Soraya Mire, with updated imagery
- Updated Concept Review and Summary Test to include new key concepts and terms with updated imagery and illustrations
- Revised Achievement section, including revised introduction about social needs and Shaquille O'Neal, new discussion on the need for achievement and entrepreneurship, updated discussion of Intel Science Talent Search and winner Nithin Tumma in discussion of cognitive influences of achievement with updated imagery
- New Application: Dieting & Eating Disorders feature, including updated discussion of Oprah Winfrey as example of difficulties with dieting, updated diet program/lifestyle discussion including examples of visualizing food as a diet program and food addiction as a lifestyle issue, new eating disorders discussion with prevalence and examples of anorexia nervosa, bulimia nervosa, and binge eating disorder, with new imagery throughout
- New Critical Thinking: Using Money to Motivate Kids to Learn feature about experiment with multiple conditions conducted with children to determine the effectiveness of monetary reward and academic performance with new imagery and questions

Module 16: Emotion

- Updated Peripheral Theories section, including revised section titles and new discussion of the Cannon-Bard theory, with new imagery throughout
- Updated Affective Neuroscience Approach section, including new landmark research study of SM and how the absence of an amygdala affects experiences of fear

- Revised Universal Facial Expressions section, including updated research about cross-cultural and genetic evidence for universal facial expressions and new discussion about criticisms of universal expressions given new research about recognition of certain expressions in young children
- Updated Happiness section, including new discussion about happiness across the lifespan, with updated imagery throughout
- Revised Cultural Diversity: Emotions across Cultures feature, including new research about outward expression of happiness and its varying perception in American and Asian cultures as well research showing that the vocalizations of negative emotion, but not positive emotions are universally recognized, with updated imagery throughout
- Updated Concept Review and Summary Test, including new key terms and imagery
- Updated Research Focus: Emotional Intelligence feature, including updated research and imagery
- Revised Application: Lie Detection feature, including new research about the accuracy and inaccuracy of lie detector tests, their use in law enforcement, and other physiological and observation-based methods that may provide more insight into lying, with updated imagery throughout

Module 17: Infancy & Childhood

- Revised Introduction section, including new subtitles, updated discussion about the lasting social deficits of a damaging orphanage environment on Romanian children, and a new definition for human development
- Revised and retitled Prenatal Development section, including new example of Yo-Yo Ma as a musical prodigy and the genetic and environmental factors affecting his talents, new discussion of epigenetics, new research on prevalence of drug abuse during pregnancy and its effect on prenatal development, with new teratogen examples of prescription painkillers and pesticides, and new discussion of partial fetal alcohol syndrome, as well as new imagery throughout
- Updated Sensory & Motor Development section, including new definition of sensory development, new titles, with new imagery and illustrations throughout
- Revised Emotional Development section, including new imagery and illustrations throughout
- Revised Cognitive Development section, including revised discussion of Piaget's theory of cognitive development and its criticisms as well as new imagery and illustrations throughout
- Revised Social Development section, including a new introductory example for Bandura's social cognitive theory and new closing research on the relationship between adverse life experiences and mental health later in life
- Newly titled Gender Development section, including discussions of gender identity and roles, social role theory, cognitive developmental theory, gender schemas, and gender traits and research on male and female differences, with new imagery throughout
- Newly titled Infancy & Childhood Review section, including discussion of sensory and motor development, emotional development, cognitive development, social development, and gender development between ages 1 month and 3 years, with new imagery and illustrations throughout
- Revised Cultural Diversity: Gender Roles feature, including new imagery throughout
- Revised Application: Child Abuse feature, including updated research on child abuse and neglect and its long-lasting effects on the psychological and neurological development of children, with new imagery throughout
- Revised Critical Thinking: Who Matters More—Parents or Peers? feature, including new imagery
- Updated Concept Review and Summary Test, including updated key terms and imagery

Module 18: Adolescence & Adulthood

- Revised Introduction, including updated case study example of Charlie Sheen, with new imagery throughout

- Revised section titles to reflect organization of module by topic, including Physical Development: Puberty, Cognitive & Emotional Development, Morality & Parenting, Personality & Social Development, Adolescence Review, and Adulthood & Aging
- Updated Physical Development: Puberty section, including new key terms *primary sexual characteristics* and *secondary sexual characteristics,* new research on environmental effects on age of menarche, updated research on trends in sexual activity and contraceptive use of teenagers, with updated imagery throughout
- New discussion of neurological gap in adolescents and updated imagery and illustrations in Cognitive & Emotional Development section
- Updated Morality & Parenting section, including completely revised discussions of authoritarian, authoritative, and permissive parenting styles as well as the parenting style's effect on the child's self-esteem, self-confidence, and achievement, with new imagery throughout
- Updated Personality & Social Development section, including new discussion of emerging adulthood and new imagery throughout
- Updated Adolescence Review section, including new discussion of Erikson's psychosocial stages of development and new imagery and illustrations throughout
- Revised Gender Roles, Love & Relationships section, including updated research on gender roles in the home and workplace for working men and women, and new research on brain scans and love, cohabitation, and socioeconomic factors in marriage and divorce, with updated imagery and illustrations throughout
- Updated Research Focus: Happy Marriages feature, including new research on successful relationships and key factors, including friendship, intimacy, constructive criticism, and shared meaning, with discussions of how to accomplish each
- Updated Cultural Diversity: Preferences for Partners feature, including new discussion of American men and women's preferences for partners and lifestyle, with updated imagery and illustrations
- Updated Adulthood & Aging section, including new research on life expectancy and population, changes in cognitive speed, brain resiliency, memory, and emotion in adulthood as well as a new discussion of death and dying and Kubler-Ross's five stages of coping, with new imagery throughout
- Updated Application: Suicide feature, including new research on suicide prevalence in the United States, the most common suicide methods, and the suicide rate in young adults and older adults as well as a new discussion on suicide prevention and identifying risk factors
- Updated Critical Thinking: Are Teens Too Young to Drive? feature, including function of executive branch of brain and common driving mistakes made by teenagers as well as research on new programs for driver's licensure involving phased driving privileges, with updated imagery
- Updated Concept Review and Summary Test, including new terminology and imagery

Module 19: Freudian & Humanistic Theories

- Revised Introduction, including new example of Greg Mathis, who went from gang member to court judge and host of an award-winning television show, with updated imagery
- Updated Divisions of the Mind section, including new imagery and research regarding defense mechanisms and denial
- Updated Developmental Stages section, including updated illustrations and new imagery
- Revised Freud's Followers & Critics section, including updated research on Freud's theory of personality and early childhood experiences with future behavior, personality, emotions, as well as how those experiences can affect genes recognized using neuroscience, with updated imagery and illustrations
- Updated Humanistic Theories section, including new introduction about Greg Mathis, new example of Yani Tseng, who knew since childhood that

she wanted to become "the world's best golfer" and is ranked No. 1 in the Women's World Golf Rankings, new positive regard example of how pet owners often live longer lives, updated information about Carrie Underwood as an example of self-actualization, and new discussion of positive psychology, with updated illustrations and imagery throughout
- Updated Concept Review and Summary Test, including updated imagery and illustrations
- Revised Research Focus: Shyness section, including definition for social cognitive theory and updated imagery

Module 20: Social Cognitive & Trait Theories
- Updated Social Cognitive Theory section, including new discussions about social cognitive theory and reciprocal determinism as well as new longitudinal research involving the children from the classic delay of gratification marshmallow study over a 40-year period, with updated imagery throughout
- Revised Trait Theory section, including a new discussion of policewomen and how their interpersonal skills are an advantage in violent situations, a new section on the Big Five personality traits and how the sizes of different regions of the brain may be associated with the Big Five, a new introduction about the behavior of infamous football coach and child molester Jerry Sandusky, whose conflicting actions provide a strong person versus situation example, updated research on heritability, and an all-new discussion on the environmental influences of shared and nonshared environments on personality development, including cultural influences, as well as updated imagery throughout
- Updated Cultural Diversity: Suicide Bombers feature, including new revised content about martyrdom, hatred, and suicide bombers, with updated imagery
- Updated Review: Four Theories of Personality section, including revised discussion of social cognitive theory with discussion of reciprocal determinism
- New Critical Thinking: More Employers Use Personality Tests in Hiring Process feature, including new discussion of industrial/organizational psychology and how the Myers-Briggs test and Minnesota Multiphasic Personality Inventory can be used in the workplace, with updated imagery
- Revised Concept Review and Summary Test, including updated questions and imagery

Module 21: Health, Stress, & Coping
- Updated Introduction section, including new discussions of stressors and coping, new research on Americans with panic disorder, and updated imagery throughout
- Revised Appraisal of Stress section, including new example of appraisals, updated section title, and updated imagery and illustrations throughout
- Updated Stress Responses section with updated section title, new discussion of tend and befriend, new discussions about the relationship between chronic illness and stress, and a new discussion of health psychology, with new imagery
- Revised Stressful Experiences section, including discussion of daily uplifts and overall functioning, updated discussion of significant causes of stress for most Americans, new real-world example of Lady Gaga and her experience with frustration, new research about violence and development of posttraumatic stress disorder (PTSD), with updated imagery and illustrations throughout
- Updated Personality & Health section, including revised information about Shaun White, updated information on the health differences of optimists and pessimists, new subsection on Bandura's self-efficacy theory, including four sources of information and student-friendly examples, updated information on negative health effects of Type D behavior, with updated imagery throughout
- Revised Coping with Stress section, including updated section title, new discussion of using problem- and emotion-focused coping and their facilitation of each other

- Revised Concept Review and Summary Test, including new key terms and updated imagery and illustrations
- New Positive Psychology section, including its definition, background, and research findings on altruism, writing exercises, and promotion of positive traits and their effect on physical and emotional health, and new imagery
- New Critical Thinking: The Positive Benefits of Social Support feature about the small town of Roseto, Pennsylvania, and the benefits of its strong social support network, how continuing research of a 40-year-old study can yield important findings, and how the Internet can provide social support, with new critical thinking questions and imagery

Module 22: Assessment & Psychological Disorders I
- Revised module title, from Assessment & Anxiety Disorders to Assessment & Psychological Disorders I
- New module-opening vignette with key term *anxiety disorder* and real-world example of Howie Mandel, comedian and actor afflicted with severe anxiety since childhood, including new imagery
- Updated Factors in Mental Disorders section, including new figure about cognitive-emotional-behavioral and environmental factors of mental disorders, with updated imagery throughout
- Revised Diagnosing Mental Disorders section, including updated history and overview of the *Diagnostic and Statistical Manual of Mental Disorders* (DSM), new section on the upcoming DSM 5, including examples of new diagnoses, an in-depth discussion of categorical versus dimensional assessments, a discussion of Howie Mandel in relation to obsessive-compulsive disorder and Axis I of the DSM, updated discussion of the frequency of mental disorders, and new imagery and illustrations throughout
- Revised Anxiety Disorders discussion, including updated research on panic disorder, updated discussion of specific phobias, expanded discussion of obsessive-compulsive disorder (OCD) using Howie Mandel's experiences as examples, revised discussion of treatment for posttraumatic stress disorder (PTSD), and updated imagery throughout
- Revised Somatoform Disorders section, including new real-world examples of mass hysteria among female high school students in New York, Vietnam, and Mexico, and updated imagery throughout
- Updated Summary Test, including revised section titles, imagery, illustrations, and key concepts
- Revised Cultural Diversity: Asian Anxiety Disorder feature, including updated research on taijin kyofusho and its occurrence in the Japanese population, with updated imagery
- Revised Application: Treating Phobias feature, including new real-world example of a woman who has a phobia of flying, with detailed descriptions of cognitive-behavioral therapy and exposure therapy as treatments for her phobia, with new imagery throughout
- Updated Concept Review and Summary Test, including new key terms and imagery

Module 23: Psychological Disorders II
- Revised Mood Disorders section, including updated discussion of bipolar disorder, its prevalence, real-world example of Catherine Zeta-Jones who has bipolar disorder, new research on genetic factors in bipolar disorder, new research on the effectiveness of antidepressants, and an updated biomedical treatment section, including discussions of electroconvulsive therapy (ECT), transcranial magnetic stimulation (TMS), and deep brain stimulation (DBS) with research on their prevalence and effectiveness, with updated imagery throughout
- Updated Personality Disorders section, including new example of Gary Ridgway, the Green River (Serial) Killer, revised list of five types of personality disorders proposed to be included in the DSM 5, a new discussion of how self-harm often becomes a part of borderline personality disorder, some causes of borderline personality disorder, and updated imagery throughout

- Revised Schizophrenia section, including the new key terms *delusion* and *flat affect,* new research on genetic markers for the condition, updated discussion of how infections may contribute to schizophrenia, new discussion of the association between brain chemistry and schizophrenia symptoms, a new discussion of how researchers are working to identify biomarkers for earlier diagnosis of the condition, and a new discussion of cognitive-behavioral therapy as treatment for schizophrenia, with updated imagery throughout
- Updated Dissociative Identity Disorder section, including new research on its prevalence and how researchers can capture personality transitions in the brain
- Updated Cultural Diversity: Interpreting Symptoms feature, including new descriptions of windigo and hikkomori as culture-specific disorders and how depression may be more prevalent in women due to biological and psychosocial factors with updated imagery
- Updated Research Focus: Exercise Versus Drugs feature, including research on how regular exercise can affect depression, with updated imagery
- Updated Application: Dealing with Mild Depression feature, including new updated imagery throughout
- Updated Critical Thinking: What Is a Psychopath? feature, including coverage of the different types of psychopaths
- Updated Concept Review and Summary Test, including new key terms and imagery

Module 24: Therapies

- Updated research on mental illness in the homeless population in the Historical Background section, with new imagery
- Revised Questions about Psychotherapy section, including the new key concept biomedical therapy and new research on the effectiveness of psychotherapy, with updated illustrations
- Revised Psychoanalysis section, including new title and updated research on the effectiveness of long-term psychoanalysis therapy on various mental disorders, with new imagery
- Revised Client-Centered Therapy section, including new discussion of the humanistic approach
- Revised Cognitive Therapy discussion, including updated illustrations and a new title
- Updated Behavior Therapy section, including new case story about a woman with phobia of flying and the use of in vivo exposure (exposure therapy) with new imagery and illustrations
- Revised Cognitive-Behavior Therapy section, including updated titles
- New section titled Common Factors and Therapy Settings, including a discussion about common factors among different therapies, new discussion of various types of group therapy, including family therapy and couple therapy, and a revised discussion of telemental health with discussion of therapy research on the prevalence of severe forms of depression in college students with apps for use on smartphones
- Revised Research Focus: EMDR feature, including new research on studies involving EMDR therapy and reducing traumatic memories in those suffering from posttraumatic stress disorder (PTSD) and updated research discussing how EMDR allows relaxation and subdues symptoms, and new discussion of the various organizations naming EMDR as an effective treatment for PTSD, with updated imagery
- Updated Cultural Diversity: Different Healer feature, including updated imagery
- New Biomedical Therapies section, including definition of the new key concept biomedical therapy, with introduction of new concepts and discussions about antidepressant drugs, antianxiety drugs, mood-stabilizer drugs, and antipsychotic drugs, with new imagery
- Updated Application: Cognitive-Behavioral Techniques, with updated imagery
- Revised Critical Thinking: Virtual Reality Can Be More than Fun & Games feature, including updated research and information about current virtual reality technology

Module 25: Social Cognition & Behavior

- New module title Social Cognition & Behavior (formerly Social Psychology)
- New Introduction section, including a discussion of a social experiment involving award-winning violinist Joshua Bell playing in a subway and a discussion of behavior in groups focusing on the hazing rituals of the "Marching 100" band from Florida A&M University (FAMU) and how it demonstrates group dynamics, with new imagery throughout
- Updated Perceiving Others section, including revised discussion about Joshua Bell, his attire in the subway performances versus music hall performances, and how appearance affects person perception, updated research examples of how physical attractiveness affects perceptions and relationships, new research on how monogamy affects looking at other attractive people, revised discussion of how cultural values and social approval contribute to stereotypes, new example of Olympian Sarah Robles as a 275-pound, 5'10" top-ranked weightlifter who hopes to change the perception of larger women in the United States, a new discussion about Jeremy Lin, the only Asian-American and Harvard grad playing in the NBA, new key concept and discussion about social cognition, with updated imagery throughout
- Updated Attributions section, including revised discussion about the glass ceiling and the number of female versus male chairpersons in the list of Fortune 500 companies, with real-world discussion about Marissa Mayer as the youngest woman to become CEO of a Fortune 500 company and believed to be the first to become CEO while pregnant
- Updated Attitudes section, including discussion of when politicians should use the central route for persuasion, with updated imagery throughout
- Updated Cultural Diversity: National Attitudes & Behaviors feature, including revised research about Egyptian women in the workforce and universities as well as their literacy, with updated imagery
- Revised Social & Group Influences section, including updated introduction about conformity and hazing using FAMU's "Marching 100" band and the death of drum major Robert Champion as an example of conformity, and updated statistics about the frequency of hazing within student organizations and athletic teams and compliance of individuals in group situations, new real-world examples of Abu Ghraib and government-sanctioned massacres in Syria and Libya as reflections of Milgram's historical obedience experiment, revised discussion of Wesley Autrey, everyday hero who protected a man who had fallen onto the subway tracks with his own body, new key concept of heroism as a form of altruism, and new real-world examples of deindividuation among Black Friday shoppers as well as how physical symbols, like clothing and gangs, help gang, fraternity, and sorority members identify with their group and feel less accountable when engaging in irrational behavior, with updated imagery throughout
- Revised Social Neuroscience section, including new research on mirror neurons and how they affect our observations, and interpretations of those in our ethnic in- and outgroups, with updated imagery
- Revised Aggression section, including updated research on adolescents and how playing violent video games can lead to either hostility or improved skills, depending on the child's personality traits, new research on sexual harassment and aggression in the United States, including statistics about the incidence of rape in men and women with new key term and definition for rape
- Updated Critical Thinking: Why the Debate over Teen Vaccination? feature, including new data on the prevalence of the HPV vaccination in teen girls as well as the recommendation to administer it to boys, with new imagery.

Now that you've read about some of the changes in the 10th edition, we'll discuss the major features of the text. ●

Distinctive Learning Approach

What's Different about This Approach?

One of the first things instructors notice about this textbook is that it looks different from more traditional texts. This book looks different because its method of presenting information is based on well-known principles of learning and memory.

One principle is that if information is presented in an interesting way, then students learn and remember the concepts much more readily. Like previous editions, the 10th edition applies this principle by integrating the text with interesting graphics so that students have visual cues to help them learn and remember. As students often say, "I'm a visual learner, so this text is perfect for me."

Another principle is that if information is organized or "chunked" into smaller units, then students learn and remember the material better. As in previous editions, the 10th edition applies this principle by organizing information into smaller and smaller segments to help students remember the hundreds of terms and concepts. As one reviewer said, "The material is broken down into small, friendly pieces that are easy for students to understand."

Thus, this text looks different because it uses visual learning, which involves the use of *VISUAL CUES* and *CHUNKING*. There is a large body of research indicating that chunking helps students better organize and store information and that visual cues help students better retrieve and remember information. The research outcomes on visual learning make complete sense when you consider that our brain is mainly an image processor (much of our sensory cortex is devoted to vision), not a word processor. In fact, the part of the brain used to process words is tiny in comparison to the part that processes visual images. Words are abstract and rather difficult for the brain to retain, whereas visuals are concrete and, as such, more easily remembered (Meier, 2000; Patton, 1991; Schacter, 1996; Verdi et al., 1997). It is for these reasons that each page of this textbook has been individually formatted to maximize visual learning.

How Are the Visuals Selected?

Every visual, whether a photo, illustration, concept map, figure, or icon, was carefully selected by the two of us in collaboration with our editorial team. As authors, we are intricately involved in decisions concerning every visual in this textbook. We work collaboratively with our photo researchers and illustrators throughout the revision process. The primary goal of each of our decisions regarding visuals is to improve student learning. If a visual doesn't clearly meet this requirement, we go back to the drawing board with our team to work toward obtaining or creating just the right visual. Based on the many hours of research for only one photo and numerous revisions of a single illustration, we're confident our team agrees that we don't settle for close enough. We believe that the right visuals can help make abstract and difficult concepts more tangible and welcoming, as well as make learning more effective and long lasting.

How Many New Visuals Have Been Added?

We have used feedback from readers and reviewers in revising and adding new photos, figures, and illustrations, which provide effective visual cues for better learning and remembering. In this revision, we added about 600 new photos and nearly 40 original illustrations. Additionally, we retained hundreds of other effective visuals from the 9th edition. ●

B Procedure: Classical Conditioning

Pavlov's Experiment

What's the procedure? Imagine that you are an assistant in Pavlov's laboratory and your subject is a dog named Sam. You are using a procedure that will result in Sam's salivating when he hears a bell, a response that Pavlov called a *conditioned reflex*. Today, we call Pavlov's procedure *classical conditioning*, which involves the following three steps.

Step 1. Selecting Stimulus and Response

Terms. Before you begin the procedure to establish classical conditioning in Sam, you need to identify three critical terms: *neutral stimulus, unconditioned stimulus,* and *unconditioned response.*

Neutral stimulus. You need to choose a neutral stimulus. A **neutral stimulus,** or **NS,** is some stimulus that causes a sensory response, such as being seen, heard, or smelled, but does not produce the reflex being tested.

Your neutral stimulus will be a tone (bell), which Sam the dog hears but which does not normally produce the reflex of salivation.

Unconditioned stimulus. You need to choose an unconditioned stimulus, or UCS.

An **unconditioned stimulus,** or **UCS,** is some stimulus that triggers or elicits a physiological reflex, such as salivation or eye blink.

Your unconditioned stimulus will be food, which when presented to Sam will elicit the salivation reflex—that is, will make Sam salivate.

Unconditioned response. Finally, you need to select and measure an unconditioned response, or UCR.

The **unconditioned response,** or **UCR,** is an unlearned, innate, involuntary physiological reflex that is elicited by the unconditioned stimulus.

For instance, salivation is an unconditioned response that is elicited by food. In this case, the sight of food, which is the unconditioned stimulus, will elicit salivation in Sam, which is the unconditioned response.

Step 2. Establishing Classical Conditioning

Trial. A common procedure to establish classical conditioning is for you first to present the neutral stimulus and then, a short time later, to present the unconditioned stimulus. The presentation of both stimuli is called a **trial.**

Neutral stimulus. In a typical trial, you will pair the neutral stimulus, the tone, with the unconditioned stimulus, the food. Generally, you will first present the neutral stimulus (tone) and then, a short time later, present the unconditioned stimulus (food).

+

Unconditioned stimulus (UCS). Some seconds (but less than a minute) after the tone begins, you present the unconditioned stimulus, a piece of food, which elicits salivation. This trial procedure is the one most frequently used in classical conditioning.

→

Unconditioned response (UCR). The unconditioned stimulus, food, elicits the unconditioned response, salivation, in Sam. Food and salivation are said to be unconditioned because the effect on Sam is inborn and not dependent on some prior training or learning.

Step 3. Testing for Conditioning

Only CS. After you have given Sam 10 to 100 trials, you will test for the occurrence of classical conditioning. You test by presenting the tone (conditioned stimulus) without showing Sam the food (unconditioned stimulus).

Conditioned stimulus. If Sam salivates when you present the tone alone, it means that the tone has become a conditioned stimulus.

A **conditioned stimulus,** or **CS,** is a formerly neutral stimulus that has acquired the ability to elicit a response that was previously elicited by the unconditioned stimulus.

In this example, the tone, an originally neutral stimulus, became the CS.

→

Conditioned response. When Sam salivates to the tone alone, this response is called the conditioned response.

The **conditioned response,** or **CR,** which is elicited by the conditioned stimulus, is similar to, but not identical in size or amount to, the unconditioned response.

One thing to remember is that the conditioned response is usually similar in appearance but smaller in amount or magnitude than the unconditioned response. This means that Sam's conditioned response will involve less salivation to the tone (conditioned stimulus) than to the food (unconditioned stimulus).

Predict. One question you may ask about classical conditioning is: What exactly did Sam learn during this procedure? One thing Sam learned was that the sound of a bell predicted the very likely occurrence of food (Rescorla, 1988). Classical conditioning helps animals and humans predict what's going to happen and thus provides information that may be useful for their survival (D. A. Lieberman, 2012).

Next, we'll use the concepts of classical conditioning to explain how Carla was conditioned to her dentist's aftershave.

MODULE 9 CLASSICAL CONDITIONING **197**

Unless otherwise noted, all images are © Cengage Learning

Integrated Custom Illustrations

Making a textbook that integrates visuals with every major concept is a massive endeavor. In fact, as authors, we spend as much time on the visual program as we do on the writing. We couldn't do this without the full support of our editorial team and the work of committed and talented photo researchers who won't stop short of finding the perfect photo. Thankfully, we have the privilege of having both.

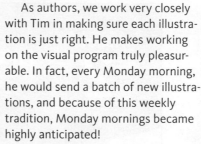

Threat to survival

Because we integrate visuals with written content to aid student learning, many times it is simply impossible to find a photo that clearly conveys a specific concept. Consequently, it is impossible to produce a text that effectively emphasizes visual learning without an extraordinarily talented illustrator, who can literally illustrate *anything* we request. We are truly fortunate to have found Tim Jacobus, an illustrator with phenomenal talent.

Humanistic approach

Tim Jacobus's work in our textbook was introduced in the 8th edition. Due to the tremendous amount of praise we received about his work, we continue to ask Tim to join us and he does in a big way. His illustrations can be found in abundance throughout the 10th edition; they include anatomy, faces, animals, objects, conceptual concepts, and so much more! In total, Tim has created nearly 300 original illustrations specifically for our textbook.

School shooter

As authors, we work very closely with Tim in making sure each illustration is just right. He makes working on the visual program truly pleasurable. In fact, every Monday morning, he would send a batch of new illustrations, and because of this weekly tradition, Monday mornings became highly anticipated!

We hope you find Tim's illustrations as amazing as we do. We are confident that your students will not only enjoy them but also learn psychological concepts easier and better because of them. Samples of Tim's illustrations are shown throughout this page, and his biography is below.

Underachiever

Elaborative rehearsal

Short-term memory

Biography of Tim Jacobus

Tim Jacobus began his art career in the early 1980s. He was taught as a traditional artist, and all of his early works were created utilizing pencils, acrylic paint, and brushes—foreign objects to most artists today.

Tim's early work was done entirely in the publishing field, designing and creating cover art. Specializing in fantasy and sci-fi work, he began to develop a style that is rich in color and extreme in depth. Tim received his greatest notoriety creating the cover art for the children's series *Goosebumps*.

After hundreds of covers, Tim broadened his scope to include the realm of digital art tools. The use of this medium helped to open a wider scope of work and subject matter, including medical illustration, character distortion, editorial concepts, and web-based animation.

Tim continues to create—unceasingly. ●

Olfaction

Adaptive theory of sleep

Artificial photoreceptors

Modules. One of the features best liked by both instructors and students is that the text is organized into smaller units called *modules,* which are shorter (20–30 pages) and more manageable than traditional chapters (45–50 pages). The 10th edition has 25 *modules* (see p. iv), which can easily be organized, omitted, or rearranged into any order. Because individual modules all have the same structure, each one can stand on its own.

Advantage. Instructors said that, compared to longer and more traditional chapters, they preferred the shorter *modules,* which allow greater flexibility in planning and personalizing one's course.

Example. The sample page on your left, which is the opening page of Module 2, Psychology & Science, shows that each *module* begins with an outline. In this outline, the heads are designated by letter (A. Answering Questions: Scientific Method) and provide students with an overview of the entire module.

Outline. Students can use the *module's* outline to organize their lecture notes as well as to find and review selected material.

MODULE
2 Psychology & Science

26

D Brain: Structures & Functions

Major Parts of the Brain

A human brain (right figure), which can easily be held in one hand, weighs about 1,350 grams, or 3 pounds, and has the consistency of firm JELL-O. The brain is protected by a thick skull and covered with thin, tough, plasticlike membranes. If shot in the head, a person may or may not die depending on which area was damaged. For example, damage to an area in the forebrain would result in paralysis, damage to an area in the midbrain would result in coma, but damage to an area in the hindbrain would certainly result in death.

Can someone be shot in the head but not die?

We'll begin our exploration of the brain by looking at its three major parts—forebrain, midbrain, and hindbrain—beginning with the forebrain.

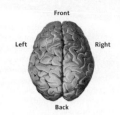
Front
Left   Right
Back

2 Midbrain

If a boxer is knocked unconscious, part of the reason lies in the midbrain.

The **midbrain** has a reward or pleasure center, which is stimulated by food, sex, money, music, attractive faces, and some drugs (cocaine); has areas for visual and auditory reflexes, such as automatically turning your head toward a noise; and contains the reticular formation, which arouses the forebrain so that it is ready to process information from the senses (Holroyd & Coles, 2002).

If the reticular formation were seriously damaged—by a blow to the head, for example—a person would be unconscious and might go into a coma because the forebrain could not be aroused (Bleck, 2007).

1 Forebrain

When you look at the brain, what you are actually seeing is almost all forebrain (figure above). The **forebrain**, which is the largest part of the brain, has right and left sides that are called hemispheres. The hemispheres, connected by a wide band of fibers, are responsible for an incredible number of functions, including learning and memory, speaking and language, having emotional responses, experiencing sensations, initiating voluntary movements, planning, and making decisions.

Side view of the brain's right hemisphere

The large structure outlined in orange to the left shows only the right hemisphere of the forebrain. The forebrain's right and left hemispheres are both shown in the figure at the top right. The forebrain is very well developed in humans.

3c Cerebellum

A person suspected of drunken driving may fail the test of rapidly touching a finger to the nose because of alcohol's effects on the cerebellum.

The **cerebellum**, which is located at the very back and underneath the brain, is involved in coordinating motor movements but not in initiating voluntary movements. The cerebellum is also involved in performing timed motor responses, such as those needed in playing games or sports, and in automatic or reflexive learning, such as blinking the eye to a signal, which is called classical conditioning (discussed in Module 9) (Gerwig et al., 2008).

3 Hindbrain

The structures and functions of the hindbrain, which are found in very primitive brains, such as the alligator's, have remained constant through millions of years of evolution. The **hindbrain** has three distinct structures: the pons, medulla, and cerebellum.

3a Pons

If someone has a serious sleep disorder, it may involve the pons. In Latin, *pons* means "bridge," which suggests its function.

The **pons** functions as a bridge to transmit messages between the spinal cord and brain. The pons also makes the chemicals involved in sleep (Monti et al., 2008).

3b Medulla

If someone dies of a drug overdose, the cause of death probably involved the medulla.

The **medulla**, which is located at the top of the spinal cord, includes a group of cells that control vital reflexes, such as respiration, heart rate, and blood pressure.

Large amounts of alcohol, heroin, or other depressant drugs suppress the functions of cells in the medulla and cause death by stopping breathing.

Because alcohol is a depressant drug and interferes with the functions of the cerebellum, an intoxicated person would experience decreased coordination and have difficulty rapidly touching a finger to the nose, which is one test for being drunk (Oscar-Berman & Marinkovic, 2007).

Of the brain's three parts, the forebrain is the largest, most evolved, and most responsible for an enormous range of personal, social, emotional, and cognitive behaviors. For those reasons, we'll examine the forebrain in more detail.

MODULE 4 INCREDIBLE NERVOUS SYSTEM 73

Visual learning. Many students who have used this text have commented that they are visual learners and that the visual layout of the text greatly helped them better understand and remember difficult concepts. The visual layout of this text involves two approaches: integrating text and graphics and using "chunking."

Text/graphic integration. Each of the 609 pages of this text has been individually formatted so that text and graphics are always integrated. An example of text/graphic integration is shown in the sample page on the right (Module 4). Students never have to search for a distant figure or graph because the text is always integrated with its related graphic.

Chunking. The second method used to help students better understand and remember the material is to break down difficult or complex concepts into smaller, more manageable "chunks." For example, in this sample page, the relatively complex structure and function of the major parts of the brain are broken down into a series of easily grasped smaller chunks or a series of steps.

Definitions. Finally, the sample page shows that students need never search for definitions because they are always **boldface and printed in blue.** Students need only look for **blue** words to easily find and review definitions.

Often-asked question. How many times have students asked, "What should I study for the test?" One way to answer this question is to tell students to complete the two built-in quizzes that appear in each module. One quiz is the *Concept Review* (shown here), and the second is the *Summary Test* (shown on p. xxxv).

Integrated approach. The sample page on the left shows a *Concept Review* (Module 16), which has the unique feature of repeating the graphics that were first linked to the major concepts discussed in the text. This repeated use of visual cues has been shown to increase the learning or encoding of information as well as to promote visual learning.

Reading versus knowing. One reason for including quizzes within the text is that students may think that they know the material because they have read it. However, studies show that students cannot judge how well they actually know the material unless they test their knowledge of specific information. The *Concept Review* serves as an interim checkpoint by giving students a chance to test their knowledge of major terms before nearing the end of the module.

Student feedback on the *Concept Review* has been very positive. Students like the visual learning approach of having the graphics integrated with the concepts, and they find that the *Concept Review* is a great way to test their knowledge.

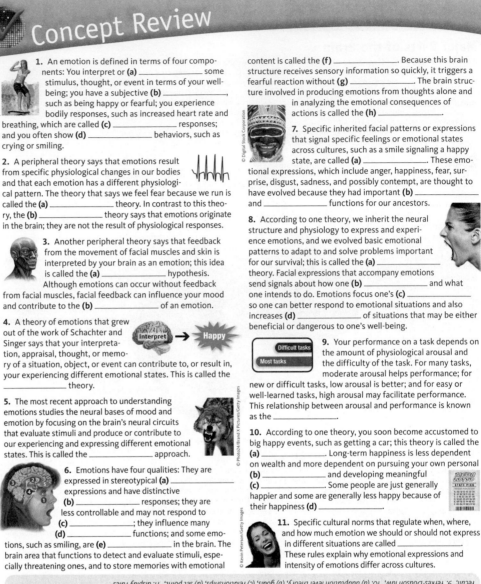

Concept Review

1. An emotion is defined in terms of four components: You interpret or **(a)** _____ some stimulus, thought, or event in terms of your well-being; you have a subjective **(b)** _____, such as being happy or fearful; you experience bodily responses, such as increased heart rate and breathing, which are called **(c)** _____ responses; and you often show **(d)** _____ behaviors, such as crying or smiling.

2. A peripheral theory says that emotions result from specific physiological changes in our bodies and that each emotion has a different physiological pattern. The theory that says we feel fear because we run is called the **(a)** _____ theory. In contrast to this theory, the **(b)** _____ theory says that emotions originate in the brain; they are not the result of physiological responses.

3. Another peripheral theory says that feedback from the movement of facial muscles and skin is interpreted by your brain as an emotion; this idea is called the **(a)** _____ hypothesis. Although emotions can occur without feedback from facial muscles, facial feedback can influence your mood and contribute to the **(b)** _____ of an emotion.

4. A theory of emotions that grew out of the work of Schachter and Singer says that your interpretation, appraisal, thought, or memory of a situation, object, or event can contribute to, or result in, your experiencing different emotional states. This is called the _____ theory.

5. The most recent approach to understanding emotions studies the neural bases of mood and emotion by focusing on the brain's neural circuits that evaluate stimuli and produce or contribute to our experiencing and expressing different emotional states. This is called the _____ approach.

6. Emotions have four qualities: They are expressed in stereotypical **(a)** _____ expressions and have distinctive **(b)** _____ responses; they are less controllable and may not respond to **(c)** _____; they influence many **(d)** _____ functions; and some emotions, such as smiling, are **(e)** _____ in the brain. The brain area that functions to detect and evaluate stimuli, especially threatening ones, and to store memories with emotional content is called the **(f)** _____. Because this brain structure receives sensory information so quickly, it triggers a fearful reaction without **(g)** _____. The brain structure involved in producing emotions from thoughts alone and in analyzing the emotional consequences of actions is called the **(h)** _____.

7. Specific inherited facial patterns or expressions that signal specific feelings or emotional states across cultures, such as a smile signaling a happy state, are called **(a)** _____. These emotional expressions, which include anger, happiness, fear, surprise, disgust, sadness, and possibly contempt, are thought to have evolved because they had important **(b)** _____ and _____ functions for our ancestors.

8. According to one theory, we inherit the neural structure and physiology to express and experience emotions, and we evolved basic emotional patterns to adapt to and solve problems important for our survival; this is called the **(a)** _____ theory. Facial expressions that accompany emotions send signals about how one **(b)** _____ and what one intends to do. Emotions focus one's **(c)** _____ so one can better respond to emotional situations and also increases **(d)** _____ of situations that may be either beneficial or dangerous to one's well-being.

9. Your performance on a task depends on the amount of physiological arousal and the difficulty of the task. For many tasks, moderate arousal helps performance; for new or difficult tasks, low arousal is better; and for easy or well-learned tasks, high arousal may facilitate performance. This relationship between arousal and performance is known as the _____.

10. According to one theory, you soon become accustomed to big happy events, such as getting a car; this theory is called the **(a)** _____. Long-term happiness is less dependent on wealth and more dependent on pursuing your own personal **(b)** _____ and developing meaningful **(c)** _____. Some people are just generally happier and some are generally less happy because of their happiness **(d)** _____.

11. Specific cultural norms that regulate when, where, and how much emotion we should or should not express in different situations are called _____. These rules explain why emotional expressions and intensity of emotions differ across cultures.

Answers: 1. (a) appraise, (b) feeling, (c) physiological, (d) observable; 2. (a) James-Lange, (b) Cannon-Bard; 3. (a) facial feedback, (b) intensity; 4. cognitive appraisal; 5. affective neuroscience; 6. (a) facial, (b) physiological, (c) reason, (d) cognitive, (e) hard-wired, (f) amygdala, (g) awareness or conscious thought, (h) prefrontal cortex; 7. (a) universal facial expressions, (b) adaptive, survival; 8. (a) evolutionary, (b) feels, (c) attention, (d) memory; 9. Yerkes-Dodson law; 10. (a) adaptation level theory, (b) goals, (c) relationships, (d) set point; 11. display rules

Unless otherwise noted, all images are © Cengage Learning

F Cultural Diversity: Differences in Episodic Memory

Euro-Americans Versus Asians

Do Asians have difficulty with episodic memory?

Cross-cultural research has found cultural differences in recalling episodic memories, which we discussed in Module 11 (see p. 246).

Episodic memory involves knowledge of specific events, personal experiences, or activities, such as naming or describing favorite restaurants, movies, songs, habits, or hobbies.

Compared to Asians, Euro-Americans have been reported to better recall autobiographical memories from childhood throughout the lifespan (Q. Wang et al., 2004; Q. Wang & Conway, 2004; Q. Wang & Ross, 2005).

There are several possible explanations for these cultural differences in episodic memory. Perhaps the importance of individuality and autonomy for Euro-Americans focuses their attention on retaining

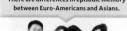

There are differences in episodic memory between Euro-Americans and Asians.

memories of life events that are associated with an individual's identity (e.g., winning a contest). In contrast, for Asians the importance of collectivism or relatedness may focus their attention on retaining more generic knowledge that is associated with their relationships with other people or their community (e.g., going to church every Sunday). Another proposed idea is that Asians may encode episodic memories as well as Euro-Americans but they have a faster rate of forgetting these memories over time.

One researcher closely examined the reasons for the differences in episodic memory between Euro-Americans and Asians (Q. Wang, 2009). We will discuss three of her studies next.

Study One

In the first study, Euro-American and Asian adults were asked to complete daily diaries for one week that listed all the events that happened to them. When participants completed this task and turned in their diaries, researchers gave them a surprise memory test by asking them to recall the events that happened during the past week (Recall 1). Then, a week later, researchers again surprised the participants by asking them to recall the events that happened to them during the week they kept their diaries (Recall 2).

Results showed that Euro-Americans recalled a greater number of specific events than did Asians at the time they turned in their diaries. The same results held true during Recall 1 and Recall 2. That is, Euro-Americans recalled a greater number of events following a one-week and a two-week delay.

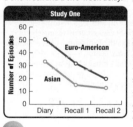

Study One

Study Two

In the second study, Euro-American and Asian adults were given a written diary kept by a fictional person during his travels. After participants read the diary, they were given another unrelated written task to complete in 5 minutes. Following this 5-minute task, participants were asked, without warning, to recall as many of the specific events from the fictional diary as they could.

Results found that in this immediate recall task in which the content is exactly the same for all participants, Euro-Americans recalled a greater number of specific events than did Asians. The results of this study are consistent with those of Study One and extend the findings by focusing on immediate recall (as opposed to recall at the end of the day, after one week, and after two weeks) and presenting all participants with the same content (as opposed to each participant having a unique set of life events to remember).

Study Two

Study Three

In the third study, Euro-American and Asian adults were given the same written diary used in Study Two, but this time they were asked to identify when one event ended and another event began. There was no recall task in this study. The aim was to determine whether Euro-Americans and Asians differ in their ability to perceive separate life events.

Results showed that Euro-Americans identified a greater number of specific events than did Asians. Asians may be more likely to perceive events as interconnected than Euro-Americans, who may tend to perceive events as being discrete or separate.

Study Three

Conclusions

Together, the findings from these three studies suggest that there are differences in perceptual and encoding processes between the two groups, as opposed to differences in the ability to remember. Asians may not be more forgetful than Euro-Americans, but rather they may perceive the world as having fewer discrete events and consequently remember fewer episodic memories.

Besides culture, other factors, such as the type of information having to be recalled, may also influence memory, as shown next in a study on recalling sexual history. ●

272 PART 6 MEMORY

Different viewpoints.

One goal of an Introductory Psychology course is to challenge and broaden students' viewpoints by providing information about other cultures. Because of their limited experience of other cultures, students may be unaware that similar behaviors are viewed very differently in other cultures. For this reason, each of the 25 modules includes a *Cultural Diversity* feature.

Example. In the sample page on the right, the *Cultural Diversity* feature (Module 12) describes differences in episodic memory between Euro-Americans and Asians.

Topics. Other *Cultural Diversity* topics include:

Module 1: Early Discrimination
Module 2: Use of Placebos
Module 4: Cultural Neuroscience
Module 7: Incidence of SAD
Module 8: Alcoholism Rates
Module 9: Conditioning Racial Prejudice
Module 15: Genital Cutting
Module 16: Emotions across Cultures
Module 17: Gender Roles
Module 21: Tibetan Monks
Module 22: Asian Anxiety Disorders
Module 24: Different Healer

The *Cultural Diversity* feature gives students a chance to see the world through very different eyes.

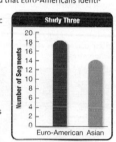

Feature. In teaching Introductory Psychology, an instructor's important but difficult goal is to explain how psychologists use a variety of research methods and techniques to answer questions. To reach this goal, each of the 25 modules includes a *Research Focus* that explains how psychologists answer questions through experiments, case studies, self-reports, and surveys.

Example. In the sample page on the left, the *Research Focus* (Module 8) explains how psychologists use research methods to examine the effects of meditation on school stress.

Topics. Other *Research Focus* topics include:

Module 2: ADHD Controversies

Module 3: What Is a Phantom Limb?

Module 5: Mind over Body?

Module 7: Circadian Preference

Module 10: Viewing Aggression

Module 12: Recalling Sexual History

Module 16: Emotional Intelligence

Module 17: Temperament

Module 19: Shyness

Module 20: 180-Degree Change

Module 22: School Shootings

Module 23: Exercise Versus Drugs

Each of the 25 modules includes a Research Focus, which discusses the research methods and techniques that psychologists use to answer questions.

B Research Focus: Meditation & School Stress

Transcendental Meditation

School stress is on the rise. A recent survey of college students' emotional health found that the percentage of students reporting good or above-average emotional health is at the lowest level in the past 25 years. Researchers find that college students are not the only ones experiencing poorer emotional health. Troubling rates of school stress are found in elementary, middle-school, and high-school students as well.

Can meditation lower school stress?

Stress can limit the ability of students to grow cognitively and psychologically. Stress in students is associated with negative school behaviors, such as absenteeism and violent behavior, and poor academic performance. The toll of stress extends to the physical body in serious ways, including increased risk for hypertension, obesity, and diabetes, which have become increasing concerns of children across the country. Stress has many other detrimental effects on our body, as we will discuss in Module 21.

Because of the association between high stress and poorer school performance and physical health, it is important to implement programs designed to lower school stress. Consequently, researchers wanted to assess the effectiveness of a stress-reduction program on school stress. They chose to use a well-established and popular type of meditation called transcendental meditation.

Transcendental meditation (TM) involves assuming a comfortable position, closing your eyes, and focusing your attention on repeating words or sounds that are supposed to help produce an altered state of consciousness.

TM is a fairly simple technique that allows the mind to experience a silent, yet awake state of consciousness. The practice of TM does not involve any changes in values, beliefs, religion, or lifestyle.

The question you might ask is: Can transcendental meditation really lower the alarming level of stress in students? This question brings us to one of the major uses of research: to evaluate the effectiveness of intervention programs that claim to change a person's well-being or behavior. Here's how and what researchers discovered when they evaluated the effectiveness of TM in easing school stress (Elder et al., 2011).

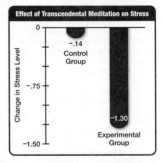

Transcendental meditation can help lower stress and produce an altered state of consciousness.

Methods and Procedures

Researchers selected 106 high-school students to participate in this study. The students were 16 to 18 years old, and there were approximately equal numbers of males and females. The students were selected from four public schools located in different areas of the country. The sample consisted of 87% racial and ethnic minorities. The researchers selected a sample with mostly racial and ethnic minority students because research data suggest that these students are at particularly high risk of experiencing school stress.

Students were divided into two groups: the experimental and control groups. The experimental group consisted of 68 students who were taught by a certified teacher how to practice TM. These students practiced TM twice a day for 10–15 minutes over a 4-month period. The control group consisted of 38 students who relaxed (such as sitting quietly or reading) but did not meditate. Stress levels were measured for all students before and after the 4-month intervention period.

Results and Conclusions

Researchers found that students in the experimental and control groups did not differ in their reported stress levels prior to beginning the intervention. Data collected after the intervention showed a clear difference between the two groups. The graph below shows a 36% reduction in stress in the students practicing TM, compared to those in the control group. The practice of TM was associated with a significant reduction in stress.

The intervention program used by these researchers teaches students a valuable skill they can use for the rest of their lives. The ongoing practice of TM is likely to continue having a positive influence on their cognitive, psychological, and physical health. TM is a fairly easy program to implement that helps improve the emotional health of students and that should thereby improve academic achievement.

Future research should extend these findings by examining the longer-term effects of TM, studying larger student samples in schools, and focusing on students of different ages, races, and ethnicities.

Next, we turn our attention to the use of drugs. ●

Effect of Transcendental Meditation on Stress

- Control Group: −.14
- Experimental Group: −1.30

Change in Stress Level: 0, −.75, −1.50

Unless otherwise noted, all images are © Cengage Learning

Application: Psychology's Practical Side

H Application: Experimental Treatments

Parkinson's Disease

Michael J. Fox is a talented actor who has starred in popular TV

Why do Michael's arms and legs shake?

series, such as *Family Ties* and *Spin City*, and numerous movies, including the *Back to the Future* trilogy. He was really good at his job until he noticed a twitch in his left pinkie (M. J. Fox, 2002). Within only 6 months, this twitch spread to his whole hand. Michael tried to conceal his symptoms from the public by using medication to calm his tremors, and he was successful doing so for the first

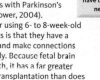

© AP Images/Charles Sykes

seven years (Dudley, 2006). However, it became increasingly difficult to hide his symptoms as he began having tremors that would shake his entire arm. Also, his legs would shake or become really stiff, making it difficult for him to walk. Eventually, these symptoms led Michael to quit his starring role in *Spin City* (Weinraub, 2000). Michael had all the symptoms of Parkinson's disease.

Parkinson's disease includes symptoms of tremors and shakes in the limbs, a slowing of voluntary movements, muscle stiffness, problems with balance and coordination, and feelings of depression. As the disease progresses, patients develop a peculiar walk and may suddenly freeze in space for minutes or hours at a time.

Michael's Parkinson's symptoms worsened because neurons in his **basal ganglia**, a group of structures located in the center of the brain that are involved in regulating movements, were running out of the neurotransmitter dopamine (see p. 55). Without a sufficient supply of dopamine in the basal ganglia, the brain loses its ability to control movement.

Like most Parkinson's patients, Michael was placed on a medication called L-dopa, which boosts the levels of dopamine in the brain, enabling him to have better control over his movements. Unfortunately, patients must take increasing amounts of L-dopa, and after prolonged use (5 to 10 years), L-dopa's beneficial effects may be replaced by unwanted jerky movements that may be as bad as those produced by Parkinson's disease (Mercuri & Bernardi, 2005). Even though Michael still takes medication, at times he has so little movement control that he cannot speak clearly, raise his arms from his side, or even smile (Dagostino, 2008). Yet, he continues to have an optimistic outlook on life and has not given up on his acting career (M. J. Fox, 2009). Most recently, he is starring in the TV drama *The Good Wife* (*People*, 2011).

In the United States, about 1.5 million adults, usually over the age of 50, have Parkinson's disease. In rare cases, such as Michael's, people are diagnosed with young-onset Parkinson's disease (Michael was only 30). To date, Parkinson's has no cure, but our knowledge of its causes, especially genetics, is continuously advancing and, as you'll see, several experimental treatments are under study (Kingwell, 2010; I. Martin et al., 2011; Mouradian, 2010).

Issues Involving Transplants

Human cells. As we learned above, the prolonged use of L-dopa to treat Parkinson's disease produces unwanted side effects. Because of these disappointing long-term results, researchers are investigating alternative

Why not just use drugs?

treatments, such as fetal brain tissue transplants. Previously, researchers had shown that when fetal rat brain tissue was transplanted into older rats, the fetal neurons lived, grew, functioned, and allowed brain damaged older rats to relearn the solutions to mazes (Shetty & Turner, 1996). Following successes in animal research, human fetal brain tissue has been transplanted into patients with Parkinson's disease (Roitberg & Kordower, 2004).

The primary reason for using 6- to 8-week-old fetal tissue for transplants is that they have a unique ability to survive and make connections in a patient's brain or body. Because fetal brain tissue is primed for growth, it has a far greater chance of survival after transplantation than does tissue from mature brains (Holden, 2002). More recently, researchers are exploring the use of stem cells to treat Parkinson's disease and spinal cord injuries.

Stem cells. About four days after a sperm has fertilized an egg, the resulting embryo, which is about the size of the period in this sentence (see p. 379), has divided and formed embryonic stem cells (shown below).

Stem cells have the amazing capacity to change into and become any one of the 220 types of cells that make up a human body, including skin, heart, liver, bones, and neurons.

The discovery of stem cells creates possibilities for treating various diseases. For example, when embryonic animal stem cells were transplanted into rats and mice with spinal cord injuries, the stem cells imitated the neighboring neurons and developed into new neurons that, in turn, helped the animals regain their lost functions (Wade, 2002). Some exciting news is that for the first time, surgeons have injected embryonic human stem cells into a patient with a spinal cord injury (Vergano, 2010a).

The use of human embryonic stem cells is controversial for ethical and political reasons. That's because these embryos, which are fertilized in laboratories and have the potential to develop into humans, are destroyed when the stem cells are removed. Because of these ethical and political problems, many scientists have turned to using **induced pluripotent stem cells (iPSCs)**, which are adult cells that have been genetically reprogrammed to be in an embryonic stem cell-like state (NIH, 2012).

There is much excitement in the scientific community about iPSCs, which, like embryonic stem cells, can turn into any type of cell in the body, but avoid the controversy. However, early research suggests that their effectiveness doesn't come close to that of embryonic stem cells (Choi, 2010; Kolata, 2010; Vergano, 2010b).

Next, we'll take a closer look at how fetal and stem cells are used in treating Parkinson's patients. We'll also learn about other experimental treatment options.

Embryonic stem cells have the ability to form new brain cells.

Real world. Students are very interested in how psychologists apply research findings and use basic principles to solve or treat real-life problems.

Example. In the sample page on the right, the **Application** (Module 3) describes the various experimental treatments available for Parkinson's disease, which include the use of human stem cells, a stereotaxic procedure to place tissue in the brain, removing part of the thalamus, and deep brain stimulation (pp. 60–61).

Topics. Other **Application** topics include:

The **Application** sections show the practical side of psychology—how psychological principles are applied to real-life situations.

Critical Thinking: Challenges Students' Minds

I Critical Thinking

Learning through Visuals

A large body of research indicates that visual cues help us to better retrieve and remember information. The research outcomes on visual learning make complete sense when you consider that our brain is mainly an image processor, not a word processor. In fact, the part of the brain used to process words is quite small in comparison to the part that processes visual images.

1 Which goal of psychology is illustrated by stating that visual learning makes sense given that our brains are mainly image processors?

2 Which area of specialization in psychology is best suited to understand how people learn through visuals?

Words are abstract and rather difficult for the brain to retain, whereas visuals are concrete and, as such, more easily remembered. To illustrate, think back to having to learn a set of new vocabulary words each week in school. Now, think back to the first kiss you had, the high school prom, or your 16th birthday party. Most likely, you had to expend great effort to remember the vocabulary words. In contrast, when you were actually having your first kiss, going to the prom, or celebrating your birthday, we bet you weren't trying to commit it to memory. Yet, you can quickly and effortlessly visualize these experiences. You can thank your brain's amazing visual processor for your ability to easily remember life experiences.

There are countless studies that have confirmed the power of visual imagery in learning. For instance, one study asked students to remember many groups of three words each, such as *dog, bike,* and *street.* Students who tried to remember the words by repeating them over and over again did poorly on recall. In comparison, students who made the effort to make visual associations with the three words, such as imagining a dog riding a bike down the street, had significantly better recall.

3 Which career setting is a psychologist who examines the effectiveness of visual learning most likely to be in?

Various types of visuals can be effective learning tools: photos, illustrations, icons, symbols, sketches, and figures, to name only a few. Consider how memorable the visual graphics are in logos, for example. You recognize the brand by seeing the visual graphic, even before reading the name of the brand. This type of visual can be so effective that Starbucks recently simplified its logo by dropping the printed name and keeping only the graphic image of the popular so-called mermaid (technically, it's a siren). We can safely assume that Starbucks Corporation must be keenly aware of how our brains have automatically and effortlessly committed the graphic image to memory.

So powerful is visual learning that we embrace it in the writing of this textbook. Each page of this textbook has been individually formatted to maximize visual learning. We believe the right visuals can help make abstract and difficult concepts more tangible and welcoming, as well as make learning more effective and long lasting. This is why we scrutinize every visual used in our writing to make sure it is paired with content in a clear, meaningful manner.

4 Which of the modern approaches to psychology is best suited to study how the brain performs during visual learning?

5 How do visual learning and academic performance relate to the definition of psychology?

As you see the visuals in this textbook, remember that, based on research outcomes, learning through visuals can decrease learning time, improve comprehension, enhance retrieval, and increase retention.

6 "Visual learning will improve academic performance" illustrates which goal of psychology?

Adapted from McDaniel & Einstein, 1986; Meier, 2000; Patton, 1991; Schacter, 1996; Verdi et al., 1997.

Summary Test

A Physical Development: Puberty

1. Girls and boys experience three major biological changes as they go through a period called **(a)** _____. For both girls and boys, one of these changes is the development of **(b)** _____ maturity, which for girls includes the first menstrual cycle, called **(c)** _____, and for boys includes the production of sperm. These physical changes in girls and boys are triggered by a portion of the brain called the **(d)** _____. A second change is the development of **(e)** _____ sexual characteristics, such as pubic hair and gender-specific physical changes. A third change is a surge in **(f)** _____ growth, especially height. The changes for girls tend to start about two years earlier than those for boys.

B Cognitive & Emotional Development

2. Piaget's fourth cognitive stage, which begins in adolescence and continues into adulthood, is called the **(a)** _____ stage. During this stage, adolescents and adults develop the ability to think about **(b)** _____ concepts, plan for the future, and solve abstract problems. One reason adolescents engage in more risky behaviors is that they have an underdeveloped **(c)** _____ but a fully functioning emotional center, called the **(d)** _____.

C Morality & Parenting

3. According to Kohlberg's theory, moral reasoning can be classified into three levels, and everyone progresses through the levels in the same order. However, not all adults reach the higher stages. The first level, the **(a)** _____ level, has two stages. In stage 1, moral decisions are determined primarily through fear of punishment, while at stage 2 they are guided by satisfying one's self-interest. The second level, the **(b)** _____ level, also has two stages. In the first of these, stage 3, people conform to the standards of others they value; in stage 4, they conform to the laws of society. In the third level, the **(c)** _____ level, moral decisions are made after thinking about all the alternatives and striking a balance between human rights and the laws of society.

4. Making impersonal moral decisions, such as keeping the money found in a stranger's wallet, involves areas of the brain associated with retrieving **(a)** _____. In comparison, making personal moral decisions, such as keeping the money found in a fellow worker's wallet, involves areas of the brain associated with **(b)** _____.

5. Parenting styles affect many aspects of adolescents' development. Parents who attempt to shape and control their children in accordance with a set standard of conduct are termed **(a)** _____. Parents who attempt to direct their children's activities in a rational and intelligent way and are supportive, loving, and committed are called **(b)** _____. Parents who are less controlling and behave with a nonpunishing and accepting attitude toward their children's impulses are called **(c)** _____.

D Personality & Social Development

There are 30 million of us.

6. How you describe yourself, including your values, goals, traits, interests, and motivations, is a function of your sense of **(a)** _____ which is part of the problem to be faced in stage 5 of Erikson's eight **(b)** _____ stages. Those who are unsuccessful in resolving the problems of this stage will experience **(c)** _____, which results in low self-esteem, and may become socially withdrawn.

7. An adolescent's feeling of worth, attractiveness, and social competence is called _____, which is influenced particularly by physical appearance, social acceptability, and management of public behaviors (anxiety and stress).

8. The challenges of adulthood are covered in the last three of Erikson's eight **(a)** _____ stages. According to his theory, in stage 6, young adults face the problems of intimacy versus **(b)** _____. In stage 7, middle adults face problems of generativity versus **(c)** _____. In stage 8, older adults reflect on their lives; if they feel positive and content about how they lived and what they accomplished, they will have a feeling of satisfaction or **(d)** _____; if not, they will have a feeling of regret and **(e)** _____.

F Gender Roles, Love & Relationships

9. During childhood and adolescence, males and females experience pressures and expectations from parents, peers, and society to behave in different ways. These expected patterns of behavior and thought, called _____, influence cognitive, personality, and social development.

MODULE 18 ADOLESCENCE & ADULTHOOD   **429**

Problem. How often have you heard students say, "I read the material three times but still did poorly on the test"? The problem is that students may think they know the material because they have a general idea of what they have read. However, researchers found that students are poor judges of how well they really know material unless they test themselves on specific questions.

Remembering. The sample page on the left shows part of the *Summary Test* (Module 18), which gives students a chance to test their knowledge by answering specific questions. The reason the *Summary Test* (and the *Concept Review*) uses fill-in-the-blank questions instead of multiple choice is that fill-in-the-blank questions require recall, while multiple-choice questions require only recognition. Thus, fill-in-the-blank questions are a better test of a student's memory.

Two tests. Each module contains two tests. The first is the *Concept Review* (discussed on p. xxx), which occurs toward the end of each module and allows students to test their knowledge of major concepts.

The second is the *Summary Test,* which occurs at the end of each module and allows students to check their knowledge of the entire module. Students' comments indicate that they like the *Summary Test* because it's a great way to review all the material.

Links to Learning: More Opportunities

Links to Learning offers students the following opportunities:

Key Terms/Key People allows students to check and review all the important concepts in the module.

Psychology CourseMate provides students with an interactive eBook, glossaries, flashcards, quizzes, videos, and more.

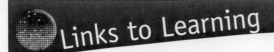 Links to Learning

Key Terms/Key People

achievement need, 348
AIDS, 345
androgens, 339
anorexia nervosa, 353
arousal theory, 330
binge-eating disorder, 353
biological hunger factors, 334, 335
biological needs, 332
biological sex factors, 338
biosocial theory, 342
bisexual orientation, 341
body mass index (BMI), 334
bulimia nervosa, 353
central cues, 335
cognitive factors in motivation, 350
double standard for sexual behavior, 342
estrogens, 339
evolutionary theory, 342

extrinsic motivation, 331, 350
fat cells, 335, 336
fear of failure, 349
fixed action pattern, 330
gender dysphoria, 340
gender identity, 340
gender identity disorder, 340
gender roles, 341
genetic hunger factors, 334, 336
genetic sex factors, 338
genital cutting, 346
heterosexual orientation, 341
high need for achievement, 348
HIV positive, 345
homosexual orientation, 341
hypothalamus, 335, 339
incentives, 331
inhibited female orgasm, 344
instincts, 330
interactive model of sexual orientation, 341

intestines, 335
intrinsic motivation, 331, 350
Klinefelter's syndrome, 339
lateral hypothalamus, 335
liver, 335
maintenance program, 352
Maslow's hierarchy of needs, 332, 333
metabolic rate, 336, 352
motivation, 329
obesity, 334
optimal or ideal weight, 334
organic factors, 344
paraphilias, 344
peripheral cues, 335
premature or rapid ejaculation, 344
psychological factors, 344
psychological sex factors, 338, 340

psychosocial hunger factors, 334, 337
reward/pleasure center, 330
self-determination theory, 331
self-handicapping, 349
sensation seeker, 330
set point, 336, 352
sex chromosome, 338
sex hormones, 339
sexual dysfunctions, 344
sexual orientation, 341
social needs, 332, 348
stomach, 335
Thematic Apperception Test, or TAT, 348
underachievers, 349
ventromedial hypothalamus, 335
weight-regulating genes, 336
Yerkes-Dodson law, 330

Media Resources

Go to **CengageBrain.com** to access Psychology CourseMate, where you will find an interactive eBook, glossaries, flashcards, quizzes, videos, answers to Critical Thinking questions, and more. You can also access Virtual Psychology Labs, an interactive laboratory experience designed to illustrate key experiments first-hand.

Supplements

The 10th edition of *Introduction to Psychology* is accompanied by a wide array of supplements developed to create the best teaching and learning experience inside as well as outside the classroom, in part by extending the book's visual approach to its supplemental materials. All of the continuing supplements have been thoroughly revised and updated, and some new supplements have been added. Cengage Learning prepared the following descriptions. We invite you to start taking full advantage of the teaching and learning tools available to you by reading this overview. Please contact your local representative if you would like copies of any of the following supplements.

Instructor's Resource Manual
1-285-17801-1

Written by Kelly Bouas Henry of Missouri Western State University, the manual includes teaching tips for new instructors, module outlines, student projects, suggested videos and films, handouts, and more.

Test Bank
1-285-17804-2

Written by Jason Spiegelman of Community College of Baltimore County, this test bank includes 150 multiple-choice, 25 true/false, and 10 short answer questions per module. Also available in Exam-View electronic format.

PowerLecture with ExamView
1-285-17737-3

This one-stop digital library and presentation tool includes preassembled Microsoft® PowerPoint® lecture slides. In addition to a full Instructor's Manual and Test Bank, PowerLecture also includes ExamView® testing software with all the test items from the printed Test Bank in electronic format, enabling you to create customized tests in print or online, and all of your media resources in one place including an image library with graphics from the book itself and videos.

CourseMate
1-285-17796-7

Psychology CourseMate is a valuable online learning resource for your students. It includes an interactive eBook and interactive teaching and learning tools such as quizzes, flashcards, videos, and more. Engagement Tracker, a first-of-its-kind tool, monitors student engagement in the course.

WebTutor on WebCT or Blackboard

Jumpstart your course with customizable, rich, text-specific content within your Course Management System. Whether you want to Web-enable your class or put an entire course online, WebTutor™ delivers. WebTutor™ offers a wide array of resources including access to the eBook, glossaries, flashcards, quizzes, videos, and more.

Guide to Wadsworth Videos for Introductory Psychology

Please contact your local representative if you would like to receive copies of any of the following videos:

ABC® DVD: Introduction to Psychology
Volume 1: 0-495-50306-1
Volume 2: 0-495-59637-X
Volume 3: 0-495-60490-9

ABC Videos feature short, high-interest clips from current news events as well as historic raw footage going back 40 years. Perfect to start discussion or to enrich your lectures and spark interest in the material in the text, these brief videos provide students with a new lens through which to view the past and present, one that will greatly enhance their knowledge and understanding of significant events and open up new dimensions in learning. Clips are taken from such programs as "World News Tonight," "Good Morning America," and "Nightline," as well as numerous ABC News specials and material from the Associated Press Television News and British Movietone News collections.

Wadsworth Psychology: Research in Action
Volume 1: 0-495-60490-9
Volume 2: 0-495-59813-5

The *Research in Action* video collections feature the work of research psychologists to give students an opportunity to learn about cutting-edge research—not just who is doing it, but also how it is done, and how and where the results are being used. By taking students into the laboratories of both established and up-and-coming researchers, and by showing research results being applied outside of the laboratory, these videos offer insight into both the research process and the many ways in which real people's lives are affected by research in the fields of psychology and neuroscience.

Psych in Film
0-618-27530-4

PSYCH IN FILM® DVD contains 35 clips from Universal Studios films, illustrating key concepts in psychology. Film clips are combined with commentary and discussion questions to help bring psychology alive for students and demonstrate its relevance to contemporary life and culture. Teaching tips are correlated with specific text chapters and concepts and are available on the instructor website.

Wadsworth Guest Lecture Series
0-547-00401-X

The Guest Lecture Series features many talented teachers sharing their teaching tips and best practices on a wide range of topics, including: Rational Emotive Behavior Theory, Blogging as an Effective Tool, How to Teach Writing in Psychology, and more.

Reviewers & Many Thanks

We especially want to thank the many reviewers who put in an amazing amount of time and energy to consider and comment on various aspects of this textbook.

We would like to explain why we were not able to include all your valuable suggestions.

Sometimes your suggestions were great but required inserting material for which there simply was no room.

Other times, one reviewer might suggest changing something that another reviewer really liked, so we tried to work out the best compromise.

Still other times, reviewers forcefully argued for entirely different points so that we felt like the proverbial starving donkey trying to decide which way to turn between two stacks of hay.

For all these reasons, we could not make all your suggested changes but we did give them a great deal of thought and used as many as we possibly could.

We do want each reviewer to know that his or her efforts were invaluable in the process of revising and developing a textbook. If it were within our power, we would triple your honorariums and give you each a year-long sabbatical.

Glen Adams, Harding University
Nelson Adams, Winston-Salem State University
Marlene Adelman, Norwalk Community Technical College
Aneeq Ahmad, Henderson State University
Edward Aronow, Montclair State University
Irwin Badin, Montclair State University
George Bagwell, Colorado Mountain College–Alpine Campus
Roger Bailey, Southwestern College
Susan Barnett, Northwestern State University
Beth Barton, Coastal Carolina Community College
Beth Benoit, University of Massachusetts–Lowell
John B. Benson, Texarcana College
Joan Bihun, University of Colorado at Denver
Kristen Biondolillo, Arkansas State University
Angela Blankenship, Halifax Community College
Pamela Braverman Schmidt, Salem State College
William T. Brown, Norwalk Community College
Linda Brunton, Columbia State Community College
Alison Buchanan, Henry Ford Community College
Lawrence Burns, Grand Valley State University
Ronald Caldwell, Blue Mountain Community College
James Calhoun, University of Georgia
Peter Caprioglio, Middlesex Community Technical College
Donna M. Casperson, Harrisburg Area Community College
Ili Castillo, Houston Community College
Hank Cetola, Adrian College
Larry Christensen, Salt Lake Community College
Saundra K. Ciccarelli, Gulf Coast Community College
Gerald S. Clack, Loyola University
J. Craig Clarke, Salisbury State University
Randy Cole, Piedmont Technical College
Jay Coleman, University of South Carolina, Columbia
Richard T. Colgan, Bridgewater State College
Lorry J. Cology, Owens Community College
Laurie Corey, Westchester Community College
Rita A. Creason, Campbellsville University
Shaunna Crossen, Penn State University, Berk-Lehigh Valley College
Sandy Deabler, North Harris College
Paul H. Del Nero, Towson State University
Julile P. Dilday, Halifax Community College
Bradley Donohue, University of Nevada, Las Vegas
Michael Durnam, Adams State College
Laura Duvall, Heartland Community College
Jean Edwards, Jones County Junior College
Tami Eggleston, McKendree College

Nolen Embry-Bailey, Bluegrass Community and Technical College
Charles H. Evans, LaGrange College
Melissa Faber, Lima Technical College
Mike Fass, Miami-Dade Community College, North Campus
Diane Feibel, Raymond Walters College
Bob Ferguson, Buena Vista University
Michael Firmin, Cedarville University
Rita Flattley, Pima Community College
Mary Beth Foster, Purdue University
Jan Francis, Santa Rosa Junior College
Joyce Frey, Pratt Community College
Meredith C. Frey, Otterbein College
Grace Galliano, Kennesaw State College
John T. Garrett, Texas State Technical College
Robert Gates, Cisco Junior College
Andrew Getzfeld, New Jersey City University
Marjan Ghahramanlou, The Community College of Baltimore, Catonsville
Kendra Gilds, Lane Community College
Philip Gray, D'Youville College
Troianne Grayson, Florida Community College at Jacksonville, South Campus
Charles M. Greene, Florida Community College at Jacksonville
Mike Grevlos, Southeast Technical Institute
Lynn Haller, Morehead State University
Chuck Hallock, Pima Community College
Verneda Hamm Baugh, Kean University
Bill Hardgrave, Aims Community College
Sheryl Hartman, Miami-Dade Community College
Matthew W. Hayes, Winthrop University
Roger Hock, Mendocino College
Steven J. Hoekstra, Kansas Wesleyan University
Quentin Hollis, Bowling Green Community College
Debra Lee Hollister, Valencia Community College
Donna Holmes, Becker College
Tonya Honeycutt, Johnson County Community College
Lucinda Hutman, Elgin Community College
Terry Isbell, Northwestern State University
Wendy Jefferson-Jackson, Montgomery College
Charles Jeffreys, Seattle Central Community College
Eleanor Jones, Tidewater Community College
Linda V. Jones, PhD, Blinn College
Joanne Karpinen, Hope College
Stan Kary, St. Louis Community College at Florissant Valley
Paul Kasenow, Henderson Community College

Don Kates, College of DuPage
Mark Kavanaugh, Kennebec Community College
Mark Kelland, Lansing Community College
Arthur D. Kemp, PhD, Central Missouri State University
Richard Kirk, Texas State Technical College
Dan Klaus, Community College of Beaver City
Gail Knapp, Mott Community College
John C. Koeppel, University of Southern Mississippi
Jan Kottke, California State University–San Bernardino
Joan Krueger, Harold Washington College
Matthew Krug, Wisconsin Lutheran College
Doug Krull, Northern Kentucky University
Diane J. Krumm, College of Lake County
Raymond Launier, Santa Barbara City College
Kristen Lavallee, Penn State University
Eamonn J. Lester, St. Philips College
Irv Lichtman, Houston Community College
John Lindsay, Georgia College & State University
Alan Lipman, Georgetown University
Karsten Look, Columbus State Community College
Jerry Lundgren, Flathead Valley Community College
Linda V. Jones, PhD, Blinn College
Frank MacHovec, Rappahannock Community College
Sandra Madison, Delgado Community College
Laura Madson, New Mexico State University
Ernest Marquez, Elgin Community College
Peter Matsos, Riverside Community College
Ann McCloskey, Landmark College
Grant McLaren, Edinboro University
Mary Lee Meiners, San Diego Miramar College
Diane Mello-Goldner, Pine Manor College
Laurence Miller, Western Washington University
Lesley Annette Miller, Triton College
Malcolm Miller, Fanshawe College
Gloria Mitchell, De Anza College
Alinde Moore, Ashland University
Therese Nemec, Fox Valley Technical College
John T. Nixon, SUNY–Canton
Peggy Norwood, Community College of Aurora
Art Olguin, Santa Barbara City College
Carol Pandey, Pierce College
Christine Panyard, University of Detroit Mercy
Jeff Parsons, Rockefeller University
Ron Payne, San Joaquin Delta College
Bob Pellegrini, San Jose State University
Julie Penley, El Paso Community College
Judith Phillips, Palomar College
James Previte, Victor Valley College
Joan Rafter, Hudson Community College
Robert R. Rainey, Jr., Florida Community College at Jacksonville
Chitra Ranganathan, Framingham State College
Lillian Range, University of Southern Mississippi
Joseph Reish, Tidewater Community College
S. Peter Resta, Prince George's Community College
Melissa Riley, University of Mississippi
Vicki Ritts, St. Louis Community College, Meramac
Bret Roark, Oklahoma Baptist University
Ann E. Garrett Robinson, Gateway Community Technical College
John Roop, North Georgia College and State University

Matt Rossano, Southeastern Louisiana University
John Santelli, Fairleigh Dickinson University
Harvey Schiffman, Rutgers University Piscataway Campus
Michael Schuller, Fresno City College
Alan Schultz, Prince George's Community College
Robert Schultz, Fulton Montgomery Community College
Debra Schwiesow, Creighton University
Harold Siegel, Rutger's University Newark Campus
N. Clayton Silver, University of Nevada, Las Vegas
Kimberly Eretzian Smirles, Emmanuel College
James Spencer, West Virginia State College
Deborah Steinberg, Jefferson Community College
Mark Stewart, American River College
Kimberly Stoker, Holmes Community College
Julie Stokes, California State University–Fullerton
Ted Sturman, University of Southern Maine
Clayton N. Tatro, Garden City Community College
Annette Taylor, University of San Diego
Clayton Teem, Gainesville College
Andy Thomas, Tennessee Technical University
Cicilia Ivonne Tjoefat, Rochester Community and
    Technical College
Larry Till, Cerritos College
Daniel J. Tomasulo, New Jersey City University
Susan Troy, Northeast Iowa Community College
Deborah Van Marche, Glendale Community College
Jane Vecchio, Holyoke Community College
Randy Vinzant, Hinds Community College
Jeff Wachsmuth, Napa Valley College
Benjamin Wallace, Cleveland State University
James Ward, Western New England College
Janice Weaver, Ferris State University
Stephen P. Weinert, Cuyamaca College
Mary Scott West, Virginia Intermont College
Fred W. Whitford, Montana State University
John Whittle, Northern Essex Community College
Ellen Williams, Mesa Community College
Melissa Wright, The Victoria College
Matthew J. Zagumny, Tennessee Technological University
Gene Zingarelli, Santa Rosa Community College

Special help on the 10th edition:

Linda Alvira, Rockland Community College
Mary Beth Mitchel, Purdue University, North Central
Pamela Auburn, University of Houston, Downtown
William Burgan, Columbus Technical College
Douglas McHugh, Indiana University
Rachel Hemphill, Kent State University
Amber Chenoweth, Hiram College
Scott Cohn, Western State College of Colorado
Cheree Madison, Lanier Technical College
Patrice M. Olsenc, Humphreys College
Deborah Miller, The Ohio State University at Newark
Henry Pomerantz, Sussex County Community College
Stacey Williams, Southern Polytechnic State University
Tawnda Bickford, Hennepin Technical College
Richard G. Kensinger, Mount Aloysius College
Angelica (Kelly) Rea, Costal Bend College
Sue Leung, Portland Community College

Acknowledgments & Many Thanks

After more than 20 years of working on my own, I decided that it was time to cut back on my workload and take on a coauthor for my 8th edition. The coauthor I chose has such unique qualifications that if I had told you about them, you might have thought I made them up. For that reason, I will let my coauthor, Haig Kouyoumdjian, tell you his own story and, after reading it, you will understand why he is so ideally and perfectly suited for this project (even though I still have trouble pronouncing his name).

—Rod Plotnik

When I took my first college psychology class at Diablo Valley College, I used *Introduction to Psychology* by Rod Plotnik. I can still recall the many conversations I had with peers and family members sharing the fascinating stories I read about and my overall enthusiasm for the textbook. For the first time ever, I did the unimaginable; that is, I began reading ahead because I was impatient to read the next great story and learn the next interesting concept. Plotnik's text sparked my interest in psychology, and I went on to pursue a Bachelor of Science degree at Saint Mary's College of California, a liberal arts college in the San Francisco Bay Area.

My interest in psychology continued to deepen while in college, and I went on to receive a Master of Arts degree in psychology at San Diego State University, where I had the unique experience of working closely with Rod Plotnik, a professor in the department and supervisor of the graduate teaching associates training program. Under Plotnik's close supervision, I began teaching Introduction to Psychology courses at the university using his textbook.

Following my education and training at San Diego State University, I attended University of Nebraska–Lincoln, where I received a PhD in Clinical Psychology. While there, I continued to teach Introduction to Psychology courses using Plotnik's text.

After receiving my PhD, I worked in a clinical setting providing mental health services to youths, adults, and families, and continued to teach undergraduate psychology courses. Most recently, I was a full-time faculty member at Mott Community College in Flint, Michigan.

My teaching experiences have strengthened my interest in the practice and study of teaching. I especially enjoy stimulating students by using visual learning approaches, such as breaking educational content into small, meaningful chunks of information and presenting visual cues to help students better process, retrieve, and remember information.

Rod Plotnik's influence on my interest in psychology began when I read his textbook as an undergraduate and developed as he trained me in how to become an effective instructor and later carefully guided me through revisions of this text. It is with much appreciation and pleasure that I help to continue his vision in *Introduction to Psychology*.

—Haig Kouyoumdjian

In revising the 10th edition, I worked with a remarkable group of creative and talented people, each of whom deserves special thanks.

Executive Editor. This edition continued to benefit from Jaime Perkins, who believes in the vision of this textbook and supported major updates to its content, design, and visual program to make this edition the best it could possibly be. This textbook would not be where it is now without the past support from Vicki Knight.

Developmental Editors. New to the team are Trina McManus and Tangelique Williams, who both skillfully coordinated many aspects of this revision. But, more important, they supported my vision while making valuable contributions that took the textbook beyond my aim. The content and visual program of this edition benefited tremendously from the attention to detail and sharp visual sense of Trina McManus.

Designers. As always, Vernon Boes does excellent work as our senior art director. Picture Mosaic is the creative team that did the wonderful cover image, Cheryl Carrington did a fantastic cover design, and Diane Beasley provided our new interior design, which so perfectly captures the personality of the textbook.

Concept Illustrator. Once again Tim Jacobus had a vital role in making this textbook visually breathtaking. He is incredibly talented and knows exactly what this textbook needs.

Photo and Text Researcher. New to this edition is the talented Terri Wright, who helped us find about 600 new photos that truly enhanced the visual learning focus of this book. I am very thankful for her patience and determination to find just the right photos, which can be quite time-consuming.

Manuscript Editor. We continued to have the best manuscript editor ever in Carol Reitz, whose editorial skills really did improve the book.

Production. Keeping track of everything at Cengage Learning were Pat Waldo and Carol Samet, who both made sure that everything got done on time and was where it should be. Paige Larkin of diacriTech made sure the individual pages were turned into a complete book. Paige's work is exceptional. The first-pass pages she presents to us could be mistaken for final pages…they are that good! Her strong sense for design and layout helped to make this book so visually appealing.

Sales. I have been fortunate to continue to have Liz Rhoden take the lead in marketing this book. She makes sure that all sales representatives know what the book is about and how to describe it to potential adopters. She is really committed to continuing the success of this book.

And finally… Writing a textbook inevitably asks family members to make sacrifices for an extended period of time. There is absolutely no way I could have revised this textbook without their help and understanding. My two lovely daughters, Sosi and Ani, were great at giving their baba quiet time in his office as well as spoiling me with plenty of hugs and laughs when I needed them the most. A special thank you to my wife, Zepure, who has a demanding medical career and yet somehow managed to find the time and energy to take care of many of my family responsibilities to allow me to focus on writing. She demonstrated as much of a commitment to the quality of this revision as I did.

—Haig Kouyoumdjian

Unless otherwise noted, all images are © Cengage Learning

To the Student: A Different Kind of Textbook

Looks different. This textbook looks different because it uses visual learning techniques, such as breaking material into smaller units and integrating text and graphics. Every definition is boldface and printed in **blue** so that you can identify it easily.

Concept Review. This is a test of how well you remember some of the key concepts. As you fill in the blanks of the Concept Review, you'll be learning important terms and concepts.

Critical Thinking. Near the end of each module are several Critical Thinking questions about an interesting newspaper article.

Summary Test. This lets you check how well you remember the material from the entire module. Taking the Summary Test is also an excellent way to review all the major terms discussed in the module.

Key Terms/Key People. There's a list of key terms/people (with page numbers) at the end of each module.

B Neurons: Structure & Function

Parts of the Neuron

Why could Charles think, move, and talk?

Before Charles developed Alzheimer's disease, he was able to engage in an incredible variety of cognitive and physical behaviors. He was able to think, remember, walk, smile, and speak—all because of the activity of millions of microscopic brain cells called neurons. We'll examine the neuron, which comes in many wondrous shapes and sizes and has only three basic structures—cell body, dendrites, and axon.

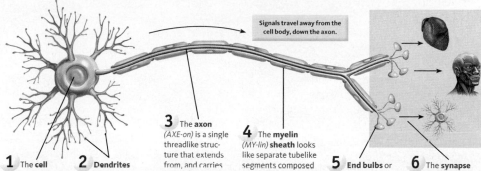

Signals travel away from the cell body, down the axon.

1 The **cell body** (or soma) is a relatively large, egg-shaped structure that provides fuel, manufactures chemicals, and maintains the entire neuron in working order.

In the center of the cell body is a small oval shape representing the nucleus, which contains genetic instructions (in the form of DNA) for both the manufacture of chemicals and the regulation of the neuron.

2 **Dendrites** *(DEN-drites)* are branchlike extensions that arise from the cell body; they receive signals from other neurons, muscles, or sense organs and pass these signals to the cell body.

At the time of birth, a neuron has few dendrites. After birth, dendrites undergo dramatic growth that accounts for much of the increase in brain size. As dendrites grow, they make connections and form communication networks between neurons and other cells or organs.

3 The **axon** *(AXE-on)* is a single threadlike structure that extends from, and carries signals away from, the cell body to neighboring neurons, organs, or muscles.

Here the axon is indicated by an orange line inside the tube composed of separate gray segments. Axons vary in length from less than a hair's breadth to as long as 3 feet (from your spinal cord to your toes). An axon conducts electrical signals to a neighboring organ (heart), a muscle, or another neuron.

4 The **myelin** *(MY-lin)* **sheath** looks like separate tubelike segments composed of fatty material that wraps around and insulates an axon. The myelin sheath prevents interference from electrical signals generated in adjacent axons and helps signals travel much faster through the axon.

The axons of most large neurons, including motor neurons, have myelin sheaths. You may have heard the brain described as consisting of gray and white matter. Gray is the color of cell bodies, while white is the color of myelin sheaths.

5 **End bulbs** or **terminal bulbs** look like tiny bubbles that are located at the extreme ends of the axon's branches. Each end bulb is like a miniature container that stores chemicals called neurotransmitters, which are used to communicate with neighboring cells.

End bulbs reach right up to, but do not physically touch, the surface of a neighboring organ (heart), muscle (head), or another cell body.

6 The **synapse** *(SIN-apse)* is an infinitely small space (20–30 billionths of a meter) that exists between an end bulb and its adjacent body organ (heart), muscles (head), or cell body.

When stimulated by electrical signals from the axon, the end bulbs eject neurotransmitters into the synapse. The neurotransmitters cross the synapse and act like switches to turn adjacent cells on or off. Below we'll take a closer look at the synapse.

Synapse: Close-up look. The right figure shows a close-up look of a synapse (small space) between the end bulb of one neuron (top) and the dendrites of an adjacent neuron (bottom). When stimulated, the end bulbs eject neurotransmitters (orange circles) that cross the synapse and act to either excite (turn on) or inhibit (turn off) adjacent cells. Later in the module, we'll discuss this process in more detail and describe several important neurotransmitters (see p. 54).

We have discussed the structure and function of neurons, but it is important not to confuse neurons (in your brain and spinal cord) with nerves (in your body). ●

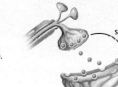

Synapse

Growing Up in a Strange World

When Donna was about 3 years old, she ate lettuce because she liked rabbits and they ate lettuce. She ate jelly because it looked like colored glass and she liked to look at colored glass.

Why did Donna avoid social interaction?

She was told to make friends, but Donna had her own friends. She had a pair of green eyes named Willie, which hid under her bed, and wisps, which were tiny, transparent spots that hung in the air around her.

When people spoke, their words were strange sounds with no meaning, like mumble jumble. Donna did learn the sounds of letters and how they fit together to make words. Although she didn't learn the meanings of words, she loved their sounds when she said them out loud. As a child, she was tested for deafness because she did not use language like other children. She did not learn that words had meaning until she was a teenager.

When people talked to Donna, especially people with loud or excited voices, she heard only "blah, blah, blah." Overstimulation caused Donna to stare straight ahead and appear to be frozen. Donna later called this state "involuntarily anesthetized."

Donna was in and out of many schools because she failed her exams, refused to take part in class activities, walked out of classes she didn't like, and sometimes threw things. When Donna did make a friend, she tried to avoid getting a friendly hug, which made her feel as if she were burning up inside and going to faint. (D. Williams, 1992). Donna Williams had symptoms of autism.

Autism is marked by especially abnormal or impaired development in social interactions, such as hiding to avoid people, not making eye contact, and not wanting to be touched. Autism is marked by difficulties in communicating, such as grave problems in developing spoken language or in initiating conversations. Individuals with autism are characterized by having very few activities and interests, spending long periods repeating the same behaviors, or following the same rituals. Signs of autism usually appear when a child is 2 or 3 years old (American Psychiatric Association, 2000).

Although it was once thought to be a rare disorder, estimates of autism disorders are now as high as 1 in every 110 births. Autism affects 3 to 4 times as many boys as girls, occurs in all parts of the world, and is thought to be 10 times more prevalent now than it was 20 years ago (CDC, 2009; NICHD, 2005).

Some parents blamed the increase in autism on childhood vaccinations, but after a thorough investigation, a U.S. federal court ruled this is not true (USCFC, 2009). More recently, the original research study linking vaccines to autism, and consequently spreading fear worldwide, was declared "an elaborate fraud" after it was discovered the researcher falsified data (Godlee et al., 2011). The most probable explanation for the increase in autism is better awareness on the part of doctors and parents as well as various environmental and genetic factors (Durand, 2011; Hall-mayer et al., 2011; Kogan et al., 2009; Pinto et al., 2010).

Though researchers have made great strides in understanding the genetic links to autism, they report there is still much to learn and there are likely to be hundreds of genetic factors involved (Gaidos, 2010; Schaaf & Zoghbi, 2011).

A very small percentage of individuals with autism are called *savants* because they have incredible math skills, spatial abilities, musical talent, or near picture-perfect memory. For example, one savant memorized 7,600 books; another plays 7,000 songs; another lists world events that happened on any given day; another performs amazing calculations, such as doubling 8,388,628 twenty-four times in only seconds (answer: 140,737,488,355,328) (D. S. Fox, 2009; Treffert, 2006; Treffert & Wallace, 2002).

Donna Williams is an example of a savant who developed exceptional language skills. In her four autobiographies (D. Williams, 1992, 1994, 1999, 2004), Donna describes how common sights, sounds, and images become strangely distorted, which makes getting through an ordinary day like finding one's way out of a terribly complex maze. Donna has also written four textbooks (D. Williams, 1996, 1998, 2008a, 2008b) that have influenced the treatment and educational environments of people with autism.

As we describe Donna's experiences, you'll see how psychologists try to answer questions about complex behaviors, such as autism, as well as countless other behaviors discussed throughout this text. For example, one question that psychologists have studied involves the problem of test anxiety.

Donna Williams had symptoms of autism beginning in childhood.

Courtesy of Chris Samuel, by permission of Chris Samuel

Test Anxiety

If you're like many other students, you probably experience some degree of test anxiety.

Why are your hands sweating?

Test anxiety is a combination of physiological, emotional, and cognitive components that are caused by the stress of taking exams and may interfere with one's concentration, planning, and academic performance (Flippo et al., 2009).

For some students, test anxiety is an unpleasant experience but doesn't necessarily interfere with exam performance. For other students, test anxiety not only is an unpleasant experience but also seriously interferes with doing well on exams. We'll discuss what psychologists have discovered about test anxiety, why students differ in how much test anxiety they feel, and, perhaps most important, how to decrease test anxiety.

There are several ways to decrease test anxiety.

© Wavebreak Media/Thinkstock

What's Coming

In this module, we'll explore the goals of psychology, the major approaches that psychologists use to understand behavior and answer questions, the historical roots of psychology, current research areas, and possible careers in the broad field of psychology. Let's begin with how psychologists study complex problems, such as Donna's autistic behaviors. ●

Definition of Psychology

When you think of psychology, you may think of helping people who have mental problems. However, psychologists study a broad range of behaviors, including Donna's autistic behaviors and students' test anxiety, as well as hundreds of others. For this reason, we need a very broad definition of psychology.

What do psychologists study?

Psychology is the systematic, scientific study of behaviors and mental processes.

What's important about this definition is that each of its terms has a broad meaning. For example, *behaviors* refer to observable actions or responses in both humans and animals. Behaviors might include eating, speaking, laughing, running, reading, and sleeping. *Mental processes,* which are not directly observable, refer to a wide range of complex mental processes, such as thinking, imagining, studying, and dreaming. The current broad definition of psychology grew out of discussions and heated arguments among early psychologists, who defined psychology much more specifically, as we'll discuss later in this module.

Although the current definition of psychology is very broad, psychologists usually have four specific goals in mind when they study some behavior or mental process, such as Donna's autistic experiences.

Goals of Psychology

What are some of Donna's unusual behaviors?

Donna (photo below) knows that she has some unusual behaviors. For example, she says that she doesn't like to be touched, held, or hugged, doesn't like to make eye contact when speaking to people, hates to talk to someone who has a loud voice, and really dislikes meeting strangers. If you were a psychologist studying Donna's unusual behaviors, you would have the following four goals in mind: to describe, explain, predict, and control her behavior.

1 Describe Donna says that when she was a child, she wondered what people were saying to her because words were just lists of meaningless sounds. When people or things bothered her, she would endlessly tap or twirl her fingers to create movements that completely held her attention and helped her escape from a world that often made no sense.

The first goal of psychology is to describe the different ways that organisms behave.

As psychologists begin to describe the behaviors and mental processes of autistic children, such as difficulties in learning language, they begin to understand how autistic children behave. After describing behavior, psychologists try to explain behavior, the second goal.

2 Explain Donna's mother believed that autism was caused by evil spirits. Donna thinks her autism may result from metabolic imbalance.

The second goal of psychology is to explain the causes of behavior.

The explanation of autism has changed as psychologists learn more about this complex problem. In the 1950s, psychologists explained that children became autistic if they were reared by parents who were cold and rejecting (Blakeslee, 2000). In the 1990s, researchers discovered that autism is caused by genetic and biological factors that result in a maldeveloped brain (Courchesne et al., 2003). Being able to describe and explain behavior helps psychologists reach the third goal, which is to predict behavior.

Psychology's goals are to describe, explain, predict, and control Donna's autistic behaviors.

Courtesy of Chris Samuel, by permission of Chris Samuel

3 Predict Donna says that one of her biggest problems is being so overloaded by visual sensations that she literally freezes in place. She tries to predict when she will freeze up by estimating how many new stimuli she must adjust to.

The third goal of psychology is to predict how organisms will behave in certain situations.

However, psychologists may have difficulty predicting how autistic children will behave in certain situations unless they have already described and explained their behaviors. For example, from the first two goals, psychologists know that autistic children are easily overwhelmed by strange stimuli and have difficulty paying attention. Based on this information, psychologists can predict that autistic children will have difficulty learning in a school environment because there are too many activities and stimuli in the classroom (Heflin & Alaimo, 2006; M. Pittman, 2007). However, if psychologists can predict behavior, then they can often control behavior.

4 Control Donna knows one reason she fears meeting people is that social interactions cause a tremendous sensory overload that makes her freeze up. She controls her social fear by making a rule to meet only one person at a time.

For some psychologists, the fourth goal of psychology is to control an organism's behavior. However, the idea of control has both positive and negative sides. The positive side is that psychologists can help people, such as Donna, learn to control undesirable behaviors by teaching better methods of self-control and ways to deal with situations and relationships (Hanley, 2011; Taubman et al., 2011). The negative side is the concern that psychologists might control people's behaviors without their knowledge or consent. In Module 2, we'll discuss the strict guidelines that psychologists have established to prevent the potential abuse of controlling behavior and to protect the rights and privacy of individuals, patients, and participants in experiments.

Because many behaviors, such as autism, are enormously complex, psychologists use a combination of different approaches to reach the four goals of describing, explaining, predicting, and controlling behavior. To reach these goals, psychologists may use one or a combination of the following eight approaches. ●

B Modern Approaches

Answering Questions

Psychologists have many questions about Donna's unusual behaviors. For example, why did Donna believe objects were alive and made their own sounds? "My bed was my friend; my coat protected me and kept me inside; things that made noise had their own unique voices, which said vroom, ping, or whatever" (Blakely, 1994, p. 14).

How do psychologists answer questions?

Why did Donna initially hear words as meaningless sounds that people were constantly saying to her? Why did she develop her own signaling system, such as scrunching her toes to signal that no one could reach her? Why did she freeze up when staring at soap bubbles in the sink? In trying to answer questions about Donna's strange and intriguing behaviors, psychologists would use a combination of approaches.

An **approach** is a focus or perspective that may use a particular research method or technique.

The eight approaches to understanding behavior are the *biological, cognitive, behavioral, psychoanalytic, humanistic, sociocultural, evolutionary,* and *biopsychosocial.* We'll summarize these approaches below and discuss them on the following pages.

1 As a child, was Donna unable to learn that words had meaning because of some problem with the development of her brain?

The *biological approach* focuses on how our genes, hormones, and nervous system interact with our environments to influence learning, personality, memory, motivation, emotions, and coping techniques.

2 How was Donna able to develop her own signaling system that involved gestures instead of words?

The *cognitive approach* examines how we process, store, and use information and how this information influences what we attend to, perceive, learn, remember, believe, and feel.

3 Why did Donna make it a rule to avoid leaving soap bubbles in the sink?

The *behavioral approach* studies how organisms learn new behaviors or modify existing ones, depending on whether events in their environments reward or punish these behaviors.

4 Why did Donna develop alternate personalities, such as Willie, who had "hateful glaring eyes, a rigid corpselike stance, and clenched fists"?

The *psychoanalytic approach* stresses the influence of unconscious fears, desires, and motivations on thoughts, behaviors, and the development of personality traits and psychological problems later in life.

5 How was Donna able to write several books and create beautiful paintings?

The *humanistic approach* emphasizes that each individual has great freedom in directing his or her future, a large capacity for personal growth, a considerable amount of intrinsic worth, and enormous potential for self-fulfillment.

6 Why did Donna's mother believe autism was caused by evil spirits? What do other people and cultures believe causes autism?

The *sociocultural approach* studies the influence of social and cultural factors on psychological and behavioral functioning.

7 How might Donna's unique behaviors help her to adapt to the environment? How did autism evolve during the course of our human ancestry?

The *evolutionary approach* studies how evolutionary ideas, such as adaptation and natural selection, explain human behaviors and mental processes.

8 How might Donna's symptoms of autism be a result of biological, psychological and social factors?

The *biopsychosocial approach* studies how biological, psychological, and social influences explain human health and illness.

The first six approaches are well-established and are commonly used to understand behavior. We'll use the problems of autism and test anxiety to show how each of these approaches examines these problems from a different perspective. Then, we'll provide more information about the more recent evolutionary and biopsychosocial approaches.

Biological Approach

As Donna explains, autism has a huge effect on all parts of her life. "Autism makes me feel everything at once without knowing what I am feeling. Or it cuts me off from feeling anything at all" (D. Williams, 1994, p. 237). Donna's description of how autism so drastically affects her life raises questions about whether her brain has developed normally or functions differently. To answer these questions, researchers use the biological approach.

Are their brains different?

The **biological approach** examines how our genes, hormones, and nervous system interact with our environments to influence learning, personality, memory, motivation, emotions, and other traits and abilities.

Autism is thought to originate in early brain development. In children with autism, brain cells appear to connect irregularly, leading to abnormal functioning in brain areas responsible for thoughts, movement, and emotions. These abnormalities may explain why these children seem uninterested in their environment and in social interaction. Brain imaging research has shown that children with autism show different brain activity than other children while looking at faces (D. S. Fox, 2009). For example, the top figure shows that the normal brain uses one area (blue—fusiform gyrus) to process *faces* of people and a different area (red—inferior temporal gyrus) to process inanimate *objects,* such as a chair. The bottom figure shows that the autistic brain uses the area that processes inanimate objects (red—inferior temporal gyrus) to also process human faces (R. T. Schultz et al., 2000). This study uses the biological approach to look inside the brain to explain why people with autism show little interest in looking at a person's face during social interactions or in identifying facial emotional expressions.

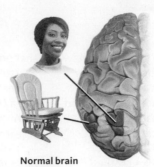

Normal brain

Autistic brain

Also using the biological approach, researchers found that social problems associated with autism are likely linked to less activity in brain cells responsible for human empathy (mirror neurons). These cells allow us to put ourselves in other people's shoes and experience how they feel. Though there is some disagreement among researchers, many report that reduced activity in these cells may help explain why children with autism misunderstand verbal and nonverbal cues suggesting different emotions felt by others, including joy, sadness, and anger, and why they have difficulty empathizing with others (Dapretto et al., 2006; Dinstein et al., 2010; Iacoboni, 2008a; 2010).

Psychologists who use the biological approach are now collaborating more and more with specialists in other biological disciplines, such as genetics, neuroanatomy, neurophysiology, neurochemistry, and neuropharmacology. Such collaboration results in the field of neuroscience.

Neuroscience is an interdisciplinary field of scientific study that examines the structure and function of all parts of the nervous system, including the brain, spinal cord, and networks of brain cells (SFN, 2012).

Like the biological approach, neuroscience studies the processes underlying cognition and behavior, but it also includes more detail about anatomy, physiology, and chemistry.

The biological approach can be used to study an experience that is familiar to many students, test anxiety.

Biological Approach to Test Anxiety

You've probably experienced one component of test anxiety, called the emotional component. This component includes a variety of physiological responses, such as increased heart rate, dry mouth, and sweaty palms. An interesting feature of sweaty palms, called palmar sweating, is that it is caused by stressful feelings and is not related to changes in room temperature (L. A. Goldsmith, 2008). In fact, palmar sweating is one of the measures used in the lie detector test, which we'll discuss in Module 16.

Why do my hands sweat?

As you take an exam—or even think about taking one—your stressful thoughts trigger the emotional component, which can interfere with processing information and increase your chances of making mistakes (Cassady & Johnson, 2002).

Sweaty hands often indicate stress.

The graph on the right shows how easily your stressful thoughts can trigger palmar sweating, which is one measure of the emotional component of test anxiety. As subjects listened to instructions telling them to do mental arithmetic, which involved them counting backward from 100 in steps of 7, there was a significant increase in palmar sweating. Then, once subjects started to actually do the mental arithmetic, their palmer sweating increased even more (Kobayashi et al., 2003). If merely listening to instructions about having to do the simple task of counting backward increased palmar sweating, a sign of physiological and emotional arousal, imagine the increased arousal that occurs while taking an exam!

In fact, symptoms of test anxiety may include shaky legs, sweating, racing heart, fidgeting, physical illness, or even crying during an exam (Cizek & Burg, 2006; Strauss, 2004). In Module 21, we'll describe methods of controlling stress to help manage the emotional component of test anxiety.

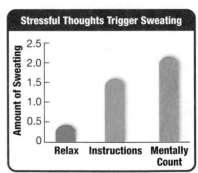

Graph data from "Arithmetic calculation, deep inspiration or handgrip exercise-mediated pre-operational active palmar sweating responses in humans," by Masayoshi Kobayashi, Noriko Tomioka, Yoshihisa Ushiyama and Toshio Ohhashi *Autonomic Neuroscience*, Volume 104, Issue 1, pp. 58–65.

Unless otherwise noted, all images are © Cengage Learning

Cognitive Approach

Individuals with autism usually have difficulty developing language skills. For example, Donna writes, "Autism makes me hear other people's words but be unable to know what the words mean. Autism stops me from finding and using my own words when I want to. Or makes me use all the words and silly things I do not want to say" (D. Williams, 1994, p. 237). Although Donna did not understand words until she was an adolescent, she eventually learned to both speak and write, has written several creative books (D. Williams, 1992, 1994, 1999, 2004), and has learned French and German. Because of her remarkable language abilities, Donna is said to be a high-functioning autistic, or *savant*. To discover why individuals with autism differ in their language and social skills, psychologists use the cognitive approach.

Was Donna an unusual autistic?

The **cognitive approach** focuses on how we process, store, and use information and how this information influences what we attend to, perceive, learn, remember, believe, and feel.

Unlike Donna Williams, who speaks fluently and is considered a high-functioning autistic, the photo on the right shows Tito Mukhopadhyay, a teenager with severe autism who often seems overcome by various movements, whose speech is virtually unintelligible, but who has the unusual ability to answer questions or explain what he's thinking or doing by writing or typing on the keyboard he is holding. For example, when Tito was being tested in a laboratory, he repeatedly stopped and started bursts of activity, standing and spinning, making loud smacking noises, or flapping his fingers. When asked why he does this, Tito didn't answer verbally but wrote, "I am calming myself. My senses are so disconnected I lose my body, so I flap. If I don't do this, I feel scattered and anxious" (Blakeslee, 2002, p. D1). Tito has written books inviting others to share in his inner life (Mukhopadhyay,

Tito is severely autistic but can type answers to questions.

2000, 2003, 2008). In his writings, he explains that his brain has difficulty processing different senses at the same time, such as sound, sight, and touch. This is the reason he avoids eye contact when talking with people, as he usually chooses to focus on hearing (McEdwards, 2008). Thus, there is a cognitive difference between normal individuals who can respond simultaneously to more than one sensory input, such as seeing and hearing, and individuals with autism who are limited to concentrating on one sense at a time.

Some cognitive researchers combine the study of cognitive skills with identifying their corresponding areas in the brain. This exciting new approach is called cognitive neuroscience (Purves et al., 2012).

Cognitive neuroscience involves taking pictures and identifying the structures and functions of the living brain during the performance of a variety of mental or cognitive processes, such as thinking, planning, naming, and recognizing objects.

For example, when listening to a conversation, 95% of right handers use primarily the left sides of their brains and very little of the right sides to process this verbal information. In contrast, researchers found that individuals with autism used primarily the right sides of their brains and very little of the left sides when listening to a conversation (E. J. Flagg et al., 2005). This reversing of brain sides as well as difficulties in processing verbal information may help explain why autistic individuals have problems acquiring cognitive, language, and communication skills.

Recently, the cognitive approach and its newer relative, cognitive neuroscience, have become popular because they have proved useful in answering questions about emotions, personality, cognitive skills, and social behaviors (Banich & Compton, 2011; Gazzaniga, 2009). For example, the cognitive approach has much to say about test anxiety, especially about worrying too much.

Cognitive Approach to Test Anxiety

Students who experience test anxiety must deal with two components. The first component, which we already described, is increased physiological arousal, which is the emotional component. The second component is the cognitive component, which is excessive worrying, usually about doing poorly on exams.

Can you worry too much?

Excessive worrying about your performance can interfere with your ability to read accurately, understand what you are reading, and identify important concepts (Cassady & Johnson, 2002). Thus, it is easy to see how excessive anxiety and

worrying can decrease students' confidence and impair their studying and academic performance (Flippo et al., 2009; Miesner & Maki, 2007; Rana & Mahmood, 2010).

Related to test anxiety is anxiety about specific academic content areas, such as math and writing. One study examined the influence of perfectionism on math anxiety and writing anxiety in high school students. Results showed that students with higher levels of passive perfectionism, meaning they avoid trying to meet their high standards, have higher math anxiety and higher writing anxiety than students with lower levels of passive perfectionism. The same study found that for girls, math anxiety decreased as they demonstrated higher active perfectionism, meaning they engage in behaviors aimed at reaching their high standards (K. Moore, 2010).

The above studies suggest that the cognitive characteristics of excessive worrying and perfectionism may either help or hinder cognitive performance depending on how the worries and perfectionism are channeled.

Behavioral Approach

If Donna happened to leave soap suds in the sink, she might see

Why have a "no soap suds" rule?

a rainbow of colors reflected in the bubbles. She would become so completely absorbed in looking at the brilliant colors that she could not move; she would be in a state of temporary paralysis. Donna made her "no soap suds" rule to prevent the environment from triggering an autistic behavior—temporary paralysis. Donna and her husband, who is also autistic, have developed many rules to control some of their unwanted behaviors. Here are some of their rules: *No lining feet up with furniture; No making the fruit in the bowl symmetrical; No reading newspaper headlines in gas stations or at newsstands* (Blakely, 1994, p. 43). These rules, which help Donna and her husband avoid performing repetitive and stereotyped behaviors, illustrate the behavioral approach.

The **behavioral approach** analyzes how organisms learn new behaviors or modify existing ones depending on whether events in their environments reward or punish these behaviors.

Donna and her husband's rules are examples of a basic behavioral principle: Rewards or punishments can modify, change, or control behavior. Psychologists use behavioral principles to teach people to be more assertive or less depressed, to toilet train young children, and to change many other behaviors. Psychologists use behavioral principles to train animals to press levers, to use symbols to communicate, and to perform behaviors on cue in movies and television shows.

Seeing a dazzling rainbow in soap suds stopped Donna in her tracks.

Largely through the creative work and original ideas of B. F. Skinner (1989), the behavioral approach has grown into a major force in psychology. Skinner's ideas stress the study of observable behaviors, the importance of environmental reinforcers (reward and punishment), and the exclusion of mental processes. His ideas, often referred to as strict behaviorism, continue to have an impact on psychology. In Module 10, we'll explain how Skinner's ideas were integrated into a program that taught autistic children new social behaviors that enabled them to enter and do well in public grade schools.

B. F. Skinner

However, some behaviorists, such as Albert Bandura (2001a), disagree with strict behaviorism and have formulated a theory that includes mental or cognitive processes in addition to observable behaviors. According to Bandura's *social cognitive approach,* our behaviors are influenced not only by environmental events and reinforcers but also by observation, imitation, and thought processes. In Module 10, we'll discuss how Bandura's ideas explain why some children develop a fear of bugs.

Behaviorists have developed a number of techniques for changing behaviors that can be applied to both animals and humans. Next, you will see how they have used a simple behavioral intervention to reduce the cognitive component of test anxiety.

Behavioral Approach to Test Anxiety

We discussed how excessive worrying and perfectionism, which are cognitive components of anxiety, may either help or hinder cognitive performance depending on how the

Can I redirect my worrying?

worries and perfectionism are channeled. We've also discussed how anxiety can impair academic performance. Now we'll focus on how a simple behavioral technique has been shown to prevent test anxiety from lowering test performance. If you are one of the many students who experience test anxiety, we think you will find this technique worth trying.

In a recent study, researchers measured students' test anxiety several weeks before students were to take their first final exam. Then, immediately before they took their final exam, students were randomly given envelopes with directions to either write about their feelings about the final exam or think about topics that would not be covered on the exam. Results indicated that for those students who didn't write about their feelings, there was a strong relationship between test anxiety and final exam performance (the higher the test anxiety, the lower the performance). However, for those students who did write about their feelings about the exam, the highly anxious students performed just as well as the less anxious students. Here, previous anxiety did not

predict performance, as it did with the group of students who did not engage in the writing task (Ramirez & Beilock, 2011).

A simple behavior, writing about your worries, may prevent all of the built-up test anxiety from interfering with your test performance. Given that excessive worrying can negatively influence performance of varying types, such as playing in a competitive athletic match, competing in a music contest, or interviewing for a job, writing about our worries may be an effective way to improve performance in a variety of situations.

In later modules, we'll give many examples of how other behavioral interventions can be used to modify a wide range of behaviors and thought patterns.

Psychoanalytic Approach

When she was about 3 years old, Donna faced a number of personal problems: having an alcoholic mother who hit and verbally abused her, having a father who was often gone, and being sent to a "special needs" school. Apparently in trying to deal with these problems, Donna developed other personalities. One personality was Willie, a child with "hateful glaring eyes, a pinched-up mouth, rigid corpselike stance, and clenched fists," who stamped and spit but also did well in school. The other was Carol, a charming, cooperative little girl who could act normal and make friends (S. Reed & Cook, 1993). Why Donna developed other personalities to deal with difficult childhood experiences would be carefully looked at in the psychoanalytic approach (Lanyado & Horne, 1999).

How was Donna's childhood?

The **psychoanalytic approach** is based on the belief that childhood experiences greatly influence the development of later personality traits and psychological problems. It also stresses the influence of unconscious fears, desires, and motivations on thoughts and behaviors.

In the late 1800s, Sigmund Freud, a physician, treated a number of patients with psychological problems. On the basis of insights from therapy sessions, Freud proposed some revolutionary ideas about the human mind and personality development. For example, one hallmark of Sigmund Freud's psychoanalytic approach is the idea that the first five years have a profound

Donna had an alcoholic and verbally abusive mother and a mostly absent father.

effect on later personality development. According to the psychoanalytic approach, Donna's first five years with a verbally abusive mother and mostly absent father would profoundly affect her later personality development.

In addition, Freud reasoned that thoughts or feelings that make us feel fearful or guilty, that threaten our self-esteem, or that come from unresolved sexual conflicts are automatically placed deep into our unconscious. In turn, these unconscious, threatening thoughts and feelings give rise to anxiety, fear, or psychological problems. Because Freud's patients could not uncover their unconscious fears, he developed several techniques, such as dream interpretation, to bring hidden fears to the surface. Freud's belief in an unconscious force that influenced human thought and behavior was another of his revolutionary ideas (Fayek, 2005). We'll discuss Freud's theory of personality in more detail in Module 19.

© Bettmann/CORBIS

Sigmund Freud

Unlike the biological, cognitive, and behavioral approaches, the psychoanalytic approach would search for hidden or unconscious forces underlying test anxiety

Psychoanalytic Approach to Test Anxiety

We discussed two components of test anxiety—excessive worrying and increased physiological responses—that can impair a student's performance on exams. Researchers also found that students with high test anxiety are much more likely to procrastinate than students with low test anxiety (N. A. Milgram et al., 1992).

Is test anxiety related to procrastination?

Procrastination is the tendency to always put off completing a task to the point of feeling anxious or uncomfortable about one's delay.

Researchers estimate that about 20% of adults are chronic procrastinators and from 80 to 95% of students procrastinate or deliberately delay completing assignments or studying for exams (Gura, 2008b; E. Hoover, 2005; Steel, 2007). Some of the more obvious reasons students give for procrastinating include being lazy or undisciplined, lacking motivation, and not knowing how to organize their time or set deadlines (Ariely & Wertenbroch, 2002).

However, the psychoanalytic approach would look beneath these obvious reasons and try to identify unconscious personality problems that may underlie procrastination and test anxiety. Because unconscious reasons for procrastination and test anxiety are difficult to uncover, psychologists use a variety of standard personality tests in their research.

Based on personality tests, researchers concluded that students who are regular

procrastinators may have low self-esteem, are too dependent on others, or have such a strong fear of failure that they do not start the task (Blunt & Pychyl, 2000). Personality tests also show that neuroticism (persistent anxiety—see p. 463) and an external locus of control (feeling little control over events—see p. 459) are associated with test anxiety (Carden et al., 2004; Chamorro-Premuzic et al., 2008). Thus, the psychoanalytic approach points to underlying personality problems as the probable cause of procrastination and test anxiety.

The best thing for you to do is to put off doing anything for a few more days.

The psychoanalytic approach would also study how childhood experiences may have led to procrastination. For instance, researchers found that procrastinators tend to be raised by authoritarian parents who stress over-achievement, set unrealistic goals for their children, or link achievement to giving parental love and approval. A child who is raised by parents like these may feel anxious when he or she fails at some task and will be tempted to put off such tasks in the future (Pychyl et al., 2002).

Psychologists know that ingrained personality characteristics, such as procrastination, remain relatively stable and persist across time unless a person makes a deliberate effort to change them. In Modules 21, 23, and 24, we'll discuss several methods that psychologists have developed to change personality characteristics.

Humanistic Approach

What was Donna's potential?

Donna says that one reason she wrote her books was to escape her prison of autism. Autism has trapped her in a world where she sometimes blinks compulsively, rocks back and forth, freezes up, stares off into space without being able to stop herself, hates to be touched, cannot stand to enter public places, and hates to make eye contact with others (D. Williams, 1992).

Even though Donna has serious life challenges, she strives toward reaching her potential. She has published autobiographies and textbooks on autism. Her creative paintings and sculptures can be seen at exhibits. Donna is also a singer–songwriter who has released two albums. Also, she married a man she refers to as a "diamond of a person" (D. Williams, 2009).

Donna's painting, titled "Believe," reflects the humanistic approach's emphasis on personal freedom and growth.

Donna's struggle to free herself from autism, develop close personal relationships, and reach her potential characterizes the humanistic approach.

The **humanistic approach** emphasizes that each individual has great freedom in directing his or her future, a large capacity for achieving personal growth, a considerable amount of intrinsic worth, and enormous potential for self-fulfillment.

Humanists believe that, like Donna, we may have to struggle to reach our potential, but we have control of our fate and are free to become whatever we are capable of being. The humanistic approach emphasizes the positive side of human nature, its creative tendencies, and its inclination to build caring relationships. This concept of human nature—freedom, potential, creativity—is the most distinctive feature of the humanistic approach and sets it far apart from the behavioral and psychoanalytic approaches (Giorgi, 2005).

Abraham Maslow

The humanistic approach officially began in the early 1960s with the publication of the *Journal of Humanistic Psychology*. One of the major figures behind establishing the journal and the humanistic approach was Abraham Maslow, who had become dissatisfied with the behavioral and psychoanalytic approaches. To paraphrase Maslow (1968), the humanistic approach was to be a new way of perceiving and thinking about the individual's capacity, freedom, and potential for growth. Many of humanism's ideas have been incorporated into approaches for counseling and psychotherapy.

Because of its emphasis on free will and lack of experimental methods, many of today's psychologists regard humanism as more of a philosophy of life than a science of human behavior. However, the humanistic approach has helped to inspire the scientific research area known as positive psychology.

Positive psychology is the scientific study of optimal human functioning, focusing on the strengths and virtues that enable individuals and communities to thrive.

Positive psychology aims to better understand the positive, adaptive, and fulfilling aspects of human life. We will discuss positive psychology in more detail in Module 21.

Now, we'll discuss how the humanistic approach applies to dealing with the problems some students have with test anxiety and academic performance.

Humanistic Approach to Test Anxiety

The first year of college can be a difficult adjustment for many students, since it is more demanding and stressful than high school.

How can students reach their potentials?

Researchers wanted to learn which specific factors lead to high academic performance and successful adjustment among first-year college students. They found that students who were confident in their academic abilities performed significantly better than students who were less confident, and they adjusted better to college. Also, students who had higher expectations for academic success, such as performing well in courses, received better grades (Chemers et al., 2001). Based on these findings, it is evident that believing in one's abilities and potential is an important factor in being a successful student. These results may be useful for educators in helping students who do poorly in school to not give up but rather try to develop their academic potential.

Psychologists have also studied students whose academic performance ranged from poor to very good in order to develop a profile of a successful student. Studies showed that successful students share a number of similar characteristics: they feel competent about meeting the demands of their classes; they believe they can handle test situations; they are very good at organizing their study time; and they prepare themselves for tests and do not procrastinate (Kleijn et al., 1994).

Based on studies of students' performances, the humanistic approach would say that just as successful students found ways to reach their academic potential, all students should search for ways to reach their own potentials. The humanistic approach emphasizes that students have the capacity to choose, that each person is unique or special, and that students should have faith in their personal or subjective feelings (Hansen, 2000).

Sociocultural Approach

Autism is believed to exist in every culture (Grinker 2007). Let's look at how different cultures perceive autism.

How is autism perceived in other cultures?

United States. A psychologist in the United States first described the symptoms of autism about 70 years ago (Kanner, 1943). Then autism was thought to be caused by environmental factors, such as having "cold" parents. In the 1960s, the focus changed to searching for biological causes (Rimland, 1964). Today, researchers believe the probable causes of autism include both environmental and genetic factors (Hallmayer et al., 2011; Matson & Sturmey, 2011).

There are between 1 million and 1.5 million Americans with autism (ASA, 2012). While the diagnosis of autism usually is made between ages 2 and 3, the American Academy of Pediatrics (2007) is now recommending screening children as young as 18 months, recognizing the importance of early intervention. Treatment is provided by psychiatrists and other physicians, psychologists, teachers, speech therapists, play therapists, and other professionals who understand autism.

South Korea. The precise number of people with autism in South Korea is unknown, as the disorder has a terrible stigma and children with autism are often kept at home hidden from the public. Parents in South Korea may fear that their family will lose face if people know a family member has autism and that marriage prospects for their other children will be negatively affected as a result of having a child with an abnormality. However, a recent study estimates that a startling number of children in South Korea have autism, 2.64% or about 1 in 38. Researchers worry that many children with autism have not been counted in previous studies (Y. S. Kim et al., 2011).

One reason to explain why many children with autism have not been included in previous estimates is that physicians in South Korea usually diagnose what would be considered autism in the United States as reactive attachment disorder (see p. 377), which South Koreans interpret as "lack of love." This is a less stigmatizing diagnosis, as parents believe they can help their child by providing more love. Also, it doesn't negatively harm the family as much as a genetic disease might. The unfortunate result, however, is that children with autism do not get the treatment they need. Within only the past several years, the perceptions of autism have begun to positively change in South Korea, resulting in new social opportunities for children. For instance, some children with autism are now going to school and walking out in public with their families (Grinker, 2007).

The differences in how autism is perceived and treated in the United States and South Korea illustrate the use of the sociocultural approach in psychology (Matsumoto & Juang, 2012; Valsiner & Rosa, 2007).

The **sociocultural approach** studies the influence of social and cultural factors on psychological and behavioral functioning.

We will be highlighting sociocultural research throughout this book. There are also differences in how other cultures experience test anxiety.

Sociocultural Approach to Test Anxiety

How do other cultures deal with test anxiety?

Culture plays an important role in determining the intensity and expression of test anxiety, and test anxiety has been examined in countries across the globe (Bodas & Ollendick, 2005).

The development and severity of test anxiety appear to be different between Asian and non-Asian students. For example, students in India experience heightened test anxiety due to several factors, including the cultural emphasis on academic achievement, parental and social pressures to perform, and the stressful, competitive nature of exams. In contrast, American students don't experience as much test anxiety, in part because parents are less involved with their children's schoolwork and they promote independence and personal responsibility. A related sociocultural difference is how children express test anxiety. Indian students express their anxiety through physical symptoms, whereas American students experience more cognitive symptoms, such as excessive worrying (Bodas & Ollendick, 2005; Verma et al., 2002).

This research shows how the sociocultural approach provides different and interesting answers to the same question.

Evolutionary Approach

A recent modern approach to psychology emerges out of evolutionary theory and is called the evolutionary approach.

The **evolutionary approach** studies how evolutionary ideas, such as adaptation and natural selection, explain human behaviors and mental processes.

Although the evolutionary approach is relatively new, research has already examined how evolution influences a variety of behaviors and mental processes, such as aggression, mate selection, fears, depression, and decision making (Buss, 2004, 2007, 2009). We'll discuss the evolutionary approach again in Module 4 (p. 69) and include some of the exciting research resulting from this approach throughout the text.

Biopsychosocial Approach

An integrative approach to psychology is the biopsychosocial approach.

The **biopsychosocial approach** studies how biological, psychological, and social factors influence human development.

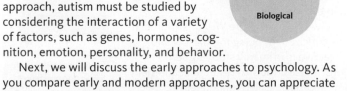

According to the biopsychosocial approach, autism must be studied by considering the interaction of a variety of factors, such as genes, hormones, cognition, emotion, personality, and behavior.

Next, we will discuss the early approaches to psychology. As you compare early and modern approaches, you can appreciate how much psychology has changed since its beginnings. ●

How did psychology begin?

Imagine living in the late 1800s and early 1900s, when the electric light, radio, and airplane were being invented and the average human life span was about 30 years. This was the time when psychology broke away from philosophy and became a separate field of study. As they developed this new area, early psychologists hotly debated its definition, approach, and goals (Benjamin, 2000). We'll highlight those early psychologists whose ideas and criticisms shaped the field. We'll begin with the person considered to be the father of psychology, Wilhelm Wundt.

Structuralism: Elements of the Mind

Who established the first lab?

There were no bands or celebrations when Wilhelm Wundt established the first psychology laboratory in 1879, in Leipzig, Germany. In fact, his laboratory was housed in several rooms in a shabby building that contained rather simple equipment, such as platforms, various balls, telegraph keys, and metronomes. The heavily bearded Wundt, now considered the father of psychology, would ask subjects to drop balls from a platform or listen to a metronome (figure below) and report their own sensations. Wundt and his followers were analyzing their sensations, which they thought were the key to analyzing the structure of the mind (Hergenhahn, 2009). For this reason they were called structuralists and their approach was called structuralism.

Wilhelm Wundt
1832–1920

Structuralism was the study of the most basic elements, primarily sensations and perceptions, that make up our conscious mental experiences.

Just as you might assemble hundreds of pieces of a jigsaw puzzle into a completed picture, structuralists tried to combine hundreds of sensations into a complete conscious experience. Perhaps Wundt's greatest contribution was his method of introspection.

Introspection was a method of exploring conscious mental processes by asking subjects to look inward and report their sensations and perceptions.

For example, after listening to a beating metronome, the subjects would be asked to report whether their sensations were pleasant, unpleasant, exciting, or relaxing. However, introspection was heavily criticized for being an unscientific method because it was solely dependent on subjects' self-reports, which could be biased, rather than on objective measurements. Although Wundt's approach was the first, it had little impact on modern psychology. The modern-day cognitive approach also studies mental processes, but with different scientific methods and much broader interests than those of Wundt.

It wasn't long before Wundt's approach was criticized for being too narrow and subjective in primarily studying sensations. These criticisms resulted in another new approach, called functionalism.

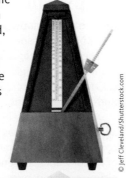

Can you describe each sensation you hear?

Functionalism: Functions of the Mind

Who wrote the first textbook?

For twelve years, William James labored over a book called *The Principles of Psychology,* which was published in 1890 and included almost every topic that is now part of psychology textbooks: learning, sensation, memory, reasoning, attention, feelings, consciousness, and a revolutionary theory of emotions.

For example, why do you feel fear when running from a raging wolf? You might answer that an angry wolf (figure below) is a terrifying creature that causes fear and makes you run—fear makes you run. Not so, according to James, who reasoned that the act of running causes a specific set of physiological responses that your brain interprets as fear—running makes you afraid. According to James, emotions were caused by physiological changes; thus, running produced fear.

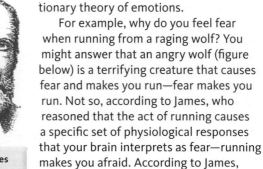

William James
1842–1910

You'll find out whether James's theory of emotions was correct in Module 16.

Unlike Wundt, who saw mental activities as composed of basic elements, James viewed mental activities as having developed through ages of evolution because of their adaptive functions, such as helping humans survive. James was interested in the goals, purposes, and functions of the mind, an approach called functionalism.

Functionalism, which was the study of the function rather than the structure of consciousness, was interested in how our minds adapt to our changing environment.

Functionalism did not last as a unique approach, but many of James's ideas grew into current areas of study, such as emotions, attention, and memory (Hergenhahn, 2009). In addition, James suggested ways to apply psychological principles to teaching, which had a great impact on educational psychology. For all these reasons, James is considered the father of modern psychology.

Notice that James disagreed with Wundt's structural approach and pushed psychology toward looking at how the mind functions and adapts to our ever-changing world. About the same time that James was criticizing Wundt's structuralism, another group also found reasons to disagree with Wundt; this group was the Gestalt psychologists.

Does running from an angry wolf cause fear?

Gestalt Approach: Sensations Versus Perceptions

Who said, "Wundt is wrong"?

When you see a road hazard sign like the one in the photo below, you think the lights forming the arrow are actually moving in one direction. This motion, however, is only an illusion; the lights are stationary and are only flashing on and off.

The illusion that flashing lights appear to move was first studied in 1912 by three psychologists: Max Wertheimer, Wolfgang Köhler, and Kurt Koffka. They reported that they had created the perception of movement by briefly flashing one light and then, a short time later, a second light. Although the two bulbs were fixed, the light actually appeared to move from one to the other. They called this the *phi phenomenon;* today it is known as *apparent motion.*

Wertheimer and his colleagues believed that the perception of apparent motion could not be explained by the structuralists, who said that the movement resulted from simply adding together the sensations from two fixed lights. Instead, Wertheimer argued that perceptual experiences, such as perceiving moving lights, resulted from analyzing a "whole pattern," or, in German, a *Gestalt.*

**Max Wertheimer
1883–1943**

The **Gestalt approach** emphasized that perception is more than the sum of its parts and studied how sensations are assembled into meaningful perceptual experiences.

In our example, Gestalt psychologists would explain that your experience of perceiving moving traffic lights is much more than and very different from what is actually happening—fixed lights flashing in sequence. These kinds of findings could not be explained by the structuralists and pointed out the limitations of their approach (D. P. Schultz & Schultz, 2012).

After all these years, many principles of the Gestalt approach are still used to explain how we perceive objects. We'll discuss many of the Gestalt principles of perception in Module 6.

Why do blinking lights seem to move?

© Philip James Corwin/CORBIS

Behaviorism: Observable Behaviors

Who offered a guarantee?

"Give me a dozen healthy infants, well-formed, and my own special world to bring them up in and I'll guarantee to take any one at random and train him to become any type of specialist I might select—doctor, lawyer, artist…" (Watson, 1924).

These words come from John B. Watson, who published a landmark paper in 1913 titled "Psychology as a Behaviorist Views It." In it, he rejected Wundt's structuralism and its study of mental elements and conscious processes. He rejected introspection as a psychological technique because its results could not be scientifically verified by other psychologists. Instead, John Watson boldly stated that psychology should be considered an objective, experimental science, whose goal should be the analysis of observable behaviors and the prediction and control of those behaviors (Harzem, 2004). It is a small step from these ideas to Watson's boast, "Give me a dozen healthy infants . . .," which illustrates the behavioral approach.

**John B. Watson
1878–1958**

The **behavioral approach** emphasized the objective, scientific analysis of observable behaviors.

From the 1920s to the 1960s, behaviorism was the dominant force in American psychology. Part of this dominance was due to the work of B. F. Skinner and other behaviorists, who expanded and developed Watson's ideas into the modern-day behavioral approach, which is fully discussed in Module 10. However, beginning in the 1970s and continuing into the present, behaviorism's dominance was challenged by the cognitive approach, whose popularity now surpasses behaviorism (Evans, 1999; Glassman & Hadad, 2004).

Can anyone guarantee what I will become?

© Image Source Black/Alamy

Survival of Approaches

Which approaches survived?

The survival of each approach—structuralism, functionalism, Gestalt, and behaviorism—depended on its ability to survive its criticisms. Criticisms of Wundt's structural approach gave rise to the functional approach of James and the Gestalt approach of Wertheimer, Köhler, and Koffka. Criticisms of all three approaches—structural, functional, and Gestalt—gave rise to Watson's behavioral approach. Another approach, Sigmund Freud's psychoanalytic approach (see p. 9), which emphasized the influence of unconscious processes, disagreed with Watson's strict behavioral approach and developed largely in parallel with these other approaches. These disagreements in approaches resulted in heated debates among early psychologists, but they helped psychology develop into the scientific field it is today (Evans, 1999).

Although early American psychologists differed in their approaches, they shared one underlying theme that was a sign of their times. They discriminated against women and minorities in both academic and career settings. Such discriminatory practices were widespread in early times, and we'll examine that issue next. ●

Because psychologists focus on studying and understanding human behavior, you would expect them to be among the first to recognize the mistreatment of and discrimination against other groups. However, psychologists are human and, being human, they knowingly or unknowingly adopted and carried out the discriminatory practices that were operating at the time. This means that, for the first 75 of its more than 100 years of existence, the academic policies and career opportunities of American psychology were determined by White males, who both intentionally and unintentionally discriminated against women and people of color. Here are just a few examples.

Women in Psychology

The reason Mary Calkins (right) could not enter graduate school was that she was a woman, and many universities (Johns Hopkins, Harvard, Columbia) would not admit women. Since Calkins was a faculty member and had established a laboratory in psychology at Wellesley College in 1891, she petitioned and was allowed to take seminars at Harvard. There, she completed all requirements for a PhD and was recommended for a doctorate by her professors, but the Harvard administration declined to grant it because she was a woman (Furumoto, 1989). It was not until 1908 that a woman, Margaret Washburn, was awarded a PhD in psychology.

Why couldn't she enter graduate school?

Courtesy, Margaret Clapp Library Archives, Wellesley College, photo by Patridge

Mary Calkins was not given a PhD because she was a woman.

During the past 40 years, women have made great progress in the field. In 1970, about 20% of graduate students receiving PhDs were women, and by 2007, the number had increased to 73% (USDE, 2009). However, even though women currently earn more PhDs in psychology than men, female psychologists have lower incomes (on average) than male psychologists, fewer women are tenured faculty members at graduate schools, and fewer women are editors of psychology journals (APA, 2007b; 2007a; Cynkar, 2007).

Not only did women face discrimination in psychology, but so did people of color.

Minorities in Psychology

Why so few minority students?

In psychology's early days, only a few northern White universities accepted Black students, while all southern White universities denied admission to Black students.

The first African American woman to receive a PhD in psychology was Inez Prosser, who graduated from the University of Cincinnati in 1933. Her career was spent teaching at Black colleges and helping Black students obtain financial aid to attend college (Benjamin, 2008).

Between 1920 and 1966, only 8 PhDs in psychology were awarded to Black students, compared to 3,767 doctorates to Whites (R. V. Guthrie, 1976). In 1996, 168 PhDs were awarded to African Americans, 183 to Hispanics, 23 to Native Americans, 131 to Asians, and 2,939 to Whites (Rabasca, 2000b).

During the early 1900s, few degrees were awarded to Hispanics. One exception was George Sanchez (on right), who conducted pioneering work on the cultural bias of intelligence

George Sanchez found intelligence tests were culturally biased.

© AP Images/Cynthia Kennedy

tests given to minority students. Sanchez criticized the claim that Mexican Americans were mentally inferior, saying the claim was based solely on intelligence tests. He showed that intelligence tests contained many questions that were biased against minorities and thus resulted in their lower scores (R. V. Guthrie, 1976).

In more recent years, psychology has made great progress in encouraging more minorities to join the American Psychological Association and to earn psychology degrees. From the founding of the American Psychological Association in 1892 to 1990, its cumulative membership was 128,000. Of those members, only 700 were African American, 700 were Latino, and 70 were Native American.

Between 1997 and 2004, 20% of new members of the American Psychological Association were ethnic minorities. Also, between 1996 and 2004, there was a 90% increase in the number of ethnic minorities who earned psychology master's degrees and a 36% increase in the number earning bachelor's degrees (APA, 2008c).

Righting the Wrongs

Today, people of color are still underrepresented in academic departments and in graduate programs in psychology, although their numbers and influence are increasing (APA, 2008a).

How much success?

The American Psychological Association (APA) recognized the need to recruit more ethnic minorities and formed a special group to reach this goal. The group established numerous journals to promote the causes of women and ethnic minorities (DeAngelis, 1966) and sponsored a program to visit high schools and teach minority students about careers in psychology (APA, 2009b). The APA has an official policy supporting equal opportunities "for persons regardless of race, gender, age, religion, disability, sexual orientation and national origin" (Tomes, 2000).

Psychology departments are actively searching for ways to recruit minority students (M. R. Rogers & Molina, 2006). ●

Concept Review

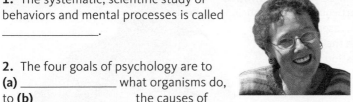

1. The systematic, scientific study of behaviors and mental processes is called _____.

8. The approach that studies the influence of social and cultural factors on psychological and behavioral functioning is called the _____ approach.

2. The four goals of psychology are to **(a)** _____ what organisms do, to **(b)** _____ the causes of behavior, to **(c)** _____ behavior in new situations, and to **(d)** _____ behavior, which has both positive and negative aspects.

Courtesy of Chris Samuel, by permission of Chris Samuel

9. Wundt studied the elements that made up the conscious mind and called this approach **(a)** _Structualism_. Subjects were asked to observe the workings of their minds, a technique that Wundt called **(b)** _introspection_. Modern-day psychologists who study mental activities with more objective and scientific methods are said to use the **(c)** _Modern-day cognitive_ approach.

© Jeff Cleveland/Shutterstock.com

3. The approach that focuses on how one's nervous system, hormones, and genes interact with the environment is called the _____ approach.

10. William James disagreed with Wundt's structuralism and instead emphasized the functions, goals, and purposes of the mind and its adaptation to the environment; he called this approach **(a)** _functionalism_. James also applied the principles of psychology to teaching, so his approach had a great effect on the field of **(b)** _educational_ psychology.

© Keith Szafranski/iStockphoto

4. The approach that studies how people think, solve problems, and process information is called the _____ approach.

© Dana Fineman/Vistalux

5. The approach that analyzes how environmental rewards and punishments shape, change, or motivate behavior is called the _____ approach.

11. Some psychologists disagreed with Wundt's approach of structuralism and instead believed that perceptions are more than the sum of many individual **(a)** _parts_. These psychologists called their approach the **(b)** _Gestalt_ approach, which studied how sensations were assembled into meaningful **(c)** _perceptual experiences_

© Philip James Corwin/CORBIS

6. The approach that stresses the influence of unconscious feelings, fears, or desires on the development of behavior, personality, and psychological problems is called the **(a)** _____ approach. This approach also emphasizes the importance of early **(b)** _____ experiences.

12. John Watson disagreed with Wundt's approach, which was called **(a)** _structuralism_, and disagreed with Wundt's technique of studying the mind, which was called **(b)** _Introspection_ Instead, Watson emphasized the objective, scientific analysis of observable behaviors, which was known as the **(c)** _behavioral_ approach. Later, this approach became a dominant force in psychology through the work of behaviorist **(d)** _B.F. Skinner_.

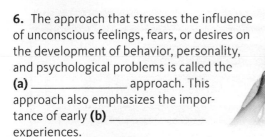

© Donna Williams

7. The approach that emphasizes freedom of choice, self-fulfillment, and attaining one's potential is called the **(a)** _____ approach. Many of this approach's concepts have been taken up and used in **(b)** _____.

© Image Source Black/Alamy

Answers: 1. psychology; 2. (a) describe, (b) explain, (c) predict, (d) control; 3. biological; 4. cognitive; 5. behavioral; 6. (a) psychoanalytic, (b) childhood; 7. (a) humanistic, (b) counseling or psychotherapy; 8. sociocultural; 9. (a) structuralism, (b) introspection, (c) cognitive; 10. (a) functionalism, (b) educational; 11. (a) sensations, (b) Gestalt, (c) perceptions; 12. (a) structuralism, (b) introspection, (c) behavioral, (d) B. F. Skinner

E Research Focus: Taking Class Notes

Best Strategy for Taking Class Notes?

How good are your class notes?

As you listen to lectures in class, you'll probably be taking notes. But how do you know if you're using the best system or strategy? To research some particular behavior, such as note-taking, psychologists first ask a very specific research question: Which system or strategy for taking notes results in the best performance on tests? One researcher answered this question by using a combination of behavioral and cognitive approaches (A. King, 1992). As we describe this interesting study, notice how it involves the four goals of psychology, beginning with the first goal, describing behavior.

1st Goal: Describe Behavior

The researcher divided college students into three different groups. Each group was given a different method or strategy for taking notes. As described below, students practiced three different strategies for taking notes: review notes, summarize notes, and answer questions about notes.

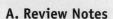

A. Review Notes

The strategy that most students use is to try to write down as much as possible of what the professor says. Then, before exams, students review their notes, hoping they took good class notes.

B. Summarize Notes

Students took notes as usual but, after the lecture, used their notes to write a summary of the lecture in their own words.

Students were shown how to identify a main topic and, in their own words, write a sentence about it. Then they identified a subtopic and wrote a sentence that related it to the main topic. When linked together, these sentences created a summary of the lecture, written in the students' own words.

C. Answer Questions about Notes

Students took notes as usual but, after the lecture, used their notes to ask and answer questions about the lecture material. Students were given a set of 13 general questions, such as: **What is the main idea of …? How would you use …to …? What is a new example of …? What is the difference between … and …?** Students answered each of these questions using their class notes.

After practicing one of these three note-taking strategies, students watched a videotaped lecture and used their particular strategy for taking notes.

2nd Goal: Explain Behavior

A week after each group had watched a videotaped lecture, they were given an exam. The graph on the right shows that the group who used the strategy of taking notes plus answering questions scored significantly higher than the other two groups. The researcher explained that students who took notes and then answered questions about their notes retained more information than students who employed the other two strategies (A. King, 1992).

Note-Taking Strategy & Average Exam Score	
Review notes	34
Summarize notes	45
Answer questions	51

3rd Goal: Predict Behavior

On the basis of these results, the researcher predicts that students who use the strategy that combines note-taking with answering questions are likely to retain more information and perform better on exams than students who use traditional note-taking methods, such as writing as much as they can and then reviewing their notes before exams.

4th Goal: Control Behavior

Students can increase their chances of getting better grades by taking the time to learn a better note-taking strategy. This new strategy involves taking notes and then answering, in their own words, a series of general questions about the lecture material. Although this new note-taking strategy takes a little time to learn, the payoff will be better performance on exams. This and other research show the connection between good note-taking skills and higher test performance (Peverly et al., 2003).

Purpose of the Research Focus

This study shows how psychologists answered a very practical and important question about how best to take lecture notes. We'll use the Research Focus to show how psychologists use different approaches and research techniques to answer a variety of interesting questions about human behavior.

Although a large percentage of psychologists engage in research, you'll see next how many others work in a variety of career settings that may or may not involve research. ●

Psychologist Versus Psychiatrist

Many students think psychologists are primarily counselors and therapists, even though degrees in psychology are awarded in many areas. Obtaining an advanced degree in psychology requires that one finish college and spend two to three years in postgraduate study to obtain a master's degree or four to five years in postgraduate study to obtain a PhD. Some careers or work settings require a master's degree, while others require a PhD. Many students are confused about the difference between a psychologist, a clinical or counseling psychologist, and a psychiatrist.

What's a psychologist?

A **psychologist** is usually someone who has completed four to five years of postgraduate education and has obtained a PhD, PsyD, or EdD in psychology.

A **clinical psychologist** has a PhD, PsyD, or EdD, has specialized in a clinical subarea, and has spent an additional year in a supervised therapy setting to gain experience in diagnosing and treating a wide range of abnormal behaviors.

Psychiatrist: MD or DO
Psychologist: PhD, PsyD, or EdD

© Jose Gil/Shutterstock.com
© Robert Kreschke/Shutterstock.com

Similar to clinical psychologists are **counseling psychologists,** who provide similar services but usually work with different problems, such as those involving marriage, family, or career counseling.

Until recently no psychologists in the United States have been able to prescribe drugs. Now, psychologists in New Mexico and Louisiana who complete special medical training can prescribe drugs as psychiatrists do. Several other states may pass similar legislation, giving psychologists the right to prescribe medication (R. E. Fox et al., 2009; Munsey, 2008).

A **psychiatrist** is a physician (medical doctor) who has a MD or DO and has spent several years in clinical training, which includes diagnosing possible physical and neurological causes of abnormal behaviors and treating these behaviors, often with prescription drugs.

Psychologists can work in the following career settings.

Many Career Settings

As you can see in the pie chart below, the majority (49%) of psychologists are therapists, while the rest work in four other settings.

Are psychologists usually therapists?

In the United States and Canada, most psychologists have a PhD, PsyD, or EdD, which requires four to five years of study after college. In many other countries, most psychologists have a college degree, which requires four to five years of study after high school (Helmes & Pachana, 2005).

The employment opportunities for psychologists are expected to grow by about 12% through the year 2018. The increased demand for psychological services in schools, hospitals, mental health centers, substance abuse treatment centers, and social service agencies helps explain the need for more trained psychologists (U.S. Department of Labor, 2012).

Here's recent data showing the breakdown of where psychologists in the United States work.

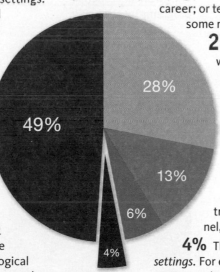

Data from "Psychological Science Around the World," by M. R. Rosenzweig, 1992, *American Psychologist, 47,* 718–22.

49% The largest percentage (49%) of psychologists work as clinical or counseling psychologists in either a *private practice* or *therapy setting,* such as a psychological or psychiatric clinic; a mental health center; a psychiatric, drug, or rehabilitation ward of a hospital; or a private office. The duties of clinical or counseling psychologists might involve doing individual or group therapy; helping patients with problems involving drugs, stress, weight, family, or career; or testing patients for psychological problems that developed from some neurological problem.

28% The second largest percentage (28%) of psychologists work in the *academic settings* of universities and colleges. Academic psychologists often engage in some combination of classroom teaching, mentoring or helping students, and doing research in their areas of interest.

13% The third largest percentage (13%) of psychologists work in a variety of other kinds of jobs and *career settings.*

6% The fourth largest percentage (6%) of psychologists work in *industrial settings,* such as businesses, corporations, and consulting firms. These psychologists, often called industrial/ organizational psychologists, may work at selecting personnel, increasing production, or improving job satisfaction.

4% The smallest percentage (4%) work in *secondary schools and other settings.* For example, school psychologists conduct academic and career testing and provide counseling for a variety of psychological problems (learning disabilities, attention-deficit/hyperactivity disorder) (D. Smith, 2002).

If you are thinking of entering the field of psychology today, you have a wide and exciting range of career choices. Your career choices are almost limitless! For example, in addition to the many work settings discussed above, psychologists are working in the Department of Defense, Department of Homeland Security, and National Institutes of Health. They are also working with attorneys, engineers, physicians, and computer scientists (DeAngelis, 2008). For those who decide to engage in research, we'll next discuss popular research areas that psychologists choose. ●

Areas of Specialization

As you proceed through your introductory psychology course, you'll find that the world of psychology has been divided into at least eight general areas. And, if you go on and enter graduate school in psychology, you'll be expected to specialize in one of these areas. Students often find it difficult to choose only one special area of psychology, since they may be interested in two or three. The reason graduate students are asked to choose one area is that there is such an enormous amount of information that it takes great effort to master even one area. As you read about each research area, think about which one you might prefer.

Which area should I choose?

Clinical/Counseling

Which type of therapy is most effective?
How do people develop phobias?

You would be asking these kinds of questions if you were a clinical or counseling psychologist.

Clinical and counseling psychology includes the assessment and treatment of people with psychological problems, such as grief, anxiety, or stress.

Some clinical and counseling psychologists work with a variety of populations, whereas others may specialize in specific groups like children or the elderly. They may work in hospitals, community health centers, private practice, or academic settings.

Developmental

Why do some babies cry more than others?
What happens to our sex drive as we age?

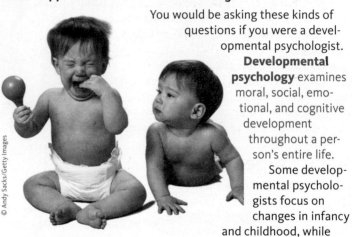

You would be asking these kinds of questions if you were a developmental psychologist.

Developmental psychology examines moral, social, emotional, and cognitive development throughout a person's entire life.

Some developmental psychologists focus on changes in infancy and childhood, while others trace changes through adolescence, adulthood, and old age. They work in academic settings and may consult on day care or programs for the aging.

Social

How does being in a group affect one's behavior?
How can people make a good impression on others?

These kinds of questions interest social psychologists.

Social psychology involves the study of social interactions, stereotypes, prejudices, attitudes, conformity, group behaviors, aggression, and attraction.

Many social psychologists work in academic settings, but some work in hospitals and federal agencies as consultants and in business settings as personnel managers.

Experimental

Why does an animal press a bar to obtain food?
Can learning principles be used to discipline children?

These kinds of questions interest experimental psychologists.

Experimental psychology includes the areas of sensation, perception, learning, human performance, motivation, and emotion.

Experimental psychologists conduct much of their research under carefully controlled laboratory conditions, with both animal and human subjects. Most work in academic settings, but some also work in business, industry, and government.

Biological

**How do brain cells change during Alzheimer's disease?
How do genes affect your intelligence?**

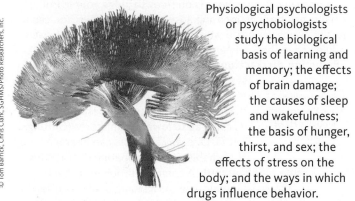

Physiological psychologists or psychobiologists study the biological basis of learning and memory; the effects of brain damage; the causes of sleep and wakefulness; the basis of hunger, thirst, and sex; the effects of stress on the body; and the ways in which drugs influence behavior.

Biological psychology or **psychobiology** involves research on the physical and chemical changes that occur during stress, learning, and emotions, as well as how our genetic makeup, brain, and nervous system interact with our environments and influence our behaviors.

Psychobiologists work in academic settings, hospitals, and private research laboratories.

Cognitive

**What's the best way to learn new information?
Do men and women think differently?**

If these questions interest you, think about being a cognitive psychologist.

Cognitive psychology involves how we process, store, and retrieve information and how cognitive processes influence our behaviors.

Cognitive research includes memory, thinking, language, creativity, and decision making. Earlier we discussed a relatively new area that combines cognitive and biological approaches and is called cognitive neuroscience.

Psychometrics

**What do college entrance tests show?
What career best fits my abilities?**

These questions introduce an area called psychometrics, which involves the construction, administration, and interpretation of psychological tests.

Psychometrics focuses on the measurement of people's abilities, skills, intelligence, personality, and abnormal behaviors.

To accomplish their goals, psychologists in this area focus on developing a wide range of psychological tests, which must be continually updated and checked for usefulness and cultural biases. Some of these tests are used to assess people's skills and abilities, as well as to predict their performance in certain careers and situations, such as college or business.

Industrial/Organizational

**How can we increase the productivity of workers?
How can we select employees who will be successful?**

If you have an interest in psychology and business, you may wish to consider becoming an industrial/ organizational psychologist.

Industrial/organizational psychology examines the relationships of people and their work environments.

These psychologists may be involved in personnel selection, help improve employee relationships, or increase employee job satisfaction. Industrial/organizational psychologists usually work in businesses, industry, and academic settings.

Making Decisions

If you decide to become a psychologist, you will need to make a series of decisions. The first is whether to obtain a master's degree or a PhD. The next decision involves which setting to work in: choosing among private practice, clinic or hospital setting, academic research and/or teaching, industry/business, or counseling and testing in a school setting. You'll also need to specialize in one of the eight areas described above. After making these decisions, you are on your way to an interesting and exciting career.

What should I do?

Next, we're going to use research findings from several research areas, including experimental and cognitive, and give you tips on how to improve your study skills. ●

Improving Study Habits

What study problems do most freshmen report?

In a survey of college freshmen, only 16% reported they had very good study habits and only 24% said they were very good at managing their time (HRSDC, 2007). We'll discuss ways you can improve your study habits and time management to help you be a successful college student.

Common complaint. The most common student complaint we hear after exams is, "I read the book and went over my notes three times and still got a C." This complaint points to the most common mistake students make in studying for exams. Because students read the material and go over their notes several times, they may have a general feeling they know the material. For example, you have just read about the modern approaches, the historical approaches, and the differences between a psychologist and psychiatrist. Having read this material, you may generally feel that you know it. However, researchers have discovered a startling fact: There is almost no relationship between how well students think they know material and how well they perform on an exam (Eva et al., 2004; Tousignant & Des-Marchais, 2002).

Poor judges. The reason students tend to be poor judges of what they know is that they base their judgments more on what they *generally* know than on what they *specifically* remember (Glenberg et al., 1987). For example, you might generally remember the modern approaches. However, on an exam you will be asked for specific information, such as names and definitions. One way to judge how prepared you are for an exam is to test yourself

How do I know when I've studied enough to take a test?

© lenetstan/Shutterstock.com

and get feedback from answering specific questions. For instance, can you list the modern approaches and define each one? Because answering specific questions is one way to judge your learning, we built specific questions and answers into this text. You can test yourself by answering questions in the Concept Review in each module and in the Summary Test at the end of each module.

Reducing distractions. When we ask students about their study habits, we often learn they listen to music, watch TV, answer phone calls, or use the Internet while studying. These study habits can lead to lower exam scores (Gurung, 2005). One way students can improve their study habits is by eliminating distractions.

Time management. A common problem students have is managing their time. As a result, students often fall behind in classes and then must cram for exams. Intense studying before an exam may help you pass, but your time could be much better spent. Did you know that spreading out your studying can help you better remember information? In fact, dividing your studying into two sessions with time between them has been shown to result in twice as much learning as one study session of the same length! This is because your brain remembers information longer if it has time to process what you've learned (Aamodt & Wang, 2008). Next, we'll discuss another useful way to better manage your time.

> **Remember:**
> To judge how well prepared you are for an exam, ask yourself specific questions about the material. You can do that by taking the tests built into each module—Concept Review and Summary Test.

Setting Goals

What's the best kind of goal to set?

Another way to better manage your study time is to set the right goals, which can vary from studying for a certain period of time to studying until you feel you are well prepared (Flippo & Caverly, 2000, 2009). Which of the following goals do you think would make your study time more efficient and improve your test performance?

1 Set a **time goal,** such as studying 10 hours a week or more, and then keep track of your study time during the semester.

Should my goal be to study 10 hours a week?

© marco mayer/Shutterstock.com

2 Set a **general goal,** such as trying to study hard and stay on schedule; then, try to reach this goal during the semester.

3 Set a **specific performance goal,** such as answering at least 80% of the Summary Test questions correctly for each module.

To determine which of these three goals leads to more effective studying, researchers told three different groups of students to set time goals, general goals, or specific performance goals when they studied on their own. The researchers found that students who set specific performance goals did significantly better on the final exam than students who set time or general goals (M. Morgan, 1985). Thus, if you want to improve your study skills, you should think less about the total time you study and concentrate more on reaching a specific performance goal every week. For example, the first week your goal might be to correctly answer 80% of the Summary Test questions. Once you have reached this goal, you could aim to answer 90% of the questions correctly. Following a study plan based on specific performance goals is the key to better time management (Wolters, 2003).

As you'll see next, one way to motivate yourself to reach your performance goals is to reward yourself at the right times.

> **Remember:**
> One way to make your study time more efficient is to set a specific performance goal and keep track of your progress.

Rewarding Yourself

One problem many students have is getting and staying motivated. One reliable solution is to give yourself a reward when you reach a specific goal, such as answering 80% of the questions correctly.

What if you reach a goal?

The reward may be a special treat (such as a CD, meal, movie, or time with friends) or a positive statement (such as "I'm doing really well" or "I'm going to get a good grade on the test"). Giving yourself a reward (self-reinforcement) is an effective way to improve performance (Allgood et al., 2000).

Motivate yourself with rewards.

> **Remember:**
> Immediately after you reach a specific goal, give yourself a reward, which will both maintain and improve your motivation.

Taking Notes

Another way to improve your performance is to take great notes. Students generally make two kinds of mistakes in taking notes. One is to try to write down everything the instructor says, which is impossible and leads to confusing notes. The other is to mechanically copy down terms or concepts that they do not understand but hope to learn by memorization, which is difficult. Researchers have four suggestions for taking good notes (Armbruster, 2000, 2009):

1 Write down the information in your own words. This approach will ensure that you understand the material and will increase your chances of remembering it.

2 Use headings or an outline format. This method will help you better organize and remember the material.

3 Try to associate new lecture or text material with material that you already know. It's easier to remember new information if you can relate it to your existing knowledge. That is the reason we have paired terms in the Concept Review section with illustrations, drawings, and photos that you are familiar with from earlier in the text.

4 As we discussed in the Research Focus (p. 16), you can improve your note-taking by asking yourself questions, such as: What is the main idea of …? What is an example of …? How is … related to what we studied earlier? Writing the answers in your own words will give you a better chance of remembering the material (A. King, 1992).

Even though you may take great notes and set performance goals, if you procrastinate and put off getting started, as about 70% of students report doing, your best-laid plans will come to nothing (E. Hoover, 2005).

> **Remember:**
> Go through your lecture notes, ask questions, and write down answers in your own words.

Taking Tests

Believe it or not, taking tests is not solely for the purpose of an instructor assessing your learning. Taking tests can actually help you learn! One study had a group of students read a passage and then take a test asking them to recall what they read. Those students remembered about 50% more of the information one week later compared to students who repeatedly studied the material (similar to cramming for a test) and those who drew diagrams about what they read (Karpicke & Blunt, 2011). Recalling information helps us retain more information.

In each of the modules in this textbook, there is a Concept Review and Summary Test (indicated by the right visual icon) that will ask you to recall key terms and other content from what you have just read. Your completion of these sections should help you retain more information when it comes time to taking your instructor's tests.

> **Remember:**
> Taking tests can be an effective learning strategy. Complete the Concept Review and Summary Test sections in each module.

Stopping Procrastination

Some students find the task of reading assignments, studying for exams, or writing papers so difficult that they cannot bring themselves to start. If you have problems with procrastinating, here are three things you should do to get started (Ariely & Wertenbroch, 2002; Blunt & Pychyl, 2000):

How do you get started?

1 *Stop thinking about the final goal*—reading 30 pages or taking two midterm exams—which may seem too overwhelming.

2 Break the final assignment down into *smaller goals* that are less overwhelming and easier to accomplish. Work on the first small goal, and when you finish it, go on to the next small goal. Continue until you have completed all the small goals. Thinking about study tasks in specific ways makes you feel like the tasks can be completed sooner and reduces procrastination (S. M. McCrea et al., 2008). Setting smaller goals is a way to think of tasks in a specific way.

3 Write down a *realistic schedule* for reaching each of your smaller goals. This schedule should indicate the time and place for study and what you will accomplish that day. Use a variety of self-reinforcements to stay on your daily schedule and accomplish your specific goals.

These 3 steps helped me overcome procrastination!

If you adopt these tested methods for improving your study skills, you'll greatly increase your chances of being a successful student (Flippo & Caverly, 2009). ●

> **Remember:**
> One of the most effective ways to start a large assignment is to break it down into a series of smaller goals and work on each goal separately.

Learning through Visuals

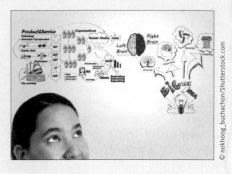

A large body of research indicates that visual cues help us to better retrieve and remember information. The research outcomes on visual learning make complete sense when you consider that our brain is mainly an image processor, not a word processor. In fact, the part of the brain used to process words is quite small in comparison to the part that processes visual images.

1 Which goal of psychology is illustrated by stating that visual learning makes sense given that our brains are mainly image processors?

2 Which area of specialization in psychology is best suited to understand how people learn through visuals?

Words are abstract and rather difficult for the brain to retain, whereas visuals are concrete and, as such, more easily remembered. To illustrate, think back to having to learn a set of new vocabulary words each week in school. Now, think back to the first kiss you had, the high school prom, or your 16th birthday party. Most likely, you had to expend great effort to remember the vocabulary words. In contrast, when you were actually having your first kiss, going to the prom, or celebrating your birthday, we bet you weren't trying to commit it to memory. Yet, you can quickly and effortlessly visualize these experiences. You can thank your brain's amazing visual processor for your ability to easily remember life experiences.

There are countless studies that have confirmed the power of visual imagery in learning. For instance, one study asked students to remember many groups of three words each, such as *dog, bike,* and *street.* Students who tried to remember the words by repeating them over and over again did poorly on recall. In comparison, students who made the effort to make visual associations with the three words, such as imagining a dog riding a bike down the street, had significantly better recall.

3 Which career setting is a psychologist who examines the effectiveness of visual learning most likely to be in?

Various types of visuals can be effective learning tools: photos, illustrations, icons, symbols, sketches, and figures, to name only a few. Consider how memorable the visual graphics are in logos, for example. You recognize the brand by seeing the visual graphic, even before reading the name of the brand. This type of visual can be so effective that Starbucks recently simplified its logo by dropping the printed name and keeping only the graphic image of the popular so-called mermaid (technically, it's a siren). We can safely assume that Starbucks Corporation must be keenly aware of how our brains have automatically and effortlessly committed the graphic image to memory.

So powerful is visual learning that we embrace it in the writing of this textbook. Each page of this textbook has been individually formatted to maximize visual learning. We believe the right visuals can help make abstract and difficult concepts more tangible and welcoming, as well as make learning more effective and long lasting. This is why we scrutinize every visual used in our writing to make sure it is paired with content in a clear, meaningful manner.

4 Which of the modern approaches to psychology is best suited to study how the brain performs during visual learning?

5 How do visual learning and academic performance relate to the definition of psychology?

As you see the visuals in this textbook, remember that, based on research outcomes, learning through visuals can decrease learning time, improve comprehension, enhance retrieval, and increase retention.

6 "Visual learning will improve academic performance" illustrates which goal of psychology?

Adapted from McDaniel & Einstein, 1986; Meier, 2000; Patton, 1991; Schacter, 1996; Verdi et al., 1997.

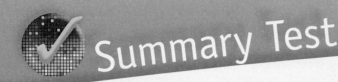

Summary Test

A Definitions & Goals

1. The broad definition of psychology is the systematic, scientific study of **(a)** _behaviors_ and **(b)** _mental processes_. The term in **(a)** refers to observable responses of animals and humans, and the term in **(b)** refers to processes that are not directly observable, such as thoughts, ideas, and dreams.

Courtesy of Chris Samuel, by permission of Chris Samuel

2. All psychologists agree that the first three goals of psychology are to **(a)** _describe_ what organisms do, to **(b)** _explain_ how organisms behave as they do, and to **(c)** _predict_ how they will respond in the future and in different situations. Some psychologists add a fourth goal, which is to **(d)** _control_ behavior and thus curb or eliminate psychological and social problems.

B Modern Approaches

3. Because behavior is often so complex, psychologists study it using eight different approaches. The approach that focuses on how a person's genetic make-up, hormones, and nervous system interact with the environment to influence a wide range of behaviors is called the _biological_ approach.

4. The approach that studies how organisms learn new behaviors or change or modify existing ones in response to influences from the environment is called the **(a)** _behavioral_ approach. There are two versions of this approach. One that primarily studies observable behaviors and excludes mental events is called **(b)** _strict behaviorism_ and is best expressed by the ideas of B. F. Skinner; the other, which includes observable behaviors plus cognitive processes, is called the **(c)** _social cognitive_ approach and is expressed by the ideas of Albert Bandura and his colleagues.

5. An approach that examines how our unconscious fears, desires, and motivations influence behaviors, thoughts, and personality and cause psychological problems is called the _psychoanalytic_ approach. Sigmund Freud developed this approach, as well as the technique of dream interpretation, to bring unconscious ideas to the surface.

6. The approach that investigates how people attend to, store, and process information and how this information affects learning, remembering, and believing is called the _cognitive_ approach.

7. The approach that emphasizes people's capacity for personal growth, freedom in choosing their future, and potential for self-fulfillment is called the _humanistic_ approach.

8. The approach that studies the influence of social and cultural factors on psychological and behavioral functioning is called the _sociocultural_ approach.

9. The approach that studies how evolutionary ideas, such as adaptation and natural selection, explain human behaviors and mental processes is called the _evolutionary_ approach.

10. The approach that studies how biological, psychological, and sociocultural factors influence human development is called the _____ approach.

C Historical Approaches

11. Considered the father of psychology, Wilhelm Wundt developed an approach called **(a)** _structuralism_. This approach studied the elements of the conscious mind by using a self-report technique called **(b)** _introspection_. Wundt's approach was the beginning of today's cognitive approach.

© Keith Szafranski/iStockphoto

12. Disagreeing with Wundt's approach, William James said that it was important to study functions rather than elements of the mind. Accordingly, James studied the functions of consciousness as well as how mental processes continuously flow and adapt to input from the environment. This approach is called _functionalism_. James's ideas contributed to the modern area of psychology and influenced educational psychology.

13. Also disagreeing with Wundt's approach was a group of psychologists, led by Wertheimer, Köhler, and Koffka, who stated that perceptions cannot be explained by breaking them down into individual elements or sensations. Instead, they believed that perceptions are more than the sum of individual sensations, an idea called the _Gestalt_ approach.

14. Another psychologist who disagreed with Wundt's approach was John B. Watson. He stated that psychology should use scientific principles to study only observable behaviors and not mental events, an approach called _behaviorism_. Watson's approach gave rise to the modern behavioral approach.

D Cultural Diversity: Early Discrimination

15. During the first 75 of its more than 100 years of existence, the field of psychology discriminated against **(a)** _women_ and **(b)** _minorities_, as indicated by the very limited number of these individuals who were granted PhDs or offered positions in major universities. During the past 40 or

Courtesy, Margaret Clapp Library Archives, Wellesley College, photo by Patridge

so years, the American Psychological Association, minority organizations, and most universities and colleges have been actively recruiting minorities and helping them enter the field of psychology.

E Research Focus: Taking Class Notes

16. Three different strategies for note-taking were studied: note-taking plus review, which means writing down almost everything the instructor says; note-taking plus questions, which means asking and answering questions about the lecture material; and note-taking plus summary, which means writing a summary of the lecture in your own words. The note-taking strategy that resulted in the highest exam grades involved **(a)** _____, and the note-taking strategy that resulted in the lowest exam grades involved **(b)** _____.

F Careers in Psychology

17. There are five major settings in which psychologists work and establish careers. The largest percentage of psychologists work in private practice or **(a)** _____ settings, where they diagnose and help clients with psychological problems. The second largest group work in **(b)** _____ settings, doing a combination of teaching and research. The third largest group work in a **(c)** _____ of settings. The fourth largest group work in **(d)** _____ settings, where they are involved in selecting personnel, increasing job satisfaction, and improving worker–management relations. The smallest group work in other settings, such as **(e)** _____, where they do academic testing and counseling.

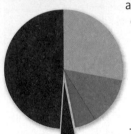

G Research Areas

18. There are eight common subareas in which psychologists specialize. Psychologists interested in the assessment and treatment of people with psychological problems, such as anxiety or stress, specialize in **(a)** _____ psychology. Those who are interested in prejudice, attitudes, and group behaviors specialize in **(b)** _____ psychology. Those interested in social, emotional, and cognitive changes

across the life span specialize in **(c)** _____ psychology. Those interested in studying sensation, perceptions, and learning, often under laboratory conditions, specialize in **(d)** _____ psychology. Those interested in the interaction among genes, the nervous system, and the environment choose **(e)** _____ psychology. Those interested in how people process, store, and retrieve information choose **(f)** _____ psychology. Those interested in the measurement and testing of skills, abilities, personality, and mental problems specialize in **(g)** _____, and those interested in the relationships of people and their work specialize in **(h)** _____ psychology.

H Application: Study Skills

19. Another common mistake that students make is that they think they know the material after reading the text and reviewing their notes. A better way to judge how prepared you are for an exam is to ask yourself specific **(a)** _____ rather than to trust your judgment about what you think you know. A good way to make your study time more efficient is to set specific **(b)** _____ and keep track of your progress. Immediately after you reach a specific performance goal, give yourself a **(c)** _____, which will both maintain and improve your motivation. To improve your lecture notes, try to associate new lecture material with what you already know, and use your notes to ask and answer **(d)** _____ in your own words. One of the most effective ways to overcome a strong tendency to delay starting a task, known as **(e)** _____, is to stop thinking about the final goal. Instead, break down a large assignment into a series of smaller goals and work on each goal separately. Finally, it's best to set a realistic **(f)** _____ in order to accomplish each of the smaller goals.

Answers: 1. (a) behaviors, (b) mental processes; 2. (a) describe, (b) explain, (c) predict, (d) control; 3. biological; 4. (a) behavioral, (b) strict behaviorism, (c) social cognitive; 5. psychoanalytic; 6. cognitive; 7. humanistic; 8. sociocultural; 9. evolutionary; 10. biopsychosocial; 11. (a) structuralism, (b) introspection; 12. functionalism; 13. Gestalt; 14. behaviorism; 15. (a) women, (b) minorities; 16. (a) answering questions, (b) reviewing notes; 17. (a) therapy or clinical, (b) academic, (c) variety, (d) industrial, (e) schools; 18. (a) clinical and counseling, (b) social, (c) developmental, (d) experimental, (e) biological or psychobiology, (f) cognitive, (g) psychometrics, (h) industrial/organizational; 19. (a) questions, (b) performance goals, (c) reward, (d) questions, (e) procrastination, (f) schedule

Links to Learning

Key Terms/Key People

academic settings, 17
apparent motion, 13
approach, 5
autism, 3
autistic savants, 3, 7
Bandura, Albert, 8
behavioral approach, 8, 13
biological approach, 6
biological psychology, 19
biopsychosocial approach, 11
Calkins, Mary, 14
career settings, 17
clinical and counseling
  psychology, 18
clinical psychologist, 17
cognitive approach, 7
cognitive neuroscience, 7

cognitive psychology, 19
counseling psychologists, 17
developmental psychology, 18
evolutionary approach, 11
experimental psychology, 18
Freud, Sigmund, 9
functionalism, 12
Gestalt approach, 13
goals of psychology, 4
humanistic approach, 10
industrial/organizational
  psychology, 19
industrial settings, 17
introspection, 12
James, William, 12
Koffka, Kurt, 13
Köhler, Wolfgang, 13

Maslow, Abraham, 10
neuroscience, 6
palmar sweating, 6
phi phenomenon, 13
positive psychology, 10
Principles of Psychology, 12
private practice, 17
procrastination, 9, 21
Prosser, Inez, 14
psychiatrist, 17
psychoanalytic approach, 9
psychobiology, 19
psychologist, 17
psychology, 4
psychometrics, 19
rewarding yourself, 21
Sanchez, George, 14

savants, 3
secondary schools, 17
setting goals, 20
Skinner, B. F., 8, 13
social cognitive approach, 8
social psychology, 18
sociocultural approach, 11
stopping procrastination, 21
structuralism, 12
taking notes, 16, 21
test anxiety, 3
therapy setting, 17
time management, 20
Watson, John, 13
Wertheimer, Max, 13
Wundt, William, 12

Media Resources

Go to **CengageBrain.com** to access Psychology CourseMate, where you will find an interactive eBook, glossaries, flashcards, quizzes, videos, answers to Critical Thinking questions, and more. You can also access Virtual Psychology Labs, an interactive laboratory experience designed to illustrate key experiments first-hand.

Psychology & Science

introduction

Blake's Problem

When Blake was 3 years old, he crawled into a *T. rex* display at a museum and set off blaring alarms.

What's wrong with Blake's behavior? As a child, he was easily bored, couldn't focus on anything for very long, and never sat still for more than a second. Blake admits that he gets bored easily and is often so desperate to find something interesting to do that he goes "full steam ahead without thinking." One day, to keep himself entertained, he launched rockets (accidentally) into the neighbor's swimming pool! Blake's mother describes him as "exhausting" and "off the wall." "Within minutes, he'd go from concocting baking-soda volcanoes to dumping out all the Lego and K'nex sets, to emptying out the linen closet in order to build a tent city," says his mother (Taylor-Barnes, 2008) (adapted from B. E. S. Taylor, 2007).

At age 5, Blake was diagnosed with a behavioral problem that has been surrounded with controversy. Blake was diagnosed as being hyperactive and inattentive, a problem that is officially called attention-deficit/hyperactivity disorder, or ADHD (American Psychiatric Association, 2000).

Attention-deficit/hyperactivity disorder, or ADHD, is not diagnosed by any medical tests but on the basis of the occurrence of certain behavioral problems. A child must have six or more symptoms of inattention, such as making careless mistakes in schoolwork, not following instructions, and being easily distracted, and six or more symptoms of hyperactivity, such as fidgeting, leaving classroom seat, and talking excessively. These symptoms should have been present from an early age, persisted for at least six months, and contributed to maladaptive development.

One controversy surrounding ADHD involves diagnosis. Since ADHD is based not on medical tests but rather on the occurrence of certain behavioral problems, how can parents and teachers distinguish children with ADHD from those who are naturally outgoing and rambunctious (West et al., 2005)? Because of this difficulty, the American Academy of Pediatrics has issued guidelines for diagnosing ADHD (AAP, 2011). These guidelines stress that, before the diagnosis of ADHD is made, a number of the symptoms described above should be present for at least six months. The guidelines focus on children as young as 4 and up to 18 years of age. For young children the AAP advises physicians to look for evidence of consistent and persistent inattentive or hyperactive behavior. These guidelines aim to improve the accuracy of diagnosis and consequently help to prevent merely rambunctious youngsters from being overmedicated while ensuring that children with ADHD get the help they need.

Another controversy is how to treat children with ADHD. To help control Blake's ADHD, he was given a popular drug that is a relatively powerful stimulant, called Adderall. With the continued aid of medication, Blake became a successful student at the University of California at Berkeley and wrote his own memoir.

Blake, now a young adult, was diagnosed with ADHD at age 5.

Reprinted with permission by New Harbinger Publications, Inc., *ADHD & Me* by Blake E. S. Taylor

Researchers do not completely understand why stimulant drugs, such as Adderall or Ritalin, decrease activity in children. But drugs used to treat ADHD are undeniably popular, and spending on these medications has exceeded $3 billion a year (GIA, 2010). Perhaps the major questions surrounding the use of Ritalin concern whether it is being overprescribed, whether it is the most effective treatment, and how long a child with ADHD should remain on the drug. In addition, Ritalin, especially in larger doses, does have side effects that may include loss of appetite and problems with sleeping. A related question is whether children with ADHD should be kept on a diet free of artificial dyes, sweeteners, and sugar, which some parents claim worsen the symptoms. We'll answer these questions in this module.

We're going to use Blake's problem with ADHD to show how researchers pursue the four goals of psychology that we discussed in Module 1. In Blake's case, the four goals are (1) to describe Blake's symptoms, (2) to explain their causes, (3) to predict their occurrence, and (4) to control Blake's behavior through some behavioral therapy or drug treatment.

Centipedes and Cough Medicine

Can beliefs cure like real medicine? One interesting aspect of trying to control unwanted symptoms with a drug treatment is that sometimes the drug is not really a drug because it has no proven medical effects. For example, in many parts of Asia, people believe powdered tablets made from centipedes are medicine for treating a variety of physical problems. Similarly, in the United States, people spend billions of dollars a year on over-the-counter cough medicines, including cough syrups and cough drops, even though there is no reliable scientific evidence that cough medications work (J. W. Payne, 2006).

The use of centipedes and cough medicine, both questionable medical treatments, raises the interesting question of how much one's mind or one's beliefs contribute to the development or treatment of physical symptoms. We'll discuss methods that researchers use to decide whether the effectiveness of a treatment is due to a drug's medical effect or the person's beliefs.

© fivespots/Shutterstock.com

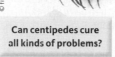

Can centipedes cure all kinds of problems?

What's Coming

Our main goal in this module is to explore the methods that researchers use to answer questions, such as how to treat ADHD and why placebos work. Specifically, we will discuss descriptive, correlational, and experimental research methods. We'll explain which research procedures can identify cause-and-effect relationships and which cannot. We'll begin by explaining the multistep process psychologists use to answer research questions. ●

Scientific Method

There are of course different ways to answer questions. If we were to answer questions about human behavior and mental processes in an informal manner, we would be engaging in what's referred to as armchair psychology.

How do psychologists answer questions?

Armchair psychology is the practice of answering questions about human behavior and mental processes through informal observation and speculation.

Sometimes we get the answer correct by using armchair psychology. But sometimes we can be wrong in our assumptions about human behavior.

The founders of the science of psychology, such as Wilhelm Wundt and William James, realized that armchair psychology could be improved by treating our speculations as hypotheses

Wilhelm Wundt

William James

that could be subjected to scientific scrutiny. Over and over again, psychologists have been surprised to find that what was once thought to be self-evident turned out, on closer examination, to be false. Scientific methods provide us with a more reliable method to answer questions.

Even though there is an endless array of questions we could ask about people's mental processes and behaviors, psychologists follow the same basic approach to answer each question. This approach is called the scientific method.

The **scientific method** is a multistep technique of gathering information and answering questions so that errors and biases are minimized.

The scientific method includes six steps:

1 Review the literature: The researcher reads the scientific literature to learn what has already been published on the subject or content he or she is interested in examining.

2 Formulate a hypothesis: The researcher makes an educated guess about some phenomenon and states it in a very precise way to rule out confusion or error in the meanings of its terms. To test a hypothesis, the variables must have operational definitions, which means they need to be described in a specific, objective manner that allows them to be measured.

3 Design the study: The researcher selects the research method that best tests the hypothesis. In this module, you'll learn about several research methods, including surveys, case studies, observations, correlations, and experiments.

4 Collect the data: The researcher now begins conducting the study and collecting the data. There are various methods of collecting data. Some examples are questionnaires, observations, interviews, psychological tests, and physiological measurements. The choice a researcher makes depends primarily on the topic being studied. For example, questionnaires are best suited to assess attitudes and beliefs, whereas physiological measurements, such as brain scans, are best suited to tell us what is happening in the brain during a specific activity.

5 Draw conclusions: First the collected data must be analyzed using appropriate statistical techniques. Then the researcher can determine whether or not the data support the hypothesis.

6 Report the findings: The final step in the scientific method is to summarize the research project and its results, and then submit the findings to a professional journal. By doing so, researchers contribute to the progression of their specific field of study and science in general. Once their research is published, other researchers can learn from their results as well as replicate their study, critique it, or pursue research that furthers knowledge of the topic.

Advantages

The scientific method has a few key advantages or strengths. First, it is specific and precise. The scientific method precisely states hypotheses and operational definitions, which makes what the researchers are examining completely clear to others. Second, the scientific method is an empirical process that ultimately reduces error by making the research findings available to others who can replicate and critique them. This promotes discussion within the scientific community and progresses knowledge in the field. Last, the scientific method can be used for any of the four goals of psychology. For instance, if a researcher is addressing the goal of prediction, then the hypothesis will state what the researcher expects to find. The researcher then chooses a research method, data collection technique, and statistical analysis that best test the hypothesis.

Now that you've learned the foundation for conducting research in psychology, we'll discuss various research methods, all of which can be used in the scientific method. To help you better understand these research methods, we're going to apply each method to the same specific topic, attention-deficit/hyperactivity disorder (ADHD). We'll begin by discussing three types of descriptive research methods: survey, naturalistic observation, and case study. ●

B Descriptive Research

Survey

Suppose you wish to know how many children have ADHD, whether it occurs more in boys or girls, which treatment is the most popular, and how many children continue to have problems when they become adults. Researchers obtain this information with surveys.

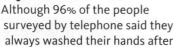

What do surveys tell us?

A **survey** is a method used to obtain information by asking many individuals—either person to person, by telephone, by mail, or by the Internet—to answer a fixed set of questions about particular subjects.

Almost every day the media report some new survey. Although surveys tell us what others believe or how they behave, survey questions can be written to bias the answers; moreover, people may not always answer truthfully (J. Wright & Marsden, 2010). For example, how many people do you think always wash their hands after going to the bathroom? We'll sample some surveys and then discuss their disadvantages and advantages.

Do you wash your hands?

Although 96% of the people surveyed by telephone said they always washed their hands after using a public bathroom, direct observation of 6,028 people in four major cities found that only 85% really do and that more women (93%) wash their hands than men (77%) (ASM, 2010).

How many children are diagnosed with ADHD?

Recent telephone surveys of parents report that 5% of U.S. children between 6 and 17 years old are diagnosed with ADHD. Boys are reported to be diagnosed with ADHD twice as often as girls. ADHD is reported to be more common among adolescents than younger children, and more common among White and African American children than Hispanic children (CDC, 2008a).

These examples show that surveys provide a great deal of useful information. However, surveys have potential problems with accuracy (as in the hand-washing survey) and, as you'll see next, with how questions are worded and who asks the questions.

Disadvantages

How questions are worded

You may be surprised to learn that surveys may get very different results depending on how questions are worded. Here are two examples:

QUESTION: "Would you say that **industry** contributes more or less to air pollution than **traffic**?"	**QUESTION:** "Would you say that **traffic** contributes more or less to air pollution than **industry**?"
Traffic contributes more: **24%**	**Traffic** contributes more: **45%**
Industry contributes more: 57%	**Industry** contributes more: 32%

These two examples indicate that the way questions are phrased and the way the possible answers are ordered can greatly influence people's responses and, in this case, produce opposite results (reported in *U.S. News & World Report,* Dec. 4, 1995, p. 55).

Who asks the questions

You may also be surprised to learn that the sex or race of the questioner can also affect how people answer the questions.

QUESTION: "The problems faced by Blacks were brought on by Blacks themselves."
When the interviewer was **White, 62%** of Whites who were interviewed agreed.
When the interviewer was **Black, 46%** of Whites who were interviewed agreed.

These two examples indicate that when asked about sensitive or emotional issues, people take into account the race of the interviewer and tend to give socially acceptable rather than honest answers (*U.S. News & World Report,* Dec. 4, 1995, p. 55).

In conclusion, surveys can be biased because people may not answer questions truthfully, may give socially acceptable answers, or may feel pressured to answer in certain ways. Also, surveys can be biased by how questions are worded and by interviewing a group of people who do not represent the general population (Gravetter & Forzano, 2012; S. L. Jackson, 2012). Despite these potential problems, surveys have advantages.

Advantages

While guarding against error and bias, surveys can be a useful research tool to quickly and efficiently collect information on behaviors, beliefs, experiences, and attitudes from a large sample of people and can compare answers from various ethnic, age, socioeconomic, and cultural groups.

For example, surveys suggest that ADHD interferes with performance in school settings, decreases the chances of graduating from high school, and may lead to conduct disorder problems in adolescence as well as continued problems in adulthood (Barkley et al., 2010; Root & Resnick, 2003).

Because surveys indicate that children with ADHD have major problems in school settings, psychologists are developing methods for improving performance. These methods include teaching children with ADHD how to organize their work, giving them constant feedback on reaching their goals, and starting programs that train teachers and families to work together to help children with ADHD control their disruptive behaviors (Hechtman et al., 2004; Matson, 2010). Thus, another advantage of surveys is their ability to identify problems and evaluate treatment programs.

However, if researchers wish to observe behavior, rather than simply ask about behavior, they use naturalistic observation.

Naturalistic Observation

How do psychologists observe behavior?

In trying to understand the kinds of problems faced by children with ADHD, psychologists study these children in different research settings, which may include observing them in the home, in the classroom, on the playground, at the store, or at their workplace.

Parents and teachers often ask whether children with ADHD have different problems at home than in school or in other settings. Researchers answer the question of whether children act differently in different settings by conducting naturalistic observations.

A **naturalistic observation** is a method researchers use to gather information by observing individuals' behaviors in a relatively normal environment without attempting to change or control the situation.

For example, naturalistic observations of children with ADHD in school settings indicate that they have difficulty remaining in their seats, don't pay attention to the teacher, can't sit still, rudely interrupt the teacher or other students, and get angry when they don't get their way (Junod et al., 2006). Parents report that, at home, children with ADHD do not respond when called, throw tantrums when frustrated, and have periods of great activity (Hancock, 1996).

Based on these naturalistic observations, researchers and pediatricians have developed a list of primary symptoms of ADHD (AAP, 2011). Similarly, psychologists study how normal people behave in different naturalistic settings, including schools, workplaces, college dormitories, bars, and sports arenas.

Home

School

Store

Park

Disadvantages

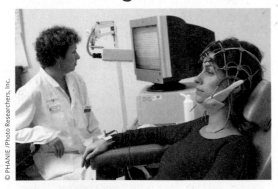

One problem with naturalistic observations is that the psychologists' own beliefs or values may bias their observations and cause them to misinterpret behaviors. Another problem is that conducting a naturalistic observation can be very time-consuming and requires much training and effort. Last, because naturalistic settings are uncontrolled and anything can happen, researchers find it difficult to identify what causes what. For this reason, researchers may have to investigate some questions in a more controlled setting, such as a laboratory.

A laboratory setting provides more control than a naturalistic setting.

Advantages

One advantage of naturalistic observations is the opportunity to study behaviors in real-life situations and environments, which cannot or would not be duplicated in the laboratory. Naturalistic observations allow researchers to get a close-up look at everyday life, which means they can be confident that this is really the way people typically behave. Also, because people don't know they are being observed, they often are not motivated to do what they think the observer or researcher wants them to do. Last, data are collected by firsthand observation and are not based on people's recollections, which at times can be far from accurate.

Naturalistic observation is a method used to study behaviors. If researchers are interested in an in-depth analysis of a single individual (thoughts, emotions, behaviors, etc.), then they would use a case study, our next topic.

Behaviors are observed in real-life situations.

Case Study

Sometimes researchers answer questions by studying a single individual in great detail, which is called a case study.

What's a case study?

A **case study** is an in-depth analysis of the thoughts, feelings, beliefs, or behaviors of a single person.

We discussed the case of Blake Taylor at the start of this module. From the age of 3, Blake has had problems paying attention and completing tasks. Throughout his childhood, he felt no one understood the challenges he endured. To help others understand what it's like to live with ADHD, he wrote his autobiography called *ADHD & Me* (right image). In it, he discusses the challenges he faced from early childhood through the present. He talks about how he must

take his ADHD medication, keep a daily routine, and make sure to get 9 hours of sleep each night to keep his ADHD symptoms from getting out of control. As a result of his motivation and self-discipline, Blake enjoys a balanced college life spent studying, working out, playing music, socializing, volunteering, and, of course, getting enough sleep (Anwar, 2008; B. E. S. Taylor, 2007). Sometimes case studies help answer questions, but case studies can also result in wrong or biased answers.

Disadvantages

One disadvantage of the case study is that some of the data rely on people's recollections, which can be inaccurate or incomplete. Another problem is that the motives of a researcher may bias the questioning of the person being studied, even though the researcher's intent is to be objective. Also, because case studies focus on individual cases, the results can be misleading if the individual being studied is atypical.

Last, results from case studies may be misinterpreted if the observer has preconceived notions of what to look for. For example, beginning in the mid-1970s, parents were told that food with artificial additives, dyes, and preservatives could cause hyperactivity in children (Feingold, 1975). Shortly after, parents reported that, yes indeed, artificial additives caused a sudden increase in restlessness and irritability in their hyperactive children (Feingold, 1975). The parents' reports and beliefs that additives cause hyperactivity are examples of a testimonial.

A **testimonial** is a statement in support of a particular viewpoint based on detailed observations of a person's own personal experience.

However, contrary to the parents' testimonials, researchers have generally found that amounts of artificial additives within a normal range do not cause hyperactivity (Kinsbourne, 1994; B. A. Shaywitz et al., 1994).

One of the major problems with testimonials is that they are based on our personal observations, which have great

Parents mistakenly believed that artificial sweeteners caused ADHD.

potential for error and bias. For example, if parents reported that sweeteners increased their son's activity, we would have to rule out personal beliefs and self-fulfilling prophecies.

Personal beliefs. If parents hear that artificial sweeteners may cause physical or psychological problems, they may interpret their child's problems as caused by artificial sweeteners. Because of biased perceptions, parents may overlook other potential causes, such as frustration, anger, or changes in the child's environment, and make the error of focusing only on artificial sweeteners. If we believe strongly in something, it may bias our perception and cause us to credit an unrelated treatment or event as the reason for some change.

Self-fulfilling prophecy. If parents believe that artificial sweeteners cause problems, they may behave in ways—being more strict or less sympathetic—that cause the problems to occur. This phenomenon is called a self-fulfilling prophecy.

A **self-fulfilling prophecy** involves having a strong belief or making a statement (prophecy) about a future behavior and then acting, usually unknowingly, to fulfill or carry out the behavior.

If we strongly believe that something is going to happen, then we may unknowingly behave in such a way as to make it happen (R. Rosenthal, 2003). Self-fulfilling prophecies reinforce testimonials and thus keep our biased beliefs alive.

In this module's Cultural Diversity section, we'll discuss how testimonials are a popular source of information, especially when we are talking about placebos.

Advantages

One of the major advantages of a case study is that it enables psychologists to obtain detailed descriptions and insights into aspects of an individual's life and behaviors that cannot be gained in other ways. This information may point to potential answers or lead to future studies. Consequently, case studies are useful in psychology to understand the development of a personality or psychological problem or to examine a person's behavior across his or her life span.

In conclusion, the purpose of descriptive research methods—survey, naturalistic observation, and case study—is to describe behavior, which, as we learned earlier, is the first goal of psychology. After the Cultural Diversity section, we'll discuss correlational research, which addresses the predictive goal of psychology. ●

Examples of Mind over Body

Psychologists are interested in how the mind influences the body, such as happens when someone takes a pill that happens to be a placebo.

Have you taken a placebo?

A **placebo** is some intervention, such as taking a pill, receiving an injection, or undergoing an operation, that resembles medical therapy but, in fact, has no medical effects.

The **placebo effect** is a change in the patient's illness that is attributable to an imagined treatment rather than to a medical treatment.

Research data reveal that placebos have helped alleviate a variety of medical problems, such as pain, headaches, depression, asthma, gastric reflux, high blood pressure, inflammatory disorders, Parkinson's disease, and even cancer (Begley, 2008b; Niemi, 2009).

You may be wondering how placebos can be so effective. Placebos may work because beliefs and thoughts are powerful enough to produce the same relief that is provided by real drugs (Ariely, 2008; Kluger, 2009). For instance, researchers in one study injected participants with a pain-inducing solution and then falsely told participants they had been injected with pain-relieving medication (placebo).

The power of placebos is in the mind.

© Andy Ryan/Getty Images

Pictures of participants' brains were then taken (PET—see p. 71), and results showed that for those people who said they felt less pain, their brain released natural painkillers after the placebo was injected (Haslinger, 2005). Our beliefs can actually change what is happening in our brain!

Recent research has shown what many would consider to be unthinkable: The placebo effect works even when people are told they are receiving a placebo. In this study, researchers divided patients with irritable bowel syndrome (IBS) into two groups. One group received no treatment. The other received twice-a-day pills described as "like sugar pills" and "placebo" was written on the pill bottles. Researchers even told participants the pills had no medical ingredient. Results indicated that 59% of those who received placebos reported relief (similar to research data on the effectiveness of real IBS medications) compared with only 35% of those who received no treatment (Kaptchuk et al., 2010). This study reveals how mysterious and powerful the placebo effect is.

As you'll see, testimonials from around the world claim that different kinds of placebos can cure a wide variety of symptoms.

Garlic

Millions of people in China claim that eating garlic prevents them from getting the H1N1 swine flu virus. People eat bulbs of garlic every day because they believe it kills the bacteria that cause swine flu. The demand for garlic in China is so high that prices have skyrocketed, rising more sharply than the prices of both gold and stocks. Despite the healing claims of garlic, there is no scientific evidence for its flu-killing powers. Even though the Chinese government tells its people about the lack of supportive data, people still adamantly believe garlic prevents swine flu (Macleod, 2009).

© Oliver Hoffmann/Shutterstock.com

Centipedes

In parts of Asia, a popular "medicine" to treat many kinds of physical problems is a tablet made from the Korean centipede. It is believed to cure arthritis, kidney stones, malaria, skin diseases, and severe scars. Folk logic seems to guide the use of centipedes as "medicine." For instance, centipedes have many legs and are used to treat leg problems (Pemberton, 2005; SACU, 2001).

In fact, centipede poison may cause pain, nausea, and fatal cases of organ failure (Norris, 2008; Yuen et al., 2006).

© fivespots/Shutterstock.com

Tiger Bones

There has been a massive decline in the tiger population in Asia because tiger bones are used to treat ulcers, typhoid, malaria, joint pain, and burns; to increase longevity; to improve sexual desire; and to cure devil possession (Friend, 1997; Sylvester, 2009). Wealthy Taiwanese pay $320 for a bowl of tiger penis soup that is thought to increase flagging libidos (Nagarahole, 1994). Tiger bones and penises function as powerful placebos in traditional Asian medicine.

© Eric Isselee/Shutterstock.com

Cough Medication

When we have a cold with a relentless cough, many of us purchase cough syrup. In the United States, billions of dollars are spent every year

© R-photos/Shutterstock.com

on cough medications (cough syrups and lozenges), yet there is no scientific evidence that these over-the-counter medications work (Ignelzi, 2006a; J. W. Payne, 2006).

Conclusion: Testimonials and Placebos

The main reason placebos are used worldwide is that their beneficial "medical" effects are supported by countless testimonials, which are convincing because they are based on the real-life experiences of friends, peers, and parents, who are honest and believable. However, it

Why are placebos so popular?

is common for even honest and trustworthy people to unknowingly make a mistake and conclude that garlic, a centipede, a tiger bone, or cough medication is producing a beneficial "medical" effect when the beneficial effect is actually being caused by the individual's thoughts influencing the brain or body's functioning (Ariely, 2008; Benedetti, 2009).

As you'll see next, people may make mistakes about the effect of placebos because there is often no way to figure out what causes what. ●

Concept Review

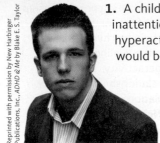

1. A child who has six or more symptoms of inattention and six or more symptoms of hyperactivity that last for at least 6 months would be diagnosed with _____.

2. The process of answering questions about human behavior and mental processes through informal observation and speculation is called **(a)** _____. The multistep technique of gathering information and answering questions so that errors and biases are minimized is called the **(b)** _____.

3. The six steps of the scientific method are:

> **1** Review
> **2** Formulate
> **3** Design
> **4** Collect
> **5** Draw
> **6** Report

1. Review the **(a)** _____.
2. Formulate a **(b)** _____.
3. Design the **(c)** _____.
4. Collect the **(d)** _____.
5. Draw **(e)** _____.
6. Report the **(f)** _____.

4. When psychologists obtain information by asking a fixed set of questions, it is called a _____.

5. When researchers gather information by observing individuals' behaviors in a relatively normal environment without attempting to change or control the situation, they are conducting a _____.

6. If psychologists obtain information through an in-depth analysis of the thoughts and behaviors of a single individual, this method is called a _____.

7. A statement that supports a particular viewpoint and is based on a person's own experience is called a **(a)** _____, which has two potential sources of error and bias. First, strongly held personal beliefs may bias an individual's **(b)** _____ of events. Second, believing strongly that something will happen and then unknowingly acting in such a way as to make that something occur can cause an error called **(c)** _____. This source of error is one of the major reasons that people believe their **(d)** _____ are true.

8. An intervention that is designed to look like a medical treatment but has no actual medical effect is called a **(a)** _____. When a change in a patient's illness is due to a supposed treatment and not to any medical therapy, it is called the **(b)** _____.

Answers: 1. attention-deficit/hyperactivity disorder or ADHD; 2. (a) armchair psychology (b) scientific method; 3. (a) literature, (b) hypothesis, (c) study, (d) data, (e) conclusions, (f) findings; 4. survey; 5. naturalistic observation, 6. case study; 7. (a) testimonial, (b) perceptions, (c) self-fulfilling prophecy, (d) testimonials. 8. (a) placebo, (b) placebo effect

Reprinted with permission by New Harbinger Publications, Inc., *ADHD @ Me* by Blake E. S. Taylor

© naenaz2/iStockphoto

© Jutta Klee/Getty Images

© Andy Ryan/Getty Images

Reprinted with permission by New Harbinger Publications, Inc., *ADHD @ Me* by Blake E. S. Taylor

ADHD&me
what I learned from lighting fires at the dinner table
blake e. s. taylor

Correlations

Research suggests that ADHD has a genetic basis.

What's a correlation?

The photo on the left shows a boy who is demonstrating hyperactive behavior. Researchers would like to know if this boy's hyperactivity has a genetic basis. One way to identify genetic factors is to study identical twins because they share almost 100% of their genes. Suppose you were studying the occurrence of ADHD in identical male twins and found that about 75% of the time, if one identical twin had ADHD so did the second twin (Faraone et al., 2005). This strong relationship between behaviors in identical twins suggests a genetic basis for ADHD. Such a relationship is called a correlation.

A **correlation** is an association or relationship between the occurrence of two or more events.

For example, if one twin has hyperactivity, a correlation will tell us the likelihood that the other twin also has hyperactivity. The likelihood or strength of a relationship between two events is called a correlation coefficient.

A **correlation coefficient** is a number that indicates the strength of a relationship between two or more events: the closer the number is to –1.00 or +1.00, the greater is the strength of the relationship.

We'll explain correlation coefficients in more detail because they can be confusing.

Correlation Coefficients

What are these numbers?

There are two major points to understand about correlations:

First, a correlation means there is an association between two or more events. For example, there is an association, or correlation, between the sex of a child and the occurrence of ADHD; four to five times more boys are diagnosed with ADHD than girls.

A second point to understand about correlations is that the strength of the relationship or association is measured by a number called a correlation coefficient. Because the correlation coefficient ranges from +1.00 to –1.00, its meaning can be confusing. In the boxes on the right, we'll describe what correlation coefficients mean, beginning at the top of the scale with a +1.00.

+1.00

+0.50

0.00

−0.50

−1.00

If each of 20 identical pairs showed equal levels of hyperactivity, the correlation coefficient would be positive and perfect and would be indicated by a +1.00 correlation coefficient.

A **perfect positive correlation coefficient** of +1.00 means that an increase in one event is always matched by an equal increase in a second event. For example, if one identical twin has hyperactivity, then the other twin always has hyperactivity. A correlation of +1.00 is virtually never found in applied psychological research (Hemphill, 2003).

If some identical pairs but not all 20 pairs were similar in hyperactivity, the result would be a positive correlation coefficient, which can range from +0.01 to +0.99.

A **positive correlation coefficient** indicates that as one event tends to increase, the second event tends to, but does not always, increase.

As the coefficient increases from +0.01 to +0.99, it indicates a strengthening of the relationship between the occurrence of two events.

If one twin of 20 pairs showed hyperactivity while the other twin sometimes did and sometimes did not show hyperactivity, the result would be no association, or zero correlation (0.00).

A **zero correlation** indicates that there is no relationship between the occurrence of one event and the occurrence of a second event.

If, in some identical pairs, one twin showed an increase while the other showed an equivalent decrease in activity, the result would be a negative correlation coefficient, which can range from –0.01 to –0.99.

A **negative correlation coefficient** indicates that as one event tends to increase, the second event tends to, but does not always, decrease.

As the coefficient increases in absolute magnitude from –0.01 to –0.99, it indicates a strengthening in the relationship of one event increasing and the other decreasing.

If one twin of 20 identical pairs showed hyperactivity and the second twin always showed decreased activity, the correlation coefficient would be negative and perfect and would be indicated by a –1.00 correlation coefficient.

A **perfect negative correlation coefficient** of –1.00 means that an increase in one event is always matched by an equal decrease in a second event. For example, if one identical twin has hyperactivity, then the other twin always has decreased activity. A correlation of –1.00 is virtually never found in applied psychological research (Hemphill, 2003).

The media often headline interesting findings: Thin people live longer than heavier ones; overweight people earn less money than their peers; wearing school uniforms decreases violence. Before you assume that one event causes the other, such as thinness causing one to live longer, you must check to see what researchers did. If researchers measured only the relationship between two events, such as thinness

Can you recognize a correlation?

and length of life, then it's a correlation. In fact, all three findings reported here are correlations. The reason you should check whether some finding is a correlation is that correlations have one very important limitation: They do not identify what causes what. For example, let's look closely at findings about kindergarten test scores and adult earnings.

Disadvantage

The biggest mistake people make in discussing correlations is assuming that they show cause and effect. For instance, many parents have been told that early childhood education has lasting positive effects. The graph on the right shows that kindergarten test scores are correlated with increased earnings during adulthood. Because higher kindergarten test scores are associated with higher earnings, this is a positive correlation (Chetty et al., 2011).

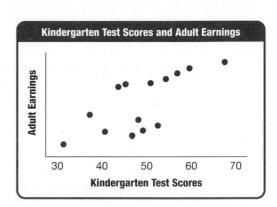

Although the correlation between kindergarten test scores and adult earnings is impressive, you must keep in mind that even though kindergarten performance may cause the increase in earnings, correlations themselves cannot demonstrate cause and effect between variables.

Correlations cannot determine if your kindergarten experience increases your adult earnings.

Let's think carefully about what is actually causing the higher earnings. Are children who do well in kindergarten destined to do better in adulthood based on who they are? Or, are their kindergarten teachers and peers changing them? Is it possible that children who do well in kindergarten come from families that provide them with ongoing opportunities to challenge their academic skills? The correlation findings leave many questions unanswered.

Although correlations cannot indicate cause-and-effect relationships, they do serve two very useful purposes: Correlations help predict behavior and also point to where to look for possible causes, as has happened in the case of lung cancer.

Advantages

Although cigarette smoking was positively correlated with lung cancer deaths (right graph), it was unknown whether smoking was the *cause* of cancer. Acting on the clue that some ingredient of cigarette smoke might trigger the development of lung cancer, researchers rubbed tar, an ingredient of cigarette smoke, on the skin of animals. After repeated applications over a period of time, the animals developed cancerous growths. This research proved that tar could cause cancer. Later, researchers discovered that one particular ingredient of cigarette smoke (benzo[a]pyrene) turns off a gene that normally suppresses tumors. When that particular gene is turned off by cigarette smoke, lung cancer develops (Z. Liu et al., 2005). In this case, correlations told researchers where to look for causes of lung cancer. Correlations can provide clues to the actual causal relationship.

Do IQ scores predict academic success?

A second advantage of correlations is that they help predict behavior. One way to predict how well students will do in academic settings is by looking at their IQ scores. For example, there is a positive correlation, from +0.24 to +0.38, between IQ scores and performance in academic settings (Chamorro-Premuzic & Furnham, 2008; D. M. Higgins et al., 2007). Thus, we would predict that individuals who score high on IQ tests have the skills to do well in college. However, IQ scores are only relatively good predictors for any single individual because doing well in college involves not only academic skills but also other motivational, emotional, and personality factors that we'll discuss in Module 13.

So far, we've discussed three descriptive research methods that describe behavior and correlational research that predicts behavior. Psychologists who want to explain behavior, which is another goal of psychology, must use the experimental research method, which we discuss next. ●

© Serhiy Kobyakov/Shutterstock.com

© Brand X/SuperStock

E Experimental Research

Experiment

How do researchers reduce error and bias?

Remember that information from surveys, case studies, and naturalistic observation has considerable potential for error and bias. Remember too that information from correlations can suggest, but not pinpoint, cause-and-effect relationships. One way to reduce error and bias and identify cause-and-effect relationships is to do an experiment.

An **experiment** is a method for identifying cause-and-effect relationships by following a set of rules and guidelines that minimize the possibility of error, bias, and chance occurrences.

An experiment is the most powerful method for finding what causes what. If we wanted to find out whether medication improves the behavior of children with ADHD, we would want to do an experiment. We will divide an experiment into seven rules that are intended to reduce error and bias and identify the cause of an effect.

Conducting an Experiment: Seven Rules

Why seven rules?

Some researchers and parents claimed that diets without sugar, artificial colors, and additives reduced ADHD symptoms, but most of these claims proved false because the rules to reduce error had not been followed (Kinsbourne, 1994). Here are seven rules that reduce error and bias and that researchers follow when conducting an experiment.

Rule 1: Ask

Every experiment begins with one or more specific questions that are changed into specific hypotheses.

A **hypothesis** is an educated guess about some phenomenon and is stated in precise, concrete language to rule out confusion or error in the meaning of its terms.

Researchers develop different hypotheses based on their own observations or previous research findings. Following this first rule, researchers change the general question—Does Ritalin help children with ADHD?—into a very concrete hypothesis (see below).

Hypothesis:
Ritalin will increase positive classroom behaviors of children diagnosed with ADHD.

Rule 2: Identify

After researchers make their hypothesis, they identify a treatment that will be administered to the participants. This treatment is called the independent variable.

The **independent variable** is a treatment or something that the researcher controls or manipulates.

The independent variable may be a single treatment, such as a single drug dose, or various levels of the same treatment, such as different doses of the same drug.

In our experiment, the independent variable is administering three different doses of Ritalin and a placebo.

After researchers choose the treatment, they identify the behavior(s) of the participants, called the dependent variable, that will be used to measure the effects of the treatment.

The **dependent variable** is one or more of the participants' behaviors that are used to measure the potential effects of the treatment or independent variable.

The dependent variable, so called because it is dependent on the treatment, can include a wide range of behaviors, such as observable responses, self-reports of cognitive processes, or recordings of physiological responses from the body or brain. In the present experiment, the dependent variable is the teacher's rating of the child's positive classroom behaviors.

RITALIN

Independent Variable: Drug treatment

Dependent Variable: Child's positive classroom behaviors

Rule 3: Choose

After researchers identify the independent and dependent variables, they choose the participants for the experiment. Researchers want to choose participants who are representative of the population.

A **population** is every person that exists in the world that matches the criteria the researchers are interested in studying.

Because it is impossible to test the entire population, researchers select a sample of participants.

A **sample** is the portion of the population selected to participate in the study.

Researchers select their sample through a process called random selection.

Random selection means that each participant in a sample population has an equal chance of being selected for the experiment.

Examples of random selection include the way lottery numbers are drawn and selecting people using a random number table.

The reason researchers randomly select participants is to avoid any potential error or bias that may come from their knowingly or unknowingly wanting to choose the "best" participants for their experiment.

Random Selection

Unless otherwise noted, all images are © Cengage Learning

Rule 4: Assign

After randomly choosing the participants, researchers randomly assign participants to different groups, either an experimental group or a control group.

Experimental Group

The **experimental group** is composed of those participants who receive the treatment.

The **control group** is composed of participants who undergo all the same procedures as the experimental participants except that the control participants do not receive the treatment.

In this study, some of the children are assigned to the experimental group and receive Ritalin; the other children are assigned to the control group and receive a similar-looking pill that is a placebo.

Control Group

The reason participants are randomly assigned to either the experimental or control group is to take into account or control for other factors or traits, such as intelligence, social class, age, sex, and genetic differences. Randomly assigning participants reduces the chances that these factors will bias the results.

Rule 5: Manipulate

After assigning participants to experimental and control groups, researchers manipulate the independent variable by administering the treatment (or one level of the treatment) to the experimental group. Researchers give the same conditions to the control group but give them a different level of the treatment, no treatment, or a placebo.

In this study, researchers give the experimental group a pill containing Ritalin, while the control group receives a placebo. Drugs and placebos are given in a double-blind procedure.

A **double-blind procedure** means neither participants nor researchers know which group is receiving which treatment.

A double-blind procedure is essential in drug research to control for self-fulfilling prophecies (see p. 31), placebo effects (see p. 32), and possible influences or biases of the experimenters.

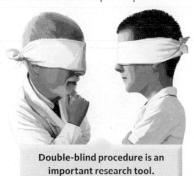

Double-blind procedure is an important research tool.

Rule 6: Measure

By manipulating the treatment so that the experimental group receives a different treatment than the control group, researchers are able to measure how the independent variable (treatment) affects those behaviors that have been selected as the dependent variables.

For example, the hypothesis in this study is: Ritalin will increase the positive classroom behaviors of children with ADHD. Researchers observe whether treatment (Ritalin or placebo) changes positive behaviors of children with ADHD in the classroom. Positive behaviors include following a variety of classroom rules, such as remaining in seat, not disturbing others, not swearing or teasing, and following instructions. As the graph at the right indicates, children with ADHD given placebos follow classroom rules 69% of the time, compared with 87% for the children given

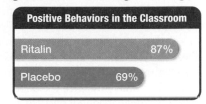

Positive Behaviors in the Classroom	
Ritalin	87%
Placebo	69%

Ritalin (Pelham et al., 2005). Thus, compared to placebos, Ritalin increases positive behaviors in the classroom. However, to be absolutely sure, researchers must analyze the results more carefully by using statistical procedures.

Rule 7: Analyze

Although there appears to be a large increase in positive behaviors, from 69% for the placebo control group to 87% for the Ritalin experimental group, researchers must analyze the size of these differences with statistical procedures.

Statistical procedures are used to determine whether differences observed in dependent variables (behaviors) are due to independent variables (treatment) or to error or chance occurrence.

Using statistical procedures, which are described in Appendix A, researchers compared the effect of the placebo with that of Ritalin on positive behaviors. They concluded that, compared with the placebo, Ritalin significantly increased positive behaviors. In this case, significantly means there was a 95% likelihood that it was Ritalin and not some error or chance occurrence that increased positive behaviors (Pelham et al., 2005).

Statistical analysis shows if the result occurred by chance.

These significant findings support the hypothesis that Ritalin increases positive classroom behaviors of children with ADHD.

Discussion

What does an experiment tell you?

By following these seven rules for conducting an experiment, researchers reduced the chances that error or bias would distort the major finding, which was that Ritalin increased the positive behaviors of children with ADHD in the classroom. This example shows that when an experiment is run according to these seven rules, it is a powerful method for identifying cause-and-effect relationships. Even so, researchers usually repeat experiments many times before being confident that the answers they found are correct.

As you can already see, experimental research, like other research techniques, has advantages and disadvantages, both of which we discuss next.

Advantages

By following the seven rules for conducting an experiment, researchers reduce the chances that error or bias will distort their findings. When an experiment is conducted according to the seven rules, one of its greatest strengths is that it is a much more powerful method for identifying cause-and-effect relationships than are surveys, case studies, observations, or correlations. An experiment can identify cause-and-effect relationship more reliably than other research methods because it allows researchers to examine the relationship between the independent and dependent variables while controlling for extraneous variables.

What are the advantages of an experiment?

Extraneous variables are variables other than the independent variable that may influence the dependent variable in a study.

By randomly assigning participants to the experimental and control groups, researchers reduce the likelihood of extraneous variables influencing the dependent variable. Even so, researchers usually repeat experiments many times before they can be truly confident that the answers they found are correct. That's why a newly reported finding, no matter how significant, is usually

regarded as questionable until other researchers have been able to repeat the experiment and replicate the finding. Still, because an experiment allows anyone interested to verify its findings by repeating it using the same seven steps, this is an advantage of an experiment.

Another advantage of experiments is they can be used to examine variables precisely because researchers are able to control the variables. For example, in the research example we used to teach you the seven steps of an experiment, researchers were able to use three different doses of Ritalin, rather than simply comparing a single dose of Ritalin to a placebo.

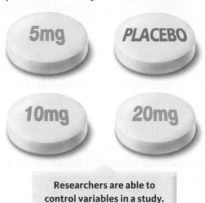

Researchers are able to control variables in a study.

Disadvantages

As wonderful as experiments are, they do have their challenges. One challenge occurs when the participant populations are limited. For instance, many research studies are conducted using college students as their participants. Although college students represent much diversity, there can be some limitations in how well the results of such a study accurately represent the general population.

What are the disadvantages of an experiment?

Another disadvantage is the possibility of experimenter bias.

Experimenter bias refers to the expectations of the experimenter that participants will behave or respond in a certain way.

Experimenter bias is a problem because it can potentially affect the participants. It is possible, for instance, that experimenters may unconsciously communicate their expectations to participants. They may do so through their facial expression, tone of voice, or choice of words.

To reduce the risk of experimenter bias, the use of a *double-blind procedure* is advised. Remember, a double-blind procedure means neither the participants nor the researchers know which group is receiving which treatment.

In addition to the possibility of experimenter expectations

presenting problems, participant expectations can present challenges. It is well known that if we strongly believe something is going to happen, we may unknowingly behave in such a way as to make it happen (*self-fulfilling prophecy*—see p. 31).

Researchers must try to prevent participant expectations. In the research example we used to teach you the seven steps in an experiment, researchers prevented participant expectations by giving all groups pills that looked and tasted the same. As a result, participants think they're getting the same drug even though some are taking a placebo.

Last, a major disadvantage of an experiment is that it cannot be used to study certain research questions due to ethical concerns. For instance, what if researchers wanted to study the effects of lead exposure on long-term cognitive functioning? They could not use an experiment because randomly assigning participants to a group in which they are forced to consume lead would be harmful.

Later in this module, we'll discuss how psychologists conducting research must follow ethical guidelines to protect participants from physical and psychological harm. But, first, we'll wrap up our discussion of ADHD by looking at three of its major controversies. ●

Eat lead so I can study its effects on your brain.

Ethics prevent researchers from studying certain research questions.

Unless otherwise noted, all images are © Cengage Learning

Why do controversies still remain?
You might ask why, after so many years of research, there are still controversies over how to diagnose and treat ADHD. Although researchers have reached the first goal of psychology, which is to describe ADHD, they have not reached the second goal, which is to explain the causes of ADHD, which will lead to better treatment. Explaining the causes of ADHD means combining biological, psychological, behavioral, and cultural factors, which is a slow process. We'll review the current controversies involving ADHD to show how far researchers have come and how far they have to go.

Controversy: Diagnosis

In the United States, as many as 7.6% of school-age children are diagnosed with ADHD (Boyle et al., 2011). There is much controversy about the accuracy and reliability of how ADHD is diagnosed. The controversy arises from the fact that the diagnosis of ADHD is based solely on reported and observed behavioral symptoms rather than on medical or laboratory tests (P. J. Frick et al., 2010). Because the behavioral symptoms vary in severity (more or less), setting (home versus school), and culture (fewer Asian American children than African American), there is the potential for misdiagnosis (Root & Resnick, 2003). For example, parents or teachers may label a child as having ADHD if the child is overwhelmed by the demands of school and acts rambunctious or is difficult to discipline

ADHD diagnosis is based on observations, not medical testing.

© Paffy/Shutterstock.com

(Sinha, 2001). Sometimes children with problems in learning, vision, or hearing are misdiagnosed with ADHD (Hillier, 2004; Lyle, 2003).

Because of diagnostic difficulties, pediatricians and family doctors have been given guidelines for diagnosing ADHD. These guidelines stress that, before a diagnosis is made, a number of the symptoms should be present for at least six months and children should exhibit symptoms in two or more settings (AAP, 2011). The purpose of the guidelines is to prevent the merely rambunctious child from being diagnosed with ADHD and given unnecessary drugs.

Controversy: Treatment

The second controversy involves how best to treat ADHD. As we discussed earlier (p. 31), researchers found that using diets with no artificial flavors and colors, preservatives, artificial sweeteners, and sugars did little to reduce hyperactive behaviors (Kinsbourne, 1994). More recently, researchers have compared nondrug and drug treatments for ADHD and made the following recommendations.

Nondrug, Behavioral Treatment

There is a nondrug, behavioral treatment program that involves changing or modifying undesirable behaviors by using learning principles (p. 232). Such a behavioral treatment program, which requires considerable efforts by the parents and teachers, has been effective in reducing ADHD symptoms (Barkley, 2006; DuPaul et al., 2011).

Experts in the treatment of ADHD recommend that a behavioral treatment program be used for preschool children with ADHD, for milder forms of ADHD, for children who also have deficits in social skills, and when the family prefers the nondrug, behavioral treatment.

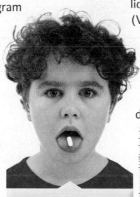

ADHD medication sales are $3.3 billion in U.S.

© Jacek Chabraszewski/iStockphoto

Combined Drug and Behavioral Treatment

A combination of Ritalin (methylphenidate) and behavioral treatment is recommended when children have severe ADHD, such as when ADHD symptoms cause a major disruption at home or in school (Barkley, 2006). ADHD medication sales have risen at an alarming rate to a total of $3.3 billion in the United States alone (Alonso-Zaldivar, 2006; GIA, 2010). Currently, more than 2.5 million Americans aged 19 or younger are using ADHD medications (Vitiello & Towbin, 2009).

ADHD medications help decrease children's hyperactivity and increase their concentration; however, they may cause side effects, including sleeping and eating problems, irritability, slowed growth rate, and in rare cases, sudden death (M. S. Gould et al., 2009; Millichap, 2011). ADHD medications don't improve some of the skill deficits of these children, such as difficult interactions with peers and parents (Fabiano, 2008). Because of the risk for serious side effects and the increase in Ritalin use, the Food and Drug Administration recommended that Ritalin and other similar drugs include a warning (*New York Times*, Feb. 12, 2006). The use of drug and/or behavioral treatment for ADHD depends on an accurate diagnosis, the severity of symptoms, and concerns of teachers and parents.

Controversy: Long-Term Effects

The third controversy involves the long-term effects of ADHD. It used to be thought that children outgrew ADHD, but researchers have found that even when children with ADHD are treated with Ritalin, 50% continue to have problems as adults. In fact, about 1.5 million adults in the United States take ADHD medication (Alonso-Zaldivar, 2006). Adults with ADHD are more likely to have school, work, and relationship problems (Barkley et al., 2008; Fayyad et al., 2007). Because ADHD is a continuing

problem, the use of medication and/or behavioral programs that focus on setting goals, establishing rules, and rewarding performance should be encouraged to help those with ADHD deal with adolescence and adulthood (Barkley, 2006, 2009).

The controversies surrounding ADHD point out the difficulties in understanding, explaining, and treating complex human problems, such as ADHD. Using Ritalin to treat children also raises questions about the rights of subjects, both humans and animals, in research. ●

Concerns about Being a Participant

When you hear about a new research finding—such as a drug to control weight or treat depression, or the discovery of a gene related to happiness, or ways to improve memory—you rarely think about the treatment of the participants, humans and animals, used in these experiments.

What's it like to be a participant?

For example, if you were asked to volunteer to be a participant, you would certainly be concerned about whether someone has checked to ensure that the experiment is safe, that there are safeguards to protect you from potential psychological or physical harm, and that you won't be unfairly deceived or made to feel foolish. These are all real concerns, and we'll discuss each one in turn.

Additionally, a separate and controversial question concerns the use of animals in research. We'll answer this question in some detail, since there are many misconceptions about the use and misuse of animals in research.

We'll begin by considering the concerns of human participants.

© Ryan Klos/iStockphoto

Code of Ethics

If you are a college student, there is a good possibility that you will be asked to participate in a psychology experiment. If you are considering becoming a participant, you may wonder what kinds of safeguards are used to protect participants' rights and privacy.

The American Psychological Association has published a code of ethics and conduct for psychologists to follow when doing research, counseling, teaching, and related activities (American Psychological Association, 2002). This code of ethics spells out the responsibilities of psychologists and the rights of participants.

Besides having to follow a code of ethics, psychologists must submit the details of their research programs, especially those with the potential for causing psychological or physical harm, to university and/or federal research committees (institutional review boards). The job of these research committees is to protect the participants (human or animal) by carefully

Are my rights protected?

© Yuri Arcurs/Shutterstock.com

checking the proposed experiments for any harmful procedures (Breckler, 2006).

Experiments are not approved unless any potentially damaging effects can be eliminated or counteracted. Counteracting potentially harmful effects is usually done by thoroughly describing the experiment, a process called debriefing.

Debriefing includes explaining the purpose and method of the experiment, asking the participants their feelings about being participants in the experiment, and helping the participants deal with possible doubts or guilt that arise from their behaviors in the experiment.

During the debriefing sessions, researchers will answer any questions or discuss any problems that participants may have. The purpose of debriefing is to make sure that participants have been treated fairly and have no lingering psychological or physical concerns or worries that come from participating in an experiment (Aronson et al., 2004).

Role of Deception

When recruiting participants for their experiments, psychologists usually give the experiments titles, such as "Study of eyewitness testimony" or "Effects of alcohol on memory." The reason for using such general titles is that researchers do not want to create specific expectations that may bias how potential participants will behave. It is well known that an experiment's results may be biased by a number of factors: by participants' expectations of how they should behave, by their unknowingly behaving according to self-fulfilling prophecies, or by their efforts to make themselves look good or to please the experimenter.

One way that researchers control for participants' expectations is to use bogus procedures or instructions that prevent participants from learning the experiment's true purpose. However, before researchers can use bogus or deceptive methodology, they must satisfy the American

Will they try to trick or deceive me?

© Jack Hollingsworth/Getty Images

Psychological Association's (2002) code of ethics. For example, researchers must justify the deceptive techniques by the scientific, educational, or applied value of the study and can use deception only if no other reasonable way to test the hypothesis is available (APA, 2002).

Another way to avoid bias from participants' expectations is to keep both the researcher and participants in the dark about the experiment's true purpose by using a double-blind procedure.

As discussed earlier (p. 37), a double-blind procedure means that neither participants nor researchers are aware of the experiment's treatment or purpose.

Thus, researchers must be careful not to reveal too many details about their experiments lest they bias how potential participants may behave.

Ethics of Animal Research

How many animals are used in research?

It is estimated that over 20 million animals are used each year in biomedical research, which includes the fields of psychology, biology, medicine, and pharmaceuticals (Humane Society, 2012). Although these numbers seem large, they are small in comparison to the 5 billion chickens eaten annually by people in the United States. However, it is the use of animals in research that has generated the most concern and debate (Rowan, 1997).

In the field of psychology, about 7 to 8% of research involves the use of animals. Over 90% of the nonhuman animals used by researchers are rats, mice, and other rodents, while the remaining fewer than 10% are other animals such as cats, dogs, and primates (C.A.R.E., 2012). We'll examine the justification for using animals in research and how their rights are protected.

Are research animals mistreated?

You may have seen a disturbing photo or heard about a laboratory animal being mistreated. The fact is that, of the millions of animals used in research, only a few cases of animal mistreatment have been confirmed. That is because scientists know that proper care and treatment of their laboratory animals are vital to the success of their research. Responsible scientists do not want to use animals or cause them any unnecessary harm if it can be avoided. Therefore, scientists accept controls on the use of animals in research and support the Animal Research Act, which balances the rights of animals to be treated with care with the needs for advancing the medical, physiological, and psychological health of humans (T. D. Albright et al., 2005; Festing & Wilkinson, 2007).

Is the use of animals justified?

Adrian Morrison, director of the National Institute of Mental Health's Program for Animal Research Issues, offers this view: "Because I do experimental surgery, I go through a soul-searching every couple of months,

The small print in the poster reads, "Without animal research, we couldn't have put an end to polio, smallpox, rubella and diphtheria. Now, some would like to put an end to animal research. Obviously, they don't have cancer, heart disease or AIDS."

The small print in the poster reads, "Recently, a surgical technique perfected on animals was used to remove a malignant tumor from a little girl's brain. We lost some lab animals. But look what we saved."

asking myself whether I really want to continue working on cats. The answer is always yes because I know that there is no other way for medicine to progress but through animal experimentation and that basic research ultimately leads to unforeseen benefits" (Morrison, 1993).

According to Frederick King, the former chair of the American Psychological Association's Committee on Animal Research and Experimentation, animal research has resulted in major medical advances, new treatments for human diseases, and a better understanding of human disorders (F. A. King et al., 1988).

In the field of psychology, animal research has led to a better understanding of how stress affects one's psychological and physical health, mechanisms underlying learning, the development and treatment of depression, anxiety, and schizophrenia, and critical information about sensory processes of taste, vision, hearing, and pain perception, to mention but a few (C.A.R.E., 2012).

Who checks on the use of animals in research?

Numerous government and university regulations ensure the proper care and humane treatment of laboratory animals. For example, the U.S. Department of Agriculture conducts inspections of all animal research facilities to ensure proper housing and to oversee experimental procedures that might cause pain or distress. Also, universities have committees with authority to decide whether sufficient justification exists for using animals in specific research projects (Kalat, 2013).

How do we strike a balance?

One of the basic issues in animal research is how to strike a balance between animal rights and research needs. Based on past, present, and potential future benefits of animal research, many experts in the scientific, medical, and mental health communities believe the responsible use of animals in research is justified. This is especially true in light of recent rules that regulate the safe and humane treatment of animals kept in laboratories or used in research (C.A.R.E., 2012; OACU, 2012). ●

Does Binge Drinking Cause Later Health Problems?

It is well known that adolescent drinking causes plenty of immediate health problems such as sleeplessness, fatigue, headaches, and lower cognitive functioning. But does adolescent binge drinking (having at least five alcoholic drinks on one occasion) have any long-term effects on health? According to a recent study, the answer is yes. Binge drinking during adolescence was found to have a variety of long-term, negative health consequences, and the risks remained even for people who stopped drinking during their teenage years.

Researchers at the University of Washington followed 808 people (about equal numbers of males and females) from ages 10 to 24, interviewing them numerous times asking about their drinking and other drug use, exercise habits, and health. They identified four types of teenage drinkers: nonbinge drinkers (including nondrinkers), who never or rarely engaged in binge drinking; chronic heavy drinkers, who drank throughout adolescence; escalators, who started drinking in mid-adolescence and quickly increased their alcohol use; and late onsetters, who began drinking late in their teenage years.

1 What are the three major methods for answering questions in psychology, and which method was used in this study?

2 Do the results of this study show a cause-and-effect relationship between teenage binge drinking and poorer health for young adults? Why or why not?

Findings showed that non-binge drinkers were in the best health at age 24, based on weight, physical activity, blood pressure, and number of times they got sick. Chronic heavy drinkers were in the worst physical health. For example, compared to nonbinge drinkers, they were almost four times as likely to be overweight and to have high blood pressure. Also, late onsetters were more likely to get sick than nonbinge drinkers, but surprisingly escalators were not found to have poorer health than teens who did not binge drink.

3 Why were "escalators" found not to have poorer health than "nonbinge drinkers"?

The researchers adjusted the study's statistical analyses to account for factors that might

4 What should alcohol prevention programs emphasize to help reduce teenage binge drinking?

explain the findings, such as income level, gender, ethnicity, and level of drinking at age 24. Even so, they still found teenage binge drinking to be associated with later health problems. These results

© Image Source/Getty Images

support the role of alcohol in long-term health risk.

Although these findings are impressive, the researchers cannot conclude that adolescent binge drinking causes later health problems. Instead, they state that those who binge drink may choose certain lifestyles and engage in certain behaviors that more directly contribute to poorer health. When these factors are better understood, interventions can be more effective in reducing the occurrence of teenage binge drinking.

5 What are the advantage and disadvantage of this study?

6 What bias or error may explain why an adult blames his recent headaches and sleeping problems on the binge drinking he did during adolescence?

Adapted from Oesterle et al., 2004; Querna, 2004

Summary Test

A Answering Questions: Scientific Method

1. The process of answering questions about human behavior and mental processes through informal observation and speculation is called **(a)** _Armchair_. The multistep technique of gathering information and answering questions so that errors and biases are minimized is called the **(b)** _Scientific meth_. The advantages of the scientific method include that it is specific and **(c)** _precise_, it's an **(d)** _empirical_ process, and it can be used for any of the four **(e)** _goals_ of psychology.

1	Review
2	Formulate
3	Design
4	Collect
5	Draw
6	Report

B Descriptive Research

2. An in-depth analysis of a single person's thoughts and behaviors is called a _case study_. One advantage of this method is that researchers obtain detailed information about a person, but one disadvantage is that such information may not apply to others.

3. A statement that supports a particular viewpoint and is based on a person's own experience is called a **(a)** _testimonial_, which has two potential sources of error and bias. First, strongly held personal beliefs may bias an individual's **(b)** _self perception_ of events. Second, believing strongly that something will happen and then unknowingly acting in such a way as to make that something occur can cause an error called a **(c)** _self fulfm_. This source of error is one of the major reasons that people believe that **(d)** _testimonials_ are true.

4. The method of learning the attitudes, beliefs, and behaviors of a large sample of individuals by asking a fixed set of questions is called a _Survey_. One advantage of this method is that psychologists can quickly and efficiently collect information about a large number of people. One disadvantage is that people may answer in a way that they think is socially acceptable.

5. The method of gathering information by observing individuals' behaviors in a relatively normal environment without attempting to change or control the situation is called _Naturalistic_. One advantage of this method is that it provides an opportunity to study behaviors in real-life situations and environments. One disadvantage is that psychologists' own beliefs or values may bias their observations.

C Cultural Diversity: Use of Placebos

6. An intervention that resembles a medical therapy but, in fact, has no medical effect is called a **(a)** _Placebo_. If a person reports an improvement in some medical condition that is due to a supposed treatment rather than to some medical therapy, that is called the **(b)** _placebo effect_. One reason people around the world believe in placebos is that people give **(c)** _testimonials_ to their effectiveness.

D Correlational Research

| +1.00 |
| +0.50 |
| 0.00 |
| −0.50 |
| −1.00 |

7. If two or more events are associated or linked together, they are said to be **(a)** _correlated_. The strength of this association is indicated by a number called the **(b)** _correlation coefficient_, which has a range from −1.00 to +1.00.

8. If there were a perfect association between two events—for example, when one increased, the other did also—this would be called a **(a)** _perfect positive_. If an increase in one event is usually, but not always, accompanied by an increase in a second event, this is called a **(b)** _positive corr_. If an increase in one event were always accompanied by a decrease in a second event, this would be called a **(c)** _negative_. If an increase in one event is usually, but not always, accompanied by a decrease in a second event, this is called a **(d)** _perfect negative_.

9. Although a correlation indicates that two or more events are occurring in some pattern, a correlation does not identify which event may **(a)** _cause_ the other(s). Although correlations do not identify cause-and-effect relationships, they do provide **(b)** _clues_ about where to look for causes and they help to **(c)** _predict_ behavior.

E Experimental Research

10. An experiment offers a set of rules or guidelines on how to conduct research with a minimum of error or bias. We have divided these guidelines into seven rules.

Rule 1 is to make a statement in precise, concrete terms. Such a statement is called a **(a)** _hypothesis_, which researchers often develop based on previous observations or studies.

Rule 2 is to identify the treatment or something the experimenter manipulates, which is called the **(b)** _independent variable_. In addition, the experimenter selects behaviors that are to be used to measure the potential effects of the treatment. These selected behaviors are called the **(c)** _dependent_, and they may include a wide range of behaviors, such as cognitive processes, observable behaviors, or measurable physiological responses.

Rule 3 is to choose participants so that each one in a sample has an equal chance of being selected. One procedure for doing so is called **(d)** _random selection_.

Rule 4 is to assign participants randomly to one of two groups. The group that will receive the treatment is called the **(e)** _experimental_, and the group that will undergo everything but the treatment is called the **(f)** _control_.

Rule 5 is to manipulate the **(g)** _experimental_ by administering it (or one level of it) to the experimental group but not to the control group. The procedure for preventing both researchers and participants from knowing who is getting the treatment is called the **(h)** _double blind procedure_.

Rule 6 is to measure the effects of the independent variable on behaviors that have been selected as the **(i)** _dependent_.

Rule 7 is to analyze differences between the behaviors of participants in the experimental group and those in the control group by using various **(j)** _stat. proc_, which determine whether differences were due to the treatment or to chance occurrences. By following these seven rules, researchers reduce the chances that **(k)** _error or bias_ caused their results.

11. One advantage of experiments is they can be **(a)** _replicated_ by other researchers. One disadvantage of experiments is the possibility of **(b)** _experimenter bias_, which refers to the expectations of the experimenter that participants will behave or respond in a certain way.

F Research Focus: ADHD Controversies

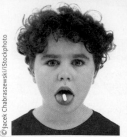
©Jacek Chabraszewski/iStockphoto

12. One controversy over ADHD is that, as of this writing, the diagnosis of ADHD is based on **(a)** _____ observations, which are not always clear-cut, rather than on more reliable **(b)** _____ tests. Another controversy involves how best to treat ADHD. For more severe ADHD, researchers recommend a combination of **(c)** _____ and **(d)** _____ treatment. However, even though Ritalin can decrease hyperactivity in children and increase their ability to pay **(e)** _____, Ritalin does not necessarily improve reading or social skills and does not necessarily reduce problems occurring during adolescence and adulthood.

G Application: Ethics in Doing Research

13. One method of counteracting potential harmful effects on experimental participants is by thoroughly _____ them. This includes explaining the purpose and method of the experiment, asking participants about their feelings, and helping participants deal with possible doubts or problems arising from the experiment.

14. The justification for using _____ in research is that it has resulted in major medical advances, treatments for diseases, and understanding of human disorders.

©Ryan Klos/iStockphoto

Links to Learning

Key Terms/Key People

Animal Research Act, 41

animal research, ethics, 41

armchair psychology, 28

attention-deficit/hyperactivity disorder (ADHD), 27

case study, 31

control group, 37

correlation, 34

correlation coefficient, 34

debriefing, 40

dependent variable, 36

double-blind procedure, 37

experiment, 36

experimental group, 37

experimenter bias, 38

extraneous variables, 38

hypothesis, 36

independent variable, 36

naturalistic observation, 30

negative correlation coefficient, 34

perfect negative correlation coefficient, 34

perfect positive correlation coefficient, 34

placebo, 32

placebo effect, 32

population, 36

positive correlation coefficient, 34

random selection, 36

sample, 36

scientific method, 28

self-fulfilling prophecy, 31

statistical procedures, 37

survey, 29

testimonial, 31

zero correlation, 34

Media Resources

Go to **CengageBrain.com** to access Psychology CourseMate, where you will find an interactive eBook, glossaries, flashcards, quizzes, videos, answers to Critical Thinking questions, and more. You can also access Virtual Psychology Labs, an interactive laboratory experience designed to illustrate key experiments first-hand.

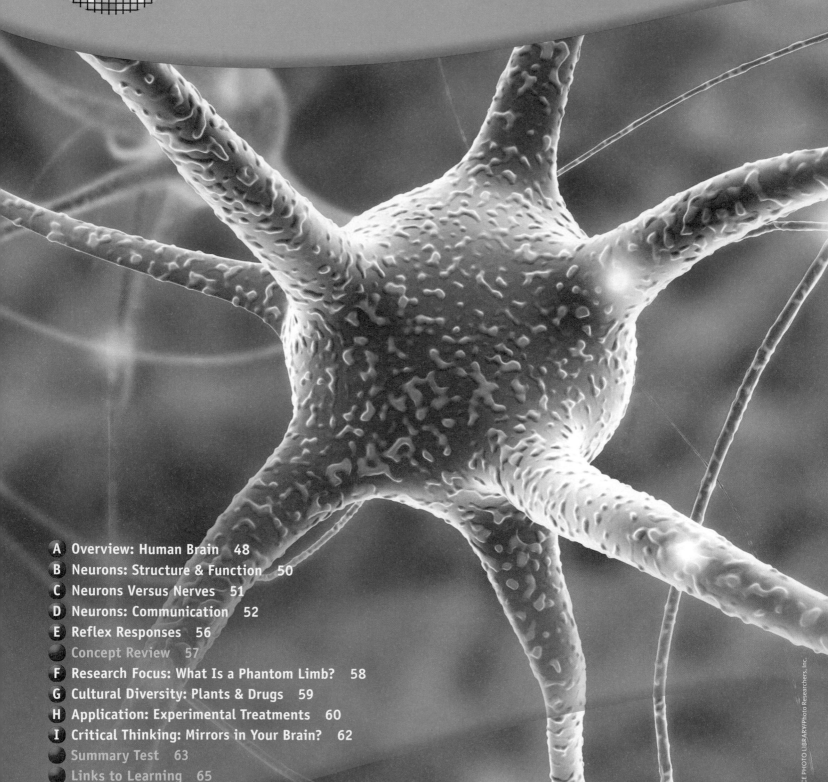

MODULE 3

Brain's Building Blocks

46

© PASIEKA/SCIENCE PHOTO LIBRARY/Photo Researchers, Inc.

Losing One's Mind

Why does Charles have Post-it® Notes everywhere?

Charles Schneider had an impressive career—a police officer, firefighter, and private investigator. He was also quite the craftsman, remodeling houses and building sturdy fences. He had a loving wife, two children, and five grandchildren. In his early fifties, Charles had everything he could ever want in life.

But that was before he started to forget things. Why could he no longer remember his lock combination at the firehouse? Why did he have to open every compartment in the firetruck to find the tools he needed? Why did the names of people he knew so well escape him? Why couldn't he remember his home phone number?

When Charles saw a neurologist, he was diagnosed with Alzheimer's *(ALTS-hi-mers)* disease.

Alzheimer's disease is an irreversible, progressive brain disease that slowly destroys an individual's memory and thought processes. Initially, someone begins forgetting and repeating things, getting lost, and being mildly confused. The person may also have problems with language, difficulties in recognizing objects, and inability to plan and organize tasks. Over a period of five to ten years, these symptoms worsen and result in profound memory loss, failure to recognize family and friends, deterioration in personality, and emotional outbursts (NIH, 2011).

In the United States, Alzheimer's is one of the leading causes of death among adults. Currently, there are more than 5 million people 65 years and older in the United States with Alzheimer's disease (Alzheimer's Association, 2011). The number of patients is projected to rise dramatically in the coming decades as people are expected to live longer (Alzheimer's Association, 2012).

Charles is an example of how someone in his fifties can develop Alzheimer's disease, which is often incorrectly associated with only elderly people. In about 10% of cases, however, Alzheimer's disease begins before the age of 65.

As expected with this devastating disease, Charles's condition is worsening over time. Charles is never without a pen and pad to write down things he doesn't want to forget, and he has Post-it Notes with written reminders in his pockets and placed throughout his house. He now has trouble completing even very simple tasks. He describes Alzheimer's disease as a "cloud over the brain. The simplest things take extreme effort" (C. Schneider, 2006b) (adapted from Fischman, 2006; C. Schneider, 2006a).

Because this disease is progressive and has no cure, for Charles, the worst is yet to come.

These handwritten notes serve as reminders for Charles.

Diagnosis and Causes

Alzheimer's is typically diagnosed by identifying a combination of behavioral, neurological, physical, and psychological symptoms. Recently, there has been great success in diagnosing Alzheimer's by identifying brain damage from pictures of living brains (MRI and PET scans—see pp. 70–71). Also, data from recent advances in blood tests and spinal fluid tests show that these tests may be up to 90% accurate in diagnosing the disease, possibly even a few years before memory loss occurs (De Meyer, et al., 2010; C. Larson, 2008; Park, 2010b; Reddy et al., 2011).

There are genetic, neurological, and possible environmental causes of Alzheimer's disease.

Genetic factors appear to have the upper hand as they account for about 70% of the risk for Alzheimer's (Gatz, 2011a, 2011b). Scientists have now identified ten specific genes that are associated with Alzheimer's disease (Naj et al., 2011). Certain chemicals (proteins and peptides) that occur naturally in all brains multiply and destroy brain cells and are believed to also be a cause.

Researchers are optimistic about finding the causes of and developing treatments for Alzheimer's. New treatments are needed because current drugs cannot reverse the brain damage and cognitive impairments caused by Alzheimer's; they only treat its symptoms. Drugs that attack the suspected causes of Alzheimer's are now in clinical trials (J. Chen et al., 2010; J. Chu & Pratico, 2011; Kounnas et al., 2010). By giving drugs sooner and tailoring the drugs to specific changes in the brain, treatment and potentially prevention may be more successful (Belluck, 2010).

The study of Alzheimer's disease is an example of neuroscience.

Neuroscience is an interdisciplinary field of scientific study that examines the structure and function of all parts of the nervous system, including the brain, spinal cord, and networks of brain cells (SFN, 2012).

One of the greatest accomplishments of neuroscience is mapping where neural (brain cell) signals are routed to result in speech, thoughts, feelings, and other mental processes. In the left figure, we've highlighted the mapping of some mental processes.

What's Coming

Modules 3 and 4 focus on our nervous system. We will use several conditions, such as Alzheimer's disease, to help you understand the structure and function of the various parts of our nervous system. In this module, we'll explain the two groups of brain cells—glial cells and neurons—that make up the building blocks that form the brain's informational network. We'll discuss how neurons receive and send information. You'll discover how brain cells communicate with chemicals that can start or stop the flow of information. Finally, we'll explain an experimental treatment of implanting neurons to treat brain diseases. ●

Neuroscientists have mapped the brain.

© colorFrame/Shutterstock.com

In Charles's case, Alzheimer's disease has progressed to the point that he can no longer get through his day without Post-it Note reminders placed throughout his house. We'll use Charles's brain and his current problems with Alzheimer's disease to answer four related questions: Why isn't the brain a nose? What's in your brain? Can neurons grow or repair themselves? How does Alzheimer's affect the brain?

Development of the Brain

Why isn't the brain a nose? The fact that your brain does not develop into a nose is because of instructions contained in your genes.

Genes are chains of chemicals arranged like rungs on a twisting ladder (right figure). There are about 20,000–25,000 genes that contain chemical instructions equal to about 300,000 pages of typed instructions (IHGSC, 2004). The chemical instructions in the genes program the development of millions of individual parts into a complex body and brain.

An amazing feature of the 20,000–25,000 genes is they are contained in a fertilized egg, which is a single cell about the size of a grain of sand. We'll explain more about the genes and their chemical instructions in the next module (see p. 68).

In the brain's early stages of development, it looks nothing like the final product. For example, the figure below looks more like some strange animal than what it really is, a six-week-old human embryo with a developing brain.

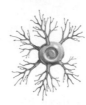

Chemical instructions

Six-Week-Old Brain. This drawing represents a greatly enlarged six-week-old human embryo. The three labeled areas (in three colors) will eventually develop into the three major divisions of the mature human brain that is shown below.

Mature Brain. The three labeled areas represent the three major divisions of the mature brain that we'll discuss in the next module. The mature human brain (side view) weighs almost 3 pounds and contains about 1 trillion cells (Ropper & Samuels, 2009).

Three major divisions of 6-week-old brain

In the case of Charles, who developed Alzheimer's disease, researchers think some of his genetic instructions were faulty. The faulty instructions resulted in an abnormal buildup in the brain of amyloid, a protein that is a gluelike substance that gradually destroys brain cells. Next, we'll explain the two different kinds of brain cells and which ones are destroyed by Alzheimer's disease.

Back

Front

Three major divisions of adult brain

Brain Cells: Glial Cells

What's in your brain? On the right is a top view of a human brain. It is shaped like a small wrinkled melon, weighs about 1,350 grams (less than 3 pounds), has a pinkish-white color, and has the consistency of firm JELL-O®. Your brain is fueled by sugar (glucose) and has about 1 trillion cells that can be divided into two groups—glial cells and neurons.

The most numerous brain cells, about 900 billion, are called glial (*GLEE-all*) cells.

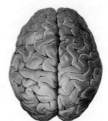

Top view of human brain

Glial cells (astrocytes) have at least three well-established functions: providing scaffolding to guide the growth of developing neurons and support mature neurons; wrapping around neurons to form insulation to prevent interference from other electrical signals; and releasing chemicals that influence a neuron's growth and function.

Glial cell

Glial cells grow throughout one's lifetime. Until recently, glial cells were believed to have only supportive functions, but research now shows that some glial cells may transmit electrical signals, which is the major function of neurons (discussed below and on the next page) (R. D. Fields, 2010; Zimmer, 2009a).

Researchers report that glial cells send messages slowly using chemicals that diffuse throughout the brain, which results in their ability to influence many brain regions. Think about how this information transforms our understanding of the brain's abilities. Glial cells make up 90% of our brain cells, and until only recently, we believed they didn't have the ability to process information.

One research finding that supports the role of glial cells in communication is that glial cells help control breathing, a fundamental physiological reflex (Gourine et al., 2010).

Brain Cells: Neurons

Can neurons grow or repair themselves? The second group of brain cells, which number about 100 billion, are called neurons (*NER-ons*).

A **neuron** is a brain cell with two specialized extensions. One extension is for receiving electrical signals, and a second, longer extension is for transmitting electrical signals.

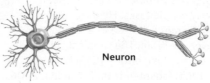

Neuron

Depending on their size, neurons receive and transmit electrical signals at speeds of up to 268 miles per hour over distances from a fraction of an inch to over 3 feet, such as from your toe to your spinal cord (V. Ross, 2011).

Neurons form a vast, miniaturized informational network that allows us to receive sensory information, control muscle movement, regulate digestion, secrete hormones, and engage in complex mental processes such as thinking, imagining, and dreaming. To appreciate the complexity of this informational network, you should know that each neuron makes about 1,000 connections with other neurons. Given that there are about 100 billion neurons, this means there are approximately 100 trillion neural connections in our brain (Zimmer, 2011)! It is estimated that brain cells send 8.6 quadrillion messages each day. For comparison, each day the entire global population places calls, e-mails, and texts that add up to less than 1/200 of 1% of your daily brain signals (K. McGowan, 2011)!

In the case of Alzheimer's disease, neurons are being destroyed faster than the brain's limited capacity for regrowth, repair, or rewiring. Why neurons do not usually repair or replace themselves is our next topic.

Growth of new neurons. If you had a bird's brain, you could grow new neurons every spring. A male canary learns to sing a breeding song in the spring, but when breeding season is over, the ability to sing the song disappears. However, come next spring, an adult canary's brain begins growing about 20,000 new neurons a day, and, during this short period, the bird relearns the breeding song. These new neurons result in a 50% or greater increase in neurons in two areas of the canary's brain that control singing (G. Miller, 2003).

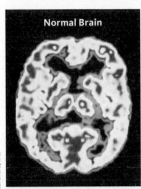

Does the fact that adult canaries as well as adult mice, rats, and other animals can grow new neurons also hold true for adult human brains (Barinaga, 2003)? Researchers believe that, with few exceptions, the brains of humans develop almost all their neurons at birth and adult brains do not grow new neurons. However, some exciting findings have recently been reported about neurogenesis in humans.

Neurogenesis is the process of developing new neurons.

It turns out that new neurons do grow in two areas of the adult human brain—the hippocampus (p. 80) and olfactory bulb (p. 107). Researchers have concluded that adult human brains are capable of growing a limited number of new neurons throughout adulthood and that some of these new neurons play an important role in memory, learning, and smell (Blaiss et al., 2011; Gage et al., 2008; Sahay et al., 2011; Seki et al., 2011). These findings have launched another inquiry—whether people can eat and exercise their way to neurogenesis. Research findings on mice are promising, but researchers are far from knowing whether the results apply to humans (Creer et al., 2010).

Repairing the brain. Besides having a limited capacity to grow new neurons, mature human brains also have a limited capacity to replace, rewire, or repair damaged neurons, such as after a stroke, gunshot wound, or blow to the head (SFN, 2007; J. Silver & Miller, 2004). This limited capacity of the brain to rewire itself by forming new connections helps explain why people may recover some, but rarely all, of the functions initially lost after brain damage.

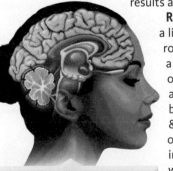

Growth of new neurons is found in two areas of the adult human brain.

Brain and Alzheimer's Disease

How does Alzheimer's affect the brain?

In Charles's case, as Alzheimer's disease destroys his brain, he also loses more and more of his mental activities, such as knowing, thinking, and deciding.

Brain activity. Researchers can study a person's mental activities by taking brain scans of the neural activities going on inside the living brain (brain scans are discussed on pp. 70–71). For example, the top left brain scan shows a great amount of neural activity occurring inside a normal brain (red/yellow indicate most neural activity, blue/green indicate least activity). In comparison, the bottom left brain scan shows relatively little neural activity and thus relatively little mental activity occurring inside an Alzheimer's brain. These kinds of brain scans show that neural activities and mental activities are closely linked, and researchers are studying how these links occur (E. L. Diamond et al., 2007; Mosconi et al., 2005).

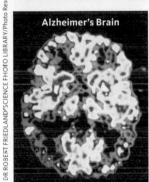

Normal Brain

Alzheimer's Brain

Brain cells. As we discussed earlier, in Alzheimer's disease there is an excessive buildup of a protein called amyloid that gradually destroy neurons. It turns out that most people with Alzheimer's disease produce a normal amount of amyloid, but they cannot get rid of it, which results in the protein accumulating into balls of plaque and destroying many neurons (Mawuenyega et al., 2010). The destruction of neurons causes the brain to actually shrink, as shown by the very deep creases in the Alzheimer's brain (picture below).

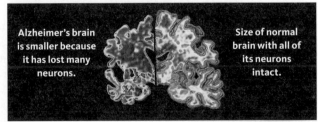

Alzheimer's brain is smaller because it has lost many neurons.

Size of normal brain with all of its neurons intact.

Researchers have been testing experimental medications and vaccines that may help stop or prevent the buildup of amyloid. Even if they successfully develop such an intervention, whether removing the amyloid plaques results in improved brain function is a separate research question that will need to be addressed later (G. Miller, 2009b; Park, 2010b).

Knowing how important neurons are to your mental and physical functions, we next examine them in detail. ●

B Neurons: Structure & Function

Parts of the Neuron

Why could Charles think, move, and talk?

Before Charles developed Alzheimer's disease, he was able to engage in an incredible variety of cognitive and physical behaviors. He was able to think, remember, walk, smile, and speak—all because of the activity of millions of microscopic brain cells called neurons. We'll examine the neuron, which comes in many wondrous shapes and sizes and has only three basic structures—cell body, dendrites, and axon.

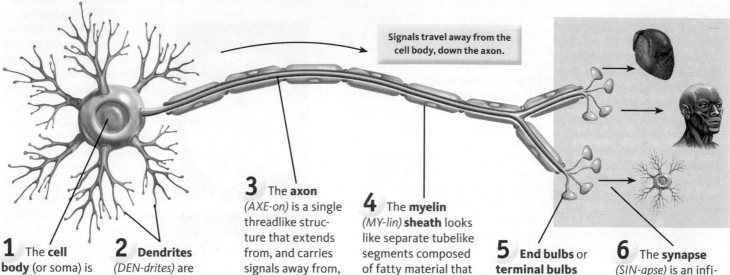

Signals travel away from the cell body, down the axon.

1 The **cell body** (or soma) is a relatively large, egg-shaped structure that provides fuel, manufactures chemicals, and maintains the entire neuron in working order.

In the center of the cell body is a small oval shape representing the nucleus, which contains genetic instructions (in the form of DNA) for both the manufacture of chemicals and the regulation of the neuron.

2 **Dendrites** *(DEN-drites)* are branchlike extensions that arise from the cell body; they receive signals from other neurons, muscles, or sense organs and pass these signals to the cell body.

At the time of birth, a neuron has few dendrites. After birth, dendrites undergo dramatic growth that accounts for much of the increase in brain size. As dendrites grow, they make connections and form communication networks between neurons and other cells or organs.

3 The **axon** *(AXE-on)* is a single threadlike structure that extends from, and carries signals away from, the cell body to neighboring neurons, organs, or muscles.

Here the axon is indicated by an orange line inside the tube composed of separate gray segments. Axons vary in length from less than a hair's breadth to as long as 3 feet (from your spinal cord to your toes). An axon conducts electrical signals to a neighboring organ (heart), a muscle, or another neuron.

4 The **myelin** *(MY-lin)* **sheath** looks like separate tubelike segments composed of fatty material that wraps around and insulates an axon. The myelin sheath prevents interference from electrical signals generated in adjacent axons and helps signals travel much faster through the axon.

The axons of most large neurons, including motor neurons, have myelin sheaths. You may have heard the brain described as consisting of gray and white matter. Gray is the color of cell bodies, while white is the color of myelin sheaths.

5 **End bulbs** or **terminal bulbs** look like tiny bubbles that are located at the extreme ends of the axon's branches. Each end bulb is like a miniature container that stores chemicals called neurotransmitters, which are used to communicate with neighboring cells.

End bulbs reach right up to, but do not physically touch, the surface of a neighboring organ (heart), muscle (head), or another cell body.

6 The **synapse** *(SIN-apse)* is an infinitely small space (20–30 billionths of a meter) that exists between an end bulb and its adjacent body organ (heart), muscles (head), or cell body.

When stimulated by electrical signals from the axon, the end bulbs eject neurotransmitters into the synapse. The neurotransmitters cross the synapse and act like switches to turn adjacent cells on or off. Below we'll take a closer look at the synapse.

Synapse: Close-up look. The right figure shows a close-up look of a synapse (small space) between the end bulb of one neuron (top) and the dendrites of an adjacent neuron (bottom). When stimulated, the end bulbs eject neurotransmitters (orange circles) that cross the synapse and act to either excite (turn on) or inhibit (turn off) adjacent cells. Later in the module, we'll discuss this process in more detail and describe several important neurotransmitters (see p. 54).

We have discussed the structure and function of neurons, but it is important not to confuse neurons (in your brain and spinal cord) with nerves (in your body). ●

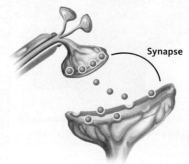

Synapse

C Neurons Versus Nerves

Reattaching Limbs

John Thompson was 18 when a farm machine ripped off both of his arms just below his shoulders.

What's unusual about John's arms?

When the paramedics arrived, he reminded them to get his two arms, which were still stuck in the farm equipment. John was taken to the hospital, where doctors reattached both arms (indicated by red arrows in left photo).

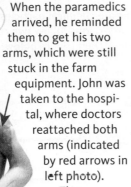

Both his arms were torn off and then reattached.

Three months later, John could raise his arms up but could not move them below his elbows. After several years of physical therapy and 20 operations, John can now raise his reattached arms over his head, make fists, and grip with his hands. John must constantly work at maintaining mobility and strength in his arms (J. Thompson & Grosinger, 2001).

Transplanting Limbs

Not only can one's own limbs be reattached, but donor limbs can be transplanted onto another person.

Can donor arms be transplanted onto another person?

In one case, for instance, donor hands were attached to the arms of a person whose own hands were severed (*USA Today,* May 7, 2009).

In another case, the first of its kind, a double arm transplant was completed on Karl Merk, a 54-year-old man who lost his arms below the shoulder in a farm accident (Associated Press, 2009; Reichert, 2008).

People with limb transplants have shown remarkable recoveries, including being able to move their arms and hands in a functional manner.

If limbs can be transplanted, can the same success be achieved by transplanting a face?

Transplanting a Face

In 2005, doctors removed facial tissue from a dead woman's face and transplanted it onto Isabelle, a 38-year-old woman whose face had been severely disfigured by a dog. She received a new nose, lips, and chin during the surgery (Gorman, 2005b). A few months after the surgery, Isabelle said, "I can open my mouth and eat. I feel my lips, my nose and my mouth" (Doland, 2006). Her ability to experience facial sensations and control facial muscles continues to improve now years later. There is still the risk her body will reject the donor's facial tissue (it has already done so twice), but so far the surgery has been a great success (Dubernard et al., 2007).

Can parts of your face be transplanted onto someone else's?

The fact that severed nerves in the arms, hands, and face can be reattached but neurons in a severed spinal cord are difficult to reattach illustrates a major difference between the peripheral and central nervous systems.

Isabelle with makeup one year after face transplant.

Peripheral Nervous System

Why can limbs be reattached?

Severed limbs can be reattached and regain movement and sensation because their nerves are part of the peripheral nervous system.

The **peripheral nervous system** is made up of nerves, which are located throughout the body except in the brain and spinal cord.

Nerves are stringlike bundles of axons and dendrites that come from the spinal cord and are held together by connective tissue (shown in orange in right figure). Nerves carry information from the senses, skin, muscles, and the body's organs to and from the spinal cord. Nerves in the peripheral nervous system have the ability to regrow or reattach if severed or damaged.

The remarkable ability of nerves to regrow and be reattached distinguishes them from neurons.

Peripheral nerves can be reattached.

Central Nervous System

People may have numbness or paralysis after damage to their brain or spinal cord because of what neurons cannot easily do.

The **central nervous system** is made up of neurons located in the brain and spinal cord (shown in yellow in left figure).

The adult human brain has a limited capacity to grow new neurons and make new connections. Once damaged, neurons usually die and are not replaced.

Why is damage to the central nervous system so serious?

Because neurons have a limited capacity for repair and regrowth, people who have an injured or damaged brain or spinal cord experience some loss of sensation and motor movement, depending upon the severity of the damage. For example, if damage is done to the myelin sheaths of neurons, the result may be multiple sclerosis (S. L. Hauser & Goodin, 2012).

Multiple sclerosis is a disease that attacks the myelin sheaths that wrap around and insulate cells in the central nervous system.

Myelin sheath is damaged in multiple sclerosis.

As a result of this damage, messages between the brain and other parts of the body are disrupted, often causing problems in motor coordination, strength, and sensation.

Because neurons do not generally regrow or repair themselves, research is aimed at discovering techniques to successfully stimulate the regrowth or repair of damaged neurons. One experimental approach is to replace damaged neurons by transplanting fetal tissue or stem cells (taken from embryos) into the damaged area. This method has great potential for treating brain and spinal cord diseases, such as Alzheimer's and multiple sclerosis (Karussis & Kassis, 2007; A. M. Wong et al., 2005). We'll discuss stem cell transplants in the Application section.

Now that you know the structure of the neuron, we'll explain how neurons communicate or send information. ●

D Neurons: Communication

Sequence: Action Potential

1 Feeling a Sharp Object

When you step on a sharp object, you seem to feel the pain almost immediately because neurons send signals at speeds approaching 200 mph. To feel the pain involves the following series of electrochemical events:

A. Some stimulus, such as a tack, causes a change in physical energy. The tack produces mechanical pressure on the bottom of your foot.

B. Your skin has sensors that pick up the mechanical pressure and transform it into electrical signals. (We'll discuss various kinds of sensors in Module 5.)

C. The sensors' electrical signals are sent by the neuron's axon to various areas in the spinal cord and brain.

D. Finally, your brain interprets these electrical signals as "pain."

We're going to focus on step C and explain how axons send electrical signals by using the analogy of a battery. We'll begin by enlarging the inside of an axon.

2 Axon Membrane: Chemical Gates

Just as a battery has a protective covering, so too does the axon. Think of an axon as a long tube that is not only filled with fluid but also surrounded with fluid. The axon's tube is formed by a thin membrane, similar to a battery's outside covering, which keeps the fluid separate and also has special gates.

The **axon membrane** has chemical gates (shown in red) that can open to allow electrically charged particles to enter or can close to keep out electrically charged particles.

Just as a battery's power comes from its electrically charged chemicals, so does the axon's power to send information. In fact, the axon's electrically charged particles are the key to making it a living battery.

3 Ions: Charged Particles

The fluid inside and outside the axon contains ions.

Ions are chemical particles that have electrical charges. Ions follow two rules: Opposite charges attract (figure below), and like charges repel.

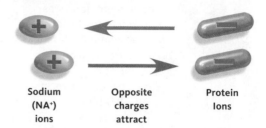

| Sodium (NA⁺) ions | Opposite charges attract | Protein Ions |

The fluid contains several different ions, such as sodium, potassium, chloride, and protein. The axon's function is often explained by discussing sodium and potassium ions. However, it is simpler and easier to focus on just sodium ions, which have positive charges and are abbreviated Na^+, and large protein ions, which have negative charges and are labeled $protein^-$. Because they have opposite charges, Na^+ ions are attracted to $protein^-$ ions (figure above).

Because the axon's membrane separates the positive sodium ions from the negative protein ions, we have the makings of a living battery, as shown in section 4 on the next page.

Sequence: Nerve Impulse

6 Sending Information

One mistake students make is to think that the axon has ONE action potential, similar to the bang of a gunshot. However, unlike a gunshot, the axon has numerous individual action potentials that move down the axon, segment by segment; this movement is called the nerve impulse.

The **nerve impulse** is a series of separate action potentials that take place segment by segment as they move down the length of an axon.

Thus, instead of a single bang, a nerve impulse goes down the length of the axon very much like a lit fuse. Once lit, a fuse doesn't go off in a single bang but rather burns continuously until it reaches the end. This movement of a nerve impulse all the way down to the end of an axon is actually a natural law.

7 All-or-None Law

Why does a nerve impulse travel down the axon's entire length? The answer is the all-or-none law.

The **all-or-none law** says that, if an action potential starts at the beginning of an axon, the action potential will continue at the same speed, segment by segment, to the very end of the axon.

You'll see how the all-or-none law works in the next figure.

8 Nerve Impulse

Notice in this drawing, which continues on the next page, that the nerve impulse is made up of a sequence of six action potentials, with the first action potential occurring at the beginning of the axon.

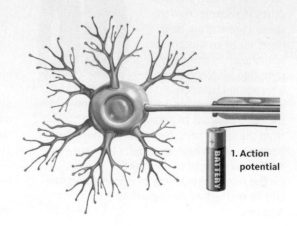

1. Action potential

Unless otherwise noted, all images are © Cengage Learning

4 Resting State: Charged Battery

The axon membrane separates positively charged sodium ions on the outside from negatively charged protein ions on the inside. This separation produces a miniature chemical battery that is not yet discharging and, thus, is said to be in its resting state.

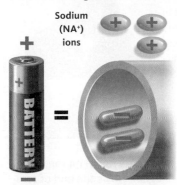

Sodium (NA⁺) ions

The **resting state** means that the axon has a charge, or potential; it resembles a battery. The charge, or potential, results from the axon membrane separating positive ions on the outside from negative ions on the inside (left figure).

The axon membrane has a charge across it during the resting state because of several factors, the primary one being the sodium pump. (To simplify our explanation of the resting state, we won't discuss other pump or transport systems.)

The **sodium pump** is a transport process that picks up any sodium ions that enter the axon's chemical gates and returns them back outside. Thus, the sodium pump is responsible for keeping the axon charged by returning and keeping sodium ions outside the axon membrane.

In the resting state, the axon is similar to a fully charged battery. Let's see what happens when the resting state is disrupted and the battery discharges.

5 Action Potential: Sending Information

If a stimulus, such as stepping on a tack, is large enough to excite a neuron, two things will happen to its axon. First, the stimulus will eventually open the axon's chemical gates by stopping the sodium pump. Second, when the stoppage of the sodium pump causes the gates to open, thousands of positive sodium ions will rush inside because of their attraction to the negative protein ions. The rush of sodium ions inside the axon is called the action potential.

The **action potential** is a tiny electric current that is generated when the positive sodium ions rush inside the axon. The enormous increase of sodium ions inside the axon causes the inside of the axon to reverse its charge. The inside becomes positive, while the outside becomes negative.

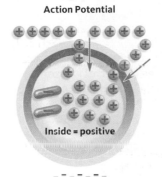

Action Potential

Inside = positive

‒ ‒ ‒ ‒ ‒ ‒
Outside = negative

5a Just as a current flows when you connect the poles of a battery, current also flows when sodium ions rush through the opened gates of the axon membrane.

5b During an action potential, the inside of the axon changes to positive and the outside changes to negative. Immediately after the action potential, the sodium pump starts up and returns the axon to the resting state.

At this point, imagine that an action potential has started at the beginning of an axon. How action potentials whiz at race-car speeds down the entire length of an axon is what we'll examine next in the section below, Sequence: Nerve Impulse.

8a According to the all-or-none law, once a nerve impulse begins, it goes to the end of the axon. This means that when action potential 1 occurs, it will be followed in order by potentials 2, 3, 4, 5, and 6. After the occurrence of each action potential, the axon membrane at that point quickly returns to its resting state.

8b Notice that the *myelin sheath* has regular breaks where the axon is bare and uninsulated. It is at these bare points that the axon's gates open and the action potential takes place.

9 End Bulbs and Neurotransmitters

Once the nerve impulse reaches the end of the axon, the very last action potential, 6, affects the end bulbs, which are located at the very end of the axon. This last action potential triggers the end bulbs to release their neurotransmitters. Once released, neurotransmitters cross the synapse and, depending upon the kind, they will either excite or inhibit the function of neighboring organs (heart), muscles (head), or cell bodies.

As you can now see, neurotransmitters are critical for communicating with neighboring organs, muscles, and other neurons. We'll examine transmitters in more detail and show you how they excite or inhibit.

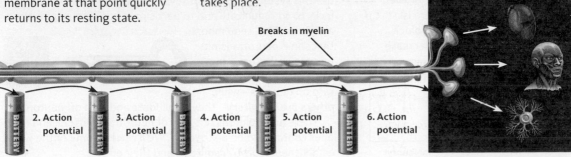

Breaks in myelin

2. Action potential   3. Action potential   4. Action potential   5. Action potential   6. Action potential

Transmitters

What makes your heart pound?

There's no doubt that you have felt your heart pounding when you are afraid, stressed, or angry. One reason for your pounding heart has to do with transmitters.

A **transmitter** is a chemical messenger that carries information between nerves and body organs, such as muscles and heart.

Everything you do, including thinking, deciding, talking, and getting angry, involves transmitters. For example, imagine seeing someone back into your brand new car and then just drive away. You would certainly become angry and your heart would pound. Let's see why getting angry can increase your heart rate from a normal 60 to 70 beats per minute to over 180.

Why does my heart rate increase when I get angry?

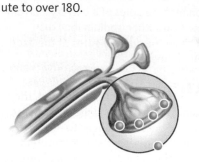

1 In the figure on the left, you see the end of an axon with three branches. At the end of the bottom branch is a greatly enlarged **end bulb.** Inside the bulb are four colored circles that represent transmitters.

Transmitters

2 When the action potential hits the **end bulb,** it causes a miniature explosion, and the transmitters are ejected outside. Once ejected, transmitters cross a tiny space, or synapse, and, in this case, reach the nearby heart muscle. Think of transmitters as chemical keys that fit into chemical locks on the surface of the heart muscle. End bulbs usually hold either excitatory or inhibitory transmitters, which have opposite effects.

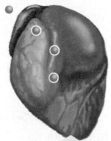

Transmitters can increase or decrease heart rate.

3 Strong emotions cause the release of **excitatory transmitters,** which open chemical locks in the heart muscle and cause it to beat faster (left figure). When you get very angry, excitatory transmitters may cause your heart rate to double or even triple. When you start to calm down, there is a release of **inhibitory transmitters,** which block chemical locks in the heart muscle and decrease its rate (right figure). Think of transmitters acting like chemical messengers that either excite or inhibit nearby body organs (heart), neurons, or muscle fibers. One special class of transmitters that are made in the brain are called neurotransmitters.

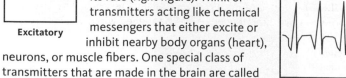

Excitatory

Inhibitory

Neurotransmitters

What makes your brain work?

Writing a paper on a computer requires your brain to use millions of neurons that communicate with one another by using chemicals called neurotransmitters.

Neurotransmitters are about a dozen different chemicals that are made by neurons and then used for communication between neurons during the performance of mental or physical activities.

Since billions of neurons that are packed tightly together use different neurotransmitters for eating, sleeping, talking, thinking, and dreaming, why don't neurotransmitters get all mixed up? The answer is that neurotransmitters are similar to chemical keys that fit into only specific chemical locks.

What happens in my brain when I use my computer?

1 The figure on the left again shows the end of an axon with three branches. We have again enlarged one **end bulb** to show that it contains neurotransmitters (four colored circles).

2 The action potential causes the end bulbs to eject their neurotransmitters (yellow circles), which, in turn, cross the synapse and, in this case, land on the surface of nearby dendrites. The surface of one dendrite is enlarged (right figure) to show its **receptors** (white notches), which are special areas that function like chemical locks.

Neurotransmitters

Receptors

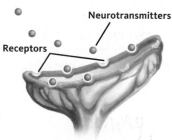

Receptors on dendrites are like chemical locks.

3 Although there are many different neurotransmitters, each one has a unique chemical key that fits and opens only certain chemical locks, or receptors. Thus, billions of neurons use this system of chemical keys that open or close matching locks to communicate and to participate in so many different activities. Also, remember that some neurotransmitters are **excitatory**—they open receptor locks and turn on neurons—while others are **inhibitory**—they close locks and turn off neurons.

There are hundreds of types of neurotransmitters, and new ones continue to be discovered. We'll review some of the well-established neurotransmitters and their effects.

The following is some well-known neurotransmitters and a brief description of their effects (Purves et al., 2012; von Bohlen und Halbach & Dermietzel, 2007):

Acetycholine is an excitatory neurotransmitter that affects neurons involved in movement, learning, memory, and emotion.

Dopamine is an excitatory neurotransmitter that affects neurons involved in voluntary movement, learning, memory, emotion, sleep, motivation, and reward.

Glutamate is the most common excitatory neurotransmitter that affects neurons involved in learning and memory.

Norepinephrine is an excitatory neurotransmitter that affects neurons involved in arousal, sleep, and emotion.

Serotonin is an inhibitory neurotransmitter that affects neurons involved in mood, sleep, appetite, and pain suppression.

Gamma-aminobutyric acid (GABA) is the most common inhibitory neurotransmitter that affects neurons throughout the nervous system.

Why do I feel different after drinking?

To help you better understand how neurons use neurotransmitters to communicate, we'll use the example of how alcohol affects GABA neurotransmitters, which ultimately changes how the brain functions and how we feel, think, and behave.

Alcohol and GABA

Drinking alcoholic beverages usually raises the level of alcohol in the blood, which is measured in terms of blood alcohol content (BAC). For example, at low to medium levels (0.01–0.06 BAC), alcohol causes friendliness, loss of inhibitions, decreased self-control, and impaired social judgment; after three or four drinks, the average person's BAC will range from 0.08 to 0.1, which meets the legal definition of drunkenness in most states. (Alcohol is discussed more fully in Module 8.)

Alcohol (ethyl alcohol) is a psychoactive drug that is classified as a depressant, which means that it depresses the activity of the central nervous system.

We'll discuss one of the major effects alcohol has on the brain.

GABA neurons. Alcohol affects the nervous system in a number of ways, blocking some neural receptors and stimulating others. For example, some neurons are excited by the neurotransmitter GABA *(GAH-bah),* which the brain normally manufactures. This means that GABA neurons (figure above) have chemical locks that can be opened by chemical keys in the form of the neurotransmitter GABA (Purves et al., 2012).

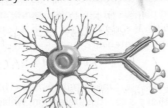

GABA keys. Now here's the interesting part. Alcohol molecules so closely resemble those of the GABA neurotransmitter that alcohol can function like GABA keys and open GABA receptors (right figure). Opening GABA receptors excites GABA neurons. Although it seems backward, when GABA neurons are *excited,* they *decrease* neural activity and produce inhibitory effects, such as a loss of inhibitions and self-control as well as reduced anxiety. In fact, one reason alcohol has become so popular is that many people drink alcohol to feel less anxious and more relaxed. It is interesting that there appears to be a biological link between alcohol and anxiety. Researchers found that a deficiency in a specific brain protein is associated with high anxiety and excessive alcohol use (Wand, 2005).

Alcohol mimics neurotransmitter.

GABA receptor

The important point to remember about neurotransmitters is that their system of chemical keys and locks permits very effective communication among billions of neurons, which allow us to move, sense, think, feel, and perform hundreds of other functions.

Other chemicals involved in neural communication are called neuropeptides.

Neuropeptides

Chemicals that are smaller than neurotransmitters yet are also used by neurons to communicate with each other are called neuropeptides (von Bohlen und Halbach & Dermietzel, 2007).

Neuropeptides are small proteinlike molecules used by neurons to communicate with each other, distinct from the larger neurotransmitters.

Neuropeptides influence the activity of the brain in specific ways and are consequently involved in particular brain functions, such as reward, eating, learning, and memory. These molecules are produced primarily in the brain, although almost every tissue in the body produces and exchanges neuropeptides.

An example of a neuropeptide is the chemical made by our brains that acts as a painkiller and is very similar in structure and function to opiates, such as morphine. This neuropeptide is called endorphin.

Endorphins *(en-DOOR-fins)* are chemicals produced by the brain and secreted in response to injury or severe physical or psychological stress.

Later, in Module 5 (p. 113), we'll provide a more detailed discussion of endorphins and how they act to reduce pain during times of physical or psychological stress.

Now that you are familiar with neurons and the chemicals they use to communicate, we'll explain a response that many of you have experienced—what happened when you touched a hot object. ●

E Reflex Responses

Definition and Sequence

Can you move without thinking? If you accidentally touched a hot light bulb, your hand would instantly jerk away, without any conscious thought or effort on your part. This is an example of a reflex.

A **reflex** is an unlearned, involuntary reaction to some stimulus. The neural connections or network underlying a reflex is prewired by genetic instructions.

Efferent, or motor, neuron

3. Interneuron makes connections between neurons, which carry message to the brain.

Afferent, or sensory, neuron

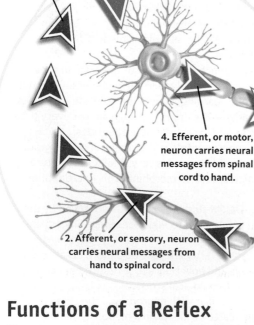

4. Efferent, or motor, neuron carries neural messages from spinal cord to hand.

2. Afferent, or sensory, neuron carries neural messages from hand to spinal cord.

In some cases, such as when a doctor taps your knee, the knee-jerk reflex is controlled by the spinal cord. In other cases, such as when someone shines a bright light into your eye, the pupillary reflex causes the pupil to constrict. We are all born with a number of programmed reflexes, and all reflexes share the same two or three steps, depending upon how they are wired in the nervous system.

One reason reflexes occur so quickly is that they are genetically programmed and involve relatively few neural connections, which saves time. Here's the sequence for how a reflex occurs:

1 **Sensors.** The skin of your fingers has specialized sensors, or receptors, that are sensitive to heat. When you touch a hot light bulb, these skin sensors trigger neurons that start the withdrawal reflex.

2 **Afferent neuron.** From the receptors in your skin, long dendrites carry "pain information" in the form of electrical signals to the spinal cord. These dendrites are part of sensory, or afferent, neurons (red arrows).

Afferent (*AFF-er-ent*), or **sensory, neurons** carry information from the senses to the spinal cord.

Sensory neurons may have dendrites 2 to 3 feet long, to reach from the tips of your fingers to the spinal cord. When the pain information enters the spinal cord, it is transmitted to a second neuron.

3 **Interneuron.** Once the afferent neuron reaches the spinal cord, it transmits the pain information to a second neuron, called an interneuron.

An **interneuron** is a relatively short neuron whose primary task is making connections between other neurons.

In this example, an interneuron transmits the pain information to a third neuron, called the efferent, or motor, neuron.

4 **Efferent neuron.** Inside the spinal cord, an interneuron transfers information to a third neuron, called an efferent, or motor, neuron (blue arrows).

Efferent (*EFF-er-ent*), or **motor, neurons** carry information away from the spinal cord to produce responses in various muscles and organs throughout the body.

From the spinal cord, an efferent (motor) neuron sends electrical signals on its 2- to 3-foot-long axon to the muscles in the hand. These electrical signals contain "movement information" and cause the hand to withdraw quickly and without any thought on your part.

In addition, an interneuron will send the pain information to other neurons that speed this information to different parts of the brain. These different parts interpret the electrical signals coming from your hand as being hot and painful. At this point your brain may direct motor neurons to move your facial and vocal muscles so that you look pained and yell "Ouch!" or something much more intense.

Functions of a Reflex

The primary reason you automatically withdraw your hand when you touch a hot object, turn your head in the direction of a loud noise, or vomit after eating tainted food has to do with survival. Reflexes, which have evolved through millions of years, protect body parts from injury and harm and automatically regulate physiological responses, such as heart rate, respiration, and blood

pressure. One primitive reflex that is no longer useful in our modern times is called piloerection, which causes the hair to stand up on your arms when you are cold. Piloerection helped keep heat in by fluffing hair for better insulation, but clothes now do a better job.

After the Concept Review, we'll discuss a very strange neural phenomenon that you may have heard of—phantom limb. ●

Unless otherwise noted, all images are © Cengage Learning

Concept Review

1. The structure that nourishes and maintains the entire neuron is the **(a)** _____. Branchlike extensions that receive signals from senses and the environment are called **(b)** _____. A single threadlike extension that speeds signals away from the cell body toward a neighboring cell is the **(c)** _____. A tubelike structure that insulates the axon from interference by neighboring signals is the **(d)** _____. Tiny swellings at the very end of the axon are called **(e)** _____, which store neurotransmitters. The process of developing new neurons is called **(f)** _____.

2. Chemicals that have electrical charges are called **(a)** _____. They obey the rule that opposite charges attract and like charges repel. Although the fluid of the axon contains a number of ions, we have focused on only two, a positively charged **(b)** _____ ion, whose symbol is Na⁺, and a negatively charged **(c)** _____ ion.

3. If an axon membrane has a potential similar to a charged battery, the axon is in the **(a)** _____. During this state, the ions outside the membrane are positively charged **(b)** _____ ions; the ions inside the membrane are negatively charged **(c)** _____ ions.

4. If an axon membrane is in a state similar to a discharging battery, the axon is generating an **(a)** _____. During this potential, the chemical gates open and positively charged **(b)** _____ rush inside, changing the inside of the membrane to a **(c)** _____ charge, while the outside of the membrane has a **(d)** _____ charge. As the action potential moves down the axon, it is called an **(e)** _____. Once it is generated, the impulse travels from the beginning to the end of the axon; this phenomenon is referred to as the **(f)** _____.

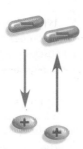

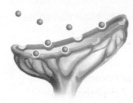

5. The end bulbs of one neuron are separated from the dendrites of a neighboring neuron by an extremely small space called the **(a)** _____. Into this space, end bulbs release chemicals, called **(b)** _____, which open/ excite or block/inhibit neighboring receptors.

6. From end bulbs, chemical keys or **(a)** _____ are secreted into the synapse. These chemical keys open matching locks called **(b)** _____, which are located on the surface of neighboring dendrites, muscles, or organs. Neurotransmitters that open a receptor's lock are called **(c)** _____; neurotransmitters that block a receptor's lock are called **(d)** _____.

7. Neurons in the brain and spinal cord make up the **(a)** _____. If neurons are damaged, they have little ability to **(b)** _____ and usually die. The mature human brain has a limited ability to regrow **(c)** _____ throughout adulthood. Information from the body's senses, skin, organs, and muscles is carried to and from the spinal cord by nerves that make up the **(d)** _____. If this nervous system is damaged, **(e)** _____ in this system have a remarkable ability to regrow and make new connections. If your finger were accidentally cut off, it could be **(f)** _____ and there is a good chance that your finger would regain most of its sensory and motor functions.

8. If you touch a sharp object, your hand automatically withdraws because of a prewired reflex response. Neurons that carry "pain information" to the spinal cord are called **(a)** _____ neurons. Inside the spinal cord, there are short neurons, called **(b)** _____, that make connections between other neurons that carry information to the brain. Neurons that carry information away from the spinal cord to muscles or organs are called **(c)** _____ neurons.

Answers: 1. (a) cell body or soma, (b) dendrites, (c) axon, (d) myelin sheath, (e) end bulbs, (f) neurogenesis; 2. (a) ions, (b) sodium, (c) protein; 3. (a) resting state, (b) sodium, (c) protein; 4. (a) action potential, (b) sodium ions, (c) positive, (d) negative, (e) impulse, or nerve impulse, (f) all-or-none law; 5. (a) synapse, (b) neurotransmitters; 6. (a) neurotransmitters, (b) receptors, (c) excitatory, (d) inhibitory; 7. (a) central nervous system, (b) regrow, repair, or reconnect, (c) neurons, (d) peripheral nervous system, (e) nerves, (f) reattached; 8. (a) sensory, or afferent, (b) interneurons, (c) motor or efferent

Case Study

A puzzling question for researchers to answer is: How can someone feel a phantom limb?

Why does Christian feel pain in his missing toes?

This question applies to Sgt. Christian Bagge, who was hit by two roadside bombs in Iraq. The next thing he remembers is waking up in a hospital with one leg amputated above the knee and the other below the knee. He didn't realize the worst of his condition until a short while later when he suddenly felt a crushing pain in his toes (which were no longer there!) (Bierma & Woolston, 2006). Christian describes the intense pain by saying it "feels like someone is smashing my toes with a hammer." He goes on to say, "On the pain scale of one to 10, I'd say it was a six or a seven. But then again, my '10' is getting both of my legs blown off" (Bagge, 2006).

Despite frequent episodes of excruciating pain, Christian wants to do everything he did before the injury. With the use of his artificial legs (left photo), he is doing just that. For instance, one year after his injury, Christian ran side by side with former President George W. Bush (Gehlert, 2006). Christian's case introduces you to the strange phenomenon of phantom limb.

Christian feels "real" pain coming from his amputated legs.

© Getty Images

Definition and Data

What is phantom limb?

Very few symptoms have so surprised doctors as when patients reported feeling strange sensations or movements in arms or legs that had been amputated, a phenomenon called phantom limb.

Phantom limb refers to feeling sensations or movements coming from a limb that has been amputated. The sensations and movements are extremely vivid, as if the limb were still present.

As the graph on the right shows, the vast majority of individuals feel sensations ("pins and needles") or intense pain coming

from their removed limbs (A. Hill et al., 1996). In other cases, amputees felt their removed limbs were not only still present but stuck in certain positions, such as permanently twisted in a spiral, painfully pinned to their backs, or sticking straight out from their bodies, so they felt they had to be careful not to hit their phantom limbs when going through doorways (Katz & Melzack, 2003; Nicolelis, 2007).

Scientists have been struggling for many years to better understand what causes the feelings of sensations and movements coming from phantom limbs.

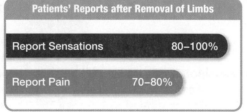

Patients' Reports after Removal of Limbs	
Report Sensations	80–100%
Report Pain	70–80%

Answers and Treatment

Answers. Early researchers thought the phantom limb sensations came from cut nerves remaining in the stump or from the spinal cord. Researchers now believe the origin of phantom limb sensations must be the brain itself (Purves et al., 2012). But, researchers are puzzled about how the brain generates these sensations.

The newest and most supported answer about the origin of phantom limb sensations comes from researcher Ronald Melzack, who has been studying this problem for over 40 years (Melzack, 1989, 1997). He states that each of us has a genetically programmed system of sensations that results in our knowing where our body parts are and in our developing an image of our body. Based on sensations from body parts, Melzack believes the brain pieces together a complete body image. Thus, having a body image, the brain can generate sensations as coming from any body part, even if that part is a phantom limb. With time, the brain can correct its representation of the body to acknowledge the loss of a limb, which could explain why phantom sensation is most severe at first and then decreases in intensity over time (Purves et al., 2012).

Because traditional medical treatment has had limited success in treating phantom limb pain, researchers are looking for more creative and effective treatments.

Treatment. One interesting treatment method has been to create an illusion that the phantom limb exists. This has been done by having people with amputations of the arm and phantom limb pain place their arm inside a mirror box. Looking into the box, they see the reverse image of their remaining arm on the mirror, rather than a missing limb (right picture). By helping patients recreate a complete body image, the use of mirrors has had success in reducing phantom pain in lower and upper limb amputations (Brodie et al., 2007; Chan et al., 2007; Maclachlan et al., 2003). Virtual reality is also being used to reduce phantom limb pain (J. Cole et al., 2009; Diers, 2011; Ramachandran & Rogers-Ramachandran, 2008).

The phantom limb phenomenon points out that the brain sometimes functions in mysterious ways. Less mysterious is how certain drugs affect the functioning of the brain and the body. ●

This mirror box can help to reduce phantom limb pain.

Based on an illustration in *Scientific American Mind*, April/May, 2006, p. 18 by Jason Lee. By permission of Jason Lee.

Unless otherwise noted, all images are © Cengage Learning

G Cultural Diversity: Plants & Drugs

Where did the first drugs come from?

The very first drugs that affected neurotransmitters came from various plants, which people used long before researchers knew what those plants contained. We'll discuss three such drugs—cocaine, curare, and salvia—which come from plants found in different parts of the world. We'll explain what these plants contain and their actions on the nervous systems.

Cocaine: Blocking Reuptake

Coca leaves

For almost 3,500 years, South American Indians have chewed leaves of the coca plant. Following this ancient custom, adult Indians habitually carry bags of toasted coca leaves, which contain cocaine. Throughout the day, they chew small amounts of coca leaves to relieve fatigue and feelings of hunger. Here's how cocaine affects neurotransmitters.

The drawing on the right shows a neuron's end bulb containing the neurotransmitter dopamine *(DOPE-ah-mean)*. Once released, dopamine (orange circles) reaches the dendrite's receptors, opens their chemical locks, and activates the neuron. However, after a short period of time, the neurotransmitter is normally removed by being transported back into the end bulb through reuptake.

Reuptake is a process through which some neurotransmitters, such as dopamine, are removed from the synapse by being transported back into the end bulbs.

If reuptake does not occur, the released neurotransmitter would continually affect the neuron by remaining longer in the synapse. What cocaine does is block reuptake so that dopamine remains longer in the synapse (Iversen et al., 2009). This results in the physiological arousal and feelings of euphoria that are associated with cocaine usage. Researchers now understand why South American Indians chewed coca leaves. The cocaine released from chewing coca leaves blocked the reuptake of dopamine, which in turn caused physiological arousal that relieved fatigue and feelings of hunger.

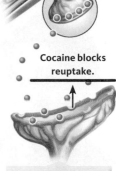

Cocaine blocks reuptake.

Cocaine works by blocking reuptake.

Curare: Blocking Receptors

Curare

When hunting animals, the Indians of Peru and Ecuador coat the ends of blow-darts with the juice of a tropical vine that contains the paralyzing drug curare.

Curare *(cure-RAH-ree)* is a drug that enters the bloodstream, reaches the muscles, and blocks receptors on muscles. As a result, the neurotransmitter that normally activates muscles, which is called acetylcholine, is blocked, and muscles are paralyzed (M. R. Lee, 2005).

Curare is an example of a drug that stops neural transmission by blocking the muscles' receptors. Today, the purified active ingredient in curare (tubocurarine chloride) is used to induce muscle paralysis in humans, such as when doctors insert a breathing tube down a patient's throat. Curare doesn't easily enter the brain because the body's blood must go through a filtering system before it can enter the brain. This filtering system, called the **blood-brain barrier,** prevents some, but not all, potentially harmful substances in the body's blood supply from reaching the brain.

Why did Indians coat blowdarts with curare?

Salvia: Mimicking a Neurotransmitter

Salvia

A member of the sage family called salvia, also known as "magic mint" or "Sally-D," has historically been used by Mazatec Indians in Mexico for relief from diarrhea and headaches as well as for religious rituals (Maisto et al., 2011; Sanders, 2011).

Salvia is a drug that causes uncontrollable laughter and vivid hallucinations. Salvia's chemical keys are similar to that of endorphins (see p. 55). Because salvia's chemical keys open the same chemical locks (receptors) as endorphins, salvia produces its effects by mimicking the actions of endorphins.

Most states currently allow the use, sale, and purchase of salvia. However, its growing popularity and concerns about safety will very likely change state laws. Thousands of YouTube videos show people using it, including a video of Miley Cyrus (actor, singer) showing her smoking salvia on her 18th birthday (TMZ, 2010). In the video she is laughing hysterically and speaking gibberish, and she thinks someone on television looks like an ex-boyfriend.

Conclusion. These three plants—cocaine, curare, and salvia—contain potent drugs that illustrate three different ways of affecting the brain. Neurotransmitters are the keys that turn the brain's functions on and off. For example, Alzheimer's disease interferes with neurons and neurotransmitters and turns off the brain's functions. Such is the case with another terrible disease, called Parkinson's, which we'll discuss next. ●

Why did Miley Cyrus smoke salvia?

Parkinson's Disease

Michael J. Fox is a talented actor who has starred in popular TV series, such as *Family Ties* and *Spin City,* and numerous movies, including the *Back to the Future* trilogy. He was really good at his job until he noticed a twitch in his left pinkie (M. J. Fox, 2002). Within only 6 months, this twitch spread to his whole hand. Michael tried to conceal his symptoms from the public by using medication to calm his tremors, and he was successful doing so for the first seven years (Dudley, 2006). However, it became increasingly difficult to hide his symptoms as he began having tremors that would shake his entire arm. Also, his legs would shake or become really stiff, making it difficult for him to walk. Eventually, these symptoms led Michael to quit his starring role in *Spin City* (Weinraub, 2000). Michael had all the symptoms of Parkinson's disease.

Why do Michael's arms and legs shake?

© AP Images/Charles Sykes

Parkinson's disease includes symptoms of tremors and shakes in the limbs, a slowing of voluntary movements, muscle stiffness, problems with balance and coordination, and feelings of depression. As the disease progresses, patients develop a peculiar walk and may suddenly freeze in space for minutes or hours at a time.

Michael's Parkinson's symptoms worsened because neurons in his **basal ganglia**, a group of structures located in the center of the brain that are involved in regulating movements, were running out of the neurotransmitter dopamine (see p. 55). Without a sufficient supply of dopamine in the basal ganglia, the brain loses its ability to control movement.

Like most Parkinson's patients, Michael was placed on a medication called L-dopa, which boosts the levels of dopamine in the brain, enabling him to have better control over his movements. Unfortunately, patients must take increasing amounts of L-dopa, and after prolonged use (5 to 10 years), L-dopa's beneficial effects may be replaced by unwanted jerky movements that may be as bad as those produced by Parkinson's disease (Mercuri & Bernardi, 2005). Even though Michael still takes medication, at times he has so little movement control that he cannot speak clearly, raise his arms from his side, or even smile (Dagostino, 2008). Yet, he continues to have an optimistic outlook on life and has not given up on his acting career (M. J. Fox, 2009). Most recently, he is starring in the TV drama *The Good Wife* (*People,* 2011).

In the United States, about 1.5 million adults, usually over the age of 50, have Parkinson's disease. In rare cases, such as Michael's, people are diagnosed with young-onset Parkinson's disease (Michael was only 30). To date, Parkinson's has no cure, but our knowledge of its causes, especially genetics, is continuously advancing and, as you'll see, several experimental treatments are under study (Kingwell, 2010; I. Martin et al., 2011; Mouradian, 2010).

Issues Involving Transplants

Human cells. As we learned above, the prolonged use of L-dopa to treat Parkinson's disease produces unwanted side effects. Because of these disappointing long-term results, researchers are investigating alternative treatments, such as fetal brain tissue transplants. Previously, researchers had shown that when fetal rat brain tissue was transplanted into older rats, the fetal neurons lived, grew, functioned, and allowed brain-damaged older rats to relearn the solutions to mazes (Shetty & Turner, 1996). Following successes in animal research, human fetal brain tissue has been transplanted into patients with Parkinson's disease (Roitberg & Kordower, 2004).

Why not just use drugs?

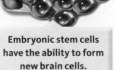

Embryonic stem cells have the ability to form new brain cells.

The primary reason for using 6- to 8-week-old fetal tissue for transplants is that they have a unique ability to survive and make connections in a patient's brain or body. Because fetal brain tissue is primed for growth, it has a far greater chance of survival after transplantation than does tissue from mature brains (Holden, 2002). More recently, researchers are exploring the use of stem cells to treat Parkinson's disease and spinal cord injuries.

Stem cells. About four days after a sperm has fertilized an egg, the resulting embryo, which is about the size of the period in this sentence (see p. 379), has divided and formed embryonic stem cells (shown below).

Stem cells have the amazing capacity to change into and become any one of the 220 types of cells that make up a human body, including skin, heart, liver, bones, and neurons.

The discovery of stem cells creates possibilities for treating various diseases. For example, when embryonic animal stem cells were transplanted into rats and mice with spinal cord injuries, the stem cells imitated the neighboring neurons and developed into new neurons that, in turn, helped the animals regain their lost functions (Wade, 2002). Some exciting news is that for the first time, surgeons have injected embryonic human stem cells into a patient with a spinal cord injury (Vergano, 2010a).

The use of human embryonic stem cells is controversial for ethical and political reasons. That's because these embryos, which are fertilized in laboratories and have the potential to develop into humans, are destroyed when the stem cells are removed. Because of these ethical and political problems, many scientists have turned to using **induced pluripotent stem cells (iPSCs)**, which are adult cells that have been genetically reprogrammed to be in an embryonic stem cell-like state (NIH, 2012).

There is much excitement in the scientific community about iPSCs, which, like embryonic stem cells, can turn into any type of cell in the body, but avoid the controversy. However, early research suggests that their effectiveness doesn't come close to that of embryonic stem cells (Choi, 2010; Kolata, 2010; Vergano, 2010b).

Next, we'll take a closer look at how fetal and stem cells are used in treating Parkinson's patients. We'll also learn about other experimental treatment options.

Unless otherwise noted, all images are © Cengage Learning

Experimental Treatments

Placing tissue in the brain. A neurosurgeon can transplant fetal cells or stem cells into a precise location in either animal or human brains by using the stereotaxic procedure.

The **stereotaxic procedure** (right figure) involves fixing a patient's head in a holder and drilling a small hole through the skull. The holder has a syringe that can be precisely guided to inject cells into a predetermined location in the brain.

In the figure, a large part of the skull has been removed to show the brain, but in actual surgery, only a small, pencil-sized hole is drilled in the skull. A long needle from the syringe is inserted into the patient's brain area that is involved with regulating movement, the basal ganglia. The surgeon injects fetal or stem cells into the designated brain area.

The advantages of the stereotaxic procedure are that a thin syringe can be placed in precise locations in the brain and that it causes relatively little damage to the brain. The stereotaxic procedure can be used to either inject solutions or, as we'll later learn, destroy diseased brain tissue.

Based on a number of experimental treatments, researchers learned that when injected into a human adult brain, fetal tissue does survive and function. Fetal tissue transplants have benefited some people, but others have reported serious side effects. Therefore, critics suggest that researchers identify the best location for injecting the tissue into the brain and aim to prevent the unwanted motor side effects by determining the optimum number of fetal cells to inject (Sanberg, 2007).

Stem cell research is still in its infancy, but already some success has been reported in using stem cells to treat people with Parkinson's disease. Recently, a case study found that adult stem cell transplantation improved motor functioning in a patient with Parkinson's disease by 80% over a three-year period (Levesque et al., 2009). Researchers are hopeful that the use of stem cells will help replace cells damaged during the progression of Parkinson's disease and consequently restore lost function (such as motor control) (Sonntag et al., 2005).

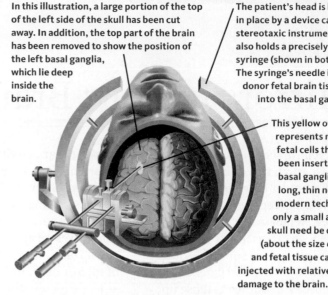

In this illustration, a large portion of the top of the left side of the skull has been cut away. In addition, the top part of the brain has been removed to show the position of the left basal ganglia, which lie deep inside the brain.

The patient's head is held firmly in place by a device called the stereotaxic instrument, which also holds a precisely guided syringe (shown in bottom left). The syringe's needle injects donor fetal brain tissue exactly into the basal ganglia.

This yellow oval represents millions of fetal cells that have been inserted into the basal ganglia by using a long, thin needle. With modern techniques, only a small area of the skull need be opened (about the size of a pencil), and fetal tissue can be injected with relatively little damage to the brain.

Removing part of the brain. People with Parkinson's disease have regained control over their limbs after having part of their thalamus (see p. 80) removed. The thalamus is an oval structure (see left) in the brain that closely interacts with the basal ganglia. One of its functions is to help make voluntary motor movements, such as when a person wants to move a leg to walk (S. M. Sherman & Guillery, 2009).

Michael J. Fox chose to have a thalamotomy, a surgery that removed part of his thalamus. During the surgery, the stereotaxic procedure was used to drill a hole in his skull and apply heat to destroy very precise sections of his thalamus. Michael's surgeon warned him that the procedure would not cure his Parkinson's, but if successful, it would stop the severe tremors in his arm. The surgery was a success in Michael's case, as most of his severe tremors went away. He now takes medication to control his milder tremors (M. J. Fox, 2002).

Thalamotomy has proven to have a high success rate, but there are serious risks, including paralysis, coma, and death. Therefore, this procedure is used only in severe cases of Parkinson's, such as Michael's. Doctors treated Michael with medication for several years before suggesting he undergo a dangerous surgery (M. J. Fox, 2002).

Thalamus

Michael J. Fox chose to have part of his thalamus removed.

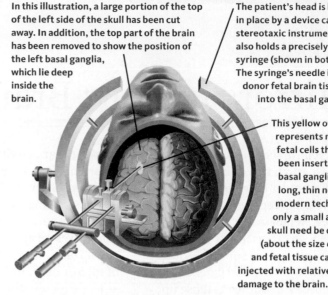

Brain stimulation. About 70,000 people with Parkinson's disease have received deep brain stimulation (DBS), a surgical procedure that involves implanting electrodes into the thalamus and placing a battery-powered stimulator under the collarbone. The electrodes are wired to the stimulator, which provides electrical stimulation to the thalamus. The patient controls the stimulation by using a remote control to turn it on and off. This procedure helps the thalamus function better and, as a result, reduces or eliminates tremors (Hendrick, 2010; Marks, 2011). An advantage of DBS is being able to modify the level of stimulation as needed. Also, patients receiving DBS show greater improvement than patients receiving only medication (F. M. Weaver et al., 2009). The limitation of this procedure is that the batteries must be surgically replaced every few years (Pahwa & Lyons, 2003). There is also a risk of dangerous bleeding and getting an infection (Kringelbach & Aziz, 2008; F. M. Weaver et al., 2009). Newer DBS systems are being developed to be smaller and more effective and decrease the chance of infection (*Science Illustrated,* 2011b; M. G. Sullivan, 2012). In addition, because Parkinson's disease is degenerative, DBS controls the tremors for only about five years (Bronstein et al., 2011).

Given its effectiveness and relatively minimal risk, researchers believe DBS will be effective in treating a variety of health problems. DBS is currently being investigated in the treatment of depression, anxiety, phantom limb pain, comas, and Alzheimer's disease (Kluger, 2007b; Kringelbach & Aziz, 2008; K. McGowan, 2010; G. Miller, 2009a; Mullins, 2008; N. D. Schiff et al., 2007). ●

Electrodes implanted in the thalamus provide stimulation to reduce tremors.

Mirrors in Your Brain?

When we see someone yawn, we yawn too. When we watch a spider crawl up someone's leg, we get creepy sensations on our leg. When we see someone in danger, we experience a wave of fear. When we see someone's arm get jabbed with a sharp needle, the muscles in our arms tense up and our breathing intensifies. When we watch our favorite Olympic athlete near the finish line to win first place, our heart races with excitement.

How can simply observing others lead us to experience such intense responses so similar to those experienced by the people we are observing? The answer is found in our brain cells. A type of neuron, called a mirror neuron, helps explain how we effortlessly "read" other people's minds and empathize with them—feel what they do. Mirror neurons automatically put us in somebody else's shoes. Not convinced? Consider brain scan research that finds that romantic partners who observe loved ones in pain

1 How might mirror neurons explain the social problems of people with autism?

2 In what type of research setting do brain scan studies take place? What are an advantage and disadvantage of this type of research setting?

show similar activity in their emotional brain areas as that experienced by the loved ones. It turns out that when we empathize with someone's pain, on some level we actually feel pain!

One fascinating characteristic of mirror neurons is that they are the only brain cells that are activated the same way whether we are "seeing" or "doing." These special neurons mirror what the other person is doing. For instance, when we see someone smiling, our mirror neurons for smiling get activated, which triggers neural activity leading to feelings associated with smiling, such as happiness. In other words, we get all the benefits of smiling without making even the slightest movement of our lips!

Mirror neurons also help us understand someone's intentions. They get activated when we watch someone do something, which helps us predict what their goal is and what they may do next. For example, if you see a boy begin to reach for candy on the counter

3 How are mirror neurons different from nerves?

4 What would it be like to have no mirror neurons?

5 How might mirror neurons be involved in the enjoyment of watching pornography?

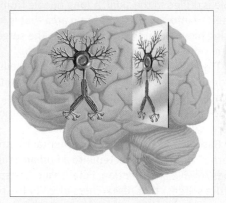

in front of him, you have a copy of what he is doing in your brain, which helps you to understand his goal (getting the candy).

Research on mirror neurons is still in its infancy, and much has yet to be learned. But, for now, those of us who are embarrassed by our free-flowing tears during dramatic scenes in television programs, movies, and, yes, sometimes even commercials should be relieved to know that the emotions we experience may be out of our control; that is, we may not be able to contain our tears after all.

6 Which modern approaches to psychology are best suited to study mirror neurons?

(Adapted from Blakeslee, 2006a; Blakeslee & Blakeslee, 2007; Ehrenfeld, 2011; Iacoboni, 2008a, 2008b; Iacoboni & Mazziotta, 2007; Ramachandran & Oberman, 2006; Rizzolatti, 2011; T. Singer et al., 2004; Winerman, 2005)

A Overview: Human Brain

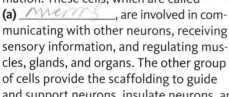

1. The brain is composed of a trillion cells that can be divided into two groups. One group of cells has specialized extensions for receiving and transmitting information. These cells, which are called **(a)** _neurons_, are involved in communicating with other neurons, receiving sensory information, and regulating muscles, glands, and organs. The other group of cells provide the scaffolding to guide and support neurons, insulate neurons, and release chemicals that influence neuron functions. These cells are much more numerous than neurons and are called **(b)** _glial cells_.

2. There is a major difference between the growth of neurons in the brains of humans and in the brains of birds. A mature human brain is normally not capable of developing new **(a)** _neurons_, which are almost all developed at the time of birth. In contrast, a mature **(b)** _bird_ brain has the capacity to develop new neurons.

3. Research shows that neurons grow in two areas of the adult human brain. This process of developing new neurons is called _neurogenesis_.

B Neurons: Structure & Function

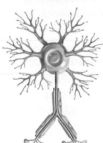

4. Although neurons come in wondrous shapes and sizes, they all share three structures. The structure that maintains the entire neuron in working order, manufactures chemicals, and provides fuel is called the **(a)** _cell body_. The structure with many branchlike extensions that receive signals from other neurons, muscles, or organs and conduct these signals to the cell body is called a **(b)** _dendrite_. The single threadlike extension that leaves the cell body and carries signals to other neurons, muscles, or organs is called the **(c)** _axon_. At the very end of this structure are individual swellings called **(d)** _end bulbs_, which contain tiny vesicles filled with **(e)** _neurotransmitters_.

5. Surrounding most axons is a fatty material called the **(a)** _myelin sheath_. This material acts like **(b)** _insulation_ and diminishes interference from electrical signals traveling in neighboring axons.

6. Neurons do not make physical contact with one another or with other organs. Instead, there is an infinitely small space between a neuron's end bulbs and neighboring dendrites, cell bodies, or other organs. This space is called the **(a)** _synapse_. When an axon's end bulbs secrete

a neurotransmitter, it flows across this space and affects the **(b)** _membrane_ on the neighboring membrane.

C Neurons Versus Nerves

7. There are major differences between neurons and nerves. Cells with specialized extensions for conducting electrical signals are called **(a)** _neurons_. These cells, which are located in the brain and spinal cord, make up the **(b)** _central_ nervous system. Stringlike bundles of neurons' axons and dendrites, which are held together by connective tissue, are called **(c)** _nerves_. These stringlike bundles, which are located throughout the body, make up the **(d)** _peripheral_ nervous system. Nerves carry information back and forth between the body and the spinal cord. If a neuron in the central nervous system is damaged, it normally does not have the capacity to **(e)** _regrow_. In comparison, a nerve in the **(f)** _peripheral_ nervous system has the capacity to regrow or reattach if cut or damaged. The mature human brain has a limited ability to regrow **(g)** _neurons_ throughout adulthood.

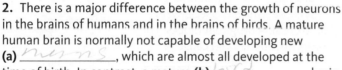
© Taro Yamasaki

D Neurons: Communication

8. The axon membrane has **(a)** _chemical gates_ that can be opened or closed. These gates keep some ions inside the membrane and other ions outside. If the axon is ready to conduct but not actually conducting an impulse, the axon is said to be in the **(b)** _resting_ state. In this state, most of the positively charged **(c)** _sodium_ ions are on the outside of the membrane and all the negatively charged **(d)** _protein_ ions are trapped inside. In the resting state, the outside of the membrane has a **(e)** _positive_ charge compared to the **(f)** _negative_ charge on the inside. The process responsible for picking up and transporting sodium ions from the inside to the outside of the axon membrane is called the **(g)** _sodium pump_.

Action Potential

9. If a stimulus is strong enough to excite a neuron, two things happen to its axon. First, the stimulus will eventually open the axon's **(a)** _gates_. Second, after the gates are opened, the **(b)** _sodium_ pump is stopped, and all the positive **(c)** _sodium_ ions rush inside because they are attracted to the negatively charged protein ions. The rush of sodium ions inside generates a tiny electric current that is called the **(d)** _depolarization_. When this current is generated, the inside of the axon membrane changes to a **(e)** _positive_ and the outside changes to a **(f)** _negative_ charge.

10. Once an action potential starts in the axon, it continues, segment by segment, down the entire length of the axon, creating the **(a)** _____. Once an action potential is triggered in the segment at the beginning of the axon, other action potentials will be triggered in sequence down the entire length of the axon; this phenomenon is called the **(b)** _____.

11. Once started, the action potential will reach the end bulbs at the end of the axon. The action potential excites the end bulbs and causes them to secrete **(a)** _____ that were stored in the end bulbs. Neurotransmitters function like chemical keys that unlock chemical locks or **(b)** _____, which are located on neighboring neurons, muscles, or other organs. If neurotransmitters open the receptors' locks on neighboring cells, they are said to be **(c)** _____. If neurotransmitters block the receptors' locks, they are said to be **(d)** _____. Because of these different actions, neurotransmitters can cause different and even opposite responses in neurons, muscles, or organs. Chemicals that are smaller than neurotransmitters yet are also used by neurons to communicate with each other are called **(e)** _____.

E Reflex Responses

12. The movement of automatically withdrawing your hand after touching a hot object is called a **(a)** _____, which involves several or more neurons. Information is carried to the spinal cord by the **(b)** _____ neuron. Information is carried from the spinal cord to the muscle by the **(c)** _____ neuron. Connections between efferent (motor) and afferent (sensory) neurons are made by relatively short **(d)** _____, which also send signals to the brain. The functions of reflexes include protecting body parts from **(e)** _____ and automatically regulating the **(f)** _____ responses of the body.

F Research Focus: What Is a Phantom Limb?

13. The experience of sensations from a limb that has been amputated is called the **(a)** _____ phenomenon. About 70–80% of patients report sensations of intense pain coming from limbs that have been amputated. A recent explanation of phantom limb sensations is that they arise from the brain's genetically programmed system of sensations that allows the brain to know the locations of all the body's **(b)** _____.

G Cultural Diversity: Plants & Drugs

14. One of cocaine's effects on the nervous system is to block the process of **(a)** _____ so that the neurotransmitter remains longer in the synapse, which causes physiological arousal. A drug that blocks receptors on muscles and causes muscle paralysis is **(b)** _____. A drug that has chemical keys similar to endorphins and causes uncontrollable laughter and vivid hallucinations is **(c)** _____.

H Application: Experimental Treatments

15. The tremors and rigidity of Parkinson's disease result when a group of structures that regulate movement, called the **(a)** _____, lose their supply of dopamine. In experimental treatment, fetal brain cells or stem cells can be transplanted into a precise location of a patient's brain by a technique called the **(b)** _____ procedure. Cells that have the amazing capacity to develop into any of the 220 types of cells that make up the human body are called **(c)** _____. These cells can be used to treat spinal cord injuries and diseases like Alzheimer's and Parkinson's because stem cells can develop into **(d)** _____.

Answers: 1. (a) neurons, (b) glial cells; 2. (a) neurons, (b) bird; 3. neurogenesis; 4. (a) cell body, or soma, (b) dendrite, (c) axon; 5. (a) myelin sheath, (b) insulation; (d) end bulbs, (e) neurotransmitters; 6. (a) synapse, (b) receptors; 7. (a) neurons, (b) central, (c) nerves, (d) peripheral, (e) regrow, (f) peripheral, (g) neurons; 8. (a) chemical gates, (b) resting, (c) sodium, (d) protein, (e) positive, (f) negative, (g) sodium pump; 9. (a) chemical gates, (b) sodium, (c) sodium, (d) action potential, (e) positive, (f) negative; 10. (a) nerve impulse, (b) all-or-none law; 11. (a) neurotransmitters, (b) receptors, (c) excitatory, (d) inhibitory, (e) neuropeptides; 12. (a) reflex, or reflex response, (b) sensory, or afferent, (c) motor, or efferent, (d) interneurons, (e) injury or harm, (f) physiological; 13. (a) phantom limb, (b) parts; 14. (a) reuptake, (b) curare, (c) salvia; 15. (a) basal ganglia, (b) stereotaxic, (c) stem cells, (d) neurons

Key Terms/Key People

acetycholine, 55
action potential, 53
afferent neurons, 56
alcohol, 55
all-or-none law, 52
Alzheimer's disease, 47
axon, 50
axon membrane, 52
basal ganglia, 60
birds' brains, 49
cell body, 50
central nervous system, 51
cocaine, 59
curare, 59
dendrites, 50
dopamine, 55

efferent neurons, 56
end bulbs, 50, 54
endorphins, 55
excitatory transmitters, 54
fetal tissue transplants, 60
GABA neurons, 55
gamma-aminobutyric acid
  (GABA), 55
gene, 48
glial cell, 48
glutamate, 55
induced pluripotent stem cells
  (iPSCs), 60
inhibitory transmitters, 54
interneuron, 56
ions, 52

mature brain, 48
multiple sclerosis, 51
myelin sheath, 50
nerve, 51
nerve impulse, 52
neurogenesis, 49
neuron, 48
neuropeptides, 55
neuroscience, 47
neurotransmitter, 54
norepinephrine, 55
Parkinson's disease, 60
peripheral nervous system, 51
phantom limb, 58
primate brains, 49
reattaching limbs, 51

reflex, 56
reflex functions, 56
reflex sequence, 56
repair of neurons, 51
repairing the brain, 49
resting state, 53
reuptake, 59
salvia, 59
serotonin, 55
six-week-old brain, 48
sodium pump, 53
stem cells, 60
stereotaxic procedure, 61
synapse, 50
transmitter, 54

Media Resources

Go to **CengageBrain.com** to access Psychology CourseMate, where you will find an interactive eBook, glossaries, flashcards, quizzes, videos, answers to Critical Thinking questions, and more. You can also access Virtual Psychology Labs, an interactive laboratory experience designed to illustrate key experiments first-hand.

Living with a Brain Disease

Throughout his life, Stu Bryant was kind, well-mannered, and respectful to others. He was known to have a "quick smile and an easy laugh." But, at about the age of 60, his behavior began to change in ways that frustrated and concerned his family.

Why is Stu acting rude and impulsive?

For instance, when standing in line behind a woman with tattoos, Stu shouted, "Wow, that's a lot of tattoos." Also, he was repeatedly caught on video camera stealing muffins and cheesecakes from a local mini-mart. Then, there's the times he entered a house that was being built even though there was a fence surrounding the house and a "No Trespassing" sign.

> I have something wrong with my brain.

Stu's inappropriate and puzzling behavior wasn't limited to strangers; his family was personally affected by his behaviors as well. One day, his wife came home to find Stu packing up a truck and moving out with no explanation for his decision. Another time he went on a bike ride with his daughter and, when he disappeared for two hours, he didn't care that his daughter was concerned about his whereabouts and safety.

Courtesy Maureen Bryant

Because of Stu's increasingly odd behaviors, his family took him to see a neurologist. After a comprehensive examination that included a brain scan to peek inside the structures of his brain, the neurologist diagnosed Stu with *frontotemporal disease* (Hodges, 2011; Roberson, 2011).

Like Alzheimer's disease, which we discussed in Module 3, frontotemporal disease is the result of damage to neurons caused by an excessive buildup of proteins in the brain. The disease affects the frontal and temporal lobes, which are brain areas responsible for social emotions. In this module, you will learn more about the frontal and temporal lobes as well as many other structures and functions of the brain. You'll learn how damage to areas of the brain results in changes in cognitive, emotional, social, and physical functioning.

As the frontotemporal disease progresses, more significant changes in personality take place. People like Stu, who were once agreeable and respectful, begin to act rudely and impulsively. They will eventually lack feelings of empathy, embarrassment, guilt, and shame. The disease has been progressing for Stu, and he has become unable to understand why insulting strangers, stealing, and trespassing are wrong (adapted from Curwen, 2012).

Diagnosis and Causes

Researchers are investigating the connection between changes in the brain and in people's behavior. This type of study is an example of research in the field of cognitive neuroscience. As we discussed in Module 1, **cognitive neuroscience** involves taking pictures and identifying the structures and functions of the living brain during the performance of a variety of mental or cognitive processes, such as thinking, planning, naming, and recognizing objects (Purves et al., 2012).

© ka i9/iSto<kphoto

Brain scans look at the structures and functions of the brain.

In this module, we will discuss different techniques used to look inside of the brain to examine its structures and functions, including the brain scan Stu received during his visit to the neurologist.

While some researchers study what happens on a biological level once someone develops frontotemporal disease, other researchers are interested in studying its causes. We already know that frontotemporal disease is associated with an excessive build-up of certain proteins in the brain, but researchers are searching for more answers.

© luchscher/Shutterstock.com

Scientists want to know how genes are responsible for brain abnormalities.

For instance, they want to learn how genetic instructions may be responsible for the disease.

In this module, we will provide an overview of how genetic instructions are written and what happens when they have errors.

There is currently no cure for frontotemporal disease—only treatments that can help to decrease the impulsive behaviors associated with it. Perhaps, with new findings about its causes, new, more effective treatments will be developed to help those who are living with the disease.

What's Coming

The biological bases of behaviors are complex and fascinating. Module 3 discussed our brain's building blocks, and Module 4 discusses our incredible nervous system. We will begin with how genetic instructions are written and how they have evolved. Next, we'll describe how scientists look inside the living brain. Last, we'll spend much of this module describing the parts of the nervous system, including the amazing 3-pound human brain. ●

What makes brains different? Your brain and body developed according to complex chemical instructions that were written in a human cell no larger than a grain of sand. The reason brains and bodies have different shapes, colors, and abilities is that they develop from different instructions, which are written at the moment of fertilization.

1 Fertilization.

Human life has its beginnings when a father's sperm, which contains 23 chromosomes, penetrates a mother's egg (ovum), which contains 23 chromosomes. The result is a fertilized cell called a zygote (shown below).

Sperm   Ovum   Zygote

2 Zygote.

A zygote, which is about the size of a grain of sand, is the largest human cell.

A **zygote** is a cell that results when an egg is fertilized. A zygote contains 46 chromosomes arranged in 23 pairs.

A zygote contains the equivalent of 300,000 pages of typewritten instructions. For simplicity, the zygote shown above has only 1 pair of chromosomes instead of the usual 23 pairs.

3 Chromosomes.

Inside the very tiny zygote are 23 pairs of chromosomes, which contain chemical instructions for development of the brain and body.

A **chromosome** is a short, rodlike, microscopic structure that contains tightly coiled strands of the chemical DNA, which is an abbreviation for deoxyribonucleic (*dee-ox-ee-RYE-bow-new-CLEE-ick*) acid. Each cell of the human body (except for the sperm and egg) contains 46 chromosomes arranged in 23 pairs.

For the sake of simplicity, the cell above contains only 2 pairs of chromosomes instead of the usual 23 pairs.

4 Chemical alphabet.

Each chromosome contains a long, coiled strand of DNA, which resembles a ladder (left figure) that has been twisted over and over upon itself.

Each rung of the DNA ladder is made up of four chemicals. The order in which the four different chemicals combine to form rungs creates a microscopic chemical alphabet. This chemical alphabet is used to write instructions for the development and assembly of the 100 trillion highly specialized cells that make up the brain and body.

5 Genes and proteins.

On each chromosome are specific segments that contain particular instructions. In the chromosome on the right, each segment represents the location of a gene.

A **gene** is a specific segment on the long strand of DNA that contains instructions for making proteins. Proteins are chemical building blocks from which all the parts of the brain and body are constructed.

For example, genes determine physical traits (eye color, shape of ear lobes) as well as contribute to the development of emotional, cognitive, and behavioral traits (Angier, 2003). When researchers discover a new gene, it means they have identified the exact location of the gene on its chromosome.

6 Polymorphic genes.

Although there is only one version of about 99% of our genes, some of our genes have more than one version.

A **polymorphic gene** is a gene that has more than one version.

Polymorphic genes help explain some of the differences in physical appearance and behaviors in people. For example, there is a polymorphic gene that influences eye color. Depending on which combination of these genes each sibling receives from the parents, two siblings may have different eye colors.

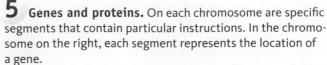

7 Dominant and recessive genes.

Because we can inherit different versions of genes for a particular characteristic (such as eye color) from each parent, conflicts between polymorphic genes can occur. The conflict is resolved by identifying the dominant and recessive genes. In terms of eye color, the gene for brown eyes is dominant and the gene for blue eyes is recessive.

A **dominant gene** is a type of polymorphic gene that determines the development of a specific trait even if it is paired with a recessive gene. A *recessive gene* is a type of polymorphic gene that determines the development of a specific trait only when it is inherited from both parents.

If you inherit a gene for brown eyes from your father and a gene for blue eyes from your mother, the dominant gene will determine your eye color. The gene for brown eyes is dominant, so you will develop brown eyes.

8 Genome.

Because genes determine a multitude of traits, scientists have long been interested in mapping our genes. The Human Genome Project, which began in 1995 and cost over $2.7 billion, reached its first goal in 2003 of mapping all the human genes (Mestel, 2003a). Unlike earlier estimates of 100,000 human genes, researchers found only 20,000–25,000 human genes on the 23 pairs of chromosomes (IHGSC, 2004). Despite this enormous effort to quantify the number of human genes, estimates continue to fluctuate. Research now suggests the number of genes may vary from human to human (Balasubramanian et al., 2010; Pertea & Salzberg, 2010). Researchers are now working to understand how humans develop physical and psychological traits, identify sources of genetic diseases, develop new drugs, and use gene therapy to treat genetic problems (Kolata, 2006, 2007, 2011). Next, we'll learn what happens when there are errors in the genetic instructions.

Errors in Genetic Instructions

When Ming was born, he weighed about 9 pounds and his doctor stated he was a very healthy baby. Everything was fine at first as Ming often smiled and cooed, and he slept and ate well. But soon Ming's parents began to worry because he was not reaching many of his developmental milestones on time, such as sitting and crawling.

As Ming got older, more problems became evident. He was hyperactive and had frequent, uncontrollable tantrums. Also, he didn't begin speaking until age 3, and he continued to fall behind in school. An examination of Ming's genetic makeup revealed he had an inherited genetic disorder called fragile X syndrome (B. O. Berg, 2007; Ropper & Samuels, 2009).

Ming has fragile X syndrome.

Fragile X syndrome, an inherited developmental disability, is due to a defect in the X chromosome (the pinched end of the X chromosome). It can result in physical changes, such as a relatively large head with protruding ears, as well as mild to profound mental retardation.

Fragile X syndrome, which can cause changes in both physical features and brain development, illustrates what happens when there is an error in the genetic instructions. Another example of an error in the genetic instructions is Down syndrome.

Down syndrome results from an extra 21st chromosome and causes abnormal physical traits (a fold of skin at the corner of each eye, a wide tongue, heart defects) and abnormal brain development, resulting in degrees of mental retardation.

Genetic Testing

Genetic testing is used to detect genes associated with a specific disease or disorder (such as fragile X syndrome and Down syndrome) as well as for paternity testing and forensics (NHGRI, 2011).

© Darren Baker/Shutterstock.com

Genetic testing involves taking a sample from someone's blood, hair, skin, or other body parts and then examining the person's genes to look for signs that he or she may be at risk for specific diseases or disorders (NLM, 2012).

Genetic testing and genetic research have a tremendous influence on psychology. One major goal for researchers is to understand how genes interact with the environment to result in mental retardation, personality traits, mental disorders, and various cognitive abilities (Flint et al., 2010; Rutter, 2006).

Next, we'll discuss how genetic changes are thought to have affected brain development over millions of years.

Evolution of the Human Brain

What is evolution?

In 1859, Charles Darwin stunned much of the Western world by publishing *On the Origin of Species*, a revolutionary book on how species originate, which was the basis for his now-famous theory of evolution.

The **theory of evolution** says that different species arose from a common ancestor and that those species that survived were best adapted to meet the demands of their environments.

According to the theory of evolution, humans descended from a creature that split off from apes.

Darwin's theory of evolution has received broad scientific support from fossil records and examination of genetic similarities and differences among species (Mayr, 2000; Zimmer, 2009a). The belief of many scientists in the theory of evolution clashes with deeply held religious beliefs that place humans on a family tree of their own. According to the theory of evolution, present-day humans descended from a creature that split off from apes millions of years ago. Supporting this theory is the finding that humans and chimpanzees share at least 98% of their DNA or genetic instructions. Research suggests that when and how much genes are activated may be what helps set humans apart from chimpanzees (Ehrenberg, 2008). Other research suggests that humans are more intelligent than chimpanzees not because of more sophisticated neurons; rather, an enormous number of basic neurons and countless more interactions between neurons are responsible for making humans so brainy (Sapolsky, 2006).

Two forces are thought to be responsible for the evolution of the human brain: (1) **genetic mutations,** which are accidental errors in genetic instructions that lead to a change, and (2) **natural selection,** which means the genes for traits that help an organism survive and reproduce **(adaptive genes)** will be selected and will continue in a species, whereas the genes for traits that prevent survival and reproduction **(maladaptive genes)** will not be selected and will be eliminated in a species (Balter, 2002; Toner, 2006).

The process of natural selection produces **adaptations,** which are common features of a species that provide it with improved function. Examples of adaptations include a behavior that helps the organism better escape a predator and a physical characteristic that provides it with an advantage, such as opposable thumbs for gripping.

A relatively new modern approach to psychology emerges from the theory of evolution and is called the evolutionary approach.

The **evolutionary approach** studies how evolutionary ideas, such as adaptation and natural selection, explain human behaviors and mental processes. This approach provides rather persuasive theories about sexual conflict, mating, sexuality, families, social conflict, aggression, morality, depression, and anxiety (Nesse, 2005; Pinker, 2002). In one instance of human evolution, scientists found a set of genes among Tibetans that they developed as recently as 3,000 years ago to help them cope with the low oxygen levels in the air they breathe. This finding may be the most recent example of human evolution and yet another example of natural selection (Wade, 2010).

Research in evolutionary psychology relies on cognitive neuroscience (see p. 7), which means it uses pictures of the living brain (Tooby & Cosmides, 2006). We'll now describe how researchers study our modern brains through the use of impressive brain images. ●

Studying the Living Brain

We have explained how genetic instructions guide the development and assembly of billions of parts that make up the human brain. We have discussed genetic mutations and natural selection as the forces responsible for the evolution of the human brain. Now we begin exploring the structures and functions of your own brain.

Can we look inside the human skull?

Looking at the skull on the right raises an interesting question: How can researchers look inside the half-inch-thick skull and study the living brain

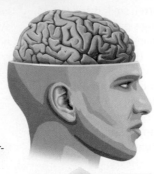

New techniques can take pictures through the skull.

without causing any damage? The answer is that during the past 10 years, researchers have developed several brain-scanning techniques that can look through the thick skull and picture the brain with astonishing clarity yet cause no damage to the extremely delicate brain cells. By using these almost science-fiction techniques, researchers are mapping a variety of cognitive functions (attention, language, memory, motor skills) as well as sites of emotional feelings and appetite (Banich & Compton, 2011; Purves et al., 2012). We'll discuss some brain-scanning techniques that take pictures through the skull.

Brain Scans: Looking at Structure

Phillipa was a healthy, intelligent, well-educated woman who loved her job as a schoolteacher. She was a positive, pleasant person who never seemed to get irritated, even when her children would act up while she still had hours of lesson planning remaining for the next morning.

Why would Phillipa have an MRI?

But Phillipa changed in many drastic ways after she was brutally assaulted by a mugger as she was walking to her car after a late night of grading her students' papers. She was hit hard on the front of her head with a steel rod. Phillipa was in excruciating pain and unable to move as she was taken to the hospital, unaware of the serious damage caused by the assault.

The neurologist at the hospital told Phillipa that the front part of her skull was shattered and the front area of her brain had serious, irreparable damage. The neurologist identified the exact location and extent of the damaged area by using a brain-scanning technique called MRI (picture at right).

What happened to Phillipa's brain that made her yell and swear at strangers?

MRI, or **magnetic resonance imaging,** involves passing nonharmful radio frequencies through the brain. A computer measures how these signals interact with brain cells and then transforms this interaction into an incredibly detailed image of the brain (or body). MRIs are used to study the structures of the brain.

During an MRI procedure, Phillipa would lie with her head in the center of a giant, donut-shaped machine. This is the same machine that was used for Stu, the gentleman we discussed at the start of the module, to enable his neurologist to diagnose his frontotemporal disease.

Reflections from the radio waves passed through the brain are computer analyzed and developed into very detailed pictures of the living brain, as shown in the scan (picture at right).

Brain damage. During Phillipa's MRI scan, images of her brain—slice by slice—appeared on a television screen. Suddenly, standing out from the normal grayish image was a large unusual area that indicated a skull fracture and brain damage (red area on left of MRI scan). Because the damage was located in a brain area involved with carrying out motor movements, behaving normally in social situations, performing emotional behaviors, and maintaining a healthy personality, Phillipa had impaired motor movements, inappropriately yelled at others with rude remarks, and broke social guidelines (such as undressing herself in front of strangers). However, since only the front area of her brain was affected, many other functions, such as seeing, feeling, speaking, hearing, and understanding, were normal (adapted from J. A. Ogden, 2005).

Next, we'll discuss brain-scanning techniques that measure the cognitive functioning of the brain. The first scan we'll discuss is a newer and different version of the MRI, called the fMRI.

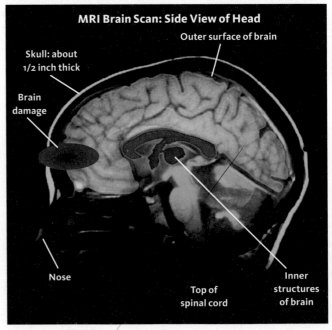

MRI Brain Scan: Side View of Head

Outer surface of brain

Skull: about 1/2 inch thick

Brain damage

Nose

Top of spinal cord

Inner structures of brain

Graphic data courtesy of Dr. Ahmad Hariri

Brain Scans: Looking at Function

Are there pictures of thinking?

Whereas the MRI examines the structures of the brain, the fMRI examines the functioning of the brain.

The "f" in **fMRI** (functional magnetic resonance imaging) stands for *functional* and measures the changes in activity of specific neurons that are functioning during cognitive tasks, such as thinking, listening, or reading.

For example, the fMRI on the right shows that while children were watching violence on TV, an increase in activity occurs in an area of the brain called the amygdala (see p. 80), which researchers believe is involved in evaluating emotional situations, especially fear and threat

(J. P. Murray et al., 2006). Notice that **fMRI** scans can map activities of neurons that are involved in various cognitive **functions**. In comparison, **MRI** scans show the location of **structures** inside the brain as well as identify tumors and sites of brain damage, as we saw in Phillipa's MRI.

The advantage of the two kinds of MRI scans is that they use nonharmful radio frequencies and give very detailed views of structures and functions inside the living brain (Ropper & Samuels, 2009).

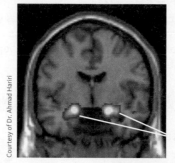

Courtesy of Dr. Ahmad Hariri

This fMRI scan shows how the amygdala responds to watching televised violence.

Another type of brain scan that also literally lights up your thoughts and feelings is called the PET scan.

A **PET scan,** or **positron emission tomography,** involves injecting a slightly radioactive solution into the blood and then measuring the amount of radiation absorbed by brain cells called neurons. Very active neurons absorb more radioactive solution than less active ones. Different levels of absorption are represented by colors—red and yellow indicate maximum activity of neurons, while blue and green indicate minimal activity.

Pictures of speaking and signing. The PET scan at the top left shows that when subjects look at an object and identify it by speaking, most neural activity occurs in the areas of the brain responsible for speaking, seeing, and understanding. The PET scan at the bottom shows that when deaf people look at an object and identify it by signing, most neural activity occurs in the same areas as when speaking, but one other area responsible for monitoring self-generated movements, such as signing, is also highly activated (Emmorey et al., 2007).

PET scans are slowly being replaced by the newer fMRI scans because fMRI scans do not require the injection of slightly radioactive solutions (Ropper & Samuels, 2009). It may simply be a matter of time before fMRIs are replaced with something even better. Already, some researchers are using a newer brain scan, called a *MEG scan* or *magneto-encephalography,* which examines how the networks in the brain are communicating with each other in real time, as opposed to the slight delay present in fMRI and PET scans.

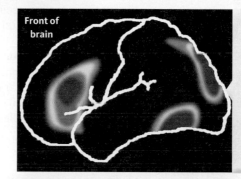

Front of brain

PET scan indicates that when you SPEAK a word, maximum neural activity—areas of red and yellow—occurs in three major areas of your brain.

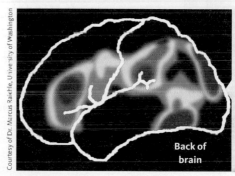

Courtesy of Dr. Marcus Raichle, University of Washington

Back of brain

PET scan indicates that when you SIGN a word, maximum neural activity occurs in the same areas as SPEAKING and one additional major area of your brain.

Another technique used to study brain activity is called an EEG.

An **EEG,** or electroencephalograph, involves placing many electrodes on the scalp, which measure changes in electrical voltages at points along the scalp and provide information about brain wave activity.

EEGs can reveal areas of the brain that are most active during certain cognitive tasks (such as speaking or reading), the presence of abnormal brain activation caused by problems with the brain (such as tumors or seizures), and changes in mental states (such as sleeping or meditation).

By using these brain-scanning techniques, researchers have been able to identify and map the living brain's neural activity as a person performs complex behavioral and cognitive tasks, such as seeing, moving, thinking, speaking, trusting, and empathizing (McCarthy, 2005).

An EEG involves electrodes being placed on the scalp (left) to provide information about electrical activity in different brain areas. The results are shown as brain wave patterns (right).

Now that you are familiar with ways to study the living brain, we can examine the brain's specific structures and interesting functions. ●

Divisions of the Nervous System

How many nervous systems do you have?

Because you have one brain, you may think that means you have one nervous system. In fact, your brain is much more complex: It has two major nervous systems, one of which has four subdivisions. We'll explain the overall organization of the brain's several nervous systems, beginning with its two major divisions: the central and peripheral nervous systems.

A. Major Divisions of the Nervous System

Central Nervous System—CNS

You are capable of many complex cognitive functions—such as thinking, speaking, and reading, as well as moving, feeling, seeing, and hearing—because of your central nervous system.

The **central nervous system** is made up of the brain and spinal cord. From the bottom of the brain emerges the spinal cord, which is made up of neurons and bundles of axons and dendrites that carry information back and forth between the brain and the body.

We'll discuss the major parts of the brain throughout this module.

Peripheral Nervous System—PNS

You are able to move your muscles, receive sensations from your body, and perform many other bodily responses because of the peripheral nervous system.

The **peripheral nervous system** includes all the nerves that extend from the spinal cord and carry messages to and from various muscles, glands, and sense organs located throughout the body.

The peripheral nervous system has two subdivisions: the somatic and autonomic nervous systems.

B. Subdivisions of the PNS

Somatic Nervous System

The **somatic nervous system** consists of a network of nerves that connect either to sensory receptors or to muscles that you can move voluntarily, such as muscles in your limbs, back, neck, and chest. Nerves in the somatic nervous system usually contain two kinds of fibers. Afferent, or sensory, fibers carry information from sensory receptors in the skin, muscles, and other organs to the spinal cord and brain. Efferent, or motor, fibers carry information from the brain and spinal cord to the muscles.

For example, this gymnast controls her muscles, knows where her arms and legs are located in space, and maintains her coordination and balance because the somatic nervous system sends electrical signals back and forth to her brain.

ANS—Autonomic Nervous System

The **autonomic nervous system** regulates heart rate, breathing, blood pressure, digestion, hormone secretion, and other functions. The autonomic nervous system usually functions without conscious effort, which means that only a few of its responses, such as breathing, can also be controlled voluntarily.

The autonomic nervous system also has two subdivisions: the sympathetic and parasympathetic divisions.

C. Subdivisions of the ANS

Sympathetic Division

The **sympathetic division,** which is triggered by threatening or challenging physical or psychological stimuli, increases physiological arousal and prepares the body for action.

For example, the sight of a frightening snake would trigger the sympathetic division, which, in turn, would arouse the body for action, such as fighting or fleeing.

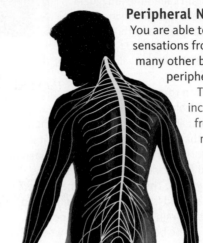

© fivespots/Shutterstock.com

Parasympathetic Division

The **parasympathetic division** returns the body to a calmer, relaxed state and is involved in digestion.

For example, when you are feeling calm and relaxed or digesting food, your parasympathetic system is activated.

Now that you know the overall organization of the nervous system, we'll focus on major parts of the brain. ●

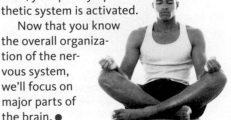

© nicolas hansen/iStockphoto

Unless otherwise noted, all images are © Cengage Learning

D Brain: Structures & Functions

Major Parts of the Brain

A human brain (right figure), which can easily be held in one hand, weighs about 1,350 grams, or

Can someone be shot in the head but not die?

3 pounds, and has the consistency of firm JELL-O. The brain is protected by a thick skull and covered with thin, tough, plasticlike membranes. If shot in the head, a person may or may not die depending on which area was damaged. For example, damage to an area in the forebrain would result in paralysis, damage to an area in the midbrain would result in coma, but damage to an area in the hindbrain would certainly result in death.

We'll begin our exploration of the brain by looking at its three major parts—forebrain, midbrain, and hindbrain—beginning with the forebrain.

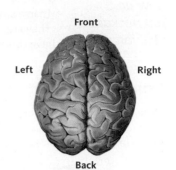

Front
Left   Right
Back

2 Midbrain

If a boxer is knocked unconscious, part of the reason lies in the midbrain.

The **midbrain** has a reward or pleasure center, which is stimulated by food, sex, money, music, attractive faces, and some drugs (cocaine); has areas for visual and auditory reflexes, such as automatically turning your head toward a noise; and contains the reticular formation, which arouses the forebrain so that it is ready to process information from the senses (Holroyd & Coles, 2002).

If the reticular formation were seriously damaged—by a blow to the head, for example—a person would be unconscious and might go into a coma because the forebrain could not be aroused (Bleck, 2007).

1 Forebrain

When you look at the brain, what you are actually seeing is almost all forebrain (figure above). The **forebrain,** which is the largest part of the brain, has right and left sides that are called hemispheres. The hemispheres, connected by a wide band of fibers, are responsible for an incredible number of functions, including learning and memory, speaking and language, having emotional responses, experiencing sensations, initiating voluntary movements, planning, and making decisions.

The large structure outlined in orange to the left shows only the right hemisphere of the forebrain. The forebrain's right and left hemispheres are both shown in the figure at the top right. The forebrain is very well developed in humans.

Side view of the brain's right hemisphere

3c Cerebellum

A person suspected of drunken driving may fail the test of rapidly touching a finger to the nose because of alcohol's effects on the cerebellum.

The **cerebellum,** which is located at the very back and underneath the brain, is involved in coordinating motor movements but not in initiating voluntary movements. The cerebellum is also involved in performing timed motor responses, such as those needed in playing games or sports, and in automatic or reflexive learning, such as blinking the eye to a signal, which is called classical conditioning (discussed in Module 9) (Gerwig et al., 2008).

Because alcohol is a depressant drug and interferes with the functions of the cerebellum, an intoxicated person would experience decreased coordination and have difficulty rapidly touching a finger to the nose, which is one test for being drunk (Oscar-Berman & Marinkovic, 2007).

Of the brain's three parts, the forebrain is the largest, most evolved, and most responsible for an enormous range of personal, social, emotional, and cognitive behaviors. For those reasons, we'll examine the forebrain in more detail.

3 Hindbrain

The structures and functions of the hindbrain, which are found in very primitive brains, such as the alligator's, have remained constant through millions of years of evolution. The **hindbrain** has three distinct structures: the pons, medulla, and cerebellum.

3a Pons

If someone has a serious sleep disorder, it may involve the pons. In Latin, *pons* means "bridge," which suggests its function.

The **pons** functions as a bridge to transmit messages between the spinal cord and brain. The pons also makes the chemicals involved in sleep (Monti et al., 2008).

3b Medulla

If someone dies of a drug overdose, the cause of death probably involved the medulla.

The **medulla,** which is located at the top of the spinal cord, includes a group of cells that control vital reflexes, such as respiration, heart rate, and blood pressure.

Large amounts of alcohol, heroin, or other depressant drugs suppress the functions of cells in the medulla and cause death by stopping breathing.

Overall View of the Cortex

How do you package 1 trillion cells?

How would you design a brain to hold 1 trillion cells (100 billion neurons and 900 billion glial cells) and be no bigger than a small melon and weigh no more than 3 pounds? You would need to make the cells microscopic in size, which they are, and to organize the billions of cells into different but interconnected areas, which they are. But would you have thought to make the brain's surface very wrinkled? Here's why.

Wrinkled Cortex

In the photo below, you see a computer-enhanced picture of the outside of an adult human brain, which has a very wrinkled surface that is called the cortex (in Latin, *cortex* means "cover").

The **cortex** is a thin layer of cells that essentially covers the entire surface of the forebrain. The vast majority of our neurons are located in the cortex, which folds over on itself so that it has a large surface area.

To understand the advantage of having a wrinkled cortex, just imagine having to put a large sheet of paper about 18 inches square into a small match box that is 3 inches square. One solution is to crumple (wrinkle) the sheet of paper until it easily fits into the tiny match box. Similarly, imagine many billions of neurons laid on a sheet of paper about 18 inches square. When this large sheet of neurons is wrinkled, the cortex can fit snugly into our much smaller, rounded skulls.

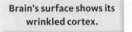

Brain's surface shows its wrinkled cortex.

Early researchers divided the wrinkled cortex into four different areas, or lobes, each of which has different functions.

Four Lobes

As you look at the brain's cortex, you see a wrinkled surface of peaks and valleys with very few distinguishing features. However, the cortex's appearance is deceiving because its hundreds of different functions are organized into four separate areas called lobes.

The cortex is divided into four separate areas, or **lobes,** each with different functions: the **frontal lobe** is involved with personality, emotions, and motor behaviors; the **parietal** *(puh-RYE-it-all)* **lobe** is involved with perception and sensory experiences; the **occipital** *(ock-SIP-pih-tull)* **lobe** is involved with processing visual information; and the **temporal** *(TEM-purr-all)* **lobe** is involved with hearing and speaking.

The one brain structure that most clearly distinguishes you from other animals is your well-developed cortex, which allows you to read, understand, talk about, and remember the concepts in this text. To understand what life would be like without a cortex, we'll introduce the case of Baby Theresa, who was born without any lobes and thus no cortex.

Cortex is divided into four different areas, or lobes.

Baby Theresa's Brain: A Fatal Defect

Baby Theresa was born with almost no brain and died only nine days after birth. Her rare condition, caused by errors in genetic instructions, is called anencephaly (Ropper & Samuels, 2009).

Anencephaly *(an-in-CEPH-ah-lee)* is the condition of being born with little or no brain. If some brain or nervous tissue is present, it is totally exposed and often damaged because the top of the skull is missing. Survival is usually limited to days; the longest has been two months.

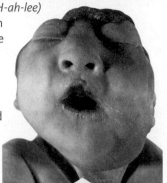

This child has anencephaly, meaning little or no brain.

Anencephaly is always fatal because it also includes other serious physical defects, such as damage to the skull (R. J. Cook et al., 2008). Baby Theresa, who survived only nine days, had almost no brain tissue and almost no skull. Lacking most of a brain means that she would be incapable of perceiving, thinking, speaking, planning, or making decisions.

The figure below shows that a baby born with anencephaly has no forebrain. One reason babies with anencephaly may survive for days or weeks is that they may have parts of their hindbrain. As discussed earlier, the hindbrain contains the pons and medulla. The medulla controls vital reflexes, such as breathing, heart rate, and blood pressure, which together can maintain life for a period of time.

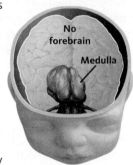

The medulla kept Theresa alive.

This example of anencephaly shows that without the forebrain, a baby may be physiologically alive but show no signs of having a mind or possessing cognitive abilities associated with being human. In a real sense, it is the functions of the forebrain's four lobes that define us as human and distinguish us from all other creatures.

Because the four lobes are vital to our existence as humans, we'll discuss each lobe in turn. We'll begin with the frontal lobe and a tragic accident.

Frontal Lobe: Functions

What does the biggest lobe do?

The frontal lobe (right figure) is the largest of the brain's lobes and has many important functions (J. H. Friedman & Chou, 2007; B. L. Miller & Cummings, 2007).

The **frontal lobe,** which is located in the front part of the brain, includes a huge area of cortex. The frontal lobe is involved in many functions: performing voluntary motor movements, interpreting and performing emotional behaviors, behaving normally in social situations, maintaining a healthy personality, paying attention to things in the environment, making decisions, and executing plans. Because the frontal lobe is involved in making decisions, planning, reasoning, and carrying out behaviors, it is said to have executive functions, much like the duties of a company's executive officer.

Our first clue about the functions of the frontal lobe came from an unusual accident in 1848; our more recent knowledge comes from research using brain scans (fMRI and PET scans). Let's first go back in time and meet Phineas Gage, whose accident led to the discovery of one of the frontal lobe's important functions.

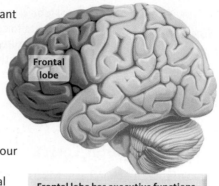

Frontal lobe

Frontal lobe has executive functions.

A Terrible Accident

The accident occurred at about half past four on the afternoon of September 13, 1848, near the small town of Cavendish, Vermont. Railroad crewmen were about to blast a rock that blocked their way. Foreman Phineas Gage filled a deep, narrow hole in the rock with powder and rammed in a long iron rod to tamp down the charge before covering it with sand. But the tamping iron rubbed against the side of the shaft, and a spark ignited the powder. The massive rod—3½ feet long, 1¼ inches in diameter, and weighing 13 pounds— shot from the hole under the force of the explosion. It struck Phineas just beneath his left eye and tore through his skull. It shot out the top of his head and landed some 50 yards away.

Phineas survived, but, following the accident, his personality changed: He went from being a popular, friendly foreman to acting impatient, cursing his workers, and refusing to honor his promises.

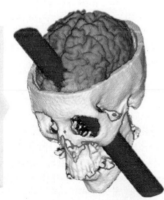

A massive rod weighing 13 pounds was accidentally driven through the front part of Phineas Gage's frontal lobe. The result, which was similar to having a frontal lobotomy, caused Phineas to have emotional outbursts and problems in making decisions, something he did not experience before this accident.

From: H Damasio, T Grabowski, R Frank, AM Galaburda, AR Damasio, The return of Phineas Gage: Clues about the brain from a famous patient. *Science, 264:* 1102–1105, 1994. Copyright © 1994 by the American Association for the Advancement in Science. Reprinted with permission of author and publisher.

Researchers recently used Phineas's preserved skull to reconstruct the site and extent of his brain damage. As the figure above shows, the iron rod had passed through and extensively damaged Phineas's frontal lobe. Researchers concluded that Phineas had suffered a crude form of frontal lobotomy, which caused deficits in processing of emotion and decision making that result after damage to the frontal lobe (H. Damasio et al., 1994).

Beginning in the 1930s, doctors performed thousands of lobotomies to treat various mental and behavioral problems.

Frontal Lobotomy

In 1936, Egas Moniz, a Portuguese neurologist, used an untested surgical treatment, frontal lobotomy, to treat individuals who had severe emotional problems (Tierney, 2000; A. P. Weiss et al., 2007).

A **frontal lobotomy** was a surgical procedure in which about one-third of the front part of the frontal lobe (figure below) was cut away from the rest of the brain.

Moniz first reported that frontal lobotomies did reduce emotional problems in about 35% of severely agitated human patients, although he did no controlled or follow-up studies to check long-term effects (D. R. Weinberger et al., 1995). Based on Moniz's reports of success, about 18,000 frontal lobotomies were performed in the 1940s and 1950s on emotionally disturbed patients who were primarily confined to state mental hospitals that offered no other treatments.

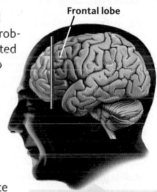

Frontal lobe

Red line indicates where lobe was severed.

Results of Lobotomies

Initially, neurologists reported good short-term effects, but better controlled, long-term studies on frontal lobotomies found mixed results: Some patients did become less violent, but others showed no improvement and some became worse. Even those whose social-emotional behaviors improved were often left with serious problems in other areas, such as having difficulty making and carrying out plans, adjusting to new social demands, or behaving with appropriate emotional responses in social situations (Mashour et al., 2005).

Two things happened in the early 1950s that ended the use of frontal lobotomies to treat social-emotional problems. First, follow-up research indicated that lobotomies were no more successful in relieving social-emotional problems than doing nothing. Second, antipsychotic drugs were discovered and showed greater success in treating serious social-emotional problems (Mashour et al., 2005).

From using frontal lobotomies as treatment, researchers learned two things: (1) careful follow-up work is essential before declaring a treatment successful, and (2) the frontal lobe has many different, important functions, which we'll look at next.

Frontal Lobe: Functions

The organization of the frontal lobe is somewhat confusing because it has such a wide range of functions, from motor movements to cognitive processes. We'll first focus on motor movements, which have a very unusual feature.

How do you move your right hand?

In the figure on the right, notice that nerves from the left hemisphere (blue) cross over and control the movements of the right hand and right side of the body; nerves from the right hemisphere (red) cross over and control the movements of the left hand and left side of the body. The ability to move your hand or any other part of your body depends on the motor cortex in the right and left frontal lobes.

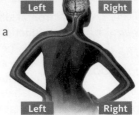

Location of Motor Cortex

To move your right hand, you will use the motor cortex in your left frontal lobe.

The **motor cortex** is a narrow strip of cortex that is located on the back edge of the frontal lobe and extends down its side. The motor cortex is involved in the initiation of all voluntary movements. The right motor cortex controls muscles on the left side of the body, and vice versa.

You can move any individual part of your body at will because of how the motor cortex is organized.

Organization and Function of Motor Cortex

The figure on the right shows an enlarged part of the motor cortex, which is organized in two interesting ways.

First, a larger body part (notice huge hand area) indicates relatively more area on the motor cortex and thus more ability to perform complex movements. A smaller body part (notice small knee area) indicates relatively less area on the motor cortex and thus less ability to perform complex movements. This unusual drawing, which uses sizes of body parts to show the ability to perform complex movements, is called the **motor homunculus. Second,** each body part has its own area on the motor cortex. This means that damage to one part of the motor cortex could result in paralysis of that part yet spare most other parts. However, recent studies indicate that the motor cortex is not as discretely organized as once believed. Instead of each body part having a different discrete area, there is considerable overlap among body parts in the motor cortex (Purves et al., 2012). Finally, notice that the motor cortex makes up only a relatively small part of the entire frontal lobe.

Next, we'll explain the frontal lobe's other functions.

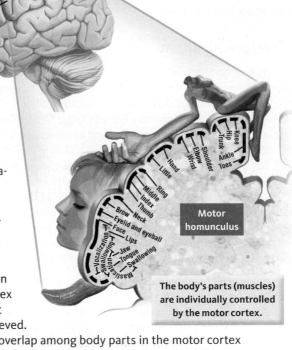

Motor homunculus

The body's parts (muscles) are individually controlled by the motor cortex.

Other Functions of Frontal Lobe

Executive function. Much of our knowledge of other frontal lobe functions comes from brain scans on both individuals who had damage to that area and healthy individuals. Researchers have found that the frontal lobes are involved in paying attention, organizing, planning, making decisions, and carrying out cognitive and social-emotional behaviors, including self-control. Frontal lobes are said to have an **executive function**—that is, act similar to a smart, successful executive of a large organization (B. L. Miller & Cummings, 2007; von Hippel, 2007).

At the beginning of the module, we discussed the case of Stu, who had frontotemporal disease. You'll recall that he had self-control problems, such as yelling at strangers, stealing, trespassing, and moving away from his wife for no apparent reason. As part of his disease the frontal lobe was damaged, which explains why he had difficulty with executive functions.

Memory. Brains scans used on individuals with no brain damage have led to interesting discoveries about frontal lobe functions.

Frontal lobe

Maximum activity

Back of brain

Courtesy of J.A. Fiez, Dept. of Neurology, Washington University School of Medicine

For example, after subjects were shown a series of word pairs, such as *ordeal* and *roach,* they were shown one word from each pair *(ordeal)* and asked to either think about or avoid thinking about the associated word *(roach)*. Brain scans, such as the one shown below, indicated that people who best avoided thinking about the associated word had maximum activity in the frontal lobe. This means the frontal lobe is involved in memory, specifically intentional forgetting (M. C. Anderson et al., 2004).

Aging. The frontal lobes shrink as we age, creating impairment in our executive functions, such as inhibiting unwanted speech (a type of self-control). Although older adults understand social rules, they often inappropriately ask others embarrassing questions in public settings and talk at great length about topics irrelevant to a conversation, both of which demonstrate executive function impairments (Begley, 2007b; von Hippel, 2007).

Immediately behind the frontal lobe is the parietal lobe, which, among other things, keeps track of your body's limbs.

Parietal Lobe: Functions

Every second of every minute of every day, your brain must keep track of what's touching your skin, where your feet and hands are, and whether you're walking or running. All this is automatically and efficiently done by your parietal lobe (right figure).

How do you know where your feet are? The **parietal lobe** is located directly behind the frontal lobe. The parietal lobe's functions include processing sensory information from body parts, which includes touching, locating positions of limbs, and feeling temperature and pain, and carrying out several cognitive functions, such as attending to and perceiving objects.

For example, the ability to know what you're touching involves the parietal lobe's somatosensory cortex.

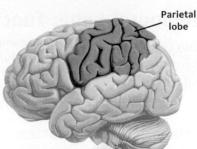

Parietal lobe processes information from body parts.

Location of Somatosensory Cortex

Knowing what you're touching or how hot to make the water for your shower involves the somatosensory cortex.

The **somatosensory cortex** is a narrow strip of cortex that is located on the front edge of the parietal lobe and extends down its side. The somatosensory cortex processes sensory information about touch, location of limbs, pain, and temperature. The right somatosensory cortex receives information from the left side of the body, and vice versa.

Your lips are much more sensitive than your elbows because of the way the somatosensory cortex is organized.

Organization of Somatosensory Cortex

The large figure on the right shows an enlarged part of the somatosensory cortex, which is also cleverly organized.

First, notice the different sizes of the body parts drawn on top of the somatosensory cortex. A larger body part (notice large area for lips) indicates relatively more area on the somatosensory cortex and thus more sensitivity to external stimulation. A smaller body part (notice small nose area) indicates relatively less area on the somatosensory cortex and thus less sensitivity to external stimulation. This unusual drawing, which uses sizes of body parts to indicate amount of sensitivity to external stimulation, is called the ***sensory homunculus*** (ho-MONK-you-luss). In Latin, *homunculus* means "little man." Notice that the somatosensory cortex makes up only a small part of the parietal lobe.

Second, notice that each body part has its own area on the somatosensory cortex. This means that damage to one part of the somatosensory cortex could result in loss of feeling to one part of the body yet spare all others. Next, we'll explain the parietal lobe's other functions.

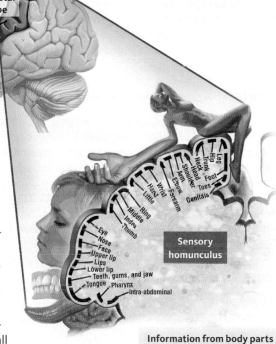

Sensory homunculus

Information from body parts (skin, muscles, etc.) is individually processed by the somatosensory cortex.

Other Functions of Parietal Lobe

Sensory integration. When you put your hand in your pocket, you can easily distinguish a key from a stick of chewing gum because your parietal lobe digests information about texture, shape, and size and "tells you" what the object is. However, patients with damage to the back of their parietal lobes cannot recognize common objects by touch or feel (Bear et al., 1996). Evidence that the parietal lobes are involved in other cognitive processes comes from studies using brain scans.

Spatial orientation. The parietal lobe is involved in processing spatial information (P. H. Weiss et al., 2006). For example, when you are judging the location and distance you must throw a football, your parietal lobe is working to enable you to complete a successful throw.

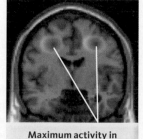

Maximum activity in parietal lobe.

Language abilities. People were asked to participate in a writing exercise while researchers investigated changes in their brain activity. fMRI scans, such as the one shown here, indicated that maximum activity during this task occurred in the parietal lobe (Menon & Desmond, 2001). Another fMRI study on people who fluently speak a second language indicated that the parietal lobe was more developed (or larger) than in those who spoke only one language (Mechelli et al., 2004).

Other functions. Research using brain scans shows that the parietal lobes are involved in additional cognitive functions, such as visual and auditory attention, memory, and numerical processing (counting) (Hao et al., 2005; Hubbard et al., 2005; Shomstein & Yantis, 2006; Simons et al., 2008).

Immediately below the parietal lobe is the temporal lobe, which we'll examine next.

Temporal Lobe: Functions

Did you hear your name? You recognize your name when you hear it spoken; because of the way sound is processed in the temporal lobe, you know it's not just some meaningless noise.

The **temporal lobe** is located directly below the parietal lobe and is involved in hearing, speaking coherently, and understanding verbal and written material.

As you'll see, the process of hearing and recognizing your name involves two steps and two different brain areas.

Primary Auditory Cortex

The first step in hearing your name occurs when sounds reach specific areas in the temporal lobe called the primary auditory (hearing) cortex; there is one in each lobe.

The **primary auditory cortex,** which is located on the top edge of each temporal lobe, receives electrical signals from receptors in the ears and transforms these signals into meaningless sound sensations, such as vowels and consonants.

At this point, you would not be able to recognize your name because the primary auditory cortex only changes electrical signals from the ears into basic sensations, such as individual sounds, clicks, or noises. For these meaningless sound sensations to become recognizable words, they must be sent to another area in the temporal lobe, called the auditory association area (D. H. Whalen et al., 2006).

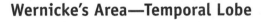

Temporal lobe

Temporal lobe processes auditory (hearing) information.

Auditory Association Area

The second step in recognizing your name is when the primary auditory cortex sends its electrical signals to the auditory association area; there is one in each lobe.

The **auditory association area,** which is located directly below the primary auditory cortex, transforms basic sensory information, such as noises or sounds, into recognizable auditory information, such as words or music.

It is only after auditory information is sent by the primary auditory cortex to the auditory association area that you would recognize sounds as your name, or words, or music (D. H. Whalen et al., 2006). So, it is safe to say that you hear with your brain rather than your ears.

Besides being involved in hearing, the temporal lobe has other areas that are critical for speaking and understanding words and sentences (Tanner, 2010).

Broca's Area—Frontal Lobe

Just as hearing your name is a two-step process, so is speaking a sentence. The first step is putting words together, which involves an area in the frontal lobe called Broca's *(BROKE-ahs)* area.

Broca's area, which is usually located in the left frontal lobe, is necessary for combining sounds into words and arranging words into meaningful sentences. Damage to this area results in **Broca's aphasia** *(ah-PHASE-zz-ah),* in which a person cannot speak in fluent sentences but can understand written and spoken words.

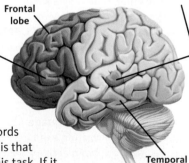

Frontal lobe

Temporal lobe

The reason that saying words and putting words into sentences come naturally to small children is that Broca's area is genetically programmed to do this task. If it is damaged, people with Broca's aphasia have difficulty putting words into sentences. For example, a patient was asked, "What have you been doing in the hospital?" The patient answered, "Yes, sure. Me go, er, uh, P.T. non o'cot, speech…two times…read…wr…ripe, er, rike, er, write…practice…get-ting better" (H. Gardner, 1976, p. 61). The patient was trying to say, "I go to P.T. (physical therapy) at one o'clock to practice speaking, reading, and writing, and I'm getting better."

A patient with Broca's aphasia cannot speak fluently but can still understand words and sentences because of a second area in the temporal lobe—Wernicke's area (Swanberg et al., 2007).

Wernicke's Area—Temporal Lobe

The first step in speaking is using Broca's area to combine sounds into words and arrange words into sentences. The second step is to understand sentences, which involves Wernicke's *(VERN-ick-ees)* area.

Wernicke's area, which is usually located in the left temporal lobe, is necessary for speaking in coherent sentences and for understanding speech. Damage to this area results in **Wernicke's aphasia,** which is a difficulty in understanding spoken or written words and in putting words into meaningful sentences.

For example, a patient with Wernicke's aphasia said, "You know, once in awhile I get caught up, I mention the tarripoi, a month ago, quite a little, I've done a lot well" (H. Gardner, 1976, p. 68). As this meaningless sentence shows, Wernicke's area is critical for combining words into meaningful sentences and being able to speak coherently (Mesulam, 2008).

We have discussed some of the major functions of the temporal lobe. Some if its other functions have to do with social and emotional behavior, such as feeling empathy and understanding social communication. As you know, Stu, whom we discussed earlier, had damage to his temporal lobe and thus had difficulty feeling empathy and interacting appropriately in social situations.

Compared to many other animals, humans rely heavily on visual information, which is processed in the occipital lobe, our next topic.

Occipital Lobe: Functions

Dogs have poor color vision and rely more on their sense of smell. In comparison, all primates, which include monkeys, apes, and humans, have a relatively poor sense of smell and rely more on vision for gathering information about their environments.

Can you see better than dogs?

If you have ever been hit on the back of the head and saw "stars," you already know that vision is located in the occipital lobe.

The **occipital lobe** is located at the very back of the brain and is involved in processing visual information, which includes seeing colors and perceiving and recognizing objects, animals, and people.

Although you see and recognize things with great ease, it is actually a complicated two-step process. Here, we'll give only an overview of that process; we'll go into more detail in Module 5.

Vision

Occipital lobe

Occipital lobe processes visual (seeing) information.

When you look in the mirror and see your face, you don't realize that seeing your face involves two steps and two different areas in the occipital lobe (Maldonado et al., 1997). The first step in seeing your face involves the primary visual cortex.

The **primary visual cortex,** which is located at the very back of the occipital lobe, receives electrical signals from receptors in the eyes and transforms these signals into meaningless basic visual sensations, such as lights, lines, shadows, colors, and textures.

Since the primary visual cortex produces only meaningless visual sensations (lights, lines, shadows), you do not yet see your face. Transforming meaningless visual sensations into a meaningful visual object occurs in the visual association area (Kiernan, 2008).

The **visual association area,** which is located next to the primary visual cortex, transforms basic sensations, such as lights, lines, colors, and textures, into complete, meaningful visual perceptions, such as persons, objects, or animals.

When the second step works properly, there is increased activity in the visual association area and decreased activity in the primary visual cortex as basic sensations are turned into meaningful perceptions (S. O. Murray et al., 2002). If there are problems in the second step, the person can still see parts of objects but has difficulty combining the parts and recognizing the whole object (B. J. Osborne et al., 2007; Purves et al., 2012).

We'll discuss two unusual visual problems that result from damage to association areas.

Visual Agnosia

Since the visual association area is critical for recognizing faces, shapes, and objects, damage to this area results in difficulties of recognition, a condition called visual agnosia *(ag-NO-zee-ah)*.

In **visual agnosia,** the individual fails to recognize some object, person, or color, yet has the ability to see and even describe pieces or parts of some visual stimulus.

Here's what happened when a patient with damage to the visual association area was asked to simply copy an object.

A patient who has visual agnosia was asked to make a copy of this horse, something most everyone can do.

The patient drew each part of the horse separately and could not combine individual parts into a meaningful image.

From "Language Specificity and Elasticity: Brain and Clinical Syndrome Studies," by M. Maratsos and L. Matheny, 1994, *Annual Review of Psychology, 45,* 487–516

Patients with visual agnosia can see individual parts of an object, such as a horse's leg, but, because of damage to visual association areas, have great difficulty combining the parts to perceive or draw a complete and recognizable image, such as a complete horse (Farah, 2004; S. Schwartz, 2010). Damage to association areas can also result in seeing only half of one's world.

Neglect Syndrome

Individuals who have damage to association areas, usually in the occipital and parietal lobes, and usually in the right hemisphere, experience a very strange problem called the neglect syndrome.

The **neglect syndrome** refers to the failure of a patient to see objects or parts of the body on the side opposite the brain damage. Patients may dress only one side of their body and deny that opposite body parts are theirs ("that's not my leg").

Here's how a patient with neglect syndrome drew an object.

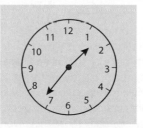

A patient with neglect syndrome caused by right-sided brain damage was asked to copy this clock.

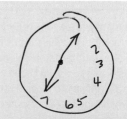

The patient drew only the right side of the clock because he did not see or recognize things on his left side.

Adapted from *Left Brain, Right Brain,* by S. P. Springer and G. Deutsch, 4/e, 1989, W. H. Freeman Company.

After a stroke or other damage, usually to the occipital and parietal association areas in the right hemisphere, patients may behave as if the left sides of objects or their own bodies no longer exist: they may not shave or dress the left sides of their bodies, which they do not recognize. Neglect syndrome shows the important function of association areas in recognizing things (Danckert & Ferber, 2006).

Now we'll journey beneath the cortex and explore a group of structures that existed in evolutionarily very old, primitive brains. ●

Structures and Functions

Your cortex is involved in numerous cognitive functions, such as thinking, deciding, planning, and speaking, as well as other sensory and motor behaviors. But what triggers your wide range of emotional experiences, such as feeling happy, sad, or angry? The answer lies deeper inside the brain, where you'll find a number of interconnected structures that are involved in emotions and are called the limbic system (J. H. Friedman & Chou, 2007; Ropper & Samuels, 2009).

How are you like an alligator?

The **limbic system** is a group of about half a dozen interconnected structures that make up the core of the forebrain. The limbic system's structures are involved with regulating many motivational behaviors such as obtaining food, drink, and sex; with organizing emotional behaviors such as fear, anger, and aggression; and with storing memories.

The limbic system is often referred to as our primitive, or animal, brain because its same structures are found in the brains of animals that are evolutionarily very old, such as alligators. The alligator's limbic system, which essentially makes up its entire forebrain, is involved in smelling out prey, defending territory, hunting, fighting, reproducing, eating, and remembering. The human limbic system, which makes up only a small part of our forebrain, is involved in similar behaviors.

Alligators and humans have limbic systems.

We'll discuss some of the major structures and functions of the limbic system. The drawing below shows the right hemisphere (the left hemisphere is cut away). Notice that the limbic structures are surrounded by the forebrain, whose executive functions regulate the limbic system's emotional and motivational behaviors.

Important Parts of the Limbic System

1 One limbic structure that is a master control for many emotional responses is the hypothalamus *(high-po-THAL-ah-mus)*.

The **hypothalamus** regulates many motivational behaviors, including eating, drinking, and sexual responses; emotional behaviors, such as arousing the body when fighting or fleeing; and the secretion of hormones, such as occurs at puberty.

In addition, the hypothalamus controls the two divisions of the autonomic nervous system discussed on the next page.

The next limbic structure, the amygdala, is also involved in emotions but more in forming and remembering them.

2 The **amygdala** *(ah-MIG-duh-la),* located in the tip of the temporal lobe, receives input from all the senses. It plays a major role in evaluating the emotional significance of stimuli and facial expressions, especially those involving fear, distress, or threat.

The amygdala is critical in recognizing emotional facial expressions, including happy faces but especially faces indicating fear, distress, or threat; evaluating emotional situations, especially those that involve threat or danger; and adding emotional feelings to happy or sad events (remembering a joke, going to a funeral) (Hooker et al., 2006; Salzman & Fusi, 2010).

When the amygdala is damaged, people have difficulty recognizing emotional facial expressions and animals do not learn to fear or avoid dangerous situations. In a rare genetic disease, a woman was found not to have an amygdala, which makes her immune to fear even in the most terrifying circumstances imaginable (Feinstein et al., 2010).

3 This limbic structure, which is like a miniature computer that gathers and processes information from all of your senses (except smell), is called the thalamus *(THAL-ah-mus)*.

The **thalamus** is involved in receiving sensory information, doing some initial processing, and then relaying the sensory information to areas of the cortex, including the somatosensory cortex, primary auditory cortex, and primary visual cortex.

For example, if the thalamus malfunctions, you might have difficulty processing sensory information (hearing or seeing).

Our last limbic structure, the hippocampus, is involved in saving your memories.

4 The **hippocampus,** which is a curved structure inside the temporal lobe, is involved in saving many kinds of fleeting memories by putting them into permanent storage in various parts of the brain.

For example, humans with damage to the hippocampus have difficulty remembering new facts, places, faces, and conversations because these new events cannot be placed into permanent storage (Rolls, 2007). Think of the hippocampus, which is involved in saving things in long-term storage (see p. 268), as functioning like the "Save" command on your computer.

Limbic system versus frontal lobe. Some of the basic emotional feelings triggered by the limbic system (anger, rage, fear, panic) carry the potential for self-injury or injury to others. Researchers found that our larger and evolutionarily newer frontal lobe, which is involved in thinking, deciding, and planning, plays a critical role in controlling the limbic system's powerful urges (Banks et al., 2007; Crews & Boettiger, 2009).

One particular structure in the limbic system, the hypothalamus, also has an important role in regulating the autonomic nervous system, which we'll examine next.

Autonomic Nervous System

You are unaware of what regulates your breathing, heart rate, hormone secretions, and body temperature. You're not concerned about these vital functions because they are usually controlled by a separate nervous system, called the autonomic nervous system, which, in turn, is regulated by a master control center, the hypothalamus (discussed on the preceding page).

Why don't you worry about breathing?

The autonomic nervous system, which regulates numerous physiological responses, has two divisions: the sympathetic and parasympathetic nervous systems. The sympathetic division is activated when you suddenly see a snake; then the parasympathetic division helps you relax (Purves et al., 2008). We'll explain some of the specific and automatic functions of the sympathetic and parasympathetic divisions.

Sympathetic Nervous System

If you were on a nature hike and suddenly saw a snake, your cortex would activate the hypothalamus, which in turn would trigger the sympathetic division of the autonomic nervous system (A. Siegal & Sapru, 2010).

The **sympathetic division,** which is one part of the autonomic nervous system, is triggered by threatening or challenging physical stimuli, such as a snake, or by psychological stimuli, such as the thought of having to give a public speech. Once triggered, the sympathetic division increases the body's physiological arousal.

All of the physiological responses listed in the left-hand column under **Sympathetic,** such as increased heart rate, inhibited digestion, and dilated pupils, put your body into a state of heightened physiological arousal, which is called the fight-flight response.

The **fight-flight response,** which is a state of increased physiological arousal caused by activation of the sympathetic division, helps the body cope with and survive threatening situations.

You have no doubt experienced the fight-flight response many times, such as when you felt your heart pound and your mouth go dry. Later, we'll discuss the role of the fight-flight response in stressful situations and in psychosomatic diseases (see pp. 484–489).

© fivespots/shutterstock.com

© nicolas hansen/iStockphoto

Parasympathetic Nervous System

After you have been physiologically aroused by seeing a snake, it usually takes some time before your body returns to a calmer state. The process of decreasing physiological arousal and calming down your body is triggered by the hypothalamus, which activates the parasympathetic division.

The **parasympathetic division,** which is the other part of the autonomic nervous system, decreases physiological arousal and helps return the body to a calmer, more relaxed state. It also stimulates digestion during eating.

As shown in the right column under the heading *Parasympathetic,* the parasympathetic division, once activated, decreases physiological arousal by decreasing heart rate, stimulating digestion, and constricting pupils. These responses result in the body returning to a more relaxed state.

For dealing with stress, we'll discuss many relaxation techniques (see pp. 502–503), such as the relaxation response, various forms of meditation, and biofeedback, which help increase parasympathetic activity, decrease body arousal, and thus help you calm down after stressful experiences.

Sympathetic		Parasympathetic
Pupils dilated, dry; far vision	*Eyes*	Pupils constricted, moist; near vision
Dry	*Mouth*	Salivation
Goose bumps	*Skin*	No goose bumps
Sweaty	*Palms*	Dry
Passages dilated	*Lungs*	Passages constricted
Increased rate	*Heart*	Decreased rate
Supply maximum to muscles	*Blood*	Supply maximum to internal organs
Increased activity	*Adrenal glands*	Decreased activity
Inhibited	*Digestion*	Stimulated
Climax	*Sexual functions*	Arousal

Homeostasis

One problem that some students face is becoming too stressed or upset by life's events. Because it is potentially harmful to your body to stay stressed or aroused, the autonomic nervous system tries to keep the body's arousal at an optimum level, a state called homeostasis.

Homeostasis *(ho-me-oh-STAY-sis)* means that the sympathetic and parasympathetic systems work together to keep the body's level of arousal in balance for optimum functioning.

© Michael Dunning/Getty Images

Homeostasis—physiological arousal kept in balance

For instance, your body's balance, or homeostasis, may be upset by the continuous stress of final exams or a difficult relationship. Such stress usually results in continuous physiological arousal and any number of physical problems, including headaches, stomachaches, tight muscles, or fatigue. These physical symptoms, which are called psychosomatic problems, may result in real pain. We'll discuss these problems in Module 21.

Besides triggering your autonomic nervous system, the hypothalamus is also involved in regulating a complex hormonal system, which we'll examine next. ●

Definition

What is your chemical system?

You have two major systems for sending signals to the body's muscles, glands, and organs. We have already discussed the nervous system, which uses neurons, nerves, and neurotransmitters to send information throughout the body. The second major system for sending information is called the endocrine system (Hinson et al., 2010).

The **endocrine system** is made up of numerous glands that are located throughout the body. These glands secrete various chemicals, called **hormones,** that affect organs, muscles, and other glands in the body.

The locations and functions of some of the endocrine system's glands are shown in the figure below.

Control Center

In many ways, the **hypothalamus,** which is located in the lower middle part of the brain, controls much of the endocrine system by regulating the pituitary gland, which is located directly below and outside the brain. The hypothalamus is often called the control center of the endocrine system.

Hypothalamus

Anterior pituitary **Posterior pituitary**

The drawing on the left shows that the hypothalamus is connected to the pituitary gland.

Other Glands

We'll describe some of the endocrine system's major glands as well as their dysfunctions.

The **pituitary gland,** a key component of the endocrine system, hangs directly below the hypothalamus, to which it is connected by a narrow stalk. The pituitary gland is divided into anterior (front) and posterior (back) sections.

Posterior pituitary. The rear portion of the pituitary regulates water and salt balance.
Dysfunction: Lack of hormones causes a less common form of diabetes.

Anterior pituitary. The front part of the pituitary regulates growth through secretion of growth hormone and produces hormones that control the adrenal cortex, pancreas, thyroid, and gonads.
Dysfunction: Too little growth hormone produces dwarfism; too much causes gigantism. Other problems in the pituitary cause problems in the glands it regulates.

Pancreas. This organ regulates the level of sugar in the bloodstream by secreting insulin.
Dysfunction: Lack of insulin results in the more common form of diabetes, while too much causes hypoglycemia (low blood sugar).

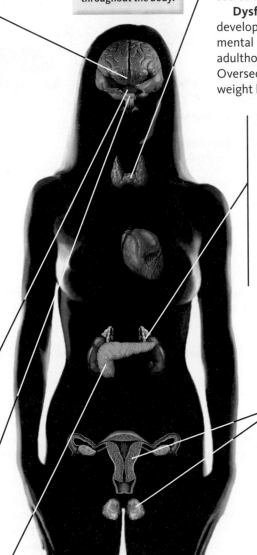

The endocrine system controls glands located throughout the body.

Thyroid. This gland, which is located in the neck, regulates metabolism through the secretion of hormones.
Dysfunction: Hormone deficiency during development leads to stunted growth and mental retardation. Undersecretion during adulthood leads to reduced motivation. Oversecretion results in high metabolism, weight loss, and nervousness.

Adrenal glands. The adrenal cortex (outside part) secretes hormones that regulate sugar and salt balances and help the body resist stress; they are also responsible for growth of pubic hair, a secondary sexual characteristic. The adrenal medulla (inside part) secretes two hormones that arouse the body to deal with stress and emergencies: epinephrine (adrenaline) and norepinephrine (noradrenaline).
Dysfunction: With a lack of cortical hormones, the body's responses are unable to cope with stress.

Gonads. In females, the ovaries produce hormones that regulate sexual development, ovulation, and growth of sex organs. In males, the testes produce hormones that regulate sexual development, production of sperm, and growth of sex organs.
Dysfunction: Lack of sex hormones during puberty results in lack of secondary sexual characteristics (facial and body hair, muscles in males, breasts in females).

Up to this point, we have examined many of the structures and functions that make up the incredible nervous and endocrine systems. After the Concept Review, we'll discuss a question that students often ask: Do the brains of males differ from those of females? ●

Unless otherwise noted, all images are © Cengage Learning

Concept Review

1. A hairlike structure that contains tightly coiled strands of the chemical DNA (deoxyribonucleic acid) is called a **(a)**_____. A specific segment on the strand of DNA that contains instructions for making proteins is called a **(b)**_____. A theory that different species arose from a common ancestor and that those species survived that were best adapted to meet the demands of their environments is called the theory of **(c)**_____.

2. There are several techniques for studying the living brain. One method for identifying structures in the brain involves measuring nonharmful radio frequencies as they pass through the brain; this is called an **(a)**_____ scan. Another method that is used to study functions of the brain involves measuring the amounts of low-level radioactive substances absorbed by brain cells; this is called a **(b)**_____ scan. A method that involves placing electrodes on the scalp and measuring changes in brain wave activity is called an **(c)** _____.

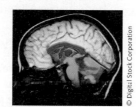

© Digital Stock Corporation

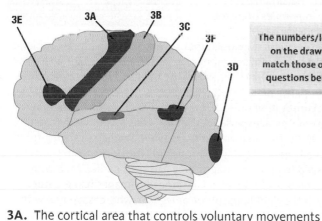

The numbers/letters on the drawing match those of the questions below.

3A. The cortical area that controls voluntary movements is called the **(a)**_____ and is located in the **(b)**_____ lobe.

3B. The cortical area that receives input from sensory receptors in the skin, muscles, and joints is called the **(a)**_____ and is located in the **(b)**_____ lobe.

3C. The cortical area that receives input from sensory receptors in the ears is called the **(a)**_____ and is located in the **(b)**_____ lobe.

3D. The cortical area that receives input from sensory receptors in the eyes is called the **(a)**_____ and is located in the **(b)**_____ lobe.

3E. The cortical area that is necessary to produce words and arrange them into sentences is called **(a)**_____ and is located in the **(b)**_____ lobe.

3F. The cortical area that is necessary for understanding spoken and written words and putting words into meaningful sentences is called **(a)**_____ and is located in the **(b)**_____ lobe.

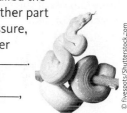

4. The two major divisions of the nervous system are the **(a)**_____ and the **(b)**_____. In turn, the peripheral nervous system has two parts: one part is a network of nerves that are connected either to sensory receptors or to muscles that you can move voluntarily and is called the **(c)**_____; another part regulates heart rate, breathing, blood pressure, digestion, secretion of hormones, and other functions and is called the **(d)**_____. The brain itself is divided into three major parts: **(e)**_____, _____, and_____.

© fivespots/Shutterstock.com

5. The old brain that is involved with many motivational and emotional behaviors is called the **(a)**_____. One structure of the limbic system, the hypothalamus, controls the autonomic nervous system, which has two divisions. The division that responds by increasing the body's physiological arousal is called the **(b)**_____. This division triggers a state of increased physiological arousal so that the body can cope with threatening situations; this state is called the **(c)**_____. The other division of the autonomic nervous system that is primarily responsible for returning the body to a calm or relaxed state and is involved in digestion is called the **(d)**_____.

© nicolas hansen/iStockphoto

6. A system made up of numerous glands that are located throughout the body and that secrete various hormones is called the **(a)**_____. The brain area that can be considered the master control for this system is the **(b)**_____. This brain area is connected to and controls one of the endocrine system's major glands that has an anterior and posterior part and is collectively called the **(c)**_____.

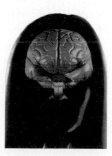

Answers: 1. (a) *chromosome*, (b) *gene*, (c) *evolution;* 2. (a) *MRI*, (b) *PET*, (c) *EEG;* 3A. (a) *motor cortex*, (b) *frontal;* 3B. (a) *somatosensory cortex*, (b) *parietal;* 3C. (a) *primary auditory cortex*, (b) *temporal;* 3D. (a) *primary visual cortex*, (b) *occipital;* 3E. (a) *Broca's area*, (b) *frontal;* 3F. (a) *Wernicke's area*, (b) *temporal;* 4. (a) *central nervous system*, (b) *peripheral nervous system*, (c) *somatic nervous system*, (d) *autonomic nervous system*, (e) *forebrain, midbrain, hindbrain;* 5. (a) *limbic system*, (b) *sympathetic nervous system*, (c) *fight-flight response*, (d) *parasympathetic nervous system;* 6. (a) *endocrine system*, (b) *hypothalamus*, (c) *pituitary gland*

Scientific Debate

Throughout history, the issue of sex differences in the brain has received much attention and debate. In the 1980s and 1990s,

Is this kind of research sexist?

research on sex differences was criticized as "sexist" because it went against the "politically correct" belief that male and female brains are essentially the same (Azar, 1997). More recently, then Harvard University President Lawrence Summers announced that women are less likely than men to succeed in science and mathematics primarily because fewer females have "innate ability" in these fields. Immediately following this statement,

a national debate took place about whether sex differences in the brain explained why fewer women reached high levels of success in science and mathematics (B. Bower, 2007; D. F. Halpern et al., 2007).

To examine the differences in the structures and functions of male and female brains, which are called sex differences, researchers use brain scans (Lenroot & Giedd, 2010; Savic-Berglund, 2010).

Sex, or **gender, differences** refer to structural or functional differences in cognitive, behavioral, or brain processes that arise from being a male or a female.

Here are some interesting sex differences.

Differences in Solving Problems

The rotating figure problem is a rather difficult spatial problem, as follows. First, study the target figure on the left. Then, from the three choices at the right, identify the same figure, even though it has been rotated.

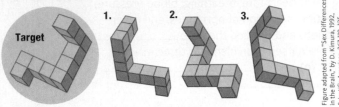

Figure adapted from "Sex Differences in the Brain," by D. Kimura, 1992, *Scientific American, 267,* 119–125.

The key to solving this problem is the ability to rotate the target figure in your mind until it matches the rotation of one of the three choices. Researchers consistently report faster or more accurate performance by males than by females in solving rotating figure problems, even as early as infancy (B. Bower, 2008d; D. F. Halpern et al., 2007). (The correct answer is 1.) There are other tasks at which women perform better than men.

Based on data from *Sex Differences in Cognitive Abilities*, by D. F. Halpern, 2000. Lawrence Erlbuam Associates

For example, look at the house outlined in black (figure left) and find its twin among the three choices. Women are generally faster on these kinds of tests, which measure perceptual speed. In addition, women usually score higher on tests of verbal fluency, in which you must list as many words as you can that begin with the same letter, as in the figure below (D. F. Halpern, 2000).

Researchers have now begun to look for sex differences in how the brain itself functions.

Limp, Livery, Love, Laser, Liquid, Low, Like, Lag, Live, Lug, Light, Lift, Liver, Lime, Leg, Load, Lap, Lucid, . . .

Based on data from *Sex Differences in Cognitive Abilities*, by D. F. Halpern, 2000. Lawrence Erlbuam Associates

Differences between Female and Male Brains

To check for sex differences between male and female brains, researchers took brain scans while the study participants were solving rotating figure problems.

Problem solving. As seen in the right figure, brain scans taken during problem solving showed that maximum neural activity in *males* occurred in the right frontal area. In contrast, maximum neural activity in *females* occurred in the right parietal-temporal

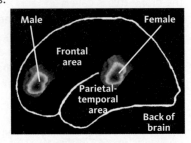

area. Researchers concluded that solving rotating figure problems showed a significant sex difference in terms of which brain areas were activated, which in turn may be the basis for sex differences in performance on this task (Alivisatos & Petrides, 1997).

Emotional memories. How do men and women remember intense emotional experiences? Brain scans (fMRI) were taken while men and women viewed images they rated as ranging from emotionally neutral to highly arousing. Two weeks later, subjects were asked to pick out images they had seen earlier. Men with better memories for emotionally arousing images had greater activity in the right hemisphere amygdala, whereas women with better memories for emotionally arousing images had greater activity in the left hemisphere amygdala. Researchers concluded that there are sex differences in how the amygdala remembers emotionally arousing experiences (Cahill et al., 2004).

Movement and coordination. Researchers found a difference in how male and female brains make a major neurotransmitter (dopamine), which is responsible for controlling movement and coordination. This may help explain why men are more likely than women to develop Parkinson's disease (see p. 60) (Gramling, 2006).

Conclusion

Researchers warn that although there are sex differences in the brain, we cannot conclude that they are the only cause of differences in ability between males and females. After all, environmental experiences influence the development of the brain, including its structures and functions, and it is entirely possible that sex differences in the brain are due to differences in socialization and learning between males and females. In fact, most sex differences begin small and become amplified as children interact in their gender-biased environment. For instance, parents may encourage boys more than girls to engage in physical activities such as throwing and navigating through action-oriented video games, which in turn may account for boys' better performance in spatial problem solving, such as the rotating figure problem described above. Research indicates that environment accounts for some of the sex differences in the brain (Eliot, 2009, 2010). ●

Unless otherwise noted, all images are © Cengage Learning

We have discussed the field of neuroscience throughout the book. One of its subfields is **cultural neuroscience**, the study of how cultural values, practices, and environment shape and are shaped by the brain (Chiao & Ambady, 2007; Chiao et al., 2010). In other words, cultural neuroscience examines the bidirectional interactions between culture and the biology of the brain. This new field has begun transforming the way scientists think about the brain. In this section, we will present recent research from the field of cultural neuroscience. First, though, we're going to go back to 1839, a time when there was no formalized field of study on cultural differences in the brain, but when one scientist took on the task anyway.

Early Research: Brain Size and Race

Which race had the biggest brain?

When he died in 1851, *The New York Times* proudly said that Samuel George Morton, scientist and physician, had one of the best reputations among scholars throughout the world. Morton had spent his lifetime collecting skulls of different races to determine which race had the biggest brain. During Morton's time, it was generally accepted that a bigger brain meant greater intelligence and innate mental ability.

No significant differences in brain size among races

Results in 1839. Morton estimated the size of a brain by pouring tiny lead pellets into each skull and then measuring the pellets. By using this procedure, he arrived at the following ranking of brain sizes in different races, from biggest to smallest: 1-Caucasian, 2-Mongolian, 3-American Indian, and 4-Negro. Along with his racial ranking of decreasing brain size, Morton also believed there was a corresponding decrease in behavioral and cognitive skills (Morton, 1839, cited in S. J. Gould, 1981).

Reanalyzed in 1980. Stephen Jay Gould, a renowned evolutionary biologist, reanalyzed Morton's data on brain size and, unlike Morton's findings, found *no significant difference* in brain size among the four races. Furthermore, Gould concluded that Morton's strong biases that Caucasians should have the biggest brains had unknowingly swayed his scientific judgment to fit his racial prejudices of the 1800s (S. J. Gould, 1981).

Major error. Morton's major error was that he included skulls that matched his personal biased expectations and omitted skulls that did not support his racial beliefs. That is, Morton chose bigger skulls to match his bias of Whites being more intelligent and smaller skulls for other races, whom he considered to be less intelligent (S. J. Gould, 1994).

Although Morton had the reputation for being a respected scholar and although he had asked a legitimate research question—Are there differences in brain size?—he was unable to prevent his strong personal beliefs from biasing his research and finding what he strongly but mistakenly believed.

One way current researchers guard against the problem of biasing their results is by having scientists in other laboratories repeat their studies. If the original findings are repeated in other laboratories, then scientists can be reasonably confident that their original results are valid.

Current Research: Cultural Neuroscience

What have we learned from cultural neuroscience?

Cultural neuroscience uses brain-imaging technology (see pp. 70–71) to help understand how cultural factors, such as environment, values, and beliefs, can shape cognitive functioning. By using brain-imaging technology, cultural neuroscientists have been finding that, although the brains of people from different cultures do not exhibit large structural differences, there are clear differences in their patterns of activity. Scientists have confirmed that these differences in brain activity can influence our behaviors, emotions, and thoughts (Blanding, 2010).

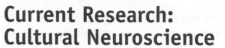

Here is a sample of cultural neuroscience findings: Americans and Japanese use different parts of their brains to complete the same simple task (drawing lines); native Japanese in Japan and Caucasians in the United States show greater activity in the amygdala (p. 80) in response to fear expressed by members of their own cultural group; when Americans think about their own honesty versus thinking about another person's honesty, they use different brain areas, whereas for Chinese people, their brains look identical when thinking about their own honesty and the honesty of others (Chiao et al., 2008; Hedden et al., 2008; Y. Zhu et al., 2007).

In just a short time, the field of cultural neuroscience has significantly influenced our understanding of brain processes. Scientists are optimistic that the developing field will make other powerful discoveries about the interactions between culture and the brain.

Before we complete our journey through the brain, we'll take you on one last trip, perhaps the most interesting of all. We'll see what happens when the brain is literally cut in two. ●

Definition and Testing

Since about the age of 6, Victoria had seizures (also called epileptic seizures). During the seizures, she would lose consciousness and fall to the floor. Although her muscles would jerk uncontrollably, she felt no pain and would remember nothing of the experience. She was given anticonvulsant medicine, which prevented any further seizures until she was 18.

Why did Victoria choose a split brain?

Split-brain operation. When Victoria was 18, for some unknown reason, her seizures returned with greater intensity. And to her dismay, anticonvulsant medication no longer had any effect. The seizures continued for ten years. Finally, when she was 27, she decided that her best chance of reducing her frightening, uncontrollable seizures was to have an operation that had a high probability of producing serious side effects. In this operation, a neurosurgeon would sever the major connection between her right and left hemispheres, leaving her with what is called a split brain (figure below).

Having to choose between a future of uncontrollable seizures and the potential problems of having a split brain, Victoria chose the operation (Sidtis et al., 1981).

In addition to Victoria (identified as V.P. in published reports), dozens of other individuals have also chosen to have a split-brain operation when they found that medicine no longer prevented their severe seizures (Gazzaniga, 2008b).

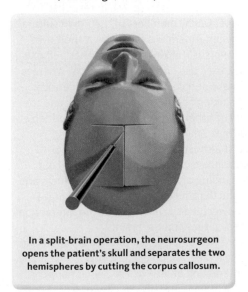

In a split-brain operation, the neurosurgeon opens the patient's skull and separates the two hemispheres by cutting the corpus callosum.

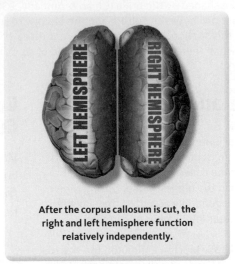

After the corpus callosum is cut, the right and left hemisphere function relatively independently.

A **split-brain operation** involves cutting the wide band of fibers, called the corpus callosum, that connects the right and left hemispheres (figure above). The corpus callosum has 200 million nerve fibers that allow information to pass back and forth between the hemispheres.

A split-brain operation not only disrupts the major pathway between the hemispheres but also, to a large extent, leaves each hemisphere functioning independently. In many split-brain patients, severing the corpus callosum prevented the spread of seizures from one hemisphere to the other and thus reduced their frequency (Gazzaniga, 2008b).

Major breakthrough. It was 1961 when researcher Michael S. Gazzaniga and his colleagues tested the first split-brain patient, known as W.J. in the literature. Researchers first flashed on a screen a number of colors, letters, and pictures of objects. These stimuli were flashed so that they went only to W.J.'s left hemisphere, and he had no difficulty naming them. Then researchers flashed the same stimuli so that they went only to W.J.'s right hemisphere, and W.J. seemed to see nothing, to be blind (Gazzaniga et al., 1962). Gazzaniga calls the discovery that W.J.'s right hemisphere was saying nothing "one of those unforgettable moments in life." Was it true that W.J.'s left hemisphere could talk but not his right?

Testing a patient. To determine what each hemisphere can and cannot do, we can watch as Gazzaniga tests Victoria after her split-brain operation.

Victoria is asked to stare at the black dot between *HE* and *ART* as the word *HEART* is displayed on a screen. Because Victoria's hemispheres are split, information from each side of the black dot will go to only the opposite hemisphere (figure below). This means that Victoria's left hemisphere will see only the word *ART* and her right hemisphere will see only the word *HE*.

When asked, "What did you see?" Victoria says that she saw the word *ART* because it was projected to the left hemisphere, which has the ability to speak.

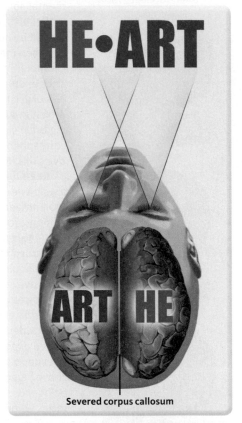

Severed corpus callosum

Although Victoria's right hemisphere saw the word *HE,* the right hemisphere turns out to be mute, meaning that it cannot say what it saw. However, Victoria can point with her left hand to a photo of a man *(HE),* indicating that the right hemisphere understood the question and saw the word *HE.* (Victoria points with her left hand because her right hemisphere controls the left side of the body.) Although the effects of having a split brain are obvious under special testing, the effects are not so apparent in everyday life.

Behaviors Following Split Brain

How does a split brain affect behavior?

Initially after her operation, Victoria reported that when she would choose clothes from her closet, her right hand would grab a blouse but then her left hand would put it back. However, these obvious conflicts between hemispheres are rare and disappear with time.

Four months after her operation, Victoria was alert and talked easily about past and present events. She could read, write, reason, and perform everyday functions such as eating, dressing, and walking, as well as carry on normal conversations. For Victoria with her split brain, as well as for most of us with normal brains, only the left hemisphere can express itself through the spoken word (Gazzaniga, 2000). If the speech area is in the left hemisphere, the right hemisphere is usually mute. (For a small percentage of left-handers, the speech area is in the right hemisphere and the left hemisphere is usually mute.) After testing split-brain patients, researchers discovered that each hemisphere is specialized for performing certain tasks (Gazzaniga, 2005, 2008a).

Different Functions of Hemispheres

Before observing split-brain patients, researchers knew very little about how each hemisphere functioned. But after studying the behaviors of split-brain patients, researchers gained a whole new understanding of what task each hemisphere does best (Borst et al., 2011).

Verbal. The left hemisphere is very good at all language-related abilities: speaking, understanding language, carrying on a conversation, reading, writing, and spelling.

Mathematical. The left hemisphere is very good at mathematical skills: adding, subtracting, multiplying, dividing, solving complex problems in calculus and physics, and so on. Generally, the right hemisphere can perform simple addition and subtraction but not more complex mathematics (Sperry, 1974).

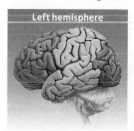
Left hemisphere

Analytic. The left hemisphere appears to process information by analyzing each separate piece that makes up a whole. For example, the left hemisphere would recognize a face by analyzing piece by piece its many separate parts: nose, eyes, lips, cheeks, and so on—a relatively slow process (J. Levy & Trevarthen, 1976).

Recognizing self. The left hemisphere is primarily involved in identifying one's own face, distinguishing one's face from others, and having memories and knowledge of oneself. Thus, the left brain contributes to the conscious understanding of oneself (Turk, 2002).

Nonverbal. Although usually mute, the right hemisphere has a childlike ability to read, write, spell, and understand speech (Gazzaniga, 1998). For example, when spoken to, the right hemisphere can understand simple sentences and read simple words.

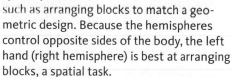
Right hemisphere

Spatial. The right hemisphere is very good at solving spatial problems, such as arranging blocks to match a geometric design. Because the hemispheres control opposite sides of the body, the left hand (right hemisphere) is best at arranging blocks, a spatial task.

Holistic. The right hemisphere appears to process information by combining parts into a meaningful whole. For this reason, the right hemisphere is better at recognizing and identifying whole faces (J. Levy et al., 1972). The right hemisphere is also good at recognizing emotions in people's gestures and tone of voice (Adolphs et al., 2002).

Recognizing others. The right hemisphere is involved in recognizing familiar faces but not in recognizing one's own face, which primarily involves the left hemisphere (Turk, 2002).

After comparing the left and right hemispheres' functions, you can see that each hemisphere has specialized skills and is better at performing particular tasks. Some hemisphere specializations begin very early in life. For example, left-brain specialization for language appears as early as 2 to 3 months of age (B. Bower, 2003a). These differences raise a popular question: Am I right-brained or left-brained?

Left- or Right-Brained?

The popular press has exaggerated the idea that you are either "right-brained"—creative and intuitive—or "left-brained"—reasonable, logical, and rational.

According to Jerre Levy (1985), who has devoted her career to studying how the brain's hemispheres interact, these distinctions are much too simple. She believes that we are constantly using both hemispheres, since each hemisphere is specialized for processing certain kinds of information. For example, when you read a novel, you are probably using programs in the left hemisphere that allow you to understand language in written form. But at the same time, you are using programs in the right hemisphere to keep track of the overall story, appreciate its humor and emotional content, and interpret any illustrations. Although hemispheres may sometimes work alone, they share much of their information by passing it quickly back and forth through the corpus callosum (Zimmer, 2009b).

How is my brain organized? Michael Gazzaniga (1998, 2008a), a cognitive neuroscientist who has studied split-brain patients for over 45 years, believes that each hemisphere of the brain has many different mental programs, such as sensing, thinking, learning, feeling, and speaking, all of which can function simultaneously. For example, when you see someone smile, your brain uses dozens of mental programs from each hemisphere to receive, interpret, and respond to this relatively simple emotional facial expression.

According to Gazzaniga, the brain and mind are built from separate units or modules that are interconnected and work together to carry out specific functions, much as your computer uses many separate programs to perform many different tasks. ●

Consciousness during Coma

In this article, we'll describe two fascinating, tragic, and well-publicized cases of people in comas. These cases represent two very different types of comas, yet pose the same fundamental question: Does this person experience consciousness?

1 What area of the brain is responsible for consciousness?

We'll begin with the case of Terri Schiavo, a 27-year-old woman who suffered a heart attack that resulted in her losing consciousness. During the next 15 years, she never regained consciousness. She could still breathe without a respirator and at times even opened her eyes. Despite these abilities, however, Terri remained completely unaware of her surroundings.

2 What part of the brain allows Terri to breathe?

Doctors describe Terri's condition as a persistent vegetative state, meaning she has severe brain damage to the cortex, resulting in long-term loss of cognitive function and awareness, but she retains basic physiological functions, such as breathing.

As a result of being in a vegetative state for more than a decade, Terri's brain severely deteriorated. All that remained was enough of a brain stem (includes midbrain, pons, and medulla—see p. 73) to keep certain basic life functions working (e.g., heart rate, breathing, arousal, visual and auditory

3 Which type of brain scan would a neurologist use to determine how much of Terri's cortex is present?

reflexes). After she died, her autopsy showed she had massive and irreversible brain damage that shrunk her cortex. It's certain that Terri had been unconscious for a long time.

4 Do Terri's abilities to function fit with severe damage to the cortex?

The second case is Jean-Dominique Bauby, a 43-year-old man who suffered a devastating stroke. It took him nearly three weeks to wake up, and when he did, he was almost completely paralyzed. He could only open and close his left eyelid.

Doctors describe Jean-Dominique's condition as a locked-in syndrome, meaning he remains completely conscious but is almost totally unable to move or speak. Jean-Dominique lived in a locked-in state for the final 15 months of his life. During this time, he learned to communicate with others by blinking his left eye. With his creativity and determination, as well as the help of an assistant, he dictated a best-selling book about his experience of being in a locked-in state: *The Diving Bell and the Butterfly.*

5 What explains why Jean-Dominique had the thinking abilities required to write a book?

Although both Jean-Dominique and Terri lacked the ability to speak or communicate readily with others, Jean-Dominique retained full consciousness and Terri's level of consciousness was severely impaired. These cases raise the question of how doctors can determine the level of consciousness in people who cannot communicate.

The presence or absence of consciousness is typically measured through behavioral criteria, which is difficult and can lead to misdiagnosis. Past brain-imaging techniques used to assess consciousness had limitations, such as requiring patients to comprehend or carry out instructions. Very recently, transcranial magnetic stimulation (TMS) combined with electroencephalography (EEG) has been used to noninvasively measure the electrical response of the brain. TMS sends signals to activate the brain, and EEG records the brain's activity. This combined technique evaluates brain activity without requiring the active participation of patients. Therefore, it can be used to detect and track recovery in brain-injured patients who are unable to understand, communicate, or move. The use of this combined technique may prevent patients who retain some level of consciousness but cannot communicate (such as Jean-Dominique) from being misdiagnosed as being in a vegetative state.

6 What type of brain-imaging technique could be used to assess consciousness in people who can comprehend and carry out instructions?

Adapted from Associated Press, 2005a, 2005b; Bauby, 1997; Rosanova et al., 2012; S. Russell, 2005; Schrock, 2007

Unless otherwise noted, all images are © Cengage Learning

A Genes & Evolution

1. A fertilized egg, which is called a **(a)** _zygote_, contains 46 chromosomes arranged in 23 pairs. A hairlike structure that contains tightly coiled strands of the chemical DNA (deoxyribonucleic acid) is called a **(b)**_____. A specific segment on the strand of DNA that contains instructions for making proteins is called a **(c)**_____.

2. In 1859, Charles Darwin published the revolutionary theory of **(a)** _evolution_, which said that different species arose from a common **(b)** _ancestor_ and that those species survived that were best adapted to meet the demands of their **(c)** _environment_.

B Cognitive Neuroscience

3. There are several recently developed techniques for studying the living brain. One technique, which measures nonharmful radio frequencies as they pass through the brain, is called an **(a)** _MRI_ and is used to identify structures in the living brain. Another technique measures how much of a radioactive substance is taken up by brain cells and is called a **(b)** _PET scan_. This kind of scan is used to study brain function and identify the most and least active parts. Another technique measures brain wave activity by placing electrodes on the scalp and is called a **(c)** _eeg_.

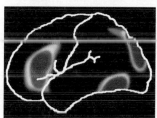

C Nervous System: Divisions & Functions

4. The human nervous system is divided into two major parts. The brain and spinal cord make up the **(a)**_____. The network of nerves outside the brain and spinal cord makes up the **(b)**_____.

5. The peripheral nervous system is further divided into two parts. One part is made up of a network of nerves that either carry messages to muscles and organs throughout the body or carry input from sensory receptors to the spinal cord; this is called the **(a)**_____. The second part of the peripheral nervous system, which regulates heart rate, breathing, digestion, and related responses, is called the **(b)**_____.

D Brain: Structures & Functions

6. The human brain is divided into three major parts. The largest part is involved in cognitive responses that we characterize as most human. This part is called the **(a)** _forebrain_,

which is divided into right and left hemispheres. The part that is involved in controlling vital reflexes, sleeping, and coordinating body movements is called the **(b)** _hindbrain_. The part that is involved in visual and auditory reflexes, as well as alerting the brain to incoming sensations, is called the **(c)** _midbrain_.

7. Beginning in the midbrain and extending downward is a long column of cells called the _reticular formation_ that alerts the forebrain to incoming sensory information.

8. The hindbrain consists of three structures. The structure that serves as a bridge to connect the brain and body and also manufactures chemicals involved in sleep is called the **(a)**_____. The structure that controls vital reflexes, such as heart rate, blood pressure, and respiration, is called the **(b)**_____. The structure that was assumed to be involved primarily in coordinating body movements but has recently been found to have a role in cognitive functions, such as short-term memory, following rules, and carrying out plans, is called the **(c)**_____.

9. The thin outside layer of cells that has a wrinkled look and covers almost the entire forebrain is called the **(a)**_____. This layer of cells is divided into four separate areas or lobes: **(b)**_____, _____, _____, and _____.

10. The lobe that is involved in controlling social-emotional behaviors, maintaining a healthy personality, and making and carrying out plans is called the _____ lobe.

11. At the back edge of the frontal lobe is a continuous strip called the _____, which controls the movement of voluntary muscles. Body parts that have greater capacity for complicated muscle movement have more area on the motor cortex devoted to them.

12. Along the front edge of the parietal lobe is a continuous strip that receives sensations from the body and is called the _____. Body parts with greater sensitivity have more area on the somatosensory cortex devoted to them.

13. An area on the upper edge of the temporal lobe that receives signals from receptors in the ears and changes them into basic auditory sensations is called the **(a)**_____. For most individuals, an area in the left temporal lobe is involved in understanding and speaking coherently; it is called **(b)**_____ area. Damage to this area results in inability to understand spoken and written speech or to speak coherently, a problem called **(c)**_____. An area in the frontal lobe, called **(d)**_____, is necessary for producing words and arranging them into fluent sentences. If this area is damaged, the result is a speech problem called **(e)**_____.

14. An area at the very back of the occipital lobe that receives signals from receptors in the eyes and changes them into basic visual sensations is called the _____.

15. The vast majority of the cortex making up the four lobes is involved in adding meaning, interpretations, and associations to sensory stimuli, as well as in many cognitive functions. Together, these areas are called _____ areas.

E Limbic System: Structures & Functions

16. Inside the forebrain is a central core of interconnected structures known as the primitive, or "animal," brain or, more technically, the **(a)**_____. Four of the areas that make up the limbic system are the **(b)** _____, _____, _____, and _____, which are all involved in motivational and emotional behaviors.

© Ron Dahlquist/Getty Images

17. One structure of the limbic system, the hypothalamus, controls the autonomic nervous system, which has two divisions. The one that arouses the body, increases physiological responses (such as heart rate and blood pressure), and prepares the body for the fight-flight response is called the **(a)**_____. The division that calms down the body and aids digestion is called the **(b)**_____. These two divisions work together to keep the body's internal organs in a balanced physiological state, which is called **(c)**_____.

F Endocrine System: Structures & Functions

18. Besides the nervous system, a network of glands regulates organs through the secretion of hormones. This chemical system is called the **(a)**_____. A major gland that controls other glands in this system is the **(b)**_____ gland, which has an anterior and posterior parts.

G Research Focus: Sex Differences in the Brain?

19. Structural or functional differences in the brain that arise from being male or female are called _____. One example of sex differences in the brain is that males primarily use the frontal area to solve spatial problems, while females use the parietal-temporal area.

Figure adapted from "Sex Differences in the Brain," by D. Kimura, 1992, *Scientific American, 267,* 119–125.

H Cultural Diversity: Cultural Neuroscience

20. In the 1800s, one scientist measured skull size and concluded that a larger brain indicated more intelligence and that the races could be ranked by brain size. However, further analysis of this researcher's data indicated that there was no basis for ranking races by **(a)**_____. The study of how cultural values, practices, and environment shape and are shaped by the brain is called **(b)**_____.

I Application: Split Brain

21. The two hemispheres are connected by a major bundle of fibers that is called the _____. Severing this structure produces a condition called a split brain.

22. For most individuals, mental programs for language, speech, and mathematics, as well as for distinguishing one's face from others and for memories and knowledge of oneself, are located in the **(a)**_____; mental programs for solving spatial problems, processing emotional responses, and recognizing familiar faces are located in the **(b)**_____. In addition, the hemispheres process information in different ways. The left hemisphere processes information in a more piece-by-piece fashion or **(c)**_____ way. In comparison, the right hemisphere processes information as a meaningful whole; that is, it uses a more **(d)**_____ approach.

23. One theory of brain organization says that your brain has many separate but interconnected _____ programs that function and work together so that you can perform many cognitive skills.

Unless otherwise noted, all images are © Cengage Learning

Links to Learning

Key Terms/Key People

adaptations, 69
adaptive genes, 69
adrenal glands, 82
amygdala, 80
anencephaly, 74
anterior pituitary, 82
auditory association area, 78
autonomic nervous system, 72
Broca's aphasia, 78
Broca's area, 78
central nervous system, 72
cerebellum, 73
chromosome, 68
cognitive neuroscience, 67
cortex, 74
cultural neuroscience, 85
DNA, 68
dominant gene, 68
Down syndrome, 69
EEG, 71
endocrine system, 82

evolutionary approach, 69
evolution theory, 69
fight-flight response, 81
fMRI scan, 71
forebrain, 73
fragile X syndrome, 69
frontal lobe, 75
frontal lobotomy, 75
frontotemporal disease, 67
gene, 68
genetic mutations, 69
genetic testing, 69
gonads, 82
hindbrain, 73
hippocampus, 80
homeostasis, 81
hormones, 82
hypothalamus, 80, 82
left hemisphere, 87
limbic system, 80
lobes, 74

maladaptive genes, 69
medulla, 73
MEG scan, 71
midbrain, 73
motor cortex, 76
motor homunculus, 76
MRI scan, 70
natural selection, 69
neglect syndrome, 79
occipital lobe, 79
ovum, 68
pancreas, 82
parasympathetic division, 72, 81
parietal lobe, 77
peripheral nervous system, 72
PET scan, 71
pituitary gland, 82
polymorphic gene, 68
pons, 73
posterior pituitary, 82
primary auditory cortex, 78

primary visual cortex, 79
recessive gene, 68
right hemisphere, 87
sensory homunculus, 77
sex or gender differences, 84
somatic nervous system, 72
somatosensory cortex, 77
sperm, 68
split-brain operation, 86
sympathetic division, 72, 81
temporal lobe, 78
thalamus, 80
thyroid, 82
visual agnosia, 79
visual association area, 79
Wernicke's aphasia, 78
Wernicke's area, 78
zygote, 68

Media Resources

Go to **CengageBrain.com** to access Psychology CourseMate, where you will find an Interactive eBook, glossaries, flashcards, quizzes, videos, answers to Critical Thinking questions, and more. You can also access Virtual Psychology Labs, an interactive laboratory experience designed to illustrate key experiments first-hand.

MODULE 5 Sensation

Artificial Eye: Life-Changing Results

Terry Byland began having difficulty seeing in dim light, which made driving at night a serious problem. When he went to his eye doctor, he was given news no one is ever prepared to hear. The doctor told Terry he had an eye disease that would eventually lead to blindness. His vision worsened gradually over time, leaving him blind just 7 years later at the young age of 45.

Can Terry see without his eyes?

After living in total darkness for 11 years, Terry volunteered to have experimental surgery in which a microchip with 16 electrodes was implanted into his eye. By wearing a tiny camera built on a pair of glasses that carries signals to the damaged area of his eye, incredibly, Terry gained vision. He can now see very rough forms of motion, lights, and objects. For example, he now sees light glowing from the chandelier when he flips on the light switch and action figures move across a TV screen. Terry

He can "see" representations of motion, lights, and objects.

describes how the surgery enabled him to see something even more special—the shadow of his 18-year-old son as he walked by: "It was the first time I had seen him since he was five years old. I don't mind saying, there were a few tears wept that day" (Byland, 2008). Terry couldn't be more pleased with the results of his surgery (adapted from *Science Illustrated*, 2008a; USDEOS, 2007).

What's Coming

We'll discuss the major human senses—seeing, hearing, taste, smell, touch, balance, and the sense that informs us about our body's positions relative to gravity. We'll also explain how you see color, why some long-playing rock-and-roll musicians have become partially deaf, why you get motion sickness, and why your sense of taste decreases when you have a cold. Although your sense organs—eye, ear, nose, skin, and tongue—look so very different, they all share the three characteristics defined next.

Characteristics of Sense Organs

What are the five sense organs?

Your eyes, ears, nose, skin, and tongue are complex, miniaturized, living sense organs that automatically gather information about your environment. We begin with three definitions that will help you understand sensation.

 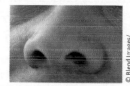

1 Transduction. The first thing each sense organ must do is to change or transform some physical energy, such as molecules of skunk spray, into electrical signals, a process called transduction.

Electrical signal

Transduction is the process by which a sense organ changes, or transforms, physical energy into electrical signals that become neural impulses, which may be sent to the brain for processing. For example, transduction occurs when a skunk's molecules enter your nose, which transforms the molecules into electrical signals, or impulses, that are interpreted by your brain as the very unpleasant odor of a skunk.

2 Adaptation. A short period of time after putting on glasses, jewelry, or clothes, you no longer "feel" them, a process called adaptation.

Adaptation refers to the decreasing response of the sense organs, the more they are exposed to a continuous level of stimulation.

For example, the continuous stimulation of glasses, jewelry, or clothes on your skin results in adaptation so that soon you no longer feel them. Adaptation occurs as neurons decrease their signals in response to an unchanging stimulus, such as jewelry left on your skin. However, sense organs do not adapt to intense forms of stimulation because such stimulation may cause physical damage. Instead, intense stimulation, such as from a very hot shower, may cause pain, which warns us of possible injury.

3 Sensations versus perceptions. Gathering information about the world involves two steps. In the first step, electrical signals reach the brain and are changed into sensations.

Sensations are relatively meaningless bits of information (left figure) that result when the brain processes electrical signals that come from the sense organs.

In the second step, the brain quickly changes sensations, which you're not aware of, into perceptions.

Perceptions are meaningful sensory experiences (right figure) that result after the brain combines hundreds of sensations.

For example, visual sensations would resemble the top figure, showing meaningless lines, colors, and shapes. Visual perceptions would be like the bottom figure, showing a complete "sad-happy" face.

While all sensations begin with step 1, transduction, sense organs use different mechanisms to do it. We'll start with how the visual system works. ●

A Vision

Stimulus: Light Waves

Why can't you see radio waves?

Each sense organ has a different shape and structure; it can receive only a certain kind of stimulus, or physical energy. For instance, the reason you cannot see radio waves is that their waves are not the right length. Although radio waves, along with light waves from the sun, are all forms of electromagnetic energy, they vary in wavelength. For example, the figure below shows that X rays are very short and AM radio waves are very long. Notice that only a small, specific range of wavelengths that come from a light source, called the visible spectrum, is able to excite receptors in your eyes.

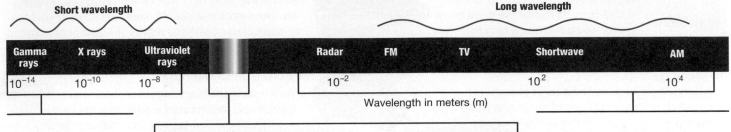

Short wavelength   Long wavelength

Gamma rays	X rays	Ultraviolet rays		Radar	FM	TV	Shortwave	AM
10^{-14}	10^{-10}	10^{-8}		10^{-2}			10^2	10^4

Wavelength in meters (m)

Violet   Blue   Green   Yellow   Red

400   500   600   700

Wavelength in nanometers (nm)

Invisible—too short. On this side of the electromagnetic energy spectrum are shorter wavelengths, including gamma rays, X rays, and ultraviolet rays. These waves are invisible to the human eye because they are too short to stimulate our receptors. However, some birds (such as hummingbirds) and insects can see ultraviolet rays to help them find food.

© Steve Byland/ Shutterstock.com

Visible—just right. Near the middle of the electromagnetic spectrum is a small range of waves that make up the visible spectrum.

The **visible spectrum** is one particular segment of electromagnetic energy that we can see because these waves are the right length to stimulate receptors in the eye.

The reason you can see a giraffe is that its body reflects light waves from the visible spectrum back to your eyes. One function of the eyes is to absorb light waves that are reflected back from all the objects in your environment.

Invisible—too long. On this side of the electromagnetic spectrum are longer wavelengths, such as radio and television waves. These waves are invisible to the human eye because they are too long to stimulate the receptors in the eye. Imagine the awful distraction of seeing radio and television waves all day long!

Stimulus. Thus, the most effective stimulus for vision is energy (light waves) from the visible spectrum. However, for you to see anything, reflected light waves must be gathered and changed into electrical signals, and for that process—transduction—we must look inside the eye itself.

Structure and Function

How can you see a giraffe?

For you to see a 16-foot-tall giraffe, your eyes perform two separate processes. First, the eyes gather and focus light waves into a precise area at the back of your eyes. Second, this area absorbs and transforms light waves into impulses, a process known as transduction. We'll follow the path of light waves from the giraffe to the back of your eyes in a series of seven steps.

1 **Image reversed.** Notice that, at the back of the eye, the giraffe appears upside down. Even though the giraffe is focused upside down in the eye, somehow the brain turns the giraffe—and all other objects we see—right side up so that we see the world as it really is.

2 **Light waves.** The problem with light waves is that after they strike an object, such as a giraffe, they are reflected back in a broad beam. You cannot see the giraffe unless your eyes change this broad beam of light waves into a narrow, focused one. Your eye has two structures, the cornea and the lens, that bring an image into focus, much as a camera does.

The giraffe's image is reflected upside down on the back of the eye.

3 Cornea. The broad beam of light reflected from the giraffe passes first through the cornea.

The **cornea** is the rounded, transparent covering over the front of your eye. As the light waves pass through the cornea, its curved surface bends, or focuses, the waves into a narrower beam.

4 Pupil. After passing through the cornea, light waves next go through the pupil.

The **pupil** is a round opening at the front of your eye that allows light waves to pass into the eye's interior.

Your pupil grows larger or smaller because of a muscle called the iris.

5 Iris. The opening of the pupil is surrounded by the iris.

The **iris** is a circular muscle that surrounds the pupil and controls the amount of light entering the eye. In dim light, the iris relaxes, allowing more light to enter— the pupil dilates; in bright light, the iris constricts, allowing less light to enter— the pupil constricts. The iris muscle contains the pigment that gives your eye its characteristic color.

If you look in a mirror in bright light, you will see that the iris is constricted and that your pupil—the black dot in the center of your eye—is very small.

6 Lens. After passing through the cornea and pupil, light waves reach the lens.

The **lens** is a transparent, oval structure whose curved surface bends and focuses light waves into an even narrower beam.

The lens is attached to muscles that adjust the curve of the lens, which in turn adjusts the focusing. This process of adjustment is called visual accommodation.

Visual accommodation is the process of the lens bending to focus light waves on the retina.

For the eye to see distant objects, light waves need less bending (focusing), so muscles automatically stretch the lens so that its surface is less curved. To see near objects, light waves need more focusing, so muscles relax and allow the surface of the lens to become very curved. Making the lens more or less curved causes light waves to be focused into a very narrow beam that must be projected precisely onto an area at the very back of the eye, called the retina.

7 Retina. Although light waves have been bent and focused, transduction hasn't yet occurred. That is about to change as light waves reach the retina.

The **retina**, located at the very back of the eyeball, is a thin film that contains cells that are extremely sensitive to light. These light-sensitive cells, called photoreceptors, begin the process of transduction by absorbing light waves.

On the following page, we'll describe the two kinds of photoreceptors, how they absorb light waves, and how they carry out the process of transduction. For some people, light waves cannot be focused precisely on the retina because of a problem with the shape of their eyeballs.

Eyeball's Shape and Laser Eye Surgery

Eyeball. Some of us are born with perfectly shaped eyeballs, which contributes to having almost perfect vision. Others, however, are born with eyeballs that are a little too long or too short, resulting in two common visual problems: nearsightedness and farsightedness.

Normal vision. The shape of your eyeball is primarily determined by genetic instructions. If your eyeball is shaped so that objects are perfectly focused on the back of your retina (**black X**), then both the near and distant objects will appear clear and sharp and you will have very good vision (20/20).

Nearsighted. If you inherit an eyeball that is too long, you are likely nearsighted.

Nearsightedness (myopia) results when the eyeball is too long so that objects are focused at a point in front of the retina (**black X**). In this case, near objects are clear, but distant objects appear blurry.

Common treatments involve corrective lenses or eye surgery.

Farsighted. If you inherit an eyeball that is too short, you are likely farsighted.

Farsightedness (hyperopia) occurs when the eyeball is too short so that objects are focused at a point slightly behind the retina (**black X**). In this case, distant objects are clear, but near objects appear blurry.

Common treatments involve corrective lenses or eye surgery.

Eye surgery. Currently, a popular and successful treatment to correct nearsighted vision is called LASIK. In this procedure, the surface of the eye is folded back and a laser is used to reshape the exposed cornea so that light waves are correctly bent and focused on the retina (FDA, 2011).

Next, we'll examine the retina more closely and see exactly how transduction occurs.

Retina: Miniature Camera–Computer

What happens to light waves?

Some miniaturized electronic cameras can record amazingly detailed video pictures. But they are primitive compared to the retina, whose microscopic cells can transform light waves into impulses that carry detailed information to the brain about all kinds of shapes, shadows, sizes, textures, and colors. Think of the retina as a combination of a video camera and a computer whose batteries never run out as it transforms light waves into impulses—the process of transduction. And here's how transduction occurs.

You already know that an object, such as a giraffe, reflects light waves that enter the eye and are bent, focused, and projected precisely on the retina, at the very back of the eyeball.

The **retina** has three layers of cells. The back layer contains two kinds of photoreceptors that begin the process of transduction, changing light waves into electrical signals. One kind of photoreceptor with a rodlike shape is called a rod and is located primarily in the periphery of the retina. The other photoreceptor with a conelike shape is called a cone and is located primarily in the center of the retina in an area called the **fovea** (FOH-vee-ah).

We have enlarged a section of retina to show that it has three layers. We'll explain the function of each layer. Start with 1, located below the figure on the far right, and move left to 3.

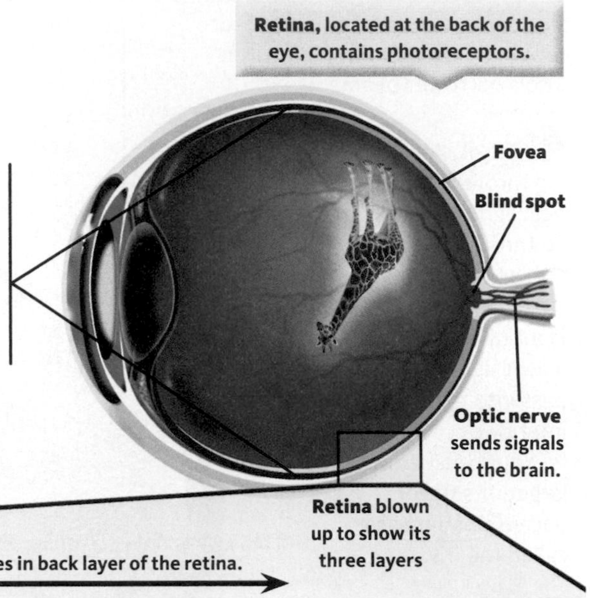

Retina, located at the back of the eye, contains photoreceptors.

Fovea

Blind spot

Optic nerve sends signals to the brain.

Retina blown up to show its three layers

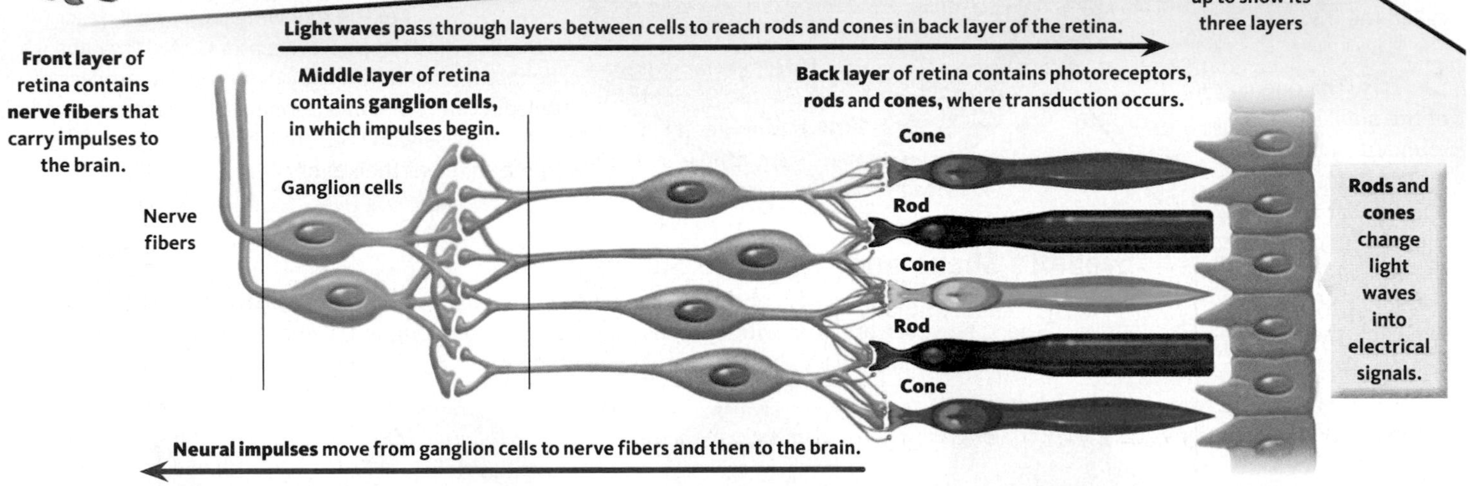

Light waves pass through layers between cells to reach rods and cones in back layer of the retina.

Front layer of retina contains **nerve fibers** that carry impulses to the brain.

Nerve fibers

Middle layer of retina contains **ganglion cells,** in which impulses begin.

Ganglion cells

Back layer of retina contains photoreceptors, **rods** and **cones,** where transduction occurs.

Cone

Rod

Cone

Rod

Cone

Rods and **cones** change light waves into electrical signals.

Neural impulses move from ganglion cells to nerve fibers and then to the brain.

3 *Nerve impulses* generated in ganglion cells exit the back of the eye through the *optic nerve,* which carries impulses through the retina's blind spot toward the brain.

The **blind spot** is the point where the optic nerve exits the eye and where there are no photoreceptors (rods or cones).

You don't notice the blind spot because your eyes are continually moving.

The eye is a sophisticated computer for transduction, changing light waves into impulses. For you to "see something," impulses must reach the visual areas in the brain, our next stop.

2 The process of *transduction* begins when chemicals in the rods and cones break down after absorbing light waves. This chemical breakdown generates a tiny electrical force that, if large enough, triggers *nerve impulses* in neighboring *ganglion* cells; now, transduction is complete.

1 Each eye has about 120 million rods, most located in the retina's periphery.

Rods are photoreceptors that contain a single chemical, called rhodopsin (row-DOP-sin), which is activated by small amounts of light. Because rods are extremely sensitive to light, they allow us to see in dim light, but to see only black, white, and shades of gray.

To see color, we need the cones. Each eye has about 6 million cones, most located in the retina's fovea (Goldstein, 2010).

Cones are photoreceptors that contain three chemicals called opsins (OP-sins), which are activated in bright light and allow us to see color. Unlike rods, cones are wired individually to neighboring cells; this one-on-one system of relaying information allows us to see fine details.

Next, we finally get to transduction, which begins in the rods and cones.

Visual Pathways: Eye to Brain

There is a lot of truth to the old saying, "Seeing is believing," but most people don't realize that the "seeing" takes place in the brain, not in the eye. So far, we have traced the paths along which light waves enter the eye, are focused on the retina, are changed into impulses, and leave the eye on the optic nerve. Now we will follow the optic nerve as it reaches its final destination in the occipital lobe, at the back of the brain. There, the occipital lobe changes light waves into colorful rock stars.

How do you see rock stars?

1 Optic nerve. Nerve impulses flow through the optic nerve as it exits from the back of the eye. This exit point creates a blind spot that we do not normally see because our eyes are constantly moving and cover any areas that might be in the blind spot.

The optic nerves partially cross over and make a major stop in the *thalamus*, which does some initial processing. The thalamus relays the impulses to the back of the occipital lobe in the right and left hemispheres.

2 Primary visual cortex. At the very back of each occipital lobe lies a primary visual cortex, which transforms nerve impulses into simple visual sensations, such as texture, lines, and colors. At this point, you would report seeing only these basic sensations (left figure), not the complete figure of a rock star.

Researchers estimate that about 25% of the entire cortex is devoted to processing visual information, more area than to any other sensory input (Goldstein, 2010). The visual cortex contains many different cells that respond to many different kinds of visual stimulation.

Meaningless stimuli

Specialized cells. From the Nobel Prize–winning research of David Hubel and Torsten Wiesel (1979), we know that different cells in the *primary visual cortex* respond to specific kinds of visual stimuli. For example, some cortical cells respond to lines of a particular width, others to lines at a particular angle, and still others to lines moving in a particular direction. These specialized cortical cells transform different stimuli into simple visual sensations, such as shadows, lines, textures, or angles.

Blindness. If part of your primary visual cortex were damaged, you would have a blind spot in the visual field, similar to looking through glasses with tiny black spots painted on the lens. Damage to the entire primary visual cortex in both hemispheres would result in almost total blindness; the ability to tell night from day might remain.

However, to make sense of what you see, such as a rock star, nerve impulses must be sent from the primary visual cortex to neighboring visual association areas.

3 Visual association areas. The primary visual cortex sends simple visual sensations (actually, impulses) to neighboring association areas, which add meaning or *associations* (Kiernan, 2008). In our example, the association area receives sensations of texture, line, movement, orientation, and color and assembles them into a meaningful image of a complete rock star (left figure). There are visual association areas in each hemisphere. If part of your visual association area were damaged, you would experience *visual agnosia*, which is difficulty in assembling simple visual sensations into more complex, meaningful images (Ropper & Samuels, 2009). For instance, a person with visual agnosia could see pieces of things but would have difficulty combining pieces and recognizing them as whole, meaningful objects (see p. 79).

Meaningful rock star

Researchers can use brain scans to show actual neural activity that is occurring in the visual association areas.

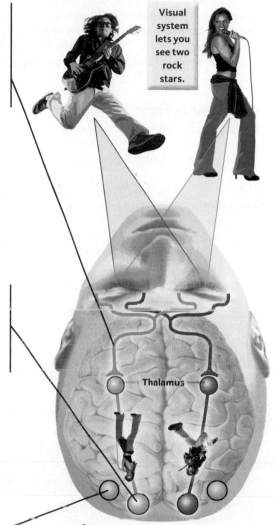

Visual system lets you see two rock stars.

Thalamus

4 This brain scan shows that when a subject is silently looking at and reading words, maximum neural activity occurs in the primary visual cortex and nearby visual association areas (red and yellow indicate maximum neural activity; blue and green indicate least). These visual areas are located in the occipital lobe (back of the brain). The visual association areas are involved in many visual activities, such as reading, writing, and perceiving objects, animals, people, and colors (Gaillard et al., 2006; Storbeck et al., 2006).

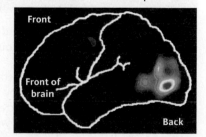

Front

Front of brain

Back

Next, we'll explain how the visual system transforms light waves into all the colors of the rainbow.

Color Vision

Debra was born with opaque films over her lenses (cataracts) that made her almost totally blind. For her first 28 years, she could tell night from day but see little else.

What is red? When a newly developed operation restored much of her vision, she cried with delight as she looked around her hospital room and saw things she had only imagined. "Colors were a real surprise to me," Debra said. "They were so bright. You can't conceive what colors are until you've seen them. I couldn't imagine what a red apple looked like and now I can hold one and actually see red" (*San Diego Tribune*, April 3, 1984).

Red is actually long light waves.

Like Debra, you might assume that a red apple is really red, but you are about to discover otherwise. Objects, such as a red apple, do not have colors. Instead, objects reflect light waves whose different wavelengths are transformed by your visual system into the experience of seeing colors. So, what is red? The answer is that the color red is actually produced by a certain kind of wavelength.

How light waves are turned into millions of colors is a wondrous and interesting process, which begins with a ray of sunlight.

Making Colors from Wavelengths

1. A ray of sunlight is called white light because it contains all the light waves in the visible spectrum, which is what humans can see.

2. As white light passes through a prism, it is separated into light waves that vary in length. Nature creates prisms in the form of raindrops, which separate the passing sunlight into waves of different lengths, creating a spectrum of colors that we call a rainbow.

3. Our visual system transforms light waves of various lengths into millions of different colors. For example, in the figure below, notice that the numbers, which vary from about 400 to 700 (nanometers, or nm), indicate the length of light waves. We see shorter wavelengths as shades of violet, blue, and green, and longer wavelengths as shades of yellow, orange, and red (Silbernagl & Despopoulous, 2009).

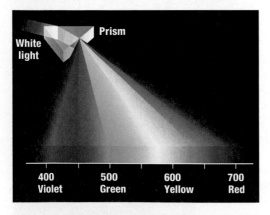

| 400 Violet | 500 Green | 600 Yellow | 700 Red |

You see an apple as red because the apple reflects longer light waves, which your brain interprets as red.

Actually, how our visual system transforms light waves into color is explained by two different theories—the trichromatic and opponent-process theories—which we'll examine next.

Trichromatic Theory

The explanation of how you see the many colors in the native face (left photo) began over 200 years ago with the early work of a British physicist, Thomas Young. It was his research that laid the basis for a theory of how you see colors, called the trichromatic *(TRI-crow-MAH-tic)* theory of color.

All colors are made from mixing three primary colors: red, green, and blue.

The **trichromatic theory** says that there are three different kinds of cones in the retina, and each cone contains one of three different light-sensitive chemicals, called opsins. Each of the three opsins is most responsive to wavelengths that correspond to each of the three primary colors: blue, green, and red. All other colors can be mixed from these three primary colors.

According to the recent version of the trichromatic theory, you see the red around the man's eyes because this area reflects light waves of a longer wavelength. You see the green in the feathers because they reflect light waves of medium length. You see the blue in the headband because it reflects light waves of shorter length. The different lengths of light waves are absorbed by three different cones whose chemicals (opsins) are most sensitive to one of the three primary colors—red, green, and blue (right figure). Thus, wavelengths of different lengths are changed into one of the three primary colors, which are mixed to produce all colors (Goldstein, 2010).

Until recently, color vision was believed to involve only three genes, one each to code the three primary colors of red, green, and blue. Researchers have now discovered that we have as many as two to nine genes (thus two to nine cones) that code the longer wavelengths involved in seeing red (Neitz & Neitz, 1995). This means that seeing a particular color, such as red, depends on how many color genes you have inherited. For example, which bar on the TV (below) you label as "red" depends

We have three types of cones.

on which of the genes (two to nine) you've inherited. One person may label deep scarlet as "red" while another sees a pale red. This means that different people may see and label the "same" color, red, very differently (scarlet to pale red), and this difference explains why people may not agree about adjusting the color (red) on their television sets (Lipkin, 1995; Yanoff et al., 2003). Thus, your perception of the color red may differ from someone who has different "color genes."

To understand how color coding occurs in the brain, we need to examine the second theory of color vision, the opponent-process theory.

People do NOT all see the same color of red.

Opponent-Process Theory

If you stare at a red square for about 20 seconds and then immediately look at a white piece of paper, you'll see a green square, which is called an afterimage.

An **afterimage** is a visual sensation that continues after the original stimulus is removed.

And if you stare at a blue square, you'll see a yellow afterimage. On the basis of his work with afterimages, physiologist Ewald Hering suggested that the visual system codes color by using two complementary pairs—red-green and blue-yellow. Hering's idea became known as the opponent-process theory.

The **opponent-process theory** says that ganglion cells in the retina and cells in the thalamus of the brain respond to two pairs of colors—red-green and blue-yellow. When these cells are excited, they respond to one color of the pair; when inhibited, they respond to the complementary pair.

For example, some ganglion and thalamic cells use a *red-green* paired combination: they signal red when excited and green when inhibited.

Other ganglion and thalamic cells use a *yellow-blue* paired combination: they signal blue when excited and yellow when inhibited.

Thus, different parts of the visual system use different methods to code different colors.

Theories Combined

Because we see colors so automatically and naturally, we don't realize it involves both the opponent-process and trichromatic theories. Here's what happens when we combine the two theories to explain color vision.

First, the trichromatic theory says that there are usually three different kinds of cones (there may be as many as nine) in the retina. Each cone absorbs light waves of different lengths, which correspond to the three primary colors of blue, green, and red. Second, when electrical signals (color information) reach the ganglion cells in the retina and neurons in the thalamus, they use the opponent-process theory, which involves a pair of colors: Activation results in one color of a pair, and inhibition results in the other color. Third, nerve impulses carry this color information to the visual cortex, where other neurons respond and give us the experience of seeing thousands of colors, which can be made by combining the three primary colors of red, green, and blue.

Although most of us have good color vision, some individuals have varying degrees of color blindness.

Color Blindness

This is normal color vision.

The vast majority of us have normal color vision. We see the vibrant colors of the leaves on the left—green, red, and yellow. However, about 8% of men and fewer than 1% of women in the United States see these same leaves in shades of blue and yellow (photo below) because they have inherited the most common form of color blindness (C. Koch, 2010).

Color blindness is the inability to distinguish two or more shades in the color spectrum.

There are several kinds of color blindness.

Monochromats (MOHN-oh-crow-mats) have total color blindness; their worlds look like black-and-white movies. This kind of color blindness is rare and results from individuals having only rods or only one kind of functioning cone (instead of three).

Dichromats (DIE-crow-mats) usually have trouble distinguishing red from green because they have just two kinds of cones. This is an inherited genetic defect, found mostly in males, that results in seeing mostly shades of blue and yellow (right photo), but it differs in severity (Gerl & Morris, 2008).

This is red-green color blindness.

People don't always realize they have color blindness. For example, a little boy came home complaining about being chased by a green dog. The dog really looked green to the little boy; he did not know he had a form of color blindness.

People in some occupations, such as electrical technicians, are screened for color blindness because they must identify differently colored wires.

Below, you see two circles filled with colored dots that are part of a test for color blindness. An individual taking this test is asked to look at each circle and identify what, if any, number is formed by the colored dots.

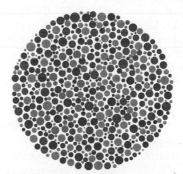

Individuals with normal vision see the number 96, while people with red-green color deficits find this number difficult or impossible to see.

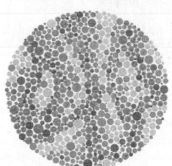

Those with normal color vision and total color blindness should not be able to read any number. The majority of those with red-green deficiencies should read the number 5.

From our discussion of the eye's structure and function, you can see that the eye is an engineering marvel that makes even the most sophisticated video camera seem like an expensive toy.

Next, we'll examine an equally astonishing sense organ, the ear, and learn about audition. ●

© Wilm Ihlenfeld/Photos.com

Ishihara Tests for Colour Blindness, Courtesy of Graham-Field, Inc.

Stimulus: Sound Waves

What happens when someone yells?

When a cheerleader gives a big yell, she is actually producing the yell by letting out air so that it is alternately compressed and expanded into traveling waves, called sound waves.

Sound waves, which are the stimuli for hearing (audition), resemble ripples of different sizes. Similar to ripples on a pond, sound waves travel through space with varying heights and frequency. Height, which is the distance from the bottom to the top of a sound wave, is called **amplitude.** The **frequency** of sound waves refers to how many sound waves occur within 1 second.

We'll demonstrate the concept of amplitude by comparing the sound waves of a cheerleader's yell with a child's whisper.

Amplitude and Loudness

Yell. As a cheerleader yells, she lets out an enormous amount of air that is compressed and expanded into very large traveling waves (shown below). Large sound waves are described as having high amplitude, which the brain interprets as loud sounds.

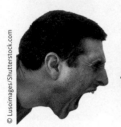

High amplitude means big sound waves and loud sounds.

Whisper. As a child whispers a secret to his friend, he lets out a small amount of air that is compressed and expanded into very small traveling waves. Small sound waves are described as having low amplitude, which the brain interprets as soft sounds.

whisper

Low amplitude means small sound waves and soft sounds.

Relationship of amplitude and loudness. You have no difficulty distinguishing between a cheerleader's yell and a child's whisper because your auditory system automatically uses the amplitude of the sound waves to calculate loudness (K. E. Barrett et al., 2009).

Loudness is your subjective experience of a sound's intensity. The brain calculates loudness from specific physical energy, in this case the amplitude of sound waves.

A whisper, which results in low-amplitude sound waves, is just above our threshold of hearing. The loudest yell on record, which resulted in high-amplitude sound waves, was about as loud as sound heard near speakers at a rock concert.

If the brain uses amplitude to calculate loudness, what does it use to calculate a sound's low or high pitch?

Frequency and Pitch

Screech or boom. As you listen to someone playing a keyboard, you can tell the difference between high and low notes because your brain is continually discriminating between high and low sounds, which is called pitch.

High frequency means sound waves are close together, resulting in high sounds or pitch.

Low frequency means sound waves are far apart, resulting in low sounds or pitch.

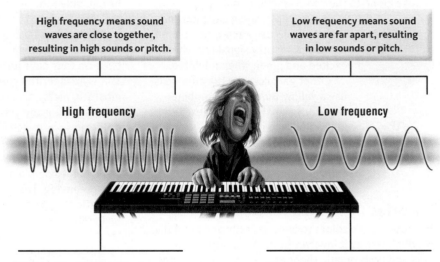

High frequency

Low frequency

High note. Striking the top key on a keyboard produces sound waves that travel rapidly and are described as having high frequency. The brain interprets high frequency as high notes or high pitch.

Low note. Striking the bottom key on a keyboard produces sound waves that travel slowly and are described as having low frequency. The brain interprets low frequency as low notes or low pitch.

Relationship of frequency and pitch. When you hear a sound, your auditory system automatically uses frequency to calculate pitch (K. E. Barrett et al., 2009).

Pitch is our subjective experience of a sound being high or low, which the brain calculates from specific physical stimuli, in this case the speed or frequency of sound waves.

The keyboard's highest key produces sound waves with a high frequency, which results in high sounds or high pitch; the keyboard's lowest key produces sound waves of lower frequency, which results in low sounds or low pitch.

Hearing range. Humans hear sounds within only a certain range of frequencies, and this range decreases with age. For example, infants have the widest range of hearing, from frequencies of 20 to 20,000 cycles per second. For college students, it is 30 to 18,000 cycles per second. With further aging, the hearing range decreases, so that by age 70, many people can't hear sounds above 6,000 cycles per seconds. Some college students are now using an ear-splitting ring tone with a frequency of 17,000 cycles per second so they can hear the ring but their parents and professors cannot (M. Block, 2006; Vitello, 2006).

Next, we'll see how loud a jet plane is compared to a whisper.

Measuring Sound Waves

At what loudness does hearing loss begin?

By comparing the sounds of a jet plane and a whisper, we are essentially asking how they compare in loudness, which is measured in decibels (dB).

A **decibel** is a unit to measure loudness, just as an inch is a measure of length. Our threshold for hearing ranges from 0 decibels, which is absolutely no sound, to 140 decibels, which can produce pain and permanent hearing loss.

The table contains common sounds with their decibel levels. Notice especially those sound levels that can cause permanent hearing loss.

Decibel (dB) level	Sounds and their decibel levels	Exposure time and permanent hearing loss
140	Jet engine, gun muzzle blast, firecracker explosion	Any exposure to sounds this loud is painful and dangerous. That's why aircraft ground personnel must wear ear protectors.
120	Rock concert near speakers, thunderclap, record-setting human yell (115 dB)	Exposure for 15 minutes or less can produce hearing loss. Rock musicians and fans who do not use ear plugs risk hearing loss.
100	Chain saw, jackhammer, baby screaming, inside of racing car	Exposure for 2 hours or more can cause hearing loss. Workers using loud power tools who do not use ear protectors risk hearing loss.
80	Heavy city traffic, alarm clock at 2 feet, subway, MP3 player/iPod	Constant exposure for 8 hours can produce hearing loss. Music lovers should know that stereo headphones can produce sounds from 80 to 115 dB.
60	Conversation, air conditioner at 20 feet	Aging decreases hearing sensitivity, and that's why older adults may ask, "What did you say?" indicating that they may not easily hear normal conversations.
30	Whisper, quiet library, gasoline-only car idling in neutral (45 dB)	Today's cars are engineered for quietness. At idle, many cars are almost as quiet as a library, and at 65 mph (70 dB), they are not much louder than a conversation.
0	Threshold of hearing, hybrid car operating on battery only (3–5 dB)	If you were standing next to an idling hybrid car, you might wonder, "Is this car turned on?" You wouldn't ask this question when standing next to a louder gasoline-only car.

(Caption within table image: Shish, Please Do Not Talk Above 30 Decibels)

Decibels and Deafness

As indicated in the table, continuous exposure to sounds with high decibel levels for long periods of time can produce permanent hearing loss. People should always take precautions against high decibel levels, especially if they are frequently exposed to such loud sounds for extended periods of time.

Although many college students think they can hear just fine, about 20–25% of today's young adults may actually have early hearing loss (Le Prell et al., 2011; Shargorodsky et al., 2010). One possible reason for this high percentage is that many young adults are listening to loud MP3 players for extended periods of time (Godlasky, 2008).

At the end of this module (p. 115) we'll discuss different causes of deafness and treatment. Now, we'll take you inside the ear and explain how it turns sound waves into wonderful sounds.

Outer, Middle, and Inner Ear

Is that the Rolling Stones or a barking dog?

Most of us think that we hear with our ears and that's how we tell the difference between, for example, the music of the Rolling Stones and the barking of a dog. But nothing is further from the truth. What really happens is that both music and a dog's barks produce only sound waves, which are just the stimulus for hearing (audition). Your ears receive sound waves, but it is your brain that actually does the hearing, distinguishing the difference between the Stones' song "(I Can't Get No) Satisfaction" and a dog's barks. It's a complicated journey; the first step begins in the outer ear.

1 Outer Ear

The only reason your ear has that peculiar shape and sticks out from the side of your head is to gather in sound waves. Thus, sound waves produced by the Rolling Stones are gathered by your outer ear.

The **outer ear** consists of two structures: the pinna and the auditory canal.

The **pinna** is an oval structure that protrudes from the side of the head. The function of the pinna is to pick up sound waves and send them down a long, narrow tunnel called the auditory canal.

1a

The **auditory canal** is a long tube that funnels sound waves down its length so that the waves strike a thin, taut membrane—the eardrum, or tympanic membrane.

In some cases, the auditory canal may become clogged with ear wax, which interferes with sound waves on their way to the eardrum. Ear wax should be removed by a professional so as not to damage the fragile eardrum.

2 Middle Ear

The boundary between the outer ear and the middle ear is called the eardrum or tympanic membrane.

The **eardrum** is a taut, thin structure, also referred to as the tympanic *(tim-PAN-ick)* membrane. Sound waves strike the eardrum and cause it to vibrate. The eardrum passes the vibrations on to the first of three small bones to which it is attached, which are part of the middle ear.

The middle ear functions like a radio's amplifier; it picks up and increases, or amplifies, vibrations.

The **middle ear** is a bony cavity that is sealed at each end by membranes. The two membranes are connected by three small bones.

The three tiny bones are collectively called **ossicles** *(AW-sick-culls)* and, because of their shapes, are referred to as the **(a) hammer, (b) anvil,** and **(c) stirrup.** The first ossicle—hammer—is attached to the back of the eardrum. When the eardrum vibrates, so does the hammer. In turn, the hammer sends the vibrations to the attached anvil, which further sends the vibrations to the attached stirrup. The stirrup makes the connection with the end membrane, the **(d) oval window.** The three ossicles act like levers that greatly amplify the vibrations, which in turn cause the attached oval window to vibrate.

Thus, the function of the middle ear is to pick up vibrations produced by the eardrum, amplify these vibrations, and pass them on to the oval window, which marks the end of the middle ear and beginning of the inner ear.

Sound waves

3 Inner Ear

The **inner ear** contains two main structures that are sealed in bony cavities: the cochlea, which is involved in hearing, and the semicircular canals, which are involved in balance.

We'll discuss the semicircular canals and their involvement in our sense of balance on page 105; now, we'll focus on the cochlea.

The **cochlea** *(KOCK-lee-ah),* located in the inner ear, has a bony coiled exterior that resembles a snail's shell. The cochlea contains the receptors for hearing, and its function is transduction—transforming vibrations into nerve impulses that are sent to the brain for processing into auditory information.

Researchers liken the cochlea to an exquisite miniature box that is made of bone and contains precious jewels, which in this case are miniature cells that are the receptors for hearing.

On the next page, we have enlarged and opened the cochlea so you can see the auditory receptors.

Unless otherwise noted, all images are © Cengage Learning

3 Inner Ear *(continued)*

3a If you were to take two drinking straws, hold them side by side, and then wind them around your finger, you would have a huge model of a cochlea. The cochlea consists of two long narrow tubes (straws) separated by membranes (basilar and tectorial) but joined together and rolled up, or coiled. The beginning of the coiled compartments is sealed by a membrane, the oval window. So when the ossicles vibrate the oval window, the oval window vibrates the fluid in the cochlea's tubes, where the auditory receptors are located.

3b The auditory receptors, called **hair cells**, are miniature hair-shaped cells that stick up from the cochlea's bottom membrane, called the **basilar** *(BAZ-ih-lahr)* **membrane**. Vibration of fluid in the cochlear tubes causes movement of the basilar membrane, which literally bends the hair cells. The mechanical bending of the hair cells generates miniature electrical forces that, if large enough, trigger nerve impulses (transduction). Nerve impulses leave the cochlea as explained at right in 3c.

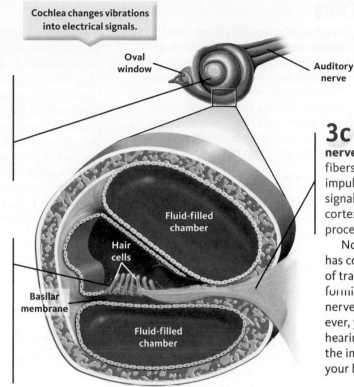

Cochlea changes vibrations into electrical signals.

Oval window

Auditory nerve

Fluid-filled chamber

Hair cells

Basilar membrane

Fluid-filled chamber

Cross Section of Cochlea

3c The **auditory nerve** is a band of fibers that carry nerve impulses (electrical signals) to the auditory cortex of the brain for processing.

Now the cochlea has completed its role of transduction—transforming vibrations into nerve impulses. However, you won't report hearing anything until the impulses reach your brain.

Auditory Brain Areas

How do we tell noise from music? Just as your eye does not see, your ear does not hear. Rather, sense organs, such as the ear, perform only transduction—transform physical energy into nerve impulses. You don't hear or recognize sound as noise, music, or words until nerve impulses are processed by various auditory areas in the temporal lobes of your brain.

4 **Sensations and Perceptions**
After nerve impulses reach the brain, a two-step process occurs in which nerve impulses are transformed first into meaningless bits of sounds and then into meaningful sounds. The first step occurs in the primary auditory area, explained in 4a.

4a The **primary auditory cortex**, which is located at the top edge of the temporal lobe, transforms nerve impulses (electrical signals) into basic auditory sensations, such as meaningless sounds and tones of various pitches and loudness.

Next, the primary auditory cortex sends impulses (sensations) to the auditory association area, explained in 4b.

SOUND WAVES

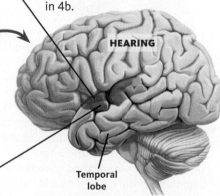

TRANSDUCTION

HEARING

Temporal lobe

4b The **auditory association area** receives meaningless auditory sensations in the form of neural impulses from the neighboring primary auditory cortex. The auditory association area combines meaningless auditory sensations into perceptions, which are meaningful melodies, songs, words, or sentences.

It takes only a moment from the time sound waves enter your ear until you say, "That's the Stones' song '(I Can't Get No) Satisfaction.'" But during that amazing moment, sound waves were changed into impulses, impulses into sensations, and finally, sensations into perceptions (Goldstein, 2010).

Now we'll explain how the brain uses nerve impulses to calculate where a sound is coming from, whether it is a high or low sound, and whether it is a loud or soft sound.

Auditory Cues

If someone yelled "Watch out!" you would immediately turn your head toward the source of the sound because your brain automatically calculates the source's location. The brain calculates not only the source of the voice but also whether the voice calling your name is high or low and loud or soft. Thus, sound waves contain an amazing amount of information. We'll begin with how your brain calculates the direction of where a sound is coming from.

Where's the sound coming from?

Calculating Direction

You automatically turn toward the source of the yell "Watch out!" because your brain instantly calculates the direction or source.

The brain determines the **direction of a sound** by calculating the slight difference in time (see 1 in right figure) that it takes sound waves to reach the two ears, which are about 6 inches apart (see 2 in right figure) (Goldstein, 2010).

If you have difficulty telling where a sound is coming from, the sound is probably arriving at both ears simultaneously. To locate the direction, you can turn your head from side to side, causing the sound to reach one ear before the other.

The brain uses other cues to calculate a sound's high or low pitch.

1. Source
A sound coming from the right reaches your right ear before it reaches your left ear. The brain automatically interprets this difference in timing as a signal that the source of the sound is to the right. You will automatically turn your head to the right, to the source of the sound.

Sound waves blocked by head

Right ear   Left ear

WATCH OUT!

2. Time difference
Sound waves reach the left ear this much later than they reach the right ear.

Calculating Pitch

Imagine the low, menacing growl of a lion and then the high screech of fingernails on the chalkboard. Your subjective experience of a sound being high or low is referred to as pitch. Exactly how the cochlea codes pitch and the brain interprets the code is rather complicated. We'll focus on two better-known theories of pitch: the frequency and place theories.

The **frequency theory,** which applies only to low-pitched sounds, says that the rate at which nerve impulses reach the brain determines how low the pitch of a sound is.

For example, the brain interprets a frequency of 50 impulses per second as a lower sound than one with a frequency of 200 impulses per second. Hearing the low-pitched roar of a lion involves the frequency theory. Hearing higher-pitched sounds, however, such as the screech of fingernails on a chalkboard, involves another theory, the place theory.

The **place theory** says that the brain determines medium- to higher-pitched sounds on the basis of the place on the basilar membrane where maximum vibration occurs.

The frequency and place theories explain how we perceive pitch.

For example, lower-pitched sounds cause maximum vibrations near the beginning of the cochlea's basilar membrane, while higher-pitched sounds cause maximum vibrations near the end of the membrane. Our auditory system combines the frequency and place theories to transform sound waves into perceptions of low- to high-pitched sounds (Goldstein, 2010).

The brain does one more thing: It calculates how loud a sound is.

Calculating Loudness

You can easily tell the difference between a yell and a whisper because your auditory system transforms the intensity of sound waves into the subjective experiences of a soft whisper or a loud yell. This transformation occurs inside the cochlea.

Compared to a yell, a whisper produces low-amplitude sound waves that set off the following chain of events: fewer vibrations of the tympanic membrane, less movement of fluid in the cochlea, less movement of the basilar membrane, fewer bent hair cells, less electrical force, and finally, fewer nerve impulses sent to the brain, which interprets these signals as a soft sound.

The brain calculates **loudness** primarily from the frequency or rate of how fast or how slowly nerve impulses arrive from the auditory nerve.

For example, the brain interprets a slower rate of impulses as a softer tone (whisper) and a faster rate as a louder tone (yell) (Goldstein, 2010).

Earlier, we said that there are two structures in the inner ear, the cochlea and the vestibular system. If you have ever stood on your head, you have firsthand experience with the vestibular sense, our next topic. ●

The brain calculates loudness from frequency of nerve impulses.

C Vestibular & Kinesthetic Senses

Vestibular Sense

What else is in the inner ear?

We guarantee that one question you never ask is "Where is my head?" Even though your head is in a hundred different positions throughout the day, you rarely forget to duck as you enter a car or forget whether you're standing on your feet or your hands. That's because the position of your head is automatically tracked by another sense, called your vestibular sense.

The **vestibular sense** includes sensing the position of the head, keeping the head upright, and maintaining balance. The vestibular sense relies on the semicircular canals to provide it with information on the position of your head and whether you're standing on your hands or feet.

The **semicircular canals** are located above the cochlea in the inner ear and resemble bony arches that are set at different angles (right figure). Each of the semicircular canals is filled with fluid that moves in response to movements of your head. In the canals are sensors (hair cells) that respond to the movement of the fluid.

A gymnast (left figure) relies heavily on his or her vestibular sense to keep balance. Sometimes an inner ear infection affects the vestibular sense and results in dizziness, nausea, and the inability to balance.

And, as you'll see next, the vestibular sense is involved in motion sickness.

Vestibular sense says you're upside down and helps maintain balance.

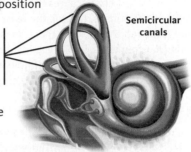

Semicircular canals

Motion Sickness

One of my (R.P.) terrible childhood memories is sitting in the back seat of a moving car and after 30 minutes of curving roads feeling a cold sweat followed by nausea, dizziness, and an extreme desire to lie down anywhere—stationary. Along with about 25% of the U.S. population, I experienced moderate to severe signs of motion sickness. About 55% of people experience only mild symptoms, while the remaining 20% are lucky and rarely experience any. Researchers think that motion sickness results when information provided by the vestibular sense doesn't match information coming from other senses (Ignelzi, 2006b).

Why am I getting sick?

Motion sickness, which includes feelings of discomfort, nausea, and dizziness in a moving vehicle, is believed to develop when there is a sensory mismatch between the information from the vestibular sense—that your head is physically bouncing around—and the information reported by your eyes—that objects in the distance look fairly steady.

Infants rarely have motion sickness, but susceptibility increases from age 2 to 12. After 12, susceptibility decreases in both men and women. Researchers suspect that genetic and not personality factors determine susceptibility to motion sickness (Ignelzi, 2006b).

Motion sickness results from a mismatch between vestibular and visual senses.

Kinesthetic Sense

How do acrobats make such dangerous moves?

As you walk, without conscious thought, you are aware of where your head, arms, and legs are in relation to the ground. You can thank your kinesthetic sense for not having to stare down at the ground for each step you take.

The **kinesthetic sense** informs us about our bodies' positions and motions relative to gravity.

As our bodies move, sensory information is sent to the brain from sensory organs in the muscles, tendons, joints, and skin. When you tighten the muscles in your leg or arm, for instance, the sensations of tightness are due to your kinesthetic sense. When we move parts of our bodies, the sensory organs send information through the spinal cord and then to the brain. Specifically, the signal will reach the somatosensory cortex and cerebellum (both discussed in Module 4), which together are responsible for the coordination of motor movements.

Athletes, such as gymnasts, acrobats, and dancers, rely heavily on their kinesthetic sense so they know where there bodies are positioned during their complex physical routines. The kinesthetic sense acts quickly so that athletes know precisely where their bodies are relative to gravity at all times during their performance.

We will now discuss another category of senses called the chemical senses, which include taste and smell. ●

Kinesthetic sense informs this acrobat about the rapidly changing position of his body as he leaps into the air.

D Chemical Senses

Taste

You rarely think about the thousands of chemicals you put into your mouth every day, but you do know when something tastes very good or very bad.

How does your tongue taste? **Taste** is called a chemical sense because the stimuli are various chemicals. On the surface of the tongue are receptors, called taste buds, for five basic tastes: sweet, salty, sour, bitter, and umami. The function of taste buds is to perform transduction, which means transforming chemical reactions into nerve impulses.

Of all the senses, taste is the least well understood in terms of how it is represented in the brain. A recent study showed that in mice there are separate groups of brain cells that each respond to a different type of taste (X. Chen et al., 2011). The results do not necessarily apply to humans, but exploring this possibility may lead to a new understanding of how we experience taste.

As you imagine biting into and chewing a very bitter slice of lemon, we'll explain how your tongue tastes.

© Gelpi/Shutterstock.com

1 Tongue: Five Basic Tastes

You're probably familiar with four basic tastes—*sweet, salty, sour,* and *bitter.* There now appears to be a fifth, called *umami,* a meaty-cheesy taste found in cheese, meat, pizza, and MSG (A. Gilbert, 2008). The right figure shows the areas on the tongue that have the most sensors or taste buds.

Scientists believe there are only a few types of sensors for four of the five tastes: sweet, salty, sour, and umami. There are many more sensors for bitter (Weir, 2010). Our increased sensitivity for bitter may have an evolutionary origin because many poisonous substances taste bitter. Humans, as well as most animals, avoid bitter-tasting substances, which may very well be advantageous to survival.

Tasting begins with what happens in the trenches on the surface of your tongue.

2 Surface of the Tongue

As you chew the lemon, its chemicals, which are the *stimuli* for taste, break down into molecules. In turn, these molecules mix with saliva and run down into narrow trenches on the surface of the tongue. Once inside the trenches, the molecules stimulate the taste buds.

3 Taste Buds

Buried in the trenches on the surface of the tongue are many hundreds of bulblike taste buds.

Taste buds, which are shaped like miniature onions, are the receptors for taste. Chemicals dissolved in the saliva activate the taste buds, which produce nerve impulses that eventually reach areas in the brain's parietal lobe. The brain transforms these nerve impulses into sensations of taste.

Taste buds live in a relatively toxic environment and are continuously exposed to heat, cold, spices, bacteria, and saliva. As a result, taste buds wear out and are replaced about every ten days. The human tongue can have as many as 10,000 taste buds and as few as 500; the number remains constant throughout life (Goldstein, 2010).

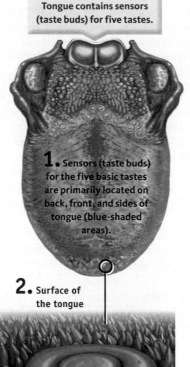

Tongue contains sensors (taste buds) for five tastes.

1. Sensors (taste buds) for the five basic tastes are primarily located on back, front, and sides of tongue (blue-shaded areas).

2. Surface of the tongue

Trench contains buried taste buds.

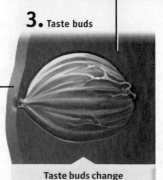

3. Taste buds

Taste buds change dissolved chemicals into electrical signals.

4 All Tongues Are Not the Same

In rare cases, individuals are born without any taste buds and cannot taste anything because they have a genetically determined disorder (Mass et al., 2005). In contrast, about 25% people are *supertasters,* which means they have two to three times as many taste buds as normal, which results in increased sensitivity to sweet, bitter, sour, and salty (Bartoshuk, 2010). For example, supertasters taste sugar to be twice as sweet as most people and get more intense oral burning sensations from the chemical (capsaicin) in chili peppers. Supertasters find grapefruit juice too bitter and don't like broccoli because they also contain a bitter chemical (Bhattacharya, 2003).

Researchers found that being a supertaster is an inherited trait and believe it may have had some evolutionary advantage. For example, supertasters would be better able to identify unsafe foods and toxins, such as whether fruits or berries are poisonous (Bartoshuk, 1997; BBC, 2008b). For all of us, our ability to taste is greatly affected by our ability to smell.

5 Flavor: Taste and Smell

If taste receptors are sensitive to only five basic tastes, how can you tell the difference between two sweet tastes, such as a brownie and vanilla ice cream, or between two sour tastes, such as lemon juice and vinegar? The truth is that a considerable percentage of the sensations we attribute to taste are actually contributed by our sense of smell (*Science Illustrated,* 2011a).

We experience **flavor** when we combine the sensations of taste and smell.

You have no doubt experienced the limitations of your taste buds' abilities when you had a cold, which blocks the nasal passages and cuts out the sense of smell. Without smell, foods we usually love now taste very bland.

Since our taste of foods is greatly enhanced by the sense of smell, we'll examine smell, or olfaction, next.

Smell, or Olfaction

How does your tongue taste?

You may have been impressed that your tongue has up to 10,000 taste buds, but that number pales in comparison to the nose's millions of receptor cells (Ganong, 2005; Glausiusz, 2008). That's why the sense of smell (olfaction) is 10,000 times more sensitive than taste (Lindstrom, 2005).

Olfaction is called a chemical sense because its stimuli are various chemicals that are carried by the air. The upper part of the nose has a small area that contains receptor cells for olfaction. The function of the olfactory receptors is transduction, to transform chemical reactions into nerve impulses.

We'll explain the steps for olfaction by having you imagine crossing paths with an angry skunk.

1 Stimulus

An angry skunk protects itself by spraying thousands of molecules, which are carried by the air and drawn into your nose as you breathe. The reason you can smell substances such as skunk spray is that these substances are volatile. A volatile substance is one that can release molecules into the air at room temperature. For example, volatile substances include skunk spray, perfumes, and warm brownies, but not glass or steel. We can smell only volatile substances, but first they must reach the olfactory cells in the nose.

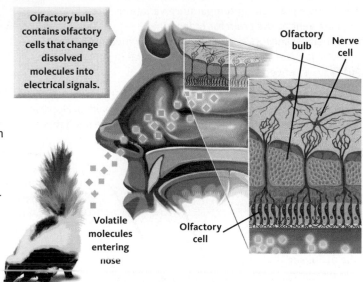

Olfactory bulb contains olfactory cells that change dissolved molecules into electrical signals.

Volatile molecules entering nose

Olfactory bulb

Nerve cell

Olfactory cell

2 Olfactory Cells

Olfactory cells are the receptors for smell and are located in two 1-inch-square patches of tissue in the uppermost part of the nasal passages. Olfactory cells are covered with mucus, a gluelike film into which volatile molecules dissolve and stimulate the underlying olfactory cells. The olfactory cells trigger nerve impulses that travel to the brain, which interprets the impulses as different smells.

As you breathe, a small percentage of the air entering your nose reaches the upper surface of your nasal passages, where the olfactory receptors are located. People can lose their sense of smell if a virus or inflammation destroys the olfactory receptors, or if a blow to the head damages the neural network that carries impulses to the brain. About 5% of all people have no sense of smell, and people lose their ability to smell as they age. For instance, 25% of people older than 60 lose their sense of smell (Raloff, 2007; von Bothmer, 2006). You don't actually smell anything until neural impulses reach your brain.

3 Sensations and Memories

Nerve impulses from the olfactory cells travel first to the *olfactory bulb*, which is a tiny, grape-shaped area (light orange structure in diagram of nose) that lies directly above the olfactory cells at the bottom of the brain. From here, *nerve cells* relay impulses to the *primary olfactory cortex*, which is located underneath the brain. This cortex transforms nerve impulses into the olfactory sensations of a skunk's spray or a sweet perfume (von Bothmer, 2006).

Although we can identify as many as 10,000 different odors, we soon stop smelling scents we are repeatedly exposed to (deodorants, perfumes) because of decreased responding, called adaptation, in the olfactory cells (Jacob et al., 2006).

Smell, in terms of evolution, is a very primitive sense and has important functions.

4 Functions of Olfaction

One function of smell is to intensify the taste of food. For example, you could not tell a piece of licorice from a jelly bean with your nose held closed. A second function is to warn of potentially dangerous foods; the repulsive odor of spoiled or rotten food does this effectively. A third function is to elicit strong memories, often associated with emotional feelings (Ropper & Samuels, 2009). This function is so strong that the smell memories a newborn forms within a week after birth are remembered more than a year later. Toddlers, for instance, prefer odors they smelled during the first week of their lives (Delaunay-El Allam et al., 2010). A fourth function may be to aid us in choosing a mate, much as smells do for animals. Human females seem to have a distinct ability to smell biological information in sweat or body odor, which may guide them in selecting a mate (Wysocki et al., 2009). Also, the human brain uses different areas to process body odors versus everyday scents, which reinforces the important evolutionary function of olfaction (Lundstrom et al., 2008).

Smells good, I'll buy something!

The power of olfaction is so strong that marketing companies work with retailers to use smell to improve our mood and influence us to purchase products. For instance, Bloomingdale's, a luxury department store, has been known to infuse the baby department with the scent of baby powder, the intimate apparel department with lilac, and the swimsuit department with coconut (Newman, 2011). Also, supermarket bakeries and fast-food restaurants use artificial fresh-cooked food smells to whet your appetite and get you to open your wallet (Lindstrom, 2008). Scent marketing is clever because smell, more than any other sense, is connected to our limbic system (see p. 80), where our motivations and emotions are processed. Consequently, the feelings we get from smells are intense and immediate. This means if businesses use attractive scents, we may make purchases based more on instinct than on rational thought, which is exactly what they want us to do (R. Baron, 2008; Herz, 2008).

Next, we discuss touch and explain what happens when you pet a cat. ●

Photodisc/Getty Images

E Touch

Definition

If you were to draw your hand across the surface of a cat, you would have the sensations of touching something soft and furry. These sensations are part of the sense of touch.

What happens when fingers feel fur?

The sense of **touch** includes pressure, temperature, and pain. Beneath the outer layer of skin are a half-dozen miniature sensors that are receptors for the sense of touch. The function of the touch sensors is to change mechanical pressure or temperature variations into nerve impulses that are sent to the brain for processing. We'll examine several miniature mechanical sensors and explain how they function.

© Royalty-Free/Alamy

Receptors in the Skin

If you were to closely examine the surface of your skin, you would see a relatively smooth membrane covered in some places with hair. Some "touch" sensors are wound around hair follicles (the backs of your arms) and are slightly different from the sensors in skin without hair (your palms). However, before we discuss several major touch receptors, we need to examine the different layers of the skin.

1 **Skin.** The skin, which is the body's largest organ, has three layers. The **outermost layer** of skin is a thin film of dead cells containing no receptors. Immediately below the dead layer are the first receptors, which look like groups of threadlike extensions. In the **middle and fatty layers** of skin are a variety of receptors with different shapes and functions. Some of the major sensors in the middle layer of skin are hair receptors.

2 **Hair receptors.** In the middle layer are free nerve endings that are wrapped around the base of each hair follicle; these are called **hair receptors.** Hair receptors respond or fire with a burst of activity when hairs are first bent. However, if hairs remain bent for a period of time, the receptors cease firing, an example of **sensory adaptation.** When you first put on a watch, it bends hairs, causing hair receptors to fire; your brain interprets this firing as pressure on your wrist. If you keep the watch on and it remains in place, keeping the hairs bent, the hair receptors adapt or cease firing, and you no longer feel pressure from your watch, even though it is still there. Your skin contains some receptors that adapt rapidly (hair receptors) and others that adapt slowly. Adaptation prevents your sense of touch from being overloaded.

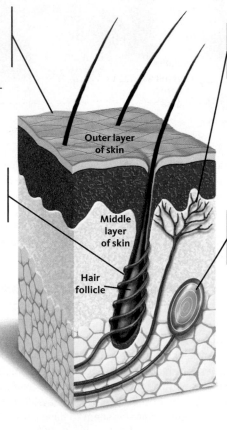

Outer layer of skin

Middle layer of skin

Hair follicle

3 **Free nerve endings.** Near the bottom of the outer layer of skin is a group of threadlike extensions called **free nerve endings** because they have nothing protecting or surrounding them. Interestingly, the same free nerve ending can transmit information about both temperature and pain. Researchers think different patterns of neural activity may signal different sensations—for example, slow bursts of firing for temperature and fast bursts for pain.

4 **Sensory receptors.** In the fatty layer of skin is the largest touch sensor, called the **Pacinian corpuscle** (pa-SIN-ee-in CORE-pus-uhl). This receptor, which has layers like a slice of onion, is highly sensitive to touch, is the only receptor that responds to vibration, and adapts very quickly. Another touch sensor is called the **Merkel cell,** which is located primarily on the palm side of our fingertips and is sensitive to gentle, localized touch. On average, women have a finer sense of touch than men because they have smaller fingertips yet the same number of Merkel cells. The more densely packed Merkel cells give female hands the ability to distinguish among finer textures (R. M. Peters et al., 2009).

Unless otherwise noted, all images are © Cengage Learning

Brain Areas

Did I touch my nose or my toe?

When pressure (touch), temperature, or pain stimulates the skin's receptors, they perform transduction and change these forms of energy into nerve impulses. The impulses go up the spinal cord and eventually reach the brain's somatosensory cortex.

The **somatosensory cortex,** which is located in the parietal lobe, transforms nerve impulses into sensations of touch, temperature, and pain. You know which part is being stimulated because, as we explained earlier (see p. 77), different parts of the body are represented on different areas of the somatosensory cortex.

Compared with touch and temperature, the sense of pain is different because it has no specific stimulus and can be suppressed by psychological factors. We'll discuss these interesting aspects of pain later in this module. But first, try out your memory on the Concept Review and then learn how psychological factors can make foods that we think are disgusting become delicacies in other parts of the world. ●

Somatosensory cortex

Parietal lobe

Concept Review

EYE: Numbers on the eye match the numbers of the questions.

1. A transparent, curved structure at the front of the eye, called the _____, focuses or bends light waves into a more narrow beam.

2. A round opening at the front of the eye that allows varying amounts of light to enter the eye is called the _____.

3. A circular, pigmented muscle that dilates or constricts, thus increasing or decreasing the size of the pupil, is called the _____.

4. The function of the transparent, oval structure called the _____ is to bend light waves into a narrower beam of light and focus the beam precisely on a layer of cells at the very back of the eye.

5. Lining the back of the eye are filmlike layers called the **(a)** _____. The back layer of cells has two kinds of photoreceptors, called **(b)** _____ and **(c)** _____.

6. This band of nerve fibers, called the **(a)** _____, exits from the back of the eye and carries impulses to the brain. The point at which this nerve exits is called the **(b)** _____ because it contains no rods or cones.

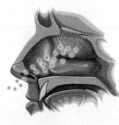

EAR: Numbers on the ear match the numbers of the questions.

1. The funnel-like structure called the _____ gathers in sound waves from the environment.

2. The short tunnel called the _____ carries sound waves that strike a membrane.

3. The thin, taut membrane at the end of the auditory canal, called the _____, transforms sound waves into vibrations.

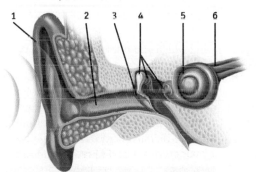

4. The three small bones (hammer, anvil, and stirrup) called the **(a)** _____ are part of the middle ear. They transform vibrations of the tympanic membrane into mechanical movements, which in turn vibrate a second membrane, called the **(b)** _____.

5. The coiled, fluid-filled structure called the **(a)** _____ is one part of the inner ear. It contains auditory receptors called **(b)** _____ that are attached to the basilar membrane.

6. The band of fibers called the _____ carries nerve impulses from the cochlea to the brain.

7. The inner ear contains a group of structures shaped like three tiny arches set at different angles. These structures signal body movement and position and are called **(a)** _____. The **(b)** _____ provides information on the position of the head and maintains balance. The **(c)** _____ provides information on our bodies' positions and motions relative to gravity.

8. Sensors that are located on the surfaces of the tongue respond to five basic tastes, which are **(a)** _____, _____, _____, _____, and the newly found taste called _____. The sensors or receptors for taste are called **(b)** _____.

9. Substances give off volatile molecules that are drawn into the nose, dissolve in mucus, and activate the **(a)** _____. The function of these cells is to produce **(b)** _____ that are sent to the olfactory bulb and then to the brain for processing.

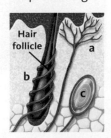

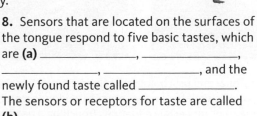

Hair follicle

10. There are several kinds of touch receptors: the **(a)** _____ is fast adapting; the **(b)** _____ is also fast adapting; the **(c)** _____ responds to both touch and vibration, and the **(d)** _____ responds to gentle, localized touch primarily on the palm side of our fingertips.

Answers: EYE: 1. cornea; 2. pupil; 3. iris; 4. lens; 5. (a) retina, (b) rods, (c) cones; 6. (a) optic nerve, (b) blind spot; **EAR:** 1. external ear; 2. auditory canal; 3. tympanic membrane (eardrum); 4. (a) ossicles, (b) oval window; 5. (a) cochlea, (b) hair cells; 6. auditory nerve; 7. (a) semicircular canals, (b) vestibular sense, (c) kinesthetic sense; 8. (a) sweet, salty, sour, bitter, umami, (b) taste buds; 9. (a) olfactory cells, (b) nerve impulses; 10. (a) free nerve ending, (b) hair receptor, (c) Pacinian corpuscle, (d) Merkel cell

Psychological Factors

Would you eat a cockroach?

We discussed how senses transform physical energy into impulses, which become sensations and then perceptions. However, your perceptions are usually influenced by psychological factors, such as learning, emotion, and motivation.

If offered a cockroach to eat, most of us would react with great disgust. The facial expression for disgust (left photo) is similar across cultures.

Disgust is triggered by the presence of a variety of contaminated or offensive things, including foods, body products, and gore. We show disgust, which is a universally recognized facial expression, by closing the eyes, narrowing the nostrils, curling the lips downward, and sometimes sticking out the tongue.

Disgust is a universally recognized facial expression.

Most people are disgusted by cockroaches. But, what if you were offered a glass of juice that just had a sterilized cockroach dipped in it? If the thought "EWWW!" just crossed your mind, you have helped us demonstrate that when something repulsive (cockroach) touches something pleasant (juice), it contaminates the pleasant object, even if it is unchanged (remember, the cockroach is harmless because it was sterilized). You still feel disgust (Rozin, 2007).

Disgust has a powerful influence on our behaviors (Herz, 2012). Consider, for example, how disgust influences whom we kiss, whom we sit next to, and whom we shun. Disgust also influences our hygiene behaviors. For example, a public health slogan that read "Don't bring the toilet with you" was effective in getting people to wash their hands before leaving the bathroom (Curtis, 2012).

Although disgust is considered a basic emotion and people around the world express disgust in the same way, cultural factors influence what we perceive to be disgusting (Rozin et al., 2000). Consider how sensitive you are to disgust. If you are like the typical college student, you likely use antibacterial soap and sanitizer every day. College students in the United States today may be some of the most disgust-sensitive people in the world (Fessler, 2010). Keep this in mind as you read the examples below.

Cultural Factors

Your particular culture has a strong influence on which foods you learn to perceive as disgusting and which you think are delicious. We'll describe some foods that are considered delicious in some cultures and disgusting in others.

Plump Grubs

For most U.S. citizens, eating a round, soft, white worm would be totally unthinkable. For the Asmat of New Guinea, however, a favorite delicacy is a plump, white, 2-inch larva—the beetle grub. The natives harvest dozens of the grubs, put them on bamboo slivers, and roast them. A photographer from the United States who did a story on the Asmat tried to eat a roasted grub, but his American tastes would not let him swallow it (Kirk, 1972).

Whale Skin

Although some Americans have developed a taste for raw fish (sushi), a common dish in Japan, most would certainly gag at the thought of eating the raw skin and blubber of a long-toothed whale. Yet for some Inuits (Eskimos), the raw skin and blubber of these whales is by far their most favorite food. Here you see a man using the Inuits' all-purpose knife to carve out his prized meal.

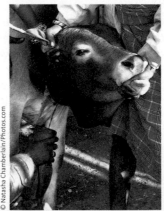

Milk and Blood

Some tribes in East Africa supplement their diet with blood that is sometimes mixed with milk. They obtain the blood by puncturing a cow's jugular vein with an arrow. A cow can be bled many times and suffer no ill effects. The blood-milk drink is a rich source of protein and iron.

Cultural Influences on Disgust

The reaction of U.S. college students to eating white, plump grubs or cold, glassy fish eyes or having a warm drink of blood mixed with milk is almost always disgust. Researchers believe that showing disgust originally evolved to signal rejection of potentially contaminated or dangerous foods. For example, gagging in disgust at the smell of rotten eggs discourages people from eating spoiled food that could make them very sick. Today, however, because of cultural and psychological influences, we may show disgust for eating a variety of noncontaminated foods (cat, dog, or horse meat) or for certain situations (touching a dead person) (Rozin et al., 2000). The fact that the same things are viewed as all right in one culture but as disgusting in another graphically shows how much cultural values can influence and bias perceptions.

Just as psychological factors are involved in perceiving taste, they are also involved in experiencing pain. ●

Definitions

One of the truly amazing research findings is how sugar pills or placebos can somehow "trick" us into feeling or getting better. For example, because many of us

Can sugar pills reduce pain?

believe that we will be helped by taking pills, about one-third of the population report feeling much better or having less pain after taking a pill, not knowing that it was only a sugar pill—a placebo.

A **placebo** is some intervention, such as taking a pill, receiving an injection, or undergoing an operation, that resembles medical therapy but that, in fact, has no medical effects.

A **placebo effect** is a change in the patient's illness (for better or worse) that is due to the patient's beliefs or expectations rather than the medical treatment.

One of the strongest and most studied placebo effects is the ability of placebos to relieve pain (G. A. Hoffman et al., 2005). For example, if people take a pill for headache pain and *believe* or *expect* that the pill will decrease their pain, about 30 to 60% of people will actually feel less pain after taking a placebo (Talbot, 2000).

Because the placebo effect can occur after taking any pill (injection or medical procedure), researchers needed to find a method that could separate a person's expectations and beliefs from the actual effects of a new drug or medical treatment.

REAL MEDICINE? SUGAR PILL?

Only a double-blind procedure can tell if a treatment is real or a placebo.

Power of Pricing

Is a more expensive pill better?

Is a cheaper pill less effective than a more expensive one? Do we believe that a higher price translates into higher quality, and if we do, can our belief or expectation make the drug more effective? Logic should tell us that the price of a pill does not determine its level of effectiveness.

10¢ $2.50

Researchers examined this fascinating question and their results may surprise you. Researchers asked participants to rate the pain caused by electric shocks applied to their wrist before and after taking a new painkiller. Half of the participants were told the new pill costs 10 cents, and half were told it costs $2.50. In fact, all the participants received a placebo. Results showed that 85% of those using the expensive pill felt less pain, compared to 61% of those using the cheaper pill. Thus, the pricier the pill, the higher the expectation of its effectiveness, and the stronger the placebo effect (Ariely, 2008; Waber et al., 2008).

Next we review three major conclusions about placebos.

Research Methods

The procedure used to separate a person's expectations (placebo effect) from the effects of a pill or medical treatment is called double-blind.

In a **double-blind procedure,** neither the researchers ("blind") nor the participants in the study ("blind") know who is receiving what treatment. Because neither researchers nor participants know who is receiving which treatment, the researchers' or participants' expectations have a chance to affect both treatments (drug and placebo) equally.

For example, in a double-blind design, headache sufferers would be told they will be given one of two kinds of pills to decrease pain. Unknown to the participants ("blind") and the researchers ("blind"), one of the pills is a drug and one is a placebo. If the participants taking the drug report the same decrease in pain as those taking the placebo, researchers conclude the drug is no better than a placebo. If the participants taking the drug report less pain than those taking the placebo, researchers conclude the drug is medically useful because it is better than a placebo.

Over the past 25 years, hundreds of double-blind experiments have found that 30 to 98% of people have reported beneficial effects after taking placebos (Talbot, 2000). For example, 85% of patients reported a reduction in pain from *Herpes simplex* (cold sores and genital sores) after a placebo drug treatment. Also, 98% of patients reported marked or complete relief of pain from ulcers after placebo treatment (Turner et al., 1994). There are hundreds of other examples that are just as incredible!

What follows is a research study that examines whether the cost of a treatment influences its effectiveness—another possible placebo effect. This promises to be interesting…let's learn what the researchers found.

Conclusion: Mind over Body!

Based on the results of decades of research, three major conclusions about placebos have been reached (Ariely, 2008; de Groot et al., 2011; Niemi, 2009).

First, potentially powerful placebo effects, such as reducing pain or speeding recovery from medical procedures, have been underestimated.

Second, both medication and fake surgeries can produce significant placebo effects, such as reducing pain, in 30 to 98% of patients.

Third, placebos indicate a powerful mind-over-body interaction, which explains why people may experience health benefits from taking placebos.

Recently, neuroscientists have mapped the brain processes underlying the placebo response. They found that the mere expectation that a treatment will work increases activity in the brain area responsible for higher mental function, which then signals the release of the brain's own opioids to relieve physical pain (Benedetti, 2009).

Thus, there is no question that our minds have powerful effects on our bodies! In fact, doctors are so aware of the power of placebos that 45 to 85% of them have prescribed a placebo to their patients (Vance, 2010).

Next, we'll examine pain in more detail and see how mental factors can affect the perception of pain. ●

Placebos work because of the power of our mind.

H Pain

Definition

What causes pain?

All of us can relate to pain because at one time or another we have felt various degrees of pain. **Pain** is an unpleasant sensory and emotional experience that may result from tissue damage, one's thoughts or beliefs, or environmental stressors.

Pain receptors send nerve impulses to the somatosensory and limbic areas of the brain, where impulses are changed into pain sensations. Pain is essential for survival: It warns us to avoid or escape dangerous situations and makes us take time to recover from injury.

The definition of pain differs from the other senses in three ways. First, pain results from many different stimuli (physical injury, psychological and social stressors), whereas the other senses respond primarily to a single stimulus. Second, pain's intensity depends not only on the physical stimulus but also on social and psychological factors. Third, the treatment of pain depends not only on treating any physical injury but also on reducing emotional distress associated with the painful sensations (Kerns, 2006, 2007).

Examples of social, psychological, and emotional factors involved in pain perception are religious beliefs and whether the harm was caused intentionally. For instance, practicing Catholics perceive electric shocks as less painful when they are looking at an image of the Virgin Mary (Wiech et al., 2008). Other research found that people who believe they are receiving an electric shock from another person on purpose, as opposed to accidentally, rate the same shock as more painful (Gray & Wegner, 2008). Also, love may actually decrease a person's perception of physical pain. Researchers found that when people in love had to hold a heat probe, they reported feeling less physical pain when they looked at pictures of their loved one than they did when viewing pictures of a platonic (nonromantic) friend (Younger et al., 2010). These studies show that the psychological experiences of pain are different even when the physical sensations are the same!

Even placebo treatments can result in a lower perception of pain. For example, after men had hot metal plates placed on their hands, they were given an injection of either a painkiller or a placebo (they did not know which—double-blind procedure). Brain scans showed that the placebo injections that had reduced pain activated pain-reducing brain circuits similar to the circuits activated by the real painkillers (Petrovic et al., 2002; Ploghaus et al., 2003). This and other studies demonstrate how one's beliefs can activate circuits in the brain that, in turn, result in changes in perception (decreased pain) (Erdmann, 2008; Scott et al., 2007; Younger et al., 2010).

Other psychological factors, such as changes in attention, can also alter perception of pain and answer an interesting question: Why do headaches come and go, depending on what you are doing?

© Yuri Arcurs/Shutterstock.com

Unless otherwise noted, all images are © Cengage Learning

Gate Control Theory

How does the mind stop pain?

Although a headache is painful, the pain may come and go as you shift your attention or become absorbed in some project. This phenomenon is explained by the gate control theory of pain (Melzack & Katz, 2004).

The **gate control theory** of pain says that nonpainful nerve impulses (shifting attention) compete with pain impulses (headache) in trying to reach the brain.

This competition creates a bottleneck, or neural gate, that limits the number of impulses that can be transmitted. Thus, shifting one's attention or rubbing an injured area may increase the passage of nonpainful impulses and thereby decrease the passage of painful impulses; as a result, the sensation of pain is dulled. The neural gate isn't a physical structure but rather refers to the competition between nonpainful and painful impulses as they try to reach the brain.

The gate control theory explains how a professional football quarterback was able to play the last six minutes of an important football game with a broken ankle (Associated Press, 2002). The gate control theory says that the football player's intense attentional and emotional involvement in the game caused his brain to send nonpainful impulses that closed neural gates in the spinal cord. The closed neural gates blocked impulses

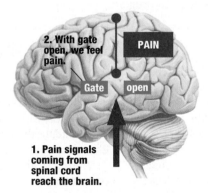

2. With gate open, we feel pain.

PAIN

Gate open

1. Pain signals coming from spinal cord reach the brain.

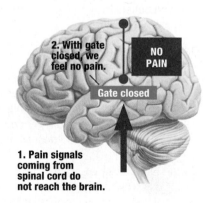

2. With gate closed, we feel no pain.

NO PAIN

Gate closed

1. Pain signals coming from spinal cord do not reach the brain.

from a painful ankle from reaching his brain and thus prevented feelings of pain (right figure above: NO PAIN). Later, when the game was over, the quarterback's attentional and emotional states calmed down, the neural gates opened, impulses from his broken ankle reached his brain, and he felt lots of pain (left figure above: PAIN). This same process explains why you may not notice the pain from your headache when you are involved in another activity.

Pain: Physical and Psychological

According to the gate control theory, your perception of pain depends not only on a stressful mental state or physical injury but also on a variety of psychological, emotional, and social factors, which can either decrease or increase your perception of pain (Pincus & Morley, 2001).

Your perception of pain from a serious injury can also be reduced by your brain's ability to secrete its own pain-reducing chemicals, called endorphins.

Endorphins

Does the brain make its own painkillers?

Someone who has experienced a serious injury—in football, for example—will usually report that initially the pain was bearable but with time the pain became much worse. One reason pain seems less intense immediately after injury is that the brain produces endorphins.

Endorphins (*en-DOOR-fins*) are chemicals produced by the brain and secreted in response to injury or severe physical or psychological stress.

The pain-reducing properties of endorphins are similar to those of morphine, a powerful painkilling drug (Ropper & Samuels, 2009). The brain produces endorphins in situations that evoke great fear, anxiety, stress, or bodily injury, as well as after intense aerobic activity. For example, participants with severe jaw pain produced increased levels of endorphins after they received a placebo injection, and participants who reported the greatest

Brain releases endorphins in times of great pain, stress, or fear.

pain relief showed the greatest endorphin release (Zubieta et al., 2005). In other research, patients showed increased levels of endorphins after bandages were removed from badly burned areas of their bodies or after nerves of their teeth were touched (Szyfelbein et al., 1985). Overall, there is a strong relationship between an increase in endorphin release and a decrease in pain perception (Zubieta, 2007). These studies indicate that the brain produces endorphins to reduce pain during times of intense physical stress.

Next, we'll look at the connection between dread and your brain's pain center.

Dread

How is dread related to pain?

Dread seems to be connected to the pain centers of the brain. One study placed participants into a brain scanner (fMRI) and offered them the choice of receiving a stronger shock now or a weaker shock in the future. Some participants dreaded the shock so much that they chose to receive the stronger shock instead of waiting to receive a weaker one. Brain imaging of these "extreme-dreaders" showed heightened activity in the brain's pain center. Thus, dread is not simply an emotional response to fear or anxiety; rather, a significant component of dread involves devoting attention to the expected and unpleasant physical threat (in this case shock) (Berns el al., 2006). These results suggest that when it comes to getting root canal surgery or receiving a painful shot, it is not the actual procedure people dread most, but rather the waiting time (Blakeslee, 2006b).

Don't make me wait for my root canal.

Next, we'll learn how having thin needles inserted into your body can help reduce pain.

Acupuncture

Can an ancient technique reduce pain?

Initially, scientists trained in the rigorous methods of the West (in particular, the United States) expressed doubt about an ancient Chinese pain-reducing procedure called acupuncture.

Acupuncture is a procedure in which a trained practitioner inserts thin needles into various points on the body's surface and then manually twirls or electrically stimulates the needles.

After 10–20 minutes of needle stimulation, patients often report a reduction in pain. The mysterious part of this procedure is that the points of insertion—such as those shown in the photograph on the right—were mapped thousands of years ago and, as researchers now know, are often far removed from the sites of injury.

Today, modern scientists have explained some of the mystery surrounding acupuncture. First, the points of needle insertion, which seem unrelated to the points of injury, are often close to known pathways that conduct pain. Second, there is some evidence from brain scans that stimulation of these points stimulates brain regions that trigger the secretion of endorphins, which we know can reduce pain (Cloud, 2011; H. Hall, 2008). Third, brain scans show that acupuncture decreases neural activity in brain areas involved in pain sensations (Aamodt & Wang, 2008; Ulett, 2003).

Acupuncture is effective for nausea, headaches, and some kinds of pain.

Acupuncture has been shown to relieve some kinds of pain (back and knee pain, dental treatment) and nausea (from chemotherapy or morning sickness), but there is no persuasive evidence that it is effective in other conditions, such as headache or drug addiction (Aamodt & Wang, 2008; Comarow, 2008; H. Hall, 2008).

One interesting study examined the impact of a placebo treatment (fake acupuncture treatment) by applying equal amounts of heat to people's right and left arms. Researchers then told participants they were being given acupuncture treatment on their right arm, but what participants didn't know was that the treatment was a sham. People reported feeling less pain in their right arms than in their left arms even though equally intense heat was applied to both arms (Kong et al., 2006). This study suggests that the power of people's belief in acupuncture is strong enough to change their perception of pain.

Many researchers insist it doesn't matter where needles are placed or whether needles are used at all; the only thing that matters, they say, is that a person believes he or she is getting real acupuncture. Furthermore, the stronger the belief, the more frequent the treatment sessions, the more interaction with the treatment provider, and the more painful the procedure, the better the results (Cochrane Collaboration, 2011; H. Hall, 2008; D. D. Madsen et al., 2009; Price et al., 2008).

Next, we turn to a very practical question: Can a sense be replaced if it is damaged? Of the five major senses—vision, audition, taste, olfaction, and touch—damage to vision and audition is especially disastrous to the quality of life. Therefore, researchers are trying to develop artificial eyes and ears. ●

I Application: Artificial Senses

Artificial Visual System

Is an artificial eye possible?

The cause and degree of blindness depend on which part of the visual system is affected. For example, a person would be totally blind if the photoreceptors (rods and cones) in the retina were destroyed (retinitis pigmentosa, an inherited disease) or if the entire retina or optic nerve were damaged. First, we'll look at a microchip that could be implanted into the retina to replace photoreceptors damaged by disease.

Artificial photoreceptors. At the beginning of this module, we told you about Terry, who was completely blind. In Terry's case, he was blind because the photoreceptors (rods and cones) in his retina were damaged by a genetic disease. For individuals like Terry who have problems with their photoreceptors, researchers have developed a microchip the size of a match head that is implanted in the back of the retina. This microchip sends impulses that travel on to the brain for visual processing. Although this microchip does not restore full vision, it allows people who are totally blind to see rough forms of light, movement, and objects. The illustration to the right shows how this amazing procedure works.

For individuals who are blind because their entire eye or optic nerve is damaged, researchers are developing a complete artificial eye that would send impulses directly to the brain.

1 Terry scans surroundings with a glasses-mounted camera.

2 Data travel from the glasses through a wire behind his ear to a microcomputer to get processed.

3 Processed data go to a wireless transmitter and then to a receiver implanted behind his ear.

4 Data then go to a microchip implanted in his eye. Normal visual processes occur next. Data are transmitted by the optic nerve to the brain's visual center.

Special glasses and eye implants work together to allow Terry to "see."

Brain implant. In an attempt to restore some vision, a blind patient was fitted with a miniature camera that sent electrical signals to 100 electrodes that were implanted directly into the visual cortex, located in the occipital lobe (figure at left). When activated, the electrodes stimulated neurons in the visual cortex and produced 100 tiny spots of light. This patient could see the letter S when some of the 100 electrodes were stimulated (LaFee, 2000). Although the 100 electrodes in this patient's visual cortex provided more visual information than did Terry's 16 electrodes, neither patient was able to see the outlines of objects or walk around without using a cane.

However, recently, researchers made a significant step forward in developing an artificial visual system.

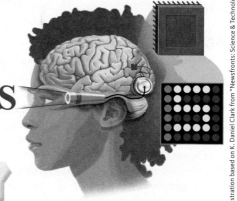

Camera sent electrical signals directly to brain.

Illustration based on K. Daniel Clark from "Newsfronts: Science & Technology," by Dawn Stover, *Popular Science*, August 1997, p. 29. Reprinted by permission.

Unless otherwise noted, all images are © Cengage Learning

Functional vision. The major goal in developing an artificial visual system is to provide enough visual information so that a blind person has meaningful visual function, such as reading letters and avoiding objects while walking around a room. Researchers have been making huge strides toward reaching this goal. Let's looks at one success story.

Erik Weihenmayer has climbed the Seven Summits, the tallest peak on every continent, and he did so without sight. Erik has been blind since the age of 13. His achievements are truly amazing. Researchers have been working with Erik to help him gain functional vision. Erik is now using a high-tech tool called the BrainPort, which is a tongue-camera device. He wears a headband with a camera that sends signals to a probe on his tongue, which contains 400 electrodes. Remember that in normal vision, the eye receives visual information, converts it into electrical impulses, and sends them to the brain for interpretation. With BrainPort, the electrical impulses are sent to the brain through nerves in the tongue instead of the optic nerve in the eye. The BrainPort essentially provides Erik with a tactile image that he interprets. At first, the images in his brain appeared as unidentifiable shapes and lines, but with practice, his brain now interprets the sensations on his tongue as recognizable patterns and symbols. He is getting pretty good at identifying the size, shape, and location of objects (A. T. Collins, 2012; Kean, 2009; B. Levy, 2010).

Erik Weihenmayer

© Scott Wintrow/Getty Images

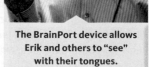

Courtesy Wicab Inc.

The BrainPort device allows Erik and others to "see" with their tongues.

Researchers have also developed devices for people who have hearing impairments, such as an artificial cochlea for the inner ear that has already benefited many thousands of people around the world.

Kinds of Deafness

What causes deafness? There are two major kinds of deafness that have different effects, causes, and treatments. The most severe kind of deafness is caused by damage to the inner ear and is called neural deafness. A less severe kind of deafness is caused by problems in the middle ear and is called conduction deafness.

Conduction Deafness

More than 28 million Americans, almost 10% of the population, have hearing loss called conduction deafness (R. J. Ruben, 2007).

Conduction deafness can be caused by wax in the auditory canal, injury to the tympanic membrane, or malfunction of the ossicles. All of these conditions interfere with the transmission of vibrations from the tympanic membrane to the fluid of the cochlea, resulting in degrees of hearing loss.

Conduction deafness, occurring in 30–40% of adults over 65, can often be treated with a hearing aid, which replaces the function of the middle ear. Hearing aids pick up sound waves, change them to vibrations, and send them through the skull to the inner ear.

Neural Deafness

Helen Keller, who was born deaf and blind, said, "To be deaf is a greater affliction than to be blind." Hellen Keller had neural deafness, which, unlike conduction deafness, is not helped by hearing aids.

Neural deafness can be caused by damage to the auditory receptors (hair cells), which prevents the production of impulses, or by damage to the auditory nerve, which prevents nerve impulses from reaching the brain.

Since neither hair cells nor auditory nerve fibers regenerate, neural deafness was generally untreatable until the development of the cochlear implant. Currently, the only approved treatment for certain kinds of neural deafness is the cochlear implant described below.

Cochlear Implants

Cochlear implant: How it works

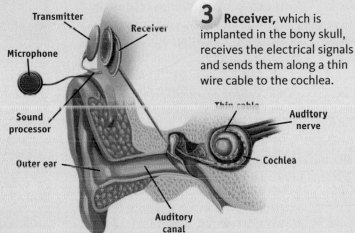

1 **Microphone**, which is worn behind the ear, gathers and sends sound waves to a sound processor.

2 **Sound processor** transforms sound waves into electrical signals, which are sent to a tiny transmitter.

3 **Receiver**, which is implanted in the bony skull, receives the electrical signals and sends them along a thin wire cable to the cochlea.

4 **Thin cable** is threaded into a fluid-filled tube of the cochlea until it makes contact with the auditory nerve. When the receiver sends electrical signals through the wire cable, the signals trigger impulses in the auditory nerve.

5 **Auditory nerve** carries the "manufactured" impulses to the auditory areas in the brain, which interpret and transform impulses into auditory impulses.

Can deaf people hear? If the auditory nerve is intact, a cochlear implant (figure above) can be used to treat neural deafness that is caused by damage to the ear (Ohl & Scheich, 2007).

The **cochlear implant** is a miniature electronic device that is surgically implanted into the cochlea. The cochlear implant changes sound waves into electrical signals that are fed into the auditory nerve, which carries them to the brain for processing.

As you proceed step by step through the figure above, notice that the cochlear implant first changes sound waves into electrical signals (1, 2, and 3) and then sends the electrical signals into the auditory nerve (4), which sends impulses to the brain (5).

About 150,000 people worldwide have received cochlear implants (M. B. Marcus, 2009). In the United States alone, 30,000 to 40,000 adults and approximately 30,000 children have received cochlear implants (Niparko, 2009; Weise, 2011).

Using the newest cochlear implants (cost up to $100,000 each), adults who had learned to speak before becoming deaf could understand about 80% of sentences without any facial cues and from 90 to 100% of sentences when watching the speaker's face and lips (speech reading). Many could converse on the telephone (Stone, 2002; Svirsky et al., 2000).

Advances in screening for hearing impairments in newborns have made cochlear implants for infants a welcome new trend. The FDA approves them for children as young as 1 year, and data show that cochlear implants are more effective when implanted by age 18 months. That's because the brains of younger children are more flexible or plastic, which means younger brains are better able to develop neurological responses to auditory information and learn to hear and speak (Niparko, 2011). Delaying implantation until after 18 months still shows positive results; however, it deprives children of exposure to speech and sounds during an important time in their language development (Niparko et al., 2010).

Other recent trends include placing cochlear implants in both ears, using the combination of cochlear implant and hearing aid, and implanting in older adults who no longer benefit from hearing aids (J. E. Brody, 2008; Niparko, 2009).

As we end this module, notice that we primarily discussed how senses transform energy into electrical impulses. Next, in Module 6, we'll focus on how "meaningless" sensations turn into meaningful perceptions. ●

What Would It Be Like Never to Feel Pain?

© Courtesy Tara Blocker, painlessbuthopeful.org

At the age of 5, Ashlyn Blocker has already experienced many serious physical injuries. She had a massive abrasion to the cornea of her eye, terrible burns, and hundreds of bite marks from fire ants. She also severely damaged her tongue, cheek, and lips, knocked out most of her front teeth, and crushed her fingers in a door frame. Other children would scream in pain from experiencing any of these injuries, but Ashlyn never yelled, nor did she shed a tear. "I can't feel my boo-boos," she said (Tresniowski et al., 2005). Ashlyn is different from most other children because she cannot feel pain.

Ashlyn has a rare and incurable genetic disorder called CIPA (congenital insensitivity to pain with anhidrosis). People with CIPA lack pain and temperature sensation yet have no other sensory deficits. These individuals cannot feel pain and temperature because they lack nerve fibers responsible for carrying the sensation of pain, heat, and cold to the brain. Anhidrosis, or the inability to sweat, can cause life-threatening problems such as developing dangerously high fevers because people aren't able to lower their body temperature by sweating.

Living life without feeling pain is not as wonderful as one might think. Pain serves an important function by telling our brain that something is wrong and something needs to be done to correct it. Imagine having appendicitis and not feeling pain. Appendicitis is especially dangerous for people with CIPA because they wouldn't know a problem existed until after their appendix had burst. Also, while most people shift their body weight when feeling pain in their joints, CIPA prevents people from sensing this pain and often results in joint problems. Lack of pain sensitivity can lead to other problems including bone fractures and infections. For example, Ashlyn had tonsillitis that went undetected for six months.

Despite the daily challenges Ashlyn faces, she looks like an ordinary girl who enjoys doing the same things others her age do. As a child, she liked to swing on the playground and enjoyed being tickled and hugged by her parents. Now, as a teenager, Ashlyn's parents try to encourage her to engage in safe activities, such as band, as opposed to gymnastics. Her parents remain cautious because even though they train her to be aware of warning signs for possible injuries, her inability to feel pain, regardless of any amount of training, places her at an increased risk of injury.

Ashlyn has impressed those who know her ever since she was a young child. "There is no reason to think she won't have a normal life," said Dr. Lawrence Shapiro, an internationally recognized child psychologist. Ashlyn's parents say she has the "best laugh in the world" and state "she's going to conquer the world" (Tresniowski et al., 2005).

1 What type of research method would you use to learn about the life of a person who cannot feel pain?

2 What type of neuron is responsible for people experiencing pain, heat, and cold?

3 What is the name for the optimum state of body arousal Ashlyn cannot achieve as a result of not sweating? Which areas of our brain and body help maintain this optimum level of arousal?

4 How might CIPA affect Ashlyn's ability to learn from her mistakes of injuring herself?

5 How helpful would acupuncture be as a treatment for people with CIPA?

6 Why is it that Ashlyn cannot sense pain or heat, but she can feel her parents tickling and hugging her?

Adapted from FoxNews, 2010; Morton, 2004; Tresniowski et al., 2005

Unless otherwise noted, all images are © Cengage Learning

Summary Test

A Vision

1. Waves in about the middle of the electromagnetic spectrum are visible because they can be absorbed by the human eye. These waves make up the _____ and can be absorbed by receptors at the back of the eye.

2. Upon entering the eye, light waves pass first through a curved, thin, transparent structure called the **(a)** _____, whose function is to bend or focus light waves into a narrower beam. Next, light waves pass through an opening in the eye called the **(b)** _____. Around this opening is a circular, pigmented muscle called the **(c)** _____; its function is to dilate or constrict, thus increasing or decreasing the amount of entering light. Finally, light waves pass through a transparent, oval structure called the **(d)** _____, whose function is to further focus light waves precisely on the photosensitive back surface of the eye, which is called the **(e)** _____.

3. The retina has several layers of cells, but only the very back layer contains photoreceptors. The photoreceptors that are used to see in dim light and transmit only black, white, and shades of gray are called **(a)** _____. Photoreceptors that are used to see in bright light and transmit colors are called **(b)** _____.

4. When rods absorb light waves, a chemical called **(a)** _____ breaks down and in turn generates tiny electrical forces that trigger **(b)** _____ in neighboring cells. Similarly, when cones absorb light waves, chemicals called **(c)** _____ break down and generate tiny electrical forces.

5. Nerve impulses generated in the eye travel along fibers that combine to form the **(a)** _____ nerve. This nerve carries nerve impulses to an area in the back of each occipital lobe called the **(b)** _____, which transforms impulses into simple visual **(c)** _____, such as lines, shadows, colors, and textures. If the primary visual cortex were totally damaged, the person would be essentially blind. Simple, meaningless sensations are transformed into complete, meaningful images when nerve impulses reach an area of the brain known as **(d)** _____.

6. We see color because our eyes absorb light waves of different **(a)** _____, which are transformed by the visual system into our experience of seeing colors. One theory of color applies to how the cones function; this is the **(b)** _____ theory. A second theory of color applies to how the ganglion and thalamic cells function; this is called the **(c)** _____ theory of color.

B Audition

7. The stimuli for hearing, or audition, are sound waves, which have several physical characteristics. The physical characteristic of amplitude or height of sound waves is transformed into the subjective experience of **(a)** _____, which is measured in units called **(b)** _____. The frequency of sound waves (cycles per second) is transformed into the subjective experience of **(c)** _____, which for humans ranges from about 20 to 20,000 cycles per second.

8. The outer ear is composed of a funnel-like shape, called the external ear, whose function is to gather **(a)** _____. These waves travel down a short tunnel called the **(b)** _____ and strike a thin, taut membrane called the **(c)** _____, whose function is to transform sound waves into **(d)** _____.

9. The middle ear has three tiny bones (hammer, anvil, and stirrup), which together are called **(a)** _____. Vibrations in the tympanic membrane produce mechanical movements in the ossicles, the third of which is attached to another thin membrane, called the **(b)** _____, which is made to vibrate.

10. Of several structures in the inner ear, one is a coiled, fluid-filled, tubelike apparatus called the **(a)** _____, which contains the auditory receptors, called **(b)** _____. Movement of the fluid in the tube causes movement of the basilar membrane, which in turn causes bending of the hair cells, generating a tiny **(c)** _____. If this is large enough, it will trigger nerve impulses, which leave the cochlea via the **(d)** _____ and travel to the brain.

11. Nerve impulses are transformed into rather simple, meaningless auditory sensations when they reach the **(a)** _____, which is located in the temporal lobe. These sensations are transformed into meaningful and complete melodies, songs, words, or sentences by the auditory **(b)** _____.

12. To tell the direction of a sound, the brain analyzes the differences in time and intensity between **(a)** _____ arriving at the left and right ears. The brain determines degrees of loudness by using the **(b)** _____ of the arriving impulses. The discrimination of different tones or pitches is explained by the **(c)** _____ and _____ theories.

C Vestibular & Kinesthetic Senses

13. Besides the cochlea, the inner ear contains three arch-shaped, fluid-filled structures called _____. The movement of fluid in these organs provides signals that the brain interprets in terms of the movement and position of the head and body.

14. Because of the workings of your _____, you are aware of where your head, arms, and legs are in relation to the ground.

D Chemical Senses

15. Sensors on the tongue respond to five basic tastes: **(a)** _____, _____, _____, _____, and _____. The receptors for taste, which are called **(b)** _____, trigger nerve impulses that travel to the brain, which then transforms them into the sensations of taste.

16. Volatile airborne substances are drawn into the upper part of the nose, where they dissolve in a thin film of mucus. Underneath the mucus are layers of receptors for olfaction (smell), which are called **(a)** _____. These receptors trigger impulses that travel to an area underneath the brain called the **(b)** _____. This area transforms impulses into hundreds of different odors.

E Touch

17. The sense of touch actually provides information on three different kinds of stimuli: **(a)** _____, _____, and _____. The various layers of skin contain different kinds of touch receptors that have different speeds of adaptation. Receptors for the sense of touch trigger nerve impulses that travel to an area in the brain's parietal lobe, called the **(b)** _____. This area transforms impulses into sensations of pressure, temperature, and pain. The more sensitive the area of the body is to touch, the larger is its area on the cortex.

Hair follicle

F Cultural Diversity: Disgust

18. A universal facial expression that indicates rejection of food is called **(a)** _____. Besides our innate preferences for sweet and salty foods and avoidance of bitter substances, most of our tastes are **(b)** _____ and particular to our culture. The fact that foods considered fine in one culture may seem disgusting to people in another culture indicates how much psychological factors influence taste.

© Natasha Chamberlain/Photos.com

G Research Focus: Mind over Body?

19. In order to control for the placebo effect, researchers use an experimental design in which neither the researchers nor the participants in the study know who is receiving what treatment. This is the _____ design, which controls for the expectations of both researchers and participants.

H Pain

20. After an injury, you feel two different kinds of pain sensations: at first, there is sharp, localized pain, which is followed by a duller, more generalized pain. The receptors for pain are **(a)** _____, which send impulses to two areas of the brain, specifically the **(b)** _____ and _____. If you rub an injured area or become totally absorbed in another activity, you may experience a reduction of pain, which is explained by the **(c)** _____. Immediately following a serious injury or great physical stress, the brain produces pain-reducing chemicals called **(d)** _____.

I Application: Artificial Senses

21. There are two basic causes of deafness. If the cause is wax in the auditory canal, injury to the tympanic membrane, or malfunction of the ossicles, it is called **(a)** _____ deafness. If the cause is damage to hair cells in the cochlea or to the auditory nerve, it is called **(b)** _____ deafness. One treatment for neural deafness is to use a **(c)** _____, which is more effective if individuals have learned to speak before becoming deaf.

Answers: 1. *visible spectrum;* 2. (a) *cornea,* (b) *pupil,* (c) *iris,* (d) *lens,* (e) *retina;* 3. (a) *rods,* (b) *cones;* 4. (a) *rhodopsin,* (b) *impulses,* (c) *opsins;* 5. (a) *optic,* (b) *primary visual cortex,* (c) *sensations,* (d) *association areas;* 6. (a) *lengths,* (b) *trichromatic,* (c) *opponent-process;* 7. (a) *loudness,* (b) *decibels,* (c) *pitch;* 8. (a) *sound waves,* (b) *auditory canal,* (c) *eardrum or tympanic membrane,* (d) *vibrations;* 9. (a) *ossicles,* (b) *oval window;* 10. (a) *cochlea,* (b) *hair cells,* (c) *electrical force,* (d) *auditory nerve;* 11. (a) *primary auditory cortex,* (b) *association areas;* 12. (a) *sound waves,* (b) *rate,* (c) *frequency, place;* 13. *semicircular canals;* 14. *kinesthetic sense;* 15. (a) *bitter, sour, salty, sweet, umami,* (b) *taste buds;* 16. (a) *olfactory cells,* (b) *primary olfactory cortex;* 17. (a) *pressure, temperature, pain,* (b) *somatosensory cortex;* 18. (a) *disgust,* (b) *learned;* 19. *double-blind;* 20. (a) *free nerve endings,* (b) *somatosensory area, limbic system,* (c) *gate control theory,* (d) *endorphins;* 21. (a) *conduction,* (b) *neural,* (c) *cochlear implant*

Links to Learning

Key Terms/Key People

acupuncture, 113
adaptation, 93
afterimage, 99
amplitude, 100
anvil, 102
auditory association area, 103
auditory canal, 102
auditory nerve, 103
basilar membrane, 103
blind spot, 96
cochlea, 102
cochlear implant, 115
color blindness, 99
conduction deafness, 115
cones, 96
cornea, 95
decibel, 101
dichromats, 99
direction of sound, 104

disgust, 110
double-blind procedure, 111
dread, 113
eardrum, 102
endorphins, 113
farsightedness, 95
flavor, 106
fovea, 96
frequency, 100
frequency theory, 104
gate control theory, 112
hair cells, 103
hammer, 102
inner ear, 102
iris, 95
kinesthetic sense, 105
lens, 95
loudness, 100, 104
Merkel cell, 108

middle ear, 102
monochromats, 99
motion sickness, 105
nearsightedness, 95
neural deafness, 115
olfaction, 107
olfactory cells, 107
opponent-process theory, 99
optic nerve, 97
ossicles, 102
outer ear, 102
oval window, 102
pain, 112
perceptions, 93
pinna, 102
pitch, 100
place theory, 104
placebo, 111
placebo effect, 111

primary auditory cortex, 103
primary visual cortex, 97
pupil, 95
retina, 95, 96
rods, 96
semicircular canals, 105
sensations, 93
somatosensory cortex, 108
sound waves, 100
stirrup, 102
taste, 106
taste buds, 106
touch, 108
transduction, 93
trichromatic theory, 98
vestibular sense, 105
visible spectrum, 94
visual accommodation, 95
visual agnosia, 97
visual association areas, 97

Media Resources

Go to **CengageBrain.com** to access Psychology CourseMate, where you will find an interactive eBook, glossaries, flashcards, quizzes, videos, answers to Critical Thinking questions, and more. You can also access Virtual Psychology Labs, an interactive laboratory experience designed to illustrate key experiments first-hand.

MODULE 6 Perception

Silent Messages

Although it seemed like an ordinary week, Maria and her 7-year-old daughter, Gabrielle, would be involved in three relatively normal events that could change their lives forever.

How can I be more confident?

On Tuesday, Maria's new boss unfairly criticized her work and made her feel insecure and unsure of herself. During her lunch hour, Maria browsed through an mp3 audio library to find something on building confidence. She was intrigued by a download titled "Improve Self-Esteem." The instructions read, "The listener hears only relaxing music, but the unconscious hears and automatically processes subliminal messages that boost self-esteem. In a few short weeks, the listener is guaranteed to have more confidence and self-esteem." Maria had heard about audio files with subliminal messages from a friend who claimed that she used a weight-reduction mp3 that helped her lose 20 pounds. Because it worked so well for her friend and she was in desperate need to improve her self-esteem, Maria purchased and downloaded the audio file on her mp3 player. She was already beginning to feel a little more confident.

Can subliminal messages change a person's behaviors?

Nice Dog, Mean Dog

On Saturday afternoon, Maria took her daughter, Gabrielle, to play at the local park, which had slides, swings, ropes, and even a small trampoline. As Gabrielle was walking toward the trampoline, she saw a beautiful white and brown dog sitting by its owner. Gabrielle loved animals, and she ran toward the dog. The dog's owner was deep in conversation and did not notice the cute little girl running toward the beautiful dog. As Gabrielle came closer, she thrust out her hands to pet the dog's smooth black nose. The movement of Gabrielle's hands startled the dog, who reflexively snarled and then snapped at the hands coming at its nose. Gabrielle felt the pain as the dog's teeth nipped two of her fingers, which immediately started to bleed. The owner turned to see what had happened and quickly pulled the dog away as Maria came running. Maria took Gabrielle in her arms, soothed her, and then examined the small cuts on her fingers. Gabrielle looked at her bleeding fingers and then at the big, ugly, white and brown dog that had bit her and said in a tearful voice, "I hate that dog. Bad dog." Seeing her daughter's reaction, Maria began to have doubts about her plans to surprise Gabrielle with a cute little puppy for her birthday.

What's a mean dog?

How does a bad experience create a bad perception?

White Spot

Can the doctor be sure?

On Friday, Maria had to take time from work for her annual physical exam, which included a mammogram. In the past, the doctor had simply said that the results of her mammogram were negative. This time, the doctor brought in her mammogram, which looked like an X ray. He pointed to a small white spot and said in a concerned voice, "I'm afraid that this tiny white dot may be a cancerous tumor." The doctor's words took her breath away. Finally, Maria asked in a terrified whisper, "Are you absolutely sure that spot is cancer?" The doctor paused for a minute, looked again at the mammogram, and said, "I can't be absolutely sure the spot is cancerous until we do a biopsy. All I can say is that there is a good possibility that it is." As Maria scheduled her biopsy, she would never forget seeing that white spot on the mammogram.

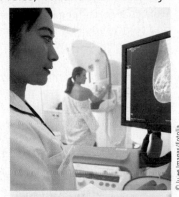

Why should two doctors read each mammogram?

Perceiving Things

What are the three questions?

At first glance, these three events—downloading an mp3 file with a subliminal message, being bitten by a dog, and seeing a spot on a mammogram—seem to have nothing in common. In fact, these events raise three basic questions about how we perceive things.

Maria's mp3 file with a subliminal message raises the first question: Are there things that we perceive but are not aware of, and can these things influence our behaviors?

Maria's mammogram raises the second question: How large or unusual must things be before our senses can detect them? This is a very important question, since the answer may have serious health consequences (Grady, 2008).

Finally, Gabrielle's painful experience with a dog raises the third question: How much are the things we perceive influenced or biased by our cultural, learning, emotional, and personal experiences (Goldstein, 2010)? These three questions are the key to understanding how we perceive our world.

What's Coming

We'll discuss what thresholds are, how sensations differ from perceptions, how sensations are combined to form perceptions, how objects can undergo great changes yet appear the same to us, how our senses are fooled by illusions, how cultural experiences change perceptions, whether there is good evidence for ESP (extrasensory perception), and whether the newest kind of perceiving, called virtual reality, can fool our senses into believing we're in a three-dimensional world.

Let's start with the first and most basic perceptual question: At what point do you become aware of seeing, hearing, smelling, tasting, or feeling some stimulus, object, or event? ●

© Juice Images/Fotolia

Becoming Aware of a Stimulus

Imagine suddenly becoming deaf or blind, unable to hear what people are saying or to see where you are going. Only then would

When do you know something is happening?

you realize that your senses provide a continuous stream of information about your world. Your senses tell you that something is out there, and your perceptions tell you what that something is. However, there are some sounds and objects you may not be aware of because the level of stimulation is too low and does not exceed the threshold of a particular sense.

Threshold is the point above which a stimulus is perceived and below which it is not perceived. The threshold determines when we first become aware of a stimulus.

Subliminal means a person is not consciously aware of a stimulus.

For example, Maria is not aware of, or does not hear, subliminal messages recorded on the mp3 audio file because these messages are below her absolute threshold for hearing. To understand how the absolute threshold is determined, imagine that Maria is presented with a series of auditory messages that slowly increase in intensity. Maria is asked to press a button when she first hears a message. You may think that there will be a certain level or absolute value of intensity (loudness) at which Maria will first report hearing a tone. The idea that there is an absolute threshold was proposed by Gustav Fechner (1860), an important historical figure in perceptual research. However, as you'll see, Fechner had difficulty identifying the absolute threshold as he defined it.

Absolute Threshold

At first, *Gustav Fechner* (FECK-ner) defined the absolute threshold as the smallest amount of stimulus energy (such as sound or light) that can be observed or experienced.

According to Fechner's definition, if Maria's hearing could always be measured under exactly the same conditions, her absolute threshold would always remain the same. Although Fechner tried various methods to identify absolute thresholds, he found that an individual's threshold was not absolute and, in fact, differed depending on the subject's alertness and the test situation. Because of this variability in measurement, researchers had to redefine absolute threshold.

Absolute threshold is the minimum amount of stimulus energy that a person can detect 50% of the time.

Psychologists have studied absolute thresholds for each of our five senses and the results demonstrate the sensitivity of our senses. Here are the absolute thresholds for human senses (Galanter, 1962):

Seeing—a candle flame seen at 30 miles away on a dark, clear night

Hearing—a ticking watch that is 20 feet away

Taste—one teaspoon of sugar dissolved in 2 gallons of water

Smell—one drop of perfume diffused into a six-room apartment

Touch—the wing of a fly falling on your cheek from a distance of 1 centimeter

The concept of an absolute threshold has very real consequences. Let's consider the case of breast cancer.

Doctors read 35 million mammograms (X rays of breasts) each year to look for white spots that stand out on a black background; these white spots indicate tumors (right photo) (Grady, 2008). However, some women have so much connective breast tissue, which also appears white, that tiny white tumors go undetected. These women are at an increased risk of having cancer, yet it is 17 times more likely to not be detected

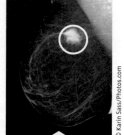

Possible cancerous breast tumor stands out as a white spot.

using mammograms (Boyd, 2007). This problem, combined with doctors' lack of expertise, results in mammograms missing up to 30% of tumors (Pisano et al., 2005).

Researchers are constantly looking for ways to lower the threshold for detecting cancerous tumors and thus save patients' lives (Shute, 2011). The accuracy of identifying cancerous tumors increases when mammograms are read independently by two doctors or when one doctor and a new computer program designed to detect tumors read them (BBC, 2008a; M. Healy, 2000). Also, digital mammograms, which allow for images to be enhanced or magnified on a computer screen, have been found to be better at detecting cancerous tumors in women who have a lot of connective tissue (Grady, 2008; Kincaid, 2007).

Subliminal Stimulus

Stimulation that is below the absolute threshold, meaning it is too weak or brief to reach our awareness, is referred to as a subliminal stimulus.

A **subliminal stimulus** has an amount of stimulus energy that is below a person's absolute threshold and consequently the person is not consciously aware of the stimulus.

The controversy over subliminal stimuli began in the 1950s, when an executive began inserting hidden messages, such as "Eat popcorn," on a movie theater screen to increase popcorn sales.

Since then, subliminal stimuli have been the center of controversy in areas such as music, religion, and marketing. More recently, researchers have found physiological support that subliminal images attract the brain's attention on a subconscious level (Bahrami et al., 2007).

We'll continue our discussion of whether subliminal messages can change behavior and cognitive processes in the Research Focus (p. 134). Next, we'll discuss how we know a stimulus has changed in intensity.

Becoming Aware of a Difference in Stimulus

Why is that music still too loud?

Suppose people are playing music too loud and you ask them to turn down the volume. Even after they turn it down, it may still seem just as loud as before. The explanation for this phenomenon can be found in the work of another historical figure in perception, E. H. Weber (VEY-ber).

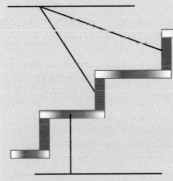

Just Noticeable Difference

Weber worked on the problem of how we judge whether a stimulus, such as loud music, has increased or decreased in intensity. This problem involves measuring the difference in thresholds between two stimuli, such as very loud music and not-quite-so-loud music. To solve this problem, Weber (1834) developed the concept of a just noticeable difference.

A **just noticeable difference (JND,** or the **difference threshold)** refers to the smallest increase or decrease in the intensity of a stimulus that a person is able to detect 50% of the time.

Smallest detectable increase or decrease in sound is a JND.

For example, to measure a just noticeable difference in weight, Weber asked people to compare stimuli of varying intensities and indicate when they could detect a difference between them. He discovered that if he presented two stimuli with very low intensities, such as a 2-ounce weight versus a 3-ounce weight, people could easily detect the difference between them. However, if he presented stimuli with high intensities, such as a 40-pound weight versus a 41-pound weight, people could no longer detect the difference. For higher-intensity stimuli, such as heavy weights, a much larger difference in intensity was required for the difference to be noticed (Kantowitz et al., 2009).

Every year, industry and business spend billions of dollars to make sure that consumers can detect just noticeable differences between this year's and last year's cars, shampoos, cereals, and fashions. For example, consumers spend millions of dollars each year on fabric softeners, which are added during washing and are claimed to make clothes feel softer. To test such claims, researchers asked people to feel towels washed with and without a fabric softener and rate the softness of the towels on a scale from 1 (hard) to 30 (very soft). The people gave an average softness rating of 5 to towels washed repeatedly without softener and an average rating of 18 to towels washed with softener. Researchers concluded that fabric softeners worked, since people could easily detect a just noticeable difference in softness (S. I. Ali & Begum, 1994). This is but one practical application of the just noticeable difference (JND) in industry.

Judging the softness of towels involves noting the JND.

Weber's Law

Weber's observations on what it takes to detect just noticeable differences were the basis for what became known as Weber's law.

Weber's law states that the increase in intensity of a stimulus needed to produce a just noticeable difference grows in proportion to the intensity of the initial stimulus.

We'll use Weber's law to explain how if someone is playing the stereo very loud, it must be turned down a great deal, usually more than the person prefers to turn it down, for you to detect a just noticeable decrease in volume.

Weber's law explains that, at lower intensities, small changes between two stimuli can be detected as just noticeable differences (JNDs); however, at higher intensities, only larger changes between two stimuli can be detected as JNDs.

Stimulus: Lower →→→ *Higher*

1 **JND.** The same height of each step illustrates your ability to detect "one sensory unit" of a *just noticeable difference* between the loudness of two sounds.

2 **Lower intensities.** The small width of this step indicates that, at lower intensities, you need only a *small difference* in order to detect a just noticeable difference between the loudness of two sounds. This statement follows from Weber's law, which says that only a small difference in intensity is required for you to detect a just noticeable difference when judging stimuli of lower intensity.

3 **Higher intensities.** The considerable width of this step indicates that, at higher sound intensities, you need a *larger difference* to detect a just noticeable difference between the loudness of two sounds. This statement follows from Weber's law, which says that a larger difference in intensity is required for you to detect a just noticeable difference when judging stimuli of higher intensity.

Besides explaining the problem with loud stereos, Weber's law has many practical applications, such as how to detect a difference in the softness of towels.

So far, we've focused on how you become aware of and detect stimuli and distinguish between their intensities. Next, we'll discuss one of the most interesting questions in perception: How do you change meaningless bits of sensations into meaningful and complete perceptions? ●

Basic Differences

Much of your success in being happy and successful depends on your ability to respond intelligently and adapt appropriately to changes in your environment (NAMHC, 1996). The first step in responding and adapting involves gathering millions of meaningless sensations and changing them into useful perceptions. Because your brain changes sensations into perceptions so quickly, automatically, and with very little awareness, you might assume that what you see (sense) is what you perceive. However, the process of changing sensations

How can I be successful and happy?

into perceptions is influenced by whether you are alert, sleepy, worried, emotional, motivated, or affected by the use of a legal or illegal drug. For example, drinking alcohol causes perceptions in social situations to be less rational and more uninhibited, causing people under its influence to act aggressively, make terrible decisions, create problems, or say really dumb things (Maisto et al., 2011). As you are about to discover, sensing and perceiving are as different as night and day.

For example, quickly glance at the black-and-white figure below on the left and then look away and describe what you saw.

Sensations

Initially, the left figure appears to be a bunch of meaningless lines, spaces, and blobs, which, for the sake of simplicity, we'll take the liberty of calling visual sensations. In real life, we rarely if ever experience sensations because, as we'll explain on the next page, they are immediately turned into perceptions.

A **sensation** is our first awareness of some outside stimulus. An outside stimulus activates sensory receptors, which in turn produce electrical signals that are transformed by the brain into meaningless bits of information.

Sensations are MEANINGLESS bits of information.

You can approximate how visual sensations may look by placing half of a ping-pong ball over your eye. As you look through this nearly opaque ping-pong ball, you'll see shadows, textures, and dark shapes but nothing meaningful; these are similar to sensations.

Another example that illustrates the difference between sensations and perceptions is the photo below. Your first impression consists of meaningless shapes, textures, and blotches of color, which we'll again take the liberty of calling visual sensations. However, you can turn these meaningless sensations into a meaningful image—a perception—by using the following clues. This photo is an ultrasound image of a fetus in the womb. The fetus is lying on his back with his rounded tummy on the left and his large head on the right. Above his head is the right arm and hand, and you can even count the five tiny fingers. You can also see that the fetus is sucking on his thumb. Once you know what to look for, you automatically change the random blotches of colors and shapes into the perception of a fetus.

Obviously, it would be impossible to respond, adapt, and survive if you had to rely only on sensations. You can now appreciate the importance of changing sensations into perceptions.

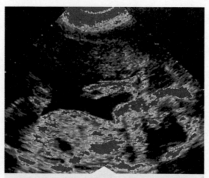

You can turn this sensation into a perception by reading the text (left).

Perceptions

As you look at the right stimulus, your brain is processing many thousands of visual sensations involving lines, curves, textures, shadows, and colors. Then, instantaneously, automatically, and without awareness, your brain combines these thousands of sensations into a perception—an orange tiger's face against a green background.

A **perception** is the experience we have after our brain assembles and combines hundreds of individual, meaningless sensations into a meaningful pattern or image. However, our perceptions are rarely exact replicas of the

Perceptions are MEANINGFUL patterns, images, or sounds.

original stimuli. Rather, our perceptions are usually changed, biased, colored, or distorted by our unique set of experiences. Thus, perceptions are our personal interpretations of the real world.

If you now look at the black-and-white drawing on the upper left, your brain will automatically combine the formerly meaningless shapes and blobs into a tiger's face. This is an approximate example of how meaningless sensations are automatically combined to form meaningful perceptions.

One important feature of perceptions is that they are rarely exact copies of the real world. For example, people who listen to the same song or music can react very differently (happy, relaxed, agitated, bored). To study how personal preferences for music can bias our perceptions, researchers assigned students who preferred listening to classical music over other types of music to groups that were instructed to sit and relax while listening to either 20 minutes of classical music or 20 minutes of rock music. Researchers used physiological measures to record anxiety levels both before and after the participants listened to music. Findings showed that only those people who listened to their favorite kind of music (classical music) had a decrease in anxiety levels (Salamon et al., 2003).

To show that no two individuals perceive the world in exactly the same way, we'll explain how your personal experiences change, bias, and even distort your perceptions.

Custom Medical Stock Photo

Changing Sensations into Perceptions

It is most unlikely that you have ever experienced a "pure" sensation because your brain automatically and instantaneously changes sensations into perceptions. Despite what you may think, perceptions do not exactly mirror events, people, situations, and objects in your environment. Rather, perceptions are interpretations, which means that your perceptions are changed or biased by your personal experiences, memories, emotions, and motivations. For example, at the beginning of this module we told you

How does a "nice" doggie become a "bad" doggie?

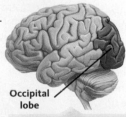

There are five steps in forming perceptions.

how 7-year-old Gabrielle's perception of a dog was changed from "nice" to "bad" by her personal experience of being bitten. The next time Gabrielle sees a dog, she won't see just a four-legged creature with ears, nose, and tail; she will see a "bad" four-legged creature. To understand how sensations become perceptions, we have divided the perceptual process into a series of discrete steps that in real life are much more complex and interactive.

1 Stimulus. Since normally we experience only perceptions, we are not aware of many preceding steps. The first step begins with some **stimulus,** which is any change of energy in the environment, such as light waves, sound waves, mechanical pressure, or chemicals. The stimulus activates sense receptors in the eyes, ears, skin, nose, or mouth. In Gabrielle's case, the stimuli are light waves reflecting off the body of a dog.

A stimulus (dog) activates receptors in the senses.

2 Transduction. After entering Gabrielle's eyes, light waves are focused on the retina, which contains photoreceptors that are sensitive to light. The light waves are absorbed by photoreceptors, which change physical energy into electrical signals in a process called **transduction.** The electrical signals are changed into impulses that travel to the brain. Sense organs do not produce sensations but simply transform energy into electrical signals.

Senses change stimulus into electrical signals.

3 Brain: primary areas. Impulses from sense organs first go to different *primary areas* of the brain. For example, impulses from the ear go to the temporal lobe, from touch to the parietal lobe, and from the eye to areas in the occipital lobe. When impulses reach primary areas in the occipital lobe, they are first changed into sensations. However, Gabrielle would not report seeing sensations.

Occipital lobe

Primary areas of brain change electrical signals into sensations.

4 Brain: association areas. Each sense sends its particular impulses to a different primary area of the brain where impulses are changed into sensations, which are meaningless bits of information, such as shapes, colors, and textures (top right). The "sensation" impulses are then sent to the appropriate *association areas* in the brain. The association areas change meaningless bits into meaningful images, called perceptions, such as a dog (bottom right).

In Gabrielle's case, impulses from her eyes would be changed into visual sensations by the primary visual area and into perceptions by the visual association areas. However, Gabrielle's perception of a dog would be changed, biased, and even distorted by many psychological, emotional, and cultural factors.

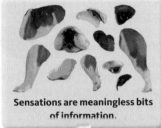

Sensations are meaningless bits of information.

Association areas change sensations into perceptions—dog.

5 Personalized perceptions. Each of us has a unique set of personal experiences, emotions, and memories that are automatically added to our perceptions by other areas of the brain. As a result, our perceptions are not a mirror but a changed, biased, or even distorted copy of the real world (Goldstein, 2010). For example, the visual areas of Gabrielle's brain automatically assemble many thousands of sensations into a meaningful pattern, which in this case is a dog. Now, however, Gabrielle doesn't see just an ordinary white and brown dog because other brain areas add her emotional experience of being bitten. Thus, Gabrielle perceives this white and brown, four-legged creature to be a "bad dog." For this same reason, two people can look at the same dog and have very different perceptions, such as cute dog, great dog, bad dog, smelly dog, or friendly dog. Thus, we have *personalized perceptions*, rather than true copies of objects, animals, people, and situations in the real world.

Perceptions do not mirror reality but rather include our biases, emotions, and memories to reflect reality.

As you'll see next, the process of assembling and organizing sensations into perceptions was of great interest to early psychologists. ●

Top-Down Versus Bottom-Up Processing

How are perceptions organized? In the preceding section, we discussed how sensations are turned into perceptions. Specifically, you learned that our brain's association areas transform meaningless bits of information into meaningful perceptions.

This section focuses on how perceptions are organized. Let's begin by using an example: I (H.K.) am looking at a picture of my dog, Cocoa. How does my brain know I'm seeing Cocoa?

Top-Down Processing

Because I've seen Cocoa countless times and have stored what she looks like in my memory, I use top-down processing to interpret this stimulus (right photo).

Top-down processing is when perception is guided by previous knowledge, experience, beliefs, or expectations to recognize the whole pattern.

It's "top" first because we begin with brain processes. We use our cognitive processes to apply context to the information we are sensing.

Top-down processing also helps us fill in missing gaps. For instance, in the photo of Cocoa, I can't see her tail. But, I know that she does have a tail, and therefore I will safely assume her tail is not missing.

Top-down processing cannot occur on its own; it relies on bottom-up processing, which we will discuss next.

Bottom-Up Processing

Try reading this sentence: Th- bo-s w-nt -o t-e p-rk -o p-ay -oc-er. Although you may have had to slow down your reading and pay more attention to the sentence, you probably were able to figure out that the sentence was "The boys went to the park to play soccer" without too much effort.

You were able to determine what the sentence stated because of your previous reading experiences. Also, you may have had expectations that we wouldn't have you read a very challenging or complex sentence. Thus, you may have been correctly thinking the sentence would be rather straightforward and simple. This is an example of top-down processing.

However, the task of reading the fragmented sentence demonstrates that top-down and bottom-up processing occur together.

Bottom-up processing is when perception begins with bits and pieces of information that, when combined, lead to the recognition of a whole pattern.

It's "bottom" first because we begin with the raw, sensory information. We use the information we take in and try to bring meaning to it.

Without being able to recognize the bits and pieces of information (e.g., curves, lines) about the stimuli, in this case letters, we would not be able to recognize the sentence (J. C. Johnston & McClelland, 1974).

Just as in the case of reading, top-down and bottom-up processing work together to help us accurately perceive countless aspects of the world around us. For example, let's consider the perceptual process that occurs as a child looks at a parrot (left photo); it involves both bottom-up and top-down processing. First, raw sensory information, which in this case is the image on the child's retina created by light being reflected off of the parrot, provides incoming information (bottom-up processing). Then, the knowledge the child already has about parrots influences his perception (top-down processing).

Perception helps us make sense of our sensations. Top-down and bottom-up processing is only one example of perceptual organization. We'll present various other ways our perceptions are organized, such as those proposed by Gestalt psychologists.

Gestalt Psychologists

In the early 1900s, psychologists engaged in a heated debate over how perceptions are formed. Some psychologists, called *structuralists,* strongly believed that we added together thousands of sensations to form a perception. Others, called Gestalt psychologists, believed just as strongly that sensations were not added but rather combined according to a set of innate rules to form a perception (M. A. Peterson et al., 2007). The Gestalt psychologists won the debate.

Gestalt psychologists believed that our brains follow a set of rules that specify how individual elements are to be organized into a meaningful pattern, or perception.

Gestalt psychologists said that perceptions result from our brain's ability to organize sensations according to a set of rules, much as our brain follows a set of rules for organizing words into meaningful sentences (Donderi, 2006; Quinn et al., 2008).

So how would Gestalt psychologists explain your perception of the scene on the right? They would say that your perception was not formed by simply adding bits of tile, steel, and foliage into a whole image. Rather, your brain automatically used a set of rules to combine these elements to form a unified whole. To emphasize their point, Gestalt psychologists came up with a catchy phrase, "The whole is more than the sum of its parts," to mean that perceptions are not merely combined sensations. The Gestalt psychologists went one step further; they came up with a list of organizational rules, which we discuss next.

According to Gestalt psychologists, your brain has rules for forming perceptions.

Organizational Rules

It is very hard to believe that the scene on the preceding page (repeated here on the right) was actually painted on a flat wall.

How many rules are there?

One reason you perceive this scene as complex and three-dimensional is that the painter followed many of the Gestalt rules of organization (Han & Humphreys, 1999).

Rules of organization, which were identified by Gestalt psychologists, specify how our brains combine and organize individual pieces or elements into a meaningful perception.

Painting by Richard Haas, photo © Bill Horsman

As you look at the scene, your brain automatically organizes many hundreds of visual stimuli, including colors, textures, shadows, bricks, steel, glass, leaves, and branches, according to one or more of the six perceptual rules of organization described below. We'll use a relatively simple figure to illustrate each rule.

Figure-Ground

One of the most basic rules in organizing perceptions is picking out the object from its background. As you look at the figure on the left, you will automatically see a white object standing out against a red background, which illustrates the figure-ground rule.

The **figure-ground rule** states that, in organizing stimuli, we tend to automatically distinguish between a figure and a ground: The figure, with more detail, stands out against the background, which has less detail.

There is some evidence that our ability to separate figure from ground is an innate response. For example, individuals who were blind from an early age and had their sight restored as adults were able to distinguish between figure and ground with little or no training (Senden, 1960). The figure-ground rule is one of the first rules that our brain uses to organize stimuli into a perception (Vecera, 2002). This particular image is interesting because, as you continue to stare at it, the figure and ground will suddenly reverse and you'll see profiles of two faces. However, in the real world, the images and objects we usually perceive are not reversible because they have more distinct shapes (Humphreys & Muller, 2000).

Similarity

As you look at this figure filled with light and dark blue dots, you see a dark blue numeral 2.

The **similarity rule** states that, in organizing stimuli, we group together elements that appear similar.

The similarity rule causes us to group the dark blue dots together and prevents us from seeing the figure as a random arrangement of light and dark blue dots.

Closure

Although the lines are incomplete, you can easily perceive this drawing as a cat or dog.

The **closure rule** states that, in organizing stimuli, we tend to fill in any missing parts of a figure and see the figure as complete.

For example, the closure rule explains why you can fill in letters missing on a sign or pieces missing in a jigsaw puzzle.

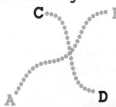

Proximity

Notice that although there are exactly eight circles in each horizontal line, you perceive each line as formed by a different number of groups of circles.

The **proximity rule** states that, in organizing stimuli, we group together objects that are physically close to one another.

You automatically group circles that are close together and thus perceive the first line as composed of three groups (Kubovy & Wagemans, 1995).

Simplicity

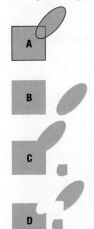

Look at figure A and then decide if it is made up of the pieces shown in figure B, C, or D. Almost everyone sees figure A as made up of the pieces in figure B—an oval with an overlapping square.

The **simplicity rule** states that stimuli are organized in the simplest way possible.

For example, almost no one sees figure A as having been formed from the complicated pieces shown in figure C or figure D. This rule says that we tend to perceive complex figures as divided into several simpler figures (Shimaya, 1997).

Continuity

As you scan this figure, keep track of the path that your eyes follow. Most people's eyes will move from left to right in a continuous line, following the path from A to B or from C to D.

The **continuity rule** states that, in organizing stimuli, we tend to favor smooth or continuous paths when interpreting a series of points or lines.

For example, the rule of continuity predicts that you do not see a line that begins at A and then turns abruptly to C or to D.

Conclusion. These figures demonstrate the Gestalt rules of organizing stimuli into perceptions. Young children slowly learn these perceptual rules and begin to use them as early as infancy (Quinn et al., 2008). As adults we use these rules to organize thousands of stimuli into perceptions, especially stimuli in print and advertisements. For doctors who read mammograms and other X rays, Gestalt rules such as figure-ground, similarity, and proximity are essential in their daily work (Koontz & Gunderman, 2008).

Next, we examine the question: How can objects change yet appear to remain the same? ●

D | Perceptual Constancy

Size, Shape, Brightness, & Color Constancy

Why don't speeding cars shrink?

The study of perception is full of interesting puzzles, such as how cars, people, and pets can change their shapes as they move about yet we perceive them as remaining the same size and shape. For example, a car doesn't grow smaller as it speeds away, even though its shape on your retina grows smaller and smaller. A door doesn't become a trapezoid as you walk through it, even though that's what happens to its shape on your retina. These are examples

of how perceptions remain constant, a phenomenon called perceptual constancy.

Perceptual constancy refers to our tendency to perceive sizes, shapes, brightness, and colors as remaining the same even though their physical characteristics are constantly changing.

We'll discuss four kinds of perceptual constancy—size, shape, brightness, and color.

Size Constancy

Imagine a world in which you perceived that every car, person, or animal became smaller as it moved away. Fortunately, we are spared from coping with so much stimulus change by perceptual constancy, one type of which is size constancy.

Size constancy refers to our tendency to perceive objects as remaining the same size even when their images on the retina are continually growing or shrinking.

As a car drives away, it projects a smaller and smaller image on your retina (left figure). Although the retinal image grows smaller, you do not perceive the car as shrinking because of size constancy. A similar process happens as a car drives toward you.

As the same car drives closer, notice in the figure below how it projects a larger image on your retina. However, because of size constancy, you do not perceive the car as becoming larger.

Size constancy is something you have learned from experience with moving objects. You have learned that objects do not increase or decrease in size as they move about. For example, an individual who was blind since birth and had his vision restored as an adult looked out a fourth-story window and reported seeing tiny creatures moving on the sidewalk. Because he had not learned size constancy, he did not know the tiny creatures were full-size people (R. L. Gregory, 1974).

We also perceive shapes as remaining the same.

Shape Constancy

Each time you move a book, its image on your retina changes from a rectangle to a trapezoid. But you see the book's shape as remaining the same because of shape constancy.

Shape constancy refers to your tendency to perceive an object as retaining its same shape even though when you view it from different angles, its shape is continually changing its image on the retina.

The figure below shows that when you look down at a rectangular book, it projects a rectangular shape on your retina.

However, if you move the book farther away, it projects trapezoidal shapes on your retina (figure below), but you still perceive the book as rectangular because of shape constancy.

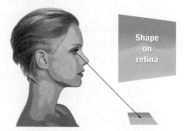

Besides size and shape constancy, there is also brightness and color constancy.

Brightness and Color Constancy

If you look into your dimly lit closet, all the brightly colored clothes will appear dull and grayish. However, because of brightness and color constancy, you still perceive brightness and colors and have no trouble selecting a red shirt.

Brightness constancy refers to the tendency to perceive brightness as remaining the same in changing illumination.

Color constancy refers to the tendency to perceive colors as remaining stable despite differences in lighting.

For example, if you looked at this boy's shirt in bright sunlight, it would be a bright yellow.

If you looked at his same yellow shirt in dim light, you would still perceive the color as a shade of yellow, although it is duller. Because of color constancy, colors seem about the same even when lighting conditions change.

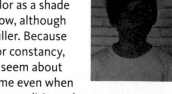

However, if the light is very dim, objects will appear mostly gray because you lose color vision in very dim light.

Perceptual constancy is important because it transforms a potentially ever-changing, chaotic world into one with stability and comforting sameness.

Our next perceptual puzzle is how our eyes can see only two-dimensional images but our brain can transform them into a three-dimensional world. ●

E Depth Perception

Binocular (Two Eyes) Depth Cues

Normally, movies are shown in only two dimensions: height and width. But if you have ever seen a movie in 3-D (using special glasses to see three dimensions: height, width, and depth), you know the thrill of watching objects or animals leap off the screen so realistically that you duck or turn your head. You may not have realized that your eyes automatically give you a free, no-glasses, 3-D view of the world. And the amazing part of seeing in 3-D is that everything projected on the retina is in only two dimensions, height and width, which means that your brain combines a number of different cues to add a third dimension—depth (J. M. Harris & Dean, 2003).

How can you see in three dimensions?

Depth perception is the ability of your eye and brain to add a third dimension, depth, to all visual perceptions, even though images projected on the retina are in only two dimensions, height and width.

© Laurent davoust/Photos.com

Seeing in 3-D means seeing length, width, and depth.

It is impossible for most sighted people to imagine a world without depth, since they rely on depth perception to move and locate objects in space. The cues for depth perception are divided into two major classes: binocular and monocular.

Binocular depth cues depend on the movement of both eyes (*bi* means "two"; *ocular* means "eye").

We'll start with two binocular cues: convergence and retinal disparity.

Convergence

When you have an eye exam, the doctor usually asks you to follow the end of her finger as she holds it a few feet away and then slowly moves it closer until it touches your nose. This is a test for convergence.

Convergence is a binocular cue for depth perception based on signals sent from muscles that turn the eyes. To focus on near or approaching objects, these muscles turn the eyes inward, toward the nose. The brain uses the signals sent by these muscles to determine the distance of the object.

During convergence the eyes turn inward to see objects up close.

© RubberBall/SuperStock

The woman in the photo at the left is demonstrating the ultimate in convergence as she looks at the bubble. You can experience convergence by holding a finger in front of your nose and slowly bringing it closer to your nose. Your finger appears to move closer to your nose because the muscles that are turning the eyes inward produce signals corresponding to convergence. The more your eyes turn inward or converge, the nearer the object appears in space. The woman in the photo sees the bubble because of convergent clues from her turned-in eyes.

The second binocular cue comes from having an eye on each side of your face.

Retinal Disparity

One reason it's an advantage to have an eye on each side of your face is that each eye has a slightly different view of the world, which provides another binocular cue for depth perception called retinal disparity.

Retinal disparity is a binocular depth cue that depends on the distance between the eyes. Because of their different positions, each eye receives a slightly different image. The difference between the right and left eyes' images is the retinal disparity. The brain interprets a large retinal disparity to mean a close object and a small retinal disparity to mean a distant object.

The figure at the left shows how retinal disparity occurs: The difference between the image seen by the left eye (1) and the one seen by the right eye (2) results in retinal disparity (3).

1. **Left eye sees a slightly different image of the fly.**

3. **Brain combines the two slightly different images from left and right eyes and gives us a perception of depth.**

2. **Right eye sees a slightly different image of the fly.**

Another example of retinal disparity occurs when viewers wear special glasses to watch a 3-D movie, which has width, height, and depth. Standard 3-D glasses use a red and a green lens, which is a technique to allow the right and left eyes to perceive slightly different views of the same scene. As a result, the brain receives two slightly different images. As the brain automatically combines the slightly different images, we get the feeling of depth—for example, seeing a mad dog jump out of the movie screen into the audience (followed by much screaming).

Individuals who have only one eye still have depth perception because there are a number of one-eyed, or monocular, cues for depth perception, which we'll explain next.

Monocular (One Eye) Depth Cues

Could a Cyclops land an airplane?

A mythical creature called the Cyclops had only one eye in the middle of his forehead. Although a Cyclops would lack depth perception cues associated with retinal disparity, he would have depth perception cues associated with having one eye, or being monocular (*mon* means "one"). This means that a Cyclops or an

I could land an airplane with one eye!

individual with only one good eye could land an airplane because of monocular depth cues.

Monocular depth cues are produced by signals from a single eye. Monocular cues most commonly arise from the way objects are arranged in the environment.

We'll show you seven of the most common monocular cues for perceiving depth.

Linear perspective makes you see the road as going on forever.

© Iakov Kalinin/Photos.com

1 Linear Perspective

As you look down a long stretch of road, the parallel lines formed by the sides of the road appear to come together, or converge, at a distant point. This convergence is a monocular cue for distance and is called linear perspective.

Linear perspective is a monocular depth cue that results as parallel lines come together, or converge, in the distance.

Relative size makes you see the larger towers as closer and the smaller towers as farther away.

© walter matheson/Photos.com

2 Relative Size

You expect the electric towers in the photo above to be the same size. However, since the electric towers in the front appear larger, you perceive them as closer, while the electric towers in the back appear smaller and thus farther away. The relative size of objects is a monocular cue for distance.

Relative size is a monocular cue for depth that results when we expect two objects to be the same size and they are not. In that case, the larger of the two objects will appear closer and the smaller will appear farther away.

Interposition makes you see the fish in front as closer and those in back as farther away.

© Digital Stock Corporation

3 Interposition

As you look at the school of fish in the photo above, you can easily perceive which fish are in front and which are in back, even though all the fish are about the same size. You can identify and point out which fish are closest to you and which are farthest away by using the monocular depth cue of overlap, which is called interposition.

Interposition is a monocular cue for depth perception that comes into play when objects overlap. The overlapping object appears closer, and the object that is overlapped appears farther away.

Light makes the outlines of the footprints appear closer, while shadow makes the imprints seem farther away.

4 Light and Shadow

Notice how the brightly lit edges of the footprints appear closer, while the shadowy imprint in the sand appears to recede. Also, the sunny side of the sand dune seems closer, while the back side in shadows appears farther away. The monocular depth cues shown here involve the interplay of light and shadows.

Light and shadow make up monocular cues for depth perception: Brightly lit objects appear closer, while objects in shadows appear farther away.

Texture gradient makes you see the sharply detailed plants as being closer.

5 Texture Gradient

You can't help but notice how the detailed plants and wide gaps between them seem closer, while the less detailed plants and narrower gaps appear farther away. These sharp changes in surface details are monocular depth cues created by texture gradients.

Texture gradient is a monocular depth cue in which areas with sharp, detailed texture are interpreted as being closer and those with less sharpness and poorer detail are perceived as more distant.

6 Atmospheric Perspective

One of the depth cues you may have overlooked is created by changes in the atmosphere. For example, the trees that are clearly visible appear much closer than the trees in fog-shrouded hills and landscape in the background. These monocular depth cues are created by changes in the atmosphere.

Atmospheric perspective is a monocular depth cue that is created by the presence of dust, smog, clouds, or water vapor. We perceive clearer objects as being nearer, and we perceive hazy or cloudy objects as being farther away.

Atmospheric perspective makes clear objects seem nearer and hazy objects appear farther away.

7 Motion Parallax

In this photo, you can easily tell which runners seem closer to you and which appear farther away. That's because you perceive fast-moving or blurry objects (runners on the right) as being closer to you and slower-moving or clearer objects (runners on the left) as being farther away. These monocular depth cues come from the way you perceive motion.

Motion parallax makes blurry objects appear closer and clear objects appear farther away.

Motion parallax is a monocular depth cue based on the speed of moving objects. We perceive objects that appear to be moving at high speed as closer to us than those moving more slowly or appearing stationary.

Conclusion. We have just discussed seven monocular cues involved in perceiving depth and distance accurately. Because they are monocular cues—needing only one eye—it means that people with only one eye have depth perception good enough to land a plane, drive a car, or play various sports such as baseball and tennis. If you wish to try some of these monocular cues, just hold your hand over one eye and see if you can avoid objects as you walk around a room.

Already in the module we've discussed various aspects of perception. Next, we'll learn how cultural values and experiences can unknowingly change what we perceive. ●

What Do Cultural Influences Do?

If you visit ethnic sections of large U.S. cities, such as Chinatown or Little Italy, or visit foreign countries, you become aware of cultural differences and influences. For example, this photo shows two Indian women selecting a sari (a traditional garment) at a local shop, which symbolizes the different cultural influences of India compared to Western countries.

Cultural influences are persuasive pressures that encourage members of a particular society or ethnic group to conform to shared behaviors, values, and beliefs.

What if you were raised in a different culture?

© Yamini Chao/Thinkstock

No one doubts that cultural influences affect the way people eat, dress, talk, and socialize. But you are less likely to notice how cultural influences also affect how you perceive things in your own environment.

For example, cultural anthropologists, who study behaviors in natural settings in other cultures, have reported intriguing examples of how cultural experiences influence perceptual processes. We'll begin with a remarkable finding about the role of cultural influences in how people recognize faces.

Perception of Faces

It is generally believed that basic visual processes, such as recognizing faces, are common to all people, regardless of their culture. People all around the world are able to quickly recognize whether a face is familiar or not, but new research shows that people's culture influences the process they use to recognize faces.

Researchers recorded eye movements of Western Caucasians (English, French, German) and East Asians (Chinese, Japanese) while they looked at Western Caucasian and East Asian faces. The results showed that the eye movements of Western Caucasians followed a triangular pattern, focusing on the eyes and mouth (see red areas in right photos), whereas East Asians

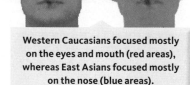

Western Caucasians focused mostly on the eyes and mouth (red areas), whereas East Asians focused mostly on the nose (blue areas).

Courtesy of Roberto Caldara

looked at only the central region of faces, focusing mostly on the nose (see blue areas in left photos). The results were the same whether the faces they looked at were of Western Caucasian or East Asian males (Blais et al., 2008).

One possible explanation for the cultural differences in how people perceive faces has to do with the value placed on eye contact. Eye contact is important in Western culture but inappropriate and even improper in many Asian cultures. It is possible that Asians are taught to recognize faces without looking into others' eyes (Blais et al., 2008).

How we describe images is another example of how culture influences what we perceive.

Perception of Images

Please look at the photo below for a few seconds and then close your eyes and describe what you saw. Richard Nisbett (2000) and colleagues found that what you see or think about depends, to a large extent, on your culture.

For example, after looking at the underwater scene, Americans tended to begin their descriptions by focusing on the largest fish and making statements like "There was what looked like a trout swimming to the left." Americans are more likely to zero in on the biggest fish, the brightest object, the fish moving the fastest.

Compared to Americans, Japanese subjects were much more likely to begin by setting the scene, saying, for example, "The bottom was rocky." On average, Japanese subjects made 70% more statements about how the background looked than Americans did and twice as many statements about the relationships between the fish and the backgrounds. For instance, Japanese subjects were more likely to say, "The big fish swam past the gray seaweed."

Generally, Americans analyze objects separately, which is called analytical thinking—seeing a forest and focusing more on separate trees. In comparison, Easterners tend to think more about the relationship between objects and backgrounds, which

Look at the photo briefly and then close your eyes and describe it.

By courtesy of Takahiko Masuda and Dr. Richard Nisbett, University of Michigan

is called holistic thinking—seeing a forest and thinking about how trees combine to make up a forest (Chua et al., 2005).

These differences in thinking and perceiving (analytical versus holistic) have been thought to primarily come from differences in culture, including social and religious practices, languages, and even geography (Nisbett, 2007; Nisbett & Miyamoto, 2005). Research has even shown that an individual's cultural background influences brain activity during simple tasks. For instance, one study involved two tasks assigned to East Asians and Americans. In one task, people estimated the length of a line—an easier task for Americans. In another, they estimated the line's length relative to the size of a square—an easier task for East Asians. Even though no difference in performance was found between the two groups, the level of brain activity differed, suggesting varying amounts of effort. Brain activity was greater for the tasks each group found to be more difficult (Hedden et al., 2008).

Thus, cultural differences in people's perceptions are based not only on differences in thinking and perceiving, but also on actual differences found in the brain.

Cultures also influence how we see cartoons.

Perception of Motion

For just a moment, look at the picture of the dog (below) and notice what its tail is doing. Then look at the female figure (right)

and describe what the figure is doing. Most people in Western cultures immediately perceive what is happening: the dog is wagging its tail, and the figure is spinning. Because of our Western cultural experience with pictures, we have learned to recognize that certain kinds of repeated images (the dog's tail) and certain lines and circles (the dancing figure) indicate movement. We have learned and become so accustomed to seeing these kinds of pictures indicate motion that the tail and the dancer really do seem to be in motion.

What is the dog's tail doing?

However, people from non-Western cultures, who have no experience with these pictures, do not perceive the dog's tail or the figure as moving. Non-Westerners see only an unusual dog that has three tails and a strange figure that is surrounded by circles; they do not perceive any indication of movement in these drawings (S. Friedman & Stevenson, 1980). This is a perfect example of how Western cultural influences shape our perceptions, often without our realizing.

If part of your cultural experience involves seeing three-dimensional objects in books, you won't be able to draw the next figure.

What is this dancer doing?

Perception of Three Dimensions

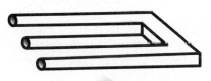

Can you draw this impossible figure?

Look carefully at the figure above. You will find that if you look at the right end of this tuning fork, it appears to have two prongs. But if you look at the left end, it appears to have three prongs. You're looking at a figure that most of us cannot draw because it seems impossible.

An **impossible figure** is a perceptual experience in which a drawing seems to defy basic geometric laws.

As you look at the figure, it changes almost magically back and forth from a two-pronged to a three-pronged tuning fork. The middle fork is unreal because it seems to come out of nowhere.

When people from industrialized nations try to draw this figure from memory, they almost surely fail. What is interesting is that Africans who have no formal education perceive only a two-dimensional pattern of flat lines, which they find easy to draw from memory. In contrast, people with formal education, who have spent years looking at three-dimensional representations in books, perceive this object as having three dimensions, a pattern that is almost impossible to draw (Coren & Ward, 1993).

Perception of Beauty

Do you think this woman is attractive?

In the past, when Burmese girls were about 5 years old, a brass coil one-third-inch wide was placed around their necks. As they grew older, girls added more brass coils until they had from 19 to 25 wrapped around their necks, sometimes weighing over 10 pounds. The appearance of long necks, caused by the brass coils, was perceived as being very attractive by Burmese people, who live in Southeast Asia. This custom eventually declined as neck coils were no longer considered beautiful, just cruel and uncomfortable. Recently, however, the custom has been revived because now tourists come and pay about $6 to see and take photos of women with brass neck coils (Moe & Son, 2005).

This example illustrates how cultural values influence our perceptions of personal beauty.

Perceptual Sets

From our previous cultural experiences with images and objects, we develop certain expectations about how things should be; these expectations are called perceptual sets.

Perceptual sets are learned expectations that are based on our personal, social, or cultural experiences. These expectations automatically add information, meaning, or feelings to our perceptions and thus change or bias our perceptions.

For example, as you look at this bodybuilder, you automatically add personal feelings, such as like/dislike and approve/

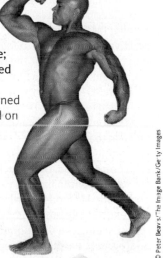

Do you think this muscular body is beautiful?

disapprove, as well as impressions of physical characteristics: height, about 6 feet, and weight, about 225 pounds. Because of your perceptual set for bodybuilders, you expect them to be large, and so you will be surprised to learn that this bodybuilder is only 5 feet 2 inches tall and weighs 182 pounds.

One function of perceptual sets is to automatically fill in information or add feelings that can greatly modify our perceptions. The discussion of the bodybuilder is an example of top-down processing, a type of perceptual organization we discussed earlier. Remember, **top-down processing** is when perception is guided by previous knowledge, experience, beliefs, or expectations to recognize the whole pattern.

These examples show that we rarely perceive the world exactly as it is. Rather, our perceptions can be changed, biased, or distorted by experiences, such as cultural influences and perceptual sets.

Next, we'll discuss the possibility of perception occurring without our conscious awareness. ●

Can Perception Occur without Conscious Awareness?

Why did people buy more popcorn? Sometimes research questions come from unusual places—in this case, a movie theater. In the late 1950s, moviegoers were reported to have bought 50% more popcorn and 18% more Coca-Cola when the words "Eat popcorn" and "Drink Coca-Cola" were projected subliminally (1/3,000 of a second) during the regular movie (J. V. McConnell et al., 1958). To this day many advertisers continue to claim that subliminal messages can change specific behaviors.

In this section, we will examine whether subliminal messages can change specific behavior. But, before we do, let's take a step back and consider how much perception, if any, can take place below our conscious awareness.

Perception and the Unconscious Mind

Earlier in this module, we learned about the concept of a *subliminal stimulus,* a stimulus that has an intensity below a person's absolute threshold, which means the person does not have conscious awareness of its occurrence. Now we're going to present a novel research study that aimed to determine whether the unconscious mind could integrate information in a visual image in a coherent and complete manner (Mudrik et al., 2011). If the research findings are positive, it means that at least some types of visual perception can occur without the need for conscious awareness. Let's begin by taking a look at the research design.

Method. Participants were presented with a series of rapidly changing random patterns in one eye, while a photograph of a person engaging in a specific task was very gradually faded in to the other eye. There were two categories of photos: realistic scenes and unnatural scenes. In the beginning of each presentation, the participant saw only the random patterns as the photo had not yet become visible. Over time the photo faded in more, allowing the participant to see it.

Results. The amount of time it took participants to report seeing the photograph depended on the type of photograph. Participants reported seeing the unnatural scenes in less time than the realistic scenes. For example, participants reported seeing the photo of a woman putting a chessboard in the oven (below left) sooner than the realistic photo of her baking cookies (below right).

The unconscious mind knows if there is something unnatural in visual scenes.

The results suggest that the unconscious mind detected something wrong with the unnatural photos. More specifically, it means the analysis of whether an object matches its context or situation may occur without conscious awareness. The findings imply that visual perception can take place on an unconscious level.

Next, we'll explore whether unconscious perception can influence specific behaviors.

Changing Specific Behaviors

At the beginning of this module, we told you about Maria, who, like millions of other Americans, downloaded an mp3 audio file because it claimed to contain subliminal persuasion that would effortlessly change her behavior.

To answer the research question, Can subliminal messages change specific behaviors?, researchers conducted a well-designed experiment that used a double-blind procedure.

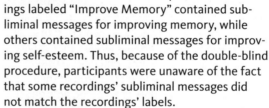

Labels did not match subliminal messages.

Method. For several weeks, participants listened to two different recordings titled either "Improve Self-Esteem" or "Improve Memory." Then they rated any improvement in these behaviors.

Double-blind procedure. Researchers had to control for any possible placebo effects, such as participants showing improvement because they believed they were hearing powerful subliminal messages. Therefore, participants were not told which subliminal messages the recordings contained.

For example, some recordings labeled "Improve Memory" contained subliminal messages for improving memory, while others contained subliminal messages for improving self-esteem. Thus, because of the double-blind procedure, participants were unaware of the fact that some recordings' subliminal messages did not match the recordings' labels.

But, subjects believed what the labels said.

Results. About 50% of participants reported improvements in either self-esteem or memory. However, participants reported improvements in behavior based on what the *recordings' labels promised* rather than on what the subliminal messages were. For example, a person who listened to a recording labeled "Improve Self-Esteem" reported improvements in self-esteem even though the recording contained subliminal messages for improving memory. These results suggest a self-fulfilling prophecy at work.

Self-fulfilling prophecies involve having strong beliefs about changing some behavior and then acting, unknowingly, to change that behavior.

Researchers concluded that subliminal messages in self-help recordings did not affect the behavior they were designed to change. Instead, any changes in behavior resulted from listeners' beliefs that the recordings would be effective (Epley et al., 1999). Most research, in fact, suggests that subliminal messages cannot change our behaviors in any significant way (Dijksterhuis et al., 2007; Greenwald et al., 2002).

After the Concept Review, we'll turn to occasions where our perceptual system does strange things, such as seeing still images move and no longer recognizing familiar faces. ●

1. This figure illustrates the concept of the _____, which is defined as the intensity level of a stimulus such that a person can detect 50% of the time.

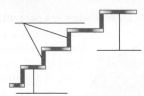

2. The smallest increase or decrease in the intensity of a stimulus that a person can detect 50% of the time is called a **(a)** _____. The increase in intensity of a stimulus needed to produce a just noticeable difference grows in proportion to the intensity of the initial stimulus; this is called **(b)** _____ law.

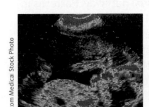

3. Our first awareness of sensory information, in the form of meaningless bits of information, is called a **(a)** _____. When many bits of sensory information have been assembled into a meaningful image, it is called a **(b)** _____, which can be biased or distorted by our unique set of experiences.

4. Early psychologists discovered a set of rules that our brains use to automatically group or arrange stimuli into perceptual experiences. These early researchers, who were called _____ psychologists, disagreed with other early psychologists, who were called structuralists.

5. You automatically separate an image into a more dominant, detailed figure and a less detailed background according to the _____ rule.

6. You fill in missing parts to form a complete image as a result of the _____ rule.

7. You see this image as formed by an oval and an overlying square because of the _____ rule.

8. You divide each line of this figure into separate groups of objects according to the _____ rule.

9. In this figure, you see a blue numeral 2 instead of light and dark blue circles because of the _____ rule.

10. In this figure, you see a continuous line from A to B, rather than a line from A to C, following the _____ rule.

11. Although the physical qualities of stimuli may change, you may perceive them as remaining the same because of **(a)** _____. For example, as a car drives away from you, its image on your retina becomes smaller but you know that the car does not shrink in size because of **(b)** _____ constancy. When you close a door, its shape on your retina changes from a rectangle to a trapezoid, but you perceive the door as remaining the same because of **(c)** _____ constancy. If you had a bright red car, it would appear red in bright light and still appear to be red in dimmer light because of **(d)** _____ constancy.

12. Cues for depth perception that depend on both eyes are called **(a)** _____ cues. Cues for depth perception that depend on a single eye are called **(b)** _____ cues. The binocular cue that occurs when your eyes move inward to track a fly landing on your nose is called **(c)** _____. The binocular cue that occurs when each eye receives a slightly different image is called **(d)** _____.

⭐13. Monocular cues for depth perception include: cues from overlapping objects, called **(a)** _____; cues from two parallel lines converging, called **(b)** _____; cues from larger and smaller images, called **(c)** _____; cues from the presence of dust and smog, called **(d)** _____; and cues from nearer and farther objects moving at different speeds, called **(e)** _____.

14. Persuasive pressures that encourage members of a particular society or ethnic group to conform to shared behaviors, values, and beliefs are called _____.

15. When perception is guided by previous knowledge, experience, beliefs, or expectations to recognize the whole pattern, it is called _____.

Answers: *1. absolute threshold; 2. (a) just noticeable difference, (b) Weber's; 3. (a) sensation, (b) perception; 4. Gestalt; 5. figure-ground; 6. closure; 7. simplicity; 8. proximity; 9. similarity; 10. continuity; 11. (a) perceptual constancy, (b) size, (c) shape, (d) color; 12. (a) binocular, (b) monocular, (c) convergence, (d) retinal disparity; 13. (a) interposition, (b) linear perspective, (c) relative size, (d) atmospheric perspective, (e) motion parallax; 14. cultural influences; 15. top-down processing*

Custom Medica Stock Photo

Painting by Richard Haas, photo © Bill Horsma

© Yamini Chao/Thinkstock

© Khoo Eng Yow/Photos.com

Illusions

What is an illusion?

There are two reasons that much of the time your perceptions of cars, people, food, trees, animals, furniture, and professors are reasonably accurate reflections but, because of emotional, motivational, and cultural influences, never exact copies of reality.

First, we inherit similar sensory systems whose information is processed and interpreted by similar areas of the brain (Franz et al., 2000). However, damage to sensory areas of the brain can result in very distorted perceptions, such as the neglect syndrome (see p. 79), in which people do not perceive one side of their body or one side of their environment. The second reason our perceptions are reasonably accurate is that we learn from common experience about the sizes, shapes, and colors of objects. But we've already discussed how perceptions can be biased or distorted by previous emotional and learning experiences, such as perceiving dogs differently after being bitten by one. Now we come to another way that perceptions can be distorted: by changing the actual perceptual cues so you perceive something unlikely, which is called an illusion.

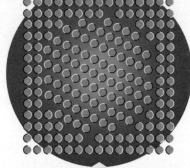

Eyes see circles moving in this illustration, even when movement doesn't really exist!

An **illusion** is a perceptual experience in which you perceive an image as being so strangely distorted that, in reality, it cannot and does not exist. An illusion is created by manipulating the perceptual cues so that your brain can no longer correctly interpret space, size, and depth cues.

For example, if you look at the illustration to the left, you'll notice the orange circles are moving right before your eyes! You have to admit this is a fun and impressive illusion. But how can the circles appear to be moving when it's actually a still illustration? In this case, we do not know for sure. The illustration somehow activates motion-detecting neurons in the visual pathway. Patterns in illustrations like this one fool the visual system into seeing motion when it doesn't really exist (Ramachandran & Rogers-Ramachandran, 2007). The motor perception area of the brain actually shows heightened activity as people move their eyes while looking at these types of illusions (Kuriki et al., 2008). (If you cannot see the circles move, please don't worry; some people with otherwise normal vision cannot see movement in this illustration.)

One of the oldest illusions that you have often experienced is the moon illusion, which also has proven very difficult to explain (H. E. Ross & Plug, 2002).

Moon Illusion

Moon appears to be huge when it's near the horizon.

© Jupiterimages/Photos.com

Moon appears 50% smaller when it's high in the sky.

© Jupiterimages/Photos.com

The moon illusion has intrigued people for centuries because it is so impressive. The left photo shows that when a full moon is near the horizon, it appears (or gives the illusion of being) as much as 50% larger than when it is high in the sky (right photo). Here's the interesting part: You perceive this 50% increase in size even though the size of both moons on your retinas is exactly the same.

For over 50 years, researchers have proposed different theories for the moon illusion. Currently, no single theory can explain the moon illusion completely and it is believed that several factors contribute to it. The most important factor has to do with how the view of the landscape surrounding the moon influences our depth perception (H. E. Ross & Plug, 2002).

When we view the moon on the horizon, we see it in relation to the landscape (trees, mountains, buildings), which consists of depth information. In contrast, because we view the elevated moon through empty space, there are no cues to indicate distance. Thus, our brains perceive the moon on the horizon to be farther away than the elevated moon. Consequently, since the size of both moons on our retinas is exactly the same and the moon on the horizon is perceived as being farther away, our brain compensates to correct this inconsistency by inflating our perception of the size of the moon on the horizon. Consistent with this theory, researchers found that people estimated the horizon moon to be much farther away and interpreted its size as being larger. Likewise, people estimated the elevated moon to be closer and perceived it as being smaller (L. Kaufman, 2000).

Besides naturally occurring illusions, there are others that humans have created. One of the most interesting illusions comes from looking inside the Ames room.

Unless otherwise noted, all images are © Cengage Learning

Ames Room

Boy appears smaller than girl even though they are the same height.

In the Ames room (left photo), you perceive the girl on the right to be twice as tall as the boy on the left. In fact, the boy and girl are about the same height. The girl appears larger because of the design of the Ames room.

The **Ames room,** named after its designer, shows that our perception of size can be distorted by changing depth cues.

The reason the girl appears to be twice as tall as the boy is that the room has a peculiar shape and you are looking in from a fixed peephole. To see how the Ames room changes your depth cues, look at the diagram of the Ames room in the drawing below. If you view the

Ames room from the fixed peephole, the room appears rectangular and matches your previous experience with rooms, which are usually rectangular. However, as the right figure shows, the Ames room is actually shaped in an odd way: The left corner is twice as far away from the peephole as the right corner. This means that the boy is actually twice as far away from you as the girl. However, the Ames room's odd shape makes you think that you are seeing the two people from the same distance, and this (illusion) makes the boy appear to be shorter than the girl (Goldstein, 2010).

The next two illusions either change your perceptual cues or rely too much on your previous perceptual experiences.

Ponzo Illusion

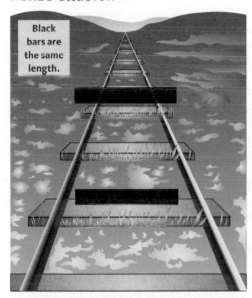

Black bars are the same length.

In the figure above, the top black bar appears to be much longer than the bottom black bar. However, if you measure these two bars, you will discover that they are exactly the same size. This is the *Ponzo illusion.* We clearly remember measuring the first time we saw this picture because we couldn't believe the bars were the same size. You perceive the top bar as being farther away, and you have learned from experience that if two objects appear to be the same size but one is farther away, the more distant object must be larger; thus, the top bar appears longer.

Müller-Lyer Illusion

The figures at the left and right illustrate the *Müller-Lyer illusion.* Notice that the left arrow appears noticeably shorter than the right arrow. However, if you measure them, you'll prove that the arrows are of equal length.

One explanation for this illusion is that you are relying on size cues learned from your previous experience with corners of rooms. You have learned that if a corner of a room extends outward, it is closer; this experience distorts your perception so that the left arrow appears to be shorter. In contrast, you have learned that if a corner of a room recedes inward, it is farther away, and this experience makes you perceive the right arrow as longer (Goldstein, 2010). Illusions are fun, but what have we learned?

Left and right arrows are the same length.

Learning from Illusions

Most of the time, you perceive the world with reasonable accuracy by using a set of proven perceptual cues for size, shape, and depth. However, illusions teach us that when proven perceptual cues are changed or manipulated, our reliable perceptual processes can be deceived, and we see something unreal or an illusion. Illusions also teach us that perception is a very active process, in which we continually rely on and apply previous experiences with objects when we perceive new situations. For example, you'll discover later (p. 140) how the entertainment industry changes the perceptual rule of closure to create movies, whose motion is a brilliant illusion. Next, we'll discuss a controversial kind of perception that goes by the initials ESP.

ESP: Extrasensory Perception

What are psychic powers?

No one doubts your ability to receive information through one or more of your major senses—seeing, hearing, tasting, smelling, and touching—because this ability has been repeatedly demonstrated and reliably measured. In comparison, most research psychologists do not believe you can receive information outside normal sensory channels, which is called extrasensory perception, because this phenomenon has been neither repeatedly demonstrated nor reliably measured (D. J. Bem & Honorton, 1994).

Extrasensory perception (ESP) is a group of psychic experiences that involve perceiving or sending information (images) outside normal sensory processes or channels.

ESP includes four general abilities—telepathy, precognition, clairvoyance, and psychokinesis.

Telepathy is the ability to transfer one's thoughts to another or to read the thoughts of others. **Precognition** is the ability to foretell events. **Clairvoyance** is the ability to perceive events or objects that are out of sight. **Psychokinesis** is the ability to exert mind over matter—for example, by moving objects without touching them.

Together, these extrasensory perceptions are called psi phenomena.

The term **psi** refers to the processing of information or transfer of energy by methods that have no known physical or biological mechanisms and that seem to stretch the laws of physics.

According to the Gallup polls, 41% of adult Americans believe in ESP, 31% believe in communication between minds without the use of regular senses, 21% believe they can communicate mentally with someone who has died, and as many as 55% believe in psychics (D. W. Moore, 2005). In fact, only 7–10% of Americans do not believe in any of these extrasensory perceptions (Begley, 2007c,

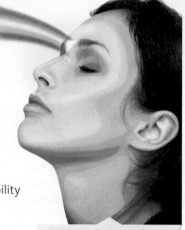

Psi refers to getting information by methods that defy the laws of physics.

2008c). The reason so many Americans but so few research psychologists believe in ESP is that researchers demand hard, scientific evidence rather than evidence from testimonials (see p. 30), which are based on personal beliefs or experiences and have a high potential for error and bias. There are many examples of testimonials that, when evaluated with scientifically designed experiments, were found to be unproven. Questioning testimonial evidence applies especially to ESP, which is outside normal senses, defies physical and biological explanations, and stretches the laws of physics (P. Kurtz, 1995; Nisbet, 1998).

Researchers have been studying the brain to better understand ESP. In one study, two groups of people, believers and nonbelievers in ESP, were shown rapidly displayed images of real faces and scrambled faces as well as real words and nonwords (Begley, 2007c). Their task was to identify real faces and words. Nonbelievers identified more real faces as scrambled faces and more real words as nonwords than believers in ESP. Even more fascinating is that when these nonbelievers in ESP were given a drug that increases levels of the neurotransmitter dopamine, they identified more faces and words as real, even those that weren't. It turns out that having more of a neurotransmitter found in all of our brains may make us more likely to believe in the supernatural!

Another reason researchers demand reliable and repeatable evidence to prove the existence of ESP is that some demonstrations of psi phenomena have involved trickery or questionable methodology. For example, one well-known researcher has used trickery and magic to duplicate many of the better-known demonstrations of ESP, such as mentally bending spoons, moving objects, and reading messages in sealed envelopes. This researcher's name is the Amazing Randi.

Trickery and Magic

According to James Randi, known as the Amazing Randi (photo below), and others acquainted with magic, much of what passes for extrasensory perception is actually done through trickery (Randi, 2005, 2009; Ybarra, 1991). For example, to show how easily people may be fooled, Randi sent two young magicians to a lab that studied psychic phenomena. Instead of admitting they were magicians, the pair claimed to have psychic powers and to perform psychic feats, such as mentally bending keys and making images on film. After 120 hours of testing, the lab's researchers, who had carefully conducted and supervised the ESP demonstrations, concluded that the two did indeed have genuine psychic abilities. The lab's researchers were not expecting trickery, had not taken steps to prevent it, and were thus totally fooled into believing they were witnessing ESP.

The Amazing Randi, professional magician, shows people how ESP is done through trickery.

Many years ago, a television show under the supervision of James Randi offered $100,000 to anyone who could demonstrate psychic powers. Twelve people claimed to have psychic powers, such as identifying through interviews the astrological signs under which people were born, seeing the auras of people standing behind screens, and correctly reading Zener cards (showing five symbols: square, circle, wavy lines, plus sign, and star). Of the 12 people who claimed psychic powers, none scored above chance on any of these tasks (Steiner, 1989). Although people may claim psychic powers, most cannot demonstrate such powers under controlled conditions that eliminate trickery, magic, and educated guessing.

To eliminate any trickery, claims of psychic abilities must withstand the scrutiny of scientific investigation. Let's see how a controlled ESP experiment is designed and conducted.

ESP Experiment

One of the more common demonstrations of psychic ability is to use Zener cards, which show five symbols—circle, waves, square, plus sign, and star (on right). A researcher holds up the back of one card and asks a person to guess the symbol on the front.

How do researchers study psychic abilities?

If there were 100 trials, the person could identify 20 symbols correctly simply by guessing (chance level). However, if a person identifies 25 symbols correctly, which is above chance level, does that mean the person has psychic powers? This is a simplified example of a very complicated statistical question: How can we determine whether a person has psychic powers or is just guessing correctly? Therefore, to solve one major problem in psi research—how to eliminate guesswork and trickery—researchers use a state-of-the-art method called the Ganzfeld procedure.

The **Ganzfeld procedure** is a controlled method for eliminating trickery, error, and bias while testing telepathic communication between a sender—the person who sends the message—and a receiver—the person who receives the message.

In the Ganzfeld procedure, the receiver is placed in a reclining chair in an acoustically isolated room. Translucent ping-pong ball halves are taped over the eyes, and headphones are placed over the ears. The sender, who is isolated in a separate soundproof

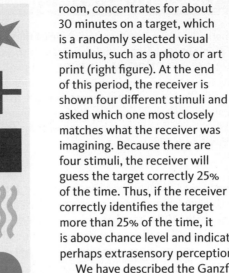

Symbols used to study ESP

room, concentrates for about 30 minutes on a target, which is a randomly selected visual stimulus, such as a photo or art print (right figure). At the end of this period, the receiver is shown four different stimuli and asked which one most closely matches what the receiver was imagining. Because there are four stimuli, the receiver will guess the target correctly 25% of the time. Thus, if the receiver correctly identifies the target more than 25% of the time, it is above chance level and indicates something else is occurring, perhaps extrasensory perception (D. J. Bem & Honorton, 1994).

Ganzfeld procedure involves mentally sending this picture to a person in another room.

We have described the Ganzfeld procedure in detail to illustrate the precautions and scientific methodology that researchers must use to rule out trickery, error, and bias. One of the biggest problems with ESP is that those who claim to have it are rarely subjected to scientific study. Such is the case with so-called psychic hotlines. There is no scientific evidence that self-proclaimed psychics are better at knowing or predicting the future than would occur by chance (Sheaffer, 1997).

The last topic in this section is a rare perceptual problem that results in the inability to recognize people's faces, even familiar ones.

Strange Perception Problems

What is face blindness?

Imagine being able to see a person's eyes, nose, and mouth but not be able to put these features together to recognize the person's face. As strange as this may sound, scientists estimate that 2–3% of people have difficulty recognizing faces. These individuals have a condition called prosopagnosia, also known as face blindness.

Prosopagnosia is a condition marked by a difficulty or inability to recognize faces.

Some people with this condition cannot recognize their own spouses, parents, or children, while others have milder cases, perhaps not recognizing the faces of people they see only rarely. In very extreme cases, some people cannot recognize that the arrangement of facial features constitutes a face at all, and still others can't recognize even their own face!

What's especially interesting in people with prosopagnosia is that they see perfectly well; they do not have a vision problem. Scientists have been exploring the possible causes of prosopagnosia. They know that sometimes the condition exists from birth, while other times it's a result of a stroke or brain injury. Given that the condition runs in some families and some people have the condition since birth, scientists suspect a genetic involvement. They think the genetic link is a mutation in a single gene, but they are not certain.

People with prosopagnosia have a difficulty or inability to recognize faces.

Although there is no definitive cause or cure, people who have prosopagnosia can benefit from intense exposure to computer-generated faces that have slight variations in the distance between features, such as the eyes and eyebrows. Outside of formal intervention, people with prosopagnosia report being able to distinguish people through the use of cues other than faces, such as hairstyle, voice, clothing, body shape, and body movement (Barrow, 2011; Grueter, 2007; *National Geographic*, 2011; *Science Illustrated*, 2008b; S. Song, 2006c).

There are other known perception problems that you may also find strange. Consider, for instance, the inability to recognize familiar voices even though the person hears and understands the words being spoken. Imagine a loved one speaking to you and you not recognizing the voice. The inability to recognize voices would certainly make phone conversations challenging, since hearing is the only sensory cue that can be used when communicating by phone.

Later, in the Critical Thinking article (p. 142), we'll explore the topic of strange perceptions further by discussing how some people hear colors, smell sounds, and taste shapes.

Next, we'll discuss other forms of perceptions that fool our senses into believing that fixed things are moving. ●

I Application: Creating Perceptions

Can we create new perceptions?

About 20,000 years ago, early humans *(Homo sapiens)* created some of the earliest images by using earth pigments to paint prancing horses on the sides of their caves (right photo) (S. Fritz, 1995). About 3,000 years ago, Egyptians created some of the most impressive images with their enormous and long-lasting pyramids. Today, computer researchers are using virtual reality techniques to develop new images and perceptions that can put you in the middle of a mind-blowing three-dimensional world. We'll begin our look at how perceptions are created with an old perceptual device that is used in modern billboards.

Painted 20,000 years ago

Creating Movement

The father of the flashing lights used in today's billboards, movie marquees, and traffic arrows was a distinguished Gestalt psychologist named Max Wertheimer. In the early 1900s, Wertheimer spent a considerable amount of time in a darkened room, where he experimented with flashing first one light and then a second light that was positioned some distance away. He discovered that if the time between flashing one light and then the other was adjusted just right, the two flashes were actually perceived as a moving spot of light rather than as two separate flashes. He called this illusion phi movement.

Neon billboards use flashing lights to create the illusion of movement.

Phi movement refers to the illusion that lights that are actually stationary seem to be moving. This illusory movement, which today is called apparent motion, is created by flashing closely positioned stationary lights at regular intervals.

Each time you pass a traffic arrow composed of flashing lights or perceive a moving string of lights used in an advertising sign, you are seeing a practical application of Wertheimer's phi movement. This phi movement was one of the first examples of how ordinary visual stimuli could be adjusted to create an illusion.

Another example of creating wonderful moving illusions with stationary visual stimuli came from the remarkable genius of Thomas Edison, who invented motion pictures in 1893.

Creating Movies

Movies create the illusion of motion by showing a series of fixed images.

If you attend a bicycle racing competition and then, minutes later, watch a videotaped replay of the same race, you perceive motion produced in two very different ways. One kind of motion is real, while the other is an illusion.

Real motion is your perception of any stimulus or object that actually moves in space.

As you watch a live bicycle race, you are perceiving real motion. However, when you watch a replay of that same race, you are seeing apparent motion.

Apparent motion is an illusion that a stimulus or object is moving in space when, in fact, the stimulus or object is stationary. The illusion of apparent motion is created by rapidly showing a series of stationary images, each of which has a slightly different position or posture than the one before.

The principle for creating apparent motion is deceptively simple and can be easily discovered by examining the positions of the bicyclist in each frame of the time-lapse photo shown above.

Beginning on the left side of the photo, notice that each frame shows only a slight change in the position of the bicyclist. However, if these frames were presented rapidly—for example, at the movie standard of 24 frames per second—you would perceive the illusion of a bicyclist jumping between hills.

In a series of ingenious experiments, researchers discovered that several complex mechanisms built into our visual system detect cues that produce the illusion of motion (Ramachandran & Anstis, 1986). One such cue is the closure principle, which means that our brains fill in the motion expected to occur between images that vary only slightly in position and are presented in rapid sequence. Without apparent motion, there would be no movies, television, or flip books.

Now, researchers have developed a procedure that creates a three-dimensional perceptual experience of walking through a house, dissecting a frog, or doing complicated human surgery. This is the brave new world of virtual reality.

Creating Virtual Reality

What is a surgical robot?

The invention of the movie camera was revolutionary because it created a new perceptual experience: the illusion that still pictures moved. Currently, another perceptual revolution is under way, and it's called virtual reality.

Virtual reality is a perceptual experience of being inside an object, moving through an environment, or carrying out some action that is created or simulated by computer.

Remote and robotic surgery. In a medical application of virtual reality, surgeons can now practice their skills with surgical simulators on virtual cadavers. Research shows that the use of virtual reality significantly improves surgeons' skills, reduces their error rates, and brings reduced pain and quicker recovery for patients (Dellorto, 2008; *Science Daily,* 2008). Virtual reality is also being used on real patients. For example, a surgeon can insert and maneuver a tiny camera and surgical tools in patients through pencil-thin incisions. The surgeon operates by maneuvering robotic arms (photo below), which are steadier and more precise than human arms. Robotic surgery has already been performed more than 70,000 times in many procedures, including the removal of prostate cancers and brain tumors, as well as heart surgery, middle-ear surgery, and pediatric surgeries (Berlinger, 2006; Dellorto, 2008; J. Fox, 2005; *Science Illustrated,* 2011c; von Drehle, 2011). Another truly amazing

Doctors use virtual reality to guide a robot to perform operations.

advance in surgical technology is the ability for a surgeon to perform remote surgery using a robot (Berlinger, 2006). For instance, one surgeon in New York robotically removed a gallbladder from a patient in France with no complications!

Psychotherapy. In a psychological application of virtual reality, clients with such fears as spiders, flying, or heights are exposed to the feared stimuli in a three-dimensional environment where everything appears very real.

In this photo, a client is being treated for fear of spiders. She wears a plastic helmet that contains a computer monitor that puts her inside a virtual reality kitchen in which she sees, touches, and kills spiders. For example, Joanne Cartwright suffered a debilitating fear of spiders. "I washed my truck every night before I went to work in case there were webs," she said. "I put all my clothes in plastic bags and taped duct tape around my doors so spiders couldn't get in. I thought I was going to have a mental breakdown" (Robbins, 2000, p. D6). After receiving 12 virtual reality sessions to decrease her fear, Joanne said, "I'm amazed because I am doing all this stuff I could never do—camping, hunting and hiking" (Carlin, 2000). Psychotherapists report success in using virtual reality therapy to treat a wide variety of phobias, posttraumatic stress disorder (PTSD), and drug addictions (Barnes, 2010; Culbertson et al., 2010; Mozes, 2008; A. Rizzo, 2006; Z. Rosenthal, 2007).

Therapists use virtual reality to treat phobias.

The next topic focuses on how much your first impressions of other people depend on your perceptions of their physical appearances.

Creating First Impressions

What's your impression of the White and Black family pictures?

Social psychologists have discovered that facial features have a significant effect on our first impressions and perceptions of people.

For example, we tend to perceive an attractive person as being interesting, sociable, intelligent, outgoing, and kind (Lemley, 2000). Similarly, first impressions are also influenced by racial stereotypes, both positive and negative, based on physical features such as skin color and hairstyle. Hollywood hairstylists know very well that the kind, amount, color, and style of actors' hair can radically change their appearance and our impressions of them. Besides hair color and style, skin color has a considerable impact on first perceptions and impressions.

To illustrate how skin color can greatly change your perceptions of people, please look at the two photos on the right and think about your first impressions of each person. Did you notice anything peculiar about the two pictures? You'll likely be surprised to

© David Livingston/Getty Images

© Robert Zuckerman/Time & Life Pictures/Getty Images

learn the two pictures show the same people. Both pictures are of the Wurgel family (mom, dad, and daughter), all of whom are White. The Wurgel family participated in a TV reality series called *Black.White.* and underwent elaborate makeup transformations to change their racial complexions (Associated Press, 2006a; Gliatto, 2006; T. Patterson, 2006). The real pictures of the Wurgel family are on the top, and their transformation pictures are on the bottom!

Now that you have seen the dramatic effect race can have on our impressions of others, you can judge for yourself how skin color influences your perceptions of others. We'll discuss how we perceive people and form impressions in Module 25.

The factors involved in forming first impressions as well as in creating moving lights, movies, and virtual reality illustrate an important underlying principle of perception: Our perceptions, which may be changed or biased by personal experiences, are interpretations rather than exact copies of reality. ●

Taste Shapes? Hear Colors? Smell Sounds?

When Carol Crane hears the sound of guitars, she feels as if someone is blowing on her ankles. Hearing the piano gives her a tapping sensation on her chest. Hearing jazz music makes her feel as if heavy, sharp raindrops are falling all over her body! When Carol looks at the number 4, she sees red, and when she looks at the letter b, she sees blue. Carol is different from most other people because of the complex way she experiences many sensations.

1 If researchers wanted to better understand how Carol's brain processes sensory experiences, which type(s) of brain scan should they use?

Carol has an uncommon condition called synesthesia, which means when one of her senses gets stimulated, another sense automatically, involuntarily gets stimulated too. Perceiving colors with letters and numbers is the most common form of synesthesia. Less common types include experiencing sounds with smells and shapes with flavors. Sometimes, the associations are reasonable or logical, such as the smell of lemons leading people to see yellow. But, other times, the associations are surprising, such as the smell of lavender leading people to see green and to feel stickiness.

2 Is synesthesia a type of illusion?

Many people with synesthesia enjoy their special abilities; however, there is a real downside for others. Some people experience unpleasant associations, such as the awful taste of earwax when hearing certain words. As you can imagine, this can make reading very unpleasant! As a result of having multiple senses stimulated, people can experience distractions at work, while reading or studying, or while driving and looking at road signs. These unique experiences can be frustrating because they are frequent and automatic, making them very difficult to prevent or stop.

3 Does having synesthesia help improve your memory?

Researchers have been studying people with synesthesia and have learned some fascinating things. In people with synesthesia, the signals that come from sensory organs, such as the eyes and ears, travel to places in the brain they shouldn't necessarily be going to, which leads to the signals being interpreted as multiple sensations. For example, when people experience color sensations when hearing words, hearing words activates areas of the brain responsible for both hearing and vision.

4 Which part of the neuron is responsible for taking signals that come from sensory organs to multiple areas of the brain?

Other biological research suggests that synesthesia runs in families. Researchers have identified specific chromosomal regions associated with auditory-visual synesthesia, which is when people see colors in response to sounds. Still, the genetic basis for synesthesia is complex and understanding how it develops requires much further study. Researchers are hopeful that understanding the genetic involvement in synesthesia will also help them better understand how the brain is organized and how different areas are connected, ultimately leading to a better understanding of human perception.

5 Which brain areas are responsible for hearing words and seeing colors?

6 Which modern approach to psychology is used to study the genetic involvement of synesthesia?

The seemingly endless variations of synesthesia highlight the differences in how individuals perceive the world. The research on synesthesia confirms that the brain filters what it perceives and that perception is a highly individualized process.

Adapted from Asher et al., 2009; Callejas, 2008; Cytowic, 1999; Cytowic & Eagleman, 2010; Hitti, 2006b; Hubbard & Ramachandran, 2005; Lemley, 1999; Nunn et al., 2002; Rouw & Scholte, 2007; Steven et al., 2006; Weir, 2009

A Thresholds

1. We discussed three basic questions that psychologists ask about perception. Our first question—At what point are we aware of a stimulus?—can be answered by measuring the threshold of a stimulus, which is a point above which a stimulus is perceived and below which it is not. The intensity at which a person can detect the stimulus 50% of the time is called the _____.

2. Our second question—At what point do we know a stimulus intensity has increased or decreased?—can be answered by measuring the smallest increase or decrease in the intensity of a stimulus that a person can detect 50% of the time; this is called a **(a)** _____. It has been found that the increase in stimulus intensity needed to produce a just noticeable difference increases in proportion to the intensity of the initial stimulus; this is called **(b)** _____ law.

B Sensation Versus Perception

3. Our third question—How are meaningless sensations combined into meaningful perceptions?—can be answered by analyzing our own perceptual experiences. Our first awareness of some outside stimulus is called a **(a)** _____. This awareness results when some change in energy activates sensory receptors, which produce signals that, in turn, are transformed by the brain into meaningless sensory experiences. When many individual sensations are assembled into a meaningful experience, image, or pattern, it is called a **(b)** _____. The latter is not an exact replica of the real world but rather a copy that has been changed, biased, or distorted by our unique set of **(c)** _____. Our brain transforms sensations into perceptions instantaneously, automatically, and without our awareness.

C Perceptual Organization

4. When perception is guided by previous knowledge, experience, beliefs, or expectations, it is called **(a)** _____. When perception begins with bits and pieces of information that, when combined, lead to the recognition of the whole pattern, it is called **(b)** _____.

5. The **(a)** _____ psychologists stated that the formation of perceptions cannot be understood by simply breaking perceptions down into individual components and then studying how we reassemble them. They argued that "the whole is more than the sum of its parts," by which they meant that perceptions are more than a combination of individual elements. The Gestalt psychologists believed that the brain has rules for assembling perceptions, which they called principles of **(b)** _____.

6. Many of the rules of perceptual organization involve ways of grouping or arranging stimuli. According to one of these rules, the first thing we do is automatically separate an image into two parts: the more detailed feature of an image becomes the **(a)** _____ and the less detailed aspects become the **(b)** _____. According to the **(c)** _____ rule, stimuli tend to be organized in the most basic, elementary way. According to the **(d)** _____ rule, stimuli that appear the same tend to be grouped together. According to the **(e)** _____ rule, stimuli that are near one another tend to be grouped together. According to the **(f)** _____ rule, stimuli that are arranged in a smooth line or curve tend to be perceived as forming a continuous path. According to the **(g)** _____ rule, we tend to fill in the missing parts of a figure and perceive it as complete.

D Perceptual Constancy

7. Although the size, shape, brightness, and color of objects are constantly changing, we tend to see them as remaining the same, a phenomenon that is called **(a)** _____. A person walking away does not appear to grow smaller, even though the image on the retina is decreasing in size, because of **(b)** _____ constancy. Even though the image of a door that is opened and closed changes on the retina from a rectangle to a trapezoid, we see it as retaining its rectangular outline because of **(c)** _____ constancy. Even though the color and brightness inside a car are altered when we drive from bright into dim light, we tend to see little change because of **(d)** _____ and _____ constancy.

E Depth Perception

8. The visual system transforms the two-dimensional image (height and width) of stimuli projected onto the retina into a three-dimensional experience by adding depth. Cues for depth that are dependent on both eyes are called **(a)** _____; cues for depth that are dependent on only a single eye are called **(b)** _____. The binocular cue for depth that arises when muscles turn your eyes inward is called **(c)** _____. The binocular cue for depth that arises because the two eyes send slightly different images to the brain is called **(d)** _____.

9. There are a number of monocular cues for depth. When an object appears closer because it overlaps another, the cue is called **(a)** _____. When parallel lines seem to stretch to a point at the horizon and create a sense of distance, the cue is called **(b)** _____. When two figures are expected to be the same size but one is larger and thus appears closer, the cue is called **(c)** _____. If dust or smog makes objects appear hazy and thus farther away, the cue is called **(d)** _____. As texture changes from sharp and detailed to dull and monotonous, it creates the impression of distance; this cue is called **(e)** _____. The play of light and shadow gives objects a three-dimensional look, a cue that is called **(f)** _____. As you ride in a car, the impression that near objects are speeding by and far objects are barely moving is called **(g)** _____.

F Cultural Diversity: Influence on Perceptions

10. Experiences that are typical of a society and shared by its members are called _____ influences. These influences have significant effects on the perception of images, constancy, depth, and motion.

© Yamini Chao/Thinkstock

11. Because of cultural influences, Americans tend to engage more in **(a)** _____ thinking, while Easterners (Japanese) engage more in **(b)** _____ thinking.

G Research Focus: Unconscious Perceptions

12. A brief auditory or visual message that is presented below the absolute threshold, which means the person is not consciously aware of the stimulus, is called **(a)** _____. Researchers have concluded that any behavioral changes attributed to subliminal messages actually result because listeners' strong belief that a behavior will change leads them to act, unknowingly, to change that behavior; this is called a **(b)** _____.

IMPROVE SELF-ESTEEM

H Strange Perceptions

13. For much of the time, our perceptions are relatively accurate reflections of the world (except for anything added by our attentional, motivational, or emotional filters). However, if perceptual cues that we have learned to use and rely on are greatly changed, the result is a distorted image, called an _____. Although illusions are extreme examples, they illustrate that perception is an active, ongoing process in which we use past experiences to interpret current sensory experiences.

14. The perception and transmission of thoughts or images by other than normal sensory channels are referred to as psychic experiences or **(a)** _____ phenomena. ESP, which stands for **(b)** _____, includes four psychic abilities. The ability to transfer one's thoughts to another or read another's thoughts is called **(c)** _____. The ability to foretell events is called **(d)** _____. The ability to perceive events or objects that are out of sight is called **(e)** _____. The ability to move objects without touching them is called **(f)** _____. Two reasons many researchers are skeptical of psychic abilities are that some supposedly psychic phenomena were actually accomplished with **(g)** _____ and some previous studies that supported ESP had questionable **(h)** _____.

15. A perception problem marked by the difficulty or inability to recognize faces is called _____.

I Application: Creating Perceptions

16. When you view objects moving in space, it is called **(a)** _____ motion. When you view images of stationary objects that are presented in a rapid sequence, it is called **(b)** _____ motion, which is the basic principle used to create movies. The illusion that stationary lights are moving can be traced to the work of Max Wertheimer, who called this phenomenon **(c)** _____ movement. A perceptual experience that is created by allowing the viewer to enter and participate in computer-generated images is called **(d)** _____; it breaks down some of the traditional boundaries between reality and fantasy. Virtual reality has been applied to treat excessive fear of spiders, flying, or heights, which are called **(e)** _____.

Ames Research Center/NASA, photo by Walt Sisler

Answers: 1. *absolute threshold;* 2. (a) *just noticeable difference,* (b) *Weber's;* 3. (a) *sensation,* (b) *perception;* 4. (a) *top-down processing,* (b) *bottom-up processing;* 5. (a) *Gestalt,* (b) *perceptual organization;* 6. (a) *figure,* (b) *ground,* (c) *simplicity,* (d) *similarity,* (e) *proximity,* (f) *continuity,* (g) *closure;* 7. (a) *perceptual constancy,* (b) *size,* (c) *shape,* (d) *color, brightness;* 8. (a) *binocular,* (b) *monocular,* (c) *convergence,* (d) *retinal disparity;* 9. (a) *interposition,* (b) *linear perspective,* (c) *relative size,* (d) *atmospheric perspective,* (e) *texture gradient,* (f) *light and shadow,* (g) *motion parallax;* 10. *cultural* 11. (a) *analytical,* (b) *holistic;* 12. (a) *subliminal,* (b) *self-fulfilling prophecy;* 13. *illusion;* 14. (a) *psi,* (b) *extrasensory perception,* (c) *telepathy,* (d) *precognition,* (e) *clairvoyance,* (f) *psychokinesis,* (g) *trickery,* (h) *methodology;* 15. *prosopagnosia;* 16. (a) *real,* (b) *apparent,* (c) *phi,* (d) *virtual reality,* (e) *phobias*

Links to Learning

Key Terms/Key People

absolute threshold, 122
Ames room, 137
apparent motion, 140
atmospheric perspective, 131
binocular depth cues, 129
bottom-up processing, 126
brain: association areas, 125
brain: primary areas, 125
brightness constancy, 128
clairvoyance, 138
closure rule, 127
color constancy, 128
continuity rule, 127
convergence, 129
cultural influences, 132
depth perception, 129

extrasensory perception, 138
Fechner, Gustav, 122
figure-ground rule, 127
Ganzfeld procedure, 139
Gestalt psychologists, 126
illusion, 136
impossible figure, 133
interposition, 130
just noticeable difference (or
    difference threshold), 123
light and shadow, 131
linear perspective, 130
monocular depth cues, 130
moon illusion, 136
motion parallax, 131
Müller-Lyer illusion, 137

perception, 124
perceptual constancy, 128
perceptual sets, 133
personalized perceptions, 125
phi movement, 140
Ponzo illusion, 137
precognition, 138
prosopagnosia, 139
proximity rule, 127
psi, 138
psychokinesis, 138
real motion, 140
relative size, 130
retinal disparity, 129
rules of organization, 127
self-fulfilling prophecies, 134

sensation, 124
shape constancy, 128
similarity rule, 127
simplicity rule, 127
size constancy, 128
stimulus, 125
subliminal stimulus, 122, 134
telepathy, 138
texture gradient, 131
threshold, 122
top-down processing, 126, 133
transduction, 125
virtual reality, 141
Weber's law, 123

Media Resources

Go to **CengageBrain.com** to access Psychology CourseMate, where you will find an interactive eBook, glossaries, flashcards, quizzes, videos, answers to Critical Thinking questions, and more. You can also access Virtual Psychology Labs, an interactive laboratory experience designed to illustrate key experiments first-hand.

MODULE 7

Sleep & Dreams

© Jolin Lund/Getty Images

introduction

Living in a Cave

The advertisement read: "We are looking for a hardy subject to live alone in an underground cave for four months. We'll provide board, room, and a monthly allowance. It will be necessary to take daily physiological measurements, measure brain waves, and collect blood samples."

Would you answer this ad?

Twenty people answered this ad, but researchers selected Stefania because she seemed to have the inner strength, motivation, and stamina to complete the entire four months. On the chosen day, Stefania crawled 30 feet underground with her favorite books into a 20-by-12-foot Plexiglas module (photo below), which had been sealed off from sunlight, radio, television, and other time cues.

Stefania lived inside this Plexiglas module placed underground without any time cues (clocks, sunshine, radio, TV).

During her first month underground, Stefania's concentration seemed to come and go. She appeared depressed, and she snapped at researchers when they asked her to do routine measurements. She had strange dreams—for example, that her computer monitor had turned into a TV that was talking to her. After several months, however, she became more comfortable with her underground isolation. She followed a regular routine of taking her body temperature, heart rate, and blood pressure and typing the results into a computer monitor, her only link with the outside world.

Without clocks, radio, television, or the sun, Stefania found it difficult to keep track of time, which seemed to have slowed down. When told she could leave her underground cave because her 130 days were up, she felt certain she had been underground only about 60 days. Her time underground allowed researchers to closely monitor her sleeping and waking behaviors in the absence of all light and time cues (adapted from *Newsweek*, June 5, 1989).

Asking Stefania to live in a cave for months was a way to answer questions about how long a day is and how much one sleeps when there are no light cues. Later in this module (p. 150), we will discuss the preferred length of day and the biological clock that regulates our sleep-wake cycle.

Movements during Sleep

Why are your eyes moving?

In the early days of sleep research, psychologists were observing changes in people as they slept and noticed that during a certain stage of sleep a person's eyes suddenly began to move rapidly back and forth. This back-and-forth eye movement can actually be seen under the eyelids in the photos at the right. Even more interesting, when people were awakened during rapid eye movement, they usually reported that they had been dreaming. This chance observation of rapid eye movement and its high association, or correlation, with dreaming gave researchers a reliable method to identify and study dreaming in the laboratory (Dement & Kleitman, 1957).

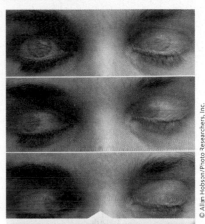

During one kind of sleep (REM—rapid eye movement sleep), the eyes dart back and forth beneath the eyelids.

Even though our eyes move during dream sleep, which is referred to as REM (rapid eye movement) sleep, our muscles become paralyzed during this stage, which prevents us from moving other areas of our body, such as our legs and arms. However, in rare instances, people's muscles do not become paralyzed, so they can act out their dreams. We'll describe this condition, known as *REM behavior disorder,* later in this module (p. 153). In an entirely different stage of sleep, some people sleepwalk. Sleepwalking is especially interesting because it occurs during the deepest level of sleep. We'll discuss sleepwalking further later in this module (p. 163). The facts that some people can walk while sleeping and others can move while they are dreaming are just a couple of reasons why the study of sleep and consciousness is so fascinating.

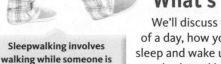

Sleepwalking involves walking while someone is in a deep level of sleep.

What's Coming

We'll discuss the preferred length of a day, how you know when to sleep and wake up, what happens to your body and brain during sleep, how much sleep you need, why you sleep, and common sleep problems and their treatments. We'll also discuss the one question students always ask: What do dreams mean? All these areas fit neatly under a much broader phenomenon that we call awareness, or consciousness, and that is where we'll begin. ●

A Continuum of Consciousness

Different States

One curious and amazing feature of consciousness is that, at some point, a person is actually observing himself or herself (Rochat, 2003). For example, how do you know that at this very moment you are conscious?

Are you conscious now?

Consciousness is different levels of awareness of one's thoughts and feelings. It may include creating images in one's mind, following one's thought processes, or having unique emotional experiences.

One way you know that you are conscious is that you are aware of your own thoughts and existence (Pinker, 2000). You may think that when awake you are conscious and when asleep you are unconscious, but there is actually a continuum of consciousness.

The **continuum of consciousness** is a wide range of experiences, from being acutely aware and alert to being totally unaware and unresponsive.

We'll summarize some of the experiences that make up the continuum of consciousness.

Controlled Processes

A problem with cell phones is that we have the ability to focus all of our attention on only one thing at a time, which is an example of controlled processes.

Controlled processes are activities that require full awareness, alertness, and concentration to reach some goal. The focused attention required in carrying out controlled processes usually interferes with the execution of other ongoing activities.

Talking on a cell phone while driving is a controlled process.

A controlled process such as talking on a cell phone while driving involves focusing most of your attention on talking and little on driving. There's less problem if the driving is easy, but if you need to take quick action, your driving will likely suffer because your attention is primarily focused on your phone conversation (P. J. Cooper et al., 2003). In fact, listening to a conversation while driving increases brain activity in language areas and decreases brain activity in spatial areas involved in driving (Just, 2008). Ray LaHood, the U.S. Transportation Secretary, said, "Distracted driving has become a deadly epidemic on America's roads" (LaHood, 2011). For these reasons, handheld cell phones are banned in nine states and efforts are under way to place a national ban on talking on cell phones and texting while driving (GHSA, 2012; NTSB, 2012).

Automatic Processes

Eating while reading is an automatic process.

Since this man's attention is focused primarily on reading an important report, he is almost automatically eating the sandwich; this is an example of an automatic process.

Automatic processes are activities that require little awareness, take minimal attention, and do not interfere with other ongoing activities.

Examples of automatic processes include eating while reading or watching television and driving a car along a familiar route while listening to the radio or thinking of something else.

Although we seem to concentrate less during automatic processes, at some level we are conscious of what is occurring. For instance, as we drive on automatic pilot, we avoid neighboring cars and can usually take quick evasive action during emergencies.

Daydreaming

Many of us engage in a form of consciousness called daydreaming.

Daydreaming is an activity that requires a low level of awareness, often occurs during automatic processes, and involves fantasizing while awake.

We may begin daydreaming in a relatively conscious state and then drift into a state between sleep and wakefulness. Usually we daydream in situations that require little attention or during repetitious or boring activities.

Most daydreams are rather ordinary, such as planning where to eat or thinking

Daydreaming isn't always a pleasant distraction.

about what happened the day before. These kinds of daydreams serve as a way for us to reflect on past actions or plan for the future.

Contrary to popular belief, daydreaming is often associated with less happiness than focusing on the present moment. When our mind daydreams, it often wanders off to unpleasant topics (Killingsorth & Gilbert, 2010).

Altered States

Over 3,000 years ago, Egyptians brewed and drank alcohol to reach altered states of consciousness (Samuel, 1996).

Altered states of consciousness result from using any number of procedures—such as meditation, psychoactive drugs, hypnosis, or sleep deprivation—to produce an awareness that differs from normal consciousness.

For example, this woman is using meditation to focus her attention on a single image or thought, free her mind from external restraints, and enter an altered state of consciousness.

Meditation is an altered state.

In an interesting series of studies on himself, neuro-psychologist John Lilly (1972) repeatedly took LSD (when it was legal) and reported that it caused unusual, bizarre, and sometimes frightening altered states of consciousness. For example, he described leaving his body, seeing it from above, and being afraid he would not be able to return safely to it.

The chief characteristic of altered states, whichever way they are produced, is that we perceive our internal and external environments or worlds in ways different from normal perception.

Sleep and Dreams

We enter an altered state of consciousness every night when we go to sleep.

Sleep consists of five different stages that involve different levels of awareness, consciousness, and responsiveness, as well as different levels of physiological arousal. The deepest state of sleep borders on unconsciousness.

Because of our decreased awareness, 8 hours of sleep may seem like one continuous state. However, it is actually composed of different states of body arousal and consciousness (Morin & Espie, 2012). One interesting sleep state involves dreaming.

Dreaming is a unique state of consciousness in which we are asleep but experience a variety of astonishing visual, auditory, and tactile images, often connected in strange ways and often in color. People blind from birth have only auditory or tactile dreams.

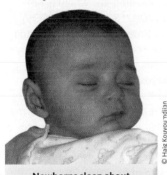

Newborns sleep about 17 hours a day.

During the initial stage of sleep, we are often aware of stimuli in our environment. However, as we pass into the deepest stage of sleep, we may sleeptalk or sleepwalk and children may experience frightening night terrors but have no awareness or memory of them.

Most of this module focuses on waking, sleeping, and dreaming.

Unconscious and Implicit Memory

We told you that one of Sigmund Freud's revolutionary ideas was his concept of the unconscious (see pp. 9, 434–437).

According to Freud's theory, when we are faced with very threatening wishes or desires, especially if they are sexual or aggressive, we automatically defend our self-esteem by placing these psychologically threatening thoughts into a mental place of which we are not aware, called the **unconscious.** We cannot voluntarily recall unconscious thoughts or images.

Freud believed that we can become aware of our unconscious thoughts only through a process of free association or dream interpretation, both of which are explained on page 435.

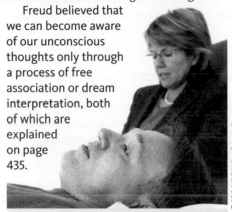

Freud's idea of the unconscious is different from implicit memory.

Somewhat related to Freud's theory of the unconscious is a new concept developed by cognitive neuroscientists called implicit or nondeclarative memory (Frensch & Runger, 2003).

Implicit or nondeclarative memory means learning without awareness, such as occurs in emotional situations or in acquiring habits. We are unaware of such learning, which can influence our conscious feelings, thoughts, and behaviors.

For example, you cannot describe the complex motor movements your feet make as they walk down stairs because such motor memories are stored in implicit memory, which you are unaware of and cannot voluntarily recall. Implicit memory explains why people cannot recall and are unaware of why or how they learned to fear a tiny spider, fell in love, fainted at the sight of blood, or learned (classically conditioned) to make a happy or sad facial expression (Reder et al., 2009). Implicit memory emphasizes the learning and influence of many different kinds of motor and emotional memories and is different from Freud's unconscious, which focuses on the influence of threatening memories (Kihlstrom, 1993).

Unconsciousness

If you have ever fainted, gotten general anesthesia, or been knocked out from a blow to the head, you have experienced being unconscious or unconsciousness.

Unconsciousness, which can result from disease, trauma, a blow to the head, or general medical anesthesia, is total lack of sensory awareness and complete loss of responsiveness to one's environment.

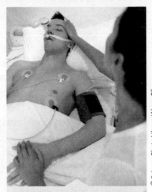

Unconsciousness results from a head knock, disease, or general anesthesia.

For example, a boxer's goal is to knock out the opponent with a quick blow to the head that produces a temporary state of unconsciousness. Being in an accident can damage the brain and cause different levels of unconsciousness and result in different kinds of comas. In some comas, a person appears to be asleep and has absolutely no awareness or responsiveness; this is called a vegetative state. People in vegetative comas are unconscious and in some cases brain-dead, which means they will never again regain consciousness.

Several Kinds

Consciousness is so mysterious because it is a continuum of states, which range from the tragic unconsciousness of being in a vegetative coma to the keen alertness of controlled processes during a final exam. Although it is difficult to define consciousness, you know what it feels like to be conscious and aware of your thoughts and surroundings. Neuroscientists find there is no single seat of consciousness; rather it results from interactions among many different areas of the brain, depending upon the kinds of thoughts, images, or stimuli to which you are attending (Baars & Gage, 2010).

Why is it so mysterious?

Although you have experienced having conscious beliefs and desires, Freud believed that there was also an active, unconscious psychological process that defended you against threatening sexual and aggressive thoughts, of which you are totally unaware. In partial support of Freud's theory, cognitive neuroscientists use the concept of implicit or nondeclarative memory to explain how you can be unaware of perceiving various stimuli, such as words, objects, faces, and emotional events, and even learn simple responses (classical conditioning). Although you are not aware of this unconscious learning, you can be unknowingly influenced by the thoughts, memories, feelings, and behaviors stored in your implicit memory (Baars & Gage, 2010; Petty et al., 2006).

One obvious sign of consciousness is being awake, which is regulated by a clock in the brain, our next topic. ●

B Rhythms of Consciousness

Biological Clocks

Sleep researchers studied Stefania living in a Plexiglas module (photo below) for 130 days. Stefania was asked to

How long is a day?

live underground so researchers could study her biological clocks.

Biological clocks are internal timing devices that are genetically set to regulate various physiological responses for different periods of time.

Stefania's sleep-wake cycle underground was regulated by a biological clock.

Biological clocks can be set for hours (secretion of urine), for a single day (rise and fall in internal body temperature), or for many days (women's 28-day menstrual cycle). We are interested in a biological clock that is set for a single day and produces what is called a circadian *(sir-KAY-dee-un)* rhythm (*circa* means "about"; *diem* means "day").

A **circadian rhythm** refers to a biological clock that is genetically programmed to regulate physiological responses within a time period of 24 hours (about one day).

Length of day. You are most familiar with the circadian rhythm that regulates your sleep-wake cycle. In previous studies, when researchers

removed all time cues (light, clock, radio, television) from people who lived underground, like Stefania, the circadian clock day was believed to lengthen from 24 hours to about 25 hours (M. W. Young, 2000). However, in a better controlled study, researchers reported that for both young (mean age 24) and older (mean age 67) adults, the sleep-wake circadian clock is genetically set for a day lasting an average of 24 hours and 18 minutes (Czeisler et al., 1999).

Resetting the circadian clock. Because your circadian clock is genetically set for about 24 hours, 18 minutes, it must be reset each day to match our agreed-upon 24-hour-long day. The resetting stimulus is morning sunlight, which stimulates newly discovered light-detecting cells in the eye's retina (see p. 96) (Purves et al., 2012). These *retinal cells,* which are involved in sensing the amount of light and are not involved in seeing, send electrical signals to the brain's circadian clock (described below) and reset it by about 18 minutes each day (Purves et al., 2012).

Problems. If your circadian clock is not properly reset each day,

Length of Day

| 24 hr, 18 min Body's circadian clock | 24 hr Industrial world's clock |

you may have problems getting to sleep, getting over jet lag, and adjusting to working the night shift (see next page). Although the circadian clock was long known to exist, only recently have researchers identified its exact location in the brain.

Location of Biological Clocks

Where is the circadian clock?

It may seem strange to think of having clocks in your brain. Actually you have several clocks, including the biological circadian sleep-wake clock located in a group of cells in the brain's suprachiasmatic *(SUE-pra-kye-as-MAT-ick)* nucleus (Dijkn & Lazar, 2012; Lee-Chiong, 2008).

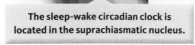

Suprachiasmatic nucleus

Optic nerve

The sleep-wake circadian clock is located in the suprachiasmatic nucleus.

The **suprachiasmatic nucleus** is one of many groups of cells that make up the hypothalamus, which lies in the lower middle of the brain. The suprachiasmatic nucleus is a sophisticated biological clock that regulates a number of circadian rhythms, including the sleep-wake cycle. Because this nucleus receives direct input from the eyes, the suprachiasmatic cells are highly responsive to changes in light.

Since light regulates sleep-wake circadian rhythms, the absence of light should disrupt circadian rhythms in blind people and cause sleep problems. Researchers found that many blind people do report sleep problems (Lamberg, 2006; Moreno, 2006). However, some people who are completely blind report no sleep problems because the pathway for transmitting light from

their eyes directly to the suprachiasmatic nucleus, which is not involved in seeing, is intact (Barinaga, 2002; R. G. Foster, 2009).

Being exposed to light at unnatural times may alter the regulation of circadian rhythms. For instance, scientists recently discovered that exposure to light at night leads to changes in feeding behaviors in mice. The research is interesting because the mice exposed to light at night gained weight, even though they were eating and exercising the same amount as mice exposed to normal light and dark daily cycles. Researchers believe that exposure to light at night may disrupt the feeding behaviors (e.g., eating more at night) and the metabolic activity of animals, and likely humans, which could lead to weight gain (Fonken et al., 2010).

The connection between light and feeding behaviors leads us to discuss a biological clock that is actually regulated by food.

The **food-entrainable circadian clock** (also referred to as the **midnight-snack clock**) regulates eating patterns in people and animals and might be responsible for late-night eating in people. Thus, obese people, many of whom eat more than half their calories at night, may have an abnormality in their clock, which is located in the hypothalamus (see p. 80) (C. Brownlee, 2006; Mieda et al., 2006).

Walking around with several fine-tuned biological clocks in your head is great for timing activities. However, if your circadian sleep-wake clock is interfered with or not properly reset, you may have various sleep-wake problems.

Circadian Problems and Treatments

What if your circadian clock is upset?

Here's the basic problem: For most of the industrial world, a day is agreed to be exactly 24 hours long, but for your genetically set sleep-wake circadian clock, a day is an average of 24 hours and 18 minutes. This difference means your sleep-wake clock must be reset about 18 minutes each day. The resetting stimulus is morning sunlight, which our eyes send directly to the suprachiasmatic nucleus. This daily resetting of our sleep-wake clocks by about 18 minutes usually occurs automatically. However, if our circadian clocks are not properly reset, we may experience decreased cognitive performance, work-related and traffic accidents, jet lag, and various sleep disorders (Aamodt & Wang, 2008; Morin & Espie, 2012).

Shift Workers

Staying awake when your sleep-wake clock calls for sleep results in decreased performance in cognitive and motor skills (Monk, 2012; M. P. Walker, 2012). For example, employees who work the graveyard shift (about 1–8 A.M.) experience the highest number of accidents, reaching their lowest point, or "dead zone," at about 5 A.M., when it is very difficult to stay alert (Stutts et al., 2002).

The reason shift workers and late-night drivers have more accidents is that their sleep-wake clocks have prepared their bodies for sleep, which means they feel sleepy, are less attentive and alert, and are often in a lousy mood (Akerstedt & Kecklund, 2012; Vila, 2011). Frequent major changes in working hours will likely cause much stress on the body and brain (Aamodt & Wang, 2008).

Next, we'll see how circadian rhythms can also create problems for long-distance travelers, including flight attendants who frequently travel across many time zones.

Jet Lag

If you flew from west coast to east coast, you experienced a 3-hour time difference and most likely had jet lag.

Jet lag is the experience of fatigue, lack of concentration, and reduced cognitive skills that occurs when travelers' biological circadian clocks are out of step or synchrony with the external clock times at their new locations.

Generally, it takes about one day to reset your circadian clock for each hour of time change.

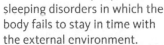

Jet lag occurs when a body's circadian clock gets out of synchrony.

Consider how severe jet lag can be for flight attendants who frequently make long trips. Those who do not take breaks to allow their circadian clocks to readjust experience impaired cognitive skills (Aamodt & Wang, 2008).

After 3 months in space, astronauts experience "space lag" or sleeplessness because their circadian clocks are not being reset (Monk et al., 2001).

Next, you'll see how researchers are studying ways to more effectively reset our biological clocks.

Resetting Clocks

Researcher Charles Czeisler (1994) spent ten years convincing his colleagues that light could reset circadian clocks. After he finally succeeded, other researchers used his and their own research to obtain patents for light therapy (Nowak, 1994).

Light therapy is the use of bright artificial light to reset circadian clocks and to combat the insomnia and drowsiness that plague shift workers and jet-lag sufferers. It also helps people with sleeping disorders in which the body fails to stay in time with the external environment.

For example, researchers report that workers who had been exposed to bright light and then shifted to night work showed improvement in alertness, performance, and job satisfaction (Czeisler et al., 1995). Exposure to bright light (about 20 times brighter) at certain times reset the workers' suprachiasmatic nucleus and resulted in a closer match between their internal circadian clocks and their external shifted clock times.

Light therapy has enormous potential for resetting our sleep-wake clocks, and more recently it has been used to treat depression (APA, 2011).

Another factor involved in setting the sleep-wake clock is a hormone from a gland that was once thought useless.

Melatonin

The discovery of a use for melatonin has been a big scientific breakthrough (Kraft, 2007).

Melatonin is a hormone that is secreted by the pineal gland, an oval-shaped group of cells that is located in the center of the human brain. Melatonin secretion increases with darkness and decreases with light. The suprachiasmatic nucleus regulates the secretion of melatonin, which plays a role in the regulation of circadian rhythms and in promoting sleep.

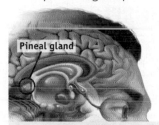

Pineal gland

Melatonin is a hormone secreted by the pineal gland.

Although early testimonials and studies claimed that melatonin reduced jet lag, a later double-blind study reported that melatonin was no better than a placebo in reducing jet lag (Spitzer et al., 1999). However, melatonin helped individuals with medical problems resulting from chronically disrupted circadian clocks sleep better and experience less fatigue (Nagtegaal et al., 2000).

A new experimental drug has shown initial promise in resetting the circadian clock, which may bring relief to shift workers and jet-lag sufferers (Rajaratnam et al., 2009).

Next, we'll examine what happens inside the brain and body during sleep. ●

Stages of Sleep

Does my brain sleep?

The first thing to know about sleep is that your brain never totally sleeps but is active throughout the night. To track your brain's activity during sleep, researchers would attach dozens of tiny wires or electrodes to your scalp and body and record electrical brain activity as you passed through the stages of sleep.

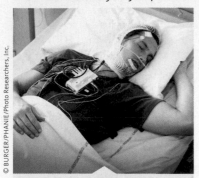

Brain activity is measured to understand sleep stages.

The **stages of sleep** refer to distinctive changes in the electrical activity of the brain and accompanying physiological responses of the body that occur as you pass through different phases of sleep.

As shown in the graph at the top, brain waves are described in terms of frequency (speed) and amplitude (height). They are recorded by a complex

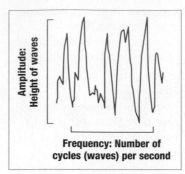

Frequency: Number of cycles (waves) per second

The **alpha stage** is marked by feelings of being relaxed and drowsy, usually with the eyes closed. Alpha waves have low amplitude and high frequency (8–12 cycles per second).

After spending a brief time relaxing in the alpha stage, you enter stage 1 of non-REM sleep.

machine called an EEG, or electroencephalogram. Each stage of sleep can be recognized by its distinctive pattern of EEGs, which we'll explain here.

Alpha Stage

Before actually going into the first stage of sleep, you briefly pass through a relaxed and drowsy state, marked by characteristic alpha waves.

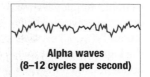

Alpha waves (8–12 cycles per second)

Non-REM Sleep

What happens during sleep?

The second thing to know about sleep is that it is divided into two major categories, called non-REM and REM. We'll discuss non-REM first.

Non-REM sleep is where you spend approximately 80% of your sleep time. Non-REM is divided into sleep stages 1, 2, 3, and 4; each stage is identified by a particular pattern of brain waves and physiological responses. (REM stands for rapid eye movement.)

You begin in sleep stage 1 and gradually enter stages 2, 3, and 4.

Stage 1

This is the lightest stage of sleep.

Stage 1 sleep is a transition from wakefulness to sleep and lasts 1–7 minutes. In it, you gradually lose responsiveness to stimuli and experience drifting thoughts and images. Stage 1 is marked by the presence of theta waves, which are lower in amplitude and lower in frequency (4–7 cycles per second) than alpha waves.

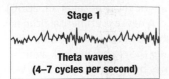

Theta waves (4–7 cycles per second)

Although stage 1 is usually labeled a sleep stage, some individuals who are aroused from it feel as if they have been awake.

Next, you enter stage 2 sleep.

Stage 2

This is the first stage of what researchers call real sleep.

Stage 2 sleep marks the beginning of what we know as sleep. EEG tracings show high-frequency bursts of brain activity called sleep spindles.

As you pass through stage 2, your muscle tension, heart rate, respiration, and body temperature gradually decrease, and it becomes

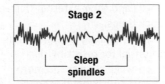

Stage 2

Sleep spindles

more difficult for you to be awakened. In fact, the more sleep spindles your brain makes, the more likely you will stay asleep when exposed to noise (Dang-Vu et al., 2010).

Stages 3 and 4

About 30–45 minutes after drifting off into sleep, you pass through stage 3 and then enter into stage 4 sleep.

Stage 3 sleep is when you begin showing some presence of slow brain-wave patterns, called delta waves.

Delta waves are large, slow brain waves, meaning they have very high amplitude and very low frequency (less than 4 cycles per second).

When you begin to show an increased presence of delta waves, you have entered stage 4 sleep.

Stage 4 sleep is characterized by a consistent pattern of delta waves. Stage 4 is often considered the deepest stage of sleep because it is the most difficult from which to be awakened. During stage 4, heart rate, respiration, temperature, and blood flow to the brain are reduced, and there is a marked secretion of GH (growth hormone), which controls levels of metabolism, physical growth, and brain development.

After spending a few minutes to an hour in stage 4, you will backtrack through stages 3 and 2 and then pass into a new stage, called REM sleep, which is associated with dreaming.

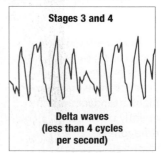

Stages 3 and 4

Delta waves (less than 4 cycles per second)

REM Sleep

When do you dream? We have discussed one major category of sleep, non-REM, and now move on to the second major category of sleep, which goes by the initials REM.

REM sleep makes up the remaining 20% of your sleep time. It is pronounced "rem" and stands for rapid eye movement sleep because your eyes move rapidly back and forth behind closed lids. REM brain waves have high frequency and low amplitude

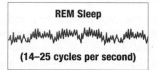

REM Sleep

(14–25 cycles per second)

and look very similar to beta waves, which occur when you are wide awake and alert. During REM sleep, your body is physiologically very aroused, but all your voluntary muscles are paralyzed. REM sleep is highly associated with dreaming.

You pass into REM sleep about five or six times throughout the night with about 30 to 90 minutes between periods. You remain in each period of REM sleep for 15 to 45 minutes and then pass back into non-REM sleep.

Physiological Responses: Brain and Body

Although you are asleep during REM, your body and brain are in a general state of physiological arousal (Aserinsky & Kleitman, 1953). For example, during REM sleep, your heart rate and blood pressure are significantly higher than during non-REM sleep (L. Rosenthal, 2006).

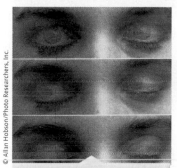

Eyes dart back and forth as a sign of REM sleep.

Because of this strange combination of being asleep yet physiologically aroused, REM sleep is often called *paradoxical sleep*. (A *paradox* is something with contradictory qualities.)

Another unusual feature of REM sleep is that its brain waves are very similar to those recorded when a person is wide awake and alert. By looking at brain-wave recordings alone, researchers cannot tell whether a person is in REM sleep or wide awake. Only the additional recording of rapid eye movements indicates the occurrence of REM sleep. Another characteristic of the brain during REM sleep is that brain areas responsible for logical thinking and disinhibition are much less active than when awake, which likely contributes to our creative thinking during dreaming (D. Barrett, 2011).

Although many physiological responses are greatly increased during REM sleep, you completely lose the muscle tension in your neck and limbs, so you are essentially paralyzed. However, involuntary muscles that regulate the heart, lungs, and other organs continue to function. Researchers think humans evolved muscle paralysis of their limbs during REM sleep so they would not act out violent dreams by running, fighting, or jumping about and injuring themselves (Schenck, 2003). In fact, this actually happens in REM behavior disorder.

In **REM behavior disorder,** which usually occurs in older people, voluntary muscles are not paralyzed, and sleepers can and do act out their dreams, such as fighting off attackers in dreams. People with this condition have been known to break a hand, punch a wall, or hurt a spouse (Seppa, 2009).

So not only is REM a paradoxical sleep but it also signals dreaming.

Dreaming and Remembering

Dreaming. One of the biggest breakthroughs in dream research was the finding that about 80–90% of the times when subjects are awakened from a REM period, they report having vivid, complex, and relatively long dreams (Dement, 1999). In contrast, only about 10% of subjects awakened from non-REM sleep report similar kinds of dreams.

One of the first questions asked was what happens when people are deprived of REM sleep and dreaming. Many subjects have been deprived of REM sleep and dreaming without showing any major behavioral or physiological effects (Bonnet, 2005). However, suppressing REM sleep does produce a curious phenomenon called REM rebound.

Dreaming usually occurs during REM sleep.

REM rebound refers to individuals spending an increased percentage of time in REM sleep if they were deprived of REM sleep on the previous nights.

Remembering. The occurrence of REM rebound suggests a need for REM sleep, and one such need involves memory. In one study, participants learned to press a button when they spotted a moving target on a screen. Participants tested on the same day as training showed a modest improvement. However, when participants were tested the next day, those who were allowed to get the most REM sleep (slept 8 hours) showed the greatest improvement compared to those who got the least REM (slept 6 hours) (Stickgold, 2000, 2005). Researchers conclude that REM sleep helps us store or encode information in memory and advise students to get a good night's sleep so that what they studied the previous day has a chance to be stored in the brain's memory (Mednick, 2010; Wilhelm et al., 2011).

Awake and Alert

A short time after awakening from sleep, you enter a state of being awake and alert. This state has distinctive brain activity called beta waves, which are characterized by high frequency and low amplitude and are very similar to those waves observed during REM sleep.

Awake and Alert

Beta waves (14–25 cycles per second)

REM Sleep

REM waves (14–25 cycles per second)

Beta waves and REM waves are very similar.

How alert you feel in the morning depends partly on whether you are a morning or an evening person, which we'll discuss in the Research Focus on page 155.

Although you now have an overview of the different sleep stages, you may be surprised to discover that how you go through the different stages is somewhat like riding a roller coaster.

Sequence of Stages

When you go to sleep at night, you may think that you simply sleep for 8 hours, perhaps toss and turn a little, and even do some dreaming. But sleep is not one unbroken state; rather, it is a series of recurring stages, similar to the ups and downs of a roller-coaster ride. We'll describe a typical night's pattern for George, a college sophomore, who goes to bed about 11 P.M. and gets up about 7 A.M. As we take you through the figure below, notice that non-REM sleep is indicated by the wide blue line and REM sleep is indicated by red inserts. The numbers 1 to 4 refer to sleep stages 1, 2, 3, and 4 of non-REM sleep, which we discussed earlier.

Why is sleep like a roller-coaster ride?

Researchers have studied and plotted changes in brain waves, physiological arousal, and dreaming as people progressed through the stages of sleep (L. Rosenthal, 2006). Here's what George will experience on a typical roller-coaster-like ride through the different stages of a night's sleep.

A night's sleep is like a roller-coaster ride through different stages of sleep.

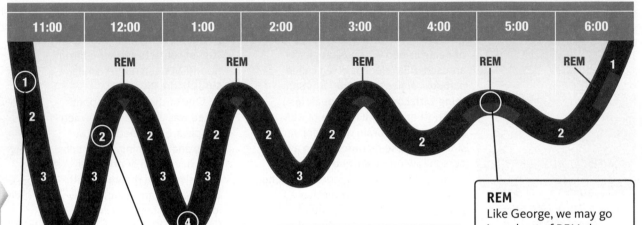

| 11:00 | 12:00 | 1:00 | 2:00 | 3:00 | 4:00 | 5:00 | 6:00 |

Here's what happens during a normal night's sleep.

Stage 1

As George becomes drowsy, he will enter non-REM stage 1, which is the transition between being awake and asleep.

As sleep progresses, he will continue to the next stage, non-REM stage 2, which is the first stage of real sleep. During stage 2, he may experience short, fragmented thoughts, so that if he is awakened, he may think he was dreaming.

He will continue through non-REM stage 3 and finally reach non-REM stage 4. When George enters non-REM stage 4, which is slow-wave, or delta, sleep, he will be very difficult to waken. After staying in stage 4 for some minutes to an hour, he will backtrack to stages 3 and 2.

Stage 2

After George reaches non-REM stage 2, he does not awaken but rather enters REM sleep. He will remain in REM for 15–45 minutes and, if awakened, will likely report dreaming. When in REM, his body is in a high state of physiological arousal, but his voluntary limb muscles are essentially paralyzed. If George experiences nightmares during REM, he will not act them out or injure himself because he cannot move.

After the REM period, he goes back down through non-REM stages 2, 3, and 4.

Stage 4

It is during stage 4 that George may sleepwalk, sleeptalk, or perform other activities, such as partially awakening to turn off the alarm, pull up the covers, or get up and go to the bathroom. However, George will remember nothing of what happens in non-REM stage 4, such as sleeptalking with his roommate or walking to the kitchen and getting a snack. He will remain in stage 4 for a period of time before again backtracking to non-REM stages 3 and 2, and then to his second REM period of the night.

Children sometimes wake up terrified during non-REM stage 4. These experiences are called night terrors (see p. 163), but the children will have no memory of them the next day. Also, bedwetting, a condition in which children are unable to control urination while asleep, occurs during non-REM stage 4.

REM

Like George, we may go in and out of REM sleep five or six times, with REM periods becoming longer toward morning. If George wants to remember his dreams, he should try when he first wakes up, since his last REM period may have occurred only minutes before.

Research findings indicate that getting as many REM periods as possible is important in helping the brain store material learned the previous day (Stickgold, 2000).

If George has a difficult time awakening from sleep, it may be because he was in stage 4, the hardest stage to awaken from.

Like George, we all go through the sleep stages in about the same sequence. However, there's a reason that some of us hate mornings more than others. ●

Unless otherwise noted, all images are © Cengage Learning

Are You a Morning or Evening Person?

Are you an early bird or a night owl?

Some students are early birds and seem to like morning classes, while night owls hate them. Researchers studied differences between early birds and night owls by developing and using a questionnaire.

A **questionnaire** is a method for obtaining information by asking subjects to read a list of written questions and check off or rate their preferences for specific answers.

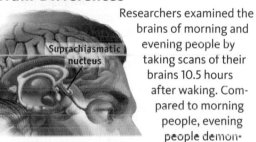

Morning person

The morning/evening questionnaire asked subjects to rate their preferred times for going to bed, getting up, and engaging in physical and mental activities, as well as their feelings of alertness in the morning and evening. The graph here shows the results from this questionnaire.

Score on Morning/Evening Questionnaire

Morning person	74
Evening person	45

Morning persons (score above 74) prefer to get up earlier, go to bed earlier, and engage in morning activities. **Evening persons** (score below 45) prefer to get up later, go to bed later, and engage in afternoon--evening activities. Those individuals who scored between 45 and 74 did not express a strong morning or evening preference (J. P. Guthrie et al., 1995).

Researchers found that there was a morning/evening continuum with strong preferences on either end and mixed or no preferences in the middle (Andershed, 2005). A combination of genetics, lifestyle, and age is believed to influence an individual's preference for mornings or evenings. Next, we'll take a close look at the brain differences between morning and evening people.

Evening person

Brain Differences

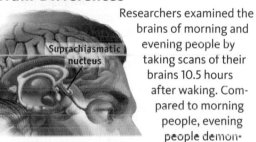

Suprachiasmatic nucleus

Researchers examined the brains of morning and evening people by taking scans of their brains 10.5 hours after waking. Compared to morning people, evening people demonstrated increased activity in the suprachiasmatic nucleus, an area that regulates the sleep-wake cycle. This suggests that evening people are not as susceptible to fatigue, which gives them the advantage in stamina. These results indicate that the preference for morning or evening may, at least in part, be explained by differences in the activity of the suprachiasmatic nucleus (Schmidt et al., 2009).

The preference for morning or evening may also be explained by changes that take place across the life span.

Changes across the Life Span

When we are young adults, most of us prefer the evenings. We tend to be most alert around 6 P.M., prefer exercising at night, and enjoy our dinner meal the most. We may need several alarms to ensure that we wake up on time in the morning. Midlife brings about an equal balance of morning people and evening people. Then, as we enter later adulthood, most of us tend to shift toward having a morning preference. We tend to be most alert around noon, prefer exercising in the morning, and enjoy our breakfast meal the most. Because we wake up early naturally during this life stage, there isn't any real need to set a morning alarm (Painter, 2011; Smolensky & Lamberg, 2001).

In addition to the differences described thus far, there are several other behavioral and cognitive differences, which we discuss next.

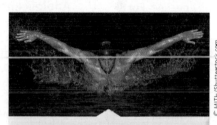

Young adults prefer exercising at night.

Older adults prefer exercising in the morning.

Behavioral and Cognitive Differences

Researchers found that students who were morning people reported being more alert at 8 A.M., took more morning classes, performed better in morning classes, and studied more in the morning than did students who were evening people (Duffy, 2002; J. P. Guthrie et al., 1995). Students who were evening people but began classes in the morning had more attention problems and poorer performance and complained of daytime sleepiness (Giannotti et al., 2002). The best time for creative thinking, such as brainstorming, is the early morning hours for morning people and the late evening hours for evening people (*Time,* 2006).

Adjust class schedule to your preference for morning or evening.

When looking at personality differences, researchers found that morning people tend to be conscientious introverts while evening people tend to be impulsive extroverts (K. Gilbert, 2006).

Finally, there are no differences between sexes in their preferences for being a morning or evening person (Duffy, 2002).

Although people differ in being morning or evening persons, they do share similar brain structures involved in putting them to sleep and waking them up, our next topic. ●

E Questions about Sleep

Most adults need 7–8 hours of sleep.

By the time you are 25 years old, you have fallen asleep over 9,000 times and have spent about 72,000 hours asleep. There are usually four questions that students ask about sleep: How much sleep do I need? Why do I sleep? What happens if I go without sleep? What causes sleep? We'll discuss each of these questions in turn.

How Much Sleep Do I Need?

What's the best amount for me?

According to a national survey, 16% of adults sleep less than 6 hours a night, 24% sleep 6–6.9 hours, 31% sleep 7–7.9 hours, and 26% sleep 8 or more hours (NSF, 2005). Overall, adults in America sleep an average of about 8 hours a night (NSF, 2008; Robinson & Martin, 2007). If we took a survey of babies, the time spent sleeping would be dramatically different, as shown in the pie charts below. Beginning at birth and continuing through old age, there is a gradual change in the total time we spend sleeping, the percentage of time we spend in REM sleep, and the kinds of sleep problems we have.

Infancy and Childhood

From infancy to adolescence, the total amount of time spent in sleep and the percentage spent in REM sleep gradually decline. For example, a newborn sleeps about 17 hours a day, and 50% of that time is spent in REM; a 4-year-old sleeps about 10 hours a day, and 25–30% of that time is spent in REM.

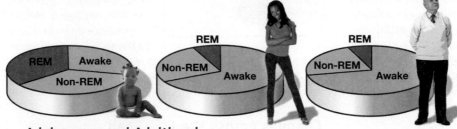

Adolescence and Adulthood

Researchers recently found that, compared to adults, adolescents need more sleep (about 9 hours) and their circadian clocks favor going to bed later and getting up later (Hathaway, 2006; MFMER, 2005). Researchers concluded that adolescents who must get up early (6 or 7 A.M.) for classes are often sleep deprived, which may interfere with their performance (L. Epstein & Mardon, 2007; NSF, 2006). One solution is for high-school classes to start an hour later so adolescents can get sufficient sleep. At about age 20, adolescents adopt the sleep pattern of adults, which is to get approximately 7–8 hours of sleep a night, with about 20% or less being REM sleep.

Old Age

Upon reaching our sixties, total sleep time drops to about 6.5 hours a day, but the percentage of REM sleep remains about the same (20%) (Ropper & Samuels, 2009). Other changes are that older people spend less time per cycle in each of sleep's stages and many experience fragmented sleep patterns, such as having to wake up more often during the night to use the bathroom (Kurdziel & Spencer, 2011).

Why Do I Sleep?

Is my brain being repaired?

Why we sleep remains one of the greatest mysteries of nature (Saey, 2009b). One reason we know sleep is important is because we can't live long without it. So far, the longest a human has voluntarily gone without sleep is 11 days (discussed on the next page). There are many theories of why we spend so much of our day asleep, none of which have been accepted as providing a complete explanation (Kurtzleben, 2011). We'll discuss two popular theories—the repair and adaptive theories.

The **repair theory** suggests that activities during the day deplete key factors in our brain or body that are replenished or repaired by sleep. The repair theory says that sleep is primarily a restorative process.

The repair theory is supported by three findings. First, during sleep there is a marked secretion of growth hormone, which controls aspects of metabolism, physical growth, and brain development (Pandi-Perumal et al., 2008). Second, during sleep there is increased production of immune cells to fight infection (Barth, 2009; M. R. Irwin et al., 2008). Third, during wakefulness there is a decline in the brain's energy stores (glycogen), which are restored during sleep and needed for normal functioning (Geiger, 2002). The brain needs sleep to grow, repair its immune system, and restore its energy and chemicals (J. M. Siegel, 2003).

Repair theory says sleep restores brain and body.

The **adaptive theory** suggests that sleep evolved because it prevented early humans and animals from wasting energy and exposing themselves to the dangers of nocturnal predators (W. B. Webb, 1992).

Support for the adaptive theory comes from observations that large predatory animals, such as lions, sleep a lot and wherever they wish, while prey animals, such as antelope, sleep far less and in protected areas. Many birds sleep with only one hemisphere at a time, to guard against predators (Sillery, 2002). Animals (humans) that rely primarily on visual cues and have little night vision have evolved a circadian clock for sleeping at night and thus avoid becoming prey (Hirshkowitz et al., 1997).

The adaptive and repair theories are not really at odds. Both have support but just focus on different reasons for sleep.

Adaptive theory says sleep helps us avoid dangers.

What If I Miss Sleep?

Can you go without sleep?

One method of investigating why sleep is important is to study people or animals who are sleep deprived. The record for sleep deprivation was set by a young adult who went without sleep for 11 days, or 264 hours (L. C. Johnson et al., 1965). On his 11th day without sleep, this young man beat the researcher in a pinball game, which indicates he was still awake and alert. Here's what happens when people are sleep deprived.

Effects on the Body

Sleep deprivation, even for 264 hours, has minimal effect on physiological functions controlled by the autonomic nervous system, such as heart rate and blood pressure (Kato et al., 2000). However, sleep deprivation can lead to serious health problems (Saey, 2009a). Sleep deprivation may compromise our immune system, which increases an individual's vulnerability to viral infections and may lead to inflammation-related diseases (Dement, 1999; M. R. Irwin et al., 2008). Also, sleep deprivation increases the production of stress hormones, elevates blood pressure, and increases plaque in coronary arteries, which are major risk factors for health conditions such as heart disease and stroke (C. R. King, 2008; R. Stein, 2005a). Sleep deprivation has been linked to changes in appetite-related hormones and elevated amounts of the hormone insulin. Researchers have concluded that sleep deprivation increases the risk for obesity and diabetes (L. J. Epstein, 2010).

Effects on the Brain

Sleep deprivation can deplete the brain's vital energy stores (glycogen) and interfere with completing tasks that require vigilance and concentration, such as recalling and recognizing words and doing math problems (Geiger, 2002; Ropper & Samuels, 2009). Sleep deprivation increases activity of the emotional centers of the brain, leading to irritability as well as interfering with the ability to make rational or logical decisions (Yoo et al., 2007).

Scientists recently found that the brains of rats who are kept awake longer than usual turn themselves off even though the rat is still awake. Researchers believe it's likely that the same occurs in humans and that it has negative consequences on our cognitive and motor functioning (Vyazovskiy et al., 2011). These results suggest that our peak performance is early in the day and the longer we stay awake, the more our performance declines.

What Causes Sleep?

How do you go to sleep?

After getting into bed, most of us fall asleep within 5–30 minutes and sleep an average of 7–8 hours (range about 6–10 hours). Going to sleep involves a very complicated process during which different areas of the brain are activated or deactivated. The whole sleep process begins with something flipping the master switch for sleep.

Master Sleep Switch

The master switch for sleep is in a nucleus of the brain called the ventrolateral preoptic nucleus (Purves et al., 2012).

VLPO is sleep switch.

The **ventrolateral preoptic nucleus (VLPO)** is a group of cells in the hypothalamus that act like a master switch for sleep. When turned on, the VLPO secretes a neurotransmitter (GABA) that turns off areas that keep the brain awake. When the VLPO is turned off, certain brain areas become active and you wake up.

Researchers don't know precisely how the VLPO in humans is turned on and off, but they recently found that histamine may play a role in how the VLPO regulates wakefulness (Y. Liu et al., 2010).

Next, we'll look at one brain area the VLPO turns off.

Reticular Formation

In order for the forebrain to receive and process information from the senses, it must be aroused and alerted by the reticular formation.

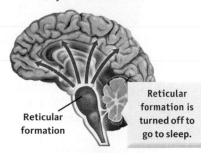

Reticular formation

Reticular formation is turned off to go to sleep.

The **reticular formation,** a column of cells that stretches the length of the brain stem, arouses and alerts the forebrain and prepares it to receive information from all the senses.

The reticular formation is important in keeping the forebrain alert and in producing a state of wakefulness (Brodal, 2010). If the reticular formation is stimulated in sleeping animals, they awaken; if it is seriously damaged in animals or humans, they lapse into permanent unconsciousness or coma.

Going to Sleep

The master sleep switch and the reticular formation are but two of the factors regulating sleep. Here is the probable sequence for going to sleep.

First, the time of day you go to sleep is regulated by the circadian clock, which is influenced by the suprachiasmatic nucleus of the hypothalamus (R. Y. Moore, 2006).

Second, something turns on your master sleep switch, which is located in the VLPO (ventrolateral preoptic nucleus). In turn, the VLPO turns off areas that arouse your brain, such as the reticular formation (Garcia-Rill et al., 2006).

Third, a number of different chemicals and neurotransmitters, some of which are manufactured in the pons, regulate when you go into and out of non-REM and REM sleep and when you awaken (Czeisler et al., 2006).

Fourth, the circadian rhythm that regulates your body temperature is tied in with sleep, since you go to sleep when your temperature falls and wake up when your temperature rises (Ropper & Samuels, 2009).

Thus, the reasons you go to sleep and wake up involve a complex interaction among the circadian clock, brain areas, sleep-inducing chemicals, and body temperature.

Four factors for sleep

After the Concept Review, we'll describe a psychological problem whose cause seems related to decreased sunlight. ●

Concept Review

1. The various levels of awareness of one's thoughts and feelings, as well as of other internal and external stimuli, are referred to as **(a)** _____. This experience varies on a continuum from very aware and alert to totally unaware and unresponsive. Activities that require full awareness and alertness and may interfere with other ongoing endeavors are called **(b)** _____. In comparison, activities that require little awareness and minimal attention and that do not interfere with other ongoing endeavors are called **(c)** _____.

2. The biological clock that is set for a day of about 24 hours is called a **(a)** _____. This rhythm regulates our sleep-wake cycle, which is set to an average day of 24 hours and 18 minutes. Our circadian clock is reset by 18 minutes each day to match our agreed-upon 24-hour day. The circadian clock is located in the brain's hypothalamus, in a small part called the **(b)** _____.

3. If your circadian rhythm is out of step with local time, you may feel fatigued and disoriented, a traveler's complaint called **(a)** _____. Workers and drivers have more accidents during the early-morning hours because their sleep-wake clock is telling them it's time to **(b)** _____. Researchers have reset circadian rhythms by exposing participants and night workers to periods of bright light; this is called **(c)** _____ therapy.

4. Near the center of the human brain is an oval group of cells, collectively called the pineal gland, that secrete a hormone called **(a)** _____. The gland secretes the hormone during dark periods and stops when it gets light. In many animals, this hormone plays a major role in the regulation of **(b)** _____ rhythms.

5. During a night's sleep, we gradually pass through five stages. Stage 1, which is a transition between waking and sleeping, has brain waves known as **(a)** _____. Stage 2 has

brain waves with bursts of activity that are called **(b)** _____. Stage 3 and especially stage 4 are marked by high-amplitude, low-frequency **(c)** _____. Stage 4 is often considered the deepest stage of sleep because it is the most difficult from which to be awakened. During stage 4, heart rate, respiration, temperature, and blood flow to the brain are **(d)** _____. Together, stages 1, 2, 3, and 4 are referred to as **(e)** _____, in which we spend about 80% of our sleep time. About five or six times throughout the night, we enter a paradoxical state called **(f)** _____, which accounts for the remaining 20% of our sleep time. This stage is characterized by increased physiological arousal, "alert and awake" brain waves, and vivid dreaming.

6. From birth through old age, there is a decrease in total sleep time, from about 17 hours in newborns to 6.5 hours after age 60. In addition, one stage of sleep, called _____, decreases from 50% of sleep time in infancy to 20% in adulthood.

7. There are two different but not incompatible theories of why we sleep. The theory that says the purpose of sleep is to restore factors depleted throughout the day is the **(a)** _____. The theory that says sleep is based on an evolutionary need to conserve energy and escape nocturnal harm is the **(b)** _____.

8. Going to sleep is regulated by the following factors. An area in the hypothalamus that is the master sleep switch is called the **(a)** _____. An area in the hypothalamus that regulates circadian rhythms is called the **(b)** _____ nucleus. A brain area that contributes to our staying awake by sending neural signals that alert and arouse the forebrain is called the **(c)** _____. Several different sleep chemicals and **(d)** _____, some of which are made in the pons, regulate going into and out of the stages of sleep. In addition, we go to sleep several hours after a fall in body **(e)** _____ and get up when it starts to rise.

Answers: 1. (a) consciousness, (b) controlled processes, (c) automatic processes; 2. (a) circadian rhythm, (b) suprachiasmatic nucleus; 3. (a) jet lag, (b) sleep, (c) light; 4. (a) melatonin, (b) circadian; 5. (a) theta waves, (b) sleep spindles, (c) delta waves, (d) reduced, (e) non-REM sleep, (f) REM sleep; 6. REM sleep; 7. (a) repair theory, (b) adaptive theory; 8. (a) VLPO, or ventrolateral preoptic nucleus, (b) suprachiasmatic, (c) reticular formation, (d) neurotransmitters, (e) temperature

Seasonal Affective Disorder

For many animals, including humans, sunlight has a direct influence on resetting the circadian clock and affecting circadian rhythms. However, it was only recently that researchers found a direct nerve connection from receptors in the retina, which is located in the back of the eye, to a nucleus in the brain (suprachiasmatic nucleus in the hypothalamus—see p. 150). This particular nerve pathway is not involved with seeing things but only with sensing the presence and amount of light, either sunlight or artificial light (M. W. Young, 2000). This means that humans have a neural pathway that is very responsive to the presence of light and may be involved in a mental health problem called seasonal affective disorder, or SAD.

Does light affect your mood?

Seasonal affective disorder, or **SAD,** is a pattern of depressive symptoms, such as loss of interest or pleasure in nearly all activities. Depressed feelings cycle with the seasons, typically beginning in fall or winter and going away in spring, when days are longer and sunnier. Along with depression are lethargy, excessive sleepiness, overeating, weight gain, and craving for carbohydrates. Recently, SAD has become a subtype (Seasonal Pattern Specifier) of major depression (American Psychiatric Association, 2000).

Light therapy is an effective treatment for seasonal affective disorder (SAD).

© Bruno Boissonnet/Photo Researchers, Inc.

What might trigger SAD is the amount of a brain neurotransmitter, serotonin, and the amount of a hormone made mostly at night, melatonin. Researchers suggest that the decreased sunlight in fall and winter causes a decrease in the amount of serotonin and an increase in melatonin, which may both act to trigger SAD (Anstett, 2006; G. W. Lambert et al., 2002).

A nondrug treatment for SAD involves exposing a person to bright light in the morning for about one hour (Westrin & Lam, 2007). This treatment has received much support as an effective way to manage the depressive symptoms of SAD (Partonen et al., 2011). Unlike medication, which can require days or weeks to take effect, researchers recently found that patients with SAD who were exposed to one hour of light therapy reported an immediate improvement in depressive symptoms (Reeves et al., 2012).

Because decreased sunlight appears to trigger SAD, you would expect the fewest cases of SAD in southern Florida, more cases in northern New Hampshire with its gloomy winters, and even more cases in northern Iceland, which has harsh winters with little or no sunlight.

Occurrence of SAD

As predicted, the graph shows that the incidence of SAD is very low (1.4%) among people who live in sunny Florida but about five times higher (7.3%) among people who live under the gray winter skies of northern New Hampshire (Magnusson, 2000). However, far north of New Hampshire is Iceland, which has far less sunlight in fall and winter than New Hampshire. In spite of having less sunlight, Icelanders have only about half the incidence of SAD (3.6%) compared to residents of New Hampshire (Axelsson et al., 2002).

Where is the highest rate of SAD?

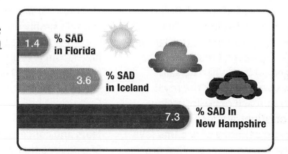

1.4 % SAD in Florida

3.6 % SAD in Iceland

7.3 % SAD in New Hampshire

When researchers try to explain any unusual or unpredicted findings, they first check the methods and procedures used to measure the dependent variable, which in this case is the occurrence of SAD. However, researchers in Iceland used the same methods (questionnaires) and procedures that were used by researchers in the United States (Magnusson, 2000). If research methods and procedures were similar, what else would explain why the highest incidence of SAD was reported in New Hampshire and not in Iceland?

Cultural Differences

What's different about Icelanders?

Why did Icelanders report less than half the incidence of SAD, even though they have far less sunlight in fall and winter than residents of New Hampshire?

Researchers concluded that differences in methods, questionnaires, and residents' lifestyles or occupations could not explain this discrepancy. Rather, there may be two other explanations that involve cultural and genetic differences.

For 1,000 years, Icelanders have lived rather isolated in a very demanding, low-sunlight environment. Because of very harsh and unyielding environmental demands, Icelanders may have developed an emotional hardiness to deal with especially gloomy winters that trigger almost twice as many cases of SAD

among residents of the northeastern United States. Another explanation for Icelanders' low incidence of SAD may involve genetic factors. For example, researchers studied a population of immigrants in Canada who were wholly of Icelandic descent. The incidence of SAD in the Icelandic immigrants was unexpectedly much lower than found in other residents of the same general area. Researchers concluded that the lower frequency of SAD in Icelanders is puzzling and may reflect both genetic and cultural differences, such as learning how to deal with isolation and living in harsh environments (Axelsson et al., 2002; Magnusson & Partonen, 2005).

Next, we'll discuss four explanations for something most of us experience every night—dreaming. ●

Although some people insist that they never dream, research suggests that everyone dreams during the night. In sleep laboratories, people awakened from REM periods report 80–100% of the time that they were having dreams with vivid, colorful, even bizarre images. Less frequently, people awakened from non-REM sleep or right after going to sleep report dreaming of dull, repetitive thoughts or of the colorful images reported after REM sleep (Domhoff, 2003). However, what you think of as dreaming usually occurs during REM sleep.

What do dreams mean?

Everybody dreams, but what do dreams mean? Figuring out the meaning of dreams is a popular and scholarly activity for the more than 400 psychologists, physiologists, anthropologists, artists, "dream workers," and swamis who attend the annual meeting of the Association for the Study of Dreams. The focus of this group is to discover meaning in dreams—no easy task, since there are many theories.

Dreaming of a plane crash creates as much anxiety as hearing about a real crash.

© GY1 NSEA/iStockphoto

We know these 400 scholars take dream interpretation seriously, but do others? Researchers surveyed people in India, South Korea, and the United States about the meaning of dreams and found that most people from these countries believe dreams contain hidden meanings. This prompted the next question: Are people affected by their dreams? Researchers found that dreaming of a plane crash created greater anxiety than consciously thinking about a plane crash or hearing that the terrorist threat level had been raised, and the same level of anxiety as hearing about an actual crash that took place on the route they planned to take (Morewedge & Norton, 2009).

It seems the majority of people believe dreams have meaning, but how does one go about interpreting dreams? We'll discuss four currently popular psychological theories of dream interpretation: Freud's theory of dream interpretation, extensions of waking life, activation-synthesis theory, and threat simulation theory.

Freud's Theory of Dream Interpretation

In the preface to his famous book *The Interpretation of Dreams*, Freud (1900) wrote, "This book contains, even according to my present-day judgment, the most valuable of all the discoveries it has been my good fortune to make. Insight such as this falls to one's lot but once in a lifetime." Before 1900, psychologists believed that dreams were meaningless and bizarre images. However, Freud 's theory changed all that when he said dreams were a way ("the royal road") to reach our unconscious thoughts and desires.

Freud believed dreams reveal repressed desires.

Freud's theory of dreams says that we have a "censor" that protects us from realizing threatening and unconscious desires or wishes, especially those involving sex or aggression. To protect us from having threatening thoughts, the "censor" transforms our secret, guilt-ridden, and anxiety-provoking desires into harmless symbols that appear in our dreams and do not disturb our sleep or conscious thoughts.

As you can see, Freud separated dreams into two levels and he called these the manifest content and latent content.

The **manifest content** is the portion of the dream that the person remembers, which are the harmless symbols.

The **latent content** is the hidden element of the dream that is determined by unconscious forces and of which the person is unaware.

Freud made two main points no one had made before: Dreams contained symbols that had meaning, and dreams could be interpreted. For example, Freud (1900) said male sex symbols are long objects, such as sticks, umbrellas, and pencils; female sex symbols are hollow things, such as caves, jars, and keyholes. Freud believed a psychoanalyst's (Freudian therapist's) task was to interpret dream symbols and to uncover a client's threatening but unconscious desires, needs, and emotions (B. Bower, 2001).

Extensions of Waking Life

Many therapists believe that dreams are extensions of waking life (Kramer, 2006b; Pesant & Zadra, 2006).

The theory that **dreams are extensions of waking life** means that our dreams reflect the same thoughts, fears, concerns, problems, and emotions that we have when awake.

Therapist and researcher Rosalind Cartwright (1988) says, "People simply don't remember their dreams very well. The therapist's task is often like trying to reconstruct a 500-page novel from just the last page. But dreams collected from a single night in the sleep lab read like chapters in a book. They illuminate current concerns and the feelings attached to them" (p. 36). Cartwright believes that patients suffering from depression or marital problems cope by repeating their fears and concerns in their dreams. She advises that as soon as you awaken from a reoccurring bad dream, you should figure out why the dream is upsetting and then visualize how you would like the dream to end the next time it occurs. With practice, people can gain control over reoccurring bad dreams. Cartwright concludes that there is little reason to pay attention to dreams unless they keep you from

Therapists believe dreams reflect waking concerns.

sleeping or cause you to wake up in a panic (Cartwright, 2002). In these cases, therapists find dream interpretation a useful tool in helping clients better understand the personal and emotional problems that are contributing to their bad dreams.

Other researchers believe that dreams have a variety of uses, ranging from dealing with threatening situations, resolving personal and emotional problems, sparking artistic creativity, to even solving scientific, mathematical, or other kinds of puzzles (B. Bower, 2001).

The next theory looks at dreams as reflecting neural activity.

Unless otherwise noted, all images are © Cengage Learning

Activation-Synthesis Theory

In the late 1970s, psychiatrist and neurophysiologist J. Allan Hobson published a new theory of dreams that totally disagreed with many therapists' as well as Freud's theory of dreams. Recently, Hobson (2002) published a revised version of this 1970s theory.

The **activation-synthesis theory** says that dreaming occurs because brain areas that provide reasoned cognitive control during the waking state are shut down. As a result, the sleeping brain is stimulated by different chemical and neural influences that result in hallucinations, delusions, high emotions, and bizarre thought patterns that we call dreams.

Unlike Freud, Hobson believes that dream interpretation is questionable, since there is no way to know whether dreams are just bizarre events or contain useful or valid information about a person's problems.

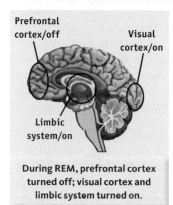

Prefrontal cortex/off

Visual cortex/on

Limbic system/on

During REM, prefrontal cortex turned off; visual cortex and limbic system turned on.

The bases for Hobson's revised theory come from brain scans of neural activity taken while people were in REM sleep. Researchers reported that during REM sleep, the area responsible for executive functions (prefrontal cortex), such as thinking, planning, and reasoning, had reduced activity, while areas involved in emotions (limbic system) and visual experiences (visual cortex) had increased activity (A. R. Braun et al., 1998). Hobson believes that this pattern of brain activity explains why dreams are emotional (limbic system/on) and full of visual images (visual cortex/on) but are often strange, bizarre, and poorly planned or thought out (prefrontal cortex/off) (Domhoff, 2003). Similar to the other dream theories, the activation-synthesis theory also has critics (Kramer, 2006a). They believe the content of dreams can contain useful and meaningful information about a person's life (Domhoff, 2005a, 2005b).

The fourth theory looks at dreams as having an important evolutionary function.

Threat Simulation Theory

Currently, there is one well-known and well-researched evolutionary dream theory that was developed by a Finnish researcher named Antti Revonsuo and is called threat simulation theory (Revonsuo, 2000a, 2000b).

The **threat simulation theory** says that dreaming serves a biological function by repeatedly simulating events that are threatening in our waking lives so our brain can practice how it perceives threats and so we can rehearse our responses to these events.

I dreamed of a dangerous bear to rehearse my response to this threat so I was prepared for my upcoming camping trip.

Based on this theory, our ancestors would have dreamed about threatening life events and used their dreams to rehearse the skills needed for survival. This theory may explain why I (H. K.) dreamed of an angry, dangerous bear approaching me just before my planned camping trip in the woods.

Much research has been done to carefully test this theory, and the results have been mixed (Zadra et al., 2006). Research shows that childhood trauma and recurrent dreams are associated with more threatening dreams (Valli et al., 2005; Valli & Revonsuo, 2009). But we all seem to have dreams that do not involve any threatening events (Malcolm-Smith et al., 2008).

Next, we'll examine what people dream about.

Typical Dreams

What do people dream about?

Although many animals, including bats, whales, monkeys, moles, dogs, and cats (but not snakes), have REM sleep, we do not know if they dream. We know that humans dream because they tell us. Thousands of descriptions of dreams have been obtained from people who had just been aroused from REM sleep and others who were asked to record their dreams at home. One researcher (Van de Castle, 1994) has catalogued these descriptions and found that typical dreams have the following characteristics:

- Dreams have several characters.
- They involve motion such as running or walking.
- They are more likely to take place indoors than outside.
- They are filled with visual sensations but rarely include sensations of taste, smell, or pain.
- They seem bizarre because we disregard physical laws by flying or falling without injury.
- They may be recurrent—for example, dreams of being threatened, being pursued, or trying to hide.
- They more frequently involve emotions of anxiety or fear than joy or happiness.
- They rarely involve sexual encounters and are almost never about sexual intercourse.

Many people dream about flying, running, falling, or hiding.

- Rarely can we control or dream about something we intend to.
- Dreams usually have visual imagery and are in color in sighted people, but in people blind from birth, dreams are never visual but only tactile, olfactory (smell), or gustatory (taste).

Researchers conclude that although individual dreams represent unique experiences, the format in which we dream, such as flying, falling, running, or hiding, is shared by others (Domhoff, 2003). One common question is: Why do some better remember their dreams? One researcher found that the ability to remember dreams was positively related or correlated with how well one can create mental images during waking and was not related to verbal ability, which might influence dream recall (Foulkes, 2003).

Sometimes dreams can turn into nightmares, which we'll discuss next in considering sleep problems and treatments. ●

© Scott E Read/Shutterstock.com

© HomeArt/Shutterstock.com

Insomnia

How big is the problem? In the United States, nearly 30% of people report experiencing some kind of sleep problem (NSF, 2009). For example, some adults stop breathing in their sleep (sleep apnea); some have trouble going to or staying asleep (insomnia); a small percentage go from being wide awake to a very deep sleep quickly and without warning (narcolepsy); and 69% of all children experience some type of sleep disturbance at least a few nights a week (Carskadon, 2006). We'll discuss a number of these sleep problems as well as possible treatments, beginning with one of the more common problems, insomnia.

Definition and Causes

In the United States, about 33% of adults report some type of insomnia (Ohayon & Guilleminault, 2006).

Insomnia refers to difficulties in either going to sleep or staying asleep through the night. Insomnia is associated with a number of daytime complaints, including fatigue, impairment of concentration, memory difficulty, and lack of well-being.

Psychological causes. Common psychological causes of insomnia include experiencing an overload of stressful events, worrying about personal or job-related difficulties, grieving over a loss or death, and coping with mental health problems. For many middle-aged working people, job stress is a major cause of insomnia and other sleep problems (Kalimo et al., 2000). For students, common causes of insomnia are worry about exams, personal problems, and changes in sleep schedule, such as staying up late Saturday night and sleeping late on Sunday morning. Then Sunday night students are not tired at the usual time and may experience insomnia.

Physiological causes. Common physiological causes of insomnia include changing to night-shift work, which upsets circadian rhythms, having medical problems or chronic pain, and abusing alcohol or other substances (sedatives). All can disrupt going to and staying asleep.

There are effective nondrug (psychological) and drug treatments for bouts of insomnia.

Nondrug Treatment

Nondrug treatments for insomnia may differ in method, but all have the same goal: to stop the person from excessive worrying and reduce tension, which are major psychological causes of insomnia. Research has found that up to 80% of people with insomnia can benefit from cognitive-behavioral therapy (CBT) (Lyon, 2009b). The cognitive component of CBT addresses the unhelpful attitudes and beliefs that cause anxiety, arouse the body, and make sleep difficult. For instance, someone may lie awake thinking, "I have to get 8 hours of sleep tonight or I'll be a complete wreck tomorrow." The behavioral piece helps change maladaptive sleep patterns. For instance, a person may be spending too much time in bed or not exercising at all during the day (Alderman, 2009; Lyon, 2009b).

One proven CBT method to reduce insomnia is to establish an optimal sleep pattern (Bootzin & Rider, 1997). The eight guidelines in establishing an optimal sleep pattern are described below and will help make sleeping more regular and efficient.

1. Go to bed only when you are sleepy, not by convention or habit.

2. Put the light out immediately when you get into bed.

3. Do not read or watch television in bed, since these are activities that you do when awake.

4. If you are not asleep within 20 minutes, get out of bed and sit and relax in another room until you are tired again. Relaxation can include tensing and relaxing your muscles or using visual imagery, which involves closing your eyes and concentrating on some calm scene or image for several minutes.

5. Repeat step 4 as often as required, and also if you wake up for any long periods of time.

6. Set the alarm to the same time each morning, so that your time of waking is always the same. This step is important because oversleeping or sleeping in is one of the primary causes of insomnia the next night.

7. Do not nap during the day because it will throw off your sleep schedule that night.

8. Follow this program rigidly for several weeks to establish an efficient and regular pattern of sleep.

Serious problems with chronic insomnia may be treated in the short term with drugs, but in the long run, people need to change their sleep habits (Morin, 2009).

Drug Treatment

Many stressful situations, such as losing a loved one, going through a divorce, or dealing with a physical injury, may result in chronic insomnia, which is defined as lasting longer than three weeks. In these cases, doctors may prescribe one of the following sleep-inducing drugs.

Benzodiazepines (*ben-zo-die-AS-ah-peens*) (Dalmane, Xanax, Restoril) reduce anxiety, worry, and stress and are effective and relatively safe when taken in moderate doses in the short-term (2–4 weeks) treatment of insomnia (Czeisler et al., 2006).

However, prolonged use of benzodiazepines, especially at higher doses, may lead to dependence on the drug and serious side effects, such as memory loss and excessive sleepiness. Reduced side effects are one advantage of the next drugs.

Nonbenzodiazepines (Ambien, Sonata, Lunesta) are rapidly becoming popular sleeping pills because they are fast acting, reduce daytime drowsiness, have fewer cognitive side effects, and are less likely to lead to dependence (Lee-Chiong & Sateia, 2006).

In the United States alone, about 56 million sleeping pill prescriptions are filled each year (IMS Health, 2009). However, studies have found that cognitive-behavioral therapy is either as effective as or superior to sleeping pills in treating and reducing chronic insomnia (Perlis et al., 2003; Sivertsen et al., 2006).

Sleep Apnea

In the United States, about 20 million adults have insomnia because they stop breathing, a problem called sleep apnea.

Sleep apnea refers to repeated periods during sleep when a person stops breathing for 10 seconds or longer. The person may repeatedly stop breathing, momentarily wake up, resume breathing, and return to sleep. Repeated awakenings during the night result in insomnia and leave the person exhausted during the day but not knowing the cause of the tiredness.

The chances of developing sleep apnea increase if a person is an intense and frequent snorer, is overweight, uses alcohol, or takes sedatives (benzodiazepines) (Chokroverty, 2000). Some people with sleep apnea may wake up an astonishing 200–400 times a night, which also results in insomnia (Czeisler et al., 2006).

The simplest treatment for sleep apnea is to sew tennis balls into the back of a pajama top so the person cannot lie on his or her back, which increases the chances of sleep apnea. For more severe cases, the most effective therapy is a device that blows air into a mask worn over the nose that helps keep air passages open (see photo below). An alternative treatment is for people to wear a mouth device that helps to move the lower jaw forward and thus open the airway (H. Fields, 2006). In severe cases, people may undergo surgery to remove tonsils or alter the position of the jaw (A. E. Sher, 2006).

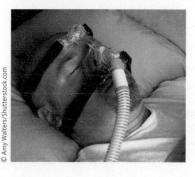

Narcolepsy

As a child, Rainer would nod off in classes. As an adult, he may fall asleep in the middle of a meeting, during a conversation, or while driving! He has fleeting urges to sleep throughout the day and always feels fatigued (Marschall, 2007). Rainer has narcolepsy.

Narcolepsy *(NAR-ko-lep-see)* is a chronic disorder that is marked by excessive sleepiness, usually in the form of sleep attacks or short periods of sleep throughout the day. The sleep attacks are accompanied by brief periods of REM sleep and loss of muscle control (cataplexy), which may be triggered by big emotional changes.

Narcoleptics describe their sleep attacks as irresistible. They report falling asleep in very inappropriate places, such as while carrying on a conversation or driving a car. In many cases, these sleep attacks make it difficult for narcoleptics to lead normal lives.

Like humans, some dogs get narcolepsy. Researchers discovered that narcolepsy occurred in dogs and mice when certain brain cells, called hypocretin neurons, either were absent or did not respond normally (Mignot, 2000). More recently, researchers found that these same neurons die in people who have narcolepsy, and they are now beginning to identify the genetic links of this condition (Hallmayer et al., 2009).

Researchers believe a hypocretin-based medicine could soon be on the market and provide a new and effective way to treat narcolepsy, which affects about 150,000 Americans (Marschall, 2007).

Other Sleep Disturbances

Night Terrors

A 4-year-old boy sits up in the night and begins screaming. This is an example of a night terror.

Night terrors, which occur during stage 3 or 4 (delta sleep), are frightening experiences that often start with a piercing scream, followed by sudden waking in a fearful state with rapid breathing and increased heart rate. However, the

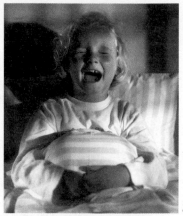

next morning the child has no memory of the frightening experience. About 3–7% of children have night terrors.

A child in the grip of night terrors is difficult to calm and, even if severely shaken, may need several minutes to regain full awareness. Night terrors are most common in children aged 5–7 and disappear by adolescence (Heussler, 2005). Caregivers should take enough time to comfort and soothe the frightened child, who usually will go back to sleep.

Nightmares

Besides night terrors, about 25–70% of all children aged 3–6 have nightmares, and about 47% of college students report having them once a month (Picchioni et al., 2002).

Nightmares, which occur during REM sleep, are very frightening and anxiety-producing images that occur during dreaming. Nightmares usually involve great danger—being attacked, injured, or pursued. Upon awakening, the person can usually describe the nightmare in great detail.

Nightmares usually stop when the person wakes, but feelings of anxiety or fear may persist for some time. One effective treatment for nightmares is cognitive-behavioral therapy, which teaches people how to change harmful thought patterns and take control of their dreams (Krakow, 2009).

Sleepwalking

One of the more unusual sleep disturbances is sleepwalking.

Sleepwalking usually occurs in stage 3 or 4 (delta sleep) and consists of getting up and walking while literally sound asleep. Sleepwalkers generally have poor coordination, are clumsy but can avoid objects, can engage in very limited conversation, and have no memory of sleepwalking.

Occasional sleepwalking is considered normal in children; frequent sleepwalking in adults may be caused by increased stress, sleep deprivation, or mental problems (Cartwright, 2006). Sleepwalking can be a serious problem because of the potential for injury and harm to oneself and others (imagine sleepwalking out of the house onto the highway).

Sleep researchers estimate that as many as 70 million Americans have one or more of the sleep problems discussed above. Sleep disorders clinics have been set up to treat the more serious problems (R. S. Rosenberg, 2006). ●

Texting: How Distracting Can It Be?

YouTube has videos of young adults texting while driving, and Facebook has a group called *I Text Message People While Driving and I Haven't Crashed Yet!* Many people are routinely texting while on the move, whether it's waiting in line for coffee, walking across the street, or driving.

1 Which type of brain wave occurs when you are text messaging?

Is texting a big enough distraction to put people at risk of danger? The American College of Emergency Physicians believes so. They report that many people arrive in the emergency department with serious, sometime fatal injuries because they weren't paying attention to their surroundings while texting.

2 How is walking across the street while using your cell phone different from walking while chewing gum?

Be honest—how many times have you been texting while driving and looked up only to be surprised you haven't been paying attention to the road? The dangers of texting while driving are so serious that 35 states and the District of Columbia have laws banning text messaging for all drivers. Though no state

3 Why have you forgotten that you're driving while talking or texting?

entirely bans the use of cell phones while driving, nine states and the District of Columbia ban drivers from using handheld cell phones while driving. It seems that the restrictions on using phones while driving will only become more strict. For instance, the Transportation Department has recently proposed guidelines aimed at disabling test messaging, Internet browsing, navigation destination entry, and phone dialing if the car is not in the Park position.

The use of a cell phone in any way while driving increases the risk of an accident, and texting is more dangerous than talking. A driver's risk of getting into an accident is believed to increase sixfold when texting and fourfold when talking on a handheld cell phone. One study reported that texting increases the risk of a near-crash by up to 23 times. Another study found that cell phone use caused distractions comparable to those that occur while driving intoxicated.

4 How might perception explain why drivers are more likely to getting into accidents while texting?

5 What type of research setting would researchers use to compare the driving abilities of cell phone users and people who are intoxicated?

Not only is texting distracting during our waking day, but for

some, it can be a problem during sleep. Teens and young adults, in particular, go to sleep with their phones plugged in right by their beds. With every beep of a new text message, they awaken, disrupting their sleep and thereby affecting their cognitive and physical performance the next day. There have even been rumors of sleep texting—that is, texting during sleep only to discover in the morning the texts sent in the middle of night.

6 What stage of sleep must people be in if they're unknowingly texting during the night?

The dangers of texting seem countless: injuring oneself or others, death, and tremendous embarrassment (who knows what you might text while asleep!).

Adapted from ACEP, 2008; Copeland, 2010; Drews et al., 2009; S. Flagg, 2008; GHSA, 2012; Jansen, 2011; Leming, 2008; Novotney, 2009a; U.S. Department of Transportation, 2012; Villarreal, 2008; Virginia Tech Transportation Institute, 2009

A Continuum of Consciousness

1. The awareness of our own thoughts and feelings, as well as of other internal and external stimuli, is called **(a)** _____, which occurs on a continuum from being very alert to being very unresponsive. Those activities that require our full awareness and concentration to reach some goal are called **(b)** _____. Those activities that require little awareness and minimal attention and that do not interfere with other ongoing activities are called **(c)** _____.

© Rich Legg/iStockphoto

2. Fantasizing or dreaming while awake, which often occurs during automatic processes, is called **(a)** _____. If, under the influence of drugs, meditation, or hypnosis, we perceive our internal and external environments in ways that differ from normal, we may be said to have entered **(b)** _____ of consciousness. Sigmund Freud suggested that we push unacceptable wishes or desires into our **(c)** _____. A blow to the head or general anesthesia can produce complete loss of awareness, which is called **(d)** _____. Mental and emotional processes that, although we are unaware of them, influence our conscious thoughts and behaviors form a kind of memory called **(e)** _____.

B Rhythms of Consciousness

© NASA

3. A biological clock that is set to run on a time cycle of 24–25 hours is called a **(a)** _____. In animals (and probably humans) the biological clock for the sleep-wake cycle is located in a part of the hypothalamus called the **(b)** _____.

4. If we travel across time zones and our circadian rhythm gets out of phase with the local clock time, we experience difficulty in going to sleep and getting up at normal times, a condition known as **(a)** _____. Researchers have been able to reset circadian rhythms in workers by exposing them to bright light during certain times; this is called **(b)** _____ therapy.

5. In the center of the animal and human brain is the pineal gland, a small group of cells that secrete the hormone _____. This hormone has a major role in regulating the sleep-wake cycle in animals; its role in humans is less clear.

C Stages of Sleep

6. Researchers study sleep and wakefulness by recording the activity of brain cells and muscles. Electrical brain activity is recorded in tracings called an **(a)** _____. The height of a wave is called its **(b)** _____, and the number of wave cycles that occur in one second is called the **(c)** _____.

7. If you are awake and alert, your brain waves have a very high frequency and low amplitude and are called **(a)** _____ waves. If you close your eyes and become relaxed and drowsy, your brain waves remain low in amplitude but decrease slightly in frequency; these are called **(b)** _____ waves.

8. Researchers divide sleep into five stages. Stage 1, the transition from wakefulness to sleep, is marked by **(a)** _____ waves and a feeling of gradually losing responsiveness to the outside world. Stage 2 represents the first real phase of sleep and is marked by high-frequency bursts of brain activity called **(b)** _____. In stage 3 and especially stage 4, there are high-amplitude, low-frequency brain waves called **(c)** _____. Stage 4 may be considered the deepest stage of sleep, since it is the most difficult from which to wake someone. Together, stages 1, 2, 3, and 4 are referred to as **(d)** _____ sleep, which makes up about 80% of sleep time.

9. About every 30–90 minutes throughout sleep, you leave stage 4 (delta sleep) and progress backward to stage 2. From stage 2, you enter a new stage of sleep marked by high-frequency, low-amplitude brain waves that look identical to **(a)** _____ waves. This stage is called **(b)** _____ sleep because your eyes move rapidly back and forth underneath closed eyelids. During this stage, you are asleep and lose muscle tension in the neck and limbs. However, your brain waves are like those when you are awake and alert, and there is increased arousal of many physiological responses. When awakened from this stage, people usually (80–90% of the time) report that they have been **(c)** _____.

D Research Focus: Circadian Preference

10. People who prefer to get up earlier, go to bed earlier, and engage in morning activities and whose body temperature rises more quickly in the morning and peaks earlier at night are called **(a)** _____. People who prefer to get up later, go to bed later, and engage in afternoon-evening activities and whose body temperature rises more slowly in the morning and peaks later at night are called **(b)** _____.

E Questions about Sleep

11. Going to sleep is regulated by the following factors. An area in the hypothalamus that is the master sleep switch is called the **(a)** _____. An area in the hypothalamus that regulates circadian rhythms is called the **(b)** _____. A brain area that contributes to our staying awake by sending neural signals that alert and arouse the forebrain is called the **(c)** _____. Several different sleep chemicals and **(d)** _____, some of which are made in the pons, regulate going into and out of the stages of sleep. In addition, we go to sleep several hours after a fall in body **(e)** _____ and get up when it starts to rise.

12. From infancy through old age, there is a gradual reduction in total **(a)** _____ time, from about 17 to 6.5 hours, and a reduction in the percentage of **(b)** _____ sleep, from about 50% to 20%.

13. The theory that says we sleep because we use up vital factors during the day that must be replaced at night is called the **(a)** _____ theory. The theory that says we sleep to conserve energy and avoid potential harm and injury from nocturnal predators is called the **(b)** _____ theory.

14. When we are sleep deprived, the next day we have difficulty performing tasks that require **(a)** _____. Sleep deprivation also affects the body by compromising our **(b)** _____ system, which increases our vulnerability to viral infections.

F Cultural Diversity: Incidence of SAD

15. The occurrence of a pattern of depressive symptoms that generally begin in the fall and winter and disappear in the spring is called **(a)** _____. Although the incidence of this disorder is lower in Florida and higher in the northeastern United States, it is not higher in Iceland, which is much farther north than New Hampshire. One reason Icelanders report a lower incidence of SAD is because of their **(b)** _____ values.

G Theories of Dream Interpretation

16. According to Freud's theory, we have a "censor" that protects us from **(a)** _____. This involves transforming threatening, unconscious desires into harmless symbols. According to Hobson's revised theory, called the **(b)** _____, the sleeping brain produces hallucinations, delusions, high emotions, and bizarre thoughts that we call dreams. During REM sleep, some parts of the brain are turned on, **(c)** _____, and some are turned off, **(d)** _____. According to many therapists and sleep-dream researchers, such as Cartwright, dreams are **(e)** _____ of waking thoughts and concerns, especially emotional ones, and provide clues to a person's problems. An evolutionary dream theory developed by Revonsuo is **(f)** _____ theory.

H Application: Sleep Problems & Treatments

17. A common sleep problem that includes difficulty in going to sleep or remaining asleep throughout the night is called **(a)** _____. A nondrug treatment is to use a proven **(b)** _____ method. Drug treatment for insomnia usually involves prescribing **(c)** _____. Insomnia caused when the sleeper stops breathing and wakes up is called **(d)** _____.

18. If children wake up screaming and in a great fright, they have experienced **(a)** _____ but will remember nothing the next morning. When adults experience emotionally charged, frightening images during their dreams, they are having **(b)** _____. If a person walks or carries out other behaviors during sleep, it is called **(c)** _____, which may be caused by increased stress. A relatively rare condition that involves irresistible attacks of sleepiness, brief periods of REM, and often loss of muscle control is called **(d)** _____.

Answers: 1. (a) consciousness, (b) controlled processes, (c) automatic processes; 2. (a) daydreaming, (b) altered states, (c) unconscious, (d) unconsciousness, (e) implicit or nondeclarative memory; 3. (a) circadian rhythm, (b) suprachiasmatic nucleus; 4. (a) jet lag, (b) light; 5. melatonin; 6. (a) electroencephalogram, or EEG, (b) amplitude, (c) frequency; 7. (a) beta, (b) alpha; 8. (a) theta, (b) sleep spindles, (c) delta waves, (d) non-REM; 9. (a) beta, (b) REM, (c) dreaming; 10. (a) morning people, (b) evening people; 11. (a) ventrolateral preoptic nucleus, (b) suprachiasmatic nucleus, (c) reticular formation, (d) neurotransmitters, (e) temperature; 12. (a) sleep, (b) REM; 13. (a) repair, (b) adaptive; 14. (a) concentration, (b) immune; 15. (a) SAD, or seasonal affective disorder, (b) cultural; 16. (a) threatening desires/wishes, (b) activation-synthesis theory, (c) limbic system and visual cortex, (d) prefrontal cortex, (e) extensions, (f) threat simulation; 17. (a) insomnia, (b) cognitive-behavioral, (c) benzodiazepines or nonbenzodiazepines, (d) sleep apnea; 18. (a) night terrors, (b) nightmares, (c) sleepwalking, (d) narcolepsy

Links to Learning

Key Terms/Key People

activation-synthesis theory, 161
adaptive theory of sleep, 156
alpha stage, 152
altered states of consciousness, 148
automatic processes, 148
benzodiazepines, 162
biological clocks, 150
circadian rhythm, 150
consciousness, 148
continuum of consciousness, 148
controlled processes, 148
daydreaming, 148
delta waves, 152
dreaming, 149
drug treatment for insomnia, 162

evening person, 155
extensions of waking life theory of dreams, 160
food-entrainable circadian clock (midnight-snack clock), 150
Freud's theory of dreams, 160
Freud's unconscious, 149
implicit or nondeclarative memory, 149
insomnia, 162
jet lag, 151
latent content, 160
light therapy, 151
manifest content, 160
melatonin, 151
morning person, 155

narcolepsy, 163
night terrors, 163
nightmares, 163
nonbenzodiazepines, 162
nondrug treatment for insomnia, 162
non-REM sleep, 152
questionnaire, 155
REM behavior disorder, 153
REM rebound, 153
REM sleep, 153
repair theory of sleep, 156
reticular formation, 157
seasonal affective disorder, SAD, 159
sleep, 149

sleep apnea, 163
sleep deprivation—effects on body, 157
sleep deprivation—effects on brain, 157
sleepwalking, 163
stage 1 sleep, 152
stage 2 sleep, 152
stage 3 sleep, 152
stage 4 sleep, 152
stages of sleep, 152
suprachiasmatic nucleus, 150
threat simulation theory, 161
unconsciousness, 149
VLPO—ventrolateral preoptic nucleus, 157

Media Resources

Go to **CengageBrain.com** to access Psychology CourseMate, where you will find an interactive eBook, glossaries, flashcards, quizzes, videos, answers to Critical Thinking questions, and more. You can also access Virtual Psychology Labs, an interactive laboratory experience designed to illustrate key experiments first-hand.

MODULE 8 Hypnosis & Drugs

© Sodapix/Corbis

Hypnosis

Consider the experience of one of us (R. P.) some years ago. One night a friend and I were sitting in the front row of one of the longest-running nightclub acts in San Diego. We were going to

Why do people do stupid things?

watch a psychologist-turned-performer who entertained locals and tourists by hypnotizing volunteers from the audience and asking them to perform funny, strange, and somewhat embarrassing acts on a stage. Before the hypnotist appeared, my friend Paul repeated for the tenth time that nothing would get him up on that stage.

Finally the lights dimmed, and the hypnotist appeared. He was a very good performer and soon had the audience laughing at his jokes and believing that he was a wonderful, trustworthy human being.

"Now we come to the interesting part," the hypnotist said in a low, soothing voice. "Just sit back and relax and, if you wish, follow my suggestions." The hypnotist slowly repeated a list of suggestions: "You cannot bend your right arm...you cannot close your eyes...your left arm will become rigid and slowly rise above your head." As I looked around the dimly lit room, a number of rigid left arms were slowly rising. To my surprise, one of those arms was Paul's. (I could not or would not raise my arm, for fear that some of my students were in the audience and would never let me forget whatever foolish behavior I might have performed.)

At the end of the show, we all filed out. Paul said nothing until we were in the car. Then he turned and asked, "Why did you let me get on stage and be hypnotized? You better not tell anyone."

After being hypnotized, shy Paul imitated Elvis.

I smiled and replied, "You were terrific. That was the best imitation of Elvis Presley ever done by a reluctant friend." Then I added, "I might have been tempted to try Mick Jagger."

Although I have changed Paul's name and minor details to protect his pride and reputation, his story is essentially true and illustrates some of the strange behaviors that occur under hypnosis.

For over 200 years, psychologists have puzzled over what hypnosis really is (Lynn et al., 2007a). Some believe hypnosis is a special state during which individuals experience hallucinations (seeing an imaginary fly), carry out suggestions (swatting an imaginary fly), or report decreased pain after receiving a painful stimulus (M. R. Nash, 2001). Recently, researchers have questioned whether hypnosis is a special state, since they found that nonhypnotized individuals responded to imaginative suggestions (see an imaginary fly) just as if they were hypnotized (Kirsch & Braffman, 2001). We'll discuss the debate over what hypnosis really is.

Local newspapers often carry ads claiming that hypnosis can help you stop smoking, lose weight, get rid of phobias, induce immediate relaxation, reduce pain, or increase motivation to tackle difficult projects. We'll discuss whether these claims for hypnosis are true as well as current medical uses of hypnosis.

Drugs

Although only some psychologists believe that hypnosis may change a person's state of consciousness, most agree that there are a number of drugs, legal and illegal, that can alter consciousness. One example of

What was the first bicycle trip?

how a drug greatly altered consciousness happened quite by chance and began with a bike ride.

On April 19, 1943, Albert Hofmann left his laboratory, got on his bike, and began pedaling his regular route home. As Albert pedaled, the world around him began to change into threatening, wavering forms that appeared distorted, as if he was looking into a curved mirror.

Once he reached home and entered his house, the familiar objects and pieces of furniture assumed grotesque and threatening forms that were in continual motion. After a while, the threatening forms disappeared, and he began to enjoy an incredible display of visual sensations and illusions. Albert saw fantastic images that opened and closed in circles and spirals that seemed to explode into colored fountains. Even stranger, sounds such as the passing of a car or opening of a door were transformed into visual images with changing forms and colors (adapted from A. Hofmann, 1983).

The cause of Albert Hofmann's startling visual experiences

Albert Hofmann tried out his newly discovered drug (LSD) and watched his furniture change into strange shapes.

was a drug that Hofmann had previously discovered in his laboratory and had taken before his bike ride. The drug was LSD (*d*-lysergic acid diethylamide) and is now well known to cause strange and bizarre visual experiences, called hallucinations. Because Hofmann had not known about LSD's great potency (compared to other drugs, a very small dose of LSD has a very large effect), he had actually taken a dose that was four times the usual amount. We will discuss LSD as well as other illegal and legal drugs that can alter consciousness.

What's Coming

We'll discuss what hypnosis is, how a person is hypnotized, what a person does and does not do under hypnosis, and the uses of hypnosis. We'll examine the use and abuse of both legal and illegal drugs, such as stimulants, hallucinogens, opiates, marijuana, and alcohol. We'll discuss how drugs affect the nervous system, their dangers, and the treatments for drug abuse.

Let's begin with an interesting and supposedly mind-altering force called animal magnetism. ●

A Hypnosis

Definition

What is hypnosis?

In the late 1700s, Anton Mesmer was the hit of Paris, France, as he claimed to cure a variety of symptoms by passing a force into a patient's body; he called this force animal magnetism. So many patients testified to the success of animal magnetism as a treatment that a committee of the French Academy of Science was appointed to investigate. The committee concluded that many of Mesmer's patients were indeed cured of various psychosomatic problems. However, the committee thought it safer to ban the future use of animal magnetism because they could neither identify what it was nor verify Mesmer's claims that such a force existed (Shermer, 2002). Mesmer's name lives on in our vocabulary: We

© Andresr/Shutterstock.com

use the term *mesmerized* to describe someone who is acting strangely because he or she has been spellbound or hypnotized.

Today we know that Mesmer was not creating animal magnetism but rather was inducing hypnosis. Here's the definition agreed to by the American Psychological Association's Division of Psychological Hypnosis (1993):

Hypnosis is a procedure in which a researcher, clinician, or hypnotist suggests that a person will experience changes in sensations, perceptions, thoughts, feelings, or behaviors.

We'll begin by answering three questions that are often asked about hypnosis.

Who Can Be Hypnotized?

Despite what you may have seen on television or at a stage show, not everyone can be easily hypnotized.

Adults and Hypnosis	
High susceptibility	10–15%
Medium susceptibility	65–70%
Low susceptibility	20%

As shown in the graph, there is considerable variation in susceptibility to being hypnotized: About 20% of adults have low susceptibility to hypnosis, which means that they cannot be easily hypnotized. About 65–70% of adults have medium susceptibility, and the remaining 10–15% have high susceptibility to being hypnotized (S. Song, 2006a; Spiegel, 2005).

Hypnotic susceptibility is not correlated with introversion, extraversion, social position, intelligence, willpower, sex, compliance, gullibility, being highly motivated, or being a placebo responder (Kirsch & Lynn, 1995; M. R. Nash, 2001).

The one trait that is highly correlated with susceptibility to hypnosis is a remarkable ability to respond to imaginative suggestions. Individuals who have this trait are highly susceptible to being hypnotized (Kirsch & Braffman, 2001).

Who Is Susceptible?

The standard test for susceptibility is to hypnotize a person and then give a fixed set of suggestions (Weitzenhoffer, 2002). The best-known test is the Stanford Hypnotic Susceptibility Scale, which asks the individual to carry out a series of both simple suggestions—for example, "Your arm is moving up"—and complex suggestions—for example, "Your body is heavy and you cannot stand up."

For instance, the person in the photo below is carrying out the hypnotic suggestion, "Your right arm is weightless and moving up." One such scale has a series of 12 activities.

This man is being tested for susceptibility to being hypnotized.

Individuals who score high on the Stanford scale are usually easily hypnotized and tend to remain so throughout their lifetimes (M. R. Nash, 2001).

The process used to hypnotize a person is called hypnotic induction.

How Is Someone Hypnotized?

Although different procedures are used, most use some of the following suggestions for hypnotic induction.

Hypnotic induction refers to inducing hypnosis by first asking a person to either stare at an object or close his or her eyes and then suggesting that the person is becoming very relaxed.

For example, here is a commonly used method for hypnotic induction:

1. The hypnotist creates a sense of trust, so that the individual feels comfortable.
2. The hypnotist suggests that the subject concentrate on something, such as the sound of the hypnotist's voice, an object, or an image.
3. The hypnotist suggests what the subject will experience during hypnosis—for example, becoming relaxed, feeling sleepy, or having a floating feeling. The hypnotist may say, "I am going to count from one to ten, and with each count you will drift more and more deeply into hypnosis" (B. L. Bates, 1994).

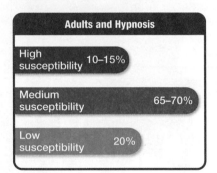

Inducing hypnosis may involve three steps.

© Rudyanto Wijaya/iStockphoto

This procedure works on both individuals and groups, provided the individuals are all susceptible to hypnosis.

During hypnosis, people are not asleep, keep their ability to control their behaviors, are aware of their surroundings, adhere to their usual moral standards, and are capable of saying no or of stopping hypnosis. For these reasons, hypnosis is not a dangerous procedure when used by an experienced researcher or clinician, and hypnosis has useful medical and therapeutic benefits (Lynn & Cardena, 2007; Sandor & Afra, 2005).

Perhaps the biggest debates surrounding hypnosis are what actually happens when a person is hypnotized and whether hypnotic induction is even needed. These are our next questions.

Theories of Hypnosis

What happens during hypnosis?

The explanation of why Paul got on the stage and imitated Elvis has changed significantly over the past 50 years. Early on, being hypnotized was believed to put a person into a trancelike state. In the late 1990s, the trancelike state was dropped for lack of evidence and some believed that being hypnotized put individuals into an altered state of consciousness. More recently, researchers believe that some individuals, hypnotized or not, have the amazing personal ability to respond to imaginative suggestions (Lynn et al., 2007a). We'll discuss these two different views of hypnosis.

Altered State Theory of Hypnosis

Perhaps Paul got on stage and imitated Elvis because hypnosis put him into an altered or disconnected state (Naish, 2006).

The **altered state theory of hypnosis** holds that hypnosis puts a person into an altered state of consciousness, during which the person is disconnected from reality and so is able to experience and respond to various suggestions (M. R. Nash, 2001).

Researcher Michael Nash (2001), former editor-in-chief of *The International Journal of Clinical and Experimental Hypnosis,* believes hypnosis disconnects an individual from reality so that the individual does things without conscious intent. Nash explains that with hypnosis, scientists can temporarily create hallucinations, compulsions, certain types of memory loss, false memories, and delusions (bee buzzing around your head).

Explanation: Altered or disconnected state. Here's how the altered or disconnected state theory of hypnosis explains why shy Paul got on stage and imitated Elvis Presley.

> **1. Hypnotic induction.** The hypnotist uses hypnotic induction: "Just sit back, relax, and follow my suggestions." The hypnotist slowly repeats a list of suggestions: "You cannot bend your right arm...you cannot close your eyes...your left arm will become rigid and slowly rise above your head...," and so on.

> **2. Susceptibility.** Paul easily responds to the hypnotist's suggestion and, without conscious intent, raises his left arm. This means that he is one of the 10–15% who are easily hypnotized and would score high on a hypnotic susceptibility scale.

> **3. Hypnosis.** According to the altered state theory, hypnosis disconnects Paul from reality. In this state, he may automatically and without conscious intent follow a wide range of suggestions, such as getting up on stage and imitating Elvis.

Conclusion. Recent case study research examining eye movements during hypnosis supports the altered state theory of hypnosis. In this research, the pupils of a hypnotized woman were smaller than in normal conditions and she demonstrated an abnormal pattern of very small eye movements. Researchers believe these eye movements cannot be imitated or faked, and occur only during an altered state of consciousness (Kallio et al., 2011).

Next, we'll learn about a theory that states hypnosis is a normal state of consciousness.

Sociocognitive Theory of Hypnosis

Perhaps Paul got on stage and imitated Elvis because of personal abilities and social pressures—the sociocognitive theory (Lynn, 2007).

The **sociocognitive theory of hypnosis** says that behaviors observed during hypnosis result not from being hypnotized, but rather from having the special ability of responding to imaginative suggestions and social pressures (Kirsch & Braffman, 2001).

Psychologist Irving Kirsch, who has published more than 85 articles on hypnosis, found that all the phenomena produced during hypnosis have also occurred in people who were not hypnotized.

Explanation: Special abilities and social pressures. Here's how the sociocognitive theory of hypnosis explains why shy Paul got on stage and imitated Elvis Presley.

> **NO hypnotic induction.** According to the sociocognitive theory of hypnosis, individuals do not have to be hypnotized because about 30% or more already have a special and amazing ability called imaginative suggestibility (Lynn & Kirsch, 2006; Lynn et al., 2008).

> **1. Imaginative suggestibility.** The reason Paul does NOT need to be hypnotized is that he is one of those 30% or more who have imaginative suggestibility. This is a special ability to alter one's experiences and produce hallucinations, experience partial paralysis, have selective amnesia, and reduce pain. Individuals who have imaginative suggestibility can perform these unusual behaviors from suggestion alone, without having to go through formal hypnotic induction (being hypnotized) (Kirsch & Braffman, 2001).

> **2. Imaginative suggestions without hypnosis.** According to the sociocognitive theory, Paul is one of those individuals who has the special ability to respond in a totally focused way to imaginative suggestions, such as getting up on stage and imitating Elvis.

Conclusion. Even though hypnotized people may believe they are in an altered state, brain research does not show altered patterns of activity (Lynn et al., 2007b). So, some researchers believe that hypnosis occurs mostly as a result of people's expectations about hypnosis, rather than being an altered hypnotic state. As research continues, we'll learn more about what happens during hypnosis.

Next, we'll discuss some of the unusual behaviors that can be experienced and performed by individuals who, according to one theory, have been hypnotized or, according to another theory, have the trait of imaginative suggestibility.

Behaviors

What are some of the unusual behaviors?

Stage hypnotists can get volunteers to perform a variety of unusual behaviors, such as pretending they are chickens, falling asleep after counting to 5, or singing like Elvis. However, keep in mind that individuals responsive to hypnosis most likely have the trait of imaginative suggestibility, which means that they can perform these behaviors with or without being hypnotized (Kirsch & Braffman, 2001).

Hypnotic Analgesia

NO PAIN

Hypnosis has long been known to reduce pain; this is called hypnotic analgesia.

Hypnotic analgesia *(an-nall-GEEZ-ee-ah)* refers to a reduction in pain reported by clients after they had undergone hypnosis and received suggestions that reduced their anxiety and promoted relaxation.

Researchers used PET scans to show that hypnosis reduced people's unpleasant feelings of pain though not the sensations of pain (Rainville et al., 1997). When people put their hands into hot water, they felt pain as usual but, depending on the hypnotic suggestions, reported it as more or less unpleasant. Hypnotic analgesia proved useful in helping patients cope with painful medical and dental treatments (F. J. Keefe et al., 2005; Milling et al., 2006; Montgomery, 2008).

Posthypnotic Suggestion

If people perform some behavior on cue after hypnosis, it's called a posthypnotic suggestion.

A **posthypnotic suggestion** is given to a person during hypnosis about performing a particular behavior to a specific cue when the person comes out of hypnosis.

Some believe that people who follow posthypnotic suggestions are acting automatically in response to a predetermined cue, such as laughing when they hear the word *student*. However, researchers have shown that people perform posthypnotic suggestions if they believe it is expected of them but stop performing if they believe the experiment is over or they are no longer being observed (Spanos, 1996).

Posthypnotic Amnesia

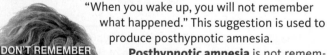
DON'T REMEMBER

"When you wake up, you will not remember what happened." This suggestion is used to produce posthypnotic amnesia.

Posthypnotic amnesia is not remembering what happened during hypnosis if the hypnotist suggested that, upon awakening, the person would forget what took place during hypnosis.

One explanation is that the person forgets because the experiences have been repressed and made unavailable to normal consciousness. However, there is good evidence that, after they come out of hypnosis, what people remember or forget depends on what they think or believe the hypnotist wants them to remember or forget (Spanos, 1996). For instance, people who are instructed to not remember anything usually report not remembering, but when pressed, many of these same people admit they do in fact remember the information (Kirsch & Lynn, 1998).

Age Regression

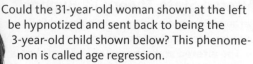

Could the 31-year-old woman shown at the left be hypnotized and sent back to being the 3-year-old child shown below? This phenomenon is called age regression.

Age regression refers to people under hypnosis being asked to regress, or return in time, to an earlier age, such as early childhood.

Researchers have found that during age regression, hypnotized people do not relive their earlier experiences as some believe but rather play the role of being a child. After an exhaustive review of more than 100 years of hypnosis research on age regression, one researcher concluded that there was no evidence that adults actually went back or regressed in time (Kirsch et al., 1993). Thus, researchers believe that, during age regression, hypnotized adults are not reliving childhood experiences but merely acting as they expect children to behave (Lynn et al., 2009).

Imagined Perception

When a hypnotized person responds to a suggestion such as "Try to swat that fly," it is called an imagined perception.

An **imagined perception** refers to experiencing sensations, perceiving stimuli, or performing behaviors that come from one's imagination.

Hypnotherapists use many forms of imagined perceptions in treating clients' problems. For example, one client imagined he was an armored knight on a great horse. After several therapy sessions, the therapist asked the client to remove the armor and discover his true self, which turned out to be a person afraid of his flaws (Eisen, 1994).

Conclusions

Researchers agree that people under hypnosis are not faking or acting out their responses but seem to be actually experiencing such behaviors as hypnotic analgesia, imagined perception, age regression, and posthypnotic suggestion and amnesia. What researchers disagree about is why these behaviors occur. Some researchers believe that these behaviors occur because hypnosis puts individuals into an altered or disconnected state (M. R. Nash, 2001). Other researchers believe that individuals who are highly susceptible to hypnosis have a trait called imaginative suggestibility, which allows these individuals to totally focus and carry out suggestions, whether or not they are hypnotized (Kirsch & Braffman, 2001).

Next, we'll examine some of the uses of hypnosis.

Medical and Therapeutic Applications

How is hypnosis used? You have probably seen hypnosis used in entertainment, such as when people in the audience volunteer to come up on stage and be hypnotized and then perform unusual and often funny behaviors, such as Paul's wild imitation of Elvis. However, there are also serious and legitimate uses of hypnosis in medical, dental, therapeutic, and behavioral settings.

Medical and Dental Uses

In both medical and dental settings, hypnosis can be used to reduce pain through hypnotic analgesia, to reduce fear and anxiety by helping individuals relax, and to help patients deal with health problems by motivating them to make the best of a difficult situation (D. R. Patterson & Jensen, 2003). Also, those clients who are highly susceptible to hypnosis are better able to respond to suggestions for pain reduction than are clients who have low susceptibility (Milling, 2008).

Client is hypnotized before painful dental work.

Hypnosis has benefited many patients undergoing painful surgeries. In research experiments, hypnotized patients undergoing surgery required less pain medication and even recovered sooner than surgical patients who did not receive hypnosis (Askay & Patterson, 2007; Spiegel, 2007).

Hypnosis can also be helpful in preparing people for anxiety-provoking procedures. For instance, the woman above seeks hypnosis to help cope with her fear about having painful dental work performed. As part of her hypnosis, she hears, "Your jaw, mouth, gums, and throat become so relaxed that the muscles get soft...and as your jaw is opened gently and your gums are examined, your entire body will feel more and more relaxed."

Next, we'll look at what happens in the brain during hypnotic analgesia.

Brain scans. Researchers used PET scans (see p. 71) to measure activity in different parts of the brain after study participants were hypnotized and told to place their hands in lukewarm (95°F) or "painfully hot" (115°F) water. Hypnotic suggestions to think of pain as *more unpleasant* (more painful) resulted in *decreased* brain activity in the frontal lobe (anterior cingulate cortex), while hypnotic suggestions to think of pain as *less unpleasant* (less painful) resulted in *increased* brain activity in the same area. In comparison, hypnotic instructions that pain was more or less unpleasant did not increase or decrease brain activity in the parietal lobe (somatosensory cortex), which indicates the reception of pain sensations (Rainville et al., 1997). Researchers concluded that hypnotic suggestions can change a person's *perception* of pain as more or less unpleasant, but hypnotic suggestions do not affect *receiving* pain sensations. This means that during hypnotic analgesia, people feel pain, but how much it bothers them depends on whether hypnotic suggestions are to think of pain as being more or less unpleasant. That is, the hypnotized people's thoughts or expectations actually change their perceptions of pain (Ploghaus et al., 2003).

Therapeutic and Behavioral Uses

Hypnosis has been used in therapy for the past 100 years. In the early 1900s, Sigmund Freud (1905) used hypnosis with his patients. More recently, Milton Erickson (1980/1941), who is generally acknowledged to be the world's leading practitioner of therapeutic hypnosis, said that hypnosis made clients more open and receptive to alternative ways of problem solving. However, hypnosis is not for all clients; some people find hypnosis frightening because they fear losing control or because they believe it indicates a lack of willpower (Kirsch, 1994).

Therapists who often use hypnosis along with other techniques generally report that it is very useful in helping clients reveal their personalities, gain insights into their lives, and arrive at solutions to their problems. Research on hypnotherapy indicates that hypnosis can be a powerful tool that leads to successful outcomes when used in therapeutic settings (M. R. Nash, 2001).

Clients who are highly susceptible to hypnosis generally respond better to suggestions aimed at treating a wide range of psychosomatic problems, which involve mind-body interactions. For example, hypnosis has been successfully used to reduce pain, decrease asthma attacks, and relieve tension. But hypnosis is not as successful with problems of self-control, such as helping clients quit smoking, stop overeating, or stop excessive drinking (Patterson, 2010; B. L. Bates, 1994; Green & Lynn, 2000; B. L. Smith, 2011).

The graph below shows the percentages of participants who continued to smoke after receiving three different treatment programs. Notice that after three weeks of treatment, hypnosis was not statistically more successful in motivating people to stop smoking than was health education or behavior modification. From these results, we can conclude that all three programs were about equally effective and significantly better than controls (no treatment program) (Green & Lynn, 2000; Rabkin et al., 1984). Clinicians generally conclude that hypnosis by itself is not a miracle treatment but can be a useful technique when combined with other procedures (Lynn et al., 2000).

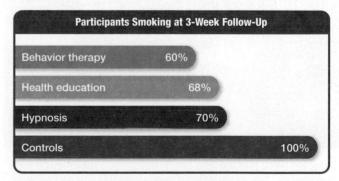

Participants Smoking at 3-Week Follow-Up

Behavior therapy	60%
Health education	68%
Hypnosis	70%
Controls	100%

Although hypnosis may be helpful in a therapeutic setting, evidence obtained under hypnosis is not allowed in most U.S. courts. That's because an examiner's questions or suggestions may bias or mislead a hypnotized witness into agreeing to something that did not occur (Lynn et al., 2009).

Next, we'll discuss another technique used to produce an altered state of consciousness—meditation. ●

Transcendental Meditation

School stress is on the rise. A recent survey of college students' emotional health found that the percentage of

Can meditation lower school stress?

students reporting good or above-average emotional health is at the lowest level in the past 25 years. Researchers find that college students are not the only ones experiencing poorer emotional health. Troubling rates of school stress are found in elementary, middle-school, and high-school students as well.

Stress can limit the ability of students to grow cognitively and psychologically. Stress in students is associated with negative school behaviors, such as absenteeism and violent behavior, and poor academic performance. The toll of stress extends to the physical body in serious ways, including increased risk for hypertension, obesity, and diabetes, which have become increasing concerns of children across the country. Stress has many other detrimental effects on our body, as we will discuss in Module 21.

Transcendental meditation can help lower stress and produce an altered state of consciousness.

Because of the association between high stress and poorer school performance and physical health, it is important to implement programs designed to lower school stress. Consequently, researchers wanted to assess the effectiveness of a stress-reduction program on school stress. They chose to use a well-established and popular type of meditation called transcendental meditation.

Transcendental meditation (TM) involves assuming a comfortable position, closing your eyes, and focusing your attention on repeating words or sounds that are supposed to help produce an altered state of consciousness.

TM is a fairly simple technique that allows the mind to experience a silent, yet awake state of consciousness. The practice of TM does not involve any changes in values, beliefs, religion, or lifestyle.

The question you might ask is: Can transcendental meditation really lower the alarming level of stress in students? This question brings us to one of the major uses of research: to evaluate the effectiveness of intervention programs that claim to change a person's well-being or behavior. Here's how and what researchers discovered when they evaluated the effectiveness of TM in easing school stress (Elder et al., 2011).

Methods and Procedures

Researchers selected 106 high-school students to participate in this study. The students were 16 to 18 years old, and there were approximately equal numbers of males and females. The students were selected from four public schools located in different areas of the country. The sample consisted of 87% racial and ethnic minorities. The researchers selected a sample with mostly racial and ethnic minority students because research data suggest that these students are at particularly high risk of experiencing school stress.

Students were divided into two groups: the experimental and control groups. The experimental group consisted of 68 students who were taught by a certified teacher how to practice TM. These students practiced TM twice a day for 10–15 minutes over a 4-month period. The control group consisted of 38 students who relaxed (such as sitting quietly or reading) but did not meditate. Stress levels were measured for all students before and after the 4-month intervention period.

Results and Conclusions

Researchers found that students in the experimental and control groups did not differ in their reported stress levels prior to beginning the intervention. Data collected after the intervention showed a clear difference between the two groups. The graph below shows a 36% reduction in stress in the students practicing TM, compared to those in the control group. The practice of TM was associated with a significant reduction in stress.

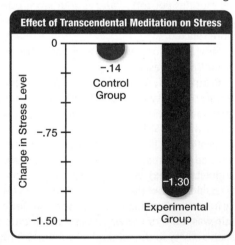

Effect of Transcendental Meditation on Stress

Change in Stress Level

0

−.14 Control Group

−.75

−1.30 Experimental Group

−1.50

The intervention program used by these researchers teaches students a valuable skill they can use for the rest of their lives. The ongoing practice of TM is likely to continue having a positive influence on their cognitive, psychological, and physical health. TM is a fairly easy program to implement that helps improve the emotional health of students and that should thereby improve academic achievement.

Future research should extend these findings by examining the longer-term effects of TM, studying larger student samples in schools, and focusing on students of different ages, races, and ethnicities.

Next, we turn our attention to the use of drugs. ●

C Drugs: Overview

Reasons for Use

For the past 6,000 years, humans have used legal and illegal drugs, and current usage continues to increase, as do drug-related problems. For example, more than 20 million Americans abuse legal and illegal drugs, and the resulting problems—personal, medical, legal, and job related—cost society a whopping $500 billion a year (Jason & Ferrari, 2010).

Why do people use drugs?

The reasons people use drugs include obtaining pleasure, joy, and euphoria; meeting social expectations; giving in to peer pressure; dealing with or escaping stress, anxiety, and tension; avoiding pain; and achieving altered states of consciousness (R. Goldberg, 2010).

In the sections that follow, we'll discuss stimulants (such as caffeine and cocaine), depressants (such as alcohol and barbiturates),

Americans spend $150 billion annually on drugs.

© Aydin Mutlu/Photos.com

opiates (such as morphine and heroin), and hallucinogens (such as LSD and marijuana).

Psychoactive drugs are chemicals that affect our nervous systems and, as a result, may alter consciousness and awareness, influence how we sense and perceive things, and modify our moods, feelings, emotions, and thoughts.

Psychoactive drugs are both licit (legal)—coffee, alcohol, and tobacco—and illicit (illegal)—marijuana, heroin, cocaine, and LSD.

Although all psychoactive drugs affect our nervous systems, how they affect our behaviors depends on our psychological state and other social factors, such as peer pressure and society's values. To illustrate how drug usage involves both pharmacological and psychological factors, we'll describe a famous person who had a serious drug problem.

Definition of Terms

When this famous person was 38, his doctor told him to stop smoking because it was causing irregular heart beats.

What famous therapist had a drug problem?

Although he tried to cut down, he was soon back to smoking his usual 20 cigars a day. When his heart problems grew worse, he stopped again. However, he experienced such terrible depression and mood swings that he started smoking to escape the psychological torture. When he was 67, small sores were discovered in his mouth and diagnosed as cancer. During the next 16 years, he had 33 operations on his mouth and jaw for cancer but continued smoking.

Freud died of cancer caused by 45 years of nicotine addiction.

By age 79, most of his jaw had been removed and replaced by an artificial one. He was in continual pain and was barely able to swallow or talk. However, he continued to smoke cigars. In 1939, at age 83, he died of cancer caused by 45 years of heavy smoking (Brecher, 1972; E. Jones, 1953).

Our famous person is none other than Sigmund Freud, the father of psychoanalysis. Freud had a serious drug problem most of his professional life—he was addicted to tobacco (nicotine). Freud's struggle with smoking illustrates four important terms related to drug use and abuse—addiction, tolerance, dependency, and withdrawal symptoms (American Psychiatric Association, 2000).

Addiction

One reason Freud continued to smoke despite a heart condition was that he had an addiction.

Addiction is a behavioral pattern of drug abuse that is marked by an overwhelming and compulsive desire to obtain and use the drug; even after stopping, the person has a strong tendency to relapse and begin using the drug again.

The reason Freud relapsed each time he tried to give up smoking was that he was addicted to nicotine.

Tolerance

One reason Freud smoked as many as 20 cigars daily was that he had developed a tolerance to nicotine.

Tolerance means that after a person uses a drug repeatedly over a period of time, the original dose of the drug no longer produces the desired effect, so that a person must take increasingly larger doses of the drug to achieve the same behavioral effect.

Becoming tolerant was a sign that Freud had become dependent on nicotine.

Dependency

Another reason Freud found it difficult to quit smoking was that he had developed a dependency on nicotine. There are two types of substance dependence—physiological dependence and psychological dependence.

Physiological dependence is a change in the nervous system so that a person now needs to take the drug to prevent the occurrence of painful withdrawal symptoms.

In some instances, the body may not be dependent on the drug, but the person may continue to use the drug because the person thinks he needs it.

Psychological dependence refers to feeling the need to experience the drug's effects in order to achieve psychological or emotional well-being.

Addiction and dependency combine to make stopping doubly difficult.

Withdrawal Symptoms

Being dependent on nicotine, Freud had withdrawal symptoms when he stopped smoking.

Withdrawal symptoms are painful physical and psychological symptoms that occur after a drug-dependent person stops using the drug.

Freud described his withdrawal symptoms as being depressed, having images of dying, and feeling so tortured that it was beyond his human power to bear (E. Jones, 1953).

Next, we'll examine a number of specific drugs that people use.

Use of Drugs

Which drugs do people use? The use of drugs often begins at a young age. The graph on the right shows the prevalence of drug use among young adults in the United States (SAMHSA, 2011b).

Recent national statistics show that almost 20 million Americans spend over $64 billion on illegal drugs each year (ONDCP, 2001; SAMHSA, 2008b).

Because drug treatment programs are more cost-effective than imprisonment, many health professionals recommend reducing illegal drug use by spending more on drug education, counseling, and treatment (Caulkins et al., 2005; Vastag, 2003).

Because of the cost and relative ineffectiveness of the current "drug war," doctors, federal judges, and political writers have proposed controlling illegal drugs either by legalization, which

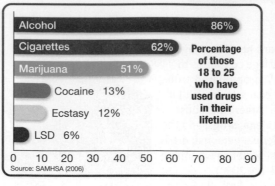

Alcohol	86%
Cigarettes	62%
Marijuana	51%
Cocaine	13%
Ecstasy	12%
LSD	6%

Percentage of those 18 to 25 who have used drugs in their lifetime

Source: SAMHSA (2006)

means illegal drugs can be used but with age restrictions, or by decriminalization, which means drugs remain illegal but criminal penalties are replaced with fines. No one knows the effect drug legalization or decriminalization might have on drug use or related personal and social problems in a country as large as the United States (Huggins, 2005).

Whether legal or illegal, psychoactive drugs alter one's consciousness, emotions, and thoughts by affecting the brain's communication network.

Effects on Nervous System

How do drugs work? You may remember from Module 3 that the nervous system communicates by using chemical messengers called neurotransmitters. You can think of neurotransmitters as acting like chemical keys that open or close chemical locks on neighboring neurons (right figure). Many drugs act by opening or closing chemical locks, which in turn results in increased or decreased neural activity. However, how drugs affect each person's nervous system partly involves genetic factors. For example, researchers found that identical twins, who share 100% of their genes, were much more similar in their use and abuse of

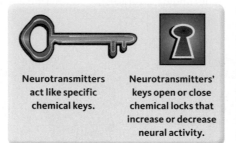

Neurotransmitters act like specific chemical keys.

Neurotransmitters' keys open or close chemical locks that increase or decrease neural activity.

drugs than fraternal twins, who share only 50% of their genes. This result is the same in countries where there are high rates of drug problems (United States) and in those with low rates (Norway) (Kendler et al., 2000a, 2006). This means that genetic factors influence the development and functioning of the nervous system, which in turn can increase or decrease the risk of a person using and abusing drugs. We'll discuss ways that drugs affect the nervous system and activate the brain's reward/pleasure center to cause addiction and dependency.

Drugs Affect Neurotransmitters

Your nervous system makes several dozen neurotransmitters as well as many other chemicals (neuromodulators) that act like chemical messengers. After neurons release neurotransmitters, they act like chemical keys that search for and then either open or close chemical locks to either excite or inhibit neighboring neurons, organs, or muscles. For example, morphine's chemical structure closely resembles that of the neurotransmitter endorphin (see p. 113). As a result of this similarity, morphine acts like, or mimics, endorphin by affecting the same chemical locks, which decreases pain. Thus, some drugs produce their effects by *mimicking* the way neurotransmitters work (Ropper & Samuels, 2009).

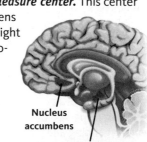

Morphine and heroin are similar to brain's neurotransmitters.

After being excited, neurons secrete neurotransmitters, which move across a tiny space (synapse) and affect neighboring neurons' receptors (see p. 54). However, after a brief period, the neurotransmitters are reabsorbed back into the neuron. The action by which neurotransmitters are removed from the synapse through reabsorption is called *reuptake.* If reuptake did not occur, neurotransmitters would remain in the synapse, and neurons would be continuously stimulated. Thus, some drugs, such as cocaine, block reuptake, which leads to increased neural stimulation that causes increased physiological and psychological arousal (Mendelson et al., 2006).

Some drugs have a powerful effect on the brain's reward/pleasure center.

Drugs Affect Brain's Reward/Pleasure Center

Many drugs, especially cocaine and methamphetamine, activate the brain's *reward/pleasure center.* This center includes the nucleus accumbens and ventral tegmental area (right figure) and involves the neurotransmitter dopamine (Saey, 2008). These drugs produce their effects by directly activating the brain's reward/pleasure center.

Some drugs activate the reward/pleasure center by increasing dopamine levels. However, repeated drug usage can decrease the number of dopamine transporters (proteins that help move dopamine into and out of neurons), which results in lower dopamine levels and a less responsive reward/pleasure center (Volkow, 2010). Consequently, the user must continue to use more drugs to activate the reward/pleasure center. When the reward/pleasure center becomes dependent on outside drugs, the user is addicted and dependent. Thus, drug addiction and dependency involve real changes in the brain's chemistry (Lemonick, 2007b).

Next, we'll examine the more frequently used drugs. ●

Nucleus accumbens

Ventral tegmental area

Unless otherwise noted, all images are © Cengage Learning

Definition

What are stimulants?

"Two pills beat a month's vacation." This marketing slogan was used to sell amphetamines in Sweden in the 1940s. It resulted in epidemic usage that peaked in the mid-1960s.

In the 1940s, American doctors prescribed amphetamines as safe energizers, mood enhancers, and appetite suppressants. By the 1960s, billions of doses of amphetamines were being used in the United States and their usage had become a serious problem.

In the 1940s, Japanese workers used amphetamines to keep factory production high during World War II. After the war, many students, night workers, and people displaced by the war began to use "wake-amines." Amphetamine use spread until, in 1954, 2 million Japanese had become abusers and addicts (Brecher, 1972).

Amphetamine slogan in the 1940s: "Two pills beat a month's vacation."

By the early 1970s, most countries had brought amphetamine usage under control by regulating prescriptions, decreasing supply, and imposing stiffer penalties. However, at present, amphetamine-like stimulants, such as methamphetamine (crystal) and cocaine, are widely available on the black market.

All **stimulants,** including cocaine, amphetamines, caffeine, and nicotine, increase activity of the central nervous system and result in heightened alertness, arousal, euphoria, and decreased appetite. Dose for dose, cocaine and amphetamines are considered powerful stimulants because they produce a strong effect with a small dose; caffeine and nicotine are considered mild stimulants.

We'll discuss the more widely used stimulants—amphetamines, cocaine, caffeine, and nicotine.

Amphetamines

Is it still a problem?

During the 1960s, amphetamine pills were heavily prescribed to treat a wide range of problems, including fatigue, depression, and being overweight. This was also the time young adults, called "flower children," took large doses of amphetamines that caused true paranoid psychotic symptoms, which resulted in their being called "speed freaks." Amphetamine usage peaked in the mid-1960s, when over 31 million prescriptions were written for dieting and about 25 tons of legitimately manufactured amphetamines were diverted to illegal sales (G. R. Hanson & Venturelli, 1998). Finally, in 1971, the Food and Drug Administration (FDA) outlawed the prescription of amphetamines for everything except attention-deficit/hyperactivity disorder (ADHD) (p. 39) and narcolepsy (p. 163).

Following a "drug war" on cocaine in the 1980s, there was a dramatic increase in using a form of amphetamine called methamphetamine, which is manufactured in illegal home laboratories. In many countries, the possession or use of methamphetamine is illegal, and yet the use of methamphetamine is quickly spreading in the United States and worldwide. Karen Tandy, a U.S. drug enforcement official, commented on the nation's use of methamphetamine: "Meth has spread like wildfire across the Unites States. It has burned out communities, scorched childhoods, and charred once happy and productive lives beyond recognition" (Eggen, 2005). In Japan, methamphetamine has become the most popular illegal drug (Ujike & Sato, 2004).

Drug

In 2001, authorities raided about 8,000 illegal crystal methamphetamine laboratories in the United States. Methamphetamine labs are becoming increasingly common in the West, Southwest, and Midwest (Crea, 2003; Sanchez, 2001).

Methamphetamine (D-methamphetamine) is close to amphetamine in both its chemical makeup and its physical and psychological effects. Unlike amphetamine, which is taken in pill form, methamphetamine (meth, speed, crank, crystal, ice) can be smoked or snorted and produces an almost instantaneous high. Both amphetamine and methamphetamine cause marked increases in blood pressure and heart rate and produce feelings of enhanced mood, alertness, and energy. However, both have a high risk for addiction and dependency.

"It's the ultimate high.... It makes you feel so powerful. You have tons of energy.... I loved it. I craved it" (Witkin, 1995, p. 50). So said 23-year-old Tara, who became addicted to and dependent on meth and whose euphoria eventually turned into a terrible nightmare.

Nervous System

The primary effect of amphetamines and related drugs (methamphetamine) is to increase release of the neurotransmitter dopamine and also to block its reuptake (Mendelson et al., 2006). Researchers are learning that the release of dopamine occurs during a wide range of pleasurable activities, such as sex (Esch & Stefano, 2005). Thus, drugs like methamphetamine are both desirable and dangerous because they increase the release of dopamine, which causes very pleasurable feelings (Bamford et al., 2008).

Dangers

At first, users of methamphetamine have periods of restless activity and perform repetitive behaviors. Later, the initial euphoria is replaced with depression, agitation, insomnia, and true paranoid feelings. Methamphetamine users have been found to have 15% fewer dopamine receptors, which are involved in the reward/pleasure center (Riddle et al., 2006; Volkow et al., 2003). Fewer dopamine receptors decrease one's ability to experience normal pleasures and contribute to further drug usage. Long-term risks include stroke, liver damage, heart disease, memory loss, and extreme weight loss (Dickerson, 2007; Jefferson, 2005). Large doses of methamphetamine can overstimulate the brain, leading to severe convulsions and possibly death (Iversen, 2008).

Another powerful stimulant is cocaine, which we'll discuss next.

© Hemera/Thinkstock

Cocaine

Why has it been used for 3,000 years?

For 3,000 years, the ancient Incas and their descendants, the indigenous Andean people of Peru, have chewed coca leaves as they made demanding journeys through the high mountains. Some minutes after chewing the leaves, which contain cocaine, they reported feeling more vigor and strength and less fatigue, hunger, thirst, and cold. Coca leaves contain very little cocaine and produce stimulation equivalent to that experienced by coffee (caffeine) drinkers (McCarry, 1996). Few psychological or physical problems are observed in those who chew coca leaves, partly because they consume very little cocaine and because this activity is part of their culture. However, natives who have switched from chewing coca leaves to using the more concentrated cocaine powder have reported many more problems (R. K. Siegel, 1989).

In the United States, an increase in usage of one illegal drug is partly due to which other drug is being targeted for enforcement. For example, the U.S. government's crackdown on amphetamine usage in the 1970s was largely responsible for the increased popularity of cocaine, whose usage reached epidemic proportions in the 1980s. Despite the efforts of U.S. law enforcement to eliminate the use of cocaine, it remains a $35-billion-a-year illegal industry with about 1.5 million current users (Brodzinsky, 2006; SAMHSA, 2012).

The stimulating effects of cocaine may be luring; however, it can have devastating effects on people's lives, including death. The list of celebrities who have been addicted to cocaine is lengthy, and perhaps one of the most recognized celebrities whose life was tragically affected by cocaine is the late Whitney Houston. Houston died on February 11, 2012, and toxicology results showed the presence of cocaine in her body at the time of death. Doctors believe cocaine contributed to her death by causing a heart attack, which resulted in accidental drowning in the bathtub (Gundersen, 2012; *People*, 2012).

Coca leaves contain cocaine.

Cocaine use contributed to Houston's death.

Drug

Cocaine can be sniffed or snorted, since it is absorbed by many of the body's membranes. If cocaine is changed into a highly concentrated form, which is called *crack,* it can be smoked or injected and produces an instantaneous but short-lived high.

Cocaine, which comes from the leaves of the coca plant, has physiological and behavioral effects very similar to those of amphetamine. Like amphetamine, cocaine produces increased heart rate and blood pressure, enhanced mood, alertness, increased activity, decreased appetite, and diminished fatigue. With higher doses, cocaine can produce anxiety, emotional instability, and suspiciousness.

When humans or monkeys have unlimited access to pure cocaine, they will use it continually, to the point of starvation and death. Only extreme shock will reduce an addicted monkey's use of cocaine, and only extreme problems involving health, legal, or personal difficulties will reduce an addicted human's intake.

Nervous System

The primary effect of cocaine is to block reuptake of the neurotransmitter dopamine, which means that dopamine stays around longer to excite neighboring neurons (Mendelson et al., 2006).

Cocaine excites one kind of neural receptor (dopamine) to produce pleasure/euphoria and another kind of receptor (glutamate) to produce a craving for more of the drug (Uys & LaLumiere, 2008). Like amphetamine, cocaine results in increased physiological and psychological arousal.

When applied to an external area of the body, cocaine can block the conduction of nerve impulses. For this reason, cocaine is classified as a local anesthetic and that is its only legal usage.

Dangers

In *moderate doses,* cocaine produces a short-acting high (10–30 minutes) that includes bursts of energy, arousal, and alertness. Users tend to believe they are thinking more clearly and performing better, but they overestimate the quality of their work. In *large doses,* cocaine can result in serious physical and psychological problems. An overdose can lead to death (Paulozzi, 2006).

Many physical problems result from cocaine abuse, including lack of appetite, headaches, insomnia, irritability, heart attacks, strokes, seizures, damage to cartilage of the nose (if snorted), and increased risk of HIV (if injected). Also, respiratory failure, which may lead to sudden death, can result from relatively low doses (NIDA, 2006a).

Heavy cocaine usage has been found to reduce the levels of dopamine receptors in the brain's reward/pleasure center. This reduction results in two disastrous consequences: First, the user must take larger doses of cocaine to experience the same pleasure and this continues the addiction; second, the user will find decreased pleasure in previously normal experiences (a good meal or companionship) and seek pleasure in continued use of drugs. Heavy usage also damages the brain's decision-making abilities, which leads to increased impulsivity and makes it harder to quit using the drug (T. W. Robbins, 2011).

Cocaine users often go through the vicious circle of feeling depressed as the effect wears off, wanting and using more cocaine to relieve the depression, and so on (Ropper & Samuels, 2009). Thus, heavy users often require professional help to break out of their addictive vicious circles (Lamberg, 2004).

Next, we turn to two legal drugs that are the most widely used stimulants—caffeine and nicotine.

Unless otherwise noted, all images are © Cengage Learning

Caffeine

What's the most widely used drug in the world?

Caffeine has been used for the past 2,000 years and is the most widely used psychoactive drug in the world (Peng, 2008b). In the United States, 80–90% of people routinely consume caffeine and 170 million are addicted to it (Gupta, 2007; Lemonick, 2007b; M. Price, 2008a). One 8-ounce cup of regular coffee, two cups of regular tea, two diet colas, and four regular-sized chocolate bars all contain about 100 milligrams of caffeine. The average amount of caffeine consumed in the United States is 238 milligrams per person per day, compared to 400 milligrams in Sweden and England and a worldwide average of 76 milligrams (Bowman, 2005).

Drug

Many users do not consider caffeine an addicting drug. **Caffeine,** a mild stimulant, produces physiological and psychological arousal, including decreased fatigue and drowsiness, feelings of alertness, and improved reaction times.

Moderate doses of caffeine improved performance in sleep-deprived drivers but had little effect on reducing motor impairment from alcohol (Fillmore et al., 2002; Reyner & Horne, 2000).

Nervous System

Caffeine belongs to a group of chemicals called xanthines *(ZAN-thenes),* which have a number of effects. One effect is to block certain receptors (adenosine receptors) in the brain, which results in stimulation and mild arousal (Keisler & Armsey, 2006).

Dangers

Researchers found that mild to heavy doses of caffeine (125–800 milligrams; two cups of coffee = 200 mg) can result in addiction and dependency similar to those produced by alcohol, nicotine, and cocaine (Strain et al., 1994). The high doses of caffeine in today's energy drinks (up to 500 mg) place people at particular risk for caffeine's dangerous side effects (J. E. Brody, 2011; Griffiths, 2008).

For 40–70% of people who abruptly stop the consumption of caffeine, especially medium to heavy doses, a number of uncomfortable withdrawal symptoms occur, such as headaches, fatigue, jitteriness, nausea, cramps, tremors, and sleeplessness (Gupta, 2007; Lemonick, 2007b). Obviously, caffeine is a real drug, as is the nicotine in tobacco products.

Nicotine

After caffeine, nicotine is the world's most widely used psychoactive drug (Julien, 2005). In the United States, over 20% of adults are active cigarette smokers, and about 1,000 children and teenagers take up the habit every day (CDC, 2010b).

What causes the most deaths?

Cigarette smoking is the leading cause of preventable death in the United States, causing about 443,000 deaths each year and costing the country over $96 billion a year in treatment expenses (CDC, 2010b; G. Harris, 2010). For this reason, the U.S. Surgeon General concluded that cigarette smoking is the most important public health issue of our time (USDHHS, 2006). The U.S. Food and Drug Administration agrees, which is why it has advocated for new warning labels on cigarette packaging (Reardon, 2011).

New graphic warning labels would cover 50% of cigarette packaging.

Drug

Nicotine has long been classified as a stimulant drug, but not until 1997 was it officially classified as an addictive drug (Koch, 2000).

Nicotine is a stimulant because it triggers the brain's reward/pleasure center to produce good feelings. In low doses, nicotine improves attention, concentration, and short-term memory. Regular use of nicotine causes addiction and dependency, and stopping leads to withdrawal symptoms.

Researchers now think they know why about 30 million American smokers try to quit each year and fail.

Nervous System

Nicotine stimulates the production of dopamine, which is used by the brain's reward/pleasure center to produce good feelings. Nicotine also stops other controlling cells from turning off the pleasure areas, so the overall result is that smoking produces a relative long-lasting good feeling (Mansvelder et al., 2003). Thus, smokers find it so difficult to quit because they are addicted to nicotine and really crave the good feeling.

Dangers

Nicotine is a very addicting drug, and it has serious health consequences. For instance, smoking causes 87% of lung cancer deaths, doubles or triples the risk of dying from heart disease, and elevates blood sugar levels, which can lead to insulin resistance (M. B. Marcus et al., 2010).

Secondhand smoke is also very dangerous. More than 600,000 people worldwide die each year as a result of secondhand smoke exposure (WHO, 2010). There is no safe level of secondhand smoke exposure (ALA, 2006; O'Neil, 2006).

Because nicotine is addictive, a habitual smoker will experience withdrawal symptoms when trying to quit. Withdrawal symptoms range in severity and include irritability, attentional deficits, cramps, sleep disturbances, increased appetite, and a strong craving to light up again (NIDA, 2006b). Stop-smoking programs, including counseling and some combination of nicotine patch, pill, or gum, are all about equally effective—only 10 to 25% remained smoke free one year later (Vergano, 2001).

Unlike stimulants, the next group of drugs, called depressants, produces the opposite effect. ●

E Depressants

Alcohol

What if alcohol was banned?

Drugs that have an opposite effect on the nervous system than stimulants are called depressants.

Depressants are a class of drugs that slow the central nervous system.

The most commonly used depressant is alcohol.

The first brewery appeared in Egypt in about 3700 B.C., making alcohol the oldest drug to be made by humans (Samuel, 1996). Alcohol has grown in popularity, and its usage has been associated with a wide range of problems, such as motor coordination (right figure). If alcohol causes so many problems, why not just ban it?

In 1919, the U.S. Congress passed the Eighteenth Amendment, which prohibited the sale and manufacture of alcohol. However, Americans did not want to give up alcohol, so a lucrative black market developed and supplied

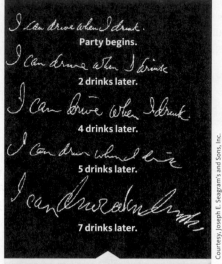

Party begins.

2 drinks later.

4 drinks later.

5 drinks later.

7 drinks later.

Courtesy, Joseph E. Seagram's and Sons, Inc.

Impairment of motor coordination is one of many problems caused by alcohol.

illegal alcohol. After 14 years of black-market alcohol and failed prohibition, the U.S. Congress repealed prohibition in 1933. The lesson learned from prohibition was that it is impossible to pass a law to ban a drug that is so popular and widely used (Musto, 1996).

In 2007, about 127 million Americans age 12 and older drank alcohol. Of these, 23% were binge drinkers (consumed five drinks in a row on the same occasion), and about 7% were heavy drinkers (five drinks in a row on five different days in the past month). The heavy drinkers are most likely to be alcoholics, who develop a variety of behavioral, neurological, social, legal, and medical problems (SAMHSA, 2008b).

We'll discuss alcoholism in the Cultural Diversity section (p. 182), but first we'll explain alcohol's effects on the user's brain, body, and behaviors.

Although we'll use the term *alcohol,* we actually mean *ethyl alcohol,* which is safe to drink. The level of alcohol is measured in percentage in the blood, which is called blood alcohol content, or BAC. For example, after three or four drinks in an hour, the average person's BAC will range from 0.08 to 0.1. The national legal definition of being drunk is now 0.08. A drink is defined as one cocktail, one 5-ounce glass of wine, or one 12-ounce bottle of beer (Gelles, 2009). It makes no difference whether you drink hard liquor, wine, or beer, since they all contain ethyl alcohol, which affects the nervous system and results in behavioral and emotional changes.

Drug

© Featureflash/Shutterstock.com

Alcohol is not a stimulant but a depressant.

Alcohol (ethyl alcohol) is a psychoactive drug that is classified as a depressant, which means it depresses activity of the central nervous system. Initially, alcohol seems like a stimulant because it reduces inhibitions, but later it depresses many physiological and psychological responses.

The effects of alcohol depend on how much a person drinks. After a couple of drinks (0.01–0.05 BAC), alcohol causes friendliness and loss of inhibitions. After four or five drinks (0.06–0.10 BAC), alcohol seriously impairs motor coordination (driving), cognitive abilities, decision making, and speech. After many drinks (0.4 BAC and higher), alcohol may cause coma and death. For example, singer and songwriter Amy Winehouse (pictured above) died as a result of alcohol poisoning. At the time of death, her BAC was 0.416, more than five times the legal limit for driving (Dover, 2011).

Nervous System

Alcohol affects many parts of the nervous system. For example, alcohol stimulates the brain's GABA *(GAH-bah)* neural receptors, which leads to feeling less anxious and less inhibited (Schuckit, 2006). Alcohol also impairs the anterior cingulate cortex, which monitors the control of motor actions. When this area is impaired, drinkers will fail to recognize their impaired motor performance (driving a car) and continue to drive (Ridderinkhof et al., 2002). In very high doses (0.5 BAC), alcohol depresses vital breathing reflexes in the brain stem (medulla), and this may totally stop breathing and result in death.

Dangers

The morning after a bout of heavy drinking (three to seven drinks), a person usually experiences a *hangover,* which may include upset stomach, dizziness, fatigue, headache, and depression. There is presently no cure for hangovers, which are troublesome and painful but not life threatening.

Repeated and heavy drinking can result in tolerance, addiction, and dependency. *Tolerance* means that a person must drink more to experience the same behavioral effects. *Addiction* means an intense craving for alcohol, and *dependency* means if the person stops drinking, he or she will experience serious *withdrawal symptoms,* which may include shaking, nausea, anxiety, diarrhea, hallucinations, and disorientation.

Another serious problem is *blackouts,* which occur after heavy and repeated drinking. During a blackout, a person seems to behave normally but when sober cannot recall what happened. If the blackout lasts for hours or days, it is probable that the person is an alcoholic.

Repeated and heavy drinking can also result in liver damage, alcoholism, and brain damage.

Risk Factors

Of the 126 million Americans who drink alcohol, almost 19 million will develop alcoholism. Researchers believe that a number of psychological and genetic risk factors increase the chances that a person will drink alcohol AND become an alcoholic. For example, one's risk of becoming an alcoholic is three to four times higher if one comes from a family whose parents are alcoholic. However, it's important to remember that risk factors increase the chances but do not guarantee that someone who drinks will become an alcoholic.

Who's at risk for becoming an alcoholic?

We'll discuss both genetic and psychological risk factors that may lead to a person abusing alcohol.

Nearly 19 million alcoholics in the United States

Psychological Risk Factors. Researchers found that children whose parents (either or both) are alcoholics develop a number of unusual, abnormal, or maladaptive psychological and emotional traits that are called *psychological risk factors* (Schuckit, 2000). For example, these childhood risk factors include being easily bored, engaging in risk-taking or sensation-seeking behaviors, and acting impulsively or overemotionally when faced with stressful situations (Legrand et al., 2005; S. Song, 2006b).

When children with these psychological risk factors become adults, they may have a tendency to imitate the behavior of their alcoholic parent and abuse alcohol when faced with personal, social, stressful, or work-related difficulties. However, besides psychological risk factors for abusing alcohol, there are also genetic risk factors (Edenberg & Foroud, 2006).

Genetic Risk Factors. Besides psychological risk factors, there are also *genetic risk factors,* which are inherited biases or predispositions that increase the potential for alcoholism. For example, if one identical twin is an alcoholic, there is a 39% chance that the other twin is also. In comparison, if one fraternal twin is an alcoholic, there is a 16% chance that the other twin is also. Based on genetic studies, researchers estimate that genetic factors contribute 50–60% to the reasons a person becomes an alcoholic (M. Price, 2008b; Schuckit, 2006).

One way genetic factors work is by making a person more or less sensitive to the effects of alcohol, meaning a person has to drink more or less to feel its effects. Recent research identified a gene that affects how people respond to alcohol. Specifically, the 10 to 20% of people who carry this gene are especially sensitive to alcohol and less likely to develop alcoholism than those who need to drink excessively to feel drunk (A. Webb et al., 2011). Other research found that genes set a person's sensitivity by affecting a number of neurotransmitter systems (GABA, NMDA, dopamine, and serotonin) (DePetrillo, 2003; Li, 2000). Researchers caution there is not one "alcoholic" gene that puts one at risk for alcoholism, but many genes, which in turn interact with the environment to increase the risk for alcoholism (Edenberg & Foroud, 2006).

Because neither every child of an alcoholic parent nor both members of a pair of identical twins become an alcoholic, genetic risk factors alone do not lead to alcoholism. Rather, researchers believe that alcoholism results from the interaction between genetic and psychological risk factors (Lesch, 2005).

Next, we'll discuss barbiturates and tranquilizers, two others types of depressants.

Barbiturates and Tranquilizers

What are other types of depressants?

Commonly referred to as sleeping pills are barbiturates.

Barbiturates are depressant drugs that have a sedative effect.

Barbiturates, such as phenobarbital, decrease the activity of the nervous system. Moderately high doses result in drowsiness, motor impairment, and poor judgment. Taken in larger doses, they can be fatal, which explains why they are often used in suicide attempts. Combining the use of barbiturates with another depressant, such as alcohol, is especially dangerous. Barbiturates are highly addictive. Withdrawal symptoms can be severe and include the possibility of convulsions, coma, and death. Because of the dangers associated with barbiturates, they have in large part been replaced with tranquilizers.

Tranquilizers are depressant drugs that reduce anxiety and stress.

Tranquilizers are considered to be much safer than barbiturates and are now commonly prescribed to help manage sleep, anxiety, and stress. Some of the common tranquilizers include Xanax, Valium, and Ativan. Even though tranquilizers are relatively safe, there is still risk for addiction and withdrawal symptoms. Also, large doses can be dangerous, especially when taken with alcohol or another depressant drug. Tranquilizers, like barbiturates, have the potential to suppress the central nervous system and consequently cause death.

Next, we'll return to discussing alcohol by taking a look at alcoholism rates across the world. ●

Taken in large doses, barbiturates and tranquilizers can be deadly.

F Cultural Diversity: Alcoholism Rates

Definition and Differences in Rates

One of the interesting questions that applies to all drugs is why some people can use a drug usually in moderation and rarely abuse it, while others use the same drug but often abuse it and usually develop serious problems. For example, of the approximately 127 million Americans age 12 and older who drink alcohol, 18 to 19 million abuse it, drink to excess, and develop alcoholism (SAMHSA, 2010).

What is alcoholism?

Alcoholism involves heavy drinking (sometimes a quart a day) for a long period of time, usually many years. Alcoholics are addicted (have intense craving) and are dependent on alcohol (must drink to avoid

© Arthur Kwiatkowski/iStockphoto

First signs of alcoholism appear in the early twenties.

withdrawal symptoms). They continue to use alcohol despite developing major substance-related life problems, such as neglecting family, work, or school duties, having repeated legal incidents, and experiencing difficulties in personal or social relationships (American Psychiatric Association, 2000).

One answer to why only certain drinkers abuse the drug and become alcoholics comes from studying various risk factors, such as psychological and genetic influences, which we discussed earlier. Now, we'll examine another risk factor—cultural influences.

Genetic Risk Factors

After the very first drink of alcohol, some individuals respond with a sudden reddening of the face. This reaction is called *facial flushing* and is caused by the absence of a liver enzyme involved in metabolizing alcohol.

Facial flushing from alcohol is a genetic trait and rarely occurs in Caucasians (Whites) but does occur in about 30–50% of Asians (photo below) (Schuckit, 2000). Asians with significant facial flushing, such as Taiwanese, Chinese, and Japanese, tend to drink less and have lower rates of alcoholism than Asians who show less facial flushing, such as Koreans (Assanangkornchai

© Phil Date/Shutterstock.com

Asians with most facial flushing have lower rates of drinking and alcoholism.

et al., 2003). These findings show that facial flushing, which occurs in some cultures more than others, is linked to a *genetic risk factor* that influences the chances of becoming an alcoholic.

Cultural Risk Factors

Different cultures have different values and pressures that may encourage or discourage alcohol abuse. For instance, researchers studied 48,000 adults (age 18 and older) in six different cultures to answer two questions: Do rates of alcoholism differ across cultures? What cultural values influence the rate of alcoholism?

The answer to the first question is shown in the graph below. Rates of alcoholism did differ across cultures, from a low of 0.5% among Taiwanese to a high of 22% among Koreans (Helzer & Canino, 1992).

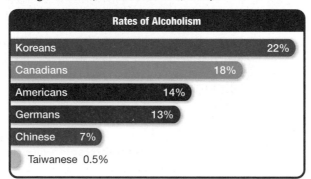

Rates of Alcoholism

Koreans	22%
Canadians	18%
Americans	14%
Germans	13%
Chinese	7%
Taiwanese	0.5%

The answer to the second question—What cultural values influence the rate of alcoholism?—was also partly answered. For example, the high rate of alcoholism in Korea was almost entirely in men, who are encouraged by cultural pressures to drink heavily in certain social situations, such as at the end of the workday, when co-workers are encouraged to have drinking contests. The medium rate of alcoholism found in Germany, the United States, and Canada was related to the stresses of living in heavily industrialized societies. The below-average rate of alcoholism found in China and especially Taiwan was influenced by the Confucian moral code, which has strong cultural-religious taboos against drinking or showing drunken behavior in public. These findings indicate that *cultural risk factors* can either encourage or discourage the development of alcoholism.

However, despite the different rates of alcoholism across cultures, there are some striking similarities.

Across Cultures

Although rates of alcoholism differed widely across cultures, from 0.5 to 22%, researchers found many similarities in how people developed alcoholism and the problems they had (Helzer & Canino, 1992; Peele, 1997). Here are some similarities that occurred across cultures:

• The average age when the first symptoms of alcoholism appear was in the early twenties or mid-twenties.

• The average number of major life problems among alcoholics was four to six.

• The average duration of alcoholism was 8–10 years.

• The average pattern of drinking involved daily heavy drinking, often a quart a day.

• Men were five times more likely to develop alcoholism than were women.

• Depression was about twice as likely to be diagnosed in alcoholics as in nonalcoholics.

• The overall mortality rate from alcoholism did not differ among cultures.

Researchers concluded that although cultural—genetic and psychological—risk factors had a significant influence on the *rate* of alcoholism, cultural factors had little effect on the *development,* symptoms, sex differences, and mental disorders associated with alcoholism.

Next, you'll have a chance to test your knowledge with the Concept Review. ●

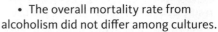

Unless otherwise noted, all images are © Cengage Learning

© Rudyanto Wijaya/iStockphoto

1. Under hypnosis, individuals may think they return to an earlier stage in life, which is called **(a)** _____; they may experience a reduction in pain, which is called **(b)** _____; or they may experience loss of memory, called **(c)** _____. Hypnotized individuals may perceive stimuli that do not exist, which is called **(d)** _____, or they may perform some behavior after coming out of hypnosis, which is called a **(e)** _____.

2. According to the **(a)** _____ theory, hypnotized people perform suggested behaviors because they are in a special state. According to the **(b)** _____ theory, people perform suggested behaviors because of social pressures and because they have the ability to respond to imaginative suggestions.

© takayuki/Shutterstock.com

3. Assuming a comfortable position, closing your eyes, and focusing your attention on repeating words or sounds that are supposed to help produce an altered state of consciousness are steps involved in _____.

4. After using a drug repeatedly, a person must take increasingly larger doses to achieve the original behavioral effect; this is called **(a)** _____. A change in the nervous system that requires a person to take a drug to prevent the occurrence of painful withdrawal symptoms is called **(b)** _____. A behavioral pattern of drug abuse that is marked by a person's overwhelming and compulsive desire to obtain and use the drug is called an **(c)** _____. Painful physical and psychological symptoms that occur after a drug-dependent person stops using the drug are called **(d)** _____.

5. Drugs that affect the nervous system and result in altered awareness and consciousness, as well as changes in mood, cognition, and perception, are called _____.

© Aydin Mutlu/Photos.com

6. Some drugs act like **(a)** _____ keys that are so similar to neurotransmitters that these drugs open the chemical **(b)** _____ of nearby neurons by acting like or **(c)** _____ the action of regularly occurring neurotransmitters. Some drugs prevent the neuron's reabsorption of neurotransmitters by slowing down a process called **(d)** _____. Some drugs act on the nucleus accumbens and ventral tegmental area, which are parts of the brain's **(e)** _____ center.

© Fedor Kondratenko/Shutterstock.com

7. Those drugs that result in increased arousal, alertness, and euphoria are called **(a)** _____. The potent stimulant that comes from a plant, can be sniffed or smoked, and produces short-acting alertness and euphoria is **(b)** _____. The potent stimulant that is a form of amphetamine, is smoked, and produces longer-lasting alertness and euphoria is known on the street as **(c)** _____. The world's most widely used stimulant, which produces mild arousal and alertness, is **(d)** _____. The drug that is the single greatest avoidable cause of death in the United States is **(e)** _____. This drug triggers dopamine, which stimulates the brain's reward/pleasure center.

8. The psychoactive drug that depresses the functions of the central nervous system is **(a)** _____. At low doses, it causes friendliness and loss of **(b)** _____; at medium doses, it impairs social **(c)** _____; and, at higher doses, it seriously impairs **(d)** _____ coordination.

© Bjorn Heller/Shutterstock.com

9. Certain individuals may develop or inherit different factors that make them at risk for becoming alcoholics. For example, a child raised by alcoholic parents may develop unusual, abnormal, or maladaptive psychological and emotional traits; these are called **(a)** _____ risk factors. In addition, a child may inherit predispositions for abusing alcohol, such as being less sensitive to alcohol; these are called **(b)** _____ risk factors.

10. Depressant drugs that have a sedative effect are **(a)** _____. Depressant drugs that reduce anxiety and stress are **(b)** _____.

© Darrin Henry/Shutterstock.com

© Aydin Mutlu/Photos.com

G Hallucinogens

Definition

In many parts of the world and in many different cultures, plants and fungi (mushrooms) have long been used to produce visions or hallucinations as part of cultural or religious experiences. However, Caucasians in the United States rarely used hallucinogens until the 1950s and 1960s, when these drugs gained popularity as part of the hippie subculture. Researchers have once again begun to study the potential therapeutic uses of hallucinogens, which have also gained back some of their former popularity (Golub et al., 2001).

What is a hallucinogen?

Hallucinogens are psychoactive drugs that can produce strange and unusual perceptual, sensory, and cognitive experiences, which the person sees or hears but knows that they are not occurring in reality. Such nonreality-based experiences are called *hallucinations.*

We'll focus on four of the more commonly used hallucinogens: LSD, psilocybin, mescaline, marijuana, and a designer drug called ecstasy.

LSD

What does LSD do?

At the beginning of this module, we told you about the strange bike ride of Albert Hofmann, who in 1943 discovered LSD (*d*-lysergic acid diethylamide). However, LSD did not become popular in America until the mid-1960s. In 2007, there were about 279,000 new LSD users (age 12 and older), compared to the 906,000 who began using cocaine (SAMHSA, 2008b). Possession or use of LSD is illegal.

Drug

LSD is a very potent drug because it produces hallucinogenic experiences at very low doses.

LSD produces strange experiences, which include visual hallucinations, perceptual distortions, increased sensory awareness, and intense psychological feelings.

An LSD experience, or "trip," may last 8–10 hours.

Nervous System

LSD resembles the naturally occurring neurotransmitter serotonin. LSD binds to receptors that normally respond to serotonin, and the net effect is increased stimulation of these neurons (D. L. Nelson, 2004). The majority of serotonin receptors are located on neurons in the brain's outermost layer, the cerebral cortex, which is involved in receiving sensations, creating perceptions, thinking, and imagining.

Dangers

LSD's psychological effects partially depend on the setting and the person's state of mind. If a person is tense or anxious or in an unfamiliar setting, he or she may experience a bad trip. If severe, a bad trip may lead to psychotic reactions (especially paranoid feelings) that require hospitalization. Sometime after the hallucinogenic experience, users may experience frightening flashbacks that occur for no apparent reason. There have been no reports of physical addiction to LSD or death from overdose, but users do quickly develop a tolerance to LSD (R. Goldberg, 2010).

Psilocybin

What are "magic mushrooms"?

Magic or psychedelic mushrooms are native to Mexico and have earned the "magic" name due to the mystical experiences they cause people to have (Talan, 2006b). According to one researcher, people who used magic mushrooms "had a sense of pure awareness.

They described feeling infinite love, tenderness, and peace. Everything was experienced in the present; the past and future had no meaning" (Griffiths, 2006). However, some people have adverse reactions to magic mushrooms, such as intense fears and paranoia (Griffiths, 2006). Possession or use of psilocybin is illegal.

Drug

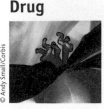

The active ingredient in magic mushrooms is psilocybin.

Psilocybin in low doses produces pleasant and relaxed feelings; medium doses produce perceptual distortions in time and space; high doses produce distortions in perceptions and body image and sometimes hallucinations.

Nervous System

Psilocybin is chemically related to LSD and, like LSD, binds to serotonin receptors. The hallucinatory effects produced by psilocybin are comparable to those from LSD but last half as long (Carter et al., 2005).

Dangers

The dangers of psilocybin come not from physical harm to the brain or body but rather from its potential for inducing psychotic states that may persist long after the experience is expected to end (Espiard et al., 2005). In addition, accidental poisonings are common among those who eat poisonous mushrooms, mistaking them for magic mushrooms.

Mescaline

What is peyote?

In the 1500s, Spanish soldiers noted that the Aztec Indians of South America ate peyote cactus as part of their religious ceremonies. Peyote cactus contains about 30 psychoactive chemicals; one of the more potent is the drug mescaline.

In 1965, the Native American Church of North America won a battle in the U.S. Supreme Court for the legal right to use peyote as a sacrament in their Christian ritual. Participants in this ritual usually sit around a fire and eat peyote buttons. This is followed by meditation, during which the participants feel removed from earthly cares and experience unusual visual perceptions, such as seeing a vast field of golden jewels that move and change (Liska, 1994). Beginning about 15 years ago, Native American Indians in the U.S. armed forces were allowed to use peyote in religious rituals (A. Gardner, 2005).

The possession or use of mescaline is illegal for all except those who belong to the Native American Church.

Drug

Mescaline is about 2,500–4,000 times less potent than LSD. **Mescaline** is the active ingredient in the peyote cactus. At high doses, mescaline produces very clear and vivid visual hallucinations, such as latticework, cobweb figures, tunnels, and spirals, which appear in various colors and intense brightness. Mescaline does not impair the intellect or cloud consciousness.

As with most hallucinogens, the setting and user's psychological state influence the experience.

Nervous System

Mescaline reaches maximum concentration in the brain about 2–4 hours after someone eats buttons of peyote cactus. Mescaline primarily increases the activity of the neurotransmitters norepinephrine and dopamine (S. M. Stahl, 2000). In addition, mescaline activates the sympathetic nervous system to produce physiological arousal, such as increased heart rate and temperature and sometimes vomiting.

Dangers

During a mescaline experience, which can last 6–8 hours, users may experience headaches and vomiting. When street samples of mescaline were analyzed in a number of cities, researchers found that the chemical was rarely mescaline. Instead "street mescaline" was usually other hallucinogens, such as LSD or PCP (G. R. Hanson et al., 2006).

Designer Drugs

Can hallucinogens be made?

The mid-1980s saw the appearance of so-called designer drugs.

Designer drugs are manufactured or synthetic drugs that are designed to resemble already existing illegal psychoactive drugs and to produce or mimic their psychoactive effects.

A drug designer can start with an amphetamine molecule and alter it in hundreds of ways. Because designer drugs are manufactured in home laboratories, users have no guarantees these drugs are safe to use. Of the many designer drugs available, we'll focus on MDMA, which was first used in the 1970s with the street name "ecstasy." In the late 1990s, ecstasy increased in popularity across the United States.

Today, ecstasy is the most popular hallucinogen, accounting for half (500,000) of all hallucinogen users (age 12 and older) (SAMHSA, 2008b). Ecstasy is the drug of choice at rave parties (image below), which feature all-night music and dancing.

The U.S. government banned research on MDMA in 1985, and only recently have researchers received permission to study its effects (Kohn, 2004). The first government-approved trial evaluating the therapeutic effects of MDMA included people who had developed treatment-resistant post-traumatic stress disorder. The results of this one study are promising, and other researchers are examining whether the results can be replicated (D. J. Brown, 2009; Mithoefer, 2009).

Drug

After alcohol and marijuana, ecstasy is often the drug of choice among teens. **MDMA,** or **ecstasy,** resembles both mescaline (hallucinogen) and amphetamine (stimulant). MDMA heightens sensations, gives a euphoric rush, raises body temperature, and creates feelings of warmth and empathy.

For these reasons, some suggest that ecstasy may be useful in some kinds of therapy (D. J. Brown, 2007).

Nervous System

MDMA causes neurons to release large amounts of two neurotransmitters, serotonin and dopamine, which stimulate the brain's reward/pleasure center. Afterward, users may feel depressed and have attention and memory deficits. The worry is that MDMA may cause brain damage (Kohn, 2004).

Dangers

In recreational doses, MDMA trips can last 6 hours and include euphoria, high energy, jaw clenching, teeth grinding, increased body temperature, and insomnia. At higher doses, trips include panic, rapid heart beat, high body temperature, paranoia, and psychotic-like symptoms (Baylen & Rosenberg, 2006). Also, MDMA depletes some of the brain's transmitters (serotonin and dopamine) (Montoya et al., 2002).

Longer-term, heavy use of MDMA can lead to serious cognitive impairments, such as memory loss, weakened immune system, and depression (Falck et al., 2006; Laws & Kokkalis, 2007; Schilt et al., 2007; J. Ward et al., 2006).

Next, we'll focus on the most widely used illegal drug in the United States.

Marijuana

The most widely used illegal drug in the United States is marijuana.

What's the most widely used illegal drug?

In this country, 33% of people have tried marijuana and 14.4 million are current users (SAMHSA, 2008b; Volkow, 2011). A recent poll found that half of Americans support the legalizing of marijuana use (Gallup, 2011). At least part of the reason for this record-high number of supporters is the increasing awareness and knowledge of the medicinal benefits of marijuana.

Medical marijuana. Research shows that marijuana can be effective in treating nausea and vomiting associated with chemotherapy, appetite loss in AIDS patients, eye disease (glaucoma), muscle spasticity, multiple sclerosis, inflammatory conditions, and some forms of pain (S. O. Cole, 2005; Seppa, 2010). Tests on the effects of marijuana use on cancer tumors, diabetes, stroke, epilepsy, depression, and

© Rachel Whenman/Alamy

schizophrenia, among other health conditions, are currently under way (Seppa, 2010).

Because of the accumulating research on the medical benefits of marijuana, 13 states have passed laws and others are considering laws that allow marijuana to be prescribed by doctors and used legally for medical problems.

Gateway effect. One reason for enforcing tough penalties against marijuana usage is the *gateway effect,* which says that using marijuana leads young people to try harder drugs (cocaine, heroin). For instance, there's data that suggest teenagers who used marijuana are more likely to become dependent on other drugs. However, other research shows that genetic and environmental predispositions explain equally well why some marijuana users go on to try harder drugs (Morral et al., 2002).

In any case, marijuana is illegal and, despite its potential medicinal benefits, it can cause a variety of serious problems.

Drug

© RayArt Graphics/Alamy

As is true of many psychoactive drugs, some of marijuana's effects depend on the user's initial mood and state of mental health. For example, older patients who used marijuana to treat glaucoma or nausea complained about its "strange side effect," which was feeling high or euphoric, which is the very effect that young users seek in smoking marijuana (Tramer et al., 2001).

Marijuana is a psychoactive drug whose primary active ingredient is THC (tetrahydrocannabinol), which is found in the leaves of the cannabis plant.

The average marijuana cigarette ("joint") contains 2.5–11.0 mg of THC, which is a tenfold increase over the amount of THC found in marijuana in the 1970s. THC is rapidly absorbed by the lungs and in 5–10 minutes produces a high that lasts for several hours. The type of high is closely related to the dose: Low doses produce mild euphoria; moderate doses produce perceptual and time distortions; and high doses may produce hallucinations, delusions, and distortions of body image (G. R. Hanson et al., 2002).

Depending on the user's state of mind, marijuana can either heighten or distort pleasant or unpleasant experiences, moods, or feelings (Moreira & Lutz, 2008).

Nervous System

In 1964, researchers identified and synthesized THC, the main mind-altering substance in marijuana.

In 1990, researchers discovered a specific receptor for THC in the brains of rats and humans (Matsuda et al., 1990). These THC receptors are located throughout the brain, including the hippocampus, which is involved in short-term memory; the cerebral cortex, which is involved in higher cognitive functions; the limbic system, which is involved in emotions; and the cerebellum and basal ganglia, which are involved in motor control, timing, and coordination (Iversen, 2000; Volkow, 2011). Mammalian brains (such as humans) contain extremely high levels of THC receptors, which suggests they may be involved in important brain functions (Iversen, 2000).

In 1993, researchers found that the brain itself makes a chemical, called anandamide, that stimulates THC receptors. Anandamide, a naturally occurring brain chemical, has been shown to be one of the brain's neurotransmitters, whose actions are currently under study (Piomelli, 1999).

Thus, the brain not only has receptors for THC but also makes a THC-like chemical, called anandamide.

Dangers

Marijuana can cause temporary changes in cognitive functioning, such as interfering with short-term memory and ability to drive a car, boat, or plane, because it impairs reaction time, judgment, and peripheral vision (Schuckit, 2000). Long-term frequent doses may cause toxic psychoses, including delusions, paranoia, and feelings of terror, and are associated with depression and anxiety (Fergusson et al., 2005; W. Hall, 2006; R. M. Murray et al., 2007). However, there is no conclusive evidence that prolonged marijuana use causes permanent brain or nervous system damage (Cloud, 2002).

Marijuana causes many of the same kinds of respiratory problems as tobacco, including bronchitis and asthma attacks. Because marijuana smoke contains 50% more cancer-causing substances and users hold smoke in their lungs longer, the effects of smoking one joint of marijuana are similar to those of smoking five cigarettes (*Time,* 2007c).

Some, but not all, regular heavy users of marijuana develop addiction and dependency. And when heavy users stop, some experience withdrawal symptoms, including irritability, restlessness, and anxiety as well as strong cravings for more (N. T. Smith, 2002; Wolfing et al., 2008).

Now we'll examine the group of drugs called opiates. ●

H Opiates

Opium, Morphine, Heroin

Beginning in 6000 B.C., opiates have been used around the world. Opiates were legal in the early 1800s, when

How popular is heroin?

the active ingredient in the juice of the opium poppy was found to be morphine. In the late 1800s, morphine was chemically altered to make heroin, which like opium is addictive. Law enforcement agencies usually refer to opiates as *narcotics*.

Narcotics are drugs that are used to relieve pain and induce sleep.

In the early 1900s, the sale and use of narcotics (opium, morphine, and heroin) were made illegal and a wildly lucrative opium black market began. In spite of restrictive laws and billions spent on enforcement,

Heroin use is on the rise among young adults.

opiates are still readily available in most major U.S. cities (Schuckit, 2000). In fact, the production of illegal opiates has reached record levels (*Time,* 2007a).

In 1980, heroin was about 7% pure, but current heroin is about 50% pure, which means instead of being injected, it can be smoked or snorted. A recent trend in heroin use is its increasing popularity with young people who prefer to smoke or snort the drug rather than inject it (SAMHSA, 2008a).

Heroin is one of the drugs most frequently reported by medical examiners in drug abuse deaths (SAMHSA, 2008a). The possession or use of opium, morphine, and heroin is illegal.

Drug

All opiates produce similar effects, but some users prefer to inject heroin because it reaches the brain more quickly and produces the biggest "rush."

Opiates, such as opium, morphine, and heroin, produce three primary effects: analgesia (pain reduction); opiate euphoria, which is often described as a pleasurable state between waking and sleeping; and constipation. Continued use of opiates results in tolerance, addiction, and dependency.

One rock star (Anthony Kiedis of "Red Hot Chili Peppers") described using heroin for the first time as "a great feeling.... It's like you're opening a door that leads you into a different world. You discover a brand new universe" (*NY Rock,* 2002). However, with constant usage, his brain developed a tolerance to heroin, which means he had to take larger and larger doses to achieve a high and ended up developing many life problems (Kiedis, 2004).

Nervous System

In the 1970s, researchers discovered that the brain has naturally occurring receptors for opiates (Pert et al., 1974). When morphine reaches the brain's receptors, it produces feelings of euphoria and analgesia. In addition, the gastrointestinal tract has opiate receptors whose stimulation results in constipation.

Researchers discovered that the brain not only has its own opiate receptors but also produces its own morphinelike chemicals. These chemicals, which function as neurotransmitters, are called *endorphins* and are found to have the same analgesic properties as morphine (Pleuvry, 2005).

Dangers

Anthony Kiedis, who injected heroin, said, "If you haven't ever put a needle in your arm, don't ever do it... it's horrible, and I don't want anyone to ever have to feel like I'm feeling right now. Let me do the suffering for you" (Kiedis, 2004, p. 179).

After several weeks of regular opiate use, a person's brain produces less of its own endorphins and relies more on the outside supply of opiates. As a result, a person becomes addicted to taking opiates and must administer one or more doses daily to prevent withdrawal symptoms.

Withdrawal symptoms, which include hot and cold flashes, sweating, muscle tremors, nausea, and stomach cramps, are not life threatening and last 5–8 days. An overdose of opiates depresses the neural control of breathing, and a person dies from respiratory failure (Mendelson et al., 2006).

Treatment

In Great Britain, where heroin addiction is considered a health problem, heroin addicts who chose methadone injections instead of heroin use showed significant reductions in drug use and crime during a 12-month period (Metrebian et al., 2001). In contrast, in the United States, heroin addiction is considered a criminal problem, and addicts have typically had limited access to regular medical treatment. In a 33-year follow-up study of heroin addicts in the United States, researchers reported that only 6% were in a medical treatment program, 40% had used heroin in the past year, and many had severe health problems or spent time in prison (Hser et al., 2001). Researchers concluded that, if heroin users do not quit by age 30, they are unlikely ever to stop. The most common treatment for heroin addiction

Opium poppy contains morphine.

is to maintain addicts on methadone, which is an addictive, synthetic drug similar to opium. Methadone treatment programs, which are becoming widely available, can be relatively effective in preventing heroin use, reducing criminal activities, and preventing loss of employment (Vocci et al., 2005).

A recent treatment for heroin addiction in the United States is a new federally approved drug (buprenorphine) that blocks the craving for heroin. This drug has several advantages, including increased accessibility (it is given in a doctor's office), lower risk of overdose, and about equal effectiveness as methadone (Kakko et al., 2007).

Next, we'll discuss other types of treatment for drug abuse. ●

Developing a Problem

Here's a case study that shows how psychological risks helped push Martin into abusing alcohol and becoming an alcoholic.

What are the risks for drug abuse?

In high school, Martin got good grades but still felt insecure, especially about his sexual abilities. His solution was to act like a "rugged, hard-drinking person." But, instead of helping, hard drinking made him feel more insecure in relationships and made it more difficult for him to perform sexually.

When Martin entered college, he continued to have low self-esteem and feared that someone would discover that his sexual performance did not match his bragging. As he had done in high school, he buried his fears in having five to ten drinks on weekends.

Despite his drinking bouts, Martin's knack for learning helped him finish college with good grades and even get into medical school. However, between college and medical school, he took a job driving a beer truck and drank half a dozen beers after work.

In medical school, Martin drank regularly because alcohol reduced his feelings of "self-loathing" and gave him an "instant" sense of self-worth. Despite heavy drinking, Martin's talents for mastering academic subjects helped him finish medical school.

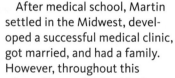

Many start out believing that alcohol is the solution.

After medical school, Martin settled in the Midwest, developed a successful medical clinic, got married, and had a family. However, throughout this period, he continued to drink heavily and began having blackouts. His wife could stand his drinking no longer, and one day she took the children and left. Martin began using painkillers, writing his own prescriptions.

Finally, one cold afternoon as Martin sat home with his booze and painkillers, the police arrested him for writing illegal prescriptions. Martin was forced to enter a psychiatric hospital for drug treatment (adapted from Khantzian & Mack, 1994).

Some of the psychological risks that pushed Martin to become a drug abuser are clear: For most of his life, he suffered from feelings of low self-esteem, worthlessness, and fears of not performing sexually. Hoping to solve his problems with drugs, Martin instead made them worse with substance abuse, the most common mental health problem among men (Kessler et al., 1994).

Many scientists now believe the process of a voluntary drug user turning into an addict, as happened to Martin, results from a combination of psychological risk factors and actual changes inside the brain. Based on considerable research, it has been found that changes in the brain's structure and function from heavy drug use result in making a person more sensitive to stress and more likely to use drugs again to reduce anxiety (Wenner, 2008b). For this reason, scientists caution against blaming addicts for their drug addiction. Instead they recommend programs that treat both the brain disease by reducing drug usage and the psychological problems by actively involving the user in returning to normal functioning without drugs (Leshner, 2001).

Substance Abuse and Treatment

Like Martin, about 5–15% of those who use legal or illegal drugs develop a serious drug problem called substance abuse.

What is a drug problem?

Substance abuse is a maladaptive behavioral pattern of using a drug so frequently that significant problems develop: failing to meet major obligations and having multiple legal, social, family, health, work, or interpersonal problems. These problems must occur repeatedly during the same 12-month period (American Psychiatric Association, 2000).

Substance abuse is one of the most challenging behaviors to change (Ray & Hutchinson, 2007). Most substance abusers need professional treatment to get straightened out. Martin entered a treatment program based on the Minnesota model, which is used in 95% of inpatient drug treatment centers in the United States. The *Minnesota model* recognizes that the drug user has lost control over drugs, may be vulnerable to using other substances, cannot solve the drug problem alone, must rebuild his or her life without drugs, and must strive for abstinence (McElrath, 1997; Owen, 2003).

Individuals with substance abuse usually need professional help.

We'll follow Martin's progress as he goes through a typical drug treatment program based on the Minnesota model.

Step 1. Admit the Problem

Why don't people seek treatment?

The fact that Martin did not seek help for his drug problem until he was arrested points out an important difference between most individuals treated for drug problems and those treated for mental health problems.

Generally, individuals with mental health problems seek help voluntarily because they want to stop their suffering or unhappiness. In contrast, many individuals with drug problems do not recognize that they have a problem and do not seek help voluntarily. In fact, of the nation's 7.4 million adults (age 21 to 64) who have an untreated alcohol abuse disorder, only 7.8% believe they need treatment (SAMHSA, 2011a).

Because of the resistance to acknowledge the existence of a problem, the first step in getting treatment is admitting that one does in fact have a drug problem. Although this step appears obvious, in reality it represents a hurdle that many drug abusers have a difficult time getting over. What happens is that drug users believe that drugs are the solution to their problems, fears, insecurities, and worries. Convincing heavy drug users to seek treatment often requires the efforts of their family, loved ones, and employer, as well as a judge or doctor (Schuckit, 2000).

Alcoholics deny that they have a problem.

Step 2. Enter a Program

Every day in the United States, about 2.7 million people receive treatment for alcoholism in either an inpatient (hospital) or outpatient (clinic) setting (SAMHSA, 2008b). In Martin's case, he was required to enter an inpatient (hospital) drug treatment program because he was both addicted and depressed, would not admit to having a problem, and would not seek help on his own. In comparison, most alcoholics (85%) are treated in clinics as outpatients.

Most in- or outpatient drug treatment programs involve the following steps and goals: Martin receives a complete medical checkup and a two-week period of detoxification (getting drug free), and then a team consisting of a physician, psychologist, counselor, and nurse discusses the treatment's four goals with Martin (Winters et al., 2000).

First goal. Help Martin face up to his drinking problem. It is not uncommon for a drug abuser to deny that he or she has a problem with drugs, even though it is obvious to everyone else.

Second goal. Have Martin begin a program of stress management, so that he can reduce his anxiety and tension without drinking. Stress management involves the substitution of relaxation exercises and other enjoyable activities (sports, hobbies) for the escape and enjoyment that alcohol has provided.

Third goal. Give Martin an opportunity to share his experiences in group therapy. Group sessions helped Martin realize that he was not suffering alone, that it was important for him to make plans for the future, and that he might have to make new, nondrinking friends once he left the program.

Fourth goal. Perhaps the most important goal is to help Martin face and overcome his psychological risk factors, which include personal and social problems that had contributed to his drug abuse.

Three different therapies, including AA, were equally effective.

Step 3. Get Therapy

Regarding the fourth goal, you may wonder which kind of therapy is most effective in helping drug abusers. One answer comes from a 8-year study on over 1,700 individuals, all diagnosed as alcohol-dependent. This study compared the effectiveness of three different programs.

Three therapies. After volunteering for this study, individuals were randomly assigned to a 12-week treatment program that involved one of the following three therapies. *Cognitive-behavioral therapy* focuses on helping patients develop skills to control their thoughts about alcohol and learn to control their urges to drink. *Motivational therapy* helps clients recognize and utilize their personal resources and encourages them to take personal responsibility to abstain from drinking. The *12-step approach* is used in traditional Alcoholics Anonymous (AA) programs. The AA therapy or program promotes spiritual awakening, and its 12 steps serve as a guide for recovery and abstinence. AA believes that drug abuse is a disease, that a person must surrender to and ask God for help, and that total abstinence is the only solution.

Effectiveness. Researchers found that, before therapy, all individuals drank heavily on about 25 days per month. In comparison, a year after finishing therapy, 35% reported not drinking at all, while 65% had slipped, or relapsed, into drinking again. Of the 65% who had relapsed, 40% reported periods of at least three consecutive days of heavy drinking.

There was little difference in the effectiveness of the three programs, which was somewhat surprising in view of their different approaches to drug treatment (Project Match Research Group, 1997). The effectiveness of a drug treatment program is measured by how many clients remain abstinent (do not use drugs) for a period of one year. Success rates range from 30 to 45%, which means that 55 to 70% relapse or return to drinking during the year following treatment (Fuller & Hiller-Sturmhofel, 1999). For most drug treatment programs, the goal is total abstinence. However, there is an ongoing debate over whether alcoholics can learn to use drugs in moderate amounts.

New drugs. Medications approved to treat alcoholism include naltrexone and acamprosate, which reduce cravings, and Antabuse, which makes people physically ill if they consume alcohol (K. Hobson, 2006). These drugs have shown modest success when used alone and greater success when combined with therapy to help alcoholics rebuild their lives (K. Hobson, 2006; Schuckit, 2002).

Vaccines. The newest treatment for substance addiction is vaccinating people so they produce antibodies against particular drugs to prevent them from reaching the brain. Ultimately, these vaccines aim to prevent users from feeling a high or having a rewarding experience by using particular drugs (Janda, 2011; Kosten, 2009; Volkow, 2009). The vaccines are early in their development but show promise.

Step 4. Stay Sober

After treatment, recovering alcoholics as well as other drug addicts are encouraged to join a community support group to help fight relapse, or returning to drugs. The most popular and successful aftercare program for alcoholics is Alcoholics Anonymous (AA); a similar program for other drug users is Narcotics Anonymous (NA). After drug treatment, AA and NA provide programs to help prevent relapse, which occurs in 55–70% of former drug users.

Relapse can be triggered by a single exposure to the drug, by being with people or in places associated with using the drug, or by acute and chronic stressors.

To help patients deal with relapse, therapists have developed a program called relapse prevention therapy, which includes helping patients recognize high-risk situations that might trigger relapse, rehearsing strategies for dealing with high-risk situations, such as avoiding old drinking buddies, and learning how to deal with drug cravings. Because the majority of drug users relapse, this therapy also helps patients recover from a relapse (Foxhall, 2001).

© pixhook/iStockphoto

About 55–70% of recovering alcoholics suffer relapse.

Thus, a person with a drug problem initially needs help to get off a drug, then treatment to recover, then a support group, and finally relapse therapy to deal with relapse and try to remain drug free. ●

Brain-Boosting Drugs: Myth or Fact?

Currently, there is major controversy among scientists, educators, and others over the rapidly increasing number of healthy people turning to "brain-boosting" drugs to enhance their mental performance. The main drugs being used for this purpose are Ritalin

1 Which illegal drug is Ritalin most similar to?

("Vitamin R"), which is used to treat ADHD, and Provigil, which is used to treat sleep disorders. College campus surveys show that nearly 25% of college students use these medications without a prescription, not

2 What are an advantage and disadvantage of the survey research method?

while partying to get a high but to help with studying.

These drugs can improve a variety of mental skills in healthy people, such as increasing concentration time on a task, reducing time needed to solve puzzles, and improving memory of a series of numbers. Provigil can even help people go for days

3 What are some of the dangers of sleep deprivation?

without sleeping, all while improving their mental performance. As impressive as these drugs may sound, their long-term risks on healthy people are unknown.

Of course, dosing up on stimulant medications to improve focus and energy is nothing new.

4 How do stimulant drugs work?

Amphetamines and other stimulant drugs have long been used for this purpose. And let's remember that almost all of us drink caffeinated beverages to feel more upbeat, alert, and focused. Many college students drink caffeinated beverages, sometimes caffeine-pumped energy drinks, to stay awake studying for an exam or completing a term paper. But how much does caffeine actually boost our brains?

Research shows that after consuming caffeine (two cups of coffee), people have faster reaction times and increased activity in the areas of the brain responsible for memory and attention.

5 Which type of research method must be used to conclude that caffeine, and not something else, was the cause of improved memory?

The data are so strong that the U.S. military now provides pilots with caffeinated gum in the cockpit and provides troops with caffeinated meals.

6 Can drinking more than two cups of coffee improve these intellectual functions even more?

Drinking small to moderate amounts of caffeine may improve your memory and attention, but this doesn't mean caffeine makes us smarter. As a

research psychologist, Harris Lieberman, says, "I use the word intelligence as an inherent trait, something permanently part of your makeup" (Lemonick, 2006, p. 95). He explains that caffeine cannot change intelligence, but what it can do is improve your attention, mood, and energy level. For instance, when you're feeling drowsy and you take caffeine, many intellectual functions, such as attention, logical reasoning, and reaction time, improve. Thus, though caffeine cannot make you more intelligent, it can help you to better use the intellectual abilities you already have. The same can be said about other so-called brain-boosting drugs, such as Ritalin and Provigil.

Adapted from S. Baker, 2009; Billingsley, 2005; Davenport, 2011; Greely et al., 2008; Hibbert, 2007; M. A. Howard & Marczinski, 2010; Koppelstaetter et al., 2005; Lemonick, 2006; Raloff, 2011; Steenhuysen, 2008; Talbot, 2009; Wire Reports, 2007

Summary Test

A Hypnosis

1. Hypnosis is defined as an altered state of awareness, attention, and alertness, during which a person is usually much more open to the **(a)** _____ of a hypnotist or therapist. About 10–15% of adults are easily hypnotized, while 20% are difficult to hypnotize. The procedure used to hypnotize someone is called **(b)** _____.

© Rudyanto Wijaya//iStockphoto

2. Under hypnosis, individuals will experience or perform the following _____: age regression, imagined perception, posthypnotic amnesia, posthypnotic suggestions, and hypnotic analgesia.

3. According to the **(a)** _____ theory, hypnotized people perform suggested behaviors because they are in a special state. According to the **(b)** _____ theory, people perform suggested behaviors, not because they are hypnotized, but because these individuals have the amazing ability of responding to imaginative suggestions and because of social pressures.

4. In dental and medical settings, hypnosis is used to help patients deal with painful procedures by producing **(a)** _____. In therapeutic settings, hypnosis is used in combination with other behavioral and cognitive treatments to help clients reveal their personalities and gain insights. However, hypnosis is not very successful in dealing with problems that involve **(b)** _____.

B Research Focus: Meditation & School Stress

© takayuki/Shutterstock.com

5. Researchers assessed the effectiveness of a stress-reduction program on school stress. With the goal of reducing stress, researchers trained students to practice _____, which involves focusing your attention on repeating words or sounds that are supposed to help produce an altered state of consciousness.

C Drugs: Overview

6. Regular use of a drug usually results in one or more of the following: A behavioral pattern of drug abuse that is marked by an overwhelming and compulsive desire to obtain and use the drug is called an **(a)** _____. If the nervous system becomes accustomed to having the drug and needs the drug for normal functioning, the user is said to have developed a **(b)** _____. If a habitual user suddenly stops taking the drug, he or she will experience unpleasant or painful

(c) _____. After using a drug over a period of time, a person must take a larger dose to achieve the original behavioral effect because this person has developed a **(d)** _____ for the drug.

7. Drugs that affect the nervous system by altering consciousness, awareness, sensations, perceptions, mood, and cognitive processes are called _____ drugs.

8. Some drugs act like **(a)** _____ keys that open neurons' chemical **(b)** _____, and some prevent the neuron's reabsorption of neurotransmitters, called **(c)** _____. Some drugs act on the brain's powerful **(d)** _____ center.

D Stimulants

9. Drugs that increase the activity of the nervous system and result in heightened alertness, arousal, and euphoria and decreased appetite and fatigue are called _____.

© Fedor Kondrate·tko/Shutterstock.com

10. In moderate doses, cocaine produces short-lived enhancement of _____. In heavy doses, it can produce addiction; serious psychological effects, such as frightening hallucinations; and serious physical problems, such as heart irregularity, convulsions, and death.

11. A form of amphetamine called _____ produces a quick high, is very addictive, and has become a major drug problem.

12. The most widely used legal psychoactive drug in the world is _____, which affects brain receptors and, depending on the dose, produces physiological arousal, a mild feeling of alertness, increased reaction time, and decreased fatigue and drowsiness.

13. The legal drug that is second to caffeine in worldwide usage is _____, which triggers the production of dopamine.

E Depressants

14. Alcohol is classified as a **(a)** _____ because it decreases the activity of the central nervous system by stimulating neural receptors called **(b)** _____ receptors. Heavy and repeated drinking can result in periods of seemingly normal behavior that the drinker, when sober, cannot recall at all; these periods are called **(c)** _____.

© Bjorn Heller/Shutterstock.com

15. A drinker's risk of becoming an alcoholic increases three to four times if members of his or her family are alcoholics. The risk of developing alcoholism is increased by having difficulties in showing trust and being overdependent in relationships, which are called **(a)** _____ factors, and also by the inheritance of predispositions for alcoholism, which are called **(b)** _____ factors.

F Cultural Diversity: Alcoholism Rates

16. People who have drunk heavily for a long period of time, are addicted to and have an intense craving for alcohol, and have developed major life problems because of drinking are _____.

Rates of Alcoholism

Koreans	22%
Canadians	18%
Americans	14%
Germans	13%
Chinese 7%	
Taiwanese 0.5%	

17. One reason the Chinese and Taiwanese have low rates of alcoholism is that these societies are heavily influenced by the Confucian moral code, which discourages _____ in public.

G Hallucinogens

18. Drugs that act on the brain (and body) to produce perceptual, sensory, and cognitive experiences that do not match the external reality are called **(a)** _____. Sometime after using LSD, a user may suddenly have a frightening, drug-related experience called a **(b)** _____. Examples of hallucinogenic drugs are LSD, psilocybin, and mescaline. Drugs that are manufactured or altered to produce psychoactive effects are called **(c)** _____; an example is **(d)** _____.

© RayArt Graphics/Alamy

19. The most widely used illegal drug in the United States is **(a)** _____. In low doses it produces mild euphoria, in moderate doses it produces distortions in perception and time, and in high doses it may produce hallucinations and delusions. Researchers discovered that the brain has neural locks, or THC **(b)** _____, that are highly concentrated in the brain and respond to the THC in marijuana. The brain makes its own chemical, called **(c)** _____, which is one of the brain's own **(d)** _____ and closely resembles THC. Throughout the brain are many THC receptors that are involved in a number of behaviors, including **(e)** _____.

H Opiates

© mafoto/iStockphoto

20. All opiates produce three primary effects: a reduction in pain, which is called **(a)** _____; a twilight state between waking and sleeping, which is called **(b)** _____; and **(c)** _____, which permits their use as a treatment for diarrhea. With continued use of opiates, users develop tolerance, addiction, and an intense craving for the drug. The brain also produces its own morphinelike chemicals, called **(d)** _____.

I Application: Treatment for Drug Abuse

21. A maladaptive pattern of continued usage of a substance—drug or medicine—that results in significant legal, personal, or other problems over a 12-month period is called _____.

22. Programs that treat drug abusers have four steps: The first step is admitting that one has a **(a)** _____. The second step is entering a **(b)** _____, which has four goals. The third step is to get **(c)** _____ to help overcome drug abuse. The fourth step is to remain **(d)** _____.

23. Researchers found that three different kinds of therapy—cognitive-behavioral, motivational, and AA's 12-step approach—were about **(a)** _____ in helping alcoholics stop drinking. Although about 35% of individuals stopped drinking, about 65% started drinking again, which is called **(b)** _____. Part of recovery is learning how to deal with relapse, called **(c)** _____ therapy. In addition, recovering addicts are encouraged to join a community **(d)** _____ group, which helps them remain drug free.

Answers: 1. (a) suggestions, (b) hypnotic induction; 2. behaviors; 3. (a) altered state, (b) sociocognitive; 4. (a) analgesia, (b) self-control; 5. transcendental meditation; 6. (a) addiction, (b) physiological dependence, (c) withdrawal symptoms, (d) tolerance; 7. psychoactive; 8. (a) chemical, (b) locks, (c) reuptake, (d) reward/pleasure; 9. stimulants; 10. activity, mood, or energy; 11. methamphetamine; 12. caffeine; 13. nicotine; 14. (a) depressant, (b) GABA, (c) blackouts; 15. (a) psychological risk, (b) genetic risk; 16. alcoholics; 17. drunkenness; 18. (a) hallucinogens, (b) flashback, (c) designer drugs, (d) MDMA, or ecstasy; 19. (a) marijuana, (b) receptors, (c) anandamide, (d) neurotransmitters, (e) memory, emotions, motor control, higher cognitive functions; 20. (a) analgesia, (b) opiate euphoria, (c) constipation, (d) endorphins; 21. substance abuse; 22. (a) drug problem, (b) treatment program, (c) therapy, (d) drug free; 23. (a) equally effective, (b) relapse, (c) relapse, (d) support

Links to Learning

Key Terms/Key People

AA—12-step approach, 189
addiction, 175
age regression, 172
alcohol, 180
alcoholism, 182
altered state theory of hypnosis, 171
barbiturates, 181
blackouts, 180
caffeine, 179
cocaine, 178
cognitive-behavioral therapy, 189
cultural risk factors, 182

depressants, 180
designer drugs, 185
ecstasy (MDMA), 185
gateway effect, 186
genetic risk factors, 181
hallucinogens, 184
hangover, 180
heroin, 187
hypnosis, 170
hypnotic analgesia, 172
hypnotic induction, 170
imagined perception, 172
LSD, 184
marijuana, 186

marijuana—medical uses, 186
mescaline, 185
methamphetamine, 177
mimicking, 176
morphine, 179, 187
motivational therapy, 189
narcotics, 187
nicotine, 179
nucleus accumbens, 176
opiates, 187
physiological dependence, 175
posthypnotic amnesia, 172
posthypnotic suggestion, 172
psilocybin, 184

psychoactive drugs, 175
psychological dependence, 175
psychological risk factors, 181
reuptake, 176
reward/pleasure center, 176
sociocognitive theory of hypnosis, 171
stimulants, 177
substance abuse, 188
tolerance, 175
tranquilizers, 181
transcendental meditation, 174
ventral tegmental area, 176
withdrawal symptoms, 175

Media Resources

Go to **CengageBrain.com** to access Psychology CourseMate, where you will find an interactive eBook, glossaries, flashcards, quizzes, videos, answers to Critical Thinking questions, and more. You can also access Virtual Psychology Labs, an interactive laboratory experience designed to illustrate key experiments first-hand.

MODULE 9 Classical Conditioning

© Mark Andersen/Age fotostock

It's Only Aftershave

What happened to Carla?

"I've got an unusual problem and I thought you might be able to explain what happened." Carla, one of my (R. P.) students, looked troubled.

"I'll help if I can," I replied, and asked her to sit down.

"It all started when my dentist told me that I needed a lot of work on my teeth and gums. I spent many mornings in the dentist's chair, and even though he gave me Novocain, it was painful and very uncomfortable. But here's the strange part that I wish you would explain. I had recently bought my boyfriend a new aftershave, and as the dentist worked on my teeth, I noticed that he was using the same one. You'll think this is silly, but now when I smell my boyfriend's aftershave, I start to feel tense and anxious."

Carla stopped and waited to see if I would tell her that she was just being silly. I didn't, and she continued.

"Finally, I told my boyfriend that he would have to stop using the aftershave I had bought him because it was the same as my dentist's and the smell made me anxious. Well, we got into a big argument because he said that he was nothing like my dentist and I was just being silly. So now my teeth are great, but I feel myself getting anxious each time we get close and I smell his aftershave."

How can smelling aftershave cause anxiety?

I assured Carla that she was not being silly and that many people get conditioned in the dentist's chair. In fact, patients have reported feeling anxious when they enter the dentist's office, smell the antiseptic odor, or hear the sound of the drill (Settineri et al., 2005; Taani et al., 2005). I explained that, without her knowing, she had been conditioned to feel fear each time she smelled her dentist's aftershave and how that conditioning had transferred to her boyfriend's aftershave. Before I explained how to get "unconditioned," I told her how after only one terrifying experience, I too had been conditioned.

It's Only a Needle

What happened to Rod?

I (R. P.) was about 8 years old when I had to get an injection from my local doctor, whom I really liked. He warned me in a kindly way that the injection might hurt a little. I was feeling OK until I saw the long needle on the syringe. I tried to be brave and think of my fuzzy dog, but as soon as I felt that long needle enter my little butt, everything started to spin. I remember sinking slowly to the floor, and then everything went dark. When I came to, the doctor told me that I had fainted.

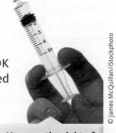

© James McQuillan/iStockphoto

How can the sight of a syringe and needle cause terror?

Even after all these years, the sight of a needle can still strike terror into me. To prevent fainting, I always lie down when getting an injection or giving blood. But I'm not alone in my fear of needles and injections; about 10 to 20% of the general population report a similar fear and many others have some aversion to needles (Page et al., 1997; Sibbitt, 2006).

Besides learning to fear needles and blood, people can unknowingly learn to feel sick and nauseated, just as Michelle did.

It's Only Dish Soap

What happened to Michelle?

Michelle was nervous and afraid as the nurse put a needle into the vein in her left arm and then opened a valve that allowed chemicals to drip into her bloodstream. Michelle was in the process of receiving chemotherapy to treat her cancer. One serious side effect of chemotherapy is severe nausea, which Michelle experienced after each treatment.

What Michelle wasn't prepared for was how other things could trigger her nausea. In one case, the odor of her dishwashing liquid, which smelled similar to the chemotherapy room, made her feel nauseated. She had to change her brand of detergent because its odor made her salivate, which was the first sign of oncoming nausea (Wittman, 1994). Without her awareness, Michelle had been conditioned to feel nauseated by numerous stimuli involved in her chemotherapy (McRonald & Fleisher, 2005).

How can smelling dish soap cause nausea?

The cases of Michelle, Carla, and Rod show how we can be conditioned to fear relatively ordinary things, such as aftershave lotion, needles, and the smell of detergent. This conditioning illustrates one kind of learning.

Learning is a relatively enduring or permanent change in behavior or knowledge that results from previous experience with certain stimuli and responses. The term **behavior** includes any observable response (fainting, salivating, vomiting).

In all three cases, conditioning resulted in a relatively enduring change in behavior. In fact, mine has lasted for more than 50 years. What happened to each of us involved a particular kind of learning, called classical conditioning, which we'll discuss in this module.

What's Coming

We'll first discuss three different kinds of learning and then focus on one, classical conditioning. We'll examine how classical conditioning is established and tested, how we respond after being classically conditioned, what we learn during classical conditioning, and how classical conditioning is used in therapy. Let's begin with a look at three different kinds of learning. ●

A Three Kinds of Learning

Why is some learning easier? Some things are difficult to learn, such as all the terms in this module. Other things are easy to learn, such as fear of an injection. To understand why some learning is easy and some hard, we'll visit three different laboratories. You'll see how psychologists identified three different principles that underlie three different kinds of learning: classical conditioning, operant conditioning, and cognitive learning.

Classical Conditioning

It is the early 1900s, and you are working as a technician in Russia in the laboratory of Ivan Pavlov. He has

Why does the dog salivate?

already won a Nobel Prize for his studies on the reflexes involved in digestion. For example, he found that when food is placed in a dog's mouth, the food triggers the reflex of salivation (Evans, 1999).

As a lab technician, your task is to place various kinds of food in a dog's mouth and measure the amount of salivation. But soon you encounter a problem. After you have placed food in a dog's mouth on a number of occasions, the dog begins to salivate merely at the sight of the food.

At first, Pavlov considered this sort of anticipatory salivation to be a bothersome problem. Later, he reasoned that the dog's salivation at the sight of food was also a reflex, but one that the dog had somehow *learned.*

In a well-known experiment, Pavlov rang a bell before putting food in the dog's mouth. As shown in this graph, after a

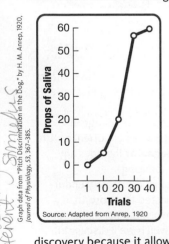

Graph data from "Pitch Discrimination in the Dog," by H. M. Anrep, 1920, *Journal of Physiology*, 53, 367–385.

number of trials of hearing a bell paired with food, the dog salivated at the sound of the bell alone, a phenomenon that Pavlov called a *conditioned reflex* and today is called classical conditioning. Classical conditioning was an important discovery because it allowed researchers to study learning in an observable, or objective, way (Honey, 2000).

Classical conditioning is a kind of learning in which a neutral stimulus acquires the ability to produce a response that was originally produced by a different stimulus.

Next, we'll visit a lab in the United States and observe a different kind of learning.

Operant Conditioning

It is the late 1800s, and you are now working in the laboratory of the American psychologist E. L. Thorndike. Your

Why does the cat escape?

task is to place a cat in a box with a door that can be opened from the inside by hitting a simple latch. Outside the box is a fish on a dish. You are to record the length of time it takes the cat to hit the latch, open the door, and get the fish.

Thorndike studied how a cat learned to open a cage to get nearby food.

On the first trial, the cat sniffs around the box, sticks its paw in various places, accidentally hits the latch, opens the door, and gets the fish. You place the cat back into the box for another trial. Again the cat moves around, accidentally strikes the latch, and gets the fish. After many such trials, the cat learns to spend its time around the latch and eventually to hit the latch and get the fish in a very short time.

To explain the cat's goal-directed behavior, Thorndike formulated the law of effect.

The **law of effect** says that if some random actions are followed by a pleasurable consequence or reward, such actions are strengthened and will likely occur in the future.

Thorndike's law of effect was important because it identified a learning process different from Pavlov's conditioned reflex. Today, the law of effect has become part of operant conditioning (Bouton, 2007).

Operant conditioning is a kind of learning in which the consequences that follow some behavior increase or decrease the likelihood of that behavior's occurrence in the future.

We will discuss operant conditioning in Module 10. Our next lab has a big plastic doll and a bunch of kids.

Cognitive Learning

It is the 1960s, and you are in Albert Bandura's laboratory, where children are watching a film

Why do they punch the doll?

of an adult who is repeatedly hitting and kicking a big plastic doll. Following this film, the children are observed during play.

Bandura found that children who had watched the film of an adult modeling aggressive behavior played more aggressively than children who had not seen the film (Bandura et al., 1963). The children's change in behavior, which was increased aggressive responses, did not seem to be based on Pavlov's conditioned reflexes or Thorndike's law of effect. Instead, the entire learning process appeared to take place in the children's minds, without their performing any observable responses or receiving any noticeable rewards. These mental learning processes are part of cognitive learning, which is a relatively new approach that began in the 1960s (Chance, 2009).

Cognitive learning is a kind of learning that involves mental processes, such as attention and memory; may be learned through observation or imitation; and may not involve any external rewards or require the person to perform any observable behaviors.

Bandura's study demonstrated a third principle of learning, which essentially says that we can learn through observation or imitation. *We will discuss cognitive learning in Modules 10, 11, and 12.*

Now, let's return to Pavlov's laboratory and examine his famous discovery in greater detail. ●

© Craig McClain

Unless otherwise noted, all images are © Cengage Learning

B Procedure: Classical Conditioning

Pavlov's Experiment

What's the procedure?

Imagine that you are an assistant in Pavlov's laboratory and your subject is a dog named Sam. You are using a procedure that will result in Sam's salivating when he hears a bell, a response that Pavlov called a **conditioned reflex**. Today, we call Pavlov's procedure **classical conditioning**, which involves the following three steps.

Step 1. Selecting Stimulus and Response

Terms. Before you begin the procedure to establish classical conditioning in Sam, you need to identify three critical terms: *neutral stimulus, unconditioned stimulus*, and *unconditioned response*.

Neutral stimulus. You need to choose a neutral stimulus. A **neutral stimulus, or NS,** is some stimulus that causes a sensory response, such as being seen, heard, or smelled, but does not produce the reflex being tested.

Your neutral stimulus will be a tone (bell), which Sam the dog hears but which does not normally produce the reflex of salivation.

Unconditioned stimulus. You need to choose an unconditioned stimulus, or UCS.

An **unconditioned stimulus, or UCS,** is some stimulus that triggers or elicits a physiological reflex, such as salivation or eye blink.

Your unconditioned stimulus will be food, which when presented to Sam will elicit the salivation reflex—that is, will make Sam salivate.

Unconditioned response. Finally, you need to select and measure an unconditioned response, or UCR.

The **unconditioned response, or UCR,** is an unlearned, innate, involuntary physiological reflex that is elicited by the unconditioned stimulus.

For instance, salivation is an unconditioned response that is elicited by food. In this case, the sight of food, which is the unconditioned stimulus, will elicit salivation in Sam, which is the unconditioned response.

Step 2. Establishing Classical Conditioning

Trial. A common procedure to establish classical conditioning is for you first to present the neutral stimulus and then, a short time later, to present the unconditioned stimulus. The presentation of both stimuli is called a **trial**.

Neutral stimulus. In a typical trial, you will pair the neutral stimulus, the tone, with the unconditioned stimulus, the food. Generally, you will first present the neutral stimulus (tone) and then, a short time later, present the unconditioned stimulus (food).

+

Unconditioned stimulus (UCS). Some seconds (but less than a minute) after the tone begins, you present the unconditioned stimulus, a piece of food, which elicits salivation. This trial procedure is the one most frequently used in classical conditioning.

→

Unconditioned response (UCR). The unconditioned stimulus, food, elicits the unconditioned response, salivation, in Sam. Food and salivation are said to be unconditioned because the effect on Sam is inborn and not dependent on some prior training or learning.

Step 3. Testing for Conditioning

Only CS. After you have given Sam 10 to 100 trials, you will test for the occurrence of classical conditioning. You test by presenting the tone (conditioned stimulus) without showing Sam the food (unconditioned stimulus).

Conditioned stimulus. If Sam salivates when you present the tone alone, it means that the tone has become a conditioned stimulus.

A **conditioned stimulus, or CS,** is a formerly neutral stimulus that has acquired the ability to elicit a response that was previously elicited by the unconditioned stimulus.

In this example, the tone, an originally neutral stimulus, became the CS.

→

Conditioned response. When Sam salivates to the tone alone, this response is called the conditioned response.

The **conditioned response, or CR,** which is elicited by the conditioned stimulus, is similar to, but not identical in size or amount to, the unconditioned response.

One thing to remember is that the conditioned response is usually similar in appearance but smaller in amount or magnitude than the unconditioned response. This means that Sam's conditioned response will involve less salivation to the tone (conditioned stimulus) than to the food (unconditioned stimulus).

Predict. One question you may ask about classical conditioning is: What exactly did Sam learn during this procedure? One thing Sam learned was that the sound of a bell predicted the very likely occurrence of food (Rescorla, 1988). Classical conditioning helps animals and humans predict what's going to happen and thus provides information that may be useful for their survival (D. A. Lieberman, 2012).

Next, we'll use the concepts of classical conditioning to explain how Carla was conditioned to her dentist's aftershave.

Terms in Classical Conditioning

What happened to Carla? After many trips to her dentist, Carla unknowingly experienced classical conditioning, which explains why she now feels anxious and tense when she smells a certain aftershave lotion. As we review the steps involved in classical conditioning, you will see how they apply to Carla's situation.

Step 1. Selecting Stimulus and Response

Terms. To explain how classical conditioning occurs, it's best to start by identifying three terms: *neutral stimulus, unconditioned stimulus,* and *unconditioned response.*

The *neutral stimulus* in Carla's situation was the odor of the dentist's aftershave lotion, which she smelled while experiencing pain in the dentist's chair. The aftershave is a neutral stimulus because although it affected Carla (she smelled it), it did not initially produce feelings of anxiety. In fact, initially Carla liked the smell.

The *unconditioned stimulus* for Carla was one or more of several dental procedures, including injections, drillings, and fillings. These dental procedures are unconditioned stimuli (UCS) because they elicited the unconditioned response (UCR), which was feeling anxious and tense.

The *unconditioned response* was Carla's feeling of anxiety, which is a combination of physiological reflexes, such as increased heart rate and blood pressure and rapid breathing, as well as negative emotional reactions. Carla's unconditioned response (anxiety) was elicited by the unconditioned stimulus (painful dental procedure).

Step 2. Establishing Classical Conditioning

Trial. One procedure to establish classical conditioning is for the neutral stimulus to occur first and be followed by the unconditioned stimulus. Each presentation of both stimuli is called a *trial.*

In Carla's case, the *neutral stimulus* was smelling the dentist's aftershave while she was experiencing a number of painful dental procedures.

+

Carla's many trips to the dentist resulted in her having repeated trials that involved occurrence of the *neutral stimulus,* smelling the dentist's aftershave, and occurrence of the *unconditioned stimulus,* having painful dental procedures.

→

The painful dental procedures elicited the *unconditioned response* (feelings of anxiety) as well as other physiological responses, such as increases in heart rate, blood pressure, and breathing rate.

Step 3. Testing for Conditioning

Only CS. A test for classical conditioning is to observe whether the neutral stimulus, when presented alone, elicits the conditioned response.

Conditioned stimulus. When Carla smelled her boyfriend's aftershave, which was the same as the dentist's, she felt anxious. The aftershave's smell, formerly a neutral stimulus, had become a *conditioned stimulus* because it elicited anxiety, the conditioned response.

→

Conditioned response. Whenever Carla smelled the aftershave (conditioned stimulus) used by both her dentist and her boyfriend, it elicited the *conditioned response,* feeling anxious. However, remember that the conditioned response is similar to, but of lesser intensity than, the unconditioned response. Thus, the anxiety elicited by smelling the aftershave was similar to, but not as great as, the anxiety Carla felt during painful dental procedures.

Acquisition. Through classical conditioning, Carla learned that the smell of a certain aftershave (NS) predicted the likely occurrence of a painful dental procedure (UCS) and made her feel anxious. This learning process is called acquisition.

Acquisition is the initial process of forming new responses through the repeated pairing of the NS and the UCS.

Researchers suggest that people who developed an extreme fear or phobia of dental procedures, such as Carla, learned such fears through classical conditioning (Coelho & Purkis, 2009; Klaassen et al., 2008). Next, we'll describe several other behaviors that are associated with classical conditioning. ●

C Other Conditioning Concepts

What else happened to Carla? Carla's experience in the dentist's office of being classically conditioned to feel anxious when she smelled a particular aftershave has some other interesting features. Carla found that similar odors also elicited anxious feelings but that other odors did not; her anxiety when smelling her boyfriend's aftershave gradually decreased, but accidentally meeting the dentist and smelling his aftershave triggered some anxiety. Pavlov found that these phenomena were associated with classical conditioning, and he named them generalization, discrimination, extinction, and spontaneous recovery.

Generalization

During Carla's conditioning trials, the neutral stimulus, which was the odor of the dentist's aftershave, became the conditioned stimulus that elicited the conditioned response, anxiety. However, Carla may also feel anxiety when smelling other similar odors, such as her own hair shampoo; this phenomenon is called generalization.

Why her shampoo?

Reacting to similar odors is generalization.

Generalization is the tendency for a stimulus that is similar to the original conditioned stimulus to elicit a response that is similar to the conditioned response. Usually, the more similar the new stimulus is to the original conditioned stimulus, the larger will be the conditioned response.

Pavlov suggested that generalization had an adaptive value because it allowed us to make an appropriate response to stimuli that are similar to the original one. For example, although you may never see your friend's smiling face in exactly the same situation, generalization ensures that the smiling face will usually elicit positive feelings.

Discrimination

Why not her nail polish? Carla discovered that smells very different from that of the aftershave did not elicit anxiety; this phenomenon is called discrimination.

Discrimination occurs during classical conditioning when an organism learns to make a particular response to some stimuli but not to others.

Not reacting to a new odor is discrimination.

For example, Carla had learned that a particular aftershave's smell predicted the likelihood of a painful dental procedure. In contrast, the smell of her nail polish, which was very different from that of the aftershave, predicted not painful dental procedures but nice-looking fingernails.

Discrimination also has an adaptive value because there are times when it is important to respond differently to related stimuli. For example, you would respond differently to the auditory stimulus of a police siren than to the auditory stimulus of a baby's cries.

Extinction

What about her boyfriend? If Carla's boyfriend did not change his aftershave and she repeatedly smelled it, she would learn that it was never followed by painful dental procedures, and its smell would gradually stop making her feel anxious; this phenomenon is called extinction.

Extinction is the procedure in which a conditioned stimulus is repeatedly presented without the unconditioned stimulus and, as a result, the conditioned stimulus tends to no longer elicit the conditioned response.

Not reacting to a previously powerful stimulus is extinction.

The procedure for extinguishing a conditioned response is used in therapeutic settings to reduce fears or phobias. For example, clients who had a conditioned fear of needles and receiving injections were repeatedly shown needles and given injections by qualified nurses. After exposure to the conditioned stimuli during a 3-hour period, 81% of the clients reported a significant reduction in fear of needles and receiving injections (Ost et al., 1992). This kind of exposure therapy is a practical application of Pavlov's work and will be discussed more fully in Module 22.

Spontaneous Recovery

Would the anxiety come back? Suppose Carla's conditioned anxiety to the smell of the aftershave had been extinguished by having her repeatedly smell her boyfriend's lotion without experiencing any painful consequences. Some time later, when Carla happened to accidentally meet her dentist in the local supermarket, she might spontaneously show the conditioned response and feel anxiety when smelling his aftershave; this is called spontaneous recovery.

Spontaneous recovery is the tendency for the conditioned response to reappear after being extinguished even though there have been no further conditioning trials.

Spontaneous recovery of the conditioned response will not persist for long and will be of lesser magnitude than the original conditioned response. If the conditioned stimulus (smell of aftershave) is not presented again with the unconditioned stimulus (painful dental procedure), the spontaneously recovered conditioned response will again undergo

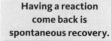

Having a reaction come back is spontaneous recovery.

extinction and cease to occur. Thus, once Carla had been classically conditioned, she would have experienced one or more of these four phenomena.

Now that you are familiar with the procedure and concepts of classical conditioning, we'll explore its widespread occurrence in the real world. ●

D Adaptive Value & Uses

Pavlov believed that animals and people evolved the capacity for classical conditioning because it had an adaptive value (Nettle, 2009).

How useful is classical conditioning?

Adaptive value refers to the usefulness of certain abilities or traits that have evolved in animals and humans and tend to increase their chances of survival, such as finding food, acquiring mates, and avoiding pain and injury. We'll discuss several examples, such as learning to avoid certain tastes, salivating at the sight of food, and avoiding pain, that support Pavlov's view that classical conditioning is useful because it has an adaptive value.

Taste-Aversion Learning

What do you learn from getting sick?

Rat exterminators have firsthand knowledge of classical conditioning's adaptive value. Exterminators find that while some rats eat enough bait poison to die, others eat only enough to get sick. Once rats get sick on a particular bait poison, they quickly learn to avoid its smell or taste, called *bait shyness*, and never again eat that bait poison. This kind of learning is a form of classical conditioning called taste-aversion learning (I. L. Bernstein & Koh, 2007).

Taste-aversion learning is associating a particular sensory cue (smell, taste, sound, or sight) with getting sick and thereafter avoiding that particular sensory cue in the future.

Taste-aversion learning is how rats avoid poison.

The adaptive value of taste-aversion learning for rats is obvious: By quickly learning to avoid the smells or taste associated with getting sick, such as eating poison bait, they are more likely to survive.

Humans. It is likely that in your lifetime, you too will experience taste-aversion learning. For example, if you have eaten something and gotten sick after taking a thrill ride, you may avoid the smell or taste of that particular food. Similarly, people who get sick from drinking too much of a particular alcoholic drink (often a sweet or distinctive-tasting drink) avoid that drink for a long period of time (Reilly & Schachtman, 2009). Taste-aversion learning may also warn us away from eating poisonous plants that cause illness or even death, such as certain varieties of mushrooms. All these examples of taste-aversion learning show the adaptive value of classical conditioning, which is to keep us away from potentially unpleasant or dangerous situations, such as taking thrill rides, overdrinking, or eating poisonous plants.

As many people have learned, taste-aversion learning can develop after a single experience and may last weeks, months, years, or forever (Reilly & Schachtman, 2009). The study of taste-aversion learning changed two long-held beliefs about classical conditioning.

I'm starting to get a sick feeling!!!

© jabiru/Shutterstock.com

Explanation

Is only one trial enough?

For a long time, psychologists believed that bait shyness was not due to classical conditioning. They were sure that classical conditioning required many trials (not a single trial of getting sick) and that the neutral stimulus (smell or taste) must be followed within seconds by the unconditioned response (nausea), and certainly not hours later (getting sick). Psychologist John Garcia thought otherwise.

One-trial learning. Garcia showed that taste-aversion learning did occur in one trial and, surprisingly, did occur even though there was an hour or more delay between the neutral stimulus (smell or taste) and the unconditioned response (sickness or vomiting). Garcia's findings proved that taste-aversion learning is a form of classical conditioning (I. L. Bernstein & Koh, 2007; Reilly & Schachtman, 2009).

PhotoDisc, Inc.

Taste-aversion learning occurs in one trial.

Preparedness. An interesting finding was that animals acquired taste aversion differently. For example, rats, which have poor vision but great senses of taste and olfaction (smell), acquired taste aversion easily to smell and taste cues but were rarely conditioned to light cues (Garcia et al., 1966). Similarly, quails, which have poor olfaction but great vision, acquired taste aversion more easily to visual cues (Wilcoxon et al., 1971). Garcia concluded that, depending on the animal, different stimuli or cues have different potentials for becoming conditioned stimuli. These findings challenged the long-standing belief in classical conditioning that all stimuli (smell, taste, visual, auditory) have an equal chance of becoming conditioned stimuli. Garcia's finding that some stimuli were more easily conditioned than others is called preparedness (Seligman, 1970).

Preparedness is the phenomenon in which animals and humans are biologically prepared to associate some combinations of conditioned and unconditioned stimuli more easily than others.

The idea of preparedness means that different animals are genetically prepared to use different senses to detect stimuli that are important to their survival and adaptation. For example, John Garcia and his colleagues (1974) applied their knowledge of preparedness and taste aversion to the problem of sheep-killing by coyotes. They baited grazing areas with pieces of sheep flesh laced with a chemical that caused coyotes to become nauseated and ill. As a result, coyotes that had acquired a taste aversion showed an estimated 30–60% reduction in sheep-killing (B. Bower, 1997; Gustavson et al., 1976). Taste-aversion learning has applications for sheep ranchers and for people who get sick from overdrinking or eating before going on thrill rides (Loy & Hall, 2002; Reilly & Schachtman, 2009).

Cynthia Kidwell/Shutterstock.com

Taste-aversion learning is used to stop coyotes from eating sheep.

Unless otherwise noted, all images are © Cengage Learning

Classical Conditioning and Adaptive Value

Taste-aversion learning helps rats survive by alerting them to the smell and taste of poison, and it also warns blue jays, which feast on butterflies, not to eat monarch butterflies. Monarch butterflies, which have a distinctive coloring pattern, contain a chemical that, when eaten, will make birds sick. Through taste aversion, blue jays learn that the distinctive color pattern of monarch butterflies predicts getting sick, and so blue jays avoid eating monarch butterflies. Thus, classically conditioned taste aversion has survival value for animals. In contrast, things that taste good can produce a classically conditioned response in humans that is also adaptive.

Why do blue jays avoid monarchs?

Hot fudge sundaes. The next time you enter a restaurant, read the menu, think about food, and see people eating, notice that you are salivating even though you have no food in your own mouth. Just as Pavlov's dog was conditioned to salivate at the sound of a bell, we have also become conditioned to salivate when only thinking about, imagining, smelling, or seeing food. This is a clear example of how many different kinds of neutral stimuli, such as reading a menu, seeing people eat, or imagining food, can become conditioned stimuli that elicit a conditioned response—salivation.

Salivation serves a useful purpose: It lubricates your mouth and throat to make chewing and swallowing food easier. Thus, being classically conditioned to salivate when reading a menu prepares your mouth for the soon-to-arrive food. Conditioned salivation and taste-aversion learning are examples of how classical conditioning has an adaptive value (Aamodt & Wang, 2008; D. A. Lieberman, 2004).

Next, we'll examine how emotional responses can be classically conditioned.

Through taste-aversion learning blue jays learn to avoid monarchs.

Does thinking about food make you salivate?

Classical Conditioning and Emotions

Why do people fear needles?

At the beginning of this module, I told a true childhood story of getting an injection that elicited such pain and fear that I fainted. Even more than 50 years later, I still fear injections and needles and always lie down to avoid fainting. In my case, you can easily identify each element of classical conditioning: The neutral stimulus is the sight of the needle; the unconditioned stimulus is the injection; and the unconditioned response is pain and fear. After a painful injection, the formerly neutral stimulus, the needle, becomes a conditioned stimulus and elicits the conditioned response, which is fear and even fainting. Because this situation involved the conditioning of an emotional response, my fear of injections and needles is called a conditioned emotional response (Barad et al., 2006).

A **conditioned emotional response** is feeling some positive or negative emotion, such as happiness, fear, or anxiety, when experiencing a stimulus that initially accompanied a pleasant or painful event.

Conditioned emotional responses can have survival value, such as learning to fear and avoid stimuli that signal dangerous situations, like the sound of a rattlesnake or wail of a siren (McNally & Westbrook, 2006). Conditioned emotional responses can also signal pleasant situations. For example, many couples have a special song that becomes emotionally associated with their relationship. When this song is heard by one in the absence of the other, it can elicit strong emotional and romantic feelings. Thus, different kinds of stimuli can be classically conditioned to elicit strong conditioned emotional responses.

This situation can condition fear of needles or injections.

Classical Conditioning in the Brain

Where does it happen?

The man in the photo below is wearing head gear that delivers a tone (conditioned stimulus) followed by a puff of air (unconditioned stimulus) that elicits his eye blink reflex (unconditioned response). With this classical conditioning procedure, individuals learn to blink about 90% of the time to the tone alone (conditioned response), before the air puff occurs. Classical conditioning of the eye blink requires the cerebellum (right figure). Lacking the cerebellum, neither humans nor animals can acquire the conditioned eye blink reflex, which is a highly specific motor response (Gerwig et al., 2003).

In contrast to the classically conditioned eye blink reflex, which is a *motor response,* the young boy on the right is acquiring a classically conditioned emotional response—fear of needles and injections. Acquiring a conditioned

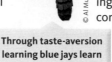

emotional response, especially involving fear, involves a different brain structure called the amygdala (see p. 80) (Calandreau et al., 2006; LaBar & Cabeza, 2006). Thus, classically conditioning responses involves different areas of the brain, depending on whether the responses are motor or emotional.

Recent research found that specialized "fear neurons" located in the amygdala fire in response to a stimulus during and after the conditioning of an emotional response. Then, when the conditioned emotional response undergoes extinction, only "extinction neurons" fire in response to the same stimulus (Herry et al., 2008).

Next, we'll examine how and why classical conditioning works. ●

Amygdala
Cerebellum

Conditioning eye blink reflex

Conditioning emotional response

Do you salivate when thinking of pizza?

Although most of us have had the experience of salivating when thinking about or seeing a favorite food, such as a pizza, researchers have given different explanations of what is learned during conditioning. We'll discuss three theories—stimulus substitution, contiguity theory, and cognitive perspective—that offer different explanations of why nearly all of us salivate when only thinking about or seeing a delicious pizza.

Stimulus Substitution and Contiguity Theory

Does the bell substitute for food?

The first explanation of classical conditioning came from Pavlov, who said the reason a dog salivated to a tone was that the tone became a substitute for the food, a theory he called stimulus substitution.

Stimulus substitution means that a neural bond or association forms in the brain between the neutral stimulus (tone) and the unconditioned stimulus (food). After repeated trials, the neutral stimulus becomes the conditioned stimulus (tone) and acts like a substitute for the unconditioned stimulus (food). Thereafter, the conditioned stimulus (tone) elicits a conditioned response (salivation) that is similar to that of the unconditioned stimulus.

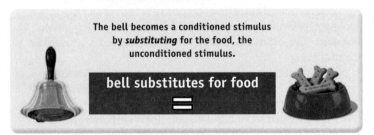

The bell becomes a conditioned stimulus by *substituting* for the food, the unconditioned stimulus.

bell substitutes for food
=

According to stimulus substitution theory, you salivate when you see a pizza because the act of seeing a pizza (conditioned stimulus) becomes bonded in your nervous system to the pizza itself (unconditioned stimulus). Because of this neural bond or association, the sight of a pizza substitutes for the pizza, so that just the sight of a pizza can elicit salivation (conditioned response).

However, researchers discovered that the responses elicited by the unconditioned stimulus were often slightly different from those elicited by the conditioned stimulus. For example, following the unconditioned stimulus, a dog salivated and always chewed, but, following the conditioned stimulus, it salivated but rarely chewed (Zener, 1937). As a result of this and other criticisms of Pavlov's stimulus substitution theory, researchers suggested a different explanation, the contiguity theory.

The **contiguity theory** says that classical conditioning occurs because two stimuli (neutral stimulus and unconditioned stimulus) are paired close together in time (are contiguous). As a result of this contiguous pairing, the neutral stimulus becomes the conditioned stimulus, which elicits the conditioned response.

The contiguity theory says that because seeing a pizza is paired closely in time with eating it, the sight alone begins to elicit salivation. Contiguity theory was the most popular explanation of classical conditioning until the 1960s, when it was challenged by the clever research of psychologist Robert Rescorla (1966).

Cognitive Perspective

Does the bell predict food is coming?

To the surprise of many researchers, Robert Rescorla (1966, 1987, 1988) showed that an association between neutral and unconditioned stimuli did not necessarily occur when the two stimuli were closely paired in time. Instead, he found that classical conditioning occurred when a neutral stimulus contained information about what was coming next; this explanation is called the cognitive perspective.

The **cognitive perspective** says that an organism learns a predictable relationship between two stimuli such that the occurrence of one stimulus (neutral stimulus) predicts the occurrence of another (unconditioned stimulus). In other words, classical conditioning occurs because the organism learns what to expect.

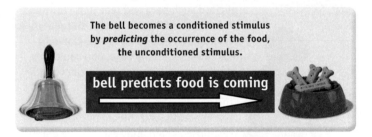

The bell becomes a conditioned stimulus by *predicting* the occurrence of the food, the unconditioned stimulus.

bell predicts food is coming →

For example, the cognitive perspective theory would explain that you salivate at the sight of a pizza because you have learned a predictable relationship: Seeing a pizza (conditioned stimulus) often leads to eating one (unconditioned stimulus), and your expectation causes salivation (conditioned response).

Support for the cognitive perspective comes from a number of findings. For example, classical conditioning works best if the neutral stimulus (tone) occurs slightly before the unconditioned stimulus (food). In this sequence, the organism learns a relationship between two stimuli: Tone predicts food. However, if the sequence is reversed and the unconditioned stimulus appears before the neutral stimulus, this is called *backward conditioning* and does not usually result in classical conditioning.

The cognitive perspective would explain that backward conditioning makes it impossible to predict a relationship between the neutral and unconditioned stimuli and thus does not usually result in classical conditioning. Currently, there is widespread support for the cognitive perspective, which says that classical conditioning involves learning about predictable relationships, or learning about cause and effect (S.G. Hofmann, 2008).

After the Concept Review, we'll discuss a well-known study of classical conditioning that involves the famous "Little Albert." ●

Concept Review

1. In classical conditioning, one of the stimuli that is chosen has two characteristics: The stimulus, such as a tone, must cause some reaction, such as being heard, seen, tasted, or smelled, but it must not elicit the unconditioned response. A stimulus with these two characteristics is called a _____.

2. In classical conditioning, a second stimulus is chosen that can elicit an unlearned, involuntary physiological reflex, such as salivation. This stimulus is called an _____.

3. In classical conditioning, the unconditioned stimulus elicits an unlearned, involuntary physiological reflex, such as salivation, which is called the _____.

4. A typical trial in classical conditioning involves first presenting the (a) _____ and then, a short time later, presenting the (b) _____.

5. On the very first conditioning trial, the neutral stimulus (tone) did not itself elicit the unconditioned response (salivation). However, on the first trial, the presentation of food, which is called the (a) _____, did elicit salivation, called the (b) _____.

6. After a dozen trials that paired the tone with the food, you noticed that as soon as the tone was presented, the dog salivated. Because the tone itself elicited a response similar to that elicited by the unconditioned stimulus (food), the tone is called the (a) _____. The salivation elicited by the tone itself is called the (b) _____.

7. During classical conditioning, there is a tendency for a stimulus similar to the original conditioned stimulus to elicit a response similar to the conditioned response. This tendency is called _____.

8. During classical conditioning, an organism learns to make a particular response to some stimuli but not to others; this phenomenon is called _____.

9. If a conditioned stimulus is repeatedly presented without the unconditioned stimulus, there is a tendency for the conditioned stimulus to no longer elicit the conditioned response. This phenomenon is called _____.

10. The tendency for the conditioned response to reappear some time later, even though there are no further conditioning trials, is called _____.

11. The kind of learning in which the cues (smell, taste, auditory, or visual) of a particular stimulus are associated with an unpleasant response, such as nausea or vomiting, is called (a) _____. This kind of learning can even occur after only a single (b) _____.

12. According to Pavlov's original explanation, classical conditioning occurs because of (a) _____, which means that the conditioned stimulus (tone) bonds to the unconditioned stimulus (food). Through this bond, or association, the conditioned stimulus (tone) elicits the conditioned response (salivation) by substituting for the (b) _____ (food). Pavlov's explanation of classical conditioning was criticized, and researchers suggested instead that conditioning occurs because two stimuli are paired close together in time. This explanation, which is called (c) _____ theory, has been challenged, in turn, by more recent explanations.

13. The current and widely accepted explanation of classical conditioning, which is called the (a) _____ perspective, states that animals and humans learn a predictable relationship between stimuli. According to this explanation, a dog learns predictable relationships, such as a tone predicting the occurrence of (b) _____.

Answers: 1. neutral stimulus; 2. unconditioned stimulus (UCS); 3. unconditioned response (UCR); 4. (a) neutral stimulus, (b) unconditioned stimulus (UCS); 5. (a) unconditioned stimulus (UCS), (b) unconditioned response (UCR); 6. (a) conditioned stimulus (CS), (b) conditioned response (CR); 7. generalization; 8. discrimination; 9. extinction; 10. spontaneous recovery; 11. (a) taste-aversion learning, (b) trial; 12. (a) stimulus substitution, (b) unconditioned stimulus, (c) contiguity; 13. (a) cognitive, (b) food

Can Emotional Responses Be Conditioned?

Why did Little Albert fear white animals?

One of the first attempts to study the development of emotional responses, such as becoming fearful, occurred in the 1920s. At this time, psychologists did not yet know if emotional responses could be conditioned. John Watson realized that he could use Pavlov's conditioning procedure to study the development of emotional behaviors in an objective way. As you may remember from Module 1, John Watson (see p. 13) was a strong supporter of behaviorism, which emphasized the study of observable behaviors and the rejection of unobservable mental or cognitive events.

What follows is a first in psychology: an important classic experiment on conditioning emotions that John Watson and his student assistant, Rosalie Rayner, published in 1920.

Method: Identify Terms

Watson questioned whether conditioning played a role in the development of emotional responses in children. To answer his question, Watson (photo) tried to classically condition an emotional response in a child.

Subject: Nine-month-old infant.

The subject, known later as Little Albert, was described as healthy, stolid, and unemotional, since "no one had ever seen him in a state of rage and fear. The infant practically never cried" (Watson & Rayner, 1920, p. 3).

Neutral stimulus: White rat.

Watson briefly confronted 9-month-old Albert with a succession of objects, including a white rat, a rabbit, and a dog. "At no time did this infant ever show fear in any situation" (Watson & Rayner, 1920, p. 2).

Rat is neutral stimulus.

Unconditioned stimulus: Noise.

Standing behind Albert, the researchers hit a hammer on a metal bar, which made a loud noise and elicited startle and crying. "This is the first time an emotional situation in the laboratory has produced any fear or crying in Albert" (Watson & Rayner, 1920, p. 3).

Bang is UCS.

Unconditioned response: Startle/cry.

Startle and crying were observable and measurable emotional responses that indicated the baby was feeling and expressing fear.

After Watson identified the three elements of classical conditioning, he and his assistant, Rayner, began the procedure for classical conditioning.

Fear is UCR.

Procedure: Establish and Test for Classical Conditioning

Establish. At the age of 11 months, Albert was given repeated trials consisting of a neutral stimulus, a white rat, followed by an unconditioned stimulus, a loud noise. During early trials, he startled at the sight of the rat and on later trials he also cried.

© PhotoDisc, Inc.

Rat (neutral stimulus) plus loud bang (UCS) elicits fear response (UCR).

Test. When first presented with the rat alone (no noise), Albert only startled. Then he was given additional conditioning trials and retested with the rat alone (no noise). "The instant the rat was shown the baby began to cry" (Watson & Rayner, 1920, p. 5). Thus, Watson had succeeded in classically conditioning Albert's emotional response (fear).

© PhotoDisc, Inc.

Classical conditioning: rat (CS) alone elicits fear response (CR).

Results and Conclusions

Watson and Rayner had shown that Albert developed a conditioned emotional response of startle and crying to the sight of a rat, which lasted about a week and then diminished, or underwent *extinction.*

After Albert was conditioned to fear a white rat, he was shown other objects to test for *generalization.* For example, he crawled away and cried at the sight of a rabbit, and he turned away and cried at the sight of a fur coat. But he showed no fear of blocks, paper, or Watson's hairy head, which indicates *discrimination.*

Watson's conditioning of Albert was more of a demonstration than a rigorously controlled experiment (Field & Nightingale, 2009). For example, Watson and Rayner did not use a standardized procedure for presenting stimuli, and they sometimes removed Albert's thumb from his mouth, which may have made him cry. Watson was also criticized for not unconditioning Albert's fears before he left the hospital.

Rabbit elicits fear (CR) is an example of generalization.

Although other researchers failed to replicate Watson and Rayner's results, this was the first demonstration that emotional responses could be classically conditioned in humans (Samelson, 1980). Watson's demonstration laid the groundwork for explaining how people can acquire conditioned emotional responses, such as developing a fear of needles (Field & Nightingale, 2009).

We've discussed how emotional responses can be conditioned; next, we'll discuss how peoples' attitudes about others can also be conditioned. ●

Unless otherwise noted, all images are © Cengage Learning

Classical Conditioning and Racial Prejudice

Negative attitudes toward others are all too common in today's society, as well as throughout our history. One *What is prejudice?* type of negative attitude toward others is prejudice. **Prejudice** is an unfair, biased, or intolerant attitude toward another group of people.

Unfortunately, prejudice can develop at an early age. In a classic study conducted in the 1930s, researchers studying preschool children found that when offered a choice, both white and black children preferred white dolls to black dolls. The researchers asked the children which doll was good and which was bad. Both white and black children answered that the white doll was good and nice, whereas the black doll was bad, ugly, and dirty. The

Good
Nice

Bad
Ugly
Dirty

explanation provided by the researchers was that the children had already learned at a young age to associate positive qualities with light-colored skin and negative qualities with dark-colored skin (K. B. Clark & Clark, 1939).

Certainly, our society has made progress in minimizing the prevalence of racial prejudice; however, there is no denying its continued existence. For instance, members of ethnic minority groups continue to experience discriminatory practices in education, employment, and housing, as well as discriminatory treatment in many social encounters (Swim et al., 2003). Consequently, it is important to understand how psychological theory explains the development of racial prejudice and how its research findings can help in the prevention and reduction of racial prejudice.

Conditioning Prejudice

One psychological theory that explains the development of racial prejudice is classical conditioning. The *How is prejudice conditioned?* power of classical conditioning in predicting how racial prejudice develops is both impressive and worrisome.

The conditioning of racial prejudice can take place through *direct, observational,* and *verbal experiences* that pair racially different people with aversive or unpleasant stimuli. For example, an individual may develop racial prejudice after directly experiencing a naturally traumatic, painful, or bad experience involving a racially different person. Such an experience may involve a person stealing from or acting aggressively toward another person. Racial prejudice can also be learned observationally, as in the case of an individual who sees a racially different person steal or act aggressively toward another person. Last, racial prejudice may develop through verbal experiences, such as hearing about a

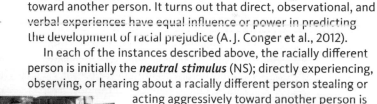

Racial prejudice can be learned through direct, observational, or verbal experiences.

racially different person stealing from or acting aggressively toward another person. It turns out that direct, observational, and verbal experiences have equal influence or power in predicting the development of racial prejudice (A. J. Conger et al., 2012).

In each of the instances described above, the racially different person is initially the *neutral stimulus* (NS); directly experiencing, observing, or hearing about a racially different person stealing or acting aggressively toward another person is the *unconditioned stimulus* (UCS); and fear and anxiety are the *unconditioned response* (UCR). After repeated pairings of the NS with the UCS, racially different people, the *conditioned stimulus* (CS), become associated with fear and anxiety, now the *conditioned response* (CR).

In conclusion, negative emotional reactions, such as fear and anxiety, become elicited (CR) by individuals of another race (CS) who should be perceived as being neutral (NS).

Unconditioning Prejudice

Unfortunately, a learned response to one stimulus, such as a single person of another race, can easily spread *How can prejudice be unconditioned?* to all similar stimuli, meaning all people of that particular race or a similar race. This is an instance of *generalization*. One way to reduce the severity and spread of racial prejudice after people have already established a negative reaction to racially different others is to provide them with repeated experiences with racially different people with no negative events taking place. This process will facilitate

Racial prejudice can be unconditioned through efforts to facilitate extinction.

extinction, which is when racially different people (now the CS) once again becomes a NS.

It is important to remember that in any prevention or reduction strategy, attention must be given not only to the direct aversive experiences but also to observations and verbal experiences, such as those portrayed on television or in movies (A. J. Conger et al., 2012).

Next, we'll examine another terrible problem that also involves classical conditioning—conditioned nausea as a result of chemotherapy treatment for cancer. ●

Examples of Classical Conditioning

Why do people faint from fear?

At the beginning of this module, I related my childhood experience of receiving an injection and then fainting. This one trial of classical conditioning resulted in my fear of needles, which remains with me to this present day. My experience illustrates the powerful effect

Conditioned emotional response

that conditioned emotional responses can have on our behavior. If you still doubt that relatively non-threatening stimuli (needle, blood) can be conditioned to elicit such a powerful physiological response as fainting, you'll be convinced by the next study (Page, 2003).

Conditioned Emotional Response

About 5–20% of adults report a fear of needles, injections, or seeing blood that often began before the age of 10 (Vogele et al., 2003). Wondering why some people feel faint at the sight of blood, researchers asked 30 such people to watch a movie on open-heart surgery as their heart rates were monitored. During the movie, 4 of the 30 participants unexpectedly fainted.

For example, the graph shows that after 4 minutes of watching the open-heart surgery movie, one participant became so fearful and anxious that his body went into mild shock and he

fainted. The reason this person fainted from simply watching a movie on open-heart surgery was that he had developed a conditioned emotional response, intense fear, to the sight of blood (Steptoe & Wardle, 1988). Intense fear triggers tremendous changes in heart rate and blood pressure that can cause many physiological changes, including fainting.

Classical conditioning can also trigger nausea to a particular odor.

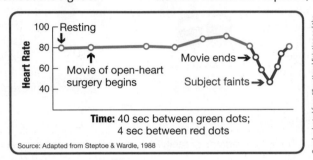

Graph adapted from "Emotional Fainting and the Psychophysiologic Response to Blood and Injury: Autonomic Mechanisms and Coping Strategies," by A. Steptoe and J. Wardle, 1988, *Psychosomatic Medicine, 50*, 402–417.

Time: 40 sec between green dots; 4 sec between red dots

Source: Adapted from Steptoe & Wardle, 1988

Anticipatory Nausea

Anticipatory nausea is an example of classical conditioning.

At the beginning of this module, we told you about Michelle, who was receiving chemotherapy treatment for breast cancer. One side effect of the powerful anticancer drugs used in chemotherapy is nausea, which may be accompanied by severe vomiting that lasts 6–12 hours.

As Michelle received additional chemotherapy injections, she experienced nausea when she smelled the treatment room or smelled her dish soap, which smelled like the treatment room. Michelle's problem is called anticipatory nausea.

Anticipatory nausea is feelings of nausea that are elicited by stimuli associated

with nausea-inducing chemotherapy treatments. Patients experience nausea after treatment but also before or in anticipation of their treatment. Researchers believe that conditioned nausea occurs through classical conditioning.

For example, by their fourth injection, 25–30% of patients who receive chemotherapy experience anticipatory nausea when they encounter smells, sounds, sights, or images related to treatment (Roscoe et al., 2011). Even 1 to 2 years after treatment ends, patients may continue to experience anticipatory nausea if they encounter cues associated with chemotherapy (Fredrickson et al., 1993). Conditioned nausea is especially troublesome because current medications do not always control it (Hesketh, 2012; NCI, 2008).

First we'll discuss how conditioned nausea occurs and then how it can be controlled with a nonmedical treatment.

Conditioning Anticipatory Nausea

A few weeks after beginning her chemotherapy, Michelle began to experience anticipatory nausea that was triggered by a number of different stimuli, including the smell of her dish detergent, which smelled similar to the treatment room. Now that you know her situation, perhaps you can identify the terms and explain how classical conditioning occurred.

- **Neutral stimulus** is the smell of the treatment room and her dish detergent, which initially did not cause any nausea.
- **Unconditioned stimulus** is the chemotherapy, which elicits nausea and vomiting.
- **Unconditioned responses** are the nausea and vomiting that were elicited by chemotherapy, the unconditioned stimulus.

- **Conditioning trials** involve presenting the neutral stimulus, the smell of the treatment room (same as her detergent), with the unconditioned stimulus, the chemotherapy.
- **Conditioned stimulus** (smell of the treatment room or detergent), when presented by itself, now elicits the conditioned response (nausea).

Once conditioning is established, anticipatory nausea can be very difficult to treat and control with drugs (Brennan, 2004). Even after chemotherapy ends, anticipatory nausea may reappear for a while, which is an example of spontaneous recovery.

However, there is a nonmedical treatment for anticipatory nausea, which is also based on classical conditioning. This treatment is called systematic desensitization, which we'll discuss next.

Dish soap is CS.

Systematic Desensitization

Can you "uncondition" fearful things?

Because of repeated chemotherapy sessions, Michelle developed anticipatory nausea, which was not relieved by medication. She is now going to try a nonmedical treatment called systematic desensitization.

Systematic desensitization is a procedure based on classical conditioning, in which a person imagines or visualizes fearful or anxiety-evoking stimuli and then immediately uses deep relaxation to overcome the anxiety. Systematic desensitization is a form of counterconditioning because it replaces, or counters, fear and anxiety with relaxation.

Essentially, systematic desensitization is a procedure to "uncondition," or overcome, fearful stimuli by pairing anxiety-provoking thoughts or images with feelings of relaxation. Systematic desensitization was developed by Joseph Wolpe in the early 1950s and has become one of the most frequently used nonmedical therapies for relief of anxiety and fears in both children and adults (M. A. Williams & Gross, 1994). Just as anticipatory nausea is based on Pavlov's classical conditioning, so too is systematic desensitization (Thorpe & Sigman, 2008).

In Michelle's case, she will try to "uncondition," or override, the anxiety-producing cues of chemotherapy, such as smells and sights, with feelings of relaxation. The procedure for systematic desensitization involves the three steps described below (Wolpe & Lazarus, 1966).

Systematic Desensitization Procedure: Three Steps

Step 1. Learning to relax

Michelle is taught to relax by tensing and relaxing sets of muscles, beginning with the muscles in her toes and continuing up to the muscles in her calves, thighs, back, arms, shoulders, neck, and finally face and forehead. She practices doing this intentional relaxation for about 15 to 20 minutes every day for several weeks.

1st step is learning to relax on cue.

After learning how to relax her body at will, she goes on to Step 2.

Step 2. Making an anxiety hierarchy

Michelle makes up a list of 7–12 stressful situations associated with chemotherapy treatment.

Most Stressful
8. Vomiting
7. Feeling nausea
6. Receiving injection
5. In treatment room
4. Smelling chemicals
3. In waiting room
2. Entering clinic
1. Driving to clinic

2nd step is making a list of items that elicit anxiety.

As shown above, she arranges her list of situations in a hierarchy that goes from least to most stressful. For example, the least stressful situations are driving to and entering the clinic, and the most stressful are nausea and vomiting. Now she's ready for Step 3.

Step 3. Imagining and relaxing

Michelle *first* puts herself into a deeply relaxed state and then vividly imagines the least stressful situation, driving to the clinic. She is told to remain in a relaxed state while imagining this situation. If she becomes anxious or stressed, she is told to stop imagining this situation and return instead to a relaxed state. Once she is sufficiently relaxed, she again imagines driving to the clinic. If she can imagine driving to the clinic while remaining in a relaxed state, she goes to the next stressful situation.

She then imagines entering the clinic, while remaining in a relaxed state. She continues up the anxiety hierarchy, imagining in turn each of the eight stressful stimuli while keeping herself in a relaxed state. At the first sign of feeling anxious, she stops and returns to a relaxed state. After returning to a relaxed state, she continues with this procedure until she reaches the most stressful situation in her anxiety hierarchy.

Most Stressful
8. Vomiting
7. Feeling nausea
6. Receiving injection
5. In treatment room
4. Smelling chemicals
3. In waiting room
2. Entering clinic
1. Driving to clinic

3rd step is combining relaxation with items in anxiety hierarchy.

Effectiveness of Systematic Desensitization

As Michelle associates relaxation with each stressful situation in the hierarchy, she overcomes, or counterconditions, each stimulus. In other words, systematic desensitization can be thought of as using relaxation to get rid of the stressful and anxious feelings that have become associated with the stimuli that are listed in the hierarchy.

Systematic desensitization has been found to be very effective in treating a variety of fearful and anxiety-producing behaviors, including conditioned nausea and fear of blood, injections, snakes, and speaking in public (Aapro et al., 2005; Head & Gross, 2009; Spiegler & Guevremont, 2010).

We have discussed the many sides of classical conditioning, from salivation to fainting, from taste aversion to little Albert's conditioned emotional responses, from bait shyness in rats to prejudice in humans, from anticipatory nausea to systematic desensitization. It's evident that classical conditioning has a considerable influence on many of our thoughts, emotions, and behaviors. ●

Marketing Changes Your Brain

What guides your preference for Coke or Pepsi? McDonald's or Burger King? Can these choices be explained as a matter of taste preference, or is there something occurring in the brain that makes us choose one over the other? Neuroscientists have been discovering how marketing companies direct us to choose their products.

Take, for instance, Coke® and Pepsi®, which are almost identical chemically and physically, yet people usually have a strong preference for one over the other. In one study, researchers found that when participants didn't know which brand of cola they were drinking, they were equally likely to choose Coke or Pepsi as their favorite. Also, the part of the brain that responds to rewards or pleasure was activated as they drank either cola. When participants had knowledge about which cola they were drinking, they were more likely to prefer Coke and their brain activity explains why—not only was there increased activity in the part of the brain that responds to rewards, but memory-related brain regions involved in recalling cultural influences were also activated. The same was not true for Pepsi.

1 Why was the part of the brain that responds to rewards activated?

2 Why were the memory-related brain regions activated when participants knew they were drinking Coke, but not when participants knew they were drinking Pepsi?

These results suggest that the marketing messages about brands of cola influence our brains in a way that likely alters our taste perception or preference.

3 How might these results be useful to companies interested in developing a cola to compete with Coke or other products similar to those that have strong brand images?

We've seen how marketing influences us to purchase a particular cola, but are marketing techniques aimed to get us to quit using addictive drugs powerful enough to change our behavior? Researchers found that warning labels on cigarette packs actually stimulate the pleasure area of the brain, which brings on cigarette cravings. The warning labels are aimed to reduce smoking, but they may just increase profits for tobacco companies!

4 Which structures make up the pleasure area of the brain?

Marketing companies also take advantage of our hearing to get us to make purchases. In one study, shoppers purchased wines from different countries based on the music being played at the store. Shoppers were more likely to purchase French wine when French music was played and more likely to purchase German wine when German music was played.

And, let's not forget about smell. Smell, more

5 How is this type of marketing strategy similar to auditory subliminal messages?

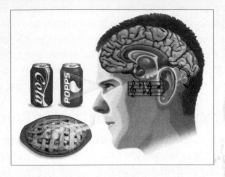

than any other sense, is connected to the brain areas that process motivations and emotions. This means that if businesses use attractive scents, we may make purchases based on impulse rather than rational thought. This is why supermarkets place their bakery near the entrance. The smell of fresh oven-baked bread or pies puts a big smile on our faces and activates the emotional centers in our brain. Consequently, we are likely to spend more money while shopping.

6 What can explain why the smell of fresh baked goods makes us smile?

By applying neuroscience to marketing, we now better understand the complex, mostly unconscious forces that influence our preferences and purchase decisions. The question remains, however: Now that we know about these clever marketing techniques, can we resist these powerful influences when making purchasing decisions, or will many of our buying decisions continue to take place deep below our conscious awareness?

Adapted from R. Baron, 2008; Herz, 2008; Lindstrom, 2008; McClure et al., 2004a, 2004b; Park, 2007

Summary Test

A Three Kinds of Learning

1. A relatively permanent change in behavior that involves specific stimuli and/or responses that change as a result of experience is a definition of _____. The change in behavior includes both unobservable mental events and observable behavioral responses.

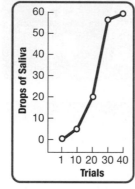

Graph: Drops of Saliva (0–60) vs Trials (1 10 20 30 40)

2. Psychologists have identified three different principles that are the basis for three different kinds of learning. One kind of learning can be traced to Pavlov's well-known experiment in which a bell was sounded and then food was placed in a dog's mouth. After a number of trials in which the bell and food were presented, the dog began to salivate to the bell alone. Pavlov called this kind of learning a conditioned reflex, which today is called _____.

3. A second kind of learning grew out of Thorndike's observations of cats learning to escape from a box. To explain a cat's goal-directed behavior of hitting a latch to get food, Thorndike formulated a principle of learning called the **(a)** _____. This law states that if certain random actions are followed by a pleasurable consequence or reward, such actions are strengthened and will likely occur in the future. Today, the law of effect has become part of the second kind of learning that is called **(b)** _____.

4. A third kind of learning involves mental processes, such as attention and memory; may be learned through observation or imitation; and may not involve any external rewards or require the person to perform any observable behaviors. This kind of learning is called _____.

B Procedure: Classical Conditioning

5. Suppose you wanted to classically condition your roommate to salivate at the sight of a psychology textbook. One procedure for establishing classical conditioning would be to present two stimuli close together in time. The presentation of the two stimuli is called a trial. In our example, a typical trial would involve first presenting a psychology textbook, initially called the **(a)** _____, which does not elicit salivation. A short time later, you would present a piece of brownie, called the **(b)** _____ stimulus, which elicits salivation. Salivation, an innate, automatic, and involuntary physiological reflex, is called the **(c)** _____.

6. After giving your roommate about a dozen trials, you observe that, as soon as you show him the psychology text, he begins to salivate. Because the sight of the psychology textbook itself elicits

salivation, the psychology text has become a **(a)** _____. The roommate's salivation at the sight of the psychology book, presented alone, is called the **(b)** _____. You know that classical conditioning is established when the neutral stimulus becomes the **(c)** _____ and elicits the **(d)** _____. Compared to the unconditioned response, the conditioned response is usually similar in appearance but smaller in amount or magnitude.

C Other Conditioning Concepts

7. The more similar the new stimulus is to the original conditioned stimulus, the stronger or larger the conditioned response will usually be. During classical conditioning, there is a tendency for a stimulus similar to the original conditioned stimulus to elicit a response similar to the conditioned response. This tendency is called _____.

8. During classical conditioning, an organism learns to make a particular response to some stimuli but not to others; this phenomenon is called _____.

9. If a conditioned stimulus is repeatedly presented without the unconditioned stimulus, there is a tendency for the conditioned stimulus to no longer elicit the conditioned response; this phenomenon is called **(a)** _____. However, if some time later you again presented the psychology text to your roommate without giving him a brownie, he would show salivation, the conditioned response. This recurrence of the conditioned response after it has been extinguished is called **(b)** _____.

D Adaptive Value & Uses

10. After receiving an injection, people may develop fear or anxiety in the presence of stimuli associated with the treatment. If we feel fear or anxiety in the presence of some stimulus that precedes a painful or aversive event, we are experiencing a _____.

11. A powerful form of classical conditioning occurs in real life when a neutral stimulus is paired with an unpleasant response, such as nausea or vomiting. The result of this conditioning is called _____. This form of classical conditioning is unusual in two ways: It may be acquired in a single trial and may last a relatively long period of time; and there may be a considerable lapse of time between the presentations of the two stimuli.

12. We now know that animals and humans are biologically prepared to associate certain combinations of conditioned and unconditioned stimuli more easily than others. This phenomenon is called _____.

Unless otherwise noted, all images are © Cengage Learning

13. Classical conditioning of the eye blink reflex, which is a motor response, requires a brain structure called the **(a)** _____. Acquiring a classically conditioned emotional response, especially involving fear, involves a different brain structure called the **(b)** _____.

14. The occurrence of salivation in response to the thought, sight, or smell of food is helpful to digestion and shows that classical conditioning has an _____ role or value.

E Theories of Classical Conditioning

15. According to Pavlov's explanation, classical conditioning occurs because a neural bond or association forms between the conditioned stimulus and the unconditioned stimulus so that the conditioned stimulus eventually substitutes for the unconditioned stimulus. Pavlov's explanation is called _____.

16. The explanation that says that classical conditioning occurs because two stimuli (the neutral and unconditioned stimuli) are paired close together in time is called the _____ theory. However, researchers have shown that contiguity or simply pairing stimuli close together does not necessarily produce classical conditioning.

17. The explanation of classical conditioning that says that an organism learns a relationship between two stimuli such that the occurrence of one stimulus predicts the occurrence of the other is called the **(a)** _____. This theory is supported by the idea that classical conditioning is not usually learned if the unconditioned stimulus appears before the neutral stimulus, a procedure that is called **(b)** _____.

F Research Focus: Conditioning Little Albert

18. An emotional response, fear, was classically conditioned in Little Albert by presenting a white rat, which was the **(a)** _____, and then making a loud noise, which was the **(b)** _____; in turn, the loud noise elicited crying, which was the **(c)** _____. Albert's conditioned emotional response, crying, also occurred in the presence of stimuli similar to the white rat, such as a rabbit; this phenomenon is called **(d)** _____. Albert did not cry at the sight of blocks or papers; this phenomenon is called **(e)** _____. Watson and Rayner were the first to demonstrate that **(f)** _____ responses could be classically conditioned in humans.

© PhotoDisc, Inc.

G Cultural Diversity: Conditioning Racial Prejudice

© Clive Chilvers/Shutterstock.com

19. An unfair, biased, or intolerant attitude toward another group of people is called **(a)** _____. In racial prejudice, negative emotional reactions, such as fear and anxiety, become **(b)** _____ by individuals of another race who should be perceived as being **(c)** _____.

H Application: Conditioned Fear & Nausea

20. During chemotherapy, 60–70% of the patients develop nausea in anticipation of, or when encountering stimuli associated with, the actual treatment. This type of nausea, which is called _____, cannot always be treated with drugs and may persist long after the chemotherapy ends. Researchers believe that conditioned nausea is learned through classical conditioning.

Most Stressful

8. Vomiting
7. Feeling nausea
6. Receiving injection
5. In treatment room
4. Smelling chemicals
3. In waiting room
2. Entering clinic
1. Driving to clinic

21. A nondrug treatment for conditioned nausea involves a procedure based on classical conditioning in which a person imagines or visualizes fearful or anxiety-evoking stimuli and then immediately uses deep **(a)** _____ to decrease the anxiety associated with these stimuli. This procedure, which is called **(b)** _____, is a form of counterconditioning because it uses deep relaxation to replace or decrease the fear or anxiety with particular **(c)** _____ that are arranged in a hierarchy.

Answers: 1. learning; 2. classical conditioning; 3. (a) law of effect, (b) operant conditioning; 4. cognitive learning; 5. (a) neutral stimulus, (b) unconditioned stimulus, (c) unconditioned response; 6. (a) conditioned stimulus, (b) conditioned response, (c) conditioned stimulus; 7. generalization; 8. discrimination; 9. (a) extinction, (b) spontaneous recovery; 10. conditioned emotional response; 11. taste-aversion learning; 12. preparedness; 13. (a) cerebellum, (b) amygdala; 14. adaptive, or survival; 15. stimulus substitution; 16. contiguity; 17. (a) cognitive perspective, (b) backward conditioning; 18. (a) neutral stimulus, (b) unconditioned stimulus, (c) unconditioned response, (d) generalization, (e) discrimination, (f) conditioned emotional response; 19. (a) prejudice, (b) elicited, (c) neutral; 20. anticipatory nausea; 21. (a) relaxation, (b) systematic desensitization, (c) stimuli or situations

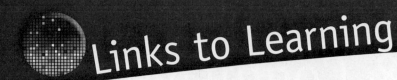
Links to Learning

Key Terms/Key People

acquisition, 198
adaptive value, 200
anticipatory nausea, 206
anxiety hierarchy, 207
behavior, 195
classical conditioning, 196
cognitive learning, 196
cognitive perspective, 202

conditioned emotional response, 201
conditioned response, 197
conditioned stimulus, 197
contiguity theory, 202
discrimination, 199
extinction, 199
generalization, 199

law of effect, 196
learning, 195
Little Albert, 204
neutral stimulus, 197
operant conditioning, 196
Pavlov's experiment, 197
prejudice, 205
preparedness, 200

spontaneous recovery, 199
stimulus substitution, 202
systematic desensitization, 207
taste-aversion learning, 200
unconditioned response (UCR), 197
unconditioned stimulus (UCS), 197

Media Resources

Go to **CengageBrain.com** to access Psychology CourseMate, where you will find an interactive eBook, glossaries, flashcards, quizzes, videos, answers to Critical Thinking questions, and more. You can also access Virtual Psychology Labs, an interactive laboratory experience designed to illustrate key experiments first-hand.

MODULE 10 Operant & Cognitive Approaches

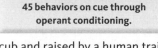

introduction

Learning 45 Commands

How did Bart become a movie star?

It was an unusual movie for two reasons. First, there was almost no dialogue: Human actors spoke only 657 words. Second, the star of the movie was a nonspeaking, nonhuman, 12-year-old, 10-foot-tall, 1,800-pound, enormous brown Kodiak bear named Bart (shown on the left). Bart was one of the world's largest land-dwelling carnivores and could, with one swipe of his massive 12-inch paw, demolish anything in his path. Yet, in the movie, there was big bad Bart, sitting peacefully on his haunches, cradling a small bear cub in his arms. "So what?" you might say, but what you may not know is that, in the wild, a Kodiak bear normally kills and eats any cub it encounters.

Bart the bear learned to perform 45 behaviors on cue through operant conditioning.

Because Bart was found as a cub and raised by a human trainer, Bart grew to act more like an overgrown teddy bear than a natural-born killer. For his role in the movie *The Bear,* Bart learned to perform 45 behaviors on cue, such as sitting, running, standing up, roaring, and, most difficult of all, cradling a teddy bear, which is not what an adult bear does in the wild.

The training procedure seems deceptively simple: Each time Bart performed a behavior on cue, the trainer, Doug Seus, gave Bart an affectionate back scratch, an ear rub, or a juicy apple or pear. For example, when the trainer raised his arms high in the air, it was the signal for Bart to sit and hold the teddy bear. After Bart correctly performed this behavior, Doug would give him a reward. After Bart learned to perform all these behaviors with a stuffed teddy bear, a live bear cub was substituted and the scene was filmed for the movie (Cerone, 1989).

Bart learned to perform 45 behaviors on cue through a kind of learning called operant conditioning.

Operant conditioning, also called instrumental conditioning, is a kind of learning in which an animal or human performs some behavior, and the following consequence (reward or punishment) increases or decreases the chance that an animal or human will again perform that same behavior.

For example, if Bart performed a particular behavior, such as picking up a teddy bear, the consequence—getting a rewarding apple—increased the chance that Bart would again pick up the teddy bear. Because of what Bart learned through operant conditioning, he starred in 20 movies and became the highest paid animal actor, making about $10,000 a day (Brennan, 1997). That's a salary that most of us would be very happy to bear!

Operant conditioning seems rather straightforward. You perform an action or operate on your environment, such as studying hard. The consequence of your studying, such as how well you do on exams, increases or decreases the likelihood that you will perform the same behavior—studying hard—in the future. Besides learning by having your behaviors rewarded or punished, you can also learn in a very different way.

Learning to Skateboard

What did Tony Hawk learn from just watching?

In operant conditioning, the learning process is out in the open: Bart performs an observable behavior (holds a teddy bear), which is followed by an observable consequence (gets an apple). But there is another kind of learning that involves unobservable mental processes and unobservable rewards that you may give yourself. This kind of learning, called cognitive learning, is partly how Tony Hawk learned to skate.

Tony Hawk is recognized as the greatest skateboarder of all time. But Tony did not always have a talent for skating. When Tony was 9 years old, his brother gave him his old skateboard. Tony had seen his brother skate before, and he tried to skate just like him. Tony then visited a skate park, where he was awed by how quickly skaters went up, down, and around walls. He was also amazed at how they daringly spun while high up in the air. Tony wanted to be as talented as the skaters at the park, and he went on to practice every chance he had. When Tony was asked why he enjoyed skating as a child, he replied, "I liked that no one was telling me how to do it" (CBS News, 2004a). Instead, Tony learned by observing how his friends and professionals skated at the park: "I would watch them and try to learn from them. I'd imitate them" (Hawk, 2002, p. 30). On his own initiative and without any special guidance, Tony learned to skate by imitating others.

The process Tony used to learn skateboarding is very different from the operant conditioning procedure used to teach Bart new behaviors. During operant conditioning, Bart performed observable behaviors that were influenced by observable consequences.

Tony Hawk learned to skateboard partly from watching others.

In comparison, Tony learned how to skateboard through observation and imitation, which involved unobservable mental processes and is called cognitive learning. We'll discuss cognitive learning later in this module.

What's Coming

In the first half of this module, we'll discuss the history and procedure of operant conditioning, how operant conditioning differs from classical conditioning, how consequences or reinforcers work, and other examples of operant conditioning. In the second half of this module, we'll explain the history of cognitive learning, the theory behind observational learning, and the role of insight learning.

We'll begin with an important study that involved a cat, a puzzle box, and a smelly fish. ●

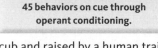

© Evan Agostini/Getty Images

A Operant Conditioning

Background: Thorndike and Skinner

We told you how a trainer used operant conditioning to teach Bart to perform 45 different behaviors on cue. Operant conditioning has now been applied to many different settings, such as training animals to perform, training children to use the potty, stopping retarded children from injuring themselves, and helping autistic children learn social behaviors. However, the discovery of operant behavior involved two different researchers who worked in two different laboratories on two different kinds of problems. So that you can appreciate the thinking that led to operant conditioning, we'll visit the laboratories of the two important researchers—E. L. Thorndike and B. F. Skinner.

How did Bart become a movie star?

Thorndike's Law of Effect

E. L. Thorndike (1874–1949)

It's the late 1800s, and we're in the laboratory of E. L. Thorndike, who is interested in animal intelligence—specifically, in measuring their capacity for reasoning.

Unlike pet owners who assume from anecdotal observations that their animals are intelligent, Thorndike devised a simple but clever way to measure reasoning in a more objective way. He built a series of puzzle boxes from which a cat could escape by learning to make a specific response, such as pulling a string or pressing a bar. Outside the puzzle box was a reward for escaping—a piece of fish.

We watch Thorndike place a cat in the puzzle box and record its escape time. After Thorndike graphs the data (graph below), we see a gradual lessening in the time needed to escape. Notice that on the first trial the cat needed over 240 seconds to hit the escape latch, but by the last trial, the cat hits the escape latch in less than 60 seconds.

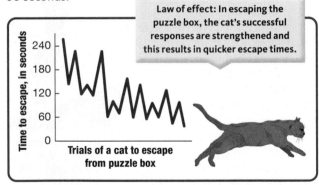

Law of effect: In escaping the puzzle box, the cat's successful responses are strengthened and this results in quicker escape times.

Time to escape, in seconds

Trials of a cat to escape from puzzle box

Thorndike explains that, with repeated trials, the cat spends more time around the latch, which increases the chances of finding and hitting the latch and more quickly escaping to get the fish. To explain why a cat's random trial-and-error behaviors gradually turned into efficient, goal-directed behaviors, Thorndike formulated the law of effect.

The **law of effect** states that behaviors followed by positive consequences are strengthened, while behaviors followed by negative consequences are weakened.

Thorndike's (1898) findings were significant because they suggested that the law of effect was a basic law of learning and provided an objective procedure to study it. Thorndike's emphasis on studying the consequences of goal-directed behavior was further developed and expanded by B. F. Skinner.

Skinner's Operant Conditioning

B. F. Skinner (1904–1990)

It's the 1930s, and we're in the laboratory of B. F. Skinner, who is interested in analyzing ongoing behaviors of animals. Skinner explains that Thorndike's law of effect is useful, since it describes how animals are rewarded for making particular responses. However, in order to analyze ongoing behaviors, you must have an objective way to measure them. Skinner's clever solution is a unit of behavior he calls an operant response (Skinner, 1938).

An **operant response** is a response that can be modified by its consequences and is a meaningful unit of ongoing behavior that can be easily measured.

For example, suppose that out of curiosity Bart picks up a teddy bear. His picking up the teddy bear is an example of an operant response because Bart is acting or operating on the environment. The consequence of his picking up the teddy bear is that he receives an apple, which is a desirable effect. This desirable effect modifies his response by increasing the chances that Bart will repeat the same response.

By measuring or recording operant responses, Skinner can analyze animals' ongoing behaviors during learning. He calls this kind of learning *operant conditioning,* which focuses on how consequences (rewards or punishments) affect behaviors.

A simple example of operant conditioning occurs when a rat in an experimental box accidentally presses a bar. If the bar press is followed by food, this consequence increases the chance that the rat will press the bar again. As the rat presses the bar more times, more food follows, which in turn increases the chances that the rat will continue to press the bar (indicated by the rise of the red line in the figure below).

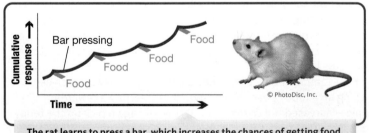

Bar pressing

Cumulative response

Food

Food

Food

Food

Time

© PhotoDisc, Inc.

The rat learns to press a bar, which increases the chances of getting food.

Using his newly developed procedure of operant conditioning, B. F. Skinner spent the next 50 years exploring and analyzing learning in rats, pigeons, schoolchildren, and adults.

The 1920s and 1930s gave learning a mighty jolt with the discovery of two general principles—Pavlov's classical conditioning and Skinner's operant conditioning. For the first time, psychologists had two methods to analyze learning processes in an objective way.

Now we'll examine Skinner's ingenious procedure for studying operant conditioning.

Unless otherwise noted, all images are © Cengage Learning

Graph based on data from *Behavior of Organisms,* by B. F. Skinner, 1938. Appleton-Century-Crofts.

Principles and Procedures

Why does a rat press a bar?

A rat may initially press a bar out of curiosity, and whether it presses the bar again depends on the consequences. To show how consequences can affect behavior, imagine that you are looking over Skinner's shoulder as he places a rat into a box. The box is empty except for a bar jutting out from one side and an empty food cup below and to the side of the bar (above figure). This box is called a Skinner box.

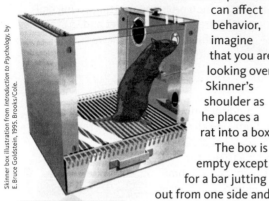

Skinner box illustration from *Introduction to Psychology*, by E. Bruce Goldstein, 1995. Brooks/Cole.

Skinner box contains bar and food cup.

A **Skinner box** is a small enclosure that is automated to record an animal's bar presses and deliver food pellets as a consequence.

The Skinner box is an efficient way to study how an animal's ongoing behaviors may be modified by changing the consequences of what happens after a bar press.

Skinner explains that the rat is a good subject for operant conditioning because it can use its front paws to manipulate objects, such as a bar, and it has a tendency to explore its environment, which means that it will eventually find the bar, touch it, or even press it.

Skinner goes on to explain the following three factors that are involved in operantly conditioning a rat to press a bar in the Skinner box.

1 The rat has not been fed for some hours so that it will be active and more likely to eat the food reward. A hungry rat tends to roam restlessly about, sniffing at whatever it finds.

2 The goal is to condition the rat to press the bar. By pressing the bar, the rat operates on its environment; thus, this response is called an *operant response.*

3 Skinner explains that a naive rat does not usually waltz over and press the bar. In conditioning a rat to press a bar, Skinner will use a procedure called shaping.

Shaping is a procedure in which an experimenter successively reinforces behaviors that lead up to or approximate the desired behavior.

For example, if the desired behavior is pressing the bar, here's how shaping works.

Shaping: Facing the Bar

Skinner places a white rat into the (Skinner) box, closes the door, and watches the rat through a one-way mirror. At first, the rat wanders around the back of the box, but when it turns and faces the bar, Skinner releases a food pellet that makes a noise as it drops into the food cup. The rat hears the pellet drop, approaches the food cup, then sees, sniffs, and eats the pellet. After eating, the rat moves away to explore the box. But, as soon as the rat turns and faces the bar, Skinner releases another pellet. The rat hears the noise, goes to the food cup, sniffs, and eats the pellet. Shaping is going well.

Shaping: Touching the Bar

As shaping continues, Skinner decides to reinforce the rat only when it actually moves toward the bar. Skinner waits and as soon as the rat faces and then moves toward the bar, Skinner releases another pellet. After eating the pellet, the rat wanders a bit but soon returns to the bar and actually sniffs it. A fourth pellet immediately drops into the cup, and the rat eats it. When the rat places one paw on the bar, a fifth pellet drops into the cup. Notice how Skinner has shaped the rat to spend all its time near the bar.

Shaping: Pressing the Bar

As soon as the rat actually puts its paws on the bar, Skinner releases a pellet. After eating, the rat puts its paws back on the bar and gets a pellet. Now Skinner waits until the rat puts its paws on the bar and actually happens to press down, which releases another pellet. Soon, the rat is pressing the bar over and over to get pellets. Notice how Skinner reinforced the rat's behaviors that led up to or approximated the desired behavior of bar pressing.

Immediate Reinforcement

Depending on the rat and the trainer's experience, it may take from minutes to an hour to shape a rat to press a bar. Skinner explains that in shaping behavior, the food pellet, or *reinforcer,* should follow *immediately* after the desired behavior. By following immediately, the reinforcer is associated with the desired behavior and not with some other behavior that just happens to occur. If the reinforcer is delayed, the animal may be reinforced for some undesired or superstitious behavior.

Superstitious behavior is a behavior that increases in frequency because its occurrence is accidentally paired with the delivery of a reinforcer.

When I (R. P.) was a graduate student, I conditioned my share of superstitious rat behaviors, such as making them turn in circles or stand up instead of pressing the bar. That's because I accidentally but immediately reinforced a rat after it performed the wrong behavior.

Humans, especially professional baseball players, report a variety of superstitious behaviors that were accidentally reinforced by getting a hit (Burger & Lynn, 2005). For example, a five-time batting champion (Wade Boggs) ate chicken every day he played, allowed no one else to touch his bats, and believed each bat had a certain number of hits. Once a batter's superstitious behaviors are reinforced, especially by getting a big hit or home run, superstitious behaviors tend to persist and can be very difficult to eliminate. You probably have some of your own!

Next, we'll discuss some interesting examples of operant conditioning in very young humans.

Examples of Operant Conditioning

Have you been operantly conditioned?

Without realizing it, you may be performing many behaviors learned through operant conditioning. For example, operant conditioning was involved if you learned to drive through a yellow traffic light to avoid stopping, study for hours to get good grades, or give flowers to your honey to see him or her smile. And you may continually perform these behaviors because they are followed by reinforcers that increase the chances that

© Jason Stitt/Shutterstock.com

you will perform these same behaviors again. We'll discuss how the procedures and principles of operant conditioning have been used by parents to solve two relatively common problems: getting young children to use the toilet and to stop refusing to eat a wide variety of healthy foods.

Toilet Training

Imagine that you are a parent of 3-year-old Sheryl, who is physically mature enough to begin toilet training. Here's how operant conditioning techniques can be applied to teach toilet training.

© Luca Cappelli/iStockphoto

Four steps in toilet training

1. **Target behavior.** The target behavior or goal is for Sheryl to urinate in the toilet.

2. **Preparation.** Before training begins, put all of Sheryl's toys away so that she will not be distracted. Then give her a large glass of apple juice, so that she will have to urinate soon.

3. **Reinforcers.** Select reinforcers, which can be candy, verbal praise, or a hug. Each time Sheryl performs or emits a desired behavior, you immediately reinforce it. The reinforcer increases the likelihood that the behavior will be repeated.

4. **Shaping.** Just as Skinner used the shaping procedure in conditioning a rat to press a bar, you can use a similar shaping procedure in conditioning Sheryl to use the toilet. Each time Sheryl performs a behavior that leads to the target behavior (using the toilet), give her a treat, verbal praise, or a hug. For instance, when Sheryl says that she has to go potty, say, "That's great." When Sheryl enters the bathroom, say, "What a good girl." When she lowers her pants by herself, say, "You're doing really well." After Sheryl urinates into the toilet, give her a big hug and perhaps a treat.

Mothers who were supervised as they used this training procedure needed 4–18 hours to toilet train their 2- to 3-year-olds (Berk & Patrick, 1990; Matson & Ollendick, 1977). However, children vary in when they are ready to begin toilet training and operant conditioning. Researchers advise that "in most cases there's no clear benefit to starting training before 24 to 27 months and in fact kids who start early often take longer to finish" (N. Blum, 2003).

Another difficulty parents face is when children eat only one or two favorite foods and refuse all others.

Food Refusal

Some young children with no medical problems may develop a habit of eating only certain foods and refusing all others, which may result in an unhealthy diet or low weight (Patel et al., 2002). Researchers taught parents how to use the principles of operant conditioning to overcome food refusal in their young children.

1. **Target behavior.** The target behavior or goal was for the child to taste, chew, and eat a food (usually fruits or vegetables) that she or he has persistently refused to eat.

2. **Preparation.** Researchers first showed mothers how to shape and reinforce target behaviors. Next, each mother shaped the target behavior in her child in the home setting.

3. **Reinforcers.** Each time the child performed or emitted a target behavior, the mother immediately reinforced the child with a positive reinforcer, such as praise, attention, or a smile.

4. **Shaping.** The shaping procedure consisted of having the child notice the food and let it be placed in his or her mouth, letting the child taste the food, and, finally, having the child chew and swallow the food.

The graph below explains and shows the success of using operant conditioning to overcome food refusal in young children (Werle et al., 1993).

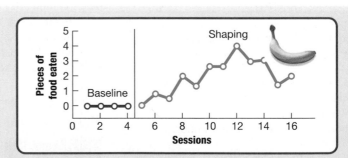

Baseline: During these four sessions, the mother offered nonpreferred food to her child, who refused the food each time.

Shaping: During these sessions, the mother shaped the child to accept nonpreferred food by giving praise, attention, and smiles each time her child made a response that was similar to or approximated the target behavior (chewing and swallowing food). Shaping proved effective in overcoming the child's habit of food refusal. Compare the child's food refusal during baseline to that during shaping sessions.

Notice that the same principles of operant conditioning apply whether the goal is to condition a child to use the potty, to overcome food refusal, or to train Bart the bear to pick up and hold a teddy bear.

Next, we'll compare the principles of operant and classical conditioning.

Adapted from "Treating Chronic Food Refusal in Young Children: Home-Based Parent Training," by M. A. Werle, T. B. Murphy & K. S. Budd, 1993, *Journal of Applied Behavior Analysis, 26*, 421–433.

Unless otherwise noted, all images are © Cengage Learning

Operant Versus Classical Conditioning

Earlier in this module, we discussed how Bart the bear was operantly conditioned to hold a teddy bear—something he would never do in the wild. As you may remember from Module 9, we discussed how Sam the dog was classically conditioned to salivate to the sound of a bell—something he would not usually do. Although both operant and classical conditioning lead to learning, they have very different procedures and principles, which may be a little confusing. We'll try to clear up any confusion by doing a side-by-side comparison of the principles and procedures of operant and classical conditioning using the same participant, Bart, one of the world's largest participants.

How are they different?

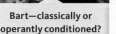

Bart—classically or operantly conditioned?

Operant Conditioning

1 Goal. The goal of operant conditioning is to ***increase or decrease the rate*** of some response, which usually involves shaping. In Bart's case, the goal was to increase his rate of holding a teddy bear.

2 Voluntary response. Bart's behavior of holding a teddy bear is a voluntary response because he can perform it at will. Bart must first perform a voluntary response before getting a reward.

3 Emitted response. Bart voluntarily performs or emits some response, which Skinner called the operant response (holding the teddy bear). Skinner used the term ***emit*** to indicate that the organism acts or operates on the environment. In most cases, animals and humans are shaped to emit the desired responses.

4 Contingent on behavior. Bart's performance of the desired response depends on, or is ***contingent*** on, the consequences, or what happens next. For example, each time Bart holds the teddy bear, the consequence is that he receives an apple. The apple, which is a reward (reinforcer), increases the chances that Bart will perform the desired response In the future.

The reinforcer must occur ***immediately after*** the desired response. In Bart's case, the reinforcer (apple) would be given immediately after Bart holds the teddy bear. If the reinforcer occurs too late, the result may be the conditioning of unwanted or superstitious responses.

5 Consequences. An animal or human's performance of some behavior is dependent or contingent on its ***consequences***—that is, what happens next. For example, the consequence of Bart's picking up and holding a teddy bear was to get an apple.

Thus, in operant conditioning, an animal or human learns that performing or ***emitting*** some behavior is followed by a ***consequence*** (reward or punishment), which, in turn, increases or decreases the chances of performing that behavior again.

Classical Conditioning

1 Goal. The goal of classical conditioning is to create a new response to a ***neutral stimulus***. In this example, Bart will make a new response, salivation, to the sound of a horn, which is the neutral stimulus because it does not usually cause Bart to salivate.

2 Involuntary response. Salivation is an example of a ***physiological reflex***. Physiological reflexes (salivation, eye blink) are triggered or elicited by some stimulus and therefore called involuntary responses.

3 Elicited response. As Bart eats an apple, it will trigger the involuntary physiological reflex of salivation. Thus, eating the apple, which is called the ***unconditioned stimulus,*** triggers or elicits an involuntary reflex response, salivation, which is called the ***unconditioned response.***

© Alex Staroseltsev/ Shutterstock.com

4 Conditioned response. Bart was given repeated trials during which the neutral stimulus (horn's sound) was presented and followed

© Alex Staroseltsev/ Shutterstock.com

by the unconditioned stimulus (apple). After repeated trials, Bart learned a relationship between the two stimuli: The horn's sound is followed by an apple. The horn's sound, or neutral stimulus, becomes the ***conditioned stimulus*** when its sound alone, before the occurrence of the apple, elicits salivation, which is the ***conditioned response.***

For best results, the neutral stimulus is presented slightly before the unconditioned stimulus. If the unconditioned stimulus is presented before the neutral stimulus, this is called ***backward conditioning*** and produces little if any conditioning.

5 Expectancy. According to the ***cognitive perspective*** of classical conditioning, an animal or human learns a predictable relationship between, or develops an expectancy about, the neutral and unconditioned stimuli. This means Bart learned to ***expect*** that the neutral stimulus (horn's sound) is always followed by the unconditioned stimulus (apple). Thus, in classical conditioning, the animal or human learns a ***predictable relationship*** between stimuli.

One major difference between operant and classical conditioning is that in operant conditioning, the performance of some response depends on its consequence (rewards or punishment). We'll discuss the effects of different kinds of consequences next. ●

B Reinforcers

Consequences

Why are consequences important?

When I (H. K.) began learning to ride a bicycle, I remember taking a turn too quickly, losing my balance, and scraping my knees on the hard pavement. My behavior illustrates a key principle of operant conditioning, which is that **consequences are contingent on behavior.** In this case, I fell and scraped my knees (consequence) when I went too quickly around a curve (behavior). Furthermore, this consequence made me think twice before repeating this careless behavior. Thus, consequences affect behavior, and in operant conditioning, there are two kinds of consequences—reinforcement and punishment.

Reinforcement is a consequence that occurs after a behavior and increases the chance that the behavior will occur again.

For example, one of the main reasons you study hard for exams is to get good grades (reinforcement). The consequence of getting a good grade increases the chances that you'll study hard for future exams.

Punishment is a consequence that occurs after a behavior and decreases the chance that the behavior will occur again.

For example, schools may use punishment to reduce students' absentee rates. The consequence of a high absentee rate could be the loss of desired privileges (such as not being permitted to attend school sporting events or dances).

Sometimes reinforcement and punishment are used together to control some behavior, as was done in treating a serious behavioral disorder called pica.

Pica is a behavioral disorder, often seen in individuals with intellectual impairment, that involves eating inedible objects or unhealthy substances. This can result in serious physical problems, including lead poisoning, intestinal blockage, and parasites.

Here's an example of how reinforcement and punishment were used to treat pica.

Reinforcement

Punishment

Changing the Consequences

Walt was 15 years old and suffered from severe intellectual impairment. One of Walt's problems was pica, which included eating bits of paper and clothing, metal and plastic objects, and especially paint chips, from which he had gotten lead poisoning.

To control his pica, Walt was given a tray containing nonfood items (fake paint chips made from flour) and food items (crackers). Each time Walt chose a food item, he received a reinforcement—verbal praise. When Walt chose a paint chip, he received a mild punishment—having his face washed for 20 seconds. The graph below shows how the consequences (reinforcement or punishment) greatly modified Walt's pica behavior (C. R. Johnson et al., 1994).

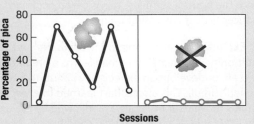

Baseline: During these sessions, Walt chose the nonfood items 10–80% of the time. Compare the baseline with training sessions.

Training: During these sessions, Walt was reinforced with praise for choosing food items and punished with face washing for choosing nonfood items. These consequences greatly modified his behaviors so that he chose primarily food items.

In this study, reinforcement and punishment proved to be an effective combination to treat a potentially dangerous problem. Next, we'll discuss two kinds of reinforcements.

Reinforcement

How are an apple and an "F" alike?

Although getting an apple and getting a grade of "F" seem very different, they are both consequences that can increase the occurrence of certain behaviors. There are two kinds of reinforcements, or consequences—positive and negative—that increase the occurrence of behaviors.

Positive Reinforcement

Immediately after Bart the bear emitted or performed a behavior (holding a teddy bear), the trainer gave him an apple to increase the likelihood of his repeating that behavior. This situation is an example of positive reinforcement.

Positive reinforcement is the presentation of a stimulus that increases the probability that a behavior will occur again.

For example, if you ask a friend for money and get it, the money is a positive reinforcer that will increase the chances of your asking again. There's also a second kind of reinforcement, called negative reinforcement.

Negative Reinforcement

If you have a headache and take an aspirin to get rid of it, your response of taking an aspirin is an example of negative reinforcement.

Negative reinforcement is an aversive (unpleasant) stimulus whose removal increases the likelihood that the preceding response will occur again.

If taking an aspirin removes your headache (aversive or unpleasant stimulus), then your response of taking an aspirin is negatively reinforced because it removes the headache and thus increases the chances of your taking an aspirin in the future.

Don't be confused by the fact that both positive and negative reinforcers *increase* the frequency of the responses they follow.

Next, we'll learn about reinforcers, including primary reinforcers, such as food, and secondary reinforcers, such as money and coupons.

Reinforcers

How are chocolate and a coupon alike?

Chocolate and coupons are examples of reinforcers.

A **reinforcer** is a stimulus that increases the likelihood that the response preceding it will occur again. Although chocolate and coupons are both reinforcers, they are examples of two different types of reinforcers—primary reinforcers and negative reinforcers.

Primary Reinforcers

If you made yourself study for 2 hours before rewarding yourself with chocolate, you would be using a primary reinforcer.

A **primary reinforcer** is a stimulus, such as food, water, or sex, that is innately satisfying and requires no learning on the part of the subject to become pleasurable.

Food: primary reinforcer

Primary reinforcers, such as eating, drinking, or having sex, are unlearned and innately pleasurable. Brain scans (see p. 70) showed that these activities, including eating chocolate, activate the brain's built-in or inherited reward/pleasure center (Belin & Rauscent, 2006). Although brain scans were discovered after Skinner, they have proven him right: Primary reinforcers are innately satisfying and require no training because they automatically activate the brain's built-in reward/pleasure center. In our example, chocolate is a primary reinforcer for studying. However, many behaviors are aided or maintained by secondary reinforcers.

Secondary Reinforcers

If a schoolteacher gave each child a coupon good for fun prizes if the child ate fruits and vegetables during lunch, the teacher would be using a secondary reinforcer.

A **secondary reinforcer** is any stimulus that has acquired its reinforcing power through experience; secondary reinforcers are learned, such as by being paired with primary reinforcers or other secondary reinforcers.

Coupons, money, grades, and praise are examples of secondary reinforcers because their value is learned or acquired through experience (Delgado et al., 2006; S. B. Klein, 2009). For example, children learned that coupons were valuable because they could be redeemed for fun prizes. The coupons became secondary reinforcers that encouraged children to eat fruits and vegetables during lunch at school (Hendy et al., 2005, 2007).

Unlike primary and secondary reinforcers, which are consequences that increase behaviors, punishment has a very different effect.

Coupons, or secondary reinforcers, encourage children's good behaviors.

Punishment

Are there different kinds of punishment?

Although placing a child in time-out and giving a child an electric shock seem very different, they are both consequences that can decrease the occurrence of certain behaviors.

There are two kinds of punishment or consequences—positive and negative—that decrease the occurrence of behaviors. Both positive and negative punishments function as "stop signs"; they stop or decrease the occurrence of a behavior.

Positive Punishment

There is a school in Massachusetts that uses a controversial method of punishment to discourage students from engaging in dangerous behaviors. Many of the children at this school have severe behavior problems, such as hitting strangers in the face, biting others or themselves, and eye gouging. The school requires students to wear backpacks, which contain an electric device that allows staff members to apply a shock to electrodes attached to the student's body whenever the student engages in dangerous or prohibited behaviors (Hinman & Brown, 2010; L. Kaufman, 2007). The goal is to decrease the occurrence of certain behaviors, and the method used is an example of positive punishment.

Positive punishment refers to presenting an aversive (unpleasant) stimulus after a response. The aversive stimulus decreases the chances that the response will recur.

The aversive stimulus in the example is electric shock, which decreases the chances that dangerous and self-destructive behaviors will occur.

There's a second type of punishment, called negative punishment, that can also be used to decrease children's undesirable behaviors.

Negative Punishment

One kind of undesirable behavior in young children is the persistent refusal of parental requests, a problem called noncompliance.

Noncompliance refers to a child refusing to follow directions, carry out a request, or obey a command given by a parent or caregiver.

One method used to decrease children's noncompliance is time-out.

Time-out removes reinforcing stimuli after an undesirable response. This removal decreases the chances that the undesired response will recur.

Time-out is an example of negative punishment.

Negative punishment refers to removing a reinforcing stimulus (such as a child's allowance) after a response. This removal decreases the chances that the response will recur.

In time-out, the reinforcing stimulus being removed is the freedom to play and the undesirable behavior being decreased is noncompliance. In the Application section of this module, we'll discuss the pros and cons of positive and negative punishment.

Although somewhat confusing, remember that positive and negative punishment *decrease* the likelihood of a behavior occurring again, while positive and negative reinforcement *increase* the likelihood of a behavior occurring again. ●

C Schedules of Reinforcement

Skinner's Contributions

On September 20, 1971, *Time* magazine recognized B. F. Skinner's influence and accomplishments in psychology and education by putting him on its cover. Just a year earlier, the *American Psychologist* rated B. F. Skinner second, after Freud, in influence on 20th-century psychology.

Why are consequences important?

Skinner is perhaps best known for his discovery of operant conditioning, which is a powerful method for analyzing the individual behaviors of animals and humans. Part of his method was to study how different kinds of consequences or reinforcements affected behavior, and this led to his study of different schedules of reinforcement.

B. F. Skinner (1904–1990)

© Bettmann/CORBIS

A **schedule of reinforcement** is a program or rule that determines how and when the occurrence of a response will be followed by a reinforcer.

Skinner pointed out many examples of how schedules of reinforcement both maintained and controlled behaviors. For example, slot machine players don't realize that they are paid off according to a schedule of reinforcement that encourages rapid responding.

Skinner was able to study how different schedules of reinforcement affected behavior because he developed a clever method to record ongoing, individual behaviors. His method included the use of the now-famous "Skinner box" and something called the cumulative record.

Measuring Ongoing Behavior

Skinner showed how different schedules of reinforcement affected an animal's or a human's ongoing behavior with something called a cumulative record.

A **cumulative record** is a continuous written record that shows an animal's or a human's individual responses and reinforcements.

Skinner box illustration from *Introduction to Psychology*, by E. Bruce Goldstein, 1995, Brooks/Cole.

Rat in a Skinner box

A rat in a Skinner box is shown on the left, and a cumulative record is shown below. When the rat is not pressing the bar, a pen draws a straight line on a long roll of paper that unwinds slowly and continuously to the left. When the rat presses the bar, the pen moves up a notch. When the rat makes numerous responses, the pen moves up many notches to draw a line that resembles a stairway going up. If the rat presses the bar slowly, the pen notches up gradually, resulting in a gentler slope. If the rat responds quickly, the pen notches up more quickly, resulting in a steeper slope.

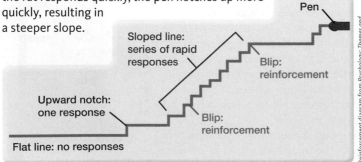

Sloped line: series of rapid responses

Blip: reinforcement

Pen

Upward notch: one response

Blip: reinforcement

Flat line: no responses

Reinforcement diagram from *Psychology: Themes and Variations*, by Wayne Weiten, 2nd ed., figure 6.13. Copyright © 1992 by Wadsworth, Inc. Reproduced by permission.

A downward blip indicates that the rat received a food pellet, or reinforcement (only two are shown). The cumulative record shows an animal's ongoing responses and reinforcements across time.

We'll first look at how two general schedules of reinforcement—continuous and partial reinforcement—can greatly affect ongoing behavior.

Schedules of Reinforcement

When I (H. K.) first began training my dog to "shake hands," I gave her a treat each time she responded to my command by shaking my hand. Later on, when she had mostly learned to shake hands, I gave her a treat only some of the time. These situations illustrate two general schedules of reinforcement—continuous and partial.

Continuous Reinforcement

Giving my dog a treat each time she responded to my command by shaking my hand illustrates the schedule of continuous reinforcement.

Continuous reinforcement means that every occurrence of the operant response results in delivery of the reinforcer.

Every response is reinforced.

In the real world, relatively few of our behaviors are on a continuous reinforcement schedule because very few things or people are as reliable as my dog. Continuous reinforcement is often used in the initial stages of operant conditioning because it results in rapid learning of some behavior.

Partial Reinforcement

After my dog had mostly learned to shake hands on command, I gave her a treat about every fifth time, which illustrates the schedule of partial reinforcement.

Partial reinforcement refers to a situation in which responding is reinforced only some of the time.

Only some responses are reinforced.

In the real world, many of our behaviors are on a partial reinforcement schedule, which is very effective in maintaining behavior over the long run. My dog keeps shaking my hand on command because some of the time she gets a treat.

We'll discuss the four common schedules of partial reinforcement and show how differently they affect behavior.

Unless otherwise noted, all images are © Cengage Learning

Partial Reinforcement Schedules

Which schedule are you on?

We'll discuss four different schedules of partial reinforcement, each of which has a different effect on controlling and maintaining animal and human behaviors.

Fixed-Ratio Schedule

If factory workers are paid after packing six boxes, they are on a fixed-ratio schedule.

Fixed-ratio schedule means that a reinforcer occurs only after a fixed number of responses are made by the participant.

A fixed-ratio schedule is often used to pay assembly-line workers because it results in fast rates of work.

Fixed-Interval Schedule

If a surfer gets a big wave to ride (the reinforcer) every 30 seconds (waves come in regular sets of big and small), he is on a fixed-interval schedule.

Fixed-interval schedule means that a reinforcer occurs following the first response that occurs after a fixed interval of time.

A fixed-interval schedule has slow responding at first, but as the time for the reinforcer nears, responses increase.

Variable-Ratio Schedule

If a slot machine pays off after an average of 25 pulls, the gambler is on a variable-ratio schedule.

Variable-ratio schedule means that a reinforcer is delivered after an average number of correct responses has occurred.

The variable-ratio schedule produces a high rate of responding because the person (gambler) doesn't know which response will finally produce the payoff.

Variable-Interval Schedule

251 252 254 257 259 260 262 263 268

If a bus arrives (the reinforcer) at your stop an average of 7 minutes late but at variable intervals, the bus rider is on a variable-interval schedule. This reinforces your arriving just a few minutes late for your bus.

Variable-interval schedule means that a reinforcer occurs following the first correct response after an average amount of time has passed.

A variable-interval schedule results in a more regular rate of responding than does a fixed-interval schedule.

In the real world, many of our behaviors are maintained on one or more of these four schedules of partial reinforcement.

Next, we'll describe an interesting and unusual application of Skinner's principles of operant conditioning.

Applying Skinner's Principles

How smart are dolphins?

After the Gulf War, ships carrying food and medicine had to wait outside the ports until the many underwater mines were located. Because the water was dark and murky, human divers could not easily detect the mines, but dolphins had no difficulty, since they can "see" by using sound waves or echolocation to find objects. Dolphins are trained to detect mines similarly to how dogs are trained to detect explosives: Their trainers applied Skinner's principles of operant conditioning.

Based on data from the U.S. Department of the Navy and an illustration by Suzy Parker, *USA TODAY*, March 27, 2003, p. 8D.

1 A dolphin has been trained to wait and circle around an inflatable boat. On the trainer's signal, the dolphin dives and uses echolocation to find the mine in the murky water. Echolocation involves emitting sound waves (too high for humans to hear) and analyzing the waves that are reflected back from objects. The dolphin's echolocation is so sensitive that it can detect a quarter-sized metal disk 100 feet away, no matter how murky the water is.

2 After locating the mine, the dolphin returns to the surface and is trained to touch a rubber disk at the front of the boat. The trainer rewards the dolphin with a fish for this and many other behaviors.

3 The trainer places on the dolphin's nose a hollow cone attached to a plastic cylinder that rides on the dolphin's back. Again, the dolphin dives and echolocates the mine, but it has been trained not to touch the mine. When close to the mine, the dolphin is trained to release the nose cone, and the cylinder break opens and releases an anchor.

4 The anchor (sound transmitter) falls to the bottom while the cylinder rises to the surface to mark the location of the mine. Human divers use the cylinder to locate and then detonate the mine. The dolphin is always removed from the area before the mine is detonated. A Navy spokesperson says that the dolphins are well cared for and, for that reason, live in captivity as long as or longer than in the wild (Friend, 2003).

Through operant conditioning, dolphins learned to perform this complex series of behaviors. During operant conditioning, a number of other things are also happening. ●

D Other Conditioning Concepts

What else did Bart learn?

During the time that Bart was being operantly conditioned to pick up and hold a teddy bear to a hand signal, he simultaneously learned a number of other things, such as to hold a bear cub, not to obey commands from a stranger, and to stop picking up the teddy

bear if he was no longer given apples (reinforcers). You may remember these phenomena—generalization, discrimination, extinction, and spontaneous recovery—from our discussion of classical conditioning in Module 9 (see p. 199). We'll explain how the same terms also apply to operant conditioning.

Generalization

In the movie, Bart was supposed to pick up and hold a bear cub on command. However, in the wild, adult male Kodiak bears don't pick up and hold cubs; instead, they usually kill them.

Generalization: Bart transfers his response from teddy bear to live cub.

Although Bart was relatively tame, his trainer took no chances of Bart's wilder nature coming out and killing the bear cub. For this reason, the trainer started by conducting the initial conditioning with a stuffed teddy bear. Only after Bart had learned to pick up and hold the teddy bear on cue did the trainer substitute a live bear cub. As the trainer had predicted, Bart transferred his holding the teddy bear to holding the live bear cub, a phenomenon called generalization.

In operant conditioning, **generalization** means that an animal or person emits the same response to similar stimuli.

In classical conditioning, **generalization** is the tendency for a stimulus similar to the original conditioned stimulus to elicit a response similar to the conditioned response.

A common and sometimes embarrassing example of generalization occurs when a young child generalizes the word "Daddy" to other males who appear similar to the child's real father. As quickly as possible, embarrassed parents teach their child to discriminate between the real father and other adult males.

Discrimination

Since Bart had been raised and trained by a particular adult male, he had learned to obey and take cues only from his trainer and not from other males. This is an example of discrimination.

In operant conditioning, **discrimination** means that a response is emitted in the presence of a stimulus that is reinforced and not in the presence of unreinforced stimuli.

In classical conditioning, **discrimination** is the tendency for some stimuli but not others to elicit a conditioned response.

One problem with Bart was that he would repeatedly pick up and hold the teddy bear to receive an apple. To control this problem, the trainer used a cue—raising his arms in the air—to signal that only then would Bart receive an apple for his behavior. This is an example of a discriminative stimulus.

A **discriminative stimulus** is a cue that a behavior will be reinforced.

Discriminative stimulus: Bart receives an apple only when the trainer's arms are in the air.

If you pay close attention to an animal trainer, you'll notice that discriminative stimuli, such as a hand signal or whistle, are used to signal the animal that the next behavior will be reinforced.

Young children learn to discriminate between stimuli when their parents reinforce their saying "Daddy" in the presence of their real fathers but do not reinforce their children when they call strangers "Daddy."

Extinction and Spontaneous Recovery

Even after filming ended, Bart continued to perform his trained behaviors for a while. However, after a period of time when these behaviors were no longer reinforced, they gradually diminished and ceased. This is an example of extinction.

In operant conditioning, **extinction** refers to the reduction in an operant response when it is no longer followed by the reinforcer.

In classical conditioning, **extinction** refers to the reduction in a response when the conditioned stimulus is no longer followed by the unconditioned stimulus.

After undergoing extinction, Bart may show spontaneous recovery.

In operant conditioning, **spontaneous recovery** is a temporary recovery in the rate of responding.

In classical conditioning, **spontaneous recovery** is the temporary occurrence of the conditioned response in the presence of the conditioned stimulus.

Remember that all four phenomena—generalization, discrimination, extinction, and spontaneous recovery—occur in both operant and classical conditioning.

One distinctive characteristic of operant conditioning is that it usually has an observable response and an observable reinforcer. Next, we turn to cognitive learning, which may have neither observable response nor observable reinforcer. ●

Extinction: Bart stops behaviors if reinforcers stop. Spontaneous recovery: After extinction, Bart's behavior returns.

E Cognitive Learning

Three Viewpoints of Cognitive Learning

© Evan Agostini/Getty Images

At the beginning of this module, we told you about Tony Hawk,

How did Tony Hawk learn?

who as a child loved to watch skateboarders at the park. He began to practice skateboarding every chance he had so that he could imitate what he saw. Tony learned how to skateboard not from classical or operant conditioning but from another kind of learning process called cognitive learning.

Cognitive learning, which involves mental processes such as attention and memory, says that learning can occur through observation or imitation and such learning may not involve any external rewards or require a person to perform any observable behaviors.

The roots of cognitive learning extend back to the work of Wilhelm Wundt in the late 1800s (see p. 12) and Edward Tolman in the 1930s. It died in the 1950s, was reborn in the 1960s, and became popular in the 1990s. Currently, cognitive learning is extremely useful in explaining both animal and human behavior and was vital to the development of a new area called cognitive neuroscience (see p. 71) (Bandura, 2001a). We'll begin by discussing what three famous psychologists had to say about cognitive learning.

He learned by observing.

Against: B. F. Skinner

Eight days before his death, B. F. Skinner was honored by the American Psychological Association (APA) with the first APA Citation for Outstanding Lifetime Contribution to Psychology. In his acceptance speech to over 1,000 friends and colleagues, Skinner spoke of how psychology was splitting between those who were studying feelings and cognitive processes and those who were studying observable behaviors, such as animals

Skinner box illustration from *Introduction to Psychology*, by E. Bruce Goldstein, 1995. Brooks/Cole.

under controlled conditions (figure at right). In a sharp criticism of cognitive learning, Skinner said, "As far as I'm concerned, cognitive science is the creationism [downfall] of psychology" (Vargas, 1991, p. 1).

In the 1950s and 1960s, Skinner had advocated that psychology's goal should be to study primarily observable behaviors rather than cognitive processes.

However, psychologists gradually discovered that cognitive processes played a major role in human and animal activities and that such activities could not be understood or explained from observable behaviors alone. Today, the study of cognitive processes is a major goal of psychology (Bandura, 2001a).

In Favor: Edward Tolman

At about the same time that Skinner was emphasizing observable behaviors, Edward Tolman was exploring hidden mental processes. For example, he placed rats individually in a maze, such as the one shown below, and allowed each rat time to explore the maze with no food present. Then, with food present in the maze's food box, he tested the rat to see which path it took. The rat learned very quickly to take the shortest path. Next, Tolman blocked the shortest path to the food box. The first time the rat encountered the blocked shortest path, it selected the next shortest path

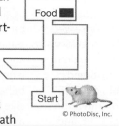

© PhotoDisc, Inc.

to the food box. According to Tolman (1948), the rat selected the next shortest path because it had developed a cognitive map of the maze.

A **cognitive map** is a mental representation in the brain of the layout of an environment and its features.

Tolman showed that the rats must have learned the layout of the maze while they wandered around trying to make their way through the maze. Therefore, the rats had demonstrated learning without evidence of performance, which is referred to as latent learning.

Latent learning is learning that is not demonstrated in behavior until its application becomes useful.

Tolman also showed that rats learned the layout of a maze without being reinforced, a position very different from Skinner's.

Psychologists continue to study cognitive processes in animals (J. Fischer & Menzel, 2011; Shettleworth, 2010). Tolman's animal research laid the groundwork for the study of cognitive processes in humans, which we discuss next.

In Favor: Albert Bandura

Albert Bandura began as a behaviorist in the Skinnerian tradition, which means focusing on observable behaviors and avoiding the study of mental events. Since then he has almost entirely shifted to a cognitive approach. In many of his studies, Bandura (1986) has focused on how humans learn through observing things. For example, Bandura says that a child can learn to hate spiders simply by observing the behaviors of someone who shows a great fear of spiders. This is an example of social cognitive learning.

© Michael Wesemann/Shutterstock.com

Social cognitive learning results from watching, imitating, and modeling and does not require the observer to perform any observable behavior or receive any observable reward.

Just as Tolman found that learning occurred while rats were exploring, Bandura found that humans learned while observing and that much (most) of human learning takes place through observation. Observational learning, which involves numerous cognitive processes, is a 180-degree change from Skinner's position, which had emphasized observable, noncognitive behaviors.

Following the death of Skinner in 1990, the study of cognitive processes has ballooned in popularity and usefulness. We'll introduce you to cognitive learning by describing one of Bandura's best-known studies, which involved a doll and a considerable amount of kicking and screaming.

Observational Learning

Do children learn by watching?

Perhaps a dozen experiments in psychology have become classics because they were the first to demonstrate some very important principles. One such classic experiment demonstrated the conditioning of emotional responses in "Little Albert" (see p. 204). Another classic is Albert Bandura (1965) and his colleagues' demonstration that children learned aggressive behaviors by watching an adult's aggressive behaviors. Learning through watching is called observational learning, which is a form of cognitive learning.

Bobo Doll Experiment

One reason this Bobo doll study is a classic experiment is that it challenged the idea that learning occurred through classical or operant conditioning. Children learned to perform aggressive responses simply from watching.

Why did children kick the Bobo doll?

Procedure. In one part of the room, preschool children were involved in their own art projects. In another part of the room, an adult got up and, for the next 10 minutes, kicked, hit, and yelled ("Hit him! Kick him!") at a large, inflated Bobo doll. Some children watched the model's aggressive behaviors, while other children did not.

© pzAxe/Shutterstock.com
© Craig McClain

After watching, children imitated adults kicking the doll.

Each child was later subjected to a frustrating situation and then placed in a room with toys, including the Bobo doll. Without the child's knowledge, researchers observed the child's behaviors.

Results. Children who had observed the model's aggressive attacks on the Bobo doll also kicked, hit, and yelled ("Hit him! Kick him!") at the doll. Through observational learning alone, these children learned the model's aggressive behaviors and were now performing them. In comparison, children who hadn't observed the model's behaviors didn't hit or kick the Bobo doll after they had been mildly frustrated.

Conclusion. Bandura's point is that children learned to perform specific aggressive behaviors not by practicing or being reinforced but simply by watching a live model perform behaviors. Observational learning is called modeling because it involves watching a model and imitating the behavior.

It turns out that observational learning may have a biological foundation. Recent research on mirror neurons (see p. 6) shows that they become activated when we observe others perform behaviors, which suggests we are biologically programmed to learn through observation (Iacoboni, 2008a; Van Gog et al., 2009).

Another finding of the Bobo doll study is that a child may learn by observing but then not perform the behavior. This is called the *learning–performance distinction.*

Learning Versus Performance

Is it possible that people learn by observing but do not necessarily perform what they have learned? To answer this question, Bandura and colleagues asked children to watch a movie in which someone hit and kicked a Bobo doll. However, after hitting and kicking the doll, the person in the film was punished by being criticized and spanked. Next, each child was left alone in a room filled with toys, including a Bobo doll.

Do you learn but not show it?

As the experimenters watched each child through a one-way mirror, they found that more boys than girls imitated the model and performed aggressive behaviors on Bobo. But not all the children imitated the model's aggressive behaviors. Next, each child who had not imitated the model's aggressive behaviors on Bobo was offered a reward (a sticker or some fruit juice) to imitate the model's behavior. With the promise of a reward, all of the children imitated the model's aggressive behaviors. We'll examine in more detail the girls' imitated aggressive behaviors, which were similar to the boys' but more dramatic.

As the graph below shows, girls imitated an average of 0.5 aggressive behaviors after watching a film of a model who performed aggressive behaviors on Bobo and then was punished for being aggressive. In other

Average Number of Aggressive Responses	
0.5 Watched punished model	
Rewarded for imitating	3.0

© Craig McClain

words, after observing a model being punished for aggressive behaviors, girls imitated almost none of the model's aggressive behaviors. However, when the same girls were promised a reward for imitating the model's aggressive behaviors, these girls imitated an average of 3.0 aggressive behaviors (Bandura, 1965).

So what does this experiment show? It shows that the girls had actually *learned* the model's aggressive behaviors through observation but that some did not *perform* these behaviors until they were rewarded for doing so (Bandura, 1965). This is an example of the learning–performance distinction.

The **learning–performance distinction** means that learning may occur but may not always be measured by, or immediately evident in, performance.

S _ _ T

Child imitates adult's speech.

The learning–performance distinction may be demonstrated by young children, often to the embarrassment of their parents. For instance, a young child may overhear a "dirty" word but not repeat the word until out in public. Repeating a "dirty" word shows that the child had learned the word through observation but waited until later to imitate the parent and actually say (perform) the "dirty" word.

Based on the Bobo doll study and others, Bandura developed a theory of cognitive learning that we'll examine next.

Bandura's Social Cognitive Theory

Would you hold this spider?

The idea that humans gather information about their environments and the behaviors of others through observation is a key part of Bandura's (2001a) social cognitive theory of learning.

Social cognitive theory emphasizes the importance of observation, imitation, and self-reward in the development and learning of social skills, personal interactions, and many other behaviors. Unlike operant and classical

© Michael Wesemann/Shutterstock.com

conditioning, this theory says that it is not necessary to perform any observable behaviors or receive any external rewards to learn.

Bandura believes that four processes—attention, memory, imitation, and motivation—operate during social cognitive learning. We'll explain how these processes operate in decreasing fear of spiders and snakes.

Social Cognitive Learning: Four Processes

1 Attention

The observer must pay attention to what the model says or does. In the photo at right, a nonfrightened person (model) holds a huge spider while a woman (observer) looks on in fear.

© Dirk Freder/iStockphoto

2 Memory

The observer must store or remember the information so that it can be retrieved and used later. The observer in the photo will store the image of seeing a nonfrightened person (model) holding a spider.

After observing the fearless model, the woman may learn not to fear spiders.

3 Imitation

The observer must be able to use the remembered information to guide his or her own actions and thus imitate the model's behavior. The observer in the photo will later try to imitate the model's calm behavior when holding a spider.

4 Motivation

The observer must have some reason or incentive to imitate the model's behavior. The observer in the photo is motivated to overcome her fear of spiders because she wants to go on camping trips. If this observer can successfully imitate the model's calm behavior, then she will overcome her fear of spiders and be able to go camping with her friends. This example shows how Bandura's four mental processes operate during social cognitive learning.

© Andrei Zarubaika/Shutterstock.com

The next study by Bandura shows how social cognitive learning, which usually takes some time and effort, decreased fear of snakes.

Social Cognitive Learning Applied to Fear of Snakes

Background. Although most people are wary of snakes, some develop an intense fear of them. Bandura and colleagues recruited study participants who had developed such an intense fear of snakes that they avoided many normal outdoor activities, such as hiking or gardening (Bandura et al., 1969). The participants' fear of snakes was objectively measured by noting how many of 29 steps of increasingly frightening actions they would perform. For example, step 1 was approaching a glass cage containing a snake; step 29 was putting the snake in their laps and letting it crawl around while holding their hands at their sides.

Treatment. One group of participants watched as a model handled a live, 4-foot, harmless king snake. After watching for 15 minutes, the participants were invited to gradually move closer to the snake. Then the model demonstrated touching the snake and asked the participants to imitate her actions. As the model held the snake, the participants were encouraged to touch the snake with a gloved hand. Another group of participants, who also reported an intense fear of snakes, received no treatment (control group).

Social cognitive learning helped this woman overcome her fear of snakes.

Results and conclusion. As the graph below shows, the participants who watched a live model handle a snake and who imitated some of the model's behaviors scored an average of 27 on the 29-step approach scale.

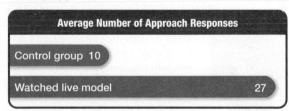

Average Number of Approach Responses	
Control group	10
Watched live model	27

Bar graph data from "Relative Efficacy of Densensitization and Modeling Approaches for Inducing Behavior, Affective and Attitudinal Changes," by A. Bandura, E. B. Blanchard & B. Ritter, 1969, *Journal of Personality and Social Psychology, 13*, 173–179.

In contrast, the participants in the control group scored an average of only 10 approach behaviors on the 29-step scale. This study clearly showed that behavior can be greatly changed through social cognitive learning, which emphasizes observation and imitation.

Bandura believes that humans acquire a great amount of information about fears, social roles, discrimination, and personal interactions through social cognitive learning. We'll discuss other aspects of cognitive learning and memory in Modules 11 and 12.

Next, we'll describe another kind of cognitive learning that involves what is often described as the "aha!" feeling.

Insight Learning

Earlier we told you that Thorndike studied how cats learned to escape from a puzzle box to get a piece of fish. Thorndike concluded that learn-

What is a flash of insight?

ing occurred through a process of trial and error as cats gradually formed associations between moving the latch and opening the door. None of the cats showed any evidence of suddenly discovering the solution of how to escape the box.

About the same time that Thorndike in America was studying the trial-and-error learning of cats escaping from a puzzle box, Wolfgang Köhler in

Aha!

Flash of insight

Germany was studying how chimpanzees learned to obtain bananas that were out of reach. Köhler challenged Thorndike's conclusion that animals learned only through trial and error. Köhler suggested instead that cats and other animals that were observed under the proper circumstances could solve a problem in a sudden flash, known as insight or the "aha!" experience (G. Cook, 2002).

Insight is a mental process marked by the sudden and unexpected solution to a problem: a phenomenon often called the "aha!" experience.

Here's an example of Köhler's chimp, Sultan, who showed insight in getting a banana that was hanging out of reach.

Köhler and Sultan the Chimp

How did the chimp get the banana?

This classic experiment in psychology suggested a new kind of learning.

What Köhler (1925) did was to hang a banana from the ceiling in a room that had a box placed off to one side. The banana was too high for Sultan the chimp to grab by reaching or jumping. When Sultan first entered the room, he paced restlessly for about 5 minutes. Then he got the box, moved it toward the banana, climbed onto the box, jumped up, and seized the banana. On his second try, Sultan quickly moved the box directly beneath the banana and jumped up to get it.

What intrigued Köhler about Sultan's problem-solving behavior was that it seemed to differ greatly from the random trial-and-error behavior of Thorndike's cats. Before Sultan arrived at a solution, he might pace about, sit quietly, or vainly grasp at the out-of-reach banana. Then, all of a sudden, he seemed to hit on the solution and immediately executed a complicated set of behaviors, such as standing on a box, to get the banana. Köhler believed that Sultan's sudden solution to a problem was an example of *insight,* a mental process quite different from what Thorndike had observed in the random trial-and-error learning of cats.

However, critics of Köhler's insight studies pointed out that he did not explain how chimps solved problems; rather, he simply described the process. Köhler replied that his studies on insight were more a way to study problem solving than an explanation of what was happening in the chimp's head. The significance of Köhler's work was

Chimp stood on a box and jumped up to reach the banana.

that it represented a method for studying learning that was different from either classical conditioning or trial-and-error learning (Pierce, 1999). Since the early 1990s, there has been a renewed interest in studying the workings of the animal mind, which is called animal cognition (Shettleworth, 2010; Wynne, 2001).

Next, we'll take a closer look at the "aha!" experience.

Characteristics of the "Aha!" Experience

What's the "aha!" experience?

Just as Sultan the chimp seemed to suddenly arrive at a solution to a problem, humans also report the experience of suddenly and unexpectedly solving a challenging or difficult problem. We call this phenomenon the "aha!" experience or a flash of insight.

Researchers generally agree that there are four main characteristics of the "aha!" experience (Topolinski & Reber, 2010):

1 Suddenness
The solution to a problem one has been trying to solve for some time pops into the mind abruptly and unexpectedly.

2 Ease
However difficult it was to try to solve the problem before, the solution is now processed easily and quickly.

3 Positive affect
Immediately as the solution enters the mind, the person feels genuinely positive.

4 Truth and confidence
Upon having an insight or an "aha!" experience, the person evaluates the solution as being true and expresses confidence in the accuracy of the solution.

Although researchers have been trying to identify the brain processes that result in an insight, they have yet to formulate a coherent, thorough explanation. However, they have reported some interesting findings regarding the association between brain activity and "aha!" experiences. For example, researchers found that there is a clear shift in neural activity during insight. Neurons that are active before the "aha!" moment calm down, whereas neurons that are only minimally active fire up. Researchers do not yet know whether the change in brain activity causes the insight or the insight causes the change in brain activity (Durstewitz et al., 2010).

We have discussed three examples of cognitive learning: Tolman's idea of cognitive maps, Bandura's theory of social cognitive learning, and Köhler's study of insightful problem solving. After the Concept Review, we'll explain why biological factors make some things easier and some things harder to learn. ●

Concept Review

Skinner box illustration from Introduction to Psychology, by E. Bruce Goldstein, 1995. Brooks/Cole.

1. The kind of learning in which the consequences that follow some behavior increase or decrease the likelihood that the behavior will occur in the future is called _____.

2. In operant conditioning, the organism voluntarily performs or **(a)** _____ a behavior. Immediately following an emitted behavior, the occurrence of a **(b)** _____ increases the likelihood that the behavior will occur again.

3. Because an organism may not immediately emit the desired behavior, a procedure is used to reinforce behaviors that lead to or approximate the final target behavior. This procedure is called _____.

4. In operant conditioning, the term *consequences* refers to either **(a)** _____, which increases the likelihood that a behavior will occur again, or **(b)** _____, which decreases the likelihood that a behavior will occur again.

© Alex Staroseltsev/Shutterstock.com

5. If the occurrence of some response is increased because it is followed by a pleasant stimulus, the stimulus is called a **(a)** _____. An increase in the occurrence of some response because it is followed either by the removal of an unpleasant stimulus or by avoiding the stimulus is called **(b)** _____.

© Roman Sonetov/Shutterstock.com

6. A stimulus, such as food, water, or sex, that is innately satisfying and requires no learning to become pleasurable is a **(a)** _____. A stimulus, such as grades or praise, that has acquired its reinforcing power through experience and learning is a **(b)** _____.

7. The various ways that reinforcers occur after a behavior has been emitted are referred to as **(a)** _____ of reinforcement. For example, if each and every target behavior is reinforced, it is called **(b)** _____ reinforcement. If behaviors are not reinforced each time they occur, it is called **(c)** _____ reinforcement.

8. When an organism emits the same response to similar stimuli, it is called **(a)** _____. When a response is emitted in the presence of a stimulus that is reinforced and not in the presence of unreinforced stimuli, it is called **(b)** _____.
© DPS/Shutterstock.com

A decrease in emitting a behavior because it is no longer reinforced is called **(c)** _____. If an organism performs a behavior again without its being reinforced, it is called **(d)** _____.

9. A kind of learning that involves mental processes, that may be learned through observation and imitation, and that may not require any external rewards or the performance of any observable behaviors is referred to as _____.

10. Tolman studied the behavior of rats that were allowed to explore a maze without any reward given. When food was present, rats quickly learned to select the next shortest path if a previously taken path was blocked. Tolman said that rats had developed a mental representation of the layout, which he called a _____.

11. Although an organism may learn a behavior through observation or exploration, the organism may not immediately demonstrate or perform the newly learned behavior. This phenomenon is known as the _____ distinction.
© Craig McClain

12. According to Bandura, one form of learning that develops through watching and imitation and that does not require the observer to perform any observable behavior or receive a reinforcer is called **(a)** _____ learning. Bandura believes that humans gather much information from their **(b)** _____ through social cognitive learning.
© Lana Langlois/Shutterstock.com © Melinda Fawver/Shutterstock.com

13. Bandura's theory of social cognitive learning involves four mental processes. The observer must pay **(a)** _____ to what the model says or does. The observer must then code the information and be able to retrieve it from **(b)** _____ for use at a later time. The observer must be able to use the coded information to guide his or her **(c)** _____ in performing and imitating the model's behavior. Finally, the observer must be **(d)** _____ to perform the behavior, which involves some reason, reinforcement, or incentive.
© Michael Wesemann/Shutterstock.com

14. In Köhler's study of problem solving in chimps, he identified a mental process marked by the sudden occurrence of a solution, which he termed **(a)** _____. This phenomenon is another example of **(b)** _____ learning.
© Maridav/Shutterstock.com

Answers: 1. operant conditioning; 2. (a) emits, (b) reinforcer or reinforcer; 4. (a) reinforcement, (b) punishment; 5. (a) positive reinforcer, (b) negative reinforcement; 6. (a) primary reinforcer, (b) secondary reinforcer; 7. (a) schedules, (b) continuous, (c) partial; 8. (a) generalization, (b) discrimination, (c) extinction, (d) spontaneous recovery; 9. cognitive learning; 10. cognitive map; 11. learning–performance; 12. (a) social cognitive, (b) environments; 13. (a) attention, (b) memory, (c) motor control, (d) motivated; 14. (a) insight, (b) cognitive

F Biological Factors

Definition

You may remember having difficulty learning to read, write, ride a bike, drive a car, put on makeup, or shave. But

Why do monkeys play with objects?

do you remember having problems learning to play? For a young child, playing just seems to come naturally. Just as children engage in play behavior with little or no encouragement, reward, or learning, so too do monkeys. For example, young monkeys are often observed interacting with objects for apparently no other reason than play (right photo). In fact, most young mammals engage in various play behaviors, which are not easily explained by the three traditional learning procedures—classical conditioning, operant conditioning, and cognitive learning (S. Brownlee, 1997). Observations of animals and humans indicate that some behaviors, such as play, are easily and effortlessly learned partly because of innate biological factors.

© Ilya D. Gridnev/Shutterstock.com

Animals have innate tendencies, such as playing with objects.

Biological factors are innate tendencies or predispositions that may either facilitate or inhibit certain kinds of learning.

Researchers suggest that animals and humans may have evolved biological predispositions to learn play behaviors because they have adaptive functions—for example, developing social relationships among peers and learning behaviors useful for adult roles (Burghardt, 2005; Dugatkin & Bekoff, 2003). This means that animals and humans have innate biological factors or predispositions that make certain kinds of learning, such as play behavior, very easy and effortless.

Besides play behavior, we'll discuss two other examples of learning—imprinting and preparedness—that are learned early and easily because of biological factors.

Imprinting

Soon after they hatch and without any apparent learning, baby chicks follow their mother hen.

Why do young chicks follow their mother?

This following behavior was not explained by any of the principles of learning identified by Pavlov (classical conditioning), Thorndike (trial-and-error learning), or Skinner (operant conditioning). The baby chick's seemingly unlearned behavior of following its mother was a different kind of learning that was first identified by ethologists.

Ethologists are behavioral biologists who observe and study animal behavior in the animal's natural environment or under relatively naturalistic conditions.

For example, an Austrian ethologist, Konrad Lorenz (1952), studied chicks, goslings, and ducks, which can all move around minutes after hatching. He discovered that these baby animals followed the first moving object they saw, which was usually their mother. This following behavior is an example of imprinting.

© PhotoDisc, Inc.

Baby ducks automatically follow the first moving object.

Imprinting refers to inherited tendencies or responses that are displayed by newborn animals when they encounter certain stimuli in their environment.

Imprinting is an unlearned behavior that is based on biological factors and that has great survival value: It increases the chances that newly hatched birds will remain with and follow their parent instead of wandering off into the waiting jaws of predators. Besides being unlearned, Lorenz noted two other major differences between imprinting and other kinds of learning.

Sensitive period. Unlike classical conditioning, operant conditioning, and cognitive learning, which occur throughout an animal's life, imprinting occurs best during the first few hours after hatching. This brief time period is called the critical, or sensitive, period.

The **critical,** or **sensitive, period** is the relatively brief time during which learning is most likely to occur.

Normally, the first object that newly hatched ducks see is their parent, upon whom they imprint. Thus, imprinting is a way for newly hatched animals to establish social attachments to members of their species. Although newly hatched birds will imprint on almost any moving object that they first see, including a human, a colored ball, or a glove, they imprint more strongly on moving objects that look or sound like their parent. Only birds that can walk immediately after hatching show imprinting, which promotes their survival (Bateson, 1991).

Irreversible. Unlike classical conditioning, operant conditioning, and cognitive learning, whose effects are usually reversible, imprinting is essentially irreversible. Most likely, imprinting evolved to be irreversible so that a young duck would not imprint on its mother one week and then imprint on a sly fox the next week.

In a program to prevent the California condor from becoming extinct, condor chicks are hatched at the San Diego Zoo and raised by humans. Because imprinting occurs very early and is irreversible, special precautions are taken so that the condor will not imprint on humans.

For example, the young condor chick shown on the right is being fed by a puppet that resembles an adult condor's head rather than a human's hand. The "puppet mother" helps the young condor imprint on real condor characteristics. When this condor grows up and is introduced into the wild, it will establish social relationships with, and attempt to mate with, its own species.

© ZSSD/MINDEN PICTURES/National Geographic Stock

"Puppet mother" feeds baby condor.

Another example of how biological factors increase the ease and speed of learning is evident in something called prepared learning.

Prepared Learning

Why was learning to talk so easy? You easily learned to talk but probably had trouble learning to read because of how your brain is organized, which illustrates the importance of biological factors. We'll discuss how biological factors help humans learn to speak different languages and birds learn to remember thousands of places where they hid food.

Incredible Memory

How do birds remember?

Remembers thousands of hidden food places

There are small birds, called Clark's nutcrackers, that live in an area where almost no food is available in the winter. During autumn, nutcrackers hide stores of food in underground places in perhaps as many as 2,500 to 6,000 different locations. During winter, nutcrackers survive by finding and digging up their hidden stores of food. How do nutcrackers locate their thousands of hidden stores? One explanation is preparedness, which we discussed earlier (see p. 200).

Preparedness, or **prepared learning,** is the innate or biological tendency of animals to recognize, attend to, and store certain cues over others, as well as to associate some combinations of conditioned and unconditioned stimuli more easily than others.

Under somewhat natural conditions, researchers observed the amazing ability of nutcrackers to hide and find hundreds of hidden stores of food. Researchers found that nutcrackers use natural landmarks (trees, stones, bushes) to form cognitive maps that help them remember the locations of their hidden stores (B. M. Gibson & Kamil, 2001; B. M. Gibson & Wilks, 2008).

One reason nutcrackers have such phenomenal memories is that the areas of their brains involved in memory are larger than the same areas in birds that do not store food. Specifically, the hippocampus, which is involved in transferring short-term memories into long-term memories, is larger in nutcrackers than in nonstoring birds (S. D. Healy et al., 2005). Thus, the nutcracker is biologically prepared for surviving winters by having a larger hippocampus (right figure), which helps it better remember the locations of thousands of food stores.

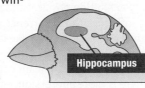

Hippocampus

Just as some birds are biologically prepared to remember the locations of critical hidden stores, humans are biologically prepared to make sounds and speak at least one of 6,800 different languages.

Incredible Sounds

How do infants make "word" sounds?

In the late 1940s, two psychologists raised a chimp in their home, along with their own child, because they wanted to know if this "speaking" environment would help a chimp learn to speak. However, after 6 years of trying, the chimp had learned to say a grand total of three words: "mama," "papa," and "cup" (Hayes & Hayes, 1951). At that time, these two psychologists did not know that the chimp's vocal apparatus and brain were not biologically prepared to produce the sounds and words necessary for human speech (see the discussion of animal language on pp. 322–323).

Chimp does not have vocal structures to speak.

The reason humans but not chimps or other animals learn to speak so easily is that humans' vocal apparatus and brains are biologically prepared, or innately wired, for speaking (Pinker, 1994).

Infant's brain is prewired for speaking.

For example, the brain of a newborn infant is biologically prepared to recognize the differences in human speech sounds. Researchers discovered this ability by playing speech sounds to infants whose rate of sucking on a nipple was being recorded. After newborns heard the sound "ba" over and over, their rate of sucking slowed, indicating that they were paying little attention to the sound. But, as soon as researchers played the sound "pa," the infants' rate of sucking increased, indicating that they had noticed the relatively small change between the sounds "ba" and "pa." This study showed that infants' brains are prewired or biologically prepared (figure below) to recognize and discriminate among sounds that are essential for learning speech (Buonomano & Merzenich, 1995). In fact, infants all around the world make similar babbling sounds, which indicates the influence and importance of biological factors in learning to speak.

Conclusion. The learning principles of Pavlov, Thorndike, and Skinner do not, by themselves, explain how rats form cognitive maps, how infants easily produce and discriminate among human speech sounds, how nutcrackers remember thousands of hiding places for stored food, why monkeys engage in play behavior, and why newborn chicks follow the first moving object. All these examples indicate how innate biological factors, such as differences in size or organization of brain structures, play a major role in preparing and helping animals and humans learn certain kinds of behaviors that are useful for their maintenance and survival.

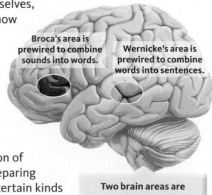

Broca's area is prewired to combine sounds into words.

Wernicke's area is prewired to combine words into sentences.

Two brain areas are prewired for speaking.

Next, we'll return to observational learning and discuss the effects of viewing relational and physical aggression in the media. ●

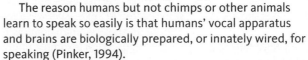

Relational and Physical Aggression in the Media

Can watching meanness make you aggressive?

Earlier in this module, we discussed observational learning, which is when an individual learns specific behaviors simply by watching someone engage in the behaviors.

Researchers have long been interested in whether watching aggression or violence in the media (television, movies) makes people more aggressive. Numerous studies have found that watching physical aggression in the media does in fact increase physical aggression in viewers. However, physical aggression

is not the only type of violence portrayed in the media. For example, relational aggression, such as verbal bullying, ostracizing peers, and spreading rumors, is also frequently portrayed. Is it possible that viewing relational aggression, such as meanness, can increase people's relational aggression behaviors or even their physical aggression behaviors? Researchers explored this very question (S. M. Coyne et al., 2008).

> Observing physical aggression in the media increases physically aggressive behaviors in viewers.

Study: Effects of Viewing Physical and Relational Aggression in the Media

Participants. They were 53 female university students with an average age of 23.

Procedure. The women were randomly assigned to one of three groups, each to watch a different video. One video featured physical aggression (a knife fight from *Kill Bill*), another featured relational aggression (a collection of scenes from *Mean Girls*), and a third featured no aggression (a scene from *What Lies Beneath* showing people engaging in a ritual to communicate with spirits).

After watching the videos, all participants completed a questionnaire about their past aggressive behaviors. As the women left the room to go home, another researcher asked if they would participate in a second study (it's actually part of the original study). The women were told this second study would examine their reaction times in completing puzzle tasks. Once participants said yes and began working on the puzzles, the researcher intentionally behaved in a very rude manner by telling them to hurry, pacing with a stopwatch, and sighing loudly. When the participants later expressed low confidence about their performance, the researcher blamed them for ruining her study. She was doing a great job of acting rude!

Participants were then asked to engage in a competitive reaction time test (pushing buttons really fast) and to choose from ten noise levels to be administered to their opponent each time they lose the button-pushing contest. At the very end, participants completed evaluation forms for the rude experimenter.

Results. Participants who viewed the videos featuring physical and relational aggression reacted in aggressive ways. When instructed to administer a loud, sharp noise to their opponent, these women administered a louder noise than women who watched a video with no aggression (example of physical aggression). On a questionnaire to be used supposedly to help decide whether the rude researcher should be hired, these women rated the rude researcher lower than the women who did not watch aggression (example of relational aggression) (S. M. Coyne et al., 2008; Toppo, 2008).

Physical Aggression   **Relational Aggression**

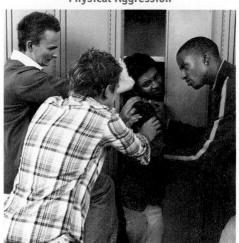

> Participants who viewed either physical or relational aggression were more likely to subsequently engage in physical and relational aggression than participants who didn't view any aggression.

Conclusion. Viewing either physical or relational aggression in the media leads to an increased likelihood of people subsequently exhibiting physical and relational aggression. Also, watching one form of aggression can influence the occurrence of other forms of aggression. For example, observing relational aggression can make it more likely for someone to subsequently engage in physical aggression.

The popularity of reality television shows may have significant consequences on viewers' aggressive behavior. This is because there is more aggression, especially relational aggression, in reality programs than in nonreality programs. Also, the aggression seen on reality programs may be the most likely to be imitated, given the realistic portrayal of the aggression (S. M. Coyne et al., 2010). For these reasons it is important for researchers to study the effects of viewing aggression in reality programs.

Another example of how learning principles can be applied to human behavior is learning to play the violin, which we'll discuss next. ●

Suzuki Method

What's the Suzuki method? In the 1940s, a violin player and teacher from Japan, Shinichi Suzuki, developed a remarkably successful method for teaching violin playing to very young children (S. Suzuki, 1998). His method, called the *Suzuki method,* was brought to the United States in the mid-1960s and has generated incredible enthusiasm among children, parents, and music teachers ever since (Gokturk, 2008).

It's interesting to learn that the basic principles of the Suzuki method for teaching young children to play the

Suzuki's method of teaching young children to play musical instruments has many similarities with Bandura's principles of social cognitive learning.

violin are very similar to Bandura's four mental processes for social cognitive learning. What's different is that Suzuki developed his learning principles after years of actually teaching young children to play the violin, whereas Bandura developed his four mental processes of observational learning after years of research with young children. We'll discuss how even though Suzuki the teacher and Bandura the researcher lived in very different cultures thousands of miles apart, their experiences led them to similar conclusions about how children learn.

Different Cultures but Similar Learning Principles

1 Attention

Bandura states that the observer must pay attention to what the model says and does.

Similarly, Suzuki advises parents to teach violin information only when the child is actually looking at and watching the parent. Parents are told to stop teaching and wait if the child rolls on the floor, jumps up and down, walks backward, or talks about unrelated things.

The recommended age for starting a child with the Suzuki method is 3 for girls and 4 for boys. Parents are cautioned, however, that the attention span of the 3- to 4-year-old child is extremely limited, usually from 30 seconds to at most several minutes at a time.

2 Memory

Bandura says that the observer must code the information in such a way that it can be retrieved and used later.

Similarly, Suzuki tells parents that they should present information in ways that a young child can understand (Bandura would say code). Because a 3- to 4-year-old child does not have fully developed verbal skills or memory, little time is spent giving verbal instructions. Instead, the young child is given violin information through games and exercises. For example, children are taught how to hold the violin, use the bow, and press the strings by first playing games with their hands. Children are taught how to read music (notes) only when they are older and have gained some technical skill at playing the violin.

3 Imitation

Bandura says the observer must be able to use the information to guide his or her own actions and thus imitate the model's behavior.

Similarly, Suzuki suggests that children start at about 3 or 4 years old, the earliest age when they can physically perform the required movements and imitate their parents and teachers. Girls can start earlier than boys because girls physically mature earlier. For other instruments, the starting times are different—piano, 4–5 years; cello, 5 years; flute, 9 years—because these instruments require more physical dexterity. As you have probably guessed, 3- and 4-year-olds start with miniature violins and move up to bigger ones as they develop.

4 Motivation

Bandura says that the observer must have some reason, reinforcement, or incentive to perform the model's behaviors.

Similarly, Suzuki emphasizes that the most important role of the parent is to constantly reward and reinforce the child for observing and "doing what Mommy or Daddy is doing." Suzuki recommends several ways to keep motivation high in young children: Be an active and interested model for the child, play violin games that are fun for the child, avoid games or lessons that involve competition, and never push the child beyond the level that he or she is capable of reaching (Slone, 1985).

Social cognitive learning involves attention, memory, imitation, and motivation.

Conclusion. Parents and teachers who have used the Suzuki method report great success (Lamb, 1990). As you can judge, the basic principles of the Suzuki method for teaching violin are quite similar to Bandura's four mental processes for social cognitive learning. Both Suzuki and Bandura recognized the importance of observational learning and how much information children can learn from watching and imitating models. Suzuki's successful method of teaching young children to play the violin provides support for Bandura's four mental processes that he believes are involved in social cognitive learning.

Next, we'll discuss how operant learning principles were used to develop a method for teaching autistic children. ●

I Application: Behavior Modification

Definitions

What is behavior mod?

In this module, we have discussed how operant conditioning principles are used to decrease food refusal in young children (p. 216), to toilet train children (p. 216), to prevent children from eating paint chips (p. 218), and to stop children from engaging in dangerous behaviors (p. 219). These are all examples of behavior modification (Miltenberger, 2007).

Behavior modification is a treatment or therapy that changes or modifies problems or undesirable behaviors by using principles of learning based on operant conditioning, classical conditioning, and social cognitive learning.

For over 40 years, psychologist and researcher Ivar Lovaas of the University of California at Los Angeles has used behavior modification or, more colloquially, behavior mod to treat autism.

Autism is a condition marked by poor development in social relationships, such as not wanting to be touched, not making eye contact, and hiding to avoid people (see drawing); great difficulty

Behavior mod is used to treat autism.

developing language and communicating; very few activities and interests; and long periods of time spent repeating the same behaviors or motor patterns, or following rituals that interfere with more normal functioning. Symptoms range from mild to severe and usually appear when a child is about 2 to 3 years old (American Psychiatric Association, 2000). (We discussed the symptoms and causes of autism more thoroughly in Module 1.)

Parents, doctors, and policy makers all agree that the best method to address the above symptoms, especially deficits in forming relationships and communicating, in autistic children is to enroll them in intensive behavioral treatment (between 20 and 40 hours a week) as early as possible (Ingersoll, 2011). There is no evidence that any treatment leads to a complete recovery, but without treatment, many autistics will remain socially unresponsive (Carey, 2004; Kabot et al., 2003). We'll discuss the behavior mod treatment developed by Ivar Lovaas, who combined principles of operant conditioning and social cognitive learning (Lovaas & Buch, 1997; Lovaas Institute, 2012).

Behavior Modification and Autism

Lovaas's program at UCLA, which is called the Young Autism Project, treats 2- to 3-year-old autistic children with a 40-hour-per-week program that runs for 2 to 3 years. Here's part of the program.

What kind of training?

Program. Lovaas's training program actually consists of hundreds of separate teaching programs, many of them using principles of operant conditioning: Select a specific **target behavior, shape the behavior,** and use **positive reinforcers** of praise and food that are given immediately after the child emits the desired behavior. For example, here's a program to increase making eye contact.

Target behavior is getting the child to make eye contact following the command "Look at me."

Shaping the behavior involves two steps.

Step 1. Have the child sit in a chair facing you. Give the command "Look at me" every 5–10 seconds. When the child makes a correct response of looking at you, say "Good looking" and simultaneously reward the child with food.

Step 2. Continue until the child repeatedly obeys the command "Look at me." Then gradually increase the duration of the child's eye contact from 1 second to periods of 2 to 3 seconds.

Using this behavior mod program, therapists and parents have had success in teaching autistic children to make eye contact, to stop constant rocking, to respond to verbal requests such as "Wash your hands," to interact with peers, to speak, and to engage in school tasks such as reading and writing (Lovaas, 1993).

Results. Lovaas and his colleagues did a long-term study of 19 children diagnosed as autistic. Behavior modification training went on for at least 40 hours per week for 2 years or more. At the end of the training, 47% (9/19) of the autistic children reached normal status (Lovaas, 1987). These children acquired sufficient language, social, and self-help behaviors to enter preschool and successfully complete first

47% reach normal status after behavior mod training.

grade in public school. Many of the children did so well that the teachers didn't know they were autistic.

However, even with intensive training, 40% of autistic children continued to have mild intellectual impairment, and 10% continued to have severe intellectual impairment. In comparison, in a control group of autistic children who received only minimal treatment, only 2% achieved normal intellectual and educational functioning, while 45% continued to have mild intellectual impairment and 53% continued to have severe intellectual impairment (Eikeseth, 2001; Lovaas & Buch, 1997; McEachin et al., 1993). Researchers concluded that without intensive behavior modification treatment, autistic children will continue to show severe behavioral deficits.

Follow-up. A six-year follow-up study of the nine children who had reached normal status found that they had kept their gains and were still functioning normally (Lovaas, 1999). A later follow-up study of the same nine children, then 20 to 30 years old, showed that eight appeared normal—that is, did not score differently from other normal adults on a variety of tests—while one had personality problems but would not be classified as autistic (Lovaas, 1999).

Health care specialists concluded that autism therapy can be effective provided it begins early (child 2–3 years old) and includes one-on-one training for a minimum of 25 hours a week, 12 months a year for several years (Tarkan, 2002). However, such therapy is so costly ($72,000 a year) that fewer than 10% of autistic children are receiving the recommended level of treatment (Lord, 2002; Wallis, 2006). It can cost over $2 million to take care of a person with autism over his or her lifetime, and the societal costs of caring for people with autism exceeds $126 billion a year, more than triple the cost in 2006 (Autism Speaks, 2012; HSPH, 2006).

As you'll learn next, behavior modification is an effective treatment program for many other conditions in addition to autism.

Contingency Management

How is it used? A type of behavior modification based on operant conditioning principles, which is often used in mental health and substance abuse treatment programs, is contingency management.

Contingency management is the systematic reinforcement of desired behaviors and the withholding of reinforcement or punishment of undesired behaviors.

Earlier in this module (p. 219) we discussed how children earned coupons for eating fruits and vegetables at lunch during school. They could exchange the coupons for fun prizes. This is an example of contingency management. Children were systematically reinforced with coupons after demonstrating the desired behavior of eating fruits and vegetables.

The use of contingency management has been shown to be especially effective in drug treatment and company wellness programs. For instance, contingency management has helped homeless people with HIV remember to take their medication, cocaine addicts to improve their punctual arrival to work, and workers to improve their health by spending more time exercising in the gym (Dingfelder, 2011). Let's take a look at a few research studies.

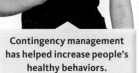

I earned money for eating healthfully.

Contingency management has helped increase people's healthy behaviors.

A drug treatment program that paid an average of $5 per day to HIV-positive methadone patients who took their medication increased pill taking from 56% to 78% (Sorensen et al., 2007). These results are impressive and important because failure to take these medications can be life threatening. There are numerous other studies supporting the effectiveness of contingency management in drug treatment programs (Schumacher et al., 2007). Also, the use of contingency management in drug courts has been shown to reduce the number of repeat offenses by nearly 35% (Marlowe, 2011).

In an effort to improve people's health, researchers paid participants to eat more healthfully. The participants who received money for healthy eating lost an average of eight more pounds during the study than the participants who didn't receive any pay for their healthy eating (John et al., 2011). In an effort to keep their health insurance costs down while improving the health of their employees, many companies are implementing various types of contingency management programs.

Our last example of behavior modification deals with concerns about using punishment to decrease undesirable behaviors.

Pros and Cons of Punishment

About 61% of parents believe that spanking is an acceptable form of discipline for young children, and 94% of 3- and 4-year-olds have been spanked during the past year (O'Callaghan, 2006). Since spanking may immediately stop undesirable behaviors, it has been and remains a popular form of discipline. But spanking is surrounded with controversy because it is associated with numerous negative side effects and may be a less desirable form of punishment (discipline) than the time-out procedure. We'll discuss the pros and cons of each.

Should it be used?

Spanking is associated with undesirable side effects.

Spanking: Positive Punishment
Since spanking involves the presentation of an aversive stimulus (pain), it is an example of positive punishment. Researchers disagree on the use of spanking. Some argue that all spanking is bad because many studies have shown that it can lead to increased aggression, physical injury, antisocial behavior, anxiety, and other mental health problems (B. L. Smith, 2012; C. Taylor, 2012). For instance, researchers found that those children who were spanked most frequently at age three were more likely to be aggressive at age 5 (C. A. Taylor et al., 2010). Others agree that severe spanking administered by harsh parents is always bad, but they think that mild to moderate spanking used as one form of discipline by loving parents does not necessarily have undesirable or negative side effects (Baumrind et al., 2002). Yet others state that although spanking can work temporarily to stop undesirable behavior, spanking does not work in the long term (Graham-Bermann, 2012).

The American Academy of Pediatrics (AAP) states that it is never appropriate to use spanking. They report it is a form of punishment that becomes less effective the more it is used. Instead, they recommend the use of time-out (AAP, 1998).

Time-Out: Negative Punishment
Another form of discipline is time-out, which was discussed earlier (see p. 219). Time-out is an example of negative punishment because it involves the removal of a reinforcing stimulus (desirable reward) so that some undesirable response will not recur. For example, after misbehaving, a child is given a time-out period (stays in a corner without games, books, or toys). Time-out is most effective when used consistently and combined with teaching the child alternative desired behaviors using positive reinforcers (J. Taylor & Miller, 1997).

Compared to spanking, time-out has fewer undesirable side effects; it does not provide a model of aggression and does not elicit severe negative emotional reactions. Thus, when it is necessary to discipline a child, care should be taken in choosing between positive punishment (spanking) and negative punishment (time-out). Although both kinds of punishment stop or suppress undesirable behaviors, spanking has more negative side effects than time-out, and time-out has been shown to be effective in eliminating undesirable behaviors. Both kinds of punishment are best used in combination with positive reinforcers so the child also learns to perform desirable behaviors (Nichols, 2004). ●

Time-out has fewer undesirable side effects than spanking.

How Do You Train a Killer Whale?

If you have ever been to a marine park, then you most certainly have been entertained by watching the marvelous marine animal performances. In one show an enormous killer whale jumps through a ring suspended in air, waves to audience members with its fins, swims backward while standing up on its tail, and gently kisses a brave volunteer. Whales are taught to perform these impressive behaviors with the use of operant and classical conditioning techniques.

Operant conditioning is used to train whales because when the consequences of performing a specific behavior are reinforcing, the whale will likely repeat the behavior. Positive reinforcers for whales may include food, toys, back scratches, being sprayed with a hose, or another favorite activity. Giving the whale positive reinforcers immediately after it performs a specific behavior makes it likely that the behavior will increase in frequency, duration, and intensity in a similar situation.

1 How do we know what a reinforcer is for a whale?

2 Why isn't punishment used to train a whale to perform behaviors?

The use of classical conditioning is also necessary to teach a whale to perform complex behaviors. Because it is not always possible to reinforce the whale immediately after it performs a specific behavior, trainers must use a signal (whistle) to provide the whale with immediate feedback that it has correctly performed the desired behavior. A whale learns the meaning of the whistle by the trainer whistling before giving the whale food. Over the course of several trials, the whale comes to associate the whistle with receiving food and the whale performs the behavior to get the reinforcement.

3 Why is it important to reinforce the whale *immediately* after it performs a desired behavior?

Once the association between the whistle and the reinforcer is established, whales can be taught to perform complex behaviors. First, the whale is taught to follow a target, such as a long stick with a ball at the end. The target guides the whale in a direction, and when the target touches the whale, the trainer blows the whistle and reinforces the whale. After this is done several times, the target is moved farther away and the trainer waits for the whale to touch it before providing reinforcement. The whale learns that making contact with the target results in being reinforced. Now, when the whale performs a behavior that is close to the desired behavior, the trainer whistles and the whale approaches to receive a positive reinforcer.

4 In this training example, what is the neutral stimulus? Unconditioned stimulus? Conditioned stimulus?

5 What should a trainer do if a whale performs a behavior incorrectly?

© Mike Price/Shutterstock.com

Teaching whales to perform behaviors may appear like a relatively easy task while watching the trainers and whales interact on stage, but the truth is that training whales to perform is challenging and dangerous work. Trainers need to be committed, patient, and friendly to earn the whale's trust, and even then it can take months or even years to teach a whale a complex set of behaviors. Also, the deadly killer whale attack on his longtime trainer that took place at SeaWorld is a tragic reminder of the "killer" in even the best-trained whales.

6 Can whales learn to do tricks by just watching other whales perform?

Adapted from Animal training at SeaWorld, 2002; *Aqua facts: Training marine mammals,* 2006; Chua-Eoan, 2010

Unless otherwise noted, all images are © Cengage Learning

Summary Test

A Operant Conditioning

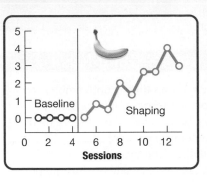

Adapted from "Treating Chronic Food Refusal in Young Children: Home-Based Parent Training," by M.A. Werle, T.B. Murphy & K.S. Budd, 1993, *Journal of Applied Behavior Analysis, 26, 421–433.*

1. A kind of learning in which the consequences that follow some behavior increase or decrease the likelihood that the behavior will occur again is called _____.

2. To explain how random trial-and-error behaviors of cats became goal-directed behaviors, Thorndike formulated the _____, which says that behaviors are strengthened by positive consequences and weakened by negative consequences.

3. Skinner used the term *operant* **(a)** _____ to describe something that can be modified by its consequences. Operant responses provide one way to separate ongoing behaviors into units that can be observed and measured. Skinner believed that Pavlov's conditioning, which involves physiological **(b)** _____, was not very useful in understanding other forms of ongoing behaviors.

4. Suppose you wished to operantly condition your dog, Bingo, to sit up. The procedure would be as follows. You would give Bingo a treat, which is called a **(a)** _____, after he emits a desired behavior. Because it is unlikely that Bingo will initially sit up, you will use a procedure called **(b)** _____, which is a process of reinforcing those behaviors that lead up to or approximate the final desired behavior—sitting up. Immediately after Bingo emitted a desired behavior, you would give him a **(c)** _____.

5. Any behavior that increases in frequency because of an accidental pairing of a reinforcer and that behavior is called a _____ behavior.

6. The essence of operant conditioning can be summed up as follows: Consequences or reinforcers are contingent on _____.

7. If you compare classical and operant conditioning, you will find the following differences. In classical conditioning, the response is an involuntary **(a)** _____ that is elicited by the **(b)** _____. In operant conditioning, the response is a voluntary **(c)** _____ that is performed or **(d)** _____ by the organism. In classical conditioning, the unconditioned stimulus is presented at the beginning of a trial and elicits the **(e)** _____. In operant conditioning, the organism emits a behavior that is immediately followed by a **(f)** _____.

B Reinforcers

8. In operant conditioning, the term *consequences* refers to what happens after the occurrence of a behavior. If a consequence increases the likelihood that a behavior will occur again, it is called a **(a)** _____. If a consequence decreases the likelihood that a behavior will occur again, it is called a **(b)** _____.

9. If a stimulus increases the chances that a response will occur again, that stimulus is called a **(a)** _____. If the removal of an aversive stimulus increases the chances that a response will occur again, that aversive stimulus is called a **(b)** _____. Both positive and negative reinforcements **(c)** _____ the frequency of the response they follow. In contrast, punishment is a consequence that **(d)** _____ the likelihood that a behavior will occur again.

10. The stimuli of food, water, and sex, which are innately satisfying and require no learning to become pleasurable, are called **(a)** _____. The stimuli of praise, money, and good grades have acquired their reinforcing properties through experience; these stimuli are called **(b)** _____.

C Schedules of Reinforcement

11. A program or rule that determines how and when the occurrence of a response will be followed by a reinforcer is called a _____.

12. If you received reinforcement every time you performed a good deed, you would be on a **(a)** _____ schedule. This schedule is often used at the beginning of operant conditioning because it results in a rapid rate of learning. If your good deeds were not reinforced every time, you would be on a **(b)** _____ schedule. This schedule is more effective in maintaining the target behavior in the long run. There are four kinds of partial reinforcement schedules.

D Other Conditioning Concepts

13. The phenomenon in which an organism emits the same response to similar stimuli is called **(a)** _____. If a response is emitted in the presence of a reinforced stimulus but not in the presence of unreinforced stimuli, the organism is exhibiting **(b)** _____. If an organism's response is no longer reinforced, it will stop emitting this behavior, which is an example of **(c)** _____. However, even without reinforcement, an organism may perform the behavior again, which is an example of **(d)** _____.

E Cognitive Learning

14. The kind of learning that involves mental processes such as attention and memory, that may be learned through observation and imitation, and that may not involve any external rewards or require the person to perform any observable behaviors is called **(a)** _____. According to Tolman, rats developed a mental representation of the layout of their environment, which he called a **(b)** _____.

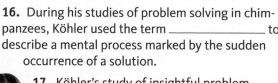

15. If an observer learns a behavior through observation but does not immediately perform the behavior, this is an example of the _____ distinction.

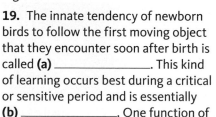

16. During his studies of problem solving in chimpanzees, Köhler used the term _____ to describe a mental process marked by the sudden occurrence of a solution.

17. Köhler's study of insightful problem solving, Bandura's theory of observational learning, and Tolman's idea of cognitive maps represent three kinds of _____ learning.

F Biological Factors

18. Innate tendencies or predispositions that may either facilitate or inhibit learning are referred to as _____.

19. The innate tendency of newborn birds to follow the first moving object that they encounter soon after birth is called **(a)** _____. This kind of learning occurs best during a critical or sensitive period and is essentially **(b)** _____. One function of imprinting is to form social attachments between members of a species.

20. The innate tendency of animals to recognize, attend to, and store certain cues over others and to associate some combinations of conditioned and unconditioned stimuli is referred to as _____. An example of this tendency is observed in Clark's nutcrackers, which are preprogrammed to bury and remember thousands of hidden stores of food.

G Research Focus: Viewing Aggression

21. Verbal bullying, ostracizing peers, and spreading rumors are all examples of _____.

22. Female university students who viewed either physical or relational aggression were _____ to subsequently engage in physical and relational aggression than women who did not view any aggression.

H Cultural Diversity: Teaching Music

23. Suzuki's method and Bandura's theory both emphasize observation, modeling, and imitation. Specifically, both Suzuki and Bandura focus on four concepts: paying **(a)** _____ to the model, placing the information in **(b)** _____, using the information to **(c)** _____ the model's actions, and having **(d)** _____ to perform the behavior.

I Application: Behavior Modification

24. Using principles of operant conditioning to change human behavior is referred to as _____.

25. The systematic reinforcement of desired behaviors along with the withholding of reinforcement or punishment of undesired behaviors is called _____.

26. If an aversive stimulus is presented immediately after a particular response, the response will be suppressed; this procedure is called **(a)** _____. If a reinforcing stimulus is removed immediately after a particular response, the response will be suppressed; this procedure is called **(b)** _____.

Answers: 1. *operant conditioning;* 2. *law of effect;* 3. (a) *response,* (b) *reflexes;* 4. (a) *reinforcer,* (b) *shaping,* (c) *reinforcer;* 5. *superstitious;* 6. *behavior;* 7. (a) *reflex,* (b) *unconditioned stimulus,* (c) *behavior,* (d) *emitted,* (e) *unconditioned response,* (f) *reinforcer;* 8. (a) *reinforcer,* (b) *punishment;* 9. (a) *positive reinforcer,* (b) *negative reinforcer;* 10. (a) *primary reinforcers,* (b) *secondary reinforcers;* 11. *schedule of reinforcement;* 12. (a) *continuous reinforcement,* (b) *partial reinforcement;* 13. (a) *generalization,* (b) *discrimination,* (c) *extinction,* (d) *spontaneous recovery;* 14. (a) *social cognitive learning,* (b) *cognitive map;* 15. *learning–performance;* 16. *insight;* 17. *cognitive;* 18. *biological factors;* 19. (a) *imprinting,* (b) *irreversible;* 20. *prepared-ness, or prepared learning;* 21. *relational aggression;* 22. *more likely;* 23. (a) *attention,* (b) *memory,* (c) *imitate,* (d) *motivation;* 24. *behavior modification;* 25. *contingency management;* 26. (a) *positive punishment,* (b) *negative punishment*

Links to Learning

Key Terms/Key People

autism, 232

behavior modification, or behavior mod, 232

biological factors, 228

Bobo doll experiment, 224

cognitive learning, 223

cognitive map, 223

contingency management, 233

continuous reinforcement, 220

critical or sensitive period, 228

cumulative record, 220

discrimination, 222

discriminative stimulus, 222

ethologists, 228

extinction, 222

fixed-interval schedule, 221

fixed-ratio schedule, 221

generalization, 222

imprinting, 228

insight, 226

latent learning, 223

law of effect, 214

learning–performance distinction, 224

negative punishment, 219

negative reinforcement, 218

noncompliance, 219

operant conditioning, 213

operant response, 214

partial reinforcement, 220

pica, 218

positive punishment, 219

positive reinforcement, 218

preparedness, or prepared learning, 229

primary reinforcer, 219

punishment, 218

reinforcement, 218

reinforcer, 219

schedule of reinforcement, 220

secondary reinforcer, 219

shaping, 215

Skinner box, 215

social cognitive learning, 223

social cognitive theory, 225

spontaneous recovery, 222

superstitious behavior, 215

time-out, 219

variable-interval schedule, 221

variable-ratio schedule, 221

Media Resources

Go to **CengageBrain.com** to access Psychology CourseMate, where you will find an interactive eBook, glossaries, flashcards, quizzes, videos, answers to Critical Thinking questions, and more. You can also access Virtual Psychology Labs, an interactive laboratory experience designed to illustrate key experiments first-hand.

MODULE 11 Types of Memory

Incredible Memory

What's a super memory? Daniel Tammet stood before the packed house at the Museum of History and Science in Oxford. He recited, from memory, the first 22,514 digits of pi, which is often rounded off to two decimal places, or 3.14. He completed this amazing feat in 5 hours and 9 minutes and made no mistakes.

Scientists describe Daniel's memory as nothing less than extraordinary. In fact, Daniel is one of only a half-dozen people worldwide with such gargantuan memory powers. He currently holds the European record for reciting digits of pi, but people elsewhere have broken his record. For instance, Akira Haraguchi correctly repeated the first 100,000 digits of pi (Associated Press, 2006d). Later in this module, we'll learn about the memory technique Daniel uses to remember so many digits.

Daniel recited 22,514 digits of pi in exact order.

Despite Daniel's unbelievable ability to memorize numbers, he faces a number of life challenges. He can't drive, doesn't tolerate shopping well, and avoids the beach because of his compulsion to count every grain of sand. As a child, he struggled to learn spelling and even simple mathematics because the techniques being taught didn't match his unique way of thinking (Schorn, 2007; Tammet, 2007, 2009).

Few people have such incredible memories and, unfortunately, many others have memory problems. Next, we'll learn about a man who has very serious problems with his memory.

Defining Memory

What are the three processes? Daniel's amazing ability to recall thousands of digits and Clive's very serious memory problems involve three different memory processes.

Memory is an active system that allows people to retain information over time.

The model that many researchers believe best explains how memory works is called the information-processing model.

The **information-processing model** states that the ability to retain information over time involves three processes: encoding, storage, and retrieval.

We'll briefly define each of the three memory processes because they are the keys to understanding the interesting and complex process of how we remember and thus create the world we live in.

1 Encoding

Daniel developed a method or code to form memories for digits, a process called encoding.

Encoding is the process of making mental representations of information so that it can be placed into our memories.

For example, Daniel encodes numbers by visualizing each number as having a different shape, color, and texture. Such vivid mental representations help him to store numbers in his memory.

Memory Problem

Imagine what life would be like without memory. For Clive Wearing, that's a grim reality.

How important is memory? At age 40, Clive Wearing, a musician, got a disease that caused brain damage resulting in severe memory impairment. For instance, despite having written a book on a classical composer, he cannot remember any information about the composer. Clive can no longer enjoy reading books or watching movies because he is unable to follow the plot. Each time Clive sees his wife, he excitedly greets her as if he has not seen her in years, even though she may have left the room for only a moment. He cannot recall his wedding day or the names of his children.

The disease did spare Clive some of his memory. Even though Clive cannot remember being educated in music, he remembers how to play the piano, conduct an orchestra, and sing.

Clive has very serious memory problems caused by a disease that damaged his brain.

When Clive tells others about his life, he says it is "precisely like death. I'd like to be alive" (J. Goodwin, 2006, p. 125). He does not feel alive because for the past 25 years, his memory problems have robbed him of a past and future. Clive lives in a never-ending present. His wife describes his memory by explaining, "It's as if Clive's every conscious moment is like waking up for the first time" (J. Goodwin, 2006, p. 126). Clive's problems with memory really affect his quality of life and demonstrate the importance of memory (Baddeley, 2009d; Sacks, 2008).

2 Storage

Daniel used associations to encode information because associations are also useful for storing information.

Storage is the process of placing encoded information into relatively permanent mental storage for later recall.

New information that is stored by making associations with old or familiar information is much easier to remember, or retrieve.

1 Encoding

2 Storage

3 Retrieval

3 Retrieval

Daniel was able to recall, or retrieve, 22,514 digits in order.

Retrieval is the process of getting or recalling information that has been placed into short-term or long-term storage.

Only a few people in the entire world can match Daniel's feat of encoding, storing, and retrieving thousands of digits in order.

What's Coming

We'll discuss three stages of memory, how memories are encoded, why emotional memories are long-lasting, the issue of repressed memories, and some unusual memory abilities. ●

A Three Stages of Memory

What are the three stages?

Traditionally, memory has been explained as involving three stages. The **three-stages model** divides memory into three sequential stages: sensory, short-term, and long-term memory (R. C. Atkinson & Shiffrin, 1968).

To illustrate each of these stages, we'll examine what happens as you walk through a shopping mall.

Sensory Memory

As you walk through a busy mall, you are bombarded by hundreds of sights, smells, and sounds, including the music of a lone guitarist playing for spare change. Many of these stimuli reach your sensory memory.

Sensory memory is an initial process that receives and holds environmental information in its raw form for a brief period of time, from an instant to several seconds.

For example, after reaching your ears, the guitarist's sounds are held in sensory memory for a second or two. What you do next will determine what happens to the guitarist's sounds that are in your sensory memory.

If you pay no more attention to these sounds in sensory memory, they automatically *disappear* without a trace.

However, if you pay attention to the guitarist's music, the auditory information in sensory memory is transferred into another memory stage called short-term memory (Baddeley, 2009c).

© William Perugini/Shutterstock.com

Short-Term Memory

Because a few notes of the guitarist's song sounded interesting, you shifted your attention to that particular information in sensory memory. Paying attention to information in sensory memory causes it to be automatically transferred into short-term memory.

Short-term memory is a process that can hold only a limited amount of information—an average of seven items—for only a short period of time, 2 to 30 seconds.

Once a limited amount of information is transferred into short-term memory, it will remain there for up to 30 seconds. If during this time you become more involved in the information, such as humming to the music, the information will remain in short-term memory for a longer period of time.

However, the music will *disappear* after a short time unless it is transferred into permanent storage, called long-term memory (Squire & Kandel, 2009).

Long-Term Memory

If you become mentally engaged in whistling along or wondering why the guitarist's music sounds familiar, there is a good chance that this mental activity will transfer the music from short-term into long-term memory.

Long-term memory is the process of storing almost unlimited amounts of information over long periods of time.

© fotofreaks/Shutterstock.com

For example, you have stored hundreds of songs, terms, faces, and conversations in your long-term memory—information that is potentially available for retrieval. However, from personal experience, you know that you cannot always retrieve things you learned and know you know. In Module 12, we'll discuss reasons for forgetting information stored in long-term memory.

Now that you know what the three memory stages are, we'll explain how they work together.

Overview

1 **Sensory memory.** We'll explain how the three stages of memory described above work and how paying or not paying attention to something determines what is remembered and what is forgotten.

Imagine listening to a lecture. All the information that enters your sensory memory remains for seconds or less. If you *do not pay attention* to information in sensory memory, it is forgotten. If you *do pay attention* to particular information, such as the instructor's words, this information is automatically transferred into short-term memory.

2 **Short-term memory.** If you *do not pay attention* to information in short-term memory, it is not encoded and is forgotten. If you *do pay attention* by rehearsing the information, such as taking notes, the information will be encoded for storage in long-term memory. That's why it helps to take lecture notes.

3 **Long-term memory.** Information that is encoded for storage in long-term memory will remain there on a *relatively permanent basis.* Whether or not you can recall the instructor's words from long-term memory depends partly on how they are encoded, which we'll discuss later. This means that poor class notes may result in poor encoding and poor recall on exams. The secret to great encoding and great recall is to associate new information with old, which we'll also discuss later.

Now that we have given you an overview of memory, we'll discuss each of the three stages of memory in more detail. ●

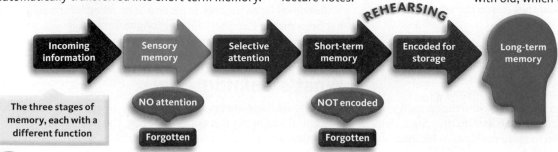

The three stages of memory, each with a different function

Incoming information → Sensory memory → Selective attention → Short-term memory → **REHEARSING** → Encoded for storage → Long-term memory

NO attention → Forgotten

NOT encoded → Forgotten

B Sensory Memory: Recording

Do you have a mental video recorder?

Your brain has a mental video-audio recorder that automatically receives and holds incoming sensory information for only seconds or less. This brief period provides just enough time for you to decide whether some particular incoming sensory information is important or interesting and therefore demands your further attention. We'll examine two different kinds of sensory memory: visual sensory memory, called iconic memory, and auditory sensory memory, called echoic memory.

Iconic Memory

What happens when you blink?

About 14,000 times a waking day, your eyes blink and you are totally blind during the blinks (Casselman, 2006; Garbarini, 2005). However, the world doesn't disappear during the eye blinks because of a special sensory memory, which is called iconic (*eye-CON-ick*) memory.

Iconic memory is a form of sensory memory that automatically holds visual information for about a quarter of a second or more; as soon as you shift your attention, the information disappears. (The word *icon* means "image.")

You don't "go blind" when both eyes close completely during a blink (about one-third of a second) because the visual scene is briefly held in iconic memory (O'Regan et al., 2000). When your eyes reopen, you don't realize that your eyes were completely closed during the blink because "you kept seeing" the visual information that was briefly stored in iconic memory. Without iconic memory, your world would disappear into darkness during each eye blink.

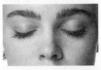

© PhotoDisc, Inc.

Iconic memory briefly holds visual information during eye blink.

Identifying Iconic Memory

Here's the first study that showed the existence and length of iconic memory.

Procedure. Individual study participants sat in front of a screen upon which 12 letters (three rows of four letters) appeared for a very brief time (50 milliseconds, or 50/1,000 of a second). After each presentation, participants were asked to recall a particular row of letters.

Results and conclusion. As shown in the graph below, if participants responded immediately (0.0-second delay) after seeing the letters, they remembered an average of nine letters. However, a delay of merely 0.5 second reduced memory to an average of six letters, and a delay of 1.0 second reduced memory to an average of only four letters (Sperling, 1960). Notice that a longer delay in responding resulted in participants remembering fewer letters, which indicated the brief duration of iconic memory—seconds or less.

This study demonstrated a sensory memory for visual information, which was called iconic memory. The sensory memory for auditory information is called echoic memory.

Number of Letters Remembered

Delay in Seconds	
0.0	9 letters
0.5	6 letters
1.0	4 letters

Echoic Memory

What did you hear?

Without realizing, you have already experienced auditory sensory memory, which is called echoic (*eh-KO-ick*) memory.

Echoic memory is a form of sensory memory that holds auditory information for 1 or 2 seconds.

For instance, suppose you are absorbed in reading a novel and a friend asks you a question. You stop reading and ask, "What did you say?" As soon as those words are out of your mouth, you realize that you can recall, or play back, your friend's exact words. You can play back these words because they are still in echoic memory, which may last as long

Echoic memory briefly holds sounds.

as 2 seconds. In addition to letting you play back things you thought you did not hear, echoic memory lets you hold speech sounds long enough to know that sequences of certain sounds form words (Norman, 1982). Researchers discovered that the length of echoic memory increases as children grow into adults (Gomes et al., 1999).

Here's a quick review of the functions of iconic and echoic memories.

Functions of Sensory Memory

1 Prevents being overwhelmed. Sensory memory keeps you from being overwhelmed by too many incoming stimuli because any sensory information you do not attend to will vanish in seconds.

Incoming information → Sensory memory → NO attention → Forgotten

2 Gives decision time. Sensory memory gives you a few seconds to decide whether some incoming sensory information is interesting or important. Information you pay attention to will automatically be transferred into short-term memory.

3 Provides stability, playback, and recognition. Iconic memory makes things in your visual world appear smooth and continuous, such as "seeing" even during blinking. Echoic memory lets you play back auditory information, such as holding separate sounds so that you can recognize them as words.

If you attend to information in sensory memory, it goes into short-term memory, the next topic. ●

Definition

What was that phone number?

You have just looked up a phone number, which you keep repeating as you dial to order a pizza. After giving your order and hanging up, you can't remember the number. This example shows two characteristics of short-term memory.

Short-term memory is a process that can hold a limited amount of information—an average of seven items—for a limited period of time, 2 to 30 seconds.

For good reason, telephone numbers and postal ZIP codes are seven numbers or fewer because that is about the limit of short-term memory.

Short-term memory does more than simply store information; it actively processes the information it contains at any given moment. For this reason, short-term memory is also referred to as working memory.

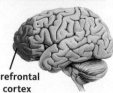

Clive Wearing's prefrontal cortex is damaged.

Prefrontal cortex

Working memory is a more recent understanding of short-term memory that involves the active processing of incoming information from sensory memory and the retrieval of information from long-term memory.

When you are paying attention and using working memory to perform a variety of cognitive tasks, maximum neural activity occurs in areas of the prefrontal cortex (Pessoa & Ungerleider, 2004). The prefrontal cortex of Clive Wearing, discussed in the beginning of this module, is damaged and he can remember certain types of information for only 7 seconds. His working memory is impaired and he cannot remember a phone number for longer than a few seconds.

Although very useful, working or short-term memory has limited duration and limited capacity.

Two Features

Limited Duration

The new telephone number that you looked up will remain in short-term memory for a brief time, usually from 2 to 30 seconds, and then disappear. However, you can keep information longer in short-term memory by using maintenance rehearsal.

Maintenance rehearsal is the practice of intentionally repeating or rehearsing information so that it remains longer in short-term memory.

Researchers studied how long information is remembered without practice or rehearsal by asking participants to remember a series of consonants composed of three meaningless letters, such as CHJ. Participants were prevented from rehearsing, or repeating, these consonants by having to count backward immediately after seeing the groups of three letters. As the graph below shows, 80% of the participants recalled the groups of three letters after 3 seconds. However, only 10% of the participants recalled the groups of three letters after 15 seconds (L. R. Peterson & Peterson, 1950). Since almost all the participants had forgotten the groups of three letters after 15 seconds (if they were prevented from rehearsing), this study clearly showed that information disappears from your short-term memory within seconds unless you continually repeat or rehearse the information.

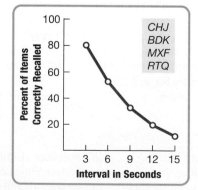

Short-term memory holds items for 2–30 seconds.

You can increase the time that information remains in short-term memory by using maintenance rehearsal. However, during maintenance rehearsal, which involves repeating the same thing over and over, new information cannot enter short-term memory.

Not only does short-term or working memory have a limited duration, but it also has a limited capacity.

Limited Capacity

In previous modules, we pointed out several studies that are considered classic because they challenged old concepts or identified significant new information. One such classic study is that of George Miller (1956), who was the first to discover that short-term memory can hold only about seven items or bits, plus or minus two. Although this seems like too small a number, researchers have repeatedly confirmed Miller's original finding (Baddeley, 2004). Thus, one reason telephone numbers worldwide are generally limited to seven digits is that seven matches the capacity of short-term memory.

Short-term memory holds about 7 items.

It is easy to confirm Miller's finding with a **memory span test,** which measures the total number of digits that we can repeat back in the correct order after a single hearing. For example, students make few errors when they are asked to repeat seven or eight digits, make some errors with a list of eight or nine digits, and make many errors when they repeat a list that is longer than nine digits. One of the main reasons information disappears from short-term memory is interference (M. C. Anderson, 2009a).

Interference results when new information enters short-term memory and overwrites or pushes out information that is already there.

For example, if you are trying to remember a phone number and someone asks you a question, the question interferes with or wipes away the phone number. One way to prevent interference is through rehearsal. However, once we stop rehearsing, the information in short-term memory may disappear.

Although short-term memory has limited capacity and duration, it is possible to increase both. For example, we use a classroom demonstration in which we guarantee that any student can learn to memorize a list of 23 digits, in exact order, in just 25 seconds. This impressive memory demonstration, which always works, is accomplished by knowing how to use something called chunking.

Chunking

How does Daniel remember thousands of numbers?

Although short-term memory briefly holds an average of about seven items, it is possible to increase the length of each item by using a process called chunking (Baddeley, 2009c).

Chunking is combining separate items of information into a larger unit, or chunk, and then remembering chunks of information rather than individual items.

One of the interesting things about Daniel Tammet's prodigious memory for numbers is his ability to chunk. Whereas most of us would see an endless string of random numbers when looking at the digits in pi, Daniel is able to chunk the numbers into groups, with each represented by a unique visual image. In his mind, every number up to 10,000 has a unique shape, color, and texture. When he sees a long sequence of numbers, as in pi, he effortlessly sees a "landscape of colorful shapes." Daniel describes some numbers as being beautiful (such as 333) and others as quite ugly (such as 289). He has a condition called

© Drew Farrell/Photoshot/Getty Images

Numbers have unique shapes, colors, and textures.

922 ³³ *72*
174 69
50 ⁸¹⁷ *333*
289 *460*
538 67 *209*
44

synesthesia, which we discussed in Module 6 (see p. 142). Synesthesia is when people's senses become intertwined. For example, they may hear colors, see music, or taste shapes. Synesthesia has been shown to activate more areas of people's brain, which in turn may improve their memory (Foer, 2006a; Schorn, 2007; Tammet, 2007, 2009).

The ability to use chunking is not limited to people with super memories. We all use chunking at times without thinking about it. For example, to remember the 11-digit phone number 16228759211, we break it into four chunks: 1-622-875-9211.

As first suggested by George Miller (1956), chunking is a powerful memory tool that greatly increases the amount of information that you can hold in short-term memory. Daniel's ability to chunk numbers helped him develop an incredible memory, and the use of chunking can improve your memory, too.

Next, we'll review three important functions of short-term memory.

Functions of Short-Term Memory

Why is it also called working memory?

Short-term memory is like having a mental computer screen that stores a limited amount of information that is automatically erased after a brief period of time and replaced by new information, and so the cycle continues. **Short-term memory** is also called **working memory** to indicate that it's an active process. Using brain scans, researchers found that short-term memory involves the front part of the brain, especially the prefrontal area (Pessoa & Ungerleider, 2004).

There are three important points to remember about short-term memory: 1st—paying attention transfers information into short-term memory; 2nd—after a short time, information disappears unless it is rehearsed; and 3rd—some information is eventually transferred from short-term memory into permanent storage.

1 Attending

Imagine driving along with your radio on while a friend in the passenger seat is talking about the weekend. A tremendous amount of information is entering your sensory memory, but you avoid stimulus overload because incoming information automatically vanishes in seconds unless you pay attention to it.

The moment you pay attention to information in sensory memory, that information enters short-term memory for further processing. For example, while your friend is talking, you don't pay attention to the radio until your favorite song comes on and enters sensory memory. As you pay attention, you hear the radio, even though it has been playing the whole time. One function of short-term memory is that it allows us *to selectively attend to information that is relevant and disregard everything else.*

Once information enters short-term, or working, memory, several things may happen.

2 Rehearsing

Once information enters short-term memory, it usually remains for only seconds unless you rehearse it. For example, the announcer on the car radio gives a phone number to call for free movie tickets. But unless you rehearse or repeat the number over and over, it will probably disappear from your short-term memory because of interference from newly arriving information. Another function of short-term memory is that it allows you *to hold information for a short period of time until you decide what to do with it.*

If you rehearse the information in short-term memory, you increase the chances of storing it.

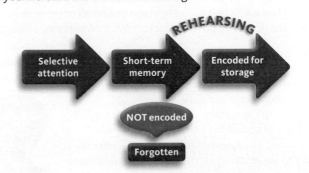

3 Storing

Rehearsing information not only holds that information in short-term memory but also helps *to store or encode information in long-term memory.* Later, we'll discuss two different kinds of rehearsing (see p. 249) and explain why one kind of rehearsing is better than the other for storing or encoding information in long-term memory.

Next, we'll describe the steps in the memory process and why some things are stored in long-term memory. ●

D Long-Term Memory: Storing

Putting Information into Long-Term Memory

Is it a thing or a process? Don't think of sensory memory, short-term memory, and long-term memory as *things* or *places* but rather as ongoing and interacting *processes*. To show how these different memory processes interact, we'll describe what happens as you hear a new song on the car radio or iPod and try to remember the song's title.

1 Sensory memory. As you drive down the highway, you're half listening to the car radio. Among the incoming information, which is held for seconds or less in sensory memory, are the words, "Remember this song, 'Love Is Like Chocolate,' and win two movie tickets."

2 Attention. If you do NOT pay attention to information about winning tickets, it will disappear from sensory memory. If the chance to win tickets gets your attention, information about the song title, "Love Is Like Chocolate," is automatically transferred into short-term memory.

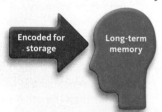

Love Is Like Chocolate

3 Short-term memory. Once the song title is in short-term memory, you have a short time (2–30 seconds) for further processing. If you lose interest in the title or are distracted by traffic, the title will most likely disappear and be forgotten. However, if you rehearse the title or, better yet, form a new association, the title will likely be transferred into and encoded in your long-term memory.

4 Encoding. You place information in long-term memory through a process called encoding.

Encoding is the process of transferring information from short-term to long-term memory by paying attention to it, repeating or rehearsing it, or forming new associations.

For example, if you simply repeat the title or don't make any new associations, the title may not be encoded at all or may be poorly encoded and thus difficult to recall from long-term memory. However, if you find the title, "Love Is Like Chocolate," to be catchy or unusual, or you form a new association, such as thinking of a heart-shaped chocolate, you will be successful in encoding this title into long-term memory.

We'll discuss ways to improve encoding information and thus improve recalling information later in this module.

5 Long-term memory. Once the song title is encoded in long-term memory, it has the potential to remain there for your lifetime.

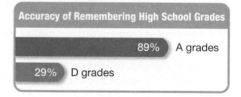

Encoded for storage → Long-term memory

Long-term memory is the process of storing almost unlimited amounts of information over long periods of time with the potential of retrieving, or remembering, such information in the future.

For example, later you may try to recall the song title from long-term memory by placing it back into short-term memory. How easily and accurately you can recall or retrieve information depends on many factors (M. C. Anderson, 2009c).

6 Retrieval. When people talk about remembering something, they usually mean retrieving or recalling information from long-term memory.

Retrieval is the process of selecting information from long-term memory and transferring it back into short-term memory.

There are several reasons you can't remember or retrieve the song's title. You may not have effectively encoded the title into long-term memory because you got distracted or neglected to form a new association (chocolate heart). The key to successfully retrieving information from long-term memory is to effectively encode information, usually by making associations between new and old information, which we'll soon discuss.

Love Is Like _____?

Features of Long-Term Memory

Capacity and permanency. *How big and how accurate?* Long-term memory has an almost unlimited capacity to store information. Anything stored has the potential to last a lifetime, provided drugs or disease do not damage the brain's memory circuits (Bahrick, 2000).

Chances of retrieval. Although all information in long-term memory has the potential to be retrieved, how much you can actually retrieve depends on a number of factors, including how it was encoded and the amount of interference from related information. The next question is: How accurate are your long-term memories?

Accuracy. Researchers found that the content and accuracy of long-term memories may undergo change and distortion across time and not always be as accurate as people think. For example, college freshmen were asked to recall their grades from all four years of high school. As the graph below shows, students accurately recalled 89% of grades of A but only 29% of grades of D. Thus, students were much

Accuracy of Remembering High School Grades

89%	A grades
29%	D grades

more accurate recalling positive events, grades of A, than they were recalling negative events, grades of D (Bahrick et al., 1996).

This and other studies show that we don't recall all events with the same accuracy, sometimes inflating positive events and eliminating negative ones, and this tendency becomes stronger as we age (M. C. Anderson, 2009b; Mather & Carstensen, 2005). The reasons we may change, distort, or forget information will be discussed in Module 12.

Next, we'll explain how psychologists demonstrated the existence of two separate memory systems: a short-term and a long-term memory.

© William Perugini/Shutterstock.com

© dgmata/Shutterstock.com

Unless otherwise noted, all images are © Cengage Learning

Separate Memory Systems

What is the evidence?

Most researchers agree that there are two memory systems Neath & Surprenant, 2013). One system involves short-term memory, which stores limited information for a brief period of time and then the information disappears. For example, a stranger tells you his or her name, but a few minutes later you have totally forgotten the name because it disappeared from short-term memory. A second system involves long-term memory, which stores large amounts of information for very long periods of time.

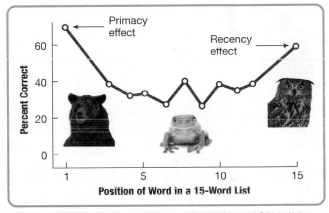

For example, you can recall in great detail many childhood memories that years ago were stored in long-term memory. Other evidence for two memory systems comes from findings that brain damage can wipe out long-term memory while completely sparing short-term memory. Still other evidence for two memory systems comes from research on how you remember items in a relatively long list. We'll give you a chance to memorize a list of items, which will show that you have two separate memory systems—short- and long-term memory.

Primacy Versus Recency

Can you remember this list?

Please read the following list only once and try to remember the animals' names:

bear, giraffe, wolf, fly, deer, elk, gorilla, elephant, frog, snail, turtle, shark, ant, owl

Immediately after reading this list, write down (in any order) as many of the animals' names as you can remember.

If you examine the list of names that you wrote down, you'll discover a definite pattern to the order of the names that you remembered. For example, here's the order in which names in the above list would most likely be remembered.

First items: Primacy effect. In studies using similar lists, participants more easily recalled the *first* four or five items (bear, giraffe, wolf, fly) because they had more time to rehearse the first words presented. As a result of rehearsing, these first names were transferred to and stored in long-term memory, from which they were recalled. This phenomenon is called the primacy effect.

The **primacy effect** refers to better recall, or improvement in retention, of information presented at the beginning of a body of information.

Middle items. Participants did not recall many items from the *middle* of the list (gorilla, elephant, frog) because they did not have much time to rehearse them. When they tried to remember items from the middle of the list, their attention and time were split between trying to remember the previous terms and trying to rehearse new ones. Less rehearsal meant that fewer middle names were stored in long-term memory; more interference meant that fewer names remained in short-term memory.

Last items: Recency effect. Participants more easily recalled the *last* four or five items (turtle, shark, ant, owl) because they were still available in short-term memory and could be read off a mental list. This phenomenon is called the recency effect.

The **recency effect** refers to better recall, or improvement in retention, of information presented at the end of a body of information.

Together, these two effects are called the serial position effect.

The **serial position effect** refers to better recall of information presented at the beginning and end of a body of information, as opposed to the middle.

As we'll explain next, the serial position effect is evidence that short- and long-term memory are two separate processes.

Short-Term Versus Long-Term Memory

Why didn't you remember "elephant"?

One reason you probably didn't remember the name "elephant" is that it came from the middle of the list. The middle section of a list is usually least remembered because that information may no longer be retained in short-term memory and may not have been encoded in long-term memory. Evidence for the serial position effect is shown in the graph below (Glanzer & Cunitz, 1966).

Position of Word in a 15-Word List (x-axis, 1 to 15); **Percent Correct** (y-axis, 0 to 60). Primacy effect labeled at position 1; Recency effect labeled at position 15.

Bear: © Eric Isselée/Shutterstock.com; Frog: © Andrew Burgess/Shutterstock.com; Owl: © Eric Isselée/Shutterstock.com

For example, participants showed better recall (70%) for the first items presented, which is the primacy effect. The primacy effect occurs because participants have more time to rehearse the first items, which increases the chances of transferring these items into long-term memory. Remember that rehearsal has two functions: keeping information longer in short-term memory and promoting encoding—the transfer of information into long-term memory.

In addition, participants showed better recall (60%) for the last items presented, which is the recency effect. Sometimes participants say that they can still "hear these words" and usually report these items first. The recency effect occurs because the last items are still in short-term memory, from which they are recalled (Glanzer & Cunitz, 1966).

The occurrence of the serial position effect suggested the existence of two separate kinds of memory processes, which we now call short-term and long-term memory (R. C. Atkinson & Shiffrin, 1968; Baddeley, 2009c).

Next, you'll discover that instead of one, there are several different kinds of long-term memory.

Declarative Versus Procedural or Nondeclarative

Why does Clive play the piano but forget names?

After brain damage, Clive Wearing (picture below left) remembered how to play the piano but forgot the names of his children and had no memory of his wedding. Clive retained some memory abilities while losing others because different types of memory are stored differently in the brain. For instance, the ability to play the piano uses one type of long-term memory, and remembering names and personal experiences uses a second type of long-term memory. The discovery that there are two kinds of long-term memory is a relatively new finding, and like many discoveries in science, it was found quite by accident.

Researchers were testing a patient, well known in memory circles as H. M., who suffered severe memory loss because of an earlier brain operation to reduce his seizures. H. M.'s task seemed simple: draw a star by guiding your hand while looking into a mirror (picture below). However, this mirror-drawing test is relatively difficult because looking into a mirror reverses all hand movements: up is down and down is up. As H. M. did this task each day, his drawing improved, indicating that he was learning and remembering the necessary motor skills.

But here's the strange part. Each and every day, H. M. would insist that he had never seen or done mirror-drawing before (N. J. Cohen, 1984).

You'll understand why H. M. could improve at mirror-drawing but not remember doing it after you learn about the two kinds of long-term memory—declarative and procedural.

Declarative Memory

Which bird cannot fly?
What did you eat for breakfast?

You recall or retrieve answers to these questions from one particular kind of long-term memory called declarative memory.

Declarative memory involves memories for facts or events, such as scenes, stories, words, conversations, faces, or daily events.

We are aware of and can recall, or retrieve, these kinds of memories. Declarative memory is a form of explicit memory.

Explicit memory is memory that is consciously known. Declarative memory includes semantic and episodic memories.

Semantic memory

"Which bird cannot fly?" asks you to remember a fact, which involves semantic *(sah-MAN-tick)* memory.

Semantic memory is a type of declarative memory that involves knowledge of facts, concepts, words, definitions, and language rules.

Most of what you *learn* in classes (facts, terms, definitions) goes into semantic memory (Eysenck, 2009c).

Episodic memory

"What did you eat for breakfast?" asks you to remember an event, which involves episodic *(ep-ih-SAW-dick)* memory.

Episodic memory is a type of declarative memory that involves knowledge of specific events, personal experiences (episodes), or activities, such as naming or describing favorite restaurants, movies, songs, habits, or hobbies.

Most of your college activities and experiences go into episodic memory (Baddeley, 2009a).

Since his brain operation, H. M. cannot remember new facts (semantic memory) or events (episodic memory). Thus, H. M. has lost declarative memory, which explains why he does not remember events, such as doing mirror-drawing (Squire et al., 2004).

However, H. M.'s motor skills improved during mirror-drawing, which indicates another kind of long-term memory.

Procedural or Nondeclarative Memory

How did you learn to play tennis?
Why are you afraid of spiders?

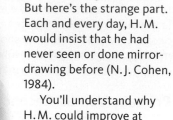

Even though you can play tennis and are afraid of spiders, you can't explain how you control your muscles to play tennis or why you're so terrified of such a tiny (usually harmless) bug. That's because motor skills and emotional feelings are stored in procedural memory.

Procedural memory, also called **nondeclarative memory,** involves memories for motor skills (playing tennis), some cognitive skills (learning to read), and emotional behaviors learned through classical conditioning (fear of spiders).

We cannot recall or retrieve procedural memories. Procedural or nondeclarative memory is a form of implicit memory.

Implicit memory is memory that is not consciously known.

Even if you have not played tennis for years, you can pick up a racket and still remember how to serve because that information is stored in procedural memory. But you cannot describe the sequence of movements needed to serve a ball because these skills are stored in procedural memory. Although procedural memories greatly influence our behavior, we have neither awareness of nor ability to recall these memories (Baddeley, 2009b).

Now we can explain H. M.'s strange behavior. He was able to improve at mirror-drawing because it involved learning a motor skill that was stored in procedural memory. But he could not talk about the skill because no one is aware of or can recall procedural memories. Although H. M. gradually improved at mirror-drawing, he could not remember the event of sitting down and drawing because that involves declarative (episodic) memories, which were damaged in his brain surgery (Hilts, 1995).

We'll discuss the brain systems underlying these types of long-term memory in Module 12. Next, we'll take a closer look at episodic memory. ●

Memories of Emotional Events

Do hormones affect memories?

Many of us have vivid memories that involve highly charged emotional situations (Goldstein, 2008). Perhaps it's the exciting moment of crossing the stage to obtain your diploma, or the moment you got married, or the first time you held your baby. For me (H. K.) I was so overwhelmed by these experiences that I could hardly contain my tears of joy. I will remember these events for the rest of my life because something happens during strong emotions that increases our chances of remembering the particular situation, person, or event.

What actually happens to improve memory during an emotional event has been studied by James McGaugh for over 40 years. Here's a summary of one of his interesting studies.

Hypothesis. McGaugh and his colleagues guessed that if a drug blocked the effects of memory-enhancing hormones normally produced during emotional situations, participants who took the drug should show poor retention for emotional events.

Participants. Those in the experimental group received a drug (propranolol) that decreases or blocks the effects of hormones (epinephrine and norepinephrine) that are normally produced during emotional states. After taking this drug, these participants would still feel emotions, but the drug would block the secretion of those emotionally produced hormones that had been shown to increase memory in animals. Participants in the control group received a placebo, but because of the double-blind procedure, no participants knew whether they were given a drug or a placebo.

Procedure. So that the drugs would have time to act, participants were given either a placebo or the drug 1 hour before seeing a series of slides. Each participant watched a series of 12 slides and heard an accompanying story. The beginning of the slide story was emotionally neutral and simply described a mother leaving home with her son to visit her husband's workplace. The middle

Hormones can "stamp in" memories.

of the slide story was emotionally charged and described the son having a terrible accident in which his feet were severed and his skull was damaged. The end of the slide story was emotionally neutral and described the mother leaving the hospital to pick up her other child from preschool. Participants were tested for retention of the slide story a week later.

Results and conclusion. Researchers found that drug and placebo participants remembered about the same number of neutral events. However, compared to participants in the placebo group (68%), those given a drug that blocked "emotional" hormones remembered fewer emotionally charged events (54%) (Cahill et al., 1994). Other studies on humans found that intense feelings triggered by emotional or stressful situations are encoded, or "carved in stone," by hormones released during emotionally charged situations and that these memories are better remembered (McGaugh, 1999). Researchers explain that these hormones cause tiny molecular changes that help brain cells form memories (Hu et al., 2007).

Although McGaugh's research shows that emotional events are easily encoded, you'll learn next that this isn't true for everyone.

Memories of Amnesia Patients

Can amnesia patients recall emotional events?

People who have amnesia experience problems recalling life events.

Amnesia, which may be temporary or permanent, is loss of memory that may occur after a blow or damage to the brain or after disease, general anesthesia, certain drugs, or severe psychological stress.

Because of an injury, Claire Robertson cannot access memories of her life experiences. Claire, like most patients with amnesia, retains the functioning of procedural memory and semantic memory. However, she has profound impairment in her episodic memory. In other words, Claire can remember how to do things, such as drive a car, and she remembers previously learned facts, such as the names of family members. However, she cannot remember personal experiences, even if they were highly charged emotional events.

Reviewing photos taken throughout the day doesn't help strengthen Claire's episodic memory.

Claire now wears a memory-enhancing camera around her neck that automatically takes photos every 30 seconds. Claire can download and review the photos at the end of the day to try to trigger what little remains of her episodic memory. Reviewing the series of photos of her daily activities allows Claire to know that she experienced a certain event, but her memory cannot store most of the pictures in a way that would allow her to actually remember experiencing the events (Harrell, 2010).

The case study of Claire shows that it is not always easy to encode emotional events. As you'll learn next, nonemotional information, such as learning terms and definitions, can be encoded only with much effort. ●

F Encoding: Transferring

Two Kinds of Encoding

How do we store memories?

It's very common for someone to say, "Let me tell you about my day," and then proceed to describe in great detail a long list of mostly bad things, including long, word-for-word conversations. You can easily recall these detailed personal experiences, even though you took no notes. That's because many personal experiences are automatically, and with no effort on your part, encoded in your long-term memory.

Encoding is the process of transferring information from short-term to long-term memory by paying attention to it, repeating or rehearsing it, or forming new associations.

> Let me tell you about my awful day. First . . .

© Konstantin Yolshin/Shutterstock.com

Why is it that detailed personal experiences and conversation seem to be encoded effortlessly and automatically and easily recalled? Why is it that much of book learning, such as memorizing terms or definitions, usually requires deliberate effort and considerable time and may still not be easily recalled when taking exams? The answer is that there are two different kinds of encoding: automatic and effortful encoding.

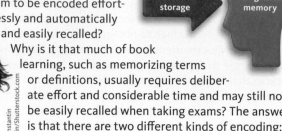
Encoded for storage → Long-term memory

Automatic Encoding

Why are some things easy to encode?

Just as most of us can easily and in great detail recall all the annoying things that happened today, the person below is recalling a long list of very detailed personal activities that were automatically encoded into his long-term memory. In fact, many personal events (often unpleasant ones), as well as things we're interested in (movies, music, sports) and a wide range of skills (riding a bike) and habits, are automatically encoded (Dere et al., 2008).

Automatic encoding is the transfer of information from short-term into long-term memory without any effort and usually without any awareness.

Personal events. One reason many of your personal experiences and conversations are automatically encoded is that they hold your interest and attention and easily fit together with hundreds of previous associations. Because personal experiences, which are examples of *episodic information,* are encoded automatically into long-term memory, you can easily recall lengthy conversations, facts about movies and sports figures, television shows, clothes you bought, or food you ate.

> My husband gave me this necklace 20 years ago for our 10 year wedding anniversary.

© Lisa F. Young/Shutterstock.com

Interesting facts. You may know avid sports fans or watchers of popular TV programs who remember an amazing number of facts and details, seemingly without effort. Because these kinds of facts *(semantic information)* are personally interesting and fit with previous associations, they are automatically and easily encoded into declarative long-term memory.

Skills and habits. Learning how to perform various motor skills, such as playing tennis or riding a bike, and developing habits, such as brushing your teeth, are examples of *procedural information,* which is also encoded automatically. For example, H. M. learned and remembered how to mirror-draw because mirror-drawing is a motor skill that is automatically encoded into procedural long-term memory.

On the other hand, factual or technical information from textbooks is usually not encoded automatically but rather requires deliberate, or effortful, encoding, which we'll discuss next.

Effortful Encoding

Why are some things hard to encode?

The person below is pulling his hair because learning unfamiliar or complicated material almost always involves *semantic information,* such as complex terms, which is difficult to encode because such information is often uninteresting, complicated, or requires making new or difficult associations. For all these reasons, semantic information, such as terms, can be encoded only with considerable concentration and effort (Squire & Kandel, 2009).

Effortful encoding involves the transfer of information from short-term into long-term memory either by working hard to repeat or rehearse the information or, especially, by making associations between new and old information.

You already know that some information, such as learning a skill, habit, or interesting personal event, is often encoded effortlessly and automatically. In contrast, semantic information, such as learning hundreds of new or difficult terms, facts, concepts, or equations, usually requires effortful encoding because you must form hundreds of new associations.

> I've been studying these terms for hours and I still can't remember their definitions.

© Ana Blazic/Photos.com

Forming new associations is often just plain hard work and is made even more difficult if you are simultaneously taking two or three difficult classes or have limited time because of other responsibilities, such as a part-time job.

Although there are two methods of effortful encoding—rehearsing and forming associations—the most effective method involves forming associations between the new information that you are trying to learn and the old information that you have already stored in long-term memory. The better the effortful encoding, the better the recall on exams. We'll explain the two methods of effortful encoding, rehearsing and forming associations, and why the second method is more effective and results in better recall.

Rehearsing and Encoding

How much do you remember?

Think of encoding information in your brain as similar to saving information on a gigantic computer hard drive. Unless you have a very good system for labeling and filing the hundreds of computer files, you will have great difficulty finding or retrieving a particular file from the hard drive. Similarly, how easily you can remember or retrieve a particular memory from your brain depends on how much effort you used to encode the information. There are two kinds of effortful encoding: maintenance rehearsal and elaborative rehearsal (Baddeley, 2009a; Kahana, 2012).

Maintenance Rehearsal

The easiest way to remember information for only a short period of time, such as a new phone number or a psychology concept, is to simply repeat or rehearse it. This kind of effortful encoding is called maintenance rehearsal.

Maintenance rehearsal involves simply repeating or rehearsing the information rather than forming any new associations.

Maintenance rehearsal works best for maintaining or keeping information longer in *short-term memory,* such as remembering a phone number for a few seconds while dialing it. However, if you want to remember the phone number later, maintenance rehearsal is not a good encoding process because it does not include a system for keeping track of how and where that particular phone number will be stored. If you need to remember phone numbers or psychology concepts for a long period of time, you'll need to use another form of effortful encoding called elaborative rehearsal.

Maintenance rehearsal is not a very effective encoding process.

Elaborative Rehearsal

There is much information in lectures and textbooks that you want to encode so that you will remember the information for long periods of time. To have the greatest chance of remembering something, it's best to encode information using elaborative rehearsal.

Elaborative rehearsal involves using effort to actively make meaningful associations between new information that you wish to remember and old or familiar information that is already stored in long-term memory.

To test the usefulness of elaborative rehearsal, students were asked to remember many groups of three words each, such as *dog, bike,* and *street.* Students who encoded the words with maintenance rehearsal (repeating words) did poorly on recall. In comparison, students who encoded the words using elaborative rehearsal—that is, taking the effort to make associations among the three words (dog rides a bike down the street)—had significantly better recall (McDaniel & Einstein, 1986).

Elaborative rehearsal is such an effective system of encoding because by making associations between new

Elaborative rehearsal is a very effective encoding process.

and old information, you create cues for locating or retrieving the new information from long-term memory. For example, thinking of the association (dog rides a bike down the street) helps you remember the three words (*dog, bike, street*). Using elaborative rehearsal will help you better encode and retrieve information for your courses than using flashcards or simply repeating information, which involves maintenance rehearsal (A. J. Greene, 2010).

Levels of Processing

How important are associations?

The poorest system for encoding information is to simply repeat the information, which is maintenance rehearsal. The best encoding system is to make associations, which is elaborative rehearsal. How much effort and time you put into encoding information is the basis for the levels-of-processing theory (Craik & Lockhart, 1972).

The **levels-of-processing theory** says that remembering depends on how information is encoded. If you encode by paying attention only to basic features (length of phone number), information is encoded at a shallow level and results in poor recall. If you encode by making new associations, this information will be encoded at a deeper level, which results in better recall.

For example, students were shown a series of words and asked a question after each one. The questions were of three types, designed to trigger three different levels of processing.

1. Shallow processing question:
"Is the word printed in capital letters?" Asks about one physical feature of the word.

2. Deeper processing question:
"Does the word rhyme with *rain?*" Asks about sound properties of the word.

3. Deepest processing question:
"Does the word fit into the sentence 'She was late for the _____'?" Asks about the meaning of the word.

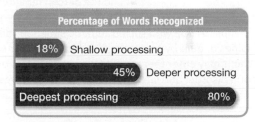

Percentage of Words Recognized

18%	Shallow processing
45%	Deeper processing
Deepest processing	80%

After students answered these questions, they were tested to see how many of the original words they recognized.

As shown in the graph above, students recognized the lowest percentage of words after shallow processing and the highest percentage after the deepest processing (Craik & Tulving, 1975).

This study clearly demonstrates that the system you use to process or encode information has a great effect on how easily you can remember or retrieve the information (M. C. Anderson, 2009a). As we'll discuss in Module 12, a major reason for forgetting is poor encoding (S. C. Brown & Craik, 2005).

Next, we'll discuss a kind of memory that has resulted in great controversy because of the difficulties in determining whether the event ever happened. ●

© Waschnig/Shutterstock.com

G Repressed Memories

Recovered Memories

Who's to blame?

The man in the picture on the right was accused by his daughter, Katrina (left picture), of allegedly molesting her as a child and being a murderer. Katrina's childhood memories first surfaced during psychiatric treatment many years later, when she was 25. She never made these accusations in a conscious state, but only while under the influence of psychiatric medication and controversial treatment methods, such as writing out her dreams using her nondominant hand (believed to prevent lying, but no scientific evidence supports this).

It was quickly discovered that the horrors Katrina was describing couldn't possibly be true, and she later withdrew the allegations. Fortunately, Katrina and her father have mended their relationship and are now closer than ever before. Katrina sued the

"He abused me."   "I did not."

psychiatrist who almost ruined her life by making her believe her so-called "repressed memories" and won a large settlement (BBC News, 2007; Madeley, 2007).

Katrina's case illustrates one of the more explosive issues in psychology: the problem of repressed and recovered memories.

Psychiatrist Harold Lief, one of the first to question the accuracy of repressed memories, said, "We don't know what percent of these recovered memories are real and what percent are pseudomemories (false).... But we do know there are hundreds, maybe thousands of cases of pseudomemories and that many families have been destroyed by them" (J. E. Brody, 2000a, p. D8).

We'll discuss four issues about repressed and recovered memories.

Definition of Repressed Memories

What's different about a repressed memory?

The idea of repressed memories is based on Sigmund Freud's theory of repression, which underlies much of his psychoanalytic theory of personality (discussed in Module 19).

Repression is the process by which the mind pushes a memory of some threatening or traumatic event deep into the unconscious. Once in the unconscious, the repressed memory cannot be retrieved at will and may remain there until something releases it and the person remembers it.

Some therapists believe that children who are sexually abused cope with such traumatic situations and their feelings of guilt by repressing the memories. For example, a client may enter therapy with sexual problems or a mood disorder and later in therapy uncover repressed memories, such as being sexually abused as a child, as the cause of her current

Repressed memories are difficult to recover.

problems. Clients usually have total amnesia (loss of memory) for the traumatic experience, their recovery of repressed memories usually occurs in the first 12 months of therapy, and recovered memories usually involve specific incidents (B. Andrews et al., 2000).

Some therapists believe that repressed memories of sexual abuse do occur; however, many others disagree. For instance, a prominent memory researcher disagrees: "The idea that forgetting in abuse survivors is caused by a special repression mechanism—something more powerful than conscious suppression—is still without a scientific basis" (Schacter, 1996, p. 264). Although there is no scientific support for the repression of traumatic experiences, therapies to recover memories are still being practiced (K. Lambert & Lilienfeld, 2007).

Therapist's Role in Recovered Memories

How does a therapist know?

Some therapists who treat survivors of incest and other traumatic situations maintain that repressed memories are so completely blocked that it may take deliberate suggestion and effort to release them, sometimes using images, hypnosis, or so-called truth serum, sodium amytal.

For example, in one case a client realized that her "memories" were created by a trusted therapist and were unreal. Through therapy she had falsely "remembered" being sexual abused by her father at a young age and then being forced to engage in bestiality and satanic rituals involving the killing and eating of human babies. Even though she was told these false memories would fade in time, she continues to have vivid memories and nightmares of the "recovered" memories. Unfortunately, there are many others who share similar stories (K. Lambert & Lilienfeld, 2007).

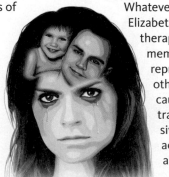

The therapist may have suggested traumatic memories.

Whatever the therapists' good intentions, researcher Elizabeth Loftus (1993, 1997b) and others wonder if some therapists are suggesting or implanting traumatic memories in their clients rather than releasing repressed ones (Loftus & Davis, 2006). Loftus and others suggest that therapists not assume that the cause of psychological problems must be an earlier traumatic experience and caution against aggressive efforts to recover traumatic memories (Geraerts et al., 2007; Loftus, 2003b). Thus, therapists are in the difficult position of distinguishing accurate accounts of repressed memories from those that may have been shaped or reinforced by the suggestions of the therapist (Baddeley, 2004).

Questions about whether suggestions can influence repressed memories raise the issue of whether false memories can be implanted.

Implanting False Memories

Do people believe "fake" memories?

Because, in some cases, it appears that therapists' suggestions may have contributed to implanting false memories, researchers studied whether fake memories could in fact be implanted and later recalled as being "true."

Researchers gave 24 adults a booklet that contained descriptions of three events that occurred when each adult was 5 years old (Loftus, 1997a). Two of the childhood events had *really happened* because they were obtained from parents or relatives. One childhood event of being lost in a shopping mall, crying, being comforted by an elderly woman, and finally getting reunited with the family had *not happened,* according to parents and relatives. After reading the three events described in the booklet, the adults (aged 18–53) were asked to write what they remembered of the event or, if they did not remember, to write "I do not remember this."

The graph above shows that 68% of the participants remembered some or most of the two *true events* from their childhood. However, about 29% also said they remembered having experienced the one *false event* of being lost in the mall at age 5 (Loftus, 1997a).

Percentage of Participants Who Remembered True and False Memories

False	29%
True	68%

Recalled events after reading booklet

About 29% of participants said that they remembered a childhood event that never happened (false) and 68% remembered childhood events that did happen (true).

Researchers concluded that although the memory of being lost in a mall is neither as terrible nor as terrifying as the memory of being abused, this study does show that false memories can be implanted through suggestion alone. Even on a follow-up interview, participants continued to insist that they remembered the false event.

There are now hundreds of studies reporting that false memories can be implanted in children and adults (Loftus, 2003a, 2005b). However, the fact that false memories can be implanted and later recalled as true does not disprove the occurrence of repressed memories. Rather, these studies simply show that a false suggestion can grow into a vivid, detailed, and believable personal memory (Loftus, 2000, 2005b). Brain imaging is now being used to examine the biological mechanisms that lead to impaired memory after exposure to misinformation (Okado & Stark, 2005).

The repeated finding that false memories can be implanted and later remembered as "true" raises a question about the accuracy of repressed memories that are later recovered and believed to be true.

Accuracy of Recovered Memories

How accurate are repressed memories?

Some individuals may initially enter therapy for help with mood disorders or eating problems, but during the course of therapy, they recover memories, apparently repressed, of childhood sexual abuse. Since researchers have shown that "false" memories can be implanted through suggestion and believed to be "true" memories, some question the accuracy of a client's recovered memories.

In a recent study, researchers examined the accuracy of recovered memories of childhood sexual abuse in 128 individuals. Over a six-month period, researchers searched for corroborating evidence for the reported recovered memories. They found corroborating evidence for 37% of memories recovered *outside* of therapy, which almost matches the corroboration rate for childhood memories we all have (45%). However, none of the memories recovered *inside* of therapy could be corroborated. These results do not necessarily indicate that memories recovered in therapy are always false, but it does suggest there is reason for some skepticism (Geraerts, 2007; Geraerts et al., 2007).

As the study above suggests, the accuracy of recovered memories often cannot be established because there is no corroborating evidence of the client's report that the traumatic event really did occur 20–30 years earlier (Roediger & McDermott, 2005). Also, there is reason to question the accuracy of recovered memories because people usually do not recall the memories on their own, but often do so with the help of therapists or support groups (Roediger & McDermott, 2005). Additionally, if the memories were obtained under hypnosis or "truth serum" (sodium amytal),

they may not be accurate, since people often become more open to suggestion and may later recall events that had been suggested during hypnosis as being true (Lynn et al., 2003).

Another reason to question the accuracy of recovered memories is reports of hundreds of clients who later retracted charges of childhood sexual abuse based on memories recovered in therapy (de Rivera, 1997; Loftus & Davis, 2006). In over a dozen other cases, including the case of Katrina (discussed on the preceding page), clients have successfully sued and won large monetary awards from their therapists for implanting false memories of child abuse (Loftus, 1999; Madeley, 2007). All these examples question the accuracy of some recovered memories.

Conclusions. Memory researcher Elizabeth Loftus (1997a, 2003a) states that there are examples of recovered memories that are accurate. However, she questions the accuracy of recovered memories for three reasons: Research has shown that memories that are very detailed but later proven false can be implanted in both children and adults; some clients later retracted their recovered memories; and memories might have been implanted by therapists' suggestions and/or the clients needed and used these memories to explain their current psychological problems. For these reasons, new guidelines caution therapists against using forceful or persuasive suggestions that might elicit memories from their clients (J. E. Brody, 2000a).

The debate over repressed and recovered memories, which reached its peak in the mid-1990s, has recently died down because some therapists have been sued by their patients over the accuracy of recovered memories and researchers have showed that false memories could be implanted in both children and adults (Lynn et al., 2003). ●

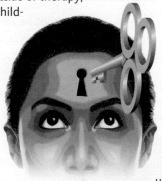

Some question the accuracy of repressed memories.

Concept Review

1. Three processes are involved in memory: The process in which information is placed or stored in memory by making mental representations is called **(a)** _____; the process of placing encoded information into a permanent mental state is called **(b)** _____; the process of getting information out of short-term or permanent storage is called **(c)** _____.

2. The initial step in memory is a process that holds visual and auditory information in its raw form for a very brief period of time, from an instant to several seconds; this process is called _____.

3. Memory that holds raw visual information for up to a quarter of a second is called **(a)** _____. Memory that holds raw auditory information for up to several seconds is called **(b)** _____. The process for controlling the transfer of information from sensory memory to the next memory process is **(c)** _____.

4. The kind of memory that has a limited capacity of about seven items (plus or minus two) and a short duration (2–30 seconds) for unrehearsed information is called either **(a)** _____ or _____ memory. One way to increase this memory capacity is by combining separate pieces of information into larger units, which is called **(b)** _____. One way to increase the duration of this memory is by repeating the information, which is called **(c)** _____.

5. The kind of memory that can store almost unlimited amounts of information over a long period of time is _____, whose accuracy may undergo change and distortion across time.

6. The process for controlling the transfer of information from short-term memory into long-term memory is called _____, which may be automatic or may involve deliberate effort.

7. The process for selecting information from long-term memory and transferring it back into short-term memory is _____.

Love Is Like Chocolate.

8. The better recall of items at the beginning of a list is called the **(a)** _____ effect. The better recall of items at the end of a list is called the **(b)** _____ effect. Evidence that there are two kinds of memory, short- and long-term, comes from the **(c)** _____ effect.

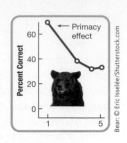

9. There are two kinds of encoding. Simply repeating or rehearsing the information is called **(a)** _____. Actively making associations between new and old information already stored is called **(b)** _____.

10. One kind of long-term memory that involves memories for facts or events, such as scenes, stories, words, conversations, faces, or daily events, is called **(a)** _____ memory. We can retrieve these memories and are conscious of them. One kind of declarative memory that involves events or personal experiences is called **(b)** _____ memory. A second kind of declarative memory that involves general knowledge, facts, or definitions of words is called **(c)** _____ memory.

11. A second kind of long-term memory that involves performing motor or perceptual tasks, carrying out habits, and responding to stimuli because of classical conditioning is called _____ memory. We cannot retrieve these memories and are not conscious of them.

12. Something happens that is so threatening, shocking, or traumatic that our mind pushes that memory into the unconscious, from which it cannot be retrieved at will. This phenomenon is called _____.

13. During very emotional or stressful situations, the body secretes chemicals called **(a)** _____ that act to make encoding very effective, and this results in vivid, long-term memories.

14. Most patients with amnesia retain the functioning of **(a)** _____ memory and **(b)** _____ memory. However, they usually have profound impairment in **(c)** _____ memory.

Unless otherwise noted, all images are © Cengage Learning

Answers: 1. (a) *encoding,* (b) *storage,* (c) *retrieval;* 2. *sensory memory;* 3. (a) *iconic memory,* (b) *echoic memory,* (c) *attention;* 4. (a) *short-term, working,* (b) *chunking,* (c) *rehearsal, or maintenance rehearsal;* 5. *long-term memory;* 6. *encoding;* 7. *retrieval;* 8. (a) *primacy,* (b) *recency,* (c) *serial position;* 9. (a) *maintenance rehearsal,* (b) *elaborative rehearsal;* 10. (a) *declarative,* (b) *episodic,* (c) *semantic;* 11. *procedural, or nondeclarative;* 12. *repression, or repressed memory;* 13. (a) *hormones;* 14. (a) *procedural,* (b) *semantic,* (c) *episodic*

H Cultural Diversity: Oral Versus Written

United States Versus Africa

What do you remember best?

If you went to grade school in the United States, you spent considerable time in your first 8 years learning to read and write. In the U.S. culture, reading and writing skills are viewed as being not only very important for personal growth and development but also necessary for achieving success in one's career. For similar reasons, the schools of many industrialized cultures place heavy emphasis on teaching reading and writing, which allow individuals to encode great amounts of information in long-term memory. In addition, reading and writing skills are necessary for being admitted to and doing well in college.

In contrast, if you went to grade school in the more rural countries of Africa, you would have spent your first 8 or so years learning primarily through the spoken word rather than the written word. In the less industrialized countries of Africa, such as Ghana, there are fewer public or private schools, fewer textbooks and libraries. As a result, these cultures are said to have a strong *oral tradition,* which means that these people have considerable practice in passing on information

In more rural parts of Africa (Ghana), children must rely more on oral than written information.

through speaking and retelling. The Ghana culture emphasizes the oral tradition, which means encoding information after hearing it rather than after reading it.

With Ghana's emphasis on oral tradition, we would expect that African people would better encode and remember information that was spoken. In comparison, with the United States' emphasis on *written tradition,* we would expect that American people would better encode and remember information that was read rather than spoken. In fact, research data support the idea that Ghanaian students demonstrate superior recall of spoken information because of their long oral tradition, which involves practicing encoding information through hearing rather than reading (B. M. Ross & Millsom, 1970). These results indicate that a culture's emphasis on how information is presented or taught can influence how information or events are encoded and how easily they can be recalled.

Next, we'll take a closer look at the oral tradition, a common way that many ancient African cultures remembered and commemorated the past.

Oral Tradition

What are griots?

The oldest way of communicating about the past is orally, and because cultures in ancient Africa did not have written language, they embraced the oral tradition.

In many parts of ancient Africa, people relied on *griots*, who were official storytellers responsible for keeping records of the history of the people. Consequently, griots were highly regarded individuals who played important roles in their community. In addition to conveying historical lessons, they imparted morals and instructions on how to behave properly. Their stories reminded people about their culture's identity and taught them how it fits into the world, in both the present and the past (Baddeley, 2004).

Although their main role was to be educators, griots were also artists and entertainers. As storytellers, they communicated historical information, often in the form of verse or song, and sometimes accompanied by musical instruments, such as drums, and dance. Griots were given flexibility to recreate the way stories were shared. Adults

A lukasa provides a conceptual map of important parts of cultural history.

and children would eagerly gather around griots to learn and be entertained (Baddeley, 2004; Goucher et al., 1998).

Although their cultural memory system was fundamentally oral, some of the tribes in ancient Africa used visual devices or objects to help them remember important information. For example, the Luba in Central Africa used a *lukasa*, which is a handheld wooden board covered with pins and beads that provides a conceptual map of important parts of cultural history. The lukasa was not meant to be read by just anyone, but rather was limited to only those trained to interpret and convey the complex meaning of its visual representations (Goucher et al., 1998).

Griots are storytellers who keep record of and convey historical information.

Whether a culture keeps a formal record of historical information through written tradition or oral tradition, the memory of cultures can be preserved. The written tradition of the United States ensures that its history is documented in written form, but it does not guarantee that people will remember the information. In fact, as we will learn in Module 12, the use of visual images, such as the lukasa, can serve as an effective way to encode and retrieve information.

Next, we'll examine some unusual cases of encoding and retrieving information. ●

I Application: Unusual Memories

Photographic Memory

Can you recall everything?

One kind of unusual memory that many of us wish we had is the ability to remember everything with little or no difficulty. Such an amazing memory is commonly called a photographic memory.

Photographic memory, which occurs in adults, is the ability to form sharp, detailed visual images after examining a picture or page for a short period of time and to recall the entire image at a later date.

There are no reports of someone developing a photographic memory and only one or two reports of adults who had a truly photographic memory (Stromeyer, 1970). Sometimes people with exceptional memories are mislabeled as having photographic memories (Adams, 2006; Foer, 2006b).

At a national memory contest (U.S. Memoriad), Tatiana Cooley (photo above) came in first by doing incredible memory feats, such as pairing 70 names and faces after studying a stack of 100 faces for just 20 minutes. As a child, Tatiana's mother would read

She could perfectly visualize her class notes so she didn't have to study for exams.

to her, and when Tatiana was 2½ years old, she read one of the books back to her mother. In college, Tatiana says, "I remember visualizing the notes that I had taken in class and being able to recall them verbatim for tests so I didn't have to study" (P. Rogers & Morehouse, 1999, p. 90). To keep her memory sharp, she spends 45 minutes each day memorizing the order in which cards appear in a freshly shuffled deck. Wow! Tatiana's ability to visually remember her notes during exams comes close to satisfying the definition of having a photographic memory.

Later in Module 14 (see p. 311), we'll introduce you to Stephen Wilshire, who has been referred to as "the human camera." Although his visual memory is truly extraordinary, it too doesn't completely satisfy the definition of having a photographic memory.

Extraordinary Episodic Memory

What did you eat for lunch when you were 14 years and 126 days old?

What would it be like to vividly remember everything you have ever experienced in your life? Jill Price, now in her forties, is known to have super-memory abilities. Interestingly, Jill doesn't have any special abilities to remember words, numbers, or factual information (types of *semantic memory;* p. 246), but she has an unsurpassed, unimaginable ability to remember her life events since the age of 14 (*episodic memory;* p. 246).

Name any date and Jill can without hesitation tell you what she did on that day, such as what she had for lunch, where she went, and whom she spoke with, as well as any significant news or world events

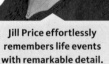

Jill Price effortlessly remembers life events with remarkable detail.

that took place on that day (provided she heard about it, of course). Jill remembers all of her life experiences in vivid detail without effort—now, that's beyond impressive!

As amazing as Jill's memory abilities are, she is constantly tormented by her memory. She describes feeling powerless because she can't stop remembering certain events no matter how much she tries. Just for a moment imagine not being able to forget all of the unpleasant life experiences you've had and have them play over and over in your mind with such clarity that you feel like you are actually reliving the moments. This is how Jill lives. She is stuck remembering both the good times and the bad (Neimark, 2009; E. S. Parker et al., 2006; J. Price, 2008).

A new super memory has recently been discovered: the extraordinary ability to recognize faces.

Super Memory for Faces

Can you remember the face of a person you saw in passing a few years ago?

Most of us cannot remember the faces of people we met a few years ago and only in passing. Recent research finds that some people (as many as 2%) in fact have this ability and are referred to as *super-recognizers,* meaning they can easily recognize someone they met in passing, even years later.

Super-recognizers have an extreme version of memory for faces. They may recognize someone they saw while shopping several months ago. They can also recognize people who have changed in appearance, such as hair color or aging. Because their memory for faces is so extreme, they often have to pretend to not recognize someone they

"Super-recognizers" easily recognize familiar faces, even in large crowds.

simply saw in passing to avoid the awkwardness of interacting with them. Imagine how awkward it would be for someone to come up and say he saw you 3 years ago at the grocery store while you were buying milk and cookies! People with this incredible memory would be great working in security and law enforcement, as well as provide trustworthy eyewitness testimony (R. Russell et al., 2009; *Science Daily,* 2009a).

Many of us have experienced a very vivid and detailed memory that is called a "flashbulb memory."

Flashbulb Memory

What makes a memory so vivid?

Although it happened over 20 years ago, I (H.K.) have a detailed memory of my cabin in the Santa Cruz Mountains of California shaking and then seesawing on the edge of a mountain during a frightening earthquake. I can play back this terrible scene in great detail and vivid color as if I were actually experiencing an earthquake. Many individuals have had a similar experience, and this kind of memory event is called a flashbulb memory (R. Brown & Kulik, 1977).

Flashbulb memories are vivid recollections, usually in great detail, of dramatic or emotionally charged incidents that are of interest to the person. This information is encoded effortlessly and may last for long periods of time.

Impact and Accuracy

Do you remember precisely what you were doing when you first learned of the 9/11 attacks? Flashbulb memories usually involve events that are extremely surprising, are emotionally arousing, or have very important meaning or consequences for the person.

Although flashbulb memories are reported with great confidence and in vivid details, this does not mean the memories are necessarily accurate (Talarico & Rubin, 2003). That's because people mistake the vividness of flashbulb memories for their accuracy.

Research examining the consistency of people's stories about their flashbulb memories of the 9/11 attacks demonstrates how faulty these recollections can be. Researchers found a significant inconsistency in people's reports made one week and then three years after the event. Examples of elements that changed included who they were with at the time they found out about the attacks and how they first found out about the attacks. The part that changed the most over the years was their reported emotions. Researchers hypothesize that people tend to project their current feelings about the event on how they felt then, when in reality their feelings have likely changed a lot since the event (Hirst et al., 2009; B. M. Law, 2011).

Most-Remembered Events

As you can see in the center table, the top five flashbulb memories of college students involved a car accident, a college roommate, high school graduation and prom, and a romantic experience, all of which are emotionally charged events.

Initially, flashbulb memories were claimed to represent a special kind of memory that was complete, accurate, vivid, and immune to forgetting (R. Brown & Kulik, 1977). Since then, several studies have investigated these claims and reported that flashbulb memories do not seem to be a separate, special kind of memory

because they are subject to inaccuracies, change with retelling, and are even forgotten over time (C. A. Weaver & Krug, 2004).

Remote Historical Events

In a study of flashbulb memory, Danes (people from Denmark) who lived through the Nazi occupation and liberation during World War II and Danes born during or after World War II were asked questions about the days of the occupation and liberation, such as what the weather conditions were like and what they were doing when they heard the news. Nearly all the older Danes reported having flashbulb memories, being able to recall detailed personal memories about the two war events. Also, the majority of older Danes but very few younger Danes accurately recalled weather conditions. These researchers concluded that flashbulb memories represent a special kind of automatic encoding that occurs when events are emotionally and personally interesting. The results of this study and other research show that flashbulb memories can last 60 years or even longer (Berntsen & Thomsen, 2005).

Brains and Hormones

Researchers think the reason flashbulb memories are so detailed and long-lasting is that their emotionally arousing content activates a special brain area and several hormones. For example, researchers believe that flashbulb memories involve a brain structure called the amygdala (see p. 80), which plays a key role in processing and encoding strong emotional experiences (Squire & Kandel, 2009).

Also, in the Research Focus on page 247, we discussed how emotionally triggered hormones are involved in encoding long-term memories as if "in stone". The secretion of these "emotional" hormones is thought to play a role in encoding emotionally charged personal experiences into long-lasting memories (Lemonick, 2007a).

Pictures Versus Impressions

Each of us has a remarkable memory system that can encode, store, and retrieve unlimited amounts of information over long periods of time. But it's important to remember that memories are not perfect pictures of objects, people, and events but rather our personal impressions of these things. This means that what you remember and recall may be changed, biased, or distorted by a wide range of emotional feelings, personal experiences, stressful situations, or social influences (Roediger & McDermott, 2005). ●

Examples of Flashbulb Memories

Cues	Percent*
A car accident you were in or witnessed	85
When you first met your college roommate	82
Night of your high school graduation	81
Night of your senior prom (if you went or not)	78
An early romantic experience	77
A time you had to speak in front of an audience	72
When you got your college admission letter	65
Your first date—the moment you met him/her	57
First time you flew in an airplane	40
Moment you opened your SAT scores	33
Your 17th birthday	30
The last time you ate a holiday dinner at home	23
Your first college class	21
The first time your parents left you alone for some time	19
Your 13th birthday	12

*Percentage of students in the memory experiment who reported that events on the experimenter's list were of flashbulb quality (D. C. Rubin & Kozin, 1984)

Adapted from "Vivid Memories," by D. C. Rubin and M. Kozin, 1984, *Cognition, 16,* 81–95. Copyright © 1984 by Elsevier Science Publishers BV. Adapted by permission from Elsevier Science.

Can Phony Memories Change Your Behavior?

It's been well established that people can be made to believe "fake" memories, but can "fake" memories change people's behavior? Research psychologist Elizabeth Loftus of the University of California–Irvine and her colleagues studied whether simply suggesting food preferences can change what people decide to eat. To answer this question, these researchers asked college-aged participants to complete questionnaires on their personalities and food experiences. As part of the questionnaires, the participants were asked about childhood food experiences, such as whether they "ate a piece of banana cream pie."

One week after completing the questionnaires, participants returned and were told that their responses were used to create a "unique" profile of their early childhood food experiences. Everyone's profile included generic statements such as they disliked spinach, enjoyed eating bananas, and felt happy when a classmate brought sweets to school. In addition, the profiles of one group of participants included one completely made-up point: "Felt ill after eating strawberry ice cream." The remaining participants were the control group and their profiles did not include a statement about getting ill as a result of eating strawberry ice cream.

1 What type of long-term memory is used to recall a bad childhood experience with food?

When participants in the false memory group were told the questionnaire results showed they had a bad childhood experience with strawberry ice cream, researchers asked several follow-up questions about the phony memory, such as where they were when they got sick and who else witnessed the event. About 41% of participants given the false memory believed they had once gotten sick from eating strawberry ice cream. Some of them even reported details about the experience such as "may have gotten sick after eating seven cups of ice cream."

During this same visit, participants completed a second questionnaire about eating preferences, and many of these "believers" (20 of the 47) now reported less preference for and less willingness to eat strawberry ice cream. In contrast, the control group, who did not receive false feedback, did not show any change in their preference for strawberry ice cream.

2 Why were researchers able to implant false memories in these people?

3 Is it possible for a person to have had a traumatic experience with strawberry ice cream as a teenager and not remember it as an adult?

4 Would the results be different if people were presented with a bowl of strawberry ice cream instead of being asked to report their preference on a questionnaire?

© Kuzmin Andrey/Shutterstock.com

As many people have learned, a strong and long-lasting aversion to a certain food can develop after only one bad childhood experience. Loftus gives an example that a novel food such as béarnaise sauce may make a person sick one time and lead to avoiding the food in the future. The current study suggests it is possible for such an aversion to occur based only on a false memory. Loftus and her colleagues are now examining whether false memories of really liking certain healthy vegetables during childhood can be implanted and make people more likely to eat such foods as adults.

5 What type of learning occurs when a person has a bad experience with food and then avoids eating it?

6 Should physicians implant false memories to help patients lose weight?

Adapted from D. M. Bernstein et al., 2005; Loftus, 2005a; Park, 2005; Skloot, 2006; M. Smith, 2005

Summary Test

A Three Stages of Memory

1. The study of memory, which is the ability to retain information over time, includes three separate processes. The first process—placing information in memory—is called **(a)** _____. The second process, which is filing information in memory, is called **(b)** _____. The third process—commonly referred to as remembering—is called **(c)** _____.

2. Although we think of memory as a single event, it is really a complex sequence that may be separated into three different kinds of memory. The initial memory process that holds raw information for up to several seconds is called _____. During this time, you have the chance to identify or pay attention to new information.

3. If you pay attention to information in sensory memory, this information is automatically transferred into a second kind of memory process, called _____ memory.

4. If you rehearse or think about information in short-term memory, that information will usually be transferred or encoded into the third, more permanent kind of memory process called _____.

B Sensory Memory: Recording

5. Visual sensory memory, known as **(a)** _____ memory, lasts about a quarter of a second. Auditory memory, known as **(b)** _____ memory, may last as long as 2 seconds. Sensory memory has many functions; for example, it prevents you from being overwhelmed by too much incoming information and gives you time to identify the incoming data and pay attention to them.

C Short-Term Memory: Working

6. If you pay attention to information in sensory memory, it is automatically transferred into short-term memory, which has two main characteristics. The first is that unrehearsed information will disappear after 2–30 seconds, indicating that short-term memory has a limited **(a)** _____. The second characteristic is that short-term memory can hold only about seven items (plus or minus two), indicating that short-term memory has a limited **(b)** _____. You can increase the length

of time that information remains in short-term memory by intentionally repeating the information, which is called **(c)** _____. You can considerably increase the capacity of short-term memory by combining separate items of information into larger units, which is called **(d)** _____.

D Long-Term Memory: Storing

7. Let's follow the progress of information from the time it enters sensory memory to its storage in long-term memory. For an instant to several seconds, incoming raw information is held in **(a)** _____. If you do not pay attention to this information, it disappears forever; if you pay attention, that information is automatically transferred into short-term memory. The transfer of Information from sensory memory into short-term memory is controlled by the process of **(b)** _____.

8. If information in short-term memory is not **(a)** _____, it will disappear in 2–30 seconds. If you rehearse or think about information in short-term memory, it may be transferred into long-term memory. The transfer of information from short-term into long-term memory is controlled by a process called **(b)** _____. In some cases, information is transferred automatically; in other cases, this transfer process may require deliberate effort.

9. The process of selecting information from long-term memory and transferring it back into short-term memory is called _____. Because information has been encoded into long-term memory does not guarantee that such information can always or easily be remembered or retrieved.

10. One demonstration of the existence of, and difference between, short-term and long-term memory is observed in the order in which people remember items from a multiple-item list. People tend to have better recall of items at the beginning of a list; this tendency is called the **(a)** _____ effect and involves long-term memory. People tend to have better recall of items at the end of the list; this tendency is called the **(b)** _____ effect and involves short-term memory. The order in which people recall items from a long list is called the **(c)** _____ effect.

11. There are two different kinds of long-term memory. One kind involves memories of facts or events, such as scenes, stories, words, conversations, faces, or daily events. We can retrieve these memories and are conscious of them; they constitute **(a)** _____ memory. There are two kinds of declarative memory. One kind consists of factual knowledge of

© fotofreaks/Shutterstock.com

© PhotoDisc, Inc.

the world, concepts, word definitions, and language rules; this is called **(b)** _____ memory. The second kind of declarative memory consists of knowledge about personal experiences (episodes) or activities; this is called **(c)** _____ memory.

12. A second kind of long-term memory involves memories for performing motor or perceptual tasks, carrying out habits, and responding to stimuli because of classical conditioning; this is called _____ memory. We cannot retrieve these memories and are not conscious of them.

E Research Focus: Strengthening Episodic Memories

13. Researchers found that during emotional or stressful situations, the body secretes chemicals called **(a)** _____, which make encoding so effective that these situations become very vivid long-term memories. A temporary or permanent loss of memory that occurs after a blow or damage to the brain or after disease, general anesthesia, certain drugs, or severe psychological stress is called **(b)** _____.

F Encoding: Transferring

14. The process of storing information in memory by making mental representations is called **(a)** _____. There are two processes for encoding information. Most procedural and episodic information is transferred from short-term into long-term memory without any effort, and usually without any awareness, through a process called **(b)** _____ encoding. Much semantic information is transferred from short-term into long-term memory by deliberate attempts to repeat, rehearse, or make associations. Together, these deliberate attempts are referred to as **(c)** _____ encoding.

15. There are two kinds of effortful encoding, which differ in their effectiveness. Encoding by simply repeating or rehearsing the information is called **(a)** _____. This method is not very effective because it involves little thinking about the information or making new associations. Encoding that involves thinking about the information and making new associations is called **(b)** _____.

16. One theory says that memory depends on how information is encoded in the mind. If we pay attention to only basic features of the information, it is encoded at a shallow level and poor memory results. If we form new associations, the information is encoded at a deeper level and good memory results. This theory is called _____.

G Repressed Memories

17. If something happens that is threatening, shocking, or traumatic, our minds may push that information deep into the unconscious, from which it may one day be released and enter consciousness. This phenomenon is called **(a)** _____ and is the theory behind the formation of **(b)** _____ memories. Unless there is corroborating evidence, the accuracy of repressed memories is difficult to establish.

H Cultural Diversity: Oral Versus Written

18. Research data finds that Ghana-ian students demonstrate superior recall of spoken information because of their **(a)** _____, which is in contrast to the United States' emphasis on **(b)** _____.

19. In many parts of ancient Africa, people relied on _____, who were official storytellers responsible for keeping records of the history of the people.

I Application: Unusual Memories

20. A person who can effortlessly remember life events that occurred many years ago with remarkable detail has extraordinary **(a)** _____ memory. In adults, the ability to form sharp, detailed visual images after a short period and recall the entire image at a later date is called **(b)** _____ memory. Memories that are vivid recollections, usually in great detail, of dramatic or emotionally charged incidents are called **(c)** _____. Although very vivid, these memories are not necessarily completely accurate.

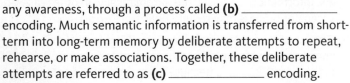

Unless otherwise noted, all images are © Cengage Learning

Links to Learning

Key Terms/Key People

amnesia, 247

automatic encoding, 248

chunking, 243

declarative memory, 246

echoic memory, 241

effortful encoding, 248

elaborative rehearsal, 249

encoding, 239, 244, 248

episodic memory, 246

explicit memory, 246

false memories: implanting, 251

flashbulb memories, 255

griots, 253

hormones and memories, 247

iconic memory, 241

implicit memory, 246

information-processing model, 239

interference, 242

levels-of-processing theory, 249

limited capacity, 242

limited duration, 242

long-term memory, 240, 244

maintenance rehearsal, 242, 249

memories of emotional events, 247

memory, 239

memory processes, 240, 244

oral tradition, 253

photographic memory, 254

primacy effect, 245

procedural or nondeclarative memory, 246

recency effect, 245

recovered memories, 250

recovered memories: accuracy, 251

repressed memories, 250

repression, 250

retrieval, 239, 244

retrieving, 244

semantic memory, 246

sensory memory, 240, 241

serial position effect, 245

short-term memory, 240, 242

storage, 239

three-stages model, 240

working memory, 242

written tradition, 253

Media Resources

Go to **CengageBrain.com** to access Psychology CourseMate, where you will find an interactive eBook, glossaries, flashcards, quizzes, videos, answers to Critical Thinking questions, and more. You can also access Virtual Psychology Labs, an interactive laboratory experience designed to illustrate key experiments first-hand.

Watching a Crime

How much can you remember? It was about nine at night when you entered the campus building, climbed one flight of stairs, and began walking down the long hallway. You had just finished your psychology paper and were going to slip it under the instructor's door. Everything happened very quickly.

From about the middle of the dimly lit hallway, a man with reddish hair and wearing a brown leather jacket jumped out from behind a half-open door and ran at you. Instinctively, you threw out your hands and tried to ward off the oncoming threat. With a quick motion, the man grabbed your blue shoulder bag and pushed you down. At that instant, your eyes met. He pointed at you with a menacing gesture and said, "Don't move or make a sound." Then he checked the hallway, stepped around you, and was gone (adapted from Buckout, 1980).

1,800 people identified the wrong mugger.

A 12-second filmed sequence with a storyline similar to this one was shown on television. In the TV film, the assailant's face was on the screen for several seconds. Next, the viewers were asked to watch a lineup of six men and then to call the TV station and identify which was the assailant. Of the more than 2,000 viewers who called in, only 200 identified the correct man; 1,800 selected the wrong one (Buckout, 1980).

Without looking back, try to answer the following questions (answers at bottom):

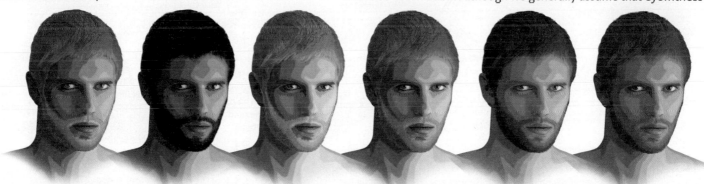

1. What color was the mugger's jacket?
2. What color and type was the student's bag?
3. Besides the bag, what else was the student carrying?
4. The mugger's exact words were "Don't make a sound." True or false?
5. When thrown down, the student yelled out "Stop!" True or false?
6. Of the 2,000 viewers who called in, 1,800 identified the correct assailant. True or false?

Answers: 1. brown; 2. blue, shoulder bag; 3. psychology paper; 4. false; 5. false; 6. false

Adapted from "Nearly 2,000 Witnesses Can Be Wrong," by R. Buckout, 1980, *Bulletin of the Psychonomic Society*, *16*, 307–310.

Recall Versus Recognition

Which is easier? You probably found the first three questions harder because they involve recall.

Recall involves retrieving previously learned information without the aid of or with very few external cues. For example, in questions 1–3, you were asked to recall colors or objects without having any choices. Students must use recall to answer fill-in-the-blank and essay questions.

You probably thought the last three questions were easier because they involve recognition.

Recognition involves identifying previously learned information with the help of external cues.

In questions 4–6, you have only to recognize whether the information provided is correct. Students use recognition to decide which of the choices is correct on multiple-choice tests. Since multiple-choice tests involve recognition, they are generally considered easier than fill-in-the-blank and essay questions, which involve recall. Later in this module, we'll discuss why recall is more difficult than recognition.

Eyewitness Testimony

Which face did you see? Question 6 asks about a very curious result. Although the assailant's face was on the television screen for several seconds, 90% of the viewers identified the *wrong* person in a six-man lineup. (For example, from the six faces below, can you identify the correct mugger? See the answer below.) How can you clearly see someone's face and not remember it? The answer to this question comes from studies on how eyewitness memories can be affected by suggestions, misleading questions, and false information. Although we generally assume that eyewitness testimony is the most accurate kind of evidence, you'll see that this is not always true. We'll discuss accuracy and problems of eyewitness testimony at the end of this module. (The mugger had reddish hair.)

What's Coming

We'll discuss how you organize thousands of events, faces, and facts and file this information in long-term memory. We'll explain the most common reasons for forgetting, the biological bases for memory, methods to improve memory, the accuracy of memory, and the accuracy of eyewitness testimony.

We'll begin with a huge problem that you face every day: How do you file away and organize your many, many thousands of memories? ●

A Organization of Memories

Filing and Organizing 87,967 Memories

How do you store memories?

One of the great puzzles of memory is how you file and store zillions of things over your lifetime. Suppose this past month you stored 91 faces, 6,340 concepts, 258 songs, 192 names, 97 definitions, 80,987 personal events, 1 dog, and 1 cat. How did you store these 87,967 memories so that you can search and retrieve one particular item from long-term memory?

There are several theories for how we file and organize memories; we'll discuss one of the more popular theories, which is called network theory (J. L. McClelland, 2005).

Network theory says that we store related ideas in separate categories, or files, called nodes. As we make associations among bits of information, we create links among thousands of nodes, which make up a gigantic interconnected network of files for storing and retrieving information.

> Network theory says we store memories by filing them into categories.

Network theory may become clearer if you imagine that the mental files, or nodes, are like thousands of cities on a map and the connections or associations among them are like roads. Just as you follow different roads to go from city to city, you follow different associative pathways to go from idea to idea. Storing new events, faces, and thousands of other things would be similar to erecting new buildings in the cities and also building new roads between the cities (B. Schwartz & Reisberg, 1991). Here's how one cognitive psychologist, Donald Norman, used network theory to explain how he retrieved a particular memory.

Network Theory of Memory Organization

Where do the roads lead?

Just as you might follow a road map to reach a particular city, cognitive psychologist Norman followed a cognitive map to remember the name of a particular store in San Diego. Although the mental roads that Norman takes may seem strange, these roads represent personal associations that he created when he filed, or stored, information in long-term memory. As he follows his associations, or mental roads, he travels the cognitive network from node to node or memory to memory in search of a particular name (Norman, 1982). Please begin reading at node 1 and continue to node 6.

1 **Norman's train of thought began with his remembering a party he had attended earlier at a friend's house.**
© Monkey Business Images/Shutterstock.com

2 **The house had associations with smoke detectors on the ceilings of the rooms.**
© Iriana Shiyan/Shutterstock.com

3 **The smoke detectors had associations with batteries, which are needed to power the detectors.**
© TerryM/Shutterstock.com

4 **The batteries had associations with a certain store in San Diego where Norman bought batteries and other items.**
© restyler/Shutterstock.com

5 **The department store had associations with many items that he bought, including trays for his slides.**
© Shawn Hempel/Shutterstock.com

6 **As Norman thought of buying slide trays, he remembered the store's name, "Nordstrom."**
NORDSTROM
© Northfoto/Shutterstock.com

Memory figure based on *Learning and Memory*, by D.A. Norman, 1982; W. H. Freeman & Company.

Norman mentally followed a cognitive map, starting with node 1 and following nodes 2, 3, 4, 5, to the name of a store at node 6.

Searching for a Memory

We've all shared Norman's problem of knowing we know something but having difficulty recalling it. This problem relates to how we store memories in long-term memory. According to the network theory of memory, we store memories in nodes that are interconnected after we make new associations. Because the network theory is somewhat complicated, we'll review how it applied to Norman's problem of trying to recall a particular memory.

Nodes. Norman organizes or stores related ideas in separate files, or categories, called nodes. We simplified this process by showing only six nodes, but there may be dozens. Nodes are categories for storing related ideas, such as birds, faces, friends, and store names.

Associations. Norman links the nodes, or categories of ideas, together by making associations or mental roads between new information and old information that was previously stored.

Network. Norman has thousands of interconnected nodes, which form an enormous cognitive network for arranging and storing files. Norman must search through this cognitive network to find a particular node or file, where a specific memory is stored.

Researchers have developed a theory of how we search through thousands of nodes to find a particular one (J. L. McClelland, 2005).

Organization of Network Hierarchy

How do you find a specific memory?

How do you find a specific memory to answer these questions: How big is a guppy? Does a rooster have feathers? Does a blue jay have skin? According to network theory, you will search for answers to these questions by using different nodes or memory files.

Nodes are memory files that contain related information organized around a specific topic or category.

According to network theory, the many thousands of nodes or memory files are arranged in a certain kind of order, which is called a network hierarchy (Diesendruck & Shatz, 2001).

A **network hierarchy** is the arrangement of nodes or memory files in a certain order or hierarchy. At the bottom of the hierarchy are nodes with very concrete information, which are connected to nodes with somewhat more specific information, which in turn are connected to nodes with general or abstract information.

For example, a partial network hierarchy for nodes or memory files containing information about animals is shown on the right. Depending on whether you're looking for a specific memory (How big is a guppy?) or a more abstract memory (Does a blue jay have skin?), you will search different nodes, as explained next.

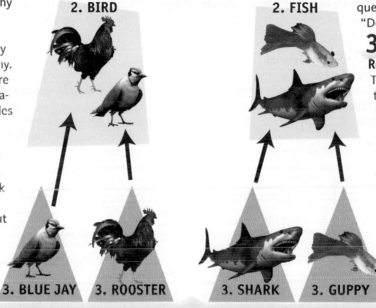

1 **Abstract: Animal**
This node, or memory file, contains information that is very abstract and applies to all animals, such as has skin, can move around, eats, and breathes. This category has answers to very general questions about animals—"Does a blue jay have skin?"

2 **More Specific: Bird or Fish**
This node, or memory file, contains information that is somewhat more specific because it applies to many fish or birds, such as has wings, can fly, and has feathers. This category has answers to somewhat specific questions about fish or birds— "Does a rooster have feathers?"

3 **Concrete: Blue Jay, Rooster, Shark, or Guppy**
This node, or memory file, contains very concrete information that applies only to a specific animal. This category has answers to very specific questions— "How big is a guppy?" "What color is a shark?"

Conclusion. Because network theory doesn't have all the answers to how you file and store information, researchers are developing more complex models, such as neural networks, that try to imitate how the brain organizes and files millions of bits of information (Ratcliff & McKoon, 2005).

Network hierarchy: Arranging memory files (nodes) so that general information is in the top file (node #1) and specific information is in the bottom files (nodes #3)

Network hierarchy based on "Retrieval time from semantic memory," by A. M. Colins and M. R. Quillian, 1969, *Verbal Learning and Verbal Behavior, 8,* 240–247. Blue jay: © Sarah Holmlund/Shutterstock.com; guppy: © Dirk Ercken/Shutterstock.com; shark: © Michael Rosskothen/Shutterstock.com; rooster: © Serg64/Shutterstock.com

---

Categories in the Brain

Does the brain come with a built-in filing system?

The network theory's idea that information is filed in interconnected nodes or categories is partly supported by findings showing that the brain seems to have its own built-in filing system. For example, researchers found that, depending on which area of the brain is damaged, patients lose the ability to identify or process information dealing with a specific category. In some cases, patients could no longer identify faces but had no problems identifying information in other categories, such as tools, animals, furniture, or plants. In other cases, patients could no longer identify plants but could identify information in different categories (tools, animals, etc.) (Schacter et al., 2005). These findings indicate that the brain has built-in categories for sorting and filing different kinds of information.

The brain seems to have built-in files or categories.

By using another research approach involving brain scans (see p. 70), researchers found further evidence that we use different areas of the brain to process different categories. For example, when people were asked to think of objects in specific categories, such as faces, tools, or furniture, researchers found that maximum neural activity occurred in different areas of the brain. As shown at the left, when people were thinking of animals, the maximum neural activity occurred in the back of the brain, while thinking of tools produced maximum neural activity in the front of the brain (A. Martin et al., 1996). The finding that the brain comes with prewired categories for processing information helps explain how you can easily sort through a tremendous amount of information and quickly find the answer to a specific question, such as "Does a camel have a hump?" (Low et al., 2003). ●

Scan: © Digital Stock Corporation; pliers: © Serg64/Shutterstock.com; camel: © tezzstock/Shutterstock.com

B Forgetting Curves

Early Memories

The earliest that people in different cultures can recall personal memories averages 3½ years old (Q. Wang, 2003). Researchers did find that children as young as 13 months can recall visual events, such as a sequence of moving toys. Also, research indicates that some basic forms of memory begin while in the womb (Springen, 2010). For example, babies have been known to calm down when they hear music that their mothers listened to during pregnancy. However, recalling moving objects and familiar sounds is different from recalling personal memories, which is based on

What's your earliest memory?

Earliest memories at about age 3½

having developed a sense of oneself (recognizing the face in the mirror as yours), which occurs after age 2 (Howe, 2003). Another reason we rarely remember personal events before age 3½ is that very young children have little or no language skills, so they cannot verbally encode early personal memories (Baddeley, 2004; Simcock & Hayne, 2002). Also, very young children have not yet developed a complete memory circuit in the brain, which is necessary for encoding and retrieving personal memories (Baddeley, 2004; Bauer, 2002). But even though you're now an adult with a completely developed memory brain circuit, why do you still forget things, especially when taking exams?

Unfamiliar and Uninteresting

Could you remember LUD, ZIB?

From your experience studying for exams, you know that just because you verbally encode information by listening, reading, or writing doesn't mean that you'll automatically recall this information on exams. The kinds of events that you are more likely to remember or forget can be demonstrated with forgetting curves.

A **forgetting curve** is a graph of the amount of previously learned information that people can recall or recognize across time.

We'll examine how two different kinds of information—unfamiliar and familiar—are remembered by using forgetting curves.

One of the earliest psychologists to study memory and forgetting was Hermann Ebbinghaus, who used himself as his only subject. He got around

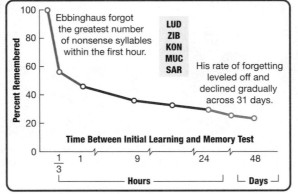

Ebbinghaus forgot the greatest number of nonsense syllables within the first hour.

LUD
ZIB
KON
MUC
SAR

His rate of forgetting leveled off and declined gradually across 31 days.

Time Between Initial Learning and Memory Test

the fact that people have better memories for more familiar events by memorizing only three-letter nonsense syllables, such as **LUD, ZIB, MUC.** He made up and wrote down hundreds of three-letter nonsense syllables on separate cards and arranged these cards into sets of varying length. To the ticking of a metronome, he turned over each card and read aloud each of the syllables until he had read all the cards in the set. He used only rote memory (made no associations) and needed only one or two readings to memorize a set of seven cards (containing seven nonsense syllables). He needed about 45 readings to memorize a set of 24 cards (Ebbinghaus, 1885/1913).

The forgetting curve on the left shows that Ebbinghaus forgot about half the unfamiliar and uninteresting nonsense syllables within the first hour.

How long do we remember familiar information?

Familiar and Interesting

Can you remember the names of your high school classmates?

Ebbinghaus's nonsense syllables are certainly uninteresting, which helps explain why he forgot half within the first hour. But what about information that is both familiar and interesting, such as the names and faces of your high school graduating class?

The graph at the right shows that even after 47 years, people correctly matched about 80% of their high school classmates' names with faces; they correctly recalled about 25% after 47 years (Bahrick et al., 1975). People did better on recognition tests (matching names to faces) because they were given clues (names). They did poorer on recall tests (seeing faces and asked to recall the names) because they were not

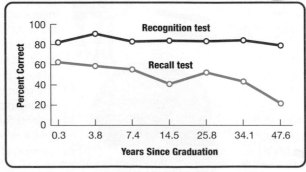

Recognition test

Recall test

Years Since Graduation

given any clues. Similarly, students also show better memory on recognition tests (multiple-choice) than on recall tests (essay or fill-in-the-blank).

Notice that even though names and nonsense syllables were both encoded verbally, people correctly recalled about 60% of familiar and interesting information (names and faces) after 7 years, while Ebbinghaus forgot about 80% of the unfamiliar and uninteresting nonsense syllables after about a week. One researcher found that, after 20 years, he best remembered those events that were vivid, rare, and emotionally intense (R. White, 2002).

These studies show that remembering is partly related to how familiar or interesting the information is. However, there are other reasons for forgetting, as you'll see next. ●

Graph data from "Fifty Years of Memory for Names and Faces," by H. P. Bahrick, P. O. Bahrick & R. P. Wittlinger, 1975, *Journal of Experimental Psychology: General, 104,* 54–75.

C Reasons for Forgetting

Overview: Forgetting

Why do I forget things?

If asked to describe what happened today, you can accurately recall many personal events, conversations, and countless irritations. However, in spite of hours of study, there are many things you seem to have forgotten when you take an exam.

Forgetting is the inability to retrieve, recall, or recognize information that was stored or is still stored in long-term memory.

We'll summarize a number of reasons people forget things.

Repression

There is a documented case of a man, J.R., who became anxious while watching a movie that featured a main character who struggled with memories of being sexually molested. Later that night, J.R. had a vivid recollection of being sexually abused by a parish priest (Schooler, 1994). J.R.'s case is an example of repression.

Repression, according to Freud, is a mental process that automatically hides emotionally threatening or anxiety-producing information in the unconscious, from which repressed memories cannot be recalled voluntarily, but something may cause them to enter consciousness at a later time.

Earlier we discussed the accuracy of recovered repressed memories involving sexual abuse (see pp. 250–251). The J.R. example suggests that a traumatic sexual event can be repressed and recovered later. However, prominent memory researchers have questioned the validity of repressed memories, pointing to the possibility that such memories may have been suggested or implanted during the therapeutic process (Lynn et al., 2003).

Poor Retrieval Cues/Poor Encoding

Studying for exams by cramming or using rote memory may lead to forgetting because these techniques result in poor retrieval cues and thus poor encoding or storing.

Retrieval cues are mental reminders that we create by forming vivid mental images or creating associations between new information and information we already know.

What if I study for 2 hours?

Many students don't realize that it's not how long but how well they study that matters. Effective studying is not only memorizing but also creating good retrieval cues. The best retrieval cues, which ensure the best encoding, are created by associating new information with information already learned.

For example, instead of just trying to remember that the hippocampus is involved in memory (see pp. 80, 84, 229), try to make a new association, such as a hippo remembered its way around campus.

We'll discuss the importance of and how to form good retrieval cues for effective encoding on page 267.

Interference

I (H.K.) often struggle to remember the correct password for a particular website. Like many other people, I frequently change my passwords to keep my private information secure. It's always a challenge to remember a new password after I've changed it. I may forget a password because of interference.

Interference, one of the common reasons for forgetting, occurs when the recall of some particular memory is blocked or prevented by other related memories.

What if you have different passwords for different websites?

Because psychologists believe that interference between material is a common cause of forgetting, we'll focus on two different kinds of interference on the next page.

Amnesia

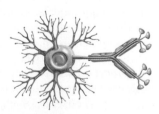

While showing off her new skates, my sister (R.P.) fell down and cracked her head on the hard Minnesota ice. She was knocked unconscious for a short time, and when she woke up the first thing she said was, "What happened?" She couldn't remember what happened because the blow had caused temporary amnesia.

Amnesia, which may be temporary or permanent, is loss of memory that may occur after a blow or damage to the brain or after disease (Alzheimer's, see p. 47), general anesthesia, certain drugs, or severe psychological trauma.

Depending on its severity, a blow to the head causes the soft jellylike brain to crash into the hard skull, and this may result in temporary or permanent damage to thousands of neurons (see p. 50), which form the communication network of the brain. The reason people who strike their heads during car accidents usually have no memories of the events immediately before and during the accident is that the brain crashed into the skull, which interferes with the neurons' communication network, disrupts memory, and results in varying degrees of amnesia (Riccio et al., 2003).

Decay

Another reason people forget things may be because they haven't used the information for a long period of time.

When we encode information, we form **memory traces,** which are physical changes in the brain that represent the memory.

If we do not access a memory, then over time the traces may **decay,** which means the memory is lost as a result of not using the memory traces.

Next, we'll more closely examine two important reasons for forgetting—interference and poor retrieval cues.

Interference

Sooner or later, every student faces the problem of having to take exams in several different courses on the same day. This situation can increase the chances of forgetting material because of something called interference.

What if you study for three exams?

The theory of **interference** says that we may forget information not because it is no longer in storage or memory but rather because old or newer related information produces confusion and thus blocks retrieval from memory.

Students who take multiple tests on the same day often complain of studying long and hard but forgetting information that they knew they knew. In this case the culprit may be interference. Similarly, if you take two or more classes in succession, you may find that information from one class interferes with learning or remembering information from the others. We'll explain the two kinds of interference—proactive and retroactive—and how each can lead to forgetting.

Proactive Interference

The first thing to remember about interference is that it can act forward, which is called proactive, or act backward, which is called retroactive. The prefix *pro* means "forward," so *proactive* interference "acts forward" to interfere with recalling newly learned information.

Proactive interference occurs when old information (learned earlier) blocks or disrupts the remembering of related new information (learned later).

Here's how proactive interference can work.

1 Psychology information.
For two hours you study for a test in psychology. The more psychology terms you store in memory, the more potential this psychology information has to "act forward" and disrupt any new and related information you study next.

2 Psychology information acts forward.
For the next two hours you study for a test in sociology. You may experience difficulty in learning and remembering this new sociology information because the previously learned psychology terms can "act forward" and interfere with remembering new and related terms from sociology.

Proactive Interference

Material learned EARLIER (psychology) interferes with learning new information (sociology).

3 Proactive interference.
When you take your sociology exam, you may forget some of the sociology terms you studied because of proactive interference: Previously learned psychology terms "act forward" to interfere with or block the recall of the more recently learned and related sociology terms (M. C. Anderson, 2009a).

Retroactive Interference

Note that the prefix *retro* means "backward," so *retroactive* interference means "acting backward" to interfere with recalling previously learned information (M. C. Anderson, 2009a).

Retroactive interference occurs when new information (learned later) blocks or disrupts the retrieval of related old information (learned earlier).

Here's how retroactive interference works.

1 Psychology information.
From 1:00 to 3:00, you study for a test in psychology. Then from 3:00 to 6:00, you study for a test in sociology.

2 Sociology information acts backward.
You may experience difficulty in remembering the psychology terms you learned earlier because the sociology terms recently learned may "act backward" and disrupt earlier learned and related psychology terms.

Retroactive Interference

Material learned LATER (sociology) disrupts learning new information (psychology).

3 Retroactive interference.
When you take the psychology exam, you may forget some of the psychology terms you studied earlier because of retroactive interference: Recently learned sociology terms "act backward" to interfere with or block the recall of earlier learned and related psychology terms.

Interference, both proactive and retroactive, is one of the two most common reasons for forgetting (Roediger & McDermott, 2005). Interference may also cause serious mistakes if eyewitnesses identify the wrong person, as happened in the study we discussed at the beginning of this module.

Why Did Viewers Forget the Mugger's Face?

We began this module by asking why only 200 out of 2,000 viewers correctly identified a mugger's face that was shown for several seconds on television. One reason viewers forgot the mugger's face is that one or both kinds of interference were operating.

If *proactive interference* was operating, it means that previously learned faces acted forward to block or disrupt remembering the newly observed mugger's face.

If *retroactive interference* was operating, it means that new faces learned since seeing the mugger's face acted

backward to block or disrupt remembering the mugger's face.

Thus, we may forget information that we did indeed store in long-term memory because of one or both kinds of interference.

Besides interference, the other most common reason for forgetting involves inadequate retrieval cues, our next topic.

Retrieval Cues

As we discussed in Module 11 (see p. 239), recalling information involves the memory process called retrieval.

Where did I park it?

Retrieval is the process of getting or recalling information that has been placed into short-term or long-term storage.

If you have ever parked your car at a shopping mall and later roamed around the lot trying to find it, you have experienced difficulty with retrieval.

In this case, the reason for your forgetting probably involved poor retrieval cues (M.C. Anderson, 2009c).

Retrieval cues are mental reminders that you create by forming vivid mental images of information or associating new information with information that you already know.

Forgetting parking places (which we have done) points to the need for creating good retrieval cues.

Forming Effective Retrieval Cues

One reason we forget things (definitions, names, phone numbers) is that we did not take the time to create effective retrieval cues (discussed on pp. 248–249). You can form effective retrieval cues by creating vivid mental images of the information, making associations between new and old information, or making somewhat bizarre but memorable associations.

For example, researchers wondered which types of sentences students would remember better: common sentences, such as "The sleek new train passes a field of fresh, juicy strawberries," or bizarre sentences, such as "The sleek new train is derailed by the fresh, juicy strawberries." As a computer randomly presented 12 common and 12 bizarre sentences, students were told to form vivid mental images of the scenes. When retested later, the students recalled significantly more bizarre than common sentences. Researchers concluded that the students remembered the bizarre sentences better because they formed better mental images or associations, which produced better retrieval cues (Robinson-Riegler & McDaniel, 1994). Poor retrieval cues may also be a problem in eyewitness testimony.

Vivid mental images make great retrieval cues.

Retrieval cues and interference. There have been cases in which eyewitnesses identified assailants who were later proven innocent based on DNA evidence. One reason eyewitnesses were mistaken is that the emotional and traumatic events prevented them from forming effective *retrieval cues.* Another reason the eyewitnesses made mistakes is *interference;* that is, the faces of the accused assailants somewhat resembled and interfered with the eyewitnesses recognizing the real assailants. These examples show that forgetting can result from poor retrieval cues, no associations, or interference.

Another example of forgetting, which involves retrieval cues and interference, usually begins with someone saying, "It's on the tip of my tongue."

Tip-of-the-Tongue Phenomenon

Most of us have had the frustrating experience of feeling we really do know the name of a movie, person, or song but cannot recall it at this moment. This kind of forgetting is called the tip-of-the-tongue phenomenon.

"It's on the tip of my tongue."

The **tip-of-the-tongue phenomenon** refers to having a strong feeling that a particular word can be recalled, but despite making a great effort, we are temporarily unable to recall this particular information.

Research shows that the tip-of-the-tongue phenomenon is nearly universal, occurs about once a week, and most often involves names of people and objects. Its frequency increases with age, and usually the information is remembered some minutes later (Branan, 2008; B.L. Schwartz, 1999).

There are a few possible explanations for the tip-of-the-tongue phenomenon. In some cases, information was encoded with inadequate retrieval cues, and so we must think up other associations (first letter of name, where last seen) for recall (Neath & Surprenant, 2013). In other cases, we have poor memory of a word because we rarely use it. Another possible explanation is that information is being blocked by interference from similar-sounding words (Vergano, 2009). Last, the brain region responsible for processing and producing sound has been reported to be less active as tip-of-the-tongue moments become more frequent (Shafto et al., 2007).

An interesting feature of retrieval cues is that such cues can also come from our states of mind.

State-Dependent Learning

When you yell at someone for doing the same annoying thing again, why is it that a long list of related past annoyances quickly comes to mind? One answer involves state-dependent learning.

What happens when you get angry?

State-dependent learning means that it is easier to recall information when you are in the same physiological or emotional state or setting as when you originally encoded the information.

For example, getting angry at someone creates an emotional and physiological state that triggers the recall of related past annoyances. Evidence for state-dependent learning comes from a wide range of studies in which

Being in the same state (emotional) improves recall.

participants (humans, dogs, rats) learned something while they used a certain drug, were in a certain mood, or were in a particular setting and later showed better recall of this information when tested under the original learning conditions (M.C. Anderson, 2009c; S.C. Brown & Craik, 2005). These state-dependent studies indicate that retrieval cues are created by being in certain physiological or emotional states or in particular settings and returning to these original states helps recall information that was learned under the same conditions.

Next, we'll look inside the brain to see what happens during remembering and forgetting. ●

Location of Memories in the Brain

Where do you put all those memories?

If you learned only 500 new things every day, that adds up to storing 180,000 new memories every year and 3,600,000 memories after twenty years. To figure out how the brain stores and files away 3,600,000 memories (a very conservative estimate), researchers have studied the formation of memories in sea slugs, which have a relatively simple nervous system, in brain-damaged individuals, who show deficits in some kinds of memory but not others, and in individuals who are having their brains scanned for neural activity while they are using different kinds of memory (Cabeza & Nyberg, 2003; Zola & Squire, 2005). Based on these studies, researchers have identified several areas of the brain that are involved in processing and storing different kinds memories. Though we do not yet fully understand the complexity of the biological bases of memory, we do know that a few key areas of the brain are involved in various memory processes.

1 Cortex: Short-Term Memories

When you look up a new phone number, you can hold it in short-term memory long enough to dial the number. Your ability to hold words, facts, and events in short-term memory depends on activity in the *cortex,* which is a thin layer of brain cells that covers the surface of the forebrain (indicated by the thin red line on the outside of the brain).

People may have brain damage that prevents them from storing long-term memories, but if their cortex is intact, they may have short-term memory and be able to carry on relatively normal conversations. However, if they cannot store long-term memories, they would not later remember having those conversations.

2 Cortex: Long-Term Memories

If you learn the words to a song, these words are stored in long-term memory. Your ability to remember or recall songs, words, facts, and events for days, months, or years depends on areas widely spread throughout the *cortex.*

People may have brain damage that prevents them from learning or remembering any new songs. However, if they have an intact cortex, they may remember the words from songs they learned before their brain damage because such information would have already been safely stored in their cerebral cortex (indicated by the thin red line on the outside of the brain).

3 Amygdala: Emotional Memories

Suppose that each time you hear a particular song associated with a special person, you have a romantic feeling. The romantic feeling associated with this emotional memory is provided by the *amygdala,* which is located in the tip of the temporal lobe and receives input from all the senses. The amygdala plays a critical role in the long-term processing of emotionally intense experiences (Squire & Kandel, 2009). For example, the amygdala helps us recognize emotional facial expressions, especially fearful or threatening ones, and adds a wide range of emotions (positive and negative) to our memories (R. J. Dolan, 2002; Ohman, 2002). So, humans with damage to the amygdala still have memories but the memories lose their emotional impact, such as no longer finding loud noises unpleasant or no longer recognizing emotional facial expressions (Hamann et al., 2002).

4 Hippocampus: Transferring Memories

Just as the "Save" command on your computer transfers a file into permanent storage on your hard drive, the *hippocampus* transfers words, facts, and personal events from short-term memory into permanent long-term memory. The hippocampus, which lies in the temporal lobe, is vital for storing certain kinds of memories. For example, individuals with hippocampal damage cannot save any declarative memories, such as new words, facts, or personal events, because the hippocampus is necessary for transferring declarative information from short-term into long-term memory (Zeineh et al., 2003). However, people with hippocampal damage CAN learn and remember nondeclarative or procedural information, such as acquiring motor skills or habits (tying one's shoes, playing tennis) (R. D. Fields, 2005). But, if asked, people with hippocampal damage CANNOT remember actually performing a motor skill (playing tennis) because performing the skill (I played tennis) is a personal event (declarative memory). Thus, the hippocampus is necessary for transferring declarative information (words, facts, and events) from short-term into long-term memory but not for transferring nondeclarative or procedural information (motor skills and habits) (Zola & Squire, 2005).

Areas of the brain involved in memory

Hippocampus: Retrieving Memories

Researchers have long assumed that the hippocampus is also somehow involved in retrieving memories. Only recently have they discovered that the storage and retrieval of memory actually involve activation of the same neurons located in the hippocampus (Gelbard-Sagiv et al., 2008).

5 Brain: Memory Model

Recent findings indicate that your *cortex* stores short-term memories as well as long-term memories; your *hippocampus* transfers or saves declarative information in long-term memory but does not transfer nondeclarative or procedural information into long-term memory; and your *amygdala* adds emotional content to positive and negative memories (Tulving & Craik, 2005).

Remember that we are still learning about the biological bases of memory. The brain areas we identified may be involved in other yet to be determined memory processes, and other brain areas may contribute to the memory processes described above. Next, we'll learn how memories are made.

© appalachian trail/Shutterstock.com
© maximma/Shutterstock.com
Save File
© Monika Olszewska/Shutterstock.com
Unless otherwise noted, all images are © Cengage Learning

Making a Short-Term Memory

How to make a short-term memory?

Suppose you just looked up the phone number 555-9013 and repeat it as you dial. Researchers believe that your brain may store that number in short-term memory by using interconnected groups of neurons that are called neural assemblies.

Neural assemblies are groups of interconnected neurons whose activation allows information or stimuli to be recognized and held briefly and temporarily in short-term memory.

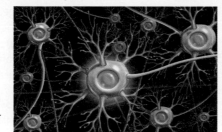

The figure below shows a very simplified neural assembly. Some information, such as repeating a phone number, activates a neural assembly that holds the phone number in short-term memory. However, if you switch your attention to something else before encoding the number in long-term memory, this neural assembly stops and the phone number is gone and forgotten. Researchers believe that neural assemblies are one mechanism for holding information in short-term memory (E. E. Smith, 2000). However, as you'll see next, permanently storing information in long-term memory involves chemical or structural changes in the neurons themselves.

Making a Long-Term Memory

How to make a long-term memory?

Besides studying memory by genetically altering mice brains, researchers also study memory in sea slugs because their nervous system contains about 20,000 neurons versus billions in the human brain. After the sea slug has learned a simple task, such as tensing its muscular foot in response to a bright light, researchers can dissect the sea slug's nervous system and look for chemical or physical changes associated with learning (Kandel & Abel, 1995). We'll focus on one mechanism—long-term potentiation, or LTP—that researchers believe is involved in forming long-term memories.

Long-Term Potentiation (LTP)

1 One way to learn the name of the large orange-beaked bird on the left is to repeat its name, "toucan," several times. After you repeat this name (repeated stimulation), some neurons in your brain actually grow and change to form new connections with other neurons (Goldstein, 2008; Stickgold & Ellenbogen, 2008). This neural change, which is involved in forming long-term memories, is part of a complicated process called LTP.

Long-term potentiation, or **LTP,** refers to changes in the structure and function of neurons after they have been repeatedly stimulated.

For example, by repeating the name "toucan," you are repeatedly stimulating neurons.

2 We'll use only two neurons (perhaps many hundreds are involved) to make the LTP process easier to understand. In the figure below, repeating the name "toucan" stimulates neuron A, which produces LTP and causes neuron A to grow and form new connections with neuron B.

3 LTP changes the structure and function of neuron A so it becomes associated with the name "toucan." To recall the name of this bird, you activate neuron A, which activates its newly formed connections with neuron B, and this combined neural activation forms the basis for your long-term memory of the name "toucan."

toucan
toucan
toucan
toucan
neuron
A
B
LTP occurs

4 Researchers found that LTP is important in the formation of long-term memory because when the occurrence of LTP was chemically or genetically blocked in sea snails or mice, these animals could not learn a classically conditioned response or a water maze (Mayford & Korzus, 2002; Tonegawa & Wilson, 1997). Blocking the occurrence of LTP blocked the formation of long-term memories. Thus, neuroscientists believe the LTP process, which changes the *structure* and function of neurons, is the most likely basis for learning and memory in animals and humans (Goldstein, 2008; Tsien, 2000).

Forgetting Unwanted Long-Term Memories

Can the brain forget bad memories?

Once a long-term memory is made, can you intentionally forget an unwanted memory? Researchers have been examining this question and have found some remarkable biological findings that suggest we do have the ability to intentionally forget bad memories.

Researchers have shown that reduced activity in the hippocampus and amygdala (brain structures responsible for consciously thinking about memories and fear conditioning) leads people to forget their unwanted memories (M. C. Anderson et al., 2004; Depue et al., 2007). Researchers can

actually predict how much forgetting people experience by examining their pattern of brain activity!

As a result of this research, we have a better understanding of how people cope with memories after traumatic experiences and the brain dysfunction that occurs in people who experience ongoing traumatic memories.

We'll further explore the topic of forgetting unwanted memories in the Critical Thinking section (p. 276). ●

Brain dysfunction may explain why this woman can't forget her bad memories.

Concept Review

1. If you retrieve previously learned information without the aid of any external cues, you are using a process of remembering called **(a)** _____. If you identify or match information that you have previously learned, you are using a process of remembering called **(b)** _____.

2. Memory files or categories that contain related information organized around a specific topic are called **(a)** _____. One theory of memory organization says that the separate memory files, or nodes, in which we file related ideas are interconnected in a gigantic system. This idea is called **(b)** _____.

1. ANIMAL

3. According to network theory, some nodes are arranged so that more concrete information is at the bottom and more abstract information is at the top; this order is called a _____.

4. A graph of the amount of previously learned information that people can recall or recognize across time is called a _____. We tend to remember information that is familiar and interesting and forget information that is unfamiliar and uninteresting.

Recognition test
Recall test

Percent Correct
0.3 3.8 7.4
Years Since Graduation

5. According to Sigmund Freud, information that is threatening to our self-concept is automatically driven into our unconscious, from which we cannot retrieve it at will. This process is called _____.

6. One common reason for forgetting is that other related memories already stored in long-term memory may interfere with or block the recall of some particular memory; this idea is called _____.

What if I have 2 exams?

7. Another reason for forgetting comes from a lack of associations between new information and information we already know; this reason has to do with the quality of the _____.

8. Brain damage, a blow to the head, drug use, or severe psychological stress may cause a form of forgetting called **(a)** _____, which results when the brain's **(b)** _____ network is temporarily or permanently disrupted.

9. When we encode information, we form **(a)** _____, which are physical changes in the brain that represent the memory. If we do not access a memory, then over time the traces may **(b)** _____, which means there is a loss of memory.

10. If we forget information not because it is lost from storage but rather because other information gets in the way and blocks its retrieval, this process is called **(a)** _____. If information learned earlier blocks, interferes with, or disrupts the retrieval of information that was learned later, it is called **(b)** _____. If information learned later blocks, interferes with, or disrupts the retrieval of information learned earlier, it is called **(c)** _____.

PSYCHOLOGY   SOCIOLOGY

11. Mental reminders that we create by making images or associating new information with information that we already know are called **(a)** _____. If you do not form effective retrieval cues when learning new information, you will likely have a difficult time **(b)** _____ this information from long-term memory.

12. Sometimes, despite making a great effort, you are temporarily unable to recall information that you absolutely know is in your memory. This is called the _____ phenomenon.

13. According to one memory model of the brain, short-term memories are formed and stored in different parts of the **(a)** _____. Long-term memories are also stored in different parts of the **(b)** _____, although these kinds of memories are not formed there. Declarative information is transferred by the **(c)** _____ into long-term memory, which is stored in different parts of the cortex. However, the hippocampus is not involved in transferring motor skills or habits, which are part of **(d)** _____ information, into long-term memory. Both positive and negative emotional associations are added to memories by an area in the temporal lobe called the **(e)** _____.

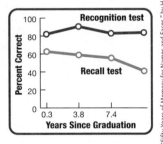

Blue jay: © Sarah Holmlund/Shutterstock.com; guppy: © Dirk Ercken/Shutterstock.com; shark: © Michael Rosskothen/Shutterstock.com; rooster: © Serg64/Shutterstock.com

Graph data from "Fifty Years of Memory for Names and Faces," by H. P. Bahrick, P.O. Bahrick & R. P. Wittlinger, 1975, *Journal of Experimental Psychology: General, 104,* 54–75.

Unless otherwise noted, all images are © Cengage Learning

Answers: 1. (a) recall, (b) recognition; 2. (a) nodes, (b) network theory; 3. hierarchy; 4. forgetting curve; 5. repression; 6. interference; 7. retrieval cues; 8. (a) amnesia, (b) communication; 9. (a) memory traces, (b) decay; 10. (a) interference, (b) proactive interference, (c) retroactive interference; 11. (a) retrieval cues, (b) recalling or retrieving or remembering; 12. tip-of-the-tongue; 13. (a) cortex, b) cortex, (c) hippocampus, (d) procedural, (e) amygdala

E Mnemonics: Memorization Methods

Improving Your Memory

Do you complain about forgetting things?

At one time or another, almost everyone complains about forgetting something. Many of our students complain about forgetting information that they really knew but couldn't recall during exams. This kind of forgetting has several causes: There may be *interference (proactive and retroactive)* from information studied for related classes; there may be *poor retrieval cues* that result from trying to learn information by using rote or straight memorization; or students may not use elaborative rehearsal (see p. 249), which involves making associations between new and old information.

After about age 40, adults begin to complain about forgetting things that they never forgot before. For example, memory researcher Daniel Schacter, at age 50, complained, "Reading a journal article 15 years ago, I would have it at my fingertips. Now,

How can I improve my memory?

if I don't deliberately try to relate it to what I already know, or repeat it a few times, I'm less likely to remember it" (Schacter, 1997, p. 56). This kind of forgetting is commonly caused by poor retrieval cues, which result from being busy or distracted and not having or taking the time to create meaningful associations.

If you hear about memory courses that claim to greatly improve your memory, what these courses usually teach are how to use mnemonic methods.

Mnemonic (ni-MON-ick) **methods** are ways to improve encoding and create better retrieval cues by forming vivid associations or images, which improve recall.

We'll discuss two common mnemonic methods—method of loci and peg method—that improve memory (M. W. Eysenck, 2009b).

Method of Loci

If you need to memorize a list of terms, concepts, or names in a particular order, an efficient way is to use the method of loci.

The **method of loci** (LOW-sigh) is an encoding technique that creates visual associations between already memorized places and new items to be memorized.

We'll use the following three steps of the method of loci to memorize names of early psychologists: Wundt, James, and Watson.

Step 1. Memorize a visual sequence of places (*loci* in Latin means "places"), such as places in your apartment where you can store things. Select easily remembered places such as in your kitchen: sink, cabinet, refrigerator, stove, and closet.

Step 2. Create a vivid association for each item to be memorized. For example, picture Wundt hanging from a bridge and saying, "I wundt jump."

Step 3. Once you have created a list of vivid associations, mentally put each psychologist in one of the selected places: Wundt goes in the sink, James in the cabinet, Watson in the refrigerator.

To recall this list of early psychologists, you take an imaginary stroll through your kitchen and mentally note the image stored in each of your memorized places.

Peg Method

Another useful mnemonic device for memorizing a long list, especially in the exact order, is the peg method.

The **peg method** is an encoding technique that creates associations between number-word rhymes and items to be memorized.

The rhymes act like pegs on which you hang items to be memorized. Let's use the two steps of the peg method to memorize our three early psychologists: Wundt, James, Watson.

Step 1. Memorize the list of peg words shown on the left, which consists of a number and its rhyming word.

> one is a bun
> two is a shoe
> three is a tree
> four is a door
> five is a hive

Step 2. Next, associate each of the items you wish to memorize with one of the peg words. For instance, imagine Wundt on a bun, James with two left shoes, and Watson stuck in a tree.

To remember this list of early psychologists, you recall each peg along with its image of an early psychologist that you placed there.

Effectiveness of Methods

A national magazine writer, who was 41 years old and complained about forgetfulness, decided to improve her memory by trying three methods (Yoffe, 1997).

First, she took a 3-hour memory-enhancement class ($49) that focused on the peg method. The magazine writer concluded that the peg method was impressive and if she were back in college, she would use it to memorize new facts.

Second, she listened to an audio program ($79) that promised to release the "perfect photographic memory" that everyone already had. The program focused on using the peg method without much application to real life. Contrary to the program's promise, researchers report that photographic memories are as rare as duck's teeth (Schacter, 1996).

Third, she read a memory-improvement book ($10) that described the peg method, how to pay attention, and the importance of creating associations and images.

As this writer's experience illustrates, improving one's memory requires making the effort to use good encoding, such as elaborative rehearsal, which means creating good associations that, in turn, produce good retrieval cues and improve memory.

As the percentage of people over 50 increases, so does interest in *memory-enhancing drugs,* such as the popular herbal supplement ginkgo. However, researchers found that ginkgo did NOT improve memory or concentration in healthy adults (Solomon et al., 2002). Still, the search for effective memory enhancers continues. Researchers have found ways to improve memory in mice, and they are now testing memory-enhancing drugs in humans (Rovner, 2007; P. J. Zhu et al., 2011).

Next, we'll discuss how cultural influences can affect what you remember. ●

Euro-Americans Versus Asians

Do Asians have difficulty with episodic memory?

Cross-cultural research has found cultural differences in recalling episodic memories, which we discussed in Module 11 (see p. 246).

Episodic memory involves knowledge of specific events, personal experiences, or activities, such as naming or describing favorite restaurants, movies, songs, habits, or hobbies.

Compared to Asians, Euro-Americans have been reported to better recall autobiographical memories from childhood throughout the lifespan (Q. Wang et al., 2004; Q. Wang & Conway, 2004; Q. Wang & Ross, 2005).

There are several possible explanations for these cultural differences in episodic memory. Perhaps the importance of individuality and autonomy for Euro-Americans focuses their attention on retaining

There are differences in episodic memory between Euro-Americans and Asians.

memories of life events that are associated with an individual's identity (e.g., winning a contest). In contrast, for Asians the importance of collectivism or relatedness may focus their attention on retaining more generic knowledge that is associated with their relationships with other people or their community (e.g., going to church every Sunday). Another proposed idea is that Asians may encode episodic memories as well as Euro-Americans but they have a faster rate of forgetting these memories over time.

One researcher closely examined the reasons for the differences in episodic memory between Euro-Americans and Asians (Q. Wang, 2009). We will discuss three of her studies next.

Study One

In the first study, Euro-American and Asian adults were asked to complete daily diaries for one week that listed all the events that happened to them. When participants completed this task and turned in their diaries, researchers gave them a surprise memory test by asking them to recall the events that happened during the past week (Recall 1). Then, a week later, researchers again surprised the participants by asking them to recall the events that happened to them during the week they kept their diaries (Recall 2).

Results showed that Euro-Americans recalled a greater number of specific events than did Asians at the time they turned in their diaries. The same results held true during Recall 1 and Recall 2. That is, Euro-Americans recalled a greater number of events following a one-week and a two-week delay.

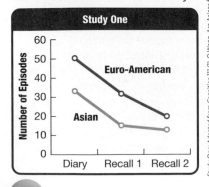

Study Two

In the second study, Euro-American and Asian adults were given a written diary kept by a fictional person during his travels. After participants read the diary, they were given another unrelated written task to complete in 5 minutes. Following this 5-minute task, participants were asked, without warning, to recall as many of the specific events from the fictional diary as they could.

Results found that in this immediate recall task in which the content is exactly the same for all participants, Euro-Americans recalled a greater number of specific events than did Asians. The results of this study are consistent with those of Study One and extend the findings by focusing on immediate recall (as opposed to recall at the end of the day, after one week, and after two weeks) and presenting all participants with the same content (as opposed to each participant having a unique set of life events to remember).

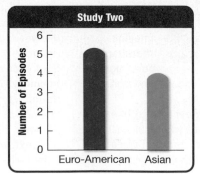

Study Three

In the third study, Euro-American and Asian adults were given the same written diary used in Study Two, but this time they were asked to identify when one event ended and another event began. There was no recall task in this study. The aim was to determine whether Euro-Americans and Asians differ in their ability to perceive separate life events.

Results showed that Euro-Americans identified a greater number of specific events than did Asians. Asians may be more likely to perceive events as interconnected than Euro-Americans, who may tend to perceive events as being discrete or separate.

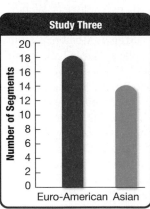

Conclusions

Together, the findings from these three studies suggest that there are differences in perceptual and encoding processes between the two groups, as opposed to differences in the ability to remember. Asians may not be more forgetful than Euro-Americans, but rather they may perceive the world as having fewer discrete events and consequently remember fewer episodic memories.

Besides culture, other factors, such as the type of information having to be recalled, may also influence memory, as shown next in a study on recalling sexual history. ●

Study One: Adapted from *Cognition 111 (1)*, Q Wang, Are Asians forgetful? Perception, retention, and recall in episodic remembering, 123-131 (2009), Fig. 2, p. 125 Research Study 1 with permission from Elsevier BV via Copyright Clearance Center.

Study Two: Adapted from *Cognition 111 (1)*, Q Wang, Are Asians forgetful? Perception, retention, and recall in episodic remembering, 123-131 (2009), Fig. 3, p. 127 Research Study 2 with permission from Elsevier BV via Copyright Clearance Center.

Study Three: Adapted from *Cognition 111 (1)*, Q Wang, Are Asians forgetful? Perception, retention, and recall in episodic remembering, 123-131 (2009), Fig. 4, p. 128 Research Study 3 with permission from Elsevier BV via Copyright Clearance Center.

Unless otherwise noted, all images are © Cengage Learning

G Research Focus: Recalling Sexual History

How Accurate Are Students' Memories?

Many schools across the United States offer sex education in an effort to reduce adolescent sexual activity.

Are students telling the truth?

Some sex education programs encourage students to take virginity pledges to abstain from sexual intercourse until marriage. These programs are considered to be so important that they are promoted by the U.S. government (Rosenbaum, 2006). But, how do we know whether or not these programs actually reduce adolescent sexual activity? Since sexual activity is not a behavior researchers can observe, research methods used to study sexual activity are limited to the survey method (see p. 28).

Using surveys to question teenagers about intimate behaviors, especially their sexual histories, is very challenging. Adolescents may deliberately report false information because they want to present a desirable self-image or because they are being influenced by social

Surveys are used to question teenagers about their sexual histories.

pressures. If adolescents' behaviors go against their moral or religious beliefs, they may falsify their answers so they are more consistent with their values. Another challenge in obtaining accurate information by using a survey is that when people are asked to report on their past experiences, their survey responses tend to be based on their current beliefs and behaviors more than on past beliefs and behaviors. Thus, if adolescents have recently changed their beliefs or their sexual behaviors, their recollection of the past may be biased (Rosenbaum, 2006).

If adolescents are inaccurately reporting their sexual histories, it becomes impossible to determine whether sex education programs are effective in reducing sexual activity. This serious concern led a researcher to study whether adolescents accurately recall their sexual histories.

Research Method to Evaluate Memory Accuracy

To answer the question of how well adolescents recall their sexual histories, Janet Rosenbaum (2006), a health policy researcher at Harvard University,

Why do so many students change their answers?

studied more than 13,000 students in grades 7 to 12 from schools across the United States.

Procedure. The students were questioned two times, a year apart. To respect students' privacy, many personal questions were asked through headphones and students typed their answers into a computer. The questions they were asked included: "Have you ever taken a public or written pledge to remain a virgin until marriage?" Students were also asked if they ever had sexual intercourse.

Results. In the first survey, about 13% of the students reported having taken a virginity pledge. In the second survey (a year later), only 6% of the students reported having ever taken a virginity pledge (see left bar graph). Thus, more than half of the students who reported having taken a virginity pledge in the first survey later denied

having done so. Also, students who reported having sexual intercourse for the first time in the second survey were more likely to deny having taken a virginity pledge than those who did not report having sexual intercourse.

When first asked about their sexual histories, about 33% of the students reported having sexual intercourse, but only 29% of the students reported having sexual intercourse when questioned during the second survey (see right bar graph). Many students who reported having had sexual intercourse during the first survey and who made a virginity pledge for the first time during the second survey denied ever having sexual intercourse. Thus, many students changed their minds about their sexual histories, especially if they recently made a virginity pledge.

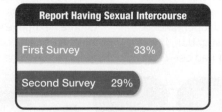

Conclusion. Many students changed their responses about their sexual histories and whether or not they had taken a virginity pledge. The results of this study show that adolescents who have sexual intercourse after making a virginity pledge are likely to deny having made a pledge. Also, adolescents who have sexual intercourse before making a virginity pledge are likely to deny their sexual histories.

These results raise concern about the reliability of surveys used to collect information about sexual activity among adolescents. One explanation for why students changed their answers is that their beliefs changed during the course of the year between the two surveys and students may recall only memories that are consistent with their current beliefs. Students may even report behaviors that never happened but that are consistent with their new beliefs. These types of reporting errors are not uncommon when using surveys to collect information. Overall, the results show that adolescents' memories for sexual behaviors are often inaccurate.

Just as adolescents may misremember information about their sexual histories, research shows that some adults have difficulty recalling their sexual histories as well (Garry et al., 2002). Adults may also misremember when giving eyewitness testimony, our next topic. ●

How Accurate Is an Eyewitness?

On a hot and humid summer night, Jennifer Thompson, a 22-year-old college student, went to bed in her apartment only to wake up frightened by a man lying on top of her holding a knife to her throat. While the man proceeded to rape her, she was committed to studying his every physical feature so she could later help police put him behind bars. When police presented Jennifer with a photo and physical lineup of suspects, she picked Ronald Cotton in both instances. When she was asked if her rapist was present in the courtroom, she again confidently pointed to Ronald Cotton.

Eyewitness testimony refers to recalling or recognizing a suspect observed during a potentially very disrupting and distracting emotional situation that may have interfered with accurate remembering.

For example, Jennifer Thompson's eyewitness testimony was the damning evidence that sent the defendant (an alleged rapist) to prison. After Ronald Cotton spent 10 years in prison, DNA evidence proved that he was not the rapist and implicated another man, Bobby Poole. The man who had been sent to prison because of the victim's eyewitness testimony was found innocent and set free (Lithwick, 2009; L. Stahl, 2009). This example points to at least three problems with eyewitness testimony.

The first problem is that juries assume eyewitness testimony is the best kind of evidence because it is so accurate and reliable. However, in the United States, 289 people have been wrongfully convicted of crimes and later freed from jail because of DNA evidence. Of the 289 convictions, nearly 75% had been based on (mistaken) eyewitness testimony (Innocence Project, 2012).

DNA evidence proved Poole (left) was the rapist, not Cotton (right), who was falsely identified through eyewitness testimony.

© AP Images/HO/Burlington Police Dept.

Own-race bias. In the rape case discussed here, the eyewitness was a White female and the accused rapist was a Black man. This case brings up another source of eyewitness error: problems in correctly identifying individuals of another race. For example, researchers found that an eyewitness of one race is less accurate when identifying an accused person of another race (Scheck, 2008; G. Wells, 2009). The finding that people better recognize faces of their own race than faces of other races is called ***own-race bias,*** which can distort and decrease the accuracy of eyewitness testimony (Ferguson et al., 2001). For instance, when White people see the faces of Cotton and Poole (left photos), they report the faces look very similar, but when Black people look at the pictures, they say the two men look nothing alike (G. Wells, 2009).

A second problem with eyewitness testimony is that the police and juries generally assume that the more confident an eyewitness is, the more accurate is the testimony. For example, the witness in this rape case was very confident when she pointed at the accused man and said, "There is no doubt in my mind." However, there is only a moderate association or correlation (+0.37) between how correct the identification of an eyewitness is and how much confidence the eyewitness feels about his or her identification (G. L. Wells & Olson, 2003). This means that an eyewitness's confidence is not a good indication of accuracy.

A third problem is eyewitnesses may make errors if law enforcement officials ask misleading or biased questions or make suggestions about the perpetrator's identification. In these cases, eyewitnesses may unknowingly accept the misinformation as fact and give unreliable testimony (B. Bower, 2003b).

Next, we'll look at the accuracy of a group of eyewitnesses.

Can a Group of Eyewitnesses Be Wrong?

During the late afternoon of September 12, 2008, a commuter train collided with a freight train near Los Angeles. The results were devastating as parts of both trains derailed. In all, 25 people were killed and 102 people injured. The estimated cost of damage was over $12 million, not including the lawsuit damages that may be awarded to the families of those passengers who died or to those who were injured.

Investigators had to decide if the conductor of the commuter train legally passed through a green light or illegally passed through a red light. The conductor died in the crash, so he could not be questioned. There were four eyewitnesses who each stated that the signal was green. Given the agreement among the eyewitnesses, you may think this was a straightforward, open-and-shut investigation. However, after a thorough investigation, it was concluded that the signal was red and the engineer had been text

messaging, which likely played a significant role in the accident (National Transportation Safety Board, 2010).

How is it possible that all of the eyewitnesses were wrong? There are a multitude of reasons why eyewitnesses, even an entire group of them, can be wrong. In addition to the problems with eyewitness testimony discussed above, you must consider that eyewitnesses are often called upon to remember details they observed during a very stressful situation, sometimes weeks, months, or years after the actual event. Also, sometimes the information they are exposed to after the event (e.g., other witnesses' reports, news stories) alters their memory of the event (Frenda et al., 2011).

On the next page we'll continue to discuss how eyewitness testimony may be inaccurate. We'll begin with how an eyewitness's memory can become altered based on misinformation.

© ssuaphotos/Shutterstock.com   © Kaspri/Shutterstock.com   © ssuaphotos/Shutterstock.com   © ssuaphotos/Shutterstock.com

Did the conductor pass through a green light or a red light?

Can Questions Change the Answers?

Because of concern about the reliability of eyewitness testimony, Elizabeth Loftus (1979, 2003a) studied whether people can be misled and do misremember, especially if they are given false information. We'll describe some of Loftus's experiments that demonstrate how people misremembered what they saw or heard.

Did the Car Pass the Barn?

In one experiment, participants watched a film of an automobile accident and then were questioned about what they saw. One of the questions contained a false piece of information: "How fast was the red sports car going when it passed the barn while traveling along the country road?" Although there was no barn in the film, 17% of the participants said they had seen a barn, indicating that people may believe misinformation if it fits the overall scene or pattern (Loftus, 1975).

Was There a Stop Sign?

In a well-known study by Loftus and colleagues, participants were first shown slides of a traffic accident involving a stop sign and then asked a series of questions about the accident. Some of the questions were not misleading and asked about the presence of a stop sign. Other questions were deliberately misleading and did not mention the stop sign but asked about the presence of a yield sign. Later, when participants were asked whether they had seen a stop sign or a yield sign, those participants who had been misled by earlier questions about a yield sign were more likely to report seeing a yield sign than participants who were not misled (Loftus et al., 1978). These results, which show that people can be misled by being given false but related information, have been replicated by many other researchers (Frenda et al., 2011; Stark et al., 2010).

How Does False Information Alter Memory?

Based on many such studies, Loftus and Hoffman (1989) concluded that if misleading information is introduced during questioning after an event, people may believe this misinformation and report events that they did not see. This change in memory is explained by the misinformation effect.

The **misinformation effect** is when misleading or false information changes a person's memory of the actual event.

According to Loftus, eyewitnesses believe the false information they are told, rather than what they saw, because the false information alters or overwrites their original, true memory (Loftus & Loftus, 1980). This explanation, which has generated much research and debate, says that people misremember because of a memory impairment: the true memory was erased or overwritten (D. G. Payne et al., 1994). Whatever the cause, these many studies indicate that people (witnesses) do misremember when given misleading information.

Is What You Say, What You Believe?

The debate over whether false information overwrites the original memory has not been settled. However, what has been settled is that sometimes people do come to believe that they actually remember seeing things that were merely suggested to them; this phenomenon is called source misattribution.

Source misattribution is a memory error that results when a person has difficulty deciding which of two or more sources a memory came from: Was the source something the person saw or imagined, or was it a suggestion?

For example, suppose you saw a hit-and-run accident involving a dark red car. During questioning, you are asked the color of the car that drove off. As you're thinking that the car was dark red, you remember hearing another bystander say, "The car was dark blue." Source misattribution would occur if you said that the car was dark blue (suggestion you heard) rather than dark red (something you saw). Researchers have found that false suggestions, misleading questions, and misinformation can result in source misattribution and create false memories (Roediger & McDermott, 2005). False memories that can result from source misattribution, such as suggestions or misleading questions, are one reason that court officials may question the accuracy of eyewitness testimony.

Did you see a red or blue car?

Which Interview Technique Works Best?

Suppose you witnessed a robbery but had trouble picking the suspect out of a police lineup. To help you provide reliable information about the suspect, you might be questioned using a procedure called the cognitive interview (M. W. Eysenck, 2009a).

The **cognitive interview** is a technique for questioning people, such as eyewitnesses, by having them imagine and reconstruct the details of an event, report everything they remember without holding anything back, and narrate the event from different viewpoints.

The cognitive interview has proved very useful in police interrogation: Detectives trained in cognitive interview techniques obtained 47–60% more information from victims and suspects than detectives using the standard police interrogation method (Gwyer & Clifford, 1997). The cognitive interview is a very effective way to increase correct recall and avoid making suggestions that might create false memories and increase errors of source misattribution in children, adults, and senior citizens from varying educational backgrounds (R. P. Fisher et al., 2011; Memon et al., 2009; L. M. Stein & Memon, 2006).

Psychologists have answered many questions about how eyewitnesses can be misled as well as how to improve the reliability of their testimony, which may result in life-or-death decisions. Because most jurors do not know that eyewitness testimonies are unreliable, many courts in the United States allow experts to testify about the reliability of eyewitnesses so juries are made aware of the same studies and findings that you have just read (McVeigh, 2006; Pezdek, 1995). ●

A cognitive interview is a more effective method for questioning eyewitnesses.

Can Bad Memories Be Erased?

Imagine a world where no one had any bad memories. New research discoveries suggest that such a world may not be so implausible. For people who are frequently haunted by painful, unpleasant memories, there may be a simple way to alter or even erase the events from their mind.

Scientists believe that after a person experiences a traumatic event, the body releases stress hormones, which act to make the bad memory stronger. To test this theory, Roger Pitman, a scientist, found patients who had just experienced a traumatic event and gave some of them a drug called propranolol, which blocks the release of stress hormones, and others a placebo. Patients also tape-recorded their recollection of the traumatic experience in detail. Months later, patients listened to the tapes. Over half of the placebo patients exhibited intense physical symptoms of anxiety and fear (high heart rate, sweaty palms), whereas none of the patients who received propranolol had such responses.

Other research also supports the use of propranolol to decrease fear associated with bad memories. For instance, Merel Kindt and her colleagues created fearful memories in participants by administering shocks when they looked at pictures of spiders while instructed to "actively remember" the pictures. One day later, half of the participants were given propranolol and half a placebo. All were shown pictures of spiders again, and the participants given medication showed less fearful responses.

The almost magical effects of propranolol occur because the drug affects brain cells in the amygdala, a critical brain structure involved in the processing of emotions in memories and learning fear responses. Using propranolol while actively remembering traumatic events seems to break down unpleasant memories by removing the fear responses associated with them.

More recently, scientists have made strides in substantially decreasing the intensity of people's bad memories without the use of drugs. Scientists found that when we recall a memory, a brief window of opportunity presents itself when we can add to, alter, or possibly even erase that memory. If people are given new information during this brief time when they are actively recalling a memory, then it is the new, pleasant story that gets saved into long-term memory.

1 What type of long-term memory includes our recollection of traumatic events we experienced?

2 In this research example, what is the neutral stimulus? Unconditioned stimulus? Conditioned stimulus?

3 Why are scientists primarily focusing on using a drug that targets brain cells in the amygdala and not the hippocampus?

4 Research shows it's more difficult to erase bad memories than to forget good memories. What explains this?

The future of memory research is full of possibilities. There are, of course, many ethical concerns. For instance, what if murderers and rapists were able to erase from their memory the horrific actions they committed? They would thereby eliminate any feelings of guilt or remorse. Also, people could interfere with the justice system by erasing the memories of important eyewitnesses. Then, there's always the risk of erasing positive, wanted memories in the process.

For now, scientific advances do help remove the trauma and fear associated with these memories. However, it may not be long before a scientific breakthrough makes it possible to completely erase memories in humans.

5 Does the phenomenon of source misattribution apply to a person whose memory of the witnessed event gets erased? Why or why not?

6 It's possible to make a memory weaker or even disappear, but is it possible to create false memories and have people believe them to be true?

Adapted from Adler, 2012; Kalb, 2009; Kindt et al., 2009; Lemonick, 2007a; K. McGowan, 2009; L. Phelps, 2010; Piore, 2012; Schiller, 2009

✓ Summary Test

A Organization of Memories

1. If you are asked to retrieve previously learned information without the aid of external cues, you are using a process of remembering called **(a)** _____, which is generally more difficult. If you are asked to answer multiple-choice questions, you can identify or match information and use a process of remembering called **(b)** _____, which is generally less difficult.

1. ANIMAL

(image credits, rotated left margin of figure): Blue jay: © Sarah Holmlund/Shutterstock.com; guppy: © Dirk Ercken/Shutterstock.com; shark: © Michael Rosskothen/Shutterstock.com; rooster: © Serg64/Shutterstock.com

2. According to one theory of memory organization, we encode or file related ideas in separate categories called _____.

3. We form links between nodes by forming associations. The idea that the interconnected nodes form a gigantic system is called _____ theory.

4. An arrangement in which nodes are organized in a logical manner, with more concrete information at the bottom and more abstract information at the top, is called a _____.

B Forgetting Curves

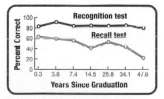

5. If the amount of previously learned information that people can recall or recognize across time is plotted, the resulting graph is called a _____. For example, Ebbinghaus demonstrated that the majority of nonsense syllables are forgotten relatively quickly—within hours. However, other studies showed that more relevant and interesting information may be remembered for many years.

C Reasons for Forgetting

6. If you forget because other memories interfere with or prevent retrieval of some particular memory, it is called **(a)** _____. If you forget because information that was learned earlier interferes with information learned later, it is called **(b)** _____ interference. If you forget because information that was learned later interferes with information learned earlier, it is called **(c)** _____ interference.

PSYCHOLOGY   SOCIOLOGY

7. Forgetting information because it was poorly encoded means that you failed to form new associations or reminders, which results in poor or inadequate _____.

8. Freud said you may forget information that is threatening to your self-concept because it is automatically pushed into your unconscious, from which you cannot retrieve it at will. This idea of Freud's is called _____.

9. If a person experiences a blow to the head, has severe psychological trauma, or takes or is given certain drugs, that person may forget things because of having _____.

10. Another reason people forget things may be because they haven't used the information for a long period of time. If we do not access a memory, then over time the memory traces may _____, which means the memory is lost as a result of not using the memory traces.

11. To increase the chances of remembering items from long-term memory, we can create reminders that associate new information with information that we already know; these reminders are called _____.

12. There are times you are absolutely sure that certain information is stored in memory but you are unable to retrieve it. This experience is called the _____ phenomenon.

13. Besides creating retrieval cues, it may also be easier to recall information when you are in the same physiological or emotional state as when you originally learned it; this phenomenon is called _____.

D Biological Bases of Memory

14. Different areas of the brain are involved in different memory processes. For example, the ability to hold words, facts, or events (declarative information) in short-term memory depends on activity in the **(a)** _____. The ability to transfer information about words, facts, and events (declarative information) from short-term into long-term memory depends on activity in the **(b)** _____. If this structure were damaged, a person could carry on a conversation but would not **(c)** _____ the conversation the next day.

15. The ability to recall words, facts, and events (declarative information) from the past involves activity in the outer covering of the brain, which is called the **(a)** _____. For example, if patients have an intact cortex, they can remember past events because these events are already stored in the cortex. However, they may have difficulty remembering any new words, facts, or events (declarative information) because of damage to their **(b)** _____.

16. The ability to transfer motor skills and habits, which is part of _____ memory, does not involve the hippocampus. Even though a person with damage to the hippocampus can store procedural information, that person would have no memory of having engaged in that event (declarative information).

17. The area of the brain that adds emotional feelings to memories is called the _____. This area is involved in forming a wide range of happy, sad, and fearful memories.

18. Researchers believe that the brain forms and briefly stores short-term memories by using a circuit of interconnected neurons called _____. When these interconnected neurons stop being activated, the short-term memory vanishes unless it has been encoded in long-term memory.

19. Researchers have evidence that the formation and storage of long-term memories involve the repeated stimulation of neurons, which in turn causes neurons to grow and change to form new connections with other neurons; this phenomenon is called **(a)** _____. When this process was chemically or genetically blocked, animals were unable to form **(b)** _____, which points to the importance of LTP in forming long-term memories.

E Mnemonics: Memorization Methods

20. Although we have the capacity to store great amounts of information, we may not be able to recall some of this information because of forgetting. Techniques that use efficient methods of encoding to improve remembering and prevent forgetting are called **(a)** _____. The major function of these techniques is to create strong **(b)** _____ that will serve as effective **(c)** _____.

21. A method that creates visual associations between memorized places and items to be memorized is called the **(a)** _____. With another method, one creates associations between number-word rhymes and items to be memorized; this method is called the **(b)** _____.

F Cultural Diversity: Differences in Episodic Memory

22. Cross-cultural research has found cultural differences in recalling **(a)** _____, which involves knowledge of specific events, personal experiences, or activities. One researcher conducted three studies to examine the reasons for the differences in episodic memory between Euro-Americans and Asians. The results suggest that there are differences in **(b)** _____ and **(c)** _____ processes between the two groups, as opposed to differences in the ability to **(d)** _____.

G Research Focus: Recalling Sexual History

23. Since sexual activity is not a behavior researchers can observe, research methods used to study sexual activity are limited to the **(a)** _____. Janet Rosenbaum at Harvard University asked more than 13,000 adolescents questions about their sexual histories and whether or not they had ever taken a virginity pledge. Overall, the results of this study show that adolescents' memories for sexual behaviors are often **(b)** _____.

H Application: Eyewitness Testimony

24. In nearly 75% of 289 cases, wrongful convictions have been based on eyewitness testimony, which indicates that such testimony is not always **(a)** _____. Another problem is that the accuracy of an eyewitness is only moderately related to the how much **(b)** _____ the eyewitness feels. Eyewitnesses have difficulty identifying a suspect of another race; this is called **(c)** _____. Eyewitness testimony may not be reliable because witnesses may be influenced by officials who ask **(d)** _____ questions.

25. When a person has difficulty deciding which of two or more sources is responsible for a memory, it is called **(a)** _____. Researchers found that misleading questions and false information can cause people to **(b)** _____ events.

26. The recall of eyewitnesses may be improved by having them imagine and reconstruct the details of an event, report everything that they remember, and report things from different viewpoints. This method is called the **(a)** _____. With this method, eyewitnesses remember much more information about the event than they do when asked standard questions. This questioning procedure also helps to eliminate suggestions or source misattributions, which can result in implanting **(b)** _____ in witnesses.

Links to Learning

Key Terms/Key People

amnesia, 265
amygdala: emotional
  memories, 268
cognitive interview, 275
cortex: long-term
  memories, 268
cortex: short-term
  memories, 268
decay, 265
episodic memory, 272
eyewitness testimony, 274, 275

forgetting, 265
forgetting curve, 264
hippocampus: retrieving
  memories, 268
hippocampus: transferring
  memories, 268
interference, 265, 266
long-term potentiation,
  or LTP, 269
memory-enhancing drugs, 271
memory trace, 265

method of loci, 271
misinformation effect, 275
mnemonic methods, 271
network hierarchy, 263
network theory, 262
neural assemblies, 269
nodes, 263
own-race bias, 274
peg method, 271
proactive interference, 266

recall, 261
recognition, 261
repression, 265
retrieval, 267
retrieval cues, 265, 267
retroactive interference, 266
source misattribution, 275
state-dependent learning, 267
tip-of-the-tongue
  phenomenon, 267

Media Resources

Go to **CengageBrain.com** to access Psychology CourseMate, where you will find an interactive eBook, glossaries, flashcards, quizzes, videos, answers to Critical Thinking questions, and more. You can also access Virtual Psychology Labs, an interactive laboratory experience designed to illustrate key experiments first-hand.

Mirror, Mirror, on the Wall, Who Is the Most Intelligent of Them All?

Who is the most intelligent?

For the past 200 years, psychologists have been involved in defining and measuring intelligence, which turns out to be a very complicated business. For example, after reading about the five individuals described below, rank them according to your idea of intelligence. After you have read the module, come back to your ranking and see if you would make any changes.

Based on my idea of intelligence, here's how I have ranked the five individuals: #1___, #2___, #3___, #4___, #5___.

A. John Grisham

While working as a criminal attorney and serving in the House of Representatives, John Grisham began his writing career. Since then, he has written 25 novels and all of them have become international bestsellers. His books have been translated into 29 languages and together have sold over 250 million copies worldwide. Also, nearly half of his books have been adapted into films.

B. Halle Berry

At age 46, she has already starred in over 40 Hollywood movies and become the highest paid African American actress in Hollywood. Not only has she earned an Emmy and a Golden Globe award for her acting, but she also won Best Actress at the Academy Awards in 2002, making her the first African American woman to ever win an Oscar for best actress.

C. Mark Zuckerberg

At the age of 28, his worth reached nearly $20 billion. He is best known as a co-founder of Facebook, which has about 600 million users worldwide. He helped launch Facebook while attending Harvard University (he later dropped out). He soon became known as a programming prodigy. In 2008, he became the youngest billionaire in the world, and in 2010, he was TIME's person of the year.

D. Alia Sabur

At only 8 months, Alia began reading. She graduated from college at age 14 with highest honors, becoming the youngest female college graduate in American history. Her IQ is off the charts. Alia is the youngest person to ever receive awards from the U.S. Department of Defense, U.S. National Science Foundation, and NASA. At the age of 19, she became the world's youngest professor in history.

E. Jeremy Lin

At age 21, he graduated from Harvard University and soon became a professional basketball player. He is the first player in the NBA who has graduated from Harvard since the 1950s. He is now a point guard for the New York Knicks. After leading his team to six consecutive wins, he developed a global following. In his first five starts with the Knicks, he scored an impressive 136 points, breaking an NBA record.

The problem you faced in trying to rank the intelligence of the above five individuals—Grisham, Berry, Zuckerberg, Sabur, and Lin—is similar to what psychologists faced in having to define and measure intelligence. As you will learn, there is no agreed-upon definition of intelligence.

Generally, **intelligence** is a person's ability to adapt to the environment and learn from experience (R. J. Sternberg & Detterman, 1986).

Measuring intelligence is part of an area of psychology that is called psychometrics.

Psychometrics, which is a subarea of psychology, is concerned with developing psychological tests that assess an individual's abilities, skills, beliefs, and personality traits in a wide range of settings—school, industry, or clinic.

As you'll discover in this module, the measurement of intelligence and the development of intelligence tests are still being debated (Gill et al., 2009; Urbina, 2011).

What's Coming

We'll discuss the different theories of intelligence, how intelligence is measured, the meaning of IQ scores, the problems with intelligence tests, how genetics and environment influence intelligence, and ways to improve environmental opportunities.

We'll begin with a very old but very basic question: How do we define intelligence? ●

A Defining Intelligence

Problem: Definition

What is intelligence?

John Grisham: author of 25 bestselling novels

Halle Berry: Oscar-winning actress

Mark Zuckerberg: co-founder of Facebook; worth $20 billion

Alia Sabur: "off the charts" IQ; professor

Jeremy Lin: NBA player; Harvard University grad

When college students were asked to estimate their overall IQs, men's reports of IQ were higher than estimates given by women, and both men and women reported higher IQs for their fathers than for their mothers (Petrides et al., 2004). In fact, over the past 20 years, men have consistently overestimated and women have consistently underestimated their IQs, even though researchers find no sex differences in IQ scores (Colom et al., 2000).

People generally believe IQ scores measure intelligence. But it's not so simple. For example, how did you rank the intelligence of the five individuals in the left photos, each of whom shows a different yet extraordinary skill or talent? Do these examples point to the existence of different kinds of intelligence (H. Gardner, 2006)?

Many psychologists believe intelligence is best defined by measuring a variety of cognitive abilities, which is what most intelligence tests measure. For example, based on an intelligence test, Alia Sabur received an IQ score so high it was "off the charts." Others argue that a definition of intelligence based entirely on cognitive abilities is much too narrow. Instead, they believe there are many kinds of intelligence, such as involving acting skills (Halle Berry), athletic abilities (Jeremy Lin), verbal skills (John Grisham), or solving problems (Mark Zuckerberg) (E. Benson, 2003a; H. Gardner, 2006).

More recently, researchers have pointed to the importance of emotional intelligence, which involves how well people perceive, express, and regulate emotions in themselves and others (Salovey et al., 2008). Award-winning actors (Halle Berry) certainly have high emotional intelligence. We'll discuss emotional intelligence in Module 16.

Here we'll examine three popular definitions of intelligence, beginning with the oldest and perhaps the most widely accepted definition, the general intelligence theory.

General Intelligence Theory

What is g?

In 1904, Charles Spearman reported that he had measured intelligence in an objective way. Spearman was one of the first to use the psychometric approach.

The **psychometric approach** measures or quantifies cognitive abilities or factors that are thought to be involved in intellectual performance.

Spearman (1904) reasoned that by measuring related cognitive factors he would have an objective measure of intelligence. This idea led to his general intelligence theory of intelligence.

Spearman's general intelligence theory (or **g-factor theory**) says that intelligence has a general mental ability factor, **g**, that represents what different cognitive tasks have in common.

Spearman believed that factor **g**, or general mental ability, represented a person's mental energy. Today, factor **g** is defined and measured by a person's performance in various and related cognitive abilities. In other words, modern intelligence tests have essentially changed or transformed Spearman's **g** into an objective score, which is commonly known as the IQ score. Today, many psychologists believe that **g**, as represented by IQ scores, is a good measure of a person's general intelligence (Jenson, 2005).

On the basis of Spearman's general intelligence theory, which of the five individuals (left photos) is most intelligent?

Many psychologists believe that **g** is the definition of general intelligence, which can be measured by an IQ test and represented by an IQ score. Thus, one way to compare people on intelligence is by using scores from IQ tests. Ranking intelligence by using IQ scores would favor Sabur ("off the charts" IQ score) and probably Grisham (attorney and author of 25 international bestselling novels) and Zuckerberg (programming prodigy). However, although Berry (Oscar-winning actress) and Lin (professional athlete) might score high on IQ tests, they would get little or no credit for having exceptional motor or acting skills.

Advantages and Disadvantages

One advantage of **g** is that it can be objectively defined and measured by an IQ test, which gives a single IQ score that is presumed to reflect a person's general intelligence. Another advantage is that **g** is a good predictor of performance in academic settings and has some success in predicting performance in certain careers (discussed later) (N. Brody, 2000).

One disadvantage of Spearman's **g** is the continuing debate over whether it is the best measure of intelligence. Or as one researcher states, "We know how to measure something called intelligence, but we do not know what has been measured" (N. Brody, 2000, p. 30). A second disadvantage of **g** is that it focuses on cognitive abilities but neglects motor, perceptual, musical, practical, and creative abilities, which some believe indicate other kinds of intelligence (H. Gardner, 2006). A third disadvantage is that **g** and its focus on cognitive abilities are popular in Western cultures but not in many Asian and African cultures, where being intelligent includes other abilities, such as how one relates to and understands others (E. Benson, 2003b). For these reasons, psychologists critical of **g**'s narrow approach to measuring general intelligence have proposed other definitions and ways to measure intelligence. We'll discuss two other definitions of intelligence.

Multiple-Intelligence Theory

Multiple kinds of intelligence?

Some psychologists reject the idea that intelligence can be reduced to *g* and expressed by a single number, an IQ score. Howard Gardner (1999, 2006) argues for broadening the definition of intelligence to include different kinds of abilities, an idea he calls the multiple-intelligence theory.

Howard Gardner

Gardner's multiple-intelligence theory says that instead of one kind of general intelligence, there are at least nine different kinds, which include verbal intelligence, musical intelligence, logical-mathematical intelligence, spatial intelligence, body movement intelligence, intelligence to understand oneself, intelligence to understand others, naturalistic intelligence, and existential intelligence.

Gardner states that standard IQ tests measure primarily verbal and logical-mathematical intelligence and neglect other but equally important kinds of intelligence, such as the ones listed above. Gardner (1999, 2006) arrived at his theory of multiple kinds of intelligence after studying which abilities remain following brain damage, how savants and prodigies develop their specialized kinds of intelligence, and how people in different environments develop different abilities to adapt and be successful.

On the basis of Gardner's multiple-intelligence theory, which of the five individuals (previous page) is most intelligent?

According to Gardner's multiple-intelligence theory, there isn't one kind of general intelligence for ranking all individuals. Rather, Gardner views the special abilities of Berry in acting and Lin in athletics as representing other kinds of intelligence. Gardner argues that none of the five is more intelligent but rather that each of the five individuals shows a different kind of ability or intelligence that was developed and adapted to his or her environment.

Advantages and Disadvantages

One advantage of Gardner's multiple-intelligence approach is that it does not reduce intelligence to a single IQ score but rather credits people with having different kinds of intelligence, which include their unique strengths and limitations (K. Davis et al., 2011).

Two disadvantages of this approach are not knowing the number of intelligence types and not having standard assessment techniques for the different kinds of intelligence (J. E. Davidson & Kemp, 2011).

Agreeing with Gardner that *g* is too narrow a measure of intelligence, Sternberg proposed a triarchic theory.

Triarchic Theory

Three kinds of intelligence?

Criticizing Spearman's *g* as too narrow and current IQ tests as limited to measuring only problem-solving skills and cognitive abilities, psychologist Robert Sternberg defined intelligence by **analyzing** three kinds of reasoning processes that people use in solving problems. Sternberg (2003a) calls his approach the triarchic theory of intelligence.

Robert Sternberg

Sternberg's triarchic theory says that intelligence can be divided into three different kinds of reasoning processes (*triarchic* means "three components"). The first is using analytical or logical thinking skills measured by traditional intelligence tests. The second is using creative thinking and the ability to learn from experience. The third is using practical thinking skills that help a person adjust to, and cope with, his or her sociocultural environment.

Analytical

Creative

Practical

Unlike Spearman's *general intelligence theory,* which measures general intelligence by measuring cognitive abilities, Sternberg's theory breaks intelligence down into three reasoning processes.

On the basis of Sternberg's triarchic theory of intelligence, which of the five individuals (previous page) is most intelligent?

According to Sternberg's triarchic theory, there isn't one kind of general intelligence for evaluating these five individuals but rather three different reasoning processes (analytical, creative, practical) that contribute to and predict the success of each of the five individuals.

Advantages and Disadvantages

One advantage of Sternberg's triarchic theory of intelligence is that it doesn't limit the definition of intelligence to cognitive abilities. Instead, Sternberg's theory evaluates a person's intelligence by measuring three different kinds of reasoning processes and how they contribute to a person's success. For example, a person may be "street smart" or have exceptional practical reasoning skills but may not necessarily score high on traditional intelligence tests (J. E. Davidson & Kemp, 2011).

Though the triarchic theory shows promise at broadly assessing intelligence, one disadvantage is that Sternberg's research and tests for measuring the three kinds of reasoning processes have been criticized as not providing sufficient support for his triarchic theory (J. E. Davidson & Kemp, 2011; Gottfredson, 2003).

Current Status

Western psychologists used the psychometric approach to measure cognitive abilities, which led to the development of intelligence tests and IQ scores and the concept of *g* as the best measure of intelligence (N. Brody, 2000). Standard intelligence tests remain popular because they have proved useful in predicting performance in academic settings. Critics argue that these IQ tests measure only analytical intelligence and ignore other types of intelligence (Nisbett, 2009). Newer approaches, such as Gardner's multiple-intelligence approach and Sternberg's triarchic approach, measure additional abilities and skills and represent different kinds of intelligence. They may replace *g* and its IQ score as the best measure of intelligence (H. Gardner, 2006; R. J. Sternberg & Pretz, 2005). Many educators have already adopted a multiple-intelligence approach in designing classroom curriculum (J. Chen et al., 2009; Kelly & Tangney, 2006).

To see how far intelligence testing has come, we'll go back in time and discuss early attempts to define and measure intelligence. ●

Earlier Attempts to Measure Intelligence

Head Size and Intelligence

Are bigger brains better?

Efforts to measure intelligence began in earnest in the late 1800s. That's when Francis Galton noticed that intelligent people often had intelligent relatives and concluded that intelligence was, to a large extent, biological or inherited. In trying to assess inherited intelligence, Galton measured people's heads and recorded the speed of their reactions to various sensory stimuli. However, measures proved to be poorly related to intelligence or academic achievement (S. J. Gould, 1996).

Galton switched gears and tried to correlate head size with students' grade point averages. For example, he reported that the average head size of Cambridge students who received A's was about 3.3% larger than that of students who received C's (Galton, 1888). However, a review of later studies showed a very low correlation of 0.15 between head size and intelligence (IQ scores) (Vernon et al., 2000). Such a low correlation has little practical use in measuring or predicting intelligence. For this reason, using head size as a measure of intelligence was abandoned in favor of using skull or brain size.

Brain Size and Intelligence

Efforts to measure intelligence continued with the work of Paul Broca, a famous neurologist in the late 1800s. Broca claimed that there was a relationship between brain size and intelligence, with larger brains indicating more intelligence. However, a later reanalysis of Broca's data indicated that measures of brain size proved to be unreliable and poorly correlated with intelligence (S. J. Gould, 1996).

Recently, the sizes of living brains were measured with brain scans (see p. 70), which permit more precise measurement. When researchers control for a person's sex (male brains are bigger) and age (older brains are smaller), studies using brain scans generally find weak positive correlations between brain size and intelligence (IQ scores) (Hoppe & Stojanovic, 2008; McDaniel, 2005). However, such correlations indicate only that a relationship exists; correlations cannot tell us whether bigger brains lead to increased intelligence or whether more cognitive activity leads to bigger brains. These medium-sized correlations indicate a positive relationship between brain size and intelligence (IQ scores) but are too low to have practical value in actually predicting an individual's intelligence.

Brain Size and Achievement

Early researchers were reluctant to give up the idea that bigger brains were better. They looked for a relationship between brain size and personal achievement, another measure of intelligence. However, as shown in the center illustration, there is enormous variation in brain size and achievement (S. J. Gould, 1996). Notice that Nobel Prize–winner Einstein's brain (1,230 grams) was slightly below average weight and that two famous authors, poet Walt Whitman (1,200 grams) and novelist Anatole France (1,000 grams), achieved literary fame with brains about half the weight of Jonathan Swift's (2,000 grams), one of the heaviest on record. For comparison, we have included a gorilla brain (500 grams), which is actually quite small considering the size of a gorilla head. It is difficult to test a gorilla's intelligence, but at least one is reported to have learned a vocabulary of more than 1,000 hand signs ("Koko's World," 2006).

Brain Size, Sex Differences, and Intelligence

Still believing that bigger brains are better, some researchers claimed that women had lower IQ scores than men because women's brains weigh about 10% less than men's (Holden, 1995). However, a later study of over 4,000 women and 6,000 men reported that there was little or no difference in intelligence (IQ scores) between men and women. Researchers concluded that the larger size of men's brains does not result in higher IQs (Colom et al., 2000).

Measuring Intelligence

As you have seen, there is a long history of scientists trying to measure intelligence. However, all the early attempts to use head, skull, body, or brain size to measure intelligence failed. In fact, a paper presented in 1904 to a German psychological society concluded that there was little hope of developing psychological tests to measure intelligence in an objective way (Wolf, 1973). What's interesting about this paper is that one of the authors was Alfred Binet, who went on to develop the first intelligence test.

We'll explain how Binet succeeded in developing an intelligence test when so many others had failed.

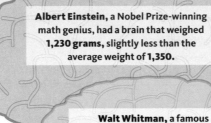

Jonathan Swift, a great 18th-century British writer who wrote *Gulliver's Travels,* had a brain that weighed **2,000 grams,** one of the largest on record.

Albert Einstein, a Nobel Prize-winning math genius, had a brain that weighed **1,230 grams,** slightly less than the average weight of **1,350.**

Walt Whitman, a famous 19th-century American poet, had a brain that weighed **1,200 grams,** within the normal range.

Anatole France, a famous 19th-century French author, had a brain that weighed **1,000 grams.**

Average size of a gorilla's brain is 500 grams.

Brain size doesn't necessarily match performance.

Binet's Breakthrough

Why did Binet develop an intelligence test?

In the late 1800s, a gifted French psychologist named Alfred Binet realized that Broca and Galton had failed to assess intelligence by measuring brain size. Binet believed that intelligence was a collection of mental abilities and the best way to assess intelligence was to measure a person's ability to perform cognitive tasks, such as understanding the meanings of words.

Binet was very pessimistic about developing an intelligence test. By a strange twist of fate, he was appointed to a commission that was instructed to develop tests capable of differentiating children of normal intelligence from those who needed special help. Binet accepted this challenge with two goals in mind: The test must be easy to administer without requiring any special laboratory equipment, and the test must clearly distinguish between normal and abnormal mental abilities (N. Brody, 1992). In 1905, Binet and psychiatrist Theodore Simon developed the world's first standardized intelligence test, the Binet-Simon Intelligence Scale (Binet & Simon, 1905).

The **Binet-Simon Intelligence Scale** contained items arranged in order of increasing difficulty. The items measured vocabulary, memory, common knowledge, and other cognitive abilities.

The purpose of this first Binet-Simon Intelligence Scale was to distinguish among mentally defective children in the Paris school system. In Binet's time, intellectually deficient children were divided into three groups: idiots (most severely deficient), imbeciles (moderate), and morons (mildest). These terms are no longer used today because they have taken on very negative meanings. The problems with this first test were that it classified children into only three categories (idiots, imbeciles, and morons) and that it did not have a way to express the results in a single score. However, several years later, Binet corrected both of these problems when he introduced the concept of mental level, or mental age.

Alfred Binet (1857–1911)

© Bettmann/Corbis

Mental Age: Measure of Intelligence

Binet and Simon revised their intelligence scale to solve several problems in their original scale. They arranged the test items in order of increasing difficulty and designed different items to measure different cognitive abilities. For each test item, Binet determined whether an average child of a certain age could answer the question correctly. For example, a child at age level 3 should be able to point to various parts of the face. A child at age level 9 should be able to recite the days of the week. Because the test items were arranged for each age level (age levels 3 to 13), this new test could identify which average age level the child performed at. If a particular child passed all the items that could be answered by an average 3-year-old but none of the items appropriate for older children, that child would be said to have a mental age of 3. Thus, if a 6-year-old child could answer only questions appropriate for a 3-year-old child, that child would be given a mental age of 3 and would be considered to have an impairment in intellectual development. Binet's intelligence test became popular because a single score represented mental age.

Which items could an average 3-year-old answer?

© Flashon Studio/Shutterstock.com

Which items could an average 9-year-old answer?

© Monkey Business Images/Shutterstock.com

Mental age is a measure that estimates a child's intellectual progress by comparing the child's score on an intelligence test to the scores of average children of the same age.

At this point, the Binet-Simon scale gave its results in terms of a mental age but not an IQ score. The idea for computing an IQ score did not occur until some years later, when the scale was revised by L. M. Terman.

Formula for IQ

What was the big change?

In 1916, Lewis Terman and his colleagues at Stanford University completed an American revision of the Binet-Simon Intelligence Scale. This revised test became known as the Stanford-Binet Intelligence Scale.

The **Stanford-Binet Intelligence Scale** was a revision of the Binet-Simon Intelligence Scale that included the addition of some test items and translation into English, as well as a new scoring system to compute the final test score.

Improving on the concept of expressing the test results in terms of mental age, Terman devised a formula to calculate an intelligence quotient (IQ) score (Terman, 1916).

Intelligence quotient (IQ) is computed by dividing a child's mental age (MA), as measured in an intelligence test, by the child's chronological age (CA) and multiplying the result by 100.

Remember that in Binet's test, mental age was calculated by noting how many items a child answered that were appropriate to a certain age. For example, if a 4-year-old girl passed the test items appropriate for a 5-year-old, she was said to have a mental age of 5. A child's chronological (physical) age is his or her age in months and years. To compute her IQ score, we use Terman's formula, shown below.

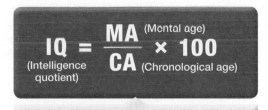

$$IQ = \frac{MA \text{ (Mental age)}}{CA \text{ (Chronological age)}} \times 100$$

(Intelligence quotient)

Formula for calculating IQ score

Thus, for the child in our example, we substitute 5 for MA, 4 for CA, and multiply by 100. We get: 5/4 = 1.25 × 100 = 125. So the child's IQ is 125. An IQ score computed in this traditional way is called a *ratio IQ* because the score represents a ratio of mental to chronological age. Today the ratio IQ has been replaced by the *deviation IQ,* whose computation is too complex to explain here. The reason for the switch from ratio IQ to deviation IQ is that deviation IQ scores more accurately reflect test performance as children get older.

Since the original Binet-Simon scale in 1905, IQ tests have become very popular and have grown into a large business. We'll look more closely at one of the most widely used IQ tests.

We are all curious to learn someone's IQ because we believe that this single score reveals a person's real intelligence. For example, try to match these IQ scores—114, 158, 160—with three famous people—Quentin Tarantino, film director, producer, and actor; Laura Shields, model on the NBC show "Deal or No Deal"; and John F. Kennedy, 35th President of the United States (answers at the right). Knowing the IQ scores of these individuals tells us something about their cognitive abilities, but some psychologists believe that cognitive abilities represent only one kind of intelligence. For example, would you expect Laura Shields and Quentin Tarantino to have about the same IQ, which is much higher than that of President Kennedy? The achievements of individuals with average or slightly above average IQs suggest that there are other kinds of intelligence, such as practical, emotional, social, and creative, which may be equally important to one's success in life and career (H. Gardner, 2003, 2006; R. J. Sternberg et al., 2003b). Now, let's see how IQ scores are measured.

Is IQ the same as intelligence?

Quentin Tarantino: film director, producer, and actor

Laura Shields: model

John F. Kennedy: 35th U.S. president

Answers: Kennedy, 114; Shields, 158; Tarantino, 160.

Examples of IQ Tests

The most widely used IQ tests are the Wechsler Adult Intelligence Scale (WAIS), for ages 16 and older, and the Wechsler Intelligence Scale for Children (WISC), for children of ages 6–16. A trained examiner administers the Wechsler scales on a one-to-one basis.

The **Wechsler Adult Intelligence Scale (WAIS)** and **Wechsler Intelligence Scale for Children (WISC)** have items that are organized into various subtests. For example, the verbal section contains a subtest of general information, a subtest of vocabulary, and others. The performance section contains a subtest that involves arranging pictures in a meaningful order, one that requires assembling objects, and one that involves using codes. The verbal and performance scores are combined to give a single IQ score.

Examples of the subtests for WAIS, currently in its fourth version, are shown on the right. The Verbal Scale (top right) emphasizes language and verbal skills. Because of this emphasis, a person from a deprived environment or for whom English is a second language might have difficulty on this scale because of lack of verbal knowledge rather than lack of cognitive ability.

In an attempt to measure nonverbal skills and rule out other cultural or educational problems, Wechsler added the Performance Scale (lower right). These performance subtests, which measure problem-solving abilities, require concentration and focused effort, which may be difficult for individuals who are very nervous, are poor test takers, or have emotional problems. Although these IQ tests carefully try to measure verbal and nonverbal abilities, you can see that part of one's success on IQ tests depends on nonintellectual factors, such as cultural, educational, or emotional factors (R. M. Kaplan & Saccuzzo, 2009). We'll discuss other problems with IQ tests later in this module.

One reason these IQ tests are widely used is that they have two characteristics of good tests: validity and reliability.

WAIS Verbal Scale: Subtests

Subtests for the verbal scale include information, comprehension, arithmetic, similarities, digit span, and vocabulary. These examples resemble the WAIS items.

Information
On what continent is France?

Comprehension
Why are children required to go to school?

Arithmetic
How many hours will it take to drive 150 miles at 50 miles per hour?

Similarities
How are a calculator and a typewriter alike?

Digit span
Repeat the following numbers backward: 2, 4, 3, 5, 8, 9, 6.

Vocabulary
What does *audacity* mean?

WAIS Performance Scale: Subtests

Subtests for the performance scale include digit-symbol coding, block design, picture completion, and cancellation test. These examples resemble the WAIS items.

Digit-symbol coding

Shown:
1 2 3 4
○ □ △ ⊙

Fill in:
1 4 3 2
_ _ _ _

Block design
Assemble blocks to match this design.

Picture completion
Tell me what is missing.

Cancellation test
When I say go, draw a line through each *red* square and *yellow* triangle.

Two Characteristics of Tests

Can you analyze handwriting?

How truthful are the claims that intelligence and other personality traits can be identified through analyzing handwriting (Searles, 1998)? For example, which one of the four handwriting samples on the right indicates the highest IQ? (Answer at bottom of page.)

Although handwriting analysis may claim to measure intelligence, research shows that

Which handwriting sample is from the person with the highest IQ?

its accuracy is usually no better than a good guess (Tripician, 2000).

The reason handwriting analysis or so-called IQ tests in popular magazines are poor measures of intelligence (IQ) is that they lack at least one of the two important characteristics of a good test. These two characteristics are validity and reliability, which mark the difference between an accurate IQ test (WAIS) and an inaccurate test (handwriting analysis).

Validity

Handwriting analysis is fun, but it is a very poor intelligence test because it lacks validity, which is one of the two characteristics of a good test.

Validity means that the test measures what it is supposed to measure.

Although the definition of validity seems simple and short, this characteristic makes or breaks a test. For example, numerous studies have shown that handwriting analysis has little or no validity as an intelligence or personality test (Basil, 1989; Tripician, 2000). Because handwriting analysis lacks the characteristic of validity, it means that this test does not accurately measure what it is supposed to measure. Thus, a test with little or no validity produces results that could be produced by guessing or by chance.

The reason handwriting analysis or tests in popular magazines are not checked for validity is that checking validity is a long, expensive, and complicated process. One way to show a test's validity is to give the new test to hundreds of people along with other tests whose validity has already been established. Then the participants' scores on the new test are correlated with their scores on the tests that have proven validity. Another way that the validity of intelligence tests, such as the WAIS, was established was to show that IQ scores correlated with another measure of intelligence, such as academic achievement (Daley & Onwuegbuzie, 2011).

However, if IQ scores are valid measures of cognitive abilities and correlate with academic performance, why do some individuals with high IQs do poorly in college? The developer of the Head Start program, Ed Zigler, believes that academic performance depends on three factors: cognitive abilities; achievement, or the amount of knowledge that a person has accumulated; and motivation (Zigler, 1995). This means that a person may have outstanding cognitive abilities but may lack either the achievement or the motivation to succeed in college.

Besides validity, a good intelligence test should also have reliability.

Reliability

If your style of handwriting remained constant over time, such as always boldly crossing your *t*'s, then this trait would be reliable.

Reliability refers to consistency: A person's score on a test at one point in time should be similar to the score obtained by the same person on a similar test at a later point in time.

For example, if boldly crossed *t*'s indicated that a person is intelligent, then this measure of intelligence would be reliable. However, there is no evidence that boldly crossed *t*'s indicate that a person is intelligent. So, in this case, handwriting analysis would be a reliable test of intelligence, but since it lacks validity (doesn't measure intelligence) it is a worthless test of intelligence.

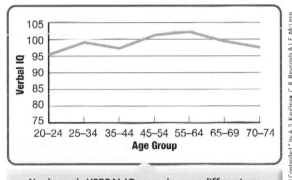

No change in VERBAL IQ scores in seven different age groups indicates that test is reliable.

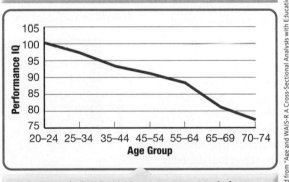

Decrease in OVERALL IQ scores across ages is due to psychological and physiological changes and not reliability problems with IQ test.

Graphs adapted from "Age and WAIS-R A Cross-Sectional Analysis with Educational Level Controlled," by A. S. Kaufman, C. R. Reynolds & J. E. McLean, 1989, *Intelligence*, 13, pp. 246, 247. Copyright © 1989 by Ablex Publishing Company. Adapted by permiss or.

Now, suppose you took the WAIS as a senior in high school and then retook the test as a junior in college. You would find that your IQ scores would be much the same because each time you would be compared with others of your same age. Because your IQ scores remain similar across time, the Wechsler scales, like other standardized IQ tests, have reliability (C. A. Berg, 2000; A. S. Kaufman, 2000).

For example, the top graph at the left shows the results of verbal IQ scores when seven different age groups were given the WAIS. Notice that verbal IQ scores are quite stable from ages 20 to 74, indicating that the Wechsler scales score high in reliability (A. S. Kaufman et al., 1989).

But notice that the lower graph shows that there is an overall decrease in performance IQ scores from ages 20 to 74 (A. S. Kaufman et al., 1989). However, this general decrease in performance scores across one's lifetime reflects changes in psychological and physiological functioning rather than a decrease in the test's reliability.

Researchers have shown that current intelligence tests, which measure primarily cognitive abilities, have relatively good validity and reliability (R. M. Kaplan & Saccuzzo, 2009). Even though IQ scores can be measured with good reliability and validity, our next question to answer is: What good or use are IQ scores? ●

(Handwriting answer: I (R. P.) wrote all four samples so that no matter which one you picked, I would come out a winner!)

Normal Distribution of IQ Scores

IQ 50–85

The left photo is of Lauren Potter, who stars in the television series "Glee." Potter has **Down syndrome,** a genetic defect that results in varying degrees of intellectual impairment and physical symptoms (slanting eyes, flattened nose, visual problems). Although Potter has a mild intellectual disability, she acts in a hit TV series and speaks in front of people throughout the country (Rice, 2012). Based on her abilities, Potter's IQ is probably between 50 and 85.

In comparison, the photo on the right is of Quentin Tarantino, who is a film director, producer, and actor and has a reported

IQ of 160. A few of the films he has worked on are *Pulp Fiction, Kill Bill,* and *Inglourious Basterds.* To compare the IQs of Potter and Tarantino with those of other people, we need to look at the distribution of IQ scores. IQ scores from established intelligence tests, such as the WAIS, are said to have a normal distribution.

A **normal distribution** is a statistical arrangement of scores that resembles the shape of a bell and, thus, is said to be a bell-shaped curve. A bell-shaped curve means the vast majority of scores fall in the middle range, with fewer scores falling near the two extreme ends of the curve.

IQ 160

For example, a normal distribution of IQ scores is shown at the left and is bell shaped. The average IQ score is 100, and about 95% of IQ scores fall between 70 and 130. An IQ of 70 and below is one sign of intellectual disability. An IQ of 130 or higher is one indication of a gifted individual. Thus, one widespread use of IQ tests is to provide general *categories* of mental abilities.

Next, we'll examine these guidelines in more detail, beginning with intellectual disability.

About 95 in 100 (95.44%) have IQ scores between 70 and 130

About 2 in 100 (2.27%) have IQ scores below 70

About 68 in 100 (68.26%) have IQ scores between 85 and 115

About 2 in 100 (2.27%) have IQ scores above 130

Number of scores

| 50 | 70 | 85 | 100 | 115 | 130 | 145 |

Intellectual Disability   **Average IQ**   **Giftedness**

Intellectual Disability: IQ Scores

One use of IQ scores has been to help identify individuals with an intellectual disability.

What is an intellectual disability?

Intellectual disability (formerly *mental retardation*) is a substantial limitation in present functioning that is characterized by significantly subaverage intellectual functioning along with related limitations in two of eleven areas, including communication, self-care, home living, social skills, academic skills, leisure, and safety (American Psychiatric Association, 2000).

In the Unites States, we have shifted from the term *mental retardation* to *intellectual disability*. The change in terminology is reflected in the name of the field's oldest and most prestigious organization, now called the American Association on Intellectual and Developmental Disabilities. More recently, *mental retardation* has been officially replaced with *intellectual disability* in most federal statutes (Hodapp et al., 2011).

The hope is that the shift away from using *retardation* will improve people's perceptions of these individuals as well as help the approximately 7.5 million Americans who have an intellectual disability to feel less stigmatized.

To test for intellectual disability, IQ tests are used in combination with observations of adaptive skills, which include social, home living, and communication skills. On the basis of IQ scores and adaptive skills, three levels of intellectual disability have been identified.

1 **Mild Intellectual Disability**

These individuals have IQs that range from 50 to 70. With special training and educational opportunities, they can learn to read and write, gain social competency, master simple occupational skills, and become self-supporting members of society. About 85% of individuals with intellectual disability are in this category.

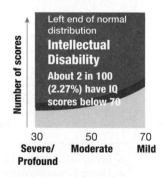

Left end of normal distribution

Intellectual Disability

About 2 in 100 (2.27%) have IQ scores below 70

Number of scores

| 30 | 50 | 70 |
| **Severe/ Profound** | **Moderate** | **Mild** |

2 **Moderate Intellectual Disability**

These individuals have IQs that range from 35 to 55. With special training and educational opportunities, they can learn to become partially independent in their everyday lives, provided they are in a family or self-help setting.

3 **Severe/Profound Intellectual Disability**

These individuals make up 5% of those with intellectual disability and have IQs ranging from 20 to 40. With special training and education, they can acquire limited skills in taking care of their personal needs. However, because of impaired motor and verbal abilities, they require considerable supervision their entire lives.

Next, we move to the middle of IQ's normal distribution.

Unless otherwise noted, all images are © Cengage Learning

Vast Majority: IQ Scores

Since the vast majority of people, about 95%, have IQ scores that fall between 70 and 130, it is interesting to see what IQ scores can tell us.

Do IQ Scores Predict Academic Achievement? Because IQ tests measure cognitive abilities similar to those used in academic settings, it is no surprise there is a medium-strength association, or correlation, between IQ scores and grades (0.50) and between IQ scores and total years of education that people complete (0.50) (N. Brody, 1997). However, based on medium-strength correlations alone, it would be difficult to predict a *specific person's academic performance* because performance in academic settings also depends on personal characteristics, such as one's interest in school, willingness to study, and belief in one's ability to succeed (Klomegah, 2007; Neisser et al., 1996).

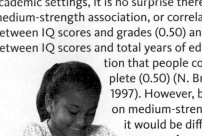

IQ scores are useful for predicting academic success.

Middle of normal distribution

About 95 in 100 (95.44%) have IQ scores between 70 and 130

Number of scores

70   85   **100**   115   130

Average IQ

Do IQ Scores Predict Job Performance? There is a low- to medium-strength correlation (+0.30 to 0.50) between IQ scores and job performance (Neisser et al., 1996). However, such correlations are not very accurate at predicting a *specific person's job performance* because several noncognitive factors that are not measured by IQ tests, such as personality traits (is a can-do person), emotional traits (can deal with stress and get along with co-workers), and practical know-how (figures out how to get the job done), play important roles in predicting job performance (Gottfredson, 2002; R. J. Sternberg, 2003b).

Now, we'll examine the right end of the normal distribution—high IQ scores.

IQ scores are somewhat useful at predicting job performance.

Giftedness: IQ Scores

Sho Yano (photo below), whose IQ is 200 plus, entered college at age 9, graduated at age 12, plays classical works on the piano, and was the youngest person ever to start a dual M.D.-Ph.D. program at the University of Chicago. Sho Yano is considered to be gifted. Although researchers and educators differ in how they define giftedness, this definition refers to academic giftedness.

Giftedness is usually defined by the approximately 2% of the population at the top end of the normal distribution having an IQ score of 130 or above.

Like Sho Yano, who excels at the piano and medicine, gifted children usually have some superior talent or skill.

When placed in *regular classrooms,* gifted children face a number of problems: They are bored by the lack of stimulation and they may feel lonely or develop social problems because they are labeled nerds or geeks. Researchers recommend that gifted children be placed in special academic programs that challenge and help them develop their potentials (Goode, 2002; Winner, 2000).

IQ of 200+ labels Sho Yano as gifted.

How Do Gifted Individuals Turn Out? In the early 1920s, Lewis Terman selected a sample of over 1,500 gifted children with IQs ranging from 135 to 200 (the average was 151) (Hulbert, 2005). Over the next 65 years, researchers repeatedly tested these individuals to determine what they had achieved and how they had adjusted. Although 10–30% more of the gifted men obtained advanced degrees compared with men in the general population, 30% never finished college, and 2% actually flunked out. Although gifted individuals generally showed better health, adjustment, life satisfaction, and achievement than people with average IQs, about 9% had serious emotional problems and 7% committed suicide (Hegarty, 2007; Holahan & Sears, 1995; Terman

Right end of normal distribution

Giftedness

About 2 in 100 (2.27%) have IQ scores above 130; about 1 in a million has an IQ above 180

Number of scores

130   145

Giftedness

& Oden, 1959). As a group, these gifted individuals were generally very successful in life but not at the extraordinary level that might have been predicted from their high IQ scores (Colangelo, 1997).

Generally, despite the stereotype that gifted people are socially awkward, research finds that most are socially well adjusted and liked by their peers (Lubinski et al., 2006). Other research shows that only gifted children who have demanding and critical parents are more likely to have social and emotional problems than children with normal intelligence (Elias, 2005).

Researchers have long been interested in brain differences between gifted people and those with normal-range intelligence and have found that the brain areas responsible for higher cognitive reasoning develop differently in highly intelligent children (see the Research Focus on p. 297) (P. Shaw et al., 2006). Recently, there has been a growing focus on the role of practice and determination in giftedness. This view holds that practice and steadfast determination, rather than innate talent, are critical factors in developing giftedness (Ericsson et al., 2007; Gladwell, 2008).

Conclusion. IQ scores, the most popular measure of intelligence, have proven moderately useful in predicting academic performance, in helping to define intellectual disability, and in identifying the gifted, but they have low to moderate success in predicting job performance. One reason IQ scores are not more predictive is that they do not measure numerous emotional, motivational, and personality factors that also influence behavior.

While IQ tests have proved useful, we'll next examine potential problems in taking and interpreting IQ tests. ●

D Potential Problems of IQ Testing

Binet's Two Warnings

You may remember that Binet's original goal was to develop a test that would distinguish between normal and abnormal mental abilities and thus identify children who were mentally retarded and needed special help and education. Although previous attempts to measure intelligence had failed, Binet and Simon succeeded in developing the first scale that identified children with varying degrees of mental retardation. Binet and Simon's scale was the beginning of the modern-day IQ test. However, even in the early 1900s, Binet realized that intelligence tests could be used in two potentially dangerous ways, so he issued the following two warnings:

What problems did Binet foresee?

Binet's Warnings

1 Binet warned that *intelligence tests do not measure innate abilities or natural intelligence;* rather, they measure an individual's cognitive abilities, which result from both heredity and environment.

2 Binet warned that *intelligence tests, by themselves, should not be used to label people* (for example, "moron," "average," "genius"); rather, intelligence tests should be used to assess an individual's abilities and used in combination with other information to make academic or placement decisions about people.

History shows that neither of Binet's warnings were heeded. In the early 1900s it became common practice to treat IQ scores as measures of innate intelligence and to use IQ scores to label people from "moron" to "genius." The U.S. Congress went so far as to pass laws that restricted immigrants based on assumed levels of innate intelligence (S. J. Gould, 1996), an issue we'll discuss in the Cultural Diversity section (see p. 296).

Along with using IQ scores to label individuals came racial and cultural discrimination, some of which continue to the present. For example, a controversial book, *The Bell Curve* (Herrnstein & Murray, 1994), suggested that racial differences in IQ scores are due primarily to genetic factors, something we'll discuss later in this module. For now, we'll examine three issues surrounding IQ tests: cultural bias, other cultures, and nonintellectual factors.

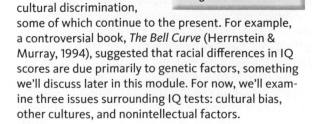

IQ tests have a history of being used to discriminate.

Racial Discrimination

There have been a number of court cases regarding the appropriate use of IQ tests. Here is one important case and the judge's ruling.

Are IQ tests racially biased?

Larry was an African American child who was assigned to special classes for the educable mentally retarded because he scored below 85 on an IQ test. However, several years later an African American psychologist retested Larry and found that his IQ score was higher than originally thought. Larry was taken out of the special classes, which were considered a dead end, and placed in regular classes that allowed for more advancement. On the basis of Larry's experience, a class action suit was brought against the San Francisco school system on behalf of all African American schoolchildren in the district. The suit was based on the finding that, although African American youngsters made up 27% of all the students enrolled in classes for the mentally retarded, they made up only 4% of the entire school population (R. M. Kaplan & Saccuzzo, 2005). African American parents wanted to know why their children were so much more numerous than White children in these special classes. They felt there must be a bias against African American children in the selection process.

IQ tests alone should not be used to define mental retardation.

Although Larry's case came to trial in the early 1970s, the final decision was given in 1979 by a judge of the federal court of appeals. The judge agreed with the African American parents and found that IQ tests being used in schools (kindergarten through grade 12) to determine intellectual disability were biased against people of color. The court ruled that California schools could not place children of color in classes for children with intellectual disability on the basis of the IQ test alone. The schools were instructed to come up with an intelligence test that does not favor Whites or else refrain from using a standardized test to identify slow learners.

Definition of intellectual disability. In other states, there is disagreement about the role of IQ tests in defining intellectual disability and making decisions about placing children in special education classes (BCSSE, 2002). Despite efforts to improve the educational opportunities for African American children in the United States, they continue to be more likely than White children to

$$IQ = \frac{MA \text{ (Mental age)}}{CA \text{ (Chronological age)}} \times 100$$

(Intelligence quotient)

be placed in classes for children with intellectual disability and less likely to be placed in classes for gifted children (R. Gardner et al., 2001; U.S. Department of Education, 2005). Critics of the special education system argue that African American students are overrepresented not because of their especially high level of disability but because of discriminatory placement procedures, such as the culturally biased IQ tests (Losen & Orfield, 2002; J. P. Shapiro et al., 1993).

Educational decisions. Based on the concerns discussed above, psychologists and educators recommend that IQ tests alone not be used as the primary basis for making decisions about a child's educational future. Instead, they suggest that educational decisions, especially about placing a child in a special education class, be made only after considering a wide range of information, which may include IQ scores but also observations and samples of the child's behavior from other situations (Palomares, 2003).

Unless otherwise noted, all images are © Cengage Learning

Cultural Bias

What kind of questions?

One criticism of IQ tests is that they are culturally biased, especially in favor of industrialized communities, such as the White middle class in the United States (Serpell, 2000).

Cultural bias means that the wording of the questions and the experiences on which the questions are based are more familiar to members of some social groups than to others.

For example, consider this question from an older version of the Wechsler Intelligence Scale for Children: "What would you do if you were sent to buy a loaf of bread and the grocer said he did not have any more?"

If you think the answer is "Go to another store," you are correct according to the developers of the Wechsler scale. However, when 200 minority children were asked this same question, 61 said they would go home. Asked to explain their answers, they gave reasonable explanations. Some children answered "Go home" because there were no other stores in their neighborhood. Yet the answer "Go home" would be scored "incorrect," despite it being correct in the child's experience (Hardy et al., 1976).

This example shows that different cultural influences and experiences may penalize some children when taking standardized tests of intelligence.

IQ tests are, to some extent, culturally biased.

In today's IQ tests, many of the above kinds of biases have been reduced (A. S. Kaufman, 2003). However, researchers still believe that it's virtually impossible to develop an intelligence test completely free of cultural bias because tests will reflect, to some degree, the concepts and values of their culture (L. A. Suzuki et al., 2011). For instance, researchers believe the reason Whites tend to score higher than African Americans on IQ tests is not differences in ability, but rather differences in knowledge. Whites may be more likely to be exposed to the information typically found on IQ tests (Fagan & Holland, 2007). This is another example of how cultural influences can affect a child's performance on standard IQ tests.

Other Cultures

Are there different definitions?

We have discussed how many Western psychologists believe the best definition of a person's intelligence is something called *g*, which is primarily measured by assessing cognitive abilities and expressed by IQ scores. However,

The definition of intelligence differs across cultures.

psychologists studying intelligence in non-Western countries, such as in Africa and Asia, find these cultures have different conceptions and definitions of intelligence.

For example, the Taiwanese conception of intelligence emphasizes how one understands and relates to others, including when and how to show intelligence (R. J. Sternberg & Yang, 2003). In Zambia (Africa), parents describe the intelligence of their children as including cognitive abilities as well as showing social responsibility, which is considered equally important (Serpell, 2003). In Micronesia, people demonstrate remarkable navigational skills as they sail long distances using only information from stars and sea currents (Ceci et al., 1997). These navigational abilities certainly indicate a high degree of intelligence that would not be assessed by traditional Western IQ tests. Thus, the definition of intelligence differs across cultures.

Nonintellectual Factors

What if a person is nervous?

Maria is 11 years old and has been in the United States for two years. She had a hard time learning English, is not doing well in school, and is terrified about taking tests. Maria comes to take an IQ test, and the psychologist tries to put her at ease. However, Maria is so afraid of failing the IQ test that she just sits and stares at the floor. The psychologist says, "I'm going to give you a word and you tell me what it means." When Maria hears the word, she is now so anxious that she can't concentrate or think of what to say. Maria will probably do poorly on this IQ test because of nonintellectual factors.

Nonintellectual factors are noncognitive factors, such as attitude, experience, and emotional functioning, that may help or hinder performance on tests.

For example, nonintellectual factors such as Maria's shyness, fear of strange situations, and anxiety about failing would certainly hinder her test performance (Oostdam & Meijer, 2003). Thus, students who have test anxiety or who come from an environment with poor educational opportunities would be disadvantaged in taking IQ tests. Also, children diagnosed with autism struggle with traditional IQ tests because they have great difficulty interacting with a stranger. One study compared the IQ scores of children with autism who took a test administered by a stranger and a test they could complete on their own. Healthy children without autism scored the same on both tests; however, children with autism scored much higher on the test they completed on their own. Clearly, nonintellectual factors play a role on a child's IQ (Begley, 2007a).

IQ scores are influenced by emotions and experience.

In comparison, a child who is experienced and confident at taking tests has nonintellectual factors that aid performance. It's well established that nonintellectual factors have a great influence on how a person performs on IQ tests (R. M. Kaplan & Saccuzzo, 2009).

Next, we'll discuss an old question about intelligence, the nature-nurture question. ●

© africa924/Shutterstock.com

© PhotoDisc, Inc.

Definitions

What is the nature-nurture question?

One of the greatest child music prodigies of our time is Lang Lang (left photo), who began playing the piano at age 3 and performing in public at age 5. His parents placed great importance and pressure on him to be "Number One." Lang accepted and enjoyed the challenge. Today he is one of the greatest pianists of our time (Lang, 2008).

Lang Lang

Another example of child prodigy is Sufiah Yusof (right photo), who had a remarkable aptitude in mathematics and entered prestigious Oxford University at the age of 13. Her parents also placed tremendous importance on her success and accomplishments. Yusof reported that the pressure to succeed was intolerable and she escaped the life her parents wanted for her. Given her intellectual abilities, she could have chosen to pursue any one of many cognitively challenging and respected careers. Her ultimate decision was to become a prostitute (A. Dolan, 2008).

Because Lang and Yusof displayed impressive talents and aptitude at such an early age, their exceptional skill was likely due to nature or heredity—that is, something they were born with. The parents of Lang and Yusof both pressured them to succeed. Whereas Lang thrived on the pressure, it devastated Yusof.

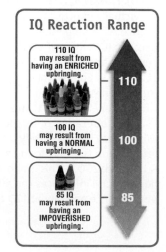

Sufiah Yusof

The different outcomes that resulted from Lang and Yusof having to balance nature or heredity factors (being a child genius) with nurture or environmental factors (facing difficult family pressures) bring us to the nature-nurture question.

The **nature-nurture question** asks how nature—hereditary or genetic factors—interacts with nurture—environmental factors—in the development of a person's intellectual, emotional, personal, and social abilities.

Today, researchers believe that nature and nurture interact and both contribute to the development of intelligence.

Interaction: Nature and Nurture

In exploring how nature and nurture contribute to and interact in the development of intelligence, researchers compared IQ scores in siblings (brothers and sisters) and in fraternal and identical twins.

How do they interact?

Fraternal twins, like siblings (brothers and sisters), develop from separate eggs and have 50% of their genes in common. **Identical twins** develop from a single egg and thus have almost identical genes, which means they have nearly 100% of their genes in common.

The graph on the right shows that the correlation in IQ scores between identical twins (0.85), who share nearly 100% of their genes, was higher than the correlation between fraternal twins (0.60), who share 50% of their genes, or between siblings (0.45), who also share 50% of their genes (Plomin & Petrill, 1997). These findings, which come from over 100 studies, indicate that genetic factors generally contribute about 50% to the development of intelligence (Plomin & Spinath, 2004).

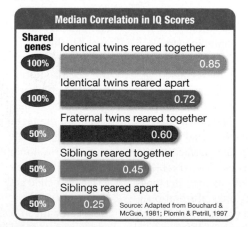

Median Correlation in IQ Scores

Shared genes		
100%	Identical twins reared together	0.85
100%	Identical twins reared apart	0.72
50%	Fraternal twins reared together	0.60
50%	Siblings reared together	0.45
50%	Siblings reared apart	0.25

Source: Adapted from Bouchard & McGue, 1981; Plomin & Petrill, 1997

When researchers report that genetic factors influence intelligence (IQ scores), they mean that genetic factors influence cognitive abilities to varying degrees, depending on the environment (Bishop et al., 2003). In the last 20 years, researchers have made significant progress in understanding the interaction of nature and nurture, and one tool they have used is a number called heritability.

Heritability is a number that indicates the amount or proportion of some ability, characteristic, or trait that can be attributed to genetic factors (nature).

For example, if the heritability (nature) for overall intelligence was about 50%, then about 50% of general cognitive ability would come from genetic factors. Researchers have calculated the heritability scores for specific cognitive abilities, such as spatial ability (32%), verbal ability (55%), and memory (55%) (McClearn et al., 1997). These studies on heritability show that genetic factors (nature) significantly contribute to a variety of cognitive abilities.

Notice that the heritability numbers above are far less than 100%, which means that genes do not determine or fix these abilities, because environmental factors have a significant influence on cognitive abilities as well. You can think of genetic factors as establishing a range of potential abilities or behaviors, which are shaped and molded through interaction with one's environment. This idea of how genetic factors operate is called the reaction range (T. J. Bouchard, 1997).

Reaction range indicates the extent to which traits, abilities, or iq scores may increase or decrease as a result of interaction with environmental factors.

Researchers estimate that the reaction range may vary up or down by as much as 10–15 points in one's IQ score.

Next, we'll take a closer look at how environment can contribute to intelligence by reviewing adoption and foster-care studies.

IQ Reaction Range

110 IQ may result from having an ENRICHED upbringing. — 110

100 IQ may result from having a NORMAL upbringing. — 100

85 IQ may result from having an IMPOVERISHED upbringing. — 85

Unless otherwise noted, all images are © Cengage Learning

Adoption and Foster-Care Studies

How much does environment contribute?

What would happen if children with limited social-educational opportunities and low IQs were adopted by parents who could provide better social-educational opportunities? Researchers reasoned that if environmental factors influence the development of intelligence, then providing more environmental opportunities should increase IQ scores.

To determine whether environment can increase IQ scores, one research study examined the IQs of African American children from impoverished environments who were adopted into middle-class families, some White and some African American; all of the families provided many social-educational opportunities for the adopted children. Researchers found that the IQs of the adopted children were as much as 10 points higher than those of African American children raised in disadvantaged homes (Scarr & Weinberg, 1976). In a follow-up study, researchers reported that the adopted children, now adolescents, had higher IQ scores than African American children raised in their own communities (Weinberg et al., 1992). Other studies also indicate that as experiences for African Americans improve, so do their IQs (W. Williams, 2009).

Children adopted into advantaged homes had higher IQ scores.

A similar study, this time focusing on children living in Romania, examined the intellectual functioning of children abandoned at birth and placed in state-run institutions (well known for not providing children with appropriate cognitive stimulation). Those children who remained in the institutions during the first several years of life demonstrated significantly poorer intellectual functioning when compared with children who soon moved into foster care. Children living in foster care are much more likely to have good educational opportunities than the children remaining in state-run institutions (C. A. Nelson et al., 2007).

These kinds of studies show that children with poor educational opportunities and low IQ scores can show an increase in IQ scores when they are provided better educational opportunities. Researchers conclude that nurture or environmental factors contribute to intellectual development (Begley, 2009a; Nisbett et al., 2012).

We'll wrap up our discussion of the nature-nurture question by taking a look some of the recent research on neuroscience and intelligence.

Neuroscience and Intelligence

How are the brain and intelligence related?

As we learned earlier, children raised in disadvantaged environments, such as poverty, are more likely to develop intellectual deficits. Recent research in the field of *neuroscience* (see p. 6) shows that the brains of children raised in poverty may not be able to process information in the same way as the brains of children raised in higher-income families.

In one study, lower brain activity was found in the *prefrontal cortex* of children from poorer homes than in the brains of children from more well-off families (Kishiyama et al., 2009). This and other research find that although children from poorer homes do not have any brain damage, their prefrontal cortex is not working as well as it should be. For instance, this area of their brains is using more energy than the brains of children from higher-income families to complete the same tasks. The result of the prefrontal cortex needing to work harder can be difficulties in paying attention, self-control, problem solving, and school performance (D'Angiulli et al., 2008; Kishiyama, 2010; Stevens et al., 2009). Researchers find that these same differences in brain activity are evident in adults who were raised in poorer homes. Consequently, the effects of poverty on the brain can be long lasting (Neville, 2011).

Fortunately, just as the brain is vulnerable to the negative effects of a disadvantaged environment, so too it is receptive to the positive effects of intervention, whether it is living in an advantaged environment or receiving special training. One neuroscientist found that training children to improve their self-control

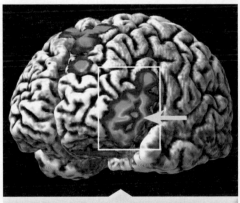
Prefrontal cortex is involved in attention, self-control, and problem solving.

and ability to pay attention through the use of specially designed games, combined with educating parents about the importance of attention and self-control in their children, resulted in significant changes in the functioning of the children's brains. The neuroscientist examined the same children again later and found that improved functioning in the prefrontal cortex continued for at least two years after the end of the intervention (Neville, 2011).

Another group of researchers studied adolescents over a four-year period and focused on the relationship between IQ scores and brain structure. These researchers found that IQ can increase or decrease during adolescence and the changes are associated with changes in brain structure. Results showed that changes in scores on the verbal scale of the IQ test were associated with changes in the brain region activated by naming, reading, and speaking, and changes in scores on the performance scale of the IQ test were associated with changes in the brain region activated by hand and finger movements. These findings support that our brains remain "plastic," meaning they can adapt and change over time depending on environmental influences, such as intense learning (Ramsden et al., 2011).

Conclusion. The studies on heritability, twins, adopted children, and neuroscience provide an answer to the nature-nurture question: Nature or heredity and environment or nurture both significantly contribute to intelligence (IQ scores).

Next, we'll examine the debate over racial differences in IQ scores.

Racial Controversy

What is the heated controversy?

In the early 1900s, psychologists believed intelligence was primarily inherited. This idea reappeared in *The Bell Curve*, by psychologist Richard Herrnstein and political scientist Charles Murray (1994). But what brought these authors the greatest publicity was their statement that racial differences in IQ scores were caused primarily by genetic or inherited factors. This and other statements from Herrnsein and Murray's book set off such a heated and often misguided public debate that the American Psychological Association (APA) formed a special task force of prominent researchers. The goal of the APA task force was to summarize what is known about intelligence (Neisser et al., 1996). We will now focus on the complex question of racial differences in IQ scores.

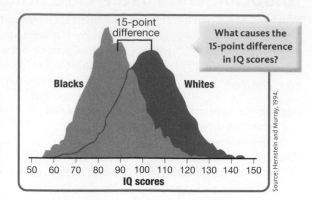

Difference between IQ Scores

Findings. To help you understand the controversy surrounding racial differences in IQ scores, please look at the figure in the upper right. Notice that there are two distributions of IQ scores: The orange bell-shaped curve shows the distribution of IQ scores for African Americans (Blacks), and the blue bell-shaped curve shows the distribution of scores for Caucasians (Whites). Although there is much overlap in IQ scores (indicated by overlapping of orange and blue areas), researchers generally agree that the average or mean IQ score for African Americans is about 15 points lower than the average IQ score for Caucasians (T. J. Bouchard, 1995). This 15-point average difference in IQ scores means that although there are many African Americans with high IQ scores, they are proportionally fewer in number compared to Caucasians.

Two explanations. There are at least two possible explanations for this 15-point difference in average IQ scores. One explanation is that the differences are due to inherited or *genetic factors:* African Americans are genetically inferior to Whites. Another explanation is that the difference is due to a number of *environmental factors:* African Americans have fewer social, economic, and educational opportunities than Whites do.

Although the authors of *The Bell Curve* emphasized the role of genetic factors, you'll see that the APA task force and many other psychologists disagreed.

How is race decided?

Cause of IQ Differences

Group differences. In a review of *The Bell Curve,* one of the leading researchers in the area of intelligence concluded that the book offered no convincing evidence that genetic factors were primarily responsible for the 15-point IQ difference between African Americans and Caucasians (R. J. Sternberg, 1995). This conclusion is based largely on the distinction between whether genetic factors can influence the development of intelligence in an individual and whether they can influence the development of intelligence among races. The APA task force said there is evidence that genetic factors play a significant role in the development of an *individual's intelligence.* However, there is no convincing evidence that genetic factors play a primary role in the differences in intelligence *among races.*

A tremendous amount of research data challenges Herrnstein and Murray's statement that IQ *differences among races* are caused primarily by genetic factors (Neisser et al., 1996; R. J. Sternberg et al., 2005). One study, for instance, examined the IQs of Black and mixed-race (Black and White) children who were adopted by middle-class families who were either Black or White (E. C. J. Moore, 1986). Both groups of children had the same average IQs. Therefore, the White genes in the mixed-race children resulted in no advantage in IQ. Moreover, children adopted by White families had IQs 13 points higher on average than children adopted by Black families, which suggests there are significant environmental differences between White and Black families.

Although the exact causes of the differences in IQ scores in the above study and the above graph are unknown, many psychologists suggest a number of environmental factors, such as differences in social-economic classes, educational opportunities, family structures, and career possibilities (Loehlin, 2000). Recent research shows that the difference in IQs between African Americans and Whites is narrowing, which suggests that environmental factors can significantly influence IQ (Nisbett et al., 2012). Thus, one of *The Bell Curve's* major conclusions—that racial differences in IQ scores are based primarily on genetic factors—is not supported by the evidence (Neisser et al., 1996).

Differences in skin color. Another problem with *The Bell Curve* is its assumption that skin color is a meaningful way to identify races. For example, based on skin color, to which race would you assign the individuals in the four photos on the left? Researchers report that skin color is not reliable in identifying racial makeup because studies on DNA (genetic instructions) indicate that people around the world are much more alike than different (Shriver, 2005). Thus, differences in skin color are not a reliable measure to assign people to different races when comparing IQ scores (Venter, 2000).

After the Concept Review, we'll discuss how early racial discrimination was based on IQ scores. ●

1. One approach to measuring intelligence focuses on quantifying cognitive factors or abilities that are involved in intellectual performance; this is called the **(a)** _____ approach. Charles Spearman used this approach to develop the general intelligence theory, which states that intelligence has a general mental ability factor known as **(b)** _____.

2. In comparison to Spearman's general intelligence theory, Howard Gardner's theory says that there are nine kinds of _____, such as verbal skills, math skills, spatial skills, and movement skills.

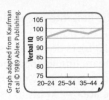

3. Another approach to measuring intelligence is by analyzing the kinds of **(a)** _____ processes that people use to solve problems. An example of this approach is Robert Sternberg's **(b)** _____ theory of intelligence.

4. Alfred Binet developed an intelligence test that estimated intellectual progress by comparing a child's score on an intelligence test to the scores of average children of the same age. Binet called this concept _____.

5. Lewis Terman revised Binet's intelligence test, and the most significant change he made was to develop a formula to compute a single score that represents a person's **(a)** _____. This formula is IQ = **(b)** _____ age divided by **(c)** _____ age, times **(d)** _____.

$$IQ = \frac{?}{?} ?$$

6. The most widely used series of IQ tests are the **(a)** _____ Intelligence Scales. These tests organize items into two subtests, which are called **(b)** _____ and **(c)** _____ scales. In an attempt to measure nonverbal skills and rule out cultural problems, Wechsler added the **(d)** _____ scale.

Block design
Assemble blocks to match this design.

Picture completion
Tell me what is missing.

7. A good psychological test has two characteristics. It should give about the same score over time, which is called **(a)** _____, and it should measure what it is supposed to measure, which is called **(b)** _____.

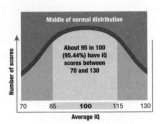

8. If IQ scores can be represented by a bell-shaped curve, the pattern is called a _____. The scores have a symmetrical arrangement, so that the vast majority fall in the middle range and fewer fall near the extreme ends of the range.

Middle of normal distribution
About 95 in 100 (95.44%) have IQ scores between 70 and 130

Left end of normal distribution
Intellectual Disability
About 2 in 100 (2.27%) have IQ scores below 70

9. An individual who has a combination of limited mental ability (usually an IQ below 70) and difficulty functioning in everyday life is said to have some degree of **(a)** _____. Individuals who have above average intelligence (usually IQ scores above 130) as well as some superior talent or skill are said to have **(b)** _____.

Right end of normal distribution
Giftedness
About 2 in 100 (2.27%) have IQ scores above 130; about 1 in a million has an IQ above 180

10. If the wording of test questions and the experiences on which they are based are more familiar to members of some social groups than to others, the test is said to have a **(a)** _____. Depending on the culture, **(b)** _____ can be defined in different ways.

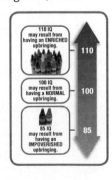

11. When we ask how much genetic factors and how much environmental factors contribute to intelligence, we are asking the **(a)** _____ question. One of the tools researchers use to study the interaction of nature and nurture is **(b)** _____, which is a number that indicates the amount or proportion of some ability, characteristic, or trait that can be attributed to genetic factors. The extent to which traits, abilities, or IQ scores may increase or decrease depending on environmental effects is called the **(c)** _____.

110 IQ may result from having an ENRICHED upbringing. 110
100 IQ may result from having a NORMAL upbringing. 100
85 IQ may result from having an IMPOVERISHED upbringing. 85

Answers: 1. (a) psychometric, (b) g; 2. intelligence; 3. (a) reasoning, (b) triarchic; 4. mental age; 5. (a) intelligence quotient or IQ, (b) mental, (c) chronological, (d) 100. 6. (a) Wechsler, (b) verbal, (c) performance, (d) performance; 7. (a) reliability, (b) validity; 8. normal distribution; 9. (a) intellectual disability, (b) giftedness; 10. (a) cultural bias, (b) intelligence; 11. (a) nature-nurture, (b) heritability, (c) reaction range

Cultural Diversity: Races, IQs, & Immigration

Misuse of IQ Tests

What were Binet's warnings about using IQ tests?

After Alfred Binet developed the first intelligence tests, he gave two warnings about the potential misuse of IQ tests. He warned that IQ tests do not and should not be used to measure innate intelligence and that IQ tests should not be used to label individuals.

However, in the early 1900s the area we know as psychology was just beginning, and American psychologists were very proud of how much they had improved IQ tests. With their improved IQ tests, American psychologists not only used IQ tests to measure what they thought was innate, or inherited, intelligence but also used IQ tests to label people (as morons or imbeciles). As if that weren't bad enough, early psychologists persuaded the U.S. Congress to pass discriminatory immigration laws based on IQ tests. As we look back now, we must conclude that the use and abuse of IQ tests in the early 1900s created one of psychology's sorriest moments. Here's what happened.

In 1924, Congress passed an immigration law to keep out those believed to have low IQs.

Innate Intelligence

One name that we have already mentioned is that of Lewis Terman, who was the guiding force behind revising Binet's intelligence test (which became the Stanford-Binet test) and also developing the formula for computing a single IQ score. Terman, who became head of the Department of Psychology at Stanford University, firmly believed that intelligence was primarily inherited, that intelligence tests measured innate abilities, and that environmental influences were far less important.

One of Terman's goals was to test all children and, on the basis of their IQ scores, to label and sort them into categories of innate abilities. Terman argued that society could use IQ scores (usually of 70 or below) to restrain or eliminate those whose intelligence was too low to lead an effective moral life (Terman, 1916).

Terman hoped to establish minimum intelligence scores necessary for all leading occupations. For example, he believed that people with IQs below 100 should not be given employment that involves prestige or monetary reward. Those with IQs of 75 or below should be unskilled labor, and those with 75–85 IQs should be semiskilled labor. In Terman's world, class boundaries were to be set by innate intelligence, as measured by his Stanford-Binet IQ test (S. J. Gould, 1996; Hunt, 1993).

Terman's belief that IQ tests measured innate intelligence was adopted by another well-known American psychologist, Robert Yerkes.

Classifying Races

Robert Yerkes was a Harvard professor who was asked to develop a test that could be used to classify applicants for the army. Under Yerkes's direction, over 1.75 million World War I army recruits were given IQ tests. From this enormous amount of data, Yerkes (1921) and his colleagues reached three conclusions:

1. They concluded that the average mental age of White American adults was a meager 13 years, slightly above the classification of a moron (a term psychologists used in the early 1900s). The reasons they gave for this low mental age were (using the terminology then current) the unconstrained breeding of the poor and feebleminded and the spread of Negro blood through interracial breeding.

2. They concluded that European immigrants could be ranked on intelligence by their country of origin. The fair peoples of western and northern Europe (Nordics) were most intelligent, while the darker peoples of southern Europe (Mediterraneans) and the Slavs of eastern Europe were less intelligent.

3. They concluded that Negroes were at the bottom of the racial scale in intelligence.

Many of Yerkes's outrageous and discriminatory views resurfaced in the book *The Bell Curve* (Herrnstein & Murray, 1994), which we discussed earlier. Following Yerkes's lead, IQ scores were next used for racial discrimination.

Immigration Laws

The fact that Yerkes ranked European races by intelligence eventually reached members of the U.S. Congress. Outraged by the "fact" that Europeans of "low intelligence" were being allowed into America, members of Congress sought a way to severely limit the immigration of people from southern and eastern Europe. In writing the Immigration Law of 1924, Congress relied, in part, on Yerkes's racial rankings and imposed harsh quotas on those nations they believed to have inferior stock (people from southern and eastern Europe, Alpine and Mediterranean nations).

Stephen Jay Gould (1996), a well-known evolutionary biologist, reviewed Yerkes's data and pointed out a number of problems: poorly administered tests, terrible testing conditions, inconsistent standards for retaking tests, written tests given to illiterate recruits (guaranteeing a low score), and no control for educational level or familiarity with the English language. As a result of these problems, Gould concluded that Yerkes's data were so riddled with errors as to render useless any conclusions about racial differences in intelligence.

Looking back, we see clearly that early psychologists badly misused IQ tests. They forgot that IQ tests are merely one of many tools to assess cognitive abilities, which many consider to be one of many kinds of intelligence (H. Gardner, 1995).

We've discussed how past IQ tests have been misused and how current IQ tests may be biased. Is there a new generation of intelligence tests on the horizon? ●

Can Genius Be Found in the Brain?

There is one question about intelligence that has especially interested researchers: How is the brain of a genius different? For example, how was Albert Einstein able to think of riding through space on a beam of light or create his famous formula ($E = mc^2$), which led to building the atomic bomb?

When Einstein died of heart failure in 1955 at age 76, Dr. Thomas Harvey, who performed the autopsy, removed Einstein's brain and kept it at Princeton University. In 1996, Harvey contacted Dr. Sandra Witelson, a neuroscientist at McMaster University, and asked if she wished to examine Einstein's brain. McMaster University in Ontario, Canada, has a bank of over 100 brains that people have donated for research. Witelson was able to compare Einstein's 76-year-old brain with brains of similar ages from 35 men and 56 women who were known to have normal intelligence when they died. The results of Witelson's examination of Einstein's brain are discussed in the figure at the right.

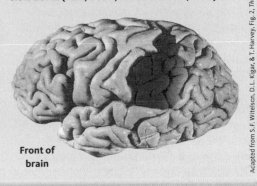

Normal brain weighs about 1,350 grams. This side view shows the wrinkled cortex, which contains separate areas for different functions (feeling, moving, reading, writing, seeing). Notice the yellow and red areas, which are part of the parietal lobe. **The red area, the inferior parietal lobe,** is especially used for thinking in visual-spatial terms, for mathematical thought, and for imaging how things move in space.

Front of brain

Einstein's brain weighed 1,230 grams, slightly less than normal. Einstein's brain was different in that it lacked the yellow area, which allowed his **red area, the inferior parietal lobe,** to be 15% wider than in normal brains. Also, his parietal lobe had rare grooves and ridges. Researchers believe that Einstein's unique parietal lobe increased his ability to think and imagine such things as space being curved and that time could slow down (Falk, 2009; Witelson et al., 1999).

Front of brain

Adapted from S.F. Witelson, D.L. Kigar, & T. Harvey, Fig. 2, *The Lancet, 353*, 1999, with permission of the authors.

Although the physical differences in Einstein's brain are obvious in the figure, Witelson cautions that they don't know if every brilliant mathematician has a larger inferior parietal lobe, which is something only further research can answer. Other researchers wonder if genius can ever be measured or located in the brain, since genius involves a mixture of creative insights, culture, and life experiences that may be unique to that person (S. C. Wang, 2000).

How Does a Prodigy's Brain Develop?

What do brain scans show?

With the recent advances in brain scans, researchers are now able to explore brain development like never before. Phillip Shaw and his colleagues (2006) at the National Institute of Mental Health and McGill University in Montreal completed a long-term study examining intelligence and brain development in children.

Method. The team of researchers followed a group of more than 300 children as they aged from 6 to 19. Each child was administered intelligence tests at the start of the study, and MRI brain scans (see p. 70) were taken about every two years to measure the size of brain structures.

Results. The thickness of the cortex (see p. 74), which is the outer layer of the brain that controls higher cognitive functioning, began thinner in highly intelligent children, but became thicker than the cortexes in children with average intelligence by adolescence. As shown in the brain above, the areas that changed the most were in the front of the brain and in a strip over the top of the brain, which are areas responsible for higher cognitive functioning, such as planning and reasoning. By the age of 19,

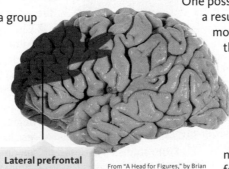

Lateral prefrontal cortex

From "A Head for Figures," by Brian Butterworth, *Science, 284*, p. 928. By permission of B. Butterworth.

the cortexes of highly intelligent children thinned such that they were equal in thickness to the cortexes of children with average intelligence.

Conclusions. This is the first study to show that the brain develops differently in highly intelligent children. However, it is uncertain what might be causing the changes in cortex thickness. One possible explanation is the thickening may be a result of highly intelligent children developing more neural connections during school years, and the later thinning of the cortex may be due to unused neural connections withering away to make cognitive functioning more efficient.

The role of genes and environment in the changes in the cortex is also unknown. Genes may play an important role as smarter children had different cortex thickness even at a young age. But environmental factors (social activities, schooling, diet) may also have an important role in the thickening of the cortex over the years (Grigorenko, 2006).

Last, this study examined only group differences, and making any predictions based on an individual child is not possible (Giles, 2006). ●

Definition of Intervention Programs

For a moment, imagine what will happen to Nancy's child. Nancy, who is in her mid-twenties, is a single mother with a 3-year-old child. Nancy lives in a lower-class neighborhood

Why might a child need a Head Start?

and earns less than $5,000 a year doing part-time work. She has completed only two years of high school and has no family and few friends. What effects do you think Nancy's background, educational level, and impoverished environment will have on her child? Psychologists would predict that Nancy's 3-year-old child will not likely acquire the social, emotional, and cognitive skills and abilities needed to do well in school or society. Her child may need outside help, which may come from an intervention program (Arnold & Doctoroff, 2003).

Intervention programs create a stimulating environment.

An **intervention program** helps disadvantaged children from low socioeconomic classes to achieve better intellectual, social, and personal-emotional development, as well as physical health. Intervention programs can give Nancy training in how to be a good parent and provide her child with educational and social opportunities. Perhaps the best-known intervention program in the United States is Head Start, which began in 1965 as a six-to-eight-week program. Researchers later discovered that was too brief to be effective. As a result, Head Start was lengthened to two years, and in 2009, the program enrolled over 900,000 3- to 5-year-olds across the United States (ACF, 2010).

We'll focus on successful intervention programs for disadvantaged children.

Parent Training

Parents can improve their children's mental abilities by better relating to them at home as learned through parent training programs.

Parent training is an intervention program in which parents are taught how to increase desirable child behavior, reduce children's misbehavior, improve parent-child interactions, and create a positive family atmosphere.

In one study, researchers tested the mental abilities of children in two different groups. The parents of one group of children participated in

Parent training benefits parents and children.

parenting skills classes to learn how to provide consistent routines at home, discipline their children in constructive ways, and better communicate with their children overall. The parents of the second group of children did not receive training in parenting skills. Results showed that for those children whose parents received parent training, the scores on tests of memory, attention, language ability, and IQ increased. Additionally, the parents of these children reported less stress at home and an improvement in their children's behavior (Downs, 2008; Stevens & Neville, 2008).

This and other research suggest that children living in disadvantaged environments can benefit from intervention programs in many ways, including an increase in IQ scores (Nisbett et al., 2012).

Next, we take a close look at Head Start.

Head Start

As mentioned above, a well-known intervention program for disadvantaged children is Head Start.

Head Start is a national child development program for children from birth to age 5 that provides services to promote academic, social, and emotional development, as well as providing social, health, and nutrition services for families whose incomes make them eligible for the program.

Since 1965, more than 27 million children have participated in Head Start (ACF, 2010). Initially, Head Start was viewed as something of a failure because two to three years after children left Head Start, few if any differences in IQ or other academic scores were found between those children and control groups (Clarke & Clarke, 1989). Although not all research finds advantages or benefits resulting from participating in Head Start, there is support for some important long-term beneficial effects (Barnett, 2004; Kirp, 2004; Zigler & Styfco, 1994):

Head Start results in long-term personal and social gains.

■ Adolescents who had been in the Head Start program were more likely to be in classes appropriate for their ages rather than to have had to repeat a class, were less likely to show antisocial or delinquent behavior, and were more likely to hold jobs.

■ Mothers whose children had been in the Head Start program reported fewer negative psychological symptoms, greater feelings of mastery, and greater current life satisfaction.

■ Children who had two years of Head Start and an additional two to seven years of educational help were much more successful in graduating from high school (69%) than a control group (49%).

■ At the age of 40, adults who had been in Head Start were more likely to have earned college degrees and to have owned a home and a car, and less likely to have criminal records and be drug users.

From studies like these we can draw two conclusions. First, often early and rather large increases (up to 10 points) in IQ scores do not last after the child leaves the intervention program. Second, programs like Head Start result in a number of long-term benefits, such as better educational achievement, employment, and social behavior (Barnett & Hustedt, 2005, Nisbett et al., 2012). These long-term effects indicate that programs like Head Start should not be evaluated solely on IQ scores but also on other personality, motivational, and psychological benefits.

Raising IQ Scores

In the early days of Head Start, psychologists were very encouraged to find that the program initially increased disadvantaged children's IQ scores by about 10 points, a significant amount. One reason IQ scores can be raised in young children from disadvantaged homes is that these children have not been exposed to and have not acquired the kinds of skills and cultural experiences assessed by IQ tests. However, when disadvantaged children are exposed to the enriched environment of Head Start, these children quickly acquire all kinds of new skills and abilities that help them score higher on IQ tests (Spitz, 1997).

For example, researchers compared two groups of disadvantaged children, all of whom had IQ scores below 80 (100 is considered the average IQ). Some of these children, called the experimental group, were placed in a special educational intervention program from ages 3 to 5. Other children, called the control group, were given no additional training and remained in their home environments.

The figure below shows that, after only one year, the children in the experimental group (intervention program) showed a significant increase in IQ scores (about 10 points) compared to the children in the control group who remained in disadvantaged home environments (Schweinhart & Weikart, 1980). However, after the children left the intervention program at the age of 5 and entered public school, their IQ scores began a slow but consistent decline. At the same time, the IQ scores of control children began a gradual increase as they benefited from attending public school. By the age of 11, there was no longer any difference in IQ scores.

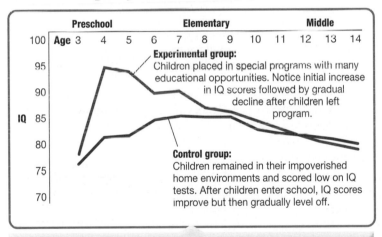

Preschool		Elementary						Middle		

Age 3 4 5 6 7 8 9 10 11 12 13 14

Experimental group: Children placed in special programs with many educational opportunities. Notice initial increase in IQ scores followed by gradual decline after children left program.

Control group: Children remained in their impoverished home environments and scored low on IQ tests. After children enter school, IQ scores improve but then gradually level off.

Initial increase in IQ scores (age 4) gradually disappears after children leave Head Start program and return to less stimulating environments.

One reason for this decline in IQ scores is that after children leave an intervention program, they usually return to less stimulating environments, which offer less educational, social, and motivational support. For this reason, researchers make two strong recommendations: First, programs like Head Start should be lengthened from three to at least five or more years so children have more time to learn and practice their newly acquired social, emotional, and academic skills; second, parents must become involved in helping their children develop cognitive skills, such as reading to their children (G. Nelson et al., 2003; Zigler & Styfco, 2001).

Finally, as we discussed earlier, intervention programs should not be evaluated solely on IQ scores but rather on other social, emotional, and psychological gains that are found to be long-lasting.

Need for Intervention Programs

The most successful intervention programs have a strong educational emphasis, well-trained teachers, and a low ratio of children to trained teachers.

Researchers make three important points about the usefulness of childhood intervention programs:

1 Currently, millions of children in the United States are living in poverty, which is known to have a devastating negative influence on a young child developing important social-emotional skills and cognitive abilities. In addition, living in poverty is known to lower academic achievement and goals, decrease motivation, and contribute to school failure and dropouts (Arnold & Doctoroff, 2003). Intervention programs help reduce the devastating effects that continuing poverty can have on families and give children a much needed head start (Zigler & Styfco, 2001).

2 In some cases, impoverished family environments lead to neglect or abuse, which has very negative effects on a child's social, emotional, and intellectual development. Intensive intervention programs during the first years of life are effective in reducing and preventing the significant intellectual dysfunction that may result from continuing poverty and lack of environmental support (Zigler & Styfco, 2001).

3 Results from the most extensive and longest-term research study of intelligence show that childhood intelligence affects physical and mental illness later in life, overall quality of life, and even an individual's life span. We have known that childhood intervention programs improve children's mental abilities, but only recently have we learned that children's mental abilities affect their lives in significant ways for years to come (Deary et al., 2009).

It is for all the reasons stated above that researchers strongly advocate for the development of well-designed childhood intervention programs. ●

Smartest or Strongest Man in America?

Smartest, definitely. Though Chris Langan can bench press a whopping 500 pounds, his intellect is far more impressive.

1 Based on Chris's IQ score, what type(s) of intelligence does he excel at?

Chris's IQ score is off the charts at an estimated 195 (average IQ score is 100). Only one in several billion people has an IQ of 195 or above. Even Einstein didn't compare, as his IQ is estimated to have been 150. Chris is surely a rocket scientist, brain surgeon, or Nobel Prize winner, right? Wrong! Let's take a look at Chris's life to understand why he hasn't achieved the extraordinary career success we expect from him.

2 Based on the normal distribution, where does Chris rank in intelligence?

Chris's childhood left much to be desired. His family was so poor he had only one outfit, which consisted of unmatched socks and a shirt, pants, and shoes, all with holes in them. His father left before his birth and his mother had four husbands, three of whom died. Chris's fourth stepfather was physically abusive toward him. For instance, he asked Chris questions and when Chris answered them correctly, he punched Chris in the mouth. Chris took up

3 Which intelligence theory takes his weight-lifting and physical strength into consideration?

weight-lifting in his early teens, and one day when his stepfather began beating him, he struck back so hard, his stepfather left and never returned.

Despite harsh living circumstances, Chris's intellect persevered. He began speaking at 6 months of age, and by age 3 he was reading. He skipped ahead in school and even then, he felt he knew more than his teachers. All he had to do to ace exams was to quickly skim his textbooks. Chris is one of the few to obtain a perfect score on the SAT, and he even squeezed in a nap during this challenging timed test.

4 Is Chris's ability to speak and read at an early age mostly attributable to nature or nurture?

Because of life circumstances, Chris never finished college. Instead, he has worked labor jobs throughout his life. Some of the jobs he's had include construction worker, lifeguard, farmhand, cowboy, factory worker, firefighter, and, for the past 20 years, a bouncer at a bar. Isn't working as a bouncer one of the last jobs you expect the smartest man in America, and quite possibly in the world, to have? So, you have to ask yourself, why did Chris end up like this? The answer is because of his disadvantaged environment. There was no one to help him. No one ever encouraged him to pursue greatness. Absolutely nothing in his background helped him take advantage of his remarkable talents.

© Mark Peterson/Corbis

Chris is now in his fifties, still lifting weights and working as a bouncer. He's also working on a theory that explains problems scientists and philosophers have been thinking about for thousands of years. He calls his theory Cognitive–Theoretic Model of the Universe (CTMU). He believes CTMU can answer all questions about reality and prove the existence of God. If anyone can answer such questions, surely Chris, with an IQ of 195, is a top contender.

5 According to Sternberg's triarchic theory, which type of intelligence stands out most for Chris?

6 Given Chris's high IQ of 195, what size brain must he have?

We have to wonder what would have happened to Chris had he been born into a wealthy, well-respected, and well-connected family. Only if he were raised in such an environment could he have become the brain surgeon or Nobel Prize winner we expect from a man with an unmatched IQ.

Adapted from Brabham, 2001; Gladwell, 2008; L. Grossman, 2008; Preston, 2008

Summary Test

A Defining Intelligence

1. A subarea of psychology that is concerned with developing psychological tests to assess an individual's abilities, skills, beliefs, and personality traits in a wide range of settings—school, industry, or clinic—is called _____.

2. Spearman's general intelligence theory says there is a general factor, called _____, that represents a person's ability to perform complex mental work, such as abstract reasoning and problem solving. The general factor underlies a person's performance across tests.

3. Gardner says that there are at least nine kinds of intelligence: verbal intelligence, musical intelligence, logical-mathematical intelligence, spatial intelligence, body movement intelligence, intelligence to understand oneself, intelligence to understand others, naturalistic intelligence, and existential intelligence. This is called the _____ theory.

4. Sternberg's triarchic theory says that intelligence can be divided into three ways of gathering and processing information (triarchic means "three"). The first is using **(a)** _____ skills, which are measured by traditional intelligence tests. The second is using **(b)** _____ skills that require creative thinking, the ability to deal with novel situations, and the ability to learn from experience. The third is using **(c)** _____ skills that help a person adjust to, and cope with, his or her sociocultural environment.

B Measuring Intelligence

5. In trying to measure intelligence, researchers through the years have learned that neither skull size nor brain weight is an accurate predictor of _____.

Block design
Assemble blocks to match this design.

Picture completion
Tell me what is missing.

6. The first intelligence test, which was developed by **(a)** _____, measured vocabulary, memory, common knowledge, and other cognitive abilities. By comparing a child's score with the scores of average children at the same age, Binet was able to estimate a child's **(b)** _____. Thus, the Binet-Simon Intelligence Scale gave its results in terms of mental age, while the IQ score was later developed by **(c)** _____, who devised a formula to calculate an individual's intelligence quotient. The formula can be written as IQ = **(d)** _____.

7. The Wechsler Adult Intelligence Scale (WAIS) and Wechsler Intelligence Scale for Children (WISC) have items that are organized into various subtests. Subtests for general information, vocabulary, and verbal comprehension are some of those in the **(a)** _____ section. Subtests that involve arranging pictures in a meaningful order, assembling objects, and using codes are examples of subtests in the **(b)** _____ section. An individual receives a separate score for each of the subtests; these scores are then combined to yield overall scores for verbal and performance abilities, which, in turn, are combined into a single score, called an **(c)** _____ score.

8. A good psychological test must have two qualities. One quality ensures that a person's score on a test at one point in time is similar to a score by the same person on a similar test at a later date; this is called **(a)** _____. The other quality ensures that a test measures what it is supposed to measure; this is called **(b)** _____. Although the results from analyzing handwriting may be consistent from time to time, this is a poor test of personality or intelligence because handwriting analysis lacks the quality of **(c)** _____.

C Distribution & Use of IQ Scores

9. Suppose IQ scores are in a statistical arrangement that resembles the shape of a bell, with the vast majority of scores falling in the middle range and fewer scores falling near the two extreme ends of the curve. This arrangement is called a _____.

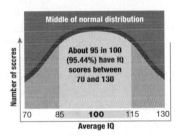

Middle of normal distribution

About 95 in 100 (95.44%) have IQ scores between 70 and 130

Average IQ

10. Substantial limitation in present functioning that is characterized by significantly below average intellectual functioning, along with related limitations in two of eleven areas, including communication, self-care, home living, social skills, and safety, is called _____.

11. Intellectual disability is reflected in IQ scores at one end of the normal distribution. The other end of the normal distribution of IQ scores represents _____. These individuals have above average intelligence (usually IQs above 130) as well as some superior talent or skill.

D Potential Problems of IQ Testing

12. Binet warned that intelligence tests should not be used to measure **(a)** _____ mental abilities because intelligence tests measure cognitive abilities, which are influenced by both heredity and environment. Binet also warned that intelligence tests, by themselves, should not be used to **(b)** _____ people—for example, a moron or a genius. Current IQ tests have been criticized for including wording or experiences that are more familiar to a particular culture, which is called **(c)** _____. The definition of intelligence differs across **(d)** _____ and may differ from the Western idea of *g.* One reason individuals may do poorly on IQ tests is noncognitive factors, such as attitude, experience, and emotional functioning, which are called **(e)** _____.

E Nature-Nurture Question

13. The **(a)** _____ question refers to the relative contributions that genetic and environmental factors make to the development of intelligence. On the basis of twin studies, researchers generally conclude that about **(b)** _____

of the contribution to intelligence (IQ scores) comes from genetic factors. Adoption and foster-care studies demonstrate that **(c)** _____ factors significantly contribute to children's intellectual development. Neuroscience research found that the **(d)** _____, which is involved in attention, self-control, and problem solving, works harder in children from poorer families than in those from higher-income families while completing the same tasks.

F Cultural Diversity: Races, IQs & Immigration

14. Early psychologists ignored Binet's warning about misusing IQ tests. For example, in the early 1900s, Terman believed that IQ tests did measure **(a)** _____ intelligence, and he wanted to use IQ tests to sort people into categories. Terman's view was adopted by Robert Yerkes, who wanted to use IQ tests to rank the intelligence of **(b)** _____ entering the United States. In the 1920s, **(c)** _____ were written to exclude citizens from certain countries because Yerkes had ranked these individuals low in intelligence.

G Research Focus: Genius & Prodigy Brains

15. In looking for physical differences in Einstein's brain, researchers found that he had a 15% wider **(a)** _____, which is involved in visual–spatial and mathematical thinking. By using MRI brain scans and intelligence tests, researchers found that the thickness of the brain's cortex began **(b)** _____ in highly intelligent children, but became **(c)** _____ than the cortexes in children with average intelligence by adolescence. By the age of 19, the cortex of highly intelligent children was **(d)** _____ in thickness to that of children with average intelligence.

Adapted from S.F. Witelson, D. L. Kigar, & T. Harvey, Fig 2, *The Lancet, 353,* 1999, with permission of the authors.

H Application: Intervention Programs

16. A program that creates an environment with increased opportunities for intellectual, social, and personality-emotional development is called an **(a)** _____ program. New research finds that parents can improve their children's **(b)** _____ by better relating to them at home. Although data indicate that IQ increases resulting from intervention programs may be short-lived, there are other long-term positive benefits, such as being more likely to graduate from high school and less likely to be involved in **(c)** _____ activities. Results from the most extensive and longest-term research study of intelligence show that childhood **(d)** _____ affects physical and mental illness later in life, overall quality of life, and even an individual's life span.

© HG Photography/Shutterstock.com

Unless otherwise noted, all images are © Cengage Learning

Answers: *1. psychometrics; 2. g; 3. multiple-intelligence; 4. (a) analytical, cognitive, or logical, (b) creative, (c) practical; 5. intelligence; 6. (a) Binet and Simon, (b) mental age, (c) Terman, (d) MA/CA × 100; 7. (a) verbal, (b) performance, (c) IQ; 8. (a) reliability, (b) validity, (c) validity; 9. normal distribution; 10. intellectual disability; 11. giftedness; 12. (a) innate, (b) label or classify, (c) cultural bias, (d) cultures, (e) nonintellectual factors; 13. (a) nature-nurture, (b) 50%, (c) environmental or nurture (d) prefrontal cortex; 14. (a) innate, (b) immigrants, (c) immigration laws, or quotas; 15. (a) inferior parietal lobe, (b) thinner, (c) thicker, (d) equal; 16. (a) intervention, (b) mental abilities, (c) antisocial, delinquent, or criminal, (d) intelligence*

Key Terms/Key People

Binet-Simon Intelligence Scale, 285

cultural bias, 291

Down syndrome, 288

fraternal twins, 292

g factor, 282

Gardner's multiple-intelligence theory, 283

giftedness, 289

Head Start, 298

heritability, 292

identical twins, 292

intellectual disability, 288

intelligence, 281

intelligence quotient (IQ), 285

intervention program, 298

mental age, 285

nature-nurture question, 292

neuroscience, 294

nonintellectual factors, 291

normal distribution, 288

parent training, 298

prefrontal cortex, 293

psychometric approach, 282

psychometrics, 281

reaction range, 292

reliability, 287

Spearman's general intelligence theory, 282

Stanford-Binet Intelligence Scale, 285

Sternberg's triarchic theory, 283

validity, 287

Wechsler Adult Intelligence Scale (WAIS), 286

Wechsler Intelligence Scale for Children (WISC), 286

Media Resources

Go to **CengageBrain.com** to access Psychology CourseMate, where you will find an interactive eBook, glossaries, flashcards, quizzes, videos, answers to Critical Thinking questions, and more. You can also access Virtual Psychology Labs, an interactive laboratory experience designed to illustrate key experiments first-hand.

Concepts

Jeff, who is only 14 months old, walks up to his mother and says, in a somewhat demanding voice, "Juice." Jeff's one-word sentence, "Juice," is shorthand for "Can I please have a glass of orange juice?" Even as a toddler, Jeff already knows a considerable number of words that represent a whole range of objects, such as cookie, car, bottle, bunny, baby, juice, ball, apple, and the most hated words of all for a young child, "wash up." So when Jeff points at an object and says, "Ball," his one-word sentence is short for "That is my ball." Jeff's use of these single-word "sentences" indicates that he is on his way to learning a very complex system of communicating by using language.

What is that four-legged thing?

Jeff also uses one-word "sentences" to ask questions. For instance, he'll point to a picture in his animal book and ask, "Name?" This means "What is the name of that animal?" Jeff has already learned that a four-legged, fuzzy-tailed, large-eared animal is a bunny; a four-legged, long-nosed animal that barks is a dog; and a four-legged, short-eared animal with a long tail that says "meow" is a cat. Perhaps when Jeff sees an animal, such as a dog, cat, or rabbit, he takes a "mental photo" that he uses for future identifications. But that would mean storing an overwhelming number of "mental photos" of all the animals, objects, and people in his environment. We'll explain a more efficient system that Jeff probably uses to identify animals, objects, and people.

Jeff learned that the object in his hands is a ball and the animal next to him is a dog.

Creativity

How does one become creative?

One of Jeff's favorite things to do is paint the animals in his picture books. Although Jeff makes a terribly wonderful mess, his parents encourage him because they hope that Jeff's early interest in painting may indicate that he has a creative talent for painting or art. How one becomes a creative person is quite a mystery. Take the case of Shawn Carter, better known as Jay-Z, for example.

Shawn Carter's early years showed no signs of his creativity. No one thought Carter would amount to much. He grew up in Brooklyn's Marcy projects, which were overrun with drugs and violence. When Carter was 11, his father left, and his mother had to raise him as well as his three older siblings. Only a year later, at the age of 12, Carter shot his brother for stealing his jewelry. He dropped out of high school to deal drugs, where he often faced dangerously close bullets. While dealing drugs, he began exploring the hip-hop scene. Even as he achieved some recognition for his music work and opportunities to pursue it became available, he was reluctant to give up the life of dealing drugs.

In his late thirties, Carter has become one of the most successful hip-hop artists and entrepreneurs in the country. He has sold nearly 50 million albums and received numerous awards for his musical accomplishments. His creativity extends beyond his musical work and includes his own line of clothing, fragrances, restaurants, and hotels. Carter passionately describes these creative accomplishments as an "extension" of him (Ali, 2006; DeCurtis, 2009).

With little formal schooling, Shawn Carter became a very creative person.

We'll discuss what creativity is and how it is measured.

Cognitive Approach

How does your mind work?

How do toddlers like Jeff learn to speak a complex language and to recognize hundreds of objects? How did Shawn Carter, with little formal schooling, develop his musical ability and express his creativity in so many ways? The answers to these kinds of questions involve figuring out how our minds work. One way to study mental processes is to use the cognitive approach.

The **cognitive approach** is one method of studying how we process, store, and use information and how this information, in turn, influences what we notice, perceive, learn, remember, believe, and feel.

Of all animals, humans have the greatest language ability.

We have already discussed several aspects of the cognitive approach: learning in Modules 9 and 10, and memory and forgetting in Modules 11 and 12. Here we'll explore two other cognitive processes: thinking and language.

Thinking or cognition involves mental processes that are used to form concepts, solve problems, and engage in creative activities.

Language is a special form of communication in which we learn and use complex rules to form and manipulate symbols (words or gestures) that are used to generate an endless number of meaningful sentences.

In fact, thinking (or cognition) and using language are two things we do much better than animals (Hoff, 2009; Woodard, 2005).

What's Coming

We'll discuss how we form concepts, solve problems, think creatively, acquire language, and make decisions. We'll examine why people have difficulty recognizing words (dyslexia) and how language used by animals is different from the language of humans.

We'll begin with the interesting question of how Jeff learned to distinguish a dog from a rabbit, and a rabbit from a cat. ●

A Forming Concepts

Is it a dog, cat, or rabbit?

During your childhood, there was a time when every animal you saw was called a "dog." As a child, you gradually learned to tell the difference between a dog, a cat, and a rabbit by forming a different concept for each animal.

A **concept** is a way to group or classify objects, events, animals, or people based on some features, traits, or characteristics that they all share in common.

How you formed the concept of a dog or cat or rabbit has two different explanations: the exemplar model and the prototype theory (Minda & Smith, 2011; Nosofsky, 2011).

Exemplar Model

You easily recognize the animals on the left, but the question is: How did you know which animal was which? Is it because your mind contains definitions of hundreds of animals?

The **exemplar model** says that you form a concept of an object, event, animal, or person by defining or making a mental list of the essential characteristics of a particular thing.

According to the exemplar model, you formed a concept of a dog, cat, or rabbit by learning its essential characteristics. The essential characteristics of a dog might include that it barks and has a long nose, two ears, two eyes, four legs, some hair, and usually a tail. Similarly, you made mental definitions for all animals. Then, when you looked at the three animals on the left, you automatically sorted through hundreds of animal definitions until you found one that included the essential properties of a dog, cat, or rabbit. Once you found the definition, you knew what the animal was.

Although the exemplar model seems like a reasonable method of forming concepts, it has two serious problems.

One way to form concepts is to make definitions.

Problems with the Exemplar Model

Too many features. In real life, it is very difficult to list all the features that define any object (Rey, 1983). For example, if your list of features to define a dog wasn't complete, the list might also apply to wolves, jackals, coyotes, and skunks. If your list of features to define a dog included every possible feature, such a mental list would be complete but take so long to go through that it would be very slow to use. And worse, you would need a long list of defining features for each and every animal, person, and object. Such a great number of mental lists would tax the best of memories.

Too many exceptions. After making a list of defining features, you would also need to list all the exceptions that do not fit into the dictionary definition of dog. For example, some dogs rarely bark, some are very tiny, some are very large, some are hairless, and some are fuzzy.

dog (dog, dag) *n.; pl.* **dogs, dog.** 1. any of a large and varied group of domesticated animals (*Canis familiaris*) that have four legs, a tail, two ears, prominent nose, a hairy coat, and a bark.

Because of these two problems, you would need to check two mental lists—a long list that contained all the defining features and another that contained all the exceptions—before finding the concept that correctly identified the animal, person, or object.

For these reasons, the exemplar model has generally been replaced by a different theory of how we form concepts: the prototype theory.

Prototype Theory

Please look at the three animals on the right, #1, #2, and #3. Despite the great differences in size, color, and facial features of these animals, prototype theory explains why you can easily and quickly recognize each one as a dog.

Prototype theory says that you form a concept by creating a mental image that is based on the average characteristics of an object. This "average" looking object is called a **prototype.**

To identify a new object, you match it to one of your already formed prototypes of objects, people, or animals.

Based on many experiences, you develop prototypes of many different objects, persons, and animals (Rosch, 1978). For example, your prototype of a dog would be a mental image of any particular animal that has *average features* (nose, tail, ears, height, weight). By using your prototype of a dog, you can easily and quickly identify all three animals on the right—the large brown mutt (#1), the tiny Chihuahua (#2), and the colorful Dalmatian (#3)—as being dogs.

Another way to form concepts is to form prototypes.

Advantages of the Prototype Theory

Average features. One advantage of the prototype theory over the exemplar model is that you do not have to make a mental list of all the defining features of an object, which is often impossible. Instead, you form a prototype by creating a mental picture or image of the object, animal, or person that has only average features.

Quick recognition. Another advantage of the prototype theory is that it can result in quick recognition, as happened when you identified these different-looking animals (#1, #2, and #3) as dogs. The more a new object resembles a prototype, the more quickly you can identify it; the less it matches your prototype, the longer it takes.

For example, what is the strange animal on the right (#4) and where is its head? Because this animal's features are not close to your dog prototype, it will take you some time to figure out that it has hair like "dreadlocks," its head is on the right, and it's an unusual dog (called a Puli).

Prototype theory, which explains that you form concepts by creating and using prototypes, is widely accepted and has generally replaced the exemplar model (Geeraerts, 2006).

Next, we'll discuss when children begin forming concepts.

Early Formation

At the beginning of this module, we described how 14-month-old Jeff had already learned a number of concepts, such as juice, cookie, car, ball, apple, cat, dog, and bunny. Many children 10 to 16 months old can form concepts; that is, they can correctly identify different living things (cat, dog, rabbit) as animals and then place each living thing in the correct category (Quinn, 2002; Quinn & Oates, 2004).

> BLOCKS

By 10 to 16 months, infants learn a number of concepts.

Children develop many concepts or categories (animal, vegetable, face) by experiencing or interacting with objects and things in their environments, and children show their grasp of concepts even before they have developed much language ability (Mareschal & Quinn, 2001). For example, as 14-month-old Jeff (above photo) plays with different objects in his environment, he will learn that one kind of object is a nonliving thing called a block. Initially, a child's categories may be very broad, such as objects, people, animals, and events.

However, as children gain more experience with objects, animals, people, and things in their environments as well as develop increased language skills, which happens around age 5 (see p. 315), they learn to form more complex concepts, such as the qualities of objects—*heavy, shiny, colorful, sweet, bitter*—and the position and placement of objects—*up, down, high, low*. The chances of a child interacting with a wide variety of objects and thus developing many concepts and categories are greatly increased by being raised in a stimulating environment, but the chances are hindered in an impoverished one (Quinn, 2002).

Thus, the development and formation of concepts depend, in large part, on the child's opportunity to interact with the environment and, as you'll see next, in part on how the brain is neatly organized to process information into categories.

Categories in the Brain

A child's ability to form and develop concepts is helped not only by having a stimulating environment but also by how the brain is organized. Brain scans and brain stimulation of normal people and tests on brain-damaged individuals showed that different visual concepts, such as animals, faces, vegetables/fruits, and nonliving things, as well as auditory concepts, such as animal, human, and tool sounds, are processed and stored in different parts of the brain (Ilmberger et al., 2002; J. W. Lewis et al., 2005). Thus, as children interact with and learn to identify different objects, they can easily place different objects into different categories because the brain is already set up to store different categories in different areas (Ilmberger et al., 2002).

This process of placing things into categories occurs very quickly. For example, you quickly and easily recognize the three objects on the right as turtle, apple, and clown, and you easily place them into three different categories: animal, fruit, and person. Researchers explain that you were able to recognize these three things by matching each to your already formed prototypes of a turtle, apple, and clown (Squire & Knowlton, 1995).

animal

fruit

person

The brain is prewired to make categories.

One reason you are not aware of forming prototypes or classifying things into categories is that these cognitive processes occur at an unconscious level, which means that you are unaware of and cannot recall what is happening (see p. 246). Evidence that forming prototypes and matching things to prototypes occur at an unconscious (implicit) level comes from studies that found that although amnesic patients were able to form prototypes and correctly match things to prototypes, they could not explain how they did it. Researchers concluded that using prototypes involves implicit processes, which we are not aware of and cannot voluntarily recall (Squire & Knowlton, 1995).

As you'll see, not being able to form concepts would make every day a very bad day.

Functions of Concepts

If you woke up one day to find that you had lost all your concepts, you would indeed have a very bad day. That's because concepts perform two important functions: They organize information and help us avoid relearning (Humphreys & Forde, 2001).

1 Organize information. Concepts allow you to group things into categories and thus better organize and store information in memory. For example, instead of having to store hundreds of mental images of many different kinds of dogs, you can store a single prototype of the average dog.

2 Avoid relearning. By having concepts that can be used to classify and categorize things, you can easily classify new things without having to relearn what each thing is. For example, once you have a concept for a dog, rabbit, cat, or cookie, you do not have to relearn what that thing is on each new encounter.

Without concepts, our cognitive worlds would consist of unconnected pieces of information. In fact, some forms of brain damage destroy a person's ability to form concepts, so that the person is unable to name or categorize what he or she sees (visual agnosia—see p. 79). By using concepts, you can identify, categorize, and store information very efficiently.

There is no doubt that concepts are useful for identifying objects and helping us make sense of our world. Next, you'll see that concepts are valuable for solving problems and thinking creatively. ●

What if you had to always relearn that this is a dog?

B Solving Problems

How do experts solve problems?

In 2006, then world chess champion Vladimir Kramnik (photo below) played a six-game match against a powerful computer named Deep Fritz. Kramnik didn't win any of the six games, but rather tied two and lost four (*Chessbase News*, 2006). This human-versus-computer chess match was all about thinking and problem solving.

Problem solving involves searching for some rule, plan, or strategy that results in reaching a certain goal that is currently out of reach.

When competing against other human chess players, Kramnik had been used to winning because he was the better thinker and problem solver. For Kramnik, as well as for most of us, problem solving involves three states: (1) the *initial state*, which is thinking about the unsolved problem; (2) the *operations state*,

> A computer that was unemotional, unconcerned, and uncaring beat me at chess!

which involves trying various rules or strategies to solve the problem; and (3) the *goal state*, which is reaching the solution. One plan used by expert problem solvers, such as Kramnik, is to think in broad terms of how to solve the problem, while less successful novices become too focused on specifics (Abernethy et al., 1994). For example, when novice players are in a difficult position, they may spend much time calculating possible moves, often planning many moves ahead, yet never find the best solution. An expert player has more knowledge of chess positions and examines fewer, but better, possibilities in much less time (P. E. Ross, 2006). Being a successful problem solver involves using different kinds of thinking, some of which can be programmed into a computer.

Different Ways of Thinking

Can a computer think?

In this man-machine chess match, Kramnik's thinking involved a combination of intuition (clever guesses based on years of experience) and creative mental shortcuts, called heuristics.

The computer's "thinking" was more fixed because it has been programmed to use a set of rules that lead to specific outcomes, called algorithms. Solving problems by using algorithms or heuristics illustrates two very different ways of thinking (Matlin, 2009).

Algorithms

If you wanted to win at a variety of games, such as chess, checkers, or bridge, you would follow a fixed set of rules that are called algorithms (*AL-go-rhythms*).

Algorithms are a fixed set of rules that, if followed correctly, will eventually lead to a solution.

For example, learning to play chess involves following algorithms that define how pieces move and the results of those moves. The reason relatively few chess players become grand masters like Kramnik is that people vary in their ability to learn and use algorithms.

Algorithms were programmed into Deep Fritz, the powerful computer, and because it worked at superfast speeds, it was able to win four of the six matches against Kramnik.

Instead of using only algorithms, chess champion Kramnik also used a set of rules called heuristics.

Heuristics

Kramnik's unique brain, together with his years of experience, allowed him to play chess using heuristics *(hyoo-RIS-ticks)*.

Heuristics are rules of thumb, or clever and creative mental shortcuts acquired through past experience, that reduce the number of operations and allow one to solve problems easily and quickly.

Until fairly recently, Kramnik's clever and creative shortcuts, or heuristics, would have given him the advantage over the fixed and not so creative algorithms of computer programs. However, computers now have been programmed with new algorithms that increase their speed of "thinking" from analyzing 100,000 chess moves per second to 2.5 million moves. As a result of this increased speed, human chess grand masters, whose thinking focuses on using clever heuristics, no longer have a clear advantage over a computer's "thinking" ability (Boyce, 2002). Still, Kramnik's use of heuristics gives him an edge over other human chess players, which is one reason he became a world chess champion.

Besides being used to solve chess problems, heuristics are often used in daily life to make decisions or draw conclusions (Manktelow, 2012). A commonly used heuristic is called the availability heuristic.

The **availability heuristic** says that we rely on information that is more prominent or easily recalled and overlook other information that is available but less prominent or notable.

For example, lottery companies show pictures of people who won millions of dollars rather than advertising the extremely low odds of winning. They do this so that "winning" is prominent or easily recalled, which leads you to overestimate your odds of winning and consequently spend more money on lottery tickets than you should.

Another commonly used heuristic is called the representative heuristic.

The **representative heuristic** says that we have a tendency to assume that an object or event belongs to a particular category because of how similar it is to the typical prototype of that category.

For example, consider David, who is 52 years old and likes to play chess, write research papers, and participate in book clubs. Which is more likely: David is a taxi driver or an Ivy League professor? People are more likely to think David is an Ivy League professor because his interests are more similar to the typical prototype of a professor, rather than the typical prototype of a taxi driver. However, people do not take into consideration that there are many more taxi drivers than Ivy League professors.

Using the availability or representative heuristic to make a decision means taking a mental shortcut. Although heuristics allow us to make quick decisions, they may result in bad decisions, since we make them using shortcuts, which limits the amount of information we use (Kahneman & Frederick, 2005).

Three Strategies for Solving Problems

What if you get stuck?

Most of us have had the experience of getting stuck while trying to solve a problem and wondering what to do next. By studying people who are good at problem solving, such as chess players, engineers, and computer programmers, psychologists have identified a number of useful strategies for solving problems. We'll discuss three problem-solving strategies—changing a mental set, using analogies, and forming subgoals. (Solutions to the first two problems appear on page 319.)

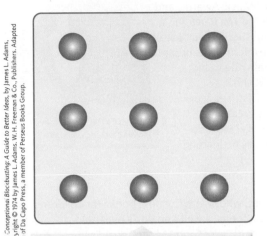

It takes new thinking to connect all dots with four straight lines without lifting the pencil.

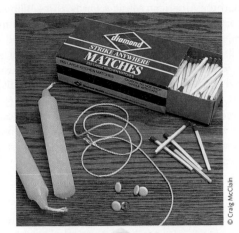

© Craig McClain

How would you mount a candle on the wall using what you see here?

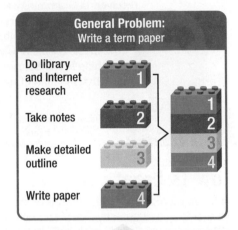

General Problem:
Write a term paper

Do library and Internet research · 1
Take notes · 2
Make detailed outline · 3
Write paper · 4

The best strategy for writing a term paper is to break the task into subgoals.

Changing One's Mental Set

Problem. Connect all nine dots shown above by drawing four straight lines without lifting your pencil from the paper or retracing any lines. If, like most people, you have difficulty solving this problem, it may be because of mental sets and functional fixedness.

A **mental set** is the tendency to use problem-solving strategies that have worked in the past.

Mental sets become an obstacle to problem solving when we continually try to use strategies that worked in the past but that simply do not work for the current problem.

For instance, you probably have a mental set that a straight line must begin and end on a dot. To solve the nine-dot problem, you need to break out of functional fixedness, which involves thinking of a line as continuing past a dot (T. C. Kershaw & Ohlsson, 2004).

Functional fixedness is a mental set that is characterized by the inability to see an object as having a function different from its usual one.

You can increase your chances of solving a problem if you consider the problem from many different viewpoints and unusual angles and if you decrease your anxiety and concern, which will in turn help you to overcome functional fixedness.

Using Analogies

Problem. Imagine that you have a box of matches, two candles, a piece of string, and several tacks, as shown in the photo above. How would you mount a candle on the wall so that it could be used as a light?

You may solve the candle problem in a flash of insight. However, most of us have to develop a strategy to solve the problem, and a good strategy may involve using an analogy.

An **analogy** is a strategy for finding a similarity between the new situation and an old, familiar situation.

If you adopt an analogy to solve the candle problem, here's how your thinking might proceed: "I'm familiar with using a shelf to hold a candle on the wall. Which of the objects—candle, string, or box—could serve as a shelf? If I remove the matches, I can tack the box to the wall."

As you gain more experience and knowledge, you become better at using analogies to solve problems. This is one reason that businesses prefer employees with experience: These employees are more likely to use analogies to solve problems.

What about the problem every student must face—writing a paper?

Forming Subgoals

Problem. Suppose your assignment is to write a term paper titled "Creativity and Madness." A useful strategy for writing this paper is to divide the assignment or general problem into a number of subgoals.

Using **subgoals** is a strategy that involves breaking down the overall problem into separate parts that, when completed in order, will result in a solution.

As shown in the figure above, the first subgoal is doing research and finding a number of articles on creativity and madness. The second subgoal is reading the articles and taking notes. The third subgoal is making a detailed outline of the whole paper. A fourth subgoal is using your outline to write the paper. The strategy of working on and completing each specific subgoal makes the overall project more manageable and reduces unproductive worrying and complaining that can interfere with starting and completing your paper.

The strategy of setting specific goals to solve a problem has some advantages: Goals direct and focus attention, help get you energized and motivated, and increase persistence and lessen procrastination (E. A. Locke & Latham, 2002).

Another problem-solving strategy is to use creative thinking, our next topic. ●

C Thinking Creatively

What does it mean to think creatively?

At the beginning of this module, we told you about Shawn Carter, better known as Jay-Z. Carter grew up living in the dangerous projects, dropped out of high school, and began dealing drugs at a young age. Despite overwhelming odds, Carter succeeded in making ten hit albums, which together have sold nearly 50 million copies. For his creative musical talent, he has received 13 Grammy Awards, three American Music Awards, three Billboard Music Awards, and countless other honors. Carter is so creative and talented that he completed *The Blueprint,* a critically acclaimed album, in only two days! His creativity has helped him succeed outside of the music business as well. Perhaps most notably, Carter's creativity is evident in his urban clothing brand Rocawear, which has become a multimillion-dollar business due to his creativity in marketing and product development (Ali, 2006; DeCurtis, 2009).

This intriguing story of Shawn Carter (Jay-Z) raises four interesting questions about creativity: How is creativity defined and measured? Is IQ related to creativity? How do creative people think and behave? Can creativity be learned?

Shawn Carter is creative as Jay-Z the rapper.

Shawn Carter is creative in his clothing business.

How Is Creativity Defined and Measured?

Although there are many definitions of creativity, we'll use the one that is agreed upon by most researchers.

Creativity is a combination of flexibility in thinking and reorganization of understanding to produce innovative ideas and new or novel solutions (R. J. Sternberg, 2001).

People can show evidence of creativity in many different ways. For example, recognized creative individuals include Albert Einstein, who formulated the theory of relativity; Michelangelo, who painted the Sistine Chapel; Sigmund Freud, who developed psychoanalysis; Dr. Seuss, who wrote rhyming books for children (and adults); the Rolling Stones, a well-known, 50-year-old rock-and-roll band; Ray Kroc, who founded McDonald's worldwide hamburger chain; and Shawn Carter (Jay-Z), who is a rapper.

Because there are so many different examples (and kinds) of creativity, psychologists have used three different approaches to measure creativity: the psychometric, case study, and cognitive approaches (R. J. Sternberg & O'Hara, 2000).

Psychometric Approach

This approach, which uses objective problem-solving tasks to measure creativity, focuses on the distinction between two kinds of thinking—convergent and divergent (Guilford, 1967; Runco, 2004).

Convergent thinking means beginning with a problem and coming up with a single correct solution.

Examples of convergent thinking include answering multiple-choice questions and solving math problems. The opposite of convergent thinking is divergent thinking.

Divergent thinking means beginning with a problem and coming up with many different solutions.

For example, the two problem-solving tasks on page 309 (nine-dot and candle-match puzzles) are used to assess divergent thinking, which is a popular psychometric measure for creativity (Amabile, 1985; Camp, 1994).

Tests of divergent thinking have good reliability, which means that people achieve the same scores across time (Domino, 1994). However, tests of divergent thinking have low validity, which means that creative persons, such as Shawn Carter, may not necessarily score high on psychometric tests of creativity (H. Gardner, 1993).

Case Study Approach

Because the psychometric approach is limited to using objective tests, it provides little insight into creative minds. In comparison, the case study approach analyzes creative persons in great depth and thus provides insight into their development, personality, motivation, and problems.

For example, Howard Gardner (1993) used the case study approach to analyze seven creative people, including Sigmund Freud. Gardner found that creative people are creative in certain areas but poor in others: Freud was very creative in linguistic and personal areas but very poor in spatial and musical areas. Although case studies provide rich insight into creative minds, their findings may be difficult to generalize: Freud's kind of creativity may or may not apply to Shawn Carter's remarkable achievements (Freyd, 1994).

Cognitive Approach

Although case studies provide detailed portraits of creative people, the findings are very personal or subjective and not easily applied to others. In comparison, the cognitive approach tries to build a bridge between the objective measures of the psychometric approach and the subjective descriptions provided by case studies. The cognitive approach, which is also the newest, identifies and measures cognitive mechanisms that are used during creative thinking (Freyd, 1994).

For example, many individuals have reported that one cognitive mechanism vital to creative thinking is the use of mental imagery, which involves thinking in images, without words or mathematical symbols (Finke, 1993). Thus, the cognitive approach involves analyzing the workings of mental imagery and its relationship to creative thinking.

Now, let's see whether creativity is related to IQ.

Is IQ Related to Creativity?

In some cases, such as Michelangelo, Sigmund Freud, and Albert Einstein, creativity seems to be linked to genius. However, creativity is not the same as intelligence, as best illustrated by savants.

Savants are about 10% of autistic individuals who show some incredible memory, music, or drawing talent.

Stephen Wiltshire (right photo) is a savant who is world famous for his architectural illustrations and incredible memory. Stephen earned the nickname "human camera" because of his extraordinary ability to look at a landscape for only minutes and then draw it from memory with exceptional detail (Sacks, 2008; Treffert, 2006).

Despite their creativity, many savants score below 70 on IQ tests (average score is 100). Savants lack verbal intelligence but

Stephen Wiltshire, "the human camera," paints an aerial view of downtown Madrid after briefly seeing it by helicopter.

excel in visual intelligence, and their right hemispheres are more active than their left during creative activities (Treffert & Wallace, 2002).

Instead of linking creativity to genius, some psychologists believe creativity involves relatively ordinary cognitive processes that result in extraordinary products (Weisberg, 1993). These creative products include inventions (Post-its, genetic crops), new drugs (Viagra), and computer software (video games). When the IQs of creative individuals are closely examined and compared to others, we find that people who are recognized as creative tend to have above average IQ scores, but those with the highest IQs are not necessarily the most creative (R. J. Sternberg & O'Hara, 2000).

How Do Creative People Think and Behave?

Researchers have studied creative individuals to identify what is unusual about their work habits and psychological traits (Helson, 1996; Simonton, 2000). Here are some of their findings.

Focus. Creative people tend to be superior in one particular area, such as dance, music, art, science, or writing, rather than in many areas. For example, Einstein was superior in the logical-spatial area—the theory of relativity ($E = mc^2$)—but poor in the personal area—developing close relationships.

Cognition. Creative individuals have the ability to change mental directions, consider problems from many angles, and make use of mental images. They are also interested in solving unusual problems.

Personality. On the positive side, creative people tend to be independent, self-confident, unconventional, risk-taking, hard-working, and obsessively committed

Creative people, such as Einstein, can consider problems from different viewpoints and are driven by strong internal goals.

to their work. On the negative side, they tend to have large egos that make them insensitive to the needs of others. They may pursue their goals at the expense of others, and they may be so absorbed in their work that they exclude others.

Motivation. They are driven by internal values or personal goals; this is called intrinsic motivation. They are less concerned about external rewards such as money or recognition, which is called extrinsic motivation. They are motivated by the challenge of solving problems; their reward is the satisfaction of accomplishment. On average, creative people work on a project for about ten years before reaching their creative peaks.

One question often asked about creativity is whether it can be learned.

Can Creativity Be Learned?

Creativity requires combining new information with old ideas. In other words, creativity involves success in using both convergent thinking and divergent thinking (see p. 310).

Although creativity cannot be learned overnight, a lifetime of consistent efforts to develop the brain's ability to think creativity can certainly pay off. Effective creativity training programs offer activities or tasks that emphasize divergent thinking combined with convergent thinking (Bronson & Merryman, 2010). An example of the type of activities that can foster creativity is asking college students to "think of all the things that could interfere with graduating from college." After students have completed their list, they are told to pick one of the problems they identified and to list as many solutions for that problem as possible (Runco, 2010). Tasks such as this one, when

Activities that require the use of convergent and divergent thinking help nurture creativity.

completed in a frequent, consistent manner, can foster creativity. Highly creative individuals will not only identify many things that can go wrong but also demonstrate flexibility in finding various creative solutions.

Efforts to teach creativity can begin early on in the home environment. Researchers find that highly creative adults tend to grow up in families who embrace opposites. These parents are responsive to their child's needs, yet challenge them to develop new skills. These parents provide stability, yet encourage uniqueness. Consequently, it is proposed that when these children are bored, they seek change; yet when they were anxious, the clear rules and structure offer them comfort (Csikszentmihalyi & Gute, 2010).

Next, we'll turn our attention to another mental process called reasoning. ●

D Reasoning & Decision Making

Reasoning

If you saw a nicely dressed older man standing in the ocean, you would naturally wonder what he was doing. To understand this man's unusual behavior, you could use the personal computer inside your brain, which has a very powerful software program called reasoning.

Reasoning is a mental process that involves using and applying knowledge to solve problems, make plans or decisions, and achieve goals.

To figure out why this normal-looking, fully dressed but shoeless man is standing in the ocean, you could use two different kinds of reasoning—deductive and inductive.

© Hans Neleman/Getty Images

Deductive Reasoning

Since you rarely see a nicely dressed older man standing in the ocean, you might assume that he is drunk. The kind of reasoning that begins with a big assumption is called deductive reasoning.

Deductive reasoning begins with making a general assumption that you know or believe to be true and then drawing specific conclusions based on this assumption—in other words, reasoning from a general assumption to particulars.

Your general assumption is that only a drunk person would gleefully walk into the ocean dressed in a suit. That's what this man is doing; therefore, he must be drunk. In its simplest form, deductive reasoning follows this formula: If you are given an

assumption or statement as true, then there is only one correct conclusion to draw. The formula is often put in this form: "If *p* (given statements), then *q* (conclusion)." For example:

Statements ("If *p*"): Only people who are over 21 years of age drink alcohol. That man is drinking alcohol. Conclusion ("Then *q*"): That man must be over 21 years of age.

One mistake people make in deductive reasoning is that they assume but do not always know if the basic statement or assumption (*p*) is true. If the basic statement is false—that is, if drunkenness is not the only explanation for the man's behavior—then so are the conclusions. Another way to figure out why the man is standing in the ocean is to use inductive reasoning.

Inductive Reasoning

Instead of just assuming that this man is standing in the ocean because he's drunk, you walk over and ask some specific questions. After listening to this man's answers, you reach a different explanation for why he's standing in the ocean. The kind of reasoning that starts with specific facts or observations is called inductive reasoning.

Inductive reasoning begins with making particular observations that you then use to draw a broader conclusion; in other words, reasoning from particulars to a general conclusion.

For example, when questioned, the man answers "No" to all the following questions: Did you drink alcohol today? Do you have a job? Are you married? Do you do this often? Have you eaten today? Are you ill? Would you like me to take you home? After

considering all these particulars, you reach a general conclusion: Either this man is suffering from Alzheimer's disease or he is lying.

Researchers use inductive reasoning when they use past experiences or observations to form a general hypothesis (J. Evans, 1993). For instance, researchers observed that when some students take exams they have rapid heart rate, sweaty palms, muscle tension, and increased blood pressure. Based on these particulars, researchers reached the general conclusion that these students have test anxiety.

One big mistake people make in inductive reasoning is jumping to a conclusion before knowing all the facts (D. Levy, 1997). As you'll learn next, sometimes people jump to a conclusion prematurely because of biased reasoning.

Confirmation Bias

Let's admit it, we all like to be correct. The problem with wanting to demonstrate to ourselves and others that we are correct is that we may overlook information that doesn't confirm our decisions and beliefs, which is called confirmation bias.

Confirmation bias is a tendency to look for information that supports our decisions and beliefs and ignore disconfirming information.

For example, imagine that you are a psychologist who is about to see a patient for the first time. The patient was referred from a primary-care physician who states that the patient needs treatment for depression. During your first appointment with the

patient, he mentions having difficulty concentrating at work and sleeping through the night. Given that these can be symptoms of depression, you conclude that the physician was correct and diagnose the patient with depression.

Because you were looking for information that supports the diagnosis of depression, you overlooked the strong possibility that the patient's problems with concentration and sleeping may be symptoms of anxiety, rather than depression.

To improve the accuracy of our decisions and beliefs we should look for both confirming *and* disconfirming evidence.

Next, we'll describe how we make decisions.

Decision Making

We make many decisions every day. Some decisions have very important consequences in our lives, such as choosing a college, career, or spouse. Other decisions have much less importance, such as choosing a flavor of ice cream, the color of a shirt, or a movie to watch. We would like to believe that we make decisions, especially important ones, based on thoughtful reasoning. But how do we actually make decisions?

How do we make decisions?

Imagine that you are in the hospital and a doctor tells you about your treatment options. One of the treatments involves surgery, and you must decide whether you want to undergo surgery. Would it influence your decision differently if a doctor tells

We often make decisions based on emotions rather than intellect.

you that the survival rate of the surgery is 80% *or* that there is a 20% chance of dying from the surgery? Even though both statements express the same risk, the 80% chance of survival sounds more appealing than the 20% chance of dying. Thinking about the success of surgery is comforting, but thinking about the failure of surgery makes us uncomfortable (De Martino, 2006a). Research shows that we often base our decisions on emotion rather than intellect (Koenigs et al., 2007; Lehrer, 2009).

Next, we'll provide an example of how the wording of instructions can also influence our decisions.

Gambling Decisions

Benedetto De Martino (2006b) and his team of researchers (2006) at the University College of London took brain scans of men and women while they were being asked to make a decision about whether or not to gamble. At the start of the study each participant was given about $100. The participants were then told that they could either *"keep"* 40% of their money or *"lose"* 60% of their money if they did not gamble. When participants were told that they could *"keep"* 40% of their money if they chose to not gamble, they gambled only 43% of the time. When told that they could *"lose"* 60% of their money if they did not gamble, the participants gambled 62% of the time. Even when the chances of winning and losing were identical, the wording of the instructions made a difference in the participants' decisions.

The wording of instructions makes a difference in gambling decisions.

The results of brain scans showed that the part of the brain responsible for strong negative emotions (amygdala) was very active while participants were making their decisions, regardless of the choice they made. Researchers concluded that emotions had a strong influence on how the participants made gambling decisions. Further support for the significant role of emotions in decision making comes from research studies showing that people who lack emotions due to brain trauma or injury often have serious difficulties making even simple decisions (A. Damasio, 2006).

Thoughts and Words

Because words are such a vital part of our reasoning and decision-making processes, we need to know how words can influence or bias our thinking.

Almost everyone has heard it said that the Inuit (Eskimos) have dozens of words for snow because their survival depends on knowing how to travel and hunt in different kinds of snow. This particular observation was first made by amateur linguist Benjamin Whorf (1956), who noticed that languages differed in their vocabularies depending on how much emphasis they gave to different objects and events in their environment. For example, Whorf reasoned that because the Inuit have many names for snow, they must be able to perceive many more kinds of snow than Americans, for whom snow conditions are less important. On the basis of these kinds of observations, Whorf formulated the theory of linguistic relativity.

The **theory of linguistic relativity** states that the differences among languages result in similar differences in how people think of and perceive the world.

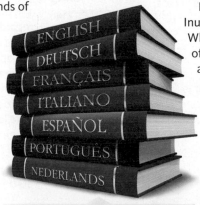

The theory of linguistic relativity states that speakers of different languages think about the world in different ways.

Therefore, the theory of linguistic relativity states that speakers of different languages think about the world in different ways. Research findings conclude that, although there is some support for language determining our thinking, there are many examples of this not being true (Davies & Corbett, 1997; Pinker, 1994).

Let's examine Whorf's famous claim that the Inuit have more words for snow than Americans do. Whorf reasoned that the Inuit's larger vocabulary of snow-related words should make them think and perceive snow very differently than most Americans. However, another linguist did a closer examination and found that Inuit and Americans both have about eight words for snow (English words for snow include *blizzard, sleet, hail, hardpack, powder, avalanche, flurry,* and *dusting*) (L. Martin, 1986). So, as it turns out, Whorf was wrong about how many words Inuit and Americans have for snow. One reason Whorf's story about differences in snow words lives on is that it's a great (but untrue) story (Pullum, 1991).

Next, we'll discuss the basics of language. ●

E Language: Basic Rules

How many languages are there?

Our ability to use language is one of the most remarkable features of our species. As of this writing, people are believed to speak 6,909 different languages, and although undiscovered languages continue to be found, about 500 languages, mostly tribal languages, are in immediate danger of becoming extinct (Harrison, 2010; *Science Illustrated,* 2011d).

Language is a special form of communication that involves learning and using complex rules to make and combine symbols (words or gestures) into an endless number of meaningful sentences.

The reason language is such a successful form of communication arises from two amazingly simple principles—words and grammar.

A **word** is an arbitrary pairing between a sound or symbol and a meaning.

For example, the word *parrot* does not look like, sound like, or fly like a parrot, but it refers to a bird we call a parrot because all of us memorized this pairing as children. Young adults are estimated to have about 60,000 such pairings or words in their mental dictionaries (Pinker, 1995). However, these 60,000 symbols

© Milena_/Shutterstock.com

Why is this called a parrot?

or words are rather useless unless the users follow similar rules of grammar.

Grammar is a set of rules for combining words into phrases and sentences to express an infinite number of thoughts that can be understood by others.

For instance, our mental rules of grammar immediately tell us that the headline "Parrot Bites Man's Nose" means something very different from "Man Bites Parrot's Nose." It may seem surprising, but speakers of all 6,909 languages learned the same four rules.

Four Rules of Language

As children, each of us learned, without much trouble, the four rules of language. Now, as adults, we use these rules without being aware of how or when we use them. To illustrate the four rules of language, we'll use the word *caterpillar.* As a child, you may have watched its strange crawling motion, or perhaps you were even brave enough to pick one up.

1 The first language rule governs phonology.

Phonology *(fuh-NAWL-uh-gee)* specifies how we make the meaningful sounds that are used by a particular language.

Any English word can be broken down into phonemes.

Phonemes *(FOE-neems)* are the basic sounds of consonants and vowels.

For example, the various sounds of **c** and **p** represent different phonemes, which are some of the sounds in the word *caterpillar.* At about 6 months old, babies begin to babble and make basic sounds, or phonemes. We combine phonemes to form words by learning the second rule.

2 The second language rule governs morphology.

Morphology *(mor-FAWL-uh-gee)* is the system that we use to group phonemes into meaningful combinations of sounds and words.

A **morpheme** *(MOR-feem)* is the smallest meaningful combination of sounds in a language.

For example, a morpheme may be

a word, such as **cat**,

a letter, such as the **s** in ca**ts**,

a prefix, such as the **un**- in **un**breakable,

or a suffix, such as the -**ed** in walk**ed**.

The word **caterpillar** is actually one morpheme, and the word **caterpillars** is two (**caterpillar**-**s**). After we learn to combine morphemes to form words, we learn to combine words into meaningful sentences by using the third rule.

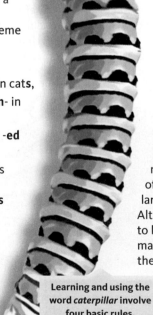

Learning and using the word *caterpillar* involve four basic rules.

3 The third language rule governs syntax, or grammar.

Syntax, or **grammar,** is a set of rules that specifies how we combine words to form meaningful phrases and sentences.

For example, why doesn't the following sentence make sense?

Caterpillars green long and are.

You instantly realize that this sentence is nonsensical or ungrammatical because it doesn't follow the English grammar rules regarding where we place verbs and conjunctions. If you apply the rules of English grammar, you would rearrange the combination of words to read: "Caterpillars are long and green." Although you may not be able to list all the rules of grammar, you automatically follow them when you speak. One way you know whether the word *bear* is a noun or a verb is by using the fourth rule.

4 The fourth language rule governs semantics.

Semantics *(si-MAN-ticks)* specifies the meanings of words or phrases when they appear in various sentences or contexts.

For instance, as you read "Did Pat pat a caterpillar's back?" how do you know what the word **pat** means, since it appears twice in succession. From your knowledge of semantics, you know that the first **Pat** is a noun and the name of a person, while the second **pat** is a verb, which signals some action.

Somehow you knew that the same word, **pat**, had different meanings depending on the context. How you know what words mean in different contexts is a very intriguing question.

Understanding Language

One of the great mysteries of using and understanding language can be demonstrated by the following two simple but very different sentences:

You picked up a caterpillar.

A caterpillar was picked up by you.

Despite a different word order, you know that these two sentences mean exactly the same thing. How you know that these different sentences mean exactly the same thing was explained by linguist Noam Chomsky (1957). We'll discuss two of Chomsky's revolutionary principles—mental grammar and innate brain program—that allow us to use and understand spoken language with relative ease (McGilvray, 2004).

Mental grammar. Almost every sentence we speak or understand is formed from a brand-new combination of words. Chomsky pointed out that the brain does not have the capacity to contain a list of all the sentences we will ever use. Instead, Chomsky argued that the brain contains a program or *mental grammar* that allows us to combine nouns, verbs, and objects in an endless variety of meaningful sentences. Chomsky's principle of mental grammar answers the question of how we can so easily create so many different sentences. The second question that Chomsky answered was: How do we acquire this mental grammar?

Broca's area is prewired to combine sounds into words.

Wernicke's area is prewired to combine words into sentences.

A child learns to speak and understand words and sentences because the brain has a built-in, or innate, language program.

Innate brain program. How is it possible that 4-year-old children, with no formal schooling, can speak and understand an endless variety of sentences? For example, the average 4-year-old child can already determine that the sentence "The caterpillar crept slowly across the leaf" is correct but that the sentence "The crept leaf caterpillar slowly the across" is meaningless. Chomsky's answer is that young children can learn these complex and difficult rules of grammar because our brains come with a built-in, or *innate, program* that makes learning the rules of grammar relatively easy (see p. 229). The brain's innate program for learning rules of grammar explains how children learn most of the complex rules by age 4 or 5 and how children who are exposed to two languages from birth learn the two distinct vocabularies and grammar rules as quickly as their monolingual peers learn the rules of one language (Kovács & Mehler, 2009). However, it is the interaction between the development of the brain's innate program and a child's range of environmental experiences that results in learning the complicated rules of grammar (Schlaggar et al., 2002).

But how does an innate grammar program, which could be used by any child in any culture, specify the rules for forming and understanding an endless number of meaningful sentences? Chomsky's answer is perhaps his cleverest contribution.

Different Structure, Same Meaning

One of the most difficult questions that Chomsky had to answer was how an idea can be expressed in several different ways, with different grammatical structures, yet mean the same thing.

He answered this question by making a distinction between two different structures of a sentence: surface structure and deep structure.

Surface structure is the actual wording of a sentence, as it is spoken.

Deep structure is the underlying meaning that is not spoken but is present in the mind of the listener.

We can illustrate the difference between surface and deep structures with our same two sentences:

You picked up a caterpillar.

A caterpillar was picked up by you.

Notice that these two sentences have different *surface structures*, which means they are worded differently. However, according to Chomsky, you are able to look underneath the different surface structures of the two sentences and recognize that they have the same *deep structure*, which is why you know they have the same meaning.

Chomsky argues that we learn to shift back and forth between surface and deep structure by applying transformational rules.

Transformational rules are procedures by which we convert our ideas from surface structures into deep structures and from deep structures back into surface ones.

For example, when you hear the two sentences about picking up the caterpillar, you transform the words into their deep

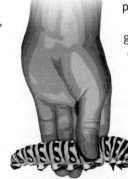

You know that the sentence "You picked up a caterpillar" means the same as "A caterpillar was picked up by you" because you recognize that both have the same deep structure.

structure, which you store in memory. Later, when someone asks what the person did, you use transformational rules to convert the deep structure in your memory back into a surface structure, which can be expressed in differently worded sentences. The distinction between surface and deep structures is part of Chomsky's theory of language.

Chomsky's theory of language says that all languages share a common universal grammar and that children inherit a mental program to learn this universal grammar.

Chomsky's theory, which is widely accepted today, was considered a major breakthrough in explaining how we acquire and understand language (Chomsky, 2011). However, one criticism of Chomsky's theory is that he downplays the importance of environmental opportunities for hearing and practicing sounds, which have been shown to interact with and influence language development (Schlaggar et al., 2002). For example, compared to infants raised in a monolingual household, bilingual infants can distinguish between two languages they have never heard before just by looking at the face of the speaker (Werker, 2011). Clearly, environmental experiences shape language abilities in significant and at times remarkable ways.

Chomsky's idea of an innate mental grammar would predict that children around the world should go through the same stages of language development. Can this be true for all 6,909 languages? ●

F Acquiring Language

What do children's brains do?

If Chomsky is correct that all children inherit the same innate program for learning grammar, then we would expect children from around the world to go through similar stages in developing language and acquiring the rules for using language. And in fact, all children, no matter the culture or the language, do go through the same stages (Pinker, 1994).

Language stages refer to all infants going through four different periods or stages—babbling, single words, two-word combinations, and sentences. All children go through these four stages in the same order, and in each stage, children show new and more complex language skills.

The occurrence of each of the four stages is associated with further development of the brain. At birth, an infant's brain has almost all of its neurons but they have not yet made all their connections (adult brains can grow some new

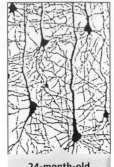

6-month-old brain has few connections.

From Conel, J. L. 1939, 1941, 1959, The Postnatal Development of the Human Cerebral Cortex, 6 Volumes, Cambridge: Harvard

neurons—see p. 49). For example, a 6-month-old infant's brain (left figure) has few neural interconnections, which are associated with performing relatively simple behaviors, such as babbling. In comparison, a 24-month-old infant's brain (right figure) has hundreds of neural interconnections, which are associated with more complex behaviors, such as using two-word combinations (Ropper & Samuels, 2009).

24-month-old brain has more connections.

From Conel, J. L. 1939, 1941, 1959, The Postnatal Development of the Human Cerebral Cortex, 6 Volumes, Cambridge: Harvard

Here are the four stages that each of us went through in learning to speak and understand the language of our parents or caregivers.

Four Stages in Acquiring Language

1 Babbling

One of the key features in human development is that infants begin to make sounds long before they can say real words. Infants repeat the same sounds over and over, and these sounds are commonly called babbling.

Babbling, which begins at about 6 months, is the first stage in acquiring language. Babbling is making one-syllable sounds, such as "dee-dee-dee" or "ba-ba-ba."

Babbling is an example of an innate "sound" program in the

Bababa

© Dereje/ Shutterstock.com

A 6-month-old brain has limited capacity for language.

From Conel, J. L. 1939, 1941, 1959, The Postnatal Development of the Human Cerebral Cortex, 6 Volumes, Cambridge: Harvard

brain that is involved in making and processing sounds that will eventually be used to form words. Scientists report that babies from around the world babble in similar ways, which further supports that babbling is an innate ability (Klass, 2010). By 6 months of age, infants have already learned to discriminate between sounds, such as *ba* from *pa,* and to distinguish sounds in their native language from those used in a foreign language (F. Bower, 2000). At about this time, in preparation for talking, infants begin to focus on speakers' mouths instead of their eyes (Lewkowicz & Hansen-Tift, 2012). At about 9 months, babbling begins to resemble the vowels and consonants that children will use in speaking their native languages.

In children who can hear, babbling is oral. In deaf children who have been exposed only to the sign language of their deaf parents, babbling is manual and not oral. That is, these babies babble by repeating the same hand sign over and over (J. L. Locke, 2006). This means that the brain has an innate program for acquiring language, whether spoken or sign language.

Through endless babbling, by about age 1, infants learn to control their vocal apparatus (mouth and tongue) and listen to the results so that they can make, change, repeat, and imitate sounds they hear from others (Hoff, 2009; Stoel-Gammon, 2010). After babbling, infants begin to say their first words.

2 Single Word

Shortly before 1 year of age, an infant usually performs a behavior that every parent has been eagerly waiting for: the first word. At about 1 year of age, infants begin not only to understand words but also to say single words.

Single words mark the second stage in acquiring language, which occurs at about 1 year of age. Infants say single words that usually refer to what they can see, hear, or feel.

An infant's ability to form sounds into words begins at about 8 months and results from an interaction between the brain's innate language program and the infant's experience with hearing sounds (Jusczyk & Hohne, 1997). At about 8 months of age, infants demonstrate the remarkable ability to learn up to ten words a day (J. Brown et al., 2010). About half the infant's single words refer to objects (juice, cookie, doll, dada), and the other half refer to actions, routines, or motions (up, eat, hot, more) (Pinker, 1994). The infant's single words, such as "Milk" or "Go," often stand for longer thoughts such as "I want milk" or "I want to go out."

Milk. Go.

A 1-year-old brain has more connections and more capacity for language.

© Royalty-Free/Masterfile

As infants learn to say words, parents usually respond in a specific way called parentese (motherese).

Parentese (formerly known as *motherese*) is a way of speaking to young children in which the adult speaks in a slower and higher than normal voice, emphasizes and stretches out each word, uses very simple sentences, and repeats words and phrases.

Researchers conclude that parentese has at least three functions: to attract and hold an infant's attention, aid comprehension, and facilitate language development (Leitzell, 2007). Also, parentese has important cross-cultural benefits. For example, researchers found that the Shuar people from South America, who don't understand or speak English, are able to understand the basic meanings of parentese among English-speaking parents in North America (Bryant & Barrett, 2007). Thus, parentese can convey meaning between people who don't speak the same language.

Next, the young child begins to combine words.

3 Two-Word Combinations

Starting around age 2, children begin using single words that they have learned to form two-word combinations.

Two-word combinations, which represent the third stage in acquiring language, occur at about 2 years of age. Two-word combinations are strings of two words that express various actions ("Me play," "See boy") or relationships ("Hit ball," "Milk gone").

Each of the two words provides a hint about what the child is saying. In addition, the relationship between the two words gives hints about what the child is communicating. For example, "See boy" tells us to look at a specific object; "Daddy shirt" tells us that something belongs to Daddy. The child's ability to communicate by combining two words and changing their order marks the start of learning the rules of grammar.

A 2-year-old brain has many connections and more capacity for language.

Scientists report that 2-year-olds understand basic rules of grammar even though they cannot yet speak in sentences. The language processing centers of their brain get organized very early, long before they produce complex sentences like adults (Bernal et al., 2010). Another example of the early development of the brain's language centers is that young children, even infants, comprehend many more words (*receptive vocabulary*) than they can speak or produce (*productive vocabulary*) (Bergelson & Swingley, 2012; Pan & Uccelli, 2009).

Although children usually go through a stage of forming single words and then two-word combinations, there is no three-word stage. Instead, at a certain point the child will begin to form sentences, which gradually increase in length through the fourth year.

4 Sentences

Children make a rather large language leap when they progress from relatively simple two-word combinations to using longer and more complex sentences.

Sentences, which represent the fourth stage of acquiring language, occur at about 4 years of age. Sentences range from three to eight words in length and indicate a growing knowledge of the rules of grammar.

However, a child's first sentences differ from adult sentences in that the child may omit the "small words" and speak in a pattern that is called telegraphic speech.

Telegraphic speech is a distinctive pattern of speaking in which the child omits articles (*the*), prepositions (*in, out*), and parts of verbs.

For example, an adult may say, "I'm going to the store." A 3- to 4-year-old child may use telegraphic speech (omit article) and say, "I go to store." However, by the time children are 4 or 5 years old, the structure of their sentences improves and indicates that they have learned the basic rules of grammar.

Basic rules of grammar are the rules for combining nouns, verbs, adjectives, and other parts of speech to form meaningful sentences.

However, as children learn the rules of grammar, they often make errors of overgeneralization.

Overgeneralization is applying a grammatical rule to cases where it should not be used.

For example, after a child learns the rule of forming the past tense of many verbs by adding a *d* sound to the end, he or she may overgeneralize this rule and add a *d* to the past tense of irregular verbs (and say, for instance, "I goed to store"). By the time children enter school, they usually have a good grasp of the general rules of their language.

A 4- to 5-year-old brain has significantly more connections so that a child can learn the basic rules of complex grammar.

Going through the Stages

How fast does a child go through the stages?

Parents or caregivers sometimes worry about whether their child is late in developing language. In the real world, normal children pass through the four stages of language at a pace that can vary by a year or more. However, as Chomsky's theory predicts and research has shown, all normal children pass through the four stages, even though some of the stages may begin later or last for shorter or longer periods of time (Pinker, 1994).

As children proceed through the stages, there is a continuous interaction between environmental stimuli and brain development. For example, researchers used brain scans to identify maximum neural activity in 3-month-old infants who were listening to recordings of human speech. The infants showed increased

neural activity in brain areas that were similar to those used by adults in speaking and understanding language (Dehaene-Lambertz et al., 2002). This study shows how environmental stimulation—hearing language sounds—activated the "language areas" of infants' brains long before infants actually begin speaking. This study is a good example of how the brain and environment interact in the development of spoken language and points out the importance of caregivers regularly talking to (verbally stimulating) their infants.

 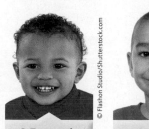 

1. Babbling   2. Single word   3. Two words   4. Sentences

Next, we'll discuss a number of innate (genetic) and environmental interactions that are important in the development of language.

It is quite amazing how children from different countries around the world, such as Bali, China, Nigeria, Sweden, United States, Mexico, France, Spain, Russia, Thailand, and Japan (right photo), can acquire the sounds, words, and rules of their particular native language. Each child learns his or her own native language because of an interaction between innate (genetic) and environmental (learning) factors.

How does a child learn a particular language?

Tanjōbi omedetō!

This boy is saying "happy birthday" in Japanese.

© miya227/Shutterstock.com

What Are Innate Factors?

All children go through the same four language stages because of innate language factors (Albert et al., 2000).

Innate language factors are genetically programmed physiological and neurological features that facilitate our making speech sounds and acquiring language skills.

We'll examine three innate language features that work together so that we can learn to speak and use language.

Innate physiological features. We have a specially adapted vocal apparatus (larynx and pharynx) that allows us to make sounds and form words. In comparison, the structures of gorillas' and chimpanzees' vocal apparatus prevent them from making the wide variety of sounds necessary to form words (Lessmoellmann, 2006; Pinker, 1994). Without specialized vocal apparatus, humans would be limited to making "animal" sounds.

Innate neurological features. When people speak or use sign language, certain brain areas are activated. The PET scan above shows a side view of the brain: red and yellow indicate the most neural activity (Petitto, 1997). These findings indicate that the left hemisphere of the brain is prewired to acquire and use language, whether spoken

The brain is genetically programmed to speak and understand.

Courtesy of Robert Zatorre, and Denise Klein, McGill University

or signed. In Module 4, we explained how damage to these same language areas (Broca's and Wernicke's areas) disrupts the use and understanding of language (see p. 78). Although your brain is prewired for language, there is a best, or critical, time for learning a language.

Innate developmental factors. Researchers have discovered that there is a critical period when acquiring language is the easiest (Shafer & Garrido-Nag, 2007).

The **critical language period** is the time from infancy to adolescence when language is easiest to learn. Language is usually more difficult to learn anytime after adolescence.

For example, immigrant children do very well learning English as a second language, while immigrant adults, who are past the critical period, have more difficulty and do less well (Jackendoff, 1994). The critical period for learning language also explains why learning your native language was easy as a child but, as an adult, learning a foreign language is many times more difficult.

Innate biological factors provide the programming so that a child can acquire any one of 6,909 languages. Which particular language the child learns depends on his or her environment.

What Are Environmental Factors?

How each child learns a particular language depends on social interactions, one of the environmental factors.

Environmental language factors are the interactions children have with parents, peers, teachers, and others who provide feedback that rewards and encourages language development, as well as provides opportunities for children to observe, imitate, and practice language skills.

What would happen if a child was deprived of almost all social interactions from ages 1 to 13? Such was the case with Genie, whose mentally disturbed father strapped her to a potty chair in a back room, punished her for making any sounds, and forbade the mother or brother to talk to her. When discovered at age 13 by a social worker, Genie could not speak a single word (Curtiss, 1977).

Genie's case illustrates that even though children are prewired by heredity to speak a language, they need certain environmental stimuli, such as listening, speaking, and interacting with others, in order to learn to speak and use language. For example, within eight months of training, Genie had acquired a vocabulary of about 200 words. However, Genie's long

Parent-child interactions provide needed stimulation and feedback.

© Temych/Shutterstock.com

period of social deprivation left its mark, and even after years of continued social interactions, her language ability did not develop much beyond that of a 2- or 3-year-old child (J. C. Harris, 1995).

Children who have the biggest vocabularies and perform best on language tests are those whose parents are the most talkative during the child's first two years (Hart & Risley, 1996). Because watching TV drastically reduces conversations between parents and child, researchers warn parents to limit their child's TV viewing, including the popular "smart baby" programs. A well-designed study found that young children who were exposed to a "smart baby" DVD for one month, either with a parent or alone, did not acquire any more new words than children who had no exposure to the video (DeLoache et al., 2010).

Another environmental language factor is whether children are raised in monolingual or bilingual environments. Research suggests that bilingual children demonstrate enhanced abilities in each language, remain more receptive to language development, and may experience other cognitive benefits throughout their lifetime (Bialystok & Craik, 2010; Petitto et al., 2012).

Together, these studies suggest that environmental and innate factors interact with and influence a child's ability to acquire language. ●

Concept Review

dog (dog, dag) *n.; pl.* **dogs, dog.**
1. any of a large and varied group of domesticated animals (*Canis familiaris*) that have four legs, a tail, two ears, prominent nose, a hairy coat, and a bark.

1. If you form a concept of an object, event, or characteristic by making a list of the properties that define it, you are forming a concept according to the _____ model.

2. If you form a concept by putting together the average characteristics of an object and then seeing whether a new object matches your average object, you are forming a concept according to **(a)** _____ theory. If you develop an idea of a dog of average age, height, weight, and color, you have formed a **(b)** _____ of a dog.

© Haig Kouyoumdjian

3. Some problems can be solved by following certain rules. If you correctly follow rules that lead to a certain solution, you are using **(a)** _____. If you follow rules that reduce the number of operations or allow you to take shortcuts in solving problems, you are using **(b)** _____.

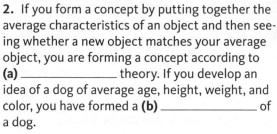
© Craig McClain

4. A combination of flexibility in thinking and reorganization of understanding to produce innovative ideas and solutions is called **(a)** _____. If you begin with a problem and come up with many different solutions, you are using **(b)** _____ thinking. The opposite of this type of thinking is beginning with a problem and coming up with the one correct solution; this is called **(c)** _____ thinking.

IMAGE ASSET MANAGEMENT/Age fotostock

5. A mental process that involves using and applying knowledge to solve problems, make plans or decisions, and achieve goals is called **(a)** _____. Sometimes people jump to a conclusion before knowing all the facts because their reasoning is biased. A tendency to seek information that supports one's decisions and beliefs and ignore disconfirming information is called **(b)** _____.

© Hans Neleman/Getty Images

6. A system of symbols that we use in thinking, solving problems, and communicating with others is called **(a)** _____. There are four rules for learning and

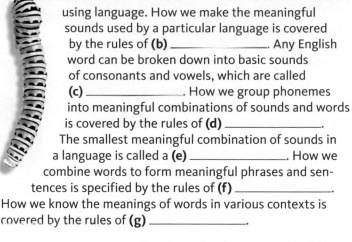

using language. How we make the meaningful sounds used by a particular language is covered by the rules of **(b)** _____. Any English word can be broken down into basic sounds of consonants and vowels, which are called **(c)** _____. How we group phonemes into meaningful combinations of sounds and words is covered by the rules of **(d)** _____. The smallest meaningful combination of sounds in a language is called a **(e)** _____. How we combine words to form meaningful phrases and sentences is specified by the rules of **(f)** _____. How we know the meanings of words in various contexts is covered by the rules of **(g)** _____.

7. Chomsky explained that a sentence can be stated in different ways and yet have the same meaning. The actual wording of a sentence is called its **(a)** _____ structure. The underlying meaning of the sentence that is not spoken but is present in the mind of the listener is called the **(b)** _____ structure. To convert our ideas from surface structures into deep structures and from deep structures back into surface ones, we use **(c)** _____ rules.

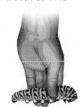
© Dereje/Shutterstock.com

8. In acquiring language, all children go through the same four stages but at different rates. Beginning at about the age of 6 months, a baby begins making one-syllable sounds, such as "bababa," which is called **(a)** _____. By about 1 year of age, a child forms **(b)** _____ words, which usually refer to what the child can see, hear, or feel. At about 2 years of age, a child makes **(c)** _____, which are strings of two words that express various actions ("Me play") or relationships ("Hit ball," "Milk gone"). At about 4 years of age, a child begins forming sentences, which range from three to eight words in length and indicate a growing knowledge of the rules of **(d)** _____.

9. One reason all children acquire a language in the same order is that there are genetically programmed physiological and neurological features in the brain and vocal apparatus. These are known as **(a)** _____ factors. Social interactions between the child and others, which offer opportunities for observation, imitation, and practice, are called **(b)** _____ factors.

© miya227/Shutterstock.com

What Kind of Problem Is Dyslexia?

Was that word "bark" or "dark"?

This Research Focus deals with a real-world problem called dyslexia.

Dyslexia is an unexpected difficulty learning to read despite intelligence, motivation, and education.

An example of a someone with dyslexia is 34-year-old Benjamin Bolger (right photo), who has earned 11 graduate degrees, including a doctorate from Harvard University. His quest for graduate degrees is nowhere near over. He is currently working on five more. Bolger's accomplishments are truly extraordinary because he reads at an elementary school level. To help him succeed, his mother reads books out loud to him and types papers that he dictates (K. Clark, 2010; R. Kaplan, 2008).

Despite having serious reading difficulties, Benjamin Bolger has 11 graduate degrees.

Courtesy Benjamin B. Bolger

Although people with dyslexia struggle with a wide range of reading difficulties, many have normal or above average IQ scores and earn high academic degrees, and some have very successful and creative careers. A few well-accomplished people with dyslexia are: Tom Cruise, movie actor; Jay Leno, TV talk-show host; Agatha Christie, author of mystery books; Walt Disney, creator of animations; and Carol Gredier, winner of a Nobel Prize in Medicine (Charkalis, 2005; *ScienceDaily*, 2009b; S. E. Shaywitz, 2009).

In studying dyslexia, researchers have investigated what happens in the brain during reading.

What's Involved in Reading?

Earlier, we explained that children usually have no difficulty learning to speak because their brains come with innate or prewired areas for speaking (see p. 318). Learning to read is entirely different from learning to speak because our brains have no innate areas dedicated specifically to reading. Instead, we must spend many years practicing how to read by learning to use three different brain areas that were originally designed to do something else (Eden, 2003).

Reading: three steps. Learning to read involves using three brain areas, each with a different function (Gorman, 2003; S. E. Shaywitz et al., 2003).

1 Phoneme (sound) producer. The first step in reading is to vocalize the word, either silently or out loud. Vocalizing involves changing the letters of each word into their basic sounds, called phonemes. For example, reading the word CAT involves vocalizing or changing the letters C-A-T into the sounds KUH-A-TUH. The phoneme producer is located in brain area #1 (left inferior frontal gyrus) (figure below).

2 Word analyzer. After we vocalize, or change a word's letters into sounds, the next step is to make a more complete analysis of a written word, such as pulling the word apart into syllables and linking syllables to their appropriate sounds. The word analyzer is located in brain area #2 (left parieto-temporal area). When first learning how to read, children rely heavily on using the phoneme producer and word analyzer.

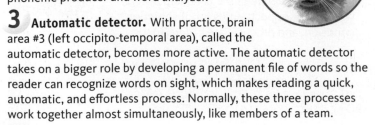

CAT

3 Automatic detector. With practice, brain area #3 (left occipito-temporal area), called the automatic detector, becomes more active. The automatic detector takes on a bigger role by developing a permanent file of words so the reader can recognize words on sight, which makes reading a quick, automatic, and effortless process. Normally, these three processes work together almost simultaneously, like members of a team.

Why Can't People with Dyslexia Read?

One problem people with dyslexia have is that their phoneme producer is faulty so they cannot easily or quickly distinguish between phonemes (*ba, pa, la*), and this results in problems distinguishing between like-sounding words (*bark, park, lark*), which makes reading difficult. Another problem people with dyslexia have is defective neural wiring between the phoneme producer (#1) and the word analyzer (#2) and automatic detector (#3). As a result, they cannot easily or quickly recognize words or their meanings, which makes reading a slow and difficult process. Once diagnosed with dyslexia, a person does not outgrow it (T. Armstrong, 2010; Ferrer et al., 2010; Gorman, 2003; S. E. Shaywitz et al., 2003).

**ba
pa
la**

Can Training Help?

Because children with dyslexia have lasting deficits in the phoneme analyzer, researchers developed computer games to improve phoneme or sound processing, which is the first step in learning to read. After children with dyslexia played computer reading games, brain scans showed that they actually had increased neural activity in brain area #1, phoneme producer, and brain area #2, word analyzer. They also developed better reading skills, listening comprehension, and word recognition (T. Armstrong, 2010; Gaab, 2008; Temple et al., 2003).

Parents should encourage their children with dyslexia to play rhyming games and have them read aloud while gently correcting their mistakes. Rhyming and reading activities help these children develop correct associations between sounds and words (Gorman, 2003). According to Sally Shaywitz (2003), the most successful dyslexia interventions use the same core elements: practice with distinguishing between phonemes, building vocabularies, and increasing comprehension.

Recent research finds that children who have reading difficulties, regardless of whether they have normal or low IQs, demonstrate the same pattern of atypical brain function. These results suggest that the interventions designed to help children with dyslexia learn to read better should also be used with children who have both reading difficulties and low IQ scores (Tanaka et al., 2011). ●

Unless otherwise noted, all images are © Cengage Learning

H Cultural Diversity: Influences on Thinking

Americans Versus Asians

How does culture influence thinking?

If you spend most of your time in one culture, you probably don't realize how much your culture influences your thinking (Hong et al., 2000). For example, look at the underwater scene at the right and then look away and describe what you saw.

When American students looked at this underwater scene and then thought about what they saw, they usually began by describing the biggest, brightest, or most outstanding feature—in this case, focusing on the fish and what they were doing (swimming to the right). In contrast, Japanese students usually began by describing the background and saying the bottom was rocky (Had you noticed?) and the water was green (Had you noticed?). They usually discussed how the fish interact with the background, such as the fish were swimming toward the seaweed. On average, Japanese students made 70% more statements about

American students' descriptions of this drawing differed from Japanese students'.

By courtesy of Takehiko Masuda and Dr. Richard Nisbett, University of Michigan

how the background looked than Americans and 100% more statements about the way the objects (fish) interact with the background.

Based on these kinds of findings, researchers concluded that Americans usually analyze each object separately, which is called analytical thinking, such as seeing a forest and focusing on the biggest or strangest trees. In comparison, Asian people (Japanese, Chinese, and Koreans) think more about the relationship between objects and backgrounds, which is called holistic thinking, such as seeing a forest and thinking about how the many different trees make up a beautiful forest (Norenzayan & Nisbett, 2000). Researchers suggest that differences in thinking between Americans and Asians—analytical versus holistic—come from differences in social and religious practices and languages (Nisbett, 2000; Nisbett & Miyamoto, 2005).

Men Versus Women

Do men and women think differently?

Just as culture influences how we think, so do gender differences. Research shows that men and women think and use language differently (Tannen, 1990, 1994).

Differences in Thinking and Use of Language

Men more frequently use language to express ideas and solve problems.	Women more frequently use language to share concerns, daily experiences, and ordinary thoughts.
Men use language to maintain their independence and position in their group.	Women use language to create connections and develop feelings of intimacy.
Men prefer to attack problems by using problem-solving strategies.	Women prefer to listen and give support.

From Shaywitz, et al.,1995, "Sex differences in the functional organization of the brain for language," *Nature, 373*, 607–609. Courtesy of NMR Research/Yale Medical School

Tannen concluded that neither the female nor the male use of language, which strongly reflects how they think, is necessarily better; the two styles are just different.

Differences in How Brains Process Words

Not only do men and women use language differently, but their brains may process language differently. Researchers used fMRI brain scans (see p. 70) to identify which brain areas were most active during language tasks. In women, activity during certain word-processing tasks occurred almost equally in the right and left hemispheres. In contrast, in men, activity during the same word-processing tasks occurred in only the left hemisphere (B. A. Shaywitz et al., 1995). Other research did not find the same hemisphere differences between men and women, but found that both use different parts of the left hemisphere when processing language (Sommer et al., 2004). Differences in brain functioning between men and women do not indicate that one brain is better than another, only that they function differently (D. Halpern, 2003).

Difference in Language, Similarity in Thought

Count without words for numbers?

Is it possible to understand the concept of numbers without words for numbers? Brazil's Pirahã people (right photo) are the first group found anywhere that lack words in their language for specific numbers. Yet, Pirahã people can identify the number of items placed in front of them by selecting a matching number of items. They have accurate knowledge of numbers without words for specific numbers. Their language has words for only relative amounts, such as "some" and "more." Contrary to prior belief, counting may not be needed when it comes to thinking about quantity (B. Bower, 2008a; M. C. Frank et al., 2008).

Next, we'll discuss the interesting question of whether animals have language and if my (R. P.) dog really understands what I say. ●

I Application: Do Animals Have Language?

Criteria for Language

What does my dog understand?

Like most pet owners, I (R. P.) talk to my dog and he usually behaves as if he understands what I say. For example, my dog Bear (photo below) behaves as if he understands "get your toy," "go for walk," "time to eat," and "watch television." The obvious question is: Has Bear learned a language? The answer to this question hinges on the difference between communication and language. Like many animals, Bear has the ability to communicate.

Communication is the ability to use sounds, smells, or gestures to exchange information.

But language is much more than just communication.

Language is a special form of communication in which an individual learns complex rules for using words or gestures to generate and understand an endless number of meaningful sentences.

Although Bear can communicate—that is, understand my commands and act accordingly—he, like most animals, shows no evidence of meeting the four *criteria for language.*

Dogs communicate but don't have a language.

1 Language, which is a special form of communication, involves *learning a set of abstract symbols* (whether words for spoken language or hand signs for sign language).

2 Language involves *using abstract symbols* (words or signs) to express thoughts or indicate objects and events that may or may not be present.

3 Language involves *learning complex rules of grammar* for forming words into meaningful phrases and sentences.

4 Language involves using the rules of grammar to *generate an endless number of meaningful sentences.*

Because some animals, such as dolphins and pygmy chimps, show an amazing ability to communicate, researchers are debating whether animals can satisfy all four criteria for language (Begley, 1998a; Savage-Rumbaugh & Lewin, 1994). We'll examine how close several animals come to satisfying the four criteria.

Dolphins

Do dolphins use language?

Dolphins are considered very intelligent, not only because of their ability to learn but also because in proportion to the size of their bodies, dolphins' brains are the largest of nonhuman mammals (smaller than human brains but larger than brains of great apes) (Tyack, 2000). Because dolphins have relatively large brains, researchers are interested in how well they communicate.

In the wild, dolphins use two kinds of sounds for communication: clicks, which they use to probe the sea and "see" their environment, and whistles, which they use in dolphin-to-dolphin communication, probably to express emotional states and identify the animal to the group (L. Herman, 1999).

In testing the ability of dolphins to communicate, psychologist Louis Herman (1999) has been training dolphins to respond to hand signals or whistles. He has taught two dolphins to respond to approximately 50 such signals (see right photos for an example).

Herman found that dolphins can understand a variety of hand signals and perform behaviors in sequence. For example, the hand signal combination "basket, right, Frisbee, fetch" means "Go to the Frisbee on the right and take it to the basket."

More recently, Herman combined "words" by using gestures or whistles in basic "sentences," such as "ball fetch surface hoop." The two dolphins responded correctly to both familiar and novel "sentences" about 85% of the time. Herman concluded that the ability of these two dolphins to pass tests of language comprehension (understanding "sentences"), which indicates an

Hand signals tell dolphin to jump high in the air.

understanding of grammar or syntax, means that dolphins have a relatively sophisticated ability to use language (L. Herman, 1999).

Other evidence for dolphins having impressive communication abilities comes from watching a pair of dolphins carry out a complex sequence of movements in synchrony (referred to as "tandem" movements). Herman described these movements by saying that dolphins "may swim in a circle, leap out of water in a spinning motion, and spit water out of their mouths together" (L. Herman, 2006, p. 150). Researchers have yet to determine how dolphins actually communicate information to each other, such as what movements they make.

Despite Herman's impressive findings, some scientists remain skeptical. For example, David Kastak, a researcher of animal cognition, said, "What dolphins do may turn out to be a lot more complex than what we thought originally, but do they have what we would call language? No. They are not animals using nouns and verbs" (Mastro, 1999, p. E4).

Although dolphins understand a variety of signals, perform behaviors in sequence, form concepts, and even understand "sentences," they show little evidence of using abstract symbols and applying rules of grammar to generate meaningful sentences to communicate information to other dolphins. It is these criteria that distinguish the ability to use language from the ability to communicate with signs, sounds, or gestures.

Next, let's turn to the apes, which in terms of evolution are the animals closest to humans.

Gorillas and Chimpanzees

What language abilities do gorillas and chimpanzees have?

Gorillas and chimpanzees have relatively large and well-developed brains. A gorilla's brain weighs about 500 grams, a chimpanzee's about 400 grams, and a human's about 1,350 grams. However, because gorillas and chimpanzees lack the vocal apparatus necessary for making speech sounds, researchers have taught them other forms of language, such as American Sign Language (P. E. Ross, 1991). We'll share with you a few impressive examples of how gorillas and chimpanzees have been trained to use language.

Koko and Washoe. Shown on the right is researcher Francine Patterson using sign language to communicate with Koko the gorilla, who has a vocabulary of about 1,000 signs (Boysen, 2009). Similarly, Beatrice and Allen Gardner (1975) taught sign language to a chimpanzee named Washoe, who learned about 250 signs and passed her language skills on to her son (*Time*, 2007b). The finding that gorillas and chimps can learn sign language raised the question of whether they use language in the same way as humans.

Nim. Psychologist Herbert Terrace (1981) analyzed videotapes of chimps using sign language with their trainers. He was particularly interested in the videotapes of a chimp named Nim, who learned more than 125 signs, such as "give orange me." After observing over 20,000 of Nim's signs on videotape, Terrace concluded that Nim was using signs more as tools to obtain things than as abstract symbols or words and that Nim never learned to form combinations of more than a few words. Perhaps the most devastating criticism was that Nim had primarily learned to imitate or respond to cues from human teachers rather than learning and using rules of grammar to initiate or produce new sentences.

About ten years later, the study of language in animals made a major breakthrough with new findings on bonobos.

Kanzi. Psychologist Sue Savage-Rumbaugh reported that Kanzi, a bonobo (commonly called a pygmy chimp), had remarkable language skills that surpassed previous accomplishments of common chimps (Savage-Rumbaugh & Lewin, 1994; Shanker et al., 1999).

Instead of using sign language, Kanzi "speaks" by touching symbols on a board (top right photo), each of which stands for a word (Boysen, 2009). For example, Kanzi (bottom right photo) might signal "Want a drink" by touching the symbol for "drink" or signal "Want to play" by touching in sequence two symbols for "hiding" and "play biting."

By the time Kanzi was 6 years old, he had a vocabulary of 90 symbols; at age 12, he knew about 190 symbols but used about 128 regularly. Even more surprising, Kanzi understands nearly 400 spoken English words, something that common chimps have failed to master (Kluger, 2010).

Francine Patterson taught Koko the gorilla a vocabulary of about 1,000 hand signs.

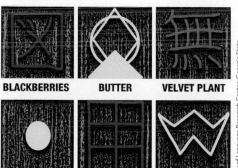

| BLACKBERRIES | BUTTER | VELVET PLANT |
| SHOT | STRING | PINE CONE |

Examples of symbols and their meanings

Kanzi has an amazing ability to use and respond to either symbols or English words.

Perhaps Kanzi's greatest accomplishment is his knowledge of word order and grammar. He can build thoughts and sentences by pointing to symbols (Kluger, 2010). Psychologists tested the ability of Kanzi to respond to 600 spoken English commands that he had not previously encountered, such as "Put the melon in the potty." Savage-Rumbaugh suggests that 17-year-old Kanzi has an ability to use abstract symbols (keyboard) and a kind of primitive grammar (word order, tense) for combining symbols that equals the language ability of a 2-year-old child (Savage-Rumbaugh, 1998).

Another chimp also communicates by using a keyboard with symbols.

Panzee. Trained to use a keyboard to press symbols that represent spoken words, Panzee recognizes 128 words. Though Panzee doesn't speak, she understands many spoken words, even when they are acoustically distorted (such as sounding fuzzy and noisy). Prior to Panzee, researchers believed that only humans could recognize distorted words. What is especially impressive is that Panzee did not need to be trained to recognize distorted words and that her accuracy is almost as good as that of humans (Heimbauer et al., 2011).

Conclusions. Although chimps can learn hundreds of symbols, string symbols together, and recognize acoustically distorted words, their language ability is nowhere near that of a high-school student, who has a vocabulary of 60,000 words and can string words together into an endless number of meaningful sentences (M. Hauser, 2003).

Researchers have examined why it is that humans developed a complex language while chimps did not. They now believe the development of human language was triggered by a major genetic change (R. Klein, 2002). This conclusion is based on the discovery of the first human gene *FOXP2* involved specifically in language. Individuals without this "language" gene are normal in other ways but not in communication; they have difficulties pronouncing words and speaking grammatically (Vargha-Khadem et al., 2005). Although ancient humans shared this gene with other animals, researchers discovered that there was an important change in this gene's structure when humans and chimps parted evolutionary company (Krause et al., 2007). The change in the structure of this "language" gene is believed by some to be the reason that humans developed complex, fluent language and chimps did not (Paabo, 2003). ●

Does Music Improve Language Skills in Children?

"Can you tell me how to get, how to get to Sesame Street?" *Sesame Street* has been using music to teach children language for over 40 years. We know children enjoy music. Infants attentively listen to their parents singing to them. Children often sing loudly to themselves and with their peers at school. They seem to be naturally wired for music. Many educators, parents, and television show creators have assumed singing helps children learn language faster. But the real question is whether music simply makes learning more accessible and entertaining for children, or whether it actually advances the learning of language.

A recent research study examined the relationship between musical training and language skills, and its results are really interesting. In this study, adults wore electrodes on their scalp to measure brain wave activity while watching and listening to a cellist perform and a person speak. The adults in the study consisted of musicians (with varying years of experience) and nonmusicians. Researchers originally expected the musicians to have an advantage (greater brain activity) only when it came to responding to the cellist and not to speech. However, the results showed that musicians had greater responses in their brains to both music and speech. Specifically, there was a positive correlation between years of musical training and activity in brain areas responsible for speech and communication.

These research findings indicate that musical training improves the same processing skills in the brain and nervous system needed for speaking and reading. If you consider the skills involved in learning music, this finding makes perfect sense. Music training requires the use of many senses, such as watching other musicians, reading lips, touching, and hearing the music. Singing, for example, is a phenomenal example of multisensory learning. When children sing, they use their ears to listen to the sounds and voices around them, their eyes to watch the movement of others, and their entire bodies to

1 What type of learning takes place as children listen to their parents sing?

2 Specifically, what is used to measure brain wave activity?

3 Does this correlation mean that a person with 20 years of musical training will have greater brain activity than a person with 5 years of musical training? Why or why not?

4 How many senses do we have? What are they? Which senses do we use when we play music?

5 According to Gardner's multiple-intelligence theory, which three types of intelligence are exhibited when children sing?

© DmitriMaruta/Shutterstock.com

develop rhythm and coordination. One beneficial outcome of this multisensory process is that it really facilitates learning. Generally, the more senses involved, the more learning takes place.

Over years of research it has become clear that musical training exercises the very same brain areas necessary for language skills. Teaching letters and words to children through songs is a very effective learning strategy and it helps make learning much more fun! Research clearly supports the work *Sesame Street* has being doing for decades: teaching children language through song and music. It turns out that *Sesame Street* and other similar children's television and DVD programs have been teaching language skills the right way all along.

6 Which type of aphasia would singing benefit most by helping people speak more fluently?

Adapted from Gadzikowski, 2007; Musacchia et al., 2007; Schon et al., 2008; Swaminathan, 2007; Tremmel, 2007; Warner, 2007

Unless otherwise noted, all images are © Cengage Learning

Summary Test

A Forming Concepts

1. There are two theories of how you have formed your concept of a dog and how you form concepts generally. If you form a concept of an object, event, or characteristic by making a list of the properties that define it, you are using the **(a)** _____ model. If you form a concept by constructing an idea of the ideal object and then seeing whether a new object matches that idea, you are using **(b)** _____ theory.

© Haig Kouyoumdjian

2. A concept is a way to group objects, events, or characteristics on the basis of some common property they all share. Concepts perform two important functions: They allow us to **(a)** _____ objects, and thus better organize and store information in memory, and to identify things without **(b)** _____.

B Solving Problems

© Craig McClair

3. The process of searching for some rule, plan, or strategy that results in reaching a certain goal that is currently out of reach is called **(a)** _____. We usually go through three states in solving problems: **(b)** _____, _____, and _____.

4. We win at games by following rules. If we correctly follow a set of rules that lead to a solution, these rules are called **(a)** _____. As you gain experience with solving problems, you may use rules of thumb that reduce the number of operations or allow you to take shortcuts in solving problems; these shortcuts are called **(b)** _____. In making everyday decisions, you rely on information that is more prominent or easily recalled and overlook other information that is available but less prominent or notable; this is an example of using the **(c)** _____ heuristic.

5. By studying how people eventually solve problems, psychologists have discovered a number of useful strategies, including changing our **(a)** _____. This often involves breaking out of a pattern called **(b)** _____, in which we cannot see an object as having a function different from its usual one.

6. A kind of thinking that is useful in solving problems is to find **(a)** _____, which are similarities between new situations and familiar situations. Still another useful strategy for solving problems is to break the problem down into a number of **(b)** _____, which, when completed in order, will result in a solution.

C Thinking Creatively

7. A combination of flexibility in thinking and reorganization of understanding to produce innovative ideas and solutions is referred to as **(a)** _____. Psychologists distinguish between two different kinds of thinking. If you begin with a problem and come up with the one correct solution, it is called **(b)** _____. If you begin with a problem and come up with many different solutions, it is called **(c)** _____, which is another definition of creative thinking.

© Victor Lerena/epa/Corbis

D Reasoning & Decision Making

© Vasi chenko Nikita/Shutterstock.com

8. Reasoning from a general assumption to particulars is called **(a)** _____. Reasoning from particulars to a general conclusion is called **(b)** _____.

9. A study on gambling found that even when people knew that their chances of winning and losing were identical, the wording of what they were told made a difference in their _____.

10. Whorf has suggested that language determines or influences the way people think and that people with different languages think and perceive their world differently. This is called the theory of _____.

E Language: Basic Rules

11. Our most impressive skill is thought to be a special form of communication in which an individual learns complex rules to manipulate symbols (words or gestures) and so generates an endless number of meaningful sentences; this form of communication is called _____.

12. All of the 6,909 known languages share four basic language rules, which are normally learned during childhood. The first language rule governs **(a)** _____, which specifies how we make meaningful sounds that are used by a particular language. The second language rule governs **(b)** _____, which specifies how we group phonemes into meaningful combinations of sounds and words. The third language rule governs **(c)** _____, which specifies how we combine words to form meaningful phrases and sentences. The fourth language rule governs **(d)** _____, which specifies the meanings of words in various contexts.

13. The linguist Noam Chomsky distinguished between how a sentence is worded, which he called the **(a)** _____ structure, and the meaning of the sentence, which he called the **(b)** _____ structure. Procedures for converting our ideas from surface structures into deep structures and from deep structures back into surface ones are called **(c)** _____.

F Acquiring Language

14. Children around the world acquire language in the same four stages that are associated with growth and development of the **(a)** _____. In the first stage, generally at about the age of 6 months, the infant makes one-syllable sounds; this is called **(b)** _____. By about 1 year of age, a child forms **(c)** _____, which usually refer to what the child can see, hear, or feel. At about 2 years of age, a child makes **(d)** _____ to express various actions or relationships. At about 4 years of age, a child is forming sentences, which range from three to eight words in length and indicate a growing knowledge of the **(e)** _____.

© Dereje/Shutterstock.com

15. A child's beginning sentences differ from adult sentences. A child's speech is called **(a)** _____ because it omits articles, prepositions, and parts of verbs. In learning the rules for combining nouns, verbs, and adjectives into meaningful sentences, children often apply a grammatical rule to cases where it should not be used. This type of error is called **(b)** _____. Although all children pass through these stages in the same order, they may go through them at different ages and speeds.

16. Children are able to acquire a language with so little formal training because of genetically programmed physiological and neurological features in the brain and vocal apparatus; these features are called **(a)** _____ factors. One innate factor is the period of time from infancy to adolescence when language is easier to learn, called the **(b)** _____. Children acquire the sounds and rules of a particular language because of their interactions with their surroundings; these interactions are called **(c)** _____ factors.

© miya227/Shutterstock.com

G Research Focus: Dyslexia

17. Dyslexia is an unexpected difficulty in **(a)** _____ despite intelligence, motivation, and education. The three steps in reading involve three different brain areas, each with a different function: Brain area #1 is called the **(b)** _____, brain area #2 is called the **(c)** _____, and brain area #3 is called the **(d)** _____. Individuals with dyslexia have a problem with changing letters into sounds or **(e)** _____ and have faulty **(f)** _____ connections between brain area #1 and brain areas #2 and #3.

ba
pa
la

H Cultural Diversity: Influences on Thinking

18. Men tend to use language to express ideas, maintain their position in the group, and solve **(a)** _____, while women use language more to share concerns and daily experiences and develop feelings of **(b)** _____.

Shaywitz, et al., 1995, Courtesy of NMR Research/Yale Medical School

19. The Pirahã people have accurate knowledge of numbers without **(a)** _____ for specific numbers. Their language has **(b)** _____ for only relative amounts.

I Application: Do Animals Have Language?

20. Many animals have the ability to use sounds, smells, or gestures to exchange information; this is the ability to **(a)** _____. Another question is whether animals can communicate with abstract symbols; this is called **(b)** _____. To decide that an animal truly uses language, researchers must show that the animal has learned complex rules of **(c)** _____ to manipulate symbols (words or gestures) and so generate an endless number of meaningful sentences.

© Michael Nichols/National Geographic Image Collection

Unless otherwise noted, all images are © Cengage Learning

Links to Learning

Key Terms/Key People

algorithms, 308
analogy, 309
availability heuristic, 308
babbling, 316
basic rules of grammar, 317
Chomsky's theory of language, 315
cognition, 305
cognitive approach, 305
communication, 322
concept, 306
confirmation bias, 312
convergent thinking, 310
creativity, 310
criteria for language, 322

critical language period, 318
deductive reasoning, 312
deep structure, 315
divergent thinking, 310
dyslexia, 320
environmental language factors, 318
exemplar model, 306
functional fixedness, 309
grammar, 314
heuristics, 308
inductive reasoning, 312
innate brain program, 315
innate language factors, 318
language, 305, 314, 322

language stages, 316
mental grammar, 315
mental set, 309
morpheme, 314
morphology, 314
overgeneralization, 317
parentese, 316
phonemes, 314
phonology, 314
problem solving, 308
productive vocabulary, 317
prototype, 306
prototype theory, 306
reasoning, 312
receptive vocabulary, 317

representative heuristic, 308
savants, 311
semantics, 314
sentences, 317
single words, 316
subgoals, 309
surface structure, 315
syntax or grammar, 314
telegraphic speech, 317
theory of linguistic relativity, 313
thinking, 305
transformational rules, 315
two-word combinations, 317
word, 314

Media Resources

Go to **CengageBrain.com** to access Psychology CourseMate, where you will find an interactive eBook, glossaries, flashcards, quizzes, videos, answers to Critical Thinking questions, and more. You can also access Virtual Psychology Labs, an interactive laboratory experience designed to illustrate key experiments first-hand.

Motivation

Why would a blind person climb the world's highest mountains?

Once a middle-school teacher and wrestling coach, Erik Weihenmayer has become one of the most respected and well known athletes in the world. In 2001, Erik climbed to the top of Mount Everest, the world's highest peak. In 2002, he stood on top of Mount Kosciuszko, completing his seven-year journey to climb the Seven Summits, the highest mountain on each of the seven continents. During these adventures, he endured severe winds, −70°F weather, and countless life-threatening situations.

Erik's quests were far from over. In 2003, he joined some of the world's best athletes to compete in the Primal Quest, the toughest multisport adventure race in the world, taking place over ten days across 457 miles of high elevation in the Sierra Nevadas. It involves intense kayaking, mountain biking, caving, whitewater rafting, and trekking. Averaging only 2 hours of sleep a night, Erik and his team became one of only about half of the teams to cross the finish line.

Erik accomplished these amazing feats while facing another major challenge: blindness. He is the only blind person in history to reach the summit of the world's highest peak, Mount Everest, and one of the youngest to climb the Seven Summits. Erik never allows his blindness to interfere with his pursuit of adventure and life fulfillment. For instance, his blindness is accompanied by increased eye pressure, which is exacerbated in high elevations. Erik described this pressure when he reached 19,000 feet during one of his climbs by saying, "It felt like someone stabbed me in the eye with a fork" (Weihenmayer, 1999). Yet, he continued to the top of the peak (adapted from Everest News, 1999; Touchthetop, 2009).

Reporters who question Erik about why he risks his life to climb and pursue dangerous adventures are really asking about his motivation.

Motivation is the various physiological and psychological factors that cause us to act in a specific way at a particular time.

When you are motivated, you usually show three characteristics:

1. You are *energized* to do or engage in some activity.
2. You *direct* your energies toward reaching a specific goal.
3. You have differing *intensities* of feelings about reaching that goal.

We can observe these three characteristics in Erik's behavior:

1. He was energized to engage in intense sport activities for ten days with little sleep or rest.
2. He directed his energy toward climbing peaks few people had ever conquered—in some cases making him the only blind person to do so.
3. He felt so intensely about reaching his goal that even when exhausted and feeling stabbing pain in his eye, he persisted in reaching the summit.

We'll discuss various motivating forces, including those involved in eating and drinking, sexual behavior, achievement, and, of course, climbing mountains.

Erik Weihenmayer, who is blind, climbed the Seven Summits, the tallest peak on every continent.

Achievement

Why did an NBA superstar pursue a doctorate degree?

Shaquille O'Neal, nicknamed "Shaq," is probably best known for his athletic achievements. He is a retired 15-time NBA all-star and played on four championship teams. In addition to his basketball career, Shaq has been an actor in several movies and has starred in his own reality show. Additionally, he has released five rap albums and has proved himself to be a successful businessman. One of Shaq's greatest achievements, however, has been his education.

Although many athletes are lured by the big money when they are recruited by a professional team and consequently discontinue their education, this was not the case with Shaq. Even after entering the NBA draft during his junior year in college, he continued to take courses to earn his bachelor's degree. More recently, Shaq went on to earn his doctorate degree in organizational learning and leadership. He is determined to continue his academic achievements by next attending law school. With pride, he insists on replacing his longtime nickname "Shaq" with "Dr. O'Neal" (ABC News Radio, 2012; O'Neal, 2012).

There is no denying that achievement is very important to Dr. O'Neal. We'll discuss the need for achievement, as well as why some people underachieve, later in this module.

Shaq's achievements have been in athletics, acting, music, business, and education.

What's Coming

We'll look at five general approaches or theories that psychologists use to explain motivation, and then focus on specific examples, including hunger, sexual behavior, and achievement. We'll examine why some people are achievers and others are underachievers. We'll discuss why people become overweight and why dieting is so difficult. We'll look at three serious eating disorders that result more from psychological than from biological factors.

We'll begin with five general theories that psychologists use to explain motivation. ●

Why does Erik climb? Many people who watch or hear about Erik engaging in his many dangerous climbs or other adventures ask, Why is he doing that? The same can be asked of you: Why are you willing to work hard for four to six years to get a college degree? These are questions about motivation. We'll discuss five general approaches or theories used to explain motivation.

Instinct Approach

Is he driven by instincts? In the early 1900s, William McDougall (1908) claimed that humans were motivated by a variety of instincts.

Instincts are innate tendencies or biological forces that determine behavior.

McDougall might have explained Erik's motivation to climb as arising from instincts involving curiosity and self-assertion. But attributing mountain climbing to an instinct is more like labeling than explaining the underlying motivation. At one point, psychologists had proposed over 6,000 instincts to explain every kind of human motivation. Although instincts proved useless in explaining human motivation, they proved useful in explaining animal behaviors because animal researchers redefined instincts as fixed action patterns (FitzGerald, 1993).

A **fixed action pattern** is an innate biological force that predisposes an organism to behave in a fixed way in the presence of a specific environmental condition.

Animals have innate biological tendencies called instincts.

For example, the above photo shows how a skunk is innately predisposed to behave in a fixed aggressive pattern—hissing, stamping its foot, raising its tail, and then releasing its powerfully scented spray—in the face of a threatening stimulus, such as a bear. Ethologists, researchers who study animal behaviors, reported that fixed action patterns help animals adapt to their natural environments. For example, in Module 10 (p. 228) we explained how birds that can walk immediately after birth become attached to, or imprinted on, the first moving object (animal, human, or basketball) that the baby bird encounters. Once imprinted, the baby bird continues to interact with that bird or object as if it were its parent. Imprinting is an example of a fixed action pattern that is extremely useful in helping young animals survive (Lorenz, 1952).

Instincts represented an early but failed attempt to explain human motivation. We'll examine more recent research that sheds a new light on human motivation.

Arousal Theory

One explanation for human motivation involves the relationship between arousal and performance; it is known as arousal theory.

What is your optimal level of arousal? **Arousal theory** states that we are motivated to seek out activities that provide a level of stimulation that allows us to maintain our optimal level of arousal.

According to arousal theory, our performance on a task may be compromised if the stimulation level is too high (such as anxiety) or too low (such as boredom). The relationship between level of arousal and performance on a task is called the Yerkes-Dodson law.

The **Yerkes-Dodson law** says that performance on a task is an interaction between the level of physiological arousal and the difficulty of the task. For difficult tasks, low arousal results in better performance; for most tasks, moderate arousal helps performance; and for easy tasks, high arousal may facilitate performance.

The graph on the right shows how the optimal level of arousal for best performance depends on the complexity of the task. We will revisit the Yerkes-Dodson law in Module 16 (see p. 365).

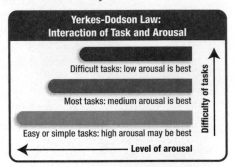

Yerkes-Dodson Law: Interaction of Task and Arousal

Difficult tasks: low arousal is best

Most tasks: medium arousal is best

Easy or simple tasks: high arousal may be best

Difficulty of tasks

Level of arousal

Why does Erik climb? The Yerkes-Dodson law would have a difficult time explaining why Erik climbs the tallest peaks on every continent, since these tasks are very difficult and involve a high level of arousal. The arousal approach would suggest that Erik is different from the average person because he is a sensation seeker.

A **sensation seeker** is someone who needs more arousal than the average person.

Sensation seekers look to engage in highly stimulating sensory experiences, such as mountain climbing, bungee jumping, skydiving, and drug use.

Reward/Pleasure Center Approach

What's his reward for climbing? During his climbs up to each of the Seven Summits, Erik was motivated to satisfy various biological needs, such as eating and drinking. One reason we are motivated to eat is that chewing on a favorite food can be so pleasurable. Researchers discovered that this "eating" pleasure comes from the brain's reward/pleasure center (Dallman et al., 2005).

The **reward/pleasure center** includes several areas of the brain, such as the nucleus accumbens and the ventral tegmental area, and involves several neurotransmitters, especially dopamine. These components make up a neural circuit that produces rewarding and pleasurable feelings.

People are motivated to eat, engage in sex, gamble, use recreational drugs, and listen to "spine-chilling" music because, as brain scans (fMRIs) have shown, all these behaviors activate the brain's reward/pleasure center (Bartels, 2002; Begley, 2001; Blood & Zatorre, 2001; K. Blum et al., 2011; Breiter et al., 2001; de Araujo et al., 2008; Grimm, 2007; Shizgal & Arvanitogiannis, 2003).

Nucleus accumbens

Ventral tegmental area

Reward/pleasure center

Why does Erik climb? Erik may climb because this behavior activates the brain's reward/pleasure center. He may also be motivated to climb by a variety of psychological factors, which we'll examine next.

Self-Determination Theory

What are psychological factors?

Motivation cannot be explained by only physiological factors, such as body arousal and activation of the reward/ pleasure center in the brain. Sometimes motivation is best explained by psychological factors, which are the focus of self-determination theory.

Self-determination theory states that as we aim to fulfill our basic needs, which include the need to feel autonomous, competent, and related to others, we experience either autonomous or controlled motivation.

When we experience autonomous motivation, our behaviors are self-motivated, whereas when we experience controlled motivation, our behaviors are motivated by external factors. Let's consider a behavior that is very familiar to you—studying. If *autonomous motivation* is the driving force behind your studying for an upcoming exam, then you are studying because you want to gain knowledge about the subject matter and do well in the course for your own satisfaction. If *controlled motivation* is the driving force behind your studying, then you are studying because you want to impress your parents, peers, or professor.

These examples of studying show that our motivation to engage in a task is related to incentives, which we'll discuss next.

Incentives

Why do you study?

Now that you're in college, what is motivating you to study for all those exams and write all those papers? One answer is that you are motivated to get a college degree because it is a very big incentive (Fiske, 2008; Petri & Govern, 2012).

The degree was worth the hard work!

Incentives are goals that can be either objects or thoughts that we learn to value and that we are motivated to obtain.

Incentives have two common features. First, they can be either thoughts ("I want to get a degree") or objects (money, clothes) that we LEARN to value. For example, when you were 5 years old, you had not yet learned the value of a good education. Second, the value of incentives can change over time. A pizza is not an incentive at 7 A.M., but it may be an important incentive at 7 P.M. Many of our behaviors are motivated by a variety of incentives, including grades, praise, money, clothes, or academic degrees. You can think of incentives as *pulling* us or motivating us to obtain them.

Why does Erik climb? Another reason Erik is motivated to climb probably involves obtaining incentives, such as recognition by national media, speaking invitations, and money from corporate sponsors and sales of his books. However, other equally powerful reasons for Erik's climbing probably involve intrinsic and extrinsic motivation, which is the original idea behind self-determination theory (Vansteenkiste et al., 2006).

Intrinsic & Extrinsic Motivation

Why do people run marathons?

Thousands of people train for months to run grueling 26-mile-long marathons, in which only the top two or three receive any prize money and the rest receive only T-shirts. What motivates people to endure such agony? The answer can be traced to the early 1960s, when psychologists began applying cognitive concepts to explain human motivation (Bandura, 1986; Deci & Ryan, 1985; Fiske, 2008; B. Weiner, 1991). These cognitive researchers said that one reason people run marathons, usually for no reward other than a T-shirt, has to do with the difference between extrinsic and intrinsic motivation.

I need to prove to myself that I can do it!

Extrinsic motivation involves engaging in certain activities or behaviors that either reduce biological needs or help us obtain incentives or external rewards.

Intrinsic motivation involves engaging in certain activities or behaviors because the behaviors themselves are personally rewarding or because engaging in these activities fulfills our beliefs or expectations.

Intrinsic motivation explains that people volunteer their services, spend hours on hobbies, run marathons, or work on personal projects because these activities are personally rewarding, fulfilling, or challenging. Intrinsic motivation emphasizes that we are motivated to engage in many behaviors because of our own personal beliefs, expectations, or goals, rather than external incentives (Linnenbrink-Garcia & Fredricks, 2008; Ryan & Deci, 2000).

Why does Erik climb? According to intrinsic motivation, another reason Erik is motivated to engage in dangerous and almost impossible climbs is that climbing itself is very rewarding to Erik. Erik began climbing to help him meet his own personal goals and expectations, which are powerful motivators. "Often," Erik said, "we are forced to throw out the expectations of others and rise to the level of our own internal potential" (Weihenmayer, 2009).

We will provide a more detailed discussion of intrinsic motivation when we discuss the cognitive factors in motivation (see p. 350).

The final explanation of human motivation we will discuss is Maslow's hierarchy of needs. As part of this discussion, we'll describe biological and social needs, which will help you to better understand Maslow's theory.

Maslow's Hierarchy of Needs

Which need gets satisfied?

You may remember from Module 1 that one of the founders of the humanistic approach in psychology was Abraham Maslow. Maslow was particularly interested in human motivation, especially in how we choose which biological or social need to satisfy. For example, should you study late for an exam and satisfy your social need to achieve, or go to bed at your regular time and satisfy your biological need for sleep? Maslow (1970) proposed that we satisfy our needs in a certain order or according to a set hierarchy (figure on opposite page).

Abraham Maslow

© Corbis

Maslow's hierarchy of needs is an ascending order, or hierarchy, in which biological needs are placed at the bottom and social needs at the top. According to Maslow's hierarchy, we satisfy our biological needs (bottom of hierarchy) before we satisfy our social needs (top of hierarchy).

Maslow hypothesized that, after we satisfy needs at the bottom level of the hierarchy, we advance up the hierarchy to satisfy the needs at the next level. However, if we are at a higher level and our basic needs are not satisfied, we may come back down the hierarchy.

Before we examine Maslow's hierarchy of needs in more detail, we'll discuss the difference between biological needs and social needs.

Do you always satisfy biological needs first?

© Ariwasabi/Shutterstock.com

Biological Needs

It's pretty obvious that the man standing in front of the refrigerator is about to satisfy his hunger, a basic biological need.

Satisfying biological needs

© Florea Marius Catalin/iStockphoto

Biological needs are physiological requirements that are critical to our survival and physical well-being.

Researchers have identified about a dozen biological needs, such as the needs for food, water, sex, oxygen, sleep, and pain avoidance, all of which help to keep our bodies functioning at their best and thus help us survive (Petri & Govern, 2012).

Biological drives are critical for survival and their automatic regulation is built into a newborn's brain. In rare cases, individuals are born with defective genes that cause biological needs to run amok. For example, some children are born with defective "eating" genes that result in never feeling full but being constantly hungry and obsessed with food and eating (Cassidy et al., 2012). Children with this genetic problem (the Prader-Willi syndrome affects the hypothalamus) can never be left alone with food because they will eat everything in sight.

Another rare genetic problem that affects only 40 families worldwide destroys the ability to sleep. As individuals with this genetic defect (fatal familial insomnia) reach their fifties, they find that one day they cannot sleep through the night and from then on they never sleep again. Over a period of several months, these individuals lose the ability to walk, speak, and think. Finally, within 15 months, their sleepless body shuts down its functions, resulting in coma and death (Grimes, 2006; Max, 2006). These two examples show that the proper regulation of biological needs is critical for healthy physiological functioning and survival.

Besides genetic defects, psychological factors can interfere with the regulation of biological needs. For example, some individuals develop the eating disorder anorexia nervosa, which involves self-starvation. Without professional help, these individuals may starve themselves to death. Eating disorders show how psychological factors can override basic biological needs. We'll discuss eating disorders in the Application section.

Although there are a relatively limited number of biological needs, there are many more social needs.

Social Needs

Getting married satisfies social needs.

© yeo2205/Shutterstock.com

One reason that about 90% of adults in the United States get married is that being married satisfies a number of social needs.

Social needs are needs that are acquired through learning and experience.

Depending on your learning and experiences, you may acquire dozens of social needs, such as the needs for achievement, affiliation (forming social bonds), fun (play), relaxation, helpfulness, independence, and nurturance (Petri & Govern, 2012).

In U.S. society, marriage satisfies a number of social needs, including affiliation, nurturance, and achievement. The need for affiliation, or forming lasting, positive attachments, is one of our stronger social needs and is important to maintaining physical health and psychological well-being (Simpson & Tran, 2006; Tay & Diener, 2011).

In some cases, the distinction between biological and social needs is blurred. For example, we may eat or drink not only to satisfy biological needs but also to make social contact or deal with stress. Similarly, we may engage in sex for reproduction, which is a biological need, or to express love and affection, which is a social need. Because we have only so much time and energy to satisfy a relatively large number of biological and social needs, how do we decide which needs to satisfy first? The answer may be found in Maslow's hierarchy.

Next, we'll examine Maslow's hierarchy of needs in more detail.

Which needs do you satisfy first? If you were very hungry and very lonely at the same time, which need would you satisfy first, your biological need (hunger) or your social need (affiliation)? One answer to this question can be found in Maslow's hierarchy of needs, which says that you satisfy your biological needs before you can turn your attention and energy to fulfilling your personal and social needs. According to Maslow, when it comes to satisfying your needs, you begin at the bottom of the needs hierarchy, with physiological needs, and then work your way toward the top. After you meet the needs at one level, you advance to the next level. For example, if your physiological needs at Level 1 are satisfied, you advance to Level 2 and work on satisfying your safety needs. Once your safety needs are satisfied, you advance to Level 3, and so forth, up the needs hierarchy.

Maslow's hierarchy of needs is represented by a pyramid and shows the order in which you satisfy your biological and social needs. The first needs you satisfy are physiological or biological ones, so please go to the bottom of the pyramid and begin reading Level 1. Then continue reading Levels 2, 3, 4, and 5, which takes you up the pyramid.

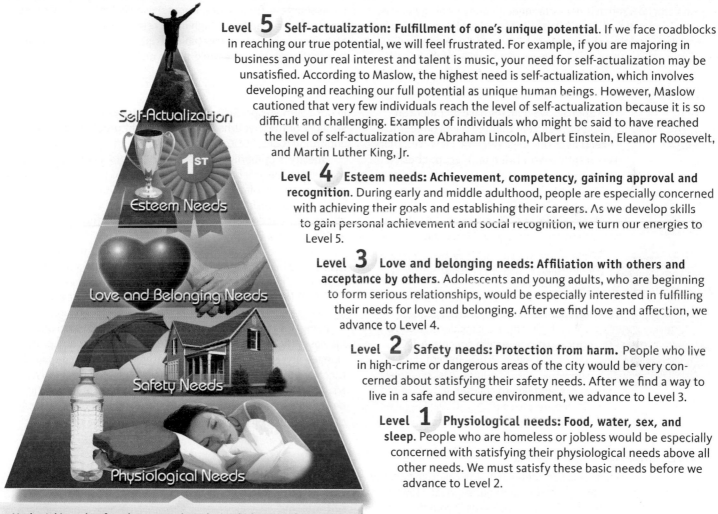

Level 5 Self-actualization: **Fulfillment of one's unique potential.** If we face roadblocks in reaching our true potential, we will feel frustrated. For example, if you are majoring in business and your real interest and talent is music, your need for self-actualization may be unsatisfied. According to Maslow, the highest need is self-actualization, which involves developing and reaching our full potential as unique human beings. However, Maslow cautioned that very few individuals reach the level of self-actualization because it is so difficult and challenging. Examples of individuals who might be said to have reached the level of self-actualization are Abraham Lincoln, Albert Einstein, Eleanor Roosevelt, and Martin Luther King, Jr.

Level 4 Esteem needs: **Achievement, competency, gaining approval and recognition.** During early and middle adulthood, people are especially concerned with achieving their goals and establishing their careers. As we develop skills to gain personal achievement and social recognition, we turn our energies to Level 5.

Level 3 Love and belonging needs: **Affiliation with others and acceptance by others.** Adolescents and young adults, who are beginning to form serious relationships, would be especially interested in fulfilling their needs for love and belonging. After we find love and affection, we advance to Level 4.

Level 2 Safety needs: **Protection from harm.** People who live in high-crime or dangerous areas of the city would be very concerned about satisfying their safety needs. After we find a way to live in a safe and secure environment, we advance to Level 3.

Level 1 Physiological needs: **Food, water, sex, and sleep.** People who are homeless or jobless would be especially concerned with satisfying their physiological needs above all other needs. We must satisfy these basic needs before we advance to Level 2.

Maslow's hierarchy of needs suggests the order in which we satisfy our needs.

Conclusion. One advantage of Maslow's hierarchy is that it integrates biological and social needs into a single framework and proposes a list of priorities for the order in which we satisfy various biological and social needs (Fiske, 2008; W. B. Frick, 2000).

One problem with Maslow's hierarchy is that researchers have found it difficult to verify whether his particular order of needs is accurate or to know how to assess some of his needs, especially self-actualization, which very few individuals are able to reach (Geller, 1982). Another problem is that people give different priorities to needs: Some may value love over self-esteem, or vice versa (Neher, 1991). We'll discuss Maslow's hierarchy of needs later on when we explain humanistic theories of personality (see p. 443). Despite criticisms of Maslow's hierarchy, it remains a useful reminder of the number and complexity of human needs.

To give you a sample of how psychologists study human motivation, we have selected two biological needs—food and sex—from Maslow's Level 1 and one social need—achievement—from Maslow's Level 4. We'll consider these needs in the following sections. ●

B Hunger

Optimal Weight

Why don't you see fat wolves?

The reason you never see fat wolves is that they, like all animals, have an inherited biological system that carefully regulates their eating so that they maintain their optimal, or ideal, weights (Kolata, 2000).

Optimal or **ideal weight** results from an almost perfect balance between how much food an organism eats and how much it needs to meet its body's energy needs.

In the wild, animals usually eat only to replace the fuel used by their bodies, and thus they rarely get fat. In addition, most wild animals use up a tremendous amount of energy in finding food.

Animals rely on a biological system to regulate weight.

© PhotoDisc, Inc.

In comparison, home pets may become fat because their owners, having the best of intentions, give the pets too much food or food so tasty that their pets eat too much. And unlike wild animals, home-bound pets may have few opportunities to run around and burn off the extra food or surplus calories.

A *calorie* is simply a measure of how much energy food contains. For example, foods high in fats (pizza, cheeseburgers, french fries, donuts) usually have several times more calories than foods high in protein (fish, chicken, eggs) or high in carbohydrates (vegetables, fruits, grains). The same factors that make pets overweight also make humans overweight.

Obesity

Why the huge increase?

Like animals, we humans have an inherited biological system that regulates hunger to keep us at our ideal weights. However, there is currently a worldwide problem of obesity.

Obesity means that a person is severely overweight, as measured by a body mass index (BMI) of 30 or higher.

Body mass index (BMI) is a number calculated from a person's weight and height. It is a measure of body fatness and is used to screen for weight categories that may lead to health problems, including underweight, overweight, and obesity.

Obesity rates in the United States have risen during the past several decades, remain high, and are considered to be a critical national health concern (CDC, 2012b; C. Ogden, 2010). Recent data show that 36% of adults, 20% of adolescents, and 18% of children in the United States are obese (CDC, 2010a; Flegal et al., 2012). The increasing rates of obesity

© Jose Manuel Gelpi Diaz/iStockphoto

36% of adult Americans are obese.

in our youth is especially concerning, as research shows that 50–80% of these youths will battle weight problems throughout adulthood (CDC, 2006a; Kotz, 2007a).

Obesity is primarily caused by two factors: eating more than is required to fuel the body's energy needs and not getting enough exercise to burn off surplus calories (CDC, 2006b). For example, some college freshmen gain 6 to 9 pounds, primarily because of all-you-can-eat dining halls and late-night junk food (Hellmich, 2008; Levitsky, 2003).

From an evolutionary perspective, consuming nutritionally dense food became necessary to provide energy needed for the demanding lifestyle of hunting and gathering. However, over time, our lifestyles have become increasingly sedentary, creating energy imbalances that explain our rising obesity rates (Leonard, 2009).

Being obese significantly shortens people's life span and increases their risk for heart disease, stroke, high blood pressure, clogged arteries, painful joints, breathing difficulties, sexual dysfunction, and adult-onset diabetes (Gorman, 2012; B. Healy, 2006; Hsu, 2006; Whitlock et al., 2009). In the United States, annual health care spending on weight-related medical issues in obese patients is $147 billion (Finkelstein et al., 2009).

Three Hunger Factors

What controls your eating?

Hunger is considered a biological drive because eating is essential to our survival. However, the way in which you satisfy your hunger drive—when, where, and how much you eat—is influenced by three different factors: biological, psychosocial, and genetic (J. O. Hill et al., 2003).

Biological hunger factors come from physiological changes in blood chemistry and signals from digestive organs that provide feedback to the brain, which, in turn, triggers us to eat or stop eating.

If your eating was regulated primarily by biological factors, as in most animals, you would keep your weight at optimal levels. The fact that so many people are obese or suffer from serious eating problems indicates the additional influence of both psychosocial and genetic factors.

Psychosocial hunger factors come from learned associations between food and other stimuli, such as snacking while watching television; sociocultural influences, such as pressures to be thin;

and various personality problems, such as depression, dislike of body image, or low self-esteem.

Genetic hunger factors come from inherited instructions found in our genes. These instructions determine the number of fat cells or metabolic rates of burning off the body's fuel, which push us toward being normal, overweight, or underweight.

© Gene Chutka/iStockphoto

Psychosocial hunger factors can override other factors.

These three hunger factors interact to influence our weight. For example, because of psychosocial factors, some of us eat when we should not, such as during stress. Because of biological factors, some of us may respond too much or too little to feedback from our digestive organs. Because of genetic factors, some of us can eat more calories and still maintain optimal weight.

We'll discuss these three hunger factors next.

Biological Hunger Factors

Why do you start eating?

A typical sumo wrestler is about 6 feet tall and weighs between 300 and 400 pounds, which is considered normal by sumo standards but obese by Western medical charts. Sumo wrestlers maintain their huge bodies by consuming up to 20,000 calories a day, which is six to seven times the amount required by an average-sized man. A sumo wrestler's eating is partly regulated by biological hunger factors, which come from peripheral and central cues (Cegla et al., 2010; K. Suzuki et al., 2010).

© J. Henning Buchholz/Shutterstock.com

Peripheral cues come from changes in blood chemistry or signals from digestive organs, which secrete various hormones.

Central cues result from activity in different brain areas, which in turn results in increasing or decreasing appetite.

Peripheral and central cues make up a complex biological system that evolved over millions of years to help humans and animals maintain their best weights for survival.

Peripheral Cues

Signals for feeling hungry or full come from a number of body organs that are involved in digestion and regulation of blood sugar (glucose) levels, which is the primary source of fuel for the body and brain.

1 When empty, the **stomach** secretes a hormone, ghrelin, which carries "hunger signals" to the brain's hypothalamus, the master control for hunger regulation (K. Suzuki et al., 2010). When the stomach is full, stretch receptors in its walls send "full signals" to the brain's hypothalamus, which decreases appetite (Chaudri et al., 2006; Kluger, 2007a).

2 The **liver** monitors the level of glucose (sugar) in the blood. When the level of glucose (blood sugar) falls, the liver sends "hunger signals" to the brain's hypothalamus; when the level of glucose rises, the liver sends "full signals" to the hypothalamus (Woods et al., 2000).

3 The **intestines** also secrete ghrelin, which carries "hunger signals" to the hypothalamus, increasing appetite. The intestines also secrete another hormone called PYY, which carries "full signals" to the hypothalamus, decreasing appetite. Finally, the intestines secrete a hormone called CCK (cholecystokinin), which signals the hypothalamus to inhibit eating (Delzenne et al., 2010).

4 **Fat cells** secrete a hormone, called leptin, that acts on the brain's hypothalamus. If levels of leptin are falling, the hypothalamus increases appetite; if levels are rising, the hypothalamus decreases appetite. The secretion of leptin helps maintain a constant level of body fat and defend against starving the body to death (Rui, 2005).

Summary. The stomach and intestines secrete a number of "hunger" or "full" hormone signals that act on the hypothalamus, which is the master control for regulating eating and produces central cues for increasing or decreasing appetite.

Central Cues

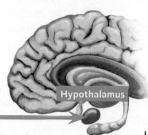
Hypothalamus

1 The brain has an area with different groups of cells that are collectively called the **hypothalamus**. Each group of cells is involved in a different kind of motivation, including regulation of thirst, sexual behavior, sleep, intensity of emotional reactions, and hunger. We'll focus on two groups of cells, the lateral and ventromedial hypothalamus, that affect hunger in opposite ways, either increasing or decreasing appetite.

2 The **lateral hypothalamus** is a group of brain cells that receive "hunger signals" from digestive organs—increase in ghrelin, fall in level of blood glucose, and fall in levels of leptin. The lateral hypothalamus interprets these "hunger signals" and increases your appetite (Kluger, 2007a; Woods et al., 2000).

For example, electrical stimulation of the lateral hypothalamus causes rats to start eating, while destruction of the lateral hypothalamus causes rats to stop eating and even starve without special feeding.

3 The **ventromedial hypothalamus** is a group of brain cells that receive "full signals" from digestive organs—a full stomach activates stretch receptors, rise in level of blood glucose, rise in levels of leptin, and increase in the hormones PYY and CCK. The ventromedial hypothalamus interprets these "full signals" and decreases appetite.

For example, stimulation of the ventromedial hypothalamus causes rats to stop eating, while destruction of the ventromedial hypothalamus causes rats to overeat. Research with rats genetically prone to obesity shows that certain brain cells in their hypothalamus don't grow much and are less sensitive to leptin, compared with other rats (Bouret et al., 2008). In addition, various chemicals affect other cells of the hypothalamus and regulate our appetites for specific foods (Kluger, 2007a).

Summary. The hypothalamus is involved in regulating different kinds of motivated behaviors; in this case, we focused on hunger. The hypothalamus has one group of cells, called the lateral hypothalamus, that respond to "hunger signals" by increasing your appetite so you start eating. The hypothalamus has another group of cells, called the ventromedial hypothalamus, that respond to "full signals" by decreasing your appetite so you stop eating. This wonderfully complex biological system for regulating hunger is hard-wired and present in a newborn's brain. Although this system is designed to keep us at our ideal weights, we'll discuss genetic and psychological factors that can interfere with this system and cause overeating and even starvation.

Genetic Hunger Factors

Researchers generally find that identical twins (photo on right), even when separated soon after birth and reared in adopted families, are much more alike in weight than fraternal twins reared apart (T. J. Bouchard et al., 1990). This similarity in weight is due to genetic hunger factors.

Are identical twins always the same weight?

Genetic hunger factors come from inherited instructions found in our genes. These instructions determine the number of fat cells or metabolic rates of burning off the body's fuel, which push us toward being normal, overweight, or underweight.

On the basis of twin studies, researchers concluded that inherited factors contribute 70–80% to

Identical twins share the same genes and thus are similar in weight.
© Cohen/Ostrow/Getty Images

the maintenance of a particular body size and weight, while environmental factors contribute the other 20–30% (Bulik et al., 2003). The finding that genetic hunger factors contribute 70–80% to having a certain body size and weight explains why identical twins have similar body types. The finding that environmental factors contribute 20–30% to body size explains why one twin may weigh a little more or less than the other.

Research shows that people who have a commonly found variation of a gene are at an increased risk of becoming obese. Scientists now believe there may be as many as 100 different fat genes and are working to identify them (C. Bouchard, 2009; Christman, 2006).

So far, psychologists have identified four genetic hunger factors.

1 We inherit different numbers of fat cells.

Fat cells, whose number is primarily determined by heredity, do not normally multiply except when people become obese. Fat cells shrink if we are giving up fat and losing weight (left) and greatly enlarge if we are storing fat and gaining weight (right) (Fried, 2008; Spalding et al., 2008).

People who inherit a larger number of fat cells have the ability to store more fat and are more likely to be fatter than average.

2 We inherit different rates of metabolism.

Metabolic rate refers to how efficiently our bodies break food down into energy and how quickly our bodies burn off that fuel.

For example, if you had a low metabolic rate, you would burn less fuel, be more likely to store excess fuel as fat, and thus may have a fatter body. In comparison, if you had a high metabolic rate, you would burn off more fuel, be less likely to store fat, and thus may have a thinner body (left figure). This means that people can consume the same number of calories but, because of different metabolic rates, may maintain, lose, or gain weight. There are only two known activities that can raise metabolic rate: exercise and smoking cigarettes. Research shows that exercise raises metabolic rate 20–30% and nicotine raises it 4–10%. That's the reason exercise helps dieters lose weight and smokers generally gain weight when they stop smoking (Aamodt & Wang, 2008; Audrain et al., 1995).

© olly/Shutterstock.com

3 We inherit a set point to maintain a certain amount of body fat.

The **set point** is a certain level of body fat (adipose tissue) that our bodies strive to maintain constant throughout our lives.

For example, a person whose body has a higher set point will try to maintain a higher level of fat stores and thus have a fatter body (right figure). In comparison, a person whose body has a lower set point will maintain a lower level of fat stores and thus have a thinner body (Woods et al., 2000). If a person diets to reduce the level of fat stores, the body compensates to maintain and build back fat stores by automatically lowering the metabolic rate and thus consuming less fuel. That's the reason dieters may lose weight for the first two or three weeks and then stop losing; the body has lowered its metabolic rate. Researchers have concluded that because the body protects its fat stores, long-term dieting will be unsuccessful in treating overweight people unless they also exercise (Leibel et al., 1995).

olly/Shutterstock.com

4 We also inherit weight-regulating genes.

Weight-regulating genes play a role in influencing appetite, body metabolism, and secretion of hormones (leptin) that regulate fat stores.

For example, the mouse on the left has a gene that increases a brain chemical (neuropeptide Y) that increased eating, so it weighs three times as much as the normal-weight mouse on the right (Gura, 1997). Researchers have also found a gene that can jack up metabolism so that calories are burned off as heat rather than stored as fat (Warden, 1997). In total, researchers have found 11 genetic mutations than can disrupt appetite regulation, leading someone to continue to eat without feeling full (Kluger, 2007a).

You have seen how genetic hunger factors are involved in the regulation of body fat and weight. But genes alone cannot explain our obesity epidemic (Gillman, 2007).

Next, we'll explore several psychological factors involved in the regulation of eating and weight.

Courtesy of Jeffrey M. Friedman, Rockefeller University

Unless otherwise noted, all images are © Cengage Learning

Psychosocial Hunger Factors

Always room for dessert? Many of us have a weakness for certain foods, and mine (H. K.) is for desserts. Even though my biological and genetic hunger factors may tell me (my brain) when to start and stop eating, I can use my large forebrain to override my innately programmed biological and genetic factors. My forebrain allows me to rationalize that one dessert can do no harm. This kind of rationalizing comes under the heading of psychosocial hunger factors.

Psychosocial hunger factors come from learned associations between food and other stimuli, such as snacking while watching television; sociocultural influences, such as pressures to be thin; and various personality traits, such as depression, dislike of body image, or low self-esteem.

We'll discuss three psychosocial hunger factors—learned associations, social-cultural influences, and personality and mood factors.

Learned Associations

The best examples of how *learned associations* influence eating are when we eat not because we're hungry but because it's "lunchtime," because foods smell good, because our friends are eating, or because we can't resist large portions (Hellmich, 2005).

It's tough to pass on supersizing, even though we don't need it all.

Americans often rely on external cues to stop eating, such as researching the end of a TV program or getting to the bottom of a soda, which, combined with a preference for large portions and tasty junk foods high in calories, has led to a rising rate of obesity in both children and adults (Hellmich, 2005; Rozin et al., 2003; Wansink et al., 2007).

One experiment demonstrated the strength of our learned association to eat until our plates are empty, no matter how large the portion. One group of people were served soup out of a self-refilling bowl that was pressure-fed from under the table and very slowly refilled without people noticing. Another group ate soup in regular bowls. The participants who ate from the self-filling bowls ate 73% more than the people in the other group, yet they didn't report feeling more full (Wansink et al., 2005).

Health professionals advise us to eat only when hungry and eat smaller portions and healthier foods (Pi-Sunyer, 2003; Story et al., 2008).

Social-Cultural Influences

Here are examples of how *social-cultural influences* affect body weight.

Czech Republic. In the 1970s, the Czech Republic government subsidized cheap fatty sausage and dairy products. The result was that 45% of Czech women and a smaller percentage of men became obese. Also, the Czech Republic has the world's highest death rates from heart disease. The government instituted programs to encourage healthier eating habits, which were effective until fast-food restaurants opened all over the country (Elliott, 1995; Jarrett, 2006).

China. In parts of China, fatty fast foods have become very popular along with a more sedentary lifestyle. This resulted in an increase in obesity rates from 12.8% in 1991 to 29% in 2006 (CDC, 2008c). In addition, there has been an alarming increase in obesity among children, who are pampered by a culture that prizes well-nourished children as indicating affluence and well-being (Mydans, 2003).

The situation is very different for women in China, who are always looking for ways to get skinnier. One of the recent diet fads, for instance, is swallowing parasites, which could cause serious health problems, including death (K. Chu, 2010). Researchers state that dieting for women in China (and other parts of Asia) is more severe than in the United States because of the cultural perceptions of beauty (K. Chu, 2010).

Some women in Asia swallow parasites to lose weight.

United States. In the United States, there are many cultural pressures on females, in particular, to be thin. For example, the mass media advertise that the ideal female is one with a slender body (think of size-0 models). As a result, many American females report being dissatisfied with their weight and see themselves as overweight even when they are not. Some also develop an eating disorder as a result (Mayo Clinic, 2006a).

Personality & Mood Factors

If a person has certain *personality traits,* he or she may be at greater risk for overeating as well as developing eating disorders, such as overeating when stressed or depressed, going on food binges (bulimia nervosa), or starving oneself (anorexia nervosa).

The particular personality traits that have been associated with eating problems include heightened sensitivity to rejection, excessive concern with approval from others, high personal standards for achievement, and the need to have control (over oneself or one's body) (Polivy & Herman, 2002). Someone with these kinds of personality traits, which are often accompanied by stress, anxiety, and emotional upset, may find it very difficult and sometimes almost impossible to control his or her eating (J. E. Brody, 2003).

Mood factors, such as stress, anxiety, and depression, can lead to bursts of overeating or indulgence in sweet and unhealthy foods. Overeating when under emotional strain is called "emotional eating" and occurs in other-wise healthy people (Macht, 2007).

Although hunger is considered a biological need, you have seen how psychosocial hunger factors can influence where, when, and how the hunger drive is satisfied. And, as we'll discuss in the Application section, there are extreme cases in which psycho-social factors can override the hunger drive.

Next, we'll discuss another very important biological need, sexual behavior. ●

I look too fat!

Personality traits influence eating habits.

C Sexual Behavior

Why do lions know how to do it?

Although we don't look, sound, or behave the same as tigers do, we share similar biological and genetic factors that regulate sexual behavior. The sexual behavior of tigers and most animals is controlled chiefly by genetic and biological factors, which means that most animals engage in sex primarily for reproduction.

Genetic sex factors include inherited instructions for the development of sexual organs, the secretion of sex hormones, and the wiring of the neural circuits that control sexual reflexes.

Biological sex factors include the action of sex hormones, which are involved in secondary sexual characteristics (facial hair, breasts), sexual motivation (more so in animals than in humans), and the development of ova and sperm.

Tigers, like most animals, generally avoid sexual interactions unless the female is in heat, which means she is ovulating and can be impregnated. In comparison, humans

In most animals, sexual behavior is regulated by genetic and biological factors.

engage in sexual behavior for many reasons, which points to psychological sex factors.

Psychological sex factors play a role in developing a sexual or gender identity, gender role, and sexual orientation. In addition, psychological factors can result in difficulties in the performance or enjoyment of sexual activities.

For example, otherwise healthy men and women may report difficulties in sexual activities arising from stress, anxiety, or guilt, which can interfere with the functioning of genetic and biological sex factors. One reason psychological factors play such an important role in human sexual behavior is that our large forebrains have the capacity to think, reason, and change our minds and thus increase, interfere with, or completely block sexual motivation, performance, or enjoyment.

As we did for the hunger drive, we'll discuss, in order, the influences of genetic, biological, and psychological factors on sexual behavior.

Genetic Influences on Sexual Behavior

Which sex organ?

How we develop a particular sex organ, male or female, is determined primarily by a genetic program that is contained in a single human cell about the size of a grain of sand (Faller et al., 2004).

Sex Chromosome

Unlike the other cells of our body, which contain 46 chromosomes (23 pairs), the sperm and egg each contain half that number and are called sex chromosomes (figure below).

The **sex chromosome,** which is in the sperm or the egg, contains 23 chromosomes,

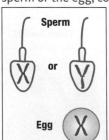

which in turn have genes that contain instructions for determining the sex of the child.

As we discussed earlier (see p. 68), each chromosome is made up of a long strand of DNA (deoxyribonucleic acid). On this long strand of DNA are hundreds of genes, which contain the chemically coded instructions for the development and maintenance of our bodies. In the figure above, notice that some sperm have an X chromosome and some have a Y, which contain different genetic instructions and, as you'll see, result in the development of different sex organs (penis or vagina).

Egg

The human egg contains one of the sex chromosomes, which is always an X chromosome. Thus, each human egg has a single X chromosome.

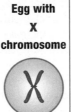

Egg with X chromosome

Fertilization

During fertilization, a single sperm penetrates an egg and results in a fertilized egg with 23 pairs of chromosomes. If the last pair has the combination **XY,** it means the egg contains the genetic instructions for developing a male's sex organs (top right figure). If the last pair has the combination **XX,** it means the egg contains the genetic instructions for developing a female's sex organs (bottom right figure).

After fertilization, the human cell, which is called a *zygote,* will divide over and over many thousands of times during the following weeks and months and eventually develop into a female body with female sex organs or a male body with male sex organs.

How an unborn infant actually develops male or female sex organs is an interesting story, especially since everyone begins as a female.

Sperm

A human sperm also contains one of the sex chromosomes. However, the sperm's chromosome can be either an X chromosome, which has instructions for the development of *female sex organs* and body, or a Y chromosome, which has instructions for male sex organs and body. Thus, the sperm (**X** or **Y**) determines the sex of the infant.

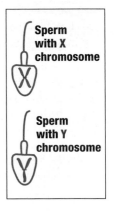

Sperm with X chromosome

Sperm with Y chromosome

Male instructions

XY

Female instructions

XX

Genetic Influences (continued)

Differentiation

Although it would seem that at fertilization you are destined to be either a male or a female, there is actually no physical difference between a male and a female embryo for the first four weeks of development in the womb. During this time period, the embryos are identical and have the potential to develop into either a male or a female. At about the fifth week, the embryo begins to differentiate into either a male or a female because of the presence or absence of certain sex hormones (Bendsen et al., 2006).

Male Sex Organ and Male Brain

XY = High Testosterone

Presence of **high** testosterone results in a male brain.

In an embryo that began from an **XY** fertilized egg, the **Y** sex chromosome has instructions for the development of male testes. At about the fifth week, the testes begin to grow and produce tiny amounts of male hormones or *androgens,* one of which most people know as *testosterone.*

The presence of high testosterone does two things: It triggers the development of the male sexual organ (penis), and it programs a particular area of the brain, called the hypothalamus, so that at puberty it triggers the pituitary gland to secrete hormones on a continuous basis, which results in the continuous production of sperm.

Female Sex Organs and Female Brain

XX = Low Testosterone

Presence of **low** testosterone results in a female brain.

In an embryo that began from an **XX** fertilized egg, the second **X** sex chromosome contains instructions for the development of ovaries.

The presence of low testosterone in the developing embryo does two things: It leads to the automatic development of female sexual organs (clitoris and vagina), and the hypothalamus, which is normally programmed for female hormonal functions, keeps its female program. Thus, at puberty, this female-programmed hypothalamus triggers the pituitary gland to secrete hormones on a cyclic basis, which results in the menstrual cycle.

Importance of Testosterone

The *presence* of testosterone, which is secreted by fetal testes, results in male sexual organs and a male hypothalamus; the *absence* of testosterone results in female sexual organs and a female hypothalamus (Kalat, 2013).

When the infant is born, the doctor identifies the infant's sex organs and says those famous words, "It's a boy" or "It's a girl." At that point a hormonal clock begins ticking and its alarm will set off biological factors at puberty.

Biological Influences on Sexual Behavior

You have seen how genetic sex factors influence the development of the body's sex organs. The next big event to affect a person's sex organs and sexual motivation occurs at puberty as a result of biological sex factors.

Sex hormones secreted during puberty both directly and indirectly affect our bodies, brains, minds, personalities, self-concepts, and mental health. We'll focus on how sex hormones affect our bodies.

Sex hormones. Before and shortly after birth, sex hormones are released in our bodies.

Sex hormones, which are chemicals secreted by glands, circulate in the bloodstream to influence the brain, body organs, and behaviors. The major male sex hormones secreted by the testes are **androgens,** such as testosterone; the major female sex hormones secreted by the ovaries are **estrogens.**

Sex hormones remain inactive until puberty, when a hormone called kisspeptin stimulates the production of androgens and estrogens to prepare the body for reproduction (Roa et al., 2008).

Male–female differences. The presence or absence of testosterone in the womb causes different neural programming so that the hypothalamus functions differently in males and females.

The *hypothalamus in males* triggers a continuous release of androgens, such as testosterone, from the testes. The increased level of androgens causes the development of male secondary sexual characteristics, such as facial and pubic hair, muscle growth, and lowered voice.

The *hypothalamus in females* triggers a cyclical release of estrogens from the ovaries. The increased level of estrogens causes the development of female secondary sexual characteristics, such as pubic hair, breast development, and widening of the hips. The cyclical release of hormones (estrogen and progesterone) also regulates the menstrual cycle.

Testosterone

Male hypothalamus triggers release of **testosterone.**

Estrogen

Female hypothalamus triggers release of **estrogen.**

Sexual Motivation

In humans, normal sexual development and motivation depend upon levels of sex hormones being within the normal range. In rare cases, males are born with an extra X chromosome, XXY or *Klinefelter's syndrome,* which results in undersized testes and penis, decreased secretion of testosterone, infertility, no development of secondary sexual characteristics at puberty, and little or no interest in sexual activity. However, when given testosterone replacement at puberty, these males regain sexual interest and drive (Lanfranco et al., 2004). Thus, the absence of sex hormones interferes with normal sexual development and motivation.

Several recent studies have found fascinating relationships between one sex's hormones or chemical signals and the other sex's level of sexual motivation and desire. For instance, researchers reported that women's ovulatory cycle affects their success as lap dancers in gentlemen's clubs. Specifically, during the time of their cycle when there is an increase in sexual hormones, women earned the most money giving men lap dances (G. Miller et al., 2007). Also, women's emotional tears have been found to contain a chemical signal that reduces sexual arousal in men, and also decreases men's testosterone levels (Gelstein et al., 2011). Last, researchers reported that women can distinguish among different types of male sweat, such as male sexual sweat, which activates several areas of their brains, including the hypothalamus (Zhou & Chen, 2008).

As genetic and biological factors guide our bodies toward physical sexual maturity, numerous psychological factors are preparing our minds for psychological sexual maturity. Next, we'll examine these psychological sex factors.

Psychological Influences on Sexual Behavior

How do boys and girls become men and women?

As boys and girls go through puberty, various genetic and biological factors prepare their bodies for sexual maturity (Ojeda et al., 2006). At the same time their bodies are developing, boys and girls are observing, imitating, and learning behaviors of their mothers, fathers, older siblings, and other adults in their environments. At this point, psychological sex factors come into play.

Psychological sex factors play a role in developing a sexual or gender identity, gender role, and sexual orientation. In addition, psychological factors can result in difficulties in the performance or enjoyment of sexual activities.

XY = Testosterone

XX = Estrogen

Sex hormones activate many physical and psychological changes.

Genetic, biological, and psychological sex factors combine and interact to result in boys and girls developing into sexually mature men and women.

Three psychological sex factors are especially important—gender identity, gender roles, and sexual orientation. We'll discuss each in turn, beginning with gender identity.

Gender Identity

Between the ages of 2 and 3, a child can correctly answer the question "Are you a boy or a girl?" The correct answer indicates that the child has already acquired the beginnings of a gender identity (Blakemore, 2003).

Gender identity, which was formerly called sexual identity, is the individual's subjective experience and feelings of being either a male or a female.

The doctor's words, "It's a girl" or "It's a boy," set in motion the process for acquiring a gender identity. From that point on, parents, siblings, grandparents, and others behave toward male and female infants differently, so that they learn and acquire their proper gender identity (C. L. Martin et al., 2002). For example, the little girl in the right photo is trying on high-heeled shoes, necklace, and purse, behaviors that she has observed her mother doing and that she is now imitating.

Gender identity is a psychological sex factor that exerts a powerful influence on future sexual thoughts and behavior, as clearly illustrated in the case of someone with a gender identity disorder.

By age 3, children know if they are boys or girls.

Gender identity disorder is commonly referred to as transsexualism. A transsexual is a person who has a strong and persistent desire to be the other sex, is uncomfortable about being one's assigned sex, and may wish to live as a member of the other sex (American Psychiatric Association, 2000).

Transsexuals usually have normal genetic and biological (hormonal) factors, but for some reason, they feel and insist that they are trapped in the body of the wrong sex and may adopt the behaviors, dress, and mannerisms of the other sex. There is no clear understanding of why transsexuals reject their biological sex; no physical cause or connection has been identified (McHugh, 2009). Because transsexuals acquire gender identities that do not match their external sex organs, they experience problems in thinking and acting and may not easily fit into or be accepted by society (Friess, 2009).

The persistent negative emotional state that occurs when there is a disconnect between a person's biological sex and gender identity is called **gender dysphoria.**

Gender dysphoria is often a factor in the decision of some transsexuals to undergo surgery to change the sex organs they were born with into those of the other sex (Bering, 2010). An example of a person with gender dysphoria is Chaz Bono, formerly named Chastity, who was the daughter, now son, of world-renowned entertainers Sonny and Cher. Chaz is a female-to-male transsexual. The process of transitioning from female to male involved breast removal and testosterone treatment, which has deepened Chaz's voice and given him facial hair. During an interview on national television, Chaz stated, "As a child, it was really clear. I felt like a boy....As you get older, it gets more confusing, because suddenly there's more pressure to fit into your assigned gender identity" (Bono, 2009). Now that he is living life as a man, Chaz has found happiness and is thankful that he can finally be who he really is (Zuckerman, 2009).

Chaz Bono is an example of a female-to-male transsexual.

Another well-known case of gender dysphoria involved doctors who, while performing a routine medical procedure to repair an 8-month-old male's foreskin, accidentally destroyed the infant's penis. As a result, doctors advised the parents to raise the boy (John) as a girl (Joan). However, since about the age of 8, Joan had been unhappy being and acting like a female and began to suspect that she was really a boy. By the time Joan was 14, she had received corrective surgery (a vagina) and hormonal treatment to physically look like a girl (developed breasts) but was so unhappy she threatened suicide and told doctors she thought she was a boy. After much discussion, doctors agreed to help Joan change back to John. In his thirties, John got married and reported that he had never liked being a female and was very happy being a male.

Researchers believe that individuals are genetically and biologically predisposed to have a male or female gender identity, which is not easily changed by being raised a certain way (boy or girl) (M. Diamond & Sigmundson, 1997).

As you acquire a male or female gender identity, you are also acquiring a matching gender role, which we'll discuss next.

Gender Roles

After the first step in becoming psychologically sexually mature, which is acquiring a male or female gender identity—"I'm a boy" or "I'm a girl"—comes the second step, which is acquiring a gender role.

Gender roles, which were formerly called sex roles, are the traditional or stereotypical behaviors, attitudes, and personality traits that society designates as masculine or feminine.

Between the ages of 3 and 4, American children learn the stereotypical or traditional expectations regarding the kinds of toys, clothes, and occupations for men and women. By the age of 5, children have acquired many of the complex thoughts, expectations, and behaviors that accompany their particular gender role of male or female (Best & Thomas, 2004).

For example, young boys learn stereotypical male behaviors, such as playing sports, competing in games, engaging in rough-and-tumble play, and acquiring status in his group. In comparison, girls learn stereotypical female behaviors, such as providing and seeking emotional support, emphasizing physical appearance and clothes, and learning to cooperate and share personal experiences (Ruble et al., 2006; Rudman & Glick, 2008).

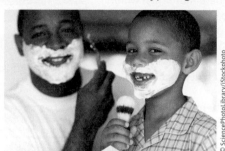

By age 5, a child knows how a boy or girl **behaves**.

As children, we all learned early on to adopt a male or female gender role, often without being aware of how subtly we were rewarded for imitating and performing appropriate sex-typed behaviors. Learning and adopting a gender role continue through adolescence and into adulthood and result in very different gender roles. For instance, adult American women tend to show stereotypical gender roles that can be described as socially sensitive, nurturing, and concerned with others' welfare. In comparison, adult American men tend to show gender roles that can be described as dominant, controlling, and independent (Eagly et al., 2004; Rudman & Glick, 2008).

A major function of gender roles is to influence how we think and behave. Notice that male gender roles—dominant, controlling, and independent—can lead to different kinds of sexual thoughts and behaviors than female gender roles—socially sensitive, nurturing, and concerned. Thus, some of the confusion, conflict, and misunderstanding over sexual behavior come from underlying differences in gender roles. A major task a couple will have in establishing a healthy, loving relationship is to work out the many differences in thoughts, beliefs, and expectations that come from combining two different gender roles.

Sexual Orientation

In answering the question "Do you find males or females sexually arousing?" you are expressing your sexual orientation, which is the third step in reaching psychological sexual maturity.

Sexual orientation, also called sexual preference, refers to whether a person is sexually aroused primarily by members of his or her own sex, the opposite sex, or both sexes.

Homosexual orientation is a pattern of sexual arousal by persons of the same sex.

Heterosexual orientation is a pattern of sexual arousal by persons of the opposite sex.

Bisexual orientation is a pattern of sexual arousal by persons of both sexes.

A review of several national surveys found that 1.7% of the American population reported having a homosexual orientation and 1.8% reported having a bisexual orientation. Clearly, the vast majority of Americans report having a heterosexual orientation (Gates, 2011).

Estimates of Americans who report having engaged in any same-sex sexual behavior and experiencing same-sex sexual attraction are much higher than the number of Americans who identify themselves as having a homosexual or bisexual orientation. About 8% of Americans report having engaged in same-sex sexual behavior and 11% report having same-sex sexual attraction during their lifetimes (Gates, 2011). Given these statistics, it makes sense that some researchers

Sexual orientation is most likely determined by a combination of genetic, biological, and psychological factors.

report that sexual orientation should not be thought of as fixed because of the somewhat flexible nature of sexual attraction (L. M. Diamond, 2008).

Of the several models that explain how we develop a particular sexual orientation, the interactive model is perhaps the most popular (Money, 1987; Zucker, 1990).

The **interactive model of sexual orientation** says that genetic and biological factors, such as genetic instructions and prenatal hormones, interact with psychological factors, such as the individual's attitudes, personality traits, and behaviors, to influence the development of sexual orientation.

There is debate over how much genetic and biological factors influence sexual orientation. Some researchers prefer the term *sexual preference* because it suggests that we have considerable freedom in choosing a sexual orientation and that genetic and biological factors do not play a major role (Baumrind, 1995; Byne, 1997). Other researchers prefer the term *sexual orientation* because they believe genetic and biological factors play a major role (M. Diamond & Sigmundson, 1997). In the end, most researchers report that sexual orientation is not the result of one factor alone, but rather a combination of genetic, biological, and psychological factors, which may vary in relative importance for each person.

Next, we'll look at male–female differences in sexual behavior.

Male–Female Sex Differences

How are men different from women?

After we have acquired a gender identity, gender role, and sexual orientation, there remain the sometimes difficult and complex decisions about when, where, and with whom sexual behavior is appropriate. Virtually every sex survey during the past few decades reports that men think about sex more, have more sexual partners, reach orgasm more, and masturbate more than women (right graph). Why men consistently report more sexual activity and are allowed more sexual freedom than women has come to be known as the double standard (M. Crawford & Popp, 2003).

The **double standard for sexual behavior** is a set of beliefs, values, and expectations that subtly encourages sexual activity in men but discourages the same behavior in women.

How these male–female differences in sexual behavior came about is explained by two different theories—the biosocial theory and the evolutionary theory.

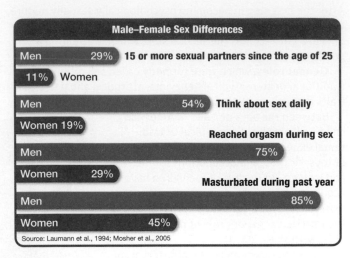

Male–Female Sex Differences

Men	29%	**15 or more sexual partners since the age of 25**
11%	Women	
Men	54%	**Think about sex daily**
Women 19%		
		Reached orgasm during sex
Men		75%
Women	29%	
		Masturbated during past year
Men		85%
Women	45%	

Source: Laumann et al., 1994; Mosher et al., 2005

Biosocial Theory

There are two major questions about male–female sexual behavior that need answering. First, why do men consistently report greater interest in sex as shown by increased frequency of sexual activities, a greater number of extramarital affairs, and a desire for more sex partners (about 18 partners) than women (about 4 or 5 partners) (Buss & Schmitt, 1993)? Second, in an international study of 37 cultures, 10,000 individuals were asked to state their top priorities in choosing a mate. Across all cultures and all racial, political, and religious groups, why do men generally value physical attractiveness more than women, while women value the financial resources of prospective mates twice as much as men do (Buss et al., 1990)? One answer to these questions comes from the biosocial theory of sexual differences.

Biosocial theory, which emphasizes social and cultural forces, says that differences in sexual activities and in values for selecting mates developed from traditional cultural divisions of labor: Women were primarily childbearers and homemakers, while men were primarily providers and protectors.

According to the biosocial theory, the double standard arose from men's roles as protectors and providers, which allowed them greater control of and access to women and in turn allowed and encouraged greater sexual freedom. In comparison, women's roles restricted and discouraged sexual activities and protected against potential problems with jealousy, which could disrupt or interfere with being successful childbearers and homemakers (right photo) (W. Wood & Eagly, 2002).

Biosocial theory focuses on the importance of different social and cultural pressures that resulted in men and women developing different social roles, which in turn led to men and women developing differences in sexual behavior, which today we call the double standard.

Provider & protector

Childbearer & homemaker

Royalty-Free

Evolutionary Theory

A different explanation for the differences in sexual behavior between men and women comes from evolutionary theory (Buss, 2009).

Evolutionary theory, which emphasizes genetic and biological forces, says that our current male–female differences in sexual behavior, which we call the double standard, arise from genetic and biological forces, which in turn grew out of an ancient set of successful mating patterns that helped the species survive.

According to evolutionary theory, men developed a greater interest in sex and desire for many attractive sex partners because it maximized their chances for reproduction. In comparison, women would not benefit from indiscriminate and frequent mating because it would place them at risk for having offspring of low quality and create an unstable environment for raising their children. Instead, women placed a high priority on finding a man who was a good protector and provider, so she and her children would have a better chance for survival (Gangestad & Simpson, 2000).

A longitudinal study examining parenthood and testosterone levels in single Filipino men adds strong support for the evolutionary theory (Gettler et al., 2011). The results showed that the men with higher testosterone levels were more likely to find partners and become fathers. Also, the new fathers experienced a decrease in testosterone levels greater than that found in men of the same age who didn't have children. Based on the results, researchers proposed that testosterone helps men find partners and have children, but that high levels of testosterone are unnecessary and perhaps detrimental to parenting. The responsibilities of fatherhood require emotional, psychological, and physical changes, and men's bodies seem capable of adapting to meet these new demands.

Evolutionary theory explains many other sexual behaviors. For example, men may deceive women about their feelings, commitment, and love to gain sexual access, and women may deceive men about their chances of gaining sexual access to evoke jealousy in existing mates and increase their perceived mate value (Buss, 2003; Haselton et al., 2005).

Next, we'll return to a controversial question in sexual behavior: Why does an individual develop a homosexual orientation?

Homosexuality

The question of whether sexual orientation is determined by choice or biological factors results in varied

Were the brothers born gay?

public opinion. One survey found that half of American adults believe sexual orientation is a result of *only* biological factors, one-third believe it is a result of choice *and* biological factors, and a smaller percentage believe it is a result of *only* choice (R. Epstein, 2006).

The acceptance of homosexuality by Americans has certainly increased in recent years, but it remains

Both brothers are gay and share similar genetic factors.

a deeply divisive issue. Many people say they would be more accepting of homosexuality if it were shown to be a genetic predisposition, since it would be similar to inheriting other preferences, such as being left-handed (Leland, 1994). We'll discuss recent genetic/biological and psychological factors that bear on the question of whether brothers Rick and Randy (photo at left) were genetically predisposed to be gay or chose to be gay.

Genetic/Biological Factors

During the past few decades, there has been a growing search for genetic and hormonal influences that contribute to the development of homosexuality. Some evidence comes from the study of sexual orientation in twins. For example, studies on identical male and female twins found that, if one male or female twin of an identical pair was gay, about 31–65% of the time so was the second twin; this compared to 8–30% for fraternal twins and 6–11% for adopted brothers or sisters (J. M. Bailey & Zucker, 1995; Kendler et al., 2000b). However, these and other twin studies are criticized because some of the twins were not reared separately, so it is impossible to determine the effects of similar environments on sexual orientation. Other research provides strong evidence that homosexual orientation has a genetic cause and that no single gene determines sexual orientation, but rather numerous genes are involved (Abrams, 2007; Rahman & Wilson, 2008).

Another kind of evidence comes from studies on genetic similarities among brothers. Researchers studied over 900 men who had at least one sibling and examined numerous factors including their sexual orientation, the number of biological and nonbiological siblings they had, and whether or not they lived with their siblings. Results found the only factor that increases the likelihood of a man having a homosexual orientation is having several older biological brothers. The rate of having a homosexual orientation for men who have several older brothers is about double the national rate of men having a homosexual orientation (Bogaert, 2006a, 2006b). These results further support the role of genetic and biological factors, such as prenatal environment, in determining sexual orientation.

To examine biological factors involved in the development of sexual orientation, one study scanned people's brains as they smelled male and female odors associated with sexual attraction. Results showed that in heterosexual men, the hypothalamus (involved in sexual responses—see pp. 80, 339) became activated only when they smelled the female odor, but in homosexual men, activation occurred only when they smelled the male odor. Thus, activation in the part of the brain involved in sexual responses is determined by sexual orientation and not biological sex. However, researchers cannot conclude whether changes in brain activity are the cause or the result of men's sexual orientation (Savic, 2005; Savic et al., 2005). Other brain research found the right hemisphere is slightly larger than the left in both men and women who are attracted to women, whereas, in men and women who are attracted to men, the brains are more symmetrical. Thus, sexual orientation may be reflected in brain structure (Savic & Lindström, 2008).

If there is a genetic/biological predisposition to homosexuality, we might expect a person would become aware of his or her homosexual orientation before learning about or engaging in homosexual behavior and despite pressure from parents, siblings, or peers to develop a heterosexual orientation. Research shows that the average age when homosexual males report beginning to have same-sex attraction is 10 and for homosexual females it is 12, which is usually before they know much about or engage in homosexual behavior (Savin-Williams, 2005).

All the above findings suggest that, to a certain extent, Rick and Randy were born with genetic or biological tendencies that played a role in the development of a homosexual orientation. Researchers continue to investigate the genetic and biological factors possibly involved in sexual orientation. There are also psychological factors worth considering.

Psychological Factors

In studying psychological factors, researchers observe the behaviors of young children and consistently find that young boys who prefer girl playmates and girls' toys, avoid rough-and-tumble play, and wear girls' clothing have a tendency to develop a homosexual orientation (Dawood et al., 2000). In addition, adult gay men and lesbian women recall engaging in more behaviors of the opposite sex as children than do heterosexual adults (J. M. Bailey & Zucker, 1995).

I knew I was gay before I did anything.

Although these studies are correlational and cannot show cause and effect, they do suggest that certain psychological factors (kinds of play behaviors and preferences) are associated with developing a homosexual orientation (Dawood et al., 2000).

One psychological factor that influenced attitudes on homosexuality was that, until the 1970s, virtually all professional health organizations considered homosexuality to be an abnormal condition that often required psychotherapy to change. However, over the past 40 years, countless studies found that homosexuals scored about the same as heterosexuals on a wide variety of mental health tests, meaning that homosexuals are as mentally healthy as heterosexuals (K. P. Rosenberg, 1994). For these reasons, most professional health organizations now consider homosexuality a normal form or expression of sexual behavior and discourage all discriminatory practices toward homosexuals.

Next, we'll discuss several of the more common sexual problems and their treatments.

Sexual Response, Problems, and Treatments

What are some of the problems?

Various surveys report that 10–52% of men and 25–63% of women aged 18 to 59, married and unmarried, experience a variety of sexual problems (Heiman, 2002). Some seek help for their problem, while others are ashamed or embarrassed and suffer in silence. There are two categories of sexual problems—paraphilias and sexual dysfunctions.

Paraphilias, commonly called sexual deviations, are characterized by repetitive or preferred sexual fantasies involving nonhuman objects, such as sexual attractions to particular articles of clothing (shoes, underclothes).

Sexual dysfunctions are problems of sexual arousal or orgasm that interfere with adequate functioning during sexual behavior.

When a person seeks help for a sexual problem, the clinician will check whether the causes are organic or psychological.

Organic factors are medical conditions or drug or medication problems that lead to sexual difficulties.

For example, certain medical conditions (such as diabetes mellitus), medications (such as antidepressants), and drugs (such as alcohol abuse) can interfere with sexual functioning.

Psychological factors are performance anxiety, sexual trauma, guilt, and failure to communicate, all of which may lead to sexual problems.

Four-stage model. To understand how psychological factors cause sexual problems, it helps to know Masters and Johnson's (1966) four-stage model of the sexual response.

Masters and Johnson proposed four stages of the human sexual response.

1st stage: Excitement. The body becomes physiologically and sexually aroused, resulting in erection in the male and vaginal lubrication in the female.

2nd stage: Plateau. Sexual and physiological arousal continues in males and females.

3rd stage: Orgasm. Men have rhythmic muscle contractions that cause ejaculation of sperm. Women experience similar rhythmic muscle contractions of the pelvic area. During orgasm, women and men report very pleasurable feelings.

4th stage: Resolution. Physiological responses return to normal.

Problems. Sexual problems can occur at different stages. For example, some individuals cannot reach stage 1, excitement, while others can reach stages 1 and 2 but not stage 3, orgasm.

There were few successful treatments for sexual problems until Masters and Johnson (1970) published their treatment program, which has several stages. First, the therapist provides basic information about the sexual response and helps the couple communicate their feelings. Then the therapist gives the couple "homework," which is designed to reduce performance anxiety. Homework involves learning to pleasure one's partner without genital touching or making sexual demands. This nongenital pleasuring is called sensate focus. After using *sensate focus,* the couple moves on to genital touching and intercourse. Sex therapists have expanded and modified Masters and Johnson's program and report considerable success with treating many sexual problems.

We'll discuss two common sexual problems and their treatments.

Premature or Rapid Ejaculation

John and Susan had been married for three years and were both 28 years old. When the clinician asked about their problem, Susan said that sex was over in about 30 seconds because that's how long it took for John to have an orgasm. John replied that he had always reached orgasm very quickly and didn't realize it was a problem. Susan said that it was a problem for her (Althof, 1995). John's problem is called premature ejaculation.

Premature or **rapid ejaculation** is the persistent or recurrent absence of voluntary control over ejaculation, in which the male ejaculates with minimal sexual stimulation before, upon, or shortly after penetration and before he wishes to.

Premature or rapid ejaculation is the most common male sexual problem and is reported by 20–40% of adult men (Lyon et al., 2008). A common treatment for it is called the squeeze technique. First, the partner stimulates the man's penis to nearly full erection. Then, the partner squeezes the head of the penis, which reduces arousal and erection. This squeeze procedure is repeated until the male develops a sense of control over arousal and ejaculation (Brannigan, 2011; Waldinger, 2008). This procedure has proved successful in treating premature ejaculation.

Inhibited Female Orgasm

Greta and Will had been married for five years and were in their late twenties. When asked about their problem, Greta said that she didn't think she had ever had an orgasm. She added that she loved Will very much but that she was becoming less interested in sex (Durand & Barlow, 2010). Greta's problem has a name; it is called inhibited female orgasm.

Inhibited female orgasm is a persistent delay or absence of orgasm after becoming aroused and excited.

About 10% of women never reach orgasm, and many others do so only occasionally (Lyon et al., 2008). Difficulty in reaching orgasm is one of the most common complaints of women seeking help for sexual problems (Laumann et al., 2005).

Psychological treatment begins with sensate focus, during which the couple learns to pleasure each other and the woman learns to relax and enjoy her body's sensations. The man is told how to help a woman reach orgasm—for example, by using his hand or, in Greta's case, using a vibrator (Durand & Barlow, 2010). This program has proved successful in treating inhibited female orgasm.

Next, we'll discuss a sexual problem that involves a potentially deadly transmitted disease—AIDS.

AIDS: Acquired Immune Deficiency Syndrome

What is AIDS?

On June 5, 1981, the U.S. Centers for Disease Control and Prevention issued a report describing five gay men in Los Angeles who had a rare form of pneumonia. Later, this rare pneumonia was determined to be one symptom of HIV.

HIV positive refers to the presence of HIV antibodies, which means that the individual has been infected by the human immunodeficiency virus (HIV), which is believed to cause AIDS.

AIDS (acquired immune deficiency syndrome) is a life-threatening condition that is present when the individual is HIV positive and has a level of T-cells (CD4 immune cells) no higher than 200 per cubic milliliter of blood or has developed one or more of 26 specified illnesses (for example, pneumonia, skin cancer). It may take years or even decades for HIV to develop into AIDS.

HIV Infections Worldwide

North America 1.2 million

Latin America and Caribbean 1.6 million

Eastern Europe & Central Asia 1.6 million

North Africa & Middle East 380,000

East, South, & Southwest Asia 4.8 million

Sub-Saharan Africa 22.5 million

The criterion of T-cell levels below 200 became a part of the definition of AIDS in 1993. T-cells are a critical part of the body's immune system, which fights against toxic agents (viruses and bacteria). Because of this change, some people who were previously defined as being HIV positive are now defined as having AIDS, even if no obvious symptoms have developed.

Researchers report that HIV originated in African monkeys, then spread to chimpanzees and, in the 1950s, to humans (Bailes et al., 2003).

About 40 million people worldwide are infected with HIV, and about 2.7 million people become newly infected each year, with people aged 13–29 being at highest risk (CDC, 2008b; U.N. AIDS, 2011). As shown in the map (above), the AIDS virus is widespread and has reached epidemic levels in Sub-Saharan Africa (U.N. AIDS, 2009). Currently, about 1.2 million people in the United States are living with HIV (CDC, 2011c).

Risk for AIDS

HIV cannot survive in air, in water, or on things that people touch. There are no reports of individuals getting AIDS through casual contact, such as through touch. HIV survives best in blood tissues and some bodily fluids, such as semen and vaginal fluids. Thus, people who come in physical contact with blood or bodily fluids (semen or vaginal fluids) from someone who has HIV are at risk for getting AIDS.

The pie chart below shows that in the United States, those people at greatest risk for AIDS are gay men and heterosexual intravenous drug users (high-risk heterosexual contact) (CDC, 2008b). In the rest of the world, about 75% of AIDS cases are spread through heterosexual intercourse (S. Sternberg, 2002).

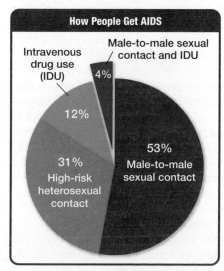

How People Get AIDS

- Intravenous drug use (IDU)
- Male-to-male sexual contact and IDU — 4%
- 12%
- 31% High-risk heterosexual contact
- 53% Male-to-male sexual contact

Progression of Disease

After infection, the AIDS virus replicates rapidly and intensively. As a result, newly infected individuals are 100–1,000 times more infectious than they are throughout the remainder of the disease (Koopman, 1995). In addition, newly infected individuals have no symptoms and the presence of antibodies to HIV cannot be confirmed biochemically for at least 60 days. Almost 20% of people with the infection don't know they are infected, don't get medication for HIV, and can unknowingly pass it along to others (CDC, 2011c). Thus, the newly infected person is regarded as a walking time bomb. In fact, one-third are diagnosed so late after the infection begins that they develop AIDS within a year. Also, people who don't know they have HIV are estimated to transmit the virus to half of all newly infected people (S. Sternberg & Gillum, 2011).

HIV destroys T-cells (CD4 cells), which are immune cells that fight off toxic agents (viruses and bacteria). It takes an average of 7 years for a person infected with HIV to develop AIDS (T-cell count below 200) and another 2 to 3 years after that to develop diseases that result in death. The reason a person with AIDS is especially susceptible to infections and diseases is that HIV slowly destroys a person's immune system's defenses, which means the body loses its ability to fight off toxic agents (infections or diseases).

Treatment

The number of AIDS-related deaths began to decrease in the late 1990s as a result of breakthroughs in drugs. The new drug treatment program has patients taking a drug "cocktail" of many pills daily, which include several new drugs (protease inhibitors and HIV-inhibiting drugs).

In many cases, these new drugs reduce HIV to undetectable levels, but the drugs still do not wipe out the virus. Instead, the virus "hides out" in the body and returns if patients stop taking the drugs, which means these drugs must be taken for life. Because the anti-HIV drugs reduce life-threatening symptoms, these drugs have enabled AIDS patients to live longer (M. May et al., 2011). The earlier patients begin HIV treatment, the better their chance of survival (S. Sternberg, 2008b).

The dramatic decreases in deaths from AIDS because of the drug cocktails used in the early 1990s have slowed greatly. That's because HIV became resistant to some of the "new" drugs and some patients stopped taking the drugs because there were too many pills to take or because of side effects (S. Sternberg, 2008a). Researchers continue to search for new drugs and vaccines to treat HIV/AIDS (Associated Press, 2012b; Park, 2010a; S. Sternberg, 2009; Wu et al., 2011).

Now, we'll discuss a cruel cultural influence on female sexual behavior. ●

Good Tradition or Cruel Mutilation?

Men have a long history of trying to control the sexual motivation of women. In many countries, men want to marry virgins and

What is genital cutting?

insist that women remain virgins until marriage, although the men do not hold themselves to the same standards. One extreme example of men controlling the sexual motivation and behavior of women is found in parts of Africa, Indonesia, and the Arabian Peninsula, where young girls undergo genital cutting before they become sexually mature (Corbett, 2008; MacInnis, 2006).

Genital cutting involves cutting away the female's external genitalia, usually including her clitoris and surrounding skin (labia minora). The remaining edges are sewn together, which leaves only a small opening for urination and menstruation.

Soraya Mire (photo at right) remembers the day her mother said, "I'm going to buy you some gifts." Soraya, who was 13, obediently got into the car with her mother and driver. They didn't go shopping but stopped at a doctor's house.

Soraya Mire speaks about her childhood genital cutting.

© Scott Gries/Getty Images

Once inside, they went into an operating room where a doctor asked Soraya to lie on the operating table. He tied her feet down with a rope so she could not move. Her mother said it was time for Soraya to become a woman and undergo genital cutting.

Like her mother and her mother's mother, Soraya underwent this ancient rite of passage. But unlike them, Soraya broke the silence to fight this cruel mutilation. At age 36, Soraya made a documentary film called *Fire Eyes* to protest the practice of genital cutting (Tawa, 1995).

About 3 million women a year and a total of 140 million women have undergone genital cutting (formerly called female circumcision), mostly in childhood and often without anesthesia or sterile procedures. Genital cutting has taken place for the past 5,000 years and is currently practiced in about 28 African countries by people of all different religious, ethnic, and cultural groups (Associated Press, 2006e; MacInnis, 2006; E. Rosenthal, 2006; WHO, 2008).

What Is Its Purpose?

In many of the poorer societies of Africa and Ethiopia, genital cutting is a common ritual to physically mark young girls and increase their chances for future marriage. Many African nations have placed government bans on genital cutting, but few are enforcing the rules (Corbett, 2008; Ras-Work, 2006).

Girls commonly under-go genital cutting before they reach puberty, usually between the ages of 4 and 10. The primary reason for genital cutting is the men's belief that if women are surgically deprived of receiving sexual pleasure, they will remain clean and virginal until marriage. Men in these societies often refuse to marry a woman who has not undergone genital cutting because they believe that she is unclean and not a virgin (Associated Press, 2006e; A. Walker & Parmar, 1993).

The male equivalent of genital cutting would be amputation of the male's penis.

Young girl is being held while undergoing genital cutting.

© Jean-Marc Bouju/Impact/HIP/The Image Works

Are There Complications?

Because of the high social status of Soraya's father, who was a general, her genital cutting was performed by a doctor. However, in the majority of cases, it is done by someone with no medical training who uses a knife, razor, or sharp stone and less than sterile procedures (Associated Press, 2006e).

Because the genital area has a high concentration of nerves and blood vessels, genital cutting results in severe pain, bleeding, and even hemorrhaging, which can lead to shock and death. Because of poor surgical procedures, girls endure many medical complications, including infections, cysts, and scarring. This procedure also makes menstruation and intercourse painful and childbirth dangerous (Nour, 2000; E. Rosenthal, 2006).

Girls submit to the fear, pain, and trauma of genital cutting for varied and complex reasons. Parents have genital cutting done in the beliefs that it is for the good of their daughters, that their religion requires it, that it will make their daughters marriageable, and that it is necessary to maintain female chastity (Corbett, 2008; Nour, 2000). However, after genital cutting many women suffer anxiety and depression from worry about their disfigured genitals, menstruation difficulties, and fear of infertility (Caldwell et al., 1997).

Is There a Solution?

The United Nations health organizations have endorsed laws against genital cutting, but such laws cannot eliminate this strong sociocultural tradition. As one supporter of genital cutting said, "This procedure helps to keep women's sexual drives at acceptable and reasonable levels" (Daniszewski, 1997). Although Westerners are horrified by this barbaric practice, many African societies consider this practice part of their culture and do it out of love for their daughters (Corbett, 2008). For example, when a newspaper in Ghana, Africa, published articles in favor of banning genital cutting, local women had great success in getting support to keep this ancient practice and reject values from the outside world.

For the past 30 years, Soraya Mire has worked to end the practice of genital cutting. In addition to her documentary film mentioned earlier, she wrote *The Girl with Three Legs: A Memoir,* in which she shares her own challenges in overcoming her childhood torture. Soraya is an activist committed to bringing awareness, education, and changes in laws regarding the practice of genital cutting. For her devoted efforts, she was given the Human Rights Award at the United Nation (Sorayamire.org, 2012).

We have discussed two biological drives—hunger and sex. After the Concept Review, we'll examine an important social need—achievement. ●

Concept Review

1. Physiological or psychological factors that cause us to act in a specific way at a particular time are included in the definition of _____.

2. Innate biological forces predispose an animal to behave in a particular way in the presence of a specific environmental condition. These ways of behaving are called _____.

3. There are several areas in the brain, including the nucleus accumbens and ventral tegmental area, that make up a neural circuit called the **(a)** _____ center. This center especially uses the neurotransmitter **(b)** _____.

4. Sometimes motivation is best explained by psychological factors, the focus of _____, which states that as we aim to fulfill our basic needs, we experience either autonomous or controlled motivation.

5. External stimuli, reinforcers, goals, or rewards that may be positive or negative and that motivate one's behavior are called **(a)** _____. When we perform behaviors to reduce biological needs or obtain various incentives, we are acting under the influence of **(b)** _____ motivation. When we perform behaviors because they are personally rewarding or because we are following our personal goals, beliefs, or expectations, we are acting under the influence of **(c)** _____ motivation.

6. Needs that are not critical to your survival but that are acquired through learning and socialization, such as the needs for achievement and affiliation, are called **(a)** _____ needs. Needs that are critical to your survival and physical well-being, such as food, water, and sex, are called **(b)** _____ needs.

7. The ascending order or hierarchy with biological needs at the bottom and social needs at the top is _____. This idea assumes that we satisfy our biological needs before we satisfy our social needs.

8. There are three major factors that influence eating. Cues that come from physiological changes are called **(a)** _____ factors. Cues that come from inherited instructions are called **(b)** _____ factors. Cues that come from learning and personality traits are called **(c)** _____ factors.

Hypothalamus

9. Biological cues for hunger that come from the stomach, liver, intestines, and fat cells are called **(a)** _____ cues. Biological cues that come from the brain are called **(b)** _____ cues.

10. The part of the hypothalamus that is involved in feelings of being hungry is called the **(a)** _____; the part that is involved in feelings of being full is called the **(b)** _____.

11. We inherit the following genetic factors involved in weight regulation: a certain number of **(a)** _____ cells that store fat; a certain **(b)** _____ rate that regulates how fast we burn off fuel; a certain **(c)** _____ point that maintains a stable amount of body fat; and weight-regulating **(d)** _____ that influence appetite, metabolism, and hormone secretion.

12. Psychological factors that influence eating include **(a)** _____ associations, **(b)** _____ influences, and **(c)** _____ variables.

13. Genetic sex factors involve the 23rd chromosome, called the **(a)** _____, which determines the sex of the child. Biological sex factors include sex hormones, which for the male are called **(b)** _____ and for the female are called **(c)** _____. Psychological sex factors include the subjective feeling of being male or female, which is called **(d)** _____; adopting behaviors and traits that society identifies as male or female, which is called **(e)** _____; and being more sexually aroused by members of the same or opposite sex, which is called **(f)** _____.

14. Findings from the sexual orientation of identical twins and the shared genetic material from gay brothers are examples of **(a)** _____ factors in the development of a homosexual orientation. Young boys who prefer girls' toys and girl playmates and engage in opposite-sex behaviors show a tendency to develop a homosexual orientation, which shows the effects of **(b)** _____ factors on sexual orientation.

15. A person who has been infected by the human immuno-deficiency virus but has not yet developed any illnesses is said to be **(a)** _____. A person whose level of T-cells has dropped to 200 per cubic milliliter of blood but who may or may not have developed an illness is defined as having **(b)** _____.

Answers: 1. *motivation;* 2. *fixed action patterns;* 3. *(a) reward/pleasure, (b) dopamine; (c) rewarded or encouraged;* 4. *self-determination theory;* 5. *(a) incentives, (b) extrinsic, (c) intrinsic;* 6. *(a) social, (b) biological; 7. Maslow's hierarchy of needs; 8. (a) biological, (b) genetic, (c) psychosocial; 9. (a) peripheral, (b) central; 10. (a) lateral hypothalamus, (b) ventromedial hypothalamus; 11. (a) fat, (b) metabolic, (c) set, (d) genes; 12. (a) learned, (b) social-cultural, (c) personality; 13. (a) sex chromosome, (b) androgens, (c) estrogens, (d) gender identity, (e) gender role, (f) sexual orientation; 14. (a) genetic, (b) psychological; 15. (a) HIV positive, (b) AIDS*

E Achievement

Need for Achievement

At the beginning of the module, we told you about Shaquille O'Neal, who has a lifetime filled with impressive achievements.

Why did Shaq succeed?

In addition to being a 15-time NBA all-star, actor, rapper, and successful businessman, he is a highly educated individual. Even after he entered the NBA draft, Shaq continued to take courses to earn his college degree. After he retired from playing basketball, Shaq went on to earn his doctorate degree in organizational learning and leadership. His next ambition is to obtain a law degree.

For Shaq, academic achievement was one of his many social needs.

Social needs, such as the desire for affiliation or close social bonds, nurturance or need to help and protect others, dominance or need to influence or control others, and

You can call me Dr. O'Neal.

achievement or need to excel, are acquired through learning and experience.

If you are working hard to achieve academic success, you are demonstrating your social need for achievement.

The **achievement need** refers to the desire to set challenging goals and to persist in pursuing those goals in the face of obstacles, frustrations, and setbacks.

The achievement need not only is a major concern of college students but also ranks high (Level 4 out of 5) in Maslow's hierarchy of needs. We'll discuss five questions related to the achievement need: How is the need for achievement measured? What is high need for achievement? What is fear of failure? What is underachievement? How is the need for achievement related to entrepreneurship?

Measuring the Need for Achievement

Do you have a strong need to achieve? Researchers David McClelland and John Atkinson tried to answer this question with a test called the Thematic Apperception Test, or TAT.

What do you think is going on in this TAT card?

The **Thematic Apperception Test,** commonly called the **TAT,** is a personality test in which participants are asked to look at pictures of people in ambiguous situations and to make up stories about what the characters are thinking and feeling and what the outcome will be.

For example, the sample TAT card on the left shows a young man with a sad expression and a bright sun and fruit tree in the background. If you were taking the TAT, you would be asked to describe what is happening in this card. To measure the level of achievement, your stories would be scored in terms of achievement themes, such as setting goals, competing, or overcoming obstacles (J. W. Atkinson, 1958; D. C. McClelland et al., 1953). The TAT assumes that the strength of your need to achieve will be reflected in the kinds of thoughts and feelings you use to describe the TAT cards. However, TAT stories are difficult to score reliably because there is no objective way to identify which thoughts and feelings indicate level of achievement (Keiser & Prather, 1990). More recently, objective ***paper-and-pencil tests*** have been developed to measure achievement motivation because these tests are easier to administer and score and have somewhat better reliability and validity than the TAT (R. M. Kaplan & Saccuzzo, 2009).

However, measuring the need for achievement has proved difficult because it relates to intrinsic motivational factors that include beliefs and expectations, which are difficult to quantify.

High Need for Achievement

There is perhaps no better example of individuals with high need for achievement than Olympic athletes. One example is Michael Phelps, who has won 22 Olympic medals, including 18 gold medals (the individual record for the most gold medals). Michael's performances have earned him countless other awards, including several World Swimmer of the Year awards. He trains for at least 5 hours a day, 6 days a week, to be the best swimmer he can be. Michael has all the traits of someone with a high need for achievement (J. W. Atkinson & Raynor, 1974; D. C. McClelland, 1985).

Michael Phelps trains 5 hours a day, 6 days a week.

High need for achievement is shown by those who persist longer at tasks; perform better on tasks, activities, or exams; set challenging but realistic goals; compete with others to win; and are attracted to careers that require initiative.

Although the vast majority of us will not make the Olympics, most of us will show varying degrees of the need to achieve by doing our best, striving for social recognition, and working to achieve material rewards (Hareli & Weiner, 2002). This need for achievement varies based on cultural factors, such as parental influence (Maehr, 2008).

The idea that there is a need for achievement and that it motivates many of our behaviors has generated a great deal of research. However, measuring a person's need for achievement and making predictions about an individual's level of achievement have proved difficult for two reasons: The TAT and paper-and-pencil tests have limited reliability and validity (see p. 287), and achievement motivation is difficult to quantify because it involves intrinsic motivation (see p. 331), which includes one's personal beliefs and expectations (Petri & Govern, 2004).

If we consider one side of a coin to be a need for achievement, then the other side is fear of failure and making excuses for failing.

Fear of Failure

Why do some fail?

Just as some individuals may be motivated by a need for achievement, others may be motivated by a fear of failure. J. W. Atkinson (1964) believed that, in order to understand why a person succeeds or fails in reaching a goal, we must examine not only a person's need for achievement but also the fear of failure.

Fear of failure is shown by people who are motivated to avoid failure by choosing easy, nonchallenging tasks where failure is unlikely to occur.

For example, fear of failure may motivate a student to study just enough to avoid failing an exam but not enough to get a good grade or set higher academic goals. In fact, the fear of failure is a good predictor of poor grades: The greater a student's fear of failure, the poorer his or her grades (W. E. Herman, 1990). Atkinson said that individuals who are motivated primarily by a fear of failure will never do as well, work as hard, or set goals as high as those who are motivated by a need for achievement. Also, the greater one's fear of failure, the greater the chances of trying to look good by engaging in self-handicapping (Zeidner & Matthews, 2005).

Self-handicapping. If a person is motivated primarily by the fear of failure, how does this individual explain his or her poor performances yet keep a good self-image? One solution is to use self-handicapping (E. Jones & Berglas, 1978).

Self-handicapping refers to engaging in tactics that contribute to failure and then using these very things, knowingly or unknowingly, as excuses for failing to achieve some goal.

For example, instead of studying for an exam, a student goes to a movie and then does poorly on the test. He excuses his bad grade by saying he didn't study, which is an example of self-handicapping. Researchers found that individuals with low self-esteem are most likely to engage in self-handicapping because it is one way to look good to their peers and thus protect their already low self-esteem (Elliot & Church, 2003). Self-handicapping excuses may involve health (missed sleep, have a cold), drug use (have a hangover), unrealistically high goals (How could I possibly do that?), or procrastination (I didn't have enough time). In the short term, self-handicapping helps preserve our positive self image and self-esteem, but in the long term, it interferes with taking personal responsibility to achieve our goals (Rhodewalt & Vohs, 2005).

One example of how fear of failure affects motivation is seen in individuals who are underachievers.

Need for Achievement and Entrepreneurship

Do entrepreneurs have a high need for achievement?

Research data generally show that a high need for achievement is a significant factor in being a successful entrepreneur (Begley, 1995; D. C. McClelland, 1961, 1965). An entrepreneur is an individual who runs a business and assumes all of the risk and reward that result from the business. Entrepreneurs prefer to engage in moderately challenging tasks, rather than simply being content with the status quo. However, they aim to choose tasks that are within their ability to complete successfully. Entrepreneurs strive to achieve success and continuously challenge themselves to reach higher standards of excellence.

Underachievement

Why do some underachieve?

One of our friends described his 14-year-old son, Rich, as having all the brains in the world but doing nothing with them. Although Rich is a computer wizard, he gets terrible grades in school, never does his homework, and doesn't seem to have any ambition. Rich might be called an underachiever.

Underachievers are individuals who score relatively high on tests of ability or intelligence but perform more poorly than their scores would predict.

$$E = mc^2$$
$$\pi = 3.14$$
$$y = mx+b$$

Underachievers have the ability but not the motivation.

The most common examples of underachievers are students who score relatively high on ability or intelligence tests but perform poorly in school or academic settings (Lupart & Pyryt, 1996). Researchers found that underachievement is not related to socioeconomic class, that there are two or three male underachievers for every female underachiever, and that about 15% of students are underachievers (McCall, 1994).

Characteristics. The psychological characteristics of underachievers include having a poor self-concept, low self-esteem, and poor peer relationships and being shy or depressed. The cognitive characteristics of underachievers include fear of failure, poor perceptions of their abilities, and lack of persistence. This means that underachievers are less likely to persist in getting their college degrees, holding on to jobs, or maintaining their marriages (McCall, 1994). Thus, underachievement reduces performance in academic, job, and marital settings, and its effects may last through adulthood.

The paradox of underachievement is that underachievers have the abilities but are not motivated to use them. Clinicians, counselors, and researchers are developing treatment programs to help underachievers change their beliefs and expectations so they will develop the motivation to use their considerable abilities (McCall, 1994).

I set challenging but realistic goals.

Some researchers believe that even though you can teach the skills involved in entrepreneurship, in order for people to actually become entrepreneurs, they must have a high need for achievement; otherwise, they won't take the necessary risks. Not surprisingly, research examining the characteristics of entrepreneurs finds that they often demonstrate the need for achievement beginning at an early age.

People become entrepreneurs because of an important cognitive factor that greatly influences motivation; that is our next topic.

© Rehan Qureshi/Shutterstock.com

Cognitive Influences

Each year, over 1,800 seniors compete in the Intel Science Talent Search to win the most prestigious high-school science award in the United States. One winner was Nithin Tumma (photo below), a senior from Michigan who has always enjoyed science, especially thinking about questions no one else can answer. Tumma's project analyzed the molecular mechanisms in cancer cells. He found that by inhibiting (turning off) certain proteins, we can slow the growth of cancer cells and decrease their malignancy (ability to spread and destroy other areas). His work may lead to less toxic and more effective cancer treatments (Intel, 2012). Tumma's love of science is a motivating force that comes from various cognitive factors.

Do you work for love or money?

Cognitive factors in motivation refer to how people evaluate or perceive a situation and how these evaluations and perceptions influence their willingness to work.

Nithin Tumma perceives science projects as interesting and works hard to complete them. He especially enjoys thinking about problems in new ways. Compared to Tumma's love of science, others find science projects hard and boring and take science courses only because they are required. The difference between taking science courses because of a love of science and because of course requirements illustrates the difference between two kinds of motivation—intrinsic motivation and extrinsic motivation (Ryan & Deci, 2000).

Intrinsic motivation involves engaging in certain activities or behaviors without receiving any external rewards because the behaviors themselves are personally rewarding or because engaging in these activities fulfills our beliefs or expectations.

Tumma's dedication to science is in large part fueled by intrinsic motivation, which is related to feeling competent, curious, and interested, having self-determination, and enjoying the task, whether it's a science project, work you like, a hobby, or volunteer work. In comparison, extrinsic motivation involves different factors.

Extrinsic motivation involves engaging in certain activities or behaviors that either reduce biological needs or help us obtain incentives and external rewards.

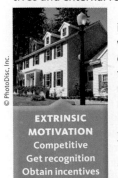

EXTRINSIC MOTIVATION
Competitive
Get recognition
Obtain incentives
Make money

If you do a job, task, or assigned work because it is required, your motivation is often extrinsic, which may involve being evaluated or competing, or seeking recognition, money, or other incentives, such as acquiring a car or home. Another major difference between intrinsic and extrinsic motivation is that working because of intrinsic motivation (loving what you're doing) makes you feel powerfully motivated. Without intrinsic motivation there would be fewer charitable donations and fewer people would volunteer their time or donate their blood (Deci et al., 1999).

So, here's an interesting question: What would happen to intrinsic motivation if you got paid for doing something that you love doing?

INTRINSIC MOTIVATION
Competent
Determined
Personally rewarding
Enjoyable

Intrinsic motivation. Would receiving money for volunteering to give blood "turn off" or decrease the intrinsic motivation of donors to the point that they might give less blood or none at all?

Researchers generally believed that if people were given external rewards (money, awards, prizes, or tokens) for doing tasks (donating blood) from intrinsic motivation, their performance of and interest in these tasks would decrease (Deci & Moller, 2005). Because of the widely held belief that external rewards decreased intrinsic motivation, many books advised that rewards should not be used in educational settings, hospitals, or volunteer organizations because such rewards would do more harm than good. Recent reviews of this issue indicate that the effects of external rewards on intrinsic motivation are more complex than originally thought.

Researchers have reached three general conclusions about the influence of external rewards on intrinsic motivation (Deci & Moller, 2005; Eisenberger et al., 1999; Lepper et al., 1999). First, giving unexpected external rewards does not decrease intrinsic motivation, but people may come to expect such rewards. Second, giving positive verbal feedback for doing work that was better than others may actually increase intrinsic motivation. Third, giving external rewards for doing minimal work or completing a specific project may decrease intrinsic motivation.

Recent studies indicate that, unlike previously thought, external rewards that are unexpected or involve positive verbal feedback may increase intrinsic motivation. External rewards that are tied to doing minimal work or completing a specific project may decrease intrinsic motivation. For example, when parents or teachers praise children, the praise is likely to increase intrinsic motivation if the praise is sincere and promotes the child's feelings of being competent and independent. In contrast, insincere praise, praise for very small accomplishments, or praise that is controlling rather than rewarding may decrease intrinsic motivation (Deci & Moller, 2005).

For a long time it was also thought that external rewards automatically decreased creative work and interest. But researchers have found that the effects of giving children a reward for completing a creative task depend on how children perceive the reward. If they perceive the reward as a treat, it will increase their intrinsic interest, but if they see the reward as external pressure to be creative, it will decrease their intrinsic interest (Eisenberger & Armeli, 1997). All these studies show that external rewards influence cognitive factors, which in turn may increase or decrease intrinsic motivation.

Next, we'll examine how poor and minority students can overcome educational disadvantages. ●

People who donate blood are usually intrinsically motivated.

Why Did Poor and Minority Students Do Well?

There has been a long history of research indicating that poor and minority children do not perform as well as their middle-class and White peers in many schools across the United States. Over many years, it has become increasingly clear that educating poor minority students to the national standards of proficiency is certainly possible, but requires considerable effort.

How should poor and minority students be educated?

In order to develop school programs to help poor and minority students overcome their academic disadvantages, education policy makers rely on research findings that identify factors that have an important influence on children's intellectual and academic achievement. For instance, researchers report that parents who are professionals speak more to their children than parents who are on welfare. Also, children of professionals hear many more words of encouragement than welfare children, and welfare children hear many more words of discouragement than children of professionals. The outcome for young children who hear fewer words spoken by their parents and receive a lot of discouragement is lower IQ scores and poorer academic success than for children who hear many words and receive a lot of encouragement (Hart & Risley, 2006).

Other related research reports that children from middle-class families have parents who are more sensitive, more encouraging, and less detached. Researchers conclude that although wealth influences children's IQs and academic success, parenting style matters even more. Thus, the advantages of middle-class children are due primarily to the language their parents use and their parents' child-rearing approach (Brooks-Gunn, 2006).

Procedure and Results

By using research findings about the disadvantages of poor and minority children to develop education programs, many schools have been able to educate these students to meet and rise above national standards of proficiency. The schools that best educate poor and minority children follow three practices. First, the school day is much longer; the first class often begins before 8 A.M., the last class ends after 4 P.M., and summer vacations are limited to one month. Second, there are clearly stated education goals and principals closely monitor whether or not teachers are achieving the goals. Teachers are very committed to these goals, and some go as far as making themselves available in the evenings to help students with their homework. Third, these schools not only are teaching students academics, but also are teaching them character, such as how to sit in class, make appropriate eye contact, and work cooperatively in a team (Tough, 2006).

Not only are students taught academics, such as reading and math, but slogans, such as REACH, are used to help them build character.

Some of the best-recognized schools for their success in educating poor and minority students are operated by KIPP (Knowledge Is Power Program). One of the slogans KIPP schools use to teach students proper classroom behavior is SLANT (Sit up, Listen, Ask questions, Nod, and Track the speaker with their eyes). Children in KIPP schools appreciate the valuable lessons they receive about respectful behavior, saying it even helps them to pay better attention to speakers. KIPP schools use other slogans too, such as the one in the above photo and "All of Us Will Learn." Research findings indicate that the "noncognitive" skills these schools are teaching students, such as patience, respect, self-control, and motivation to work hard, have an important role in children's future academic and career success (Tough, 2006).

Many of the KIPP schools have demonstrated their effectiveness by improving students' performances on state exams. For instance, recent state exam scores for middle-school students at one KIPP school in New York were 12% higher than the state average. When compared to scores from other children in their high-poverty neighborhoods, 86% of KIPP eighth-grade students scored at grade level in math, but only 16% of students attending other schools reached math proficiency. This is especially impressive because when students enter KIPP schools, they are usually at least two grade levels behind (Tough, 2006).

Conclusions

Children from poor and minority families who are behind in school need more than the same education provided to middle-class families. These children have a lot of catching up to do and therefore need a better, more intensive education. Results on the effect these special schools have on students' academic performance suggest that schools should not only focus on academics, but also include personality and behavioral curriculum. Programs like KIPP offer promise in reducing the academic achievement and IQ gap between poor and minority students and middle-class and White students. Yet, these relatively few programs are only a beginning to a large-scale educational issue that requires substantial public school reform (Tough, 2006). ●

G Application: Dieting & Eating Disorders

Dieting

Some of us have learned to eat at certain times (learned associations) or eat when stressed (personality variables), or we come from families that encourage eating to show appreciation (cultural influences). Any of these psychosocial factors—learned associations, personality variables, or cultural influences—can override our genetic and biological factors and lead us to become overweight. Losing weight is difficult because the body is genetically designed to store extra calories as fat and because our large forebrains are good at rationalizing why we need to eat another piece of pizza and have a late-night snack.

Why is dieting so difficult?

We'll use the dieting experiences of television talk-show host Oprah Winfrey to illustrate the difficulties of dieting and how best to maintain an optimal weight.

Difficulties of Dieting

As you can see in the photos below, Oprah Winfrey has had an up-and-down battle with managing her weight. In the 1970s, when Oprah Winfrey was in her twenties, she weighed 140 pounds. By the mid-1980s, Oprah weighed 190 pounds, which is considered overweight for her height and frame. When her weight reached 211, she decided it was time for a diet program (B. Greene & Winfrey, 1996).

In the 1980s, Oprah went on a diet and lost nearly 70 pounds. She pronounced she was finally cured of overeating. She was wrong. In the 1990s, Oprah did not make the necessary changes in her lifestyle and she regained all her lost weight and then some, reaching about 237 pounds (*People*, March 14, 2005, p. 148).

In 2005, through devoted dieting and exercise, Oprah got down to a trim and fit 160 pounds. She believed she was finished with her ongoing weight battle. Unfortunately, she was wrong again. She later tipped the scale at 200 pounds. She asked herself, "How did I let this happen again?" (Winfrey, 2009).

Like all bodies, Oprah's body has two physiological factors that make it difficult to keep off lost weight.

Physiological factors. One physiological factor is that Oprah's body, which is set up to store a certain amount of fat, automatically adjusts to any decrease in fat stores by lowering its *rate of metabolism* (J. M. Friedman, 2003). This results in her body more efficiently burning fuel so she must eat even less or exercise more to avoid regaining lost weight. Another physiological factor is that Oprah's body has a *genetically fixed set point*, which maintains her fat stores at a stable level. If the level of fat stores drops below her set point, her body compensates by increasing her appetite so her fat stores will return to their former level (J. M. Friedman, 2003).

Like most dieters who have regained their lost weight, Oprah admitted, "I didn't do whatever the maintenance program was. I thought I was cured. And that's just not true. You have to find a way to live in the world with food" (*People*, January 14, 1991, p. 84). After dieting, people like Oprah need to develop a *maintenance program* to eat less and exercise more.

Psychological factors. Oprah recalls a time when she was depressed and she went on a "macaroni-and-cheese-eating tailspin" (CNN, 2011). Oprah realized that food had become more than nutrition. "For me, food was comfort, pleasure, love, a friend, everything. Now I consciously work every day at not letting food be a substitute for emotions" (Tresniowski & Bell, 1996, p. 81). Thus, some dieters need a change in lifestyle so that they don't eat when stressed or depressed.

Diet Program/Lifestyle

Researchers found that an effective program of exercise and diet involves four factors: (1) changing one's attitudes toward food (making it less important); (2) changing one's eating patterns (consuming fewer calories); (3) developing a regular exercise program (a critical part of a weight program); and (4) perhaps the most important, sticking to this weight program over the long term, often for a lifetime (J. E. Brody, 2000b).

Low-fat or low-carbohydrate diet? There has been a debate over which of these diets is more effective. Dieters report that a low-fat diet works better for some, while a low-carbohydrate diet works better for others. One long-term study found that low-carb diets beat low-fat diets in weight loss, but another long-term study found no difference in weight loss between the two diets (G. D. Foster et al., 2010; Shai et al., 2008). Researchers generally report that whichever diet you choose, the ONLY reason you lose weight is that you're consuming fewer calories (Christensen, 2003). And, don't forget the exercise.

Visualizing food. Though it isn't considered a diet program, new research reports that repeatedly thinking about food, such as chocolate, will make it less appealing. Visualizing yourself eating an indulgent food helps trick your brain into substituting your thoughts for the actual experience of eating so that you have fewer cravings for and eat less of the actual food (Morewedge et al., 2010). Try repeatedly visualizing yourself eating your dessert before actually eating it, and see what happens!

Food addiction. Obesity has been suspected to be a result of an addiction to food. But neurological connections between overeating and drug addiction have only recently been found. For instance, overeaters and drug addicts have deficiencies in dopamine (a chemical that makes us feel good) (P. M. Johnson & Kenny, 2010). Researchers report that years of overeating result in less pleasure experienced in the brain's reward/pleasure center. Consequently, people have to eat more and more to experience the pleasurable feelings they once had (Stice et al., 2010). Thus, obese people may be compulsively driven to eat food.

Next, we'll discuss three eating disorders.

Eating Disorders

Must you be thin? It's common for people from time to time to be concerned about what they eat and their body image. We may have these types of concerns while going through adolescence, beginning to date someone, getting ready for our wedding day, or entering mid-life, for instance. However, eating disorders are marked by extremes. They are characterized by severe disturbances in eating or severe concern about body weight or shape (NIMH, 2012b).

As extreme as eating disorders are, they are unfortunately not rare. It is estimated that 8 million Americans have an eating disorder, 7 million women and 1 million men. Eating disorders can have severe consequences on health, as is evidenced by these types of disorders having the highest mortality rate of any mental illness, including depression (SCDMH, 2012).

We'll discuss three eating disorders: anorexia nervosa, bulimia nervosa, and binge-eating disorder.

Anorexia Nervosa

Actress Portia de Rossi now enjoys a successful career, having starred in hit TV shows including "Ally McBeal" and "Arrested Development," and a satisfying personal life, as she is happily married to Ellen DeGeneres. However, the path to reach this point in her life was filled with struggles, most notably her battle with weight and body image.

Portia de Rossi had anorexia and was never happy with her body.

In 2000, de Rossi collapsed on the set while working. At 5 feet 8 inches tall, she weighed only 82 pounds, which was the result of a diet limited to 300 calories a day and excessive exercise. Asked whether she was happy with her body image, she commented about her thighs, "Eh, they're still not good" (de Rossi, 2012).

Now the 37-year-old de Rossi has overcome her battle with weight and body image and weighs a healthy 130 pounds. She wrote a memoir called *Unbearable Lightness* in which she shares the thought processes that led her to the eating disorder called anorexia nervosa *(an-uh REX-see-ah ner-VOH-suh),* as well as her rituals around eating food (such as using a chopstick to eat so the bites would be tiny) and her overwhelming feelings of worthlessness (de Rossi, 2010; Zinko, 2010).

Anorexia nervosa is a serious eating disorder characterized by refusing to eat and not maintaining weight at 85% of what is expected, having an intense fear of gaining weight or becoming fat, and missing at least three consecutive menstrual cycles. Anorexics also have a disturbed body image: They see themselves as fat even though they are very thin (American Psychiatric Association, 2000).

Anorexia nervosa is a relatively rare disorder that affects about 0.5% to 3.7% of U.S. girls and women and a much lower percentage of boys and men (NIMH, 2008).

One risk factor for anorexia nervosa is a dysfunctional family. These children have parents who set excessively high standards that they cannot possibly achieve (Eggers & Liebers, 2007). Another risk involves personality factors, such as being very anxious, compulsive, rigid, and a perfectionist (Bulik, 2006; Gura, 2008a). Brain scan studies show that the parts of the brain that normally respond to the pleasurable, rewarding aspects of eating do not seem to work in people with anorexia (Kaye, 2008). Thus, there may be multiple risk factors for developing anorexia nervosa.

Bulimia Nervosa

Actress and singer Demi Lovato is well recognized as providing wholesome teen entertainment. She has sang herself to the top of the charts and became a Disney icon. Until recently, no one knew there were problems underneath her beautiful smile. Lovato opened up to her fans about her longtime struggle with overeating and vomiting. She reports beginning to compulsively overeat when she was 8 years old. Lovato recalls performing concerts on an empty stomach and losing her voice as a consequence of forcefully vomiting. She has since received treatment, but acknowledges that her eating disorder remains a daily battle (J. Johnston, 2011; Lovato, 2012).

Demi Lovato had bulimia nervosa and continues to struggle even after treatment.

Lovato's disorder, which is called bulimia nervosa *(boo-LEE-me-ah ner-VOH-sah),* affects about 3% of the general population (Hudson et al., 2007).

Bulimia nervosa is characterized by a minimum of two binge-eating episodes per week for at least three months; fear of not being able to stop eating; regularly engaging in vomiting, use of laxatives, or rigorous dieting and fasting; and excessive concern about body shape and weight (American Psychiatric Association, 2000).

One risk factor involves cultural pressures to develop a slim body, as seen in the increase in bulimia nervosa among Fijian girls. Another risk factor involves personality characteristics, such as being excessively concerned about appearance, being too sensitive, and having low self-esteem and high personal standards for achievement. For some, bouts of depression, anxiety, mood swings, and problems with social relationships may trigger episodes of bulimia nervosa, which may lead to obesity (Stice, 2002).

Binge-Eating Disorder

An eating disorder that resembles bulimia nervosa but is less severe and affects about 3% of the general population is called binge-eating disorder (Hudson et al., 2007).

Binge-eating disorder is characterized by recurrent binge-eating episodes during which a person feels a loss of control over his or her eating. Unlike bulimia nervosa, there is no vomiting, use of laxatives, or rigorous dieting and fasting (NIMH, 2012a).

Because people with binge-eating disorder do not engage in behaviors to rid their bodies of the calories consumed (such as vomiting or using laxatives), they tend to be overweight or obese. Their excessive eating is often triggered by stress, and they experience great distress about their overeating behaviors.

Eating disorders clearly illustrate how various personality and psychosocial factors can not only influence but even override the normal functioning of one of our basic biological needs, food. ●

Using Money to Motivate Kids to Learn

Beginning when children are very young, we reward them for good behavior. We may give them a sticker for using the toilet or a cookie for cleaning up their bedroom. As children get older, some parents may reward them for getting good grades in school by giving them cash.

1 What type of operant conditioning consequence is getting a sticker for using the toilet?

Decades of research show that providing children with rewards is an effective way to motivate them to perform desirable behaviors. Yet, there is much controversy about using monetary rewards in our educational system. Roland Fryer, Jr., a Harvard professor, boldly suggests that schools use cash as a way to motivate students to attend classes, complete their homework, and obtain high scores on standardized tests. Opponents state that students should learn for the love of learning, rather than for monetary rewards. These individuals fear that money will cheapen the act of learning and that students will stop learning when the rewards eventually go away.

2 Which cognitive factor do opponents wish to use to motivate students to learn?

Despite widespread resistance, Fryer was determined to find out if his

3 What are the experimental and control groups in these studies? What are the independent and dependent variables?

proposed system would work. He designed and carried out ambitious experiments involving thousands of children of varying ages in schools across the country. In his studies, some groups of children would earn money for performance on desired behaviors (such as reading, grades, and test scores) and other groups would not be paid for any performance.

In one of the experimental conditions, children were paid for achieving high test scores, and the results showed that money did not improve learning or grades. In a second condition, students were paid for earning good grades, and the results showed that there was an improvement in attendance and grades, but no change in standardized test scores. In a third condition, paying children on a routine basis for small accomplishments, such as attendance and behavior, resulted in increased standardized reading test scores. Last, in the fourth condition, paying students to read books dramatically improved their reading comprehension and standardized test scores, and these children continued to perform better the following year, long after the monetary rewards had ended.

Fryer explains that the reason the improvement was highest in the last condition was likely

4 What do psychologists call objects, such as money, that we learn to value? What happens to the value of these objects over time?

because students were frequently rewarded for a specific behavior that is known to improve learning—reading books. It's quite possible that many students do not really know what type of work and effort are required to learn more and perform better on assessments. The results are as strong as or even stronger than the results of studies showing the benefits of decreasing class size and enrolling students in early education intervention programs, which actually cost much more than the financial reward system used by Fryer.

In response to those who criticize Fryer's efforts because they want children to learn for the love of learning, Fryer begins by agreeing with them, but states that for that to happen, we must begin by getting students involved in learning. His research data supports his position. Remember that children continued to perform better on reading tests even during the year after the monetary reward system ended. Last, Fryer reminds us that as adults, many of us work mostly for money, so it doesn't seem fair to hold kids to a higher standard than we hold for ourselves.

5 If students were paid after each book they read, which schedule of reinforcement was used?

6 In which level(s) of Maslow's hierarchy do academic performance and job performance belong?

Adapted from Ripley, 2010.

A Theories of Motivation

1. The combined physiological and psychological factors that cause you to act in specific ways at particular times are referred to as **(a)** _____. When motivated, you usually exhibit three characteristics: you are **(b)** _____ to do something; you **(c)** _____ your energies toward a specific goal; and you have different **(d)** _____ of feelings about reaching that goal.

2. The theory of motivation that applies primarily to animal motivation involves innate biological forces that determine behavior. This is called the **(a)** _____ approach. The reward/pleasure center approach says that there are several areas in the brain, including the **(b)** _____ and _____, that especially use the neurotransmitter **(c)** _____. The theory that states we are motivated to seek out activities that provide a level of stimulation that allows us to maintain our optimal level of arousal is called the **(d)** _____ theory. Motivation cannot be explained by only physiological factors; sometimes it is best explained by psychological factors, which is the focus of **(e)** _____ theory.

3. Food, water, and sleep are examples of **(a)** _____ needs. In comparison, needs that are acquired through learning and socialization are called **(b)** _____ needs. The theory that we satisfy our needs in ascending order, with physiological needs first and social needs later, is called **(c)** _____. According to this theory, needs are divided into five levels: biological, safety, love and belongingness, esteem, and self-actualization.

B Hunger

4. If there is an almost perfect balance between how much food an organism needs to maintain the body's energy needs and how much the organism actually eats, the organism's weight is said to be **(a)** _____. People who are severely overweight, as measured by a body mass index of 30 or higher are considered to be **(b)** _____. Three different factors influence the hunger drive. Factors that come from physiological changes in blood chemistry and signals from digestive organs that provide feedback to the brain, which, in turn, triggers us to eat or stop eating, are called **(c)** _____ factors. Factors that come from learned associations between food and other stimuli, sociocultural influences, and various personality problems are called **(d)** _____ factors. Factors that come from inherited instructions contained in our genes are called **(e)** _____ factors.

5. Biological factors that influence eating come from two different sources. Cues arising from physiological changes in your blood chemistry and signals from your body organs are called **(a)** _____; cues from your brain are called **(b)** _____.

6. Genetic factors that influence hunger come from four different sources: the number of cells that store fat, which are called **(a)** _____; your rate of burning the body's fuel, which is called your **(b)** _____; the body's tendency to keep a stable amount of fat deposits, which is called the **(c)** _____; and a number of **(d)** _____ genes that influence appetite, metabolism, and secretion of hormones regulating fat stores.

C Sexual Behavior

7. Human sexual behavior is influenced by three different factors. Inherited instructions for the development of sexual organs, hormonal changes at puberty, and neural circuits that control sexual reflexes are called **(a)** _____ factors. The fact that humans engage in sexual behavior for many reasons besides reproduction and the fact that humans experience sexual difficulties that have no physical or medical basis indicate the influence of **(b)** _____ factors on sexual behavior. Factors that regulate the secretion of sex hormones, which play a role in the development of secondary sexual characteristics, influence sexual motivation (more so in animals than in humans), regulate the development of ova and sperm, and control the female menstrual cycle, are called **(c)** _____ factors.

8. Biological sex factors include the secretion of sex hormones, which is controlled by an area of the brain called the **(a)** _____. The major male sex hormones secreted by the testes are called **(b)** _____, and the major female sex hormones secreted by the ovaries are **(c)** _____. When hormone levels are within the normal range, there is little **(d)** _____ between levels of sex hormones and sexual motivation in humans.

9. Three psychological sex factors are the individual's subjective experience and feelings of being a male or a female, which is called **(a)** _____; traditional or stereotypical behaviors, attitudes, and personality traits that society designates as masculine or feminine, which are called **(b)** _____; and whether a person is sexually aroused primarily by members of his or her own sex, the opposite sex, or both sexes, which is called **(c)** _____.

© Comstock/Thinkstock

Courtesy of Jeffrey M. Friedman, Rockefeller University

XY = High Testosterone

10. The persistent negative emotional state that occurs when there is a disconnect between a person's biological sex and gender identity is called _____.

11. The findings that identical twins are often alike in their sexual orientation and that homosexual brothers shared similar inherited material indicate the influence of **(a)** _____ factors on homosexual orientation. The finding that genetic factors do not necessarily determine sexual orientation indicates the influence of **(b)** _____ factors on sexual orientation.

12. There are two kinds of sexual problems. Problems that are characterized by repetitive or preferred sexual fantasies involving nonhuman objects (articles of clothing) are called **(a)** _____. Problems of sexual arousal or orgasm that interfere with adequate functioning during sexual behavior are called **(b)** _____. When a person seeks help for a sexual problem, the clinician will check whether the causes are **(c)** _____ or _____.

13. If a person has been infected by the human immuno-deficiency virus (HIV) but has not yet developed one or more of 26 specified illnesses, that person is said to be **(a)** _____. A person whose level of T-cells (CD4 immune cells) has dropped to below 200 per cubic milliliter of blood (one-fifth the level of a healthy person) and who may or may not have any other symptoms is said to have **(b)** _____.

D Cultural Diversity: Genital Cutting

14. In some cultures the female's external genitalia, usually including her clitoris and surrounding skin (labia minora), are cut away; this practice is called _____. Girls often submit to the fear, pain, and trauma of this procedure to gain social status, please their parents, and comply with peer pressure. A number of feminists in Africa have formed a society to fight the sexual mutilation of females.

© Jean-Marc Bouju/Impact/HIP/The Image Works

E Achievement

15. High in Maslow's needs hierarchy is a desire to set challenging goals and persist in pursuing those goals in the face of obstacles, frustrations, and setbacks. This social need is called the **(a)** _____. Someone who persists longer at tasks, shows better performance on tasks, activities, or exams, sets challenging but realistic goals, competes with others to win, and is attracted to careers that require initiative is said to have a high **(b)** _____. Individuals who score relatively high on tests of ability or intelligence but perform more poorly than their scores would predict are called **(c)** _____. Individuals who choose either easy, non-challenging tasks or challenging tasks where failure is probable and expected are said to be motivated by **(d)** _____.

© PhotoDisc, Inc.

16. If you engage in behaviors without receiving any external reward but because the behaviors themselves are personally rewarding, you are said to be **(a)** _____ motivated. If you engage in behaviors to reduce biological needs or obtain external rewards, you are said to be **(b)** _____ motivated.

F Research Focus: Overcoming Educational Disadvantages

R E A C H

17. Schools that best educate poor and minority students have **(a)** _____ class days and clearly stated **(b)** _____ and teach students not only academics but also **(c)** _____. Research findings indicate that the **(d)** _____ skills these schools are teaching students, such as patience and respect, have an important effect on children's future academic and career success.

G Application: Dieting & Eating Disorders

18. A healthy weight-maintenance program, which can reduce the risk of serious medical problems of **(a)** _____ people, involves changing **(b)** _____ toward food, changing **(c)** _____ patterns, developing an **(d)** _____ program, and sticking to a long-term **(e)** _____ program. Three eating disorders are: a pattern characterized by binge-eating, fear of not being able to stop eating, and regularly purging the body, which is called **(f)** _____; a pattern of binge-eating episodes without purging the body, which is called **(g)** _____; and another pattern in which a person starves to remain thin, has a fear of being fat, and has a disturbed body image, which is called **(h)** _____.

© Helga Esteb/Shutterstock.com

Answers: 1. (a) motivation, (b) energized, (c) direct, (d) intensities; 2. (a) instinct, (b) nucleus accumbens, ventral tegmental area, (c) dopamine, (d) arousal, (e) self-determination; 3. (a) biological, (b) social, (c) psychosocial, (e) genetic; 5. (a) peripheral cues, (b) central cues; logical, (d) psychosocial, (e) genetic; 5. (a) peripheral cues, (b) central cues; (c) Maslow's hierarchy of needs; 4. (a) ideal or optimal, (b) obese, (c) bio-6. (a) fat cells, (b) metabolic rate, (c) set point, (d) weight-regulating; 7. (a) genetic, (b) psychological, (c) biological; 8. (a) hypothalamus, (b) androgens, (c) estrogens, (d) correlation or association; 9. (a) gender identity, (b) gender roles, (c) sexual orientation; 10. gender dysphoria; 11. (a) genetic, (b) psychological; 12. (a) paraphilias, (b) sexual dysfunctions, (c) psychological, physiological; 13. (a) HIV positive, (b) AIDS; 14. genital cutting; 15. (a) achievement motive, (b) need for achievement, (c) underachievers, (d) fear of failure; 16. (a) intrinsically, (b) extrinsically; 17. (a) longer, (b) education goals, (c) character, (d) noncognitive; 18. (a) overweight, (b) attitudes, (c) eating, (d) exercise, (e) maintenance, (f) bulimia nervosa, (g) binge-eating disorder, (h) anorexia nervosa

Links to Learning

Key Terms/Key People

achievement need, 348

AIDS, 345

androgens, 339

anorexia nervosa, 353

arousal theory, 330

binge-eating disorder, 353

biological hunger factors, 334, 335

biological needs, 332

biological sex factors, 338

biosocial theory, 342

bisexual orientation, 341

body mass index (BMI), 334

bulimia nervosa, 353

central cues, 335

cognitive factors in motivation, 350

double standard for sexual behavior, 342

estrogens, 339

evolutionary theory, 342

extrinsic motivation, 331, 350

fat cells, 335, 336

fear of failure, 349

fixed action pattern, 330

gender dysphoria, 340

gender identity, 340

gender identity disorder, 340

gender roles, 341

genetic hunger factors, 334, 336

genetic sex factors, 338

genital cutting, 346

heterosexual orientation, 341

high need for achievement, 348

HIV positive, 345

homosexual orientation, 341

hypothalamus, 335, 339

incentives, 331

inhibited female orgasm, 344

instincts, 330

interactive model of sexual orientation, 341

intestines, 335

intrinsic motivation, 331, 350

Klinefelter's syndrome, 339

lateral hypothalamus, 335

liver, 335

maintenance program, 352

Maslow's hierarchy of needs, 332, 333

metabolic rate, 336, 352

motivation, 329

obesity, 334

optimal or ideal weight, 334

organic factors, 344

paraphilias, 344

peripheral cues, 335

premature or rapid ejaculation, 344

psychological factors, 344

psychological sex factors, 338, 340

psychosocial hunger factors, 334, 337

reward/pleasure center, 330

self-determination theory, 331

self-handicapping, 349

sensation seeker, 330

set point, 336, 352

sex chromosome, 338

sex hormones, 339

sexual dysfunctions, 344

sexual orientation, 341

social needs, 332, 348

stomach, 335

Thematic Apperception Test, or TAT, 348

underachievers, 349

ventromedial hypothalamus, 335

weight-regulating genes, 336

Yerkes-Dodson law, 330

Media Resources

Go to **CengageBrain.com** to access Psychology CourseMate, where you will find an interactive eBook, glossaries, flashcards, quizzes, videos, answers to Critical Thinking questions, and more. You can also access Virtual Psychology Labs, an interactive laboratory experience designed to illustrate key experiments first-hand.

Emotional Experience

What did Bethany feel during a shark attack?

What happened to 13-year old Bethany Hamilton at 7:30 on a Friday morning was something she would never forget. Bethany paddled her surfboard about a quarter-mile off the north shore of Kauai, Hawaii, and as she waited to catch the best waves, she noticed the water was clear and calm, like a swimming pool. The waves turned out to be too small to ride so she relaxed by holding the surfboard with her right arm and letting her left arm dangle in the warm water. Suddenly she saw a glimmer of gray in the clear blue water. Almost instantly, Bethany felt tremendous pressure and fierce yanking on her left arm. It was then she realized that the razor-sharp teeth of a 15-foot tiger shark were wrapped tightly around her left arm. When she saw the water around her turn bright red with streaks of her blood, her heart pounded like a hammer and her adrenaline flowed like water from a fire hose. The shark eventually let go of her arm and swam away. With great courage and perseverance, Bethany paddled to the beach as quickly as she could with only her right arm. Her left arm had been violently ripped off almost to the armpit, and the shark even took a big chunk out of her surfboard!

As Bethany approached the beach, people helped her off the surfboard and called for help. She was rushed to the hospital for surgery, and about a week after her stitches were removed, Bethany began surfing again. It was difficult learning to surf with only her right arm, but her extraordinary drive helped her win several surfing competitions after the attack. Although Bethany at times experiences dread and fright that something bad is going to happen again, for the most part, she is as comfortable as other surfers are while in the water (adapted from B. Hamilton, 2004). Her life story is so extraordinary that it is portrayed in the movie *Soul Surfer* (Dodd, 2011).

Bethany experienced a variety of emotions during and after her shark attack. During the attack, she felt intense anxiety and fear for her life. When she reached the shore, she felt relieved to be alive but worried about her missing arm. Sometime later, she felt fright about surfing again, but she also felt pride and joy after catching her first big wave after the attack. Although Bethany experienced over a half-dozen emotions, they all shared the same four components (Frijda, 2008).

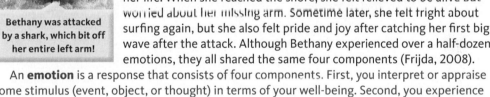
Bethany was attacked by a shark, which bit off her entire left arm!

An **emotion** is a response that consists of four components. First, you interpret or appraise some stimulus (event, object, or thought) in terms of your well-being. Second, you experience a subjective feeling, such as fear or happiness. Third, you have physiological responses, such as changes in heart rate or breathing. Fourth, you may show observable behaviors, such as smiling or crying.

Bethany's experience with the shark illustrates the four components of an emotion:

First, she *interpreted* or *appraised* the stimulus, a shark attack, as a very serious threat to her well-being and survival.

Second, she had the *subjective experience or feeling* of fear and terror.

Third, she had a variety of *physiological responses,* such as heart pounding and adrenaline pumping, which cause arousal and prepare the body for action, such as swimming away fast.

Fourth, she showed *overt* or *observable behaviors,* such as fearful facial expressions and rapid paddling to the beach. In some cases, such as playing poker, a person may experience a wide range of emotions but try to hide his or her overt behaviors by showing no facial expression, commonly known as a "poker face." In other cases, cultural factors influence overt behaviors, such as allowing American women but not usually American men to cry in public.

Although there is general agreement that emotions have four components, there is much discussion of the order in which these four components occur (Frijda, 2008). For instance, did Bethany have to think about the shark before she felt fear, or did she feel fear immediately and then think about how terrified she was? We'll discuss this as well as many other questions about emotions, such as why people can identify a fearful face quicker than a happy one.

Staying Happy

How long do emotions last?

Being attacked by a shark results in a very different emotional experience than winning big bucks in a lottery. Since lotteries began in the late 1970s, over 4,000 people have become instant millionaires. Immediately after winning, the new millionaires reported feeling intense pleasure, being ecstatic, and living in a dream world (Angelo, 1991). But what happens when a winner finally realizes that for the next 20 years he or she will receive a large monthly check? Will the emotional high continue, or will being a millionaire become a taken-for-granted experience?

Ten years after winning a $20-million lottery, would you still be very happy?

Researchers have studied lottery winners to find out what effect such an enormous windfall has had on their lives (CPO, 2006). Later in this module, we'll tell you what the researchers discovered about happiness and how it applies to lottery winners and you.

What's Coming

We'll discuss how emotions occur; how much our physiological responses, facial expressions, and interpretations contribute to emotions; whether feeling or thinking comes first in experiencing an emotion; whether there is a set of basic or universal facial expressions that occur across all cultures; what the functions of emotions are; how specific emotions work; and how emotions are used in lie detection.

We'll begin our discussion of emotions with how a swimmer's sight of a shark causes him or her to feel fear. ●

A Peripheral Theories

Studying Emotions

Why do you feel fear? Seeing a shark swimming nearby causes instant fear. Explaining how this fear arises has taken three different approaches.

© Andreas Meyer/Shutterstock.com

The **peripheral theories of emotions** emphasize how physiological changes in the body give rise to emotional feelings.

The **cognitive appraisal theory of emotions** emphasizes how interpretations or appraisals of situations result in emotional feelings.

The **affective neuroscience approach** studies the underlying neural bases of mood and emotion by focusing on the brain's neural circuits that evaluate stimuli and produce or contribute to experiencing and expressing different emotional states.

We'll begin with one of the peripheral approaches to understanding emotions, the historic James-Lange theory, which says that if you see a bear, you are frightened because you run. Is it true?

James-Lange Theory and Cannon-Bard Theory

This theory, proposed independently in the late 1800s by two psychologists, William James and Carl Lange, emphasizes specific physiological patterns as causing emotional feelings.

The **James-Lange theory** says that our brains interpret specific physiological changes as feelings or emotions and that there is a different physiological pattern underlying each emotion.

James (1884/1969) illustrated his theory with the example of seeing a bear: If you see a bear, "you are frightened because you run" rather than run because you are frightened. According to the James-Lange theory, the order for the occurrence of the four components of an emotion is shown in the figure below.

1 Stimulus (shark) triggers different physiological changes in your body.

2 Your brain interprets different patterns of physiological changes. Interpret

3 Different physiological changes produce different emotions (fear).

4 You may or may not show observable responses (scream).
© PhotoDisc, Inc.

There are three major criticisms of the James-Lange theory. First, different emotions are not necessarily associated with different patterns of physiological responses. For instance, anger, fear, and sadness share similar physiological patterns of arousal (Cacioppo et al., 2000). This particular criticism led to Walter Cannon and Philip Bard developing the Cannon-Bard theory.

The **Cannon-Bard theory** says that emotions originate in the brain; they are not the result of physiological responses.

Thus, according to the Cannon-Bard theory, James's bear example is backward: Instead of the act of running making you feel fear, you feel fear and then run.

A second criticism of the James-Lange theory is illustrated by people whose spinal cords have been severed at the neck. These individuals are deprived of most of the feedback from their physiological responses, yet they experience emotions with little or no change in intensity. This finding is the opposite of what the James-Lange theory would predict, which is that these people should experience little or no emotion (Chwalisz et al., 1988).

Third, some emotions, such as feeling guilty or jealous, may require a considerable amount of interpretation or appraisal of the situation. The sequence involved in feeling such complex emotions points to the influence of cognitive factors on emotional feelings (Clore & Ortony, 2008).

Next, we turn to the facial feedback hypothesis, which offers a different explanation of how emotions occur.

Facial Feedback Hypothesis

The idea that feedback from facial muscles causes emotional feelings originated with Charles Darwin (1872/1965) and evolved into the facial feedback hypothesis (Keltner & Ekman, 2000; Matsumoto et al., 2008).

The **facial feedback hypothesis** says that the sensations and feedback from the movement of your facial muscles and skin are interpreted by your brain as different emotions.

According to the facial feedback hypothesis, the four components of emotions occur in the order shown in the figure below.

1 Stimulus (shark) triggers changes in facial muscles and skin.

2 Your brain interprets feedback from facial muscles and skin.

3 Different facial feedback results in feeling different emotions (fear). Interpret

4 You may or may not show observable responses (scream).
© PhotoDisc, Inc.

While it is true that facial expressions of fear, happiness, sadness, and disgust involve different muscle-skin patterns, there is little evidence that it's the feedback from these different muscle groups that actually causes the emotions. For example, if feedback from facial muscles caused emotions, then individuals whose facial muscles are completely paralyzed should not be able to experience emotions, yet they do report feeling emotions (K. M. Heilman, 2000).

Although researchers have not confirmed Darwin's original idea that feedback from facial muscles *alone* is sufficient to produce emotions, they have found that feedback from facial muscles, such as those involved in smiling or crying, may influence your mood and overall emotional feeling and increase the intensity of your subjective emotional experience (Kolb & Taylor, 2000).

The peripheral theories of emotions show that physiological changes in the body and feedback from facial muscles contribute to but do not themselves cause different emotions. What can cause an emotion are the thoughts that go on inside your brain (mind). ●

B Cognitive Appraisal Theory

Thoughts and Emotions

Can thoughts cause emotions?

Suppose you won a lottery and felt very happy. Weeks later, the thought of winning still makes you feel very happy. The fact that your thoughts alone can give rise to emotions illustrates the importance of cognitive factors.

Current cognitive theories of emotions can be traced back to the original research of Stanley Schachter and Jerome Singer (1962), whose classic experiment was the first to show the importance of cognitive interpretation, or appraisal, in contributing to emotional states.

Schachter-Singer Experiment

As shown in the figure below, Schachter and Singer first injected a group of people with a hormone, epinephrine (adrenaline), that caused physiological arousal, such as increased heart rate and blood pressure. However, the participants were told that the injections were vitamins and were not told that they would experience physiological arousal. After the injections, the participants were placed in different situations—a happy one or an angry one.

Those people in the happy situation often reported feeling happy, and their observable behaviors were smiles. However, those in the angry situation often reported feeling angry, and their observable behaviors were angry facial expressions. Schachter and Singer explained that the participants did not know that their physiological arousal was caused by hormone injections and they looked around for other causes in their environment. Participants interpreted environmental cues, such as being in a happy or angry situation, as the cause of their arousal and thus reported feeling happy or angry. The Schachter-Singer cognitive theory was the first to show that cognitive factors, such as your interpretation of events, could influence emotional feelings.

The Schachter-Singer finding that your cognitive processes, such as thoughts, interpretations, and appraisals of situations, can trigger emotions became the basis for today's cognitive appraisal theory of emotions.

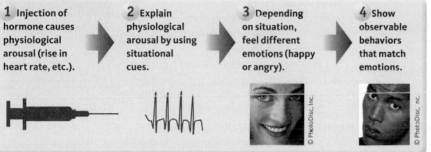

1 Injection of hormone causes physiological arousal (rise in heart rate, etc.).

2 Explain physiological arousal by using situational cues.

3 Depending on situation, feel different emotions (happy or angry).

4 Show observable behaviors that match emotions.

Cognitive Appraisal Theory

The cognitive appraisal theory began with the experiment of Schachter and Singer and was developed into its present form by many researchers (Ellsworth & Scherer, 2003; Lazarus, 2006).

The **cognitive appraisal theory** says that your interpretation or appraisal or thought or memory of a situation, object, or event can contribute to, or result in, your experiencing different emotional states.

Suppose you're thinking about having won the lottery last week and planning what to do with all that money. According to the cognitive appraisal theory, the sequence for how thinking results in feeling happy is shown in the figure on the right.

Thought then emotion. Thinking of your first serious kiss can make you feel happy, while thinking of times you were jealous can make you sad or angry. In these cases, as well as in feeling pride, envy, or compassion, the thinking or appraisal occurs before the emotion (Lazarus, 2006).

Emotion without conscious thought. Imagine being on a nature walk, turning a corner, and seeing a huge snake on the path. In this case, the feeling of fear is instant, without conscious thought or appraisal; you don't have to think "that's a dangerous snake and I better be careful." On the next page, we'll discuss how seeing a snake

can elicit fear instantaneously, before awareness or conscious thoughts can occur (Helmuth, 2003b; Zajonc, 1984). Thus, in some situations, such as those that involve personal relationships, problems at work, fond family memories, or terrible tragedies, thoughts precede and result in emotional feelings. In other situations, such as those involving attack or threat to one's personal survival, emotions can occur instantly, without conscious thought or awareness.

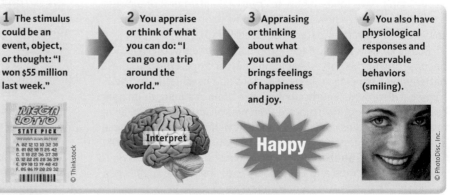

1 The stimulus could be an event, object, or thought: "I won $55 million last week."

2 You appraise or think of what you can do: "I can go on a trip around the world."

3 Appraising or thinking about what you can do brings feelings of happiness and joy.

4 You also have physiological responses and observable behaviors (smiling).

Interpret

Happy

The relatively new finding that certain emotions, especially fear, can occur without conscious thought or awareness brings us to the most recent approach to the study of emotions, called affective neuroscience, which we'll discuss next. ●

C Affective Neuroscience Approach

Four Qualities of Emotions

What emotion do you feel?

Seeing this ferocious wolf suddenly appear on your nature walk would cause instant fear. The ability of humans to sense and evaluate stimuli as being more or less favorable to their well-being is an important function of emotions, which have four unique qualities (R. J. Dolan, 2002).

1 Unlike most psychological states, emotions are felt and *expressed in stereotypical facial expressions*, such as showing a fearful expression (open mouth, raised eyebrows), and accompanied by *distinctive physiological responses* (fear is accompanied by a fast heart rate, quick shallow breathing, and sweaty palms).

How quickly would you react?

2 Emotions are *less controllable* than we might like and may *not respond to reason.* For example, advising someone to "calm down" or "control your temper" may have little effect. In fact, some people may need to attend anger management programs to help them gain some rational self-control over their hot tempers.

3 Emotions have an enormous *influence on many cognitive processes*, such as making decisions, developing personal relationships, and selecting goals. One reason for this is that you essentially have two brains: an older primitive or animal brain, called the limbic system (see p. 80), which regulates emotions, and a newer forebrain, which influences but doesn't completely control the limbic system. For example, well-known politicians, who intellectually know better, have gotten into trouble by engaging in illicit sexual activities, and some students, who intellectually know better, admit to doing badly in their freshman year and explain that they were emotionally immature.

4 Some emotions are *hard-wired in the brain.* That's why babies don't have to learn how to cry to gain attention or express basic needs or learn how to smile to show happiness and form social bonds with their parents or caretakers.

Study of emotions. Recently, the study of emotions has become one of the hottest topics in neuroscience, which studies patients who have discrete brain lesions and psychiatric and neurological disorders. Neuroscientists use brain scanning or imaging techniques to identify structures and neural activities in the living brain. These studies contribute to the new affective neuroscience approach to understanding mood and emotions (Panksepp, 2008).

The **affective neuroscience approach** studies the underlying neural bases of mood and emotion by focusing on the brain's neural circuits that evaluate stimuli and produce or contribute to experiencing and expressing different emotional states.

The word *affective* suggests affect or emotion. The word *neuroscience* suggests research methods that involve studying patients with neurological disorders and using methods that involve brain scans or imaging to identify neural activity in the living brain.

Amygdala: The Emotional Detector

Can you detect a snake quicker than a flower?

Detecting stimuli. If you were shown a number of stimuli, would you detect a snake quicker than a flower? In one study, researchers found that, compared to detecting unemotional neutral targets (flowers, mushrooms), we are faster at detecting targets with emotional meaning, such as faces with positive (smiling) or negative (fearful) expressions, and threatening things, such as snakes or spiders. However, we are fastest at identifying emotional stimuli that may pose a threat—fearful faces, snakes (M. A. Williams & Mattingley, 2006). These findings support the idea that our brains have evolved the ability to quickly recognize dangerous things in our environment and thus increase our chances for survival. Further support for this idea comes from scanning or imaging studies (see p. 70) that point to an emotional detector in the brain.

Threat to your survival

Emotional detector. Your physical survival depends in part on a brain structure about the size and shape of an almond—the amygdala (P. J. Whalen & Phelps, 2009).

The **amygdala** (*ah-MIG-duh-la*) is located in the tip of the brain's temporal lobe and receives input from all the senses. Using all this sensory input, the amygdala monitors and evaluates whether stimuli have positive (happy) or negative (fearful) emotional significance for our well-being and survival. It is also involved in storing memories that have emotional content.

One researcher said the amygdala (figure below) is like a guard dog that is constantly sniffing for threats, and this gives us an evolutionary advantage in terms of survival (LeDoux, 2003). For example, brain scans indicate that the amygdala is especially activated when we view emotional facial expressions indicating fear or distress (Ohman, 2009). When the amygdala is damaged, patients often overlook important emotional cues. For instance, they identify all faces as being more trustworthy and approachable than the rest of us do (Adolphs, 2004; Dobbs, 2006a). Similarly, when the amygdala is damaged in animals, they no longer learn to fear and avoid dangerous situations (Hamann et al., 2002).

Amygdala

Amygdala is an emotional detector.

In a rare case, researchers were able to closely study a person who has no amygdala. The patient, named "SM," demonstrates no fear of frightening stimuli, such as spiders and snakes, and repeatedly places her life in great risk. For example, she walks through a park alone at night, even though she was attacked by a man with a knife at the same park the day before (Feinstein et al., 2010).

How the amygdala detects a frightening stimulus, such as a snake, almost instantaneously is a neat trick.

Brain Circuits for Emotions

What happens when you feel fear?

Researchers use brain-scanning or imaging techniques (fMRI—see p. 70) to measure neural activity and trace neural pathways or circuits throughout the living brain. We'll focus on the neural activity that occurs when a person is confronted with a fearful stimulus, such as seeing a ferocious wolf. This neural circuit is important for our survival and has received considerable attention (Quirk, 2007; M. Siegal, 2005).

A Slower Circuit

We'll give a simplified version of the sequence of neural activity in the brain that would occur when you see a ferocious wolf. Visual information about the wolf's shape, size, and color enters the *eyes* (1), which send neural information about the "wolf" to a structure in the brain called the *thalamus* (2). In turn, the thalamus relays the neural information to another part of the brain called the *visual cortex* (3). The visual cortex transforms the neural signals into the image of a ferocious wolf and relays the "wolf" information to the *amygdala* (4). The amygdala interprets the neural information and signals the presence of a threat, which results in feelings of fear, an associated fearful facial expression, and probably a lot of yelling and running to escape from the threat. And this neural activity happens very fast, in about 0.12 second. However, there is an even faster circuit that gives a quicker warning.

B Faster Circuit

Researchers have evidence of an even faster circuit for identifying threatening stimuli. As usual, visual information about the wolf enters the *eyes* (1), which send neural information about the "wolf" to the *thalamus* (2). The thalamus sends neural information directly to the *amygdala* (4), saving time by skipping the *visual cortex* (3). This means that the amygdala recognizes the threatening wolf and triggers a fearful response almost instantly after seeing the wolf. This is an example of an emotion occurring without any awareness or conscious thought. Researchers believe that this **faster circuit** evolved because its amazingly quick warning of a threatening stimulus greatly improves our chances of avoiding and surviving dangerous stimuli.

© Photo24/Brand X Pictures/Getty Images

C Prefrontal Cortex

The part of your brain that is involved in complex cognitive functions, such as making decisions, planning, and reasoning, is called the *prefrontal cortex* (5). The prefrontal cortex has several functions: It is involved in remembering and experiencing emotions even when the fear object is not present, such as when you tell a friend about your wolf encounter and again feel fear or recall a joke and laugh; it is also involved in anticipating and analyzing the potential rewards, punishments, and emotional consequences of performing or not performing certain behaviors (Fuster, 2008). For example, the prefrontal cortex is involved in analyzing the emotional consequences, rewards, and punishments of deciding whether to go to a party instead of studying for an exam. Because reason often has less effect on emotions than you would like, you may decide to go and enjoy the party and live with the potential disappointment and unhappiness of doing poorly on the exam.

In some cases, faulty functioning of the prefrontal cortex, perhaps due to undeveloped neural connections or circuits, may result in less rational control of emotions, which in turn increases the risk for committing impulsive acts of violence or aggression (Strueber et al., 2006). Researchers warn that this finding points to the need for developing new treatments, both behavioral and drug, to help some people suppress their impulsive and violent emotions (Bradley et al., 2005; Quirk, 2007).

The kinds of studies that we have just discussed illustrate the affective neuroscience approach to understanding emotions as well as emotional disorders.

Fear and the Amygdala

Why do some have more fears?

Some individuals suffer from social phobias, which means they avoid going out in public because they have an enormous fear of being scrutinized, which would surely result in being humiliated or embarrassed. Researchers wondered if these fears might be reflected in the activity of the amygdala, which evaluates and signals threats from the environment.

Individuals with social phobias and healthy individuals were shown color photos of faces (happy, fearful, angry, and contemptuous) while researchers used brain scans (fMRIs) to record the neural activity of the amygdala. When individuals with social phobias were looking at photos of angry and contemptuous faces, there was increased neural activity in the left amygdala compared to the activity in healthy individuals. Researchers concluded that the amygdala of social phobics is particularly active when processing angry and contemptuous faces (M. B. Stein et al., 2002). This study, which is an example of the affective neuroscience approach, identified neurological factors that may be useful in evaluating and treating emotional disorders.

Phobias and other anxieties are believed to result from there being more neural connections running from the amygdala to the cortex (see p. 74) than from the cortex to the amygdala. This explains why our anxieties often control our thoughts and why our thoughts cannot always lower our anxieties (Dobbs, 2006a). ●

Social fears result in an overactive amygdala.

Definition

When did you first smile?

When you were 4–6 weeks old, you began to smile, which greatly pleased your parents. Smiling is considered one of the universal emotional expressions (Ekman, 2003).

Universal emotional expressions are specific inherited facial patterns or expressions that signal specific feelings or emotional states, such as a smile signaling a happy state.

For example, notice that although the four individuals in the photos come from four different countries, they display similar facial expressions—smiles—which you would interpret as showing happiness.

Why do people from different cultures smile the same way?

Number of expressions. Researchers generally agree that six or seven facial expressions for emotions are universal, which means they are recognized across cultures: anger, happiness, fear, surprise, disgust, sadness, and possibly contempt (Ekman, 2003; Ekman & Rosenberg, 2005; Matsumoto et al., 2008). Other emotions, such as pride, jealousy, and compassion, do not have particular facial expressions.

The existence of universal emotions was scientifically formulated by Charles Darwin (1872/1965), and his ideas have inspired modern-day researchers to study universal emotional expressions (Ekman, 2003). We'll review two kinds of evidence—cross-cultural and genetic—that support the idea of universal emotional expressions.

Cross-Cultural Evidence

How do individuals from relatively isolated cultures in New Guinea, Burma, and Borneo (photos from top to bottom) know how to smile or what a smile means? One answer is that a smile is one of the unlearned, inherited universal emotional expressions. For example, researchers showed photos of different facial expressions to individuals in 20 different Western cultures and 11 different primitive (illiterate and isolated) cultures. Researchers found that individuals in both Western and primitive cultures showed significant agreement on which facial expressions signaled which emotions. Most individuals in Western and primitive cultures agreed that a smile indicated happiness. However, only about one-third of individuals in primitive cultures agreed that an open-mouth and raised-eyebrows expression indicated surprise.

Based on the cross-cultural findings, researchers concluded that there are innately or biologically determined universal facial expressions for emotions. Universal emotional expressions are thought to have evolved because they served adaptive and survival functions for our ancestors (Ekman, 2003; Ekman & Rosenberg, 2005).

Support for universal emotional expressions also comes from genetic evidence.

Genetic Evidence

How does an infant who is born blind learn to smile? Is it possible that the programming of specific facial expressions, such as smiling, is in the DNA, which is a chemically coded alphabet that contains and writes out genetic instructions for the development of the body and brain? One answer to this question comes from observing the development of emotional expressions in infants.

Researchers found that at 4–6 weeks of age, infants begin to smile. The question is whether an infant's smiling is biologically programmed or whether the infant has learned to smile by observing and imitating the parents' facial expressions. The answer is that even infants born blind, who never observe their parents smiling, begin to smile at 4–6 weeks. This observation supports the idea that some facial expressions are biologically programmed (Eibl-Eibesfeldt, 1973).

Additional evidence for universal emotions comes from reports that infants in all cultures develop facial expressions in a predictable order. For instance, infants 4–6 weeks old begin to smile, infants 3–4 months old show angry and sad facial expressions, and infants 5–7 months old show fear (Izard, 1993; Kopp & Neufeld, 2003).

Last, research examining the facial expressions of sighted and blind individuals found that blind individuals produced the same facial expressions for anger, disgust, surprise, joy, sadness, and contempt as those who are sighted. These results provide support for facial expressions being innate or genetically programmed and not learned through observation (Matsumoto & Willingham, 2009).

Although there is evidence supporting the existence of universal emotions, there is also some research data that suggest otherwise.

Criticisms

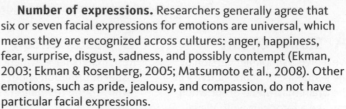

The general consensus during the past 20 years has been that emotions are genetically programmed into us and that their expressions are universal, making them recognizable across cultures all over the world. However, recent research suggests that some emotional expressions take a surprisingly long time for children to recognize. For instance, researchers found that until the age of 5, children do not understand the meaning of adults' facial expressions of disgust (J. Russell, 2010). Moreover, other researchers have reported that the interpretation of emotional expressions is highly dependent on context or situation (L. F. Barrett et al., 2011). Take a look at the left photo of Serena Williams. How do you think she is feeling? You might interpret her facial expression to mean that she is angry or in pain. But if you look at the right photo, where the face is seen in the larger context of her body, you might now see that she is really excited. ●

E Functions of Emotions

What good are emotions?

To appreciate the value and worth of emotions, try living a single day without feeling or expressing any emotions. It would be one of the worst days of your life because emotions have three important functions. Emotions send powerful *social signals* about how you feel; emotions help you *adapt and survive* in your world; and emotions *arouse and motivate* many of your behaviors. We'll examine each emotional function in turn.

Social Signals

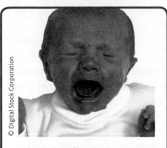

This baby's facial expression is a signal to show others that she is _____.

You would probably fill in the above blank with "distressed, unhappy, in need of something (food, dry diaper)." Thus, one function of emotions is to **send social signals** about one's feelings or needs. Because the baby's facial expression signals distress, she is likely to elicit help, sympathy, or compassion from her parents or caregiver. This is one example of how we send signals through facial expressions (Keltner et al., 2003).

Facial expressions that accompany emotions may send social signals about how we feel as well as provide social signals about what we are going to do.

For example, if you smiled at a classmate you didn't know, it may signal that you're feeling friendly and perhaps that you wish to meet this person.

In some cases, there may be gender differences in the ability to recognize facial expressions. For instance, men appear to be better than women at finding angry faces in a crowd, and women appear to be better than men in detecting facial expressions signaling happiness, sadness, surprise, and disgust (M. A. Williams & Mattingley, 2006).

Survival, Attention, and Memory

If you're walking through a strange neighborhood at night, you may feel fear. Fear is a signal that all is not well, so you should be careful. Emotions help us evaluate situations (Rothbart & Sheese, 2007).

The **evolutionary theory of emotions** says that one function of emotions is to help us evaluate objects, people, and situations in terms of how good or bad they are for our well-being and survival (Rozin, 2003).

There are many examples of emotions having *survival value:* showing anger (below photo) to escape or survive a dangerous or threatening situation, showing disgust to signal the presence of poisonous or rotten food, or feeling fear and becoming watchful when walking home at night.

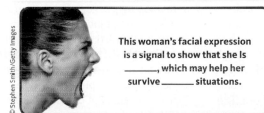

This woman's facial expression is a signal to show that she is _____, which may help her survive _____ situations.

Our facial expressions also help us manage our sensory experiences. For instance, when we express disgust, we block our nasal passages, narrow our visual field, and slow our eye movement. This helps us to not smell or see disgusting things. When we express fear, we open our nasal passages, enlarge our visual field, and quicken our eye movements, which helps us to be more aware of our surroundings (Susskind et al., 2008). Emotions also affect our attention and memory.

Attention. Feeling happy when you see your honey means he or she will get your full attention. Feeling angry when you are threatened means you're totally focused on getting out of this situation. These are examples of another function of emotions, which is to *focus one's attention* and thus better detect and respond to emotional situations (Rothbart & Sheese, 2007).

Memory. Strong emotions trigger hormone secretion that causes memories to be "carved in stone" (see p. 247). Thus, emotions help *increase memory* of emotionally charged events (Dobbs, 2006a). This results in better remembering events that are beneficial or dangerous to our well-being.

Arousal and Motivation

Earlier we discussed how Bethany's emotional reaction to seeing a shark included a variety of physiological responses, such as heart pounding and adrenaline pumping, that cause arousal. One major function of emotions is to *produce general arousal*, which prepares the body for some action (Hamm et al., 2003). In Bethany's case, maximum arousal helped her get to shore, but in other cases, such as taking a test, maximum arousal may interfere with performance.

In fact, there is a relationship between emotional arousal and performance on a task. That relationship is called the Yerkes-Dodson law.

The **Yerkes-Dodson law** says that performance on a task is an interaction between the level of physiological arousal and the difficulty of the task. For difficult tasks, low arousal results in better performance; for most tasks, moderate arousal helps performance; and for easy tasks, high arousal may facilitate performance.

If we apply the Yerkes-Dodson law to taking difficult exams, we would predict that a person with high test anxiety (high arousal) would do more poorly than someone with comparable ability but low test anxiety. Researchers confirmed this prediction by finding that students who were highly aroused because of either high test anxiety or a lot of coffee (caffeine) scored more poorly on difficult tests than students who had low test anxiety or were less aroused (less caffeine) (K. J. Anderson, 1994). The graph below shows how the optimal level of arousal for best performance depends on the complexity of the task.

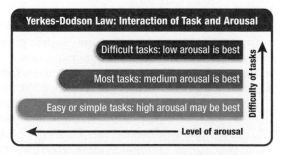

Yerkes-Dodson Law: Interaction of Task and Arousal

Difficult tasks: low arousal is best

Most tasks: medium arousal is best

Easy or simple tasks: high arousal may be best

Difficulty of tasks

Level of arousal

Besides affecting performance on various tasks, emotions also increase physiological arousal, which forms the basis for lie detector tests, discussed in the Application section (pp. 370–371).

Next, we'll turn to a positive emotion and the question: Why doesn't happiness last longer? ●

F Happiness

Positive Emotions

What makes you happy?

Pam was unmarried, eight months pregnant, and holding down two jobs when she stopped in at Jackson's Food Store for her morning orange juice and one lottery ticket. She remembers praying, "Please, God, let something happen so I can afford a small studio apartment" (S. Reed & Free, 1995, p. 63). The next day she was ecstatic when she discovered that her single lottery ticket was worth $87 million.

How long will my happiness last?

Happiness, usually indicated by smiling and laughing, is a mental state that can result from momentary pleasures, such as a funny commercial; short-term joys, such as a great date; and long-term satisfaction, such as an enjoyable relationship.

Inside the brain, the amygdala is involved in recognizing happy facial expressions and remembering happy occurrences (laughing at jokes) (W. M. Kelley, 2002; P. J. Whalen et al., 2009). In addition, the brain has a special reward/pleasure center that's involved in happiness.

The **reward/pleasure center** includes several areas of the brain, such as the nucleus accumbens and ventral tegmental area, and several neurotransmitters, especially dopamine. These and other brain areas make up a neural circuit that produces rewarding and pleasurable feelings, such as happiness.

Nucleus accumbens

Ventral tegmental area

Reward/pleasure center

Researchers found that many behaviors—eating, developing romantic attachments, engaging in sex, gambling, using recreational drugs (cocaine), looking at photos of attractive people, and listening to great music—activate the brain's reward/pleasure center (top figure) and result in happy and pleasurable feelings (Berridge, 2003; Nestler, 2005).

For example, the $87 million that Pam received activated her brain's reward/pleasure center to trigger much happiness, and this occurrence was stored as a happy memory by her amygdala. But, happiness is about more than measurable physiological processes; it is also about people's life experiences. Researchers have asked: What makes people happy in the long term?

Long-Term Happiness

How much happiness can money buy?

When researchers interviewed lottery winners 1 to 24 months after they had won large sums of money, the majority reported positive changes, such as financial security, new possessions, more leisure time, and earlier retirement. However, when asked to rate their happiness one year after winning, lottery winners were no happier than before (Diener & Diener, 1996). Sometime after winning the lottery, a woman was asked about her level of happiness and she responded, "I don't know whether 'happy' is the word. I'm still trying to grasp it" (Landau, 2011). Why the happy feeling of winning a lottery doesn't last is explained by the adaptation level theory.

The **adaptation level theory** says that we quickly become accustomed to receiving some good fortune; we take the good fortune for granted within a short period of time; and as a result, the initial impact of our good fortune fades and contributes less to our long-term level of happiness.

According to the adaptation level theory, the immediate emotional high of obtaining good fortune—such as graduating from college, getting married, getting promoted, or winning a lottery—will fade with time and contributes less and less to our long-term happiness (Brickman et al., 1978; Easterlin, 2003; Seligman, 2002).

Researchers find that happiness is not a fixed state and does not primarily result from getting more money, cars, clothes, or promotions because these achievements gradually lose their emotional appeal, as predicted by the adaptation level theory. Rather, being happy is a continuous process associated with making an effort to enjoy simple, daily pleasurable events, people, or situations. It includes a daily diet of little highs as well as pursuing personal goals,

Riches don't guarantee happiness.

developing a sense of meaningfulness, having intimate relationships, and not judging yourself against what others do but by your own yardstick (Lykken, 2003; Seligman, 2002; Wiederman, 2007).

Gender differences in happiness. Researchers report that women are, on average, happier than men in early adulthood, but men end up happier later in life. The point at which men's happiness exceeds that of women is near the age of 50. One explanation is that by age 50, men are more satisfied with their family (men are more likely to be married than women after age 34) and finances (men have greater spending power) (Plagnol & Easterlin, 2008).

Happiness across the life span. Happiness is associated with an extended life span, which makes the study of happiness across all ages especially important (Frey, 2011; Lyubomirsky, 2011). Research data show the following trends in happiness across the life span: At about age 18, young adults are rather happy, but as life begins to throw challenges at them, they report feeling less and less happy until about the age of 50, which marks a sharp turning point. Beginning at age 50, people generally report getting happier and happier until about age 75, which is then followed by a slight decrease in happiness that fortunately doesn't reach the low point experienced at age 50 (Bakalar, 2010).

Genetic differences in happiness. One reason some people are just generally happier than others is one's individual *happiness set point*. Each person has a set point for experiencing a certain level of happiness—some more and some less. Although happiness can go up or down, it generally returns to the person's set point. Researchers estimate that one's personal level for being happy is set half by inherited or genetic influences, which affect the development of helpful or hurtful cognitive and personality traits, and half by various environmental factors, such as one's career, relationships, and finances (Lykken, 2003).

Next, we'll return to the expression of emotion as we look at how the displays of emotional expressions differ across cultures. ●

Showing Emotions

Do you cover your mouth when you laugh?

When I (R. P.) visited Japan, I noticed that many Japanese women covered their mouths when laughing, something American women never do. This Japanese–American cultural difference comes from differences in emotional display rules (Ekman, 2003, 2007).

Display rules are specific cultural norms that regulate how, when, and where a person expresses emotions and how much emotional expression is appropriate.

Here are examples of how different cultures have developed different display rules for emotional expressions.

Laughing and crying. American display rules generally encourage public displays of emotions, such as open-mouth laughing. In contrast, Japanese display rules for laughing include covering one's open mouth because showing much emotion in public is discouraged (Matsumoto et al., 2002). An Inuit (Eskimo) mother may let a baby cry to send the message that her culture disapproves of the display of negative emotions (Mauss, 2005).

Smiling. Another common public display of emotion made by Americans is smiling. In contrast, Russians rarely smile in public. Does this mean Russians are less happy than Americans? Not necessarily. Russians are more likely to display their emotions in private gatherings, such as with family, but in public situations Russians control their emotions more than Americans. Interestingly, Americans may mistake the restricted emotions displayed by Russians for irritability or unhappiness, and Russians may mistake the big smiles displayed by Americans as being phony (Krakovsky, 2009).

Anger. Among the Inuit (Eskimos), feelings of anger are strongly condemned, but among certain Arab groups, a man's failure to respond with anger is seen as dishonorable (Abu-Lughod, 1986; Briggs, 1970).

These examples show how different cultures have developed different display rules for emotional expressions. One may be unaware of such display rules until visiting another culture (Marsh et al., 2003).

Potential problems. Because of different display rules for expressing emotions, people from one culture may run into problems when traveling or conducting business in another culture. For example, Westerners often make direct eye contact and may show emotions during business meetings, while Asians avoid direct eye contact and outward expressions of emotions. Because of increased international travel and business, there are now companies that give advice and training on dealing with the display rules of other cultures (www.communicaid.com).

These examples show how culture influences the expression of emotional display rules. Depending on your culture, you perceive emotions differently.

Americans **don't cover** their mouths when they laugh.

Japanese **cover** their mouths when they laugh.

Perceiving Emotions

What's the most intense emotion?

Of these five emotions—surprise, anger, happiness, disgust, and sadness—which one do you rate as the most intense?

It turns out that your rating depends very much on your culture. For example, because the Japanese have a long history of discouraging any show of emotional intensity in public, researchers guessed that their ratings of emotional intensity would be different from those of Americans, who have a history of showing emotions of all intensities in public (Reitman, 1999).

Researchers asked a group of Japanese and a group of Americans to look at photos of five emotional expressions—anger, surprise, happiness, disgust, and sadness—and rate the intensity of each. As predicted, the Japanese gave lower ratings of *emotional intensity* to all five emotional expressions than the Americans did. The Japanese rated disgust as the most intense emotion of the five, while the Americans rated happiness as the most intense (Matsumoto & Ekman, 1989). This study illustrates how cultures affect the display of emotions and our perception of an emotion's intensity (Rozin, 2003).

Another cultural difference is how cultures view the expression of certain emotions. For example, in many Asian cultures, expressing emotion in moderation is preferred to expressing happiness because happiness is perceived to be a precursor to jealousy and disharmony with friends or family. In contrast, happiness is a highly valued emotional expression in Western cultures (Leu et al., 2011).

Although there are differences in how cultures perceive emotions, there are also some similarities. The results from one study suggest that perceiving emotions in music may be a universal human ability. Cameroon's Mafa farmers and Westerners are from vastly different cultures, yet they perceive emotions in music similarly. Both groups perceive fast-paced pieces as happy and slow-paced pieces as fearful. Also, they generally agree on which passages are sad (B. Bower, 2009a; T. Fritz, 2009). Other research has found that vocalizations of negative emotions, and not positive emotions, are recognized universally. For instance, sobbing and yelping are universally recognized as sadness and fear, respectively. The results suggest that the perception of negative emotions may have a biological component (Sauter et al., 2010).

After the Concept Review, we'll discuss emotional intelligence. ●

Japanese rated *disgust* as the most intense of five emotions.

Disgust

Americans rated *happiness* as the most intense of five emotions.

Happiness

1. An emotion is defined in terms of four components: You interpret or **(a)** _____ some stimulus, thought, or event in terms of your well-being; you have a subjective **(b)** _____, such as being happy or fearful; you experience bodily responses, such as increased heart rate and breathing, which are called **(c)** _____ responses; and you often show **(d)** _____ behaviors, such as crying or smiling.

2. A peripheral theory says that emotions result from specific physiological changes in our bodies and that each emotion has a different physiological pattern. The theory that says we feel fear because we run is called the **(a)** _____ theory. In contrast to this theory, the **(b)** _____ theory says that emotions originate in the brain; they are not the result of physiological responses.

3. Another peripheral theory says that feedback from the movement of facial muscles and skin is interpreted by your brain as an emotion; this idea is called the **(a)** _____ hypothesis. Although emotions can occur without feedback from facial muscles, facial feedback can influence your mood and contribute to the **(b)** _____ of an emotion.

4. A theory of emotions that grew out of the work of Schachter and Singer says that your interpretation, appraisal, thought, or memory of a situation, object, or event can contribute to, or result in, your experiencing different emotional states. This is called the _____ theory.

5. The most recent approach to understanding emotions studies the neural bases of mood and emotion by focusing on the brain's neural circuits that evaluate stimuli and produce or contribute to our experiencing and expressing different emotional states. This is called the _____ approach.

6. Emotions have four qualities: They are expressed in stereotypical **(a)** _____ expressions and have distinctive **(b)** _____ responses; they are less controllable and may not respond to **(c)** _____; they influence many **(d)** _____ functions; and some emotions, such as smiling, are **(e)** _____ in the brain. The brain area that functions to detect and evaluate stimuli, especially threatening ones, and to store memories with emotional

content is called the **(f)** _____. Because this brain structure receives sensory information so quickly, it triggers a fearful reaction without **(g)** _____. The brain structure involved in producing emotions from thoughts alone and in analyzing the emotional consequences of actions is called the **(h)** _____.

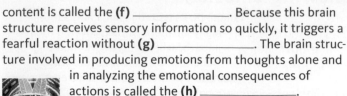

7. Specific inherited facial patterns or expressions that signal specific feelings or emotional states across cultures, such as a smile signaling a happy state, are called **(a)** _____. These emotional expressions, which include anger, happiness, fear, surprise, disgust, sadness, and possibly contempt, are thought to have evolved because they had important **(b)** _____ and _____ functions for our ancestors.

8. According to one theory, we inherit the neural structure and physiology to express and experience emotions, and we evolved basic emotional patterns to adapt to and solve problems important for our survival; this is called the **(a)** _____ theory. Facial expressions that accompany emotions send signals about how one **(b)** _____ and what one intends to do. Emotions focus one's **(c)** _____ so one can better respond to emotional situations and also increases **(d)** _____ of situations that may be either beneficial or dangerous to one's well-being.

9. Your performance on a task depends on the amount of physiological arousal and the difficulty of the task. For many tasks, moderate arousal helps performance; for new or difficult tasks, low arousal is better; and for easy or well-learned tasks, high arousal may facilitate performance. This relationship between arousal and performance is known as the _____.

10. According to one theory, you soon become accustomed to big happy events, such as getting a car; this theory is called the **(a)** _____. Long-term happiness is less dependent on wealth and more dependent on pursuing your own personal **(b)** _____ and developing meaningful **(c)** _____. Some people are just generally happier and some are generally less happy because of their happiness **(d)** _____.

11. Specific cultural norms that regulate when, where, and how much emotion we should or should not express in different situations are called _____. These rules explain why emotional expressions and intensity of emotions differ across cultures.

Unless otherwise noted, all images are © Cengage Learning

What Is Emotional Intelligence?

One of the exciting things about being a researcher is the chance to come up with new ideas. This

What is it and who has it?

happened in the early 1990s, when researchers came up with the idea of emotional intelligence, which they suggested made people more effective in social situations (Salovey & Mayer, 1990). By the mid-1990s, popular magazines, such as *TIME,* declared that emotional intelligence may redefine what it means to be smart and may be the best predictor of success in life (Gibbs, 1995).

Emotional intelligence is the ability to perceive emotions accurately, to take feelings into account when reasoning, to understand emotions, and to regulate or manage emotions in oneself and others (Salovey et al., 2008).

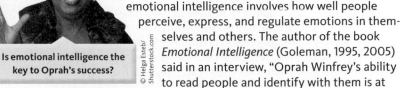
Is emotional intelligence the key to Oprah's success?
© Helga Esteb/Shutterstock.com

Unlike the traditional idea of intelligence involving performance on cognitive tests (IQ scores—see p. 282), emotional intelligence involves how well people perceive, express, and regulate emotions in themselves and others. The author of the book *Emotional Intelligence* (Goleman, 1995, 2005) said in an interview, "Oprah Winfrey's ability to read people and identify with them is at the heart of her success" (S. A. Brown, 1996, p. 85). In other words, the reason for Oprah's incredible success as a talk-show host is that she rates very high in emotional intelligence.

Since the early 1990s, researchers have been working to better understand emotional intelligence and just how important it really is (Mayer et al., 2008).

How Important Is Emotional Intelligence?

Here are some common remarks that show how emotions can influence our behaviors.

- "I was so angry, I couldn't think straight."
- "I get worse when people tell me to calm down."
- "When we argue, I get mad and say the wrong thing."
- "Sometimes I act on my feelings, right or wrong."

These kinds of self-reports point to the influence that emotions can have on what we say and do and on our success in life. According to supporters of the importance of emotional intelligence, the better our understanding of how emotions work, the more likely we are to find a compromise between our often strong emotional feelings ("I felt like doing that") and our equally strong rational thoughts ("I knew I should not have done that") (Mayer et al., 2000). However, these kinds of self-reports need to be confirmed by a more scientific technique. Emotional intelligence tests continue to be developed, and additional tests of reliability and validity (see p. 287) are necessary. Thus, the findings below are considered preliminary.

Emotional intelligence involves the ability to regulate or manage emotions.
© Jo Ann Snover/iStockphoto

Preliminary findings. Here are some findings reported from emotional intelligence tests: Youths who scored higher on emotional intelligence tests were less likely to have smoked cigarettes; schoolchildren who scored higher were rated as less aggressive by their peers and more helpful by their teachers; college-age males who scored higher were less likely to use alcohol and other drugs; and higher scores were related to being more satisfied with life (Brackett et al., 2004; Lopes et al., 2003; Salovey & Pizarro, 2003).

Emotional intelligence has also been shown to be a predictor of job performance and leadership ability, as well happiness in intimate relationships (O'Boyle et al., 2010). A study with college-age couples found that the unhappiest couples were those in which both individuals had low emotional intelligence test scores and the happiest couples were those in which both individuals scored high. Couples in which only one partner scored high on emotional intelligence, on average, fell between the other groups in terms of happiness (Brackett et al., 2005).

Researchers are only recently beginning to understand how it is that we can perceive, express, and regulate emotions. Next, we'll learn about how we perceive emotional expressions.

How Do We Perceive Emotional Expressions?

Scientists have known that we are able to detect emotions, such as fear and happiness, in people's faces almost instantly (M. A. Williams & Mattingley, 2006). Researchers now understand the brain mechanisms that permit us to very easily perceive emotions in others.

We are able to share the emotions others feel because of mirror neurons, which track the emotions of the person we are with and replicate the same emotions in us by activating our brains in the same way the other person's brain is activated (Goleman, 2006b). The discovery of mirror neurons shows us that human brains are innately prepared to connect with others in an intimate way, which enables us to share the emotions of others and be sensitive to their feelings.

When we empathize with someone, the activation pattern in our brains becomes the same as that of the person we are empathizing with (Goleman, 2006a). For instance, by using fMRI scans (see p. 70), researchers found that feeling disgust activates similar parts of the

Mirror neurons help us to share the emotions of others.
© Alliance/Shutterstock.com

brain when people smell a disgusting odor and when they observe a video of someone else feeling disgusted (Rizzolatti et al., 2006). Interestingly, people who score higher on empathy tests exhibit stronger mirror neuron reactions to others' facial expressions. Also, it appears that children with autism have mirror neuron deficiencies, which may explain why they are unable to perceive the emotional expressions of others (Binkofski & Buccino, 2007; Keysers, 2007).

Next, we'll learn about how difficult it is to accurately detect whether someone is lying. ●

I Application: Lie Detection

How did a spy pass a lie detector test twice?

For nine years, the Russians paid or promised $4.6 million to Aldrich Ames (photo on right), who was a high-level Central Intelligence Agency official. Later, Ames pleaded guilty to espionage, which involved selling secrets to the Russians. Ames is currently serving a life sentence in prison. The Ames case brings up the issue of lie detection because he reportedly passed at least two lie detector (polygraph) tests during the

> I lied, but I passed two lie detector tests.

time that he was selling U.S. secrets to Russia (R. L. Jackson, 1994). The publicity surrounding this case made people ask, "How could Ames be selling secrets and pass two lie detector tests?" The Ames case raises three questions: What is the theory behind lie detection? How is a lie detector test given? How accurate are lie detector tests?

What Is the Theory?

The lie detector test is based on the four components of an emotion that we discussed earlier. The first component of an emotion is interpreting or appraising a stimulus. In this case, Ames will need to interpret questions such as "Have you ever sold secrets to Russia?" The second component of an emotion is a subjective feeling, such as whether Ames will feel any guilt or fear when he answers "Yes" or "No" to the question "Have you ever sold secrets to Russia?" The third component of an emotion is the occurrence of various physiological responses (figure below). If Ames feels guilty about selling secrets, then his guilt feeling will be accompanied by physiological arousal, which includes increases in heart rate, blood pressure, breathing, and sweating of the hands. These physiological responses occur automatically and are usually involuntary because they are controlled by the autonomic nervous system (discussed in Module 4). The fourth component of an emotion is the occurrence of some overt behavior, such as a facial expression. Ames may be able to control his facial expressions and put on a nonemotional poker face. However, neither the presence nor the absence of expressions is critical to the theory behind lie detector tests.

Does the test measure lying?

Lie detector (polygraph) tests are based on the theory that, if a person tells a lie, he or she will feel some emotion, such as guilt or fear. Feeling guilty or fearful will be accompanied by involuntary physiological responses, which are difficult to suppress or control and can be measured with a machine called a polygraph.

A polygraph (lie detector) is about the size of a laptop computer (right figure) and measures chest and abdominal muscle movement during respiration, heart rate, blood pressure, and skin conductance or galvanic skin response.

The **galvanic skin response** is changes in sweating of the fingers (or palms) that accompany emotional experiences and are independent of perspiration under normal temperatures (Cacioppo et al., 1993).

For example, you may remember having sweaty or clammy palms when taking exams, giving a public talk, or meeting someone important, even though the temperature was not unduly hot.

We'll focus on the galvanic skin response because its changes are often the most obvious.

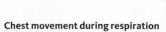

Chest movement during respiration

Abdominal movement during respiration

Heart rate and blood pressure

Skin conductance

Man hooked up to lie detector (polygraph)

Redrawn from an illustration by John Tom Seetin in "Working Knowledge," *Scientific American, 277* (6), December, 1997, p. 132. Reprinted by permission of the illustrator. All rights reserved.

What Is a Lie Detector Test?

Is the suspect lying?

Very few details have been released about how Ames, who apparently lied, passed two lie detector tests. Instead, we'll use a more detailed report of a man named Floyd, who told the truth but failed two lie detector tests.

Floyd was very surprised when two police officers came to his home. They had a warrant and arrested him for the armed robbery of a liquor store. However, the case against Floyd was weak, since none of the witnesses could positively identify him as the robber. Soon after his arrest, the prosecutor offered to drop all charges if Floyd agreed to take, and pass, a lie detector test. Floyd jumped at the chance to prove his innocence and took the test. He failed the lie detector test but insisted that he had not lied and that he be allowed to take a second one, which he also failed. Eventually Floyd was tried, found guilty, and sent to prison. He served several years behind bars before his lawyer tracked down the real robbers, which proved Floyd's innocence (*Los Angeles Times,* December 22, 1980).

Floyd was given the most commonly used procedure for lie detection in criminal investigations, which is called the *Control Question Technique* (Iacono, 2008; Iacono & Patrick, 2006).

The **Control Question Technique** is a lie detection procedure in which the examiner asks two kinds of questions: neutral questions that elicit little emotional response, and critical questions that are designed to elicit large emotional responses. The person answers only "Yes" or "No" to the questions and, if guilty, is expected to show a greater emotional response to the critical questions than to the neutral questions.

Neutral Questions

These are general questions, such as "Is your name Floyd?" or "Do you live at (a specific address)?" These questions are designed to elicit few, if any, emotional responses and are used to establish a baseline for normal physiological responding.

Critical Questions

These are specific questions about some particular crime or misconduct that only a person who committed the crime would know, such as "Did you rob the liquor store on 5th and Vine?" Critical questions are designed to elicit emotional responses, such as guilt or fear, if the person tells a lie.

As shown in the figure below, Floyd showed very little physiological arousal—as measured by the galvanic skin response—when asked a neutral question, "Is your name Floyd?" However, he showed great physiological arousal when asked a critical question, "Did you rob the liquor store?"

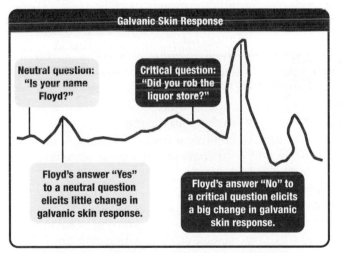

Galvanic Skin Response

Neutral question: "Is your name Floyd?"

Critical question: "Did you rob the liquor store?"

Floyd's answer "Yes" to a neutral question elicits little change in galvanic skin response.

Floyd's answer "No" to a critical question elicits a big change in galvanic skin response.

The examiner decides whether the client is lying or telling the truth by looking at the differences in physiological responses between neutral and critical questions. In Floyd's case, he answered "No" to a number of critical questions, such as "Did you rob the liquor store?" But his "No" answers were accompanied by large increases in galvanic skin response (as well as other responses). For those reasons, the examiner decided that Floyd had lied and thus failed the polygraph test. However, when the real robbers were eventually caught, tried, and sentenced, it proved that Floyd had not lied even though he failed the lie detector test twice. Floyd's case, as well as the Ames case, questions the accuracy of lie detector tests.

How Accurate Are Lie Detector Tests?

Why aren't tests allowed in most courts?

The basic problem with lie detector tests is that researchers have been unable to identify a pattern of physiological responses specific to lying. This means a number of different emotions—such as guilt, fear, or worry—can trigger physiological responses that make a person appear to be lying when he or she is telling the truth (Fiedler et al., 2002). Also, the polygrapher (person administering the polygraph test) can have a bias about the subject and not provide objective interpretations of the results (Haseltine, 2008; Vrij et al., 2010). Because of these serious problems, researchers estimate that lie detector tests are wrong 25–75% of the time (Broad, 2002; Saxe, 1994).

Innocent or faking. Besides high error scores, lie detector tests have two other problems: In one study, about 40% of participants were judged to be lying or maybe lying when they were telling the truth (Honts, 1994); and in another study, about 50% of guilty people who were told to both press their toes to the ground and bite their tongues during control questions passed lie detector tests (Honts et al., 1994). Also, many guilty people, including psychopaths, may not experience anxiety or arousal when they are lying. Consequently, the lie detector test may be more appropriately named an "arousal detector" (Lilienfeld et al., 2010).

Restrictions. Because of the above problems, federal law prohibits most employers from using polygraph tests to screen employees, and most state and federal courts prohibit the use of polygraph evidence (Frazier, 2003). In 1998, the U.S. Supreme Court ruled that polygraph evidence cannot be used in most courts. Even with these restrictions, the federal government is estimated to conduct at least 40,000 polygraph tests each year for use in police investigations, parole hearings, and security screenings of government employees (*Mental Floss*, 2011).

New tests. Although new lie detector tests are in development, it should be noted that the validity of these tests is questionable because scientists have yet to identify a single characteristic, physiological or otherwise, that is uniquely associated with lying (Vrij et al., 2010).

One of the newest tests involves using brain scans, such as the fMRI (see p. 71), to detect changes in thinking and associated neural activity that occur when lying. No area of the brain specializes in lying; however, researchers are finding increased activation in regions involved in suppressing information and resolving conflicts when an individual lies (Gamer et al., 2007; Kozel et al., 2005). Also, researchers studying structural brain abnormalities find that, compared to nonliars, pathological liars have 22% more prefrontal white matter, which is linked to the ability to deceive others (Yang et al., 2005a). Although these data are preliminary, they suggest that brain scans combined with clever questioning strategies may prove to be a more accurate and reliable way to detect lying (Gamer, 2009). However, given the lack of strong scientific evidence, a federal court ruled that these tests are not yet ready for use in the courtroom (G. Miller, 2010).

Other recently developed tests aimed at improving the accuracy of lie detection include using eye scans to measure blood flow to the eye; observing very brief, involuntary facial expression changes; analyzing the consistency and amount of detail in someone's testimony; and noticing stress in someone's voice while telling a lie (Colwell, 2009; Ehrenberg, 2010; Ekman, 2006; Kluger & Masters, 2006). ●

© SCOTT CAMAZINE/ Photo Researchers

Brain scan tests may be better than polygraph at detecting lies.

Why Do They Have to Learn to Smile?

In the United States it's very common to see people smiling in public because it's a friendly way to interact socially. In fact, many businesses insist that their salespeople smile at customers because smiling makes the customers feel more comfortable and more likely to buy something. But in Japan, people are very reluctant to show emotions in public and that's become a problem.

1 In the United States, why is smiling in social situations considered an acceptable and even desirable way to behave in public?

Japan is currently going through a recession or downturn in business, so there is increased competition to get new customers and keep current customers happy. Said one gas station attendant who is trying to learn to smile more, "In this recession, customers are getting choosy about their gas stations, so you have to think positively. Laughter and a smile are representative of this positive thinking" (Reitman, 1999, p. A1).

2 When having to make money is bucking cultural traditions, what do you think will happen?

But getting salespeople to smile is a radical change in Japan, whose cultural tradition has long emphasized suppressing any public display of emotions, be it happy, sad, or angry. For example, women never smile at their husbands and members of families rarely touch in public and never hug, even when greeting after a long separation. It's still common for women to place a hand over their mouths when they laugh, and men believe that the correct and proper behavior is to show no emotions in public. Unlike American salespeople who often smile and make eye contact with their customers, Japanese salespeople are reserved and greet customers with a simple "welcome"; smiling, up until now, was totally frowned upon.

3 Even though emotional expressions, such as smiling, are considered universal facial expressions, why don't the Japanese smile more?

Because getting salespeople to smile is going against a strong tradition, learning how to smile has grown into a big business in Japan. Employees are now being sent to "smile school," which uses various techniques to teach reluctant and bashful students to smile. For example, one technique in learning how to smile is biting on a chopstick (photo above) and then lifting the edges of the mouth higher than the chopstick. Another technique is to follow "smile" instructions: "Relax the muscle under your nose, loosen up your tongue. Put your hands on your stomach and laugh out loud, feeling the

4 Why is it so difficult for many highly motivated Japanese to learn to smile?

'poisons' escape" (Reitman, 1999, p. A1).

What is driving all this smiling in Japan is sales and morale. As is well known by American businesses, happy, friendly salespeople are usually the most successful and are great at building company morale. The same is holding true in Japan, where smiley clerks are racking up the most sales and creating a friendly morale.

5 Why do you think that smiley, friendly salespeople are more successful and better at building morale?

People in other parts of Asia, such as China, also are not accustomed to smiling in social situations. In fact, volunteers for the 2008 Olympics in Beijing were required to take classes on how to smile to ensure that they portray China as hospitable.

6 According to the facial feedback hypothesis, how would not smiling influence emotions?

Adapted from Mauss, 2005; Reitman, 1999; UPI, 2006

Summary Test

A Peripheral Theories

1. We can define an emotion in terms of four components: We interpret or appraise a **(a)** _____ in terms of our well-being; we have a subjective **(b)** _____; we experience various **(c)** _____ responses, such as changes in heart rate and respiration; and we often show **(d)** _____ behaviors, such as crying or smiling.

2. Several theories explain what causes emotions. Theories that emphasize changes in the body are called **(a)** _____ theories. One such theory states that emotions result from specific physiological changes in your body and that each emotion has a different physiological basis; this is called the **(b)** _____ theory. The major criticism of this theory is that different emotions do not always cause different patterns of physiological arousal. This particular criticism led to the **(c)** _____ theory, which states that emotions originate in the brain; they are not the result of physiological responses.

3. According to another peripheral theory, sensations or feedback from the movement of facial muscles and skin are interpreted by your brain and result in an emotion; this is called the **(a)** _____ theory. However, people with paralyzed facial muscles still experience emotions. Facial feedback may influence your **(b)** _____ as well as increase the **(c)** _____ of emotional feelings.

B Cognitive Appraisal Theory

4. A theory of emotions that grew out of the work of Schachter and Singer says that your interpretation, appraisal, thought, or memory of a situation, object, or event can contribute to, or result in, your experiencing different emotional states. This is called the _____ theory.

C Affective Neuroscience Approach

5. The most recent approach to understanding emotions studies the neural bases of mood and emotion by focusing on the brain's neural circuits that evaluate stimuli and produce or contribute to our experiencing and expressing different emotional states. This is called the _____ approach.

6. Emotions have four qualities: They are expressed in stereotypical **(a)** _____ expressions and have distinctive **(b)** _____ responses; they are less controllable and may not respond to **(c)** _____; they influence many **(d)** _____ functions; and some emotions, such as smiling, are **(e)** _____ in the brain. The brain area that functions to detect and evaluate stimuli, especially threatening ones, and to store memories with emotional content is called the **(f)** _____. Because this brain structure receives sensory information so quickly, it triggers a fearful reaction without **(g)** _____. The brain structure involved in producing emotions from thoughts alone and in analyzing the emotional consequences of actions is called the **(h)** _____.

D Universal Facial Expressions

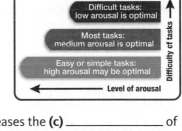

7. Specific inherited facial patterns or expressions that signal specific feelings or emotional states across cultures, such as a smile signaling a happy state, are called **(a)** _____. These emotional expressions, which are said to include happiness, surprise, fear, anger, contempt, disgust, and sadness, are thought to have evolved because they had important **(b)** _____ functions for our ancestors. Evidence for universal emotions includes that people in different cultures recognize the same **(c)** _____ expressions, that infants in different cultures show a predictable **(d)** _____ in developing facial expressions, and that even blind children, who cannot observe their parents' faces, develop smiling at the same time as sighted children.

E Functions of Emotions

8. Facial expressions that accompany emotions send signals about how one **(a)** _____ and what one intends to do. Emotions focus one's **(b)** _____ so one can better respond to emotional situations and also increases the **(c)** _____ of situations that may be either beneficial or dangerous to one's well-being.

Difficulty of tasks
Difficult tasks: low arousal is optimal
Most tasks: medium arousal is optimal
Easy or simple tasks: high arousal may be optimal
← Level of arousal

9. According to one theory of emotions, we have inherited the neural structure and physiology to express and experience emotions and we evolved basic emotional patterns to adapt to and solve problems important for our survival; this is called the _____ theory.

10. There is a relationship between emotional arousal and your performance on a task; this relationship is called the **(a)** _____ law. According to this law, low arousal results in better performance on **(b)** _____ tasks; for most tasks, **(c)** _____ arousal helps performance; and for easy tasks, **(d)** _____ arousal may facilitate performance.

© Andreas Meyer/Shutterstock.com

© Digital Stock Corporation

© Photo24/Brand X Pictures/Getty Images

F Happiness

11. Momentary pleasures, short-term joys, or long-term satisfaction can result in an emotional feeling called **(a)** _____. This emotion also stimulates the brain's reward/pleasure center, which includes several areas, such as the **(b)** _____ and _____. Researchers estimate that one's personal level of happiness is set half by **(c)** _____ influences and half by **(d)** _____ factors.

12. One theory explains that we quickly become accustomed to receiving some good fortune (money, job, car, degree) and, within a relatively short period of time, take the good fortune for granted. As a result, this good fortune contributes little to our long-term level of happiness; this is called the **(a)** _____ theory. Research shows that long-term happiness is less dependent upon **(b)** _____ because we soon adapt to our good fortunes. Instead, long-term happiness is more dependent upon pursuing our own personal **(c)** _____ and developing meaningful **(d)** _____. One reason some people are generally more happy and some are generally less happy is that each of us seems to have a happiness **(e)** _____, which is about half set or influenced by environmental factors and about half set or influenced by inherited or genetic factors.

G Cultural Diversity: Emotions across Cultures

13. Although many emotional expressions are shared and recognized across cultures, it is also true that cultures have unique rules that regulate how, when, and where we should express emotion and how much emotion is appropriate; these rules are called _____. For example, among the Inuit (Eskimos), feelings of anger are strongly condemned, but among certain Arab groups, a man's failure to respond with anger is seen as dishonorable.

14. Another example of display rules is from a study in which Americans and Japanese rated the intensity of five emotions—surprise, anger, happiness, disgust, and sadness—on a scale from 1 to 10. The emotion rated most intense by the Japanese was **(a)** _____, while the Americans rated **(b)** _____ as the most intense. This study illustrates how cultural display rules may differently influence how people perceive the **(c)** _____ of emotions.

H Research Focus: Emotional Intelligence

© Neale Cousland/Shutterstock.com

15. The ability to perceive and express emotion, understand and reason with emotion, and regulate emotion in oneself and others is called **(a)** _____. One reason researchers believe that emotional intelligence is important is that the better we understand how emotions operate, the better are our chances of finding a way to work out compromises between our strong **(b)** _____ feelings and our equally strong rational **(c)** _____. We are able to share emotions felt by others because of our **(d)** _____, which track the emotions of the person we are with and replicate the same emotions in us by activating our brains in the same way the other person's brain is activated.

I Application: Lie Detection

16. The instrument that is sometimes referred to as a lie detector is correctly called a **(a)** _____; it measures a person's heart rate, blood pressure, respiration, and emotionally induced hand sweating, which is called the **(b)** _____ response.

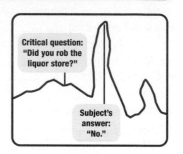

Critical question: "Did you rob the liquor store?"

Subject's answer: "No."

To determine whether a person is telling the truth or a lie, the examiner compares the person's physiological responses to **(c)** _____ and questions. The basic problem with lie detector tests is that no pattern of physiological responses has been specifically associated with lying. This means that many emotions can cause increased physiological responses that make the person appear to be lying. Because of the relatively high **(d)** _____ rate, evidence from lie detector tests is not admitted in most courts of law. The newest method to detect lies involves using brain scans to detect changes in thinking and associated **(e)** _____ that occur when people lie.

Answers: 1. (a) stimulus, (b) feeling, (c) physiological, (d) overt; 2. (a) peripheral, (b) James-Lange, (c) Cannon-Bard; 3. (a) facial feedback, (b) mood, overall feeling, (c) intensity; 4. cognitive appraisal; 5. affective neuroscience; 6. (a) facial, (b) physiological, (c) reason, (d) cognitive, (e) hard-wired, (f) amygdala, (g) awareness or conscious thought, (h) prefrontal cortex; 7. (a) universal emotions, (b) adaptive, survival, (c) facial, (d) order; 8. (a) feels, (b) attention, (c) memory, recall; 9. evolutionary; 10. (a) Yerkes-Dodson, (b) difficult, (c) medium, (d) high; 11. (a) happiness, (b) nucleus accumbens, ventral tegmental area, (c) genetic or inherited, (d) environmental; 12. (a) adaptation level, (b) wealth or material things, (c) goals, (d) relationships or friends, (e) set point; 13. display rules; 14. (a) disgust, (b) happiness, (c) intensity; 15. (a) emotional intelligence, (b) emotional, (c) thoughts, (d) mirror neurons; 16. (a) polygraph, (b) galvanic skin, (c) neutral, critical, (d) error, (e) neural activity

Links to Learning

Key Terms/Key People

adaptation level theory, 366

affective neuroscience approach, 360, 362

amygdala, 362, 363

Cannon-Bard theory, 360

cognitive appraisal theory of emotions, 360, 361

Control Question Technique, 371

display rules, 367

emotion, 359

emotional intelligence, 369

evolutionary theory of emotions, 365

facial expressions, 365

facial feedback hypothesis, 360

galvanic skin response, 370

happiness, 366

happiness set point, 366

James-Lange theory, 360

lie detector (polygraph) tests, 370

peripheral theories of emotions, 360

prefrontal cortex, 363

reward/pleasure center, 366

Schachter-Singer experiment, 361

social signals, 365

thalamus, 363

universal emotional expressions, 364

Yerkes-Dodson law, 365

Media Resources

Go to **CengageBrain.com** to access Psychology CourseMate, where you will find an interactive eBook, glossaries, flashcards, quizzes, videos, answers to Critical Thinking questions, and more. You can also access Virtual Psychology Labs, an interactive laboratory experience designed to illustrate key experiments first-hand.

Nature-Nurture Question

Will Alex ever learn to love a parent?

For the first 3 years of his life, Alex was raised in an orphanage in Romania where the number of infants and children greatly exceeded the number of caregivers. At the orphanage, Alex was given adequate nutrition, allowing him to develop well physically, but the affection, stimulation, and comfort he received were far from adequate. Alex, like other children in Romanian orphanages, spent most of his days alone in a crib with almost no interaction with others. When he cried, no one came to hold or soothe him. He was never given the opportunity to bond with a caregiver.

When Alex was 3 years old, a family living in the United States adopted him. His adoptive mother described him as being friendly and engaging, but also "self-abusive" and having a "dark side." For instance, Alex would make himself go into a seizure by slamming his head on the floor. He was also aggressive toward others, one time attacking his younger sister, "beating her senseless." When asked if he wanted his adoptive mother to love him, he said to her, "I never want you to love me." When his adoptive mother asked him if he loved her, he replied, "No, I don't love anybody." After years

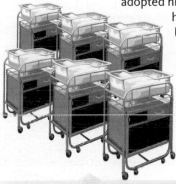

Until age 3, Alex lived in an orphanage where he didn't receive affection, stimulation, or comfort.

of exhausting every treatment option and still unable to feel loved by Alex, his adoptive parents arranged for Alex to live with another family (Jarriel & Sawyer, 1997).

Children like Alex, whose emotional needs (such as forming a stable attachment with a caregiver) are unmet during infancy and early childhood, may develop reactive attachment disorder.

Reactive attachment disorder is a psychiatric illness characterized by serious problems in emotional attachments to others beginning before age 5. Some symptoms children may show include resisting comfort and affection by parents, being superficially engaging and overly friendly with strangers, having poor peer relationships, and engaging in behavior destructive to themselves and to others (American Psychiatric Association, 2000; G. C. Keck & Kupecky, 1995).

Do all children raised in Romanian orphanages who are later adopted have attachment problems? This question brings up an interesting issue in psychology referred to as the nature-nurture question.

The **nature-nurture question** asks how much nature (genetic factors) and how much nurture (environmental factors) contributes to a person's biological, emotional, cognitive, personal, and social development.

Although the nature-nurture question seems like an abstract intellectual issue, it has very practical consequences. For example, let's consider the research findings on Romanian children who spend time in orphanages.

There are now over 10,000 Romanian children growing up in the United States, and nearly all of them initially had serious developmental problems. One researcher studying the adjustment of over 300 Romanian adoptees in the United States found that after the first year, 20% of children reached normal development, 60% showed only mild problems, and the remaining 20% had serious cognitive, behavioral, and emotional problems (Fischer, 1999). Other research found that children who spent their first two years living in the poor conditions of a Romanian orphanage have lasting social deficits, such as being unable to carry on a conversation normally. However, if the children were removed from the orphanage prior to age 2, then they were able to develop their social skills and perform as well as children who were raised in their own homes (C. Nelson, 2012).

The reason many Romanian adoptees have long-term developmental problems while others make significant improvements is complex, involving both biological (nature) and environmental (nurture) factors.

Human Development

The questions about why Romanian adoptees differ in how they are affected by being raised in an orphanage and how they later adjust to adoption illustrate the kinds of issues researchers examine in human development.

Human development involves the study of a person's biological, emotional, cognitive, personal, and social development across the life span, from infancy through late adulthood.

Later in this module, we'll explain how Alex was doing at age 7 and what it means when he is finally able to say "I love you" to a parent. From research in the field of human development, we have learned that the answer to the age-old question of whether nature or nurture is more important is that they are

7-year-old Alex still has serious problems in his emotional attachment to others.

both important and their interaction is the key to understanding how an infant develops into a very complex adult with his or her own personality, behaviors, and goals (Pinker, 2002).

What's Coming

We'll discuss how development is affected by various prenatal factors, such as alcohol and air pollutants. We'll explain the amazing abilities of newborns, the early appearance of a basic emotional makeup, the surprising growth of mental abilities, the different factors that influence social development, and the terrible occurrence of child abuse, which affects millions of children in our country.

We'll begin by telling you about a family whose young son's unusual musical abilities showed how nature and nurture interact. ●

A Prenatal Development

Nature and Nurture

By the age of 4, Yo-Yo Ma had already studied a few instruments, including the violin and viola, and decided to focus on the cello.

Was he born a cellist?

One year later, at age 5, Yo-Yo was performing in front of large audiences. His talent was recognized at a national level shortly thereafter when he was invited to perform for Presidents John F. Kennedy and Dwight D. Eisenhower at age 7. At the age of 9, Yo-Yo began his university music studies by attending several esteemed schools, including the Julliard School, Columbia University, and Harvard University.

Yo-Yo Ma, now a world-famous cellist, is a 15-time Grammy Award winner and is considered by many to be one of the best classical performers of all time.

When only 7 years old, Yo-Yo Ma performed for U.S. presidents.

The amazing musical abilities of young Yo-Yo Ma certainly classify him as a prodigy.

A **prodigy** is a child who shows an unusual talent, ability, or genius at a very early age and does not have an intellectual disability.

Because prodigies demonstrate such unusual abilities so early, they are excellent examples of the interaction between nature (genetic influences) and nurture (learned influences).

Genetic and Environmental Factors

One reason Yo-Yo Ma was a prodigy and could give an inspiring cello performance at the age of 5 was the prenatal (before birth) effects of genetic influences. Prenatal influences, in the form of genetic instructions, regulated the development of Yo-Yo's brain and body.

Parents. The father contributed half of Yo-Yo's genetic instructions (23 chromosomes), and the mother contributed half of the genetic instructions (23 chromosomes).

Yo-Yo's father and mother both had musical interests. The father was a violinist and music professor. The mother was a singer. Through their chromosomes, the parents passed some of their musical talents on to their two children, Yo-Yo and his older sister, who began violin lessons at age 3 and received music awards at age 7.

Son. Yo-Yo received half of his genetic instructions from his mother and half from his father. The unique pairing of chromosomes from the mother and father results in unique physical and mental traits for each of the two children. Because Yo-Yo and his sister, Yeou-Cheng showed great musical ability at such an early age, we can assume that their early musical ability was primarily due to genetic or inherited instructions that came from their parents' chromosomes. However, certain environmental factors, perhaps fewer opportunities for women musicians, directed Yeou-Cheng's parents' attention to fostering Yo-Yo's talents and ending her music lessons. Different environmental factors, such as continued lessons and education, encouraged Yo-Yo to develop his musical talents more fully.

Interaction. Yo-Yo Ma, who was universally hailed as a great child prodigy, developed into a legendary cellist. The development of Yo-Yo's musical talents is a perfect example of how nature and nurture interact. You can see that genetic influences (nature) played a major role in wiring his brain so that his incredible musical abilities appeared at a very early age, before he had a chance to learn them. You can also see that environmental influences (nurture), such as being encouraged to practice and take lessons, as well as to attend esteemed music programs, encouraged Yo-Yo to develop the musical talents that he had inherited from his parents.

Psychologists have long recognized the importance of learning influences, but it is only in about the past couple of decades that psychologists have also recognized the importance

Music lessons (environment) helped Yo-Yo Ma develop the musical talents he inherited (genetic) from his parents.

of genetic factors that influence almost every aspect of behavior, including cognitive, social, emotional, and personality development (C. Baker, 2004). Today, researchers no longer focus on which is more important, nature or nurture, but rather on how nature and nurture interact to influence and regulate our behaviors (Pinker, 2002). With this focus, more and more researchers are studying epigenetics.

Epigenetics is the study of how environmental factors result in changes in gene activity that do not involve alterations to the genetic instructions but are still passed down to the next generation.

It turns out that some genes are either turned on or turned off depending on environmental factors. This area of research is especially fascinating because these genes are not mutated or changed by environmental factors, but simply altered in their level of activity. Though epigenetics research has only recently begun, there have been many interesting findings, such as how long-term stress can change the way the brain responds to life experiences. Also, the more epigenetic changes that are identified, the more likely it is that scientists will be able to reverse those changes, which can offer new hopeful treatments for psychiatric conditions, such as drug addiction (Cloud, 2010; Nestler, 2011; Weir, 2012; Zimmer, 2010).

As we've learned throughout this textbook, genetic instructions from our parents can result in our having a wide range of abilities. Next, we'll explain what happens when genetic instructions are damaged—for example, if a mother uses drugs during the prenatal period.

378 PART 9 THE DEVELOPING HUMAN

Prenatal Period: Three Stages

How did you begin?

You began as a single cell about the size of a grain of sand. In this tiny cell was the equivalent of about 300,000 pages of instructions for the development of your brain and body. This single cell marks the beginning of the prenatal period.

The **prenatal period** extends from conception to birth and lasts about 266 days (around nine months). It consists of three successive phases: the germinal, embryonic, and fetal stages. During the prenatal period, a single cell will divide and grow to form 200 billion cells.

As we examine the prenatal period, we'll unravel one of the great puzzles of science—how a human being begins, develops, and is born. We'll start with the germinal stage.

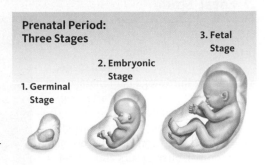

Prenatal Period: Three Stages

1. Germinal Stage
2. Embryonic Stage
3. Fetal Stage

1 Germinal Stage

The germinal stage marks the beginning of our development into a human being.

The **germinal stage** is the first stage of prenatal development and refers to the two-week period following conception.

To understand how conception occurs, we need to back up a little and explain ovulation.

Ovulation is the release of an ovum, or egg cell, from a woman's ovaries.

In most cases, only a single ovum is released during ovulation, but sometimes two ova are released. If two separate ova are released and fertilized, the result is fraternal twins, who can be two brothers, two sisters, or a brother and sister.

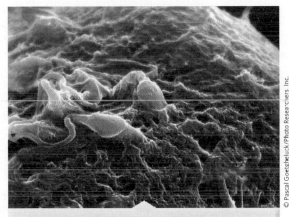

Only one of millions of sperm will fertilize this egg.

Because fraternal twins come from two separate eggs, they are no more genetically alike than any other two children of the same parents. In contrast, if a single ovum splits into two parts after fertilization, the result is identical twins, whose genes are almost indistinguishable.

How does conception take place?

If no sperm are present, there can be no fertilization, and the ovum, together with the lining of the uterus, is sloughed off in the process called *menstruation*. If, however, sperm have been deposited in the vagina (100–500 million sperm may be deposited with each act of intercourse), they make their way to the uterus and into the fallopian tubes in search of an ovum to be fertilized.

Conception, or **fertilization,** occurs if one of the millions of sperm penetrates the ovum's outer membrane. After the ovum has been penetrated by a single sperm (above photo), its outer membrane changes and becomes impenetrable to the millions of remaining sperm.

Once the ovum has been fertilized, it is called a *zygote*, which is a single cell that is smaller than the dot in the letter *i*. The zygote begins a process of repeated division and, after about a week, consists of about 150 cells. After two weeks, it has become a mass of cells and attaches itself to the wall of the uterus. Once the zygote is implanted, or attached to the wall of the uterus, the embryonic stage begins.

2 Embryonic Stage

During this next stage, the organism begins to develop body organs.

The **embryonic stage** is the second stage of the prenatal period and spans the 2–8 weeks that follow conception; during this stage, cells divide and begin to differentiate into bone, muscle, and body organs.

At about 21 days after conception, the beginnings of the spinal cord and eyes appear; at about 24 days, cells differentiate to form what will become part of the heart; at about 28 days, tiny buds appear that will develop into arms and legs; and at about 42 days, features of the face take shape.

During this stage, the embryo is very fragile, since all of its basic organs are being formed. This is the time when most miscarriages occur and when most major birth defects occur (J. M. Nash, 2002; Niebyl & Simpson, 2012).

Toward the end of the embryonic stage, the organism has developed a number of body organs, such as the heart. The embryo is only about 4 cm long but already has the beginnings of major body organs and limbs and begins to look somewhat human (Cunningham et al., 2009).

In the left photo, you can see the head as the large rounded structure at the top, and the black dot on the side of the head is the developing eye. After this second stage of development, which is called the embryonic stage, comes the last stage, which is called the fetal stage.

Embryo—about 6 weeks

3 Fetal Stage

What is the fetal stage?

The embryonic stage is followed by the fetal stage.

The **fetal stage,** which is the third stage in prenatal development, begins two months after conception and lasts until birth.

At the end of the fetal stage, usually 38–42 weeks after conception (roughly nine months), birth occurs and the fetus becomes a newborn.

During the fetal stage, the fetus develops vital organs, such as lungs, and physical characteristics that are distinctively human. For example, at about six months a fetus has eyes and eyelids that are completely formed, a fine coating of hair, relatively well-developed external sex organs, and lungs that are beginning to function.

Infants born very prematurely (under six months) will have difficulty surviving because their lungs are not completely formed and they have difficulty breathing. However, a six-month-old fetus usually has lungs well enough developed to begin to show irregular breathing and, for this reason, can survive if born prematurely.

During stage 2, the embryonic stage, and stage 3, the fetal stage, the developing organism is especially vulnerable to toxic agents and chemicals. To help keep out these potentially harmful agents, the developing organism is protected by the placenta.

Placenta and teratogens. Because the fetus experiences rapid body growth and development of the nervous system, it is highly vulnerable to the effects of drugs and other harmful agents. However, the blood supply of the fetus is partly protected by the placenta (Koren, 2007).

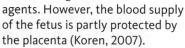

Placenta   Umbilical cord

The **placenta** is an organ that connects the blood supply of the mother to that of the fetus. The placenta acts like a filter, allowing oxygen and nutrients to pass through while keeping out some toxic or harmful substances.

However, certain viruses, such as HIV, and many drugs, including nicotine, caffeine, marijuana, cocaine, and heroin, pass from the placenta into the fetus's blood vessels and thus can affect fetal development. These potentially dangerous agents are called teratogens.

A **teratogen** (teh-RAT-oh-gen) is any agent that can harm a developing fetus (causing deformities or brain damage). It might be a disease (such as genital herpes), a drug (such as alcohol), or another environmental agent (such as chemicals).

Besides harmful chemicals, drugs, and viruses, the developing fetus can also be affected by genetic problems, especially if the parents are carriers of potentially harmful genes (Tay-Sachs) or if the mother is in her forties, which increases the risk for

Fetus in womb at 6 months

© NEIL BROMHALL/SCIENCE PHOTO LIBRARY/Photo Researchers, Inc.

certain fetal genetic problems (Down syndrome). In cases where fetal genetic problems are possible, the mother may wish to have her fetus tested by a relatively safe process called amniocentesis (M. B. Marcus, 2000).

Birth defects and amniocentesis. During the fetal stage, a number of genetic errors can be tested for by amniocentesis *(AM-nee-oh-sen-TEE-sis)*.

Amniocentesis is a medical test done between weeks 14 and 20 of pregnancy. It involves inserting a long needle through the mother's abdominal muscles into the amniotic fluid surrounding the fetus. By withdrawing and analyzing fetal cells in the fluid, doctors can identify a number of genetic problems.

One genetic problem identified by amniocentesis is Down syndrome (see p. 288).

Down syndrome results from an extra 21st chromosome and causes abnormal physical traits (a fold of skin at the corner of each eye, a wide tongue, heart defects) and abnormal brain development, resulting in degrees of intellectual disability.

Besides Down syndrome, more than 1,000 other genetic disorders can now be tested for and identified (Weil, 2006). For many years, a combination of various relatively noninvasive screening tests completed during the first and second trimesters was used to detect Down syndrome up to 96% of the time. Recently, a major diagnostic breakthrough occurred: A simple blood test taken at ten weeks after conception can detect Down syndrome with almost 99% accuracy (Palomaki et al., 2012; Skotko, 2011).

As shown in the graph below, birth defects can occur if something (toxin, drug, genetic malfunction) interferes with developing structures, especially during the embryonic stage (J. M. Nash, 2002).

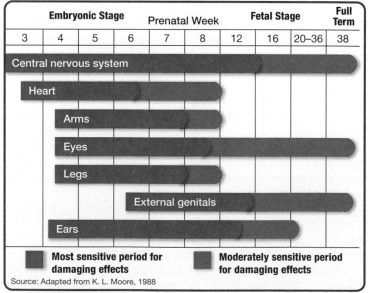

Source: Adapted from K. L. Moore, 1988

Bar graph adapted from a figure in *The Developing Human: Clinically Oriented Embryology*, 4th ed., by Keith L. Moore. W. B. Saunders Co. Copyright © 1988 by Keith L. Moore. Adapted by permission of the author.

Next, we'll discuss several teratogens (from the Greek word *tera*, meaning "monster") that can pass through the placenta and interfere with fetal growth and development.

Drugs and Prenatal Development

How well is the fetus protected? In the womb, the fetus is protected from physical bumps by a wraparound cushion of warm fluid. The fetus is also protected from various teratogens (certain chemicals and drugs) by the filtering system of the placenta (described on p. 380). However, we'll discuss several drugs, both legal and illegal, that can pass through the placenta, reach the fetus, and cause potential neurological, physiological, and psychological problems.

Drug Use and Exposure to Chemicals

Caffeine. Pregnant women who use caffeine, even as little as one cup of coffee a day, are at higher risk of having an underweight baby. Babies born underweight are more likely to have health problems as adults, such as high blood pressure and diabetes (CARE, 2008).

Smoking and nicotine. Smoking during pregnancy increases the risk of low birth weight, preterm deliveries, and possible physical problems (Cunningham et al., 2009). In addition, infants born to smoking mothers have an increased risk for developing attention-deficit/hyperactivity disorder (see p. 27), sudden infant death syndrome (SIDS), oral clefts (birth defect of mouth and lips), and respiratory infections (J. Braun et al., 2006; Dambro, 2006; G. M. Shaw et al., 2009).

Prescription painkillers. The number of infants born addicted to prescription painkillers is rapidly rising, with these addictions now affecting more than 13,000 infants a year. Many mothers who take prescription painkillers during pregnancy have an addiction and are unable to quit during pregnancy. Others simply don't know that painkillers can harm their developing baby. Infants exposed in the womb to prescription painkillers are at heightened risk of having breathing problems, low birth weight, difficulty eating, and seizures (Patrick et al., 2012).

Lead. Children exposed to large amounts of lead (paint, gasoline, industry) during pregnancy are at high risk for attention problems, hyperactivity, learning disabilities, low IQ, and even seizures (Canfield, 2003; Weise & Young, 2012). Also, lead exposure is associated with criminal and antisocial behavior in adulthood, such as assaults, robbery, arson, and disorderly conduct (J. Braun et al., 2006; Dietrich, 2003; J. P. Wright et al., 2008).

Air pollutants. Prenatal exposure to air pollutants, such as gasoline, diesel, and coal, has a negative impact on children's cognitive (attention) and psychological (anxiety, depression) development. Also, pregnant women exposed to high levels of air pollutants are more likely to have children with low birth weights, fetal growth deficiencies, and delays in physical development. Because it is not possible for pregnant women to completely avoid exposure to air pollutants, environmental changes in vehicles and power plants are important (Harder, 2006; Park, 2012; Rich et al., 2009).

Pesticides. The results of three recent studies indicate that exposure to pesticides in the womb is associated with lower average IQs in children years later. It's important to note that the exposure levels in these studies were not high, but rather were within the range of exposures considered acceptable in the United States. Other research reports that pesticide exposure after birth is not associated with lower IQs, which suggests that the chemicals are especially harmful during very early brain development (M. F. Bouchard et al., 2011).

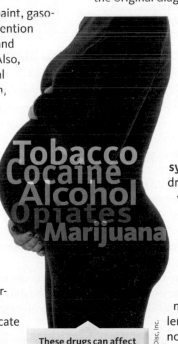

These drugs can affect the developing fetus.

Alcohol

Heavy drinking—Fetal alcohol syndrome (FAS). In the United States, alcohol is the leading known cause of intellectual disability. Alcohol (ethanol) is a teratogen that crosses the placenta, affects the developing fetus, and can result in fetal alcohol syndrome (S. L. Fryer et al., 2007; Schuckit, 2012).

Fetal alcohol syndrome, or **FAS,** results from a mother drinking heavily during pregnancy, especially in the first 12 weeks. FAS results in physical changes, such as short stature, flattened nose, and short eye openings; neurological changes, such as fewer brain connections within the brain structure; and psychological and behavioral problems, such as hyperactivity, impulsive behavior, deficits in information processing and memory, alcohol and drug use, and poor socialization.

Children with fetal alcohol syndrome continue to have problems into adolescence and adulthood. For example, follow-up studies up to 21 years after the original diagnosis indicated that FAS individuals tended to remain short, had an average IQ of 68 (normal is 100), were likely to be easily distracted and to misperceive social cues, and were at risk for developing drinking and drug problems (Baer et al., 2003; Streissguth et al., 1999). This means that various physical, neurological, psychological, and behavioral problems associated with fetal alcohol syndrome are long-lasting.

Moderate drinking—Partial fetal alcohol syndrome. Researchers found that moderate drinking (7–14 drinks per week) by pregnant women does not usually result in fetal alcohol syndrome (FAS). However, moderate drinking may result in *partial fetal alcohol syndrome*, which is less severe than fetal alcohol syndrome but more prevalent (E. P. Riley et al., 2011). Children with partial fetal alcohol syndrome have most, but not all, of the physical, neurological, psychological, and behavioral problems associated with FAS. Researchers say there is no safe level of alcohol use during pregnancy, and therefore it is recommended that women who are pregnant or are planning a pregnancy should not drink any alcohol (Gorman, 2006).

We have discussed the three stages of prenatal development, which end with the baby's birth. After the baby gets a pat on the backside and lets out a cry, he or she is ready to take on the world. ●

Facial features associated with FAS

© Teresa Kellerman, www.fasstar.com

©PhotoDisc, Inc.

Why can't a newborn walk? Some animals, such as baby elephants (150 pounds), can walk immediately after birth. In comparison, baby humans (7 pounds) cannot walk because neither their leg muscles nor brain areas are well enough developed. However, human infants are born with a surprising number of sensory and motor abilities, such as hearing, grasping, and sucking. How these abilities develop is explained by an inherited genetic program.

Genetic Developmental Program

Conception results in a fertilized egg, which has a genetic program that is equivalent to 300,000 pages of typed instructions for developing the body and brain. The mother and father each contribute 23 chromosomes, so each child receives a unique genetic program.

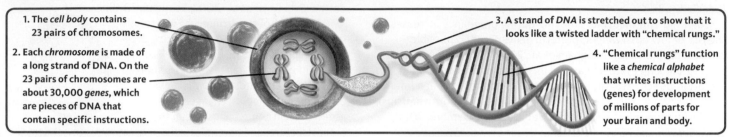

1. The *cell body* contains 23 pairs of chromosomes.

2. Each *chromosome* is made of a long strand of DNA. On the 23 pairs of chromosomes are about 30,000 *genes*, which are pieces of DNA that contain specific instructions.

3. A strand of *DNA* is stretched out to show that it looks like a twisted ladder with "chemical rungs."

4. "Chemical rungs" function like a *chemical alphabet* that writes instructions (genes) for development of millions of parts for your brain and body.

Brain growth. After birth, the genetic program regulates how the brain develops, such as making thousands of connections among neurons. For example, during the first three months of life, the most active areas of the newborn's brain are involved in processing sights, sounds, and touches, preparing the infant for dealing with sensory information from the surrounding environment.

In the figures on the right, notice that a 1-month-old brain has very few neural connections, while a 2-year-old brain has thousands. This enormous increase in neural connections partly explains why the size of a baby's brain increases about 100% in the first year and then 15% in the second year (Knickmeyer et al., 2008).

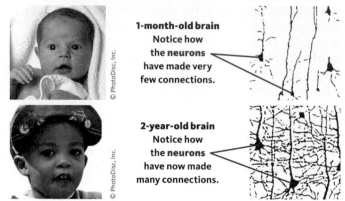

1-month-old brain Notice how the neurons have made very few connections.

2-year-old brain Notice how the neurons have now made many connections.

Sensory Development

At birth, newborns benefit from the sensory development that occurs during the prenatal period.

Sensory development is the growth of our senses—sight, hearing, touch, smell, and taste—beginning during the prenatal period and continuing on through childhood.

Here is a brief summary of an infant's sensory abilities:

Faces. Newborns show a preference for their mother's face over strangers' faces in the first few days after birth. Apparently newborns first learn to recognize a person's eyes, a process that occurs through positive stimulation, such as caressing and suckling (E. M. Blass & Camp, 2001). Beginning at 4 months of age, an infant can *visually* distinguish his or her mother's face from a stranger's or an animal's (Wingert & Brant, 2005). By 3 or 4 years of age, an infant's visual abilities are equal to those of an adult.

Hearing. One-month-old infants have very keen hearing and can discriminate small sound variations, such as the difference between *bah* and *pah*. By 6 months, infants can make all the sounds necessary to learn the language in which they are raised (Pascalis et al., 2002).

Touch. Newborns also have a well-developed sense of touch and will turn their head when lightly touched on the cheek. Touch will also elicit a number of reflexes, such as grasping and sucking.

Smell and taste. Researchers found that 1-day-old infants could discriminate between a citrus odor and a floral odor (Sullivan et al., 1991). Six-week-old infants can smell the difference between their mother and a stranger (Macfarlane, 1975). Newborns have an inborn preference for both sweet and salt and an inborn dislike of bitter-tasting things.

Depth perception. By the age of 6 months, infants have developed depth perception, which was tested by observing whether they would crawl off a visual "cliff" (E. J. Gibson & Walk, 1960).

A **visual cliff** is a glass tabletop with a checkerboard pattern over part of its surface; the remaining surface is clear glass with a checkerboard pattern several feet below, creating the illusion of a clifflike drop to the floor.

As shown in the right photo, an infant is placed on the area with the checkerboard pattern and is encouraged to creep off the cliff. Six-month-old infants hesitate when they reach the clear glass "dropoff," indicating that they have developed depth perception.

Although the genetic program is largely responsible for the early appearance of these sensory abilities, *environmental stimulation*, such as parental touch and play, encourages the infant to further develop these sensory abilities (W. A. Collins et al., 2000).

Unless otherwise noted, all images are © Cengage Learning

Motor Development

Why do infants crawl before they walk?

"Gloria just took her first step." Parents are proud to note their child's motor accomplishments, which are primarily regulated by a built-in genetic program. As infants learn to crawl and walk, they change from passive observers into very active participants in the family's social life. The first area studied by early developmental psychologists was motor skill development (Thelen, 1995).

1 The **proximodistal principle** states that parts closer to the center of the infant's body (*proximo* in Latin means "near") develop before parts farther away (*distal* in Latin means "far").

For example, activities involving the trunk are mastered before activities involving the arms and legs. For that reason, infants can roll over before they can walk or bring their arms together to grasp a bottle.

2 The **cephalocaudal principle** states that parts of the body closer to the head (*cephalo* in Greek means "head") develop before parts closer to the feet (*caudal* in Greek means "tail").

For example, infants can lift their heads before they can control their trunks enough to sit up, and they can sit up before they can control their legs to crawl. In the figure below, notice the head area (larger) developing before the feet area (smaller).

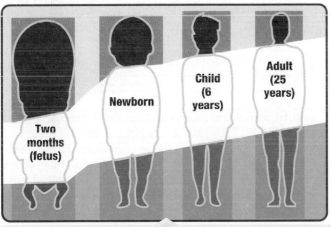

Two months (fetus)   **Newborn**   **Child (6 years)**   **Adult (25 years)**

Head size decreases in proportion to body size.

3 The cephalocaudal and proximodistal principles, which regulate the sequence for developing early motor skills, are part of a process known as maturation.

Maturation is the succession of developmental changes that are genetically or biologically programmed rather than acquired through learning or life experiences.

In developing motor skills (see the three photos on the right), such as sitting up alone, crawling, and walking, all infants in all parts of the world go through the same developmental stages at about the same times. However, if children are given more opportunities to practice their stepping reflex earlier in life, they will begin to walk at an earlier age than children who lack such opportunities (Thelen, 1995). Thus, the development of early motor skills is heavily influenced by maturation (genetic program), but the timing can be partly slowed or speeded up by experience and learning (nurture).

Motor development refers to the stages of motor skills that all infants pass through as they acquire the muscular control necessary for making coordinated movements.

Because each child has a unique genetic program, he or she will acquire motor skills at different times (Darrah et al., 2009). The development of early motor skills, such as sitting, crawling, and walking, follows two general rules, called the proximodistal and cephalocaudal principles.

Sitting up alone— average 5.5 months (range 4.5–8.0 months)

4 Parents often note the major milestones in their infants' motor development, such as their first time crawling or walking, because they want to know if their children are within the developmental norms.

Developmental norms are the average ages at which children perform various skills or exhibit certain abilities or behaviors.

Some examples of developmental norms for stages in walking accompany the three photos. Because norms for motor development represent average ages rather than absolute ages, parents should not be disturbed if their infant's motor progress does not match the norms.

By the age of 2, infants have grown into toddlers who can walk up and down stairs and use their hands to hold glasses of juice, operate toys, and, of course, get into a lot of trouble.

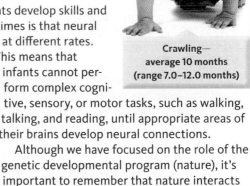

Crawling— average 10 months (range 7.0–12.0 months)

5 The reason infants develop skills and abilities at different times is that neural connections develop at different rates. This means that infants cannot perform complex cognitive, sensory, or motor tasks, such as walking, talking, and reading, until appropriate areas of their brains develop neural connections.

Although we have focused on the role of the genetic developmental program (nature), it's important to remember that nature interacts with the environment (nurture) to encourage or discourage the development of various motor, sensory, and cognitive abilities (Hadders-Algra, 2002). For example, infants need appropriate *environmental stimulation* for development of their visual systems (see things), for learning to speak (hear parents speaking), for emotional development (get loving care), and for motor development (explore objects). These examples show how the genetic program needs and interacts with environmental stimulation for the proper development of a child's sensory, motor, and cognitive abilities.

Walking alone— average 12.1 months (range 11.5–14.5 months)

Along with developing motor skills, an infant is also undergoing emotional changes. ●

C Emotional Development

Definition

Becki is describing the emotional makeup of her sextuplets (photo below). "Brenna, the oldest by 30 seconds, is the affectionate one. Julian, the second child delivered, is 'Mr. Smiley.' Quinn, the third, is sweet and generous and most adventurous. Claire, fourth oldest, is the boss, as charming as she is tough. Ian, the fifth, is the smallest and loves music, drawing, and sleep. Adrian, the youngest, is the biggest and most gentle" (S. Reed & Breu, 1995, p. 127). Each of these 2-year-old sextuplets has a unique emotional development.

How can sextuplets be so different?

Each one has a different emotional makeup.

Emotional development refers to the influence and interaction of genetic factors, brain changes, cognitive factors, coping abilities, and cultural factors in the development of emotional behaviors, expressions, thoughts, and feelings (H. H. Goldsmith, 2009).

Similar to all infants, the sextuplets initially showed a limited number of inherited emotional expressions, including interest, startle, distress, disgust, and a neonatal smile (a half-smile that appears spontaneously for no apparent reason). Also, similar to all infants, during the first two years the sextuplets developed a wide range of emotional expressions and feelings, including *social smiling* (age 4–6 weeks); *anger, surprise*, and *sadness* (age 3–4 months); *fear* (age 5–7 months); *shame* and *shyness* (age 6–8 months); and *contempt* and *guilt* (age 24 months) (Kopp & Neufeld, 2003).

A child's development of emotional expressions and feelings results from the interaction among genetic, neurological (brain), cognitive, coping, and cultural factors. The interaction of all these factors explains why each of the sextuplets has a unique emotional makeup, ranging from being sweet and gentle to being charming, adventurous, and tough.

We'll focus on one of the genetic factors involved in emotional development, which is called temperament.

Temperament and Emotions

One reason each of the sextuplets developed a unique emotional makeup so very early in life involves something called temperament.

Why did the differences show up so early?

Temperament is an individual's relatively stable and long-lasting pattern of mood and emotional behavior. The pattern emerges early in childhood because temperament is largely influenced by genetic factors.

Researchers studied differences in infants' temperaments by interviewing mothers with 2- to 3-month-old infants and then observing these same infants repeatedly over the next seven years. Researchers rated each infant on nine components of temperament, including activity level, attention span, fussiness, and mood. On the basis of these ratings, they divided infants into four categories (A. Thomas & Chess, 1977).

1 **Easy babies**, who made up 40% of the sample, were happy and cheerful, had regular sleeping and eating habits, and adapted quickly to new situations.

2 **Slow-to-warm-up babies**, who made up 15% of the sample, were more withdrawn, were moody, and tended to take longer to adapt to new situations.

3 **Difficult babies**, who made up 10% of the sample, were fussy, fearful of new situations, and more intense in their reactions. During the course of the seven-year study, difficult babies developed more serious emotional problems than the easy or slow-to-warm-up babies.

4 **No-single-category babies**, who made up 35% of the sample, had a variety of traits and could not be classified into one of the other three categories.

10–15% fearful

40% fearless

Genetic influence. Infants develop distinct temperaments very early, usually in the first 2–3 months of life, and these temperaments occur largely because of genetic factors rather than learning experiences (J. Bates, 2000). For example, about 10–15% of Caucasian babies inherit an inhibited or fearful temperament (e.g., show physiological arousal in novel situations), while about 40% inherit a fearless temperament (e.g., remain calm in novel situations) (Kagan, 2003a).

Infants with highly reactive or fearful temperaments at 4 months of age are ten times more likely to develop depression and anxiety disorders during adulthood than less reactive or less fearful infants. The adults who are highly reactive as infants have overdeveloped brain areas responsible for emotional responses, which likely interferes with the proper functioning of these brain areas, and leads to mood disorders (C. Schwartz, 2008, 2009).

Environmental influence. About 30% of infants who began with a fearful or fearless temperament remained that way emotionally into adulthood, but 70% showed moderate changes in temperament. One reason for changes in temperament involves environmental factors, such as family influence, poverty level, and educational opportunities, all of which interact with and can change the infant's initial temperament (Kagan 2003b). Thus, whether or not an infant's genetically influenced temperament persists depends to a considerable extent on the influence and interaction of environmental factors.

Because an infant's temperament influences the development of emotional behavior, it also affects the bond or attachment between parent and child, our next topic.

Attachment

Do infants and parents form a special bond?

For the first 3 years of his life, Alex (right picture) lived in an orphanage where he had no consistent, loving person to take care of him. When he was adopted at age 3, he repeatedly rejected his parents' love and he was never able to express love toward them. Living his first few years of life without close bonding to a parent or caregiver led Alex to have problems in attachment.

Attachment is a close, fundamental emotional bond that develops between the infant and his or her parents or caregiver.

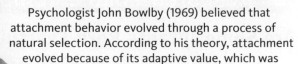

Alex lived in a Romanian orphanage until he was adopted at age 3.

Psychologist John Bowlby (1969) believed that attachment behavior evolved through a process of natural selection. According to his theory, attachment evolved because of its adaptive value, which was to give the infant a better chance of surviving because the parent was close by to provide care and protection. Much of the research on attachment was initiated by Mary Ainsworth (1989), who asked three general questions: How does attachment occur? Are there different kinds of attachment? What are the long-term effects of attachment?

How Does Attachment Occur?

According to attachment theory, babies form an attachment to their parents through a gradual process that begins shortly after birth and continues through early childhood. As newborns, infants have a powerful social signal, crying, which elicits care and sympathy. As 4- to 6-week-old infants, they begin social smiling (smiling at others), which elicits joy and pleasure in their parents. At about 6 months, infants begin to give their parents a happy greeting (smiling, holding out their arms) when they reappear after a short absence. These behaviors contribute to children expressing their needs better and understanding their parents' emotional experiences, which ultimately help to build a good parent–child attachment (R. A. Thompson, 1998, 2006).

As the infant develops a closer attachment to her parents, she also shows more distress when her parents leave; this is called separation anxiety.

Separation anxiety is an infant's distress—as indicated by loud protests, crying, and agitation—whenever the infant's parents temporarily leave.

According to Ainsworth, separation anxiety is a clear sign that the infant has become attached to one or both parents. By the end of the first year, an infant usually shows a close attachment to her parents as well as to one or more other family members.

However, depending on the infant's temperament (easy or difficult) and the mother's attitude (caring or not responsive), different kinds of attachment occur.

Are There Different Kinds of Attachment?

Ainsworth (1979) is best known for developing a method for studying infants' reactions to being separated from, and then reunited with, their mothers. She used these reactions to indicate the kind or quality of the infants' attachment. There are now four different kinds of attachment, but we'll focus on two, which are called secure (65% of infants) and insecure (20% of infants) attachment.

Secure attachment is an emotional bond characteristic of infants who use their parent or caregiver as a safe home base from which they can wander off and explore their environments.

For example, when infants are placed in an unfamiliar room containing many interesting toys, securely attached infants tend to explore freely as long as their parent looks on. If the parent leaves, most of the infants cry. On the parent's return, securely attached infants happily greet the caregiver and are easily soothed. In contrast, some infants show insecure attachment.

Insecure attachment is an emotional bond characteristic of infants who avoid or show ambivalence or resistance toward their parent or caregiver.

For example, insecurely attached infants may cling and want to be held one minute but squirm and push away the next minute, displaying a lack of trust in the parent or caregiver.

Attachments formed in infancy may also affect one's later relationships as well as mental health.

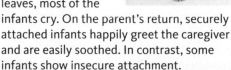

What Are the Effects of Attachment?

Because Alex never formed an attachment to a parent during infancy, he will likely have difficulty forming healthy bonds with parents or other adults in the future. As it turned out, despite being adopted by parents who cared tremendously for him and tried every day to show they loved him, Alex never bonded with them. Even at age 7, he still rejected his parents' affection and did not trust them. Because Alex never developed a secure attachment, when the time came to say good-bye to his parents and meet his new adoptive mother, he left his parents without any hesitation and he immediately called the new woman "mom" and told her "I love you."

The kind of attachment formed in infancy is thought to be associated with the success of future relationships. For example, a secure attachment is associated with being more trusting, enjoying relationships more, and dealing better with stress; an insecure attachment is associated with being dependent and having poor social relationships and poor coping skills (Burge et al., 1997; M. S. Howard & Medway, 2004).

Also, the kind of attachment formed in infancy has been shown to be associated with mental health in later years. For example, infants with a secure attachment grow up to have more positive moods and are better able to cope with stress (Fearon et al., 2010). Insecure attachment is associated with mental health disorders during adolescence (A. Lee & Hankin, 2009). Last, insecure attachment is associated with a high frequency of medical visits for unexplained physical symptoms during adulthood (R. E. Taylor et al., 2012).

The kind of attachment an infant forms is partly dependent on temperament. We'll next discuss the kinds and effects of different temperaments. ●

© Monkey Business Images/Shutterstock.com

© Jan Mika/Shutterstock.com

Are Some Infants Born Fearful?

How can children be so different?

We're going to discuss a series of classic studies by Jerome Kagan (2003a) that changed the way we think about children's temperaments. Kagan wanted to answer a question asked by many parents: Why do children raised by the same parents in the same family grow up with such different emotional makeups? For example, Eric's parents wondered why he (similar to the circled child in the right photo) was more shy and fearful than his two brothers, would never leave his mother's side to play with other children, was afraid to tell a story to his grade-school class, and feared going into the swimming pool with other children (Elias, 1989). Kagan wondered if Eric was born "fearful" and if he would change as he grew up.

Why is only one child shy?

The first problem Kagan faced was to select between two different research methods—longitudinal and cross-sectional—to study developmental changes. As we discuss the advantages and disadvantages of each method, you'll understand why Kagan selected the longitudinal method to study temperament.

Longitudinal Method

One method researchers use to study developmental changes, such as a child's temperament, is the longitudinal method.

With the **longitudinal method,** the same group of individuals is studied repeatedly at many different points in time.

For example, as shown in the figure below, researchers first study the temperaments in a group of 2-year-old children, look at this same group again at age 7, then see them again at age 12, and so on.

Disadvantages. Disadvantages are that researchers must wait many years for their participants to grow older and they must deal with the problem of participants dropping out of the study due to relocation, illness, or death.

Age	2	7	12
Year	1989	1994	1999

Advantage. A major advantage of the longitudinal method is that the same participants are used throughout the study. This means that researchers can track and analyze the development of each participant as he or she ages and confronts new environmental conditions. This ability to track each participant across time is the chief reason researchers prefer to use the longitudinal method to study developmental changes, such as changes in temperament.

Cross-Sectional Method

With the **cross-sectional method,** several groups of different-aged individuals are studied at the same time.

For example, in the figure below, researchers are using the cross-sectional method because they selected a group of 2-year-olds, a group of 7-year-olds, and a group of 12-year-olds and studied all their temperaments at the same time.

Advantage. The primary advantage of the cross-sectional method is that researchers can compare any developmental differences, such as in temperaments, across many different age groups, all at the same time. This lowers the dropout rate due to relocation, illness, or death and gives immediate results.

Age	2	7	12
Year		1999	

Disadvantage. A major disadvantage of the cross-sectional approach is that it does not track the development of the same person across time but rather compares different groups at different ages. This means that both the participants and the environmental conditions are different, which allows for more error and bias in interpreting the results.

Procedure

Choosing the longitudinal method, Jerome Kagan and his colleagues (Kagan, 2003a; Kagan & Snidman, 1991) began by studying the temperaments of 4-month-olds. These same infants would be evaluated at different ages until they reached their early 20s. The initial findings were that some 4-month-olds were fearless while others were fearful, whom Kagan called inhibited children.

Inhibited/fearful children show avoidance, anxiety, or fear (measured by avoiding or crying) when in a strange or

novel environment; they also show increased physiological arousal (increased heart rate) and brain activity (increased response of amygdala—threat detector) in novel or strange situations.

Having identified infants with two very different temperaments—inhibited/fearful and fearless—Kagan and his colleagues were able to study how these different temperaments affected emotional development by evaluating the same participants across more than 20 years. Here's what they found.

Results

How many were fearful/inhibited? Kagan and his colleagues observed several hundred 4-month-old infants and reported that about one-fourth were classified as inhibited or highly fearful (graph below). An inhibited or highly fearful *infant* showed a high degree of avoidance, fretting, and crying in novel or strange situations. A typical inhibited *child* stayed at the periphery of a large group of peers, reading a book, painting at an easel, or standing in a corner quietly watching another child. One of the best indicators of an inhibited child was that he or she spoke very little and initiated very little spontaneous conversation with unfamiliar peers or adults (Kagan et al., 1988; Kagan & Snidman, 1991).

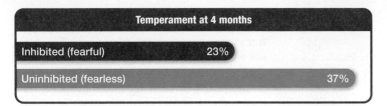

Temperament at 4 months	
Inhibited (fearful)	23%
Uninhibited (fearless)	37%

How many were fearless/uninhibited? About one-third of the *infants* were classified as uninhibited or low-fear individuals (above graph), and the remaining infants were classified in between. A typical fearless/uninhibited *child* was involved in group activities, was very talkative, initiated spontaneous interactions, engaged in conversations, often with smiling and laughter, and showed enthusiasm for social interactions not observed in inhibited children.

Based on these studies, as well as studies that compared identical twins (share nearly 100% of their genes) with fraternal twins (share 50% of their genes), researchers concluded that the influence of genetic factors on emotional development is as high as 60% (H. H. Goldsmith, 2003).

How many changed temperaments? About 18% of the very fearful infants remained highly fearful at 14 and 21 months of age and developed anxious symptoms at about 7 years, but about 80% of infants who were initially classified as very fearful did not develop into very fearful children. However, none of the very fearful children developed into completely fearless ones. This means that having a fearful temperament at infancy puts a person at risk for becoming a fearful child, but the risk for becoming fearful is not completely determined because some do become less fearful (but never fearless) (Kagan, 2003a).

What happens in the brain? Earlier we discussed the brain's emotional detector, called the amygdala (see p. 362), which signals threatening or fearful stimuli. Researchers guessed that perhaps fearful infants were born with a more active amygdala. Researchers measured the amygdala's activity (fMRI) in response to novel or familiar faces in 20-year-old adults who had been classified as either fearful or fearless at age 2. Researchers found that adults classified as *fearful* at age 2 had more activity in response to novel faces than did adults initially classified as *fearless.* Researchers suggested that an infant who is born with an overactive amygdala is at risk for having a fearful temperament and later developing into a fearful or shy person (C. E. Schwartz et al., 2003).

Amygdala

Fearful adults had more activity in the amygdala.

How can parents help a fearful/inhibited child overcome his or her fear and shyness?

Conclusions

This research answers a question asked by many parents: How can children raised by the same parents in the same family have such different temperaments? Part of the answer comes from Kagan's (2003a) series of longitudinal studies, which showed that infants have at least two distinct temperaments—fearful/inhibited or fearless/uninhibited. These two temperaments are relatively stable across time and involve observable behaviors (avoiding and crying), physiological arousal (increased heart rate), and differences in the activity of the brain's emotional detector, the amygdala.

The occurrence of different temperaments in young infants indicates the influence of genetic factors (nature). However, the finding that about 80% of the children's temperaments changed moderately indicates the influence of environmental experiences (nurture) (Pesonen et al., 2003).

Another interesting finding was that although children differed in temperament—inhibited or uninhibited—they did not differ in IQ scores, intellectual abilities, language, memory, or reasoning abilities (Kagan, 1998).

How can parents help fearful children? Researchers advise parents with fearful children to be very caring and supportive and to consistently help their inhibited children deal with minor stressors. With such support, inhibited children learned to control their initial urges to withdraw from strange people or situations. Additionally, researchers suggest that if parents avoid becoming too anxious, overprotective, or angry at their children's extreme fearfulness and timidity, there will be a better chance that the inhibited child will become less anxious in adolescence (Kagan, 1994).

Eric's parents followed this advice. As an infant and child, Eric (left photo) showed signs of being fearful or inhibited. For example, Eric spent two weeks worrying about having to give a book report, which meant standing in front of, and speaking to, the whole class. Eric was sure he couldn't do it. His parents encouraged Eric to role-play giving his book report, so Eric repeated his speech over and over at home until he felt comfortable. When Eric gave his book report to the class, he did very well and felt great afterward (Elias, 1989). With support and understanding, parents can help a fearful child to become more outgoing and less fearful.

At the same time an infant is developing emotional behaviors, he or she is also acquiring numerous cognitive skills and abilities, which we'll discuss next. ●

Being fearful is one kind of temperament.

© Manfred Rutz/Getty Images

© LWA/Dann Tardif/Getty Images

E Cognitive Development

Piaget's Theory

What are blocks for?

We have explained how a newborn's brain and senses develop relatively quickly so that an infant is soon ready to creep and walk and explore and learn about a wondrous world through a process called cognitive development.

Cognitive development refers to how a person perceives, thinks, and gains an understanding of his or her world through the interaction and influence of genetic and learned factors.

For example, if you gave blocks to Sam, who is 5 months old (top right photo), he would surely put one into his mouth. If you gave the same blocks to Sam when he was 2 years old (bottom right photo), he might stack them. If you gave the same blocks to Sam when he was an adolescent, he might play a game of throwing them into a can. What Sam does with blocks depends on his experience and level of cognitive development.

Jean Piaget. In the history of developmental psychology, the person who had the greatest impact on the study of cognitive development was Jean Piaget, who was both a biologist and a psychologist. From the 1920s to his death in 1980, Piaget (1929) studied how children solved problems in their natural settings, such as cribs, sandboxes, and playgrounds. Piaget developed one of the most influential theories of cognitive development (M. H. Bornstein & Lamb, 2011).

Piaget believed that from early on, a child acts like a tiny scientist who is actively involved in making guesses or hypotheses about how the world works. For example, when given blocks, 5-month-old Sam puts them into his mouth, while 2-year-old Sam tries to stack them, and adolescent Sam laughs and plays a game of tossing blocks into a can. Piaget believed that children learn to understand things, such as what to do with blocks, through two active processes that he called assimilation and accommodation.

Assimilation

If you gave 5-month-old Sam a block, he would first try to put it into his mouth because at that age, infants "think" that objects are for sucking on. This mouthing behavior is an example of assimilation.

Blocks are for putting in mouth.

Assimilation is the process by which a child uses old methods or experiences to deal with new situations.

At 5 months, Sam will first put a new object into his mouth because his knowledge of objects is that they are for eating or sucking. Thus, Sam will assimilate the new object as something too hard to eat but all right for sucking.

Depending on their age and knowledge, children assimilate blocks in different ways: infants assimilate blocks as something to suck; toddlers assimilate blocks as something to stack or throw; adolescents assimilate blocks as something used to play games; and adults assimilate blocks as something to give to children. The assimilation of new information leads to Piaget's next process—accommodation.

Accommodation

If you gave 2-year-old Sam the same blocks, he would not try to eat them, but he might try to stack them, which is an example of accommodation.

Accommodation is the process by which a child changes old methods to deal with or adjust to new situations.

For example, because of Sam's experience with different kinds of objects, he has learned that square, hard objects are not food but things that can be handled and stacked. Sam's learning to change existing knowledge because of new information (blocks are for stacking, not eating) is an example of accommodation, which is one way that mental growth occurs.

Blocks are for stacking.

As an infant or child is actively involved in exploring his or her environment, there are many opportunities for assimilation and accommodation, which result in different kinds of cognitive growth and development.

According to Piaget, children make big gains in reasoning, thinking, and understanding through active involvement and the processes of assimilation and accommodation. Using these two processes, children go through a series of cognitive stages.

Piaget's Stages of Cognitive Development

What is Sam thinking?

Piaget is best known for describing the changes or different stages in cognitive development that occur between infancy and adulthood (Bjorklund, 2005).

Piaget's cognitive stages are four different stages—sensorimotor, preoperational, concrete operations, and formal operations—each of which is more advanced than the preceding stage because it involves new reasoning and thinking abilities.

1 **Sensorimotor**

2 **Preoperational**

3 **Concrete**

4 **Formal**

Although Piaget believed that all people go through the same four cognitive stages, he acknowledged that they may go through the stages at different rates.

Piaget's hypothesis that cognitive development occurs in stages and that each stage involves different kinds of thinking was one of his unique contributions to developmental psychology. We'll explain Piaget's four stages by following Sam through his cognitive development.

Stage 1

Imagine Sam as a newborn infant. His primary way of interacting with the world is through reflexive responses, such as sucking and grasping. By 5 months, Sam has developed enough voluntary muscle control so that he can reach out, grasp things, and put them into his mouth to discover if the things are good to suck on. Sam is in the sensorimotor stage.

The **sensorimotor stage** (from birth to about age 2) is the first of Piaget's cognitive stages. During this stage, infants interact with and learn about their environments by relating their sensory experiences (such as hearing and seeing) to their motor actions (mouthing and grasping).

Hidden objects. At the beginning of the sensorimotor stage, Sam has one thinking problem: remembering that hidden objects still exist. For example, notice in the top left photo that 5-month-old Sam is shown a toy dog. Sam immediately tries to grab it and put part of it in his mouth. This is another example of assimilation; Sam believes that objects are mostly for mouthing.

With doggie in sight, infant tries to touch it.

With doggie hidden, infant acts as if there is no doggie.

However, notice in the bottom left photo that when a screen is placed in front of the dog, Sam looks away. He doesn't push the screen away to get at the toy because, at this point, Sam behaves as if things that are out of sight are out of mind and simply no longer exist. Sam has not learned object permanence.

Object permanence. Beginning at around 9 months, if Sam is shown a toy dog that is then covered by a screen, he will try to push the screen away and look for the dog. Sam has learned that a toy dog that is out of sight still exists behind the screen. This new concept is called object permanence.

Object permanence refers to the understanding that objects or events continue to exist even if they can no longer be heard, touched, or seen.

The concept of object permanence develops slowly over a period of about nine months. By the end of the sensorimotor period (about age 2), an infant will search long and hard for lost or disappeared objects, indicating a fully developed concept of object permanence.

At the end of the sensorimotor stage, 2-year-old Sam can think about things that are not present and can form simple plans for solving problems, such as searching for things.

According to Piaget, after the sensorimotor stage, Sam enters the next stage, called the preoperational stage.

Stage 2

As a 4-year-old, Sam is busy pushing a block around the floor and making noises as he pretends the block is a car. The cognitive ability to pretend is a sign that Sam is going through the preoperational stage.

The **preoperational stage** (from about 2 to 7 years old) is the second of Piaget's cognitive stages. During this stage, children learn to use symbols, such as words or mental images, to solve simple problems and to think or talk about things that are not present.

At this stage, Sam is acquiring the cognitive ability to pretend things and to talk about or draw things that are not physically present. Although Sam is learning to use words and images in speech and play, his thinking has a number of interesting limitations that make it different from an adult's thinking. During the preoperational stage, two of his cognitive limitations involve problems with conservation and egocentrism.

Conservation. As 4-year-old Sam watches you pour milk from a tall, thin glass into a short, wide glass, will he know that the amount of milk remains the same even though its shape changes? This is called the problem of conservation.

Conservation refers to the fact that even though the shape of some object or substance is changed, the total amount remains the same.

Here's what happens when 4-year-old Sam is faced with a conservation problem.

In photo #1, 4-year-old Sam watches as his mother fills two short, wide glasses with equal amounts of milk.

In photo #2, Sam sees his mother pour the milk from one short, wide glass into a tall, thin glass. Mother asks, "Does one glass have more milk?"

In photo #3, Sam points to the tall, thin glass as having more milk because the tall glass looks larger. He makes this mistake even though he just saw his mother pour the milk from a short, wide glass.

Sam, like other children at the preoperational stage, will not be able to solve conservation problems until the next stage.

Egocentrism. A second problem that Sam has during the preoperational stage is that he makes mistakes or misbehaves because of egocentrism.

Egocentrism (ee-goh-SEN-trism) refers to seeing and thinking of the world from only your own viewpoint and having difficulty appreciating someone else's viewpoint.

Piaget used the term *egocentrism* to mean that preoperational children cannot see situations from another person's, such as a parent's, point of view. When they don't get their way, children may get angry or pout because their view of the world is so self-centered.

Stage 3

Between the ages of 7 and 11, Sam learns that even if things change their shape, they don't lose any quantity or mass, a new concept that occurs during the concrete operations stage.

The **concrete operations stage** (from about 7 to 11 years) is the third of Piaget's cognitive stages. During this stage, children can perform a number of logical mental operations on concrete objects that are physically present.

Conservation. As you may remember, when Sam was 4 years old and in the preoperational stage, he had not mastered the concept of conservation. In the preoperational stage, Sam thought a tall, thin glass held more milk than a short, wide glass. And if 4-year-old Sam watched as a ball of clay (top left picture) was flattened into a long, thin piece (bottom left picture), he would say the long piece was larger.

Can these two pieces of clay be the same size?

However, Sam is now 10 years old and has just watched you flatten a ball of clay into a long piece. Sam now says that the long, flattened piece contains the same amount of clay as the ball, even if the shape changed. Similarly, if 10-year-old Sam watched you pour soda from a short glass into a tall glass, he would correctly answer that the amount of soda remained the same. Children gradually master the concept of conservation during the concrete operations stage, and they also get better at classification.

Classification. If you gave a 4-year-old, preoperational Sam some red and blue marbles in different sizes (picture right), he would be able to classify the pieces according to a single category, such as size. However, during the concrete operations stage, 10-year-old Sam has acquired the ability to classify the marbles according to two categories, such as color and size, indicating that he has learned a new cognitive skill.

During the concrete stage, children learn to sort objects by both size and color.

New abilities. During the concrete operations stage, children learn to classify or sort objects according to more than one category, and they learn to solve a variety of conservation problems. The reason Piaget called this the *concrete* operations stage is that children can easily classify or figure out relationships between objects provided the objects are actually physically present or "concrete."

However, children at the concrete operations stage still have difficulty figuring out relationships among objects that are not present or situations that are imaginary. Thinking about imaginary or hypothetical situations occurs in Piaget's fourth stage.

Stage 4

Sam is now 17 years old and is surfing the Web for a paper he's writing on what killed the dinosaurs. This kind of abstract thinking indicates that Sam is in the formal operations stage.

The **formal operations stage** (from about 12 years old through adulthood) is Piaget's fourth cognitive stage. During this stage, adolescents and adults develop the ability to think about and solve abstract problems in a logical manner.

Piaget believed adolescents develop thinking and reasoning typical of adults during the formal operations stage. For example, 17-year-old Sam can compare theories about why the dinosaurs died, including being destroyed by a giant asteroid, radical temperature change, or some terrible virus. During this stage, adolescents also encounter new worlds of abstract ideas and hypothetical concepts. For example, Sam can discuss abstract ideas, such as whether computer hackers should go to jail, if going steady is a good idea, and how strict parents should be.

Acquiring the ability to think in a logical, systematic, and abstract way is one of the major characteristics of the formal operations stage. In comparison, seven years ago, when Sam was in the concrete operations stage, he lacked the ability to solve abstract problems. As you may have already realized, the cognitive skills associated with the formal operations stage are the very ones you need to do well in college.

How much does the thinking of a 17-year-old differ from that of a 10-year-old?

Along with advances in cognitive abilities, the formal operations stage welcomes the return of *egocentrism*, which refers to the tendency of adolescents to believe that others are always watching and evaluating them, and the belief that everyone thinks and cares about the same things they do. Because adolescents think people are watching their every move, they act as though they are performing in front of an audience. Of course, such an audience doesn't really exist because everyone is not actually obsessed with the teen's every action. Thus, this phenomenon is named the imaginary audience.

I think everyone is always watching me.

Imaginary audience refers to the belief adolescents have that everyone is watching all of their actions.

Another aspect of adolescent thinking related to egocentrism is the personal fable.

Personal fable refers to an adolescent's belief that he or she is invulnerable, unique, and special.

This type of thinking explains why adolescents can never accept that anyone might even remotely understand how they are feeling, because after all they are unique and special (Elkind, 1967, 1998).

Evaluation of Piaget's Theory

What's happened to Piaget's theory?

We have discussed Piaget's cognitive stages in some detail, but there are three ideas that stand out (Larivee et al., 2000): (1) Children gradually and in a step-by-step fashion develop reasoning abilities through the active processes of assimilation and accommodation. (2) Children are naturally curious and self-motivated to explore their worlds and, in the process, develop numerous cognitive skills. (3) Children acquire different kinds of thinking and reasoning abilities as they go through different stages of cognitive development.

Piaget's theory has had a tremendous influence on the area of cognitive development. However, over the past 50 years, there have been numerous criticisms of Piaget's theory. We'll discuss these criticisms along with current ideas about cognitive development.

Impact and Criticisms

Impact of Piaget's theory. For three main reasons, Piaget's theory has had a huge impact on understanding cognitive development. First, his theory was far more comprehensive than any other theory at the time. Second, his theory triggered an enormous amount of research and led to the development of

© AFP/Getty Images

Jean Piaget (1896–1980)

other cognitive development theories. Third, many of Piaget's ideas have proven correct and have been replicated (R. J. Sternberg et al., 2003b).

Criticisms. There are several criticisms. First, Piaget's four stages are not as rigid or orderly as he proposed (R. J. Sternberg et al., 2003b). For example, children can solve certain kinds of problems, such as object permanence, much earlier than Piaget proposed (Birney & Sternberg, 2011).

Second, although Piaget described how children can and cannot think at different ages and stages, his theory is criticized for not explaining how or why this change occurs (Bruner, 1997). Today, researchers associate changes in thinking with changes in the brain, something unknown to Piaget (Petrill, 2003).

Third, children failed some of the Piagetian tasks not because children lacked the thinking abilities but because they did not understand the instructions. For example, preoperational children can solve some abstract problems, such as who is taller or shorter than someone else, provided the problems are presented simply. According to Piaget, preoperational children should not be able to solve these simple abstract problems.

Fourth, Piaget implied that everyone develops formal operations at about age 12 and then no significant cognitive development takes place throughout adulthood. Some researchers believe there is no denying that the cognitive development of an adult is more advanced than that of a 12-year-old (Hopkins, 2011).

Current status. Almost by himself, Piaget began the area of cognitive development. His observational methods to study children and his view that children are active explorers in discovering their worlds are still considered important ideas. However, because of criticisms and new findings on the influence of genetic and neural factors, Piaget's theory is now viewed as having historical importance but is no longer the major force in guiding research in cognitive development (Newcombe, 2002).

New Information

Since Piaget developed his theory, there have been two major changes in understanding and studying cognitive development.

1 Genetic factors. One big change involves identifying genetic factors that influence many cognitive abilities. For example, research on identical and fraternal twins shows that genetic factors account for 20–60% of the influence on verbal, spatial, and perceptual abilities (Petrill, 2003). In Piaget's time, the influence of genetic factors on cognitive abilities had not been as clearly established.

Recently, an increasing number of studies have shown how genetic factors (nature) interact with a child's environmental and learning experiences (nurture) in the development of cognitive abilities. For example, being outgoing and fearless is related to the kind of temperament an infant inherits (nature) (Kagan, 2003a). Researchers reported that children who had been rated high in seeking stimulation at age 3 scored significantly higher on IQ tests at age 11 compared to children who had been rated low in seeking stimulation at age 3. This significant difference in IQ scores (11 points) was not related to the occupation or education of their parents. Researchers concluded that children rated high in seeking stimulation (nature) were more curious and open to learning from their environments (nurture), which in turn enhanced the development of their cognitive abilities and resulted in higher scores on IQ tests (A. Raine et al., 2002). Researchers conclude that genetic factors set a range for many cognitive abilities and these abilities can be either facilitated by a stimulating environment or depressed by an impoverished environment (Bjorklund, 2012).

2 Brain development. Another major change has been our knowledge of how the brain develops. After birth and continuing through adolescence, different areas of the brain develop at different times. For example, the infant on the right doesn't know the doggie is hidden behind the screen because his prefrontal cortex is not yet well developed (Kalat, 2009). Similarly, at about age 2, a child learns on average a new word every two hours, in large part because of rapid neural

Child fails to find the doggie because his prefrontal cortex is not well developed.

© Doug Goodman/Photo Researchers, Inc.

growth in the brain's language areas (Pinker, 1994). These kinds of studies point out that cognitive development results from the interaction among genetic, neural, and environmental factors, much of which was unknown during Piaget's time.

Cognitive development is closely intertwined with and occurs at the same time as social development, which we'll examine next. ●

F Social Development

At the beginning of this module we described how Alex was raised in an orphanage until age 3, at which time he was adopted.

What will happen to Alex? Some psychologists wonder how Alex's early emotional difficulties will affect his future social development.

Social development refers to how a person develops a sense of self or a self-identity, develops relationships with others, and develops the social skills important in personal interactions.

After Alex was adopted, we know that even after a few years with his adoptive parents he never seemed to have made a good adjustment. Some psychologists would not be surprised that Alex never developed close relationships with others or that he never learned social skills important in personal interactions. This is because some psychologists believe that the first five years are the most important and that early emotional troubles may lead to later social problems.

Alex's social development is a long and complicated process, which is influenced by many of the emotional and cognitive factors that we have just discussed. We'll describe three different theories of social development, each of which emphasizes a different aspect of behavior.

Freud's Psychosexual Stages

One of the best-known theories is that of Sigmund Freud (1940/1961), who said that each of us goes through five successive psychosexual stages.

The **psychosexual stages** are five different developmental periods—oral, anal, phallic, latency, and genital stages—during which the individual seeks pleasure from different areas of the body that are associated with sexual feelings. Freud emphasized that a child's first five years were most important to social and personality development.

In Freud's theory, there is often conflict between the child and parent. The conflict arises because the child wants immediate satisfaction or gratification of his or her own needs, while the parents often place restrictions on when, where, and how the child's needs should be satisfied. For example, a

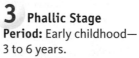
© PhotoDisc, Inc.

Does an infant's experience during breast feeding have lasting effects?

child may wish to be fed immediately, while the parent may want to delay the feeding to a more convenient time. Freud believed that interactions between parent and child in satisfying these psychosexual needs—for example, during breast feeding or toilet training—greatly influence the child's social development and future social interactions. In addition, Freud emphasized the importance of a child's first five years in influencing future social development or future personality problems.

According to Freud, Alex will go through five developmental stages, some of which contain potential conflicts between his desires and his parents' wishes. If his desires are over- or undersatisfied, he may become fixated at one of the first three stages. As you'll see, becoming fixated at one of these stages will hinder his normal social development.

---

1 **Oral Stage**

Period: Early infancy—first 18 months of life.

The **oral stage** lasts for the first 18 months of life and is a time when the infant's pleasure seeking is centered on the mouth.

Potential conflict: Pleasure-seeking activities include sucking, chewing, and biting. If Alex were locked into or fixated at this stage because his oral wishes were gratified too much or too little, he would continue to seek oral gratification as an adult.

2 **Anal Stage**

Period: Early infancy—1½ to 3 years.

The **anal stage** lasts from the age of about 1½ to 3 and is a time when the infant's pleasure seeking is centered on the anus and its functions of elimination.

Potential conflict: If Alex were locked into or fixated at this stage, he would continue to engage in behavioral activities related to retention or elimination. Retention may take the form of being very neat, stingy, or behaviorally rigid. Elimination may take the form of being generous or messy.

3 **Phallic Stage**

Period: Early childhood—3 to 6 years.

The **phallic** *(FAL-ick)* **stage** lasts from about age 3 to 6 and is a time when the infant's pleasure seeking is centered on the genitals.

Potential conflict: During this stage, Alex will compete with the parent of the same sex (his father) for the affections and pleasures of the parent of the opposite sex (his mother). Problems in resolving this competition (called the Oedipus complex and discussed in Module 19) may result in Alex going through life trying to prove his toughness.

4 **Latency Stage**

Period: Middle and late childhood—from 6 to puberty.

The **latency stage,** which lasts from about age 6 to puberty, is a time when the child represses sexual thoughts and engages in nonsexual activities, such as developing social and intellectual skills.

At puberty, sexuality reappears and marks the beginning of a new stage.

5 **Genital Stage**

Period: Puberty through adulthood.

The **genital stage** lasts from puberty through adulthood and is a time when the individual has renewed sexual desires that he or she seeks to fulfill through relationships with members of the opposite sex.

If Alex successfully resolved conflicts in the first three stages, he will have the energy to develop loving relationships and a healthy and mature personality.

According to Freud, Alex's future personality and social development will depend, to a large extent, on what he experiences during the first three psychosexual stages, which occur during his first five years. Freud's psychosexual stages are part of his larger psychoanalytic theory of personality, which we'll discuss more fully in Module 19.

Erikson's Psychosocial Stages

According to well-known psychologist Erik Erikson, Alex will encounter kinds of problems very different from the psychosexual ones proposed by Freud. Unlike Freud's emphasis on psychosexual issues, Erikson (1963, 1982) focused on psychosocial issues and said that each of us goes through eight psychosocial stages.

How important is trust?

The **psychosocial stages** are eight developmental periods during which an individual's primary goal is to satisfy desires associated with social needs. The eight periods are associated, respectively, with issues of trust, autonomy, initiative, industry, identity, intimacy, generativity, and ego integrity.

Erikson hypothesized that from infancy through adulthood we proceed through these stages, each of which is related to a different problem that needs to be resolved. If we successfully deal

Are the effects of psychosocial problems long-lasting?

© PhotoDisc, Inc.

with the potential problem of each psychosocial stage, we develop positive personality traits and are better able to solve the problem at the next stage. However, if we do not successfully handle the psychosocial problems, we may become anxious, worried, or troubled and develop social or personality problems.

Unlike Freud, Erikson believed that psychosocial needs deserve the greatest emphasis and that social development continues throughout one's lifetime. Thus, Erikson would emphasize Alex's psychosocial needs and downplay the importance of sexuality in the first five years.

We'll explain Erikson's first five stages here and discuss the remaining three stages in Module 18, which deals with social development in adolescents and adults.

Stage 1
Trust versus Mistrust
Period: Early infancy—birth through first year.
Potential problem: Alex comes into the world as a helpless infant who needs much care and attention. If his parents are responsive and sensitive to his needs, Alex will develop what Erikson calls basic trust, which makes it easier for him to trust people later in life. If Alex's parents neglect his needs, he may view his world as uncaring, learn to become mistrustful, and have difficulty dealing with the second stage. It appears that Alex did not receive the care and attention he needed during his first year of life.

Stage 2
Autonomy versus Shame and Doubt
Period: Late infancy—1 to 3 years.
Potential problem: As Alex begins walking, talking, and exploring, he is bound to get into conflict with the wishes of his parents. Thus, this second stage is a battle of wills between his parents' wishes and Alex's desires to do as he pleases. If his parents encourage Alex to explore, he will develop a sense of independence, or autonomy. If his parents disapprove of or punish Alex's explorations, he may develop a feeling that independence is bad and feel shame and doubt.

Stage 3
Initiative versus Guilt
Period: Early childhood—3 to 5 years.
Potential problem: As a preschooler, Alex has developed a number of cognitive and social skills that he is expected to use to meet the challenges in his small world. Some of these challenges involve assuming responsibility and making plans. If his parents encourage initiative, Alex will develop the ability to plan and initiate new things. However, if they discourage initiative, he may feel uncomfortable or guilty and may develop a feeling of being unable to plan his future.

Stage 4
Industry versus Inferiority
Period: Middle and late childhood—5 to 12 years.
Potential problem: Alex's grade school years are an exciting time, filled with participating in school, playing games with other children, and working to complete projects. If Alex can direct his energy into working at and completing tasks, he will develop a feeling of industry. If he has difficulty applying himself and completing homework, he may develop a feeling of inferiority and incompetence.

Stage 5
Identity versus Role Confusion
Period: Adolescence.
Potential problem: Adolescents need to leave behind the carefree, irresponsible, and impulsive behaviors of childhood and develop the more purposeful, responsible, planned behaviors of adults. If Alex is successful in making this change, he will develop a sense of confidence and a positive identity. If he is unsuccessful, he will experience role confusion, which will result in having low self-esteem and becoming socially withdrawn.

According to Erikson, Alex will encounter a particular psychosocial problem at each stage. If he successfully solves the problem, he will develop positive social traits that will help him solve the next problem. If he does not solve the problem, he will develop negative social traits that will hinder his solving a new problem at the next stage.

Evaluation of Erikson's and Freud's theories. Many psychologists agree with Erikson that psychosocial conflicts do contribute to social-emotional development (Bugental & Goodnow, 1998). Erikson said that the first five years were not necessarily the most important and that social development continues throughout one's life. In fact, longitudinal studies show that personality change and development continue well into middle adulthood (Erber, 2005).

Many psychologists also agree with Freud that childhood events are important to social development (Guterl, 2002; Sigelman & Rider, 2012). However, they criticize Freud for emphasizing childhood sexuality while neglecting the influences of social,

cultural, and cognitive factors on social development (Bugental & Goodnow, 1998; Burger, 2011). In addition, longitudinal studies show that children may overcome a variety of problems during the first five years and still have a well-adjusted personality, contrary to Freud's predictions (E. E. Werner, 1995).

The strength of Erikson's and Freud's theories is that they explain the whole of social development, from infancy through adulthood. Their weakness is that many of their concepts (trust, autonomy, oral stage, fixation) are more descriptive than explanatory and are difficult to verify or test experimentally (Burger, 2011). Next, we'll examine the social cognitive theory of social development.

Bandura's Social Cognitive Theory

After watching her daddy fish, this 4-year-old girl walked up to her daddy, pointed at the fish, and said, "I want to catch fish." Neither Freud's nor Erikson's theory

What is the 4-year-old doing?

explains why this girl wanted to learn how to fish, what motivated her to ask her daddy, or why she shouted "Caught one!" just like her daddy when he pulled up a fish with his rod. Albert Bandura (2001a) says that this little girl, like all of us, develops many of her behaviors and social skills through a variety of social cognitive processes.

The **social cognitive theory** emphasizes the importance of learning through observation, imitation, and self-reward in the development of social skills, interactions, and behaviors. According to this theory, it is not necessary that you perform any observable behaviors or receive any external rewards to learn new social skills because many of your behaviors are self-motivated, or intrinsic.

Social cognitive theory stresses how you learn by modeling and imitating behaviors you observe in social interactions and

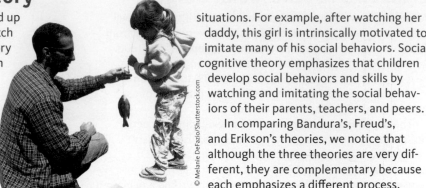

She watched her daddy fish and then she wanted to fish.

situations. For example, after watching her daddy, this girl is intrinsically motivated to imitate many of his social behaviors. Social cognitive theory emphasizes that children develop social behaviors and skills by watching and imitating the social behaviors of their parents, teachers, and peers.

In comparing Bandura's, Freud's, and Erikson's theories, we notice that although the three theories are very different, they are complementary because each emphasizes a different process. Social cognitive theory emphasizes learning through modeling; Freud's theory focuses on parent–child interactions that occur in satisfying innate biological needs; and Erikson's theory points to the importance of dealing with social needs.

We'll use these theories to explain how some children overcame terrible childhood experiences to develop normal social behaviors.

Resiliency

Based on observations of his patients, Freud concluded that social and personality development is essentially completed in the first

How do children overcome early problems?

five years. That is, even though an individual might undergo later social changes, his or her basic social and personality traits are primarily established during the first five years. One way to test Freud's hypothesis is to do a long-term study of children who are faced with major problems. One such individual is Dave Pelzer.

According to Dave's autobiographies, beginning in his early childhood, Dave's extremely disturbed, alcoholic mother did her best to put him through one life-threatening situation after another. She abused him mentally, physically, and emotionally. Some of the ways she tortured him were by denying him food, clothing, and warmth, forcing him to drink ammonia, stabbing him in his stomach, and constantly threatening to kill him. She belittled Dave by referring to him only as "It" rather than his name. Dave's father and brothers (who were not abused) did nothing to stop the horrendous abuse.

Dave had to do everything he could to survive. He stole food to eat as his mother aimed to starve him to death. When his mother burned him or stabbed him, he would take care of his wounds while in agonizing pain. The abuse Dave endured was so grave that it has been identified as one of the most serious and disturbing cases of child abuse on record.

At age 12, Dave was finally removed from his mother's custody and placed in several foster homes. He struggled to adjust to these various caregivers, but he finally developed a trusting, loving relationship with two caregivers he learned to call Mom and Dad.

Dave was exposed to very serious life stressors during his childhood. How these stressors affect children depends on each child's vulnerability and resiliency.

Vulnerability refers to psychological or environmental difficulties that make children more at risk for developing later personality, behavioral, or social problems.

Resiliency refers to various personality, family, or environmental factors that compensate for increased life stresses so that expected problems do not develop.

There is no question that Dave was extremely vulnerable. Although other children with such high vulnerability may have later developed very serious emotional or behavioral problems, Dave triumphed over seemingly insurmountable odds, displaying tremendous resiliency, and developed into a competent, courageous, and autonomous adult. He served as a member of the armed forces, where his accomplishments earned him personal commendations by three U.S. presidents. Also, Dave has authored six best-selling inspirational books, two of which were nominated for the Pulitzer Prize.

Children like Dave are called resilient, or stress-resistant. These children defy expectations because they develop into well-adapted individuals despite serious life stressors (Gorman, 2005a). For example, even though Dave experienced a severely brutal childhood, he developed into an amazing individual with high achievement motivation and deep insight into his life (Peltzer, 1995, 1997, 1999, 2000, 2003, 2009).

Adverse life experiences have long been thought to be associated with later personality, behavioral, and social problems. Thus, it comes as somewhat of a surprise to find out that a life with no adversity is not optimal either. Research shows that a history of some adversity predicts better mental health and well-being later in life, when compared to a history of high adversity and a history of no adversity. This research suggests that experiencing some life stressors during childhood may actually be advantageous (Seery, 2011). ●

Dave Pelzer overcame a truly disturbing childhood because of his incredible resilience.

G Gender Development

Gender Differences

What three words change your life forever?

When you look at the photo of the infant on the right, you can't help asking, Is it a girl or a boy? This question has great importance to social development because it involves gender identity.

Gender identity. By the age of 3, most children learn to label themselves as boys or girls and can classify others as being the same sex or the other sex (Ruble et al., 2006).

Gender identity is an individual's subjective experience and feelings of being a female or male.

Once children know their correct sex, they begin to learn and show sex-appropriate behaviors, which are called gender roles.

Gender roles. By age 2 to 3, American children have learned the preference of each traditional gender role for toys, clothes,

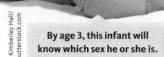

By age 3, this infant will know which sex he or she is.

© Kimberley Hall/Shutterstock.com

games, and tools. By ages 4 to 5, children have developed a clear idea of which occupations are stereotypically for men and for women. And by the relatively early age of 5, children have already learned the thoughts, expectations, and behaviors that accompany their particular gender roles (Eckes & Trautner, 2000).

Gender roles are the traditional or stereotypical behaviors, attitudes, and personality traits that parents, peers, and society expect us to have because we are male or female.

Gender roles become part of who we are and have a relatively powerful effect on how we behave, think, and act.

How children acquire gender roles is explained by two somewhat different but related theories: social role theory and cognitive developmental theory (C. L. Martin et al., 2002).

Social Role Theory

In many families, the parents expect a son to behave and act differently than a daughter. How parental expectations influence a child's gender identity is explained by the social role theory (Eagly et al., 2000).

The **social role theory** emphasizes the influence of social and cultural processes on how we interpret, organize, and use information. Applied to gender roles, it says that mothers, fathers, teachers, grandparents, friends, and peers expect, respond to, and reward different behaviors in boys than in girls. Under the influence of this differential treatment, boys learn a gender role that is different from girls'.

For example, the stereotypical gender roles for males include being dominant, controlling, and independent, while gender roles for females include being sensitive, nurturing, and concerned (Eagly & Karau, 2002; W. Wood et al., 1997).

According to social role theory, these gender differences originate, to a large extent, because mothers and fathers respond to and reward different behaviors in girls than in boys.

For instance, in playing with boys, fathers were observed to model being assertive and dominant, while in playing with girls, mothers were observed to model being concerned and nurturing (Leaper, 2000). Mothers were found to be more likely to enforce rules when their daughters misbehaved in a way that might be dangerous than when their sons misbehaved in a similar way (Morrongiello & Hogg, 2004). Parents are more likely to encourage dependence in girls, reward boys for conforming to traditional play activities, and reward girls for doing traditional household chores (Keenan & Shaw, 1997). These differences in parents' behaviors support the social role theory idea that parents encourage or discourage behaviors depending on whether these behaviors match traditional boy–girl gender roles.

One criticism of social role theory is that it focuses too much on rewarding and discouraging behaviors and too little on cognitive influences, which are emphasized in the cognitive developmental theory.

Why does she want to be a model?

© Studio 1One/Shutterstock.com

Cognitive Developmental Theory

When you were a child, you probably learned that there were rules about what boys and girls could and could not do. This childhood experience supports the cognitive developmental theory (C. L. Martin, 2000).

The **cognitive developmental theory** says that, as children develop mental skills and interact with their environments, they learn one set of rules for male behaviors and another set of rules for female behaviors.

In this view, children actively process information that results in learning gender rules regarding which behaviors are correct for girls and wrong for boys, and vice versa. On the basis of these rules, children form mental images of how they should act; these images are called gender schemas.

Gender schemas are sets of information and rules organized around how either a male or a female should think and behave (S. L. Bem, 1985).

For instance, the traditional gender schema for being a boy includes engaging in rough-and-tumble play and sports, initiating conversations, and exploring; the traditional gender schema for being a girl includes playing with dolls, expressing emotions, listening, and being dependent.

Cognitive developmental theory emphasizes that a child is an active participant in learning a male or female set of rules and schemas, which result in different gender roles (S. L. Bem, 1981).

Both social role theory and cognitive developmental theory predict that the sexes will develop different gender roles.

Why does he want to be a baseball player?

© Monkey Business Images/Shutterstock.com

Differences in Gender Traits

Girls and boys develop very different gender roles. For example, girls develop traits of being concerned, sensitive, and nurturing (left figure), while boys develop traits of being independent, controlling, and dominant (right figure) (Eckes & Trautner, 2000).

CONCERNED SENSITIVE NURTURING

These differences in gender traits are explained by two different theories.

According to **social role theory**, the expectations of parents, peers, and others *reward* or *discourage* different gender roles and behaviors for boys and girls. Social role theory focuses on boys and girls learning different gender roles and behavior because of *outside pressures* from family, peers, and society.

According to **cognitive developmental theory**, children acquire gender schemas or *cognitive rules* that indicate which gender roles and behaviors are right or wrong for boys and girls. Cognitive developmental theory focuses on boys and girls developing different gender roles because of *inside pressures*, which come from their own personal rules.

These two theories are not mutually exclusive but rather emphasize different factors in the development of gender-role differences and behaviors (C. L. Martin et al., 2002).

We'll discuss how differences in gender traits have important influences on personal, social, and career choices.

INDEPENDENT CONTROLLING DOMINANT

Male and Female Differences

Can a woman be elected president?

Career choices. As boys and girls grow into men and women, their different gender roles, which involve different ways for men and women to think, behave, interact socially, and make career choices, are further strengthened by pressures from parents, peers, and society (Eckes & Trautner, 2000). For example, until the early 1990s, gender roles for women did not include careers in law enforcement, the armed forces, fire or police departments, or management of large corporations, while gender roles for men did not include careers as nurses, secretaries, or elementary-school teachers. Since then gender roles have changed so that men and especially women have more flexibility and freedom in making job and career choices. However, gender roles still influence career choices, the most obvious being the reluctance to elect a woman as president of the United States.

Aggression. Researchers find that, from the age of 2 through college age, males tend to show more rough-and-tumble play, display more aggressive physical and verbal behavior, and commit more violent crimes than females (Kenrick et al., 2004). Sex differences in physical aggression have been found in children as young as 17 months. For example, one study found that 17-month-old boys were twice as likely as girls to hit another child frequently (Baillargeon, 2002). Twin and adoption studies indicate that the reasons for these sex differences in aggressive behavior include both genetic and environmental factors (Perusse & Gendreau, 2005). Therefore, although biological factors help to explain why boys are more aggressive than girls, psychosocial influences also play a key role. For example, researchers found that parents, peers, and society reward boys for acting out, being competitive, and settling their conflicts with fighting. In comparison, "nice girls" don't fight and they tend to settle conflicts through talking (Coie & Dodge, 1998). As a result of these biological and psychosocial influences, the gender role for males encourages aggressive behavior and helps explain why the majority of aggressive acts, both social and criminal, are committed by males (DiLalla, 2002; D. F. Halpern, 2000).

Boys and men are more aggressive.

Different brains. One reason girls and women develop traits of being concerned, sensitive, and nurturing may involve how women's brains process emotional situations. For example, researchers took brain scans (fMRI) while women and men looked at photos, which they graded from neutral (bookcase, landscape) to emotionally intense (crying people, dead body). Weeks later, when the same people were asked to pick out photos that they had earlier rated as emotionally intense, women correctly remembered 10–15% more than men did. Equally interesting, brain scans taken during viewing of the emotionally intense photos indicated that in women's brains the amygdala and additional areas were more activated than in men's brains. Researchers concluded that, compared to men, women's brains are more effectively wired for processing, coding, and remembering emotional experiences.

Amygdala

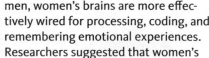

Women had more activation of brain areas.

Researchers suggested that women's greater focus on emotional events may help explain why women report higher rates of clinical depression than men (Canli et al., 2002). These findings also support the evolutionary theory of behavior, which says that in early times women developed particular emotional traits, such as being concerned, sensitive, and nurturing, because these traits were beneficial to women in maintaining a stable family structure and in raising children (Caporael, 2001).

Researchers advise against making claims that the brains of boys and girls are different; they state that at an early age the differences are small and they become magnified as children interact in the gender-influenced culture. Of course brain differences are biological; however, they are not necessarily hard-wired at birth (Eliot, 2010). As we've learned throughout this textbook, experience itself changes brain structure and function. Moreover, no amount of brain research will explain all the social differences between males and females. Many other factors, such as temperament, attachment, family background, and environment, may explain why the sexes can be so different (Tyre, 2006).

Next, we'll provide a review of infant and child development. ●

Unless otherwise noted, all images are © Cengage Learning

H Infancy & Childhood Review

The Big Picture

What's going on?

We have discussed how during infancy and childhood there are amazing increases in sensory abilities and motor skills and wondrous development of emotions, cognitive skills, social interactions, and gender roles. We'll briefly review and summarize these changes so that you can see the big picture of infant and child development.

| 1 month old | 6 months old | 10 months old | 1 year old | 3 years old |

Sensory & Motor Development

Newborns come with more sensory and perceptual abilities than previously thought. They have a well-developed sense of touch, show an innate preference for sweet and salt, and recognize (smell) their mothers' odors. In a few more months, infants can recognize their mothers' faces, produce speech sounds, and perceive depth. This new and improved version of infants' abilities better explains how they discover the world.

Infants gradually acquire the *coordinated movements* that they need to crawl, sit, stand, and walk. Many motor skills occur in a set sequence called *maturation* that is regulated by genetic programming. Two principles for motor development are that parts closest to the center of the body develop first—the

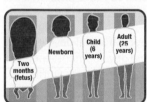

proximodistal principle—and parts closer to the head develop first—the *cephalocaudal* principle. With motor development comes the ability to get up and explore.

Emotional Development

"Good" babies and "difficult" babies show signs of differences in temperament, which is largely influenced by genetic factors. *Temperament* refers to stable differences in attention, arousal, and reaction to new situations; it also affects level of arousal and the development of emotional behaviors. Infants develop many *emotions*, which allow a wide range of wordless communications with the parent and the world. Infants form a close emotional bond with parents (caregivers). This emotional bond, which is called *attachment*, is thought to influence the development of future emotional and social behaviors.

Cognitive Development

One theory of cognitive development is *Piaget's theory*, which says that children play an active role in cognitive development by incorporating new information into existing knowledge *(assimilation)* or changing existing knowledge through experience *(accommodation)*. Children pass through four different cognitive stages—*(1) sensorimotor, (2) preoperational, (3) concrete operations*, and *(4) formal operations*—in that order but at differing rates. With

each stage, the child adds a new and qualitatively different kind of thinking or reasoning skill that helps the child make better sense of the world.

1 Sensorimotor
2 Preoperational
3 Concrete
4 Formal

Social Development

At the same time that children are developing emotionally and cognitively, they are also developing socially. *Freud* said that children develop socially by going through five *psychosexual stages* and that during the first three stages, the individual seeks pleasure from different areas of the body associated with sexual feelings. Freud's is the only theory that says the first five years are critical. *Erikson* said that children develop socially by going through eight *psychosocial stages*, during which an individual's primary goal is to satisfy desires associated with social needs. According to *Bandura's social cognitive theory*, children develop social skills through imitation, observation, and self-reward. These three theories are not mutually exclusive but rather complement each other by focusing on different factors believed to be important in social development.

Gender Development

Two somewhat different but related theories that explain how we acquire gender roles are *social role theory* and *cognitive developmental theory*. Both state that gender roles are learned over time through a series of environmental interactions. It turns out that life experiences can also shape many of the differences observed in the brains of males and females.

After the Concept Review, we'll examine an interesting and related question: Do children from very different cultures acquire similar or different gender roles and behaviors? ●

Concept Review

1. The question that asks how much genetic factors and how much environmental factors contribute to a person's biological, emotional, cognitive, personal, and social development is called the _____ question.

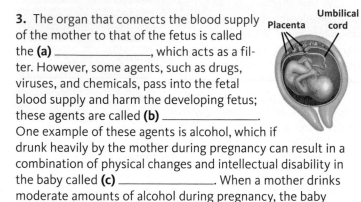

2. The prenatal period, which begins at conception and ends at birth, is composed of three different stages. The first stage of prenatal development refers to the two-week period following conception; this is called the **(a)** _____ stage. The second stage of the prenatal period spans the 2–8 weeks that follow conception; this is called the **(b)** _____ stage. The third stage of the prenatal period begins two months after conception and lasts until birth; this is called the **(c)** _____ stage.

3. The organ that connects the blood supply of the mother to that of the fetus is called the **(a)** _____, which acts as a filter. However, some agents, such as drugs, viruses, and chemicals, pass into the fetal blood supply and harm the developing fetus; these agents are called **(b)** _____. One example of these agents is alcohol, which if drunk heavily by the mother during pregnancy can result in a combination of physical changes and intellectual disability in the baby called **(c)** _____. When a mother drinks moderate amounts of alcohol during pregnancy, the baby may be born with **(d)** _____.

Placenta
Umbilical cord

4. Newborns have some visual acuity, respond to touch, and are able to hear, smell, and taste. This indicates that they have relatively well-developed _____.

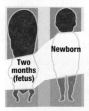

5. The acquisition of the muscular control necessary for coordinated physical activity, which is called **(a)** _____ development, follows two general principles. The principle that parts of the body closer to the head develop before parts closer to the feet is the **(b)** _____ principle. The principle that parts closer to the center of the infant's body develop before parts farther away is the **(c)** _____ principle. Development of motor skills occurs in a sequential and orderly fashion because of a genetic plan; this process is called **(d)** _____.

Two months (fetus)   Newborn

6. An individual's stable pattern of behavioral and emotional reactions that appear early and are influenced in large part by genetic factors is called his or her _____.

7. The close fundamental emotional bond that develops between the infant and his or her parent or caregiver is called **(a)** _____. Infants who use their parent as a safe home base from which they can wander off and explore their environments are said to have formed a **(b)** _____ attachment. Infants who avoid or show ambivalence toward their parents are said to have formed an **(c)** _____ attachment.

8. Piaget believed that children are actively involved in understanding their world through two basic processes: incorporating new information or experience into existing knowledge is called **(a)** _____; changing existing knowledge or experience as a result of assimilating some new information is called **(b)** _____.

9. Piaget's theory of cognitive development includes four stages, each of which is characterized by the development of particular kinds of reasoning. The first stage, during which infants learn about their environments by relating their sensory experiences (such as hearing and seeing) to their motor actions, is called the **(a)** _____ stage. The second stage, during which infants learn to use symbols to think about things that are not present and to help them solve simple problems, is called the **(b)** _____ stage. The third stage, during which children learn to perform a number of logical mental operations on objects that are physically present, is called the **(c)** _____ stage. The fourth stage, during which adolescents and adults develop the ability to think about and solve abstract problems in a logical manner, is called the **(d)** _____ stage.

10. According to Freud's theory of social development, children go through five developmental periods, which he called _____ stages. During these stages, a child's primary goal is to satisfy desires associated with innate biological needs.

11. According to Albert Bandura's social cognitive theory, we learn social skills through _____, _____, and self-reward.

12. According to Erik Erikson, a person goes through eight developmental periods during which the primary goal is to satisfy desires associated with social needs. Each of these eight periods is called a _____ stage, during which the person works to resolve a potential problem.

Answers: 1. *nature-nurture;* 2. (a) *germinal,* (b) *embryonic,* (c) *fetal;* 3. (a) *placenta,* (b) *teratogens,* (c) *fetal alcohol syndrome,* (d) *partial fetal alcohol syndrome,* (b) *accommodation.* 9. (a) *sensorimotor,* (b) *preoperational,* (c) *concrete operations,* (d) *formal operations;* 10. *psychosexual;* 11. *observation, imitation;* 12. *psychosocial*
8. (a) *assimilation,* (b) *accommodation.* 9. (a) *sensorimotor,* (b) *preoperational,* (c) *concrete operations,* (d) *formal operations;* 10. *psychosexual;* 11. *observation, imitation;* 12. *psychosocial*
syndrome; 4. *senses;* 5. (a) *motor,* (b) *cephalocaudal,* (c) *proximodistal,* (d) *maturation;* 6. *temperament;* 7. (a) *attachment,* (b) *secure,* (c) *insecure;*

I Cultural Diversity: Gender Roles

Identifying Gender Roles

Do cultures have different gender roles?

Although we know that young boys and girls acquire different gender roles, the intriguing question is, Why do little boys generally grow up to be more aggressive and independent, while little girls grow up to be less aggressive and more nurturing? To answer this question, researchers tested hundreds of 5-, 8-, and 11-year-old children in 24 countries to find out if young children from so many different cultures developed similar or different male–female gender roles and behaviors (J. E. Williams & Best, 1990).

> One of these people is a very affectionate person. When they like someone, they hug and kiss them a lot. Which person likes to hug and kiss a lot?

For younger children (5- and 8-year-olds), researchers told 32 brief stories and then asked whether the person in the story was more like a man or a woman; an example is given below. For older children (11-year-olds), researchers gave a list of 300 adjectives, such as aggressive, affectionate, calm, bossy, sensitive, loud, and helpful, and asked which adjectives were more likely to be associated with men and which with women. Unlike 5- and 8-year-old children, 11-year-olds were able to understand the meanings of the adjectives and indicate their choices by checking off adjectives that they thought best suited men or women.

Gender Roles across Cultures

Similarities. Researchers found that across the 24 countries, relatively young children showed remarkable similarities in the characteristics that they associated with gender roles.

About 57% of 5-year-old children made stereotyped responses about gender roles by associating people in the stories with a particular sex, either male or female. For example, 5-year-old children associated being strong, aggressive, and dominant with men, while they associated being gentle and affectionate with women. Eight-year-old children had learned even more

© Martin Harvey/Getty Images

Strong, aggressive, dominant, independent, coarse, loud, boastful

stereotypical behaviors. They associated being weak, emotional, appreciative, excitable, gentle, softhearted, meek, and submissive with women, while they associated being disorderly, cruel, coarse, adventurous, independent, ambitious, loud, and boastful with men (see photos). By the age of 11, the percentage of children who made stereotyped responses about gender roles jumped to 90%.

Differences. Researchers also found that across countries and cultures, interesting differences occurred in children's perceptions of gender roles. For example, in Germany, children associated being adventurous, confident, jolly, and steady with women, while in most other countries, these characteristics were typically associated with men.

In Japan, children associated being dominant and steady with women, while in other countries, these characteristics were typically associated with men.

Conclusions. Researchers concluded that children in 24 different countries and cultures developed knowledge of gender roles relatively early and showed remarkable similarities in choosing different gender roles and behaviors for men and women. Although there were some differences due to cultural values, there were generally more similarities in male–female gender roles across the 24 countries (J. E. Williams & Best, 1990).

Two Answers

We began with the question, Why do little boys generally grow up to be more aggressive and independent, while little girls grow up to be less aggressive and more nurturing? To this we add another question, Why do little boys and little girls from 24 different countries and cultures develop such similar male–female gender roles? There are two different but somewhat complementary answers.

The **social role theory** (discussed on p. 395), which emphasizes social and cultural influences, states that gender differences between men and women arise from different divisions of labor.

According to social role theory, male–female gender differences developed from traditional cultural divisions of labor, in which women were childbearers and homemakers, while men were providers and protectors (Eagly et al., 2000). Because men and women performed different duties, men and women were under different social-cultural pressures to develop different gender roles. Another answer comes from a relatively new theory.

The **evolutionary theory**, which emphasizes genetic and biological forces, says that current gender differences are a continuation of the behaviors that evolved from early men and women, who adapted these different behaviors in their attempts to survive the problems of their time.

© Howard Sayer/Shutterstock.com

Emotional, appreciative, excitable, gentle, submissive

According to evolutionary theory, men increased their chances for reproduction by being dominant, controlling, and aggressive. In comparison, women increased their chances of raising their children by being concerned, sensitive, and nurturing. According to this theory, the current male–female gender differences arise from genetic and biological forces that evolved from an ancient set of mating patterns that had initially helped the species to survive (Buss, 1999; Caporael, 2001).

Because social role theory emphasizes cultural influences and evolutionary theory emphasizes genetic and biological forces, researchers suggest that by combining the two theories we can better explain the development of our current male–female gender differences (Baldwin & Baldwin, 1997). ●

J Application: Child Abuse

People probably know Teri Hatcher best for her acting roles in "Desperate Housewives," "Lois & Clark: The New Adventures of Superman," and *Tomorrow Never Dies*. Yet, even though Teri is a famous Hollywood celebrity, there is much about her life that people have only recently learned about.

What was her terrible secret?

The story. Teri was raised in a middle-class family; her father was a nuclear physicist and her mother a computer programmer. She was an only child but had relatives visit during her childhood. One of these relatives was Richard Stone, her uncle, who went out of his way to develop a close relationship with Teri. Beginning when Teri was only 5 years old, her uncle began to sexually molest her on special rides in his car. This continued for three years, after which time, Teri never saw her uncle again.

Dealing with abuse. The experience of being sexually abused was so traumatic for Teri that she never told anyone this secret. Instead, she lived every day of her life with the haunting memories of what her uncle did to her so many times. The memories were so painful and disturbing that Teri even considered taking her own life.

At 41, Teri Hatcher admitted being sexually abused by her uncle.

Confronting her fears. About 30 years after last seeing her uncle, Teri went to her parents' house to help them with a garage sale. While there, she came across a newspaper article her mother had been saving. The article was about a 14-year-old girl who shot herself and left a suicide note that implicated Richard Stone, Teri's uncle! Teri was stunned, and tears began to pour down her face. She realized that her uncle didn't sexually abuse only her, but that he had done the same horrific thing to other young girls as well.

Teri knew she had to take quick action to help ensure that her uncle would not do the same thing to anyone ever again. Concerned that her uncle might escape charges of molestation, Teri gathered the courage to contact the district attorney handling his case. She then painstakingly revealed the details of her own abuse. Teri's statement helped to put Stone in prison for a 14-year sentence. The prosecutor said that without Teri's statement, the case would have been dismissed and her uncle would still be out possibly continuing to sexually abuse other young girls. After completing six years of his sentence, Stone died in prison (Associated Press, 2006b; Hatcher, 2007; Oprah, 2006).

Teri was a victim of one kind of child abuse—sexual abuse. There are several kinds of child abuse.

Kinds of Abuse

How many children are abused?

In the United States, allegations of childhood abuse and neglect are made for 6 million children annually (USDHHS, 2009).

Child abuse and neglect (physical and emotional) result from inadequate care or acts of the parent that put the child in danger, cause physical harm or injury, or involve sexual molestation.

The most common kind of abuse (78%) is neglect, followed in order by physical abuse and sexual abuse (USDHHS, 2009). For example, 2-year-old Brianna was left at home alone for almost three weeks and amazingly survived by drinking water from the toilet and eating any food she could find and unwrap. When the sheriff's department found Brianna, her body was smeared with ketchup and mustard, and the sheriff stated, "Feces and urine were everywhere" (Skipp & Johnson, 2003).

The second most frequently confirmed kind of child abuse (18%) is physical abuse. For example, Karen, who was 10 years old, vividly remembered how much and how often her mother beat her. Her mother would get angry over the tiniest things, grab something handy (shoes, father's belt, potato masher), and start hitting her. One time her mother beat her so hard that Karen's legs turned black and blue. When Karen threatened to tell the police, her mother

Allegations of child abuse are made for 6 million children annually.

replied in an angry voice, "Go ahead. They won't believe you and they'll put you in the darkest prison" (*TIME*, September 5, 1983).

The third most frequently confirmed kind of child abuse (10%) is sexual abuse. As in Teri's case, sexual abuse is most frequently committed by people who know the child, such as an acquaintance or family member, and many children are too fearful of the abuser to report their maltreatment (Douglas & Finkelhor, 2005; Finkelhor, 2002). National surveys of adults indicate that 9–32% of women and 5–10% of men have been sexually abused during their childhood; international surveys suggest similar rates of abuse (7–36% of women and 3–29% of men) (Douglas & Finkelhor, 2005; Emery & Laumann-Billings, 1998). These numbers indicate that sexual abuse, which may result in serious long-term behavioral, social, neural, and personality problems, is an international problem.

The remaining 8% of child abuse cases include psychological maltreatment and other kinds of abuse that do not easily fit into any category. (The percentages provided in this discussion have a sum greater than 100% because some children experience multiple types of abuse.)

We'll focus on three questions related to abuse and neglect: What problems do abused children suffer? Who abuses children? How are abusive parents helped?

What Problems Do Abused Children Have?

Children who suffer abuse may experience a number of physical, neurological, and psychological problems. The *physical problems* include stomachaches, headaches, bedwetting, and abnormal hormonal changes that indicate their systems are trying to deal with large doses of stress (Myers, 2011; Yehuda, 2000). Recent research also finds that childhood abuse can result in damage to the biochemical markers of stress (part of DNA), which is associated with a shorter lifespan (Kiecolt-Glaser et al., 2010).

Abused children also suffer a number of *psychological problems*, which include increased anxiety, social withdrawal, delays in social, cognitive, and emotional development, poor school performance, and fearful nightmares (Myers, 2011). As teenagers, abused children are at risk for continuing problems, such as low self-esteem, depression, posttraumatic stress, substance abuse, loneliness, and delinquent behaviors (CDC, 2012a; J. L. Davis & Petretic-Jackson, 2000).

Childhood abuse can also have enduring negative effects on a child's *brain development and neural functioning.* Negative effects include abnormal brain functioning, reduction in the size of brain areas that are involved in recognizing and processing emotional cues (hippocampus and amygdala), and reduction in the size of the band of fibers (corpus callosum) responsible for transferring neural information between the right and left hemispheres of the brain (Teicher, 2002). Childhood abuse can also alter the functioning of a brain area responsible for releasing hormones in response to stress, which results in individuals experiencing heightened stress throughout their life (P. O. McGowan et al., 2009).

Together, these data indicate that maltreatment or abuse at an early age can result in long-lasting deficits and problems in physical, psychological, and neurological development. However, with early intervention abused children can develop the resilience to overcome their adverse experiences (Mannarino, 2012).

Who Abuses Children?

Parents who abuse their children are likely to have low self-esteem and a wide range of personal problems. They are apt to be in distress, unemployed, unhappy, impulsive, anxious, and aggressive and to have problems with substance abuse (AAP, 2010; Emery & Laumann-Billings, 1998; J. F. Pittman & Buckley, 2006). Recent statistics show that 54% of people who abused children were women and 44% were men (2% unknown). Also, over 80% of people who abused children were parents (USDHHS, 2009).

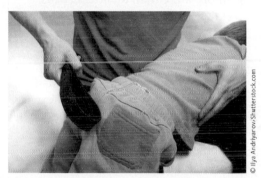

Some abused children become parents who abuse their own children; however, most do not and a number of compensatory factors can prevent this from happening (R. D. Conger et al., 2009). These *compensatory factors* include having a positive attachment to a caregiver, resolving not to repeat the abuse, having an awareness of one's early abusive experiences, having good self-esteem, and having good social support. The path from being abused to becoming an abusive parent is neither direct nor fixed and can be reversed by these compensatory factors (Glasser et al., 2001).

A child who is fussy, irritable, or sickly is more difficult to care for, especially if parents have personal problems of their own (J. R. Knutson, 1995). The interaction between a difficult child and troubled parents illustrates the principle of bidirectionality, which is one reason child abuse may occur (Maccoby, 1984).

The **principle of bidirectionality** says that a child's behaviors influence how his or her parents respond, and in turn the parents' behaviors influence how the child responds.

According to this principle, child abuse results from an interaction between a child's difficult traits, which tend to elicit maltreatment or abuse from the parents, and the parents' social-emotional and caregiving problems, which make it difficult for them to recognize and meet the needs of their child (J. Miller, 1995). Thus, the combination of a difficult child and parents who have their own personal or drug-related problems results in a potentially explosive parent–child interaction that increases the risk for child abuse.

How Are Abusive Parents Helped?

Effective therapy programs typically have two goals:

1 Overcoming the parent's personal problems. Abusive parents need help in learning about and developing social relationships, which are needed for positive bonding and attachment between parent and child. Abusive parents also need training in basic caregiving skills, which involves learning how to meet the physical, social, and emotional needs of their children. Dealing with abusive parents' personal or drug problems usually requires long-term professional therapy. As parents get their personal or marital problems under control, they can concentrate on improving their interactions with their child.

2 Changing parent–child interactions. Abusive parents are less likely to use positive behaviors (smiling, praising) and are more likely to use negative behaviors (disapproving, showing anger) when dealing with their children (Reid et al., 1981). Therefore, abusive parents need to learn more positive ways of interacting. Parent-training programs, which focus on modifying ways parents interact with their children through behavior modification techniques (discussed in Module 10), are effective in helping parents increase positive interactions with their children (Timmer et al., 2005).

Clinicians and researchers recognize that, in many countries, neglect, physical abuse, and sexual abuse are serious social problems that deserve more community-based prevention methods and treatment programs than are currently available (Coates, 2006). ●

Who Matters More—Parents or Peers?

Sigmund Freud argued that parents are to blame for the problems of children. In fact, people all around the world, many psychologists included, believe that parents are responsible, at least in some way, for children's problems. But, could this notion that seems like indisputable common sense be wrong?

Judith Harris, a researcher, argues that parents have minimal effect on their children's development, while peers have a much more influential role. Skeptical? Let's consider the changes in parenting styles over the years and the influence they have had on children's behavior. There has been a decrease in the use of physical punishment, yet children are no less aggressive than in earlier generations. Parents shower their children with more praise and affection than ever before, yet children's self-confidence, happiness, and overall mental health are no better for it. Could it be that Harris has a valid point?

1 If researchers wanted to observe how children typically behave with parents and with peers, what type of research setting should they use?

2 What is the name of the age-old question of which is more important—genetics or environment?

Harris states that genetics is responsible for half of children's personality and peers are essentially responsible for the other half. Therefore, Harris is not saying environment doesn't play a role in shaping a child's development, but rather that the environment that is important is the one outside of the home. She provides support for this position by presenting research on identical twins (genetically almost indistinguishable) raised together, which shows they are no more alike than identical twins reared apart. Also, how people behave at home with their parents does not predict how they behave with teachers or bosses, and how one behaves with siblings does not predict how they interact with peers. Together, these findings suggest that the home environment has little effect on behavior and personality development.

3 How would the evolutionary approach explain Harris's position that peers matter more than parents?

Research finds that children learn how to behave appropriately by observing their peers. If they simply imitated their parents' behaviors, their behavior would be considered quite odd. Children are motivated to be similar to their peers and at the same time to be better than them. They compare themselves to their peers to understand their strengths and weaknesses. By comparing their

4 What type of learning describes the process of learning by observing peers?

5 Which level of Maslow's hierarchy of needs best matches the need for people to gain personal achievement and competency?

© Intellistudies/Shutterstock.com © Rohit Seth/Shutterstock.com

intellectual knowledge and ability with peers, children can judge how smart they really are. After all, children don't have to know more than their parents to be considered smart; they have to know more than their peers.

Harris acknowledges that how parents interact with their child affects the child's behavior at home as well as how the child will regard the parents when he or she becomes an adult. However, she states that parents do not have a long-term effect on the type of person the child will become. There are many researchers who disagree with her. They cite studies showing that changes in the behavior of parents affect the behavior of children, even outside of the home. So then, which is more important to a child's development—parents or peers? It's difficult to answer with certainty. It seems they may be equally important, but perhaps in different ways.

6 What type of parent behavior would likely have a long-term effect on children's development?

Adapted from J. R. Harris 1998, 2006, 2007, 2009a, 2009b; Saletan, 2006

Summary Test

A Prenatal Development

1. The time from conception to birth is called the **(a)** _____ period, which is divided into three parts. The two-week period that immediately follows conception is called the **(b)** _____ period; it is marked by the zygote dividing into many cells. The period that includes the 2–8 weeks after conception, during which cells continue to divide and begin to differentiate into bone, muscle, and body organs, is called the **(c)** _____ period. The period of development that begins two months after conception and lasts for about seven months is called the **(d)** _____ period. At the end of this period, birth occurs and the fetus becomes a newborn.

Placenta
Umbilical cord

2. The development of the fetus can be interrupted or damaged by a variety of toxic agents, called **(a)** _____ which cause malformation of the brain or body and result in birth defects. For example, heavy drinking during pregnancy can cause a combination of physical and psychological deficits called **(b)** _____ which is the leading known cause of intellectual disability in the United States.

B Sensory & Motor Development

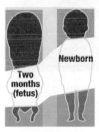

Newborn

Two months (fetus)

3. The newborn comes into the world with relatively well-developed sensory and perceptual responses. For example, the newborn can see, but his or her ability to see details, such as on **(a)** _____ is poor. Six-month-old infants will not crawl off the visual cliff, indicating that they have developed **(b)** _____ perception. Newborns have good hearing, touch, and smell and an inherited preference for sweet and salt tastes.

4. Motor development, which is the acquisition of the muscle control required for coordinated physical activity, follows two general principles. The principle that parts of the body closer to the head develop before those closer to the feet is called the **(a)** _____ principle. The principle that parts closer to the center of the body develop before those farther away is called the **(b)** _____ principle.

5. Development that occurs in a sequential and orderly fashion because of a genetic plan is called **(a)** _____. The average age at which individuals perform various kinds of motor skills or exhibit abilities or behaviors is reflected in **(b)** _____.

C Emotional Development

6. Early and stable individual differences in attention, arousal, and reaction to new things refer to an infant's _____, which is greatly influenced by genetic, or inherited, factors.

7. Newborns have a limited range of emotional expressions that include interest, startle, distress, disgust, and neonatal smile. During the first two years, infants develop a wide range of _____ expressions and feelings that signal their physiological needs and psychological moods.

8. The close emotional bond that develops between infant and parent (caregiver) is called **(a)** _____. As the infant develops a closer attachment to her parents, she also shows more distress when her parents leave; this distress is called **(b)** _____.

9. There are two kinds of attachment. Infants who use their caregiver as a safe home base from which they can wander off and explore their environments are said to be **(a)** _____ attached. This kind of attachment may contribute to better emotional bonds later in life. Infants who avoid or show ambivalence toward their caregivers are said to be **(b)** _____ attached. For example, these infants may cling and want to be held one minute but squirm and push away the next minute.

D Research Focus: Temperament

10. Researchers use two different methods to study developmental processes. Repeatedly studying the same group of individuals at different ages is using the **(a)** _____ method. Studying different groups of individuals who are of different ages is using the **(b)** _____ method.

Age   2   7

11. Researchers found that about one-fourth of infants show avoidance, anxiety, fear, and increased physiological arousal when in a strange or novel situation. These individuals are called shy or _____, and the majority remain the same into adulthood. This finding supports the idea that temperaments appear early, are stable across time, and are partially under genetic control (nature).

E Cognitive Development

12. Piaget believed that children participate in their own cognitive development by active involvement through two different processes: incorporating new information or experiences into existing knowledge is called **(a)** _____; and changing one's knowledge or experiences as a result of assimilating some new information is called **(b)** _____.

© PhotoDisc, Inc.

13. Piaget divided cognitive development into four stages. In the first, lasting from birth to about age 2, infants interact with and learn about their environments by relating their sensory experiences to their motor actions; this is called the **(a)** _____ stage. A significant development of this stage is the knowledge that objects or events continue to exist even if they cannot be heard, touched, or seen; this is called **(b)** _____.

14. In the second stage, lasting from the age of about 2 to 7, children learn to use symbols to think about things that are not present and to help solve simple problems; this is the **(a)** _____ stage. A limitation in this stage is the tendency to think of the world from only one's own viewpoint, called **(b)** _____.

15. The third stage, which lasts from the age of about 7 to 11, is called the **(a)** _____ stage. During this stage, children can perform a number of logical mental operations on concrete objects (ones that are physically present). The idea that the amount of a substance remains the same even in different shapes, known as **(b)** _____, is mastered during the third stage.

16. During the fourth and last stage, which lasts from about age 12 through adulthood, the individual develops the ability to think about and solve abstract problems logically; this is called the **(a)** _____ stage. Each of Piaget's cognitive stages is thought to be qualitatively different from the preceding one because each new stage represents the development of some new **(b)** _____ ability.

F Social Development

© Melanie DeFazio/Shutterstock.com

17. How a person develops social relationships, develops a sense of self, and becomes a social being is called **(a)** _____ development. Three theories of such development each emphasize a different aspect. According to Freud, a person goes through five developmental periods, called **(b)** _____ stages, during which the primary goal is to satisfy innate biological needs. In contrast, Erikson identified eight developmental periods, in which the primary goal is to satisfy social needs; he called these **(c)** _____ stages. Bandura emphasizes the importance of learning through imitation, observation, and reinforcement; this is called **(d)** _____ theory.

18. Freud's five psychosexual stages are called the **(a)** _____, **(b)** _____, **(c)** _____, **(d)** _____, and **(e)** _____ stages. Freud believed that the first five years leave a lasting impression on the individual's personality and social development.

19. The first five of Erikson's eight stages involve the resolution of a potential social problem between the child and his or her environment. In stage 1, the infant deals with resolving issues surrounding trust versus **(a)** _____. In stage 2, the toddler must resolve issues surrounding autonomy versus shame and **(b)** _____. In stage 3, the younger child deals with issues of initiative versus **(c)** _____. In stage 4, the older child deals with issues that involve industry versus **(d)** _____. In stage 5, the adolescent deals with issues that involve identity versus **(e)** _____.

20. Early psychological difficulties increase a child's **(a)** _____, which in turn increases the risk for developing later social or personality problems. However, certain emotional traits, family factors, and outside emotional support help a child overcome early problems and are said to help make the child **(b)** _____ and thus develop normal social behaviors.

G Gender Development

21. Expectations of how we should think or behave because we are male or female are called **(a)** _____. One theory says that these roles develop because parents or caregivers expect, treat, and reward different kinds of behaviors depending on the child's sex; this is the **(b)** _____ theory. Another theory says that children learn rules for male or female behavior through active involvement with their environments; this is the **(c)** _____ theory.

I Cultural Diversity: Gender Roles

© Martin Harvey/Getty Images

22. Although children's perceptions of gender roles show some variation across countries and cultures, it appears that their _____ of gender roles develops in a generally similar way at similar times.

J Application: Child Abuse

23. Inadequate care, neglect, or acts of the parent that put the child in danger or that cause physical harm or injury or involve sexual molestation make up the definition of **(a)** _____. According to the principle of **(b)** _____, the child's behaviors influence how the parents respond and the parents' behaviors influence how the child responds. Two goals of treatment to stop or prevent child abuse are to help parents overcome their **(c)** _____ problems and to change parent–child interactions from negative to positive.

© Suzanne Tucker/Shutterstock.com

Unless otherwise noted, all images are © Cengage Learning

Links to Learning

Key Terms/Key People

accommodation, 388
amniocentesis, 380
anal stage, 392
assimilation, 388
attachment, 385
cephalocaudal principle, 383
child abuse and neglect, 400
cognitive development, 388
cognitive developmental
  theory, 395
conception, or fertilization, 379
concrete operations stage, 390
conservation, 389
cross-sectional method, 386
developmental norms, 383
Down syndrome, 380
egocentrism, 389
embryonic stage, 379
emotional development, 384

epigenetics, 378
evolutionary theory, 399
fetal alcohol syndrome (FAS), 381
fetal stage, 380
formal operations stage, 390
gender identity, 395
gender roles, 395
gender schemas, 395
genital stage, 392
germinal stage, 379
human development, 377
imaginary audience, 390
inhibited/fearful children, 386
insecure attachment, 385
latency stage, 392
longitudinal method, 386
maturation, 383
motor development, 383
nature-nurture question, 377

object permanence, 389
oral stage, 392
ovulation, 379
partial fetal alcohol
  syndrome, 381
personal fable, 390
phallic stage, 392
Piaget's cognitive stages, 388
placenta, 380
prenatal period, 379
preoperational stage, 389
principle of bidirectionality, 401
prodigy, 378
proximodistal principle, 383
psychosexual stages, 392
psychosocial stages, 393
reactive attachment disorder, 377
resiliency, 394
secure attachment, 385

sensorimotor stage, 389
sensory development, 382
separation anxiety, 385
social cognitive theory, 394
social development, 392
social role theory, 395, 399
stage 1: trust versus mistrust, 393
stage 2: autonomy versus shame
  and doubt, 393
stage 3: initiative versus
  guilt, 393
stage 4: industry versus
  inferiority, 393
stage 5: identity versus role
  confusion, 393
temperament, 384
teratogen, 380
visual cliff, 382
vulnerability, 394
zygote, 379

Media Resources

Go to **CengageBrain.com** to access Psychology CourseMate, where you will find an interactive eBook, glossaries, flashcards, quizzes, videos, answers to Critical Thinking questions, and more. You can also access Virtual Psychology Labs, an interactive laboratory experience designed to illustrate key experiments first-hand.

Adolescence & Adulthood

introduction

Adolescence

Will Branndi become president?

"I will eventually become president... I've figured it out. I don't want people to think, 'She's just a kid. She doesn't know what's ahead of her.' I know the presidency will not come easy to me. I'm black, first of all, and I'm a woman. I want to be a lawyer, then work my way up in politics, become like mayor, then senator, then governor...

"I know people will look into my past and say, 'Years ago, she did this, she did that, blah, blah, blah.' The worst thing I've ever done is to steal two little five-cent Bazooka gums from a 7-Eleven when I was nine. I don't think they'll count that against me...

> Do not label me as anything. I'm an individual.

"Sometimes people just expect me to make trouble because I'm 'one of the black kids.' Do not label me as anything. Label me as individual....

"I want everyone to know that some 12-year-olds really do think seriously about the future. I want to be a role model. I'm glad I was born black. I want to tell others, 'Stay in there because you can do just as much good as any other person.'"

Besides talking like a philosopher, Branndi is a fun-loving adolescent who likes rap music, hanging out at the mall with her friends, and "dumb" movies. She is an above-average student, likes to write fairy tales for children, and sings in the youth choir at the neighborhood church (*Los Angeles Times,* December 22, 1991, pp. E-1, E-12).

Branndi had ambitious goals at age 12, the beginning of adolescence.

Adolescence is a developmental period, lasting from about ages 12 to 18, during which many biological, cognitive, social, and personality traits change from childlike to adultlike.

While it is true that adolescents, like Branndi, go through dramatic changes, experts now believe that adolescence is not necessarily marked by great psychological turmoil. Psychologists have learned that the majority of teenagers, unlike the terrible adolescents portrayed in the media, do develop a healthy sense of identity, maintain close relationships with their families, and avoid major emotional disorders (Gutgesell & Payne, 2004; Wallace, 2004). After making it through adolescence, most teenagers are ready to enter the adult world.

Adulthood

Did Charlie live happily ever after?

Charlie Sheen was raised among Hollywood royalty. His father is famous actor Martin Sheen, and many of his close childhood friends later became successful Hollywood actors themselves. Charlie's background provided him with great potential to enjoy a satisfying life. But as you'll soon learn, Charlie faced many challenges during his adulthood, only some of which he successfully overcame.

Back in high school, Charlie was best known as a star baseball player, but because of his low grades and poor classroom attendance, he was expelled shortly before his scheduled graduation. This is when Charlie decided to focus on an acting career and establishing a life for himself.

Some time later, Charlie got engaged, but after he accidentally shot his fiancée in the arm, she broke off the engagement. His personal life worsened when he became sexually involved with a series of prostitutes. Charlie then got married only to get divorced about a year later. Another decline in his personal life then occurred: this time a drug overdose followed by intensive rehabilitation. After he recovered, relapsed, and recovered again, Charlie fell in love again and married a Hollywood actress. He had two beautiful girls during this relationship, which also ended in divorce. Then Charlie fell in love again, got married, and had twin boys with his wife. In 2011, this marriage also ended in divorce and as a result of his continued drug use, Charlie entered drug rehabilitation yet again.

Charlie experienced the many ups and downs of adulthood.

Like his personal life, Charlie's career experienced highs and lows. Early in his career he starred in two very big films, *Platoon* and *Wall Street*. His career continued to improve until his personal problems escalated. When his personal life bounced back, so did his career. It was then he was offered the opportunity to replace Michael J. Fox in "Spin City." For his performance in this show, Charlie received a Golden Globe award. He then starred in the hit comedy series, "Two and a Half Men," which ended in him getting dismissed from the show. Currently, he is starring in a sitcom called "Anger Management" (Bowles, 2009; Cruz & Chiu, 2009; Hibberd, 2011; NNDB, 2009; Oldenburg, 2011).

As you can clearly see, Charlie has experienced many of the joys and pains of adulthood.

Major Periods of Change

Both Charlie and Branndi went through periods of great change. Each of us goes through three major developmental periods marked by significant physical, cognitive, personality, and social changes. We discussed childhood in Module 17. Now we'll turn to the other two periods: adolescence and adulthood.

What's Coming

We'll explain the personality, social, cognitive, and physical changes that individuals undergo from adolescence through adulthood and discuss some of the challenges and problems that adolescents and adults face during each of these periods.

We'll begin with perhaps the biggest change in adolescence—puberty. ●

A Physical Development: Puberty

Why is puberty such a big deal? A teenager leaves behind the mind and body of a child and begins to take on the mind and body of an adult. Perhaps the biggest event in changing from a child to an adult is the onset of puberty, which is altogether interesting, wondrous, and potentially very stressful.

Puberty is a developmental period, between the ages of 9 and 17, when the individual experiences significant biological changes that result in developing secondary sexual characteristics and reaching sexual maturity.

To understand how puberty uniquely changes the bodies of girls and boys, you need to understand the difference between primary sexual characteristics and secondary sexual characteristics.

Primary sexual characteristics are body structures that are specific to each sex and are related to reproduction. For instance, males have testes and females have ovaries.

Secondary sexual characteristics are physical characteristics other than reproductive organs that differentiate males and females.

Now we'll discuss the physical changes that occur during puberty for girls and boys, including examples of secondary sexual characteristics.

Girls during Puberty

Every girl wants to grow up so she can finally be a woman. Becoming a woman means going through puberty and experiencing three major biological changes that occur between ages 9 and 13. The onset of puberty usually occurs about two years earlier in girls (average of 10.5 years) than in boys (average of 12.5 years).

© Andrey_Popov/Shutterstock.com
© East/Shutterstock.com

1 Puberty sets off a surge in *physical growth*, which is marked by an increase in height that starts on average at 9.6 years. This growth spurt begins about 6 to 12 months before the onset of breast development.

2 Puberty triggers a physiological process that results in a girl's reaching *female sexual maturity*, which primarily involves the onset of menarche.

Menarche is the first menstrual period; it is a signal that ovulation may have occurred and the girl may have the potential to conceive and bear a child.

In the United States, menarche occurs on average at the age of 12.5 years, about 2.5 years after the beginning of breast development. Because of differences in body weight, environmental chemicals, psychosocial stress, and genes, the age of menarche varies within and across cultures and societies (S. E. Anderson et al., 2003; Chumlea et al., 2003; Szabo, 2011).

The onset of menarche is triggered by an area of the brain called the *hypothalamus*, which releases a hormone called *kisspeptin* that helps to stimulate the *pituitary gland* to produce hormones. These hormones travel throughout the bloodstream and stimulate the ovaries to greatly increase production of female hormones (Kotulak, 2006; McKie, 2005; Navarro et al., 2007).

Estrogen is one of the major female hormones. At puberty, estrogen levels increase eightfold, which stimulates the development of both primary and secondary sexual characteristics.

3 Puberty marks a major change in the girl's body as she develops female secondary sexual characteristics.

Female secondary sexual characteristics, whose development is triggered by the increased secretion of estrogen, include growth of pubic hair, development of breasts, and widening of hips.

In girls, the onset of secondary sexual characteristics begins at 10.5 years (the range is from age 7 to age 18).

Early versus late maturing. Girls who are early maturing—that is, who go through puberty early—may encounter psychological problems because they have not yet acquired the adult personality traits and social skills that are needed for normal and healthy functioning in their newly developed adult bodies (Joinson et al., 2011; Szabo, 2010).

Boys during Puberty

Every boy wants to grow up so he can finally be a man. Becoming a man means going through puberty and experiencing three major biological changes that occur between ages 10 and 14. The onset of puberty in a boy usually occurs about two years later than in a girl.

1 Puberty triggers an increase in *physical growth*, especially height, generally at 13 to 14 years of age. The increase in height may be dramatic, and a boy may feel strange as he discovers that he is taller than his mother and as tall as or taller than his father.

2 Puberty starts a physiological process that results in a boy's reaching *male sexual maturity*, which includes growth of the genital organs—testes and penis—and production of sperm. The onset of genital growth begins at around 11.5 years (the range is from age 9 to age 16) and continues for approximately three years. The production and release of sperm begin at 12 to 14 years of age.

The increase in genital growth and the production of sperm are triggered by the *hypothalamus*, which stimulates the male pituitary gland. The pituitary in turn triggers the testes to increase production of testosterone by as much as 18 times more than before puberty.

Testosterone, which is the major male hormone, stimulates the growth of genital organs and the development of secondary sexual characteristics.

3 The increased production of testosterone triggers the development of male secondary sexual characteristics.

Male secondary sexual characteristics, which are triggered by the increased secretion of testosterone, include the growth of pubic and facial hair, development of muscles, and a change (deepening) in voice.

These changes usually occur between 12 and 16 years of age, but there is a wide range in their development.

Early versus late maturing. Generally, boys who are early maturing, which means they go through puberty earlier, are found to be more confident, relaxed, socially responsible, popular, and highly regarded by their peers. In comparison, boys who go through puberty later (are late maturing) are found lacking in self-confidence and self-esteem, more dependent on their parents, and less highly regarded by peers. However, many of the psychological differences between early- and late-maturing girls and boys decrease and disappear with age (Sigelman & Rider, 2012).

Going through puberty raises difficult questions for adolescents, which we will discuss next.

Adolescent Sexual Behavior

Now what do I do?

In the United States, about 30 million youths between the ages of 10 and 17 are looking for answers to a very important and burning question: Now that I am sexually mature,

what do I do? Part of the difficulty that adolescents have in making decisions about how to behave sexually is that they receive conflicting answers.

Conflicting Answers

On the one hand, the media (movies, television, magazines), as well as peers, friends, and classmates, often discuss or portray sex in exciting ways that stimulate and encourage adolescents to try sex, often before they are emotionally ready (L. Ali & Scelfo, 2002). For example, in a study of 174 girls, most said that they had been too young (average age was 13) at the time of their first intercourse. The reasons (in order of frequency) that they gave for engaging in sex were that they were physically attracted or curious, were alone with their partner, and knew that all their friends were having sex. Looking back, most of these girls wished they had waited longer before having sexual intercourse because they had not been ready and had not appreciated the risks of pregnancy and disease (S. L. Rosenthal et al., 1997).

Advice. On the other hand, most parents, mental health organizations, and religious groups advise adolescents not to engage in sex too early and to wait until they are more emotionally mature and involved in an intimate relationship (Rabasca, 1999). Researchers advise more parent–teen discussions of sexual behavior because one study found that 50% of mothers whose 14-year-olds were sexually active mistakenly believed their teens were still virgins (R. Blum, 2002). In addition, teens often lack basic information about potential problems, as indicated by 30% of teens who had oral sex but were unaware that this activity could result in sexually transmitted diseases (J. Davis, 2003).

Approach. Trying to explain sexual development in teenagers and the complicated relationship between sex and love has given rise to the biopsychosocial model.

The **biopsychosocial approach** views adolescent development as a process that occurs simultaneously on many levels and includes hormonal, neural, sexual, cognitive, social, cultural, and personality changes that interact and influence each other (Herdt, 2004; D. L. Tolman et al., 2003).

According to the biopsychosocial approach, sexual behavior cannot be discussed independently of hormonal, cognitive, personality, and emotional factors. For example, sex hormones trigger important physical changes but also influence mood and behavioral changes, such as perceiving peers as romantically attractive (J. Schwab et al., 2001). Finding someone romantically attractive naturally leads to seeking a more intimate relationship, which raises the question of becoming sexually active.

Sexual activity of teenage boys and girls is about equal.

© Masson/Shutterstock.com

Decisions about Becoming Sexually Active

Twenty years ago, 60% of teenage males and 51% of teenage females reported engaging in sexual intercourse, but now only 42% of teenage males and 43% of teenage females report having ever engaged in sexual intercourse (CDC, 2011b). When asked whether they have had intercourse within the past 90 days, 16% of teens reported they had (Herbenick et al., 2010). Statistics reveal that older teens are more likely to have engaged in sexual intercourse than younger teens. Also, a lower percentage of teens from households with both parents present report engaging in sexual intercourse than teens from both stepparent and single-parent households (CDC, 2011b).

During the past 20 years, the number of teenagers who report NOT having sexual intercourse has risen (CDC, 2011b). Frequently reported reasons teenagers give for abstaining from sexual activity include following religious or moral teachings, not having found the right person, and not wanting to get pregnant or to get someone pregnant (CDC, 2011b).

Problems. Teenagers who do become sexually active face a number of potential problems. One problem is that the age at which teenagers engage in sexual activity is earlier than what they think is the best age. Although the median age for first intercourse was 17.4 years for girls, about half the girls (48%) said the best age for first intercourse is between 18 and 20 years. Teenage girls report that sex and pregnancy are the number one issues they face today. However, curiosity, media, and peer pressure play a large role in motivating sexual activity (L. Ali & Scelfo, 2002). Although puberty prepares teenage bodies for engaging in sexual behavior, the majority of teenagers (especially girls) report not being emotionally, psychologically, or mentally prepared to deal with strong sexual desires and feelings.

Another problem is that not all teens who become sexually active report using contraceptives every time they have intercourse. Recent data indicate that between 60–86% of teens used contraception during the most recent time they had intercourse (CDC, 2011b; Herbenick et al., 2010). The lack of consistent contraceptive use can lead to two major problems: the spread of sexually transmitted diseases (STDs), including AIDS, and unwanted pregnancies. The risk of STDs is especially high, as teens account for half of the 19 million new cases each year (B. Healy, 2008). There is some good news, however: More more teens are now using contraception than in past years, fewer teenagers are giving birth than ever before, and teens are waiting longer to become sexually active (NCHS, 2012).

It's important to point out that engaging early in sexual intercourse does not inevitably lead to problems. In fact, one research study found that teens who had sex earlier had less delinquency and antisocial behavior years later, rather than more (Harden et al., 2008).

We'll next examine a number of mental and psychological changes that accompany the teenage years. ●

Definition

When most adults and especially current parents of teenagers hear the word *adolescence,* they often get a pained look as they remember a time full of problems. Until the early 1990s, researchers

Why is Branndi's head spinning?

believed that adolescence was primarily a time of storm and stress, of intense feelings, huge mood swings, and irritating parental conflicts. However, current research paints a different picture of adolescence. Yes, storm and stress and intense mood swings and parental conflicts are likely to occur during adolescence, but they come and go, and not all adolescents have a terrible time (Arnett, 2000). Research also finds that along with the storm and stress, adolescence is a time for tremendous growth in emotional, social, and cognitive development as teenagers go from childhood to adulthood (L. Steinberg, 2011).

We have already discussed the dramatic physical changes and sexual feelings that occur during puberty and the problems adolescents have in deciding what to do with their newly developed sexual maturity. Along with sexual maturity, adolescents develop new ways of thinking and reasoning, which represents a major change in cognitive development.

Cognitive development refers to how a person perceives, thinks, and gains an understanding of his or her world through the interaction and influence of genetic and learned factors.

I believe God lets awful things happen to teach us a lesson.

© Samuel Borges/Shutterstock.com

For example, at the beginning of this module we told you that, during adolescence, Branndi (left photo) would undergo major changes in reasoning and thinking. For example, here are some of her thoughts about the condition of the world:

"I don't believe in the Pledge of Allegiance. I don't say it, because they're telling a lie—'liberty and justice for all....' My first step into politics will be mayor. I write lots of letters to Tom Bradley [former mayor of Los Angeles] about things like animal rights. But he just sent me, you know, one of those typed things. I don't think it's right...I'm very outspoken. I worry about things—sex, rape, and stuff like that...I believe in God. I believe God lets awful things happen to teach us a lesson..." (*Los Angeles Times,* December 22, 1991, p. E-13).

There's no question that 12-year-old Branndi is capable of abstract thinking, is very outspoken, and holds absolute opinions on a variety of concrete and abstract issues. Her views illustrate one of the most significant changes in cognitive development during adolescence, which is the ability to think about abstract issues, such as the meaning of liberty, justice, and God. This kind of abstract thinking indicates that Branndi is entering Piaget's fourth cognitive stage, called formal operations, which marks the beginning of thinking and reasoning like an adult.

Piaget's Cognitive Stages: Continued

What's new about a teenager's thinking?

As you may remember from Module 17, Piaget's theory of cognitive development is that we all go through four distinct *cognitive stages* (left figure). As we go through each stage, we acquire a new and distinct kind of reasoning and thinking that is different from and more advanced than the reasoning abilities we possessed at our previous stage. We discussed Piaget's four cognitive stages in Module 17, but

we'll review stage 4, the formal operations stage, because it begins in adolescence.

1 **Sensorimotor** Births to age 2

2 **Preoperational** Ages 2 to 7

3 **Concrete** Ages 7 to 11

4 **Formal** Ages 12 thru adulthood

Stage 4: Formal Operations

The fact that 12-year-old Branndi is using abstract concepts, such as liberty, justice, animal rights, and God, is good evidence that she is entering the formal operations stage.

The **formal operations stage,** the last of Piaget's four cognitive stages, extends from about age 12 through adulthood. During this stage, adolescents and adults develop the abilities to think about abstract or hypothetical concepts, to consider an issue from another's viewpoint, and to solve cognitive problems in a logical way.

Having the ability to think about and discuss abstract concepts means that adolescents can critically consider their beliefs, attitudes, values, and goals as well as discuss a wide range of topics important to their becoming adults. For instance, when adolescents were asked about their major concerns, tops on their lists were getting married, having friends, getting a good job, and doing well in school. Each of these concerns involves the ability to discuss abstract concepts, which is a cognitive skill that they are learning at the formal operations stage.

My major concerns are doing well in school and having friends.

© ZINQ Stock/Shutterstock.com

One of the interesting questions about adolescents is why some seem so slow to develop thinking and reasoning skills that prepare them to deal with typical problems and stressful situations that occur during adolescence. For example, many adolescents report that they were not prepared to have sex but it just happened, or they fight continually with their parents, or they do stupid things like drink and then drive. Researchers have only recently discovered that the answer involves the developing adolescent's brain.

Unless otherwise noted, all images are © Cengage Learning

Brain Development: Reason and Emotion

A difficult problem for parents is dealing with seemingly irresponsible or impulsive bad behaviors or decisions of their teenagers. Parents believe their teens should know better, and until recently, researchers thought that teens should know better because they believed that teenage brains were fully developed by puberty. However, new findings indicate that teenage brains are still developing, especially areas involved in clear thinking and reasoning (Crews, 2006).

Prefrontal cortex: executive functions

Every company has an executive officer who is responsible for making decisions, day-to-day planning, organizing, and thinking about the future. Similarly, our brains have an executive area, called the *prefrontal cortex*, that is involved in similar functions and is located near the front of the brain (see p. 75) (right figure).

Researchers used brain scans (see p. 70) to take pictures of the neural development of teenage brains. Unlike earlier beliefs that an adolescent's prefrontal cortex was fully developed, researchers found that the adolescent's prefrontal cortex was still developing and thus did not yet have the ability to think, reason, decide, or plan like an adult (Reyna et al., 2011; Shute, 2009).

Vulnerability. Beginning at about age 11 and continuing into young adulthood, the brain undergoes major "rewiring" and reorganization and is especially vulnerable to traumatic adolescent experiences, such as being physically or sexually abused or bullied, feeling depressed, and abusing drugs. Research suggests that alcohol causes more injury to teenage brains than it does to adult brains. These kinds of traumatic experiences can interfere with the adolescent's brain developing a healthy and reasonable executive center (Crews, 2006; Shute, 2009).

Risk-taking behavior. The finding that executive functions in the adolescent's brain are not yet fully developed helps explain many of the adolescent's seemingly irresponsible behaviors. For example, adolescents have about twice the rate of adults in transmitting venereal diseases because only 50% think to use condoms, and they have 20 times the rate of automobile accidents as adults because adolescents don't worry about drinking, driving, and speeding (C. E. Irwin et al., 2002). The earlier explanation for why adolescents engaged in risk-taking behavior was that they felt invulnerable and had no fear of injury. Researchers now explain that adolescents' tendency to take risks is due to the executive manager of their behaviors, their prefrontal cortex, being underdeveloped, which means they don't have the neural bases to analyze risks and make intelligent decisions (Luna, 2006). One researcher described the teenage brain very well by saying it "is like a car with a good accelerator but a weak brake" (L. Steinberg, 2007). We'll discuss how this brain research applies to teen driving in the Critical Thinking section on page 428.

Another reason adolescents have a tendency to engage in risk-taking behaviors involves a different part of their brain that's involved in emotional behaviors.

> As executive officer, I'm responsible for thinking, planning, and making decisions.

Limbic system: emotional behaviors

Teenagers are known to act impulsively, such as getting a tongue pierced on a dare, and they experience wide mood swings. As one parent said, "It's hot and cold, nasty and nice. One minute loving me, one minute hating me." What parents don't realize is that a teenager's prefrontal cortex, which acts like an executive officer, is not fully developed, so an adolescent has less control over his or her emotional and impulsive behaviors. This explains why teens are so easily upset when parents can't understand why (Shute, 2009).

Moody, emotional, and impulsive behaviors. As shown in the left figure, in the center of the brain is a circle of structures that make up our emotional brain, called the limbic system (see p. 80). The *limbic system* is involved in a wide range of emotional behaviors, such being ecstatic over getting a date, feeling depressed when failing a test, and getting angry when insulted. Sex hormones (testosterone in males and estrogen in females), which are secreted in abundance during puberty, increase the growth of limbic system structures (amygdala, hippocampus). Researchers believe the increased size and function of the limbic system account for a teenager's irritability and increase in talking aggressively with others, such as their parents (Whittle et al., 2008).

Conclusion. A neuroscientist explains that adolescents fall into a "neurological gap" (Casey, 2011). That is, the hormones released during puberty foster the development of the limbic system but do not aid in development of the prefrontal cortex. Consequently, the emotional center is more mature than the executive functioning area of the brain. This combination results in many of the unthinking and irritating behaviors of adolescents, such as taking risks, switching moods, and acting impulsively. Fortunately, executive functioning will mature throughout adolescence and into adulthood (Casey, 2011; Spear, 2010).

An adolescent's lack of a strong executive officer (prefrontal cortex) will also affect moral judgment, which is our next topic. ●

> I was dared to get my tongue and nose pierced.

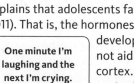

> One minute I'm laughing and the next I'm crying.

Kohlberg's Theory of Moral Reasoning

Would you steal to save a friend? Suppose your best friend is dying of cancer. You hear of a chemist who has just discovered a new wonder drug that could save her life. The chemist is selling the drug for $5,000, many times more than it cost him to make. You try to borrow the full amount but can get only $2,500. You ask the chemist to sell you the drug for $2,500 and he refuses. Later that night, you break into the chemist's laboratory and steal the drug. Should you have done that?

Three Levels of Moral Reasoning

Level **1** Self-Interest

The **preconventional level,** which represents Kohlberg's lowest level of moral reasoning, has two stages. At stage 1, moral decisions are based primarily on fear of punishment or the need to be obedient; at stage 2, moral reasoning is guided most by satisfying one's self-interest, which may involve making bargains.

For example, individuals at stage 1 might say that you should not steal the drug because you'll be caught and go to jail. Individuals at stage 2 might say that you can steal the drug and save your best friend, but in return you'll have to give up some freedom by going to jail. Most children are at the preconventional level.

Level **2** Social Approval

The **conventional level,** which represents an intermediate level of moral reasoning, also has two stages. At stage 3, moral decisions are guided most by conforming to the standards of others we value; at stage 4, moral reasoning is determined most by conforming to the laws of society.

Individuals at stage 3 might say that you should steal the drug since that is what your family would expect you to do. Individuals at stage 4 might say that you should not steal the drug because of what would happen to society if everybody took what they needed. Many adolescents and adults are at this level.

Level **3** Abstract Ideas

The **postconventional level,** which represents the highest level of moral reasoning, has one stage. At stage 5, moral decisions are made after carefully thinking about all the alternatives and striking a balance between human rights and the laws of society.

Individuals at stage 5 might say that one should steal the drug because life is more important than money. (Stage 6, which appeared in earlier versions of Kohlberg's theory, has been omitted in later versions because too few people had reached it.) Some, but not all, adults reach the postconventional level.

Kohlberg's theory has two distinct features. First, he classifies moral reasoning into three distinct levels—preconventional, conventional, and postconventional. Second, he suggests that everyone progresses through the levels in order, from lowest to highest. However, not everyone reaches the higher stages of moral development.

Next, we'll evaluate Kohlberg's theory and its present status.

Did you decide that it would be all right to steal the drug to save the life of your dying friend? If you did, how did you justify your moral decision? Lawrence Kohlberg (1984) and associates presented similar dilemmas to individuals who were asked to explain their moral decisions. On the basis of such studies, Kohlberg explained the development of moral reasoning in terms of three levels.

Evaluating Kohlberg's Theory

Stages. Kohlberg hypothesized that everyone goes through the five stages in sequence, with no skipping of stages. Researchers reviewed 45 Kohlberg-type studies conducted in 27 cultures and concluded that, as Kohlberg assumed, we go through the stages in order but not everyone reaches the higher stages (Damon, 1999; Helwig, 1997).

Thinking versus behaving. Kohlberg's stages present different kinds of moral thinking that may or may not predict how someone behaves. Thus, Kohlberg focused on the development of moral thinking, not on the development of moral behavior in real-life situations (Damon, 1999).

Carol Gilligan (1982) criticized Kohlberg's stages by saying that, in making moral decisions, women use more of a *care orientation*, which is based on caring, having concern for others, and avoiding hurt, while men use more of a *justice orientation*, based on law, equality, and individual rights. However, research shows that both men and women use a mixture of care and justice orientations, depending on the situation (Jaffee & Hyde, 2000).

Brain or neural factors. Kohlberg constructed his theory before researchers were able to study the structures and functions of the living brain (see pp. 70–71). We have explained that the teenage brain has an underdeveloped prefrontal cortex, which results in an underdeveloped executive area and limits a teenager's ability to think, reason, and make intelligent decisions needed for moral reasoning (Luna, 2006). Also supporting the role of the prefrontal cortex in moral reasoning are findings that individuals who had their prefrontal cortex damaged in infancy had difficulty learning the normal social and moral rules in childhood and adolescence (A. Damasio, 1999). More recently, researchers identified different brain areas involved in moral decisions: Making *impersonal moral decisions*, such as keeping the money found in a stranger's wallet, involved areas associated with retrieving information (see p. 242); in comparison, making *personal moral decisions*, such as keeping the money found in a fellow worker's wallet, involved areas associated with emotions. Thus, when we make moral decisions, especially those involving personal concerns (abortion, death penalty), we use not only reasoning and logic but also our gut feelings or emotions (J. D. Greene et al., 2004). Making moral decisions appears to involve some kind of unconscious process (M. Hauser, 2007).

Moral reasoning is also influenced by the kinds of rules that parents use, which is our next topic.

Parenting Styles and Effects

Were your parents easy or strict?

During adolescence, teenagers experience several major changes in cognitive and emotional development. These changes are influenced by both biological factors, such as brain development, and environmental factors, such as the influence of peers and parents.

If someone asked how your parents raised you, would you answer that they were strict, supportive, easy, or hard? How do such different styles of parenting affect adolescents' development? To answer this question, psychologist Diana Baumrind (1991, 1993) carried out a series of longitudinal studies on parent–child and parent–adolescent interactions. She has identified a number of parenting styles that are associated with different kinds of adolescent development.

Baumrind's Parenting Styles

We'll focus on three of Baumrind's parenting styles: authoritarian parents, authoritative parents, and permissive parents.

Authoritarian parents attempt to shape, control, and evaluate the behavior and attitudes of their children in accordance with a set standard of conduct, usually an absolute standard that comes from religious or respected authorities.

For these parents, obedience is a virtue, and they punish and use harsh discipline to keep the adolescent in line with their rules. These parents don't communicate well with their children. For instance, authoritarian parents don't explain the rationale behind rules or consequences. Moreover, they do not respect or care about their children's viewpoint. These parents demand complete obedience and will use force to ensure compliance.

> My parents won't listen to why I was late.

Authoritative parents attempt to direct their children's activities in a rational and intelligent way. They are supportive, loving, and committed, encourage verbal give-and-take, and discuss their rules and policies with their children.

Authoritative parents value being expressive and independent but are also reasonably demanding. Unlike authoritarian parents, who communicate poorly with their children, authoritative parents offer explanations for rules and consequences. They also encourage their children to share their viewpoint.

> I understand and respect my parents' rules.

Permissive parents are less controlling and behave with a nonpunishing and accepting attitude toward their children's impulses, desires, and actions; they consult with their children about policy decisions, make few demands, and tend to use reason rather than direct power.

Permissive parents are warm and supportive; however, they tend to not enforce rules and their communication skills are poor. Because discipline is lacking, children make up their own rules or guidelines to follow, even when they could benefit from parental direction.

> My parents let me set my own rules.

Effects of Parenting Styles

Each of Baumrind's three parenting styles has different costs and benefits.

Authoritarian parents, who are very demanding, benefit by preventing adolescent behavioral problems but at some cost to their adolescents, who tend to be more withdrawn, conforming, and dependent, as well as have lower self-esteem and difficulties with schoolwork (Rudy & Grusec, 2006).

Authoritative parents, who state their values clearly, benefit by having loving and supportive parent–teenager interactions, which further benefit their teenagers, who tend to be more friendly, cooperative, competent, self-confident, and achievement oriented (Grusec, 2006; Hickman et al., 2000; Vazsonyi et al., 2003).

Researchers generally agree that the most effective style of parenting is authoritative. The benefits of authoritative parenting have been reported in several ethnic groups in the United States (Abar et al., 2009; Cheah et al., 2009).

Permissive parents benefit by having to make fewer demands and enforce fewer rules but at some cost to their adolescents, who may be less mature, less socially assertive, and less achievement oriented than

> Which is better, being too easy or too strict?

adolescents with authoritative parents (Baumrind, 1991, 1993). These adolescents also tend to engage in impulsive behaviors and have trouble with delinquency.

Thus, different parenting styles can have significantly different effects on the cognitive, social, and personality development of adolescents.

Even though parenting styles influence adolescent development, recent research finds that siblings may have the strongest influence on who we become in the long term. This isn't too surprising, since we spend every day of our childhood with our siblings and they remain in our lives long after our parents leave us. Through all of the sibling conflict, we learn how to negotiate, compromise, and maintain lasting relationships, which can help us to have successful adult relationships, such as those with our spouse/partner and colleagues (Kluger, 2006b).

Next, we'll continue our journey of learning about adolescent and adult development by discussing personality and social changes. ●

D Personality & Social Development

Definition

Who am I? We have discussed many of the major changes that occur during adolescence. One more change is that adolescents develop a sense of who they are, which involves personality and social development.

> **Like it or not, this is the real me!**

© dean bertoncelj/Shutterstock.com

Personality and **social development** refer to how a person develops a sense of self or self-identity, develops relationships with others, and develops the skills useful in social interactions.

For example, the teenager in the left photo shows her independence and what she believes is her real identity by having a very noticeable hairstyle and piercings.

Personal identity or **self-identity** refers to how we describe ourselves and includes our values, goals, traits, perceptions, interests, and motivations.

Personal identity grows and changes as adolescents acquire new values, goals, beliefs, and interests (Bandura, 1999). Even as adolescents attain an identity, their identity may change as they continue to develop. In fact, according to some researchers, young people living in industrialized nations are now taking longer to develop their core identity. The pursuit of advanced education and careers as well as the tendency to delay getting married and having children has led to a recently proposed transitional phase of identity development called emerging adulthood (Arnett, 2007).

Emerging adulthood is a period of development in which adolescents and young adults in industrialized nations continue self-exploration as they experiment with different possibilities in work and love.

A major influence on the kind of identity young people develop is how they feel about themselves, which is called self-esteem.

Development of Self-Esteem

What influences self-esteem? Throughout this module, we have discussed 12-year-old Branndi, who, like other teenagers, has many beliefs and goals, such as being proud to be Black and female, having high hopes for her future, and wanting to be a role model. How Branndi perceives herself, which is called self-esteem, has a significant influence on her developing personality.

Self-esteem is how much we like ourselves and how much we value our worth, importance, attractiveness, and social competence.

For example, in adolescents, self-esteem is influenced by a number of factors, including how *physically attractive* and how *socially competent* they appear to their peers (DuBois et al., 2000). As teenagers develop sexually mature bodies, they wonder how physically attractive they are; as teenagers begin dating, they wonder how socially skilled they are. Researchers measure changes in adolescents' self-esteem by using longitudinal studies that begin in adolescence and continue through adulthood, such as measuring self-esteem at ages 14, 18, and 23. We'll discuss three different patterns of self-esteem development in adolescents (M. A. Zimmerman et al., 1997).

High Self-Esteem—develop and maintain high levels. A large percentage of adolescents (about 60%) develop and maintain a strong sense of self-esteem through junior high school. These individuals do well in school, develop rewarding friendships, participate in social activities, and are described as cheerful, assertive, emotionally warm, and unwilling to give up if frustrated.

Low Self-Esteem—develop and maintain low levels. A small percentage of adolescents (15%) develop and maintain a chronically low sense of self-esteem that continues through junior high school. These adolescents usually have continuing personal and social problems (shy, lonely, depressed) that have been present for some time and contribute to this low self-esteem.

Reversals—reverse levels. A moderate percentage of adolescents (about 25%) show dramatic reversals in self-esteem, either from high to low or from low to high. For example, some boys change from being stern, unemotional, and lacking social skills into being open and expressive. Researchers think that reversals in self-esteem may result from changes in peer groups, personal attractiveness, or parental relationships.

Next, we'll describe some influences on the development of self-esteem as well as the importance of self-esteem.

> **I'm proud to be Black and female.**

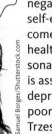
© Samuel Borges/Shutterstock.com

Importance of self-esteem. Self-esteem has been linked to important positive and negative outcomes. For example, having high self-esteem is associated with positive outcomes, such as being cheerful and happy, having healthy social relationships, and promoting personal adjustment, while having low self-esteem is associated with negative outcomes, such as depression, anxiety, antisocial behavior, and poor personal adjustment (S. L. Murray, 2005; Trzesniewski et al., 2006).

Today's adolescents are a special group of people, or at least they seem to think so. In general, today's teens think quite highly of themselves and believe they will achieve extraordinary success in their personal and work lives. One reason for this shift is that today's parents praise and possibly overpraise their children more than in earlier generations (Twenge & Campbell, 2008). Some researchers argue that this heightened self-esteem may lead to depression because of inevitable disappointment, while others believe it will protect teens against feeling the blues (Elias, 2008b).

> **There's nothing wrong with us!**

One theory of how self-esteem and personal identity develop is found in Erikson's psychosocial stages.

© Bobby Deal/RealDealPhoto/Shutterstock.com

Erikson's Psychosocial Stages

What will I have to deal with?

Adulthood has had ups and downs.

At the beginning of this module, we described how Charlie went from a Hollywood childhood and extraordinary early career success to a middle-aged adult. Along the way, he dealt with dating, getting married, having children, getting divorced, going through drug rehabilitation, and experiencing ups and downs in his career. How these life events might affect Charlie's social and personality development was something Erik Erikson (1982) tried to explain.

As you may remember from Module 17, Erikson divided life into eight *psychosocial stages*, each of which contained a unique psychosocial conflict, such as intimacy versus isolation. If Charlie successfully solved each psychosocial conflict, he would develop a healthy personality; if unsuccessful in solving these conflicts, he might develop an unhealthy personality and future psychological problems. In Module 17, we discussed Erikson's stages related to childhood; now, we'll discuss the stages related to adolescence and adulthood.

Stage **5** Identity versus Role Confusion

Period. Adolescence (12–20)
Potential conflict. Adolescents need to leave behind the carefree, irresponsible, and impulsive behaviors of childhood and develop the more purposeful, planned, and responsible behaviors of adulthood. If adolescents successfully resolve this problem, they will develop a healthy and confident sense of *identity*. If they are unsuccessful in resolving the problem, they will experience *role confusion*, which results in having low self-esteem and becoming unstable or socially withdrawn.

Stage **6** Intimacy versus Isolation

Period. Young adulthood (20–40)
Potential conflict. Young adulthood is a time for finding intimacy by developing loving and meaningful relationships. On the positive side, we can find *intimacy* in caring relationships. On the negative side,

without intimacy we will have a painful feeling of *isolation*, and our relationships will be impersonal.

Stage **7** Generativity versus Stagnation

Period. Middle adulthood (40–65)
Potential conflict. Middle adulthood is a time for helping the younger generation develop worthwhile lives. On the positive side, we can achieve *generativity* through raising our own children. If we do not have children of our own, we can achieve generativity through close relationships with children of friends or relatives. Generativity can also be achieved through mentoring at work and helping others. On the negative side, a lack of involvement leads to a feeling of *stagnation*, of having done nothing for the younger generation.

Stage **8** Integrity versus Despair

Period. Late adulthood (65 and older)
Potential conflict. Late adulthood is a time for reflecting on and reviewing how we met previous challenges and lived our lives. On the positive side, if we can look back and feel content about how we lived and what we accomplished, we will have a feeling of satisfaction or *integrity*. On the negative side, if we reflect and see a series of crises, problems, and bad experiences, we will have a feeling of regret and *despair*.

Conclusions. Erikson believed that achieving a personally satisfying identity was the very heart and soul of an adolescent's development. As adolescents developed into adults and reached middle adulthood (stage 7), Erikson described a shift from concerns about identity to concerns about being productive, creative, and nurturing (R. Coles, 2000).

Researchers have found evidence that we do go through a sequence of psychosocial stages and that how we handle conflicts at earlier stages affects our personality and social development at later stages (Van Manen & Whitbourne, 1997).

Personality Change

How much will I change?

When Mick Jagger, lead singer of the Rolling Stones, was in his early 20s (below), he boasted, "I'd rather be dead than sing 'Satisfaction' when I'm 45." Now at age 69, Jagger (right) has changed his tune; he and the Stones recently went on a world tour and sang "Satisfaction" dozens of times (L. Ali, 2005; E. Gardner, 2006). As Jagger found out, some of the things that we say and do at 20 may seem stupid at 60. The differences in Jagger at 20 and 60 raise an interesting question: How much do our personalities change and how much do they remain the same?

Researchers answer such questions with longitudinal studies, which measure personality development across time in the same group of individuals. One study found that from adolescence to middle adulthood, individuals became more trusting and intimate and developed a better sense of control and identity. Researchers also

In his 20s, he said he'd rather be dead than singing at 45.

Now almost 70, Jagger is still touring and singing.

found that possessing certain personality traits as a young adult (early 20s) led to developing related traits in middle adulthood (middle 40s). For example, individuals with a high level of identity in their early 20s showed more independence, warmth, and compassion later on in their mid-40s (Vandewater et al., 1997). From these kinds of longitudinal studies researchers draw three conclusions: First, from the end of adolescence through middle adulthood, there are less dramatic but still continuing changes in personality traits, such as becoming more trusting and intimate. Second, possessing certain personality traits in early adulthood is the foundation for developing related traits later on (Roberts et al., 2002). Third, adults appear to pass through psychosocial stages and face conflicts in personality development similar to those proposed by Erikson (Van Manen & Whitbourne, 1997). We'll discuss personality more fully in Modules 19 and 20. ●

The Big Picture

What are the major changes?

In the United States, there are about 30 million youths (ages 10 to 17) who are currently going through adolescence, a period of considerable physical, neurological (brain), cognitive, and emotional change. We'll review some of the major changes that occur during adolescence.

There are 30 million of us.

Girls during Puberty

Puberty sets off a surge in physical growth, which is marked by an increase in height that starts on average at 9.6 years of age. Puberty triggers a physiological process that results in a girl's reaching *female sexual maturity*, which involves primarily the onset of *menarche*, or the first menstrual period, at an average age of 12.5 years. The onset of menarche is triggered by the *hypothalamus*, which releases a hormone called *kisspeptin* that helps to stimulate the *pituitary gland* to produce hormones (Kotulak, 2006). These hormones stimulate the ovaries to produce female hormones including *estrogen*, which stimulates the development of both primary and secondary sexual characteristics, such as development of pubic hair and breasts.

Boys during Puberty

Puberty triggers an increase in physical growth, especially height, generally at 13 or 14 years of age. Puberty starts a physiological process that results in a boy's reaching *male sexual maturity*, which includes growth of the genital organs—testes and penis—and production of sperm at 12 to 14 years of age. The increase in genital growth and the production of sperm are triggered by the *hypothalamus*, which stimulates the male pituitary gland. The pituitary in turn triggers the testes to increase production of *testosterone*, which is the major male hormone and stimulates the growth of genital organs and the development of secondary sexual characteristics, such as growth of pubic and facial hair, development of muscles, and a change (deepening) in voice.

Piaget's Cognitive Stages

According to Piaget's theory, children pass through four different cognitive stages—(1) sensorimotor, (2) preoperational, (3) concrete operations, and (4) formal operations—in that order but at individual rates. With each stage, the child adds a new and qualitatively different kind of thinking or reasoning skill that helps the child make better sense of the world. Adolescents are entering Piaget's fourth stage, called the formal operations stage, which begins at about age 12 and extends through adulthood. During this stage, adolescents develop the abilities to think about abstract or hypothetical concepts, to consider an issue from another's viewpoint, and to solve cognitive problems in a logical way. These cognitive abilities are very useful during adulthood.

1 Sensorimotor

2 Preoperational

3 Concrete

4 Formal

Brain Development: Reason & Emotion

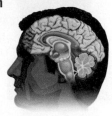

Researchers are finding that the adolescent's brain has an underdeveloped prefrontal cortex or executive officer but a well-developed limbic system or emotional center (Spear, 2010). This combination of a weak executive officer and a strong emotional center results in many of the unthinking, irresponsible, and irritating behaviors of adolescents. For example, the lack of a strong executive officer (prefrontal cortex) explains why adolescents engage in risky behaviors, switch moods suddenly, and act impulsively. As one researcher summarized, "Good judgment is learned but you can't learn it if you don't have the necessary hardware (neural development)" (Yurgelun-Todd, 1999, p. 48).

Kohlberg's Theory of Moral Reasoning

Kohlberg hypothesized that everyone goes through three levels of moral reasoning. Level 1, the preconventional level, involves stage 1 (fear of punishment) and stage 2 (self-interest). Level 2, the conventional level, involves stage 3 (conforming to the standards of others) and stage 4 (conforming to the standards of society). Level 3, the postconventional level, has only stage 5 (balancing human rights and society's laws). There is support for Kohlberg's assumption that individuals progress through the stages in order and that not everyone reaches the higher stages (Damon, 1999). Since Kohlberg's time, researchers have found several brain or neural factors (prefrontal cortex, emotional areas) that play a role in making moral decisions.

Erikson's Psychosocial Stages

According to Erikson's theory, we pass through eight different psychosocial stages throughout the life span and each stage contains a unique psychosocial conflict. Erikson proposed that during adolescence we enter stage 5, which involves the conflict between identity and role confusion. To successfully develop a confident sense of identity, adolescents must leave behind the carefree, irresponsible, and impulsive behaviors of childhood and develop the more purposeful, planned, and responsible behaviors of adulthood. Failure to resolve this conflict results in role confusion, which involves having low self-esteem and becoming unstable or socially withdrawn.

We'll discuss gender roles, love, and relationships next. ●

Gender Roles

Why couldn't women be firefighters?

As boys and girls grow to become men and women, they acquire a set of behavioral and cognitive rules called gender roles.

Gender roles are traditional or stereotypical behaviors, attitudes, values, and personality traits that society says are how males and females should think and behave.

You can become aware of gender roles by noticing how differently males and females dress, behave, think, and express emotions. Gender roles played a major part in whether firefighters could be women. Firefighters had always been men because they were considered strong and cool in the face of danger, while

Women fought for 20 years to become firefighters.

women were considered weak and nervous. In the 1970s, when women applied to become firefighters, a local paper warned against the city's "futile exercise in trying to fit women into jobs which common sense tells us are best filled by men." Only after 20 years of political and legal battles were gender roles changed and women allowed to become firefighters (S. Kershaw, 2006).

During the past years, there have been some changes in gender roles in the United States. Women can enter careers traditionally reserved for men, such as doctors, police officers, astronauts, and soldiers. And men can enter careers traditionally reserved for women, such as nurses, single parents, and grade-school teachers. We'll discuss some issues surrounding current gender roles and their development.

Gender Roles: United States

Each of us acquired a male or female gender role with little conscious effort or awareness, and we often don't notice the effect of gender roles on the development of our personality and social behaviors (Prentice & Carranza, 2002).

The influence of gender roles on personality became clear when researchers asked college students to describe the traits of a typical male and female. Students generally agreed that the female gender role included being caring, insecure, emotional, social, and shy. In comparison, students said the male gender role included being arrogant, aggressive, ambitious, unemotional, and dominant (Helgeson, 1994).

caring
insecure
helpful
emotional
social
shy

arrogant
confident
aggressive
ambitious
unemotional
dominant

The influence of gender roles in the work setting is also undeniably evident. For instance, although an increasing number of women are graduating from top business schools, women fill less than 2% of chief executive jobs at Fortune 500 companies (Creswell, 2006). Researchers do not expect gender equality in high-rank positions to occur any time soon, and there continues to be a wage gap between the sexes, with men earning more than women for the same kind of work (Judge & Livingston, 2008; Kinsman, 2006). On average, women earn about 80% of what their male colleagues earn (U.S. Department of Education, 2010).

Changes. In the United States, traditional gender roles are becoming less popular. In fact, 60% of men and women report they disagree with the idea that men should earn money and women should take care of children (Jayson, 2009b). Also, two-thirds of today's 18- to 34-year-old women report that being successful in a high-paying career is "very important" or "one of the most important things" in their lives (Pew Research Center, 2012).

As more and more women pursue higher education and high-paying professional careers, today's men are welcoming their role as fathers more than ever. Men's role as active, involved parents is becoming more of the norm than a rarity. In fact, there are now three times as many stay-at-home fathers as there were ten years ago (Anthes, 2010; Cullen & Grossman, 2007; Jayson, 2009c).

Recent changes in adult gender roles are reducing the gender wage gap, which is currently the smallest on record (Bureau of Labor Statistics, 2010). In fact, almost 40% of working wives earn more money than their husbands. If this trend continues, soon more families may be supported by women than by men (Mundy, 2012). Changes in gender roles are placing greater pressure on both sexes to balance work and family. There is some research to suggest that fathers are struggling to adapt to this change more than mothers (Baird, 2010). For instance, in dual-earner couples, 60% of fathers reported having a difficult time managing work and family responsibilities, compared to only 47% of mothers (Aumann et al., 2011).

Gender Roles: Development

The question of why gender roles develop has two different but related answers.

Evolutionary psychology theory. One answer from *evolutionary psychology theory* emphasizes genetic and biological forces and says that current gender differences are a continuation of the behaviors that evolved from early men and women who adapted these different behaviors to survive the problems of their time (Buss, 1999; Kenrick et al., 2004). According to evolutionary theory, men increased their chances for reproduction by being dominant, controlling, and aggressive. In comparison, women increased their chances of raising children by being concerned, sensitive, and nurturing.

Social role theory. A different but related answer comes from *social role theory*, which emphasizes social and cultural influences and states that gender differences between males and females arise from different divisions of labor (Eagly et al., 2004).

These two theories do not disagree but rather emphasize either biological or psychological factors.

Next, you'll see that gender roles affect our expectations about relationships.

Kinds of Love

As we acquire a male or female gender role, we also develop expectations about who we would like for an intimate relationship (Fletcher, 2002; Fletcher & Simpson, 2000). Once we find someone to experience an intimate relationship with, we may experience different kinds of love.

Which kind of love are you in?

If we consider Charlie Sheen's history of intimate relationships, we see that as time went by, his expectations for intimate relationships changed. He likely experienced various kinds of love, chose partners for different reasons, and learned some ways to develop intimate relationships. Charlie's experiences bring up three issues: kinds of love, choosing a partner, and the characteristics of a long-term commitment.

Earlier researchers had thought love too mysterious for scientific study, but current researchers have begun to classify love into various types. As a starting point, researchers distinguish between passionate and companionate love (Rapson & Hatfield, 2005).

Passionate love involves continuously thinking about the loved one and is accompanied by warm sexual feelings and powerful emotional reactions.

Companionate love involves having trusting and tender feelings for someone whose life is closely bound up with one's own.

Charlie's experienced different kinds of love.

Love Triangle — Commitment, Intimacy, Passion

Three components of love

For example, when people fall madly in love, it's usually passionate love. When mature couples talk about enjoying each other's company, it's usually companionate love, which may or may not involve sexual behaviors. Thus, love is more complex than many think. One of the better known theories of love is Robert Sternberg's (1999) triangular theory of love.

The **triangular theory of love** has three components: passion, intimacy, and commitment. **Passion** is feeling physically aroused and attracted to someone. **Intimacy** is feeling close and connected to someone; it develops through sharing and communicating. **Commitment** is making a pledge to nourish the feelings of love and to actively maintain the relationship.

What makes you feel in love is the component of passion, which rises quickly and strongly influences and biases your judgment. What makes you want to share and offer emotional and material support is the component of intimacy. What makes you want to form a serious relationship, such as getting married, and to promise support through difficult times is the component of commitment. Sternberg believes that the kind of love most of us strive for is **consummate love**, which is a balanced combination of all three components—passion, intimacy, and commitment.

Sternberg (1999) uses his triangular theory to answer some of the most commonly asked questions about love.

Is there love at first sight? Love at first sight occurs when we are overwhelmed by passion, without any intimacy or commitment. Sternberg calls this *infatuated love*, which can arise in an instant, involves a great deal of physiological arousal, and lasts varying lengths of time. Because there is no intimacy or commitment, infatuated love is destined to fade away.	**Why do some people get married so quickly?** Sternberg calls this *Hollywood love*, which is a combination of passion and commitment but without any intimacy. In Hollywood love, two people make a commitment based on their passion for each other. Unless they develop intimacy over time, the relationship is likely to fail.	**Can there be love without sex?** Sternberg calls love without sex *companionate love*, which is a combination of intimacy and commitment without any sexual passion. An example of companionate love is a married couple who are committed to each other and share their lives but whose physical attraction has waned.	**Why doesn't romantic love last?** *Romantic love*, which is a combination of intimacy and passion, usually doesn't last because there is no commitment. As soon as the passion dies and the intimacy fades, the individuals no longer feel in love and go their separate ways.

Brain in Love

Researchers took brain scans of college coeds who had been with their "one true love" for between 2 and 17 months and topped the charts on the passionate love scale (constantly think about their partners, can't sleep, feel euphoric). The coeds were shown photos of their loved ones interspersed with familiar but emotionally neutral faces. Only in response to seeing their loved ones did their brain's *reward/pleasure center* (see p. 330) show increased activity, similar to the activity seen with cocaine-produced euphoria (Helmuth, 2003a). In comparison, brain scans of partners who had been in longer relationships (average 2 years) indicated activity in additional emotional areas (insula, anterior cingulate) (H. Fisher, 2003). Researchers concluded that infatuated love primarily activates the brain's reward/pleasure center and turns down activity in brain areas responsible for reason and judgment. In comparison, a more committed love activates additional emotional brain areas, which contributes to forming a longer-lasting relationship (Carey, 2002; C. Miller, 2008).

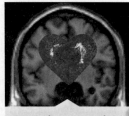

Researchers can see love in brain scans.

Is it possible for long-married couples to feel the same passion and romance as new love? Common wisdom may say no, but results from brain scans say yes! Researchers found similar brain activity in people who report being in intense love after decades of marriage and in people who only recently fell in love. By using brain scans, researchers also found that people in long-lasting marriages don't experience the obsession and anxiety of new love; instead parts of the brain associated with deep attachment are active, suggesting that these people feel more calm and secure (Acevedo, 2008a, 2008b, 2010; Acevedo et al., 2012).

After choosing a partner and falling in love, the next step is to develop a long-term relationship.

Choosing a Partner

The fact that about 90% of adults in the United States marry means that most of us will eventually select a partner for a long-term relationship. However, given that approximately half of couples divorce, we know that selecting the right partner can be a difficult and somewhat mysterious process.

What am I looking for?

Researchers suggest that one way we choose a partner for a long-term relationship is by finding someone who matches our ideal-partner schema (Fletcher & Simpson, 2000).

A **schema** is an organized mental or cognitive list that includes characteristics, facts, values, or beliefs about people, events, or objects.

An ideal-partner schema is a mental list of the most desirable characteristics we are seeking. An ideal-partner schema in order of preference for unmarried college students (averaged for men and women) is shown below (Buss, 1994). Results showed differences in how men and women form ideal-partner schemas: Men rank physical attractiveness higher and women rank earning capacity higher (Buss, 1995, 2003).

> **IDEAL PARTNER**
> 1. kind/understanding
> 2. exciting
> 3. intelligent
> 4. physically attractive (men rank higher)
> 5. healthy
> 6. easygoing
> 7. creative
> 8. wants children
> 9. earning potential (women rank higher)

One reason we date different people is to find the ideal partner who best matches the traits on our ideal-partner schema list. However, when we become passionately attracted to a person, our brain's reward/pleasure center is activated and we lose the ability to rationally decide whether a person really has the traits on our list. In this passionate state, we see our person through euphoric, rose-colored lenses that make disagreeable traits temporally disappear. However, such traits will reappear when the euphoric state fades, as it always does (H. Fisher, 2002).

After Mr. or Ms. Right is chosen, the couple is ready to make a commitment, such as living together or getting married.

Cohabiting

Why do couples cohabit?

In the United States, the number of unmarried, heterosexual couples living together, or *cohabiting,* increased from 1 million in 1960 to 13.6 million in 2008 (Jayson, 2005; USCB, 2009). Fewer unmarried people who cohabit are in homosexual relationships.

The long-standing reason given for why people chose to cohabit was to "test" the relationship. However, this turns out not to be a major reason at all. Instead, most couples report simply wanting to spend more time together as their primary reason to cohabit. Also, high housing costs and tight budgets make living with a dating partner desirable. Additionally, many homosexual couples cohabit due to laws in their states that do not permit them to marry or have civil unions (Jayson, 2009d; Smock, 2005). Last, there are some interesting gender differences in why people cohabit. For instance, men report "sex" as a reason to cohabit four times as often as women do, and women report "love" as a reason three times as often as men do (P. M. Huang et al., 2011).

What happens during the first few years of living together really matters, since most couples will either break up or marry by then. In the United States, about two-thirds of couples who marry live together first. Recent research shows that, contrary to what many may believe, the chance of divorce is not much greater for couples who cohabit prior to marriage (NCHS, 2010).

More people are choosing to cohabit.

Getting Married

Why do marriages last?

Perhaps due to the rising number of people choosing to cohabit, the average age when men and women get married is rising (26 for women and 28 for men) (USCB, 2011). For those who choose to marry, many find long-term happiness and many others find themselves getting a divorce.

To find out why some marriages succeed but others fail, researcher John Gottman analyzed videotapes of couples' social interactions and physiological responses over 14 years. Using these data, Gottman's predictions of which couples would stay together and which would divorce were 91% accurate (Gottman, 2003). As Gottman analyzed couples' social interactions, he found that couples who later divorced had four major problems: One or both partners spent too much time criticizing the other; one or both partners became too defensive when one of their faults was criticized; one or both partners showed contempt for the other; and one or both partners engaged in stonewalling or being unwilling to talk about some problem (Gottman, 2000). The continual stress arising from these problems resulted in couples becoming more unhappy through the years (Gottman, 2003).

Ongoing stress on the relationship certainly increases the likelihood of divorce. Education and income are significant factors in divorce as well. Research finds that less-educated, lower-income couples are more likely to divorce than college graduates (Amato, 2010). Additionally, as women achieve greater financial success in their careers, they don't have the same pressure to remain in an unhappy marriage. In fact, it is estimated that two-thirds of today's divorces are initiated by women (Luscombe, 2010).

Researchers agree that achieving long-term marital success takes a lot of work. Fortunately, maintaining a long-term, satisfying marriage

Having a happy marriage helps us to live longer.

does have numerous biological and psychological benefits, which are reported to add seven years to a man's life and two years to a woman's life (N. A. Christakis & Fowler, 2009). ●

Concept Review

1. Puberty is accompanied by a number of biological and physical changes, which are triggered by male or female **(a)** _____. These chemicals result in the development of male and female secondary **(b)** _____ characteristics and, for females, their first menstrual cycle, which is called **(c)** _____.

2. The idea that adolescent development consists of a number of cognitive, sexual, social, and personality changes that occur simultaneously is called the _____ model.

3. Piaget hypothesized that cognitive development is made up of four distinct stages of reasoning, each of which is qualitatively different from and more advanced than the preceding one. According to Piaget, from adolescence through adulthood, we are at the _____ stage, which involves the ability to think about hypothetical concepts, consider an issue from another's viewpoint, and solve abstract problems in a logical manner.

4. New findings indicate that teenagers do not yet have a fully developed part of their brains called the **(a)** _____, which has **(b)** _____ functions, such as thinking, planning, and making decisions.

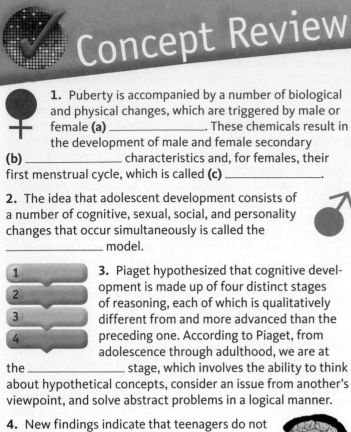

5. One reason adolescents engage in more risky behaviors is that they have an underdeveloped **(a)** _____ but a fully functioning emotional center, called the **(b)** _____.

6. The idea that moral reasoning can be classified into three distinct levels and that everyone goes through these levels in order is a theory of moral development proposed by **(a)** _____. The level of moral reasoning based primarily on punishment is called **(b)** _____; the one based on conforming to laws and society is called **(c)** _____; and the one based on balancing rights and laws is called **(d)** _____. Most research supports Kohlberg's idea that people do go through **(e)** _____ of moral development but not everyone reaches the higher stages.

7. Making impersonal moral decisions, such as keeping the money found in a stranger's wallet, involves areas of the brain associated with retrieving **(a)** _____. In comparison, making personal moral decisions, such as keeping the money found in a fellow worker's wallet, involves areas of the brain associated with **(b)** _____.

8. The development of independence and achievement during adolescence is shaped by a number of different parenting styles—in particular, **(a)** _____, **(b)** _____, and **(c)** _____—each of which has different costs and benefits to parents and adolescents.

9. How we describe ourselves, including our values, goals, traits, perceptions, interests, and motivations, is called **(a)** _____. How much we value our worth, importance, attractiveness, and social competence is called **(b)** _____. The pursuit of education and careers in industrialized nations has led to a proposed period of development called **(c)** _____, in which adolescents and young adults continue self-exploration.

10. According to Erik Erikson, across our lifetimes we proceed through eight **(a)** _____, each of which presents a particular kind of personality or social problem. For adolescents, stage 5 is most relevant and involves **(b)** _____ versus role confusion. Finding one's identity has many aspects; the aspect that involves how much we like ourselves and our feelings of worth, attractiveness, and social competence is called **(c)** _____. Erikson believed that the most important part of personality development for an adolescent was to achieve a satisfying sense of **(d)** _____, while adults are more concerned about being **(e)** _____.

11. Males and females think, act, and behave in different ways, and these are called _____, which are enforced by expectations of parents and peers and by society rewarding traditional roles and punishing roles that are different.

12. One way we select a partner is by forming a mental list of characteristics and then looking for someone who matches our mental list, which is called a _____.

13. The theory of love that has three components—passion, intimacy, and commitment—is called the _____.

14. Infatuated love primarily activates the brain's reward/pleasure center and causes feelings of **(a)** _____. In comparison, a more committed love activates additional emotional brain areas, which help in forming a longer-lasting **(b)** _____.

15. Couples are more likely to have successful long-term relationships if they learn to deal with _____ in a straightforward way.

Answers: 1. (a) hormones, (b) sexual, (c) menarche; 2. biopsychosocial; 3. formal operations; 4. (a) prefrontal cortex, (b) prefrontal cortex; 5. (a) prefrontal cortex, (b) limbic system; 6. (a) Kohlberg, (b) preconventional, (c) conventional, (d) postconventional, (e) stages; 7. (a) information, (b) emotions; 8. (a) authoritarian, (b) authoritative, (c) permissive; 9. (a) personal identity or self-identity, (b) self-esteem, (c) emerging adulthood; 10. (a) psychosocial stages, (b) identity, (c) self-esteem, (d) identity, (e) productive, creative, nurturing; 11. gender roles; 12. schema; 13. triangular theory; 14. (a) euphoria, (b) relationship; 15. conflicts.

Unless otherwise noted, all images are © Cengage Learning

G Research Focus: Happy Marriages

What's a Love Lab?

Imagine being a researcher who wants to predict one of the most complex human behaviors: Which couples will

What's the key to a successful relationship?

succeed and which will fail in long-term relationships? The fact that 40–60% of marriages fail indicates that something is leading to success or failure. How would you design a "love lab," or a research program to figure out what that "something" is?

Every research program aims for the same four goals, which are to describe, explain, predict, and control behavior. The first two goals—describe and explain—are relatively easy. However, the last two goals—predict and control—are very difficult because many human behaviors are so complex that they cannot be completely explained, much less predicted or

© Katrina Brown/Shutterstock.com

controlled. Now, along comes psychologist and researcher John Gottman, who claims that not only can he explain the "something" but he can also predict with 91% accuracy which marriages will succeed or fail (Gottman et al., 2006). Since very few human behaviors can be predicted with 91% accuracy, his claim is absolutely amazing.

In the past, researchers used primarily self-reports or questionnaires to study the success or failure of long-term relationships. However, self-reports and questionnaires are not totally reliable, since marriage partners could knowingly (out of embarrassment) or unknowingly (out of defensiveness) bias their answers. Gottman's breakthrough in studying and predicting the success or failure of long-term relationships was to develop a better research method that goes by the zany name of "Love Lab."

Method

In the Love Lab, one partner sits facing the other (photos below). For 15 minutes they discuss a topic that is a known sore point while their facial and physiological responses are recorded.

Facial responses. The advantage of recording each of the partners' nonverbal facial responses is that facial responses reflect a wide range of emotional expressions (surprise, interest, anger, disgust, contempt) that one or both partners may be unaware of or try to deny. Nonverbal behaviors are very important ways of communicating in real life. For example, it's not uncommon for one partner to notice the other partner's facial expression and ask, "What's bothering you?" By recording nonverbal facial cues, which are difficult to hide or fake by normal (untrained) individuals, Gottman can reliably determine whether certain kinds of social interactions cause problems for the partners.

Physiological responses. Gottman also wants to know how long the emotional feelings last. He measures the duration of emotional feelings by recording physiological responses (heart and breathing rate, sweating). These responses reflect the start and duration of increased physiological or emotional arousal, which one or both partners

In the Love Lab, a video camera (circled) records facial expressions, and white bands of wires (visible on her fingers and his wrist) record various physiological responses.
© Dmitriy Shironosov/Shutterstock.com

may be unaware of or try to deny. For example, if one or both partners experience frequent and long-lasting bad feelings, it often signals that the marriage is in trouble (Gottman, 1999).

Longitudinal method. So far, you can see that Gottman's Love Lab solved the problem of how to reliably measure a couple's emotional responses and feelings. But how would he know if these measures predicted a marriage's success or failure? To answer this question, Gottman used the longitudinal research method, which means he retested the same couples regularly during 14 years. By retesting the same couples over time, he could determine whether a couple's social interactions and emotional responses recorded during early sessions could be used to predict with 91% accuracy whether this particular marriage would succeed or fail.

Results and Conclusions

After retesting the same 79 couples for 14 years, Gottman (1999) reported that he could predict, based on previous observations in the Love Lab, which of the marriages would succeed or fail. Here are some of the findings that allowed him to predict with such accuracy.

Unsuccessful relationships. Gottman identified four major problems that couples experience early on and that, if not dealt with successfully, predict failure in long-term relationships. These four problems are giving too many *criticisms,* becoming too *defensive,* showing *contempt* of a partner, and *stonewalling* or refusing to settle disagreements in an open, straightforward discussion.

Successful relationships. There are three behaviors that predict successful relationships (Gottman, 2011). First, people in happy marriages demonstrate *friendship and intimacy,* which means they engage in lifelong learning about each other. They may ask questions such as "What life goals do you wish to achieve?" or "What other career would you have liked to pursue?"

Second, happy couples give each other *constructive criticism.* For example, when beginning difficult conversations, they open gently and keep the focus on their feelings rather than attacking the other person. So, rather than saying, "You are irresponsible and messy," they may say, "I'm upset the garbage hasn't been taken out as promised."

Third, happy marriages demonstrate *shared meaning,* which involves developing connection rituals that foster a sense of mutual purpose on a daily basis. For instance, couples may exercise together, engage in the same hobby, have dinner together nightly, or share family play time.

Although in the United States most people marry for love, that's not true in other cultures. ●

Measuring Cultural Influences

Can 9,000 people agree?

Imagine being born and raised in a country different from your own, such as Nigeria, Germany, China, Iran, Brazil, Japan, France, or India. Now imagine being asked to list, in order, those traits that you consider most desirable in a potential partner. How much does your culture influence the order of desirable traits? To answer this question, researchers surveyed more than

What if you were born in Egypt?
© Roger Wood/Corbis

9,000 young adults (men and women), all in their 20s, who lived in 37 different countries (Buss, 1994; Buss et al., 1990). Participants were given a list of 32 traits and asked to rank the traits from most to least desirable in a potential partner. The results indicate that 9,000 individuals from many different cultures seemed to agree reasonably well in ranking traits.

Desirable Traits

What is considered desirable in a potential partner? The list on the near right shows the most desirable traits for potential partners averaged across cultures. Men and women have similar lists of desirable traits, as indicated by a high correlation of +0.87 between lists. The numerous similarities between men's and women's lists indicate similar cultural influences.

> **Average ranking of desirable traits**
> 1 **Kind and understanding**
> 2 **Intelligent**
> 3 **Exciting personality**
> 4 **Healthy**
> 5 **Emotionally stable and mature**
> 6 **Dependable character**
> 7 **Pleasing disposition**
>
> Adapted from "Mate Preferences in 37 Cultures," by D. M. Buss, 1994. In W. J. Lonner & R. Malpass (Eds.), *Psychology and Culture.* Allyn and Bacon.

There were also some interesting differences in desirable traits between men and women. For instance, men almost always ranked physical appearance in a partner higher, while women almost always ranked earning potential in a partner higher.

Are Americans changing their preferences for partners? In the largest study of single people ever, researchers reported surprising results about men's and women's preferences for partners

(Match.com/MarketTools, 2011a, 2011b). Results indicate that men are more interested in love, marriage, and children today than in the past. Also, compared to women, men are more open to dating people of a different race or religion. Women want more independence in their relationships than ever before. More women than men place high importance on having their own personal space, hobbies or interests, and regular nights out with their friends.

This research revealed that men are expressing some traditionally female preferences for partners, whereas women are expressing preferences that have generally been attributed to men. Researchers say that today's men and women are not judging a potential partner on the basis of gender-related traits, but that they are increasingly looking for the whole package.

I want to get married.

I want to be independent.

© Kurhan/Shutterstock.com

Reasons for Marrying

How much is love valued? As the figure on the right shows, people in different countries place different values on marrying for love. In the United States and other Western countries, marrying for love is highly valued, but it is valued less in some Middle East, Asian, and African nations.

How do women decide? Some anthropologists have argued that women, who invest more time in caring for offspring, would adopt more discriminating standards for potential mates than would men, who invest less time in rearing children. Thus, women would be more careful in deciding whom to marry. This proved true: In nearly every culture, women expressed more stringent standards across a wide range of characteristics (Buss, 1994).

How do men decide? Across cultures, men generally decide to marry younger

> **How Citizens in Different Nations Ranked the Importance of Love in Choosing a Spouse**
>
> **United States: Love** ranked **FIRST**; that is, love was the most important factor in choosing a spouse.
>
> **Iran: Love** ranked **THIRD**, while ranked higher were education, ambition, chastity.
>
> **Nigeria: Love** ranked **FOURTH**, while ranked higher were good health, refinement, neatness, desire.
>
> **China: Love** ranked **SIXTH**, while ranked higher were health, chastity, homemaker.
>
> **Zulu: Love** ranked **SEVENTH**, while ranked higher were mature, emotionally stable, dependable.

women who are physically attractive. In those societies where men purchase their wives, younger women command a higher bride price. Also, across cultures, the most common reason that men use to dissolve marriages is infertility, or the inability to have children (Buss, 1994).

From surveys of desirable traits in marriage partners, researchers found many similarities across cultures, but they found considerable differences among cultures in reasons for getting married.

We have primarily discussed development in adolescents and young to middle-aged adults. Next, we'll examine the physical changes that come with aging. ●

Adapted from "International Preferences in Selecting Mates," by D. M. Buss, M. Abbott, A. Angleitner, A. Asherian, A. Biaggio, A. Blanoco-Villasenor, A. Bruchon-Scwietzer, H. Y. Ch'U, J. Czapinski, B. Deraad, B. Ekehammar, N. E. Lohamy, M. Fioravanti, J. Georgas, P. Gjerde, R. Guttmann, E. Hazan, S. Iwawaki, H. Jankiramaiah, F. Khosroshani, D. Kreitler, L. Lachenicht, M. Lee, K. Klik, B. Little, S. Mika, M. Moadel-Shahid, G. Moane, M. Montero, A. C. Mundy-Castle, T. Niit, E. Nsenduluka, R. Pienkowski, A. M. Pirttila-Backman, J. P. De Leon, J. Rousseau, M. A. Runco, M. P. Safir, C. Samuels, R. Sanitioso, R. Serpell, N. Smid, C. Spencer, M. Tadinac, E. N. Tordorova, Z. K. Troland, L. Van Den Brande, G. Van Heck, L. Van Langenhove & K. S. Yang, 1990, *Journal of Cross-Cultural Personality, 21,* 5–47, and additional data from "Mate Preferences in 37 Cultures," by D. M. Buss. In W. J. Lonner & R. Malpass (Eds.), *Psychology and Culture.* Allyn & Bacon.

Unless otherwise noted, all images are © Cengage Learning

I Adulthood & Aging

Kinds of Aging

Why do we grow old?

As you look at the photo on the right, the differences you see in grandmother, daughter, and granddaughter illustrate normal aging, which is very different from pathological aging.

© Monkey Business Images/
Shutterstock.com

Percentage of U.S. Population Over 65

1995	12.6%
2010	13.4%
2040	20.7%

Source: U.S. Census Bureau

Normal aging is a gradual and natural slowing of our physical and psychological processes from middle through late adulthood.

Pathological aging may be caused by genetic defects, physiological problems, or diseases, such as Alzheimer's (see p. 47), all of which accelerate the aging process.

One goal of the study of aging, which is called *gerontology,* is to separate the causes of normal aging from those of pathological aging.

You may find these statistics on the aging population interesting:

- Life expectancy in the United States is now a record 78 years (CDC, 2011a).
- The percentage of people in the United States over 65 is expected to exceed 20% by the year 2040 (left graph).
- The number of people age 60 and over is expected to triple worldwide by 2050 (United Nations, 2010).
- The fastest growing population worldwide is people age 80 and over. The size of this group, referred to as the "oldest old," is expected to quadruple by 2050 (United Nations, 2010).
- The number of centenarians (people 100 years and older) in the world is expected to increase nine fold by 2050 (United Nations, 2010).

We'll examine two related questions about aging: Why do our bodies age? How do our bodies and behaviors change with age?

Physiological Changes

So far, the oldest people on record have lived from 113 to 122 years. How long you will live and how fast your body will age depend about 50% on heredity (genes) and 50% on other factors, such as diet, exercise, lifestyle, and diseases (K. Wright, 2003). In the past decades, the steady increases in life expectancy came primarily from improved public health and new cures for diseases. But advances in controlling diseases are slowing, and researchers believe that even with major improvements in geriatric care, the average life expectancy will not go beyond 85 years (Olshansky, 2003). Instead, researchers believe that large increases in life expectancy must now come from slowing the aging process itself (R. Miller, 2003).

The **aging process** is caused by a combination of certain genes and proteins that interfere with organ functioning and the natural production of toxic molecules (free radicals), which in turn cause random damage to body organs and DNA (the building blocks of life). Such damage eventually exceeds the body's ability to repair itself and results in greater susceptibility to diseases and death (Olshansky et al., 2002).

Researchers found that stress—like that caused by job loss or divorce—results in the aging of DNA, and they are studying the effects that meditation and psychotherapy may have on slowing the aging of DNA (Epel & Blackburn, 2004). Human studies have identified a half-dozen genetic factors in the very old (average age 98) that seemed to have slowed the aging process (K. Wright, 2003). Although such practices as having a good diet, exercising, reducing stress, and taking vitamins or antioxidants may improve quality of life and help one live into the 100s, none of these things alone has been shown to slow the aging process and allow humans to live to 130 or beyond (Olshansky, 2003).

As our bodies age, they experience many physiological changes.

Physiological Changes: Early Adulthood

In our early to middle 20s, our immune system, senses, physiological responses, and mental skills are at their peak efficiency.

Middle Adulthood

In our 30s and 40s, we usually gain weight, primarily because we are less active. By the late 40s, there is a slight decrease in a number of physiological responses, including heart rate, lung capacity, muscle strength, and eyesight.

Late Adulthood

In our 50s and 60s, we may experience a gradual decline in height because of loss of bone density, a further decrease in output of lungs and kidneys, an increase in skin wrinkles, and a deterioration in joints. Sensory organs become less sensitive, resulting in less acute vision, hearing, and taste. The heart, which is a muscle, becomes less effective at pumping blood, which may result in as much as a 35% decrease in blood flow through the coronary arteries. A general decrease occurs in both the number and diameter of muscle fibers, which may explain some of the slowing in motor functions that usually accompanies old age.

© Nigel Riches/IMAGE SOURCE

Very Late Adulthood

In our 70s and 80s, we undergo further decreases in muscle strength, bone density, speed of nerve conduction, and output of lungs, heart, and kidneys. More than 10% have Parkinson's or Alzheimer's disease.

As many of the body's physical responses slow down with aging, there are corresponding decreases in related behaviors. Now we'll discuss changes in cognitive abilities with aging and then decreases in sexual behavior.

Cognitive and Emotional Changes

Cognitive abilities usually remain sharp through the 30s. But beginning in the 40s and continuing through the 50s and 60s, there is a gradual decline in some cognitive abilities, especially in the ability to remember things. However, our brains demonstrate impressive resiliency as we age. Also, older adults have a remarkable ability to focus their attention on positive information and positive emotions. We'll discuss some cognitive and emotional changes that occur as we age.

Changes in Cognitive Speed

From about ages 20 to 40, cognitive skills remain relatively stable. However, between 40 and 80, there is a general slowing of some cognitive processes. Beginning in the late 50s, there is a slowing of three cognitive processes:

1 There is a slowing in **processing speed,** which is the rate at which we encode information into long-term memory or recall or retrieve information from long-term memory.

2 There is a slowing in **perceptual speed,** which is the rate at which we can identify a particular sensory stimulus.

3 There is a slowing in **reaction time,** which is the rate at which we respond (see, hear, move) to some stimulus.

Why is my golf game slowing down?

This slowing in processing, perceiving, and reacting partly explains why older people react more slowly when driving a car or playing golf and are slower to make decisions or understand and follow instructions.

Although there is a slowing in cognitive speed, there is no decrease in knowledge, and in fact, vocabulary increases through at least age 60. Also, there are some adults in their 60s who perform better on problem solving and other cognitive tasks than average adults in their 20s (Begley, 2010).

Besides a slowing in cognitive speed, older adults experience a problem in remembering things.

Changes in Memory

Beginning in the 40s and continuing into old age, most people complain about not remembering things. Researchers have concluded that older adults have no trouble remembering the big picture (name of a movie) but do forget many of the small details (who played the starring role). In comparison, young adults easily remember the big picture plus all the details (Schacter, 2001). So as people move into their 50s, 60s, and 70s, their complaints are true: They forget details (names, places, groceries) that may be bothersome but are usually unimportant.

Memory differences. Young adults in their 20s excel at encoding (storing) and recalling vast amounts of detail but are not as good at making sense of what all the details mean. In comparison, mature adults in their 50s excel at making sense of information but forget many details.

Am I losing my memory?

Brain changes. Decreases in memory skills result from the slowing down of memory abilities, reasoning processes, and focusing of attention. Brain scans show that these kinds of problems, which occur throughout normal aging, result from the normal loss of brain cells in the prefrontal cortex (Milham et al., 2002).

Memory-enhancing products. Americans spend billions of dollars on memory-enhancing products, such as ginkgo biloba, which researchers have repeatedly found does NOT improve memory in healthy adults, nor does it prevent cognitive decline in older adults (Snitz et al., 2009; Solomon et al., 2002). Experts advise that the best way to combat age-related memory difficulties is to exercise physically (keep heart healthy) and mentally (engage in cognitive activities like reading, doing crosswords) (G. Cohen, 2006). By consistently engaging in these activities, you may be able to improve your memory 30–40% (B. Gordon, 2007).

Next, we'll learn how the brain changes for the better as we age.

Resiliency

Research indicates that as we age, our brains become more flexible and adaptable. Though brain cells may lose processing speed, their connections to other brain cells multiply and they form more meaningful neural connections as a result of more life experiences (Anthes, 2009; Phillips, 2011). Also, the brain's left and right hemispheres become better integrated during middle age. For instance, by using brain scans, researchers found that older adults who used both brain hemispheres during a memory task performed better than older adults who used only one brain hemisphere (Cabeza et al., 2002). These findings are encouraging because they show that the brains of older adults have the ability to compensate in order to accomplish cognitive tasks (Reuter-Lorenz, 2011).

As brains become more flexible and adaptable, they also manage emotions better.

Emotions

Older adults have a "positivity bias," which means that they pay less attention to negative information and more to positive information (Carstensen, 2011; Mather, 2011; Stawski et al., 2008). Research found that the part of the brain responsible for strong negative emotions (amygdala) becomes less active with age. This focus on the positive explains why older adults report being calmer, less neurotic, and happier than younger adults, who mostly focus on negative emotions (Cabeza, 2006, 2008; A. A. Stone et al., 2010; Reuter-Lorenz, 2011).

I focus on the positive.

Next, we'll turn to sexual changes that occur as we age.

Sexual Changes

How does sex change with aging?

People in late adulthood (ages 60–80) are often not included in surveys about sexual behavior because of the common stereotype that they no longer have any interest in sexual activity or that it is inappropriate for them to engage in sex. However, a survey of men and women over age 70 found that about 57% of men and 52% of women were sexually active (Beckman et al., 2008). This survey indicates that adults can enjoy sexual activity well into their later years, especially if they know how sexual responses change and learn ways to deal with these changes. We'll discuss some of the normal changes in sexual responses that accompany aging.

Sexual Changes in Women

The most significant effect on women's sexual behavior in later adulthood is menopause.

Menopause occurs in women at about age 50 (range 35–60) and involves a gradual stoppage in secretion of the major female hormone (estrogen), which in turn results in cessation of both ovulation and the menstrual cycle.

Menopause doesn't mean I have to stop having sex.

© PhotoDisc, Inc.

During and immediately after menopause, many women experience a variety of physical symptoms.

Physical Symptoms

Most women experience hot flashes, sleep disturbance, and dryness of the vagina, which result from a decrease and eventual stoppage in the secretion of the female hormone estrogen. A lack of estrogen results in thinning of the vaginal wall and reduction of lubrication during arousal. However, there is little or no change in the ability to become sexually aroused or to reach orgasm. Because researchers find no correlation between decreased levels of hormones and sexual activity, women's continued sexual activity after menopause is affected primarily by psychological rather than physiological factors (Crooks & Baur, 2002; Potter, 2006).

Psychological Symptoms

After studying healthy women going through menopause, researchers found that women did report psychological symptoms, such as depression, anxiety, and anger. However, these symptoms were related to other stressful issues (e.g., growing older in a society that glorifies being young), rather than to the physical symptoms of menopause. In addition, women's expectations influenced their psychological outlook during menopause. Women with positive expectations about what they hope to accomplish have few psychological symptoms, compared to women who expect their lives to be over and thus feel depressed during menopause (Dennerstein et al., 1997; Neugarten, 1994).

Sexual Changes in Men

As men reach late adulthood (60s, 70s, and 80s), they may experience some physiological changes that decrease their sexual responsiveness.

Physical Symptoms

Because many of the body's physiological responses slow down, older men may require more time and stimulation to have an erection and to reach orgasm. Upon ejaculation, there may be a reduction in the force and amount of fluid. However, healthy men usually have no difficulty in becoming sexually aroused or reaching orgasm. Some men worry that their decreased ability to have an erection or reach orgasm means an end to their sexuality (Masters & Johnson, 1981). Currently, there are a few drugs approved for the treatment of impotency, which is the inability to have an erection.

Some things may take longer, but that's OK.

© PhotoDisc, Inc.

Psychological Problems

Although older men are generally more sexually active than older women, their decreased sexual abilities can make them uncomfortable and threaten their self-esteem.

However, having longer periods of stimulation, improving intimate communication, and using more imaginative sexual activity can usually compensate for men's decreased self-confidence (Bartlik & Goldstein, 2001).

Next, we'll discuss death and dying.

Death and Dying

How can I accept dying?

Have you ever wondered about your own death? How will you accept the process of dying? Will you be able to die with integrity, or will you be left in despair? These questions are perhaps of most relevance to those who have been told they have a terminal illness. After spending hundreds of hours at the bedsides of people with terminal illnesses, Elisabeth Kübler-Ross (1969) developed her stage theory of the psychological process involved in accepting one's death:

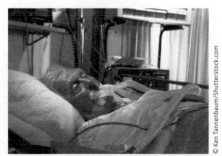

© Ken Tannenbaum/Shutterstock.com

1. Denial "This can't be happening to me." "I feel fine, there's nothing wrong with me."

2. Anger "Why me?" "How can this happen to me?" "Why couldn't it have been someone else?"

3. Bargaining "Just let me live long enough to see my daughter's marriage." "Please, I'll do anything, just give me more time!"

4. Depression "I'm losing everyone I love." "I'm so sad, what's the point of living any longer?"

5. Acceptance "I know I'm going to die soon and I'm OK with it." "There isn't much I can do to postpone death, so why not prepare for it?"

Kübler-Ross (1974) explained that some people may not go through each of these stages or they may experience a different sequence. In developing her theory, she was not trying to convey the only way or the best way for people to accept death. Rather, she described the typical response to impending death. Still, there has been much discussion during the past few decades regarding the process of death and dying, and much of this discussion is undoubtedly due to Kübler-Ross's pioneering efforts in studying the process of dying.

Next, we'll discuss a serious problem that is shared by both adolescents and seniors—a high rate of suicide. ●

Application: Suicide

Teenage/Young Adult Suicide

What is a major, preventable cause of death?

Suicide is a major, preventable cause of death. In the United States alone, there are more than 36,000 suicides each year (CDC, 2012c). The top three methods used to commit suicide are firearms (50%), suffocation (24%), and poisoning (18%) (CDC, 2012d). Among teens and young adults, the suicide rate is 6.9 and 12.7 per 100,000, respectively. People over 65 have a higher rate of suicide (14.3 per 100,000) (NIMH, 2012d).

We'll first discuss issues related to teenage and young adult suicide and then look at suicide in the elderly. We'll begin with

four real-life teenage examples that illustrate how complex the issues and causes are. In a span of only five weeks, four teenage boys—one a straight-A student, one the class clown, one deeply religious person, and one very troubled boy—committed suicide in the small southern town of Sheridan, Arkansas (adapted from *People*, May 21, 1990, pp. 56–59). Here are their sad and tragic stories.

© Sascha Burkard/Shutterstock.com

© tlorna/Shutterstock.com

© Monkey Business Images/Shutterstock.com

1 Raymond, 17 Years Old

According to the police chief, Ray had threatened to kill himself in the past, but the threats were considered teenage histrionics. He had a drinking problem, had been arrested for drunken driving, and had been sent to a rehabilitation center for several weeks. Before Ray shot himself, however, his life seemed to be improving, and he had made plans to go to college. A suicide note to his girlfriend said, "Don't blame yourself. It's nobody's fault."

© Julia Zakharova/Shutterstock.com

2 Tommy, 16 Years Old

His teenage peers considered Tommy a clown, but his best friend, Rhonda, didn't believe that. She thought Tommy's clever wit and clowning were a mask for his insecurity. On April 29, Tommy called Rhonda, which he did regularly, and told her that he was going to kill himself. Certain he would not carry out his threat, she made him promise to come to school the next day. Tommy came to school, and in one of his classes he got up and stated that he had two things to say. He said that he loved Rhonda, although they had never dated. "The other thing," he said, "is this." He pulled out a pistol and shot himself.

© Paul Matthew Photography/Shutterstock.com

3 Thomas, 19 Years Old

Thomas was a straight-A student who liked to read, listen to oldies, and hunt and fish. He did not drink, smoke, or swear. He lived too far out of town to have many buddies. His father had died when he was 9. Two years earlier, his grandfather, who had terminal cancer, committed suicide with a pistol to his head. Tommy had shot himself in the afternoon, and that very night Thomas did the same. In his suicide note he said, "Where shall I begin? I really don't know. It's hard to say what's going on anymore. A long time now I have felt like I am on the edge and slipping fast. I guess I've finally slipped over the edge."

© CREATISTA/Shutterstock.com

4 Jerry, 17 Years Old

Jerry's suicide was the last of the four and the most troubling. He was popular, gregarious, good looking, and so deeply religious that he was nicknamed "preacher boy." The night after Tommy's suicide Jerry told his mother, "I can't understand how anyone would commit suicide—that was the coward's way." That same night he called his girlfriend and said, "I love you. I'll talk to you tomorrow." The next day he stayed home from school, and around noon he shot himself in the head. The family insists that Jerry's death was accidental.

© DEKANARYAS/Shutterstock.com

Notice that in the above examples, family and friends could not believe that two of the four adolescents would ever even think of committing suicide. That's because one was a straight-A student and the other was very popular and deeply religious. In the other two cases, one adolescent had said he was thinking about suicide and one had made a previous attempt. Thus, if and when adolescents talk about committing suicide, parents and friends need to take such talk seriously. In other cases, the problems, symptoms, or events leading up to or triggering suicide may be difficult to recognize.

On the next page, we will identify various risk factors to increase your awareness and knowledge of the precipitators of suicide. But first, we'll discuss suicide in the elderly.

Suicide in the Elderly

Suicide rates in the elderly increase with age, from 14 per 100,000 for individuals aged 65–74 to as high as 48 per 100,000 for those 85 and older (NIMH, 2009b).

Why are rates so high? Common risk factors for suicide among the elderly include serious health problems, stressful life events, loneliness, and especially depression, which is present in about 90–95% of those who commit suicide (Cavanagh et al., 2003). There is also a growing trend of murder-suicide, in which one member of an elderly couple kills the other and then takes his or her own life.

One controversial method of suicide is especially relevant to the elderly and that is assisted suicide.

I have six months to live and I'm in constant pain.

© Alexander Raths/Shutterstock.com

Polls indicate that although only 12% of those surveyed think that suicide is morally acceptable (Sharp, 2003), 46% said a doctor should be allowed to help a person "commit suicide" provided that person has a painful and incurable disease (C. L. Grossman & Nichols, 2006). In the late 1990s, Oregon voters twice approved an assisted suicide law, which allows a mentally competent patient to request a lethal dose of drugs if at least two doctors determine that the person has less than six months to live. Assisted suicide is also currently legal in the Netherlands, Belgium, and Switzerland (CBS News, 2004b).

Let's take a look at both sides of the debate on assisted suicide.

Opponents of Doctor-Assisted Suicide

Opponents include religious groups that believe taking one's life should never be sanctioned, others who think doctors should not be involved in helping people take their own lives, and those who fear caretakers may coerce vulnerable people into assisted suicide to reduce the financial burden of caring for them (CBS News, 2004b; Verhovek, 2002). For example, making assisted suicide easier may increase the chances that people who are suffering from mental problems or temporary emotional difficulties will take their own lives without exploring other possibilities for living.

Proponents of Doctor-Assisted Suicide

Proponents explain that each of us has the moral right to end life if we decide that life has become unbearable for health reasons (CBS News, 2004b). The *New England Journal of Medicine* published an article by a group of doctors who proposed a policy of legalized physician-assisted death with safeguards to protect patients, preserve the integrity of physicians, and ensure that voluntary physician-assisted death occurs only as a last resort (F. G. Miller et al., 1994). Researchers reviewed the effects of Oregon's assisted suicide law and concluded that there have not been any of the abuses or problems feared by opponents and that most of the individuals who chose doctor-assisted suicide were well-educated, were mostly elderly cancer patients who had health insurance, and were concerned about loss of bodily functions, increasing pain, and being a burden on family members or caregivers (Gibbs, 2009; Wineberg & Werth, 2003).

The pros and cons of doctor-assisted suicide will continue to be debated, especially since the elderly population will almost double in the next 35 years.

Preventing Suicide

How can suicide be prevented? We've learned that suicide is a major leading cause of death among youth and adults. It is also a preventable public health program. The prevention of suicide begins with identifying its risk or warning factors.

Identify Risk Factors

The table lists some of the major risk or warning factors for suicidal behavior (NCCBH, 2012; NIMH, 2012d; Rudd, 2010):

Risk Factors for Suicidal Behavior

- Exhibiting depression or a dramatic change in mood
- Appearing agitated or angry
- Using increased amounts of alcohol or other drugs
- Having a prior suicide attempt or self-injurious behavior
- Putting affairs in order
- Behaving recklessly or engaging in risky behaviors
- Talking or writing about death, dying, or suicide
- Talking or writing about feeling worthless
- Withdrawing from friends, family, or society

Psychiatric Evaluation and Psychosocial Intervention

After risk factors are identified, the next step is a thorough medical and psychological evaluation of the individual as well as interviews with the individual's family members—with each family member being assured of confidentiality (Weller et al., 2001). Based on such information, a treatment plan is developed.

© David Castillo Dominici/Shutterstock.com

In the short term, (1) a contract is negotiated so that the person will not harm him- or herself, (2) lethal means are removed from the home (guns and drugs), and (3) support and a 24-hour contact are provided. In the long term, the individual's personal problems are addressed, which may include help with improving his or her self-image and developing better interpersonal skills and functioning. Because most suicidal individuals also have serious psychological problems (depression, loneliness, anxiety), psychotherapy and psychiatric medication are usually needed (Fristad & Shaver, 2001). ●

Are Teens Too Young to Drive?

Car crashes are the No. 1 cause of death and disability for teens, killing more than 5,000 a year and injuring 300,000 more. Teenage drivers are about four times more likely to crash than older drivers and three times more likely to die in a crash. The risk of crashes is highest for 16-year-olds; one in five will have a car crash within the first year of driving.

1 Besides traffic accidents, what are other costs or dangers of teen driving?

The possibility of raising the legal driving age has been receiving increasing attention. Proponents argue that teens are too immature to handle the responsibility of driving. In fact, a recent national survey found that nearly two-thirds (61%) of people believe that a 16-year-old is too young to have a driver's license, and more than half (53%) think teens should be at least 18 to obtain a driver's license. Opponents of raising the legal driving age argue that responsible teen drivers should not be punished for the mistakes of careless teens causing accidents.

2 What immature teen characteristics may contribute to their irresponsible driving?

The opinion of the majority of Americans about teens being too young to drive is supported by scientific findings.

3 What other irresponsible teen behaviors may be a result of an "executive branch" that is not yet fully developed?

Brain researchers report that the "executive branch" of the teen brain—the part that considers risks and consequences, makes judgments, and controls impulsive behavior—is not fully developed until age 25 and is far less developed in 16-year-olds than in older teens.

The danger involved with drivers who do not yet have a fully developed executive branch is evident in the three most common teenage driving mistakes that lead to crashes: failing to scan the road ahead, misjudging driving conditions, and becoming distracted. Planning, following rules, and paying attention are all functions of the executive branch.

4 What part of the brain is responsible for risk-taking behaviors?

A contributing factor to teens' poor judgment is that they don't understand that well-established risky driving behaviors are dangerous. For instance, only 28% of teens reported using a cell phone is a risk; only 10% said having other teens in the car is a distraction while driving; and only 50% reported not wearing a seat belt or speeding is dangerous. All these things place drivers in serious risk of harm.

Several states have imposed a graduated driver's license program, which

5 What are some factors that are not specific to teens that increase the probability of getting into a car accident?

© Rich Legg/iStockphoto

phases in driving privileges, such as driving late at night and having multiple passengers in their car, for beginning drivers as they gain experience. These restrictive programs could save the lives of as many as 2,000 teenagers each year.

6 Are stricter laws the solution to reducing the dangers of teen driving?

But, how far should lawmakers go to reduce the dangers of teen drivers? Jeffrey Runge, an emergency room doctor, has treated many teen crash victims and makes it clear that lawmakers should take the dangers of teenage drivers very seriously: "If we had any other disease that was wiping out our teenagers at the rate of thousands per year, there would be no end to what we would do as a society to stop that" (Stafford, 2005).

Adapted from Associated Press, 2006c; Brophy, 2006; CDC, 2011d; L. Copeland, 2011; R. Davis, 2005; Henderson, 2006; Lyon, 2009a; O'Donnell, 2005; Parker-Pope, 2011; Stafford, 2005; Vetter, 2008; Williamson, 2005

Summary Test

A Physical Development: Puberty

© Andrey_Popov/Shutterstock.com

1. Girls and boys experience three major biological changes as they go through a period called **(a)** _____. For both girls and boys, one of these changes is the development of **(b)** _____ maturity, which for girls includes the first menstrual cycle, called **(c)** _____, and for boys includes the production of sperm. These physical changes in girls and boys are triggered by a portion of the brain called the **(d)** _____. A second change is the development of **(e)** _____ sexual characteristics, such as pubic hair and gender-specific physical changes. A third change is a surge in **(f)** _____ growth, especially height. The changes for girls tend to start about two years earlier than those for boys.

B Cognitive & Emotional Development

2. Piaget's fourth cognitive stage, which begins in adolescence and continues into adulthood, is called the **(a)** _____ stage. During this stage, adolescents and adults develop the ability to think about **(b)** _____ concepts, plan for the future, and solve abstract problems. One reason adolescents engage in more risky behaviors is that they have an underdeveloped **(c)** _____ but a fully functioning emotional center, called the **(d)** _____.

C Morality & Parenting

© Leah-Anne Thompson/iStockphoto

3. According to Kohlberg's theory, moral reasoning can be classified into three levels, and everyone progresses through the levels in the same order. However, not all adults reach the higher stages. The first level, the **(a)** _____ level, has two stages. In stage 1, moral decisions are determined primarily through fear of punishment, while at stage 2 they are guided by satisfying one's self-interest. The second level, the **(b)** _____ level, also has two stages. In the first of these, stage 3, people conform to the standards of others they value; in stage 4, they conform to the laws of society. In the third level, the **(c)** _____ level, moral decisions are made after thinking about all the alternatives and striking a balance between human rights and the laws of society.

4. Making impersonal moral decisions, such as keeping the money found in a stranger's wallet, involves areas of the brain associated with retrieving **(a)** _____. In comparison, making personal moral decisions, such as keeping the money found in a fellow worker's wallet, involves areas of the brain associated with **(b)** _____.

5. Parenting styles affect many aspects of adolescents' development. Parents who attempt to shape and control their children in accordance with a set standard of conduct are termed **(a)** _____. Parents who attempt to direct their children's activities in a rational and intelligent way and are supportive, loving, and committed are called **(b)** _____. Parents who are less controlling and behave with a nonpunishing and accepting attitude toward their children's impulses are called **(c)** _____.

D Personality & Social Development

There are 30 million of us.

© Lucky Business/Shutterstock.com

6. How you describe yourself, including your values, goals, traits, interests, and motivations, is a function of your sense of **(a)** _____, which is part of the problem to be faced in stage 5 of Erikson's eight **(b)** _____ stages. Those who are unsuccessful in resolving the problems of this stage will experience **(c)** _____, which results in low self-esteem, and may become socially withdrawn.

7. An adolescent's feeling of worth, attractiveness, and social competence is called _____, which is influenced particularly by physical appearance, social acceptability, and management of public behaviors (anxiety and stress).

8. The challenges of adulthood are covered in the last three of Erikson's eight **(a)** _____ stages. According to his theory, in stage 6, young adults face the problems of intimacy versus **(b)** _____. In stage 7, middle adults face problems of generativity versus **(c)** _____. In stage 8, older adults reflect on their lives; if they feel positive and content about how they lived and what they accomplished, they will have a feeling of satisfaction or **(d)** _____; if not, they will have a feeling of regret and **(e)** _____.

F Gender Roles, Love & Relationships

© zuluphoto/Shutterstock.com

9. During childhood and adolescence, males and females experience pressures and expectations from parents, peers, and society to behave in different ways. These expected patterns of behavior and thought, called _____, influence cognitive, personality, and social development.

10. The kind of love that involves continually thinking about the loved one and is accompanied by sexual feelings and powerful emotional reactions is called **(a)** _____ love. The kind of love that involves trusting and tender feelings for someone whose life is closely bound up with one's own is called **(b)** _____ love. Sternberg's triangular theory of love has three components: feeling physiological aroused and attracted is **(c)** _____, feeling close and committed is **(d)** _____, and pledging to nourish feelings is **(e)** _____. Infatuated love primarily activates the brain's **(f)** _____ and causes feelings of euphoria. In comparison, a more committed love activates additional **(g)** _____ brain areas, which help in forming a longer-lasting relationship.

11. One way that we select a mate is by developing an organized mental list of desirable characteristics and then looking for someone who matches this mental list, which is called a _____.

G Research Focus: Happy Marriages

12. Gottman identified four problems that can result in the failure of a long-term relationship: these problems involve **(a)** _____, _____, _____, and _____. In successful marriages, couples demonstrate **(b)** _____, _____, and _____.

H Cultural Diversity: Preferences for Partners

13. People's lists of desirable traits for a mate show remarkable similarity across cultures. However, there are some differences in ranking between the genders; for example, men rank **(a)** _____ higher than women do, and women rank **(b)** _____ higher than men do. In the United States, today's men are expressing some traditionally female preferences for partners and women are expressing preferences that have generally been attributed to men. For instance, women want more **(c)** _____ in their relationships than ever before.

United States: Love ranked **FIRST**, that is, love was the most important factor in choosing a spouse.

Iran: Love ranked **THIRD**, while ranked higher were education, ambition, chastity.

I Adulthood & Aging

14. The gradual and natural slowing of our physical and psychological processes from middle through late adulthood is called **(a)** _____ aging. This process occurs when certain **(b)** _____ and _____ interfere with organ functioning and when the natural production of toxic **(c)** _____ (free radicals) causes random damage to body organs and to DNA (the building blocks of life).

This aging process, which decreases the effectiveness of sensory and body organs, eventually exceeds the body's ability to repair itself and results in greater susceptible to **(d)** _____.

15. If the aging process is caused by genetic defects, physiological problems, or diseases, it is called _____ aging, an example of which is Alzheimer's disease.

16. In later adulthood (about age 50), women experience a gradual reduction in the secretion of estrogen, which results in cessation of ovulation and the menstrual cycle; this is called **(a)** _____. In late adulthood (60–80), men do not stop producing testosterone, but they may experience a decrease in sexual responsiveness due to **(b)** _____ changes.

J Application: Suicide

17. The suicide rate for people age 65 and over is **(a)** _____ than the rate for teens and young adults. The most common method used to commit suicide is **(b)** _____.

18. Among the risk factors for suicide in the elderly are health problems and stressful life events, but the major contributing cause is **(a)** _____. Currently, there is considerable discussion in the United States over the right of a person with a terminal disease to end his or her life through **(b)** _____ suicide.

Unless otherwise noted, all images are © Cengage Learning

Links to Learning

Key Terms/Key People

adolescence, 407

aging process, 423

authoritarian parents, 413

authoritative parents, 413

biopsychosocial approach, 409

cognitive development, 410

commitment, 418

companionate love, 418

consummate love, 418

conventional level, 412

emerging adulthood, 414

Erikson's psychosocial stages, 415

estrogen, 408

evolutionary psychology theory, 417

female secondary sexual characteristics, 408

formal operations stage, 410

gender roles, 417

intimacy, 418

Kohlberg's theory of moral reasoning, 412

Kübler-Ross, Elisabeth, 425

limbic system, 411

male secondary sexual characteristics, 408

menarche, 408

menopause, 425

normal aging, 423

passion, 418

passionate love, 418

pathological aging, 423

perceptual speed, 424

permissive parents, 413

personal identity or self-identity, 414

personality and social development, 414

personality change, 415

postconventional level, 412

preconventional level, 412

prefrontal cortex, 411

primary sexual characteristics, 408

processing speed, 424

puberty, 408

reaction time, 424

schema, 419

secondary sexual characteristics, 408

self-esteem, 414

social role theory, 417

stage 5: identity versus role confusion, 415

stage 6: intimacy versus isolation, 415

stage 7: generativity versus stagnation, 415

stage 8: integrity versus despair, 415

testosterone, 408

triangular theory of love, 418

Media Resources

Go to **CengageBrain.com** to access Psychology CourseMate, where you will find an interactive eBook, glossaries, flashcards, quizzes, videos, answers to Critical Thinking questions, and more. You can also access Virtual Psychology Labs, an interactive laboratory experience designed to illustrate key experiments first-hand.

MODULE 19 Freudian & Humanistic Theories

Personality

How did he become a deceiver and a liar?

Ted Haggard founded New Life Church in the basement of his house 25 years ago and became a prominent author and national evangelical Christian leader with a congregation of 14,000 worshippers in the largest church in Colorado. He is married with five children and has boyish dimples and a warm smile.

In 2006, at the peak of his career, a male prostitute accused Haggard of having a three-year sexual affair with him and of using drugs. This accusation was alarming not only because Haggard was a married pastor, but also because he publicly supported a constitutional amendment banning gay marriage.

When the accusations were first broadcast on the news, Haggard confessed to church officials, saying, "Ninety-eight percent of what you know of me was the real me. Two percent of me would rise up, and I couldn't overcome it" (Haggard, 2006a). Then, in a television news interview the next morning, Haggard denied ever having sex with a male prostitute and ever using drugs. Church officials were shocked and appalled when they saw the other side of Ted during the interview as he lied while still smiling at the camera, appearing calm and assured.

At the height of his career, Ted Haggard, well-known pastor, confessed to "sexual immorality."

© Denris Oda

As evidence of Haggard having sexual encounters with a male prostitute and using drugs continued to build, he made the following public confession: "The fact is that I am guilty of sexual immorality…I'm a deceiver and a liar. There is part of my life that is so repulsive and dark that I've been warring against it all of my adult life" (Haggard, 2006a). Haggard resigned as president of the 30-million-member National Association of Evangelicals and was dismissed as senior pastor of New Life Church. In less than 24 hours, everything Haggard had worked so hard for during the past 25 years quickly slipped away from him.

Figuring someone out involves examining the puzzling, fascinating, and complex components of our innermost selves, our personalities.

Personality is a combination of long-lasting and distinctive behaviors, thoughts, motives, and emotions that typify how we react and adapt to other people and situations.

Haggard's moral public persona and dark private self raise a number of questions about personality: How does personality develop? Why do personalities differ? How well do we know ourselves? These kinds of questions are explored by theories of personality.

A **theory of personality** is an organized attempt to describe and explain how personalities develop and why personalities differ.

On the one hand, personality theories try to explain why Haggard's personality ended his career as an evangelical pastor. On the other hand, personality theories also try to explain why some individuals have personalities that help them overcome horrendous problems and achieve personal success. One such individual is Greg Mathis.

Changing Personality

Greg Mathis was raised by his mother in the very dangerous projects in Detroit. During his youth, he joined a gang called the Errol Flynns, who wore stylish three-piece suits while stealing from others. In an effort to get Greg out of the projects and away from his thuggish lifestyle, he was sent to live with his middle-class cousins. It didn't take long for Greg to persuade the local youth to commit crimes. Even spending time in jail didn't change his ways.

How did he change from a gangbanger to a judge?

The turning point for Greg took place when his mother visited him in jail and told him she had been diagnosed with cancer. Greg, who was then 17 years old, prayed to God and promised that if his mother was saved he would change his life by pursuing and staying on the right path. True to his word, Greg changed his ways as his mother recovered.

Greg began working at a fast-food restaurant while taking evening classes. He finished high school, then college, and then law school. He later became the youngest judge in Michigan history, then a district court judge, and most recently a judge on his award-winning television court show, "Judge Mathis."

Judge Mathis is committed to helping troubled youth by working to improve the community he grew up in. He opened a community center in Detroit that provides youth with career training, job opportunities, and college enrollment assistance (Mathis, 2002; *About the judge*, 2012).

Greg Mathis, formerly a violent gang member, became a respected and accomplished judge.

© AP Images/CharlesBennett

Mathis's story is an emotionally painful search for identity, culminating in the discovery and development of his legal career. We'll discuss a theory of personality that emphasizes the development of our full potential.

What's Coming

We'll discuss two very different theories of personality: Sigmund Freud's psychodynamic theory emphasizes unconscious forces, irrational thoughts, and the lasting impressions of childhood experiences, whereas humanistic theories emphasize our rational processes and our natural striving to reach our true potentials.

We'll begin with a look at Ted Haggard's problems and where his inner demons came from. ●

A Freud's Psychodynamic Theory

Definition

Why sexual immorality at age 50?

Freud's theory of personality begins with a controversial assumption that is an important key to unlocking the secrets of personality. To understand how Freud found this key idea, we'll journey back in time to the late 1800s.

At that time, Freud was wondering why several of his women patients had developed very noticeable physical symptoms, such as losing all sensation in their hands or being unable to control the movements of their legs. What most puzzled Freud, who was a medical doctor, was that despite these obvious physical complaints, he could not identify a single physical cause for these symptoms. Somehow, Freud's brilliant mind solved this problem and, in so doing, found an important key to unlocking the secrets of personality. Freud reasoned that since there were no observable physical or neurological causes of the women's physical symptoms, the causes must come from unconscious psychological forces (Westen & Gabbard, 1999).

In the 1800s, Freud's belief that human behavior was influenced by unconscious psychological forces was revolutionary, and it led to his equally revolutionary theory of personality.

The **psychodynamic theory of personality** emphasizes the importance of early childhood experiences, unconscious or repressed thoughts that we cannot voluntarily access, and the conflicts between conscious and unconscious forces that influence our feelings, thoughts, and behaviors.

Freud believed not only that unconscious psychological forces had a powerful influence on personality but also that these forces originated in early childhood. If Freud were alive today, he would

© Kevin Moloney/Getty Images

Freud would say that childhood experiences and unconscious forces played a role in Ted Haggard's "sexual immorality."

look for reasons behind Ted Haggard's self-confessed "sexual immorality" at age 50 by searching through Ted's childhood and his unconscious thoughts and forces. Here's what Freud would find.

Background. Ted Haggard was raised in a very religious family with a born-again father and a mother who counted the days to Sunday to help get Ted and his siblings excited about church. Ted remembers dressing in starched shirts and clip-on ties, clipping his nails just before church, and never missing a service. Ted wanted to attend journalism school, but his father pushed him to attend a Christian college. Soon after, Ted recalls receiving a calling from God to become a pastor (Asay, 2007; *Colorado Springs Gazette,* 2002). Even though Ted believes God wanted him to become a pastor, he admits to battling dark sexual desires throughout his adult life, which finally made him behave in inappropriate ways (Haggard, 2006a).

Freud might point to Ted's childhood, which was full of religious pressure, as greatly affecting his personality development and causing problems that eventually overwhelmed Ted. Explaining the complex development of someone's personality, such as Ted Haggard's, is such a difficult task that only a dozen or so psychologists have tried. One of the best-known attempts to explain personality is included in Sigmund Freud's (1901/1960, 1924, 1940/1961) overall theory of psychoanalysis, which includes two related theories: a method of psychotherapy, which we'll discuss in Module 24, and a theory of personality development, which we'll focus on here.

We'll begin with Freud's controversial and revolutionary assumption that unconscious psychological forces influence behavior.

Conscious Versus Unconscious Forces

Ted Haggard's life was full of inconsistencies. His public behaviors as a pastor and husband were moral and respectable, but

Why was Ted Haggard fighting his dark side?

his private behaviors of having sexual relations with a male escort were immoral and degrading to his character: "The public person I was wasn't a lie; it was just incomplete…the darkness increased and finally dominated me. As a result, I did things that were contrary to everything I believe" (Haggard, 2006a).

Ted indicated that just as he had preached all along, he believed homosexual acts were immoral and lying about a sexual affair was equivalent to "the stinking garbage of a rotting sin" (Haggard, 2006b). In doing so, he was expressing conscious thoughts.

Conscious thoughts are wishes, desires, or thoughts that we are aware of, or can recall, at any given moment.

However, Freud theorized that our conscious thoughts are only a small part of our total mental activity, much of which involves unconscious thoughts or forces (Adler, 2006; Westen et al., 2008).

Unconscious forces are wishes, desires, or thoughts that, because of their disturbing or threatening content, we automatically repress and cannot voluntarily access.

Did Ted have sexual relations with a male escort because of some unconscious forces that he was unaware of and had repressed? According to Freud, although repressed thoughts are unconscious, they may influence our behaviors through unconscious motivation.

Unconscious motivation is a Freudian concept that refers to the influence of repressed thoughts, desires, or impulses on our conscious thoughts and behaviors.

Freud used unconscious forces and motivation to explain why we say or do things that we cannot explain or understand. Once he assumed that there were unconscious forces and motivations, Freud needed to find ways to explore the unconscious.

Conscious thoughts

↓

Behavior

↑

Unconscious forces

Freud would say that unconscious thoughts, desires, and feelings influence behaviors.

Techniques to Discover the Unconscious

What was in Ted Haggard's unconscious?

It was one thing for Freud to propose the existence of powerful unconscious psychological forces and motivations, but it was quite another thing for him to show that such unconscious forces actually existed. For example, were there any signs that unconscious psychological forces were making Ted Haggard act out his sexual desires that were contrary to his conscious beliefs?

Ted's very strong religious upbringing and pressure from his father to attend a Christian college may have been too much for Ted to cope with as he was growing up. These early experiences may have served as unconscious forces that led him to act out against his Christian values, such as by having an affair with a male escort even though he was a married pastor with five children. Also, in contrast to his homosexual desires and his long-term relationship with a male escort is his strong public advocacy to ban gay marriages. The inconsistency between the values Ted learned while growing up and his sexual desires during adulthood undeniably led to Ted feeling anxious and guilty. As a way of coping with his anxiety and guilt, Ted actively condemned gay marriages, a behavior that is directly opposite to his own unacceptable thoughts and wishes.

Freud proposed ways to unlock unconscious wishes and feelings.

Because neither Ted nor any of us can easily or voluntarily reveal or talk about our unconscious thoughts and desires, Freud needed to find ways for his patients to reveal their unconscious thoughts and desires, some of which may be psychologically threatening or disturbing. From observing his patients during therapy, Freud believed he had found three techniques that uncovered, revealed, or hinted at a person's unconscious wishes and desires.

Three techniques. Freud's three techniques to uncover the unconscious were free association, dream interpretation, and analysis of slips of the tongue (commonly known as Freudian slips) (Grunbaum, 2006).

Free Association

One of Freud's techniques for revealing the unconscious was to encourage his patients to relax and to sit back or lie down on his now-famous couch and talk freely about anything. He called this process free association.

Free association is a Freudian technique in which clients are encouraged to talk about any thoughts or images that enter their head; the assumption is that this kind of free-flowing, uncensored talking will provide clues to unconscious material.

Free association, which is one of Freud's important discoveries, continues to be used today by some therapists (Lothane, 2006b). However, not all therapists agree that free associations actually reveal a client's unconscious thoughts, desires, and wishes (Grunbaum, 1993).

Dream Interpretation

Freud listened to and interpreted his patients' dreams because he believed that dreams represent the purest form of free association and a path to the unconscious.

Dream interpretation, a Freudian technique of analyzing dreams, is based on the assumption that dreams contain underlying, hidden meanings and symbols that provide clues to unconscious thoughts and desires. Freud distinguished between the dream's obvious story or plot, called manifest content, and the dream's hidden or disguised meanings or symbols, called latent content.

Exploring the unconscious with free association, dreams, and slips of the tongue

For example, Freud interpreted the hidden meaning of dreams' objects such as sticks and knives as being symbols for male sexual organs and interpreted other objects (such as boxes and ovens) as symbols for female sexual organs. The therapist's task is to look behind the dream's manifest content (bizarre stories and symbols) and interpret the symbols' hidden or latent content, which provides clues to a person's unconscious wishes, feelings, and thoughts (Lothane, 2006a).

Freudian Slips

At one time or another, most of us, according to Freud, unintentionally reveal some unconscious thought or desire by making what is now called a Freudian slip (Grunbaum, 2006).

Freudian slips are mistakes or slips of the tongue that we make in everyday speech; such mistakes, which are often embarrassing, are thought to reflect unconscious thoughts or wishes.

For example, a colleague was lecturing on the importance of regular health care. She said, "It is important to visit a veterinarian for regular checkups." According to Freud, mistakes like substituting *veterinarian* for *physician* are not accidental but rather "intentional" ways of expressing unconscious desires. As it turns out, our colleague, who is in very good health, was having serious doubts about her relationship with a person who happened to be a veterinarian.

Freud assumed that free association, dream interpretation, and slips of the tongue share one thing in common: They are all mental processes that are the least controlled by our conscious, rational, and logical minds. As a result, he believed that these three techniques allowed uncensored clues to slip out and reveal our deeper unconscious wishes and desires (Grunbaum, 2006).

According to Freud's theory, there is a continuing battle going on in our minds between conscious thoughts and unconscious forces. How our minds fight these battles is perhaps one of Freud's best-known theories, and you'll easily recognize many of the terms, including *id, ego,* and *superego.* ●

B Divisions of the Mind

Id, Ego, and Superego

Ted Haggard wrote an apology letter that was read to his congregation. Ted's letter revealed some of his problems and internal struggle. Here is an excerpt from his letter (Haggard, 2006a): "For extended periods of time, I would enjoy victory and rejoice in freedom. Then, from time to time, the dirt that I thought was gone would resurface, and I would find myself thinking thoughts and experiencing desires that were contrary to everything I believe and teach."

What was in his apology letter?

Freud might say that Haggard's immoral acts result from inner conflicts between his id and superego.

© Kevin Moloney/Getty Images

This excerpt and other quotes you've read earlier in this module suggest that Ted was fighting a number of psychological and emotional battles. After years of maintaining his privacy, Ted's problems became public when he confirmed that accusations of him having sexual relations with a male escort were true. According to Freud's theory, some of Ted's driving forces were rising from unconscious battles among three separate mental processes, which you know as the id, ego, and superego.

Iceberg example. To understand how the id, ego, and superego interact, imagine an iceberg floating in the sea. The part of the iceberg that is above water represents conscious forces of which we are aware, while the parts below the water represent unconscious forces of which we are not aware.

Freud divided the mind into three separate processes, each with a different function. Because of their different functions, Freud believed that interactions among the id, ego, and superego would result in conflicts (Westen et al., 2008).

Please begin at the top left with number **1**, the id.

1 Id: Pleasure Seeker

Freud believed that mental processes must have a source of energy, which he called the id.

The **id,** which is Freud's first division of the mind to develop, contains two biological drives—sex and aggression—that are the source of all psychic or mental energy; the id's goal is to pursue pleasure and satisfy the biological drives.

Freud assumed that the id operated at a totally unconscious level, which is analogous to an iceberg's massive underwater bulk. The id operates according to the pleasure principle.

The **pleasure principle** operates to satisfy drives and avoid pain, without concern for moral restrictions or society's regulations.

You can think of the id as a spoiled child who behaves in a totally selfish, pleasure-seeking way without regard for reason, logic, or morality. Simply following the pleasure principle leads to conflict with others (parents), and this conflict results in the development of the ego.

2 Ego: Executive Negotiator between Id and Superego

As infants discover that parents put restrictions on satisfying their wishes, infants learn to control their wishes through the development of an ego.

The **ego,** which is Freud's second division of the mind, develops from the id during infancy; the ego's goal is to find safe and socially acceptable ways of satisfying the id's desires and to negotiate between the id's wants and the superego's prohibitions.

Freud said that a relatively large part of the ego's material is conscious (iceberg above water), such as information that we have gathered in adapting to our environments. A smaller part of the ego's material is unconscious (below water), such as threatening wishes that have been repressed. In contrast to the id's pleasure principle, the ego follows the reality principle.

The **reality principle** is a policy of satisfying a wish or desire only if there is a socially acceptable outlet available.

You can think of the ego as an executive negotiator that operates in a reasonable, logical, and socially acceptable way in finding outlets for satisfaction. The ego works to resolve conflicts that may arise because of different goals of the id and superego.

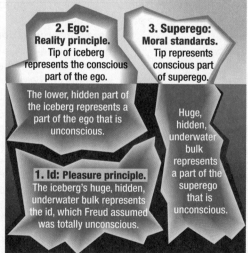

2. Ego: Reality principle. Tip of iceberg represents the conscious part of the ego.

The lower, hidden part of the iceberg represents a part of the ego that is unconscious.

3. Superego: Moral standards. Tip represents conscious part of superego.

Huge, hidden, underwater bulk represents a part of the superego that is unconscious.

1. Id: Pleasure principle. The iceberg's huge, hidden, underwater bulk represents the id, which Freud assumed was totally unconscious.

3 Superego: Regulator

As children learn that they must follow rules and regulations in satisfying their wishes, they develop a superego.

The **superego,** which is Freud's third division of the mind, develops from the ego during early childhood; the superego's goal is to apply the moral values and standards of one's parents or caregivers and society in satisfying one's wishes.

Think of the iceberg's visible tip as representing that part of the superego's moral standards of which we are conscious or aware and the huge underwater bulk as representing the part of the superego's moral standards that are unconscious or outside our awareness.

A child develops a superego through interactions with the parents or caregivers and by taking on or incorporating the parents' or caregivers' standards, values, and rules. The superego's power is in making the person feel guilty if the rules are disobeyed. Because the pleasure-seeking id wants to avoid feeling guilty, it is motivated to listen to the superego. You can think of a superego as a moral guardian or conscience that is trying to regulate or control the id's wishes and impulses.

Disagreements. Freud believed that in some situations there is little or no disagreement between the goals of the id and superego, which means a person experiences little if any conflict. However, in other situations, there could be disagreements between the goals of the id and superego, which result in the ego (executive negotiator) trying to mediate this conflict. Freud describes a number of mental processes that the ego uses to mediate conflicts between the id and superego. We'll next discuss these mental processes, called defense mechanisms.

Unless otherwise noted, all images are © Cengage Learning

Anxiety

Why do you feel anxious?

Suppose you know that you should study for tomorrow's exam but at the same time you want to go to a friend's party. Freud explained that in this kind of situation there is a conflict between the desires of the pleasure-seeking id and the goals of the conscience-regulating superego, and this conflict causes anxiety.

Anxiety, in Freudian theory, is an uncomfortable feeling that results from inner conflicts between the primitive desires of the id and the moral goals of the superego.

For example, the study-or-party situation sets up a conflict between the pleasure-seeking goal of the id, which is to go to the party, and the conscience-keeping goal of the superego, which is to stay home and study.

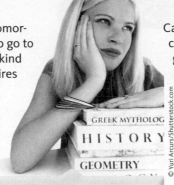

What happens if you want to party but know you should study?

Caught in the middle of this id–superego conflict is the ego, which, like any good executive, tries to negotiate an acceptable solution. However, this id–superego conflict along with the ego's continuing negotiations to resolve this conflict causes anxious feelings. Freud suggested that the ego, as executive negotiator, tries to reduce the anxious feelings by using a number of mental processes, which he called defense mechanisms (Cramer, 2006).

Defense Mechanisms

Have you ever rationalized?

Freud reasoned that anxiety is a sure sign of the id–superego inner conflict and that in order to reduce levels of anxiety, the ego may use defense mechanisms (Beresford, 2012; Cramer, 2003, 2006).

Defense mechanisms are Freudian processes that operate at unconscious levels and that use self-deception or untrue explanations to protect the ego from being overwhelmed by anxiety.

According to Freud, a student's ego has two ways to reduce anxiety over deciding whether to party or study. The student's ego can take realistic steps to reduce anxiety, such as motivating or convincing the student to stay home and study. Or the student's ego can use a number of defense mechanisms, which reduce anxiety by deceiving the student to think it's fine to party and then study tomorrow. Here is a brief summary of some of Freud's more popular defense mechanisms.

Rationalization involves covering up the true reasons for actions, thoughts, or feelings by making up excuses and incorrect explanations.

A student may rationalize that by going to a party tonight he or she will feel more motivated to study for the exam tomorrow, even if he or she will be very tired and in no mood or condition to study tomorrow.

Denial is refusing to recognize some anxiety-provoking event or piece of information that is clear to others.

Heavy smokers use denial when they disregard the scientific evidence that smoking increases the risk of lung cancer and cardiovascular disease; in addition, they use rationalization when they say they can quit any time they want.

Repression involves blocking and pushing unacceptable or threatening feelings, wishes, or experiences into the unconscious.

Having feelings of jealousy about your best friend's academic success might be threatening to your self-concept, so you unknowingly block these unwanted feelings by also unknowingly pushing them into your unconscious.

Projection falsely and unconsciously attributes your own unacceptable feelings, traits, or thoughts to individuals or objects.

Defense mechanisms function like a mental traffic cop trying to reduce conflict and anxiety.

A student who refuses to accept responsibility for cheating during exams may look at other students and decide they are cheating.

Reaction formation involves substituting behaviors, thoughts, or feelings that are the direct opposite of unacceptable ones.

A person who feels guilty about engaging in sexual activity may use reaction formation by joining a religious group that bans sex.

Displacement involves transferring feelings about, or response to, an object that causes anxiety to another person or object that is less threatening.

If you were anxious about getting angry at your best friend, you might unknowingly displace your anger by picking an argument with a safer individual, such as a salesclerk, waiter, or stranger.

Sublimation, which is a type of displacement, involves redirecting a threatening or forbidden desire, usually sexual, into a socially acceptable one.

For instance, a person might sublimate strong sexual desires by channeling that energy into physical activities.

Conclusions. Freud believed that defense mechanisms are totally unconscious, which means that, if a best friend or spouse points out that you are being defensive, you will absolutely deny it. We all use defense mechanisms at some time, and they can be helpful or harmful. For example, the occasional use of defense mechanisms is normal and helps reduce conflict and anxiety so we can continue to function as we work on the real cause of our anxiety. However, the overuse of defense mechanisms may prevent us from recognizing or working on the real causes of our anxiety. There is growing scientific evidence that we do indeed use unconscious defense mechanisms much as Freud theorized, which is to reduce anxiety and conflict. In fact, research reveals that many of us have a dominant or most-often-used defense mechanism and that our dominant defense mechanism may change across our life span. (M. C. Anderson, 2009d; Cramer, 2003, 2006). For instance, longitudinal research finds that the use of denial increases between adolescence and adulthood (Cramer, 2009, 2012).

We have discussed the three divisions of the mind—id, ego, and superego—and how the ego may use defense mechanisms to reduce anxiety. Now we'll turn to how one's ego and personality develop. ●

Development: Dealing with Conflicts

What shaped Ted's personality?

Imagine a theory so broad that it is able to describe almost exactly how and why your personality developed the way it did and why you did or did not develop certain personality problems along the way. Such is Sigmund Freud's personality theory, which can give a complex description of how each of us develops a different personality.

Case study. For example, let's return to the case of Ted Haggard. He was raised in a strong Christian family that never missed a Sunday service, and his father encouraged him to attend a Christian college. He got married and had five children while becoming the founder of the largest church in Colorado. Ted's life also had a dark side consisting of infidelity, lies, and hypocrisy, all of which made him feel anxious and guilty. He preached one thing and did the opposite behind everyone's back. When his immoral acts were discovered, he confessed to church officials but then went on a television news broadcast smiling happily and denying all accusations.

Psychosexual stages. According to Freud, the development of Ted's personality, such as being all smiles on the outside but feeling anxious and guilty internally, was primarily influenced by how he dealt with the five different kinds of conflicts that occurred at five different times or stages. According to Freud (1940), our personality develops as we pass through and deal with potential conflicts at five psychosexual stages.

1 Oral

2 Anal

3 Phallic

4 Latency

5 Genital

According to Freud, Haggard's personality developed as he passed through five psycho-sexual stages.

Psychosexual stages are five developmental periods—oral, anal, phallic, latency, and genital stages—each marked by potential conflict between parent and child. The conflicts arise as a child seeks pleasure from different body areas that are associated with sexual feelings (different erogenous zones). Freud emphasized that the child's first five years were most important in personality development.

You can think of each psychosexual stage as being a source of potential *conflict* between the child's id, which seeks immediate gratification, and the parents, who place restrictions on when, where, and how the gratification can take place. For example, the child may want to be fed immediately, while the parent may wish to delay the feeding to a more convenient time. The kind of interactions that occur between parent and child in satisfying these psychosexual needs and the way a child learns to deal with psychosexual conflicts, especially during breast feeding or toilet training, will greatly influence personality development as well as future problems and social interactions.

One of Freud's controversial ideas is the relationship between early psychosexual stages and the development of later personality, social, and emotional problems. Here is Freud's explanation of how different problems may arise.

Fixation: Potential Personality Problems

Why did Ted develop problems?

Freud explained that the way a person deals with early psychosexual conflicts lays the groundwork for personality growth and future problems. This means that, to a large extent, Ted's later personality problems grew out of early childhood experiences. Freud would say that Ted's problems in finding his identity began in childhood, likely as a result of having a specific need or wish that was either undergratified or overgratified.

Healthy personality involves resolving conflicts during the psychosexual stages.

Fixation. As an adult, there were times when Ted was happy, but at other times he was anxious and guilt-ridden. The problem for any theory of personality is to explain why problems and contradictions in personality occur. For example, why did Ted preach in front of 14,000 worshippers and become politically active, yet engage in immoral sexual conduct and then lie about it? Freud would explain that the development of Ted's personality depended, to a large extent, on the way he dealt with early psychosexual conflicts. One way a child can deal with or resolve these conflicts—wanting to satisfy all desires but not being allowed to by the parents—is to become fixated at a certain stage.

Fixation, which can occur during any of the first three stages—oral, anal, or phallic—is a Freudian process through which an individual may be locked into a particular psychosexual stage because his or her wishes were either overgratified or undergratified.

For example, if a person were fixated at the oral stage because of *too little* gratification, he might go through life trying to obtain oral satisfaction through eating too much, boasting too much, or focusing on other oral behaviors. If fixation had occurred at the oral stage because of *too much* gratification, he might focus on seeking oral gratification while neglecting to develop other aspects of his personality.

Next, we'll summarize Freud's psychosexual stages, focusing on possible parent–child conflicts, problems from fixation, and implications for future personality and social development.

Fixation at one psycho-sexual stage can cause sexual problems.

Five Psychosexual Stages

What happens during the stages?

According to Freud, every child goes through certain situations, such as nursing, bottle feeding, and toilet training, that contain potential conflicts between the child's desire for instant satisfaction or gratification and the parents' wishes, which may involve delaying the child's satisfaction. How these conflicts are resolved and whether a child becomes fixated at one stage because of too much or too little satisfaction greatly influence the development of personality and the onset of future problems.

1 Oral Stage

Time. Early infancy: first 18 months of life.

The **oral stage** lasts for the first 18 months of life and is a time when the infant's pleasure seeking is centered on the mouth.

Potential conflict. Pleasure-seeking activities include sucking, chewing, and biting. If we were locked into or fixated at this stage because our oral wishes were gratified too much or too little, we would continue to seek oral gratification as adults. *Fixation* at this stage results in adults who continue to engage in oral activities, such as overeating, gum chewing, or smoking; oral activities can be symbolic as well, such as being overly demanding or "mouthing off."

2 Anal Stage

Time. Late infancy: 1½ to 3 years.

The **anal stage** lasts from the age of about 1½ to 3 years and is a time when the infant's pleasure seeking is centered on the anus and its functions of elimination.

Potential conflict. *Fixation* at this stage results in adults who continue to engage in activities of retention or elimination. Retention may take the form of being very neat, stingy, or behaviorally rigid (thus the term *anal retentive*). Elimination may take the form of being generous, messy, or very loose or carefree (thus the term *anal expulsive*).

3 Phallic Stage

Time. Early childhood: 3 to 6 years.

The **phallic** *(FAL-ick)* **stage** lasts from the age of about 3 to 6 and is a time when the child's pleasure seeking is centered on the genitals.

Potential conflict. Freud theorized that the phallic stage is particularly important for personality development because of the occurrence of the Oedipus complex (named for Oedipus, the character in Greek mythology who unknowingly killed his father and married his mother).

The **Oedipus** *(ED-ah-pus)* **complex** is a process in which a child competes with the parent of the same sex for the affections and pleasures of the parent of the opposite sex.

According to Freud, the Oedipus complex causes different problems for boys and girls.

Boys. When a boy discovers that his penis is a source of pleasure, he develops a sexual attraction to his mother. As a result, the boy feels hatred, jealousy, and competition toward his father and has fears of castration. The boy resolves his Oedipus complex by identifying with his father. If he does not resolve the complex, fixation occurs and he may go through life trying to prove his toughness.

Girls. When a girl discovers that she does not have a penis, she feels a loss that Freud called *penis envy.* Her loss makes her turn against her mother and develop sexual desires for her father. A girl resolves her Oedipus complex, sometimes called the Electra complex (for Electra, a woman in Greek mythology who killed her mother), by identifying with her mother. If this complex is not resolved, fixation occurs and the woman may go through life feeling inferior to men.

4 Latency Stage

Time. Middle and late childhood: 6 to puberty.

The **latency stage,** which lasts from about age 6 to puberty, is a time when the child represses sexual thoughts and engages in nonsexual activities, such as developing social and intellectual skills.

At puberty, sexuality reappears and marks the beginning of a new stage, called the genital stage.

5 Genital Stage

Time. Puberty through adulthood.

The **genital stage** lasts from puberty through adulthood and is a time when the individual has renewed sexual desires that he or she seeks to fulfill through relationships with other people.

Potential conflict. How a person meets the conflicts of the genital stage depends on how conflicts in the first three stages were resolved. If the individual is fixated at an earlier stage, less energy will be available to resolve conflicts at the genital stage. If the individual successfully resolved conflicts in the first three stages, he or she will have the energy to develop loving relationships and a healthy and mature personality.

Summary. Freud's psychodynamic theory of personality development made a number of assumptions that, at the time, were revolutionary. His assumptions included the influence of unconscious forces; the division of the mind into the id, ego, and superego; the importance of resolving conflicts at five psychosexual stages; the importance of fixation; and the importance of the first five years to personality development.

Next, we'll discuss what Freud's critics have had to say about his theory and assumptions. ●

Disagreements

What did they argue about?

Because Freud's theory was so creative and revolutionary for its time, it attracted many followers, who formed a famous group called the Vienna Psychoanalytic Society. However, it was not long before members of the society began to disagree over some of Freud's theories and assumptions, such as whether Freud placed too much emphasis on biological urges (sex and aggression), psychosexual stages, and the importance of early childhood experience in personality development (Horgan, 1996; Westen et al., 2008). We'll focus on three influential followers who broke with Freud's theory.

Carl Jung

Why did Freud's "crown prince" stop talking to him?

Jung disagreed on the importance of the sex drive.

National Library of Medicine, Bethesda, MD

In 1910 Carl Jung, with the wholehearted support of Sigmund Freud, became the first president of the Vienna Psychoanalytic Society. Freud said that Jung was to be his "crown prince" and personal successor. However, just four years later, Jung and Freud ended their personal and professional relationship and never again spoke to each other.

The main reason for the split was that Jung disagreed with Freud's emphasis on the sex drive. Jung believed the collective unconscious—and not sex—was the basic force in the development of personality.

The **collective unconscious,** according to Jung, consists of ancient memory traces and symbols that are passed on by birth and are shared by all peoples in all cultures.

Jung's theory of collective unconscious and his elaborate theory of personality, called *analytical psychology,* had more influence on the areas of art, literature, philosophy, and counseling/therapy than on current areas of psychology.

Alfred Adler

Why did one of the society's presidents resign?

Adler disagreed on the importance of biological urges.

Courtesy, Adler School of Professional Psychology. Reproduced by permission of Kurt Adler.

Alfred Adler was another contemporary of Freud's who later became president of the Vienna Psychoanalytic Society. However, after Adler voiced his disagreement with Freud at one of the society's meetings, he was so badly criticized by the other members that he resigned as president.

Like Jung, Adler disagreed with Freud's theory that humans are governed by biological and sexual urges. Adler believed that the main factors influencing a child's development were sibling influences and child-rearing practices.

In contrast to Freud's biological drives, Adler proposed that humans are motivated by *social urges* and that each person is a social being with a unique personality. Adler formed his own group, whose philosophy became known as *individual psychology.* In contrast to Freud's emphasis on unconscious forces that influence our behaviors, Adler suggested that we are aware of our motives and goals and have the capacity to guide and plan our futures.

Karen Horney

What would a woman say about penis envy?

Horney disagreed on the importance of penis envy.

Courtesy, Association for the Advancement of Psychoanalysis

Karen Horney was trained as a psychoanalyst; her career reached its peak shortly after Freud's death in 1939. For many years, Horney was dean of the American Institute of Psychoanalysis in New York.

Horney strongly objected to Freud's view that women were dependent, vain, and submissive because of biological forces and childhood sexual experiences. She especially took issue with Freud's idea that penis envy affects girls' development.

In contrast to Freud's psychosexual conflicts, Horney insisted that the major influence on personality development, whether in women or men, can be found in child–parent *social interactions.* Unlike Freud, who believed that every child must experience child–parent conflicts, Horney theorized that such conflicts are avoidable if the child is raised in a loving, trusting, and secure environment. Karen Horney would now be called a feminist and is credited with founding the psychology of women.

Neo-Freudians

Karen Horney is sometimes referred to as a *neo-Freudian.*

Neo-Freudians were followers of Freud who agreed with some of his theoretical ideas but changed and renovated others to develop their own approaches.

One of the best-known neo-Freudians was Erik Erikson, who formulated his own theory of personality development, which we discussed in Modules 17 and 18. Erikson proposed that everyone goes through a series of *psychosocial* stages, rather than the *psychosexual* stages proposed by Freud.

Neo-Freudians generally agreed with Freud's basic ideas, such as the importance of the unconscious; the division of the mind into the id, ego, and superego; and the use of defense mechanisms to protect the ego. However, they mostly disagreed with Freud's placing so much emphasis on biological forces, sexual drives, and psychosexual stages. The neo-Freudians turned the emphasis of Freud's psychodynamic theory away from biological drives toward psychosocial and cultural influences (Plante, 2011).

From early on, followers of Freud criticized his theory and, as you'll see, criticisms continue to the present day.

Freudian Theory Today

What is the current status of Freud's theory?

To give you an idea of where Freud's theory stands today, we'll focus on four questions: How valid is Freud's theory? How important are the first five years? Are there unconscious forces? What was the impact of Freud's theory?

1 How Valid Is Freud's Theory?

Too comprehensive. Freud's psychodynamic theory, which includes how the mind develops (id, ego, and superego), how personality develops (psychosexual stages), and how to do therapy (psychoanalysis), is so comprehensive that it can explain almost any behavior. Advocates of Freud's theory state that it is a coherent and sophisticated view of the mind, while critics argue that Freud's theory is too comprehensive to be useful in explaining or predicting behaviors (Horgan, 1996; Kandel, 2006).

Difficult to test. Current followers agree that some of Freud's concepts, such as the id being the source of energy, the importance of the Oedipus complex in personality development, and basic drives limited to sex and aggression, have been difficult to test or verify. The same followers add that other Freudian ideas, such as the influence of unconscious forces, the long-term effects of early childhood patterns, and the existence of defense mechanisms, have been experimentally tested and received support (Fotopoulou, 2006; Ramachandran, 2006; Westen et al., 2008).

Must be updated. However, if psychoanalysis or psychodynamic theory is to survive in the 2000s, Freud's theory must continue to be tested experimentally and updated with findings from other areas of psychology. For example, Freud's theory needs to explain how **genetic factors** account for 20–50% of a wide range of behaviors and how **brain development,** which is not complete until early adulthood, is associated with and necessary for the development of related behaviors, thoughts, and feelings (Westen, 1998). Currently, neuroscientists are examining many of Freud's questions about the mind and hope to build on his theory (Solms, 2006).

2 How Important Are the First Five Years?

Based on observations of his patients, Freud concluded that personality development is essentially complete after the first five years. However, Freud never did systematic research or collected longitudinal observations to support his hypothesis that personality development is fixed during a child's first five years (Bruer, 1999). In fact, there are two lines of research showing the opposite. First, our earlier discussion of **resilient children** (see p. 394) indicated that the occurrence of serious psychological and physical problems during the first five years does not necessarily stunt or inhibit personality development, as Freud predicted.

Second, a number of **longitudinal studies** that followed children into adulthood indicate that personality development is not complete in the first five years but rather continues well into middle adulthood (Caspi & Roberts, 1999; McCrae & Costa, 2003). For these reasons, current psychologists question Freud's idea that personality development is complete in the first five years.

Theory of Personality

Unconscious forces

Id, ego, & superego

Defense mechanisms

Five psychosocial stages

During the 1990s, Freud's theory had several major revisions.

© Bettmann/CORBIS

3 Are There Unconscious Forces?

One of Freud's major assumptions was that unconscious or repressed forces influence our conscious thoughts and behaviors. Research generally supports Freud's assumption (Kandel, 2008; R. Michels, 2011). For instance, when you speak, you use correct grammar while paying little or no conscious attention to doing so.

Also, patterns of brain activity can actually reveal which choice a person is going to make before he or she is aware of it. In one study, researchers took brain scans of people while they held a button in each hand and were instructed to push either button. The brain scans revealed which hand people were going to use before the people were even aware they had made a decision (Haynes, 2008).

Although Freud's assumption has received research support, he may have overstated the extent to which unconscious forces can influence human behavior. There are conscious forces that influence many of our behaviors. For instance, reading this book and studying for your psychology class are very likely the result of conscious determination.

Related to Freud's theory of the repressed unconscious forces, cognitive neuroscientists developed a different concept, called implicit or nondeclarative memory (see p. 246) (Solms, 2006).

Implicit or **nondeclarative memory** means learning without awareness, such as occurs in experiencing emotional situations or acquiring motor habits. Although we are unaware of such learning, it can influence our conscious feelings, thoughts, and behaviors. Thus, there is evidence for the **influence of unconscious forces** on conscious thoughts, feelings, and behaviors.

4 What Was Freud's Impact?

Freud's theory has had an enormous impact on society, as can be seen in the widespread use of Freudian terms (*ego, id, rationalization*) in literature, art, and our everyday conversations. Freud's theory also has had a great impact on psychology: Many of his concepts have been incorporated into the fields of personality, development, abnormal psychology, and psychotherapy. His theory is also credited for the view that the early childhood years have a strong influence on future behavior, personality, and emotions. Neuroscientists have demonstrated that early life experiences are so powerful that they can actually influence whether or not specific genes are expressed (M. K. Raskin, 2011).

Unlike Freud's psychodynamic theory, which paints a picture of humans filled with irrational and unconscious forces with little free choice, we next discuss a family of theories—humanistic theory—that is almost the direct opposite of Freud's theory. ●

E Humanistic Theories

At the beginning of this module, we told you about two very different people. One was evangelical Christian leader Ted Haggard, who struggled with numerous

How did he develop his real potential?

personal problems. At age 50, as a husband, father, and national evangelical leader, he confessed to having sexual relations with a male escort and purchasing drugs.

The other person was Greg Mathis, who at a young age had become a violent gang member and had seen the inside of a jail cell many times. Just when most people would have given up on reforming Mathis, he began to reform himself. Inspired by a promise to God to change his ways if his mother survived cancer, he began to channel his rage against society into becoming a student and then a judge. Greg Mathis worked hard to change his life and became a very successful judge.

What Mathis and Haggard shared in common as young men was that neither showed particular evidence of having special

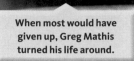

When most would have given up, Greg Mathis turned his life around.

© AP Images/CharlesBennett

talents or great potentials. Few people would have predicted that Ted Haggard, who as a teen wanted to pursue journalism, would become a nationally recognized Christian pastor. No one would have predicted that angry, tough, mean Greg Mathis would discover, of all things, the other side of a jail cell. To the surprise of many, Mathis pursued the legal profession and channeled his toughness into becoming a judge. The lives of these two men demonstrate the difficulty in predicting someone's potential and whether he or she will develop it. Developing our potential is at the heart of humanistic theories.

Humanistic theories emphasize our capacity for personal growth, development of our potential, and freedom to choose our destiny.

Humanistic theories reject the biological determinism and the irrational, unconscious forces of Freud's psychodynamic theory. Humanistic theories emphasize freely choosing to go after one's dream and to change one's destiny, as Yani Tseng is doing.

Three Characteristics of Humanistic Theories

Yani Tseng has always set high goals. As a child, she aimed to become the world's best golfer. It didn't take long for her to achieve the success she

What was her goal?

dreamed about. Yani has become the youngest player ever to win five major championships and is ranked No. 1 in the Women's World Golf Rankings (M. Elliott, 2011; Sorenstam, 2012). Even though at age 23 Yani has achieved the highest ranking and won a career's worth of tournaments and prize money, she recognizes that she still has much to learn: "Right now I'm No. 1, but I feel like I still have a long way to go. I still have so many things I need to learn, I need to achieve and I need to work on" (Tseng, 2012).

Yani Tseng's life illustrates the humanists' emphasis on developing fully one's potential to lead a rich and meaningful life and becoming the best person one can be (Moss, 2002). Yani's drive to reach her lifelong dream exemplifies the three characteristics that distinguish humanistic theories from other theories of personality. We'll describe each of the three characteristics unique to humanistic theories: a phenomenological perspective, a holistic view, and a goal of self-actualization (P. T. P. Wong, 2006).

1 Humanistic theories stress learning about the world through personal experiences, which illustrates the phenomenological *(feh-nom-in-no-LODGE-uh-cal)* perspective.

The **phenomenological perspective** is the idea that your perception or view of the world, whether or not it is accurate, becomes your reality.

For instance, Yani's phenomenological perspective of how she perceived her golfing abilities may or may not have been accurate. However, because she believed so strongly that she had the abilities, this perception became her reality. Other examples of phenomenological perspectives are long-held beliefs that women could not perform certain jobs—for example, police officer, doctor, plumber, truck driver, or lawyer. Since women have demonstrated that they can perform these jobs, this particular perception has been proven false.

Yani's life dream has been to become the world's best golfer.

© cjmac/Shutterstock.com

2 Humanistic theories emphasize looking at the whole situation or person, which illustrates the holistic *(hole-LIS-tick)* view.

The **holistic view** means that a person's personality is more than the sum of its individual parts; instead, the individual parts form a unique and total entity that functions as a unit.

For example, the holistic view would explain that Yani became the top-ranked female golfer because of her unique combination of many traits—discipline, ability, motivation, desire—rather than any single trait.

3 Humanistic theories highlight the idea of developing one's true potential, which is called self-actualization.

Self-actualization refers to our inherent tendency to develop and reach our true potentials.

By becoming a professional golfer and aiming to get better and better, Yani is an example of someone who is developing and reaching her true potential and thus is getting closer to achieving a high level of self-actualization. According to humanists, each of us has the capacity for self-actualization. Humanists believe that one's self-esteem, self-expression, sense of belonging, creativity, and love are as important to human life as the biological needs of food and water (Rabasca, 2000a).

The beginning of humanistic theories in the 1960s can be traced to two psychologists—Abraham Maslow and Carl Rogers. They had surprisingly different backgrounds but arrived at the same uplifting ideas.

Maslow: Need Hierarchy and Self-Actualization

Why did a behaviorist become a humanist?

We can trace the official beginning of the humanistic movement to the early 1960s and the publication of the *Journal of Humanistic Psychology*. One of the major figures behind establishing this journal was Abraham Maslow. Interestingly enough, Maslow was trained as a behaviorist, but along the way he felt there was too much emphasis on rewards and punishments and observable behaviors and too little emphasis on other important aspects of human nature, such as feelings, emotions, and beliefs. For these reasons, Maslow (1968) broke away from the reward/punishment/observable behavior mentality of behaviorism and developed his humanistic theory, which emphasized two things: our capacity for growth, or self-actualization, and our desire to satisfy a variety of needs, which he arranged in a hierarchy.

Maslow's Hierarchy of Needs

For just a moment, think of all the needs that you try to meet each day: eating, having a safe place to live, talking to your friends, perhaps working at a part-time job, caring for loved ones, and studying for exams. Maslow believed that you satisfy these needs in a certain order. As you may remember from Module 15 (see p. 333), Maslow arranged all human needs into a hierarchy of five major needs.

Maslow's hierarchy of needs arranges needs in ascending order (figure on left), with biological needs at the bottom and social and personal needs at the top. Only when needs at a lower level are met can we advance to the next level.

According to Maslow's hierarchy, you must satisfy your biological and safety needs before using energy to fulfill your personal and social needs. Finally, you can devote time and energy to reaching your true potential, which is called self-actualization, your highest need.

Maslow divided our needs into two general categories: deficiency and growth needs.

Deficiency needs are physiological needs (food, sleep) and psychological needs (safety, love, esteem) that we try to fulfill if they are not met.

Growth needs are those at the higher levels and include the desire for truth, goodness, beauty, and justice.

According to Maslow, we must satisfy our deficiency needs before we have the time and energy to satisfy our growth needs and move toward self-actualization.

Self-Actualization

One of the major characteristics of the humanistic movement is the emphasis on a process called self-actualization.

Self-actualization is the development and fulfillment of one's unique human potential.

Maslow (1971) developed the concept of self-actualization after studying the lives of highly productive and exceptional people, such as Abraham Lincoln, Albert Einstein, and Eleanor Roosevelt. Maslow believed that these individuals were able to reach the goal of self-actualization because they had developed the following personality characteristics.

Characteristics of Self-Actualized Individuals

- They perceive reality accurately.
- They are independent and autonomous.
- They prefer to have a deep, loving relationship with only a few people.
- They focus on accomplishing their goals.
- They report peak experiences, which are moments of great joy and satisfaction.

Maslow believed that, although very few individuals reach the level of self-actualization, everyone has a self-actualizing tendency. This tendency motivates us to become the best kind of person we are capable of being.

There is no doubt that Maslow would also have considered Martin Luther King, Jr. an example of a self-actualized person. Martin Luther King, Jr. devoted his life to achieving civil rights for all people. At left he delivers his famous "I Have a Dream" speech at a civil rights rally in Washington, D.C. He was awarded the Nobel Peace Prize at age 35. He was gunned down by an assassin's bullet at age 39. King's achievements exemplify the humanistic idea of self-actualization.

Civil rights leader Martin Luther King, Jr. is an example of a self-actualized person.

About the same time that Maslow was making this journey from behaviorism to humanism and developing the concept of self-actualization, another psychologist by the name of Carl Rogers was developing a different but related humanistic theory.

Self-Actualization

Level 5
Self-actualization: fulfillment of one's unique potential

Esteem Needs

Level 4
Esteem needs: achievement, competency, gaining approval and recognition

Love and Belonging Needs

Level 3
Love and belonging needs: affiliation with others and acceptance by others

Safety Needs

Level 2
Safety needs: protection from harm, safety and survival

Physiological Needs

Level 1
Physiological needs: food, water, sex, and sleep

Rogers: Self Theory

Carl Rogers was initially trained in the psychodynamic approach, which he used in his practice as a clinical psychologist. However, Rogers began to feel that Freud placed too much emphasis on unconscious, irrational forces and on biological urges, and too little emphasis on human potential for psychological growth. As a result, Rogers gradually abandoned the psychodynamic approach in favor of a new theory of personality that he developed in the 1960s. Rogers's new humanistic theory is often called self theory because of his emphasis on the self or self-concept.

What are the two most important concepts?

Self theory, also called *self-actualization theory,* is based on two major assumptions: that personality development is guided by each person's unique self-actualization tendency, and that each of us has a personal need for positive regard.

Rogers's first major assumption about self-actualization is similar but slightly different from Maslow's use of the term.

Rogers's **self-actualizing tendency** is an inborn tendency for us to develop all of our capacities in ways that best maintain and benefit our lives.

The self-actualizing tendency relates to *biological functions*, such as meeting our basic needs for food, water, and oxygen, as well as *psychological functions*, such as expanding our experiences, encouraging personal growth, and becoming self-sufficient.

The self-actualizing tendency guides us toward positive or healthful behaviors rather than negative or harmful ones. For example, one of the two boys in the photo below has lost the use of his legs and must use a wheelchair. Part of his self-actualizing process will include learning to deal with his disability, engaging in positive healthful behaviors, and getting to know himself.

Self or **self-concept** refers to how we see or describe ourselves. The self is made up of many self-perceptions, abilities, personality characteristics, and behaviors that are organized and consistent with one another.

Because of very different experiences, the boy in the wheelchair will develop a self-concept different from that of his friend who has normal use of his legs. According to Rogers (1980), self-concept plays an important role in personality because it influences our behaviors, feelings, and thoughts. For example, if you have a *positive self-concept*, you will tend to act, feel, and think optimistically and constructively; if you have a *negative self-concept*, you will tend to act, feel, and think pessimistically and destructively.

Sometimes a person may be undecided about his or her real self. As we discover our real self, we may undergo a number of changes in personality.

Because of different experiences, the boy in the wheelchair will likely develop a different concept of self than the other boy.

© Don Smetzer/Getty Images

Real Self Versus Ideal Self

We all change how we see ourselves but probably not as much as hip-hop star Sean Combs, who, through the years, has radically changed his appearance and even his name.

Who is the real Sean Combs?

For example, at the start of his career, Combs was known as "Puff Daddy" and his appearance (top photo) and behaviors (legal problems) might have been described as pushing some of society's limits. Now, however, Combs is known as "Diddy" and has a rather conventional appearance (bottom photo). He has donated huge amounts to charities, and he once attempted to release a gospel album, unlike his other albums that all require a "Parental Advisory" warning. The question is: Which is Combs's real self?

Carl Rogers said that his clients often asked questions related to their selves: "How do I find myself?" "Why do I sometimes feel that I don't know myself?" "Why do I say or do things that aren't really me?" Rogers developed a clever answer to these relatively common and perplexing questions. He said there are two kinds of selves: a real self and an ideal self.

The **real self,** according to Rogers, is based on our actual experiences and represents how we really see ourselves.

My ideal self is based on my hopes and wishes.

© AP Images/Jim Cooper

My real self is based on my actual experience.

© Carlo Allegri/Getty Images

The **ideal self,** according to Rogers, is based on our hopes and wishes and reflects how we would like to see ourselves.

In some cases, the hopes and wishes of one's ideal self may contradict the abilities and experiences of the real self. For example, a student's ideal self may be someone who is very responsible and studies hard, but the real self may be someone who puts things off and studies less than is required.

Contradiction between ideal and real self. According to Rogers, a glaring contradiction between the ideal and real selves can result in personality problems. Rogers suggested that we can resolve contradictions between our ideal and real selves by paying more attention to our actual experiences, working to have more positive experiences, and paying less attention to the expectations of others. In working out discrepancies between our ideal and real selves, we may undergo a variety of changes in our appearance and behaviors, such as Sean Combs experienced.

Now that you know what the self is, here's how Rogers says that it develops.

Positive Regard

One reason I (H. K.) am one of the millions of dog owners is that my dog Cocoa shows great happiness at seeing me, no matter how grouchy, distracted, or sad I may feel or act.

Why are there millions of dog owners?

In fact, researchers find that because people perceive their pets as showing appreciation, being supportive, and giving pleasure, pets are helpful in reducing stressful feelings and lowering blood pressure (K. Allen, 2003; Lilienfeld & Arkowitz, 2008; Springen, 2008).

Pets have even been shown to help us live longer. For instance, research studies that followed adults who had heart attacks over a number of years found that those who had a pet dog were more likely to be alive than those who didn't have a pet dog (NIH, 2009). Also, pets may be able to help some of us cope more effectively with stress. For example, when confronted with a stressful experience, pet owners have been found to have milder responses and speedier recovery from stress when they were with their pets, compared to being with a friend or spouse (NIH, 2009).

> It's so nice you're always glad to see me.

© Catalin Petolea/Shutterstock.com

Because pets provide constant, nonjudgmental devotion, they can be especially helpful in boosting our morale and helping us feel validated (Lloyd, 2010). As such, pets can be a great source of companionship and social support for people who are depressed or lonely (Lilienfeld & Arkowitz, 2008; *USA Today,* 2010).

The popularity of pets and their positive influence on our loves illustrate the second assumption of Carl Rogers's self theory, which is that we have a need to receive positive regard.

Positive regard includes love, sympathy, warmth, acceptance, and respect, which we crave from family, friends, and people who are important to us.

Rogers believed that positive regard was essential for the healthy development of one's self and for successful interpersonal relationships (Joseph & Murphy, 2012; Liebert & Spiegler, 1994).

Conditional and Unconditional Positive Regard

What's a big problem for teenagers?

Unlike friends and family, pets never pass judgment; they provide endless amounts of positive regard no matter how their owners look, feel, dress, or talk. In contrast, friends and family can be very judgmental and may give only conditional positive regard.

Conditional positive regard is the positive regard we receive if we behave in certain acceptable ways, such as living up to or meeting the standards of others.

For instance, one way teenagers display their independence is by choosing different (radical, awful, outrageous) hairstyles and fashions. In this case, if the teenagers receive only conditional positive regard based on conforming to the traditional fashion standards of their parents, they may develop a negative self-concept or feel bad or worthless because they displeased or disappointed their

No matter how she dresses, she hopes to get unconditional positive regard.

© Jose AS Reyes/Shutterstock.com

parents. Rogers believed that the development of a healthy and positive self-concept depends on receiving as much unconditional positive regard as possible.

Unconditional positive regard is the warmth, acceptance, and love that others show you because you are valued as a human being even though you may disappoint people by behaving in ways that are different from their standards or values or the way they think.

Parents who provide love and respect, even if a teenager does not always abide by their fashion standards, are showing unconditional positive regard, which will foster the development of a healthy self-concept.

Importance of Self-Actualization

What does it take to reach your potential?

Carrie Underwood was the winner of the fourth season of "American Idol" and has since become a multi-platinum-selling recording artist, winning awards and prestigious recognitions. For instance, her debut album, *Some Hearts,* was the fastest-selling female country album ever, and she has won numerous music awards— American Music Awards, Grammy Awards, Billboard Music Awards, Academy of Country Music Awards, and Country Music Television Awards, to list only a few.

The life of Carrie Underwood is a case study in self-actualization. Her dream since childhood was to become a professional singer, and despite years of disappointing attempts to establish a singing career, she never lost sight

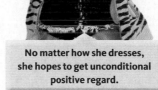

> I never gave up on my dream to be a singer.

© Peter Kramer/Getty Images

of her dream. Rogers would explain that Underwood persisted in singing because of the tendency for self-actualization, which provides direction and motivation to develop one's potential.

Rogers recognized that our tendency for self-actualization may be hindered, tested, or blocked by situational hurdles or personal difficulties, as happened to Underwood. But like Underwood, Rogers believed that we will experience the greatest self-actualization if we work hard and diligently to remove situational problems, resolve our personal problems, and, hopefully, receive tons of unconditional positive regard.

Humanistic theories contain powerful positive messages, but how do these uplifting messages work in real life?

Applying Humanistic Ideas

What problems do at-risk students face?

Unlike almost every other theory of personality, humanism holds that people are basically good and can achieve their true potentials if the roadblocks placed by society, poverty, drugs, or other evil influences are removed (Megargee, 1997). One of the primary goals of the humanistic approach is to find ways of removing blocking influences so people can grow and self-actualize.

In 1998, a racially diverse group of 150 high-school seniors walked across a graduation stage, an event few people expected to ever happen. These teenagers grew up in rough neighborhoods, witnessing and, for many, being victims of gun shootings. At the start of high school, these students made it clear they hated school and had no desire to learn. Thus, they were labeled "unteachable, at-risk" students. So, how did these 150 disadvantaged students overcome the many roadblocks on the path to graduating from high school?

Helping these students overcome roadblocks was Erin Gruwell, a dedicated teacher and role model. Erin encouraged students to think beyond the negative expectations others had of them and

The Freedom Writers shattered stereotypes because of the positive regard received from their teacher, Erin Gruwell.

to actively set life goals. By believing in each of her students, Erin helped them develop and reach their own potentials. At the heart of Erin's teaching was providing positive regard, including warmth, acceptance, and respect, to show them that someone truly cares.

With Erin's support, these students shattered stereotypes by not only graduating from high school but also going on to earn undergraduate and graduate degrees. The lives of these students had been transformed and it did not stop at their education. These 150 students are now known as the "Freedom Writers," and their mission is to teach tolerance and inspire others through their success. The Freedom Writers shared their story in the book they wrote together, *The Freedom Writers Diary*. Later, a Hollywood movie was made about their amazing success, *Freedom Writers* (Freedom Writers, 1999; Gruwell, 2007).

Next, we'll review the important humanistic concepts and discuss what critics have to say about humanistic theories.

Evaluation of Humanistic Theories

How popular is humanism?

Perhaps the main reason humanistic theories, such as those of Maslow and Rogers, continue to be popular is that they view people as basically good and believe that people can develop their true potentials (Clay, 2002).

Humanistic theories have had their greatest impact in counseling, clinical settings, and personal growth programs, where ideas like self-concept, self-actualization, and self-fulfillment have proven useful in developing healthy personalities and interpersonal relationships (Rabasca, 2000a; Soyez & Broekaert, 2005). Compared to Freud's idea that we are driven by unconscious irrational forces, humanism says we are driven by positive forces that point us toward realizing our good and true selves.

Like psychodynamic personality theory, humanistic theories have come under considerable criticism, especially by psychologists who rely on empirical research to understand personality. Because the major assumptions of self-actualization and other humanistic concepts, such as positive regard and self-worth, are difficult to demonstrate experimentally, critics argue that humanistic theories primarily describe how people behave rather than explain the causes of their behaviors. For these reasons, critics regard humanistic theories more as a wonderfully positive view of human nature or a very hopeful philosophy of life rather than as a scientific explanation of personality development (Burger, 2011).

One major problem is that humanistic theories generally ignore research

showing that 20–60% of the development of intellectual, emotional, social, and personality traits comes from genetic factors (Jang, 2005; McClearn et al., 1997; Parens et al., 2006). This means that genetic factors must be considered when discussing a person's true potential or a person's ability to achieve self-actualization.

Maslow hoped that humanistic theories would become a major force in psychology. Although the humanistic approach has not achieved Maslow's goal, humanism's ideas inspired the human potential movements in the 1960s–1970s and have been integrated into approaches for counseling, psychotherapy, and, as we learned with the Freedom Writers, education (Clay, 2002).

The influence of humanistic theories has recently been rejuvenated as empirical research in *positive psychology* (see p. 10), a relatively recent approach, is bringing humanistic ideas into the mainstream (Compton & Hoffman, 2013; Hefferon & Boniwell, 2011).

Positive psychology is the scientific study of optimal human functioning, focusing on the strengths and virtues that enable individuals and communities to thrive. It aims to better understand the positive, adaptive, and fulfilling aspects of human life.

One reason there is growing interest in positive psychology is that it provides a change from the tendency of researchers in psychology to focus more on problems or weaknesses than on strengths or virtues, which are at the core of humanistic psychology. ●

Positive psychology aims to better understand the positive, adaptive, and fulfilling aspects of human life.

1. The combination of long-lasting and distinctive behaviors, thoughts, and emotions that are typical of how we react and adapt to other people and situations forms our _____.

2. Freud's theory of personality, which emphasizes the importance of early childhood experiences and of conflicts between conscious thoughts and unconscious forces, is called a _____ theory.

3. Freud developed three techniques for probing the unconscious. A technique that encourages clients to talk about any thoughts or images that enter their head is called **(a)** _____. A technique to interpret the hidden meanings and symbols in dreams is called **(b)** _____. With a third technique, the therapist analyzes the mistakes or **(c)** _____ that the client makes in everyday speech.

4. Freud considered the mind to have three major divisions. The division that contains the biological drives and is the source of all psychic or mental energy is called the **(a)** _____. This division operates according to the **(b)** _____ principle, which demands immediate satisfaction. The division that develops from the id during infancy and whose goal is finding safe and socially acceptable ways of satisfying the id's desires is called the **(c)** _____. This division operates according to the **(d)** _____ principle, which involves satisfying a wish only if there is a socially acceptable outlet. The division that develops from the id during early childhood and whose goal is applying the moral values and standards of one's parents and society is called the **(e)** _____.

5. Conflicts between the id and the superego over satisfaction of desires may cause the ego to feel threatened. When threatened, the ego generates an unpleasant state that is associated with feelings of uneasiness, apprehension, and heightened physiological arousal; this unpleasant state is called **(a)** _____. Freud suggested that the ego may reduce anxiety by using unconscious mechanisms that produce self-deception; these are called **(b)** _____.

6. Freud proposed that the major influence on personality development occurs as we pass through five developmental periods that he called the **(a)** _____ stages, each of which results in conflicts between the child's wishes and parents' restrictions. The result

of a person's wishes being overgratified or undergratified at any one of the first three stages is called **(b)** _____.

7. Personality theories that emphasize our capacity for personal growth, the development of our potential, and freedom to choose our destinies are referred to as _____ theories.

8. Humanistic theories have three characteristics in common. They take the perspective that our perception of the world, whether or not it is accurate, becomes our reality; this is called the **(a)** _____ perspective. Humanistic theories see personality as more than the sum of individual parts and consider personality as a unique and total entity that functions as a unit; this is the **(b)** _____ view of personality. Humanistic theories point to an inherent tendency that each of us has to reach our true potential; this tendency is called **(c)** _____.

9. The idea that our needs occur in ascending order, with biological needs at the bottom and social and personal needs toward the top, and that we must meet our lower-level needs before we can satisfy higher ones is called **(a)** _____. Our physiological needs (food, sleep) and psychological needs (safety, belongingness, esteem) are called **(b)** _____ needs because we try to fulfill them if they are not met. The highest need of self-actualization, which includes the desire for truth, goodness, beauty, and justice, is called a **(c)** _____ need.

10. Carl Rogers's self theory of personality makes two basic assumptions. The first is that personality development is guided by an inborn tendency to develop our potential; this idea is called **(a)** _____. The second assumption is that each of us has a personal need for acceptance and love, which Rogers called **(b)** _____. According to Rogers, it is important that we receive love and acceptance despite the fact that we sometimes behave in ways that are different from what others think or value; this type of acceptance is called **(c)** _____.

11. Rogers proposes that we have two kinds of selves: the self that is based on real-life experiences is called the **(a)** _____ self; the self that is based on how we would like to see ourselves is called the **(b)** _____ self.

12. The scientific approach that studies optimal human functioning, focusing on the strengths and virtues that enable individuals and communities to thrive, is called _____.

Answers: 1. *personality;* 2. *psychodynamic;* 3. (a) *free association,* (b) *dream interpretation,* (c) *Freudian slips or slips of the tongue;* 4. (a) *id,* (b) *pleasure,* (c) *ego,* (d) *reality,* (e) *superego;* 5. (a) *anxiety,* (b) *defense mechanisms;* 6. (a) *psychosexual,* (b) *fixation;* 7. *humanistic;* 8. (a) *phenomenological,* (b) *holistic,* (c) *self-actualization;* 9. (a) *Maslow's hierarchy of needs,* (b) *deficiency,* (c) *growth;* 10. (a) *self-actualization,* (b) *positive regard,* (c) *unconditional positive regard;* 11. (a) *real,* (b) *ideal;* 12. *positive psychology*

Boat People: Remarkable Achievement

We have always been puzzled by why students with similar academic skills perform so differently: Some do well on our exams, while others do poorly. A humanist would look at the same differences and ask, Why are some students developing their potential, while others are not? One answer comes from studying thousands of Indo-Chinese refugees, known as the boat people, who were allowed to resettle in the United States in the 1970s and 1980s.

What was different about these children?

On their arrival in America, the boat people's only possessions were the clothes they wore. They knew virtually no English, had almost no knowledge of Western culture, and had no one to turn to for social or financial support. In spite of horrendous difficulties, refugee children achieved such remarkable academic success that American educators were scratching their heads and asking why.

Background. Researchers set out to discover why these refugee children had achieved astonishing scholastic success against overwhelming odds (N. Caplan et al., 1992). The researchers selected a random sample of 200 Indo-Chinese refugee families with a

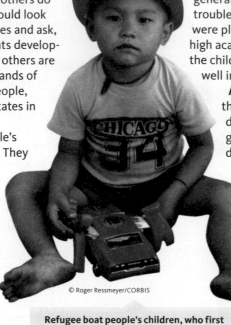
© Roger Ressmeyer/CORBIS

Refugee boat people's children, who first had to learn English, went on to achieve remarkable academic success.

total of 536 school-age children. The children had been in the United States for an average of 3½ years. They had generally lived in low-income metropolitan areas with troublesome neighborhoods and rundown schools that were plagued with problems and not known for their high academic standards. Despite all these problems, the children of the boat people performed remarkably well in school. Here's what researchers found.

Amazing success. The researchers computed the mean grade point average for the 536 children, who were fairly evenly distributed among grades 1 to 12. They found that 27% of the children had a grade point average (GPA) in the A range, 52% had a GPA in the B range, 17% in the C range, and only 4% had a GPA below C. Equally noteworthy was the children's overall performance in math: Almost 50% of the children earned A's, while another 33% earned B's. On national math tests, the Indo-Chinese children's average scores were almost three times higher than the national norm.

After analyzing all these data, researchers were able to identify several reasons immigrant Indo-Chinese students achieved such high grades.

Values and Motivation

What were their values?

Although Indo-Chinese refugee children had been in the United States for an average of only 3½ years, they were doing better in math than 90% of their peers. It could not be the quality of their schools, which were average, undistinguished low-income schools in metropolitan areas. But clearly there were powerful factors helping these children overcome the problems of learning a second language and adapting to a new culture. Researchers located these powerful factors in the values of the Asian family.

The primary values held by the Indo-Chinese families were that parents and children have mutual respect, cooperate freely, and are committed to accomplishment and achievement. A clear example of commitment to accomplishment was the amount of time Indo-Chinese children spent doing homework: They averaged about 3 hours a day, while American students averaged about 1½ hours. Thus, among refugee families, doing homework, not watching television, was the main activity; the older children helped the younger children.

Another primary value is that parents were very involved in their children's education: Over 50% of parents read aloud and helped with homework. When children were asked, "What accounts for your academic success?" the children most often checked the category "having a love of learning." Love of learning was one of the values nourished and passed on from parent to child. When children were asked, "How much do you choose your own destiny?" the children answered that they did not trust luck or fate but were the masters of their own destinies.

Parental Values

Children

Parental values on the importance of education motivated the children.

Parental Attitudes

How did parents help?

One reason Indo-Chinese children earned great academic success was the personal and cultural values transmitted by their parents, who were committed to help their children succeed through educational performance. After studying the immigrant parents' values and how they instilled these values in their children, researchers concluded that for American schools to succeed, parents must become more committed to the education of their children. In this case, Americans can truly learn from the values of these refugees.

In explaining the immigrant children's wonderful academic achievement, humanists would emphasize how parental values served to remove mental roadblocks that otherwise might have hindered their children from developing their true potentials and reaching self-fulfillment.

Next, we'll turn to a relatively common personality problem, shyness, and discuss how different theories of personality explain its causes. ●

What Is Shyness and What Causes It?

It's one thing to discuss Freud's psychodynamic theory of personality, but it's another to see it in action—in this case, to treat shyness.

What's it like to be shy?

At some time and in some situations, we have all felt a little shy. However, there are degrees of shyness, and a high degree of shyness can interfere with enjoying personal and social interactions. For example, when Alan was a child, he would walk home from school through alleys to avoid meeting any of his classmates. Although he received a perfect math score on his SAT, he dropped out of the University of Texas because he always felt like a stranger and was continually frustrated by not being able to reach out and make contact with people. He was so shy that he could not even use the Internet. Finally, feeling so lonely, Alan sought help at the Shyness Clinic, which was founded in the 1970s by well-known shyness researcher, Philip Zimbardo of Stanford University (Noriyuki, 1996).

Shyness is a feeling of distress that comes from being tense, stressed, or awkward in social situations and from worrying about and fearing rejection.

The cause and treatment for shyness depend partly on which theory of personality guides our thinking. We'll contrast answers from two different theories: Freud's psychodynamic theory and social cognitive theory.

Psychodynamic Approach

Is shyness due to unresolved conflicts?

As a practicing psychoanalyst, Donald Kaplan (1972) used his clinical experience and psychodynamic concepts to answer the question, What causes shyness? Kaplan traced the causes of shyness back to **unresolved conflicts** at one or more of Freud's psychosexual stages. For example, one very shy client reported that his mother constantly fed him so that he would never cry or whimper. As a result, Kaplan suggested that this client's unresolved conflict during the oral stage resulted in his feelings of inadequacy and shyness in later social interactions.

According to Kaplan, the symptoms of shyness include both conscious fears, such as having nothing to say, and unconscious fears of being rejected. Shy people may deal with these anxieties by using **defense mechanisms;** for example, one client reduced his anxiety through displacement, by changing his fears of being rejected into opposite feelings of self-righteousness and contempt.

One **advantage** of the psychodynamic approach is that it suggests that a number of causes, such as conscious and unconscious fears as well as unresolved psychosexual conflicts, are involved in shyness.

One **disadvantage** of the psychodynamic approach is that Freudian concepts (unconscious fears, unresolved psycho-sexual stages) are difficult to verify by experimental methods (E. F. Torrey, 2005). For example, saying that being fixated at the oral stage may result in a person becoming a shy adult is mostly a descriptive guess rather than a testable hypothesis.

A very different account of what causes shyness comes from the social cognitive theory of personality.

The cause and treatment for shyness depend partly on which theory of personality the therapist follows.

Social Cognitive Theory

What are the three factors?

Unlike the Freudian approach, which relies primarily on therapists' personal observations, social cognitive theory uses primarily experimental studies to study personality.

Social cognitive theory says that personality development is shaped primarily by three forces: environmental conditions (learning), cognitive-personal factors, and behavior, which all interact to influence how we evaluate, interpret, organize, and apply information.

Social cognitive theory breaks shyness down into three measurable or observable components—cognitive, behavioral, and environmental—which can be studied using the experimental method described in Module 2. For example, in a series of longitudinal studies, researchers found that about 10–15% of the population have a shy personality that, to a large extent, comes from **genetic factors**—for example, inheriting a nervous system that is easily aroused by novel stimuli (Battaglia, 2005; Kagan, 2003a). By observing the social interactions (the behavioral component) of shy people, researchers found that shy people have too few social and communication skills and, as a consequence, they are continually punished during social interactions (Gabrieli, 2005; Putnam, 2005). By giving personality tests (the cognitive component), researchers found that shy people are overly self-conscious, which leads to worrisome thoughts and irrational beliefs that interfere with social functioning (Romney & Bynner, 1997). Therapies based on social cognitive theory (see Module 20) have proved successful in helping shy individuals decrease their anxiety in social situations, develop better social skills, and decrease levels of shyness (Greco & Morris, 2001; Kluger, 2005).

One **advantage** of social cognitive theory is that it breaks shyness down into three measurable or observable components, which can be experimentally studied and appropriate treatments developed.

One **disadvantage** of this approach is that researchers may overlook certain influences that we are neither conscious nor aware of, such as how our brain processes emotions or experiences conditioned emotional responses, both of which can trigger shy behaviors (Theall-Honey & Schmidt, 2006; Westen, 1998).

Our discussion of shyness raises the interesting question of how psychologists measure or assess personality traits, such as shyness. ●

Definition of Projective Tests

At the beginning of this module, we discussed Ted Haggard, the 50-year-old pastor who at the height of his career confessed to committing infidelity with a male prostitute. When a close friend described Haggard's personality, he said that Ted was a family man who followed God's word (top photo) (Goodstein & Banerjee, 2006). Before the accusations against Ted were made, none of his family, friends, or colleagues described him as a deceitful, dishonest, or immoral individual (bottom photo). When friends were describing Ted's personality, they were making a kind of psychological assessment.

How did friends describe Ted's personality?

Psychological assessment refers to the use of various tools, such as psychological tests or interviews, to measure various characteristics, traits, or abilities in order to understand behaviors and predict future performances or behaviors.

Psychological tests are usually divided into ability tests and personality tests, which differ considerably. For example, when people enter a psychological or drug treatment

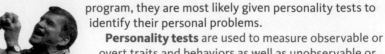

Was Ted Haggard generally an honest, righteous man or a deceitful, immoral one?

program, they are most likely given personality tests to identify their personal problems.

Personality tests are used to measure observable or overt traits and behaviors as well as unobservable or covert characteristics. Personality tests are used to identify personality problems and psychological disorders as well as to predict how a person might behave in the future.

Although you may not have taken a personality test, you certainly have taken many ability tests, such as exams.

Ability tests include achievement tests, which measure what we have learned; aptitude tests, which measure our potential for learning or acquiring a specific skill; and intelligence tests, which measure our general potential to solve problems, think abstractly, and profit from experience (R. M. Kaplan & Saccuzzo, 2009).

The primary tools of assessment are tests of ability and personality. There are two kinds of personality tests. We'll now focus on one kind, projective personality tests, and later (see p. 474) discuss objective personality tests. Personality assessment is a $500-million-a-year industry (Elejalde-Ruiz, 2006).

Examples of Projective Tests

In describing Haggard's personality, we can identify observable behaviors, such as happy, family-oriented, and friendly, as well as unobservable behaviors, such as anxious, guilt-ridden, and deceitful. In Freud's psychodynamic theory, observable behaviors reflect conscious wishes, desires, and thoughts, while unobservable behaviors may reflect unconscious forces. Freud developed three techniques for revealing unconscious forces—free association, dream interpretation, and interpretation of slips of the tongue. We now add a fourth technique to reveal hidden or unconscious forces: projective tests.

Projective tests require individuals to look at some meaningless object or ambiguous photo and describe what they see. In describing or making up a story about the ambiguous object, individuals are assumed to project both their conscious and unconscious feelings, needs, and motives.

Although Freud didn't develop projective tests, they are assumed to reveal unconscious thoughts (Butcher, 2009b; Groth-Marnat, 2009). We'll examine two widely used projective tests—the Rorschach (*ROAR-shock*) inkblot test and the Thematic Apperception Test (TAT).

Rorschach Inkblot Test

What do you see in this inkblot?

The Rorschach inkblot test, which was published in the early 1920s by a Swiss psychiatrist, Hermann Rorschach (1921/1942), contains five inkblots printed in black and white and five that have color (the inkblot shown on the left is similar to but is not an actual Rorschach inkblot).

What might this be?

The **Rorschach inkblot test** is used to assess personality by showing a person a series of ten inkblots and then asking the person to describe what he or she thinks each image is.

This test is used primarily in the therapeutic setting to assess personality traits and identify potential problems of clients (I. B. Weiner & Meyer, 2009).

Thematic Apperception Test (TAT)

What's happening in this picture?

A person would be shown a picture like the one on the right and asked to make up a plot or story about what the young man is thinking, feeling, or doing. This is an example of, but not a real, TAT card.

The **Thematic Apperception Test**, or **TAT**, involves showing a person a series of 20 pictures of people in ambiguous situations and asking the person to make up a story about what the people are doing or thinking in each situation.

What's happening in this picture?

The TAT, which was developed by Henry Murray (1943), is used to assess the motivation and personality characteristics of normal individuals as well as clients with personality problems (Butcher, 2009a; R. M. Kaplan & Saccuzzo, 2009).

Before we discuss how well the Rorschach inkblot test and the TAT assess personality traits and identify potential problems, we'll look at another personality test that you have probably heard of: handwriting analysis. How much can someone learn from just your handwriting?

Two Characteristics

What does handwriting show? Handwriting analysts (graphologists) can charge hundreds of dollars to do personality assessments that they claim reveal a person's strengths and weaknesses, which are important in selecting job applicants and identifying people who may not be trusted (M.C. Healy, 2005; Scanlon & Mauro, 1992).

However, researchers report that handwriting analysis is no better than chance at assessing personality

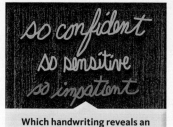

Which handwriting reveals an honest and sincere person?

characteristics, rating the success of job applicants, or identifying one's profession (M.C. Healy, 2005; Tripician, 2000). In order for handwriting analysis or any personality assessment test to be an effective personality assessment tool, it must have two characteristics: validity and reliability. Handwriting analysis is no better than chance in assessing personality because it lacks validity.

Validity

Handwriting analysis is fun but no better than chance as a personality test because it lacks validity.

Validity means that the test measures what it says it measures or what it is supposed to measure.

For example, for a personality test to be valid, it must measure personality traits specific to the person rather than general traits that apply to almost everyone. Handwriting analysis does not measure, identify, or predict traits specific to an individual, so it has no validity as a personality test (M.C. Healy, 2005; Tripician, 2000).

In addition to validity, a good personality test must have a second characteristic, reliability.

Reliability

In judging the usefulness of any personality test, the major question is always the same: How good are the test's validity and reliability?

Reliability refers to having a consistent score at different times. A person who takes a test at one point in time should receive the same score on a similar test taken at a later time.

For example, handwriting analysis may have good reliability provided your handwriting remains about the same across time. But, even if handwriting analysis has good reliability, it is still no better than chance at assessing or predicting an individual's personality traits because graphology lacks the important characteristic of validity.

This means that the usefulness of projective personality tests, such as the Rorschach test and TAT, depends on their validity and reliability.

Usefulness of Projective Tests

Are they valid and reliable? Projective tests, such as the Rorschach ink-blot test, have been used for over 90 years. However, there is still a debate between therapists, who report that projective tests are useful in assessing personality traits and problems, and researchers, who continue to disagree about the reliability and validity of projective tests (Mestel, 2003b; Society for Personality Assessment, 2005). This debate involves the advantages and disadvantages of projective tests.

Advantages

Individuals who take projective tests do not know which are the best, correct, or socially desirable answers to give because the stimuli—the inkblot or the TAT picture—are ambiguous and have no right or wrong answers. Thus, one advantage of projective tests such as the Rorschach and the TAT is that they are difficult to fake or bias, since there are no correct or socially desirable answers.

When clients respond to Rorschach's meaningless inkblots or make up stories about what is happening in TAT's ambiguous pictures, clinicians assume that clients project their hidden feelings, thoughts, or emotions onto these ambiguous stimuli. Based on this assumption, some clinicians believe that a second advantage of projective tests is that they are another method for assessing a client's hidden and unconscious thoughts and desires of which he or she is normally unaware (Groth-Marnat, 2009). Other researchers suggest that the Rorschach test is useful as an interview technique in eliciting unique information about the person (Aronow et al., 1995). Thus, the Rorschach test's advantage is obtaining information about the person in a setting where there are no right or wrong answers.

Clinicians' experience affects reliability and validity of projective tests.

Disadvantages

One disadvantage of projective tests comes from their use of ambiguous stimuli to which there are no right or wrong answers. The current method of scoring the Rorschach is based on analyzing and making judgments about so many different variables (such as content, theme, color, and detail of the cards) that disagreements often arise over interpretations and classifications (Mestel, 2003b). For example, there are several studies using the Rorschach in which clinicians scored and interpreted the results as indicating that perfectly normal individuals were classified as psychologically disordered (J.M. Wood et al., 2003). Although the Rorschach is one of the more popular personality assessment tests and some studies show it has high reliability and validity, there are other studies that point to serious problems in scoring and interpreting responses and making assessments based on the Rorschach test (Society for Personality Assessment, 2005; J.M. Wood et al., 2003, 2006).

In spite of criticisms, some experienced clinicians report that projective tests can provide reliable and valid information about a client's personality and problems, especially when combined with other assessment techniques (Exner & Erdberg, 2005). Thus, a clinician's training and experience play a major role in the accuracy of assessing a client's personality and problems using projective tests (R.M. Kaplan & Saccuzzo, 2009). ●

Can Personality Explain Obesity?

About two of every three American adults are overweight or obese. Peter Herida is one of the very few who is medically defined as "super massive morbid obese." As a 10–12-year-old child, Peter already weighed 179 pounds. At age 46, his weight reached an astonishing 863 pounds (pictured at right). His grocery bill was nearly $400 a week, and he ate over 3,000 calories at each meal. Peter took 14 different medications four times a day because of the life-threatening health damage caused by his extreme morbid obesity. Some of Peter's medical problems included heart failure, diabetes, and difficulty breathing during sleep. He became so heavy he could not walk, which resulted in him being housebound for 20 years. His mobility became so limited that a trip to the doctor's office required a wheelchair van, two fire truck crews, and one ambulance crew to transport him.

During one doctor's visit, Peter was told that unless he took radical measures to lose weight quickly, he would die soon. Peter chose to undergo gastric bypass surgery, a risky procedure that promised to make his stomach smaller so he would feel full after eating much less food. His doctor warned him that because of his weight and health problems, the operation carried a 60% chance of death. So, when Peter woke up after surgery, he promised himself, "I'm going to try and make this thing work, as I now was given a second chance at life!" (Herida, 2003).

Peter knew the operation was the easy part and the challenging part would be to make long-term lifestyle changes. After not having moved his body for 20 years, Peter spent his first 3 months learning how to walk again. He exercised and dieted for years afterward. At age 49, he swims a mile a day and works out daily. His health improved so much he takes only two medications a day compared to the 14 he took before.

1 Which part of Freud's psychodynamic theory might explain why Peter could not control his eating?

2 Does Peter have a food addiction?

3 What roles might the Freudian concepts of the id, ego, and superego have had in Peter becoming so obese that he could not walk?

4 Following Freud's psychodynamic theory, what kinds of questions might you ask or what techniques might you use to understand Peter's overeating behavior?

5 What psychological impulses or conflicts may have made losing weight difficult for Peter?

He is no longer a diabetic, he sleeps without difficulty breathing, and his heart is functioning better.

Peter's efforts helped him to lose a whopping 560 pounds during the first 10 months after surgery. His self-esteem skyrocketed and he rewarded himself by purchasing his dream car, a mint-condition 1982 Mercedes sedan, which he says "beats the heck out of a wheelchair van and emergency vehicle motorcade" (Herida, 2005). Peter became a motivational speaker to encourage others to strive to reach their potential just as he did.

6 How might humanistic theories explain Peter's obesity and then the dramatic changes he made in his life?

Adapted from Herida, 2003, 2005; *Incredible weight loss stories,* 2007; Taneeru, 2006

Summary Test

A Freud's Psychodynamic Theory

1. The lasting behaviors, thoughts, and emotions that typify how we react and adapt to other people and situations make up our **(a)** _____. An organized attempt to explain how personalities develop and why they differ is called a **(b)** _____ of personality.

2. Freud's approach, which emphasizes the importance of early childhood experiences and conflicts between conscious and unconscious forces, is called a **(a)** _____ theory of personality. According to Freud, those wishes, desires, or thoughts of which we are aware or that we can readily recall are **(b)** _____; those that we automatically repress because of their disturbing or threatening content are **(c)** _____.

3. Freud's technique of encouraging clients to talk about any thoughts or images that enter their heads is called **(a)** _____. His assumption that dreams provide clues to unconscious thoughts and desires gave rise to his technique of **(b)** _____. Mistakes that we make in everyday speech that are thought to reflect unconscious thoughts or wishes are called **(c)** _____.

B Divisions of the Mind

4. According to Freud, the biological drives of sex and aggression are the source of all psychic or mental energy and give rise to the development of the **(a)** _____. Because this division of the mind strives to satisfy drives and avoid pain without concern for moral or social restrictions, it is said to be operating according to the **(b)** _____. During infancy, the second division of the mind develops from the id; it is called the **(c)** _____. The goal of this second division is to find safe and socially acceptable ways of satisfying the id's desires. The ego follows a policy of satisfying a wish or desire only if a socially acceptable outlet is available; thus it is said to operate according to the **(d)** _____. During early childhood, the third division of the mind develops from the id; it is called the **(e)** _____. The goal of this division is to apply the moral values and standards of one's parents and society in satisfying one's wishes.

5. When the id, ego, and superego are in conflict, an unpleasant state of uneasiness, apprehension, and heightened physiological arousal may occur; this is known as **(a)** _____.

The Freudian processes that operate at unconscious levels to help the ego reduce anxiety through self-deception are called **(b)** _____; they can be helpful or harmful, depending on how much we rely on them.

C Developmental Stages

6. The essence of Freud's theory of personality development is a series of five developmental stages, called **(a)** _____, during which the individual seeks pleasure from different parts of the body. The stage that lasts for the first 18 months of life is called the **(b)** _____ stage. It is followed by the **(c)** _____ stage, which lasts until about the age of 3. The next stage, until about the age of 6, is called the **(d)** _____ stage. The stage that lasts from about 6 to puberty is called the **(e)** _____ stage; it is followed by the **(f)** _____ stage, which lasts through adulthood.

7. The resolution of the potential conflict at each stage has important implications for personality. A Freudian process through which individuals may be locked into earlier psychosexual stages because their wishes were overgratified or undergratified is called _____; it can occur at any of the first three stages.

D Freud's Followers & Critics

8. Jung believed that the basic force is not the sex drive, as Freud believed, but ancient memory traces and symbols shared by all peoples in all cultures, called the **(a)** _____. According to Adler's philosophy, each person is a social being with a unique personality and is motivated by **(b)** _____. Karen Horney disagreed with Freud's emphasis on biological urges and insisted that the major influence on personality development was **(c)** _____ between parents and child.

9. Those who generally agreed with Freud's basic ideas but disagreed with his emphasis on biological forces, sexual drives, and psychosexual stages are referred to as _____. They turned the emphasis of psychodynamic theory to psychosocial and cultural influences.

10. Criticisms of Freud's psychodynamic theory include that it is so comprehensive that it is not very useful for explaining or predicting behaviors of a specific **(a)** _____; that some Freudian ideas (Oedipal complex) are out of date because they cannot be **(b)** _____; and that psychodynamic theory must be updated with findings about **(c)** _____ factors and the association between **(d)** _____ development and related behaviors.

E Humanistic Theories

11. Humanistic theories emphasize our capacity for personal growth, development of our potential, and freedom to choose our **(a)** _____. They stress that our perception of the world becomes our reality; this is called the **(b)** _____ perspective. These theories emphasize that one's personality is unique, functions as a unit, and is more than the sum of individual parts; together these ideas make up the **(c)** _____ view. These theories also highlight the idea of an inherent tendency to reach our true potentials, which is called **(d)** _____.

12. According to Maslow, our needs are arranged in a hierarchy with **(a)** _____ at the bottom and **(b)** _____ toward the top.

13. How we see or describe ourselves, including how we perceive our abilities, personality characteristics, and behaviors, is referred to as our **(a)** _____. According to Carl Rogers, the development of self-concept depends on our interactions with others. If we receive **(b)** _____ positive regard even when our behavior is disappointing, we will develop a positive self-concept and tend to act, feel, and think optimistically and constructively.

F Cultural Diversity: Unexpected High Achievement

14. Indo-Chinese children overcame problems of language and culture and excelled in American schools in part because of the _____ held by their families, including mutual respect, cooperation, parental involvement, and the belief that they, not fate, controlled their destinies.

G Research Focus: Shyness

15. As a practicing psychoanalyst, Donald Kaplan traced the causes of shyness back to unresolved conflicts at one or more of Freud's **(a)** _____. The Freudian approach primarily uses therapists' **(b)** _____ to answer questions about personality. In comparison, social cognitive theory breaks shyness down into three measurable or observable components that can be investigated using **(c)** _____.

H Application: Assessment— Projective Tests

16. Tests that are used to measure observable traits and behaviors as well as unobservable characteristics of a person and to identify personality problems and psychological disorders are called _____ tests.

17. Achievement tests measure what we have learned; aptitude tests measure our potential for learning or acquiring a specific skill; and intelligence tests measure our general potential to solve problems, think abstractly, and profit from experience. Collectively, these are called _____ tests.

18. For a test to be useful, it must have two characteristics. First, a test must measure what it is supposed to measure; this is called **(a)** _____. Second, a person's score on a test at one point in time should be similar to the score obtained by the same person on a similar test at a later point in time; this is called **(b)** _____.

19. Typically, a combination of tests is used to assess personality. Tests that involve presenting an ambiguous stimulus and asking the person to describe it are called **(a)** _____ tests. A test used to assess personality in terms of how the participant interprets a series of inkblots is called the **(b)** _____ test. A test in which the participant is to make up a story about people shown in ambiguous situations is called the **(c)** _____.

Key Terms/Key People

ability tests, 450
Adler, Alfred, 440
anal stage, 439
anxiety, 437
collective unconscious, 440
conditional positive regard, 445
conscious thoughts, 434
defense mechanisms, 437
deficiency needs, 443
denial, 437
displacement, 437
dream interpretation, 435
ego, 436
fixation, 438
free association, 435
Freudian slips, 435
genital stage, 439

growth needs, 443
holistic view, 442
Horney, Karen, 440
humanistic theories, 442
humanistic theories, evaluation, 446
id, 436
ideal self, 444
implicit or nondeclarative memory, 441
Jung, Carl, 440
latency stage, 439
Maslow's hierarchy of needs, 443
neo-Freudians, 440
Oedipus complex, 439
oral stage, 439
personality, 433

personality tests, 450
phallic stage, 439
phenomenological perspective, 442
pleasure principle, 436
positive psychology, 446
positive regard, 445
projection, 437
projective tests, 450
psychodynamic theory of personality, 434
psychological assessment, 450
psychosexual stages, 438
rationalization, 437
reaction formation, 437
real self, 444
reality principle, 436
reliability, 451

repression, 437
Rorschach inkblot test, 450
self or self-concept, 444
self-actualization, 442, 443
self-actualizing tendency, 444
self theory, 444
shyness, 449
social cognitive theory, 449
sublimation, 437
superego, 436
Thematic Apperception Test, or TAT, 450
theory of personality, 433
unconditional positive regard, 445
unconscious forces, 434
unconscious motivation, 434
validity, 451

Media Resources

Go to **CengageBrain.com** to access Psychology CourseMate, where you will find an interactive eBook, glossaries, flashcards, quizzes, videos, answers to Critical Thinking questions, and more. You can also access Virtual Psychology Labs, an interactive laboratory experience designed to illustrate key experiments first-hand.

MODULE 20

Social Cognitive & Trait Theories

Power of Beliefs

Why did she get threatened, clubbed, and jailed?

Wangari Maathai *(wan-GAH-ree mah-DHEYE)* was born in Kenya into a family of peasant farmers. She grew up in a beautiful countryside filled with many varieties of shrubs and trees. Water cascaded down to streams where she drank to quench her thirst. According to Kenyan tradition, as the oldest daughter, Maathai spent most of her days side by side with her mother, helping her and learning from her. She later made a bold decision to break with cultural expectations and study in the United States, where she earned both bachelor's and master's degrees. Upon returning home, Maathai yet again challenged cultural expectations by becoming the first woman in Kenya to earn a Ph.D. and later the first female professor at the University of Nairobi. When Maathai returned to Kenya, she realized there were fewer and fewer of the magnificent trees that once filled the region. One day she went to her yard and planted a tree, and it was then that she founded the Green Belt Movement, an organization that helps conserve the environment, educates people about environmental issues, and trains women to have jobs as nursery managers and forest rangers. Maathai empowered women by letting them plant their own trees and make profits from the products (nuts, fruits) to support their children's education and household needs.

She chose to be tortured and jailed rather than change her major beliefs.

As Maathai began her efforts to restore nature, she quickly realized that the government in Kenya was corrupt and was largely responsible for the deforestation by illegally selling land and trees to make room for buildings. The Green Belt Movement challenged the government's abuse of power, corruption, and destruction of the environment. Maathai initiated sit-ins and a hunger strike but was attacked with tear gas and viciously clubbed by police. She received many death threats, was repeatedly arrested, and once even went into hiding.

Despite the brutality she experienced time and time again, Maathai persisted in her struggle for human rights and environmental conservation. Today, the Green Belt Movement has planted over 40 million trees in Kenya and provided work for tens of thousands of women. Up until her death in 2011, Maathai demonstrated unwavering dedication, absolute selflessness, and inspiring courage, which brought her many honors. In 2004, Maathai was honored by becoming the first African woman to win the Nobel Peace Prize (adapted from Busari, 2011; Maathai, 2004, 2005, 2006; Mjøs, 2004).

What were the forces that shaped Maathai's personality and gave her the strength and motivation to persist in the face of overwhelming adversity? In this module, we'll discuss some forces that shape and mold our personalities.

In a different nation, an ocean away, Kiran Bedi waged her own personal struggle against forces that said no Indian woman should be doing what she wanted to do.

Determination

What's unusual about this woman?

At just 5 feet 3 inches tall, Kiran Bedi wouldn't normally attract much attention. Yet, with her petite stature and only a wooden baton, she once turned back a 3,000-member, sword-wielding group of rioters by herself. Her male colleagues felt overwhelmed and ran away.

In 1972, Kiran Bedi became India's first female police officer. Sure, she faced criticism from her male counterparts who believed she didn't have the physical strength or mental toughness the job required. But, she never let their negative comments hold her back.

Bedi began her service in the traffic division and made headlines when she towed the illegally parked cars of government officials. She later worked as a narcotics officer and antiterrorist specialist. She even reformed the largest prison in Asia, and her work there has led to prison reform all over the world.

In India, a country where women struggle to achieve gender equality, Bedi's unyielding determination didn't go unnoticed. She has received many prestigious awards for her achievements, including the Asian version of the Nobel Prize. She has become a hero and role model for Indian women, as well as all women living in countries where the struggle for gender equality continues. Bedi has taught women that with determination they can overcome criticisms and stereotypes to realize their dreams (Bedi, 2006; Turnbull, 2008). After more than 35 years of police work, Bedi recently founded two organizations that reach out to improve the health care, education, and vocational skills of thousands of underserved children, men, and women (www.kiranbedi.com).

Kiran Bedi fought against stereotypes to fulfill her dream.

Kiran Bedi, like the many thousands of female officers around the world, has shown that women make good cops, partly because of their particular personality traits: Women are less authoritarian, more open, better listeners, and less likely to trigger showdowns than are their male counterparts (Lonsway et al., 2003; Munoz, 2003). Apparently, what women may lack in sheer muscle power, they make up for with a winning combination of personality traits.

In this module, we'll discuss personality traits, which are motivating forces that we all have, cannot live without, like to talk about, and are often asked to change but find it difficult to do so.

What's Coming

We'll discuss two theories of personality, each with a different emphasis. The first is social cognitive theory (previously called social learning theory), which stresses the influences of cognitive, learning, and social processes on personality development. The second is trait theory, which focuses on measuring traits and describing how traits make up our different personalities and influence our behaviors.

We'll begin with three social cognitive forces that helped shape Wangari Maathai's personality. ●

A Social Cognitive Theory

Review and Definition

What shaped her personality?

How many of us would still have fought to protect the environment after being beaten repeatedly, having our life threatened, and being imprisoned more than a dozen times, as Maathai did? What forces shaped Maathai's personality and gave her such courage, self-confidence, and perseverance? In Module 19, we discussed two approaches to this question: Freud's psychodynamic theory and humanistic theories.

Freud's psychodynamic theory said that our personality is shaped primarily by our inborn biological urges, especially sex and aggression, and by how we resolve conflicts during the psychosexual stages, especially during the first five years.

Humanistic theories, such as those of Abraham Maslow and Carl Rogers, assume that we are basically good and

Maathai won honors because of her unwavering courage.

© Tor Richardsen/AFP/Getty Images

that our personality is shaped primarily by our inborn tendency for self-actualization or self-fulfillment, which includes both biological and psychological factors.

Now we'll discuss two more answers: first, social cognitive theory and, later, trait theory.

Social cognitive theory says that our personality is influenced by our social experiences and our resulting thoughts.

Social cognitive theory grew out of the research of a number of psychologists, especially Albert Bandura (1986, 2001a). According to social cognitive theory, we are neither good nor bad but are shaped primarily by three influential factors.

Interaction of Three Factors

For over 40 years, Wangari Maathai fought for human rights and environment conservation. During this time, she suffered tremendous personal hardships, including being beaten and imprisoned. You can't help wondering what shaped her personality and gave her the strength, determination, and character to sacrifice so much to reach her goals of preserving the environment and empowering women.

According to social cognitive theory's concept of reciprocal determinism, Maathai's personality was influenced and shaped by the interactions among three significant forces.

1 Cognitive factors

2 Behaviors

3 Environmental factors

Y O U

Reciprocal determinism is the idea that personality development is shaped primarily by the interactions among three forces: environmental conditions, cognitive-personal factors, and behavior, which all influence how we evaluate, interpret, organize, and apply information. We'll apply reciprocal determinism to Maathai to help you learn how these factors can interact to shape one's personality.

Cognitive-Personal Factors

Maathai was born into a family of peasant farmers and grew up during a time when Kenya had an abundance of greenery. Her childhood experiences taught her the beauty of nature's wonders. Her family encouraged her to be self-confident, ambitious, and determined to achieve her dreams. Being born into a farming family and being taught to value nature are examples of cognitive-personal factors that helped shape Maathai's personality.

Cognitive factors include our beliefs, expectations, values, intentions, and social roles. **Personal factors** include our emotional makeup and our biological and genetic influences.

Cognitive factors guide personality development by influencing the way we view and interpret information. For example, Maathai views the world from the standpoint of someone whose livelihood depended on nature. These kinds of beliefs (cognitions) give Maathai the strength and determination to fight to plant more trees. Thus, cognitive-personal factors influence our personalities by affecting what we think, believe, and feel, which in turn affect how we act and behave.

Behaviors

During her lifetime, Maathai spoke forcefully against deforestation, founded the Green Belt Movement, and empowered women by involving them in restoring the environment. These are examples of the kinds of behaviors that also shaped her personality.

Behaviors include a variety of personal actions, such as the things we do and say.

In Maathai's case, the political and social behaviors that she engaged in to help preserve the environment in turn strengthened her belief that the government's actions to replace greenery with buildings were morally and politically wrong.

Just as behavior influences our beliefs, so too does our environment influence both.

Environmental Factors

Maathai lived in Kenya at a time of political oppression, which resulted in harsh beatings, imprisonment, and sometimes death for those who spoke out against the government's corrupt actions. These environmental factors certainly affected Maathai's personality development.

Environmental factors include our social, political, and cultural influences, as well as our particular learning experiences.

Just as our cognitive factors influence how we perceive and interpret our environment, our environment in turn affects our beliefs, values, and social roles.

We can assume that living in such an oppressive environment strengthened Maathai's determination to get a Ph.D. and to devote her life to restoring trees and empowering women.

According to Bandura (2001a), personality development is influenced by the interactions among these three factors. He especially focused on cognitive-personal factors.

Bandura's Social Cognitive Theory

Albert Bandura (1986, 2001a) originally called his theory of personality development the social learning theory.

Why are beliefs important?

However, to emphasize the importance of cognitive factors in personality development, he has changed the name to the social cognitive theory.

Bandura's social cognitive theory assumes that personality development, growth, and change are influenced by four distinctively human cognitive processes: highly developed language ability, observational learning, purposeful behavior, and self-analysis.

Bandura believes that these four cognitive processes reach their highest level of functioning in humans and that much of human personality and behavior is shaped by our own thoughts and beliefs.

Cognitive factors—beliefs, values, and goals—influence their personalities.

For example, the people in the photo on the left are members of Wangari Maathai's international Green Belt Movement. Maathai founded this organization over 40 years ago to help restore the environment all over the world while helping to empower women by getting them actively involved in the organization. According to Bandura's social cognitive theory, the personalities of these members are, to a large extent, molded by cognitive factors such as the beliefs, values, and goals of the Green Belt Movement. We'll briefly explain each of Bandura's cognitive factors.

Four Cognitive Factors

At the heart of Bandura's social cognitive theory is the idea that much of personality development is shaped and molded by cognitive processes that influence how we view and interpret the world. And, in turn, how we view and interpret the world influences how we behave. Here's how Bandura's cognitive processes apply to Green Belt Movement members.

1 Language ability. This is a powerful tool for processing and understanding information that influences personality development. We turn this information into ideas, beliefs, values, and goals, which shape, guide, and motivate our behaviors. For example, the Green Belt Movement teaches and values restoring the environment and empowering women, which helps motivate members to be more nurturing, giving, and self-confident.

2 Observational learning. Almost all of us "people watch"; we observe parents, brothers, sisters, peers, friends, and teachers. By doing so, we learn a great deal. Observational learning involves watching, imitating, and modeling. Most of the time, the observer provides his or her own reward for developing some belief or performing some behavior. For example, observational learning allows the members of the Green Belt Movement to imitate and model the personality characteristics of Wangari Maathai.

3 Purposeful behavior. Our capacity to anticipate events, plan ahead, and set goals influences our personality development, growth, and change. For instance, in working to restore the environment, members of the Green Belt Movement organize and plan ways to plant more trees and speak firmly against deforestation, which encourages them to become responsible, confident, and passionate about their cause.

4 Self-analysis. This is an internal process that allows us to monitor our own thoughts and actions. By deciding to change our goals or values, we can affect our personality development. For instance, members of the Green Belt Movement may use self-analysis to check their personal progress and to reward themselves for meeting the organization's goals.

According to Bandura's social cognitive theory, these four cognitive processes influence our personality development, growth, and change.

To make the relationship between cognitive factors and personality more concrete, we'll focus on three specific beliefs: locus of control (this page), delay of gratification, and self-efficacy (next page).

Locus of Control

Can you control when you'll graduate?

This is the kind of question that intrigued Julian Rotter (1990), who was interested in how social cognitive theory applied to human behavior. Rotter developed a well-known scale to measure a person's expectancies about how much control he or she has over situations, which Rotter called the locus of control.

Locus of control refers to our beliefs about how much control we have over situations or rewards. We are said to have an *internal locus of control* if we believe that we have control over situations and rewards. We are said to have an *external locus of control* if we believe that

Can you control when you will graduate?

we do not have control over situations and rewards and that events outside ourselves (fate) determine what happens. People fall on a continuum between internal and external locus of control.

For example, if you believe that when you graduate depends primarily on your motivation and determination, then you have more of an internal locus of control. If you believe that when you graduate depends mostly on chance or things outside your control, then you have more of an external locus of control. Having more of an internal locus of control is an advantage because hundreds of studies report a positive relationship between internal locus of control and psychological functioning. For example, people with an internal locus of control are generally higher achievers, cope better with chronic illness, and report less stress, anxiety, and depression than those with an external locus of control. Also, an internal locus of control during childhood seems to protect people against some health problems in adulthood (Burger, 2008; Gale et al., 2008; Livneh et al., 2004; Spector et al., 2001).

These findings indicate that a specific belief influences how you perceive your world, which, in turn, affects how you behave. Next, we'll examine two other beliefs that influence behavior.

Delay of Gratification

Get it now or wait for better things?

Many young children have a difficult time not grabbing their favorite candy from the low-lying shelves at checkouts in spite of parents promising they'll get candy when they get home. Likewise, adults may see something they didn't intend to buy but do so on impulse, not always getting the best product or deal. These are common examples of the struggle with a cognitive concept or belief called delay of gratification.

Delay of gratification refers to not taking an immediate but less desirable reward and instead waiting and pursuing an object or completing a task that promises a better reward in the future.

Although related to the ideas of self-control, impulsiveness, and will power, delay of gratification is defined so that it can easily be studied in the laboratory (Mischel et al., 1989). One technique to measure delay of gratification was to show children two objects, one less preferred (a single marshmallow) and one more preferred (two marshmallows). The children were told that to obtain the more preferred reward they had to wait until the experimenter, who had to leave the room, returned after some delay (about 15 minutes).

Children were free to end the waiting period by ringing a bell, but then they would get only the less preferred reward. Thus, the child had a conflict: Accept immediate gratification and take the less preferred reward, or delay gratification and obtain the more preferred reward (Mischel et al., 1989).

> Should I take one marshmallow now or wait and get two later?

Based on a longitudinal study with the children in the marshmallow experiment, researchers found that delay of gratification is a lifelong trait. Using fMRI brain imaging (see p. 71), researchers tested the original participants over a 40-year period. Those individuals who were good at delaying gratification as children demonstrated greater brain activity in regions responsible for thoughtful and rational thinking, as well as inhibition of impulsive behavior. In contrast, those individuals who were poor at delaying gratification as children had less activity in the above-mentioned regions, but more activity in areas responsible for instant gratification. Researchers concluded that delay of gratification is a stable individual characteristic (Casey et al., 2011).

Important to delay gratification? Developing the beliefs and cognitive processes involved in the ability to delay gratification can influence a variety of personal behaviors and social interactions in positive or negative ways (Francis & Susman, 2009; Peake et al., 2002). For example, 4-year-old children good at delaying gratification tended to be more intelligent, to have greater social responsibility, and to strive for higher achievement. When these very same 4-year-old children were retested at age 14, they were rated by parents as more competent, more intelligent, and better able to concentrate than those children who were not good at delaying gratification. NOT being able to delay gratification has been linked to self-regulatory problems, including impulsive violence, overeating, drug abuse, and unprotected sex.

Another cognitive process that affects personality and behavior is how much we believe in our own capabilities.

Self-Efficacy

Can I get better grades?

Students often ask about how to improve their grades. According to Albert Bandura (2004), one reason students differ in whether they receive high or low grades is self-efficacy.

Self-efficacy refers to the confidence in your ability to organize and execute a given course of action to solve a problem or accomplish a task.

For example, saying "I think that I am capable of getting a high grade in this course" is a sign of strong self-efficacy. You judge your self-efficacy by combining four sources of information (Bandura, 1999; E. T. Higgins & Scholer, 2008):

1. You *use previous experiences* of success or failure on similar tasks to estimate how you will do on a new, related task.

> Why do my friends say that I should be getting better grades?

2. You *compare* your capabilities with those of others.

3. You *listen* to what others say about your capabilities.

4. You *use feedback* from your body to assess your strength, vulnerability, and capability.

You would rate yourself as having strong self-efficacy for getting good grades if you had previous success with getting high grades, if you believe you are as academically capable as others, if your friends say you are smart, and if you do not become too stressed during exams.

Influence of self-efficacy. According to Bandura's self-efficacy theory, your motivation to achieve, perform, and do well in a variety of tasks and situations is largely influenced by how strongly you believe in your own capabilities. Some people have a strong sense of self-efficacy that applies to many situations (academic settings, sports, and social interactions), others have a strong sense that applies to only a few situations (computers but not social interactions), while still others have a weak sense of self-efficacy, which predicts having less success in many of life's tasks (Eccles & Wigfield, 2002). For example, people with higher self-efficacy had greater success at stopping smoking, losing weight, overcoming a phobia, recovering from a heart attack, performing well in school, adjusting to new situations, coping with job stress, playing video games, and tolerating pain (Caprara et al., 2004; Joseph et al., 2003; Luszczynska & Sutton, 2006).

Conclusion. So far we have discussed three important beliefs: whether you have an internal or external locus of control, how much you can delay gratification, and whether you have high or low self-efficacy. Research on these three beliefs supports the basic assumption of social cognitive theory—that cognitive factors influence personality development, which in turn affects performance and success in a variety of tasks and situations.

© PhotoDisc, Inc.

Evaluation of Social Cognitive Theory

Sometimes a person's experience better illustrates the power and importance of beliefs than all the research in the world. One

Where does he get his courage?

example of this is Michael J. Fox, a talented actor who has starred in popular TV shows, such as "Spin City," and movies, including the *Back to the Future* trilogy. At age 30, Michael was diagnosed with young-onset Parkinson's disease (see p. 60), which began with a twitch in his left pinkie and led to relentless tremors in his arms and legs. Acting was his livelihood, but the progression of his symptoms made it increasingly difficult for him to act, even with the use of powerful medications to help control his tremors (Dudley, 2006; M. J. Fox, 2002).

The worsening of his symptoms forced Michael to make a key life decision: Would he allow his disease to lower his life's ambitions *or* would he believe in his ability to fight harder than ever before to reach his life's goals? Michael was unwilling to allow Parkinson's disease to take over his life. He began fighting against the disease and did so in incredible ways. Michael has continued to act by guest starring in television shows, such as "The Good Wife," "Curb Your Enthusiasm," and "Rescue Me." Also, by starting a charitable foundation, which has become a leader in Parkinson's disease research, and speaking in favor of stem cell research, he has taken an active role in discovering a cure for Parkinson's disease.

In his memoir titled *Lucky Man* (M. J. Fox, 2002), Michael speaks of the pleasure he has had in increasing public awareness of Parkinson's disease: "The ten years since my diagnosis have been the best ten years of my life, and I consider myself a lucky man." Michael's story illustrates a major assumption of social cognitive theory: Beliefs have a great influence on personality, motivation, and behavior.

We'll evaluate social cognitive theory's approach to personality development and compare it with other theories.

1 Comprehensive Approach

Social cognitive theory focuses on the interaction of three primary forces in the development of personality: cognitive-personal factors, which include beliefs, expectations, social roles, and genetic influences; behaviors, which include actions, conversations, and emotional expressions; and environmental influences, such as social, political, and cultural forces.

> I believe I can continue to act.

Bandura (2001a) points out that other theories of personality tend to focus on one or two of these factors but neglect the interaction among all three factors. For example, Freudian and humanistic theories emphasize the effects of personal and cognitive forces on personality development but neglect the significant behavioral, learning, and environmental influences. Thus, one advantage of social cognitive theory is that its approach to personality development is more comprehensive and includes more influential factors than other theories.

2 Experimentally Based

Many of the concepts used in social cognitive theory have been developed from, and based on, objective measurement, laboratory research, and experimental studies. Because social cognitive theory's concepts—such as locus of control, delay of gratification, and self-efficacy—are experimentally based, they can be manipulated, controlled, and tested and are less subject to error and bias.

In comparison, many concepts from Freudian and humanistic theories of personality were developed from clinical interviews and practice and, for that reason, these concepts (oral stage, Oedipal complex, self-actualization, positive regard) are more difficult to test and validate and more open to error and bias.

3 Programs for Change

Because many of the concepts of social cognitive theory are experimentally based and objectively defined (observational learning, self-reward, modeling behavior, self-analysis, and planning), these concepts have been used to develop very successful programs for changing behavior and personality. For example, we earlier discussed two behavioral change programs that were based on social cognitive theory. In one study, individuals who had developed an intense fear of snakes showed decreased fear after observing a fearless model touching and handling a snake (see p. 225); in another study, children who had observed an adult's aggressive behaviors imitated and performed similar aggressive behaviors when given an opportunity (see p. 224). These are just two examples of behavioral changes that occurred after applying concepts based on social cognitive theory (Bandura, 2001a).

4 Criticisms and Conclusions

Critics say that because social cognitive concepts focus on narrowly defined behaviors, such as self-efficacy, locus of control, and delay of gratification, social cognitive theory is a somewhat piecemeal explanation of personality development. They add that social cognitive theory needs to combine these objectively but narrowly defined concepts into a more integrated theory of personality. Finally, critics contend that social cognitive theory pays too little attention to the influence of genetic factors, emotional influences, and childhood experiences on personality development (Bouchard & Loehlin, 2001; Loehlin et al., 2003).

Despite these criticisms, social cognitive theory has had a profound impact on personality theory by emphasizing the objective measurement of concepts, the influence of cognitive processes, and the application of concepts to programs for behavioral change.

Next, we'll discuss an interesting theory of personality that emphasizes describing and assessing differences between individuals and explaining why we do not always act in a consistent way. ●

© s_bukley/Shutterstock.com

B Trait Theory

Definition

At the beginning of this module, we told you about Kiran Bedi (photo below), who in 1972 became the first female police officer in India. This

Do women make better cops?

was no small achievement in a country where women struggle to break free of their second-class status, which is rooted in India's ancient culture. But, even in the United States, the land of opportunity, throughout the 1970s, 1980s, and 1990s, women had to fight against discrimination and harassment from male police officers who believed that women did not have the physical or mental strength to be police officers (Copeland, 1999). However, studies have shown that women do make good police officers and in some instances they are

Which traits of policewomen make them better at keeping the peace?

more successful than policemen because policewomen have better interpersonal skills than men (Lonsway et al., 2003).

Women's interpersonal skills can benefit the police force by reducing the number of police brutality cases resulting from undue force. In one police department, for instance, 96% of police brutality cases were a result of acts by male officers (Melnick, 2011). Policewomen seem to have an advantage in keeping potentially violent situations peaceful. For example, although we may think that the best way to control thugs is with threat or force, policewoman Kelly

rarely uses either. Kelly admits that her physical strength cannot always match that of some of the macho males she encounters. "Coming across aggressively doesn't work with gang members," Kelly explains. "If that first encounter is direct, knowledgeable, and made with authority, they respond. It takes a few more words but it works" (McDowell, 1992, p. 70). As another woman police officer said, "We've been learning our whole lives how to deal with things without having to resort to physical strength and physical violence" (Munoz, 2003, p. B2). These examples suggest that, in some situations, women make better cops than men because they have different personality traits.

Men. Traits of male officers include being assertive, aggressive, and direct, which help them act as enforcers. **Women.** Traits of female officers include being compassionate, sympathetic, and diplomatic, which help them act as peacekeepers.

The reason female police officers act more as peacekeepers and male police officers act more as enforcers may be explained by trait theory.

Trait theory is an approach for analyzing the structure of personality by measuring, identifying, and classifying similarities and differences in personality characteristics or traits.

The basic unit for measuring personality characteristics is the trait.

A **trait** is a relatively stable and enduring tendency to behave in a particular way.

For example, traits of female police officers include being compassionate, sympathetic, and diplomatic, which help them function as peacekeepers, while traits of male police officers include being assertive, aggressive, and direct, which help them function as enforcers.

Identifying Traits

How would you describe these individuals?

How would you describe the personalities of a criminal, clown, graduate, nun, and beauty queen? This seemingly impossible task was the major goal of personality researchers. They were determined to find a list of traits whose two characteristics seemed mutually exclusive: The list had to contain very few traits but at the same time be able to describe differences among anyone's and everyone's personality, from farmer to business woman, to teenage singer. The search for this elusive list began in the 1930s with, of all things, a dictionary.

How would you describe their personalities?

How many traits can there be?

In the 1930s, Gordon Allport and an associate went through the dictionary and selected every term that could distinguish differences among personalities (Allport & Odbert, 1936). They found about 18,000 terms that dealt with all kinds of personality differences; of these, about 4,500 were considered to fit their definition of personality traits. Allport defined *traits* as stable and consistent tendencies in how an individual adjusts to his or her environment. The advantage of Allport's list was that it was comprehensive enough to describe anyone's and everyone's personality. The disadvantage was that it was incredibly long and thus impractical to use in research.

Allport's search for a list of defining traits set the stage for future research. However, his list of thousands of traits needed to be organized into far fewer basic traits. This task fell to Raymond Cattell.

Aren't some traits related?

In the 1940s, Raymond Cattell (1943) took Allport's list of 4,500 traits and used factor analysis to reduce the list to the most basic traits.

Factor analysis is a complicated statistical method that finds relationships among many different or diverse items and allows them to be grouped together.

Cattell used factor analysis to search for *relationships* among hundreds of traits on Allport's list so that the original list could be reduced to 35 basic traits, which Cattell called *source traits*. He claimed that these 35 basic traits could describe all differences among personalities. Although Cattell's achievement was remarkable, his list of 35 traits—and even his further reduction of the list to 16 traits—still proved too long to be practical for research and only moderately useful in assessing personality differences. Obviously, Cattell's list needed more reducing, but that was to take another 30 years.

Finding Traits: Big Five

Can it be done with just five?

From the 1960s to the early 1990s, about a dozen researchers in several countries were using factor analysis to find relationships among lists of adjectives that described personality differences. Doing the impossible, researchers reduced the list of 35 traits to only 5, which make up the five-factor model of personality (Durrett & Trull, 2005; G. Matthews et al., 2009).

Each letter in the word OCEAN is the first letter of one of the Big Five traits.

The **five-factor model** organizes personality traits and describes differences in personality using five categories, which are **openness, conscientiousness, extraversion, agreeableness,** and **neuroticism.**

These five factors became known as the *Big Five* and are easy to remember if you note that their first letters make the acronym OCEAN. Each of the five factors actually represents a continuum of behavior, as briefly described in the figure below.

Openness

| Is open to novel experience. | Has narrow interests. |

Conscientiousness

| Is responsible and dependable. | Is impulsive and careless. |

Extraversion

| Is outgoing and decisive. | Is retiring and withdrawn. |

Agreeableness

| Is warm and good-natured. | Is unfriendly and cold. |

Neuroticism

| Is stable and not a worrier. | Is nervous and emotionally unstable. |

You can think of each Big Five factor as a *supertrait* because each factor's continuum includes dozens of related traits. For example, for conscientiousness, one end of the continuum includes the traits of being dependable, responsible, deliberate, hardworking, and precise; at the other end are the traits of being impulsive, careless, late, lazy, and aimless.

Importance of the Big Five

Researchers wondered if the structure of personality was shaped primarily by different *cultural factors* (child-rearing practices, religious and moral values, language similarities) or primarily by differences in the *basic human ways* of acting and experiencing that are universal, or similar across all peoples and countries.

Because support for the five-factor model was found in many very different countries or cultures, researchers concluded that the basic structure of human personality arises from some universal living experience or biological basis rather than being shaped by individual countries or cultures (Jang et al., 2006; R. R. McCrae & Costa, 2003; Yamagata et al., 2006). If basic human personality structure is universal, it means that the personalities of individuals in different countries can be described by using the Big Five traits.

Big Five in the Real World

Because personality similarities and differences can be described by five categories, questionnaires based on the five-factor theory can more accurately assess personality, which is one of the major tasks of therapists and psychologists.

For instance, questionnaires based on the five-factor theory reveal differences among people in the United States and in other countries. The Swiss, for instance, rate themselves as highly conscientious, while Canadians and Indians rate themselves as highly agreeable (R. McCrae, 2008). There are also regional personality differences in the United States (Rentfrow, 2010). For instance, people in the Midwest and Southeast score highest in agreeableness, people in the South and Midwest score highest in conscientiousness, and people in the Northeast and West score highest in openness (Rentfrow et al., 2008).

Researchers generally agree that the five-factor theory is a leap forward in trait theory and is useful in defining personality structures, predicting behaviors, and identifying personality problems (Burger, 2011; R. R. McCrae & Costa, 2003). Still, some researchers propose that five factors are too few, while others think that five is too many (De Young, 2006; K. Lee & Ashton, 2006; Musek, 2007).

Big Five in the Brain

Researchers have found that the sizes of different parts of our brains are associated with the Big Five traits (De Young et al., 2010). Using MRI scans (see p. 70) to examine the structures of people's brains and the results from a personality questionnaire, researchers found a few interesting outcomes. For instance, people high in conscientiousness were found to have larger areas of the brain responsible for planning and decision making. People high in neuroticism were found to have smaller brain areas known to regulate emotions. Also, people high in agreeableness had larger areas responsible for understanding others' emotions, intentions, and mental states.

The researchers caution that these findings are only suggestive and do not indicate cause-and-effect relationships. Also, they say that personality traits are not fixed at birth and can be affected by life experiences. Still, it is interesting to find personality traits to be associated with brain structures.

Although each of us possesses relatively enduring supertraits, why do we sometimes behave differently in different situations?

Person Versus Situation

How does private life compare to public life?

One of the best-known American football coaches is Jerry Sandusky, who spent most of his career coaching at Pennsylvania State University. In addition to being committed to coaching, he founded The Second Mile, a nonprofit organization aimed at helping underprivileged and at-risk youth achieve their dreams. Since its inception in 1977, The Second Mile has received great praise, notably from former U.S. President George H. W. Bush, who commended Sandusky's charitable work with youth.

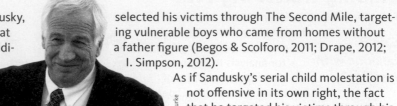

Sandusky advocated for youth in public, but in private he was a child molester.

Then, in 2011, Sandusky was arrested and charged with multiple counts of child sexual abuse spanning a 15-year period. In 2012, he was found guilty on 45 of 48 charges against him, which included indecent assault, unlawful contact with minors, endangering the welfare of children, and deviate sexual intercourse. During the criminal investigation, it was discovered that Sandusky selected his victims through The Second Mile, targeting vulnerable boys who came from homes without a father figure (Begos & Scolforo, 2011; Drape, 2012; I. Simpson, 2012).

As if Sandusky's serial child molestation is not offensive in its own right, the fact that he targeted his victims through his charitable foundation aimed at helping and protecting youth makes his acts even more unconscionable.

The observation that, like Jerry Sandusky, individuals often behave differently in different situations questions one of the basic assumptions of trait theory, which is that traits create tendencies to behave in certain consistent ways. Psychologist Walter Mischel (1968) was one of the first to conduct a series of classic experiments on why traits fail to predict the behavior of people across different situations.

Experiment: Person-Situation

To test trait theory's basic assumption that people behave consistently across situations, Walter Mischel and Philip Peake (1982) asked college students, "How conscientious are you?" If students answer that they are "very conscientious," trait theory predicts that they will behave conscientiously in many different situations. Mischel then observed how conscientious college students behaved across 19 very different situations, such as attending classes, getting homework in on time, and keeping their rooms neat.

Students who rated themselves as very conscientious behaved that way day after day in similar situations. However, these same students did not behave conscientiously across all 19 conditions. For example, very conscientious students might clean their rooms daily but not get their homework in on time, or they might attend all their classes but not clean their rooms. Researchers concluded that, as trait theory predicted, students behaved with great consistency in the *same* situation, but contrary to trait theory's prediction, students behaved *differently* or with low consistency across different situations. This finding led to what is now called the person-situation interaction.

The **person-situation interaction** means that a person's behavior results from an interaction between his or her traits and the effects of being in or responding to cues from a particular situation.

The person-situation interaction explains that even if you were an extravert, you would behave differently at a wedding than at a funeral because each of these situations creates different cues to which you respond (Mischel & Shoda, 1995). Similarly, the person-situation interaction describes how Jerry Sandusky could be a child advocate through his charitable organization, yet be a serial child molester. The person-situation interaction says that to understand or predict a person's behavior across situations, we must consider both the person's traits and the powerful cues that come from being in each different situation (Funder, 2008).

If you are open to new experiences, would you try this?

Conclusions

There is no question that humans have stable and consistent parts of their personalities, which are called traits. There is no question that personality differences can be accurately described by using the Big Five traits. However, people may act inconsistently or contradictorily because traits interact with and are partly dependent upon situational cues. Thus, even though you consider yourself open to new experiences, you might very well draw the line and say NO! to potentially dangerous rock climbing (below left photo). Although researchers have found that traits are not consistent across all situations, the concept of traits is still useful for two reasons (G. Matthews et al., 2003).

Descriptions. First, traits are useful because they provide a kind of shorthand method for describing someone's personality. In fact, if we asked you to describe your best friend, you would essentially list this person's traits.

Predictions. Second, traits are useful because they help predict someone's behavior in future situations. However, you must keep in mind the person-situation interaction, which means you must take into account how the person's traits will interact with the situation's cues. For example, my friends would predict that I (R. P.) generally try to watch my weight, but they also know that when placed in front of a dessert counter, I can easily consume my weight in chocolate. However, researchers found it is possible to significantly increase the accuracy of predicting a person's behaviors across situations if that person is actually observed in a number of different settings (G. Matthews et al., 2003).

Conclusion. Most personality researchers agree that traits, such as the Big Five, are useful in describing our stable and consistent behavioral tendencies, yet they warn that traits may not predict behaviors across different situations (Funder, 2008; G. Matthews et al., 2003).

Does saying that traits are stable and consistent mean that one's personality gradually becomes fixed?

Stability Versus Change

How changeable are your traits?

If you are now 16, 18, 20, 25, or 30, what will your personality be like when you're 40, 50, 60, 70, or 80? The question of how much your personality traits remain the same and how much they change is answered by using a research approach called the longitudinal method.

With the **longitudinal method**, the same group of individuals is studied repeatedly at many different points in time. For example, if you asked your parents to list your personality traits at age 3, would these traits match your traits at age 21? In other words, how changeable or fixed are your personality traits?

3 to 21 Years Old

To answer the question of how much personality traits change or remain the same, researchers did a longitudinal study on 1,000 children whose traits were assessed at age 3 and then reassessed when the same children were 21 years old. Based on their assessment, the personality traits of 3-year-old children were divided into five different personality groups that were labeled undercontrolled, inhibited, confident, reserved, and well-adjusted (Caspi, 2000).

Will this 3-year-old child's personality traits...

Consistency. Researchers found significant consistencies between traits assessed at 3 years and at 21 years old. For example, traits of 3-year-old children in the *undercontrolled group* included being impulsive, restless, and distractible. When these 3-year-old children were retested at age 21, their traits were similar and included being reckless, careless, and favoring dangerous and exciting activities. In comparison, traits of 3-year-old children in the *well-adjusted group* included being confident, having self-control, and easily adjusting to new or stressful situations. When these 3-year-old children were retested at age 21, their traits were similar and included being in control, self-confident, and all-around well-adjusted and normal adults. Researchers concluded that the origin or development of a person's more stable personality traits begins around age 3. This means that traits observed at age 3 predict personality traits observed later in the same young adults (Caspi, 2000).

...be similar to those he has at 21 years old?

Change. Although there were remarkable consistencies in personality traits between age 3 and age 21, researchers point out that there are often major changes in emotional traits during adolescence. During adolescence, individuals may become less responsible, less cautious, and more moody or impulsive (Caspi & Roberts, 1999).

What happens to personality development after age 21, and does personality ever stop changing?

22 to 80 Years Old

If you are 20, 25, or 30, what will your personality be like at 60, 70, or 80? Answers come from longitudinal studies, which reached the following conclusions (Caspi et al., 2005; R. R. McCrae & Costa, 1999; R. R. McCrae et al., 2000; Roberts et al., 2006; Terracciano et al., 2006; Trzesniewski et al., 2003):

1 Major changes in personality occur during childhood, adolescence, and young adulthood. Between 22 and 30, both men and women become less emotional, less likely to be thrill seekers, and somewhat more likely to be cooperative and self-disciplined. These personality changes are often associated with becoming more mature.

2 In fact, longitudinal studies find that most major changes in personality occur before the age of 30 because adolescents and young adults are more willing to adopt new values and attitudes or revise old ones.

3 Personality traits are relatively fixed by age 30, after which changes in personality are few and small. However, after 30, adults continue to grow in their ideas, beliefs, and attitudes as they respond to changing situations and environments. For example, an eager tennis player may, with age, become an eager gardener, but an eager liberal is unlikely to become an eager conservative.

4 Men and women, healthy and sick people, and Blacks and Whites all show the same stable personality pattern after age 30. Because personality is stable, it is somewhat predictable. However, individuals may struggle to overcome or change certain traits (become less shy or more confident), which brings up the question of how much personality changes during adulthood.

5 When middle-aged and older adults were asked to describe the course of their personality development, they all described increases in desirable traits (energetic, realistic, intelligent) as they grew older. But on objective tests, these same individuals showed little or no change in these same traits. These findings indicate that as people grow older, they tend to report more socially desirable or stereotypical responses rather than what actually has occurred.

Conclusions. Your personality is more likely to change the younger you are, but after age 30, personality traits are relatively stable and fixed. However, depending upon situations, stressors, and challenges, some change can occur throughout adulthood (Kluger, 2006a). Thus, personality has the interesting distinction of being both stable and changeable (up to a point). One reason personality traits remain relatively stable across time is that they are influenced by genetic factors, which we'll discuss next.

Before age 30, personality may go through major changes, but...

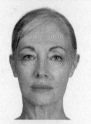

...after age 30, personality is relatively fixed and difficult to change.

Genetic and Environmental Influences on Traits

Jim Lewis (left photo) and Jim Springer (right photo) drove the same model blue Chevrolet, smoked the same brand of cigarettes, owned dogs named Toy, held jobs as deputy sheriff, enjoyed the same woodworking hobby, and had vacationed on the same beach in Florida. When they were given personality tests, they scored almost alike on traits of flexibility, self-control, and sociability. The two Jims are identical twins who were separated four weeks after birth and reared separately. When reunited at age 39, they were flabbergasted at how many things they had in common (Leo, 1987).

Why are twins so similar?

These surprising coincidences come from an ongoing University of Minnesota project on genetic factors (Bouchard, 1994; Bouchard & Loehlin, 2001). One of the project's major questions is whether the similarities between the two Jims are simply coincidence or reflect the influence of genetic factors on personality traits.

Most of us grew up hearing one or both of these phrases: "You're acting just like your father" or "You're behaving just like your mother." These phrases suggest that genetic factors we inherit from our parents influence our behaviors. Psychologists have only recently recognized the importance and influence of genetic factors, which have resulted in a new area of study called behavioral genetics.

Why did they drive the same kind of car, smoke the same cigarettes, hold the same kind of job, and both name their dogs Toy?

Behavioral genetics is the study of how inherited or genetic factors influence and interact with psychological factors to shape our personality, intelligence, emotions, and motivation and also how we behave, adapt, and adjust to our environments.

Many of us have a difficult time accepting the idea of genetic influences because we equate genetic with *fixed*. However, genetic factors do not fix behaviors but rather establish a range for a behavior, which environmental factors foster or impede. For example, a girl born with genes for shyness whose parents appropriately encourage her to socialize and interact with other children is more likely to outgrow her shyness than a girl whose parents simply believe the inherited genes for shyness indicate she will remain shy and therefore do not encourage her to interact with others (Begley, 2008d).

As we discuss studies showing that genetic factors influence and set a range for development of various personality traits, please remember that our actual traits result from the interaction between genetic factors and environmental influences.

Genetic Influences

What's in the genes?

Few studies have made as great an impact on beliefs about what shapes personality and behavior as the twin study at the University of Minnesota. Until the early 1990s, most psychologists recognized that genetic factors shaped personality but believed that genetic factors had much less impact than environmental factors. Then in 1990, Thomas Bouchard and his colleagues (1990) published results of the first study to simultaneously compare four different groups of twins: identical twins reared together, identical twins reared apart, fraternal twins reared together, and fraternal twins reared apart.

> We're identical twins, and we share nearly 100% of our genes.

Remember that identical twins share nearly 100% of their genes, while fraternal twins share only 50% of their genes and thus are no more genetically alike than ordinary brothers and sisters. This study allowed researchers to separate genetic factors (identical versus fraternal twins) and environmental factors (reared together versus reared apart).

More than 100 sets of twins in the United States, Great Britain, and many other countries participated in this initial study. Each participant was given over 50 hours of medical and psychological assessment,

This is a piece of the genetic code, which uses a chemical alphabet to write instructions that influence the development of personality traits.

including four different tests to measure personality traits. Those identical and fraternal twins who were reared apart were adopted shortly after birth and had not met their twin until this study brought them together for testing. The measure that researchers use to estimate genetic influences is called heritability.

Heritability is a statistical measure that indicates how much of some cognitive, personality, or behavioral trait is influenced by genetic factors.

Heritability is expressed on an increasing scale of influence from 0.0 to 1.0. That is, if genetic factors have no influence, the heritability is 0.0, having half the influence is indicated by 0.5, and having total control over behavior is indicated by 1.0. Researchers estimate that the heritability of personality traits ranges from 0.41 to about 0.51, which means that genetic factors contribute about 40–50% to the development of an individual's personality traits (Bouchard, 2004).

> We're fraternal twins, and we share only 50% of our genes.

Even though genetic factors are responsible for about half of each of the Big Five personality traits we develop, that still leaves about half coming from environmental factors.

Environmental Influences

We've learned that genes don't entirely explain our personality development. Consequently, environment is also an influential factor.

Which environmental factors are important?

For many years, researchers believed that the **shared environment** of the home was a major contributing factor to personality traits. It turns out that shared environments, which include the experiences you have with your parents and siblings, account for little overall influence on personality. There are instances in which parents do influence their children's personality traits, but research finds that peers generally have a stronger influence.

Once children reach school age, they begin to spend more time with their peers than with their families. Time spent with peers is in a **nonshared environment**, meaning it is away from the home environment. Though some researchers report there is no factor of greater importance than parents, others disagree. Regardless of this debate, an abundance of research shows that nonshared environmental factors have a stronger influence on personality traits than shared environmental factors.

Interaction of Genetic and Environmental Factors

What shapes personality?

As I (R. P.) was growing up, I remember hearing my parents talking (when they thought I wasn't listening) about how different I was from my older brother and sister. My parents questioned how my brother and sister and I could be so (very) different even though we had the same parents, lived in the same house in the same town, and even went to the same school and

Culture influences whether tardiness is considered acceptable or rude.

© elwynn/Shutterstock.com

Although personality may be initially influenced by genes, the effects of various environmental factors, such as parents, peers, and, perhaps most influential, culture, cannot be denied.

Earlier in this module we discussed that there are differences in the Big Five among people across the globe. Now we'll focus on only one trait, conscientiousness, to illustrate how culture can influence personality. In the United States, being on time to appointments and meetings is a sign of being conscientious, and being late is regarded as rude. In contrast, in Middle Eastern and Latin countries, it does not bother people to wait for hours after their meeting time to see someone. People in these countries understand that the person may have had family responsibilities to attend to, which are valued as being more important than being on time for an appointment or meeting.

Next, we'll summarize research data on the interaction of genetic and environmental influences on traits.

church. One reason that brothers and sisters develop such different personalities is that 50% of their genes are different (and 50% are shared). And another important reason that brothers and sisters develop different personalities is that each brother's or sister's unique set of genetic factors interacts differently with his or her environment. Researchers have broken down the contributions to personality development into the following four factors.

40% Genetic Factors

The fingerprints of the two Jims were almost identical because they shared nearly 100% of their genes, and genetic factors contribute 97% to the development of ridges on fingertips (Bouchard et al., 1990). In comparison, the two Jims' scores were similar but not identical on personality traits of self-control, flexibility, and sociability because, although they share almost 100% of their genes, genetic factors contribute about 40–50% to the kind of personality traits they developed.

27% Nonshared Environmental Factors

Although we know that the two Jims showed remarkable similarities in personality, they also displayed unique differences. Jim Lewis says that he is more easygoing and less of a worrier than his identical twin, Jim Springer. When the twins get on a plane, Jim Springer worries about the plane being late, while Jim Lewis says that there is no use worrying (*San Diego Tribune*, November 12, 1987). One of the reasons that the two Jims developed different personality traits is that about 27% of the influence on personality development comes from how each individual's genetic factors react and adjust to his or her own environment. These factors are called **nonshared environmental factors** because they involve how each individual's genetic factors react and adjust to his or her particular environment.

26% Error

About 26% of the influence on personality development cannot as yet be identified and is attributed to errors in testing and measurement procedures. As methodology improves, this error percentage will decrease and other factors will increase.

7% Shared Environmental Factors

About 7% of the influence on personality development comes from environmental factors that involve parental patterns and shared family experiences. These factors are called **shared environmental factors** because they involve how family members interact and share experiences. One of the major surprises to come out of the twin studies was how little impact parental practices and shared family experiences have on personality development. Researchers concluded that being raised in the same family contributes little (about 7%) to personality development. Far more important for personality development are nonshared environmental factors (27%), which refer to how each child's unique genetic factors react and adjust to being in that family (Bouchard & Loehlin, 2001; De Fruyt et al., 2006).

Next, we'll take a last look at the impact of trait theory.

© Grady Reese/iStockphoto

Evaluation of Trait Theory

Could we live without traits?

It would be very difficult to live without traits because you use them constantly, usually without knowing it. For example, whenever you describe someone or predict how he or she will behave, your descriptions of personality and predictions of behaviors are based almost entirely on knowing the person's traits. Online dating sites are full of personal ads, which are essentially a list of most-desired traits.

Dating profiles are based on traits.

© Peter Scholey/Getty Images RF

Although traits are very useful as a shorthand to describe a person's personality and predict a person's behaviors, critics raise three major questions about traits: How good is the list? Can traits predict? What influences traits? We'll discuss each issue in turn.

How Good Is the List?

The Big Five, or five-factor trait theory, assumes that all similarities and differences among personalities can be described by an amazingly short but comprehensive list of five traits—openness, conscientiousness, extraversion, agreeableness, and neuroticism (OCEAN). Each of the *Big Five traits* has two poles or two dimensions, which include dozens of related traits. The Big Five traits' ability to describe personality has now been verified in many different countries, with different populations and age groups (Allik & McCrae, 2004; Schmitt et al., 2007).

The Big Five traits have the ability to describe personalities of children and adults in many different countries.

Critics of the five-factor model point out that the data for the model came from questionnaires that may be too structured to give real and complete portraits of personalities. As a result, data from questionnaires may paint too simplistic a picture of human personality and may not reflect its depth and complexity (J. Block, 1995). Critics also point out that traits primarily describe a person's personality rather than explain or point out its causes (Digman, 1997).

In defense of the five-factor theory, researchers have shown that the Big Five traits provide a valid and reliable way to describe personality differences and consistencies in our own lives and in our social interactions with others (R. R. McCrae & Costa, 2003).

Can Traits Predict?

One of the more serious problems faced by early trait theory involved the assumption that, since traits are consistent and stable influences on our behaviors, traits should be very useful in predicting behaviors.

Jerry Sandusky advocated for youth in public, but in private he was a child molester.

© AP Images/Matt Rourke

But how does trait theory explain why Jerry Sandusky behaved so inconsistently? He advocated for underprivileged and at-risk youth by founding The Second Mile, a charitable organization. Yet, in his private life he sexually molested children over a 15-year period.

One explanation is that Sandusky did behave in a consistent, moral way in public situations (The Second Mile). However, in other situations, such as his private life, he had become a serial child molester. This problem of predicting behavior across situations is known as the *person-situation interaction.* Researchers found that situations may have as much influence on behavior as traits do, so situational influences must be taken into account when predicting someone's behavior (Funder, 2008). Researchers found that traits could better predict behaviors if traits were measured under different conditions and situations.

Currently, the Big Five traits are considered useful concepts for describing consistent and stable behavioral tendencies in similar situations, but traits do not necessarily predict behaviors across different situations.

What Influences Traits?

One major surprise from twin studies was what relatively little effect parental practices or shared family experiences have on personality development (graph below). Researchers concluded that parental practices or *shared factors* contributed only about 7% to personality development. In contrast, how each child personally reacts or adjusts to parental or family practices, called *nonshared factors,* contributed about 27% to personality development (Bouchard & Loehlin, 2001; Plomin & Crabbe, 2000). This finding questioned a major belief of developmental psychologists, who hold that sharing parental or family environment greatly influences personality development among siblings (brothers and sisters). Instead, twin research suggests that psychologists need to look more closely at each child's reactions to his or her family environment as a major influence on personality development.

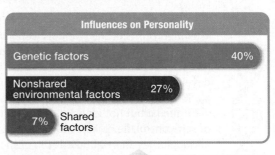

Influences on Personality

Genetic factors — 40%

Nonshared environmental factors — 27%

7% Shared factors

Personality development depends more on genetic and nonshared factors (child's individual reactions) than on shared parental influences.

According to behavioral geneticists, the idea of genes influencing complex human behaviors was unthinkable as recently as 15 years ago. Today, however, there is convincing evidence that genetic factors exert a considerable influence on many complex human behaviors, including intelligence, mental health, and personality traits (Bouchard, 2004). Yet these same researchers warn that *genetic influences* on human behavior should not be blown out of proportion. Because heritability scores generally do not exceed 50%, this means that the remaining 50% or more involves *environmental influences,* especially nonshared environmental influences. ●

Bar graph data from "Genes, Environment, and Personality," by T. J. Bouchard, 1994, *Science, 264,* 1700–1701. American Association for the Advancement of Science. Additional data from Bouchard & Loehlin, 2001; Plomin & Crabbe, 2000.

Unless otherwise noted, all images are © Cengage Learning

1. Social cognitive theory says that personality development is primarily shaped by three interacting forces: _____, _____, and _____.

1 Cognitive factors	
2 Behaviors	**Y O U**
3 Environmental factors	

2. The above three forces all interact to influence how we evaluate, interpret, and organize _____ and apply such knowledge to ourselves and others.

3. An example of the social cognitive approach is Bandura's social cognitive theory, which says that personality development, growth, and change are influenced by four distinctively human cognitive processes: highly developed **(a)** _____ ability, **(b)** _____ learning, **(c)** _____ behavior, and **(d)** _____.

4. Three different beliefs based on social cognitive theory have been shown to influence personality development and behavior. Rotter studied beliefs concerning how much control we have over situations or rewards. If we believe that we have control over situations and rewards, we are said to have an **(a)** _____. If we believe that we do not have control over situations and rewards and that events outside ourselves (fate) determine what happens, we are said to have an **(b)** _____.

5. According to Bandura, our personal beliefs regarding how capable we are of exercising control over events in our lives—for example, carrying out certain tasks and behaviors—is called **(a)** _____, which, in turn, affects our performance on a wide variety of behaviors. Mischel devised ways of measuring our ability to voluntarily postpone an immediate reward and persist in completing a task for the promise of a future reward, which is called **(b)** _____.

Should I take one marshmallow now or wait and get two later?

6. The approach to describing the structure of personality that is based on identifying and analyzing ways in which personalities differ is known as _____ theory.

7. A relatively stable and enduring tendency to behave in a particular way is called a **(a)** _____. A statistical procedure that may be used to find relationships among many different or diverse items, such as traits, and form them into selected groups is called **(b)** _____.

8. The model that organizes all personality traits into five categories that can be used to describe differences in personality is called the **(a)** _____ model. This model uses the Big Five traits, which are **(b)** _____, _____, _____, _____, and _____.

OCEAN

9. Research supports the five-factor model and the Big Five traits. Each of the Big Five traits has two poles or dimensions and represents a wide range of _____.

10. Walter Mischel said that to predict a person's behavior we must take into account not only the person's traits but also the effects of the situation; this became known as the **(a)** _____. According to this idea, a person's behavior results from an **(b)** _____ between his or her traits and the effects of being in a particular situation.

11. To investigate whether personality changes as people grow older, psychologists study the same individuals at different times; this is called a **(a)** _____ study. In general, studies have shown that personality is more likely to change if a person is under **(b)** _____ years old. After that, changes usually involve variations on the same behavioral theme or accompany changes in social roles.

12. The field that focuses on how inherited or genetic factors influence and interact with psychological factors is called **(a)** _____. A statistical measure that estimates how much of some behavior is due to genetic influences is called **(b)** _____.

13. Studies have found that about 40% of the influence on personality development comes from **(a)** _____; about 27% comes from how each person adjusts to his or her own environment, which is called **(b)** _____; and about 7% comes from parental patterns and family experiences, which are called **(c)** _____.

Answers: 1. *cognitive-personal factors, behavior, environmental influences;* 2. *information;* 3. (a) *language,* (b) *observational,* (c) *purposeful,* (d) *self-analysis;* 4. (a) *internal locus of control,* (b) *external locus of control;* 5. (a) *self-efficacy,* (b) *delay of gratification;* 6. *trait;* 7. (a) *trait,* (b) *factor analysis;* 8. (a) *five-factor,* (b) *openness, conscientiousness, extraversion, agreeableness, neuroticism;* 9. *behaviors;* 10. (a) *person-situation interaction,* (b) *interaction;* 11. (a) *longitudinal,* (b) 30; 12. (a) *behavioral genetics,* (b) *heritability;* 13. (a) *genetic factors,* (b) *nonshared environmental factors,* (c) *shared environmental factors*

Total Change in One Day?

What triggers a major change?

Sometimes researchers study unusual behaviors that seem to contradict what is known. For example, anyone who has ever tried to change some behavior finds it difficult because traits are relatively stable and enduring. For this reason, it's difficult to believe people who claim to have totally changed their personalities in minutes, hours, or a single day. Researchers call these sudden, dramatic changes quantum personality changes (W. R. Miller & C'de Baca, 1994, 2001).

A **quantum personality change** is a very radical or dramatic shift in one's personality, beliefs, or values in minutes, hours, or a day.

For example, here's the quantum personality change of Bill Wilson, who cofounded Alcoholics Anonymous (AA). He was in the depths of alcoholic despair and depression when he suddenly saw his room lit with a bright light. In his mind's eye, he saw himself on a

mountaintop and felt that spirit winds were blowing through him. Then, suddenly, a simple but powerful thought burst upon him: he was a free man (E. Kurtz, 1979). This dramatic experience changed Wilson's personality 180 degrees as he went from being a desperate and hopeless drunk to being a sober and dedicated worker who devoted his life to helping others overcome alcoholism.

Reports of sudden and major changes in personality challenge two well-established findings: First, personality traits are stable and enduring tendencies that may change gradually but rarely undergo sudden and dramatic changes; and second, even when people want to change their personalities, as in therapy, it doesn't happen overnight but takes considerable time and effort. So, how can quantum personality changes occur, often in a single day? To answer this question, researchers first had to develop a method to study quantum changes.

How much could you change in one day?

Method

Researchers found people who had experienced a quantum personality change through a feature story in the local paper (Albuquerque, New Mexico). Researchers asked for volunteers who, in a relatively short period of time, had experienced a transformation in their basic values, feelings, attitudes, or actions. Out of a total of 89 people who responded, 55 were found acceptable. These 55 participants were given a series of personality tests and structured interviews (average length 107 minutes).

Structured interviews involve asking each individual the same set of relatively narrow and focused questions so that the same information is obtained from everyone.

During the structured interviews, all the participants were asked the same detailed questions about the what, when, and where of the unusual experiences that had apparently transformed their personalities so completely.

Structured interviews use the participants' self-reports to provide information about subjective thoughts, feelings, and experiences, which are most often unobservable cognitive and emotional processes.

Results

The researchers used a variety of personality tests to make sure the participants (31 women and 24 men) performed within the normal range on personality tests and had no strange problems. In fact, based on the battery of personality tests and interviews, all the participants seemed to be normal, ordinary individuals who had had extraordinary experiences (W. R. Miller & C'de Baca, 1994). Here are some of the study's major findings:

- A majority of the participants (58%) could specify the date and time of day when the quantum experience occurred even though the experience had occurred, on average, 11 years earlier.

- A majority of the participants (75%) reported that the quantum experience began suddenly and took them by surprise. For some the experience lasted only minutes (13%), and for most it was over within 24 hours (64%). The actual experiences included being struck by an intense thought, making a total commitment, hearing a voice, and hearing God's voice.

- A majority of the participants (56%) reported a high level of emotional distress and a relatively high level of negative life experiences in the year before the quantum experience.

- Most (96%) reported that the quantum experience had made their lives better, and most (80%) stated that the changes had lasted.

All of these 55 individuals reported that they had, in a single day or less, experienced a 180-degree change in personality. For the vast majority, the quantum change in personality seems to have resulted from or been triggered by a period of bad times. After the quantum change, the participants reported that their lives had improved.

When these individuals were interviewed ten years later, researchers found that the dramatic changes continued and no one reported returning to their old ways (C'de Baca & Wilbourne, 2004).

Conclusions

The quantum personality changes reported by the participants were dramatically larger than are ordinarily observed, occurred in a shorter period of time than is normally reported, and lasted for years (C'de Baca & Wilbourne, 2004; W. R. Miller & C'de Baca, 1994).

For most of the participants, the changes represented an increased sense of meaning, happiness, and satisfaction; some reported a sense of closeness to God. This study suggests that quantum changes in personality do occur and may be one way a person solves some long-standing and stressful personal problem.

In many cases, people who experienced quantum personality changes also reported subsequent changes in behavior.

As you'll see next, how much personality influences behavior is partly dependent on one's culture. ●

D Cultural Diversity: Suicide Bombers

One of the most difficult and tragic issues for Westerners to understand is the reasons behind suicide bombers. One young woman agreed to tell her story of how she became a suicide bomber (Bennet, 2002).

Why was Arien the exception?

I believe Israeli forces killed my fiancé and I want to avenge his death.

James Bennet/*The New York Times*/Redux Pictures

Arien Ahmed (right photo) was a 20-year-old Palestinian student of business administration at Bethlehem University. Five days after she had volunteered to become a suicide bomber, she was pulled out of a marketing lecture and shown how to trigger a bomb inside a backpack. She got into an old car with another would-be killer and went on her mission dressed as an Israeli woman. As she walked through an Israeli town carrying a heavy backpack containing a bomb surrounded with nails, she began to have second thoughts. She described a kind of awakening and remembered a childhood belief "that nobody has the right to stop anybody's life." At that moment she decided not to go through with the bombing. She was later arrested by Israeli police (Bennet, 2002). Arien was a rare exception, since suicide bombers almost never fail to complete their deadly missions.

Cultural and Personal Reasons

After Arien was arrested, she said that she agreed to tell her story to discourage other Palestinians from becoming suicide bombers and to gain sympathy for herself. The Israeli Security Agency, which allowed Arien to be interviewed by newspaper reporters, appeared eager to show how easily militants manipulate susceptible people and send them to kill and die (Bennet, 2002).

What conditions lead to suicide attacks? In the mid-1990s, there were more than 20 suicide attacks throughout Turkey. The attacks stopped because the Turkish government undertook steps to satisfy the rebel forces' demands. Since 1990, Chechnyans have engaged in suicide attacks in their effort to win their independence from Russia (Zakaria, 2003). Since 2002, Palestinian women have become increasingly involved in acts of terrorism (McGirk, 2007). Let's take a look at the reasons Palestinian women choose to become suicide bombers.

What motivates a suicide bomber? Arien was motivated by both personal and cultural reasons. As she told Israeli security agents, her strong *personal reason* was that she wanted to avenge the death of her fiancé, whom she believed had been killed by Israeli forces (who said that her fiancé accidentally blew himself up). After his death, she said, "So I lost all my future." Arien's recruiters told her that dying as a suicide attacker would earn her the reward of rejoining her slain fiancé in paradise. Even though Arien now calls her attempt to be a suicide bomber a mistake, she said she understood it. "It's a result of the situation we live in. There are also innocent people killed on both sides" (Bennet, 2002, p. A1).

There are also strong Muslim *cultural influences* that encourage women, such as Arien, to become suicide bombers. For example, during the past several years, women have been increasingly involved in Palestinian terrorism largely because their involvement is unsuspected by others and their actions receive heightened media attention. The use of women as suicide bombers is also thought to convey the seriousness of the threat and to make the men involved act more aggressively (Berko & Erez, 2006; Bloom, 2005).

Suicide bombers justify killing civilians, even children, by believing that they pose a risk, now or in the future.

© David Silverman/Getty Images

There are many other reasons women become suicide bombers. For instance, 21-year-old Wafa Samir al-Biss, a burn victim, volunteered to martyr herself after she was told she would never marry due to her many scars. Some choose to become suicide bombers instead of receiving the death sentence. At least that way they will die as a proud martyr, which many believe is the reason they were created by God. Yet others become suicide bombers simply because they have a deep hatred of a specific group of people; this is the reason some of the Palestinian suicide bombers target Jews (Abdul-Zahra & Murphy, 2009; BBC News, 2008; Dviri, 2005; McGirk, 2007).

Jyad Sarraj, a Palestinian psychiatrist, states he cannot criticize the suicide bombers because their culture considers them to be martyrs and martyrs are considered prophets, who are revered (Sarraj, 2002). Other experts state the increasing number of women who are becoming suicide bombers shows that women are taking a step forward in achieving status equal to men (Bloom, 2005).

Do suicide bombers share certain traits? Almost all of the suicide bombers have been Muslim, relatively young, single, varying in education, with some knowledge of political causes and terror tactics (Bennet, 2002; Zakaria, 2003). These traits tend to be general, however, and apply to many Palestinians who do not become suicide bombers. Israel's national security force studied suicide bombers, and their results are puzzling. They didn't find any specific personality profile or traits that differentiated suicide bombers from nonbombers. However, as in Arien's case, some powerful, tragic emotional event, such as the death of her fiancé, may be the final hurt that, combined with cultural forces, led her to become a suicide bomber.

Next, we'll briefly review the four major theories of personality to help you understand their major points. ●

Psychodynamic Theory

Freud's psychodynamic theory, which was developed in the early 1900s, grew out of his work with patients.

Freud's *psychodynamic theory of personality* emphasizes the importance of early childhood experiences, the importance of repressed thoughts that we cannot voluntarily access, and the conflicts between conscious and unconscious forces that influence our thoughts and behaviors. (Freud used the term *dynamic* to refer to mental energy force.)

Conscious thoughts are wishes, desires, or thoughts that we are aware of or can recall at any given moment.

Unconscious forces are wishes, desires, or thoughts that, because of their disturbing or threatening content, we automatically repress and cannot voluntarily access.

Freud believed that a large part of our behavior was guided or motivated by unconscious forces.

Unconscious motivation is a Freudian concept that refers to the influence of repressed thoughts, desires, or impulses on our conscious thoughts and behaviors.

Freud developed three methods to uncover unconscious processes: *free association, dream interpretation,* and *slips of the tongue* (Freudian slips).

Divisions of the Mind

Freud divided the mind into three divisions: id, ego, and superego.

The first division is the *id,* which contains two biological drives—sex and aggression—that are the source of all mental energy. The id follows the pleasure principle, which is to satisfy the biological drives.

The second division is the *ego,* whose goal is to find socially acceptable ways of satisfying the id's desires within the range of the superego's prohibitions. The ego follows the reality principle, which is to satisfy a wish or desire only if there is a socially acceptable outlet available.

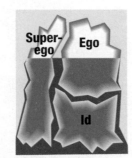

The third division is the *superego,* whose goal is to apply the moral values and standards of one's parents or caregivers and society in satisfying one's wishes.

1 Oral	
2 Anal	
3 Phallic	
4 Latency	
5 Genital	

Psychosexual Stages

Freud assumed that our personality develops as we pass through a series of *five psychosexual stages.*

During these developmental periods—the *oral, anal, phallic, latency,* and *genital stages*—the individual seeks pleasure from different areas of the body associated with sexual feelings. Freud emphasized that the child's first five years were the most important in personality development.

Humanistic Theories

Humanistic theories emphasize our capacity for personal growth, development of our potential, and freedom to choose our destiny. *Humanistic theories* stress three major ideas—phenomenological perspective, holistic view, and self-actualization.

The *phenomenological perspective* means that our perception of the world, whether or not it is accurate, becomes our reality.

The *holistic view* means that a person's personality is more than the sum of its individual parts; instead, the individual parts form a unique and total entity that functions as a unit.

Self-actualization is our inherent tendency to reach our true potentials.

Humanistic theories reject the biological determinism and the irrational, unconscious forces of Freud's psychodynamic theory. Humanistic theories emphasize freely choosing to go after one's dream and change one's destiny.

The beginning of humanistic theory can be traced to two psychologists: Abraham Maslow, who rejected behaviorism's system of rewards and punishment, and Carl Rogers, who rejected Freud's psychodynamic theory with its emphasis on unconscious forces.

Abraham Maslow

Maslow (1968) broke away from the reward/punishment/observable behavior mentality of behaviorism and developed his humanistic theory. *Maslow's humanistic theory* emphasized two things: our capacity for growth or self-actualization and our desire to satisfy a variety of needs.

Maslow's hierarchy of needs arranges needs in ascending order, with biological needs at the bottom and social and personal needs toward the top; as needs at one level are met, we advance to the next level.

Carl Rogers's Self Theory

Carl Rogers rejected the psychodynamic approach because it placed too much emphasis on unconscious, irrational forces. Instead, Rogers developed a new humanistic theory, which is called self theory. *Rogers's self theory,* also called self-actualization theory, has two primary assumptions: Personality development is guided by each person's unique self-actualization tendency, and each of us has a personal need for positive regard.

Ideal Self hopes and wishes
Real Self actual experiences

Rogers said that the *self* is made up of many self-perceptions, abilities, personality characteristics, and behaviors that are organized and consistent with one another.

Unless otherwise noted, all images are © Cengage Learning

Social Cognitive Theory

Freud's *psychodynamic theory,* developed in the early 1900s, grew out of his work with patients. Humanistic theories were developed in the 1960s by an ex-Freudian (Carl Rogers) and an ex-behaviorist (Abraham Maslow), who believed that earlier theories had neglected the positive side of human potential, growth, and self-fulfillment.

In comparison, *social cognitive theory,* which was developed in the 1960s and 1970s, grew out of a strong research background, unlike the way humanistic and Freudian psychodynamic theories were developed. Social cognitive theory emphasizes a more rigorous experimental approach to develop and test concepts that can be used to understand and explain personality development.

Reciprocal determinism is the idea that personality development is primarily shaped by three factors: environmental factors, cognitive-personal factors, and behaviors. *Behaviors* include a variety of actions, such as what we do and say. *Environmental factors* include our social, political, and cultural influences as

		YOU
1	Cognitive factors	Y
2	Behaviors	O
3	Environmental factors	U

well as our particular learning experiences. Just as our cognitive factors influence how we perceive and interpret our environment, our environment in turn affects our beliefs, values, and social roles. *Cognitive-personal factors* include our beliefs, expectations, values, intentions, and social roles as well as our biological and genetic influences. Thus, what we think, believe, and feel affects how we act and behave.

Bandura's Social Cognitive Theory

Perhaps the best example of the social cognitive approach is Bandura's social cognitive theory, which he developed in the 1970s. *Bandura's social cognitive theory* says that personality development, growth, and change are influenced by four distinctively human cognitive processes: highly developed language ability, observational learning, purposeful behavior, and self-analysis.

> Should I take one marshmallow now or wait and get two later?

Bandura's theory emphasizes *cognitive factors,* such as personal values, goals, and beliefs. Three particular beliefs have been shown to influence personality development: *locus of control,* which refers to how much control we think we have over our environment; *delay of gratification,* which involves our voluntarily postponing an immediate reward for the promise of a future reward; and *self-efficacy,* which refers to our personal beliefs of how capable we are in performing specific tasks and behaviors.

One of the basic assumptions of social cognitive theory is that our beliefs, values, and goals influence the development of our personalities, which, in turn, affects how we behave.

Trait Theory

For over 50 years, a major goal of personality researchers was to find a way to define the structure of personality with the fewest possible traits. The search for a list of traits that could describe personality differences among everyone, including criminals and nuns, began in the 1930s with a list of about 4,500 traits and ended in the 1990s with a list of only 5 traits.

In the 1990s, trait theory developed the five-factor model, which is based on laboratory research, especially questionnaires and statistical procedures. *Trait theory* refers to an approach for analyzing the structure of personality by measuring, identifying, and classifying similarities and differences in personality characteristics or traits. The basic unit for measuring personality characteristics is the trait. *Traits* are relatively stable and enduring tendencies to behave in particular ways, but behavior is not always the same across different situations.

Trait theory says relatively little about the development or growth of personality but instead emphasizes measuring and identifying differences among personalities.

Five-Factor Model

The *five-factor model* organizes all personality traits into five categories—openness, conscientiousness, extraversion, agreeableness, and neuroticism (OCEAN). These traits, which are referred to as the *Big Five traits,* raise three major issues.

First, although traits are stable tendencies to behave in certain ways, this stability does not necessarily apply across situations. According to the *person-situation interaction,* you may behave differently in different situations because of the effects of a particular situation.

Second, personality traits are both *changeable and stable:* Most change occurs before age 30 because adolescents and young adults are more willing to adopt new values and attitudes or revise old ones; most stability occurs after age 30, but adults do continue to grow in their ideas, beliefs, and attitudes.

Third, *genetic factors* have a considerable influence on personality traits and behaviors. Genetic factors push and pull the development of certain traits, whose development may be helped or hindered by environmental factors.

Traits are useful in that they provide shorthand descriptions of people and predict certain behaviors. ●

Definition

The study of traits has become big business because traits are used in constructing personality tests. For example, if you're applying for a job, you may be asked to fill out a written questionnaire, which is really a honesty or integrity test. To help employers make hiring decisions, about 6,000 companies administer integrity tests to weed out dishonest job applicants each year (Cullen, 2006). These tests aim to predict how likely an applicant is to engage in counterproductive work behaviors (e.g., stealing, arguing, lying, blaming) (C. M. Berry et al., 2007; Spector et al., 2006). Integrity tests, which are the most frequently administered psychological tests in the United States, are examples of objective personality tests (Mumford et al., 2001).

Why are traits big business?

Objective personality tests, also called **self-report questionnaires,** consist of specific written statements that require individuals to indicate, for example, by checking "true" or "false," whether the statements apply to them.

I would never give free drinks to my friends—it's against the rules.

Because objective personality tests or self-report questionnaires use very specific questions and require very specific answers, they are considered to be highly *structured,* or *objective.* In comparison, projective tests (see pp. 450–451) use ambiguous stimuli (inkblots or photos), have widely varying responses, and are considered to be *unstructured,* or *projective,* personality tests.

It is most likely that, as part of a job interview, you will be asked to take a variety of self-report questionnaires. That's because employers, clinicians, researchers, and government and law enforcement agencies use self-report questionnaires to identify and differentiate personality traits.

The basic assumption behind self-report questionnaires brings us back to the definition of traits. We defined traits as stable and enduring tendencies to behave in certain ways. Self-report questionnaires identify traits, which employers use to predict how prospective employees will behave in particular jobs or situations (D. J. Ozer, 1999).

Before we discuss how valid and reliable self-report questionnaires are in predicting behavior, we'll examine two of the more popular self-report questionnaires.

Examples of Objective Tests

How honest are most employees?

Objective personality tests are used in both business and clinical settings. In business settings, self-report questionnaires are often used in selecting employees for certain traits, such as being honest and trustworthy (C. M. Berry et al., 2007; Spector et al., 2006).

Integrity Tests

Integrity or honesty tests are supposed to assess whether individuals have high levels of the trait of honesty. Questions asked on honesty tests are similar to the following (Lilienfeld, 1993):

1. Have you ever stolen merchandise from your place of work?

2. Have you ever been tempted to steal a piece of jewelry from a store?

3. Do you think most people steal money from their workplace every now and then?

4. A person has been a loyal and honest employee at a firm for 20 years. One day, after realizing she neglected to bring lunch money, she takes $10 from her workplace but returns it the next day. Should she be fired?

People strong in the trait of honesty answer: (1) no, (2) no, (3) no, (4) yes.

Notice that some self-report questionnaires, such as the integrity test, focus on measuring a single personality trait—in this case honesty. The next self-report questionnaire, called the MMPI-2, is used primarily in clinical settings and measures a number of traits and personality problems.

Would you sign a contract with this man?

Minnesota Multiphasic Personality Inventory-2

Suppose a parole board needed to decide whether a convicted murderer had changed enough in prison to be let out on parole. To help make this decision, the board might use a test that identifies the range of normal and abnormal personality traits, such as the well-known Minnesota Multiphasic Personality Inventory-2 (MMPI-2), which has recently been updated to include fewer test items while retaining the effectiveness of the longer version (Ben-Porath, 2010). The revised test is named MMPI-2-RF (Restructured Form), but for simplicity, we will continue to refer to it as MMPI-2.

The **Minnesota Multiphasic Personality Inventory-2-RF (MMPI-2)** is a true-false self-report questionnaire that consists of 338 statements describing a wide range of normal and abnormal behaviors. The purpose of the MMPI-2 is to measure the personality style and emotional adjustment in individuals with mental illness.

The MMPI-2 asks about and identifies a variety of specific personality traits, including depression, hostility, high energy, and shyness, and plots whether these traits are in the normal or abnormal range. The statements below are similar to actual statements in the MMPI-2:

- I tire quickly.
- I am not worried about sex.
- I believe people are plotting against me.

Could a test show if a prisoner were ready for parole?

One advantage of this test is that it has three kinds of scales: *validity scales,* which assess whether the client was faking good or bad answers; *clinical scales,* which identify psychological disorders, such as depression or schizophrenia; and *content scales,* which identify specific areas, such as the anger scale, which includes references to being irritable and to difficulties controlling anger (R. M. Kaplan & Saccuzzo, 2009).

The MMPI-2 is a commonly used objective test to assess a wide range of personality traits, numerous behaviors, health and psychosomatic symptoms, and many well-known psychotic symptoms (Ben-Porath, 2010).

Another method that claims to identify your particular traits involves astrology.

Reliability and Validity

How do horoscopes work?

About 78% of women and 70% of men read horoscopes, and many believe they are so correct that they were written especially for them (D. F. Halpern, 1998). As you read the horoscope on the right, note how many traits apply to you. Because horoscopes contain general traits, people believe horoscopes were written especially for them, a phenomenon called the Barnum principle (Snyder et al., 1977).

> You are bright, sincere, and likable but can be too hard on yourself.

The **Barnum principle** (named after the famous circus owner P. T. Barnum) refers to the method of listing many general traits so that almost everyone who reads the horoscope thinks that these traits apply specifically to him or her. But, in fact, these traits are so general that they apply to almost everyone.

Astrologers claim they can identify your personality traits by knowing the zodiac sign under which you were born. However, researchers found that horoscopes do not assess personality traits for a particular individual, which means horoscopes lack one of the two characteristics of a good test—validity (Hartmann, 2006).

© Tudor Catalin Gheorghe/ Shutterstock.com

Validity

Students claim that the Scorpio horoscope, which I (R. P.) wrote, is accurate for them. The reason I can write "accurate" horoscopes is that I use the *Barnum principle,* which means that I state personality traits in a general way so that they apply to everyone.

> I read my horoscope every day, and it's always right on the mark.

Validity means that the test measures what it claims or is supposed to measure.

A personality test that has no validity is no better than chance at describing or predicting a particular individual's traits. For example, researchers found that the 12 zodiac signs were no better than chance at identifying traits for a particular individual (Svensen & White, 1994).

Because horoscopes cannot identify or predict traits for a particular person, horoscopes lack validity. The reason horoscopes remain popular and seem to be "accurate" is that astrologers essentially use the Barnum principle, which means their horoscopes are "accurate" for almost everyone. For comparison, integrity tests generally have low validity, while the MMPI-2 has good validity, which means it can describe and predict behaviors for particular individuals (R. M. Kaplan & Saccuzzo, 2009). In addition to validity, a good personality test must also have reliability.

© Gelpi/Shutterstock.com

Reliability

Even though horoscopes lack validity, they may actually have the second characteristic of a good personality test—reliability.

Reliability refers to consistency: A person's score on a test at one point in time should be similar to the score obtained by the same person on a similar test at a later point in time.

Horoscopes may be reliable if the astrologer remains the same. Integrity tests and the MMPI-2 have good reliability. However, the MMPI-2 is better than integrity tests because the MMPI-2 has both good validity and reliability, while the integrity test has good reliability but low validity (R. M. Kaplan & Saccuzzo, 2009).

Usefulness

Is a monk or a devil more honest?

Self-report questionnaires and objective personality tests are popular and widely used because they assess information about traits in a structured way so that such information can be compared with others who have taken the same tests. For example, employers and government and law enforcement agencies use objective personality tests, such as integrity tests, to compare and select certain traits in job applicants (Cullen, 2006). Researchers use objective personality tests to differentiate between people's traits. Counselors and clinicians use objective personality tests, such as the MMPI-2, to identify personality traits and potential psychological problems (J. R. Graham, 2005). We'll discuss the disadvantages and advantages of objective personality tests.

Disadvantages

One disadvantage of objective personality tests is that their questions and answers are very structured, and critics from the psychodynamic approach point out that such structured tests may not assess deeper or unconscious personality factors. A second disadvantage comes from the straightforward questions, which often allow people to figure out what answers are most socially desirable or acceptable and thus bias the test results. For example, one problem with integrity tests is that the answers can be faked so that the person appears more trustworthy (compare the devil's and monk's responses on the right) (Cullen, 2006). Third, many self-report questionnaires measure specific traits, which we know may predict behavior in the same situations but not across situations. This means a person may behave honestly with his or her family but not necessarily with his or her employer.

> Of course, I'm a very, very honest person.

PhotoDisc, Inc.

> I'm not as honest as I should be.

Which of these two would you trust?

PhotoDisc, Inc.

Advantages

One advantage of objective personality tests is that they are easily administered and can be taken individually or in groups. A second advantage is that, since the questions are structured and require either a true-false or yes-no answer, the scoring is straightforward. Third, many of the self-report questionnaires have good reliability. For example, the reliability of the MMPI-2 ranges from 0.70 to 0.85 (1.0 is perfect reliability) (R. M. Kaplan & Saccuzzo, 2009). Fourth, the validity of self-report questionnaires varies with the test; it ranges from poor to good. For example, the validity of integrity tests appears to be poor: In one study, a group of monks and nuns scored "more dishonest" than a group of prisoners in jail (Rieke & Guastello, 1995). In comparison, many studies on the MMPI-2 indicate that its validity is good (R. M. Kaplan & Saccuzzo, 2009).

Because objective personality tests and projective personality tests (see pp. 450–451) have different advantages and disadvantages, counselors and clinical psychologists may use a combination of both to assess a client's personality traits and problems. ●

More Employers Use Personality Tests in Hiring Process

More and more job applicants are being required to take personality tests. Because many personality tests are available and each measures something different, employers often hire industrial/organizational psychologists, who study behavior in the workplace, to help choose personality tests to aid in personnel selection.

1 Why do some employers use both interviews and objective personality tests in deciding whom to hire?

Depending on an employer's specific needs, industrial/organizational psychologists may choose to have applicants complete the Myers-Briggs test, which measures personality traits necessary for leadership and teamwork. Alternatively, they may choose to administer the Minnesota Multiphasic Personality Inventory, which measures an individual's tendency toward substance abuse and psychopathology. Other personality tests look at a variety of additional characteristics, such as thought processes, sociability, motivation, self-awareness, emotional intelligence, stress management, dependability, and work style.

2 Why do companies look for certain traits in selecting employees, and why would Freud question the importance of selecting for traits?

Some experts believe personality tests are overused and over-interpreted. Others believe personality tests have an important place in the hiring process because the tests can predict how well an applicant "fits" with the job description. For instance, when hiring a salesperson, a company can have a list of the personality traits of successful salespeople and then match an applicant's test results against that standard.

3 If you were using the Big Five traits to design a test for salespeople who work as a team, which traits would you look for?

Many companies that have used personality tests showed a decrease in absenteeism and turnover, which means big savings for the company. Other companies have observed increases in employee retention and customer satisfaction, and reductions in absenteeism and theft.

4 What are some objections to or disadvantages of using objective personality tests in the hiring process?

Personality tests are now being used in the hiring process to narrow down the number of applicants to interview. The popularity of Internet job postings has created floods of applications that employers need to quickly narrow down, and personality tests offer an efficient

5 An applicant's behavior during an interview is important, but does it generalize to good behavior on the job? Why or why not?

© Blaj Gabriel/Shutterstock.com

way for them to review only the applicants who may be a good "fit."

So, how should you respond to test questions to be sure you get the job? Although ideal responses vary by job position and company, experts suggest that you not falsify your responses, as many personality tests have a sophisticated way of knowing if you're lying. Luis Valdes, an executive consultant, explains,

6 Which objective personality test has a scale to detect lying? Can objective personality tests prevent a person from "faking his or her character"?

"For any given character trait, say independence, there's an optimal amount. If a person seems to be really extreme, well, most people aren't that extreme, so it suggests they tried to answer all the questions in a positive but not very realistic way" (Valdes, 2006). In the case of personality tests, it appears that honesty is the best policy.

Adapted from Cha, 2005; Cullen, 2006; Frieswick, 2004; Gladwell, 2004; Gunn, 2006; C. Smith, 1997; Tahmincioglu, 2011; Valdes, 2006; Wessel, 2003

Unless otherwise noted, all images are © Cengage Learning

Summary Test

A Social Cognitive Theory

1. The social cognitive theory concept that says personality development is shaped primarily by environmental condi-

tions (learning), cognitive-personal factors, and behaviors, which all interact to influence how we evaluate, interpret, and organize information and apply that information to ourselves and others, is called _____.

2. Albert Bandura called the version of his original social learning theory the **(a)** _____ theory. Bandura's theory assumes that four distinctively human cognitive processes—highly developed language ability, observational learning, purposeful behavior, and self-analysis—influence the growth, development, and change in **(b)** _____.

3. Our highly developed **(a)** _____ ability provides us with a tool for processing and understanding information, which is critical to personality development. Our capacity for **(b)** _____ learning allows us to learn through watching, without observable behavior or a reinforcer. Our capacity for forethought enables us to plan ahead and set goals—to perform **(c)** _____ behavior. Finally, the fact that we can monitor our thoughts and actions as well as set and change goals and values gives us the capacity for **(d)** _____.

4. The power of beliefs and ideas to change the way that we interpret situations and events is one of the basic assumptions of social cognitive theories. Rotter developed a scale to measure our belief about how much control we have over situations or rewards; he called this belief **(a)** _____. If we believe that we have control over situations and rewards, we are said to have an **(b)** _____ locus of control. In contrast, if we believe that we do not have control over situations and rewards and that events outside ourselves determine what happens, we are said to have an **(c)** _____ locus of control.

5. According to Bandura, our personal belief regarding how capable we are of exercising control over events in our lives is called **(a)** _____. According to Mischel, our voluntary postponement of an immediate reward and persistence in completing a task for the promise of a future reward is called delay of **(b)** _____.

B Trait Theory

6. A relatively stable and enduring tendency to behave in a particular way is called a **(a)** _____. An approach to understanding the structure of personality by measuring,

identifying, and analyzing differences in personality is called **(b)** _____ theory. In attempting to pare down a list of traits by finding relationships among them, researchers have used a statistical method called **(c)** _____.

7. The model that organizes all personality traits into five categories is called the **(a)** _____. These five categories, known as the Big Five, are **(b)** _____, _____, _____, _____, and _____; their initial letters spell the word OCEAN.

8. Mischel questioned the basic assumption of trait theory, saying that, if traits represent consistent behavioral tendencies, they should predict behaviors across many different **(a)** _____. Instead, he found that people behaved with great consistency in the same situation but behaved with low consistency across different situations. Mischel pointed out that predicting a person's behavior must take into account not only the person's traits but also the effects of the situation; this idea became known as the **(b)** _____ interaction.

9. How inherited or genetic factors influence and interact with psychological factors—for example, the ways we behave, adapt, and adjust to our environments—is the focus of the field of behavioral **(a)** _____. Current thinking about genetic factors is that they do not fix behaviors but rather set a range for behaviors. Researchers estimate genetic influences with a measure that estimates how much of some behavior is due to genetic influences; this measure is referred to as **(b)** _____.

10. Considering the various influences on personality development, researchers estimated that about 40% of the influence comes from **(a)** _____, which are inherited. About 27% of the influence on personality development comes from environmental factors that involve how each individual reacts and adjusts to his or her own environment; these are called **(b)** _____ factors. About 7% of the influence on personality development comes from environmental factors that involve parental patterns and shared family experiences; these are called **(c)** _____ factors. The remaining 26% of the influence on personality development cannot as yet be identified and is attributed to errors in testing and measurement procedures.

© SuperStock RF/SuperStock

11. Trait theory assumes that differences among personalities can be described by a short but comprehensive list of traits. Critics of the current list, known as the **(a)** _____, point out that the data for the model may paint too simplistic a picture of human personality and may not reflect its depth and complexity. Trait theory assumes that traits are consistent and stable influences on our **(b)** _____, but critics argue that when traits are measured in one situation, they do not necessarily predict behaviors in other situations.

OCEAN

12. The biggest changes in personality occur during childhood, adolescence, and young adulthood because young men and women are somewhat more likely to be open to new ideas. Personality is less likely to change after age **(a)** _____. Observations from twin studies indicate that **(b)** _____ factors significantly influence personality traits. Critics warn that inherited factors should not be exaggerated because 50% or more of the influence on traits comes from **(c)** _____ influences.

C Research Focus: 180-Degree Change

13. If you were to experience a sudden and radical or dramatic shift in personality, beliefs, or values, you would be said to have experienced a **(a)** _____ in personality. One way researchers studied these changes in personality was to ask each individual the same set of relatively narrow and focused questions so that the same information was obtained from everyone; this method is called the **(b)** _____.

© Lilya Espinosa/Shutterstock.com

D Cultural Diversity: Suicide Bombers

14. Individuals who volunteer to become suicide bombers do so for both strong **(a)** _____ and _____ reasons. Personal reasons may include such things as wanting to avenge the death of a loved one. Almost all suicide bombers are raised in the Muslim culture, whose beliefs hold that individuals who die as suicide bombers are considered **(b)** _____, who are revered in this culture as prophets.

James Bennet/*The New York Times*/ Redux Pictures

15. In pursuing their goals, violent Muslim groups will continue to use suicide bombers because they have widespread **(a)** _____ approval and are an effective method of killing, instilling **(b)** _____, and spreading their political **(c)** _____.

E Review: Four Theories of Personality

16. How does personality grow and develop? We discussed four different answers. The theory that emphasizes the importance of early childhood, unconscious factors, the three divisions of the mind, and psychosexual stages is called **(a)** _____. The theories that focus on the phenomenological perspective, a holistic view, and self-actualization are called **(b)** _____ theories. The theory that says that personality development is shaped by interactions among three factors—environmental conditions, cognitive-personal factors, and behavior—is called **(c)** _____ theory. The theory that emphasizes measuring and identifying differences among personalities is called **(d)** _____ theory.

Super-ego   Ego

Id

Ideal Self hopes and wishes

Real Self actual experiences

F Application: Assessment— Objective Tests

17. Self-report questionnaires, which consist of specific written statements that require structured responses—for example, checking "true" or "false"—are examples of _____ personality tests.

18. A true-false self-report questionnaire containing hundreds of statements that describe a wide range of normal and abnormal behaviors is called the **(a)** _____. The purpose of this test is to distinguish normal from **(b)** _____ groups.

19. The method of listing a number of traits in such a general way that almost everyone who reads a horoscope thinks that many of the traits apply specifically to him or her is called the _____ principle.

© Tudor Catalin Gheorghe/ Shutterstock.com

Answers: 1. *reciprocal determinism;* 2. *(a) social cognitive, (b) person-ality;* 3. *(a) language, (b) observational, (c) purposeful, (d) self-analysis;* 4. *(a) locus of control, (b) internal, (c) external;* 5. *(a) self-efficacy,* (b) *gratification;* 6. *(a) trait, (b) trait, (c) factor analysis;* 7. *(a) five-factor model, Big Five, (b) openness, conscientiousness, extraversion, agreeable-ness, neuroticism;* 8. *(a) situations, (b) person-situation;* 9. *(a) genetics,* (b) *genetic, (c) environmental;* 10. *(a) genetic factors, (b) nonshared environmental,* (c) *shared environmental;* 11. *(a) Big Five, (b) behaviors;* 12. *(a) 30,* (b) *heritability;* 13. *(a) quantum change, (b) structured interview;* 14. *(a) personal, cultural, (b) martyrs;* 15. *(a) cultural, (b) fear,* (c) *message;* 16. *(a) Freud's psychodynamic theory, (b) humanistic,* (c) *social learning, (d) trait;* 17. *objective;* 18. *(a) Minnesota Multiphasic Personality Inventory-2-RF, or MMPI-2, (b) abnormal;* 19. *Barnum*

Unless otherwise noted, all images are © Cengage Learning

Links to Learning

Key Terms/Key People

agreeableness, 463

Bandura's social cognitive theory, 459, 473

Barnum principle, 475

behavioral genetics, 466

Big Five traits, 463, 473

cognitive factors, 458

conscientiousness, 463

delay of gratification, 460

environmental factors, 458

extraversion, 463

factor analysis, 462

five-factor model, 463, 473

heritability, 466

humanistic theories, 472

locus of control, 459

longitudinal method, 465

Maslow, Abraham, 472

Minnesota Multiphasic Personality Inventory-2-RF (MMPI-2), 474

Mischel, Walter, 464

neuroticism, 463

nonshared environmental factors, 467

objective personality tests, 474

OCEAN, 463

openness, 463

person-situation interaction, 464

personal factors, 458

psychodynamic theory, 472

quantum personality change, 470

reciprocal determinism, 458

reliability, 475

Rogers's self theory, 472

self-efficacy, 460

shared environmental factors, 467

social cognitive theory, 458, 473

structured interviews, 470

suicide bombers, 471

trait theory, 462, 473

traits, 462, 473

validity, 475

Media Resources

Go to **CengageBrain.com** to access Psychology CourseMate, where you will find an interactive eBook, glossaries, flashcards, quizzes, videos, answers to Critical Thinking questions, and more. You can also access Virtual Psychology Labs, an interactive laboratory experience designed to illustrate key experiments first-hand.

MODULE 21 Health, Stress, & Coping

introduction

Stress

Why does Luisa fear she will die?

One afternoon, Luisa, a 23-year-old college student, was walking on campus and she suddenly felt her heart rate rapidly accelerate, her throat tighten up, and her arms and legs tremble. She became so nauseous she almost vomited. Luisa felt she had no control over what was happening, and when she went to the doctor, she was told nothing was wrong. Then, weeks later, while at the movies, she had another episode during which she experienced dizziness, chest pain, shortness of breath, and weakness in her legs and feet. She feared she was having a heart attack and might die, but after a series of tests, her doctors found no medical problem. About a month later, Luisa had her most serious attack while sitting in her physics class. This time she had a strong desire to leave the classroom, and as soon she got outside, her legs gave in and she fell to the floor. From then on, Luisa became fearful of places that were closed in or crowded, such as shopping malls, restaurants, theaters, and even classrooms. She avoided these places in fear she would have another crisis. After this most recent episode, she was diagnosed with panic disorder (adapted from Di Salvo, 2006).

23-year-old Luisa has severe anxiety.

Panic disorder is characterized by recurrent and unexpected panic attacks (described below). The person becomes so worried about having another panic attack that this intense worrying interferes with normal psychological functioning (American Psychiatric Association, 2000).

The symptoms Luisa had while walking on campus, watching a movie, and sitting in class indicate that she was having a panic attack.

A **panic attack** is a period of intense fear or discomfort in which four or more of the following symptoms are present: pounding heart, sweating, trembling, shortness of breath, feelings of choking, chest pain, nausea, dizziness, and fear of losing control or dying (American Psychiatric Association, 2000).

In any given year, about one-third of American adults have at least one panic attack, but most of these adults never develop repeated panic attacks. Like Luisa, about 1–3% of adults in the United States suffer from panic disorder (Valentiner & Fergus, 2012). Compared with most people who may experience only mild forms of anxiety, people who have panic attacks find their experiences to be very stressful.

Stress is the anxious or threatening feeling that comes when we interpret or appraise a situation as being more than our psychological resources can adequately handle (Lazarus, 1999).

The study of stress is very much the study of how the mind and body interact. In this module, you'll learn how your mind is involved in what happens to your body during stressful situations.

Just as we can use our mind to overreact to stress, we can also use it to cope with stress, which is something Brenda must do almost every minute of her life.

Coping

How has Brenda's life changed?

As you approach Brenda Combs's third- and fourth-grade classroom, you hear her enthusiastically lead her students in joyful singing. Brenda has become an extraordinary educator of at-risk children, making a tremendous impact on the lives of her students. But, the hours are long, the stress is high, and the pay is so low she has to also work part-time jobs to make ends meet. She does this all while being a responsible and loving single mother to her son, Mycole, who suffered a massive stroke at birth and requires special care, and being a graduate school student. Brenda earned her master's degree in 2007 and her doctorate in 2011.

Brenda's story is especially impressive because about 15 years ago, she was a homeless crack addict and a petty criminal who had been shot, beaten, and raped during her years living on the streets. She was fortunate to have escaped many life-threatening moments. Most people would have expected Brenda's life to continue to spiral downward, but Brenda received a wake-up call serious enough to motivate her to drastically improve her life.

The turning point for Brenda was the morning she woke up to find that her shoes had been stolen from her feet as she slept in an alleyway. But, more than shoes were stolen from Brenda that morning—her last shred of dignity was taken too. At this point, Brenda took complete charge of her life. She is now clean of drugs, is a college faculty member, and is an inspirational role model to people everywhere (adapted from APB, 2009; Celizic, 2007; K. Miller, 2007; www.brendacombs.com).

How does Brenda cope with so many life stressors?

Brenda's adult life has presented her with a series of nonstop potential stressors.

Stressors are conditions or events that give rise to stress.

To keep these stressors from growing out of control, she uses a variety of coping techniques.

Coping is the thinking and behaviors we engage in to manage stressors.

As you can imagine, Brenda must have continually guarded against being overwhelmed by school, by work, by being a single mother, and by all the other responsibilities of life. One of the interesting topics we'll discuss in this module is the different ways to cope with stressors.

What's Coming

We'll discuss how you decide something is stressful, your physiological and psychological responses to stress, how your immune system works, how you develop psychosomatic symptoms, which situational and personality factors help or hinder your coping processes, the field of positive psychology, and how to develop a stress management program.

We'll begin with how Luisa's mind can make her physical symptoms worse for no good reason. ●

Primary Appraisals

Although Luisa believes she will die during a panic attack, in fact that is impossible ("Panic attacks," 2005). If there is no real threat to Luisa's survival, then why does she react so strongly to her physical symptoms (dizziness, trembling)? One explanation is that she may misinterpret normal physical symptoms as serious problems, which can intensify the symptoms. For example, Luisa may be nervous about school grades or going on a date and experience that nervousness physiologically (sweating, racing heart). These symptoms can make her feel more anxious ("What is wrong with me?"), escalating the physical sensations into the chest pain of a heart attack (Ham, 2005). In this example, Luisa's initial interpretation of her physical symptoms is that a stressful situation is happening ("Something is wrong with me and I could die"). The initial interpretation of a potentially stressful situation is called a primary appraisal (Lazarus, 1999, 2000).

What makes Luisa's symptoms so stressful?

Primary appraisal is our initial, subjective evaluation of a situation, in which we balance the demands of a potentially stressful situation against our ability to meet these demands. For example, there can be three different primary appraisals when experiencing a racing heart rate. If a doctor gives you medication to treat a painful headache and says you will initially feel your heart racing, your primary appraisal of your racing heart is that it is irrelevant (your real concern is your headache) and therefore mostly nonstressful. If you're running a marathon and feel your heart beating quickly, your primary appraisal is positive and mostly nonstressful because it makes you feel good. If you're trying to sleep or relax and your heart rate accelerates, your primary appraisal of this situation is stressful. Your primary appraisal that a situation is stressful involves three different interpretations: harm/loss, threat, or challenge.

Luisa's mind creates her intense fear.

Harm/Loss

If you broke your arm in a bike accident, you know that you have suffered harm or loss.

Harm/loss appraisal

A **harm/loss appraisal** of a situation means that you have already sustained some damage or injury.

Because the harm/loss appraisal *elicits negative emotions*, such as fear, depression, fright, and anxiety, you will feel stressed; and the more intense your negative emotions are, the more stressful and overwhelming the situation will seem.

Threat

If you have a terrible fear of giving blood and are asked to do so, you would automatically interpret giving blood as a threat to your well-being.

Threat appraisal

A **threat appraisal** of a situation means that the harm/loss has not yet taken place but you know it will happen in the near future.

Because a threat appraisal also *elicits negative emotions*, such as fear, anxiety, and anger, the situation or event may seem especially stressful. In fact, just imagining or anticipating a threatening situation, such as giving blood or taking a final exam, can be as stressful as the actual event itself.

Challenge

If you are working hard in college but find that you have to take two more classes, you might interpret taking these classes as a way to achieve a major goal—that is, you use a challenge appraisal.

Challenge appraisal

A **challenge appraisal** means that you have the potential for gain or personal growth but you also need to mobilize your physical energy and psychological resources to meet the challenging situation.

Because a challenge appraisal *elicits positive emotions*, such as eagerness or excitement, it is usually less stressful than a harm/loss or threat appraisal.

Situations and Primary Appraisals

Your first reaction to a potentially stressful situation, such as waiting in line, dealing with a sloppy roommate, giving blood, making a public speech, taking an exam, or being in a car accident, is to appraise the situation in terms of whether it harms, threatens, or challenges your physical or psychological well-being.

Making primary appraisals about complex situations, such as whether to take a certain job, get married, or go on to graduate school, may require considerable time as you think over the different ways a situation will affect you. In comparison, making primary appraisals about very emotional situations, such as taking a surprise quiz, presenting a

He made a primary appraisal that giving a speech was a threat to his self-esteem.

report in class, or getting into a car accident, may occur quickly, even automatically (Lazarus, 2000). However, not all appraisals neatly divide into harm/loss, threat, or challenge. Some primary appraisals are a combination of threat and challenge. For instance, if you are about to ask someone for a first date, you may feel threatened by the possibility of being rejected yet challenged by the chance to prove yourself. Depending on the kind of primary appraisal, your level of stress may either increase or decrease.

Appraisal and Stress Level

Would it stress you to watch a bloody accident?

If you were asked to watch a film of bloody accidents caused by power saws, how much would your primary appraisal affect your level of stress? This is exactly what researchers asked people to do while they recorded a major sign of physiological arousal, called the galvanic skin response.

The **galvanic skin response** is a measure of how much a person's hand sweats due to physiological arousal and not to normal temperature changes.

As participants watched the accident film, they were given instructions that would cause them to make a primary appraisal of either challenge or threat. To encourage challenge appraisals, some participants were told to watch the film objectively, to consider how these accidents might be prevented, but

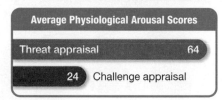

Level of stress from watching a bloody accident depended on threat or challenge appraisal.

Average Physiological Arousal Scores	
Threat appraisal	64
24	Challenge appraisal

not to identify with the injured. To encourage threat appraisals, other participants were told to put themselves in the place of men who accidentally cut off their fingers and imagine how they would feel.

As the graph below shows, people who made threat appraisals showed significantly more physiological arousal—that is, higher levels of galvanic skin responses—than those who made challenge appraisals (Dandoy & Goldstein, 1990). Researchers concluded that in threatening or disturbing situations, your feelings of stress increase with the kind of appraisal: Threat appraisals raise levels of stress more than challenge appraisals do. However, when people are asked to identify the cause of their stressful feelings, they usually—and often incorrectly—point to a particular situation rather than to their primary appraisals. As you'll see next, people often appraise the same situation in different ways.

Same Situation, Different Appraisals

How stressful is waiting in a doctor's office?

When we ask our students, "What stresses you?" they always list a variety of situations, including many of those situations listed in the table at the right. Notice especially how the same situation was stressful for some but not for others. For example, 65% said waiting for a late person was stressful, but 35% reported it wasn't. Similarly, 61% said waiting in line was stressful, but 39% said it wasn't. Because people don't agree on which situations are stressful, researchers concluded that level of stress depends not only on the kind of situation but also on the kind of *primary appraisal* one makes (G. Fink, 2007; C. Rasmussen et al., 2000). For example, you could appraise waiting in a doctor's

Why are 59% stressed by waiting in a doctor's office while 41% are not?

Situation	Percentage rating it	
	stressful	not stressful
Waiting for someone who is late	65	35
Being caught in traffic	63	37
Waiting in line	61	39
Waiting in a doctor's office	59	41
Waiting for the government to act	51	49
Waiting for a repair person	46	54
Looking for a parking space	42	58
Waiting for an airplane to take off	26	74

Situation list data from *USA Today*, August 19, 1987, p 4D.

office as a challenge (maybe you can benefit by reading magazines or brochures), which elicits positive emotions and little stress. Or, you could appraise waiting as a threat or a real test of your patience, which elicits negative emotions (growing impatient) and considerable stress. Thus, similar situations (waiting in a doctor's office) can result in different levels of stress depending on your primary appraisal.

Sequence: Appraisal to Arousal

The first step in feeling stress depends on your primary appraisal, which can be harm/loss, threat, or challenge. In turn, harm/loss and threat appraisals elicit

How does stress start?

negative emotions, which, in turn, increase levels of stress. In comparison, challenge appraisals elicit positive emotions, which, in turn, decrease levels of stress. Thus, when you say that a situation is causing you stress, such as giving blood, taking an exam, making a public speech, changing your job, asking for a date, arguing with your boss, having to move, getting married, or arguing with your roommate, you

Making a threat or harm/loss appraisal results in increased physiological arousal.

are forgetting that part of the stress is coming from whether you make a harm/loss or threat appraisal versus a challenge appraisal (Lazarus, 2000).

The moment after you make an appraisal, especially a harm/loss or threat appraisal, your body changes from a generally calm state into a state of heightened physiological arousal as it prepares to deal with the stressor, whether it involves a car accident, a mugger, a speech, or giving blood. We'll look inside the body and see what happens when you are stressed. ●

Fight-Flight Response

What happens when you're frightened?

Imagine giving a talk in class. As you look at everyone staring at you, you feel your heart pounding, mouth becoming dry, hands sweating, stomach knotting, and muscles tensing; you take in short, rapid breaths. Your body is fully aroused before you have spoken a single word (Tanouye, 1997). The thought of having to give a public speech is the No. 1 fear reported by people in the United States (Witt et al., 2006).

Since speaking in public is no threat to your physical survival and you can neither fight nor flee, why is your body in this state of heightened physiological arousal? The answer is that once you make a primary appraisal that something is a threat—whether it's giving a speech or facing a mugger—these threatening and fearful thoughts automatically trigger one of the body's oldest physiological response systems, the fight-flight response (J. M. White & Porth, 2000).

The **fight-flight response** (1) directs great resources of energy to the muscles and the brain; (2) can be triggered by either physical stimuli that threaten our survival or psychological situations that are novel, threatening, or challenging; and (3) involves numerous physiological responses that arouse and prepare the body for action—fight or flight.

© MSPhotographic/ Shutterstock.com

© SerrNovik/ Shutterstock.com

The fight-flight response helps us survive by preparing the body for action—fleeing or fighting.

We know that the fight-flight response is evolutionarily very old because it can be found in animals such as the alligator, which has been around for millions of years. We presume that our early ancestors evolved a similar fight-flight response to help them survive attacks by wild animals and enemies.

Physical stimuli. Today you have almost no need to fight wild animals or flee attacking enemies, so you rarely activate your fight-flight response for the reasons important to our early ancestors. However, you would activate the fight-flight response when faced with a potentially dangerous physical stimulus, such as a mugger, accident, police siren, snake, tornado, or other situation that threatened your physical survival.

Psychological stimuli. Today the most common reason you activate the fight-flight response is exposure to potentially bothersome or stressful psychological stimuli, such as worrying about exams, being impatient in traffic, having to wait in lines, getting angry over a putdown, or arguing with someone (Lazarus, 2000). We'll trace the sequence of how psychological or physical stimuli can trigger the fight-flight response and transform your body into a state of heightened physiological arousal (J. M. White & Porth, 2000).

Sequence for Activation of the Fight-Flight Response

Autonomic Nervous System

© luckypic/Shutterstock.com

1 Appraisal

A number of potentially dangerous physical stimuli, such as seeing a snake or being in an accident, can automatically trigger the fight-flight response. But much more common triggers of the fight-flight response are hundreds of psychological stimuli that you appraise as threatening, such as making a public speech or taking an exam. Thus, either *physically or psychologically threatening stimuli* can trigger the fight-flight response and negative emotional feelings (fear, rage).

2 Hypothalamus

If you appraise making a public speech as psychologically threatening, these thoughts activate a part of your brain called the *hypothalamus*. In turn, the hypothalamus simultaneously activates two stress-related responses: It triggers the pituitary gland to release a stress-fighting hormone called *ACTH* (adrenocorticotropic hormone), and it activates the sympathetic division of the autonomic nervous system.

3 Sympathetic Division

As we discussed earlier (see p. 81), the autonomic nervous system has two divisions. The *sympathetic division*, which is activated by the hypothalamus, triggers a number of physiological responses that make up the fight-flight response, which prepares the body to deal with potentially threatening physical or psychological stimuli. In contrast, the *parasympathetic division*, also activated by the hypothalamus, returns the body to a more calm, relaxed state.

4 Fight-Flight Response

The sympathetic division triggers a very primitive *fight-flight response* (present in crocodiles), which causes great *physiological arousal* by increasing heart rate, blood pressure, respiration, secretion of excitatory hormones, and many other responses that prepare the body to deal with an impending threat, whether speaking in public or facing a mugger.

Next, we'll describe the many interesting physiological responses that transform the body into a powerful fighting or fleeing machine.

Fight-Flight: Physiological and Hormonal Responses

I hate to speak in public!

SPEECH

Physical or psychological stimuli can trigger the fight-flight response.

It is difficult to believe that the powerful fight-flight response can be triggered just as easily by potentially threatening psychological stimuli, such as speaking in public or taking exams, as by potentially threatening physical stimuli, such as seeing a rattlesnake. Although you rarely experience potentially threatening physical stimuli, such as meeting a snake, you do face many psychological situations that you appraise as threatening—"Let me tell you about my terrible day." As soon as you appraise a situation as threatening, specific parts of your brain start the fight-flight response, which in turn prepares your body for action (Cowley, 2003). We'll describe some of the major physiological changes triggered by the fight-flight response (S. Johnson, 2003).

1 A **stress appraisal**, especially if it involves something fearful or threatening, can instantly activate the *amygdala* (light blue), which functions like a threat detector (p. 363). In turn, the amygdala activates the *hypothalamus* (red), which functions like a switch to quickly and simultaneously trigger two systems that arouse the body for action (p. 81). One system involves the *pituitary gland* (p. 82), which triggers a release of the hormone ACTH (adrenocorticotropic hormone), which acts on part of the adrenal gland (adrenal cortex) to increase fuel for quick energy. A second system involves the *sympathetic division* of the autonomic nervous system (p. 72), which increases physiological arousal by automatically increasing heart rate, blood pressure, and other responses such as releasing powerful arousing hormones from the adrenal glands (see #7 on the right).

2 **Respiration**, which is increased by the sympathetic division, is more rapid and shallow so that there is a greater flow of oxygen into the body. However, if breathing is too rapid and shallow, we may feel light-headed or "spacey" from lack of oxygen.

3 **Heart rate**, which is increased by the sympathetic division, can rocket from a normal 70–90 beats per minute to an incredible 200–220 beats per minute. Rapid heart rate increases blood flow to muscles and vital organs (lungs, kidneys). Rapid heart rate during stressful experiences can lead to a "pounding heart" and, in extreme cases, result in heart attack and death.

4 The **liver** releases its stores of blood sugar (glycogen) to provide a ready source of energy during stress. After a stressful experience, we may feel fatigued because our supply of blood sugar is low.

Stomach and **intestinal activity** is reduced by the sympathetic division. During stressful experiences, the blood that is normally used by digestive organs is rerouted to muscles and vital organs. Because the sympathetic division shuts down the digestive system, people may experience problems with digestion, such as stomach pain, constipation, and diarrhea, during stressful times.

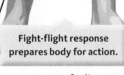

Liver

Stomach

Fight-flight response prepares body for action.

5 **Pupils** are dilated by the sympathetic division. As a result, more light enters our eyes so we can see better if we have to fight or flee in dim light. One way to check for physiological arousal is to see how much a person's pupils are dilated: More dilation usually indicates more arousal (except in the case of drug use).

6 **Hair** stands up; this is called piloerection (goose bumps) and is more noticeable in dogs and cats. Piloerection, which occurs when we are stressed (frightened or angry) or cold (fluffy fur or hair conserves heat), is triggered by the sympathetic division, which also regulates sweating. The next time you are feeling stressed, look for piloerection and sweaty hands.

7 **Adrenal glands**, which are located above the kidneys, have an outside—adrenal cortex—and an inside—adrenal medulla. The *adrenal medulla*, which is activated by the sympathetic division, secretes two powerful activating hormones, epinephrine (adrenaline) and norepinephrine. These hormones increase heart rate, blood pressure, blood flow to muscles, and release of blood sugar (glucose) as a source of energy. Epinephrine and norepinephrine may be regarded as the body's own stimulants; they can result in euphoria, loss of appetite, and sleeplessness.

The *adrenal cortex*, which is activated by the pituitary gland's release of ACTH, secretes a group of hormones called corticoids, which regulate levels of minerals and increase fuel (glucose) for energy needed to take some action.

8 **Muscle tension** is increased during stressful experiences, so that we are better able to coordinate and move quickly if needed. However, if you are feeling stressed for long periods of time, you may end up with muscle aches and pains because of increased muscle tension throughout your body.

Male–female difference. The fight-flight response is automatically triggered to increase physiological arousal and prepare our bodies for action. However, researchers found that while men are more likely to fight or flee when stressed, women show a different response to stress, called *tend and befriend,* which involves nurturing (children) and seeking social support (S. E. Taylor, 2002; S. E. Taylor & Master, 2011). Researchers suggest that this male–female difference in responding to stress may have developed from evolutionary pressures on primitive men to fight and protect their families and on primitive women to nurture their children and seek help and social support for themselves and their families.

Although the fight-flight response is designed to aid survival in stressful situations, if the fight-flight response is continuously triggered over a period of time (days, weeks), you may develop painful physical problems, which we'll describe next.

Psychosomatic Symptoms

What causes stomach pains?

As a college freshman, Joan was stressed out from having too many classes, spending 28 hours a week on homework, working another 10 hours a week at a part-time job, and not getting enough sleep. Joan is one of the 30% of college students in the United States who reported feeling "frequently overwhelmed" by all they have to do (Sax, 2002). Women report more stress (37%) than men (17%), who seem to reduce stress by exercising, partying, and playing more video games than women (Deckro, 2002; Gallagher, 2002). If stress persists for weeks and months, there is a good possibility that you will develop one of a variety of unwanted psychosomatic (also called psychophysiological) symptoms (Kemeny, 2003; Selye, 1993).

Psychosomatic *(SIGH-ko-so-MAH-tick)* **symptoms** are real and sometimes painful physical symptoms, such as headaches, muscle pains, stomach problems, and increased susceptibility to colds and flu, that are caused by increased physiological arousal that results from psychological factors, such as worry, stress, and anxiety. (The word *psychosomatic* is derived from *psyche* meaning "mind" and *soma* meaning "body.")

1. Stressful situations

2. Threat appraisal

3. Trigger fight-flight

4. Develop psychosomatic symptoms

"The fact is that we're now living in a world where our bodies aren't allowed a chance to rest…they're being driven by inadequate sleep, lack of exercise, by smoking, by isolation or frenzied competition" (McEwen, 2002). Although our bodies are cleverly designed to use the fight-flight response to deal with relatively infrequent stressors, our bodies do need time for rest and relaxation. However, for many, the busy and competitive world is filled with so many stressful situations that they are constantly appraising situations as threatening to their psychological survival and thus giving their bodies little chance to relax (Sapolsky, 2002). The result, as shown in the figure above, is that the constant use of threat appraisals continually triggers the fight-flight response. In turn, the fight-flight response produces a heightened state of physiological arousal that goes on and on and thus increases the risk of developing one or more psychosomatic symptoms (Kemeny, 2003).

We'll discuss different kinds of psychosomatic symptoms as well as why you may develop one symptom but not others.

Do you have any of these symptoms?

Doctors estimate that 60–90% of patients seen in general medical practice have stress-related, psychosomatic symptoms (H. Benson, 2008). It is estimated that 75 percent of healthcare costs are associated with chronic illnesses, and it is well documented that the main contributing factor in chronic illness is stress (N. B. Anderson, 2012). Even though stress plays a major role in the development of chronic health conditions, many adults in the United States (31 percent) report that stress has only a slight or no impact on their physical health (APA, 2012).

Some of the more common stress-related or psychosomatic symptoms are listed below. Our students (and each of us) usually report having developed at least one of these psychosomatic symptoms each semester.

> ## Common Psychosomatic Symptoms
> - **Stomach symptoms:** feelings of discomfort, pain, pressure, or acidity
> - **Muscle pain and tension:** occurring in neck, shoulders, and back
> - **Fatigue:** feeling tired or exhausted without doing physical activity
> - **Headaches:** having either tension or migraine headaches
> - **Intestinal difficulties:** having either constipation or diarrhea
> - **Skin disorders:** exaggerated skin blemishes, pimples, oiliness
> - **Eating problems:** feeling compelled to eat or having no appetite
> - **Insomnia:** being unable to get to sleep or stay asleep
> - **Asthmatic or allergic problems:** worsening of problems
> - **High blood pressure or heart pounding**
> - **Weak immune system and increased chances of getting a cold or flu**

List adapted from "The Factor Structure of Self-Reported Physical Stress Reactions," by J. C. Smith and J. M. Seidel, 1982, *Biofeedback and Self-Regulation, 7,* 35–47. Springer Netherlands.

Development of Psychosomatic Symptoms

Researchers find that whether one develops a psychosomatic symptom as well as the kind of symptom depends upon several different factors.

Genetic predisposition. Because of genetic predispositions, most of us inherit a tendency that targets a particular organ or bodily system for weakening or breaking down, such as the heart, blood vessels, stomach lining, or immune system. That's why different individuals who are in similar stressful situations experience different kinds of psychosomatic symptoms. For example, researchers found that some individuals inherit genes that protect their bodies from potentially harmful hormonal effects produced by frequent activation of the fight-flight response. As a result, these individuals may experience fewer psychosomatic symptoms (van Rossum et al., 2002).

Lifestyle. Some lifestyles, such as smoking, being overweight, not exercising, or taking little time for relaxing, promote poor health practices. Such lifestyles give the body little chance to relax and recover from the heightened state of physiological arousal that is produced when the fight-flight response is triggered.

Threat appraisals. Some of us are more likely to appraise situations as threatening, thus eliciting negative emotions, which automatically trigger the fight-flight response (Kiecolt-Glaser et al., 2002). One solution (discussed in the Application section on p. 502) is to practice changing threat appraisals, which involve negative emotions, into challenge appraisals, which involve positive emotions (N. Skinner & Brewer, 2002).

But how can worrying cause my awful stomach pains?

Later, we'll discuss how to prevent psychosomatic problems by developing an effective stress management program. Now, we'll examine in more detail how prolonged stressful experiences can affect and break down the body organs.

© Oscar C. Williams/Shutterstock.com

Unless otherwise noted, all images are © Cengage Learning

General Adaptation Syndrome

What does stress do?

One thing continued stress does is activate the fight-flight response. The continual activation of fight-flight responses results in what Hans Selye (1993) has described as the general adaptation syndrome.

The **general adaptation syndrome** (GAS) refers to the body's reaction to stressful situations during which it goes through a series of three stages—alarm, resistance, and exhaustion—that gradually increase the chances of developing psychosomatic symptoms.

Selye's general adaptation syndrome explains how coed Joan, who felt continually overwhelmed, developed a psychosomatic symptom, stomach pain.

1 Alarm Stage

As sleep-deprived Joan worries about having too little time for all she has to do, she appraises that situation as a terrible threat to her well-being, which causes her body to be in the alarm stage.

The **alarm stage** is the initial reaction to stress and is marked by activation of the fight-flight response; in turn, the fight-flight response causes physiological arousal.

Your body may go into and out of the alarm stage (fight-flight response) many times during the day as stressful experiences come and go. Normally, you do not develop psychosomatic problems during the alarm stage because the fight-flight responses come and go. However, if stress continues for a longer period of time, your body goes into the resistance stage.

Alarm: initial reaction

2 Resistance Stage

As the semester comes to an end, Joan's continual feelings of being overwhelmed cause almost continual fight-flight responses, which in turn cause her body to go into the resistance stage.

The **resistance stage** is the body's reaction to continued stress during which most of the physiological responses return to normal levels but the body uses up great stores of energy.

During the resistance stage, Joan's body will use up vital reserves of hormones, minerals, and glucose (blood sugar) because her body is almost continually in the fight-flight state. Joan doesn't realize that the resistance stage is taking a toll on her stomach by interfering with digestion and causing stomach pain, a psychosomatic symptom. If her stress continues, her body will go into the exhaustion stage and her psychosomatic symptom will worsen.

Resistance: fighting back

3 Exhaustion Stage

As Joan's feeling of being overwhelmed continues over many weeks, her body may enter the exhaustion stage.

The **exhaustion stage** is the body's reaction to long-term, continuous stress and is marked by actual breakdown in internal organs or weakening of the infection-fighting immune system.

During the exhaustion stage, Joan's stomach problems may become more serious. Extended periods of stress, such as during final exams, may cause your body to go into the stage of resistance or exhaustion. During this time you may develop a variety of psychosomatic symptoms, such as a cold, flu, cold sore, sore throat, allergy attack, aching muscles, or stomach problems. For example, researchers found that individuals who had prolonged and high levels of anxiety, signaling stages of resistance and exhaustion, were more likely to develop physical health problems than those with normal levels (Hoge et al., 2007). As you'll see, psychosomatic symptoms develop because of a mind-body interaction.

Exhaustion: breakdown in organs

Mind-Body Connection

Can your mind cause health problems?

At the beginning of this module, we learned how Luisa's mind can intensify the physical sensations she feels during a panic attack. This is a perfect example of the mind-body connection.

The **mind-body connection** refers to how your thoughts, beliefs, and emotions can produce physiological changes that may be either beneficial or detrimental to your health and well-being.

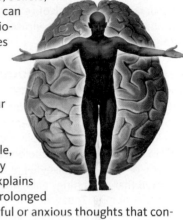

For example, the mind-body connection explains why, after a prolonged period of fearful or anxious thoughts that continually trigger the fight-flight response, there may be a breakdown in body organs and development of psychosomatic symptoms (Hoge et al., 2007). Researchers found that emotional stress, such as hearing the news of a death in the family, narrowly avoiding a car accident, or walking into a surprise party, can trigger a condition that mimics a massive heart attack. Doctors call this condition "broken-heart syndrome" and explain that when patients experience emotional shock, a sudden surge of stress hormones is released, overwhelming the heart. After the emotional stress subsides, the stress hormone levels return to normal and the heart functions properly again (Fackelmann, 2005).

Research on the importance and implications of the mind-body connection has given rise to a specialty in psychology called health psychology (S. E. Taylor, 2011).

Health psychology is the study of how psychological factors relate to the promotion and maintenance of health, as well as the prevention and treatment of illnesses.

We have already discussed how psychological factors, such as worry, stress, and anxiety, can contribute to the development of a variety of psychosomatic symptoms. We will continue our exploration of how psychological factors are associated with health conditions by discussing a field of study known as psychoneuroimmunology on the next page.

Then, later in this module, we'll discuss ways of coping with stress, including stress management programs, which at their core are based on the mind-body connection.

Immune System

Why did you get a cold?

How often have you gotten a cold, strep throat, or some other bacterial or viral infection when final exams were over? This rather common experience of "coming down with something" when exams are over indicates how prolonged stressful experiences can decrease the effectiveness of your immune system.

The **immune system** is the body's defense and surveillance network of cells and chemicals that fight off bacteria, viruses, and other foreign or toxic substances.

Getting a cold is partly due to how much stress you're under.

© leungchopan/ Shutterstock.com

For many years, researchers believed that the immune system was a totally independent bodily system with no input from the brain and certainly not influenced by one's thoughts. However, in the mid-1970s, a psychologist and an immunologist found the first good evidence of a mind-body connection—that psychological factors, such as one's thoughts, influenced the immune system (R. Ader & Cohen, 1975). Their research led to the development of an entirely new area of medical science that is called psychoneuroimmunology *(SIGH-ko-NOOR-oh-im-you-NAH-luh-gee)*, which is an example of the mind-body connection.

Psychoneuroimmunology

Researchers Ader and Cohen (1975) were trying to figure out why some of their rats were dying so young when they chanced upon one of the important scientific discoveries of the 1970s. Previously, immunologists believed the immune system operated independently of psychological influences. Then, to the surprise of all and the disbelief of many, Ader and Cohen reported that psychological factors influenced the immune system's functioning. Today, no one doubts their findings, which launched the field of psychoneuroimmunology (Daruna, 2012).

Psychoneuroimmunology is the study of the relationship among three factors: the central nervous system (brain and spinal cord), the endocrine system (network of glands that secrete hormones), and psychosocial factors (stressful thoughts, personality traits, and social influences).

For example, coming down with an illness (cold, flu) after a stressful time results from the interactions among three factors—central nervous system, endocrine system, and psychosocial factors. These three factors can suppress or strengthen the immune system and in turn make the body more or less susceptible to disease and infection (Kiecolt-Glaser et al., 2002). For instance, when stress weakens the immune system, it can reduce the number of natural killer cells known to fight cancer (Lenzer, 2007). Also, when elderly people lose their spouse, the bereavement process can take a serious toll on their body, leading to a 53–61% increased risk of death within one month (Christakis & Allison, 2006). As you can see, the effects of stress on the body can be profound.

The immune system has several ways to kill foreign invaders. In the left photo, an immune system cell sends out footlike extensions to engulf and destroy the small bacterial cell (inside the white oval).

However, the immune system's defenses can be weakened by psychosocial factors (Daruna, 2012).

An immune system cell sends out a footlike extension to destroy a bacterial cell (in white oval).

© SPL/Photo Researchers, Inc.

Evidence for Psychoneuroimmunology

Researchers were faced with a difficult question: Why doesn't everyone who is exposed to a disease virus or bacteria actually get the disease? They tackled this question by giving the same amount of cold virus to 394 individuals, all of whom were quarantined for a week. During this period, the researchers checked for symptoms of colds and related the percentage of colds to the levels of stress that participants had reported before they received the virus. As shown in the graph below, researchers found that those individuals who reported high levels of psychological stress were more likely to develop colds than were those who reported low stress levels. Researchers concluded that, with every increase in psychological stress, there's an increased likelihood of developing a cold—provided we are exposed to the cold virus (S. Cohen, 2003; S. Cohen et al., 1997).

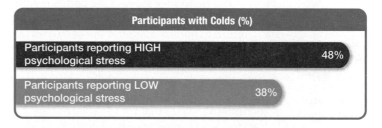

Participants with Colds (%)

Participants reporting HIGH psychological stress — 48%

Participants reporting LOW psychological stress — 38%

Fight-flight response. Other research has confirmed the link between short-term stress and physical health risks, such as increased inflammation (Chiang et al., 2012). While short-term stress can weaken the immune system, chronic stress (such as ongoing relationship conflict or unemployment) has even more severe effects on our health (Daruna, 2012). People who experience chronic stress are more susceptible to illness, including catching colds, because they are continually activating their fight-flight response (S. Cohen et al., 2012).

When the fight-flight response is activated, your body produces stress hormones, which suppress the immune system and make the body more susceptible to diseases, viruses, and other infections, as well as reduce its ability to heal from wounds and respond to vaccinations (Ebrecht et al., 2004; Kiecolt-Glaser, 2008). One psychoneurimmunology researcher described the effects of chronic stress on the body by saying, "Stress made 55-year-olds have 90-year-old immune systems" (Kiecolt-Glaser, 2008).

How psychological factors affect the immune system will become clearer as we next describe a really clever experiment.

Unless otherwise noted, all images are © Cengage Learning

Conditioning the Immune System

Could artificial flowers make you sneeze?

There is an interesting story of a woman who was in therapy for having severe allergic reactions to flowers. The therapist was curious about what caused her allergic reaction. It could be caused either by organic factors, which are the physical properties of flowers, or by psychosomatic factors, which are thoughts, beliefs, or conditioned responses to flowers. To determine whether the cause was organic or psychosomatic, one day the therapist took a dozen red roses from under her desk, gave them to the woman, and asked her what the flowers reminded her of. The woman held them for a short time and then began to have allergic responses, including nasal congestion and tears. What the woman did not know was that the flowers were artificial.

Why do artificial flowers make my nose run?

© iofoto/Shutterstock.com

The woman's allergic reaction to artificial flowers clearly demonstrated that the cause of her allergy was not physical but psychosomatic (caused by the woman's own thoughts). As the woman later explained, her husband had regularly given her flowers as a sign of affection, but now that he was seeking a divorce, the flowers had become a depressing or aversive stimulus. This means that, through classical conditioning, flowers had become conditioned stimuli capable of eliciting a conditioned response—in this case, an allergic reaction (classical conditioning is discussed on pages 197–199). Just to be sure, researchers designed the following experiment that left no doubt that the immune system could be classically conditioned (Maier et al., 1994).

Classical Conditioning Experiment

If the immune system could be classically conditioned, it would clearly show the influence of psychological factors. As explained in Module 9, classical conditioning involves changing a neutral stimulus, such as a flashing light or a humming fan, into a conditioned stimulus so that it alone can elicit a conditioned response—in this case, an allergic reaction in a rat. Here's how an immune response (allergic reaction) was classically conditioned in rats (MacQueen et al., 1989).

 Conditioned stimuli: flashing light and humming fan.

 **Unconditioned stimulus:** injection of a substance that produces allergy.

 Unconditioned response: allergic reaction elicited by injected substance.

1 For the first three trials, each rat was first presented with two conditioned (neutral) stimuli, a light flashing and a fan humming. A short time later, each rat was given an injection of an allergy-producing substance, which was the unconditioned stimulus. In turn, the unconditioned stimulus elicited an allergic reaction, which was the unconditioned response.

2 On the fourth trial, the animals were divided into two groups: control and experimental groups.

The *control group* received a trial with the regular sequence: flashing light and fan humming, then the injection of the substance, which elicited the allergic reaction.

The *experimental group* received a different trial: The rats were only exposed to the conditioned stimuli of flashing light and fan humming, with no injection.

3 The *experimental group* of animals showed a conditioned response, which means that just being given or exposed to the conditioned stimuli (flashing light and humming fan) caused the allergic reaction, which is the *conditioned response*.

4 **Discussion.** During classical conditioning, animals or people learn that the neutral or conditioned stimulus signals or predicts what will happen next. In this study, rats learned that the flashing light and humming fan predicted an allergic reaction. And in fact, by the fourth trial, the conditioned stimuli (light and fan) alone elicited the allergic reaction—the conditioned response. Researchers concluded that psychological factors can trigger an allergic reaction in animals (MacQueen et al., 1989).

5 **Conclusion.** The amazing fact that immune responses can be conditioned demonstrates a method through which purely psychological or cognitive factors can affect immune function. Although the immune system was originally thought to act independently, it is now known that psychological factors influence the immune system in both animals and humans (F. Ader, 1999).

These findings in rats explain why the woman had an allergic reaction to artificial flowers: The artificial flowers had become conditioned stimuli that, by themselves, could elicit conditioned responses—in this case, allergic reactions of congestion and tearing eyes.

The history of psychoneuroimmunology reads like a mystery story. For 50 years, researchers had written in stone that the immune system was totally independent and only a fool would believe otherwise. In the early 1970s, Ader the psychologist and Cohen the immunologist were studying something entirely different (why animals were dying prematurely) when they discovered the reason was that the animals' immune systems had been weakened through classical conditioning (R. Ader & Cohen, 1975). This revolutionary finding meant that the immune system could be influenced by psychological factors, and this led to the birth of a whole new field, called psychoneuroimmunology (Daruna, 2012).

We have discussed how stressful experiences trigger the fight-flight response and affect the immune system. Next, we'll examine which situations are the most likely to become stressful. ●

C Stressful Experiences

Kinds of Stressors

We began this module with a description of Brenda Combs's life. During her climb from homeless crack addict to college professor, Brenda encountered countless daily hassles: managing to be on time to her job and classes, completing her homework and studying, cooking, cleaning, getting her son through the many steps of his day, and managing the behavior of the children in her classroom, to list just a few. Hassles are small stressors, which can add up to make what she would probably call a "bad day."

What are Brenda's stressors?

Brenda experienced daily hassles and major life changes.

Courtesy of Brenda Combs

Besides dealing with daily hassles, Brenda also went through a number of major life changes: She quit using drugs, became a single mother, went back to college, and became a college professor. Unlike hassles, which seem relatively small, major life events have had a significant impact on Brenda's life and can be very big stressors.

Both hassles and major life events have the potential to become stressful experiences that influence mood and the development of psychosomatic problems.

Hassles

When someone asks, "And how was your day?" you usually reply with a list of hassles.

Hassles are those small, irritating, frustrating events that we face daily and that we usually appraise or interpret as stressful experiences.

For example, a nationwide survey of adults (ages 25–74) found that the most frequently reported daily hassles involved interpersonal tensions followed by work-related stressors. The most frequently reported appraisals involved danger (36%), loss (30%), or frustration (27%), and only 2% were appraised as representing opportunity or challenge. Generally, women reported the stressors as being more severe than did men. As the number of daily hassles increased, so too did the chance of developing psychosomatic problems or being in a bad mood (Almeida et al., 2002).

© jcjgphotography/Shutterstock.com

Daily hassles are related to having physical problems.

The opposite of a hassle is a good experience called an uplift.

Uplifts are those small, pleasurable, happy, and satisfying experiences that we have in our daily lives.

For many college students (and most adults), the daily hassles, which lead to having a "bad day," usually far outnumber the uplifts, which lead to having a "good day." For example, how often do you hear people say, "I had such a great day!" In contrast to hassles, daily uplifts are associated with fewer psychosomatic symptoms and better functioning (J. S. Werner et al., 2012).

Besides hassles, another source of stress involves major life events.

Major Life Events

© Christoph Wilhelm/Getty Images

Experiencing a major life event (getting married) can be stressful.

Not only do hassles increase stress levels and predict daily mood and health, but so do major life events.

Major life events are potentially disturbing, troubling, or disruptive situations, both positive and negative, that we appraise as having a significant impact on our lives.

Researchers measure life events using the ***Social Readjustment Rating Scale*** (see below) (M. A. Miller & Rahe, 1997). The number after each event rates the impact that the event would have on one's life; death of one's spouse has the highest rating (119). To obtain your score, add the numbers associated with each event you have experienced in the last year. The total reflects how much life change you have experienced. Researchers predicted that experiencing a higher number of life changes would increase levels of stress and, in turn, lead to more psychosomatic problems.

One problem with the Social Readjustment Rating Scale is that it makes no distinction between appraisals of positive events (getting married) and negative events (getting divorced). Researchers report that the appraisal of negative life events is more important in predicting illnesses or depression than are positive events (Dixon & Reid, 2000; Shimizu & Pelham, 2004).

When asked about their causes of stress, most Americans reported the following stressors to be somewhat or very significant: money, work, family responsibilities, personal relationships, and personal health concerns (American Psychiatric Association, 2012).

Adjustment Disorder. As we just learned, there are many stressors, including major life events such as getting married, moving, beginning college, and losing a job. Most of the time, people adjust to these changes within a few weeks or months. However, in some cases, these life changes may cause people to feel anxious or depressed for many months, which means they have adjustment disorder.

Adjustment disorder is a condition in which a person is unable to cope with or adjust to a major life change. The condition includes emotional (such as feeling depressed, overwhelmed) and behavioral (such as avoiding social interaction, performing poorly at school or work, making reckless decisions) symptoms.

Individuals with adjustment disorder experience an excessive reaction to a life stressor, and their symptoms cause trouble in their daily functioning.

Next, we'll discuss how stressful events are generally frustrating experiences.

Social Readjustment Rating Scale	
Life event	**Mean value**
Death of spouse	119
Divorce	98
Death of close family member	92
Fired at work	79
Personal injury or illness	77
Death of a close friend	70
Pregnancy	66
Change in financial state	56
Change in work conditions	51
Marriage	50
Sex difficulties	45
Change in living conditions	42
Change in residence	41
Beginning or ending school	38
Great personal achievement	37
Change in school	35
Trouble with boss	29
Revision of personal habits	27
Change in sleeping habits	26
Vacation	25
Minor violations of the law	22

Scale: Reprinted from "Life changes scaling for the 1990s," by M. A. Miller and R. H. Rahe, *Journal of Psychosomatic Research, 43,* 279–292, Copyright © 1997, with permission from Elsevier Science.

Situational Stressors

What makes situations stressful? We're going to examine three situations—being frustrated, feeling burned out, and experiencing interpersonal violence—that have the potential to be highly stressful. What can make these situations especially stressful is that they can all elicit very negative emotions, which can greatly increase levels of stress.

Frustration

Being a pop music star is exhausting.

In 2010, Lady Gaga, a singer-songwriter who has received numerous music awards and nominations, canceled a planned performance, complaining of "exhaustion." She felt tremendous stress resulting from her rapidly rising fame, work on an album, and the constant pressure of a worldwide concert tour spanning nearly two years (*People*, 2010). Lady Gaga's example illustrates the difficulties of having a job in which success is judged by how many albums and concert tickets you sell and awards you win.

After canceling her performance due to exhaustion, Lady Gaga tweeted to her fans: "I've been crying for hours, I feel like i let my fans down 2nite" (Gaga, 2010). Lady Gaga was clearly experiencing frustration.

Frustration is the awful feeling that results when your attempts to reach some goal are blocked.

You may be blocked from reaching a goal because of *personal limitations*, such as losing your temper, making dumb mistakes on an exam, or not having the skills to pass a course. In Lady Gaga's case, she lacked the energy and good health (paramedics reported that she had an irregular heartbeat) needed to carry through with her scheduled performance. Alternatively, you may be blocked from reaching a goal because of *social* or *environmental limitations*, such as having to work extensive hours for several consecutive days. This also applied to Lady Gaga, as she was on the road performing about 200 concerts during her worldwide tour.

The case of Lady Gaga illustrates how stress and frustration can contribute to serious psychosomatic symptoms.

If frustration lasts for a long period of time, the result can be burnout.

Burnout

About 5–20% of nurses, lawyers, police officers, social workers, managers, counselors, teachers, medical residents, and others whose jobs demand intense involvement with people suffer from burnout (Farber, 2000a, 2000b).

Burnout refers to being physically overwhelmed and exhausted, finding the job unrewarding and becoming cynical or detached, and developing a strong sense of ineffectiveness and lack of accomplishment in this particular job (Maslach, 2003).

I'm burnt out after working 10 years in social services.

Burnout is accompanied by intense feelings and negative emotions that trigger the fight-flight response, keep the body in a continual state of heightened physiological arousal, and cause most of the psychosomatic symptoms we have discussed: sleep problems, stomach disorders, headaches, muscle pain (especially lower back and neck), and frequent and prolonged colds (Melamed et al., 2006).

One way to reduce the likelihood of burnout is to take a vacation. Research shows that time spent on vacation enhances people's well-being by decreasing their complaints about health problems and exhaustion (C. Fritz & Sonnentag, 2006).

Student burnout. College counselors report that burnout often causes students to drop out of college. Counselors suggest that before students decide to drop out, they should consider ways to reduce their work and class load so that school seems less overwhelming and more manageable (Schaufeli et al., 2002).

The next situation is so stressful that it leaves a terrible, lasting mark that may trigger years of problems.

Violence

Most people experience at least one traumatic situation during their life. For example, a soldier may return from war after witnessing death in battle. A woman may be raped while walking through the city park. A man may get stuck in a building after a massive earthquake. An adolescent may have a serious car accident. A child may be a victim of physical abuse. For some people their experience is so stressful that it results in posttraumatic stress disorder (T. M. Ball & Stein, 2012).

Posttraumatic stress disorder, or **PTSD**, is a disabling condition that results from personally experiencing an event that involves actual or threatened death or serious injury or from witnessing or hearing of such an event happening to a family member or close friend. People suffering from PTSD experience a number of psychological symptoms, including recurring and disturbing memories, terrible nightmares, and intense fear and anxiety (American Psychiatric Association, 2000).

I saw my best buddy blown apart.

For example, about 32% of women report having PTSD after being raped; about 15% of soldiers report having PTSD after serving in war; and about 20% of people report having PTSD after being in a serious car accident (Elias, 2008a; Hidalgo & Davidson, 2000). These horrible memories and feelings of fear keep stress levels high and result in a range of psychosomatic symptoms, including sleep problems, pounding heart, high blood pressure, and stomach problems (Marshall et al., 2006; Schnurr et al., 2002).

Treatment. The treatment of posttraumatic stress disorder may involve drugs (SSRIs—see p. 534), but some form of cognitive-behavioral therapy (p. 568) has proved more effective in the long term (Foa et al., 2009). Cognitive-behavioral therapy provides emotional support so that victims can begin the healing process, helps to slowly eliminate the horrible memories by bringing out the details of the experience, and gradually replaces the feeling of fear with a sense of courage to go on with life (Harvey et al., 2003; Resick et al., 2008).

We'll examine two more situations with high potential for stress because they involve conflict or anxiety.

Conflict

Why are decisions so stressful? Sometimes situations can be stressful because they involve making difficult decisions. For example, what decisions would you make in the following situations?

• You can either go to a great party or see a good friend who is visiting town for just one day.
• You can study for a psychology exam or write a paper for a history class.
• You can ask a new acquaintance to have lunch, but then you risk being rejected.

In making these kinds of decisions, you are most likely to feel stressed because each involves facing a different kind of conflict.

Conflict is the feeling you experience when you must choose between two or more incompatible possibilities or options.

The reason the situations put you in conflict is that, no matter which option you choose, you must give up something you really want to get or you must do something you really want to avoid. We'll describe three common kinds of conflicts—approach-approach, avoidance-avoidance, and approach-avoidance—and some ways of dealing with conflicts.

© Laurent Renault/Shutterstock.com

© Laurent Renault/Shutterstock.com

© Laurent Renault/Shutterstock.com

Approach-approach. Deciding between going to a party and seeing a friend involves choosing between two pleasurable options.

Approach-approach conflict involves choosing between two situations that both have pleasurable consequences.

At first it seems that approach-approach conflicts are the least stressful of the three kinds because, whichever option you choose, you will experience a pleasurable consequence. But on second thought, approach-approach conflicts can be the most stressful because you must give up one of the pleasurable consequences. The result is that you will feel considerably stressed as you agonize over which one of the two great possibilities to give up.

Avoidance-avoidance. Deciding between studying for a psychology exam and writing a paper for a history class involves choosing between two undesirable options.

Avoidance-avoidance conflict involves choosing between two situations that both have disagreeable consequences.

In an avoidance-avoidance conflict, you may change your mind many times and wait until the last possible minute before making the final decision. You delay choosing as long as possible in trying to avoid the disagreeable or unpleasant outcome.

Approach-avoidance. Deciding about asking a new acquaintance to lunch and being afraid of being rejected involves a single situation that has both desirable and undesirable possibilities.

Approach-avoidance conflict involves a single situation that has both pleasurable and disagreeable aspects.

In this example, asking the person to lunch would make you feel good, but at the same time, being rejected is something you want to avoid because it makes you feel bad. Our lives are full of approach-avoidance conflicts, and trying to decide what to do about them can be very stressful.

Five Styles of Dealing with Conflict

Researchers have identified five different styles of dealing with conflict: One may be similar to yours and one is better than the rest (R. J. Sternberg & Soriano, 1984).

1 Avoidance. These individuals find dealing with conflicts unpleasant. They hope that by avoiding or ignoring the conflict it will disappear or magically go away. But, the conflict usually gets worse and will have to be dealt with eventually.

2 Accommodation. These individuals also hate conflicts and just give in to make the disagreement go away. They tend to please people and worry about approval. Unfortunately, giving in does not solve the problem, which in the long term will need to be solved.

3 Domination. In conflicts, these individuals go to any lengths to win, even if it means being aggressive and manipulative. However, aggressively solving conflicts results in hostility rather than intimate human relationships.

4 Compromise. These individuals recognize that others have different needs and try to solve conflicts through compromise. Unfortunately, they may use manipulation and misrepresentation to further their own goals, so compromise isn't always the best solution.

5 Integration. These individuals try to resolve conflicts by finding solutions to please both partners. They don't criticize the other person, they try to be open, and they emphasize similarities rather than differences.

Perhaps the best way to resolve relationship conflicts is to try to be as much of an integrator as possible because this style avoids criticism and has the best chance of pleasing both individuals (B. K. Williams & Knight, 1994).

Situations involving conflict can be very stressful because you must often make undesirable choices. The situations described next are stressful because they involve anxiety.

Anxiety

How does anxiety develop?

This module began with the story of Luisa, who experienced tremendous anxiety. Remember that Luisa had sudden and intense panic attacks for no apparent reason. Like Luisa's experiences, everyone at some time will be caught in the terrible grip of anxiety.

Anxiety is an unpleasant state characterized by feelings of uneasiness and apprehension as well as increased physiological arousal, such as increased heart rate and blood pressure.

Next, we'll learn three ways of developing anxiety: classical conditioning, observational learning, and unconscious conflict. We'll begin by sharing two personal stories about how each of us developed severe anxiety.

Classical Conditioning

I developed anxiety through classical conditioning.

I (R. P.) have a great fear of blood, which is a result of a traumatic childhood incident: I had seen my father almost cut off his thumb. For me and about 76% of people surveyed, fear of blood began with a traumatic event that involved classical conditioning (Kleinknecht, 1994). In my case, the neutral stimulus was the sight of blood. It was paired with an unconditioned stimulus—seeing my father almost cut off his thumb—that caused an unconditioned response—anxiety, fear, and the fight-flight response. After this single pairing, the sight of blood became the conditioned stimulus, which now elicits the unconditioned response—great anxiety. My fear of blood is an example of a conditioned emotional response.

A **conditioned emotional response** results when an emotional response, such as fear or anxiety, is classically conditioned to a previously neutral stimulus.

A conditioned emotional response not only is highly resistant to extinction but also can cause stressful feelings (see p. 201).

Observational Learning

When I (H. K.) was younger, I had a debilitating fear of public speaking, which came from watching some of my classmates give a speech only to be ridiculed when they made an error. My anxiety developed through observational learning in the classroom.

Observational learning, which is a form of cognitive learning, results from watching and modeling and does not require the observer to perform any observable behavior or receive a reinforcer.

My observations of classmates speaking in front of the class made me develop severe anxiety over public speaking. Since childhood, I've had to speak in public many times and my anxiety has decreased because I've had positive experiences giving speeches.

Albert Bandura (2001b) believes that the majority of human learning, including feeling anxious in specific situations, occurs through observational learning (see p. 225).

I developed anxiety from observing students get embarrassed.

Unconscious Conflict

Luisa developed anxiety through unconscious conflict.

During psychotherapy, Luisa discovered the reason for her anxiety was that she was giving up her lifelong dream of becoming a writer to respect her parents' wish for her to become a scientist.

Sigmund Freud hypothesized that there are three divisions of the mind—id, ego, and superego—that at times may be in conflict over how a need should be satisfied (see p. 436). This unconscious conflict may result in feeling anxiety.

Anxiety, according to Freud, arises when there is an unconscious conflict between the id's and superego's desires regarding how to satisfy a need, with the ego caught in the middle. The ego's solution to this conflict is to create a feeling of anxiety.

According to Freud, we may try to decrease our anxiety by using a number of *defense mechanisms* (see p. 437). Luisa had been using the defense mechanism of repression to help manage her anxiety, but this did not solve her dilemma of which career to choose. As a result, her anxiety intensified and she began having panic attacks.

Next, we'll learn about different ways stress can actually be positive.

Positive Stress

How can stress be positive?

When most people think of stress, negative thoughts immediately come to mind. But, did you know that there is a type of stress that is actually healthy and desirable? It's called eustress.

Eustress is a pleasant and desirable type of stress that is healthful and keeps us engaged in situations.

You've likely experienced eustress when purchasing a new car, applying to college, getting a promotion at work, winning first place in a competition, watching a suspenseful thriller, getting married, or having a child.

I feel great! It was worth the stress!

As a student, you can probably acknowledge that a little bit of stress in school helps motivate you to study. Just imagine if your instructor removed all of the potential stress from the course, such as not requiring you to take exams or not assigning grades! Be honest—how much would you study then?

Eustress arouses and motivates us to achieve and overcome challenges. It is one type of stress we don't want to live without.

Next, we'll examine how different kinds of personality variables can help or hinder our coping with anxiety and stress. ●

Hardiness

Shaun White, nicknamed the "Flying Tomato" for his long, curly red hair, has never been an ordinary ath-

How does he cope with the stress of competition?

lete. At the age of 6, he began skateboarding on a ramp in his backyard, and he practiced snowboarding during family trips to the mountains. By the time Shaun was 13 years old, he was a pro skateboarder and snowboarder. At age 19, he became the first athlete to compete in both the summer and winter X Games. Shaun always strives to do his very best, even under the most stressful situations. He does not allow the pressure of heated competition or the setback of an

awkward landing to compromise his determination to win. Shaun's ability to handle extreme stress is undeniable, as he has already won two Olympic gold medals (Dodd, 2010; Ruibal, 2006; *Shaun White,* 2006).

How can Shaun White, the "Flying Tomato," perform so well in extremely stressful conditions?

Why is it that certain people, like Shaun White, seem to handle stressful situations better than others? This was exactly the question researchers asked as they studied the personality characteristics of middle- and upper-level executives and lawyers who had experienced considerable stress in the past three years (Kobasa, 1982; Kobasa et al., 1982a, 1982b). Researchers discovered that those executives and lawyers who stayed healthy in spite of stressful life situations had three personality traits, which, taken together, were labeled hardiness.

Hardiness is a combination of three personality traits—control, commitment, and challenge—that protect or buffer us from the potentially harmful effects of stressful situations and reduce our chances of developing psychosomatic illnesses.

Shaun White is a great example of a hardy person who has the three Cs—control, commitment, and challenge. His disciplined practicing shows he has *commitment* to his goal of being a snowboarding legend; his participation in the Olympics shows he likes a *challenge;* and his determination to come back more focused after even the slightest error indicates his desire to be in *control* (Maddi, 2008).

Just as hardiness helps Shaun White deal with stress, hardiness helps people cope in a wide range of stressful situations, such as nurses who work with dying patients and military personnel who experience life-threatening situations (Bartone, 1999; Maddi, 2002). Researchers also reported that hardiness helps college students cope by reducing the effects of daily frustrations (Beasley et al., 2003). Hardiness is a personality factor that increases protection against stress and decreases the chances of developing psychosomatic symptoms. Being hardy motivates people like Shaun White to see stressors as opportunities for growth, which gives them a real edge in dealing with potentially stressful situations (Bonanno, 2004; Maddi, 2008).

Next, we'll discuss what researchers have learned by studying control, one of the three traits in hardiness.

Locus of Control

A daily hassle that most of us hate is having to wait for something or somebody. One reason waiting can be so

Why can waiting be such a hassle?

stressful is that we have little or no control in this situation. How much control you feel you have over a situation is a personal belief that is called locus of control.

Locus of control represents a continuum: At one end is the belief that you are basically in control of life's events and that what you do influences the situation; this belief is called an internal locus of control. At the other end is the belief that chance and luck mostly determine what happens and that you do not have much influence; this belief is called an external locus of control.

Most of us lie somewhere along the locus of control continuum, rather than being at one end or the other (Carducci, 2006). For example, when students discuss how much their studying affects their grades, they are in part talking about their locus of control, which in turn affects their stress level.

What's the use of studying when I do poorly on exams?

External locus of control. "No matter how much I study, it never seems to help," says the student with an external locus of control. This student will likely appraise exams and papers as less of a challenge and more of a threat, which in turn will generate negative emotions (fear, anxiety, anger) and increase stress levels.

Studying 15 hours a week will lead to better grades.

Internal locus of control. "If I study hard and apply myself, I can get good grades," says the student with an internal locus of control. This student will likely appraise exams and papers less as threats and more as challenges, which in turn will generate positive emotions (excitement, enthusiasm) and decrease stress levels. This means that students with internal locus of control have lower levels of stress and, as a result, report fewer psychosomatic symptoms than those with external locus of control (Ruiz-Bueno, 2000).

A cross-cultural study comparing stress and coping styles among Japanese and British people revealed interesting results about stress and a sense of control. Although Japanese people reported feeling less personal control, only British people reported that a feeling of less personal control results in increased stress. These results suggest that a sense of control may be most important in Western cultures that emphasize autonomy and personal accomplishment (O'Connor & Shimizu, 2002).

Studies on locus of control show that our personality traits influence our appraisal (more or less challenging or threatening), which, in turn, increases or decreases our feelings of stress and our chances of developing psychosomatic symptoms (Kirkcaldy et al., 2002).

Another personality trait that can influence stress levels is how pessimistic or optimistic we generally are.

Optimism Versus Pessimism

Why is it better to be an optimist?

If you want to experience more positive than negative emotions and reduce your levels of stress, try being more optimistic.

Optimism is a relatively stable personality trait that leads to believing and expecting that good things will happen. **Pessimism** is a relatively stable personality trait that leads to believing and expecting that bad things will happen.

Optimists. One way optimists reduce stress is by focusing on the good things, a process called *positive reappraisal*. Forms of positive reappraisal include discovering new opportunities for personal growth, noticing actual personal growth, and seeing how your actions can benefit others. By using positive reappraisal, you can change the meaning or appraisal of situations to seem more positive and thus feel positive emotions (Folkman & Moskowitz, 2000). Researchers found that individuals who perceive themselves as in control—that is, have an internal locus of control—are more likely to have an optimistic attitude in dealing with stressors (C. T. F. Klein & Helweg-Larsen, 2002). Generally, optimists cope more effectively with stress and experience better physical health, including fewer psychosomatic symptoms, than pessimists (Carver et al., 2010; Nes & Segerstrom, 2006; Sharot, 2011; S. E. Taylor et al., 2000). Optimists may even live longer than pessimists (DeKeukelaere, 2006; Giltay et al., 2004; R. Rubin, 2009).

I'm an optimist and believe that good things will happen.

I'm a pessimist and believe that bad things will happen.

Pessimists. Because pessimists expect bad things to happen, they are likely to change the meaning or appraisal of situations to seem more negative and thus experience more negative emotions, such as anger, rage, fear, or anxiety, and they are less able to ask for or receive social support. For example, researchers found that men with high levels of negative emotions were four times more likely to suffer sudden heart death. In comparison, optimistic patients who received heart transplants reported more positive emotions and dealt better with setbacks than patients with more pessimistic outlooks (Leedham et al., 1995).

Numerous studies associate pessimism and negative emotions with increasing stress levels, decreasing functioning of the immune system, and a wide range of psychosomatic symptoms such as high blood pressure, heart problems, headaches, allergies, and stomach problems (Vahtera et al., 2000).

Personality factors. A number of personality factors, such as optimism/pessimism, internal/external locus of control, and hardiness, have been associated with feeling more or less positive or negative emotions, which in turn are involved in increasing or decreasing stress levels and increasing or decreasing the chances of developing psychosomatic symptoms (Salovey et al., 2000).

Another characteristic that affects our experience of stress is how much we believe in our own capabilities.

Self-Efficacy

Can I get better grades?

Students often ask how they can improve their grades. According to Albert Bandura (2004), one reason students differ in whether they receive high or low grades is self-efficacy.

Self-efficacy is the confidence in your ability to organize and execute a given course of action to solve a problem or accomplish a task.

For example, saying "I think that I am capable of getting a high grade in this course" is a sign of strong self-efficacy. You judge your self-efficacy based on four sources of information (Bandura, 1999; E. T. Higgins & Scholer, 2008):

1. You *use previous experiences* of success or failure on similar tasks to estimate how you will do on a new, related task.

2. You *compare* your capabilities with those of others.

3. You *listen* to what others say about your capabilities.

4. You *use feedback* from your body to assess your strength, vulnerability, and capability.

I am capable of getting a high grade in this course.

You would rate yourself as having strong self-efficacy for getting good grades if you had previous success with getting high grades, if you believe you are as academically capable as others, if your friends say you are smart, and if you do not become too stressed during exams.

Influence of self-efficacy. According to Bandura's self-efficacy theory, your motivation to achieve, perform, and do well in a variety of tasks and situations is largely influenced by how strongly you believe in your own capabilities. Some people have a strong sense of self-efficacy that applies to many situations (academic settings, sports, and social interactions), others have a strong sense that applies to only a few situations (computers but not social interactions), while still others have a weak sense of self-efficacy, which predicts that they will have less success in many of life's tasks (Eccles & Wigfield, 2002). For example, people with higher self-efficacy had greater success at stopping smoking, losing weight, overcoming a phobia, recovering from a heart attack, performing well in school, adjusting to new situations, coping with job stress, playing video games, and tolerating pain (Caprara et al., 2004; Greven et al., 2009; Joseph et al., 2003; Luszczynska & Sutton, 2006).

I just don't have what it takes to get a passing grade in this course.

Next, we'll examine two combinations of personality traits, called Type A and Type D behavior, that have been associated with increased risk of having a heart attack.

Type A Behavior

Is there such a thing as Type A behavior?

In the mid-1970s, a new expression—"You're a Type A person"—was coined when two doctors published the book *Type A Behavior and Your Heart* (M. Friedman & Rosenman, 1974). At that time, the best-known risk factors associated with developing heart disease were diet, exercise, and smoking. This book startled the medical world by describing a combination of personality traits that made up a psychological risk factor, which was called Type A behavior.

1970S: Type A Behavior—Impatient, Hostile, Workaholic

We'll begin with the original 1970s definition of Type A behavior (M. Friedman & Rosenman, 1974).

Impatient, hostile, and workaholic

Type A behavior referred to a combination of personality traits that included an overly competitive and aggressive drive to achieve, a hostile attitude when frustrated, a habitual sense of time urgency, a rapid and explosive pattern of speaking, and being a workaholic. **Type B behavior** was characterized as being easygoing, calm, relaxed, and patient.

The reason Type A behavior made such a big scientific splash was that, compared to Type B's, Type A's were found to have experienced two to three times as many heart attacks. By 1978, Type A behavior was officially recognized as an independent risk factor for heart disease by a National Institutes of Health panel.

However, at about the same time that Type A behavior was declared a risk factor, researchers began having trouble replicating earlier findings and began to seriously question the definition of Type A behavior.

1980S–1990S: Type A Behavior—Depressed, Angry

Research in the 1980s showing that coronary disease was not associated with being impatient or a workaholic led to both traits being dropped from the new definition of Type A behavior (Booth-Kewley & Friedman, 1987; K.A. Matthews & Haynes, 1986).

Depressed and angry

Type A behavior was defined in the 1980s as being depressed, easily frustrated, anxious, and angry, or some combination of these traits.

Despite using this new and improved definition, a review of many studies between 1983 and 1992 led one researcher to conclude that the relationship between Type A behavior and cardiac disease is so weak as to have no practical meaning and that Type A behavior is no longer a valid or useful concept (Myrtek, 1995). Because of the continuing failure to replicate the original relationship, researchers again redefined Type A behavior.

The 1990s definition of **Type A behavior** specifies an individual who feels angry and hostile much of the time but may or may not express these emotions publicly.

This definition made prolonged hostility or anger (felt or expressed) the major component of Type A behavior (Leventhal & Patrick-Miller, 2000). Research indicates that angry/hostile individuals are three times more likely to have heart attacks, and individuals who are quick to anger under stress are five times more likely to develop a premature heart disease (D. Smith, 2003). Researchers concluded that individuals who either always **show** their anger/hostility or always **suppress** it have large increases in physiological arousal, which can have damaging effects on one's heart and one's health (Finney, 2003).

Type D Behavior

2000S: Type D Behavior—Chronic Distress: Negative Affectivity, Social Inhibition

What is Type D behavior?

In his work with cardiac patients, Johan Denollet, a psychologist, noticed that some heart-attack survivors remained happy and optimistic, while others became discouraged and pessimistic. He went on to describe a set of behaviors he believed to be predictive of health risk (M.C. Miller, 2005).

Type D behavior is chronic distress in terms of two emotional states: negative affectivity (worry, irritability, gloom) and social inhibition (being shy and reserved, lacking self-assurance).

People with Type D behavior tend to experience negative emotions and inhibit self-expression in social interactions. Their chronic distress and lack of strong social support help explain why they are at an increased risk for various health problems (Pelle et al., 2009; L. Williams et al., 2008). For instance, research on heart patients with Type D profiles found them to be three times as likely to have a heart attack

Negative affectivity and social inhibition

or stroke than patients without the personality profile (Denollet et al., 2010).

Even though research supports the link between Type D behavior and health problems, recall that research on Type A behavior also began strong, and yet Type A behavior had to be redefined. Type D behavior is a relatively new concept and needs more research to better determine its impact on health conditions (M.C. Miller, 2005).

In conclusion, research on Type A and Type D behavior shows that certain personality traits, such as anger/hostility and negative affectivity/social inhibition, can increase the risks of cardiovascular diseases. This means that treatment for such diseases should include not only medical treatments but also psychological interventions to decrease negative traits (Merz et al., 2002).

In this module's Critical Thinking article (see p. 504) we will discuss the influence of social factors on health. Following the Concept Review, we'll turn our attention to ways of coping with stress. ●

Concept Review

1. The cognitive and behavioral efforts that we use to manage a situation that we have appraised as exceeding, straining, or taxing our personal resources are referred to as _____.

2. Our initial, subjective evaluation of a situation, in which we balance environmental demands against our ability to meet them, is referred to as _____. We may appraise the situation in three ways: as irrelevant, positive, or stressful.

3. If we appraise a situation as stressful, we go on to determine whether it represents (a) _____, _____, or _____. If our primary appraisal is one of harm/loss or threat, we will experience more (b) _____ than if our appraisal is one of challenge, because harm/loss or threat appraisals elicit (c) _____ emotions.

4. A combination of physiological responses that arouse and prepare the body for action is referred to as the (a) _____ response. This response begins in a part of the brain called the (b) _____, which triggers the (c) _____ division of the autonomic nervous system. This response is especially triggered by threat appraisals.

5. Real and painful physical symptoms that are caused by psychological factors, such as our reactions to stress, are called _____ symptoms.

6. A series of three stages—alarm, resistance, and exhaustion—that the body goes through in dealing with stress is referred to as the (a) _____. The alarm stage is our initial reaction to stress and is marked by activation of the (b) _____. The resistance stage is the body's reaction to continued stress and is marked by most physiological responses returning to (c) _____ levels. The exhaustion stage is the body's reaction to long-term, continuous stress and is marked by the actual breakdown or weakening of (d) _____.

7. The study of how psychological factors relate to the promotion and maintenance of health, as well as the prevention and treatment of illnesses, is a specialty in psychology called _____.

8. The body's defense and surveillance network of cells and chemicals that fight off bacteria, viruses, and other foreign matter is called the _____ system.

9. The study of how three factors—the central nervous system, the endocrine system, and psychosocial factors—interact to affect the immune system is called _____.

10. Potentially disturbing, troubling, or disruptive situations—both positive and negative—that we appraise as having considerable impact on our lives are called (a) _____ events. In comparison, those small, irritating, frustrating events that we face in our daily lives are called (b) _____, and those small, pleasurable, daily experiences that make us feel happy are called (c) _____.

11. When our attempts to reach some goal are blocked, the feeling we have is called (a) _____. The feeling of doing poorly at one's job, physically wearing out, and becoming emotionally exhausted due to intense involvement with people is called (b) _____. The problem arising from direct personal experience of an event that involves actual or threatened death or serious injury or from witnessing such an event or hearing of such an event happening to a family member or close friend is called (c) _____.

12. There are three general kinds of conflict. A single situation that has both pleasurable and disagreeable aspects is called (a) _____ conflict; choosing between two options that both have pleasurable consequences is called (b) _____ conflict; choosing between two options that both have disagreeable consequences is called (c) _____ conflict.

13. We can become anxious in at least three different ways. If an emotional response is classically conditioned to a previously neutral stimulus, this procedure results in a (a) _____ response. If we become anxious through watching and do not perform any observable behavior or receive a reinforcer, this is called (b) _____ learning. If we become anxious because of unconscious conflicts between the id and the superego, this is (c) _____ explanation of anxiety.

14. A combination of three personality traits—control, commitment, and challenge—that protect or buffer us from the potentially harmful effects of stressful situations and reduce our chances of developing psychosomatic illness is referred to as (a) _____. The belief that you are basically in control of life's events and that what you do influences the situation is called an (b) _____ locus of control. The belief that chance and luck mostly determine what happens is called an (c) _____ locus of control.

Answers: 1. *stress or stressful;* 2. *primary appraisal;* 3. (a) *harm/loss, threat, challenge,* (b) *stress,* (c) *negative;* 4. (a) *fight-flight,* (b) *hypothalamus,* (c) *sympathetic;* 5. *psychosomatic;* 6. (a) *general adaptation syndrome,* (b) *fight-flight response,* (c) *normal,* (d) *internal organs or the immune system;* 7. *health psychology;* 8. *immune;* 9. *psychoneuroimmunology;* 10. (a) *major life,* (b) *hassles,* (c) *uplifts;* 11. (a) *frustration,* (b) *burnout,* (c) *posttraumatic stress disorder;* 12. (a) *approach-avoidance,* (b) *approach-approach,* (c) *avoidance-avoidance;* 13. (a) *conditioned emotional,* (b) *observational,* (c) *Freud's;* 14. (a) *hardiness,* (b) *internal,* (c) *external*

E Coping with Stress

Appraisal

Sooner or later, every couple gets into an argument. In this case, Susan complained that Bill always got home late, but Bill had had a bad day and said that he didn't want

Why is arguing stressful?

to talk about it. Bill's reply angered Susan, who complained more, which made Bill quieter and madder. One reason Bill and Susan's argument quickly became very stressful

was that each one made a *primary appraisal* of being threatened, which elicited negative emotions and triggered the fight-flight response, which in turn increased physiological arousal and further intensified their negative feelings. How Bill and Susan deal with their stressful situation depends on what kind of secondary appraisal they make next (Lazarus, 2000).

How can they best end their argument?

© Daniel Korzeniewski/ Shutterstock.com

Secondary appraisal involves deciding to deal with a potentially stressful situation by using one or both of two different coping patterns: Problem-focused coping means doing something about the particular problem, while emotion-focused coping means dealing with one's negative feelings.

Which coping strategy Bill and Susan use to deal with their stressful situation—that is, whether they use problem-focused or emotion-focused coping— will affect how their argument gets resolved and what happens to their levels of stress. We'll discuss how each coping strategy has both short- and long-term disadvantages and advantages.

Kinds of Coping

How to cope with arguing?

If Bill or Susan tried to decrease the stress by stopping arguing and making up, he or she would be using problem-focused coping.

Problem-focused coping means we try to decrease stress by solving the problem through seeking information, changing our own behavior, or taking whatever action is needed to resolve the difficulty.

For example, if Bill agreed to talk about ways of not being late, he would be using problem-focused coping. If Susan agreed to interpret Bill's being late as something he cannot always control and something not to get angry about, she would be using problem-focused coping. The *goal* of problem-focused coping is to reduce stress by solving the problem.

Another coping strategy that Bill and Susan might use to decrease stressful feelings is called emotion-focused coping.

Emotion-focused coping means that we do things primarily to deal with our emotional distress, such as seeking support and sympathy or avoiding or denying the situation.

> **Emotion-focused**
>
> ↓
>
> **Stress**
>
> **Problem-focused**

These are the two kinds of coping strategies.

For example, Bill may use emotion-focused coping to get over his anger by going to a sports bar to drink and watch television with the "boys." Susan may use emotion-focused coping to deal with her hurt feelings by calling her friends to talk about what happened and get advice, sympathy, and support.

In the short term, emotion-focused coping may help Bill and Susan deal with their negative emotions, but it doesn't usually solve the basic stressful problem, which means the problem will likely reoccur and cause more stress (Lazarus, 2000). In contrast, a big advantage of using problem-focused coping is that it's a long-term coping strategy, which can help identify and solve the underlying problem that is causing the stressful and negative emotional feelings. In addition, compared to using emotion-focused coping, using problem-focused coping is positively correlated with having and maintaining good physical and mental health (Largo-Wight et al., 2005; Penley et al., 2002).

Choosing a Coping Strategy

Which coping strategy to use?

Which coping strategy you choose depends partly on the situation and on your personality (Lazarus, 2000). For example, if you appraise a situation (being late) as something under your control, you can use primarily problem-focused coping to solve this problem. On the other hand, if you appraise a situation (dealing with your partner's complaints) as being out of your control, you may first use emotion-focused coping to get over your negative emotions (anger). Once you calm down, you can use problem-focused coping to take some direct action to solve the basic problem (being late), which may involve changing some undesirable behavior (being disorganized).

Women and men tend to use different kinds of coping strategies.

© Ljupco Smokovski/Shutterstock.com

As you may have already realized, problem-focused and emotion-focused coping can often facilitate each other. For instance, using effective problem-solving strategies tends to reduce emotional distress. And, using emotion-focused coping can help a person approach stressful situations more calmly and generate better problem-focused solutions (Carver, 2011).

Sex differences. Compared with men, women are more likely to use emotion-focused coping to seek emotional support and advice from others about dealing with stressors. Compared with women, men are more likely to withdraw or avoid problems and not talk about or engage in emotion-focused coping (Tamres et al., 2002). Thus, women appear to use more coping strategies and are more willing to talk about solving problems, while men are more likely to keep silent or avoid certain problems.

One of the newest movements in psychology focuses on the characteristics of people that enable them to effectively cope with stress and pursue their own happiness and well-being. We'll discuss this movement, called positive psychology, next. ●

F Positive Psychology

Definition and Background

Why should I focus more on the positive?

Sherrod Ballentine has a stressful job as a court mediator, and although she's not clinically depressed, she wants to learn ways to improve her mood. She takes a class called "Authentic Happiness and How to Obtain It" and learns activities that will train her mind to focus more on the positive. One activity Sherrod learns is to write down three happy events and their causes at the end of each day for a week. After completing the class, she said, "I am happier. Every day, I feel so grateful to wake up this way" (Lemley, 2006). Sherrod's new, learned skills are based on positive psychology.

Positive psychology is the scientific study of optimal human functioning, focusing on the strengths and virtues that enable individuals and communities to thrive. It aims to better understand the positive, adaptive, and fulfilling aspects of human life.

Martin Seligman

Unless otherwise noted, all images are © Cengage Learning

Although the roots of positive psychology can be traced back to the humanistic approach (see p. 10), Martin Seligman, former President of the American Psychological Association, took the initiative to formalize the discipline and deserves credit for its popularity. Seligman believed that psychology was focusing too much on the negative, such as people's problems and weaknesses, and not enough on the positive, such as people's strengths and virtues.

To help individuals and communities thrive and flourish, positive psychology embraces three main concerns. The first is the study of *positive emotions*, such as happiness, hope, love, and contentment. The second is the study of *positive individual traits*, such as altruism, courage, compassion, and resilience. The third is the study of *positive institutions*, or the strengths that promote better communities, such as justice, parenting, tolerance, and teamwork (Seligman, 2003).

Research Findings

There are many research examples showing that characteristics of positive psychology have a beneficial impact on mood and physical health. For example, a review of research data on altruism and its relationship to mental and physical health found that volunteering and other supportive behaviors (such as providing emotional support to others) are associated with greater life satisfaction as well as better physical and mental health (S. Post, 2005). Also, research on writing exercises, such as the one Sherrod did, shows impressive results. One study found that after writing about positive experiences for 20 minutes each day for three consecutive days, college students reported improved mood and had fewer health center visits for illness in the months that followed (C. M. Burton & King, 2004).

Researchers are now examining how promoting personal strengths and resources can help individuals with mental illnesses, such as depression and anxiety. This area of research is still in its infancy, and questions remain about whether the positive psychology strategies will be effective for people with chronic,

maladaptive coping strategies and high levels of stress. However, some of the available research gives reason to be optimistic about its potential to help people with mental illnesses. For example, researchers found that having highly self-critical, depressed individuals write down five things a day that they are grateful for significantly reduced their depressive symptoms and that the benefits lasted over time (Sergeant & Mongrain, 2011). Additionally, because a lack of well-being at the present time places individuals at risk for depression up to ten years later, more and more therapists are focusing on the development of positive emotions and adaptive functioning, rather than on problems and limitations (Compton & Hoffman, 2013; Joseph & Wood, 2010).

Positive psychology has shown us that the benefits of positive emotions are widespread. Results of various studies using different research methods conclude that happiness has a positive effect on longevity and health. For example, happy people report having more friends, more satisfying marriages, higher productivity and satisfaction at their jobs, and higher incomes than their unhappy peers. Also, people who experience and express positive emotions more often than those who are less positive are more likely to have better physical health, be more resistant to illnesses, and even live longer (Diener & Chan, 2011; Hales, 2008; Lyubomirsky et al., 2005).

Next, we'll continue our discussion of coping with stressful experiences by revisiting panic disorders, which we introduced at the beginning of this module. This time we'll turn our attention to how treatment can help people with panic disorder better cope with their stressful symptoms. ●

How Effective Is Treatment for Panic Disorder?

How is panic disorder best treated?

We have discussed stress and coping in general, and now we return to the case of Luisa, the 23-year-old college student with panic disorder. Remember that Luisa had unexpected episodes in which she experienced rapid heart rate, a sense of suffocation, trembling of her arms and legs, dizziness, and chest pain. She felt so frightened by these episodes that she worried she might die. Luisa's experience of having panic disorder is not uncommon. Many adults suffer from panic disorder, and fortunately there are treatment options available to them. Psychologists conduct research studies to learn which treatment or combination of treatments is most effective for problems such as panic disorder. Next, we'll discover which research methods psychologists use to determine the effectiveness of treatments, as well as discuss research findings on the treatment of panic disorder.

Research Methods

In Module 2, we discussed several ways psychologists answer questions, including case studies and experiments, each of which has advantages and disadvantages.

A **case study** is an in-depth analysis of the thoughts, feelings, beliefs, or behaviors of an individual, without much ability to control or manipulate situations or variables.

For example, much of the initial information on how the brain functions came from case studies on individuals who had tumors, gunshot wounds, or accidental damage. Similarly, psychologists can learn about how individuals cope with panic disorder by observing and questioning them as they progress through treatment to identify how they cope and adjust to their condition.

When it is possible to control or manipulate situations or variables, the preferred research method is an experiment.

An **experiment** is a method for identifying cause-and-effect relationships by following a set of guidelines that describe how to control, manipulate, and measure variables, while at the same time minimizing the possibility of error and bias.

Experiments give researchers great control over manipulating treatments and measuring individual responses. Also, they allow research data to be collected on a group of people, rather than on only one person, as in a case study, so the results can be more meaningful to a large group of people. Fortunately, psychologists can use experiments to compare the effectiveness of various treatments for panic disorder. We will learn about one such experiment, but before we do, let's learn about the most common treatments available for panic disorder.

Luisa received medication and psychotherapy.

© lilolab/Shutterstock.com

How Can Panic Disorder Be Treated?

In Luisa's case, her treatment began with medication only, and a few months later she received a combination of medication and psychotherapy. Panic disorder is usually treated with drugs—benzodiazepines (tranquilizers, such as diazepam) or antidepressants (Prozac-like drugs, which are selective serotonin reuptake inhibitors, or SSRIs)—and/or psychotherapy. Many more people with panic disorder receive drugs than psychotherapy, mostly because they seek treatment from their primary care physician rather than a psychologist. One popular type of psychotherapy used to treat panic disorder is cognitive-behavioral therapy, or CBT (see p. 559), which views the physiological arousal symptoms as a learned fear of certain bodily sensations and views the fear of being in closed or crowded situations as a behavioral response to expecting that the bodily sensations will intensify into a full-blown panic attack (Craske & Barlow, 2001). Given the various treatment options available for panic disorder, how do psychologists know for sure which treatment or combination of treatments is most effective?

Which Treatment Is Most Effective?

A comprehensive experiment including more than 300 people diagnosed with panic disorder used random assignment to place each participant in one of five treatment groups: drug only (a benzodiazepine), CBT only, placebo only, CBT plus drug, and CBT plus placebo (Craske & Barlow, 2001). The results showed that people who received drugs or CBT, as well as the combined treatments, showed more improvement than people in the placebo-only group. In regard to short-term treatment effects (measured after three months of treatment), CBT plus drugs was not better than CBT plus placebo, and people receiving combined treatments showed no more improvements than people receiving individual treatments. In regard to long-term treatment effects (six months after treatment had ended), many people in the drug-only group and CBT-plus-drug group relapsed. Thus, people treated with CBT alone or in combination with placebo did better than those who took medication. Though this study used only a benzodiazepine for drug treatment, similar research studies using an SSRI show comparable results. This suggests that CBT has a better long-term treatment benefit for panic disorder than medication.

Conclusions

By using an experiment, researchers found that CBT and drugs, either used individually or combined, worked about equally well in the short term. However, the use of CBT without drugs led to the best long-term treatment effects. It is well established that over 80% of people with panic disorder who receive CBT will be panic-free at the end of treatment, and they generally continue to show long-term treatment benefits (Craske & Barlow, 2001). Therefore, treatment for panic disorder should include CBT.

Next, we'll look at how some monks develop mind-over-body control. ●

Monks' Amazing Abilities

Tibetan monks claim that by meditating they can voluntarily control their autonomic nervous systems to perform a number of responses, such as warming their hands (graph below). Since many Western researchers believe that voluntary control of the autonomic nervous system is very, very difficult to learn, Western researcher Herbert Benson and his colleagues from Harvard Medical School traveled to India to scientifically test and verify the monks' amazing claims (H. Benson et al., 1982, 1990).

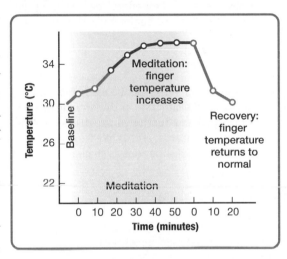

The **autonomic nervous system** has two divisions that are not usually under voluntary control: The sympathetic division causes physiological arousal by increasing heart rate, breathing, blood pressure, and secretion of hormones; the parasympathetic division calms and relaxes the body by decreasing physiological responses and stimulating digestion.

The only two responses of the autonomic nervous system that you can control *voluntarily* and *without practice* are breathing and eye blinking. All other responses of the autonomic nervous system, such as increasing or decreasing blood pressure, temperature, or heart rate and dilating or constricting blood vessels, are controlled automatically and, without considerable practice, are not under voluntary control.

If you want to voluntarily control one of your autonomic nervous system's responses, such as dilating blood vessels to warm your hands, sit quietly in a chair, close your eyes, and think relaxing thoughts. If you can think relaxing thoughts, they will activate your parasympathetic division, which will dilate blood vessels and result in warming your hands. However, the first time you try this, your hands will probably become colder because by trying so hard to relax, you may be doing the reverse: activating your sympathetic system, which causes arousal and constricts the blood vessels in your fingers.

Tibetan monks use meditation to increase hand temperature, a response very difficult to control.

Westerners find it takes considerable practice to learn to warm our hands because we usually spend little time practicing how to produce relaxing thoughts. In comparison, certain Tibetan monks, through various forms of meditation, claim that they can warm their hands and bodies to such an extent that they can actually dry wet towels that are placed on their shoulders. This was exactly the kind of claim that excited and puzzled Benson's group of researchers.

Voluntary control—hand warming. Benson's group obtained permission from three monks at a monastery in India to measure their skin temperature during heat meditation, or g Tum-mo yoga. The monks sat in the lotus position, closed their eyes, and began meditating. As shown in the left graph, within a short period of time, one monk had raised his finger temperature as much as 7–9°C (or 9–12°F) with no change in heart rate (H. Benson et al., 1982). The monks' success at warming their hands was about five times as great as Westerners, who had managed only 0.25–2°F (Freedman, 1991). However, only a small number of monks can produce this kind of hand and body warming and only after 10 to 20 years of practice.

Explanation. Westerner Benson gave a very scientific explanation: Monks are able to raise their hand temperature by using thoughts to deeply relax, which in turn activates the parasympathetic division, which dilates tiny blood vessels that lie near the surface of the skin. The Tibetan monks' explanation is much more mysterious: During their meditation, the monks gather winds that are scattered in consciousness and focus these winds into a "central channel" that can generate a great internal body heat (H. Benson et al., 1982).

Studying the mind's abilities. The monks' ability to voluntarily control their physiological responses clearly shows the mind-body interaction as they use their thoughts to influence the difficult-to-control and normally involuntary autonomic nervous system. Western scientists completed a study in which a group of Buddhist monks extensively trained in meditation and a group of volunteers without meditation experience were instructed to meditate on unconditional compassion while brain wave activity was recorded. The results showed that meditation activated the minds of the trained monks very differently from those of the volunteers. The Buddhist monks had greater activation of fast-moving and powerful *gamma brain waves* (40 cycles per second—much faster than REM brain waves; see p. 153). It is interesting that the highest gamma brain wave activity was recorded in the left prefrontal cortex, which is associated with happiness and positive thoughts. These findings suggest that Buddhist monks can rid themselves of negative emotions through gamma brain wave activity occurring during meditation (M. Kaufman, 2005; Talan, 2006a).

Although we are unlikely to ever achieve the monks' level of mind control, we'll next discuss several more easily learned techniques that can be used to reduce stress. ●

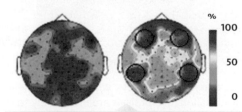

As shown in these head diagrams, volunteers (above left) had low gamma brain wave activity and the Buddhist monks (above right) had high gamma brain wave activity during the meditation task.

Graph data from "Body Temperature Changes During the Practice of g Tum-mo-Yoga," by H. Benson, J. W. Lehmann, M. S. Malhotra, R. F. Goldman, P. J. Hopkins & M. D. Epstein, 1982, Nature, 295, 234–235.

© IndiaPicture/Alamy

© Richard J. Davidson, Director, W. M. Keck Laboratory for Functional Brain Imaging and Behavior

I Application: Stress Management Programs

Definition

How can I reduce my stress levels?

One reason 30% of college freshmen feel continuously overwhelmed is that their classes, exams, papers, personal problems, and part-time jobs combine to take more time and energy than they have (Duenwald, 2003). Being overwhelmed leads to increased levels of stress and increased risk of developing psychosomatic symptoms. One way to reduce levels of stress is with a stress management program.

A **stress management program** uses a variety of strategies to reduce anxiety, fear, and stressful experiences by changing three different aspects of our lives: thoughts (appraisals), behaviors, and physiological responses.

By controlling your thoughts you can control your body.
© Nejron/Shutterstock.com

Psychologists have developed a number of very effective stress management programs that reduce stress levels, which in turn decrease the occurrence of psychosomatic symptoms. Although stress management programs have different names, they all focus on ways to change three major contributors to stressful experiences: your thoughts and beliefs (appraisals), your behaviors, and your emotional and physiological responses (Spiegler & Guevremont, 2010).

We'll describe some methods that psychologists have developed for effectively changing each of these three factors, beginning with changing your thoughts.

Changing Thoughts

Can you learn to think more positively?

Many daily hassles—dealing with long lines, slow traffic, rude people, loud neighbors, and sloppy roommates—can be made more or less stressful depending on how you appraise these situations. Since your appraisal of a situation as threatening or challenging is related to increasing or decreasing your stress levels, it follows that an effective way to decrease stressful experiences is to work at changing how you initially appraise a situation (Lazarus, 2000). We'll explain two effective strategies for changing your appraisals: thinking of potentially stressful situations as challenging rather than threatening and changing negative self-statements into positive ones.

Use Challenge Appraisals

The reason you want to think of or appraise potentially stressful situations as challenging rather than threatening is that threat appraisals elicit negative emotions (fear, anxiety, depression), which in turn raise stress levels, while challenge appraisals elicit positive emotions, which lower stress levels. For example, students who emphasize threat appraisals of exams, such as thinking they will not have time to study or expecting to do poorly, are more likely to experience negative emotions such as anxiety and fear (Shannon, 1994). In turn, anxiety and fear trigger the fight-flight response, which raises the level of stress and often leads to emotion-focused coping, such as complaining, seeking sympathy, or avoiding studying. However, emotion-focused coping does not usually motivate actions, such as studying, that are needed to prepare students for exams.

I see life as one big challenge!
© Greg Epperson/Shutterstock.com

In comparison, students who emphasize challenge appraisals of exams, such as wanting to do their best or to prove themselves, are more likely to experience positive emotions, such as excitement or eagerness, which decrease levels of stress. In turn, challenge appraisals are more likely to result in problem-focused coping, which means taking direct action to deal with the situation itself, such as developing a study program.

Thus, a good way to deal with potentially stressful situations is to focus on challenging rather than threatening appraisals (N. Skinner & Brewer, 2002).

Substitute Positive Self-Statements

Another way to prevent a situation, such as taking an exam, from becoming more stressful is to work at removing negative self-statements by substituting positive ones. Specifically, on one side of a sheet of paper write your negative self-statements; then next to them on the other side write the positive ones that you can substitute. The example below shows negative self-statements changed into positive ones.

Negative self-statements	Positive self-statements
"I know I'll do badly."	*"I know I can do OK."*
"I always get so anxious."	*"I'm going to stay calm."*
"I'm not smart enough."	*"I've got plenty of ability."*
"I'm never going to learn it."	*"I can learn the material."*

The reason you want to avoid making negative self-statements is that they elicit negative emotions (fear, anger, anxiety), which increase stress levels. By substituting positive self-statements, which elicit positive emotions, you can decrease stress levels. For example, each time you begin to think of a negative self-statement, stop yourself and substitute a positive one. For regularly occurring stressors, such as taking exams, waiting in lines, fighting with traffic, and dealing with rude people, it is best to have prepared

I know I can reach the top!
© YanLev/Shutterstock.com

a different list of self-statements to go with each different situation. Researchers found that a program of substituting positive self-statements proved very effective in helping people change their thought patterns and reduce their stress levels (Spiegler & Guevremont, 2010).

Changing Behaviors

How do you get ready for an exam?

There are generally two different ways that students get ready for exams. Some students get ready by complaining about how much work there is, making excuses about not studying, or blaming the instructor for presenting too much material. These behaviors involve *emotion-focused coping*, which in the short term serves to reduce stress by decreasing negative emotional feelings. However, in the long run, students may need to change these behaviors and engage in *problem-focused coping*, which means developing a study plan (N. Skinner & Brewer, 2002).

Because some students are not aware of whether they use emotion-focused or problem-focused coping, stress management programs include an observation period of 1 to 2 weeks. During this time, a student observes or monitors his or her own behaviors to identify emotion-focused versus problem-focused behaviors. If a student is using primarily *emotion-focused coping* (making excuses, procrastinating, or blaming others), he or she will likely do poorly on exams. Instead, a student needs to start a program of *problem-focused coping* (making a study plan, rewriting class notes) by using some of the self-reward and behavior modification techniques that we discussed in Module 10 (Spiegler & Guevremont, 2010). Thus, one way to reduce stress is to change your behaviors—that is, to emphasize problem-focused over emotion-focused activities.

Learning to Relax

Learning to relax at will is important for developing a stress management program because being able to relax is one way to turn off the fight-flight response and decrease your body's heightened arousal. But unless you practice one of the following methods, you will find it very difficult to relax at will. In fact, when someone says "Just relax," you usually get tenser because you don't know how to relax. We'll describe three techniques that have proved almost equally effective at getting you to relax, and each involves using your mind (brain) to control your body's responses (S. L. Shapiro et al., 2000).

How do you learn to relax?

Biofeedback

You could learn a relaxing response, such as decreasing muscle tension, by having small sensors placed on your forehead. The sensors are attached to a machine that records, amplifies, and displays changes in muscle tension. Each time you think thoughts or images that increase tension, you hear a high tone; if you decrease tension, you hear a low tone. This procedure is called biofeedback (M. S. Schwartz & Andrasik, 2005).

Biofeedback refers to voluntarily learning to control physiological responses, such as muscle activity, blood pressure, or temperature, by recording and displaying these responses.

After 12 to 30 biofeedback training sessions (about 20 minutes per session), most individuals have some success in turning on relaxing responses, especially after being stressed.

You could also learn to relax by using progressive relaxation.

Progressive Relaxation

Progressive relaxation involves practicing tensing and relaxing the major muscle groups of the body until you are able to relax any groups of muscles at will.

With progressive relaxation, you usually begin by first tensing and relaxing your toes and then continuing up the body, tensing and relaxing the muscles of your calves, thighs, pelvis, stomach, shoulders, arms, hands, neck, face, and forehead. After several weeks of daily practice, about 20 minutes per session, you would be able to use this exercise to relax your body at will, especially immediately after being stressed.

You could also learn to relax by using a form of meditation.

Meditation

There are various kinds of meditation exercises. We'll describe two of the more popular ones, which are Eastern forms of meditation.

Transcendental meditation (TM) and **yoga** involve assuming a comfortable position, closing your eyes, and repeating a sound or concentrating on your breathing so that you clear your head of all thoughts, worrisome and otherwise.

Because meditation involves removing all worrisome or stressful thoughts and replacing them with peaceful ones, it can be an effective method for relaxing and reducing stress. Meditation also provides some relief from anxiety and depression, and improved alertness, focus, and memory (M. Andrews, 2005; Lazar et al., 2005; Novotney, 2009b; Peng, 2008a).

However, learning to use meditation to relax at will usually requires practicing about 20 minutes a day for many weeks (J. Stein, 2003).

Stopping Stress Responses

The next time some stressor triggers the fight-flight response, you can use some form of relaxation to stop or turn down the heightened arousal caused by the fight-flight response and thus reduce your stressful or negative feelings before they result in psychosomatic symptoms, such as a headache or stomach distress. Researchers report that most relaxation techniques, whether biofeedback, progressive relaxation, or various forms of meditation (Zen, yoga, TM), are about equally effective in producing relaxation and reducing stress (Spiegler & Guevremont, 2010). More important than which relaxation technique you choose is daily practice so that you can learn to relax at will. Being able to relax at will is vital to developing an effective stress management program (M. Davis et al., 2008; J. Stein, 2003). ●

© sfam_photo/Shutterstock.com

© CLIPAREA | Custom media/Shutterstock.com

© Christopher Edwin Nuzzaco/Shutterstock.com

The Positive Benefits of Social Support

In the small town of Roseto, Pennsylvania, people were relatively obese and ate a lot of animal fat. They smoked as much and exercised as little as residents of other neighboring towns. Despite the citizens' awful diet and lifestyle, however, they had lower rates for heart attacks, ulcers, and emotional problems than people in the rest of the United States and their neighboring towns.

This puzzling question—Why do the citizens of Roseto enjoy such good physical and mental health in the face of obvious risk factors?—was answered by a study of the town's social order. "One striking feature did set Roseto apart from its neighbors," says Stewart Wolf, vice president for medical affairs at St. Luke's Hospital in Bethlehem, Pennsylvania, and a principal investigator of the Roseto phenomenon. "We found that family relationships were extremely close and mutually supportive, and this wonderful social support system extended to neighbors and to the community as a whole" (J. Greenberg, 1978, p. 378). But the story of Roseto does not have a happy ending.

1 Which type of research method was used to study Roseto families? What are its advantages and disadvantages?

As the families of Roseto prospered, they moved into larger homes in the countryside, and their social support system began to break down. Families no longer had helpful friends for neighbors, which meant fewer get-togethers and far less social support. One of the most interesting and deadly findings was that with the breakdown in social support came an increase in heart attacks. This study on families in Roseto was one of the first to suggest that dealing with stress and overcoming health risks were in large part aided by one's social support.

Social support refers to having a network of family, friends, neighbors, co-workers, and others who provide strong social attachments and with whom you can exchange helpful resources.

Forty years ago (the time of the Roseto study), no one would have thought that lack of social support was a major factor that contributed to becoming ill and developing psychosomatic symptoms. Thanks to many years of research, today we know

2 What are some possible effects of stressful experiences?

that social support decreases the effects of stressful experiences. A strong social support system is such a good predictor of physical health that it is even associated with a longer life span.

3 What type of primary appraisal would shy people likely make when confronted with having to establish social support?

Not only has our understanding of the importance of social support moved forward, but so has our ability to provide and

receive social support. In today's society, providing and receiving social support are easier than ever. Even introverted or shy people can find social support by accessing the Internet and participating in virtual support groups, which have been found to be effective in helping people cope with stress associated with psychosocial and medical problems.

4 What type of coping is facilitated by joining support groups?

5 Which personality traits help people cope with the stress of knowing they have medical problems?

Sometimes life presents us with stressors that are so great that no matter how strong our individual coping strategies are, they will not be enough to help us effectively cope. It is during these times that we gain a true appreciation for our friends, family, and others in our social circle.

6 What are some individual coping strategies that can help reduce stress?

Adapted from Høybye et al., 2005; P. D. Martin & Brantley, 2004; Marziali et al., 2006; Uchino, 2004; Uchino & Birmingham, 2011

Unless otherwise noted, all images are © Cengage Learning

© iStockphoto/Thinkstock

A Appraisal of Stress

1. The uncomfortable feeling we have when we appraise a situation as something that overloads or strains our psychological resources is called _____.

2. Our initial, subjective evaluation of a situation in which we balance various environmental demands against our ability to meet them is called _____.

3. There are three outcomes of primary appraisal. Those situations that do not matter to our well-being are called **(a)** _____; those that will enhance or preserve our well-being are called **(b)** _____; and those that overtax our resources are called **(c)** _____.

4. A stressful situation has the potential for three different kinds of personal experiences. If you have already sustained some damage or injury, this is referred to as **(a)** _____. If the injury has not yet taken place but you anticipate it in the near future, this is referred to as **(b)** _____. If you have the potential for gain or personal growth but need to use physical energy and psychological resources, this is referred to as **(c)** _____. Not all appraisals are clear-cut; some may represent a combination of threat and challenge.

B Stress Responses

5. A combination of physiological responses that arouse and prepare the body for action is called the **(a)** _____ response. Although this response originally evolved to help our ancestors survive dangerous and life-threatening situations, it can also be triggered by psychological stimuli, such as our primary **(b)** _____ of a situation as harm/loss, threatening, or challenging.

6. Threat appraisals activate two brain areas, called the **(a)** _____ and _____, which trigger two responses simultaneously. The hypothalamus causes the **(b)** _____ gland to release ACTH, which acts on the adrenal cortex to secrete hormones that regulate levels of minerals and glucose in the body. It also triggers the **(c)** _____ division of the autonomic nervous system, which causes physiological arousal.

7. Our psychological reactions to stressful situations can result in real, painful, physical symptoms called **(a)** _____ symptoms. According to Selye, we develop psychosomatic symptoms because the body's response to stress involves going through three stages that he called the **(b)** _____ syndrome. The first is called the **(c)** _____ stage, which is our initial reaction to stress and is marked by physiological arousal. The second is called the **(d)** _____ stage,

in which most physiological responses return to normal levels as the body uses up great stores of energy. The third is called the **(e)** _____ stage, which is marked by the actual breakdown in body organs or weakening of the infection-fighting immune system.

8. The body's network of cells and chemicals that automatically fight off bacteria, viruses, and other foreign matter is known as the **(a)** _____. The study of the relationships among the central nervous system, the endocrine system, and psychosocial factors is called **(b)** _____. The interaction among these factors affects the immune system and, in turn, makes the body more or less susceptible to disease and infection.

C Stressful Experiences

9. Situations that are potentially disturbing or disruptive and that we appraise as having an impact on our lives are called **(a)** _____ events. Small, irritating daily events are called **(b)** _____, and small, pleasant daily experiences are called **(c)** _____. How we cope with hassles predicts our daily mood and the occurrence of psychosomatic symptoms.

© Laurent Renault/Shutterstock.com

10. The feeling that results when our attempts to reach some goal are blocked is called **(a)** _____. Feelings of wearing out or becoming exhausted because of too many demands on our time and energy are referred to as **(b)** _____. A direct personal experience of actual or threatened death or serious injury or witnessing such an event could result in terrible stress symptoms called **(c)** _____.

11. When we must decide between two or more incompatible choices, we are in **(a)** _____, which can include at least three possibilities. If we must choose between two options with pleasurable consequences, we experience **(b)** _____ conflict. If we must choose between two options that both have disagreeable consequences, we are in **(c)** _____ conflict. If a single situation has both pleasurable and disagreeable aspects, we are in **(d)** _____ conflict.

12. An unpleasant state in which we have feelings of uneasiness and apprehension as well as increased physiological arousal is called **(a)** _____. This feeling has at least three causes. One is classical conditioning of an emotional response to a previously neutral stimulus; the result is called a **(b)** _____ response. A second cause is a form of learning that develops through watching and does not require any observable behavior or reinforcer; this is called **(c)** _____ learning. According to Freud, anxiety arises when the id and superego disagree, leading to an **(d)** _____ conflict, which results in the ego producing a feeling of anxiety.

D Personality & Health

13. Three personality traits that decrease the potentially harmful effects of stressful situations are control, commitment, and challenge, which together are called _____.

14. If you believe that what you do influences what happens, you are said to have an **(a)** _____ of control. In contrast, if you believe that chance and luck mostly determine what happens and that you do not have much influence, you are said to have an **(b)** _____ of control. People with an external locus of control experience more negative emotions, higher levels of stress, and more psychosomatic symptoms than do those whose locus of control is internal.

E Coping with Stress

15. After we make a primary appraisal, we then must decide what action to take, which is called a **(a)** _____ appraisal. This involves two different kinds of coping. If we seek information about what needs to be done, change our own behavior, or take whatever action will solve the problem, we use **(b)** _____ coping. If we use our energies to deal with emotional distress caused by a harm or threat appraisal, we are using **(c)** _____ coping. Compared to emotion-focused coping, problem-focused coping is better at reducing the long-term effects of stress because it solves the problem.

F Positive Psychology

16. Positive psychology has three main concerns. The first is the study of **(a)** _____, such as happiness and contentment. The second is the study of **(b)** _____, such as altruism and resilience. The third is the study of **(c)** _____, or the strengths that promote better communities, such as justice and teamwork.

G Research Focus: Treatment for Panic Disorder

17. Psychologists use a number of different research methods. One method is an in-depth analysis of the thoughts, feelings, beliefs, or behaviors of individuals; this is called the **(a)** _____. Another method identifies cause-and-effect relationships by following a set of guidelines that describe how to control and manipulate variables; this is called the **(b)** _____ method. Panic disorder is usually treated with **(c)** _____. By using an experiment, researchers found that cognitive-behavioral therapy and drugs, either used individually or combined, worked equally well in terms of **(d)** _____ treatment effects. Research findings showed that the most effective long-term treatment for panic disorder is **(e)** _____.

H Cultural Diversity: Tibetan Monks

18. Many of our physiological responses involved in relaxation (heart rate, blood pressure, temperature, and secretion of hormones) are not under voluntary control because they are regulated by the **(a)** _____ system. Researchers discovered that some monks have learned a method to voluntarily control temperature, which involves relaxation. This demonstrates that the **(b)** _____ can be used to control the **(c)** _____ physiological responses.

Meditation: finger temperature increases

Baseline

Recovery: finger temperature returns to normal

Meditation

Graph data from "Body Temperature Changes During the Practice of g Tum-mo-Yoga," by H. Benson, J. W. Lehmann, M. S. Malhotra, R. F. Goldman, P. J. Hopkins & M. D. Epstein, 1982, *Nature, 295,* 234–235.

I Application: Stress Management Programs

19. A program for reducing anxiety, fear, and stressful experiences by using a variety of strategies to change three different aspects of our lives—thoughts, behaviors, and physiological responses—is called a _____.

20. One component of a stress management program is learning to relax at will, which can be accomplished with three different methods. Recording and amplifying physiological signals from the body and displaying these signals so that we can learn to increase or decrease them is known as **(a)** _____. An exercise of tensing and relaxing the major muscle groups is called **(b)** _____. Meditation can take many forms. Sitting or lying in a comfortable position while repeating a meaningless sound over and over to rid oneself of anxious thoughts is called **(c)** _____.

Answers: 1. *stress;* 2. *primary appraisal;* 3. (a) *irrelevant,* (b) *positive,* (c) *stressful;* 4. (a) *harm/loss,* (b) *threat,* (c) *challenge;* 5. (a) *fight-flight,* (b) *appraisal;* 6. (a) *amygdala,* hypothalamus, (b) *pituitary,* (c) *sympathetic;* 7. (a) *psychosomatic,* (b) *general adaptation,* (c) *alarm,* (d) *resistance,* (e) *exhaustion;* 8. (a) *immune system,* (b) *psychoneuroimmunology;* 9. (a) *major life,* (b) *hassles,* (c) *uplifts;* 10. (a) *frustration,* (b) *burnout,* (c) *posttraumatic stress disorder;* 11. (a) *conflict,* (b) *approach-approach,* (c) *avoidance-avoidance,* (d) *approach-avoidance;* 12. (a) *anxiety,* (b) *conditioned emotional,* (c) *observational,* (d) *unconscious;* 13. *hardiness;* 14. (a) *internal locus,* (b) *external locus;* 15. (a) *secondary,* (b) *problem-focused,* (c) *emotion-focused;* 16. (a) *positive emotions,* (b) *positive individual traits,* (c) *positive institutions;* 17. (a) *case study,* (b) *experimental or scientific,* (c) *drugs and/or psychotherapy,* (d) *short-term,* (e) *cognitive-behavioral therapy;* 18. (a) *autonomic nervous or parasympathetic,* (b) *mind,* (c) *body's;* 19. *stress management program;* 20. (a) *biofeedback,* (b) *progressive relaxation,* (c) *transcendental meditation (TM)*

Links to Learning

Key Terms/Key People

adjustment disorder, 490
alarm stage, 487
anxiety, 493
approach-approach conflict, 492
approach-avoidance conflict, 492
autonomic nervous system, 501
avoidance-avoidance conflict, 492
biofeedback, 503
burnout, 491
case study, 500
challenge appraisal, 482
conditioned emotional response, 493
conflict, 492
coping, 481
emotion-focused coping, 498

eustress, 493
exhaustion stage, 487
experiment, 500
fight-flight response, 484
frustration, 491
galvanic skin response, 483
gamma brain waves, 501
general adaptation syndrome, 487
hardiness, 494
harm/loss appraisal, 482
hassles, 490
health psychology, 487
immune system, 488
locus of control, 494
major life events, 490
meditation, 503

mind-body connection, 487
observational learning, 493
optimism, 495
panic attack, 481
panic disorder, 481
pessimism, 495
positive psychology, 495, 499
positive stress, 493
posttraumatic stress disorder, or PTSD, 491
primary appraisal, 482
problem-focused coping, 498
progressive relaxation, 503
psychoneuroimmunology, 488
psychosomatic symptoms, 486
resistance stage, 487
secondary appraisal, 498

self-efficacy, 495
Social Readjustment Rating Scale, 490
social support, 504
stress, 481
stress appraisal, 485
stress management program, 502
stressor, 481
threat appraisal, 482
transcendental meditation, 503
Type A behavior, 496
Type B behavior, 496
Type D behavior, 496
uplifts, 490
yoga, 503

Media Resources

Go to **CengageBrain.com** to access Psychology CourseMate, where you will find an interactive eBook, glossaries, flashcards, quizzes, videos, answers to Critical Thinking questions, and more. You can also access Virtual Psychology Labs, an interactive laboratory experience designed to illustrate key experiments first-hand.

MODULE 22 Assessment & Psychological Disorders I

© RAW FILE/Masterfile

Mental Disorder

He was a loving husband, devoted father, respected church elder, and straitlaced county official. He also worked for a home security company, where he helped individuals protect them-

How did a serial killer go unnoticed?

selves from dangerous people. Until the day he was caught, he blended into the Wichita community as an average next-door neighbor. But over a period of 17 years, Dennis Rader planned and carried out the cruel murders of 10 people. He became known as the "BTK killer," which stands for Bind, Torture, and Kill, describing the methods he used with his victims.

In a very real sense, Rader led two different lives. In public, Rader seemed like a quiet, law-abiding guy who helped to protect the safety of others. However, in private, Rader would break into people's homes, hide, and then sneak up on his victims. He would proceed to tie them up, callously strangle them, and eventually murder them.

Although no two serial killers are alike, Rader fits the typical pattern. Serial killers usually look like ordinary people, often with families and good jobs. Many serial killers have experienced a traumatic childhood event and have serious personality defects, such as low self-esteem and a lifelong sense of loneliness. They are obsessed with control, manipulation, and dominance and often con their victims into agreeing to their requests. Most serial killers enjoy not the actual killing, but the ruthless torturing of their victims. This explains why serial killers feel special when their victims suffer and plead for help, and why Rader became sexually aroused as he strangled each of his victims (Hickey, 2006; Mann, 2005).

Dennis Rader, who murdered 10 people, fits the pattern of serial killers.

When Rader's trial began, his defense attorneys had to decide whether they wanted to claim he was legally insane when he committed the murders. You are probably thinking that a person who coldheartedly plans and carries out 10 violent murders must certainly be insane, but let's consider what it means to be insane.

Insanity, according to its legal definition, means not knowing the difference between right and wrong.

As inhumane as Rader's behaviors may seem, his defense did not claim he was insane. Based on Rader's testimony, it was clear he knew all along that his actions were wrong and conducted for his own selfish interests. In 2005, thirty-one years after the first BTK attacks, Rader was charged with 10 counts of first-degree murder for which he must serve 10 life sentences (Davey, 2005; O'Driscoll, 2005; Wilgoren, 2005).

When mental health professionals examine Rader's behaviors, they are trying to identify his particular mental disorder.

A **mental disorder** is generally defined as a prolonged or recurring problem that seriously interferes with an individual's ability to live a satisfying personal life and function adequately in society.

Deciding whether a person has a mental disorder can be difficult because so many factors are involved in defining what is abnormal. As you'll learn in this module, someone's behavior may be described as abnormal but the person may or may not have a mental disorder.

Anxiety Disorder

What's so scary about untied shoelaces?

There is no doubt that Dennis Rader's murder and mutilation of 10 individuals indicate extremely abnormal behavior and a severe mental disorder (Hickey, 2006). In other cases, a mental disorder may involve a relatively common behavior or event that has the power to elicit tremendous anxiety and may become an anxiety disorder.

An **anxiety disorder** is a condition characterized by an individual feeling anxiety that is out of proportion to the danger elicited by an object or situation, and the anxiety interferes with the person's normal daily functioning.

Howie Mandel, a comedian and television star (host of "Deal or No Deal" and judge on "America's Got Talent"), has experienced anxiety since childhood. As a child, for instance, when his shoelaces got untied, he wouldn't touch them because he feared they had dangerous germs from the dirty ground. Instead, he'd walk the rest of the day dragging his feet so that he wouldn't trip over his laces or lose a shoe.

As an adult, Mandel doesn't shake hands with others. If he did, he would have to wash his hands again and again to make sure his hands were no longer contaminated by germs. This process could take hours each time someone shook his hand because he would obsess about his hands not being completely clean. This obsession would be so intense that he would not be able to continue

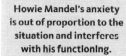

Howie Mandel's anxiety is out of proportion to the situation and interferes with his functioning.

with his day until he was absolutely sure his hands were clean (Mandel, 2009).

Mandel has an anxiety disorder because his anxiety is clearly out of proportion to the danger elicited by the situations he encounters and the anxiety interferes with his daily functioning. We'll tell you more about Mandel's anxiety disorder later in this module.

These two examples of Dennis Rader and Howie Mandel raise a number of questions about mental disorders: How do they develop? How are they diagnosed? How are they treated? We'll answer these questions as we discuss mental disorders.

What's Coming

In this module, we'll discuss three approaches to understanding mental disorders. We'll explain how mental disorders are assessed and diagnosed and present some specific examples of mental disorders, such as generalized anxiety disorder, phobias, obsessive-compulsive behaviors, and somatoform disorders. Finally, we'll discuss how common phobias, such as fear of flying, are treated.

We'll begin with the different factors that are involved in defining, explaining, and treating mental disorders, such as that of Dennis Rader. ●

Causes of Abnormal Behavior

Explanations for the causes of mental disorders have changed dramatically through the centuries. In the Middle Ages, mental disorders were thought to be the result of demons or devils who inhabited individuals and made them do strange and horrible things. In the 1600s, mental disorders were thought to involve witches, who were believed to speak to the devil. This was the case in Salem, Massachusetts, in 1692, where, in a short span of four months, 14 women and 5 men were hanged as witches on the testimony of young girls and

God-fearing adults (L. Shapiro, 1992). In the 1960s, one major cause of mental disorders was thought to be environmental factors, such as stressful events. In the 1990s came advances in studying genetic factors as well as new methods to study the structures and functions of living brains. As a result, current researchers and clinicians believe that mental disorders, such as that of Dennis Rader, result from a number of factors, which include biological, cognitive-emotional-behavioral, and environmental influences (Hersen & Thomas, 2006).

Biological Factors

Biological influences include genetic or inherited factors and various neurological factors that influence how the brain functions.

Genetic factors. As an infant, Joan would cry, show great fear, and try to avoid new or novel objects or situations. Because Joan showed great fear as an infant, researchers concluded that her fearfulness was primarily due to genetic factors (Kagan, 2003a).

Genetic factors that contribute to the development of mental disorders are unlearned or inherited tendencies that influence how a person thinks, behaves, and feels.

Genetic factors operate by affecting the developing brain and/or the neurotransmitters that the brain uses for communication. Researchers estimate that genetic factors contribute from 30% to 60% to the development of mental disorders, such as depression, schizophrenia, and anxiety disorders (Rutter & Silberg, 2002).

Neurological factors. Joan, who started life as a fearful infant, had developed a serious mental disorder called a social phobia (see p. 518) by the time she was 20. Researchers believed that one reason she developed a social phobia was that her brain's emotional detector, called the amygdala (see p. 362), was overactive and too often identified stimuli as threatening when they were only new or novel. In fact, when

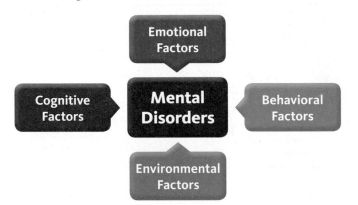

Emotional Factors → **Mental Disorders**
Cognitive Factors → **Mental Disorders** ← **Behavioral Factors**
Environmental Factors ↑

researchers measured the activity (fMRI) of Joan's amygdala, they found that her amygdala overreacted when she looked at new or novel faces, something that did not happen in the amygdalas of individuals who did not have social phobias (C. E. Schwartz et al., 2003). In a related study, individuals who had developed social phobias, like Joan, showed far more amygdala activity when they looked at angry, fearful, or disgusted faces than did individuals without social phobias (Luan et al., 2006).

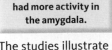

Amygdala–emotions

Very fearful adults had more activity in the amygdala.

The studies illustrate neurological factors, such as having an overactive brain structure that contributes to the development of a mental disorder by causing a person to see the world in a biased or distorted way and to see threats when none really exist.

Although these studies show that biological factors—genetic and neurological—can contribute to the development of mental disorders, not everyone with an overactive amygdala develops a mental disorder. This means that other factors are also involved in the development of mental disorders.

Cognitive-Emotional-Behavioral & Environmental Factors

Because biological factors themselves do not always explain why people develop mental disorders, psychologists point to various cognitive-emotional-behavioral factors that interact with and contribute to developing mental disorders.

Cognitive-emotional-behavioral and environmental factors that contribute to the development of mental disorders include deficits in cognitive processes, such as having unusual thoughts and beliefs; deficits in processing emotional stimuli, such as under- or overreacting to emotional situations; behavioral problems, such as lacking social skills; and environmental challenges, such as dealing with stressful situations.

For example, Dennis Rader was a shy and polite child who preferred to spend time alone. As a boy, he recalls watching his grandparents strangle chickens at their farm, and by the time he reached high school, he was strangling cats and dogs. Rader's hobby during childhood was looking at pictures of women in bondage. By his teens, he fantasized about tying up, controlling, and torturing women. He was becoming increasingly bothered by murderous impulses but did not know how to tell anyone about it (Ortiz, 2005; Singular, 2006). Rader's many maladaptive thoughts, emotions, and behaviors as well as environmental factors interacted with his biological factors and resulted in his serious mental disorder.

The answer to why Joan developed a social phobia, or Dennis Rader became a serial killer, or a family member, friend, or relative developed a mental disorder involves a number of factors—genetic, neurological, cognitive-emotional-behavioral, and environmental. As several or more of these factors interact, the result in some cases can be the development of one of the mental disorders that we'll discuss in this and the next module.

Unless otherwise noted, all images are © Cengage Learning

Definitions of Abnormal Behavior

In some cases, such as Dennis Rader's murder and mutilation of 10 individuals, we have no doubt that he demonstrated an extremely abnormal behavior pattern. In other cases, such as Howie Mandel's, we would probably say that most of his life appears to be normal except for one piece—fear of germs—that is abnormal. In still other cases, such as that of 54-year-old Richard Thompson (right photo), it is less clear what is abnormal behavior.

Is Mr. Thompson abnormal?

The City of San Diego evicted Thompson and all his belongings from his home. His belongings included shirts, pants, dozens of shoes, several Bibles, a cooler, a tool chest, lawn chairs, a barbecue grill, tin plates, bird cages, two pet rats, and his self-fashioned bed. For the previous nine months, Thompson had lived happily and without any problems in a downtown storm drain (sewer). Because the city does not allow people to live in storm drains, however, Thompson was evicted from his underground storm-drain home and forbidden to return. Although Thompson later lived in several care centers and mental hospitals, he much preferred the privacy and comfort of the sewer (Grimaldi, 1986).

There are three different ways to decide whether Richard Thompson's behavior—living in the sewer—was abnormal.

Is it abnormal to live in a storm drain if you don't bother anyone?

Statistical Frequency

Although Thompson caused no problems to others except to violate a city law against living in a storm drain, his preferred living style could be considered abnormal according to statistical frequency.

The **statistical frequency approach** says that a behavior may be considered abnormal if it occurs rarely or infrequently in relation to the behaviors of the general population.

According to statistical frequency, living in a monastery is abnormal.

By this definition, Thompson's living in a storm drain would be considered very abnormal since, out of over 300 million people in the United States, only a very few prefer his kind of home. This illustrates that even though statistical frequency is a relatively precise measure, it is not a very useful measure of abnormality. By this criterion, getting a Ph.D., being president, living in a monastery, and selling a million records are abnormal, although some of these behaviors would be considered very desirable by most people. In fact, Guinness World Records (2012) lists thousands of people who have performed some statistically abnormal behaviors and are very proud of them. We would not consider any of these individuals to necessarily have mental disorders.

As all these examples demonstrate, the statistical frequency definition of abnormality has very limited usefulness.

Deviation from Social Norms

Thompson's behavior—preferring to live in a sewer—could also be considered abnormal based on social norms.

The **social norms approach** says that a behavior is considered abnormal if it deviates greatly from accepted social standards, values, or norms.

Thompson's decision to live by himself in a storm drain greatly deviates from society's norms about where people should live. However, a definition of abnormality based solely on deviations from social norms runs into problems when social norms change with time. For example, 25 years ago, few males wore earrings, while today many males consider earrings very fashionable. Similarly, 50 years ago, a woman who preferred to be very thin was considered to be ill and in need of medical help. Today, our society pressures women to be thin like the fashion models in the media.

According to social norms, it used to be abnormal for men to wear earrings.

Thus, defining abnormality on the basis of social norms can be risky because social norms may, and do, change over time. The definition of abnormality most used by mental health professionals is the next one.

Maladaptive Behavior

The major problem with the first two definitions of abnormal behavior—statistical frequency and deviation from social norms—is that they don't say whether a particular behavior is psychologically damaging or maladaptive.

The **maladaptive behavior approach** defines a behavior as psychologically damaging or abnormal if it interferes with the individual's ability to function in his or her personal life or in society.

For example, being terrified of flying, hearing voices that dictate dangerous acts, feeling compelled to wash one's hands for hours on end, starving oneself to the point of death (anorexia nervosa), and Dennis Rader's committing serial murders would all be considered maladaptive and, in that sense, abnormal.

However, Thompson's seemingly successful adaptation to living in a sewer may not be maladaptive for him and certainly has no adverse consequences to society.

Most useful. Of the three definitions discussed here, mental health professionals find that the most useful definition of abnormal behaviors is the one based on the maladaptive definition—that is, whether a behavior or behavior pattern interferes with a person's ability to function normally in society (Sue et al., 2010).

According to the maladaptive definition, behavior is abnormal if it interferes with a person's functioning.

However, you'll see that deciding whether behavior is truly maladaptive is not always so easy. ●

Definition of Assessment

How do you find out what's wrong?

In some cases, it's relatively easy to identify what's wrong with a person. For example, it's clear that Dennis Rader was a serial killer and that Howie Mandel has an intense and irrational anxiety about germs. But in other cases, it's more difficult to identify exactly what the person's motivation and mental problem are. Take the tragic case of Susan Smith.

Susan Smith appeared on the "Today" show, crying for the return of her two little boys (right photo), Michael, 3 years old, and Alex, 14 months old, who, she said, had been kidnapped. She begged the kidnapper to feed them, care for them, and please, please, return them. And then, nine days later, after a rigorous investigation turned up doubts about the kidnapping story, the police questioned Susan again. Not only did she change her story, but she made the teary confession that she had killed her two children. She said that she had parked her car by the edge of the lake, strapped her two

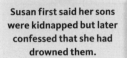

Susan first said her sons were kidnapped but later confessed that she had drowned them.

© AP Images/Lou Krasky

children into their car seats, shut the windows and doors, got out of the car, walked to the rear, and pushed the car into the lake. She covered her ears so she couldn't hear the splash. The car disappeared under the water. The two little boys, strapped into their seats, drowned.

Susan's confession stunned the nation as everyone asked, "How could she have killed her own children?" "What's wrong with Susan?" To answer these questions, mental health professionals evaluated Susan's mental health with a procedure called the clinical assessment (J. M. Wood et al., 2002).

A **clinical assessment** is a systematic evaluation of an individual's various psychological, biological, and social factors, as well as the identification of past and present problems, stressors, and other cognitive or behavioral symptoms.

A clinical assessment is the first step in figuring out which past or current problems may have contributed to Susan killing her own children (Begley, 1998b). We'll discuss how a clinical assessment is done.

Three Methods of Assessment

How was Susan evaluated?

After Susan's arrest, mental health professionals did clinical assessments to try to discover what terrible forces pushed her over the edge. Depending on their training, mental health professionals use one or more of three major techniques—neurological exams, clinical interviews, and psychological tests—to do clinical assessments.

Neurological Tests

We can assume that Susan was given a number of *neurological tests* to check for possible brain damage or malfunction. These tests might include evaluating reflexes, brain structures (MRI scans), and brain functions (fMRI scans—see p. 71).

Neurological exams are part of a clinical assessment because a variety of abnormal psychological symptoms may be caused by tumors, diseases, or infections of the brain.

Neurological tests are used to distinguish physical or organic causes (tumors) from psychological ones (strange beliefs) (Lezak et al., 2012). Susan was reported to have no neurological problems.

Clinical Interviews

As part of her clinical assessment, several psychiatrists spent many hours interviewing Susan. This method is called a clinical interview (Summerfeldt et al., 2010).

The **clinical interview** is one method of gathering information about a person's past and current behaviors, beliefs, attitudes, emotions, and problems. Some clinical interviews are unstructured, which means they have no set questions; others are structured, which means they follow a standard format of asking a similar set of questions.

During the clinical interview, Susan would have been asked about the history of her current problems, such as when they started and what other events accompanied them. The focus of the interview would have been on Susan's current problem, killing her children, especially on the details of the symptoms that led up to the killing. The clinical interview is perhaps the primary technique used to assess abnormal behavior.

Based on 15 hours of interviews, Dr. Seymour Halleck testified that Susan was scarred by her father's suicide and her stepfather sexually abusing her, which led to periods of depression (Towle, 1995).

© Lewis J Merrim/Photo Researchers

Psychological Tests

As part of her assessment, psychologists may have given Susan a number of personality tests (see pp. 450, 474).

Personality tests include two different kinds of tests: objective tests (self-report questionnaires), such as the MMPI, which consist of specific statements or questions to which the person responds with specific answers, and projective tests, such as the Rorschach inkblot test, which have no set answers but consist of ambiguous stimuli that a person interprets or makes up a story about.

As we also discussed in Modules 19 and 20, personality tests help clinicians evaluate a person's traits, attitudes, emotions, and beliefs.

Purpose. A major goal of doing a clinical assessment is to decide which mental health disorder best accounts for a client's symptoms. For example, based on her symptoms, Susan was described as having a mood disorder, which you'll see next is one of many possible mental health problems. ●

Unless otherwise noted, all images are © Cengage Learning

C Diagnosing Mental Disorders

History and Overview of the DSM

What is the DSM? Those who knew Susan tried to diagnose the problem that led to her tragic crime.

"Maybe Susan was just plain crazy." "Maybe she was too depressed to know what she was doing." "Maybe she had bad genes." "Maybe something bad happened to her as a child."

Using a more rigorous method, mental health professionals conduct clinical assessments to identify symptoms, which are then used to make a clinical diagnosis.

A **clinical diagnosis** is the process of matching an individual's specific symptoms to those that define a particular mental disorder.

Making a clinical diagnosis was very difficult prior to the 1950s because there was no uniform code or diagnostic system. However, since 1952, the American Psychiatric Association (APA) has been developing a uniform diagnostic system, whose most recent version is known as the *Diagnostic and Statistical Manual of Mental Disorders*-IV-Text Revision, abbreviated as DSM-IV-TR (American Psychiatric Association, 2000).

The ***Diagnostic and Statistical Manual of Mental Disorders*** describes a uniform system for assessing specific symptoms and matching them to different mental disorders.

With each revision of the DSM, there have been improvements in diagnosing mental disorders. For example, the DSM-II (1968) gave only general descriptions of mental problems because it was based on Sigmund Freud's general concepts

© McPHOTO/Age fotostock

- ❏ depressed mood
- ❏ sleeping difficulties
- ❏ changes in appetite
- ❏ fatigue or loss of energy
- ❏ feelings of worthlessness
- ❏ decreased concentration
- ❏ recurrent thoughts of death

To make a clinical diagnosis, a clinician must conduct an assessment (left) and match the client's specific symptoms to those that define a mental disorder (above).

of **psychoses** (severe mental disorders, such as schizophrenia) and **neuroses** (less severe forms of psychological conflict, such as anxiety). Using only general descriptions caused disagreements in diagnosing problems. The DSM-III (1980) dropped Freudian terminology and instead listed specific symptoms and criteria for mental disorders. However, these criteria were based primarily on clinical opinions, not research, so disagreements continued. A major improvement in the current DSM-IV-TR is that it establishes criteria and symptoms for mental disorders based more on research findings than on clinical opinions (L. A. Clark et al., 1995). Interestingly, the first *Diagnostic and Statistical Manual of Mental Disorders* (1952) described about 100 mental disorders, as compared to almost 300 in the most recent DSM-IV-TR (right figure).

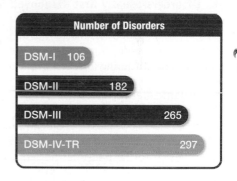

Number of Disorders

DSM-I	106
DSM-II	182
DSM-III	265
DSM-IV-TR	297

Currently, efforts are being made to revise the DSM again. We'll give you a sneak preview of some of the new features expected to be in the upcoming revision.

DSM 5

At the present time, the DSM is being revised again, and the new edition will be titled DSM 5. The DSM 5 is tentatively scheduled to be released in mid-2013. As they did with each of the earlier revisions, researchers are considering omissions of existing diagnoses, revisions to existing diagnoses, and additions of new diagnoses. The total number of diagnoses is uncertain at this time. Some new diagnoses under consideration include complex posttraumatic stress disorder, relational disorder, negativistic personality disorder, gambling addiction, and hypersexual disorder (G. Miller & Holden, 2010; R. Rubin, 2010; www.dsm5.org).

How will the DSM 5 be different?

The organization of the DSM 5 is a departure from that of earlier editions. The disorders will be organized in a developmental life span format, beginning with disorders often diagnosed in infancy and early childhood and progressing through disorders more commonly diagnosed in adulthood (www.dsm5.org).

Perhaps the most significant revision under consideration is whether to move away from the existing approach of reaching diagnoses by using a ***categorical assessment*** to using a ***dimensional assessment*** (Clay, 2011; G. Miller, 2012; G. Miller & Holden, 2010).

In *categorical assessments,* each disorder has a specific list of symptoms. An individual either has the symptom or doesn't, and a certain number of symptoms have to be checked off to make a diagnosis. Categorical assessments do not account for the severity of the symptoms or any symptoms individuals may have that are not included in their particular diagnosis.

In contrast, *dimensional assessments* permit clinicians to evaluate the severity of symptoms as well as consider "cross-cutting" symptoms (symptoms not part of the primary diagnosis). This approach encourages clinicians to document and track each of the client's symptoms, including those that are not part of their particular disorder, and note improvements even if the symptoms do not entirely disappear.

Because a transition to the use of dimensional assessments would significantly change the approach of the DSM, it is most likely that the DSM 5 will retain the categorical approach, but perhaps add the dimensional approach to some of its disorders (Regier et al., 2009). Overall, it is expected that the DSM 5 will likely be more of a "fine-tuning" than a radical transformation (Bufka, 2011).

We'll use the cases of Dennis Rader (serial killer), Susan Smith (murderer), and Howie Mandel (fear of germs) to show how mental health professionals use the current DSM (DSM-IV-TR) to make a diagnosis.

The Five Axes of the DSM

How do we make a diagnosis?

In making a clinical diagnosis, a mental health professional first assesses the client's specific symptoms and then matches these symptoms to those described in the DSM-IV-TR. The DSM-IV-TR has five major dimensions, called axes, which serve as guidelines for making decisions about symptoms. We'll first describe Axis I and show how it can be used to diagnose the very different problems of Susan Smith and Howie Mandel. (The numbered items below and on the opposite page are based on the *Diagnostic and Statistical Manual of Mental Disorders*-IV-Text Revision [2000], American Psychiatric Association.)

Axis I: Nine Major Clinical Syndromes

Axis I contains lists of symptoms and criteria about the onset, severity, and duration of these symptoms. In turn these lists of symptoms are used to make a clinical diagnosis of the following nine major clinical syndromes.

1 Disorders usually first diagnosed in infancy, childhood, or adolescence

This category includes disorders that arise before adolescence, such as attention-deficit disorders, autism, mental retardation, enuresis, and stuttering (discussed in Modules 1, 2, and 13).

2 Organic mental disorders

These disorders are temporary or permanent dysfunctions of brain tissue caused by diseases or chemicals, such as delirium, dementia (Alzheimer's—p. 50), and amnesia (p. 265).

3 Substance-related disorders

This category refers to the maladaptive use of drugs and alcohol. Mere consumption and recreational use of such substances are not disorders. This category requires an abnormal pattern of use, as with alcohol abuse and cocaine dependence (pp. 188–189).

4 Schizophrenia and other psychotic disorders

The schizophrenias are characterized by psychotic symptoms (for example, grossly disorganized behavior, delusions, and hallucinations) and by over six months of behavioral deterioration. This category, which also includes delusional disorder and schizoaffective disorder, will be discussed in Module 23.

5 Mood disorders

The cardinal feature is emotional disturbance. Patients may or may not have psychotic symptoms. These disorders, including major depression, bipolar disorder, dysthymic disorder, and cyclothymic disorder, are discussed in Module 23. Susan Smith is an example of a person with a mood disorder.

Susan Smith: Diagnosis—Mood Disorder

From childhood on, Susan's symptoms included being depressed, attempting suicide, seeking sexual alliances to escape loneliness, drinking heavily, and having feelings of low self-esteem and hopelessness, all of which match the DSM-IV-TR's list of symptoms for a mood disorder. In Susan's case, the specific mood disorder most closely matches major depressive disorder but without serious thought disorders and delusions.

Diagnosis: Mood disorder

© AP Images/Lou Krasky

In diagnosing major depression, the DSM-IV-TR distinguishes between mild and severe depression, as judged by how many episodes of depression she had and whether she showed a decreased capacity to function normally, such as the inability to work or care for children. Susan's ability to hold a job and care for her children suggests mild depression. This example shows how the guidelines of Axis I are used to arrive at one of nine major clinical syndromes—in this case, major depression.

6 Anxiety disorders

These disorders are characterized by physiological signs of anxiety (for example, palpitations) and subjective feelings of tension, apprehension, or fear. Anxiety may be acute and focused (phobias) or continual and diffuse (generalized anxiety disorder). An example of a person with an anxiety disorder is Howie Mandel.

Howie Mandel: Diagnosis—Obsessive-Compulsive Disorder

Mandel's symptoms included having recurring thoughts about germs that he was unable to control and that interfered with his normal daily functioning. Another one of his symptoms was having to wash his hands repeatedly for hours to reduce his needlessly intense anxiety about his hands not being clean.

Mandel's symptoms most closely match the DSM-IV-TR's list of symptoms for an anxiety disorder called ***obsessive-compulsive disorder*** (p. 519). The DSM-IV-TR's symptoms for obsessive-compulsive disorder include experiencing obsessive thoughts that a person is unable to control and having irresistible impulses to repeatedly perform some senseless behavior, which interferes with a person's normal daily activities.

Diagnosis: Obsessive-compulsive disorder

© Helga Esteb/Shutterstock.com

7 Somatoform disorders

These disorders are dominated by somatic symptoms that resemble physical illnesses. These symptoms cannot be accounted for by organic damage. There must also be strong evidence that these symptoms are produced by psychological factors or conflicts. This category, which includes somatization and conversion disorders and hypochondriasis, will be discussed later in this module.

8 Dissociative disorders

These disorders all feature a sudden, temporary alteration or dysfunction of memory, consciousness, identity, and behavior, as in dissociative identity disorder (discussed in Module 23).

9 Sexual and gender-identity disorders

There are three types of disorders in this category: gender-identity disorders (discomfort with one's identity as male or female), paraphilias (preference for unusual acts to achieve sexual arousal), and sexual dysfunctions (impairments in sexual functioning) (discussed in Module 15).

Syndrome titles from *Diagnostic and Statistical Manual of Mental Disorders,* Fourth Edition. Copyright © 1994 American Psychiatric Association.

We have explained how Axis I is used to make clinical diagnoses of such mental disorders as major depression (mood disorder) and specific phobias (fear of flying). Now, we'll briefly describe how the other four axes are used in diagnosing problems.

This axis refers to disorders that involve patterns of personality traits that are long-standing, maladaptive, and inflexible and involve impaired functioning or subjective distress. Examples include borderline, schizoid, and antisocial personality disorders. Personality disorders will be discussed in Module 23. An example of a person with a personality disorder is Dennis Rader.

Axis II: Personality Disorders

Dennis Rader: Diagnosis—Antisocial Personality Disorder

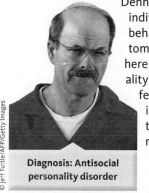

Diagnosis: Antisocial personality disorder

Dennis Rader's symptoms included torturing and killing 10 individuals, feeling no guilt or remorse, and exhibiting this behavior over a considerable period of time. Rader's symptoms may indicate a combination of mental disorders, but here we'll focus on only one from the DSM-IV-TR, a personality disorder. According to the DSM-IV-TR, the essential features of an antisocial personality disorder are strange inner experiences that differ greatly from the expectations of one's culture, that lead to significant impairment in personal, occupational, or social functioning, and that form a pattern of disregard for, and violation of, the rights of others. This list of symptoms from the DSM-IV-TR matches those of Rader.

Axis III: General Medical Conditions

This axis refers to physical disorders or conditions, such as diabetes, arthritis, and hemophilia, that have an influence on someone's mental disorder.

Axis IV: Psychosocial and Environmental Problems

This axis refers to psychosocial and environmental problems that may affect the diagnosis, treatment, and prognosis of mental disorders in Axes I and II. A psychosocial or environmental problem may be a negative life event (experiencing a traumatic event), an environmental difficulty or deficiency, a familial or other interpersonal stress, an inadequacy of social support or personal resources, or another problem that describes the context in which a person's difficulties have developed (PTSD was discussed on p. 491).

Axis V: Global Assessment of Functioning Scale

This axis is used to rate the overall psychological, social, and occupational functioning of the individual on a scale from 1 (severe danger of hurting self) to 100 (superior functioning in all activities).

Using all five axes. Mental health professionals use all five axes to make a clinical diagnosis. For example, in the case of Dennis Rader, his unusual sexual symptoms may match those of a sexual disorder in *Axis I.* His other maladaptive symptoms match those of an antisocial personality disorder in *Axis II.* Rader apparently had no related medical conditions listed in *Axis III.* Rader was a loner with poor self-esteem and struggled with his schoolwork, which match some of the psychological, social, and environmental factors listed in *Axis IV.* Amazingly, Rader functioned well enough to hold a job and go unnoticed in his neighborhood, which would be used to rate his general functioning listed in *Axis V.* As you can see, each of the five axes in the DSM-IV-TR focuses on a different factor that contributes to making an overall clinical diagnosis of a person's mental health.

Usefulness of the DSM-IV-TR

The figure below shows the steps in making a clinical diagnosis. Mental health professionals begin by using three different methods to identify a client's symptoms, a process called clinical assessment. Next, the client's symptoms are matched to the five axes in the DSM-IV-TR to arrive at a diagnosis of each client's particular mental disorder.

1 Clinical interviews

2 Psychological tests

3 Neurological tests

Clinical assessment: identify symptoms

DSM-IV-TR: Use symptoms to diagnose mental disorder

For mental health professionals, there are three advantages of using the DSM-IV-TR's uniform system to diagnose and classify mental disorders (Widiger & Clark, 2000).

First, mental health professionals use the classification system to communicate with one another and discuss their clients' problems.

Second, researchers use the classification system to study and explain mental disorders.

Third, therapists use the classification system to design their treatment program so as to best fit a particular client's problem.

Although using the DSM-IV-TR system to diagnose mental problems has advantages, it also has a number of potential problems. For example, mental health professionals do not always agree on whether a client fits a particular diagnosis. In addition, there may be social, political, and labeling problems, which we'll discuss next.

Potential Problems with Using the DSM

Is labeling a problem? It's not uncommon to hear people use labels, such as "Jim's really anxious," "Mary Ann is compulsive," or "Vicki is schizophrenic." Although the goal of the DSM-IV-TR is to give mental disorders particular diagnostic labels, once a person is labeled, the label itself may generate a negative stereotype. In turn, the negative stereotype results in negative social and political effects, such as biasing how others perceive and respond to the labeled person.

Labeling Mental Disorders

David Oaks, a sophomore at Harvard University, was having such fearful emotional experiences that he was examined by a psychiatrist. Although David believed that he was having a mystical experience, the psychiatrist interpreted and labeled David's fearful experiences as indicating a kind of short-term schizophrenic disorder (Japenga, 1994). This mental health professional made a clinical diagnosis that resulted in giving a label to David's problem.

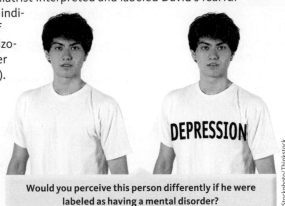

Would you perceive this person differently if he were labeled as having a mental disorder?

Labeling is the process of identifying and naming differences among individuals. The label, which places individuals into specific categories, may have either positive or negative associations.

At first David felt relieved to know that his problem had a diagnosis or label. Later he realized that his new label was changing his life for the worse. People no longer responded to him as David-the-college-sophomore but as David-with-schizophrenic-disorder.

As David's case shows, the *advantage* of diagnostic labels is their ability to summarize and communicate a whole lot of information in a single word or phrase. But, the *disadvantage* is that if the label has negative associations—for example, mentally ill, retarded, schizo—the very label may elicit negative or undesirable responses. For this reason, mental health professionals advise that we not respond to people with mental disorders by their labels and instead respond to the person behind the label (Albee & Joffe, 2004).

Social and Political Implications

Diagnostic labels can change how a person is perceived and thus have political and social implications. For instance, in the 1970s, gays protested that homosexuality should not be included in the DSM-I and II as a mental disorder. When studies found that homosexuals were no more or less mentally healthy than heterosexuals, homosexuality as a mental disorder was eliminated from the DSM-III.

In the 1980s, women protested the DSM label of self-defeating personality disorder because the label applied primarily to women who were said to make destructive life choices, such as staying in abusive relationships (Japenga, 1994). This label was dropped from the DSM-IV because it suggested that women were choosing bad relationships, which wasn't true (P. Caplan, 1994).

Despite these advances, labeling continues to be a serious problem. For instance, 68% of Americans don't want someone with a mental illness marrying into their family and 58% don't want people with mental illness at their workplace (J. K. Martin et al., 2000). Also, even though mental illness does not increase the chance of someone being violent, many Americans still believe that people with mental illness tend to behave in violent ways (Elbogen & Johnson, 2009).

Japan has a special problem with labels: Mental disorder labels have very negative connotations, which discourages Japanese from seeking professional help for mental disorders. One result is that, compared to the United States, Japan has a very high rate of suicide. That's because one risk for suicide is depression, a label the Japanese avoid and thus they do not get timely treatment. In comparison, in the United States, the label of depression is widely accepted, so people are more likely to be treated, even by doctors in general practice (Menchetti et al., 2009).

These examples illustrate the social and political implications of labeling individuals with mental disorders.

Frequency of Mental Disorders

Although labels are a fact of life, researchers and clinicians try to apply the DSM labels as fairly as possible. Researchers interviewed a national sample of 9,282 noninstitutionalized civilians aged 18 and older and diagnosed their problems using the DSM's diagnostic system. As the graph at the right shows, based on those surveyed, 51% of people will develop at least one disorder during their lifetime (Kessler et al., 2005). Other research confirms this statistic and finds that 25% of the population meets the criteria for a mental disorder in any given year (Kessler & Wang, 2008). The most common mental disorder is anxiety, followed by mood disorders and substance abuse, especially problems with alcohol.

Because mental illness affects so many people, psychologist E. Jane Costello (2012) advocates for destigmatizing mental illness and states, "We shouldn't be surprised that the brain has problems, just like the rest of the body."

Next, we'll examine the symptoms and treatment of specific disorders, beginning with anxiety. ●

Percentage Who Will Have a Mental Disorder in Their Lifetime	
Any disorder	51%
Anxiety disorders	32%
Mood disorders	28%
Alcohol use disorders	15%
Drug use disorders	9%

D Anxiety Disorders

How common is anxiety? The most common mental disorder reported by adults in the United States is any kind of anxiety disorder (Kessler et al., 2005). We have already discussed two serious anxiety problems: panic disorder (p. 481) and posttraumatic stress disorder (PTSD) (p. 491). Here we'll review panic disorder and PTSD, as well as discuss other common forms of anxiety: generalized anxiety disorder, three kinds of phobias, and obsessive-compulsive disorder.

Generalized Anxiety Disorder

During his initial therapy interview, Fred (pictured below) was sweating, fidgeting in his chair, and repeatedly asking for water to quench a never-ending thirst. From all indications, Fred was visibly distressed and extremely nervous. At first, Fred spoke only of his dizziness and problems with sleeping. However, it soon became clear that he had nearly always felt tense. He admitted to a long history of difficulties in interacting with others, difficulties that led to his being fired from two jobs. He constantly worried about all kinds of possible disasters that might happen to him (Davison & Neale, 1990). Fred's symptoms showed that he was suffering from generalized anxiety disorder.

Generalized anxiety disorder (GAD) is characterized by excessive or unrealistic worry about almost everything or feeling that something bad is about to happen. These anxious feelings occur on a majority of days for a period of at least six months (American Psychiatric Association, 2000).

About 5% of adults are reported to have GAD, but almost twice as many adult women (6.6%) report GAD as do men (3.6%) (Halbreich, 2003).

> I worry about everything and think something bad is about to happen.

Symptoms

Generalized anxiety disorder includes both psychological and physical symptoms. Psychological symptoms include being irritable, having difficulty concentrating, and being unable to control one's worry, which is out of proportion to the actual event. Constant worrying causes significant distress or impaired functioning in social, occupational, and other areas. Physical symptoms include restlessness, fatigue, sweating, flushing, pounding heart, insomnia, headaches, and muscle tension or aches (American Psychiatric Association, 2000).

Treatment

Generalized anxiety disorder is commonly treated with psychotherapy (see Module 24), with or without drugs. The drugs most frequently prescribed are tranquilizers such as alprazolam and diazepam, which belong to a group known as the ***benzodiazepines*** *(ben-zoh-die-AS-ah-peens)*. One of the limitations of these drugs is that at high doses they are addicting and interfere with the ability to remember newly learned information (Arkowitz & Lilienfeld, 2007a; Rupprecht et al., 2009). Antidepressant drugs are also used to treat GAD and have fewer side effects and a lower risk of addiction (Holmes & Newman, 2006).

Researchers found that about 40–50% of clients treated for generalized anxiety disorder with either psychotherapy (cognitive-behavioral) or drugs (tranquilizers) were free of symptoms six months to one year later (Arntz, 2003; Holmes & Newman, 2006).

Panic Disorder

One afternoon, Luisa (pictured below), a college student, was walking on campus and she suddenly felt her heart rate rapidly accelerate, her throat tighten up, and her arms and legs tremble. She became so nauseous she almost vomited. Luisa felt she had no control over what was happening. Then, weeks later, while at the movies, she had another episode during which she experienced dizziness, chest pain, shortness of breath, and weakness in her legs and feet. She feared she was having a heart attack and might die, but her doctors found no medical problem (Di Salvo, 2006). Luisa's symptoms indicate that she had a panic disorder.

Panic disorder is characterized by recurrent and unexpected panic attacks (described below). The person becomes so worried about having another panic attack that this intense worrying interferes with normal psychological functioning (American Psychiatric Association, 2000).

> I'm constantly worried about having another panic attack.

Like Luisa, about 1–4% of adults in the United States suffer from panic disorder, and women are two to three times more likely to report it than are men (Halbreich, 2003; Valentiner & Fergus, 2012). Panic disorder typically develops during late adolescence or early adulthood (McClure-Tone & Pine, 2009). People who suffer from panic disorder have an increased risk of alcohol and other drug abuse, depression, decreased social functioning, and less marital happiness.

Symptoms

Luisa's symptoms on campus and at the movies indicate that she was having a panic attack, which may occur in several different anxiety disorders but is the essential feature of panic disorder.

A **panic attack** is a period of intense fear or discomfort in which four or more of the following symptoms are present: pounding heart, sweating, trembling, shortness of breath, feelings of choking, chest pain, nausea, feeling dizzy, and fear of losing control or dying (American Psychiatric Association, 2000).

Treatment

Panic disorders are usually treated with drugs—benzodiazepines, antidepressants (Prozac-like drugs, which are selective serotonin reuptake inhibitors, or SSRIs)—and/or psychotherapy. Research indicates that psychotherapy is at least as effective as drug therapy and that drug therapy alone increases the risk of clients relapsing after treatment ends (Smits et al., 2006). Researchers found that, one year after treatment with a combination of psychotherapy and drugs, about 30–50% of clients were symptom-free (Page, 2002).

Another kind of anxiety disorder that is relatively common involves different kinds of phobias.

Phobias

Can fear go wild?

When common fears of seeing blood, spiders, or mice, having injections, meeting new people, speaking in public, flying, or being in small places turn into very intense fears, they are called phobias (over 500 phobias are listed on www.phobialist.com).

A **phobia** (*FOE-bee-ah*) is an anxiety disorder characterized by an intense and irrational fear that is out of proportion to the possible danger of the object or situation. Because of this intense fear, which is accompanied by increased physiological arousal, a person goes to great lengths to avoid the feared event. If the feared event cannot be avoided, the person feels intense anxiety.

Researchers report that because many individuals with phobias trace their onset to specific traumatic events, phobias are learned through conditioning or observing a person showing fear of something. Research also points to genetic and environmental causes of phobias. Thus, different pathways may lead to people developing phobias (Rowa et al., 2006).

We discussed fear of blood and needles earlier (pp. 195, 201, 493). Here we'll discuss three common phobias—social phobias, specific phobias, and agoraphobia.

Social Phobias

Why didn't Billy speak up in class?

In junior high school, Billy never, never spoke up in class or answered any questions. The school counselor said that Billy would be sick to his stomach the whole day if he knew that he was going to be called on. Billy began to hide out in the restrooms to avoid going to class. Billy's fear of speaking up in class is an example of a social phobia (Durand & Barlow, 2013).

Social phobias are characterized by irrational, marked, and continuous fear of performing in social situations. The individuals fear that they will humiliate or embarrass themselves (American Psychiatric Association, 2000).

As a fearful social situation approaches, anxiety builds up and may result in considerable bodily distress, such as nausea, sweating, and other signs of heightened physiological arousal. Although a person with a social phobia realizes that the fear is excessive or irrational, he or she may not know how to deal with it, other than by avoiding the situation.

Specific Phobias

Why was Rod afraid of needles?

Earlier in this book (p. 195), we told you about Rod's intense fear of needles, which dates back to his childhood. Because Rod has an excessive fear of a particular object (needles), he has a specific phobia.

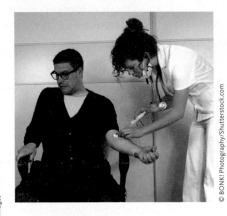

Specific phobias, formerly called simple phobias, are characterized by marked and persistent fears that are unreasonable and triggered by anticipation of, or exposure to, a specific object or situation (flying, heights, spiders, seeing blood) (American Psychiatric Association, 2000).

Among the more common specific phobias seen in clinical practice are fear of animals (zoophobia), fear of heights (acrophobia), fear of confinement (claustrophobia), fear of injury, and fear of flying (Durand & Barlow, 2013).

The content and occurrence of specific phobias vary with culture. For example, fears of spirits or ghosts are present in many cultures but become specific phobias only if the fear turns excessive and irrational (American Psychiatric Association, 2000).

Agoraphobia

Why couldn't Rose leave her house?

Fear trapped Rose in her house for years. If she thought about going outside to do her shopping, pain raced through her arms and chest. She grew hot and perspired. Her heart beat rapidly and her legs felt like rubber. She said that thinking about leaving her house caused stark terror, sometimes lasting for days. This 39-year-old mother of two is one of millions of Americans suffering from an intense fear of being in public places, which is called agoraphobia (*Los Angeles Times,* October 19, 1980).

Agoraphobia is characterized by anxiety about being in places or situations from which escape might be difficult or embarrassing if a panic attack or panic-like symptoms (sudden dizziness or onset of diarrhea) were to occur (American Psychiatric Association, 2000).

Agoraphobia arises out of an underlying fear of either having a full-blown panic attack or having a sudden and unexpected onset of paniclike symptoms.

Common places or situations that may evoke worry about having a panic attack include public transportation, tunnels or bridges, and crowds.

After any of these phobias are established, they are extremely persistent and may continue for years if not treated (M. E. Coles & Horng, 2006). We'll discuss drug and psychological treatments for phobias later in this module—in the Application section.

Next, we'll look at another form of anxiety that can be very difficult to deal with—obsessive-compulsive disorder.

Obsessive-Compulsive Disorder

Comedian and television celebrity Howie Mandel lives a life of relentless anxiety. If he shakes hands with someone, he becomes so concerned with germ contamination that he repeatedly washes his hands with almost scalding hot water while aggressively rubbing them together. Then, despite trying to move on with his day, he needs to return to repeat the process again and again. Howie is not free of this anxiety even in his home. He admits to wearing a mask and rubber gloves to avoid germ contamination from his family. Howie has also engaged in repetitive checking of doors to make sure they are locked, which may involve him getting into and out of his car more than ten times just to be sure. He recounts one time he finally made himself punch the door so that the lingering physical pain would remind him that he had checked the door enough times (Mandel, 2009).

Why doesn't Howie shake hands?

To describe the workings of his mind, Howie says, "I have uncontrollable, repetitive thoughts that just won't go away, regardless of how illogical or unreasonable they might be" (Mandel, 2009, p. 19). Howie's symptoms are consistent with obsessive-compulsive disorder.

Obsessive-compulsive disorder (OCD) consists of obsessions, which are persistent, recurring irrational thoughts, impulses, or images that a person is unable to control and that interfere with normal functioning, and compulsions, which are irresistible impulses to perform over and over some senseless behavior or ritual (hand washing, checking things, counting, putting things in order) (American Psychiatric Association, 2000).

Washing hands over and over again with nearly scalding hot water is a sign of OCD.

Many of us may have obsessions or compulsions but do not meet the criteria for OCD. For example, about 17% of adults with no mental disorder have an obsession or compulsion, yet only about 3% of adults meet the criteria for OCD (Fullana et al., 2009; Riggs & Foa, 2006).

Howie's symptoms include both obsessions—need to be very clean and need to make sure doors are locked—and compulsions—need to wash hands repeatedly and to check doors repeatedly. Some individuals have obsessions (irrational, recurring thoughts) without compulsions. Because compulsions are usually very time-consuming, they often take an hour or more to complete each day. Common compulsions involve cleaning, checking, and counting; the less common include buying, hoarding, and putting things in order. These kinds of obsessive-compulsive behaviors interfere with normal functioning and make holding a job or engaging in social interactions difficult. OCD can be a chronic problem that requires treatment with drugs, psychotherapy, or some combination (Riggs & Foa, 2006).

Treatment

About half of patients with OCD report improvement after being treated with drugs or exposure therapy (Franklin et al., 2002).

Exposure therapy involves gradually exposing the person to the actual anxiety-producing situations or objects that he or she is attempting to avoid and continuing the exposure treatments until the anxiety decreases.

For example, a client like Howie with OCD could be exposed over and over to his feared objects, such as germs, until such exposures elicit little or no anxiety (left photo).

Treatment for OCD may involve exposure therapy.

Clients who cannot tolerate or are not motivated to undergo exposure therapy may be given antidepressant drugs. However, about one-third of clients with OCD are not helped by antidepressants (Riggs & Foa, 2006).

A new, last resort treatment for OCD is deep brain stimulation (see p. 61) (DeNoon, 2009b; Talan, 2009).

Next, we'll describe how a threatening event can lead to posttraumatic stress disorder.

Posttraumatic Stress Disorder

Mark was driving home from work when a huge truck unexpectedly lost control and rammed his car. Mark had no way to escape the traumatic accident. Though he needed hospital treatment, he was lucky to walk away alive. However, since the accident Mark has become so fearful of driving that he works from home. He still experiences troublesome, recurring memories of the event and frequently has terrifying nightmares about being in a car accident. Mark's symptoms would be diagnosed as indicative of posttraumatic stress disorder.

Posttraumatic stress disorder, or PTSD, is a disabling condition that results from personally experiencing an event that involves actual or threatened death or serious injury or from witnessing or hearing of such an event happening to a family member or close friend. People suffering from PTSD experience a number of psychological symptoms, including recurring and disturbing memories, terrible nightmares, and intense fear and anxiety (American Psychiatric Association, 2000).

These horrible memories and feelings of fear keep stress levels high and result in a range of psychosomatic symptoms, including sleep problems, pounding heart, and stomach problems (Marshall et al., 2006; Schnurr et al., 2002).

Treatment

Treatment may involve drugs, but cognitive-behavioral therapy (see p. 568) or exposure therapy is more effective in the long term. The combined treatment of cognitive-behavioral therapy or exposure therapy with drugs is the most effective approach (Bolton et al., 2004; Welberg, 2012). In brief, cognitive-behavioral therapy helps change negative thinking and maladaptive behaviors by helping people learn new skills to improve their functioning (M.J. Friedman et al., 2010; Resick et al., 2008).

Next, we will discuss a set of disorders that involve anxiety about one's physical health, which can actually result in real physical symptoms with no medical cause. ●

E Somatoform Disorders

Definition and Examples

Imagine someone whose whole life centers around physical symptoms, some that are imagined and others that appear real, such as developing paralysis in one's legs. This intense focus on imagined, painful, or uncomfortable physical symptoms is characteristic of individuals with somatoform disorders.

Somatoform (*so-MA-tuh-form*) **disorders** are marked by a pattern of recurring, multiple, and significant bodily (somatic) symptoms that extend over several years. The bodily symptoms (pain, vomiting, paralysis, blindness) are not under voluntary control, have no known physical causes, and are believed to be caused by psychological factors (American Psychiatric Association, 2000).

Although not easily diagnosed, somatoform disorders are among the most common health problems seen in general medical practice (Wise & Birket-Smith, 2002). The DSM-IV-TR lists seven kinds of somatoform disorders. We'll discuss two of the more common forms—somatization and conversion disorders.

> All tests are negative.

> I have a lot of symptoms.

A psychologically distressed individual may have painful physical symptoms that have no physical causes.

Somatization Disorder

One kind of somatoform disorder, which was historically called hysteria, is now called somatization disorder and is relatively rare (2.7% of the population).

Somatization disorder begins before age 30, lasts several years, and is characterized by multiple symptoms—including pain, gastrointestinal, sexual, and neurological symptoms—that have no physical causes but are triggered by psychological problems or distress (American Psychiatric Association, 2000).

This disorder is especially common among women (P. Fink et al., 2004). Those who have somatization disorder use health services frequently and have twice the annual medical care costs of people without somatization disorder (Barsky et al., 2005). Many people with somatization disorder are raised in emotionally cold and unsupportive family environments and are often victims of emotional or physical abuse (R. J. Brown et al., 2005). Somatization disorders may be a means of coping with a stressful situation or obtaining attention (Durand & Barlow, 2013).

Conversion Disorder

Some people report serious physical problems, such as blindness, that have no physical causes and are examples of conversion disorder, a type of somatoform disorder.

A **conversion disorder** refers to changing anxiety or emotional distress into real physical, motor, sensory, or neurological symptoms (headaches, nausea, dizziness, loss of sensation, paralysis) for which no physical or organic cause can be identified (American Psychiatric Association, 2000).

Usually the symptoms of a conversion disorder are associated with psychological factors, such as depression, concerns about health, or the occurrence of a stressful situation. Recent research examining the brains of people with medically unexplainable paralysis has shown that when patients try to move their paralyzed limbs, the emotional areas of the brain are activated inappropriately and may inhibit the functioning of the motor cortex, leaving the patients unable to move their paralyzed limbs (Kinetz, 2006). The development of such physical symptoms gets the person attention, removes the person from threatening or anxiety-producing situations, and thus reinforces the occurrence and maintenance of the symptoms involved in the conversion disorder (Durand & Barlow, 2013). Researchers found that in some cultures, bodily complaints (somatoform disorders) are used instead of emotional complaints to express psychological problems (Lewis-Fernandez et al., 2005).

The same kind of painful or uncomfortable physical symptoms observed in somatoform disorders are observed in individuals suffering from mass hysteria.

Mass Hysteria

More than 20 high school girls in rural Upstate New York experienced a sudden onset of spasms, tics, and seizures. It started with one girl, then over a short period of time escalated to more than 20. Doctors ruled out medical disorders, diseases, and environmental factors. These girls had very real physical symptoms, yet no identifiable physical causes (Dominus, 2012; Hass, 2012; Jayson, 2012). Essentially each of these girls had a conversion disorder, but when conversion disorders occur in a large group, the condition is known as mass hysteria.

Mass hysteria is a condition experienced by a group of people who, through suggestion, observation, or other psychological processes, develop similar fears, delusions, abnormal behaviors, or physical symptoms.

Outbreaks of mass hysteria are uncommon and most involve teenage girls. Typically, one person develops the symptoms and spreads them to people he or she knows. One thing all of the teenage girls in Upstate New York had in common was some kind of precipitating stress in their lives, such as divorcing parents or other upsetting situations (Associated Press, 2012a).

Similar cases of mass hysteria have been identified in the recent past. For example, 50 teenage girls in Vietnam were hospitalized due to sudden fainting after watching one girl collapse and be carried away by medical personnel (IANS, 2006). Also, 600 girls suffered fever, nausea, and buckling knees at a boarding school in Mexico (Associated Press, 2012a).

Individuals who are emotionally aroused in a group may experience similar physical symptoms.

In the Middle Ages, hysteria was attributed to possession by evil spirits or the devil. Today, mass hysteria is known to involve members of a group who experience and share emotional arousal or excitement, which spreads through the group and results in its members developing *real physical symptoms* with no known physical causes (Durand & Barlow, 2013). Mass hysteria is another example of somatoform disorders.

After the Concept Review, we'll discuss how symptoms of mental disorders can vary among cultures, as we examine an anxiety disorder that seems to be unique to Asian cultures. ●

1. A prolonged or recurring problem that seriously interferes with the ability of an individual to live a satisfying personal life and function in society is called a _____.

2. Mental disorders arise from the interaction of a number of factors. Biological factors include inherited behavioral tendencies, which are called **(a)** _____ factors. These factors contribute 30–60% to the development of mental disorders. Biological factors also include the overreaction of brain structures to certain stimuli, which are called **(b)** _____ factors. Other factors that contribute to the development of mental disorders, such as having deficits or problems in thinking, reacting inappropriately to emotional stimuli, lacking social skills, and being in or seeing a traumatic event, are called **(c)** _____ factors.

© AP Images/Lou Krasky

3. There are three definitions of abnormality. A behavior that occurs infrequently in the general population is abnormal according to the **(a)** _____ definition. A behavior that deviates greatly from accepted social norms is abnormal according to the **(b)** _____ definition. Behavior that interferes with the individual's ability to function as a person or in society is abnormal according to the **(c)** _____ definition, which is used by most mental health professionals.

© San Diego Union Tribune/ZUMA Press

4. When performed by a mental health professional, a systematic evaluation of an individual's various psychological, biological, and social factors that may be contributing to his or her problem is called a clinical **(a)** _____. A mental health professional who determines whether an individual's specific problem meets or matches the standard symptoms that define a particular mental disorder is doing a clinical **(b)** _____. One of the primary techniques used to gather an enormous amount of information about a person's past behavior, attitudes, and emotions and details of current problems is the clinical **(c)** _____.

5. The manual that describes the symptoms for almost 300 different mental disorders is called the **(a)** _____. The manual's primary goal is to provide mental health professionals with a means of **(b)** _____ mental disorders and **(c)** _____ that information in a systematic and uniform way. The DSM-IV-TR has five major dimensions, called **(d)** _____, that serve as guidelines for making decisions about symptoms.

Number of Disorders	
DSM-I	106
DSM-II	182
DSM-III	265
DSM-IV-TR	297

© Ilolab/Shutterstock.com

6. There are several kinds of anxiety disorders. An anxiety disorder that is characterized by excessive and/or unrealistic worry or feelings of general apprehension about events or activities, when those feelings occur on a majority of days for a period of at least six months, is called **(a)** _____ disorder. An anxiety disorder marked by the presence of recurrent and unexpected panic attacks, plus continued worry about having another panic attack, when such worry interferes with psychological functioning, is called a **(b)** _____ disorder. Suppose a person has a period of intense fear or discomfort during which four or more of the following symptoms are present: pounding heart, sweating, trembling, shortness of breath, feelings of choking, chest pain, nausea, feeling dizzy, and fear of losing control or dying. That person is experiencing a **(c)** _____.

© 3ONKI Photography/Shutterstock.com

7. An anxiety disorder characterized by an intense and irrational fear and heightened physiological arousal that is out of proportion to the danger elicited by the object or situation is called a **(a)** _____, of which there are several kinds. Unreasonable, marked, and persistent fears that are triggered by anticipation of, or exposure to, a specific object or situation are called a **(b)** _____. An anxiety that comes from being in places or situations from which escape might be difficult or embarrassing if a panic attack or paniclike symptoms were to occur is called **(c)** _____. Irrational, marked, and continuous fear of performing in social situations and feeling humiliated or embarrassed is called a **(d)** _____.

© Jo unruh/iStockphoto

8. A disorder that consists of persistent, recurring irrational thoughts, impulses, or images that a person is unable to control and irresistible impulses to perform over and over some senseless behavior or ritual is called **(a)** _____ disorder. A nondrug treatment for this disorder, which consists of gradually exposing the person to the real anxiety-producing situations or objects that he or she is attempting to avoid, is called **(b)** _____ therapy.

© iStockphoto/Thinkstock

9. When something happens to a group of people so that all share the same fears or delusions or develop similar physical symptoms, it is called **(a)** _____. There is a disorder that involves a pattern of recurring, multiple, and significant bodily complaints that have no known physical causes. This is called **(b)** _____ disorder, and one of its more common forms is somatization disorder.

Taijin Kyofusho, or TKS

Anxiety is a worldwide concern and is a common mental disorder in the United States and several Asian nations, notably Japan. The symptoms of one kind of anxiety disorder, somatoform disorder, occur in very similar form in many cultures around the world (Lewis-Fernandez et al., 2005). However, it's also true that the unique cultural values of some countries, such as Japan, can result in the development of a unique anxiety disorder not found in Western cultures such as the United States.

Can a culture create a disorder?

If you had a **social phobia** in the United States, it would usually mean that you had a great fear or were greatly embarrassed about behaving or performing in social situations, such as making a public speech. But if you had a social phobia in several Asian cultures, especially Japan and somewhat in Korea, it might mean that you had a very different kind of fear or embarrassment, called taijin kyofusho, or TKS (Tarumi et al., 2004).

Taijin kyofusho *(tai-jin kyo-foo-show)*, or TKS, is a kind of social phobia characterized by a terrible fear of offending others through awkward social or physical behavior, such as staring, blushing, giving off an offensive odor, having an unpleasant facial expression, or having trembling hands (Dinnel et al., 2002).

Although many Westerners are also concerned or embarrassed about offending others through staring, having offensive body odors, or blushing, TKS is different in that it is an intense, irrational, morbid fear—in other words, a true phobia. Also, TKS is characterized more by fear of offending others than fear of embarrassing oneself. In desperately trying to avoid TKS symptoms, Asians may try to avoid social interactions altogether. The Japanese word *taijin-kyofu* literally means "fear of people or interpersonal relations" (D. J. Stein, 2009).

In Japan, the fear of offending others (by staring) is considered a kind of social phobia.

Occurrence. TKS is the third most common psychiatric disorder treated in Japanese college students. Its occurrence among Japanese college students is estimated at 8–19% (Kirmayer, 1991; Takahashi, 1989). TKS is more common in males than in females (D. J. Stein, 2009). Most patients have a primary symptom, such as fear of blushing or fear of making eye contact or staring (Yamashita, 1993). In comparison, making eye contact is very common in Western cultures; if you do not make eye contact in social interactions, you may be judged as being shy or lacking in social skills.

TKS begins around adolescence, when interpersonal interactions play a big role in one's life. TKS is rarely seen after the late twenties because, by then, individuals have learned the proper social behaviors. TKS seems to develop from certain cultural influences that are unique to Japan.

Cultural values. The Japanese culture places great emphasis on the appropriate way to conduct oneself in public, which means a person should avoid making direct eye contact, staring, blushing, having trembling hands, or giving off offensive odors. To emphasize the importance of avoiding these improper behaviors, mothers often use threats of abandonment, ridicule, and embarrassment as punishment. Through this process of socialization, the child is made aware of the importance of avoiding improper public behaviors, which result in a loss of face and reflect badly on the person's family and social group. Thus, from early on, Japanese children are strongly encouraged to live up to certain cultural expectations about avoiding improper public behaviors, especially staring and blushing, which are considered to be rude and disgraceful.

Social Customs

In Japan, individuals are expected to know the needs and thoughts of others by reading the emotional expressions of faces rather than asking direct questions, which is considered rude social behavior. In contrast, Westerners may ask direct questions to clarify some point and often use direct eye contact to show interest. Individuals in Japan who make too much eye contact or ask direct questions are likely to be viewed as insensitive to others, unpleasantly bold, or aggressive. In fact, Japanese children are taught to fix their gaze at the level of the neck of people they are talking to. This Japanese social custom that emphasizes not making eye contact, blushing, or having trembling hands or offensive body odors during social interactions results in about 20% of Japanese teenagers and young adults developing the intense, irrational fear called TKS. This social phobia is so common in Japan that there are special clinics devoted only to treating TKS. The Japanese TKS clinics are comparable in popularity to the numerous weight-loss clinics in the United States. Interestingly, TKS is a kind of social phobia that doesn't occur in Western cultures (Dinnel et al., 2002; Tarumi et al., 2004).

Cultural differences. Although people in many cultures report anxiety about behaving or performing in public, the particular fears that they report may depend on their own culture's values. For example, TKS is unique to Asian cultures and unknown in Western cultures. Japanese who are especially at risk for developing TKS are those who score low on independence and high on interdependence, two traits found in traditional Japanese cultural values (Dinnel et al., 2002). Clinicians emphasize the importance of taking cultural values, influences, and differences into account when diagnosing behaviors across cultures (S. G. Hofmann et al., 2010).

Next, we'll discuss a very serious problem in the U.S. culture: school shootings. ●

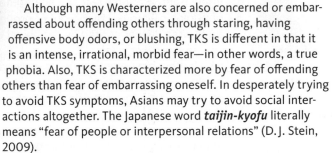

In Japan, it is very important to know and show the proper public behaviors.

© Tom Wang/Shutterstock.com

© elwynn/Shutterstock.com

G Research Focus: School Shootings

What Drove Teens to Kill Fellow Students and Teachers?

What is their problem? Sometimes researchers are faced with answering tragic questions, such as why teenagers took guns to schools and shot and killed at least 500 and wounded another 1,000. Everyone wonders what turns these teens into killers. In some cases, but not all, these adolescents might be diagnosed with conduct disorder.

Conduct disorder is a repetitive and persistent pattern of behaving that has been going on for at least a year and that violates the established social rules or the rights of others. Problems may include aggressive behaviors such as threatening to harm people, abusing or killing animals, destroying property, being deceitful, or stealing.

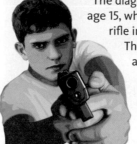

Adolescent school shooters may have conduct disorder.

The diagnosis of conduct disorder seems to apply to Kipland Kinkel, age 15, who was charged with firing 50 rounds from a semiautomatic rifle into the school cafeteria, killing 2 students and injuring 22. Those who knew him said that Kinkel had a violent temper and a history of behavioral problems, which included killing his cat by putting a firecracker in its mouth, blowing up a dead cow, stoning cars from a highway overpass, and making bombs (Witkin et al., 1998). In trying to answer the question Why did these adolescents shoot their fellow students and teachers? mental health professionals have primarily used the case study approach.

A **case study** is an in-depth analysis of the thoughts, feelings, beliefs, experiences, behaviors, and problems of a single individual.

We'll give brief case studies of two school shooters and then examine some factors that put a student at risk for becoming a shooter.

Case Studies

The first school shooting that received national attention occurred in Moses Lake, Washington, on February 2, 1996. On that date, Barry Loukaitis, 14, fired on his algebra class, killing three and wounding one. He said that he wanted to get back at a popular boy who had teased him. Loukaitis shot that boy dead. Since then, school shootings have continued at an alarming rate. Across the world, there have been at least 50 adolescents, mostly boys, who took guns to their schools, fired hundreds of shots, killed at least 500 teachers and students, and wounded about 1,000 more (IANSA, 2007).

One such shooter is 23-year-old college student Seung-Hui Cho (photo below), who in 2007 killed 32 people and wounded 25 others on the Virginia Tech campus, making it the deadliest school shooting in history. Cho was born in South Korea and immigrated to the United States when he was 8 years old. As a child, he was relentlessly teased and bullied for being shy and speaking with a strong accent. Consequently, he was isolated and developed anger toward his more "privileged" peers. He came to view himself as an avenger against those who humiliated him (White and affluent). He wanted to get even with the "rich brats" who had trust funds and drove Mercedes. In a disturbing message on the day of his shooting, he stated to the privileged, "You have never felt a single ounce of pain in your whole lives." At the end of his killing spree, Cho took his own life (Gibbs, 2007; Shute, 2007; E. Thomas, 2007).

Seung-Hui Cho committed the deadliest school shooting in history.

However, very, very few students who are picked on and bullied commit violent acts, such as shooting teachers and students. We'll examine some of the factors that put students at risk for committing violent acts.

Risks Shared by Adolescent School Shooters

Although there are differences among school shooters, researchers have identified a number of risk factors that these boys shared (FBI, 2001; Langman, 2009; R. Lee, 2005; Pollack, 2007; Robertz, 2007; Verlinden et al., 2000).

• Most of the boys (shooters) showed uncontrolled anger and depression, blaming others for problems and threatening violence. Most had poor coping skills, discipline problems at school or home, access to weapons, and a history of drug use.

• Half of the boys had been given little parental supervision, had troubled family relationships, and perceived themselves as receiving little support from their families. Most of the boys had recently experienced the breakup of a relationship, a stressful event, or loss of status.

• Most of the boys were generally isolated and rejected by their peers in school. Most had poor social skills and felt picked on, bullied, and persecuted and made friends who were also antisocial. The most commonly stated motives for shootings were to mete out justice to peers or adults who the teenage shooters believed had wronged them and to obtain status or importance among their peers. Most teenage shooters gave warning signs of their violent intentions that were not taken seriously.

Neurological factors. Although coming from a broken home, being bullied, and dealing with various life stressors are risk factors for adolescents committing violent acts, another important risk factor is inside an adolescent's brain. Everyone gets angry and has felt rage and the desire to get revenge, but most of us are able to control these violent impulses. This control involves the prefrontal cortex (p. 411), which has executive functions, such as planning, making decisions, and controlling strong emotional and violent impulses that arise from a very primitive part of the brain called the limbic system (p. 411) (right figure). The prefrontal cortex in the adolescent brain is still immature and may not

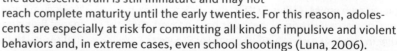

prefrontal cortex | limbic system

reach complete maturity until the early twenties. For this reason, adolescents are especially at risk for committing all kinds of impulsive and violent behaviors and, in extreme cases, even school shootings (Luna, 2006).

Gathering data about what motivates school shooters is an example of using the case study method. Next, we'll turn to explaining several ways of treating two relatively common anxiety disorders—social and specific phobias. •

Specific Phobia: Flying

About one in eight Americans are afraid to fly. The reasons for their fear include having been on a turbulent flight, hearing news of terrorist attacks, being afraid of enclosed spaces, fearing heights, and being unable to give up control, among others. People with a phobia of flying may not fly under any circumstance, may fly only when absolutely necessary, or may reluctantly fly and be anxious the entire time.

Christine is an example of someone who has an intense fear of flying, to the point of avoiding even looking at a plane. Simply seeing a plane flying in the sky could trigger a panic attack. Christine wasn't always afraid of flying; her fear developed suddenly at the age of 32 following what she recalls as a routine flight. Some

A fear of flying is an example of a specific phobia.

people, such as Christine, develop an overwhelming fear of flying without experiencing a worrisome flying event. Christine's fear developed soon after having two young children. Perhaps she became fixated on the idea that flying is dangerous and that she is not immortal.

Most phobias do not disappear without some treatment. Finally, after years of not flying, Christine joined a treatment clinic that helps people overcome their fears of flying (adapted from M. Miller, 2003). Treatment for phobias can involve psychotherapy or drugs, or some combination of them. We'll discuss psychotherapy and drug treatment, beginning with cognitive-behavioral and exposure therapy.

Cognitive-Behavioral Therapy

Christine's phobia of flying involves fearful and irrational thoughts, which in turn cause increased physiological arousal. She can learn to reduce her irrational and fearful thoughts and reduce her arousal through cognitive- behavioral therapy (J. S. Beck, 2011).

Cognitive-behavioral therapy involves using a combination of two methods: changing negative, unhealthy, or distorted thoughts and beliefs by substituting positive, healthy, and realistic ones; and changing limiting or disruptive behaviors by learning and practicing new skills to improve functioning.

Thoughts. Cognitive-behavioral therapy is useful in helping Christine control her fearful thoughts and eliminate dangerous beliefs about flying. For example, Christine believed that an airplane doesn't fly on anything; that it's just suspended in the sky. But in treatment she learned that an airplane flies on air, similar to how a boat rides on water. Thus, when a plane hits turbulence, Christine could think "water, water, water" to remind herself that the plane is being supported by air.

Behaviors. Because Christine automatically gets nervous and fearful when just thinking about flying, she is instructed to do breathing exercises that will help her calm down. Deep and rhythmic breathing is an effective calming exercise because it distracts Christine from her fears and focuses her attention on a pleasant activity. Deep breathing helps to control (relax) her body's fight-flight response, thereby reducing physiological arousal (adapted from M. Miller, 2003).

Cognitive-behavioral methods have proved effective in treating a variety of phobias (A. R. Singer & Dobson, 2006). Sometimes cognitive-behavioral therapy is combined with another kind of therapy, called exposure therapy.

Exposure Therapy

For treating phobias, cognitive-behavioral therapy is often combined with exposure therapy. The most difficult part of Christine's phobia treatment is exposure therapy, when she must actually confront her most feared situation.

Exposure therapy consists of gradually exposing the person to the real anxiety-producing situations or objects that he or she is attempting to avoid and continuing exposure treatments until the anxiety decreases.

The first part of Christine's treatment involved cognitive-behavioral therapy, in which she learned how to control her irrational thoughts and acquire some basic relaxation techniques. The second part of her treatment involves exposure therapy, in which she is required to fly on an airplane, meaning that she will be exposed to her most feared situation. To help Christine deal with her fear of flying, she is instructed to begin relaxation exercises (deep and rhythmic breathing) and to substitute positive, healthy thoughts for negative, fearful ones. After completing the treatment program, Christine has become comfortable flying and can now travel across the country to visit her family (adapted from M. Miller, 2003).

It is important to continue exposure therapy until the person's anxiety decreases.

Programs that treat specific phobias, such as fear of flying, often use some combination of cognitive-behavioral and exposure therapy, which significantly reduces fear in a majority of clients (R. A. Friedman, 2006; M. Miller, 2003).

Clients who are not helped by cognitive-behavioral or exposure therapy may be given drug therapy (see next page), or they may try virtual reality therapy.

Virtual reality therapy. Although clients never leave the ground, they sit in real airplane seats that vibrate to the sound of airplane engines. Clients wear head-mounted displays that surround them with 3-D experiences of "taking off" and "flying." Everything appears so real that clients who have a fear of flying begin to sweat and their hearts pound just as on real flights. Virtual reality therapy is a kind of exposure therapy, and it can be combined with relaxation exercises and thought substitution and be used to treat a variety of specific phobias, including fear of flying (Parsons & Rizzo, 2008; Rothbaum et al., 2006).

Social Phobia: Public Speaking

When does a fear become a phobia?

Just as specific phobias can be successfully treated with psychotherapy, so too can social phobias, such as fear of public speaking. Almost everyone is somewhat anxious about getting up and speaking in public. For a fear to become a full-blown phobia, however, the fear must be intense, irrational, and out of proportion to the object or situation. For example, individuals with social phobias have such intense, excessive, and irrational fears of doing something humiliating or embarrassing that they will go to almost any lengths to avoid speaking in public. There are a number of very effective nondrug programs for treating social phobias (fear of speaking, performing, or acting in public). These programs combine cognitive-behavioral and exposure therapies and usually include the following four components (M. E. Coles & Horng, 2006).

1 **Explain.** Clinicians *explain* to the person that, since the fears involved in social phobias are usually learned, there are also methods to unlearn or extinguish such fears. The person is told how both thoughts and physiological arousal can exaggerate the phobic feelings and make the person go to any lengths to avoid the feared situation.

2 **Learn and substitute.** Clinicians found that some individuals needed to *learn* new social skills (initiating a conversation, writing a speech) so that they could function better in social situations. In addition, individuals were told to record their thoughts immediately after thinking about being in a feared situation. Then they were shown how to *substitute* positive and healthy thoughts for negative and fearful ones.

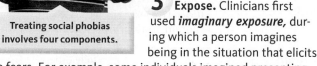

Treating social phobias involves four components.

3 **Expose.** Clinicians first used *imaginary exposure,* during which a person imagines being in the situation that elicits the fears. For example, some individuals imagined presenting material to their co-workers, making a classroom presentation, or initiating a conversation with a member of the opposite sex. After imaginary exposure, clinicians used *real (in vivo) exposure,* in which the person gives his or her speech in front of a group of people or initiates conversations with strangers.

4 **Practice.** Clinicians asked their clients to *practice* homework assignments. For instance, individuals were asked to imagine themselves in feared situations and then to eliminate negative thoughts by substituting positive ones. In addition, individuals were instructed to gradually expose themselves to making longer and longer public presentations or having conversations with members of the opposite sex.

Researchers report that programs similar to the one described above resulted in reduced social fears in about 56% of those who completed the program (Lincoln et al., 2003).

Drug Treatment of Phobias

How effective are drugs?

Imagine being told to walk into a room and meet a group of strangers while you are stark naked. For most of us, this idea would cause such embarrassment, fear, and anxiety that we would absolutely refuse. This imagined situation is similar to the terrible negative emotions that individuals with social phobia feel when they must initiate a conversation, meet strangers, or give a public presentation. As we have discussed, social phobias can be treated with cognitive-behavioral and exposure therapy. However, some individuals with social phobia do not choose to or are too fearful to complete a therapy program that includes exposure to the feared situation. Instead, these individuals may choose drug therapy, which may involve tranquilizers (benzodiazepines) or the increasingly prescribed antidepressants (Blanco et al., 2003; M. E. Coles & Horng, 2006).

Drug therapy for phobias involves tranquilizers or antidepressants.

The graphs below show the results of a double-blind study in which individuals with social phobia were given either a placebo or an antidepressant, in this case sertraline (Zoloft). After 20 weeks of treatment, individuals given antidepressants showed a significant clinical reduction in scores on both anxiety and fear tests, which means they were able to function relatively well in social situations (Van Ameringen et al., 2001). Although 34% of those on antidepressants showed a significant decrease in social anxiety, a remarkable 18% of those given placebos (sugar pills) showed a similar decrease. This means that the significant decrease in the social fears of almost one out of five individuals resulted from purely psychological factors, such as a client's expectations and beliefs ("The pill is powerful medicine and will reduce my fear").

Average Score on Fear Scale: Drug reduced fear more than placebo

Placebo	16
Drug	13

Average Score on Fear Scale: Drug reduced avoidance more than placebo

Placebo	16
Drug	13

Although drug treatments are effective in reducing social phobias, there are two potential problems. First, about 50–75% of individuals relapse when drugs are discontinued, which means that their original intense social phobic symptoms return. Second, long-term maintenance on drugs can result in tolerance and increases in dosage, which, in turn, can result in serious side effects, such as loss of memory (S. M. Stahl, 2000, 2002). Compared to drug treatment of phobias, psychotherapy programs have the advantages of no problems with tolerance and no unwanted physical side effects.

Which treatment to choose? Whether a client chooses psychotherapy or drug treatment for phobias depends to a large extent on the individual client's preference. That's because drug treatment (tranquilizers or antidepressants) and cognitive-behavioral or exposure therapy are about equally effective in the treatment of different phobias, including specific phobias, social phobias, and agoraphobia (Liebowitz et al., 1999). ●

Why Women Marry Killers behind Bars

In 2004, Scott Peterson was convicted of murdering his wife and unborn child. Within an hour of being on Death Row, he received a marriage proposal from a woman he didn't even know. As if this proposal wasn't bizarre enough, on Scott's first day at San Quentin State Prison, the warden's office received calls from over 30 women desperate to make contact with the convicted killer, many of them believing they were in love with Peterson.

1 How would clinicians decide whether women who fall in love with killers have a mental disorder?

About a decade earlier, Doreen Lioy, a 41-year-old woman, fell in love with satanic serial killer Richard Ramirez, who was convicted of torturing, sexually abusing, and murdering 13 people. Lioy described her attraction to Ramirez beginning immediately upon seeing his mug shot on TV: "I saw something in his eyes. Something that captivated me" (Warrick, 1996, E-1). Lioy began sending Ramirez letters and visiting him behind bars, and soon after they married at the prison, even though Ramirez would eventually be executed. Lioy speaks about her complete devotion to her new husband: "Because of my love for Richard,

2 Do women who almost instantly fall in love with prisoners they have never met have obsessive-compulsive disorder?

3 According to the three definitions of abnormal behavior, is Doreen Lioy abnormal?

I have given up my family, home, employment, and friends" (Warrick, 1996, E-1).

There is such a demand for prisoner romance that matchmaking websites, such as prisonpenpals.com, offer thousands of ads from inmates who want to find love outside of their cellblocks. Marriages in prisons are common enough for each prison to have its own set of regulations for inmate marriages. Some of the rules for one California prison include: "No property will be exchanged and kept by inmate after the marriage ceremony. The marriage ceremony will be conducted in the visiting area with the glass separating the couple being married" (*Inmate marriages,* 2007).

4 According to Freud's psycho-dynamic theory of personality, why is it difficult to explain why women fall in love with and marry killers?

According to Sheila Isenberg, author of *Women Who Marry Men Who Kill,* women who pursue intimate relationships with killers are usually attractive, intelligent, and accomplished. Isenberg also says that most of these women have come from loveless homes and have been abused by men

5 Which of the five axes in the DSM-IV-TR best describes the problems these women share?

A woman fell in love with a convicted and jailed killer.

earlier in their lives. Gilda Carle, a relationship adviser, explains that these women are attracted to the "bad boy syndrome" and they feel special when the man who has hurt and killed others treats them with love, kindness, and respect. In fact, the most repugnant murderers receive the most attention from women.

Women in love with convicted killers find the danger, excitement, and drama of prison romance more arousing than the routine and predictability of romance outside prison. Having an intimate relationship with a man behind bars also makes the relationship exceptionally safe.

6 What are the advantages and disadvantages of labeling these women's problems?

Adapted from Fimrite & Taylor, 2005; *Inmate marriages,* 2007; Isenberg, 1992; Warrick, 1996, 1997; Wiltenburg, 2003

Summary Test

A Factors in Mental Disorders

1. A prolonged or recurring problem that seriously interferes with an individual's ability to live a satisfying personal life and function in society is a _____. This definition takes into account genetic, behavioral, cognitive, and environmental factors, all of which may contribute to a mental disorder.

2. Mental disorders arise from the interaction of a number of factors. Biological factors include inherited behavioral tendencies, which are called **(a)** _____ factors. These factors contribute 30–60% to the development of mental disorders. Biological factors also include the overreaction of brain structures to certain stimuli, which are called **(b)** _____ factors. Other factors that contribute to the development of mental disorders, such as having deficits or problems in thinking, reacting inappropriately to emotional stimuli, lacking social skills, and being in or seeing a traumatic event, are called **(c)** _____ factors.

3. If a behavior is considered abnormal because it occurs infrequently in the general population, we are using a definition based on **(a)** _____. If a behavior is considered abnormal because it deviates greatly from what's acceptable, we are using a definition based on **(b)** _____. If a behavior is considered abnormal because it interferes with an individual's ability to function as a person or in society, we are using a definition based on **(c)** _____.

B Assessing Mental Disorders

4. A systematic evaluation of an individual's various psychological, biological, and social factors that may be contributing to his or her problem is called a **(a)** _____. The primary method used in clinical assessments is to get information about a person's background, current behavior, attitudes, and emotions and also details of present problems through a **(b)** _____. A complete clinical assessment usually includes three major methods: **(c)** _____, _____, and _____.

5. Assessing mental disorders may be difficult because **(a)** _____ vary in intensity and complexity. The assessment must take into account past and present problems and current stressors. The accurate assessment of symptoms is important because it has significant implications for the kind of **(b)** _____ that the client will be given.

C Diagnosing Mental Disorders

6. When mental health professionals determine whether an individual's specific problem meets or matches the standard symptoms that define a particular mental disorder, they are making a **(a)** _____. In trying to reach an agreement on the clinical diagnosis, mental health professionals use a set of guidelines, developed by the American Psychiatric Association, called the **(b)** _____, abbreviated as DSM-IV-TR.

7. The DSM-IV-TR is a set of guidelines that uses five different dimensions or **(a)** _____ to diagnose mental disorders. The advantage of the DSM-IV-TR is that it helps mental health professionals communicate their findings, conduct research, and plan for treatment. One disadvantage of using the DSM-IV-TR to make a diagnosis is that it places people into specific categories that may have bad associations; this problem is called **(b)** _____.

D Anxiety Disorders

8. A mental disorder that is marked by excessive and/or unrealistic worry or feelings of general apprehension about events or activities, when those feelings occur on a majority of days for a period of at least six months, is called _____. This anxiety disorder is treated with some form of psychotherapy and/or drugs known as benzodiazepines.

9. One mental disorder is characterized by recurring and unexpected panic attacks and continued worry about having another panic attack; such worry interferes with psychological functioning. This problem is called a _____ disorder.

10. Suppose you experience a period of intense fear or discomfort in which four or more of the following symptoms are present: pounding heart, sweating, trembling, shortness of breath, feelings of choking, chest pain, nausea, feeling dizzy, and fear of losing control or dying. You are having a **(a)** _____. Panic disorders are treated with a combination of benzodiazepines or antidepressants and **(b)** _____.

11. Another anxiety disorder characterized by increased physiological arousal and an intense, excessive, and irrational fear that is out of all proportion to the danger elicited by the object or situation is called a _____.

12. The DSM-IV-TR divides phobias into three categories. Those that are triggered by common objects, situations, or animals (such as snakes or heights) are called **(a)** _____ phobias.

Those that are brought on by having to perform in social situations and expecting to be humiliated and embarrassed are called **(b)** _____ phobias. Those that are characterized by fear of being in public places from which it may be difficult or embarrassing to escape if panic symptoms occur are called **(c)** _____. Once established, phobias are extremely persistent and may require treatment.

13. Persistent, recurring irrational thoughts that a person is unable to control and that interfere with normal functioning are called **(a)** _____. Irresistible impulses to perform some ritual over and over, even though the ritual serves no rational purpose, are called **(b)** _____. A disorder that consists of both of these behaviors and that interferes with normal functioning is called **(c)** _____. The most effective nondrug treatment for obsessive-compulsive disorder is **(d)** _____ therapy.

E Somatoform Disorders

14. The appearance of real physical symptoms and bodily complaints that are not under voluntary control, have no known physical causes, extend over several years, and are believed to be caused by psychological factors is characteristic of **(a)** _____ disorders. The DSM-IV-TR lists seven kinds of somatoform disorders. The occurrence of multiple symptoms—including pain, gastrointestinal, sexual, and neurological symptoms—that have no physical causes but are triggered by psychological problems or distress is referred to as **(b)** _____ disorder; a disorder characterized by unexplained and significant physical symptoms or deficits that affect voluntary motor or sensory functions and that suggest a real neurological or medical problem is called a **(c)** _____ disorder. A recent survey reported that somatoform disorders occur worldwide, although their symptoms may differ across cultures.

F Cultural Diversity: Asian Anxiety Disorder

15. A social phobia found in Asia, especially Japan, that is characterized by morbid fear of making eye contact, blushing, giving off an offensive odor, having an unpleasant or tense facial expression, or having trembling hands is called _____. This phobia appears to result from Asian cultural and social influences that stress the importance of showing proper behavior in public.

G Research Focus: School Shootings

16. A method of investigation that involves an in-depth analysis of the thoughts, feelings, beliefs, experiences, behaviors, or problems of a single individual is called a **(a)** _____. This method was used to decide whether teenage school shooters had repetitive and persistent patterns of behavior that had been going on for at least a year and involved threats or physical harm to people or animals, destruction of property, being deceitful, or stealing. These symptoms define a mental disorder that is called **(b)** _____.

H Application: Treating Phobias

17. There are several different treatments for phobias. A nondrug treatment combines changing negative, unhealthy, or distorted thoughts and beliefs by substituting positive, healthy, and realistic ones and learning new skills to improve functioning; this treatment is called **(a)** _____ therapy. Another therapy that gradually exposes the person to the real anxiety-producing situations or objects that he or she has been avoiding is called **(b)** _____ therapy. Individuals who are unwilling or too fearful to be exposed to fearful situations or objects may choose drug therapy.

18. Social and specific phobias have been successfully treated with tranquilizers called **(a)** _____. Although these drugs are effective, they have two problems: When individuals stop taking these drugs, the original fearful symptoms may return, which is called **(b)** _____; and, if individuals are maintained on drugs for some length of time, they may develop tolerance, which means they will have to take larger doses, which in turn may cause side effects such as loss of **(c)** _____. Researchers found that drug therapy was about equally effective as cognitive-behavioral or exposure therapy in reducing both social and specific phobias, including agoraphobia.

Unless otherwise noted, all images are © Cengage Learning

Links to Learning

Key Terms/Key People

agoraphobia, 518

anxiety disorder, 509

Axis I: Nine major clinical syndromes, 514

Axis II: Personality disorders, 515

Axis III: General medical conditions, 515

Axis IV: Psychosocial and environmental problems, 515

Axis V: Global assessment of functioning scale, 515

case study, 523

categorical assessment, 513

clinical assessment, 512

clinical diagnosis, 513

clinical interview, 512

cognitive-behavioral therapy, 524

cognitive-emotional-behavioral and environmental factors, 510

conduct disorder, 523

conversion disorder, 520

deviation from social norms, 511

Diagnostic and Statistical Manual of Mental Disorders, 513

dimensional assessment, 513

exposure therapy, 519, 524

generalized anxiety disorder, 517

genetic factors, 510

insanity, 509

labeling, 516

maladaptive behavior approach, 511

mass hysteria, 520

mental disorder, 509

obsessive-compulsive disorder, or OCD, 519

panic attack, 517

panic disorder, 517

personality tests, 512

phobia, 518

posttraumatic stress disorder, 519

social norms approach, 511

social phobia, 518

somatization disorder, 520

somatoform disorders, 520

specific phobia, 518

statistical frequency approach, 511

taijin kyofusho, or TKS, 522

virtual reality therapy, 524

Media Resources

Go to **CengageBrain.com** to access Psychology CourseMate, where you will find an interactive eBook, glossaries, flashcards, quizzes, videos, answers to Critical Thinking questions, and more. You can also access Virtual Psychology Labs, an interactive laboratory experience designed to illustrate key experiments first-hand.

MODULE
23 Psychological Disorders II

Mood Disorder

Why do his thoughts speed up?

Chuck Elliot (photo below) was checking out the exhibits at an electronics convention in Las Vegas when suddenly his mind seemed to go wild and spin at twice its regular speed. His words could not keep up with his thoughts, and he was talking in what sounded like some strange code, almost like rapid fire "dot, dot, dot." Then he stripped off all his clothes and ran stark naked through the gambling casino of the Hilton Hotel. The police were called, and Chuck was taken to a mental hospital. After his symptoms were reviewed, Chuck was diagnosed with what was then called manic depression.

Chuck Elliot's mind spins and whirls out of control. He was diagnosed with having bipolar I disorder.

At one time, Chuck had a very successful career. After taking postgraduate courses, he obtained a doctor of education degree (Ed.D.). He started and ran his own video production business while also designing computer software. But since that first strange episode at the computer electronics convention, Chuck has been hospitalized about twice a year when his mind races and spins wildly out of control in what are called manic episodes. He usually takes medication, but because the drug slows him down more than he likes, he stops taking his medication every so often. Without medication, his energy may come back with such force that it blasts him into superactive days and sleepless nights, and he often ends up in a psychiatric hospital.

Chuck's last regular job ended when he was in the middle of another manic attack. He was going on 100 hours without sleep when he went out to his car, grabbed a bunch of magazines, books, fruits, and vegetables, and piled them all on the desk in his office. When his boss came by and found a desk piled high with junk and Chuck sitting there with his mind spinning, the boss fired him on the spot (C. Brooks, 1994). Since that time, despite his very good academic, computer, and business qualifications, he has not been able to hold a steady job.

More recently, Chuck married a woman he had been dating for only ten days. She understands Chuck very well because she too is manic-depressive and has similar mental health problems. She hopes that they can care for each other. She says, "Chuck is the most brilliant man I have ever met. I am so lucky" (C. Brooks, 1994, p. 4).

In this module, we'll explain Chuck's illness, his treatment, and how he is dealing with his problem.

Schizophrenia

Why was he hearing voices?

When Michael McCabe was 18 years old, Marsha, his mother, thought that he was just about over his rebellious phase. She was looking forward to relaxing and enjoying herself. But then Michael said that he was hearing voices. At first Marsha thought that Michael's voices came from his smoking marijuana. But the voices persisted for two weeks, and Marsha checked Michael into a private drug treatment center. He left the center after 30 days and seemed no better off than he had been before. Several days later, Marsha found Michael in her parents' home, a couple of miles down the road from her own house. Michael was sitting on the floor, his head back, holding his throat and making grunting sounds like an animal. Marsha got really scared and called the police, but before they arrived, Michael ran off.

Michael spent time with his grandparents, who finally called Marsha and said that they couldn't take his strange behavior anymore. Once again Marsha called the police. Just as Michael (photo below) tried to run away, the police caught him and took him to the community psychiatric hospital.

Marsha received a call from a psychiatrist at the hospital, who explained that Michael had been diagnosed as having schizophrenia, a serious mental disorder that includes hearing voices and having disoriented thinking. A few days later, Michael escaped from the hospital. He was later returned by police, put into leather restraints, and given antipsychotic drugs that would also calm him down. Michael remained in the hospital and was treated with drugs for about a month, with little success.

Michael McCabe, 18 years old, began hearing voices and was diagnosed with having schizophrenia.

© Robert Gauthier

Just about the time Marsha was at her wits' end about what to do next, Michael was put on a new antipsychotic drug, clozapine. After about a month on the new drug, Michael improved enough to be discharged back into Marsha's care (C. Brooks, 1994, 1995a).

In this module, we'll explain what schizophrenia is, describe the drugs Michael was given, and report how his treatment is working.

What's Coming

We'll discuss several different mental disorders and their treatments. We'll explain mood disorders and their treatments, including the treatment of last resort for depression, electroconvulsive shock therapy. We'll also examine several personality disorders and different kinds of schizophrenia, along with old and new antipsychotic drugs. We'll end with a group of strange and unusual disorders, one of which is multiple personality disorder.

We'll begin with Chuck Elliot's problem, which is an example of one kind of mood disorder. ●

A Mood Disorders

Kinds of Mood Disorders

Depression is not choosy; it happens to about 6 million Americans a year. Major depression is one example of a mood disorder.

How bad is it? A **mood disorder** is a prolonged and disturbed emotional state that affects almost all of a person's thoughts, feelings, and behaviors.

Most of us have experienced a continuum of moods, with depression on one end and elation on the other. However, think of the depression or blues that most of us feel as having a paper cut on our finger. Then major depression is more like having to undergo open-heart surgery. It's some of the worst news that you can get.

Here we'll focus on the symptoms of three of the more common forms of mood disorders: major depressive disorder, bipolar disorder, and dysthymic disorder.

Major Depressive Disorder

Popular singer-songwriter Sheryl Crow (photo below) says that she has battled major depression most of her life.

Major depressive disorder is marked by at least two weeks of continually being in a bad mood, having no interest in anything, and getting no pleasure from activities. In addition, a person must have at least four of the following symptoms: problems with eating, sleeping, thinking, concentrating, or making decisions, lacking energy, thinking about suicide, and feeling worthless or guilty (American Psychiatric Association, 2000).

Sheryl Crow says that she had been on a world tour with Michael Jackson, singing in front of 70,000 screaming fans. When the tour ended, she was back in her lonely apartment with the anxiety of having to get a record contract. All this stress triggered her first bout of depression, which resulted in her lying in bed, hardly able to move, going unshowered, stringy-haired, and ordering take-out food for seven straight months (Hirshey, 2003). Like Crow, about 16% of U.S. adults reported at least one lifetime episode of major depression, with women outnumbering men by a ratio of 2 to 1 (Thase, 2006).

To help understand mood disorders, look at the graph below, which shows three general mood states. The top bar shows a manic episode or period of incredible energy and euphoria that we'll discuss later. The middle bar shows a normal period when a person's moods and emotions do not interfere with normal psychological functioning. However, like what happened to Crow, some event may cause a person to go from a normal period to a period of depression (bottom bar). Individuals may fluctuate between a normal period and a bout of severe depression.

Dysthymic Disorder

Another mood disorder that is less serious than major depression is called dysthymic *(dis-THY-mick)* disorder.

Dysthymic disorder is characterized by being chronically but not continuously depressed for a period of two years. While depressed, a person experiences at least two of the following symptoms: poor appetite, insomnia, fatigue, low self-esteem, poor concentration, and feelings of hopelessness (American Psychiatric Association, 2000).

Individuals with dysthymic disorder, which affects about 6% of the U.S. population, are often described as "down in the dumps." Some of these individuals become accustomed to such feelings and describe themselves as "always being this way."

Next, we'll learn about a disorder that involves alternating between two extreme moods.

Bipolar Disorder

Unlike Sheryl Crow, who has a major depressive disorder, Chuck Elliot (right photo) fluctuates between two extreme moods of depression and mania; he has what is called bipolar I disorder.

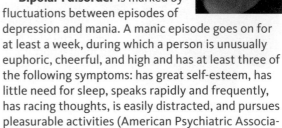

Bipolar I disorder is marked by fluctuations between episodes of depression and mania. A manic episode goes on for at least a week, during which a person is unusually euphoric, cheerful, and high and has at least three of the following symptoms: has great self-esteem, has little need for sleep, speaks rapidly and frequently, has racing thoughts, is easily distracted, and pursues pleasurable activities (American Psychiatric Association, 2000).

About 1.3% of the U.S. population suffer from bipolar I disorder (Rush, 2003).

As shown in the right graph, Chuck Elliot may have periods of being normal, which may turn into extreme manic episodes followed by periods of extreme depression.

Similar to Chuck, Oscar-winning actress Catherine Zeta-Jones experiences mood swings. However, Zeta-Jones's mood swings are not as severe. She has been diagnosed with bipolar II disorder (Cotliar & Tauber, 2011).

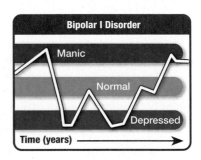

Bipolar II disorder is marked by fluctuations between episodes of depression and hypomania (mild mania). A hypomanic episode consists of the same symptoms as a manic episode, but lasts for at least four days, as opposed to one week (American Psychiatric Association, 2000).

Next, we'll examine some of the common causes of mood disorders.

Causes of Mood Disorders

Sheryl Crow says that she has had a lifelong battle with mood disorders and, contrary to popular myths, when depressed she cannot make great music or work much at anything. Crow thought her depression was due to

What caused Crow's depression?

some chemical imbalance in her brain and that depression ran in families (partly inherited or genetic) because her father suffered from similar mood problems (Hirshey, 2003). Let's see if she's right.

Biological Factors

Using recently developed techniques for studying the living brain and information from mapping the genetic code, researchers have been actively studying biological factors involved in mood disorders.

Biological factors for depression are genetic, neurological, chemical, and physiological components that may predispose or put someone at risk for developing a mood disorder.

Genetic factors. Sheryl Crow was right about depression having a genetic component. Research studies comparing depression rates of identical twins with those of fraternal twins, who share only 50% of their genes, find that 40–60% of each individual's susceptibility to depression is explained by genetics (Canli, 2008). Other research shows that the risk of bipolar disorder when both parents have the condition is 25% and when one parent has the condition the risk is 4%, compared to a risk of only 0.5% when neither parent has bipolar disorder (Gottesman et al., 2010).

Researchers believe there is no single gene but rather a combination of genes that produces a risk, or predisposition, for developing a mood disorder (B. Bower, 2009b; Levinson, 2009). One theory states that defects in specific genes affect our sensitivity to stress, which can result in depression (D. R. Weinberger, 2005). Genes play a role in developing a mood disorder because genes are involved in regulating the brain's neurotransmitter or chemical system used for communication (Canli, 2008).

Neurological factors. Sheryl Crow was also right about depression involving a chemical imbalance in her brain. A group of neurotransmitters, called the *monoamines* (serotonin, norepinephrine, and dopamine), are known to be involved in mood problems. Abnormal levels of certain neurotransmitters can interfere with the functioning of the brain's communication networks and, in turn, put individuals at risk for developing mood disorders. More recently, researchers discovered that continued stress causes the brain and the body's stress management machinery (see p. 485) to go into overdrive, which in turn alters hormonal and neurotransmitter levels and can trigger depression (Thase, 2009).

Brain scans. Researchers took photos of the structure and function of living brains and compared the brains of depressed patients with those of individuals with normal moods. Researchers reported that a brain area called the anterior cingulate cortex (figure below) was overactive in very depressed patients. When the anterior cingulate cortex is overactive, it allows negative emotions to overwhelm thinking and mood. These same researchers cured two-thirds of a group of very depressed patients who had not benefitted from years of psychotherapy, drugs, or electroconvulsive therapy (see p. 535) by electrically stimulating the brain, which led to reduced activity in the anterior cingulate cortex (Mayberg, 2006; Mayberg et al., 2005). We now know that faulty brain structure or function contributes to mood disorders (Thase, 2009).

The anterior cingulate cortex is overactive in very depressed patients, which allows negative emotions to overwhelm thoughts and mood.

Psychosocial Factors

In addition to biological factors, an individual may be at risk for depression because of psychosocial factors.

Psychosocial factors for depression, such as personality traits, cognitive styles, social supports, and the ability to deal with stressors, interact with predisposing biological factors to put one at risk for developing a mood disorder.

Stressful life events. Sheryl Crow says that her period of depression was triggered by the stress of seeing a fantastic world tour end with her living in a lonely apartment, having to wait on tables while struggling to get a record contact. Researchers found that stressful life events are related to the onset of mood disorders such as depression (Kendler et al., 2004; Monroe et al., 2009).

Negative cognitive style. There is considerable research to support Aaron Beck's (1991) idea that depression may result from one's perceiving the world in a negative way, which in turn leads to feeling depressed. We'll discuss Beck's theory later in the Application (p. 548), but just note here that having a negative cognitive style or *negative way of thinking* and perceiving can put one at risk for developing a mood disorder such as depression.

Personality factors. Individuals who are especially sensitive to and *overreact to negative events* (rejections, criticisms) with feelings of fear, anxiety, guilt, sadness, and anger are at risk for developing a mood disorder (D. N. Klein et al., 2002). Researchers also found that individuals who make their self-worth primarily dependent on what others say or think have a kind of *socially dependent personality,* which puts them at risk for becoming seriously depressed when facing the end of a close personal relationship or friendship. Some individuals have a *need for control,* which puts them at risk for depression when they encounter uncontrollable stress (Mazure et al., 2000).

Certain personality factors increase risk for mood disorders.

Depressed mothers. Research shows that a depressed mother significantly increases her child's susceptibility to depression, even if the child is adopted and shares no genes with the mother. Also, when depressed mothers receive successful treatment, their depressed children experience mood improvement without receiving therapy themselves (B. Bower, 2008b; Tully et al., 2008).

The psychosocial factors discussed above interact with underlying biological factors to increase one's risk of developing a mood disorder (Thase, 2006).

Next, we'll discuss the treatment for depression.

Treatment of Mood Disorders

What's the treatment? Because the causes of depression include both biological and psychosocial factors, the treatment for depression, depending upon the diagnosis and severity, may include psychotherapy, antidepressant drugs, or both. We'll discuss the effectiveness of drugs and psychotherapy.

Major Depressive Disorder and Dysthymic Disorder

After months of depression, Sheryl Crow's mother finally persuaded her (with threats of coming to haul her baby out of bed) to get professional treatment, which involved both psychotherapy and antidepressant drugs.

Treatment often requires professional help.

Antidepressant drugs act by increasing the levels of a specific group of neurotransmitters (monoamines—serotonin, norepinephrine, and dopamine) that are involved in the regulation of emotions and moods.

Selective serotonin reuptake inhibitors—SSRIs. About 80% of prescribed antidepressant drugs, such as Prozac and Zoloft, belong to a group of drugs called *SSRIs* (selective serotonin reuptake inhibitors) (Noonan & Cowley, 2002). The SSRIs work primarily by raising the level of the neurotransmitter serotonin. Common side effects include nausea, insomnia, sedation, and sexual problems (decreased libido, erectile dysfunction) (Gitlin, 2009; Khawam et al., 2006). Antidepressants have recently become the most commonly prescribed medication in the United States, used by 10% of the population (Olfson & Marcus, 2009).

Effectiveness of antidepressants. When depressed patients use an antidepressant, which may take up to eight weeks to work, symptoms will go away for only one-third of the patients (comparable to the recovery rate for a placebo) (Berenson, 2006). The challenge for physicians prescribing antidepressants is that for any given individual, some antidepressants work better than others, but no one antidepressant has been found to be more effective for everyone. Often, patients must try a second or third antidepressant until they find one that works well and has minimal side effects (Arkowitz & Lilienfeld, 2007b).

A review of experimental research data found that only in patients with very severe symptoms did a clinically meaningful improvement result from antidepressant use (Fournier et al., 2010). For people with mild to severe symptoms, the benefit from an antidepressant appears to be due to a placebo effect, rather than a result of an active ingredient in the pills people swallow. In contrast, psychotherapy has been shown to be effective for various levels of depression.

Psychotherapy. Researchers compared patients who had received antidepressant drugs, psychotherapy, or a combination of drugs and psychotherapy to treat major depression. For patients with less severe depression, psychotherapy was as effective as antidepressant drugs. For patients with more severe depression, a combination of antidepressant drugs (SSRIs) and psychotherapy was more effective than either treatment alone (Hollon et al., 2002).

Relapse. When patients who had recovered were followed for 18 months, the results were discouraging because, within that time, 70% of the patients had relapsed, which means they became depressed again and required additional treatment. Of those who maintained their recovery and were doing well, 30% had been treated with psychotherapy, 20% with antidepressant drugs, and 20% with placebos. Thus, patients treated with psychotherapy were somewhat less likely to relapse than those treated with drugs or placebos (Shea et al., 1992). Psychotherapy may take longer to begin working, but its strength is in reducing the likelihood of relapse (Charney, 2009).

Next, we'll discuss treatment for bipolar disorder.

Bipolar Disorder

Unlike Sheryl Crow's problem, which is major depressive disorder, Chuck Elliot has bipolar I disorder, which means he cycles between episodes of depression and mania. For example, one of Elliot's manic episodes lasted four days, during which he was in almost constant motion and did not sleep. Several times, when he lost control, he screamed at his wife and ripped the blinds from the windows. His wife called the police, who handcuffed Elliot (right photo) and drove him to a psychiatric hospital for drug treatment.

Bipolar I is treated with lithium and other drugs.

Treatment. In the past, the drug of choice to treat bipolar I disorder was a mood stabilizer called *lithium (LITH-ee-um)*. Although still used today as the drug of choice, lithium is often combined with other drugs, including antipsychotics and antidepressants, which offer more effective long-term treatment (C. F. Newman, 2006).

Lithium is thought to prevent manic episodes by preventing neurons from being overstimulated (Lenox & Hahn, 2000). When Elliot takes medication, he functions well enough that he has enrolled in law school and is working toward his degree. The problem arises when Elliot doesn't take lithium. When patients with bipolar I disorder stop taking lithium (and combined drugs), about 50% experience a manic episode (P. E. Keck & McElroy, 2003). In terms of effectiveness, 50% of bipolar patients are greatly helped with a combined drug program (lithium plus other drugs), 30% are partially helped, and 20% get little or no help (F. K. Goodwin, 2003).

Mania. Lithium has been found to be effective in treating individuals with *mania*—that is, the manic episodes without the depression (F. K. Goodwin, 2003). Because lithium prevents mania, patients may stop taking it to experience the euphoria they miss, as Elliot did several times.

Relapse. For both major depression and bipolar I disorder, 10–30% of patients receive no help from current drugs and 30–70% initially improve but later relapse. Researchers are constantly searching for new ways to treat mood disorders and prevent relapse.

For individuals with major depression who are not helped by drugs, there is something called the treatment of last resort.

© Featureflash/Shutterstock.com

© Robert Gauthier

Biomedical Treatment

There are a few biomedical treatment options for people whose
depression is not effectively treated with psychotherapy and medication. We'll begin by discussing a long-standing biomedical treatment that involves applying electric shocks to a patient's brain.

What are the biomedical treatments for depression?

Electroconvulsive therapy. If psychotherapy and medications fail to decrease depression in patients, many of them will choose to undergo electroconvulsive therapy, one of the last resort options to treat their severe depression.

Electroconvulsive therapy (ECT) involves placing electrodes
on the skull and administering a mild electric current that passes through the brain and causes a seizure. Usual treatment consists of a series of 10 to 12 ECT sessions, at the rate of about three per week.

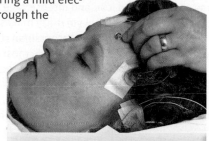

The reason ECT is the last resort for treating depression is that ECT produces major brain seizures and may cause varying degrees of memory loss. However, even as a treatment of last resort, ECT is effective in reducing depressive symptoms in about 70–90% of patients (Husain et al., 2004). For example, the graph below shows the results for eight out of nine seriously depressed patients who had received no help from antidepressants. After a series of ECT treatments, they showed a dramatic reduction in depressive symptoms and remained symptom-free after one year (Paul et al., 1981). However, the average relapse rate after ECT treatment exceeds 50%, which means patients may need antidepressant therapy following ECT treatment or additional ECT treatments for depression (Nemeroff, 2007). Researchers are not exactly sure how ECT works but suggest that it changes brain chemistry and restores a normal balance to neurotransmitters (Baldauf, 2011; Salzman, 2008).

Electrodes on this patient's forehead will carry electricity through the brain and cause a major seizure.

Recent modifications to the ECT procedure include improved placement of electrodes on the scalp and reduced levels of electric current, which have lessened the risk for complications (Nemeroff, 2007; Sackeim et al., 2000). The most common side effect of ECT is memory loss, which ranges from a loss of memory for events experienced during the weeks of treatment to events both before and after treatment. Following ECT treatment, there is a gradual improvement in memory functions, and for most patients, memory returns to normal levels. However, some patients complain of long-term memory problems (Gitlin, 2009; Sackeim & Stern, 1997).

Another biomedical treatment option for persistent depression involves sending pulses of magnetic energy into the brain.

Transcranial magnetic stimulation. For patients with treatment-resistant depression, a new treatment option is transcranial magnetic stimulation (shown below).

Transcranial magnetic stimulation (TMS) is a noninvasive technique that activates neurons by sending pulses of magnetic energy into the brain.

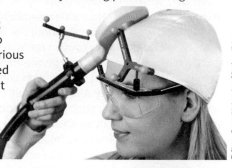

Research shows that depressed patients who did not benefit from various medications experienced significant improvement in symptoms after 40 minutes of TMS daily for four weeks (O'Reardon et al., 2007). Although side effects, such as headache, lightheadedness, and scalp discomfort, may occur, the advantages of TMS over ECT are that it is unlikely to cause seizures and does not require anesthesia (Baldauf, 2009; George, 2009).

The last type of biomedical treatment we will discuss requires surgery.

Deep brain stimulation. An invasive biomedical treatment option for people with severe, persistent depression is called deep brain stimulation (shown below).

Deep brain stimulation (DBS) is a surgical procedure that involves implanting electrodes into the brain and placing a battery-powered stimulator under the collarbone. The electrodes are wired to the stimulator, which provides electrical stimulation to the brain.

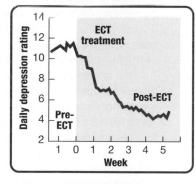

This procedure helps the brain areas where the electrodes are implanted function better and, as a result, decreases the symptoms of depression. One group of researchers has found that about 60% of their treatment-resistant patients show long-term improvement after receiving DBS (Mayberg, 2011).

An advantage of DBS is being able to modify the level of stimulation as needed (Mayberg, 2011). Also, patients who receive DBS show greater improvement than patients who receive only medication. The limitation of this procedure is that the batteries must be surgically replaced every few years (Pahwa & Lyons, 2003). There is also a risk of dangerous bleeding and infection (Kringelbach & Aziz, 2008; F. M. Weaver et al., 2009). Newer DBS systems are being developed to be smaller and more effective and decrease the chance of infection (*Science Illustrated,* 2011; M. G. Sullivan, 2012).

We've discussed psychotherapy, antidepressants, ECT, TMS, and DBS as treatments for mood disorders. Later in the Research Focus feature we will discuss how exercise can help alleviate symptoms of depression. Then in the Application feature we will discuss ways of coping with mild depression, which is commonly seen among college students.

Next, we'll discuss a disorder shared by many serial killers. ●

B Personality Disorders

Definition and Types

What are serial killers like?

We have all heard the expression "Don't judge a book by its cover." That advice proved absolutely true when we heard what their friends and neighbors said about the following individuals.

His boss said David Berkowitz was "quiet and reserved and kept pretty much to himself. That's the way he was here, nice—a quiet, shy fellow." Berkowitz, known as "Son of Sam," was convicted of killing six people.

A neighbor of Westley Allan Dodd said that he "seemed so harmless, such an all-around, basic good citizen." Dodd was executed for kidnapping, raping, and murdering three small boys.

His wife said Gary Ridgway "made me smile everyday. I had the perfect husband. Perfect life" (Mawson, 2011). Ridgway, known as the notorious "Green River Killer," confessed to murdering 49 women and is believed to have actually murdered more than 70 women.

A friend said Jeffrey Dahmer "didn't have much to say, was quiet, like the average Joe." Dahmer confessed to killing and dismembering 15 people (*Time*, July 12, 1993, p. 18).

Notice how friends and neighbors judged all these cold-blooded killers to be "quiet" and "nice" individuals. However, while these individuals appeared very ordinary in public appearance and behavior, each was hiding a deep-seated, serious, and dangerous personality disorder (Hickey, 2006).

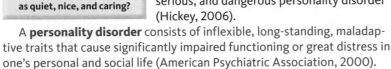

Why do friends describe serial killers, such as Dahmer, as quiet, nice, and caring?

© AP Images/Mark Elias

A **personality disorder** consists of inflexible, long-standing, maladaptive traits that cause significantly impaired functioning or great distress in one's personal and social life (American Psychiatric Association, 2000).

Currently, there are ten different personality disorders described in the DSM-IV-TR. However, it is expected that the DSM 5 will reduce the number of personality disorders to the following five types (Holden, 2010):

Schizotypal personality disorder is characterized by an acute discomfort in close relationships, distortions in thinking, and eccentric behavior (3–5% of population).

Obsessive-compulsive personality disorder is an intense interest in being orderly, achieving perfection, and having control (4% of population).

Avoidant personality disorder is characterized by social inhibition, feelings of inadequacy, and heightened sensitivity to negative evaluation (0.5–1% of population).

Borderline personality disorder is a pattern of instability in personal relationships, self-image, and emotions, as well as impulsive behavior (2% of population).

Antisocial personality disorder is a pattern of disregarding or violating the rights of others without feeling guilt or remorse (3% of population, predominantly males) (American Psychiatric Association, 2000).

Individuals with personality disorders often have the following characteristics: troubled childhoods, childhood problems that continue into adulthood, maladaptive or poor personal relationships, and abnormal behaviors that are at the extreme end of the behavioral continuum. Their difficulties arise from a combination of genetic, psychological, social, and environmental factors (Vargha-Khadem, 2000).

We'll focus on two particular personality disorders, the borderline personality and antisocial personality, because they are mentioned most often in the media.

Borderline Personality Disorder

What does it mean to be borderline?

People who have borderline personality disorder have intense, unpredictable emotional outbursts and lack impulse control, which causes them to express inappropriate anger and engage in very dangerous behaviors.

Patients with borderline personality disorder are so emotionally erratic that they are capable of expressing profound love and intense rage almost simultaneously. Such emotional volatility makes it difficult for them to maintain stable interpersonal relationships. They are terrified of losing the people most close to them, yet they ragefully attack these same people, only to later show sweetness and affection toward them (American Psychiatric Association, 2000; Cloud, 2009).

About 75% of patients with borderline personality disorder hurt themselves through cutting, burning, or other forms of self-mutilation, and another 10% eventually commit suicide. The intentional self-harm is preceded by heightened arousal and followed by a huge decrease in arousal (Nock, 2011). Self-injury seems to relieve their agonizing emotional pain by distracting them with physical pain, which is easier for them to bear.

75% of people with borderline personality disorder hurt themselves.

© Mikael Damkier/Shutterstock.com

Causes. Borderline personality disorder has both environmental and biological causes. Experiencing trauma during childhood, such as being abused or prohibited from expressing negative emotions, places individuals at risk for this condition. Brain scan studies have shown that the amygdala (emotional center of the brain) in these patients is overactive, while the brain areas responsible for controlling emotional responses are underactive. Also, these patients have a tendency to pick up on the subtle facial expressions of others. Together, these findings help explain why people with borderline personality disorder lack emotional regulation and have intense insecurities in interpersonal relationships. Though no specific genes have been identified, the major symptoms of this condition, such as impulsivity and aggression, are highly heritable (J. E. Brody, 2009; Cloud, 2009; Meyer-Lindenberg, 2009; M. K. Raskin, 2010).

Treatment. The most effective treatment for this condition is dialectical behavior therapy.

Dialectical behavior therapy is a type of cognitive-behavioral therapy that helps patients identify thoughts, beliefs, and assumptions that make their life challenging and teaches them different ways to think and react (Linehan, 1993).

Typically, intense, long-term therapy is required, as well as medication.

Antisocial Personality Disorder

The "nice," "quiet" killers we described would probably be diagnosed as having antisocial personality disorder or some combination of personality disorders. Between 50% and 80% of prisoners meet the criteria for a diagnosis of antisocial personality disorder (Ogloff, 2006). But, not all people diagnosed with antisocial personality disorder are alike, and the diagnostic symptoms vary along a continuum. At one end of the continuum are the chronic delinquents, bullies, and lawbreakers; at the other end are the serial killers.

What are people with antisocial personality disorder like?

Delinquent. An example of someone on the delinquent end of the continuum is Tom, who always seemed to be in trouble. As a child, he would steal items (silverware) from home and sell or swap them for things he wanted. As a teenager, he skipped classes in school, set deserted buildings on fire, forged his father's name on checks, stole cars, and was finally sent to a federal institution. After Tom served his time, he continued to break the law, and by the age of 21, he had been arrested and imprisoned 50 to 60 times (Spitzer et al., 1994).

Serial killer. At the other end of the psychopathic continuum is serial killer Jeffrey Dahmer, who would pick up young gay men, bring them home, drug them, strangle them, have sex with their corpses, and then, in some cases, eat their flesh. As Dahmer said in an interview, "I could completely control a person—a person that I found physically attractive, and keep them with me as long as possible, even if it meant just keep a part of them" (Gleick et al., 1994, p. 129).

Jeffrey Dahmer was diagnosed as having an antisocial personality disorder.

Causes

Antisocial personality disorder involves complex psychosocial and biological factors (Moffitt, 2005).

Psychosocial factors. Researchers have found that aggressive and antisocial children whom parents find almost impossible to control are at risk for developing an antisocial personality (Morey, 1997). Also, research shows that children who experience physical or sexual abuse are at an increased risk of developing antisocial personality disorder (D. Black, 2006). However, since many abused children do not develop an antisocial personality, it is difficult to determine how much childhood abuse contributes to the development of antisocial personality disorder.

Biological factors. Researchers suggest that the early appearance of serious behavioral problems, such as having temper tantrums, bullying other children, torturing animals, and habitually lying, indicates that underlying biological factors, both genetic and neurological, may predispose or place a child at risk for developing antisocial personality disorder (Pinker, 2008).

Evidence for ***genetic factors*** comes from twin and adoption studies that show that genetic factors contribute 30–50% to the development of antisocial personality disorder (Thapar & McGuffin, 1993). Evidence for ***neurological factors*** comes from individuals with brain damage and from MRI studies on the brains of individuals with antisocial personality disorder.

For example, researchers found that early brain damage to the ***prefrontal cortex*** (shown below) resulted in two children who did not learn normal social and moral behaviors and showed no empathy, remorse, or guilt as adults. In addition, MRI scans (see p. 70) indicated that individuals diagnosed with antisocial personality disorder had 11% fewer brain cells in their prefrontal cortex (A. Raine et al., 2000). Since the prefrontal cortex is known to be involved in important executive functions, such as making decisions and planning, researchers suggest that damage to or maldevelopment of the prefrontal cortex predisposes or increases the risk of an individual developing antisocial personality disorder. Researchers believe that biological factors can predispose individuals to act in certain ways but that the interaction between biological and psychosocial factors results in the development and onset of personality disorders (A. B. Morgan & Lilienfeld, 2000).

Prefrontal cortex

Treatment

Psychotherapy has not proved very effective in treating people with antisocial personality disorder because these individuals are guiltless, mistrusting, irresponsible, and practiced liars, who fail to see that many of their behaviors are antisocial and maladaptive. As a result, psychotherapists have a very difficult time changing their behavior (Bateman & Fonagy, 2000).

Because of the relative ineffectiveness of psychotherapy, clinicians have tried various drugs that raise levels of serotonin in the brain. Researchers believe that some abnormality in the brain's serotonin system may

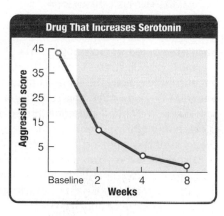

Drug That Increases Serotonin

underlie the impulsive and aggressive behaviors observed in patients with personality disorders (D. Black, 2006). As shown in the graph above, patients who took a serotonin-increasing drug (sertraline) reported significant decreases in their aggressive behaviors across eight weeks of treatment. However, researchers caution that aggressive behaviors may return once patients stop taking these serotonin-increasing drugs (Coccaro & Kavoussi, 1997). Other research shows that the use of antipsychotic medication (see p. 541) can decrease impulsivity, hostility, aggressiveness, and rage in patients with antisocial personality disorder (C. Walker et al., 2003).

Even though there are some treatment successes, researchers caution that for 69% of patients, antisocial personality disorder is an ongoing, relatively stable, long-term problem that needs continual treatment (G. Parker, 2000).

Next, we'll examine one of the most tragic mental disorders—schizophrenia. ●

© AP Images/Mark Elias

C Schizophrenia

Definition and Types

What if you lose touch with reality?

At the beginning of this module, we described 18-year-old Michael McCabe (photo below), who said that his mind began to weaken during the summer of 1992. "I totally hit this point in my life where I was so high on life, it was amazing. I had this sense of independence. I was 18 and turning into an adult. Next thing I knew I got this feeling that people were trying to take things from me. Not my soul, but physical things from me. I couldn't sleep because they [his mother and sister] were planning to do something to me. I think there was a higher power inside the 7-Eleven that was helping me out the whole time, just bringing me back to a strong mental state" (C. Brooks, 1994, p. 9).

Michael was diagnosed as having schizophrenia *(skit-suh-FREE-nee-ah)*.

Schizophrenia is a serious mental disorder that lasts for at least six months and includes at least two of the following symptoms: delusions, hallucinations, disorganized speech, disorganized behavior, and decreased emotional expression. These symptoms interfere with personal or social functioning (American Psychiatric Association, 2000).

Michael has a number of these symptoms, including delusions (higher power inside the 7-Eleven), hallucinations (hearing voices), and disorganized behavior. Schizophrenia affects about 0.2–2% of the adult population, or about 4.5 million people (equal numbers of men and women) in the United States (American Psychiatric Association, 2000).

Michael McCabe had many of the symptoms described on the right.

© Robert Gauthier

Subcategories of Schizophrenia

Michael's case illustrates some of the symptoms that occur in schizophrenia. In fact, no two patients have exactly the same set of symptoms, which are described in the list on the right. The DSM-IV-TR describes five subcategories of schizophrenia, each characterized by different symptoms. We'll briefly describe three of the more common schizophrenia subcategories.

Paranoid schizophrenia is characterized by auditory hallucinations or delusions, such as thoughts of being persecuted by others or thoughts of grandeur.

Disorganized schizophrenia is marked by bizarre ideas, often about one's body (bones melting), confused speech, childish behavior (giggling for no apparent reason, making faces at people), great emotional swings (fits of laughing or crying), and often extreme neglect of personal appearance and hygiene.

Catatonic schizophrenia is characterized by periods of wild excitement or periods of rigid, prolonged immobility; sometimes the person assumes the same frozen posture for hours on end.

Differentiating among the types of schizophrenia can be difficult because some symptoms, such as disordered thought processes and delusions, are shared by all types.

Chances of Recovery

Chances of recovery are dependent upon a number of factors, which have been grouped under two major types of schizophrenia (Crow, 1985).

Type I schizophrenia includes having positive symptoms, such as hallucinations and delusions, which are a distortion of normal functions. In addition, this group has no intellectual impairment, good reaction to medication, and thus a good chance of recovery.

Type II schizophrenia includes having negative symptoms, such as dulled emotions and little inclination to speak, which are a loss of normal functions. In addition, this group has intellectual impairment, poor reaction to medication, and thus a poor chance of recovery.

According to this classification system, the best predictor of recovery for a person with schizophrenia is his or her symptoms: Those with positive symptoms have a good chance of recovery, while those with negative symptoms have a poor chance (Dyck et al., 2000).

Next, we'll describe the major symptoms of schizophrenia.

Symptoms

Schizophrenia is a serious mental disorder that lasts for at least six months and includes at least two of the following symptoms:

1 Disorders of thought

These are characterized by incoherent thought patterns, formation of new words (called *neologisms*), inability to stick to one topic, and delusions.

Delusions are irrational beliefs that have no basis in reality and are held in spite of contrary evidence.

For example, Michael believed that his mother and sister were plotting against him.

2 Disorders of attention

These include difficulties in concentration and in focusing on a single chain of events. For instance, one patient said that he could not concentrate on television because he couldn't watch and listen at the same time.

3 Disorders of perception

These include strange bodily sensations and hallucinations.

Hallucinations are sensory experiences without any stimulation from the environment.

About 70% of schizophrenics report hearing voices that sound real and talk either to them (steal brain cells) or about them (mostly negative things, like "You have a cancer") (Thraenhardt, 2006).

4 Motor disorders

These include making strange facial expressions, being extremely active, or (the opposite) remaining immobile for long periods of time.

5 Emotional (affective) disorders

These include having emotional responses that are inappropriate to the situation—for example, laughing when told of the death of a close friend—or having a flat affect.

Flat affect is characterized by little or no emotional responsiveness when an emotional reaction would be expected.

The cause of these schizophrenia symptoms involves biological, neurological, and environmental factors.

Biological Causes

What caused Michael's problems?

When Michael was in the hospital, his mother, Marsha (photo below), began going to a support group to get help and find out about schizophrenia. At one meeting, Marsha said, "I haven't been doing very well with this, to be perfectly honest. How in the hell were we dealt this hand?" (C. Brooks, 1994, p. 8).

Marsha tries to help her son, Michael, who has schizophrenia.

The psychiatrist who led Marsha's group answered that about 1 in 100 people get schizophrenia but the odds increase to 1 in 10 if it's already in the family. If a person inherits a predisposition for schizophrenia, any number of things—such as drugs, a death in the family, growing-up problems—can trigger its onset (C. Brooks, 1994). The psychiatrist was pointing out three major factors—biological, neurological, and environmental—that interact in the development of schizophrenia. We'll begin with biological factors, specifically genetic causes.

Genetic Predisposition

In 1930, the birth of four identical baby girls (quadruplets) was a rare occurrence (1 in 16 million) and received great publicity. By the time the girls reached high school, all four were labeled "different." They sometimes broke light bulbs, tore buttons off their clothes, complained of bones slipping out of place, and had periods of great confusion. By young adulthood, all four girls, who are called the Genain quadruplets and share nearly 100% of their genes, were diagnosed with schizophrenia (Mirsky & Quinn, 1988). The finding that all four Genain quadruplets (above photo) developed schizophrenia indicates that increased genetic similarity is associated with increased risk for developing schizophrenia and suggests that a person inherits a *predisposition* for developing the disorder. Support for a genetic predisposition also comes from twin studies.

All four of these identical quadruplets developed schizophrenia.

Genetic Markers

Because researchers knew that schizophrenia might have a genetic factor, they compared rates of schizophrenia in identical twins, who share nearly 100% of their genes, with rates in fraternal twins and siblings (brothers and sisters), who share only 50% of their genes. The right graph shows the risk of developing schizophrenia for individuals who share different percentages of genes and thus have different degrees of genetic similarity. Notice that if one identical twin has schizophrenia, there is a 48–83% chance that the other twin will also develop the disorder. In comparison, if one brother or sister (sibling or fraternal twin)

has schizophrenia, there is only about a 10–17% chance that the other will develop the disorder (Gottesman, 2001). Because genetic factors are involved in developing schizophrenia, researchers are searching for the location of specific genes involved in schizophrenia; such genes are called genetic markers (Levinson, 2003).

A **genetic marker** is an identifiable gene or number of genes or a specific segment of a chromosome that is directly linked to some behavioral, physiological, or neurological trait or disease.

Researchers have made some progress in identifying genetic markers for schizophrenia, but they have also run across challenges. Researchers now believe that people may inherit a vulnerability to schizophrenia, which depends on a combination of genes, and that no one gene by itself has a strong influence (Gunter, 2009; ISC, 2009; T. Walsh et al., 2008).

We'll share some of the promising research findings on genetic markers for schizophrenia. Researchers found evidence of a slight excess of a protein in the prefrontal cortex of people with schizophrenia, resulting from a variation in a gene they believe may explain common symptoms of the disorder (Law & Weinberger, 2006). Also, researchers found that a disruption in a particular gene makes new neurons that are supposed to reach the hippocampus, an area of the brain important for memory and emotional processing, go elsewhere, causing a burst of abnormal brain activity, which may explain schizophrenia symptoms (H. Song, 2007). Other researchers found a gene linked to negative symptoms of schizophrenia (see p. 541), which suggests that researchers should seek genes responsible for specific symptoms (Fanous et al., 2005). Taken together, recent genetic studies plus earlier studies on identical twins indicate that schizophrenia has a genetic factor and that further research is warranted.

Infections

Another biological factor that may contribute to the development of schizophrenia is infections. For instance, women who get the flu during pregnancy have been found to be three times more likely to give birth to children who will develop schizophrenia (A. S. Brown, 2011). Also, results in about 250 studies find that children born in winter or early spring are 5–8% more likely to develop schizophrenia. Additionally, one specific virus called HERV-W has been found in the blood of nearly half of people with schizophrenia, compared with only 4% of people without schizophrenia (D. Fox, 2011; Perron et al., 2008; Wenner, 2008a).

However, biological factors alone cannot completely explain why individuals develop schizophrenia. As we'll discuss, environmental factors interact with biological factors.

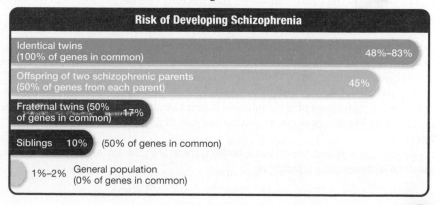

Risk of Developing Schizophrenia

Identical twins (100% of genes in common) — 48%–83%

Offspring of two schizophrenic parents (50% of genes from each parent) — 45%

Fraternal twins (50% of genes in common) — 17%

Siblings — 10% (50% of genes in common)

General population (0% of genes in common) — 1%–2%

Neurological Causes

Is the brain different?

New techniques for studying the structures and functions of the living brain (see pp. 70–71) reveal major differences between the brains of people with schizophrenia and those of mentally healthy individuals. We'll discuss three reliable differences—larger ventricles, decreased activity in the prefrontal cortex, and changes in brain chemistry.

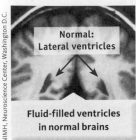

Normal: Lateral ventricles

Fluid-filled ventricles in normal brains

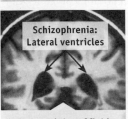

Schizophrenia: Lateral ventricles

Increased size of fluid-filled ventricles in brains of schizophrenics

Courtesy of Drs. E. Fuller Torrey & Daniel R. Weinberger, NIMH, Neuroscience Center, Washington D.C.

Ventricle Size

Most us of don't realize that our brains have four fluid-filled cavities called ventricles (left figure). The fluid in these cavities helps to cushion the brain against blows and also serves as a reservoir of nutrients and hormones for the brain. One reliable finding is that in up to 80% of the brains of people with schizophrenia, the ventricles are larger than normal (Niznikiewicz et al., 2003). Using brain scans (MRIs), researchers studied 15 pairs of identical twins; one was diagnosed with schizophrenia, while the other was mentally healthy (normal). The brains of the twins with schizophrenia had **larger ventricles** than the brains of the mentally healthy twins (left figures) (Suddath et al., 1990). However, not all brains of people with schizophrenia have larger ventricles or an overall decrease in brain size. Also, the enlarged ventricles in some people with schizophrenia may remain the same over the course of their illness, while the size of ventricles may change over time for others (DeLisi et al., 2004). Researchers conclude that some people with schizophrenia have abnormally large ventricles, which results in a reduction in brain size and in turn may contribute to the development of schizophrenia (I. C. Wright et al., 2000).

Frontal Lobe: Prefrontal Cortex

Another brain structure involved in many executive functions, such as reasoning, planning, remembering, paying attention, and making decisions, is the prefrontal cortex (figure right). Researchers report that in pairs of identical twins where one twin has schizophrenia and the other does not, the brain of the twin with schizophrenia was characterized by significantly **less activation of the prefrontal cortex** (F. E. Torrey et al., 1994). This decreased prefrontal lobe activity is consistent with the deficits in many executive functions observed in schizophrenics, such as disorganized thinking, irrational beliefs, and lack of concentration (Niznikiewicz et al., 2003).

Prefrontal cortex

Brain Chemistry

Another neurological factor that plays a role in the development of schizophrenia is brain chemistry. The neurotransmitter that has long been associated with the onset and maintenance of schizophrenia is dopamine. It was originally believed that increases in dopamine resulted in symptoms of schizophrenia. Our understanding of the relationship between dopamine and schizophrenia has advanced, and it is now believed that excess dopamine in certain brain regions and a lack of dopamine in other brain regions are associated with different types of symptoms. Also, researchers believe that other neurotransmitters, such as serotonin and glutamate, share responsibility for the symptoms of schizophrenia (Combs et al., 2012; Howes & Kapur, 2009; Javitt, 2010). We will continue to discuss the role of dopamine in schizophrenia on the next page.

Besides genetic and neurological factors, there are also environmental factors involved in developing schizophrenia.

Environmental Causes

Can stress act as a trigger?

If biological or neurological factors explained why people develop schizophrenia, then the risk for developing schizophrenia in identical twins would be almost 100% rather than 48–83%. Because biological and neurological factors alone cannot explain the development of schizophrenia, researchers look at the influence of environmental factors, such as the incidence of stressful events and how individuals cope. For example, when Michael McCabe (right photo) was 18, he began to develop symptoms of schizophrenia. The onset of these symptoms occurred after the death of his father and during the potentially stressful period of adolescence.

Stressful events may have led to his onset of schizophrenia.

© Robert Gauthier

Stressful events, such as hostile parents, poor social relationships, the death of a parent or loved one, and career or personal problems, can contribute to the development and onset of schizophrenia. This relationship between stress and the onset of schizophrenia is called the diathesis stress theory (S. R. Jones & Fernyhough, 2007).

The **diathesis** (*die-ATH-uh-sis*) **stress theory** of schizophrenia says that some people have a genetic predisposition (a diathesis) that interacts with life stressors to result in the onset and development of schizophrenia.

The diathesis stress theory assumes that biological or neurological factors have initially produced a **predisposition for schizophrenia.** If a person already has a predisposition for schizophrenia, then being faced with stressful environmental factors can increase the risk and vulnerability for developing schizophrenia as well as trigger the onset of schizophrenia symptoms (S. R. Jones & Fernyhough, 2007). Thus, the diathesis stress theory says that biological and neurological factors first create a predisposition, such as overreacting to stressful situations, that then makes a person vulnerable or at risk for developing schizophrenia.

Now we'll examine the drugs used to treat schizophrenia.

Treatment

Treatment for schizophrenia typically begins long after patients first begin to display symptoms. Consequently, it's not uncommon for there to be a gap of several years between the first signs of symptoms and treatment. Scientists are currently working to develop techniques that assess biomarkers, such as genes, which may lead to earlier diagnosis and better treatment outcomes (Vastag et al., 2011).

How is Michael treated?

The case of Michael (right photo) is an example of treatment beginning long after the symptoms of schizophrenia emerged. Michael's mother suspected something was wrong with her son long before he was taken to a psychiatric hospital. It was during his hospitalization that he was diagnosed with schizophrenia.

Schizophrenia symptoms are commonly divided into positive and negative symptoms.

Positive symptoms of schizophrenia reflect a distortion of normal functions: distorted thinking results in delusions; distorted

Michael was given a neuroleptic drug to treat his schizophrenia.

© Robert Gauthier

perceptions result in hallucinations; and distorted language results in disorganized speech.

Negative symptoms of schizophrenia reflect a decrease in or loss of normal functions: decreased range and intensity of emotions, decreased ability to express thoughts, and decreased initiative to engage in goal-directed behaviors (American Psychiatric Association, 2000).

Like most individuals diagnosed with schizophrenia, Michael had both positive symptoms, such as delusions that people were going to steal from him, and negative symptoms, such as loss of emotional expression. To reduce these symptoms, he was given haloperidol, which is an antipsychotic or neuroleptic (meaning "taking hold of the nerves") drug.

Neuroleptic drugs, also called **antipsychotic drugs,** are used to treat serious mental disorders, such as schizophrenia, by changing the levels of neurotransmitters in the brain.

There are two kinds of neuroleptic drugs: typical and atypical.

Typical Neuroleptics

> **Typical neuroleptics:** decrease dopamine

Typical neuroleptics were discovered in the 1950s and were the first effective medical treatment for schizophrenia.

Typical neuroleptic drugs primarily reduce levels of the neurotransmitter dopamine. These drugs mainly reduce positive symptoms and have little effect on negative symptoms.

Because typical neuroleptics reduce levels of dopamine, their action supports the dopamine theory of schizophrenia (Downar & Kapur, 2008).

The **dopamine theory** says that in schizophrenia, the dopamine neurotransmitter system is somehow overactive and gives rise to a wide range of symptoms.

The dopamine theory focuses on neurons in a group of brain structures called the *basal ganglia* (figure right). Typical neuroleptics block dopamine usage in the basal ganglia, which reduces communication among these neurons and in turn reduces some of the symptoms of schizophrenia. However, because 20% of people with schizophrenia are not helped by typical neuroleptics and because recent findings point to the involvement of several nondopamine neurotransmitters (serotonin and glutamate), the dopamine theory will need revision to include other neurotransmitter systems.

basal ganglia

Atypical Neuroleptics

In Michael's case and for about 20% of all schizophrenics, typical neuroleptic drugs (phenothiazines, such as haloperidol or Thorazine) have little or no effect on their symptoms. Many of these patients are being helped by newer atypical neuroleptic drugs (Downar & Kapur, 2008).

> **Atypical neuroleptics:** decrease dopamine & serotonin

Atypical neuroleptic drugs (clozapine, risperidone) lower levels of dopamine and also lower levels of other neurotransmitters, especially serotonin. These drugs primarily reduce positive symptoms, may reduce negative symptoms, and prevent relapse.

The first atypical neuroleptic, clozapine, was approved for use in schizophrenia in 1990. Since then, atypical neuroleptics have proven effective in decreasing symptoms of schizophrenia, especially in patients who were not helped by typical neuroleptics.

Michael, for example, showed little improvement with typical neuroleptics (haloperidol). However, the atypical neuroleptic clozapine reduced his positive symptoms to the point that he was allowed to leave the psychiatric hospital and return home. A year later, Michael was still taking clozapine and was making slow progress in overcoming his symptoms, such as paranoia.

On most days, Michael comes home from group therapy and job-training classes, puts on a Bob Marley record, and sits and listens, afraid to do much else. As Michael explains, "I can't go out and skate or do anything because I'm

Atypical neuroleptics helped Michael (shown with his mother and sister) reduce his symptoms.

© Robert Gauthier

afraid I'm going to have a paranoia attack" (C. Brooks, 1995b, p. D-3). Michael, as well as others with schizophrenia, face a daily struggle to overcome their symptoms, which points to the need for continued social support and psychotherapy (Bustillo et al., 2001).

Next, we'll discuss the serious side effects of typical and atypical neuroleptics.

Evaluation of Neuroleptic Drugs

What are the side effects?

The major advantage of neuroleptic drugs is that they effectively reduce positive symptoms so that many patients can regain some degree of normal functioning. However, neuroleptics also have two potentially serious disadvantages: They may produce undesirable side effects, and they may decrease but not prevent relapse or return of the original symptoms of schizophrenia.

NEUROLEPTICS

| **Typical:** decrease dopamine | **Atypical:** decrease dopamine & serotonin |

Typical Neuroleptics

Side effects. One group of typical neuroleptics, called the phenothiazines *(pheen-no-THIGH-ah-zeens),* is widely prescribed to treat schizophrenia. Phenothiazines can produce unwanted motor movements, which is a side effect called tardive dyskinesia (Dolder, 2008).

Tardive dyskinesia *(TAR-div dis-cah-KNEE-zee-ah)* involves the appearance of slow, involuntary, and uncontrollable rhythmic movements and rapid twitching of the mouth and lips, as well as unusual movements of the limbs. This condition is associated with the continued use of typical neuroleptics.

As shown in the right graph, the risk for developing tardive dyskinesia increases with use: After three months, 16% developed this side effect; after ten years, 40% developed it (Sweet et al., 1995). About 30% of patients with tardive dyskinesia will experience a reduction in symptoms if they are taken off typical neuroleptics, but the remaining 70% may continue to have the problem when the drug therapy is stopped (Roy-Byrne & Fann, 1997).

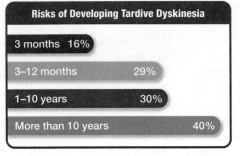

Risks of Developing Tardive Dyskinesia

3 months	16%
3–12 months	29%
1–10 years	30%
More than 10 years	40%

Effectiveness. Researchers have completed several long-term follow-up studies on patients who were treated for schizophrenia with typical neuroleptics. They found that, 2 to 12 years after treatment, about 20–30% of patients showed a good outcome, which means they needed no further treatment and had no relapse; about 40–60% continued to suffer some behavior impairment and relapse, although their symptoms reached a plateau in about 5 years and did not worsen after that; and about 20% were not helped by these drugs.

Relapse. The basic problem with taking patients off typical neuroleptics is that they may relapse. For example, after an average of about one year, 60% of patients taken off a typical neuroleptic experienced a relapse, as compared to a relapse rate of 34% for those who were maintained on an atypical neuroleptic (Csernansky et al., 2002).

Next, we'll learn about the side effects and effectiveness of the newer atypical neuroleptics.

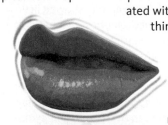

Unwanted motor movements (lip smacking) are a side effect of typical neuroleptics but less so with atypical neuroleptics.

Atypical Neuroleptics

Side effects. One advantage of atypical neuroleptics is they cause tardive dyskinesia in only about 5% of patients, compared to 1–29% of patients given typical neuroleptics (Caroff et al., 2002). However, atypical neuroleptics can cause side effects, the most serious being increased levels of cholesterol and glucose or blood sugar, weight gain, and onset or worsening of diabetes (S. Burton, 2006; Dolder, 2008). Thus, typical and atypical neuroleptics may produce serious side effects.

Effectiveness and relapse. From the 1950s through the middle of the 1990s, the drugs of choice for treating schizophrenia were typical neuroleptics. Beginning in the late 1990s and continuing to the present, there has been a general switch to atypical neuroleptics. That's because, compared to typical neuroleptics, atypical neuroleptics have generally proved to be as effective in reducing positive symptoms, more effective in reducing negative symptoms, less likely to cause tardive dyskinesia, and more effective in preventing relapse, the recurrence of schizophrenia symptoms (S. Burton, 2006; J. M. Davis et al., 2003). However, some research found that the use of typical and atypical drugs led to about equal improvement in patients with schizophrenia and similar rates of movement-related side effects, such as tardive dyskinesia (G. C. Alexander et al., 2011; J. A. Lieberman, 2005). Due to these inconsistencies, clinicians must carefully consider which type of drug to prescribe to their patients.

New direction. Because some patients with schizophrenia either do not benefit from typical or atypical neuroleptics or experience intolerable side effects, researchers have been working to create a new drug that targets a different neurotransmitter called glutamate. Glutamate may be just as important as dopamine and serotonin in schizophrenia because it is associated with perception, memory, emotion, and concentration. Scientists think drugs that target glutamate will provide patients with another treatment option that promises to be effective and have limited side effects (Berenson, 2008; Downar & Kapur, 2008; Goff, 2008; S. F. Locke, 2008).

Researchers find that, for the majority of patients, schizophrenia is a chronic or lifelong problem with a high risk for relapse. Thus, in addition to drug treatment, patients need psychotherapy and social support to improve their social interactions, work at an acceptable job, and maintain their quality of life.

Cognitive-behavioral therapy, one type of psychotherapy, has been shown to effectively treat paranoid ideas and other maladaptive thinking associated with schizophrenia by helping patients challenge these self-defeating beliefs. Family therapy is helpful in improving family members' understanding of schizophrenia, reducing the hostility and criticism they direct toward patients, and increasing the social support they provide to the patient. Together, psychotherapy and social support enable patients to be more active, social, and employable (Carey, 2011; Lauriello, 2007; Lilienfeld & Arkowitz, 2010).

After the Concept Review, we'll discuss a disorder that has a very strange symptom—the person does not know who he or she is. ●

Concept Review

1. A prolonged emotional state that affects almost all of a person's thoughts and behaviors is called a _____ disorder.

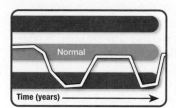

2. The most common form of mood disorder is marked by at least two weeks of daily being in a bad mood, having no interest in anything, and getting no pleasure from activities and having at least four of these additional symptoms: problems with weight or appetite, insomnia, fatigue, difficulty thinking, and feeling worthless and guilty. This problem is called _____ disorder.

3. Another depressive disorder is characterized by being chronically depressed for many but not all days over a period of two years and having two of the following symptoms: poor appetite, insomnia, fatigue, low self-esteem, and feelings of hopelessness. This problem is called _____ disorder.

4. Another mood disorder is characterized by a fluctuation between a depressive episode and a manic episode that lasts about a week, during which a person is unusually euphoric, cheerful, or high, speaks rapidly, feels great self-esteem, and needs little sleep. This problem is called _____ disorder.

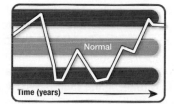

5. Underlying genetic, neurological, chemical, or physiological components may predispose a person to developing a mood disorder. Together, these components are called _____ factors.

6. Factors such as dealing with stressors and stressful life events are believed to interact with predisposing biological factors and contribute to the development, onset, and maintenance of mood disorders. These are called _____ factors.

7. One treatment for major depression involves placing electrodes on the skull and administering a mild electric current that passes through the brain and causes a seizure. Usual treatment consists of a series of 10 to 12 such sessions, at the rate of about three per week. This treatment is called _____.

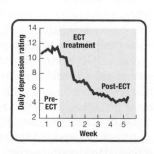

8. Certain psychoactive drugs act by increasing levels of a specific group of neurotransmitters (monoamines, such as serotonin) that are believed to be involved in the regulation of emotions and moods. These are called **(a)** _____ drugs. A mood stabilizer that is used to treat bipolar I disorder is called **(b)** _____, and it's often combined with antidepressants and antipsychotics.

9. A person who has inflexible, long-standing, maladaptive traits that cause significantly impaired functioning or great distress in his or her personal and social life is said to have a **(a)** _____ disorder. Examples of this disorder include an acute discomfort in close relationships, distortions in thinking, and eccentric behavior, which is called a **(b)** _____ personality disorder; a pattern of instability in personal relationships, self-image, and emotions, as well as impulsive behavior, which is called a **(c)** _____ personality disorder; and a pattern of disregarding or violating the rights of others without feeling guilt or remorse, which is called an **(d)** _____ personality disorder.

© AP Images/Mark Elias

10. A serious mental disturbance that lasts for at least six months and that includes at least two of the following persistent symptoms—delusions, hallucinations, disorganized speech, grossly disorganized behavior, and decreased emotional expression—is called **(a)** _____. There are subcategories of this disorder: the one characterized by auditory hallucinations or delusions, such as thoughts of being persecuted by others or thoughts of grandeur, is called **(b)** _____ schizophrenia.

© Robert Gauthier

11. Drugs that are used to treat schizophrenia and act primarily to reduce levels of dopamine are called **(a)** _____ drugs. Drugs that are used to treat schizophrenia and reduce levels of dopamine and levels of serotonin are called **(b)** _____ drugs, which are generally more effective than **(c)** _____ drugs. The theory that, in schizophrenia, the dopamine neurotransmitter system is somehow overactive and gives rise to many of the symptoms observed in schizophrenics is called the **(d)** _____ theory, which is supported by the actions of **(e)** _____ drugs but not by the actions of **(f)** _____ drugs.

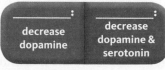

decrease dopamine : decrease dopamine & serotonin

D Dissociative Disorders

Definition

You have probably had the experience of being so absorbed in a fantasy, thought, or memory that, for a short period of time, you cut yourself off from the real world. However, if someone calls your name, you quickly return and explain, "I'm sorry, I wasn't paying attention. I was off in my own world." This is an example of a normal "break from reality," or dissociative experience, which may occur when you are self-absorbed, hypnotized, or fantasizing (Berlin & Koch, 2009; Kihlstrom et al., 1994). Now imagine a

What if you became someone else?

What if you had a split or breakdown in your self?

dissociative experience so extreme that your own self splits, breaks down, or disappears.

A **dissociative disorder** is characterized by a disruption, split, or breakdown in a person's normal integrated self, consciousness, memory, or sense of identity. This disorder is relatively rare and unusual (American Psychiatric Association, 2000).

We'll discuss three of the five more common dissociative disorders listed in the DSM-IV-TR. These are dissociative amnesia, dissociative fugue, and dissociative identity disorder (formerly called multiple personality disorder).

Dissociative Amnesia

Mark is brought into the hospital emergency room by police. He looks exhausted and is badly sunburned. When questioned, he gives the wrong date, answering September 27th instead of October 1st. He has trouble answering specific questions about what happened to him. With much probing, he gradually remembers going sailing with friends on about September 25th and hitting bad weather. He cannot recall anything else; he doesn't know what happened to his friends or the sailboat, how he got to shore, where he has been, or where he is now. Each time he is told that it is really October 1st and he is in a hospital, he looks very surprised (Spitzer et al., 1994).

I can't remember anything about the past month.

Mark is suffering from dissociative amnesia.

Dissociative amnesia is characterized by the inability to recall important personal information or events and is usually associated with stressful or traumatic events. The importance or extent of the information forgotten is too great to be explained by normal forgetfulness (American Psychiatric Association, 2000).

In Mark's case, you might think his forgetfulness was due to a blow to the head suffered on the sailboat in rough seas. However, doctors found no evidence of head injury or neural problems. To recall the events between September 25th and October 1st, Mark was given a drug (sodium amytal) that helps people relax and recall events that may be blocked by stressful experiences. While under the effect of the drug, Mark recalled a big storm that washed his companions overboard but spared him because he had tied himself to the boat. Thus, Mark did suffer from dissociative amnesia, which was triggered by the stressful event of seeing his friends washed overboard (Spitzer et al., 1994). In dissociative amnesia, the length of memory loss varies from days to weeks to years and is often associated with stressful events (Eich et al., 1997; C. A. Ross, 2009).

As we'll see next, a person may even forget who he or she is.

Dissociative Fugue

A 40-year-old man wanders the streets of Denver with $8 in his pocket. He asks people to help him figure out who he is and where he lives. He feels lost, alone, anxious, and desperate to learn his identity. He appears on news shows pleading for help: "If anybody recognizes me, knows who I am, please let somebody know" (Ingram, 2006). After his parents and fiancée see him on television, they contact the police, informing them that the man's name is Jeffrey Ingram and that he lives in Seattle. Upon reuniting with his fiancée and family, Jeffrey fails to recognize their faces. He also cannot recall anything about his past (Woodward, 2006). Jeffrey Ingram had experienced dissociative fugue.

Who am I? What's my name?

Dissociative fugue is a disturbance marked by suddenly and unexpectedly traveling away from one's home or place of work and being unable to recall one's past. The person may not remember his or her identity or may be confused about his or her new assumed identity (American Psychiatric Association, 2000).

Before clinicians diagnosed Jeffrey as suffering from dissociative fugue, they ruled out drugs, medications, and head injuries. His fiancée explained that Jeffrey had been on his way to Canada to visit his friend's wife, who was dying of cancer. She believes the stress of seeing his friend's wife dying led him to an amnesia state. Jeffrey's history is especially fascinating because he had experienced a similar dissociative fugue in 1995, when he disappeared during a trip to the grocery store and wasn't found until 9 months later. And, Jeffrey later went missing for a third time! This time, he was quickly identified because he had gotten a tattoo on his arm that gave his name and state ID number. Jeffrey is considering his options to always have GPS technology with him so his family can quickly find him if he should go missing again (M. Alexander, 2007).

As Jeffrey's case illustrates, the onset of dissociative fugue is related to stressful events. Usually, fugue states end abruptly, and individuals recall most or all of their identity and past (C. A. Ross, 2009).

In other cases, a person's self splits into two or more "true" selves or identities, which is called dissociative identity disorder.

Dissociative Identity Disorder

Is it really true?

The case in which one individual possesses two or more "different persons" who may or may not know one another and who may appear at different times to say and do different things describes one of the more remarkable and controversial mental disorders. Previously this disorder was called multiple personality disorder, but now it's called dissociative identity disorder. We'll discuss a real case of dissociative identity disorder and its possible causes.

Definition

Herschel Walker is recognized for being an NFL legend, Heisman Trophy winner, track star, Olympic competitor, and successful business-man. You would think Herschel would feel as though he was on top of the world. On the contrary, Herschel felt that his life was out of his control. He had difficulty managing his anger, he struggled to feel connected to people, and he experienced unexplained periods of memory loss.

Herschel's wife of 16 years (now divorced) also noticed several oddities about him. For instance, she described him as having many different sides, such as the side with an interest in the Marines, the side interested in ballet, the side interested in the FBI, and the side interested in sports. She even noticed that he would occasionally speak in different voices and show uniquely different physical mannerisms.

Football legend Herschel Walker is diagnosed with dissociative identity disorder, formerly called multiple personality disorder.

© Anna Webber/Getty Images

After Herschel got the courage to seek professional help to understand what had been happening to him, his therapist diagnosed him as suffering from a very rare and complex disorder called dissociative identity disorder.

Dissociative identity disorder (formerly called multiple personality disorder) is the presence of two or more distinct identities or personality states, each with its own pattern of perceiving, thinking about, and relating to the world. Different personality states may take control of the individual's thoughts and behaviors at different times (American Psychiatric Association, 2000).

As a boy, Herschel was relentlessly teased and bullied for being an overweight child who had a severe stutter. His therapist explains that Herschel developed his alter personalities to help him overcome the abuse by his peers as well as other major challenges he faced later in life.

Herschel identifies about a dozen alter personalities, including "The Hero," who came out in public appearances, and "The Warrior," who was in charge of playing football and coping with the physical pain that came with it. Herschel's therapist describes meeting the alter personalities in therapy by saying, "They will come out and say, I am so-and-so. I'm here to tell you Herschel is not doing too good…. When he finishes, it would just disappear back in him, and Herschel comes out" (Mungadze, 2008).

As in Herschel's case, the personalities are usually quite different and complex, and the original personality is seldom aware of the others. After nearly ten years of psychotherapy, Herschel managed to obtain great insight about his condition and says he is doing much better now (H. Walker, 2008; Woodruff et al., 2008).

How common is dissociative identity disorder, and what causes it?

Occurrence and Causes

The worldwide occurrence of dissociative identity disorder was very rare before 1970, with only 36 cases reported. However, an "epidemic" occurred in the 1970s and 1980s, with estimates ranging from 300 to 2,000 cases (Spanos, 1994). Reasons for the upsurge include incorrect diagnoses, renewed professional interest, the trendiness of the disorder, and therapists' (unknowing) encouragement of patients to play the roles. Whatever the reasons, the vast majority of mental health professionals are skeptical about the upsurge of dissociative identity disorder (DID), but others believe it to be a rare, but real condition (Dell, 2009; Lilienfeld et al., 1999). The patients most often diagnosed with DID are females, who outnumber males by eight to one. In addition, patients with DID usually have a history of other mental disorders.

There are two opposing explanations for DID. One is that DID results from the severe trauma of childhood abuse, which causes a mental splitting or dissociation of identities as one way to defend against or cope with the terrible trauma. A second explanation is that DID has become commonplace because of cultural factors, such as DID becoming a legitimate way for people to express their frustrations or to manipulate or gain personal rewards (Lilienfeld et al., 1999). These opposing explanations reflect the current controversy about why so many patients have been diagnosed with DID.

Researchers have found biological evidence to support the existence of dissociative identity disorder. For instance, they found that the brains of patients with the condition

Dissociative identity disorder is said to have two very different causes.

© Ren Nickel/Photolibrary

generate multiple distinct patterns of seeing, thinking, and behaving. Their physiological arousal patterns (e.g., heartbeat, brain wave activity) are different depending on which alter is present (Reinders et al., 2006). Researchers have also identified specific brain regions that are activated when a patient is in the process of switching between the alters. The activated areas include the motor cortex (see p. 76; believed to be associated with facial movements made during switching), the nucleus accumbens (see p. 330; believed to be associated with a sense of reward and pleasure during switching), and the prefrontal cortex (see p. 411; believed to be associated with the executive control involved in switching) (Savoy et al., 2012).

Dissociative disorders are no doubt fascinating. Next, in the Cultural Diversity feature, we'll discuss other intriguing and peculiar disorders. ●

Spirit Possession

Imagine being a clinician and interviewing a 26-year-old female client who reports the following experience:

How does the world view mental disorders?

"Sometimes a spirit takes complete control of my body and mind and makes me do things and say things that I don't always remember. The spirit is very powerful and I never know when it will take control. The spirit first appeared when I was 16 and has been with me ever since."

As a clinician, you would of course conduct a much more in-depth clinical interview and administer a number of psychological tests. But, on the basis of these symptoms alone, would you say that the woman has delusions and hallucinations and possibly schizophrenia or that she has multiple identities and possibly dissociative identity disorder? In this case, both diagnoses would be incorrect. This female client comes from a small village in

About 45% of the women in northern Sudan report spirit possession.

© urost/Shutterstock.com

northern Sudan, where spirit possession is part of their culture and about 45% of married women over 15 years of age report spirit possession (Boddy, 1988). Although in the United States symptoms of spirit possession would probably be interpreted as delusional and abnormal, in northern Sudan spirit possession is interpreted as a normal behavior and an expression of the women's culture. To deal with possible cultural differences, the DSM-IV-TR includes an appendix that describes how to diagnose symptoms within the context of a person's culture (American Psychiatric Association, 2000).

Spirit possession is an example of how cultural factors determine whether symptoms are interpreted as normal or abnormal. Cultural factors and gender also influence the occurrence of certain other kinds of mental disorders. We'll examine how culture and gender influence the occurrence of mental disorders.

Culture-Specific Mental Disorders

Mental illness is present across all cultures; however, cultures often differ in what they consider to be normal and abnormal. There are some mental disorders that are unique to a culture and are best understood within the context of a particular culture. They are collectively referred to as culture-specific disorders.

A **culture-specific disorder** is a pattern of mental illness or abnormal behavior that is unique to an ethnic or cultural population and does not match the Western classifications of mental disorders (American Psychiatric Association, 2007c).

Cross-cultural research has identified numerous culture-specific disorders, a few of which are described below (Gaw, 2001; Lilienfeld & Arkowitz, 2009).

© NASA

Some mental disorders are unique to specific ethnic or cultural populations.

- *Latah* involves the inability to stop copying or imitating others' behaviors, such as movements and speech. Individuals with this disorder are susceptible to doing things they wouldn't typically do, such as using intense profanity. Latah is found in Malaysian and Indonesian cultures.
- *Bibloqtoq* involves an intense urge to leave one's home, tear off one's clothes, and expose oneself to the freezing cold weather. It is found in Greenland, Alaska, and the Canadian Arctic.
- *Koro* involves the fear and sensation of one's penis retracting into the body and the belief that one will die as a result. This syndrome is found in Malaysian cultures.
- *Windigo* involves extreme anxiety and fears of cannibalizing others. It is found in central and northeast Canada and Native American populations.
- *Hikkomori* involves extreme social withdrawal, leading to isolation and confinement for extended periods of time. This syndrome is found in Japan, usually among adolescents and young adults.

These examples show the importance of cultural factors in mental disorders. Cultural factors influence not only the occurrence of disorders but also the rates of occurrence in males and females.

Gender Differences in Mental Disorders

Many mental disorders in the United States, such as bipolar disorder and personality disorders, are reported about equally by women and men (Kluger, 2003; C. F. Newman, 2006). However, as shown in the graph below, disorders such as major depression and dysthymic disorder are reported about twice as frequently by women as by men in the United States as well as in many other countries (Keita, 2007; Kessler, 2003; Thase, 2006).

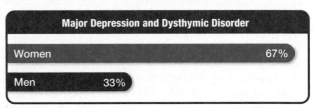

Major Depression and Dysthymic Disorder

| Women | 67% |
| Men | 33% |

Some clinicians attribute the higher percentage of women reporting depression to cultural differences in gender roles. For example, the stereotypical gender role for men is to be independent and assertive and to take control, which tends to reduce levels of stress. In comparison, the stereotypical gender role for women is to be dependent, passive, and emotionally sensitive, which reinforces women's feelings of being dependent, not having control, and being helpless, and increases levels of stress and puts women at greater risk for developing depression (Durand & Barlow, 2006). Some researchers suggest that biological (hormones, genetics, childbirth, infertility) and psychosocial (the roles and expectations of women, family responsibilities, increased rates of sexual abuse and poverty) factors may also contribute to women's higher rate of depression (MHA, 2012; NIMH, 2012e).

Next, we'll look at a very simple yet effective treatment for depression. ●

F Research Focus: Exercise Versus Drugs

Choices of Therapy for Depression

Can exercise help?

What would you think if you were in the middle of feeling very depressed and someone recommended running three times a week as a good treatment? It seems hard to believe that something as simple as exercising could be as effective as antidepressants. Remember that major depression is not how you feel after having a bad day or doing poorly on an exam. Major depression must meet the following definition.

Major depressive disorder is marked by at least two weeks of continually being in a bad mood, having no interest in anything, and getting no pleasure from activities. In addition, a person must have at least four of the following symptoms: problems with eating, sleeping, thinking, concentrating, or making decisions, lacking energy, thinking about suicide, and feeling worthless or guilty (American Psychiatric Association, 2000).

We have already discussed how psychotherapy, antidepressants, and a combination of the two have proven effective in treating major depression (Goode, 2003). Now researchers are asking whether regular exercise can also be effective in treating major depression.

This Research Focus shows how scientists used the experimental approach to answer a question that potentially has very practical, applied benefits.

Exercise Experiment: Seven Rules

Method and Results

You may remember that there are seven rules for doing an experiment (see pp. 36–37). We'll review these seven rules by showing how researchers followed them in their study (Babyak et al., 2000).

Rule 1: Ask. Every experiment asks a specific question that is changed into a hypothesis or educated guess. In this study, the **hypothesis** is that exercise will be as effective a treatment for major depression as are antidepressants.

Rule 2: Identify. Researchers *identify* the treatment, which is called the *independent variable* because researchers are able to control or administer it to the participants. Here, the independent variable has three levels of treatments: the first level is 30 minutes of exercise (stationary bike or walking/jogging) three times a week; the second level is taking antidepressants (Zoloft); and the third level is a combination of exercising and taking antidepressants.

Next, researchers *identify* the behavior(s), called the **dependent variable,** that depends on the treatment and measure its effectiveness. In this study, the dependent variable is a scale (Hamilton rating scale for depression) that measures increases or decreases in participants' depression.

Rule 3: Choose. Researchers *choose* participants, who in this study are 156 adult volunteers (50 years or older) who have been diagnosed with major depression (according to the above definition).

Rule 4: Assign. The chosen patients are *randomly assigned* to groups, which means that each of the 156 patients has an equal chance of being assigned to one of the three treatment groups.

Rule 5: Manipulate. Researchers administer or *manipulate* the three levels of the treatment by giving one level of treatment to each of the three groups of patients.

Rule 6: Measure. After 4 months of treatments, researchers use the depression scale to *measure* how effective each one of the three levels of treatment was in decreasing the patients' depression.

ZOLOFT

Antidepressants: independent variable

Exercise: independent variable

© Oleg Kozlov/Shutterstock.com

Scale to measure depression: dependent variable

© Pavel Lysenko/Shutterstock.com

Rule 7: Analyze. Researchers found that about 60% of patients in the exercise group had greatly improved, compared with 66% of patients who took antidepressants and 69% of those who combined exercise and antidepressants. Although these percentages look different, *statistical analysis* indicated that the three treatments were equally effective. This means that exercise alone was as effective in reducing depression as were antidepressants or the combination, which supports the researchers' original hypothesis.

Relapse

We discussed how, after treatment for a mental disorder, a certain percentage of patients relapse or again return to having symptoms. Of the 60–69% of patients in each of the three treatment groups who showed significant improvement (few if any depressive symptoms), some patients had relapsed during the 6-month period following treatment. Researchers reported (above graph) that 38% of patients who had received antidepressants had relapsed and 31% of patients who had received both exercise and antidepressants had relapsed. However, only 8% of patients relapsed who were in the exercise-only treatment.

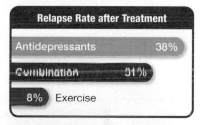

Relapse Rate after Treatment

Antidepressants	38%
Combination	31%
Exercise	8%

Conclusions

Researchers found that after 4 months of treatment for depression, patients in all three treatment groups showed improvement. However, when patients were retested 6 months later, those who had received exercise only showed less relapse. Researchers suggest that exercise helps patients develop a sense of personal mastery and positive self-regard, which helps patients get over being depressed and decreases the risk of future relapse (Babyak et al., 2000). Other research found that depressed patients who reported regular exercise one year following treatment had lower depression scores than did their less active counterparts (B. M. Hoffman et al., 2011). Also, researchers found that exercise has an immediate positive effect on mood that lasts for as long as 12 hours (Sibold, 2009). As a treatment for depression, exercise is effective and inexpensive, has no unwanted side effects, and begins improving mood right away.

Next, we'll discuss ways to overcome mild depression. ●

Mild Versus Major Depression

There is a big difference between mild and major depression. Earlier, we discussed singer Sheryl Crow, who experienced major depressive disorder. Symptoms of major depressive disorder include being in a bad mood for at least two weeks, having no interest in anything, and getting no pleasure from activities. Additionally, to be diagnosed with major depression, a person must have at least two of the following problems: difficulty in sleeping, eating, thinking, and making decisions, having no energy, and feeling continually fatigued. Compared with the symptoms of major depressive disorder, the symptoms of mild depression are milder and generally have less impact on a person's functioning. For example, take the case of Janice, who has what is often called the sophomore blues.

How does depression differ?

"At first I was excited about going off to college and being on my own," explains Janice. "But now I feel worn out from the constant pressure to study, get good grades, and scrape up enough bucks to pay my rent. I've lost interest in classes, I have trouble concentrating, I'm doing poorly on exams, and I'm thinking about changing my major—again. And to make everything even more depressing, my boyfriend just broke up with me. I sit around wondering what went wrong or what I did or why he broke it off. What did I do that was so bad? My friends are tired of my moping around and complaining, and I know they are starting to avoid me. Yeah, everyone says that I should just get over him and get on with my life. But exactly what do I do to get out of my funk?"

Depression falls along a continuum from mild depression to major depression.

Continuum. Researchers generally agree that depression is best thought of as a continuum. At one end of the continuum is mild depression, such as that experienced by many college students, which is basically similar in quality but just a milder form of major depression, which is at the other end of the continuum.

College students. Although many college students experience mild depression, a considerable number also suffer from more severe forms of depression. For instance, a national survey found that when asked about how they have felt in the past 12 months, about 30% of college students reported feeling "so depressed it's difficult to function" and another 6% reported they had "seriously considered suicide." In fact, more than 1% of students reported they had actually attempted suicide, which is the second leading cause of death among college students, compared to its ranking as the tenth leading cause of death in the general population (ACHA, 2012; AFSP, 2012). These statistics are devastating but perhaps not surprising when you consider that college students are experiencing almost all the major stressors of adulthood, including coping with a new environment, dealing with academic pressures, trying to establish intimate personal relationships, experiencing financial difficulties, and trying to achieve some independence from parents and family (Pennebaker et al., 1990).

Vulnerability. There are three major factors that increase an individual's vulnerability or risk for developing mild depression. The first factor is being a young adult who is facing new, challenging, and threatening situations and feelings. The second factor is having a high number of negative life events. Since college students experience both of these factors, they are at high risk for developing mild depression, which may lead to major depression later in life. The third factor involves an individual's pattern of thinking, which is the basis for Beck's theory of depression.

Beck's Theory of Depression

Janice thinks that her depression is caused by outside forces, such as academic pressures, financial concerns, personal difficulties, and family pressures. There is no question that stressful events or negative situations can depress Janice's mood. However, another factor that Janice may not be aware of and that may contribute to her depression is a particular pattern of thinking, which is described by Aaron Beck's (1991) cognitive theory of depression.

How much do thoughts matter?

Beck's cognitive theory of depression says that when we are feeling down, automatic negative thoughts that we rarely notice occur continually throughout the day. These negative thoughts distort how we perceive and interpret the world and thus influence our behaviors and feelings, which in turn contribute to our feeling depressed.

Often these automatic negative thoughts are centered on personal inadequacies, such as thinking one is a failure, is not liked, or never gets anything done. Beck has identified a number of *specific negative, maladaptive thoughts* that he believes contribute to developing anxiety and depression. For example, thinking "I'm a failure" after doing poorly on one test is an example of *overgeneralization*—that is, making a blanket judgment about yourself based on a single incident. Thinking "People always criticize me" is an example of *selective attention*—that is, focusing on one detail so much that you do not notice other positive events, such as being complimented. Beck believes that maladaptive thought patterns cause a distorted view of oneself and one's world, which in turn may lead to various emotional problems, such as depression. Thus, one of the things that Janice must work on to get out of her depressed state is to identify and change her negative, maladaptive thoughts.

We'll discuss how negative thoughts and two other factors maintain depression, as well as ways to change them.

Increased risk for depression

1. Academic pressures
2. Financial concerns
3. Family pressures
4. Negative thought patterns

Overcoming Mild Depression

What can one do? Once we get "down in the dumps," we are likely to stay there for some time unless we work at changing certain thoughts and behaviors, such as improving social skills, increasing social support, and eliminating negative thoughts. We'll describe several ways to "get out of the dumps" and overcome mild depression.

Improving Social Skills

Problem. In some cases, a person may feel mildly depressed because he or she has poor social skills, which lead to problems in having good social interactions.

Poor social skills can increase chances of feeling depressed.

For example, researchers found that depressed teenagers and college students may be overly dependent, competitive, aggressive, or mistrustful, which in turn caused problems in developing and maintaining close social relationships (M. K. Reed, 1994). If part of being depressed involves poor social skills, a person can learn new ways of interacting with friends.

Program. As with every behavioral change program, the first step is to monitor our social interactions to notice what we are doing wrong, such as complaining too much and irritating our friends. Once we're aware of our bad habits, such as being negative, not asking questions or showing interest, and not being sympathetic, we can begin to take positive steps. That means making a real effort to stop complaining and to show more interest in our friends' activities and to be more sensitive to their feelings. By proceeding in gradual steps, we can learn to improve our social skills and get more rewards from social interactions, which in turn will make us feel better and help us get over our mild depression (Hokanson & Butler, 1992).

Problem. Researchers find that individuals often become and remain mildly depressed because they do not give themselves credit for any success (however small), make every situation (however small) into a bad or unpleasant experience, and constantly blame themselves for every failure, which makes them more depressed and thus elicits more negative reactions from friends (Nurius & Berlin, 1994).

Program. The first step in increasing our self-esteem is to become aware of self-blame by monitoring our thoughts and noticing all the times we blame ourselves for things, no matter how small. Once we become aware of self-blame, we can substitute thoughts of our past or recent accomplishments, no matter how small. By substituting thoughts of accomplishment and focusing on recent successes, we will gradually improve our self-esteem. As our self-esteem improves, we will slowly get a more positive attitude, which increases the social support of our friends (Granvold, 1994).

Learning to take credit for our actions can help overcome feelings of mild depression.

Eliminating Negative Thoughts

Problem. According to Beck's theory of depression, a depressed person thinks negative, maladaptive thoughts, which in turn cause the person to pay attention to, perceive, and remember primarily negative and depressing situations, events, and conversations (A. T. Beck, 1991). Thus, besides improving social skills and increasing social support, depressed individuals also need to stop the automatic negative thought pattern that maintains depression.

Researchers found that depressed individuals have a tendency to select and remember unhappy, critical, or depressing thoughts, events, or remarks, remember fewer good things than bad things, and take a more pessimistic view of life (Corey, 2005).

> **After identifying negative thoughts...**

> **...substitute positive thoughts**

Although discussed later (pp. 574–575), here's a brief description of a program for changing negative thought patterns.

Program. The first step is to monitor the occurrence of negative, depressive thoughts. The second step is to eliminate depressive thoughts by substituting positive ones. This second step is difficult because it requires considerable effort to stop thinking negative thoughts ("I really am a failure") and substitute positive ones ("I've got a lot going for me"). With practice, we can break the negative thought pattern by stopping negative thoughts and substituting positive ones. These kind of "talk" programs can help a person overcome mild depression and enjoy life more (Dienes et al., 2011; Freeman et al., 2004). One reason "talk" programs can help as much as antidepressants is that "talk" programs and antidepressants produce strikingly similar changes in the brain.

Power of Positive Thinking

Everyone has heard about the power of positive thinking, and now researchers have found a concrete example. It began with the interesting and reliable finding that psychotherapy ("talk" therapy) can often reduce depressive symptoms as much as antidepressants can (Rupke et al., 2006). Wondering why psychotherapy was as powerful as drugs, researchers took brain scans (see pp. 70–71) of patients diagnosed with depression before and after 12 weeks of treatment with either psychotherapy or antidepressants. The result was that both treatments, psychotherapy and antidepressants, decreased depression. But the surprising finding was that both psychotherapy and antidepressants produced similar changes in the brain, one of which was to decrease the abnormally high activity of the prefrontal cortex (right figure) (A. L. Brody et al., 2001).

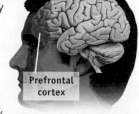

Prefrontal cortex

Several studies have now reported similar results: Talk therapy alters brain functioning (Porto et al., 2009; Roffman et al., 2005). This means that the next time you are down in the dumps, try the power of positive thinking to change your brain functioning. You may be pleasantly surprised by the happy results. ●

What Is a Psychopath?

Jeffrey Dahmer would pick up young gay men, bring them home, drug them, strangle them, have sex with their corpses, and then, in some cases, eat their flesh.

Dennis Rader would break into people's homes, tie them up, strangle them, and eventually murder them. His murder method earned him the name "BTK killer," which stands for Bind, Torture, and Kill.

1 According to the three definitions of abnormal behavior (see p. 511), are Dahmer and Rader abnormal?

Dahmer and Rader are superficially charming, unemotional, impulsive, and self-centered. They are pathological liars who constantly manipulate others. Also, both men completely lack remorse, guilt, and empathy. Finally, they have low self-esteem and a lifelong sense of loneliness. However, not all psychopaths are serial killers.

Other types of psychopaths include the corporate psychopath, the con artist, and the chronic offender. A corporate psychopath may swindle investors out of billions of dollars. The con artist may pass himself off as a doctor, attorney, or police officer to deceive and manipulate others. The chronic

2 What objective test can be used to best assess for these psychopathic personality traits?

offender is persistently in trouble with the law and gets rearrested soon after he is released.

What may seem surprising is that psychopaths can love their

3 Which trait theory can explain how an individual can display such drastically inconsistent behaviors?

family members but have great difficulty loving the rest of the world. Rader, for instance, was a loving husband and father. Yet, he seemed completely devoid of humanity as he plainly recounted the details of how he murdered his many victims.

Some of the fascinating characteristics and behaviors of psychopaths may be explained by biological and neurological factors. For example, some psychopaths have abnormalities in their limbic system, which is responsible for motivational behaviors, such as eating and sex, as well as emotional behaviors, such as fear and anger.

4 What part of the limbic system explains how psychopaths can be so cold and fearless?

Also, some psychopaths have a disruption in the communication between the hippocampus and the prefrontal cortex, which is believed to contribute to their inability to regulate aggression and their insensitivity to cues that predict they will get caught and punished. Interestingly, psychopaths also have lower

© claudia veja/Shutterstock.com

5 How would a psychopath do on a lie detector test?

autonomic arousal and consequently experience less distress when exposed to threats.

The life histories of psychopaths often include a chaotic upbringing, lack of parental attention, parental substance abuse, and child abuse. These life experiences may interact with biological or neurological factors linked to psychopathic behaviors. In other words, at least for some children, the con-

6 What is it called when someone has inherited a gene for psychopathic behaviors but develops those behaviors only if he or she has a stressful childhood?

sequences of having a stressful childhood can be deadly.

Adapted from B. Bower, 2008c; Crenson, 2005; Hickey, 2006; Larsson et al., 2006; Lilienfeld & Arkowitz, 2007; Martens, 2002; A. Raine et al., 2004; Skeem et al., 2011; Wilgoren, 2005; Yang et al., 2005b

A Mood Disorders

1. A disturbed emotional state that affects almost all of a person's thoughts and behaviors is called a _____ disorder.

2. One mood disorder is marked by being in a daily bad mood, having no interest in anything, getting no pleasure from activities, and having at least four of the following symptoms: problems with weight, appetite, sleep, fatigue, thinking, or making decisions and having suicidal thoughts. This is called **(a)** _____ disorder, which is the most common form of mood disorder. Another mood disorder is characterized by being chronically depressed for many but not all days over a long period of time and having two of the following symptoms: problems with appetite and sleep, fatigue, low self-esteem, and feelings of hopelessness. This is called **(b)** _____ disorder.

3. A mood episode that is characterized by a distinct period, lasting at least a week, during which a person is unusually euphoric, cheerful, or high and has at least three of the following symptoms—has great self-esteem, needs little sleep, speaks rapidly and frequently, experiences racing thoughts, is easily distracted—is called a **(a)** _____ episode. A disorder characterized by periods of fluctuation between episodes of depression and mania is called **(b)** _____ disorder. A disorder characterized by periods of fluctuation between episodes of depression and hypomania is called **(c)** _____ disorder.

4. Underlying genetic, neurological, or physiological components may predispose a person to developing a mood disorder. These components are called **(a)** _____ factors. Factors such as dealing with stressors and stressful life events are believed to interact with predisposing biological influences and contribute to the development, onset, and maintenance of mood disorders. These are called **(b)** _____ factors.

5. Some drugs increase levels of neurotransmitters (serotonin, norepinephrine, dopamine) called **(a)** _____. These drugs, which are involved in the regulation of emotions and moods, such as major depression, are called **(b)** _____ and may take up to 8 weeks before they begin to work. The newer and more popular antidepressants (Prozac) are called **(c)** _____, or SSRIs, and are not more effective but have fewer unwanted **(d)** _____ than older antidepressants.

6. A mood stabilizer used to treat bipolar I disorder is called **(a)** _____, and it's often combined with antidepressants and antipsychotics. This drug is also used to treat euphoric periods without depression; this disorder is called **(b)** _____.

7. If antidepressant drugs fail to treat major depression, the treatment of last resort involves placing electrodes on the skull and administering a mild electric current that passes through the brain and causes a seizure. This treatment is called **(a)** _____ therapy. A potentially serious side effect of this treatment is impairment or deficits in **(b)** _____, which usually affects events experienced during the weeks of treatment as well as events before and after treatment. However, following ECT treatment, there is a gradual improvement in memory functions.

B Personality Disorders

8. A disorder that involves inflexible, long-standing, maladaptive traits that cause significantly impaired functioning or great distress in one's personal and social life is called a **(a)** _____ disorder. Five of these disorders are expected to be in the DSM 5, including one that is characterized by social inhibition, feelings of inadequacy, and heightened sensitivity to negative evaluation, which is called **(b)** _____ disorder, and one that involves a pattern of disregarding or violating the rights of others without feeling guilt or remorse, which is called **(c)** _____ disorder. There is evidence that personality disorders develop from an interaction of **(d)** _____ and factors.

9. Evidence that genetic factors influence personality disorders comes from studies on _____, which show that genetic factors contribute 30–50% to the development of these personality disorders.

C Schizophrenia

10. Schizophrenia is a serious mental disturbance that lasts for at least six months and includes at least two of the following persistent symptoms: delusions, hallucinations, disorganized speech, grossly disorganized behavior, and decreased emotional expression. These symptoms interfere with personal or social _____.

NEUROLEPTICS

Typical: decrease dopamine	Atypical: decrease dopamine & serotonin

11. The DSM-IV-TR lists five subcategories of schizophrenia, which include the following three. A category characterized by bizarre ideas, confused speech, childish behavior, great emotional swings, and often extreme neglect of personal appearance and hygiene is called **(a)** _____ schizophrenia.

Another form marked by periods of wild excitement or periods of rigid, prolonged immobility is called **(b)** _____ schizophrenia. A third form characterized by thoughts of being persecuted or thoughts of grandeur is called **(c)** _____ schizophrenia.

12. Researchers have searched for an identifiable gene or a specific segment of a chromosome that is directly linked to developing schizophrenia. This genetic link is called a _____.

13. Two kinds of neuroleptic drugs are used to treat schizophrenia symptoms by changing levels of neurotransmitters in the brain. Drugs that act primarily to reduce levels of the neurotransmitter dopamine are called **(a)** _____ neuroleptics. An example is the phenothiazines. Drugs that lower levels of dopamine but, more important, also reduce levels of other neurotransmitters, especially serotonin, are called **(b)** _____ neuroleptics. These drugs are generally more effective in reducing schizophrenia symptoms and better at preventing **(c)** _____.

14. One side effect of the continued use of phenothiazines is the appearance of slow, involuntary, and uncontrollable rhythmic movements and rapid twitching of the mouth and lips, as well as unusual movements of the limbs. This side effect is called _____.

15. One theory of schizophrenia says that it develops when the **(a)** _____ neurotransmitter is overactive. Another related theory says that some people have a genetic predisposition, called a **(b)** _____, that interacts with life stressors to result in the onset and development of schizophrenia.

D Dissociative Disorders

16. A dissociative disorder is characterized by a **(a)** _____ in a person's normally integrated functions of memory, identity, or perception of the environment. The DSM-IV-TR lists five types of dissociative disorder, which include the following three. If a person is unable to recall important personal information or events, usually in connection with a stressful or traumatic event, and the information forgotten is too important or lengthy to be explained by normal forgetfulness, it is called **(b)** _____. If a person suddenly and unexpectedly travels away from home or place of work and is unable to recall the past and may assume a new identity, it is called **(c)** _____. If a person experiences the presence of two or more distinct identities or personality states, each with its own pattern of perceiving, thinking about, and relating to the world, it is called **(d)** _____ disorder.

17. One theory says that dissociative identity disorder (DID) develops as a way to cope with the severe trauma of childhood **(a)** _____. A second explanation is that DID has become a culturally approved way for people to express their **(b)** _____ or to control others or gain personal rewards.

E Cultural Diversity: Interpreting Symptoms

18. Spirit possession is one example of how cultural factors determine whether symptoms are interpreted as **(a)** _____ or _____. An example of how cultural factors may increase the risk for development of mood disorders can be traced to the differences in assigned **(b)** _____ roles: Males are expected to be independent and in control, and females are expected to be dependent and not have control.

F Research Focus: Exercise Versus Drugs

19. After three different treatments, including exercise only, researchers found that at least 60% of patients diagnosed with **(a)** _____ showed significant improvement. Another finding was that when patients were retested 6 months later, those who had received exercise only showed significantly less **(b)** _____. Researchers suggest that **(c)** _____ helps patients develop a sense of personal mastery and positive self-regard, which helps prevent relapse.

G Application: Dealing with Mild Depression

20. Beck's cognitive theory of depression says that when we are depressed, we have automatically occurring **(a)** _____, which center around being personally inadequate. In turn, these negative thoughts **(b)** _____ how we perceive and interpret the world and thus influence our behaviors and feelings. There are effective programs for developing better social skills and eliminating negative thoughts. Psychotherapy and antidepressant drugs both reduced depression and both produced similar changes in how the **(c)** _____ functions.

Links to Learning

Key Terms/Key People

antidepressant drugs, 534

antisocial personality disorder, 536

atypical neuroleptic drugs, 541

avoidant personality disorder, 536

Beck's cognitive theory of depression, 548

bibloqtoq, 546

biological factors for depression, 533

bipolar I disorder, 532

bipolar II disorder, 532

borderline personality disorder, 536

catatonic schizophrenia, 538

culture-specific disorders, 546

deep brain stimulation (DBS), 535

delusions, 538

dialectical behavior therapy, 536

diathesis stress theory, 540

disorganized schizophrenia, 538

dissociative amnesia, 544

dissociative disorder, 544

dissociative fugue, 544

dissociative identity disorder, 545

dopamine theory, 541

dysthymic disorder, 532

electroconvulsive therapy (ECT), 535

flat affect, 538

genetic marker, 539

hallucinations, 538

hikkomori, 546

koro, 546

latah, 546

lithium, 534

major depressive disorder, 532, 547

mania, 534

mood disorder, 532

negative symptoms of schizophrenia, 541

neuroleptic drugs, 541

obsessive-compulsive personality disorder, 536

paranoid schizophrenia, 538

personality disorder, 536

positive symptoms of schizophrenia, 541

psychosocial factors for depression, 533

schizophrenia, 538

schizotypal personality disorder, 536

selective serotonin reuptake inhibitors, 534

tardive dyskinesia, 542

transcranial magnetic stimulation (TMS), 535

Type I schizophrenia, 538

Type II schizophrenia, 538

typical neuroleptic drugs, 541

windigo, 546

Media Resources

Go to **CengageBrain.com** to access Psychology CourseMate, where you will find an interactive eBook, glossaries, flashcards, quizzes, videos, answers to Critical Thinking questions, and more. You can also access Virtual Psychology Labs, an interactive laboratory experience designed to illustrate key experiments first-hand.

Beginning of Psychoanalysis

It is the late 1800s, and we are listening to a young, intelligent woman named Anna O. She explains that she was perfectly healthy until she was 21 years old, when she began to experience strange physical symptoms. She developed a terrible squint that blurred her vision, a gagging feeling when she tried to drink a glass of water, and a paralysis in her right arm that spread down her body. These symptoms occurred at about the time her father developed a serious illness and she felt the need to care for him by spending endless hours at his bedside. When her symptoms persisted, she consulted her doctor, Joseph Breuer.

Why couldn't she drink a glass of water?

Dr. Breuer takes up Anna's story and explains that, during some of her visits, she would sit in a trancelike state and talk uninhibitedly of her past experiences. One time Anna related a childhood incident in which she had watched her governess's dog drink out of a glass. The experience was disgusting to her because she disliked both the governess and the dog. At the time of the incident, Anna had shown no emotional reaction. But as she retold her story, she let out strong emotional reactions that had been locked inside. After releasing these pent-up emotional feelings, she was once again able to drink a glass of water without gagging.

Breuer explains that sometimes hypnosis helped Anna recall painful past experiences. She told of sitting by her father's sickbed, falling asleep, and having a horrifying dream in which a snake attacked him. She could not reach out and stop the snake because her arm had fallen asleep from hanging over the chair. As Anna relived her powerful guilt feelings of not being able to protect her father, the paralysis of her right arm disappeared. Breuer describes how, each time Anna recalled a past traumatic experience, a physical symptom associated with that trauma would vanish. Breuer would often discuss Anna's case with his friend and colleague, Sigmund Freud.

Dr. Freud interpreted Anna's symptoms as being caused by strong, primitive forces, probably related to unconscious sexual desires (Breuer & Freud, 1895/1955). The case of Anna O. is important because it played a role in the development of Freud's system of psychoanalysis, which was the start of what we currently call psychotherapy.

Just as psychoanalysis had its beginning with Anna O., another very different kind of therapy had its beginning with Little Albert.

Her right arm became paralyzed with no physical or neurological cause.

Beginning of Behavior Therapy

Why was Albert afraid of a white rat?

It was the early 1900s when John Watson, an up-and-coming behaviorist, showed 9-month-old Albert a number of objects to see if any caused fear. Little Albert looked at a white rat, rabbit, dog, monkey, several masks, pieces of wool, and burning newspapers without showing the slightest sign of fear.

Later, when Albert was about 11 months old, Watson retested Albert. This time, as Albert sat on a mattress, Watson suddenly took a white rat out of a basket and showed it to Albert. At the very moment Albert touched the animal, another experimenter standing behind Albert struck a steel bar with a hammer. The sudden loud noise made Albert jump violently and fall forward into the mattress. Five more times Watson showed Albert the white rat and each time a loud sound rang out from behind. Finally, Watson showed Albert the rat but there was no loud sound. The instant the rat appeared, Albert began to cry and turn away from the rat. From this demonstration, Watson concluded that he had shown, for the first time, that an emotional reaction—in this case, fear—could be conditioned to any stimulus (Watson & Rayner, 1920).

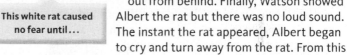

This white rat caused no fear until...

© PhotoDisc, Inc.

The case of Little Albert could be considered the starting point for a kind of psychotherapy known as behavior therapy. Behavior therapists believe that emotional problems may arise through conditioning and thus may be treated—or unconditioned—by using other principles of learning.

The cases of Little Albert and Anna O. illustrate two very different assumptions about how psychotherapy works. According to behavior therapy, emotional problems are learned and thus can be unlearned through conditioning techniques. According to psychoanalysis, emotional problems arise from unconscious fears, which can be uncovered and revealed only with special techniques. We'll discuss these two assumptions along with those of several other therapies as well as whether different therapies produce different results.

...Little Albert was classically conditioned.

What's Coming

In this module we'll discuss the history of psychotherapy and how current therapists are trained. We'll explain Freud's psychoanalysis and how those who disagreed with Freud developed their own kinds of therapies. We'll discuss three of the more popular forms of psychotherapy: behavior therapy, cognitive therapy, and humanistic therapy. Finally, we'll answer one of the most interesting questions: Do therapies differ in their effectiveness?

Let's begin with how psychotherapy came about and how it has developed into a multibillion-dollar business. ●

A Historical Background

Definition

Today, there are over 400 different forms of psychotherapy, some of them tested and some based on purely personal beliefs. For example, some states do not require the licensing of therapists; almost anyone can hang out a sign and go into practice (M. T. Singer & Lalich, 1997). The remaining states require licensing and training of therapists. There are about a dozen tested psychotherapies that may differ in assumptions and methods but generally share three characteristics.

Psychotherapy has three basic characteristics: verbal interaction between therapist and client(s), the development of a supportive relationship in which a client can bring up and discuss traumatic or bothersome experiences that may have led to current problems, and analysis of the client's experiences and/or suggested ways for the client to deal with or overcome his or her problems.

We'll discuss the major changes in treating mental disorders, including early inhumane treatments, the breakthrough in the use of drugs, and community mental health centers.

Early Treatments

From 1400 to 1700, people who today would be diagnosed as schizophrenics were considered insane and called lunatics. They were primarily confined to asylums or hospitals for the mentally ill, where the treatment was often inhumane and cruel. For example, patients were treated by being placed in a hood and straitjacket, chained to a cell wall, swung back and forth until they were quieted, strapped into a chair (right drawing), locked in handcuffs, hosed down with water until they were exhausted, or twirled until they passed out.

Why did hospitals sell tickets?

In the late 1700s, Dr. Benjamin Rush, who is considered the father of American psychiatry, developed the "tranquilizing chair" (bottom drawing). A patient was strapped into this chair and remained until he or she seemed calmed down. Dr. Rush believed that mental disorders were caused by too much blood in the brain. To cure this problem, he attempted to treat patients by withdrawing huge amounts of blood, as much as six quarts over a period of months. Dr. Rush also tried to cure patients with fright, such as putting them into coffins and convincing them they were about to die. Despite these strange and inhumane treatments, Dr. Rush encouraged his staff to treat patients with kindness and understanding (Davison & Neale, 1994).

Early treatment was to be strapped to a chair.

National Library of Medicine, #A-13392

In the 1700s, some hospitals even sold tickets to the general public. People came to see the locked-up "wild beasts" and to laugh at the tragic and pathetic behaviors of individuals with severe mental disorders. However, in the late 1700s and early 1800s, a few doctors began to make reforms by removing the patients' chains, forbidding physical punishment, and using a more psychological approach to treat mental disorders (J. C. Harris, 2003).

National Library of Medicine, # A-13394

Early treatment was to sit in a "tranquilizing chair."

Reform Movement

In the 1800s, a Boston schoolteacher named Dorothea Dix (right photo below) began to visit the jails and poorhouses where most of the mental patients in the United States were kept. Dix publicized the terrible living conditions and the lack of reasonable treatment of mental patients. Her work was part of the reform movement that emphasized moral therapy.

What did she change?

Photo by Ken Smith of painting in Harrisburg State Hospital/LLR Collection

Dorothea Dix began the humane treatment of the mentally ill.

Moral therapy, which was popular in the early 1800s, was the belief that mental patients could be helped to function better by providing humane treatment in a relaxed and decent environment.

During the reform movement, pleasant mental hospitals were built in rural settings so that moral therapy could be used to treat patients. However, these mental hospitals soon became overcrowded, the public lost interest, funds became tight, and treatment became scarce.

By the late 1800s, the belief that moral therapy would cure mental disorders was abandoned. Mental hospitals began to resemble human snake pits, in which hundreds of mental patients, in various states of dress or undress, milled about in a large room while acting out their symptoms with little or no supervision. Treatment went backward, and once again patients were put into straitjackets, handcuffs, and various restraining devices (Routh, 1994).

Freud developed the first psychotherapy.

By the early 1900s, Sigmund Freud had developed psychoanalysis, the first psychotherapy. Psychoanalysis eventually spread from Europe to the United States and reached its peak of popularity in the 1950s. However, psychoanalysis was more effective in treating less serious mental disorders (neuroses) than in treating the serious mental disorders (psychoses) that kept people in mental hospitals.

Thus, the wretched conditions and inhumane treatment of patients with serious mental disorders persisted until the early 1950s. By then, more than half a million patients were locked away. But, in the mid-1950s, two events dramatically changed the treatment of mental patients: one was the discovery of antipsychotic drugs, and the other was the development of community mental health centers.

Unless otherwise noted, all images are © Cengage Learning

Phenothiazines and Deinstitutionalization

The discovery of drugs for treating mental disorders often occurs by chance. Such was the case in the 1950s as a French surgeon, Henri Laborit, searched

What was the first breakthrough?

for a drug that would calm down patients before surgery without causing unconsciousness. He happened to try a new drug on a woman who was about to have surgery and who was also schizophrenic. To the doctor's great surprise, the drug not only calmed the woman down but also decreased her schizophrenic symptoms. This is how the drug chlorpromazine was discovered to be a treatment for schizophrenia. Chlorpromazine *(klor-PRO-ma-zeen)* belongs to a group of drugs called phenothiazines.

Phenothiazines *(fee-no-THIGH-ah-zeens),* which were discovered in the early 1950s, block or reduce the effects of the neurotransmitter dopamine and reduce schizophrenic symptoms, such as delusions and hallucinations.

After 200 years of often cruel and inhumane treatments for patients with mental disorders, chlorpromazine was the first drug shown to be effective in reducing severe mental symptoms, such as delusions and hallucinations. For this reason, the discovery of chlorpromazine is considered the first revolution in the drug treatment of mental disorders. Earlier we discussed the phenothiazines, now called typical neuroleptics, as well as the newer discovery of atypical neuroleptics (see p. 541), which are used in the treatment of schizophrenia.

In 1954, one of the phenothiazines, chlorpromazine (trade name: Thorazine), reached the United States and had two huge effects. First, it stimulated research on neurotransmitters and on the development of new drugs to treat mental disorders. Second, chlorpromazine reduced severe mental symptoms such as delusions and hallucinations to the point that patients could function well enough to be released from mental hospitals, a policy called deinstitutionalization.

Deinstitutionalization is the release of mental patients from mental hospitals and their return to the community to lead more independent and fulfilling lives.

In 1950, before the discovery of phenothiazines, there were 550,000 patients in mental hospitals in the United States. With the use of phenothiazines and deinstitutionalization, the number of patients in mental hospitals had dropped to about 150,000 in 1970 and to about 80,000 in 2000 (Manderscheid & Sonnenschein, 1992). However, deinstitutionalization has created a related problem.

About 20–80% of the homeless have some degree of mental problems.

Homeless. The goal of deinstitutionalization, which is to get patients back into the community, has been only partly realized. Some former mental patients do live in well-run halfway houses (F. R. Lipton et al., 2000). However, recent investigations have found that some halfway houses are poorly maintained, use untrained staff, and provide little or no treatment for the residents. The major problems are lack of funding and poor supervision of halfway houses.

Because there are not enough good halfway houses, many deinstitutionalized patients end up on the streets and homeless. The result is that about 20% of today's homeless individuals have serious mental disorders and receive little or no treatment (USCM, 2009). To provide mental health treatment for the homeless as well as those who are released from hospitals or too poor to pay for services, there is another place to receive help—community mental health centers.

Community Mental Health Centers

Where can they go for treatment?

There is a need for treatment of mental disorders in the homeless, county prisoners, those released from mental hospitals, as well as about 26% of Americans who experience a mental disorder in the course of a year (NIMH, 2012c). Some of these individuals may have less serious mental disorders that require professional help but not hospitalization. One way to provide professional help to individuals with less serious mental disorders is through community mental health centers.

Community mental health centers offer low-cost

Therapist is treating a client in a community mental health center, which helps those who need care but can't afford it.

or free mental health care to members of the surrounding community, especially the underprivileged. The services may include psychotherapy, support groups, and telephone crisis counseling.

Just as the 1950s saw the introduction of a new drug treatment for mental disorders (phenothiazines), the 1960s saw the growing availability of new treatment facilities—community mental health centers. The goal of these centers as well as other outpatient centers is to provide treatment for the poor and those who have no other forms of treatment for their mental health problems. These kinds of mental health centers provide briefer forms of therapy that are needed in emergencies and focus on the early detection and prevention of psychological problems. To meet these ambitious goals required an enormous increase in the number of mental health personnel (Burns, 2004; J. Rosenberg, 2006).

In the 1960s, *psychiatrists* provided the majority of psychological services, which consisted of mainly psychoanalysis and served individuals in the middle and upper social classes who were not very seriously disturbed. Because of the limited number of psychiatrists, community mental health centers turned to *clinical psychologists* and *social workers* to provide the new mental health services. This demand increased the number of clinical and counseling psychologists and social workers and stimulated the development of new therapy approaches (Garfield & Bergin, 1994).

Before discussing specific psychotherapies, we'll answer four general questions about psychotherapy. ●

What do I need to know?

If you or a family member, friend, relative, or acquaintance has a mental health problem, there are at least four questions that you might ask about seeking professional help or psychotherapy: Do I need professional help? Are there different kinds of therapists? What are the different approaches? How effective is psychotherapy? We'll answer each question in turn.

Do I Need Professional Help?

Each year, more than 30 million Americans need help in dealing with a variety of mental disorders (NIMH, 2009a). For example, a person may feel overwhelmed by a sense of sadness, depression, or helplessness so that he or she cannot form a meaningful relationship. A person may worry or expect such terrible things to happen that he or she cannot concentrate or carry out everyday activities. A person may become so dependent on drugs that he or she has difficulty functioning in personal, social, or professional situations. If these problems begin to interfere with daily functioning in social, personal, business, academic, or professional interactions and activities, then a person may need help from a mental health professional (American Psychiatric Association, 2009).

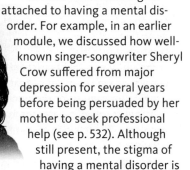

Each year, more than 30 million Americans need help in dealing with mental disorders.

One reason individuals do not seek professional help involves the social stigma attached to having a mental disorder. For example, in an earlier module, we discussed how well-known singer-songwriter Sheryl Crow suffered from major depression for several years before being persuaded by her mother to seek professional help (see p. 532). Although still present, the stigma of having a mental disorder is decreasing as people recognize the need for professional treatment (Alonso et al., 2009; Golberstein et al., 2008).

Another reason individuals do not seek professional help is that they don't realize they need it. In an earlier module, we discussed the case of Michael McCabe, who heard voices and believed people were going to steal things from him (schizophrenia); in another case, Chuck Elliot went sleepless for four nights and had trouble controlling his behavior (bipolar I disorder) (see p. 531). Although both of these individuals needed professional treatment, neither wanted or asked for it. Thus, in some cases, individuals with serious mental disorders may not be able to decide what is best, and their friends or family may need to help them get professional help.

Currently, there are a number of different kinds of mental health professionals who may provide a drug or nondrug treatment program or some combination.

Are There Different Kinds of Therapists?

We'll discuss three of the more common kinds of therapists: psychiatrists, clinical psychologists, and counseling psychologists, each of whom receives a different kind of training in psychotherapy techniques. Together, they provide psychotherapy to 3% of the U.S. population each year (Weissman et al., 2006).

Psychiatrists go to medical school, receive an MD degree, and then take a psychiatric residency, which involves additional training in pharmacology, neurology, psychopathology, and psychotherapeutic techniques.

Psychiatrists usually prescribe drugs to treat mental health disorders. Since the 1990s, psychiatrists have been providing less psychotherapy and instead focusing primarily on biological factors. Currently, less than 30% of psychiatrist office visits involve psychotherapy (Westly, 2008).

Clinical psychologists go to graduate school in clinical psychology and earn a doctorate degree (PhD, PsyD, or EdD). This training, which includes one year of work in an applied clinical setting, usually requires four to six years of work after obtaining a college degree.

Clinical psychologists focus on psychosocial and environmental factors and use psychotherapy to treat mental health disorders. They generally cannot prescribe drugs. However, in a trial program, clinical psychologists were trained in prescribing drugs for a variety of mental disorders. Evaluators of this program concluded that, with proper training, clinical psychologists can provide high-quality drug treatment for their patients (Dittmann, 2003). Since then, New Mexico and Louisiana have passed laws that allow psychologists with advanced medical training to prescribe medications for patients with mental disorders. Several other states may soon pass similar legislation giving psychologists the right to prescribe medication (R. E. Fox et al., 2009; Munsey, 2008). For political and financial reasons, psychiatrists oppose laws that allow specially trained psychologists to prescribe drugs (Munsey, 2006; R. J. Sternberg, 2003b).

College degree

Counseling psychologist has a PhD, PsyD, or EdD and counseling experience.

Clinical psychologist has a PhD, PsyD, or EdD and clinical experience.

Psychiatrist has an MD and psychiatric residency.

Counseling psychologists go to graduate school in psychology or education and earn a doctorate degree (PhD, PsyD, or EdD). This training, which includes work in a counseling setting, usually requires about four to six years after obtaining a bachelor's degree.

Counseling psychologists receive training similar to that of clinical psychologists but with less emphasis on research and more emphasis on counseling in real-world settings. Counseling psychologists, who function in settings such as schools, industry, and private practice, generally deal more with problems of living than with the mental disorders that are treated by clinical psychologists.

In addition, other mental health professionals, such as *clinical social workers* and *psychiatric nurses,* provide mental health services.

Just as there are different kinds of therapists, there are also different kinds of therapeutic approaches from which to choose.

What Are the Different Approaches?

If you were to seek professional help for a mental problem, you could choose from a number of different therapeutic approaches: Some use primarily psychotherapy, some use primarily drugs, and others use a combination of psychotherapy and drugs. These different therapies can be divided into three groups: insight therapy, cognitive-behavioral therapy, and biomedical therapy.

With **insight therapy,** the therapist and client talk about the client's symptoms and problems with the goal of reaching or identifying the cause of the problem. Once the client has an insight into the cause of the problem, possible solutions can be discussed with the therapist.

The classic example of insight therapy is psychoanalysis, whose goal is to help clients get insights into their problems. But because psychoanalysis requires hundreds of sessions, it is very costly; and because it is no more effective than other, briefer therapies, its popularity has significantly decreased since the 1950s. The next kind of therapy, called cognitive-behavioral therapy, combines some features of insight therapy with a much more directive approach.

Cognitive-behavioral therapy involves the application of principles of learning that were discussed in Modules 9 and 10. The therapist focuses on the client's problem, identifies specific thoughts and behaviors that need to be changed, and provides techniques based on learning principles to make desired changes.

Here's my problem...

There are several kinds of drug and nondrug therapies for mental disorders.

Unlike psychoanalysis, which focuses on insight and gives little direction for change, cognitive-behavioral therapy focuses on changing specific undesirable or problematic thoughts and behaviors. This approach combines techniques and ideas from cognitive therapy (p. 565) and behavior therapy (p. 566). Cognitive-behavioral therapy is an example of the most popular approach, which is used by 25–33% of therapists and is called the eclectic approach (Norcross, 2005).

The **eclectic** (e-KLEK-tik) **approach** involves combining and using techniques and ideas from many different therapeutic approaches.

For example, a therapist using an eclectic approach might combine some of the nondirective techniques from psychoanalysis with more directive techniques from cognitive-behavioral therapy. Unlike insight and cognitive-behavioral approaches, which focus on psychosocial factors, the next kind of therapy focuses on changing biological factors.

Biomedical therapy involves the use of interventions to treat mental disorders that change biological factors, such as the levels of neurotransmitters in the brain.

In Modules 22 and 23, we discussed biomedical therapies and how various psychoactive drugs are used to treat a wide variety of mental disorders, including anxiety, mood disorders, and schizophrenia. Unlike biomedical therapies, in which drugs may have undesirable physical side effects, no undesirable side effects are associated with psychotherapy. In this module, we'll focus on several psychotherapies.

With so many different therapeutic approaches, is one kind of psychotherapy more effective than another?

A number of different drugs (neuroleptics, antidepressants) may be used to treat more serious mental disorders.

How Effective Is Psychotherapy?

Sometimes when we have a problem, we might say, "I'll just wait, and maybe the problem will go away by itself." This kind of remark raises a major question: Is psychotherapy more effective than just waiting for problems to go away? To answer this question and determine the effectiveness of psychotherapy, researchers have used a complex statistical procedure called meta-analysis.

Meta-analysis is a powerful statistical procedure that compares the results of dozens or hundreds of studies to determine the effectiveness of some variable or treatment examined in these studies.

Researchers have done meta-analysis on more than 1,500 studies that examined the effects of psychotherapy on a variety of problems, such as depression, anxiety disorders, family problems, eating disorders, and headaches (Butler et al., 2006; M. Cooper, 2008; L. Luborsky et al., 2002; P. E. Nathan et al., 2000). We'll discuss three of the major findings:

• Psychotherapy was effective in relieving a wide variety of psychological and behavioral symptoms in comparison with control groups who were on a waiting list to receive therapy or who received no systematic treatment.

✔ Mood Disorder

✔ Anxiety Disorder

✔ Relationship Problem

✔ Eating Disorder

✔ Substance Use Disorder

Psychotherapy has proved effective for a wide variety of mental disorders.

• There was little or no significant difference in effectiveness among the approaches used by different therapies. In other words, the same psychological or behavioral symptoms were, in most cases, treated effectively with different approaches.

• The vast majority of patients (75%) showed measurable improvement by the end of six months of once-a-week psychotherapy sessions (24 sessions).

Thus, based on data from thousands of patients, psychotherapy has proved effective in treating many mental and behavioral problems, and the greatest improvement occurs in a relatively brief time (13 to 18 sessions) (M. J. Lambert et al., 2004). However, the amount of improvement varies across patients (G. S. Brown et al., 2005; Sotsky et al., 2006). Also, for a minority of patients, psychotherapy may not prove beneficial. In fact, it is possible for a patient's condition to worsen during treatment (M. J. Lambert & Ogles, 2004; Lilienfeld, 2007).

Although many different therapies have been shown to be about equally effective, we'll discuss why some therapeutic approaches are preferred for certain problems and why some clients may prefer one approach over another (O'Donahue & Fisher, 2009; Prochaska & Norcross, 2010).

We'll begin with one of the oldest and best-known therapy approaches—Freud's system of psychoanalysis. ●

© S. Wanke/PhotoDisc, Inc.

C Psychoanalysis

Overview

What happens in psychoanalysis?

One reason almost everyone knows the name Freud is that he constructed one of the first amazingly complete and interesting descriptions of personality development, mental disorder, and treatment, which was a monumental and revolutionary accomplishment at the time. In fact, Sigmund Freud's theory of psychoanalysis includes two related theories. The first is his comprehensive theory of personality development (id, ego, superego, and psychosexual stages), which we discussed in Module 19. His second theory involves the development and treatment of various mental disorders, which we'll examine here.

Psychoanalysis focuses on the idea that each of us has an unconscious part that contains ideas, memories, desires, or thoughts that have been hidden or repressed because they are psychologically dangerous or threatening to our self-concept. To protect our self-concept from these threatening thoughts and desires, we automatically build a mental barrier that we cannot voluntarily remove. However, the presence of these threatening thoughts and desires gives rise to unconscious conflicts, which, in turn, can result in psychological and physical symptoms and mental disorders.

Freud's psychoanalysis searches for unconscious conflicts that result in psychological problems.

Freud began developing the theory of psychoanalysis in the late 1800s. From 1902 onward, a number of young doctors and interested laypersons gathered around Freud to learn the principles and practice of psychoanalysis. In 1908, Freud was invited to America to discuss his approach. Psychoanalysis makes three major assumptions (Corey, 2009; E. B. Luborsky et al., 2008).

1 Freud believed that ***unconscious conflicts*** were the chief reason for the development of psychological problems (such as paranoia) and physical symptoms (such as loss of feeling in a hand). To overcome psychological and physical problems, patients needed to become aware of, and gain insight into, their unconscious conflicts and repressed thoughts.

2 Freud developed ***three techniques***—free association, dream interpretation, and analysis of slips of the tongue—that he believed provide clues to unconscious conflicts and repressed thoughts.

3 Freud found that at some point during therapy the patient would react to the therapist as a substitute parent, lover, sibling, or friend and, in the process, project or ***transfer*** strong emotions onto the therapist.

Freud developed these three assumptions gradually, over a period of about ten years, when he was treating patients for a variety of psychological problems and physical symptoms.

We'll explain how Freud used these three assumptions to develop the therapy he called psychoanalysis.

Therapy session. To give you an appreciation of what happens during psychoanalysis, we'll begin with an excerpt from a therapy session and then explain what goes on between client and psychoanalyst.

Henry is in his mid-forties and is well advanced in treatment. As he arrives, he casually mentions his somewhat late arrival at the analyst's office, which might otherwise have gone unnoticed.

"You will think it is a resistance," Henry remarked sarcastically, "but it was nothing of the kind. I had hailed a taxi that would have gotten me to the office on time. However, the traffic light changed just before the cab reached me, and someone else got in instead. I was so annoyed that I yelled 'F___ you!' after the cab driver."

A brief pause ensued, followed by laughter as Henry repeated "F___ you!"—this time clearly directed to the analyst.

The analyst interpreted this interaction to mean that the cabbie had represented the analyst in the first place. Henry's anger at the analyst was relieved by the opportunity to curse out the analyst (cabbie).

After another brief pause, it was the analyst who broke the silence and injected his first and only interpretation of the 50-minute session. He asserted that Henry seemed to be angry about a previously canceled therapy session.

Henry was furious over the interpretation. "Who are you that I should care about missing that session?" he stormed.

Henry paused again, and then reflected more tranquilly, "My father, I suppose."

This time it was the word *father* that served as the switch word to a new line of thought.

I was thinking how my mother didn't make me feel appreciated and how I felt bad but I still loved her and...

One of Freud's techniques was the use of free association.

"My father was distant, like you," he began. "We never really had a conversation" (adapted from S. D. Lipton, 1983).

Role of the analyst. This brief excerpt from a psychoanalytic session illustrates the basic assumptions of psychoanalysis.

• **Free association.** Notice that the patient is encouraged to free-associate or say anything that comes into his mind, while the analyst makes few comments.

• **Interpretation.** When the analyst does comment, he or she interprets or analyzes something the patient says, such as the meaning of the anger at the cab driver.

• **Unconscious conflicts.** By analyzing the client's free associations, the analyst hopes to reveal the client's unconscious and threatening desires, which are causing unconscious conflicts that, in turn, cause psychological problems.

We'll examine two of Freud's therapy techniques in more detail.

Text credit: Therapy session adapted from "A Critique of So-Called Standard Psychoanalytic Technique," by S. D. Lipton, 1983, *Contemporary Psychoanalysis, 19,* 35–52.

Unless otherwise noted, all images are © Cengage Learning

Techniques to Reveal the Unconscious

One of Freud's major challenges was to find ways to uncover unconscious conflicts, which, he believed, led to psychological problems that he labeled neuroses.

Neuroses, according to Freud, are maladaptive thoughts and actions that arise from some unconscious thought or conflict and indicate feelings of anxiety.

In order to treat neuroses or neurotic symptoms, such as phobias, anxieties, and obsessions, Freud wanted to discover what was in the patient's unconscious. To do this, he developed two major techniques: free association and dream interpretation. To show how these techniques work, we'll describe two of Freud's most famous cases, Rat Man and Wolf-Man.

Rat Man: Free Association

Freud encouraged patients to relax, sit back, or lie down on his now-famous couch and engage in something called free association.

Free association is a technique that encourages clients to talk about any thoughts or images that enter their heads; the assumption is that this kind of free-flowing, uncensored talking will provide clues to unconscious material.

For example, here is how Freud described a session with one of his most famous patients, a 29-year-old lawyer later named the Rat Man because of his obsession that rats would destroy his father and lover.

Rat Man believed that rats would destroy his father and lover.

Freud writes, "The next day I made him [Rat Man] pledge himself to submit to the one and only condition of the treatment—namely, to say everything that came into his head even if it was *unpleasant* to him, or seemed *unimportant* or *irrelevant* or *senseless.* I then gave him leave to start his communications with any subject he pleased" (Freud, 1909/1949, p. 297; italics in the original).

Freud is actually telling Rat Man to free-associate. By this means, Freud uncovered a number of Rat Man's repressed memories, such as how Rat Man, as a child, would get into rages and bite people, just like a rat.

Free association was one of Freud's important methodological discoveries. Psychoanalysts still use this technique today to probe a client's unconscious thoughts, desires, and conflicts (Corey, 2013).

Wolf-Man: Dream Interpretation

Freud listened to and interpreted his patients' dreams because he believed that dreams represent the purest form of free association.

Dream interpretation is a psychoanalytic technique based on the assumption that dreams contain underlying, hidden meanings and symbols that provide clues to unconscious thoughts and desires.

For example, here is one of the best-known dreams in psychoanalytic literature. This dream was told to Freud by a 23-year-old patient who was later named Wolf-Man because he had a phobia of wolves and other animals (P. Buckley, 1989).

"I dreamt that it was night and that I was lying in my bed. Suddenly the window opened of its own accord, and I was terrified to see that some white wolves were sitting on the big walnut tree in front of the window. There were six or seven of them. The wolves were quite white, and looked more like foxes or sheep-dogs, for they had big tails like foxes and they had their ears pricked like dogs when they are attending to something. In great terror, evidently of being eaten up by the wolves, I screamed and woke up.... I was 3, 4, or at most 5 years old at the time. From then until my 11th or 12th year I was always afraid of seeing something terrible in my dreams" (Freud, 1909/1949, p. 498).

Wolf-Man dreamed wolves were sitting in the tree outside his room.

Freud's interpretation of this dream was that, as a young boy, Wolf-Man was "transformed" into a wolf and had witnessed his parents' sexual intercourse (looking through the bedroom window). Later, sexual fears created unconscious conflicts and resulted in a phobia of wolves and other animals.

As Freud demonstrates, the psychoanalyst's task is to look behind the dream's often bizarre disguises and symbols and decipher clues to unconscious, repressed memories, thoughts, feelings, and conflicts (R. Greenberg & Perlman, 1999).

Case Studies: Anna O., Rat Man, and Wolf-Man

Case studies, such as those of Rat Man, Wolf-Man, and Anna O., whom we discussed at the beginning of the module, were very important because from these Freud developed the major concepts of psychoanalysis. For example, from cases like that of Anna O., who had physical symptoms (paralyzed arm, blurred vision) but no apparent physical causes, Freud developed the idea that repressed feelings and unconscious conflicts could affect behavior but that the person would have no awareness of this happening. In support of Freud's belief that unconscious forces were causing Anna O.'s physical problems, each time she revealed some apparently repressed emotional experience, one of her physical symptoms disappeared.

Were Anna O.'s physical symptoms caused by unconscious forces?

Freud's case studies read like mystery stories, with Freud being the master detective who searches for psychological clues that will reveal the person's repressed feelings and unconscious conflicts. At the time, Freud's assumptions and theories, such as repressed feelings and unconscious motivation, were revolutionary. However, as we'll discuss later, Freud's theories and assumptions have been very difficult to verify or prove with experimental methods.

Besides developing methods to reveal unconscious thoughts and conflicts, Freud discovered two other concepts that are central to psychoanalysis.

© Mary Evans/Sigmund Freud Copyrights/The Image Works

Problems during Therapy

Why did clients get angry? Freud was the first to notice that, during therapy, his clients became somewhat hostile toward him, a problem he called transference. He also found that patients became very resistant about dealing with their feelings. Freud believed that how these two problems, called transference and resistance, were handled determined how successful therapy would be. We'll explain these two concepts by using the cases of Rat Man and Wolf-Man.

Rat Man: Transference

Freud describes a patient, later labeled Rat Man, who expressed powerful, aggressive feelings toward him. For example, Rat Man refused to shake hands with Freud, accused Freud of picking his nose, called Freud a "filthy swine," and said that Freud needed to be taught some manners (Freud, 1909/1949).

During therapy, Rat Man called Freud a "filthy swine," which Freud believed resulted from transference.

According to Freud, Rat Man was projecting negative traits of his own very controlling mother onto Freud, who became a "substitute mother." This process of transferring feelings to the therapist is called transference.

Transference is the process by which a client expresses strong emotions toward the therapist because the therapist substitutes for someone important in the client's life, such as the client's mother or father.

Freud believed that the main part of therapy involved working through the transference—that is, resolving the emotional feelings that the client has transferred to the therapist. Freud said that if the feelings involved in transference were not worked out, therapy would stall and treatment would not occur. For this reason, Freud believed that one of the major roles of the analyst was to help the client deal with, work through, and resolve the transferred feelings. Identifying the process of transference, which occurs in many therapeutic relationships, is considered one of Freud's greatest insights (Eagle, 2000).

Wolf-Man: Resistance

For most patients, working out transference and achieving insight into their problems are long and difficult processes. One reason for the difficulty is that the client has so many defenses against admitting repressed thoughts and feelings into consciousness. These defenses lead to resistance.

Resistance is characterized by the client's reluctance to work through or deal with feelings or to recognize unconscious conflicts and repressed thoughts.

Resistance may show up in many ways: Clients may cancel sessions or come late, argue continually, criticize the analyst, or develop physical problems. For example, the patient named Wolf-Man constantly complained of severe constipation. Freud said that Wolf-Man used constipation as an obvious sign that he was resisting having to deal with his feelings (Freud, 1909/1949).

Freud overcame Wolf-Man's resistance by promising that his constipation would disappear with continued therapy, and it did (P. Buckley, 1989). Freud cautioned that the analyst must use tact and patience to break down the client's resistance so that the client faces his feelings.

During therapy, Wolf-Man complained of constipation, which Freud believed indicated resistance.

A necessary role of the analyst is to overcome the client's resistance so that the therapy can proceed and stay on course (G. Frank, 2012; E. B. Luborsky et al., 2011).

Short-Term Dynamic Psychotherapy

The cases of Rat Man and Wolf-Man illustrate two problems that psychoanalysts must solve before their clients can get better. One problem involves the strong emotional feelings that occur with transference, which must be resolved before therapy can succeed. The second problem is helping clients overcome their resistance so that they can begin to deal with threatening or undesirable feelings. Resolving the problems of transference and resistance may take 200 to 600 sessions across several years of traditional psycho-analysis. However, there is currently a strong push toward shorter versions of psychotherapy, in large part because current health insurance coverage typically pays for only 20 to 30 sessions. As a result, therapists have developed a briefer version of psychoanalysis, which is called short-term dynamic psychotherapy (Prochaska & Norcross, 2010).

How long will it take me to get over my fears?

Shorter versions of traditional psychoanalysis have proved effective.

Short-term dynamic psychotherapy emphasizes a limited time for treatment (20 to 30 sessions) and focuses on limited goals, such as solving a relatively well-defined problem. Therapists take a more active and directive role by identifying and discussing the client's problems, resolving issues of transference, interpreting the patient's behaviors, and offering an opportunity for the patient to foster changes in behavior and thinking that will result in more active coping and an improved image of oneself.

Several forms of short-term dynamic psychotherapy have recently become more popular than long-term traditional psychoanalysis. Short-term dynamic psychotherapy, which incorporates techniques of traditional psychoanalysis, has proven effective for treating a number of problems, including generalized anxiety disorder, panic, depression, and several personality disorders (A. J. Lewis et al., 2008; Milrod et al., 2007).

Next, we'll evaluate the current importance of psychoanalysis.

Psychoanalysis: Evaluation

The 50th anniversary of Sigmund Freud's death (1939) was marked by a series of articles in *Psychoanalytic Quarterly* titled, "Is There a Future for American Psychoanalysis?" One author said that such a question was unheard of in the 1950s, when psychoanalysis was at the height of its popularity (Kirsner, 1990).

However, after the 1950s, there was a decline in the popularity of psychoanalysis (R. F. Bornstein, 2001). Now, more than 150 years after Freud's birth (1856), many articles are reporting that some of his ideas are regaining popularity and describe his influence as an "inescapable force" (Adler, 2006). We'll discuss the decline in popularity of psychoanalysis following the 1950s as well as its current status.

Decline in Popularity

How did it happen that psychoanalysis, the dominant therapy in the 1950s, lost its popularity and is now struggling to compete with other therapies? Here are some of the reasons according to its practitioners (Wallerstein & Fonagy, 1999; Westen & Gabbard, 1999).

• **Lack of research.** In the 1970s, critics pointed out that almost no research had been done on whether the psychoanalytic process was an effective form of therapy. For example, psychoanalysts were very slow to analyze their own profession in terms of education—how best to train analysts—and to conduct research into what goes on during analysis and how to make it more effective. This criticism, which questioned the effectiveness of psychoanalysis, contributed to its decline in popularity.

• **Competing therapies.** Perhaps the major reason for the decrease in popularity of psychoanalysis was that, beginning in the 1970s, a number of competing psychotherapies (discussed later in this module) were developed that proved to be equally effective but had a great advantage in that they are much quicker and far less costly. For example, psychoanalysis may require 200 to 600 sessions (2 to 4 per week for several years) versus about 25 for other therapies. This last point is particularly important, since most major health insurance plans limit either the amount of money or the number of sessions (usually about 25) for treatment of psychological problems. Because of this policy, health plans would not pay the costs of therapy for patients choosing psychoanalysis.

Freud's method of psychoanalysis has declined in popularity, but his ideas have been incorporated into other therapies.

• **Psychoactive drugs.** Another reason for the decline of psychoanalysis was the discovery of many new psychoactive drugs that proved effective in treating many of the problems formerly dealt with in psychoanalysis, such as anxiety and mood disorders. Some patients preferred drugs to psychoanalysis.

All of the above factors—lack of research on its effectiveness, development of new and less costly therapies, and discovery of psychoactive drugs—resulted in psychoanalysis experiencing a great decline from its peak popularity in the 1950s.

Current Status

Beginning in the 1980s and continuing to the present, there has been a major effort by psychoanalytic societies and their members to encourage research on the methods, concepts, and outcomes of therapy. This shift toward research indicates a major turning point in psychoanalysis. Previously, psychoanalysts almost exclusively reported individual case studies; they rarely studied the psychoanalytic process or its effectiveness using the experimental approach that had been adopted by competing therapies. For example, when researchers compared long-term psychoanalysis with different kinds of short-term psychotherapies among over 1,000 patients, they found that psychoanalysis was more successful in treating a variety of mental disorders (Leichsenring & Rabung, 2008). This is one example of the current efforts to test, compare, and show that long-term psychoanalysis can produce results as successful as those found with other therapies.

Freudian concepts. Current followers agree that some of Freud's concepts, such as the id being the source of energy, the importance of the Oedipus complex in personality development, and basic drives limited to sex and aggression, have proved difficult to verify. The same followers add that other Freudian concepts, such as the influence of unconscious forces, long-term effects of early childhood patterns, and the existence of defense mechanisms, resistance, and transference, have been experimentally tested and supported (Cortina, 2010; Fotopoulou, 2006; L. Luborsky & Barrett, 2006; Westen, 2007). For example, researchers discovered we have memories, called procedural or nondeclarative (see p. 246), that are outside our awareness (unconscious) but affect various behaviors, such as acquiring strong emotional responses through classical conditioning (Mayes, 2000). Thus, two basic concepts underlying psychoanalysis—unconscious forces and defense mechanisms—have received support (Solms, 2006).

According to recent surveys, Freud's influence is very much alive in today's culture. Forty-three percent of adults in the United States believe dreams reflect unconscious desires, and nearly 30% believe that an adult's psychological problems can be traced back to his or her childhood (Adler, 2006).

Conclusion

Through the years, many ideas from Freud's classical psychoanalysis have been used to develop a kind of therapy called the psychodynamic approach. Although it shares some of its concepts with classical psychoanalysis, the psychodynamic approach has the therapist taking a more directive role that reduces the number of sessions but seems equally effective. One example of this newer approach is short-term dynamic psychotherapy (see p. 562).

Next, we'll discuss an approach developed by a clinician who had been using Freud's psychoanalytic approach but became very displeased with it. ●

D Client-Centered Therapy

Overview

What is a therapist's role?

As a therapist, Carl Rogers used the most popular therapy in his time, which was Freud's psychoanalytic approach. However, before long Rogers became dissatisfied with Freud's view that human nature was dependent on biological urges and instincts—sex and aggression—and that psychological problems arose from unconscious thoughts and desires that threatened one's self-concept. Rogers also disagreed with Freud's belief that the analyst—and not the client—was responsible for the client's progress. Instead, Rogers said that clients themselves have the capacity and are responsible for change. Rogers's ideas exemplify the humanistic approach (see p. 10).

The **humanistic approach** emphasizes that each individual has great freedom in directing his or her future, a large capacity for achieving personal growth, a considerable amount of intrinsic worth, and enormous potential for self-fulfillment.

Using these ideas, Rogers developed client-centered therapy (C. R. Rogers, 1951, 1986).

Client-centered therapy (also called person-centered therapy) assumes that each person has an actualizing tendency, which is a tendency to develop one's full potential.

Rogers believed that each person has a tendency to develop his or her potential.

The therapist's task is to be nondirective and show compassion and positive regard in helping the client reach his or her potential.

In client-centered therapy, Rogers changed the therapist's role from that of an all-knowing expert to a helper or facilitator, whose personal characteristics would foster growth and change.

Therapy session. To illustrate some of the differences between psychoanalysis and client-centered therapy, here is a brief excerpt from a client-centered therapy session where a mother is talking about her problems with letting her daughter be more independent.

Client: I'm having a lot of problems dealing with my daughter. She's 20 years old; she's in college; I'm having a lot of trouble letting her go... And I have a lot of guilt feelings about her; I have a real need to hang on to her. And it's very hard with a lot of empty places now that she's not with me.

Rogers: The old vacuum, sort of, when she's not there.

Client: Yes, yes. I also would like to be the kind of mother that could be strong and say, you know, "go and have a good life," and it's really hard for me to do that.

Rogers: It's very hard to give up something that's been so precious in your life, but also something that I guess has caused you pain when you mentioned guilt.

Client: Yeah, and I'm aware that I have some anger toward her that I don't always get what I want. I have needs that are not met. And, uh, I don't feel I have a right to those needs. You know... she's a daughter; she's not my mother—though sometimes I feel as if I'd like her to mother me... It's very difficult for me to ask for that and have a right to it.

Rogers: So it may be unreasonable, but still, when she doesn't meet your needs, it makes you mad.

Client: Yeah. I get very angry, very angry with her. *(pause)*

Rogers: You're also feeling a little tension at this point, I guess.

Client: Yeah, yeah. A lot of conflict...

Rogers: A lot of pain.

Client: A lot of pain.

Rogers: A lot of pain. Can you say anything more what that's about? (adapted from C. R. Rogers, 1989).

In this excerpt, you can see two of the hallmarks of client-centered therapy. First, Rogers avoids giving any suggestions, advice, or disapproval and primarily shows the client that he understands what the client is feeling. Second, one technique Rogers uses for showing understanding is *reflecting* or restating the client's concerns. Reflecting the client's feelings is one of the basic techniques of the person-centered approach. In addition, humanistic therapists believe that clients have the capacity to discover and reach their true potential and it is the therapist's role to help and remove any roadblocks in their paths (Prochaska & Norcross, 2010).

Therapist's traits. Rogers believed that personal characteristics of the therapist—empathy, positive regard, genuineness—would bring about the client's change. *Empathy* is the ability to understand what the client is saying and feeling. *Positive regard* is the ability to communicate caring, respect, and regard for the client. *Genuineness* is the ability to be real and nondefensive in interactions with the client.

However, numerous studies have shown that these three characteristics are not always related to successful outcomes (C. E. Hill & Nakayama, 2000). The success of client-centered therapy appears to be due more to developing a good working client–therapist partnership and to the client's attitudes of wanting to and working hard to change (Prochaska & Norcross, 2010).

> What's blocking my path to developing my true potential?

Effectiveness. Client-centered therapy has been found to be effective in producing changes in clients in comparison with no-treatment control groups, but no more or less effective than other forms of therapy (C. E. Hill & Nakayama, 2000). According to client-centered therapy, the client–therapist relationship is the main reason the approach is effective (Kirschenbaum & Jourdan, 2005). Some studies, however, report that client-centered therapists who are very reflective and give very little direction are less effective than therapists who make more suggestions and give more direction (L. S. Greenberg & Rice, 1997).

Although very few therapists currently identify themselves as primarily client-centered in their approach, the principles of client-centered therapy have greatly contributed to making therapists aware of the importance of and the need to develop a positive working relationship with their clients (Kirschenbaum & Jourdan, 2005).

The therapist takes a much more directive role in the next kind of insight therapy, called cognitive therapy. ●

Text credit: Therapy session adapted from "Person-Centered Therapy," by N. J. Raskin and C. R. Rogers, 1989. In R. J. Corsini and D. Wedding (Eds.), *Current Psychotherapies*, 4th ed. F. E. Peacock.

E Cognitive Therapy

Overview

Do negative thoughts get you down?

Similar to Carl Rogers's experience, Aaron Beck was also trained in psychoanalytic techniques and used them to treat patients, many of whom were suffering from depression. When he asked them to free-associate, he noticed that depressed patients often expressed negative or distorted thoughts about themselves—"I'm a failure, no one likes me, nothing turns out right." What really caught his attention was how patients would express a string of negative thoughts almost automatically, without paying much attention. Beck reasoned that these automatically occurring negative thoughts had a great impact on the patients' lives, such as by lowering their self-esteem and encouraging self-blame and self-criticism. Beck developed his form of cognitive therapy to stop these thoughts and so treat depression and other problems (A. T. Beck, 1976, 1991).

Cognitive therapy, as developed by Aaron Beck, assumes that we have automatic negative thoughts that we typically say to ourselves without paying much attention. By continually repeating these automatic negative thoughts, we color and distort how we perceive and interpret our world and influence how we behave and feel.

Negative messages we say to ourselves—for example, "Nothing ever goes right," "I'm a failure," or "Everybody criticizes me"—can bias and distort our thoughts and feelings. Cognitive therapy was developed to make a person aware of, and stop, negative self-statements.

Therapy session. To give you an idea of how negative thoughts occur, here is a brief excerpt from one of Dr. Beck's sessions.

The client is a 26-year-old graduate student who has bouts of depression.

Client: I get depressed when things go wrong. Like when I fail a test.

Therapist: How can failing a test make you depressed?

Client: Well, if I fail, I'll never get into law school.

Therapist: Do you agree that the way you interpret the results of the test will affect you? You might feel depressed, you might have trouble sleeping, not feel like eating, and you might even wonder if you should drop out of the course.

Client: I have been thinking that I wasn't going to make it. Yes, I agree.

Therapist: Now what did failing mean?

Why do I keep thinking all those negative thoughts?

Client: *(tearful)* That I couldn't get into law school.

Therapist: And what does that mean to you?

Client: That I'm just not smart enough.

Therapist: Anything else?

Client: That I can never be happy.

Therapist: And how do these thoughts make you feel?

Client: Very unhappy.

Therapist: So it is the meaning of failing a test that makes you very unhappy. In fact, believing that you can never be happy is a powerful factor in producing unhappiness. So, you get yourself into a trap—by definition, failure to get into

law school equals "I can never be happy" (A. T. Beck et al., 1979, pp. 145–146).

Notice how the client tries to avoid admitting that her thoughts influence her feelings. Also notice her negative self-statements, such as "I'm just not smart enough" and "I can never be happy." Beck believes that these kinds of negative self-statements will influence this client's thoughts and feelings and contribute to her major symptom, depression.

Important factors. Beck identified a number of specific maladaptive thoughts that contribute to various symptoms, such as anxiety and depression. Thus, thinking "I'm a failure" after doing poorly on one test is an example of *overgeneralization,* which is making blanket judgments about yourself on the basis of a single incident. Thinking "Most people don't like me" is an example of *polarized thinking,* which is sorting information into one of two categories, good or bad. Thinking "People always criticize me" is an example of *selective attention,* which is focusing on one detail so much that you do not notice other events, such as being complimented. Beck believes that maladaptive thought patterns cause a distorted view of oneself and one's world, which in turn may lead to various emotional problems. Thus, the primary goals of cognitive therapy are to identify and change maladaptive thoughts.

Overgeneralization	
Polarized thinking	EMOTIONAL PROBLEMS
Selective attention	

Cognitive techniques. Beck's approach, which is an example of cognitive therapy, works to change thought patterns, which, in turn, play a critical role in influencing behavior and emotions. In cognitive therapy, clients are told how their maladaptive thoughts and irrational beliefs can result in feelings of depression, anxiety, or other symptoms. Clients are shown how to monitor their thoughts and beliefs, how to recognize maladaptive thought patterns, such as overgeneralization and polarized thinking, and how to substitute rational thought patterns (A. T. Beck & Weishaar, 2008). In the Application section (p. 574), we'll give examples of specific techniques for stopping negative thoughts and substituting positive ones.

Effectiveness. Cognitive therapy has proved effective in treating a variety of symptoms. For example, it is as effective as various drugs in treating depression, bipolar disorder, general anxiety disorder, social phobia, agoraphobia, panic attacks, smoking, anger, and eating disorders. The benefits of cognitive therapy extend beyond the end of treatment. In some cases, the benefits last longer than those of other forms of therapy, including the use of medications (J. R. Ball et al., 2006; Begley, 2009b; D. M. Clark et al., 2006; DeRubeis et al., 2005; Eisendrath et al., 2011; Rupke et al., 2006).

Increasingly, methods of cognitive therapy are combined with those of the next approach, behavior therapy. The result is a very popular approach called cognitive-behavioral therapy. However, before explaining cognitive-behavioral therapy, we'll need to discuss behavior therapy, which is our next topic. ●

F Behavior Therapy

Overview

The 1950s was the time Carl Rogers developed client-centered therapy and Aaron Beck developed cognitive therapy. Both were motivated to develop new approaches because they had become disillusioned with the techniques and results of the psychoanalytic approach, which they had used in clinical practice.

What's so important about Little Albert?

This was also the time Joseph Wolpe (1958, 1990), a physician in South Africa, became disillusioned with psychoanalysis and developed a new, quicker, and more effective procedure to reduce fear and anxiety.

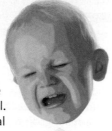

Through classical conditioning, this pet rat . . .

At the beginning of this module, we told you about Little Albert, who initially wanted to touch and play with a white rat but, after being conditioned, came to fear it (Watson & Rayner, 1920). This demonstration, which occurred in the 1920s, showed that emotional responses could be conditioned.

But it was not until the 1950s that a clinician developed a procedure to unlearn emotional responses.

In a real sense, Wolpe finished what John Watson had started: Watson had conditioned Little Albert to fear an object, while Wolpe conditioned patients to be less fearful. Wolpe's procedure was the first experimental demonstration of reducing fear through conditioning and gave a real jump-start to the development of behavior therapy (Persons, 1997).

. . . came to be feared by Little Albert.

Behavior therapy, also called behavior modification, uses the principles of classical and operant conditioning to change disruptive behaviors and improve human functioning. It focuses on changing particular behaviors rather than the underlying mental events or possible unconscious factors.

We'll first give you an example of a behavior therapy session and then describe Wolpe's conditioning procedure to reduce fear.

Therapy session. In this session, the therapist is talking to a woman who feels bad because she has great difficulty being assertive.

Client: The basic problem is that I have the tendency to let people step all over me. I don't know why, but I just have difficulty in speaking my mind.

Therapist: So you find yourself in a number of different situations where you don't respond the way you would really like to and you would like to learn how to behave differently.

Client: Yes. But you know, I have tried to handle certain situations differently, but I just don't seem to be able to do so.

Therapist: Well, maybe you tried to do too much or didn't quite know the right technique. For example, imagine yourself at the bottom of a staircase, wanting to get to the top. It's too much to ask to get there in one gigantic leap. Perhaps a better way to go about changing your reaction in these situations is to take it one step at a time.

Client: That would seem to make sense, but I'm not sure if I see how it could be done.

Therapist: Well, there are probably certain situations in which it would be less difficult for you to assert yourself, such as telling your boss that he forgot to pay you for the past four weeks.

Client: *(laughing)* I guess in that situation, I would say something. Although I must admit, I would feel uneasy about it.

Therapist: But not as uneasy as if you went in and asked him for a raise.

Client: No. Certainly not.

Therapist: So, the first situation would be low on the staircase, whereas the second would be higher up. If you can learn to handle easier situations, then the more difficult ones would present less of a problem. And the only way you can really learn to change your reactions is through practice.

Client: In other words, I really have to go out and actually force myself to speak up more, but taking it a little bit at a time?

Therapist: Exactly. And it's easier and safer to run through some of these situations here because you can't really get into trouble if you make a mistake. Once you learn different ways to speak your mind, you can try them out in the real world (adapted from Goldfried & Davison, 1976).

Notice that the behavior therapist does not encourage the client to free-associate, which is a major technique of psychoanalysis. The behavior therapist does not repeat or reflect what the client says, which is a major technique of client-centered therapy. The behavior therapist does not discuss the client's tendency to automatically think negative thoughts, which is a major technique of cognitive therapy.

Instead, the behavior therapist quickly identifies the specific problem, which is the woman's tendency to be unassertive when she really wants to speak her mind. Next, the behavior therapist will discuss a program for behavioral change that will help this woman learn to behave more assertively.

Two goals. Behavior therapy has two goals. The first is to modify undesirable behaviors, using many of the principles of operant conditioning, and teach the client how to perform new behaviors, which for this woman involves learning ways to be more assertive.

The second goal of behavior therapy is to help the client meet specific behavioral goals through constant practice and reward (Spiegler & Guevremont, 2010). For example, this woman would be asked to practice initiating conversations and stating her opinions, perhaps beginning in the safety of the therapist's office and then gradually practicing these new assertive behaviors in the more threatening situations of the real world.

Why do I let people walk all over me?

The next example of behavior therapy illustrates a specific technique that is used to help clients overcome phobias.

Therapy session adapted from *Clinical Behavior Therapy,* by M. R. Goldfried and G. C. Davison, 1976. Holt, Rinehart & Winston.

Unless otherwise noted, all images are © Cengage Learning

© PhotoDisc, Inc.

Systematic Desensitization

Case Study

Jack had developed a phobia of blood that interfered with his plans. He was a high-school senior who wanted to be an ambulance driver. But the problem was that he passed out at the sight or discussion of blood. He had been afraid of blood for years and had fainted about 20 times in science and biology classes. He even felt queasy when bloody accidents or operating-room scenes were shown on television. If his supervisor found out about his phobia, Jack might lose his chance to be an ambulance driver. Except for his phobia, Jack was happy at school, rarely became depressed, and was generally easy-going (Yule & Fernando, 1980).

Jack's fear of blood interfered with his being an ambulance driver.

Some therapies for phobias might require years of treatment; for instance, a psychoanalyst would search for unconscious conflicts causing the phobia. In contrast, behavior therapists would take a direct approach to the treatment, requiring 5 to 30 sessions. The technique used today by behavior therapists is based on the one that Wolpe (1958) developed in the 1950s and is called systematic desensitization.

Systematic desensitization is a technique of behavior therapy in which the client is gradually exposed to the feared object while simultaneously practicing relaxation. Desensitization involves three steps: learning to relax, constructing a hierarchy with the least feared situation on the bottom and the most feared situation at the top, and being progressively exposed to the feared situation.

Behavior therapists assume that since Jack's phobia was acquired through a conditioning process, his phobia can be unconditioned by gradually exposing him to the feared object through the process of systematic desensitization.

1 Relaxation

Jack, whose phobia was a fear of blood, underwent systematic desensitization, a very effective treatment for phobias (Cormier & Nurius, 2003). In the first step, Jack learned to relax by practicing progressive relaxation. This method involves tensing and relaxing various muscle groups, beginning with the toes and working up to the head. With this procedure, Jack learned how to put himself into a relaxed state. For most individuals, learning progressive relaxation requires several weeks with at least one 15-minute session every day.

2 Stimulus Hierarchy

The second step was for Jack to make a *stimulus hierarchy,* which is a list of feared stimuli, arranged in order from least to most feared. With the help of his therapist, Jack made the stimulus hierarchy shown on the right, which lists various situations associated with blood. A rating of 1 indicates little fear if confronted by this stimulus, while a rating of 7 indicates that Jack would probably pass out from this stimulus.

MOST STRESSFUL

7 Needle drawing blood

6 Finger dripping blood

5 Seeing someone cut

4 Needle entering arm

3 Watching blood on TV

2 Cutting own finger

1 Seeing word "blood"

Stimulus hierarchy ranks fearful situations from least (1) to most (7).

3 Exposure

Systematic desensitization training means that, after successfully completing steps 1 and 2, Jack was ready for step 3, which was to systematically desensitize himself by exposing himself to the fear stimuli. Desensitization occurs through relaxing while simultaneously imagining the feared stimuli.

Jack put himself into a relaxed state and then imagined the first or least feared item in his hierarchy, seeing the word *blood.* He tried to remain in a relaxed state while vividly imagining the word *blood.* He repeated this procedure until he felt no tension or anxiety in this situation. At this point, he went on to the next item in his hierarchy. Jack repeated the procedure of pairing relaxation with images of each feared item until he reached the last and most feared item.

A necessary part of therapy is exposure to the feared situation.

Through the desensitization program described here, Jack's blood phobia was treated in five one-hour sessions. A follow-up five years later indicated that Jack was still free of his blood phobia, had not developed any substitute symptoms, and was training to be an ambulance driver (Yule & Fernando, 1980).

Exposure: Imagined or In Vivo

Systematic desensitization appears to be most effective if, instead of just imagining the items on the list, which is called *imagined exposure,* clients gradually expose themselves to the actual situation, which is called *in vivo exposure* (the phrase *in vivo* is Latin for "in real life") (G. T. Wilson, 2005). For example, in Module 22 we described the case of Christine, who signed up for a course to treat her phobia of flying. In her case, a modified systematic desensitization program included in vivo exposure, which meant taking an actual flight while doing the breathing and relaxation exercises that she had learned. The in vivo exposure worked for Christine, who was able to overcome her phobia of flying.

Systematic desensitization has proved to be a very effective treatment for a variety of anxiety disorders, especially when combined with in vivo exposure (Moscovitch et al., 2008). Later, in the Critical Thinking section (p. 576), we'll discuss how systematic desensitization is being used in virtual therapy, a revolutionary new treatment approach.

It is important to continue exposure until the person's anxiety decreases.

The next therapy is actually a combination of behavior and cognitive therapies. ●

G Cognitive-Behavioral Therapy

Definition

As psychoanalysis reached its peak of popularity in the 1950s, a number of clinicians and researchers were becoming dissatisfied with its procedures, which were time-consuming, costly, and useful for treating only a limited number of clients with relatively minor problems (Franks, 1994).

Why combine two different therapies?

At this same time, there was a great increase in the popularity of learning principles that came from Pavlov's work on classical conditioning and Skinner's work on operant conditioning. Researchers and clinicians began to apply these learning principles to change human behavior with methods based on a strong experimental foundation rather than Freud's unverified beliefs about unconscious conflicts. Both behavior and cognitive therapies developed out of dissatisfaction with psychoanalysis and the belief that learning principles would provide more effective methods of changing human behavior than would the concepts of psychoanalysis.

Combining therapies. One of the interesting developments in therapy has been occurring since the late 1970s as both behavior and cognitive therapies have become increasingly popular. The major difference between them is that ***behavior therapy*** focuses on identifying and changing specific behaviors, while ***cognitive therapy*** focuses on identifying and changing specific maladaptive thought patterns. Beginning in the early 1990s, researchers and clinicians began combining the methods of behavior and cognitive therapies into what is now called cognitive-behavioral therapy (P. Grant et al., 2005).

Cognitive-behavioral therapy combines the cognitive therapy technique of changing negative, unhealthy, or distorted thought patterns with the behavior therapy technique of changing maladaptive or disruptive behaviors by learning and practicing new skills to improve functioning.

> I need to stop thinking all those negative thoughts.

Currently, the difference between cognitive therapy and behavior therapy has become blurred as techniques from these two approaches are combined into what has become a very popular therapy that is commonly called cognitive-behavioral therapy (J. S. Beck, 2011; Dobson, 2009).

Techniques. Cognitive-behavioral therapists combine a number of techniques that are designed to change both thoughts and behaviors and thus improve a person's psychological functioning. These techniques include monitoring one's own thoughts and behaviors; identifying thoughts and behaviors that need to be changed; setting specific goals that increase in difficulty; learning to reinforce oneself for reaching a goal; imitating or modeling new behaviors; substituting positive for negative thoughts; and doing homework, which involves practicing new behaviors in a safe setting before performing them in the real world (A. T. Beck & Weishaar, 2008). These cognitive-behavioral techniques are the basis for almost all *self-help programs,* which may be completed without the assistance of a therapist. For more serious problems or additional support, the aid and help of a therapist may be needed.

Kinds of problems. Throughout this text, we have discussed how behavior therapy, cognitive therapy, and the popular cognitive-behavioral therapy have been used to treat the following problems:

- **Insomnia:** A cognitive-behavioral program was as effective as drugs in helping people get to sleep (p. 162).
- **Conditioned nausea:** Individuals undergoing chemotherapy developed conditioned nausea and were treated with behavior therapy (p. 207).
- **Autistic children:** Behavior modification helped some autistic children develop sufficient academic and social skills to enter public schools and function very well (p. 232).

> I need to learn assertive behaviors.

- **Psychosomatic problems:** Behavior therapy (biofeedback) helped people decrease stress-related symptoms by reducing headaches and physiological arousal (p. 233).
- **Abusive parents:** Cognitive-behavioral therapy that involved training in social skills helped parents deal with their own personal problems as well as daily difficulties related to caring for demanding children (p. 401).
- **Stress management:** Cognitive-behavioral techniques are basic to all programs for reducing stress (p. 502).
- **Phobias:** Various phobias, such as fear of specific situations (flying, public speaking) or objects (snakes, bugs, blood), were treated with cognitive-behavioral techniques (pp. 225, 524, 525).

We'll also discuss other examples of cognitive-behavioral techniques in the Application section.

Effectiveness. Cognitive-behavioral therapy is currently being used to treat a wide variety of problems, including eating disorders, marital problems, anxiety and phobias, depression, and sexual dysfunction. Programs based on cognitive-behavioral therapy are widely used to help people stop smoking, become more assertive, improve communication and interpersonal skills, manage stress, and control anger. Researchers report that cognitive-behavioral therapy was significantly more effective in treating this wide variety of problems than were control procedures (Butler et al., 2006; Dobson, 2009). And in some cases, cognitive-behavioral therapy was as effective as drugs in treating some forms of anxiety, phobia, depression, and compulsive behavior (Butler et al., 2006; Spiegler & Guevremont, 2010).

After the Concept Review, we'll discuss some of the common factors among effective therapies as well as a few therapy settings that are alternatives to the traditional one-to-one therapy session. ●

Unless otherwise noted, all images are © Cengage Learning

Concept Review

1. If you first trained as a physician and then went into a psychiatric residency, which involves additional training in pharmacology, neurology, and psychotherapeutic techniques, you would be a **(a)** _____. If you completed a PhD program in psychology, including one year of work in a clinical setting, you would be a **(b)** _____. If you completed a PhD program in psychology or education, including work in a counseling setting, you would be a **(c)** _____.

2. A process characterized by verbal interaction between therapist and client and the development of a supportive relationship, during which a therapist may analyze or suggest ways for the client to deal with and overcome his or her problems, is called _____.

3. One approach to therapy is characterized by the idea that we have an unconscious part whose activities and

thoughts are hidden behind a mental barrier that we cannot voluntarily remove. Behind this barrier are repressed and psychologically dangerous thoughts that give rise to unconscious conflicts, which, in turn, can result in psychological and physical symptoms. This approach is called _____.

4. Freud developed two techniques to uncover unconscious thoughts. One was to encourage clients to talk about any thoughts or images that entered their heads, which is called **(a)** _____. The second technique was based on the assumption that dreams contain hidden meanings and symbols and the therapist's role was to **(b)** _____ these dream symbols.

5. Freud said that, during therapy, a patient may respond as if the therapist were a father or mother and project strong feelings toward the therapist. This process is called **(a)** _____. Also during therapy, a patient may be reluctant to work through feelings or to recognize unconscious conflicts and repressed thoughts; this is called **(b)** _____.

6. The popular approach to therapy shares many of the features of psychoanalysis—for example, discussing the client's feelings,

breaking down the client's defenses and resistances, and interpreting the client's behaviors—but may not necessarily use free association or agree that many problems result from unconscious sexual conflicts. This approach, which takes less time than psychoanalysis, is called _____ psychotherapy.

7. One approach to therapy assumes that each person has an actualizing tendency—that is, a tendency to develop his or her full potential. In this approach, the therapist's task is to show compassion and positive regard in helping the client reach his or her potential. This approach was developed by **(a)** _____ and is called **(b)** _____ therapy.

8. Another approach to therapy assumes that we have automatic negative thoughts that we say to ourselves without paying much attention. By continually repeating these automatic negative thoughts, we color and distort how we perceive and interpret our world and influence how we behave and feel. This approach to therapy was developed by **(a)** _____ and is called **(b)** _____ therapy.

9. One approach to therapy uses primarily the principles of classical and operant conditioning to change disruptive behaviors and improve human functioning. This approach, which focuses on changing particular behaviors rather than on the underlying mental events or possible unconscious factors, is called _____ therapy.

10. One approach combines changing negative, unhealthy, or distorted thoughts and beliefs by substituting positive, healthy, and realistic ones and changing one's undesirable or disruptive behaviors by learning and practicing new skills to improve functioning. This approach, which combines two therapies, is called _____ therapy.

11. There is a technique of behavior therapy in which the client is gradually exposed to the feared object while simultaneously practicing relaxation. This technique, which involves three steps—learning to relax, constructing a hierarchy with the least feared situation on the bottom and the most feared situation at the top, and being progressively exposed to the feared situation—is called _____.

12. Because of its effectiveness, cognitive-behavioral therapy has become the basis for many self-help programs to stop smoking, reduce insomnia, decrease conditioned nausea, help autistic children develop academic and social skills, and reduce intense and irrational fears called _____.

Answers: *1. (a) psychiatrist, (b) clinical psychologist, (c) counseling psychologist; 2. psychotherapy; 3. psychoanalysis; 4. (a) free association, (b) interpret; 5. (a) transference, (b) resistance; 6. psychodynamic; 7. (a) Carl Rogers, (b) client-centered; 8. (a) Aaron Beck, (b) cognitive; 9. behavior; 10. cognitive-behavioral; 11. systematic desensitization; 12. phobias*

© Cengage Learning

H Common Factors & Therapy Settings

Common Factors

If you need professional help today, you can choose from a number of different therapies. However, because therapy approaches begin with different assumptions and use different methods, you might wonder if one therapy is more effective than another. In answer to this question, researchers have consistently found, with some exception, that there is very little, if any, difference in effectiveness among various therapies (Drisko, 2004; L. Luborsky et al., 2002).

What do the different therapies have in common?

It may seem surprising that therapies with such different assumptions and techniques have been found to be equally effective. One reason different therapies using different techniques achieve the same results is that they all share common factors (L. Luborsky et al., 2002).

Common factors are basic procedures and experiences that different therapies share and that explain why different approaches are equally effective.

Common factors include the growth of a supportive and trusting relationship between therapist and client and the development of an accepting atmosphere, in which the client feels willing to admit problems and is motivated to work on changing.

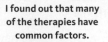

I found out that many of the therapies have common factors.

© fotoluminate/Shutterstock.com

The fact that some common factors are basic to all approaches explains why different assumptions and techniques can be combined to develop different forms of psychotherapy, all of which are about equally effective (L. Luborsky et al., 2002).

In addition to the commonalities shared among the various forms of psychotherapy, good therapists also share some characteristics. They build trust with clients, offer hope and realistic optimism, are reflective, have an acceptable and adaptive explanation for the client's conditions, have a treatment plan and allow it to be flexible, monitor the client's progress, and engage in ongoing improvement through professional development (Wampold, 2011).

Related to the commonalities shared among therapeutic approaches and good therapists is the basic assumption that therapy takes places face to face, with one therapist and one client in the same room. Next, we'll discuss how therapy can occur in groups as well as how it is possible for a client and therapist to never meet in person.

Group Therapies

The different therapeutic approaches we have discussed in this module are not limited for use in individual therapy; rather, they can be applied in a group setting.

What are the types of group therapies?

Group therapy is when psychotherapy is conducted in a group setting and involves clients receiving feedback from others in the group as well as from the therapist(s).

Group therapy can be used to place individuals with similar problems together in a group to help them feel less isolated and more supported. Group therapy is especially helpful in treating problems arising from social interactions, such as relationship conflict.

While many types of therapy may be conducted in a group setting, there are forms of therapy that take place only in groups. We will define two such types of group therapy: family therapy and couple therapy (Goldenberg & Goldenberg, 2012; Gurman, 2008; Prochaska & Norcross, 2010).

Family therapy is a form of group therapy in which all family members are treated as the client and helped to change destructive relationships and improve the way they communicate with one another.

Couple therapy is a form of group therapy in which the couple is treated as the client and helped to improve their skills in communication and conflict management.

Telemental Health

Is cybertherapy really therapy?

Our understanding of therapy has largely been based on the assumption that it must take place in person, face to face. However, psychologists are now incorporating various forms of technology to communicate with patients in a rapidly growing field called telemental health (Novotney, 2011).

Telemental health refers to providing psychological services remotely, via telephone, e-mail, or videoconferencing.

One of the major high-tech methods being used to deliver telemental health services is cybertherapy.

Cybertherapy is therapy delivered over the Internet.

Cybertherapy can range from clients e-mailing questions or concerns to a therapist, who in turn responds by e-mail, to clients sitting in front of a camera mounted on their computer and having a live online session with a therapist (right photo).

© Ingram Publishing/Alamy

The advantages of cybertherapy are that it reduces costs and improves treatment access in areas with limited availability of mental health services. Also, it may help individuals overcome barriers related to stigma by providing them with mental health treatment from the privacy of their home (Clay, 2012). The disadvantages are that cybertherapists may not have the same credentials or be as well trained as traditional therapists. Also, cybertherapists cannot clearly see body gestures or facial expressions and cannot clearly hear the emotional tone in a client's voice.

The most recent change in telemental health is the development of therapy apps to be used on smartphones to allow people to access services anytime, anywhere (Carey, 2012).

Next, we'll discuss an interesting treatment of a challenging psychological problem—getting over a traumatic situation. ●

I Research Focus: EMDR

Does EMDR Stop Traumatic Memories?

Can watching a moving hand reduce terrible memories?

In the early 1990s a new kind of psychotherapy appeared that was unlike any we have discussed. After only a few sessions, clients reported a decrease in traumatic memories, a problem very difficult to treat. This therapy was called Eye Movement Desensitization and Reprocessing (F. Shapiro, 2002).

Eye Movement Desensitization and Reprocessing, or **EMDR,** essentially involves having the client talk about or imagine a troubling traumatic memory while visually focusing on and following the back-and-forth movement of a therapist's hand. This process usually continues for several 90-minute sessions, after which the traumatic memories are greatly reduced or eliminated.

Francine Shapiro (1991) discovered EMDR after noticing that her own troubling thoughts disappeared after she associated them with her back-and-forth eye movements. Because EMDR's method and claims were so unusual, researchers wondered if it really worked.

Evidence from Case Studies

All of the early support for the effectiveness of EMDR came from testimonials and case studies, many of them as dramatic as the following:

After one individual lost both arms and hearing in a tragic fire and explosion, he experienced terrible flashbacks and nightmares for the next six years. When he finally consulted a psychiatrist, he was desperate and agreed to try the then-new EMDR procedure. During the EMDR procedure, he vividly recalled the fire, the shouts of the employees, and other terrible images, while visually following the back-and-forth movement of the therapist's hand. However, as he continued imagining terrible images and following the therapist's hand movements, he began to feel a flowing sensation of peace. Following a number of sessions, he was reported to be free of flashbacks and nightmares, had taught himself to drive a car, and had joined a group that helps children who need artificial limbs (Wartik, 1994).

Dramatic cases like this suggested that EMDR was a very simple yet effective treatment for getting rid of traumatic memories, one of the most difficult problems therapists face. In explaining how EMDR worked, Shapiro (1991) hypothesized that the eye movements during EMDR aided information processing to somehow reduce the distress accompanying traumatic events and images.

Although the effectiveness of EMDR was supported by case studies and testimonials, we must remember that such methods have great potential for error and bias and cannot demonstrate cause and effect. Thus, to evaluate the effectiveness of EMDR, researchers used a more scientific approach, the experimental method (see p. 36).

During EMDR, a client talks about a painful memory while watching a therapist's moving hand.

© CC Studio/Photo Researchers, Inc.

Evidence from Experiments

Does EMDR work? We have discussed many examples of so-called "medical treatments" (Korean centipedes, tiger bones, fake pills and injections) that, according to 30–80% of users' testimonials, reduced pain, increased sexual stamina, or cured various physical problems (see pp. 31, 111) (Talbot, 2000). These "medical treatments" are examples of the well-known *placebo effect,* which can have a powerful influence and may explain why EMDR works. Researchers have conducted about ten randomized, controlled studies on EMDR therapy and concluded that it was not simply a placebo effect but was effective in reducing traumatic memories, such as those that occur in posttraumatic stress disorder or PTSD (see p. 491). So the answer to our first question, Does EMDR work? is yes (F. Shapiro, 2012).

However, wondering if eye movement was the critical feature of EMDR therapy, researchers compared clients who moved their eyes with those who stared straight ahead. As shown in the right graph, clients who made eye movements and who fixed their stare both showed reductions in distress (Renfrey & Spates, 1994).

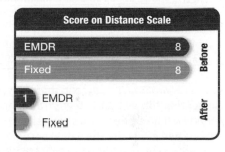

Score on Distance Scale		
EMDR	8	Before
Fixed	8	Before
EMDR	1	After
Fixed		After

Researchers now know that different kinds of stimulation (eye movements, fixed staring, hand taps) are effective as long as such stimulation occurs while clients are recalling their traumatic memories (May, 2005; F. Shapiro & Maxfield, 2002).

How does EMDR work? What researchers know is that during EMDR clients are recalling and confronting their most feared feelings, images, or situations, an established method of exposure therapy (see p. 567). Thus, many researchers suggest that EMDR may be another form of traditional exposure therapy, which is very effective for reducing fearful thoughts, images, and situations (Lilienfeld & Arkowitz, 2006). However, others suggest that the treatment process of EMDR is unique because the eye movements allow patients to enter a state of relaxation and emotionally distance themselves from the trauma experiences (C. W. Lee et al., 2006; Schubert et al., 2011).

Although there has been much controversy about EMDR, research has shown that EMDR is effective for treating the occurrence of traumatic memories (D. L. Albright & Thyer, 2010; Marsa, 2002; R. Shapiro, 2005). Consequently, organizations such as the American Psychiatric Association, the Department of Veterans Affairs and Department of Defense, and the International Society of Traumatic Stress Studies have identified EMDR as an effective treatment for posttraumatic stress disorder (F. Shapiro, 2012).

EMDR may seem strange to some, but the next treatment sounds very strange to most Westerners. ●

J Cultural Diversity: Different Healer

Case Study: Young Woman

What was her problem?

In Bali, which is a province of Indonesia, as well as in parts of Africa, China, and Fiji Islands, many psychological problems that Western clinicians would diagnose as anxiety, mood disorders, or schizophrenia are believed to be caused by possession by evil spirits (Hobart, 2003; McGrath, 2003). For example, take the case of Putu, a young unmarried woman, who was about 20 years old.

Putu lived with her family in a small village on the beautiful island of Bali. Putu's family had made her break off her loving relationship with one man and become engaged to another, whom she did not want to marry. Since her new engagement, Putu had lost all interest in things around her, ate very little, and did not take part in normal activities or conversation. Putu was taken to the local nurse, who gave an injection of multivitamins to treat her low energy level and general apathy. The injection did not help and the nurse recommended that the family take Putu to a local witch doctor or healer, who could use special rituals to cure Putu (L. Connor, 1982).

In Western terminology, clinicians would say that Putu was suffering from depression, which was most certainly brought on by having to break off her loving relationship and being forced by her family to become engaged to someone she did not like. Western therapists would have treated her depression with some form of psychotherapy and, if possible, would have brought the whole family in for therapy. However, in Bali, Putu was believed to be the victim of witchcraft, which could be cured by taking her to a traditional healer, who is called a *balian* (Keeney, 2004).

Healer's Diagnosis and Treatment

What is healing smoke?

The family took the depressed Putu to a well-respected healer, or balian. Balians believe their powers come from supernatural forces. The balians often undergo periods of fasting and isolation that induce trances through which the spirits speak to them. Balians are considered special healers who are asked to help individuals with a variety of personal and mental problems (Keeney, 2004).

In Putu's case, the balian located a small pulsation beneath Putu's jawbone that indicated the presence of an evil wind spirit. The rejected lover had placed the evil spirit into Putu's body, and there was now a great danger that this evil spirit might travel throughout her body: If it reached Putu's ears, she would go deaf; if it reached her brain, she would become violent and insane. The balian (right photo) said that he would mix a special medicine and that the family should return in two days for an exorcism of the evil wind spirit.

As part of the exorcism rites, two small human effigies, a male and a female, were made out of cooked rice and were set on the ground to the south of the girl. When the evil spirit was driven out of Putu's body by smoke, the evil spirit would be attracted to the effigies, which would then be broken to destroy the spirit.

You are possessed of an evil wind spirit.

Traditional healers, called balians, function like Western therapists.

© Dimas Ardian/Getty Images

In the morning, the balian asked Putu to stand in the middle of healing smoke. After about 40 minutes, the evil wind spirit left Putu's body and entered the small male and female rice figures, which were broken and thrown away. Then Putu's body was purified with holy water. During the course of the afternoon, Putu began to talk, show interest in food and things around her, and generally get over her former apathy.

For two more weeks, Putu stayed with the balian, who continued to perform purification ceremonies and drive away any lingering evil wind spirits. As part of the purification ceremonies, Putu was asked to take part in everyday activities, such as gathering and making food, engaging in normal conversations, washing clothes, and doing other chores. Through this process, Putu was helped and encouraged to resume her normal duties and take part in social activities.

Healers Versus Western Therapists

Is a balian a therapist?

The case of Putu shows that the beliefs and treatments used in the traditional healing practices of African and Asian balians or healers are very different from those used by Western therapists to treat psychological problems. But notice that the balian's exorcism rites, purification rituals, and herbal medicines did reduce Putu's depression. In many parts of Asia, China, Africa, Fiji Islands, and Indonesia, healers use herbal medicines, exorcism, and purification rituals to successfully treat a variety of psychological problems (McGrath, 2003; Sue & Sue, 2007).

There are two explanations of why a balian's potions and rituals are effective treatments for various mental and physical problems. First, studies on Western patients find that many patients suffering from a variety of psychological and physical problems show remarkable improvement after receiving placebo treatments (Wampold et al., 2005). The balian's rituals and herbs may function like Western placebos (see p. 111), which create positive beliefs and expectations to help individuals recover from a variety of physical and psychological problems. Second, the balian's purification ceremonies involve the development of a close relationship with the sufferer, and this relationship may involve common factors similar to those found effective in Western therapy. Thus, placebos and psychotherapy's common factors may explain the success of balians in treating a variety of mental problems in different cultures.

In this module, we've discussed various forms of therapies used to treat mental disorders. Next, we'll discuss biomedical therapies. ●

K Biomedical Therapies

Definition and Types

What are the types of biomedical therapies?

The psychotherapy approaches we have discussed in this module apply psychological principles to understanding and treating psychological disorders. People with psychological disorders may also be treated with biomedical therapies, either solely or in combination with psychotherapy.

Biomedical therapy involves the use of interventions to treat mental disorders that change biological factors, such as the levels of neurotransmitters in the brain.

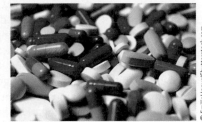

Throughout Modules 22 and 23, we discussed a variety of drug and nondrug types of biomedical therapies. For instance, we discussed medical procedures including electroconvulsive therapy (ECT), transcranial magnetic stimulation (TMS), and deep brain stimulation (DBS) (see p. 535). Also, we provided information on a variety of drugs used to treat mental disorders.

We will focus our discussion here on the most common form of biomedical therapy—drug therapies. There are various categories of drugs used to treat symptoms of mental disorders. We'll discuss antidepressant drugs, antianxiety drugs, mood-stabilizer drugs, and antipsychotic drugs.

Antidepressant Drugs

Antidepressants are the most commonly prescribed medication in the United States, used by 10% of the population (Olfson & Marcus, 2009).

Antidepressant drugs act by increasing the levels of a specific group of neurotransmitters (monoamines—serotonin, norepinephrine, and dopamine) that are involved in the regulation of emotions and moods.

About 80% of prescribed antidepressant drugs, such as Prozac and Zoloft, belong to a group of drugs called *SSRIs* (selective serotonin reuptake inhibitors) (Noonan & Cowley, 2002). The SSRIs work primarily by raising the level of the neurotransmitter serotonin.

Common side effects include nausea, insomnia, sedation, and sexual problems (decreased libido, erectile dysfunction) (Gitlin, 2009; Khawam et al., 2006).

Antianxiety Drugs

Most antianxiety drugs belong to a class of chemicals known as benzodiazepines.

Benzodiazepines *(ben-zo-die-AS-ah-peens)* (Valium, Xanax, Restoril) reduce anxiety, worry, and stress by lowering physiological arousal, which results in a state of tranquility.

Benzodiazepines provide a sense of tranquility by decreasing the activity of the sympathetic division of the central nervous system, which results in reduced heart rate, respiration, and muscle tension. In addition to being used to treat anxiety, benzodiazepines are prescribed for the treatment of sleeping problems, such as insomnia.

However, prolonged use of benzodiazepines, especially at high doses, may lead to dependence on the drug and serious side effects, such as memory loss and excessive sleepiness.

Mood-Stabilizer Drugs

People who experience the highs and lows of mood disorders (i.e., mania and depression) will likely benefit most by taking a mood-stabilizer drug.

Mood-stabilizer drugs act by adjusting the levels of neurotransmitters (e.g., norepinephrine and serotonin) to even out the highs and lows of mood disorders, such as bipolar disorder.

One example of a mood-stabilizer drug is lithium, which is used to keep people diagnosed with bipolar disorder from becoming too elated (manic) or too depressed. Also, lithium is effective in treating individuals who experience *mania*—that is, the manic episodes without the depression (F. K. Goodwin, 2003).

However, lithium is a potentially dangerous drug that can in rare cases cause death if its concentration in the blood becomes too high. Therefore, people who use lithium must undergo regular blood tests.

Antipsychotic Drugs

Most individuals diagnosed with schizophrenia are prescribed an antipsychotic or neuroleptic (meaning "taking hold of the nerves") drug.

Neuroleptic drugs are used to treat serious mental disorders, such as schizophrenia, by changing the levels of neurotransmitters in the brain.

There are two kinds of neuroleptic drugs: typical and atypical. Typical neuroleptics were the first effective medical treatment for schizophrenia.

Typical neuroleptic drugs primarily reduce levels of the neurotransmitter dopamine.

Typical neuroleptics: decrease dopamine

One group of typical neuroleptics, called the phenothiazines *(phee-no-THIGH-ah-zeens),* is widely prescribed to treat schizophrenia. Continued use of phenothiazines can produce unwanted motor movements, however, which is a side effect called tardive dyskinesia (Dolder, 2008).

Using typical neuroleptics to treat schizophrenia has been challenged by newer drugs, called atypical neuroleptics.

Atypical neuroleptic drugs (clozapine, risperidone) lower levels of dopamine and also lower levels of other neurotransmitters, especially serotonin.

Atypical neuroleptics: decrease dopamine & serotonin

Atypical neuroleptics have proven effective in decreasing the symptoms of schizophrenia, especially in patients who are not helped by typical neuroleptics (W. Carpenter, 2003).

One advantage of atypical neuroleptics is that they cause tardive dyskinesia in only about 5% of patients, compared to up to 29% of patients given typical neuroleptics (Caroff et al., 2002). However, atypical neuroleptics can cause other side effects, the most serious being increased levels of cholesterol and glucose or blood sugar, weight gain, and onset or worsening of diabetes (S. Burton, 2006; Dolder, 2008).

Next, we'll review the application of cognitive-behavioral techniques. ●

Unless otherwise noted, all images are © Cengage Learning

© EmiliaUngur/Shutterstock.com

MODULE 24 THERAPIES   **573**

L Application: Cognitive-Behavioral Techniques

Thought Problems

What's a common problem?

There are a number of psychological/behavioral problems that are not usually considered serious mental disorders but that can be very bothersome and interfere with our functioning normally.

For example, if you happened to do poorly on an exam, were criticized by someone important to you, broke up with someone, or had an accident, you may find it difficult to stop worrying and thinking about the troubling event. Researchers find a gender difference in worrying: Compared to men, women report more worrying and more recurring negative thoughts (Robichaud

How do I change negative thoughts into positive ones?

et al., 2003). Although it's good advice to "Just stop worrying about it," such advice is often very difficult to follow. The harder you try to stop worrying about something, the more you may worry about it. Fortunately, clinicians have developed a number of helpful cognitive-behavioral techniques that can be used to solve a variety of psychological or behavior problems. We'll discuss programs to stop recurring and troubling thoughts, to change negative thoughts into positive ones, and to deal with mild insomnia.

Thought-Stopping Program

Could you not think about a white bear?

Researchers asked college students to try very hard to suppress or stop any thoughts having to do with a large white bear. But researchers found that no matter how hard students tried to suppress worrisome negative thoughts, they kept coming back (Borton, 2002). These kinds of recurring and unwanted thoughts are called intrusive thoughts.

Intrusive thoughts are thoughts that we experience repeatedly, are usually unwanted or disruptive, and are very difficult to stop or eliminate.

Researchers found that just trying to stop thinking about something, called *thought suppression,* is not very effective, especially when the thoughts involve emotional situations and especially if we are under a lot of stress (G. J. Beck et al., 2006; Wenzlaff & Luxton, 2003). Instead of using thought suppression (trying not to think that thought), which is not effective, researchers suggest using a mental program that either distracts us or helps us change our goals (Wenzlaff & Wegner, 2000). For example, we'll describe a cognitive-behavioral program to identify and change intrusive thoughts. This program can be carried out on one's own or with the help and support of a therapist.

Here's a real-life example of Carol, who couldn't stop thinking about her former boyfriend, Fred, with whom she had just broken up. No matter how much she tried, she thought about Fred almost every day, and her thinking about breaking up with Fred triggered a chain of other negative thoughts about herself: "I feel that I am a failure. I feel ugly and useless. I keep thinking about not being able to have a relationship. I feel really depressed and I don't want to do anything" (G. L. Martin, 1982).

How do I stop thinking about my former boyfriend?

Carol's problem is that she has been unable to stop the intrusive thoughts about Fred, which result in her feeling depressed. An effective cognitive-behavioral technique for stopping intrusive thoughts has three steps.

1 Self-Monitoring

In all behavior-changing procedures, the first step is *self-monitoring,* which is observing one's own behavior without making any changes. In Carol's case, it meant that for one week she wrote down all depressing thoughts about Fred that lasted for more than a couple of minutes. In addition, the therapist asked Carol to bring in pictures of herself that showed her in pleasurable activities. These pictures would provide cues for thinking rational thoughts.

2 Thought Stopping

Each time Carol began to experience a disturbing thought, she would stop what she was doing, clasp her hands together, close her eyes, silently yell "Stop!" to herself, and silently count to ten. This was the *thought-stopping procedure.*

3 Thought Substitution

After counting silently to ten, she would open her eyes and take five photographs out of her purse. She would look at each photograph and read what she had written on the back. For example, one photograph showed her about to board an airplane for a trip. On the back she had written, "I'm my own boss. My life is ahead of me. I can do what I want to do." Carol would then think about the trip and how much she liked to travel. She would do the same for all five photographs.

This *thought-substituting procedure* took one or two minutes. After that, she would return to whatever she had been doing.

During Carol's first week of self-monitoring, she thought about Fred constantly and spent from 15 minutes to an hour each day crying. However, after using the thought-stopping and thought-substituting procedures for eight weeks, Carol had reduced the time thinking about Fred to the point that she rarely cried or was depressed. A follow-up interview four months after therapy revealed that Carol was no longer having intrusive thoughts about Fred, was no longer depressed, had developed no new symptoms, and had a new boyfriend (G. L. Martin, 1982).

In Carol's case, thought suppression alone (trying not to think that thought) did not stop intrusive thoughts about Fred. What Carol and most individuals with this problem need is a thought-stopping plus a substitution program, which together are very effective (Borton, 2002).

As you'll see next, thought substitution is a very useful technique for a number of problems, including fear and anxiety.

Thought Substitution

How can I change fearful thoughts?

For many years Rose was trapped in her house by intrusive thoughts that resulted in an intense fear of going out into public places, which is called *agoraphobia.* If she even thought about going outside to do her shopping, she felt pain in her arms and chest, she began to perspire, her heart beat rapidly, and her feet felt like rubber. However, after cognitive-behavioral therapy, she overcame her agoraphobia.

As part of the overall therapy program, a cognitive therapist asked Rose a number of questions to identify her irrational thoughts. For example, she may have overgeneralized, thinking, "The last time I went out I was terrified; it's sure to happen again." Or Rose may have engaged in polarized thinking: "All my happiness is right here in this house; nothing outside could give me any pleasure." Her thinking might have been distorted by selective attention, such as remembering all those activities outside the house that terrified her and forgetting all those activities that she had once found pleasurable, such as shopping and going to movies.

Rose was asked to make a list of all her irrational thoughts on one side of a sheet of paper. Then, next to each irrational thought, she was asked to write down a rational response that could be substituted for the irrational one. Here are some examples:

Irrational Thoughts	Rational Thoughts
• I am much safer if I stay at home.	• Rarely has anything bad happened when I have gone out.
• I feel more protected if I do not have to walk through crowds.	• I have never been harmed by a crowd of people
• I think something awful will occur if I go to a supermarket.	• Thousands of people go to supermarkets and do their shopping unharmed.
• I can't bear the thought of going to a movie theater.	• Many people enjoy going to movies.

Like Rose, you can follow the same three steps of the thought-substitution program, which is a very effective technique for changing feelings and behaviors.

1 Through self-monitoring, write down as many irrational thoughts as possible. If you are in a habit of thinking irrational thoughts, it may require special attention to identify them.

2 Next to the column of irrational thoughts, compose a matching list of rational thoughts. The rational thoughts should be as detailed or specific as possible.

3 Begin to practice substituting rational thoughts for irrational ones. Each time you make a substitution, give yourself a mental reward for your effort.

How do I change my fearful thoughts so I can go out in public?

One reason therapists give clients homework, such as using thought substitution in daily life, is to encourage clients to practice thinking rationally (A. T. Beck & Weishaar, 2008). Cognitive-behavioral therapists see irrational thoughts and beliefs as the primary causes of emotional and behavioral problems (J. S. Beck, 2011; Dobson, 2009).

Worrisome, annoying, and irrational thoughts are one of the major causes of insomnia, which can also be treated with a cognitive-behavioral program.

Treatment for Insomnia

How can I get to sleep?

Two major causes of insomnia are excessive worry and tension. There are several nondrug treatments for insomnia that differ in method, but all have the same goal: to stop the person from excessive worrying and reduce tension. One proven cognitive-behavioral method to reduce insomnia is to establish an optimal sleep pattern (Bootzin & Rider, 1997; Means & Edinger, 2006).

Establishing an Optimal Sleep Pattern

By following the eight steps below, your sleep pattern will become more regular and efficient and help reduce insomnia.

Cognitive-behavioral program for insomnia

1. Go to bed only when you are *sleepy,* not by convention (it's time for bed) or habit.

2. Put the *light out* immediately when you get into bed.

3. *Do not read or watch television* in bed, since these are activities that you do when awake.

4. If you are not asleep within *20 minutes,* get out of bed and sit and relax in another room until you are *sleepy and tired* again. Relaxation can include tensing and relaxing one's muscles or using *visual imagery,* which involves closing one's eyes and concentrating on some calm scene or image for several minutes.

5. *Repeat step* 4 as often as required and also if you wake up for any long periods of time.

6. *Set the alarm to the same time each morning* so that your time of waking is always the same. This step is very important because oversleeping or sleeping in is one of the primary causes of insomnia the next night.

7. *Do not nap during the day* because it will throw off your sleep schedule that night.

8. *Follow this program* rigidly for several weeks to establish an efficient and regular pattern of sleep.

Results. Nondrug treatment programs, such as the eight-step program described here, are among the most effective programs for decreasing insomnia (Means & Edinger, 2006).

We have discussed several cognitive-behavioral techniques that can be used on one's own or with the aid of a therapist. These techniques are effective for treating a wide range of mild to severe mental problems (J. S. Beck, 2011; Dobson, 2009). ●

Virtual Reality Can Be More than Fun & Games

© AP Images/Ted S. Warren

Most people experience a traumatic event at some point in their life, but for some, the trauma has lasting effects that interfere with their daily functioning. People who are plagued by nightmares, flashbacks, and constant stress as a result of a traumatic experience, such as abuse, rape, burglary, or watching a person die, are often in desperate need of treatment. For many years, therapists have been working with such clients by helping them confront their fears in a systematic, step-by-step approach.

As you may expect, many clients who have intense fears are reluctant to undergo therapy that requires them to confront the very fear they so badly want to avoid. A relatively new treatment option for these clients is virtual-reality therapy, where they can vividly experience the feared object or situation in a safe and controlled manner. That's right, virtual reality is no longer only about experiencing fun adventures or fantasies. It's a powerful treatment technique. For instance, virtual-reality therapy can help a socially anxious client speak to intimidating crowds of people, or help a client with a phobia of spiders to

1 Can virtual-reality therapy be used to treat drug addiction, even though it isn't a fear resulting from a traumatic experience? Explain.

2 What type of DSM-IV-TR disorder is fear of spiders and fear of heights?

approach and hold a hideous-looking spider, or even help a client with an intense fear of heights stand on a 30-story building and look straight down.

The virtual worlds are so realistic that when someone with social anxiety is asked a question by a virtual stranger, the resulting tension mimics that which takes place in real-life encounters. And, the reaction is the same when someone with a substance addiction is offered a virtual beer or a virtual line of cocaine.

One of the major advantages of virtual-reality therapy is that it can be used when a client's fear is not something a therapist can easily expose him or her to. For this reason, virtual-reality therapy is being used to treat Iraq war veterans diagnosed with PTSD as a result of traumatic combat experiences. Therapists use a computer program to create a virtual environment that consists of the key elements of the reported traumatic experience. The handheld joystick is used to navigate through the three-dimensional scene, and special goggles help make the scene more real. The reenactment takes place on a vibrating platform so the veteran

3 What are some other advantages of virtual-reality therapy over traditional therapy methods?

4 What type of mental health professional(s) would most likely administer virtual-reality therapy?

5 What are some of the physical symptoms you would expect these veterans to exhibit during the reenactment that seems so real?

can feel the humming of the tank's motor or the rumbling of explosives being set off. Sounds and smells (such as voices, gunshots, and odors) can be incorporated to add to the realness of the situation. This process is gradual, beginning with only a few elements of the traumatic experience and adding more elements until the scenes become gruesomely realistic, with images of people getting blown up and terrifying sounds of screaming. The goal is that eventually the veteran can go through an intense re-creation without being overcome with fear.

6 Which type of therapeutic approach and technique is virtual-reality therapy most like?

Although the current technology is not nearly as advanced as the world portrayed in *The Matrix* films, based on clients' intense reactions, the virtual scenes are sophisticated enough.

Adapted from P. L. Anderson et al., 2005; APA, 2008b; Carey, 2010; DeAngelis, 2012; H. G. Hoffman, 2004; Jardin, 2005; L. Osborne, 2002; A. Rizzo et al., 2009; S. Rizzo, 2008; Z. Rosenthal, 2007; Rothbaum, 2009; Saladin et al., 2006; J. Williams, 2009

Unless otherwise noted, all images are © Cengage Learning

Summary Test

A Historical Background

1. In the early 1800s, the popular belief that mental patients could be helped to function better by providing humane treatment in a relaxed and decent environment was called **(a)** _____. In the early 1950s, the first drugs to reduce schizophrenic symptoms were discovered. These drugs, called **(b)** _____, reduced the effects of the neurotransmitter **(c)** _____.

National Library of Medicine, #A-13392

2. Following the use of phenothiazines, many mental patients were released from mental hospitals and returned to the community to develop more independent and fulfilling lives; this process was called **(a)** _____. People with mental disorders that do not require hospitalization often seek treatment in **(b)** _____ centers.

B Questions about Psychotherapy

3. If you go to medical school, receive an MD degree, and then take a psychiatric residency, you can become a **(a)** _____. If you go to graduate school in clinical psychology and complete a PhD program, including at least one year of work in a clinical setting, you can become a **(b)** _____. If you go to graduate school in psychology or education and complete a PhD program, including work in a counseling setting, you can become a **(c)** _____.

4. Therapy in which the therapist and client talk about the client's symptoms and problems with the goal of reaching or identifying the cause of the problem is called **(a)** _____ therapy. Therapy that involves the application of learning principles and focuses on identifying and changing specific behaviors is called **(b)** _____ therapy. Therapy that involves the use of interventions to treat mental disorders that change biological factors is called **(c)** _____ therapy.

C Psychoanalysis

5. Freud developed one of the first forms of insight therapy, which he called **(a)** _____. At the core of psychoanalysis is the idea that psychological and physical symptoms arise from **(b)** _____ that a person cannot voluntarily uncover or recall.

6. Freud developed two techniques that he believed provide clues to unconscious thoughts and conflicts: When clients are encouraged to talk about any thoughts or images that enter their heads, this is called **(a)** _____ ; when a therapist looks for hidden meanings and symbols in dreams, this is called **(b)** _____.

7. During the course of therapy, a patient will project conflict-ridden emotions onto the therapist; this process is called **(a)** _____. Working through transference is one of the two essential requirements for improvement in psychoanalysis; the other is that the patient achieves **(b)** _____ into the causes of his or her problem. A patient's reluctance to work through feelings or recognize unconscious conflicts and repressed thoughts is called **(c)** _____.

8. Increasing pressure to use briefer versions of psychotherapy resulted in a shortened form of traditional psychoanalysis. This new version uses some of the same principles, such as dealing with transference, but has the therapist taking a more active role and dealing with a more specific problem; this approach is called _____ psychotherapy.

D Client-Centered Therapy

9. A form of insight therapy developed by Carl Rogers emphasizes our creative and constructive tendencies and the importance of building caring relationships. This is called **(a)** _____ therapy. One of its basic techniques is to restate or **(b)** _____ the client's concerns and feelings.

10. Rogers believed that the therapist's characteristics foster growth and change. The therapist needs to have the ability to understand what the client is saying and feeling, a trait called **(a)** _____; the ability to communicate caring, respect, and regard for the client, called **(b)** _____ ; and the ability to be real and nondefensive in interactions with the client, called **(c)** _____.

E Cognitive Therapy

11. Another form of insight therapy is the cognitive therapy developed by Aaron Beck. The basic assumption of Beck's cognitive theory is that our **(a)** _____ negative thoughts distort how we perceive and interpret things, thus influencing our behaviors and feelings. For example, making blanket judgments about yourself on the basis of a single incident is called **(b)** _____. Sorting information into one of two categories is **(c)** _____. Focusing on one detail so much that you do not notice other events is using **(d)** _____. Beck believes that maladaptive thought patterns cause a distorted view of one's world, which in turn may lead to various emotional problems.

12. Cognitive therapy has been shown to have approximately the same effectiveness as do drugs in treating major _____ and has been used effectively to treat other psychological problems.

F Behavior Therapy

13. Therapy that emphasizes the treatment of specific behaviors and working toward specific goals without focusing on mental events or underlying unconscious factors is known as behavior therapy. This form of therapy is based on **(a)** _____ and **(b)** _____ conditioning principles.

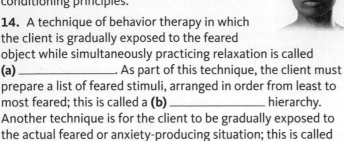

14. A technique of behavior therapy in which the client is gradually exposed to the feared object while simultaneously practicing relaxation is called **(a)** _____. As part of this technique, the client must prepare a list of feared stimuli, arranged in order from least to most feared; this is called a **(b)** _____ hierarchy. Another technique is for the client to be gradually exposed to the actual feared or anxiety-producing situation; this is called **(c)** _____ exposure.

G Cognitive-Behavioral Therapy

15. Cognitive-behavioral therapy combines two methods: changing negative **(a)** _____ by substituting positive ones, and changing unwanted or disruptive **(b)** _____ by learning and practicing new skills to improve functioning.

H Common Factors & Therapy Settings

16. One reason different therapies tend to be equally effective is that they all share _____. For example, the development of a supportive and trusting relationship between therapist and client results in an accepting atmosphere in which the client feels willing to admit problems and is motivated to work on changing.

17. Providing psychological services remotely, via telephone, e-mail, or videoconferencing, is called **(a)** _____. Specifically, delivering therapy over the Internet is called **(b)** _____.

I Research Focus: EMDR

18. Eye Movement Desensitization and Reprocessing (EMDR) involves having the client talk about or imagine a troubling traumatic memory while visually focusing on and following the movement of a therapist's **(a)** _____. Researchers believe that EMDR may work because it is similar to another therapy called **(b)** _____.

J Cultural Diversity: Different Healer

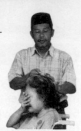

19. In many cases, the healers in Asia and Africa are as effective as Western therapists. One explanation is that these healers may rely on the **(a)** _____ effect, which is found to produce significant improvement in 10–30% of Western patients. Another is that the healers' ceremonies may involve some of the **(b)** _____ that underlie the effectiveness of Western therapy.

K Biomedical Therapies

20. Biomedical therapy involves the use of interventions to treat mental disorders that change _____ factors, such as the level of neurotransmitters in the brain.

21. Medications that reduce anxiety by lowering physiological arousal, resulting in a state of tranquility, belong to a class of chemicals known as **(a)** _____. Medications that help to even out the highs and lows of mood disorders, such as bipolar disorder, are known as **(b)** _____.

L Application: Cognitive-Behavioral Techniques

22. Behavior or cognitive-behavioral therapy usually involves three steps in changing thought patterns. The first step is observing one's own behavior without making any changes; this is called **(a)** _____. The second step is to identify those **(b)** _____ thoughts that need to be changed. The third step is to **(c)** _____ a positive thought for a negative one. Another step that is sometimes included is to actively stop **(d)** _____ thoughts.

Answers: 1. (a) moral therapy, (b) phenothiazines, (c) dopamine; 2. (a) deinstitutionalization, (b) community mental health; 3. (a) psychiatrist, (b) clinical psychologist, (c) counseling psychologist; 4. (a) insight, (b) behavior, (c) biomedical; 5. (a) psychoanalysis, (b) unconscious conflicts. 6. (a) free association, (b) dream interpretation; 7. (a) transference, (b) insight, (c) resistance. 8. short-term dynamic; 9. (a) client-centered, (b) reflect; 10. (a) empathy, (b) positive regard, (c) genuineness; 11. (a) automatic, (b) overgeneralization, (c) polarized thinking, (d) selective attention; 12. depression; 13. (a) classical, (b) operant; 14. (a) systematic desensitization, (b) stimulus, (c) in vivo; 15. (a) thoughts, (b) behaviors. 16. common factors; 17. (a) telemental health, (b) cybertherapy; 18. (a) hand, (b) exposure therapy; 19. (a) placebo, (b) common factors; 20. biological; 21. (a) benzodiazepines, (b) mood-stabilizer drugs; 22. (a) self-monitoring, (b) negative or automatic, (c) substitute, (d) intrusive or annoying

Links to Learning

Key Terms/Key People

agoraphobia, 575

antidepressant drugs, 573

atypical neuroleptic drugs, 573

balian, 572

Beck, Aaron, 565

behavior therapy, 566

benzodiazepines, 573

biomedical therapy, 559, 573

client-centered therapy, 564

clinical psychologists, 558

cognitive-behavioral therapy, 559, 568

cognitive therapy, 565

common factors, 570

community mental health centers, 557

counseling psychologists, 558

couple therapy, 570

cybertherapy, 570

deinstitutionalization, 557

dream interpretation, 561

eclectic approach, 559

empathy, 564

Eye Movement Desensitization and Reprocessing, or EMDR, 571

family therapy, 570

free association, 561

Freud, Sigmund, 560

genuineness, 564

group therapy, 570

humanistic approach, 564

imagined exposure, 567

insight therapy, 559

insomnia, 575

intrusive thoughts, 574

in vivo exposure, 567

meta-analysis, 559

mood-stabilizer drugs, 573

moral therapy, 556

neuroleptic drugs, 573

neuroses, 561

overgeneralization, 565

phenothiazines, 557

polarized thinking, 565

positive regard, 564

psychiatrists, 558

psychoanalysis, 560

psychotherapy, 556

reflecting, 564

resistance, 562

Rogers, Carl, 564

self-monitoring, 574

selective attention, 565

short-term dynamic psychotherapy, 562

stimulus hierarchy, 567

systematic desensitization, 567

telemental health, 570

thought stopping, 574

thought substitution, 574, 575

transference, 562

typical neuroleptic drugs, 573

Media Resources

Go to **CengageBrain.com** to access Psychology CourseMate, where you will find an interactive eBook, glossaries, flashcards, quizzes, videos, answers to Critical Thinking questions, and more. You can also access Virtual Psychology Labs, an interactive laboratory experience designed to illustrate key experiments first-hand.

MODULE 25

Social Cognition & Behavior

© Chris Whitehead/cultura/Corbis

introduction

Perception of Others

Why didn't more people stop to listen?

One busy morning at a subway station in Washington, DC, Joshua Bell finds a spot to settle in where every passerby is sure to see him. He puts on a baseball cap, leaves his violin case open to accept money, and begins playing the violin. Bell isn't playing just any type of music; rather, he is performing some of the most challenging classical pieces ever written. The violin he holds in his hand is worth about $3.5 million. His playing is flawless, sure to impress even the most discerning music critic.

Three minutes into his performance and after 63 people had already passed by, one person finally looked at him. Then Bell received his first donation, a dollar bill. A few minutes later, someone paused to listen to him play. In the 45 minutes Bell performed, a total of 7 people stopped to listen to him and 27 people donated money totaling about $32. More than a thousand people simply walked by without pausing to acknowledge the beautiful music being performed only a few feet away from them.

The event at the subway station was a hidden-camera experiment (Weingarten, 2010).

Joshua Bell didn't receive much attention or donations while playing in the subway station.

The experiment involved taking an accomplished musician, having him play in the subway station, and observing what happens. In real life, Joshua Bell is one of the most distinguished violinists in the world today. He has performed with many of the world's major orchestras and best conductors. He has won a Grammy Award and released numerous highly acclaimed albums. If you were to listen to his music at a symphony hall or even on your iPod, you would be in awe of his talent. Although he earned only $32 during his 45-minute subway performance, he commands about $1,000 for every minute of his professional performances.

This simple experiment demonstrates that physical appearance (wearing a baseball cap) and the situation (playing in a subway station) influenced people's judgments of Joshua Bell. People expect to see and hear panhandlers at a busy subway station. Consequently, people have learned to quickly walk by without looking at musicians or devoting much attention to them.

The subway station experiment is a study of social psychology. **Social psychology** is a broad field whose goals are to understand and explain how our thoughts, feelings, perceptions, and behaviors are influenced by the presence of, or interactions with, others.

Social psychologists study how we form impressions and perceive others, how we form attitudes and stereotypes, and how we evaluate social interactions—all of which are involved in Joshua Bell's story.

Another major topic of social psychology is how people behave in groups.

Behavior in Groups

Florida A&M University's (FAMU) "Marching 100" band is a group of hundreds of highly trained and entertaining musicians.

How do people become violent hazers?

Being a member of FAMU's marching band is reported to have more prestige than being a member of the football team. The band is so highly regarded that it has performed at Super Bowls and presidential inaugurations. The Marching 100 is said to embrace inspirational goals, including highest quality in character, attainment in leadership, and dedication to service (Copeland, 2012; FAMU, 2012).

Like many other groups across the country, the Marching 100 has its own traditions. One tradition is known as "Crossing Bus C" and involves band members walking down the aisle of the bus while their peers take turns punching them. After a football game against a rival school, Robert Champion, a drum major in the Marching 100, was beaten, kicked, and suffocated by fellow band members during their "Crossing Bus C" tradition. Champion began vomiting and complaining that he could not breathe. Soon afterwards, he died (R. Brown, 2012; Copeland, 2012).

The tradition known as "Crossing Bus C" is a form of hazing.

Hazing may be part of a group's initiation ritual during which individuals are subjected to a variety of behaviors that range from humiliating and unpleasant to potentially dangerous both physically and psychologically.

Drum major Robert Champion died as a result of hazing.

Hazing has been a national problem for many years, especially among college fraternities and athletic teams. It has been a part of the Marching 100 tradition for decades. The case involving Champion received national attention because of its severity—hazing led to his death. A total of 13 people were charged in the death of Champion, and many others faced smaller charges.

In the instance of Champion's hazing, the members of the Marching 100 strayed from their goals of dedication to character, leadership, and service. Not a single band member stepped up to try to stop the hazing.

In studying hazing, social psychologists ask What kind of group pressure causes normal people to submit to being hazed? What kind of group pressure turns normal people into violent hazers?

What's Coming

We'll discuss how we perceive people, how we explain the causes of our behaviors, why we develop attitudes, and how we respond to persuasion. We'll also explore a variety of social influences and group behaviors, such as what makes hazing so popular, how we respond to group pressures, what motivates us to help others, and why we behave aggressively.

We'll begin with Bell's story, which raises the question of how we form impressions of others. ●

MODULE 25 SOCIAL COGNITION & BEHAVIOR

581

Person Perception

How do you form first impressions?

Compare the photo of Joshua Bell on the left with the one on the right. In the left photo, your first impression is that he is a panhandler, while in the right photo, your first impression is that Bell is a talented and successful musician. Your first impressions, which were formed in seconds, with little conscious thought, and were biased by your past experiences, are part of person perception (Macrae & Quadflieg, 2010).

At the subway, very few people appreciated his talent.

Person perception refers to seeing someone and then forming impressions and making judgments about that person's likability and the kind of person he or she is, such as guessing his or her intentions, traits, and behaviors.

As you formed a first impression of Bell from each photo, several factors influenced your judgment (Macrae & Quadflieg, 2010; L. S. Newman, 2001).

Physical appearance. Your initial impressions and judgments of a person are influenced and biased by the person's physical appearance. For example, Bell makes a very different first impression when he looks like a panhandler than when he looks like a professional.

Need to explain. You don't just look at a person, but rather you try to explain why he looks, dresses, or behaves in a certain way. You might explain that Bell-as-panhandler is working to put a roof over his head, while Bell-as-professional is successfully advancing his career.

Influence on behavior. Your first impressions influence how you like or interact with a person. For example, if your first impression of Bell is as a panhandler, you interact with him very differently than if your impression of him is as a world-renowned musician.

At the musical hall, everyone appreciates his talent.

Effects of race. Members of one race generally recognize faces of their own race more accurately than faces of other races (Ferguson et al., 2001). This means we may perceive faces that are racially different from our own in a biased way because they do not appear as distinct as faces from our own race. Racial bias in first impressions is also evident in research showing that the brain area associated with emotional vigilance becomes more activated when White people view photos of unfamiliar Black, as compared to unfamiliar White, faces (Fiske, 2006).

Researchers report that first impressions, such as the one you make of Bell, usually occur automatically and function to influence or bias future social interactions in a positive or negative direction (Andersen et al., 2007; L. S. Newman, 2001).

One factor that plays a major role in person perception, especially forming first impressions, is physical attractiveness.

Physical Attractiveness

Researchers found that, for better or worse, a person's looks matter, since we tend to make more accurate and positive evaluations of people who are judged to be more physically attractive (Leary, 2010; Lorenzo et al., 2010).

What makes a face attractive?

Attractive individuals are sure to benefit from such evaluations because being evaluated by others accurately and positively is ideal in close relationships (Lackenbauer et al., 2010). Research finds that attractive adults are paid more for their work. Also, teachers favor more attractive students and judge them to be smarter. Even mothers give more attention to attractive infants (Wargo, 2011).

There has been much research to determine what makes a face attractive. In one study, researchers created faces by combining and averaging physical features taken from different faces (Langlois et al., 1994). For example, the face in the left photo, which was rated very attractive, was actually created by averaging thousands of faces (Johnston, 2000). It turns out that average faces are more attractive than the originals, and the preference for average faces begins in infancy (Langlois, 2009).

Men prefer women with "hourglass figures."

How attractive is this woman?

Evolution. Research suggests that some physical characteristics are considered more universally attractive, which lends support for an evolutionary explanation for physical attraction (Jayson, 2009a). For example, researchers found that both within and across cultures, there is strong agreement among Whites, African Americans, Asians, and Hispanics about which faces of adults and children are and are not attractive (Langlois et al., 2000). Also, evolutionary psychologists report that men are most attracted to youthful women who have an "hourglass figure" (hips larger than waist), which signals an advantage in childbirth. Women are most attracted to men who have masculine faces, with a larger jaw and greater muscle mass, which suggests higher testosterone levels (Jayson, 2009a).

According to evolutionary psychologists, judging and valuing attractiveness may have evolved and become a "built-in" ability because attractiveness was a visible sign of a person having good genes, being healthy, and becoming a good mate (Lie, 2009; Quill, 2009).

Once people have entered into a monogamous relationship, however, researchers found that they look away from attractive faces much faster than from less attractive faces. They explain the bias to look away from attractive faces by stating that it helps people stay in monogamous relationships, which gives them a reproductive advantage (Maner et al., 2008).

Women prefer men with more masculine faces.

Stereotypes

On the right are photos of actors who played the roles of patients complaining of chest pains. While describing their symptoms, the actor-patients were videotaped. These videotapes were shown to over 700 physicians who were asked to recommend treatments. Because the actor-patients all described the same physical symptoms, all the physicians should have generally recommended the same treatments. However, physicians recommended different treatments that depended on the physicians' particular sexual and racial stereotypes (Schulman et al., 1999).

What could bias medical treatment?

Stereotypes are widely held beliefs that people have certain traits because they belong to a particular group. Stereotypes are often inaccurate and frequently portray the members of less powerful, less controlling groups more negatively than members of more powerful or more controlling groups.

Which of these individuals received the best treatment for heart problems?

From "The Effect of Race and Sex on Physicians' Recommendations for Cardiac Catheterization" by K. A. Schulman et al., 1999, *The New England Journal of Medicine*, 2/5/99, pp. 621–622. Copyright © 1999, Massachusetts Medical Society. Reprinted by permission of publisher and Interactive Drama

Stereotypes played an important role in the study we just described. Although the actor-patients reported the same symptoms, physicians were 40% less likely to recommend sophisticated medical tests for women and African Americans compared to White men (Schulman et al., 1999). More recent research also found that African Americans were less likely than Whites to receive expensive medical procedures (*USA Today*, 2005).

These studies show that racial and sexual stereotypes, which may occur automatically and without awareness, may bias the physicians' perceptions and judgments (Andersen et al., 2007).

Psychologists believe that we develop stereotypes when parents, peers, teachers, and others reward us with social approval for holding certain attitudes and beliefs. There are also cultural pressures to adopt certain values and beliefs about members of different groups. Next, we'll discuss a few stereotypes that are common in the United States.

Examples of Stereotypes

In our weight-conscious culture, there is an emphasis on being thin (see Module 15), so we might expect a negative stereotype to apply to people who are overweight. For instance, we may expect our female Olympic athletes to be lean or petite. Olympian Sarah Robles (right photo) challenges this stereotype. Robles is 5 feet 10 inches tall and weighs 275 pounds. She can lift an impressive 321 pounds over her head. Robles is one of the strongest women in the world and is the top-ranked female weightlifter in the United States. Robles realizes that some people may look at her and think she is fat or lazy, but she is on a mission to change how people perceive larger women (S. Gregory, 2012b).

As we learned from the patient-doctor research discussed above, people may apply racial stereotypes when they make serious decisions that can affect an individual's life. There are countless other examples of racial stereotypes, including people of certain races being better in athletics or superior in academics. Since more than four out of five NBA All-Star players are Black, and most of the remaining are White, it's easy to see why people would stereotype Asian American Jeremy Lin (right photo) as not being a threat on the court. And, in addition, Lin is book smart; he graduated from Harvard. Lin dispelled stereotypes that Asian Americans can't succeed in the NBA and that being a successful athlete is incompatible with being excellent in academics. His winning streak on the court was so impressive during the 2011–12 season that fans and reporters stirred up their support by creating the term *Linsanity* in his honor. Lin is currently the only Asian American and the only Harvard grad in the NBA (Duncan, 2012; S. Gregory, 2012a).

© Davie Eul tt/Kansas City Star/MCT via Getty Images

© Jim McIsaac/Getty Images

Prejudice and Discrimination

Negative stereotypes, such as the ones we just discussed, are often accompanied by prejudice and discrimination (Dovidio & Gaertner, 2010).

Prejudice is an unfair, biased, or intolerant attitude toward another group of people.

An example of prejudice is believing that overweight women are not as intelligent, competent, or capable as women of normal weight.

Discrimination is specific unfair behaviors exhibited toward members of a group.

An employer's bias against hiring overweight applicants is an example of discrimination.

The history of the United States provides many examples of racist and sexist cultural stereotypes, such as beliefs that women are not smart enough to vote and that African Americans are inferior to Whites (Swim et al., 1995).

One reason we frequently use stereotypes to make judgments about people is that stereotypes save us thinking time. By using stereotypes, we make quick (and sometimes inaccurate) decisions and thus save time and energy by not having to analyze an overwhelming amount of personal and social information.

However, a major problem with stereotypes is they are difficult to change because they occur automatically and without our awareness of having used them to make judgments (D. J. Schneider, 2004). Another reason stereotypes are difficult to change is that we often dismiss information that contradicts or doesn't fit our stereotypes (Banaji, 2006). This means biased stereotypes can live on and lead to inaccurate judgments and decisions in social situations.

Another view of stereotypes is they are like having information categories in the brain, which are called schemas, our next topic.

Schemas

When Dr. Harriet Hall received her medical degree in 1970, few women were in medicine and even fewer women joined the military. Dr. Hall was the only female doctor at David Grant USAF Medical Center and the only female military doctor in Spain. Throughout her career, she had to fight for acceptance from just about everyone. Even a 3-year-old daughter of a patient said, "Oh, Daddy! That's not a doctor, that's a lady." After spending several years as a medical officer in Spain, Hall returned to the United States, learned to fly, and became a flight surgeon. Hall earned a pilot's license despite being told "women aren't supposed to fly," a phrase she chose as the title of her memoirs.

How are schemas like social filters?

With such exceptional accomplishments, Hall had to tolerate prejudice and discrimination simply because she chose to work in a male-dominated field. For instance, when she applied for specialty training as a radiologist, she was rejected because the program gave preference to males, as females were not considered to have stable, long-term careers. While married to a civilian, she was not allowed to live in base housing or receive

Why was Dr. Hall shown less respect than her male peers?

the dependent allowances that her male colleagues got because wives were classified as dependents and husbands were not (H. A. Hall, 2008). One reason people responded to Hall in sexist ways is that they had developed schemas.

Schemas are mental categories that, like computer files, contain knowledge about people, events, and concepts. Because schemas affect what we attend to and how we interpret things, schemas can influence, bias, and distort our thoughts, perceptions, and social behaviors.

Sexist schemas of women working in medical fields and in the military put women like Hall at a disadvantage compared to their male colleagues. Even today, successful women in male-dominated educational and occupational domains are often regarded more negatively than their male peers (M. E. Heilman & Okimoto, 2007; Sakalli-Uğurlu, 2010).

The study of schemas is part of a subfield of social psychology called social cognition (Fiske & Macrae, 2012).

Social cognition is the mental processes involved in the ways in which people perceive, think about, remember, and respond to other individuals or groups.

Next, we'll discuss the different kinds of schemas.

Kinds of Schemas

Schemas, which are like hundreds of different information files in your brain, are generally divided into four types: person, role, event, and self schemas.

Person schemas include our judgments about the traits that we and others possess.

For example, when meeting someone new, we may rely on person schemas to provide general information about that person. Person schemas that contain general information about people who have membership in groups are *stereotypes* (Wyer, 2007).

Role schemas are based on the jobs people perform or the social positions they hold.

The reason you often ask "What do you do?" is so that you can use your role schemas to provide missing information about the person and provide mental shortcuts about what you might say or how you might act in social situations.

Event schemas, also called scripts, contain behaviors that we associate with familiar activities, events, or procedures.

The event schema for graduation is to celebrate getting your degree. In contrast, the event schema for a college class is to be silent, pay attention, and take notes. Event schemas help us know what to expect and provide guidelines on how to behave in different kinds of situations.

Self schemas contain personal information about ourselves, and this information influences, modifies, and distorts what we perceive and remember and how we behave.

What's interesting about our self schemas is that they overemphasize our good points, which explains why being criticized in public easily hurts our feelings.

We especially look for information or feedback to support our schemas and tend to disregard information that doesn't (Wyer, 2007). For this reason, once schemas are formed, they are difficult to change (J. E. Young et al., 2006).

Person schema has information on how to act with a new date.

Advantages and Disadvantages

There are two *disadvantages* of schemas. First, schemas may *restrict, bias,* or *distort* what we attend to and remember and thus cause us to overlook important information (Devine et al., 1994). For example, if your self schema is being a good student, you may not pay attention to suggestions from parents or teachers that may make you a better student.

The second disadvantage is that schemas are *resistant to change* because we generally select and attend to information that supports our schemas and deny information that is inconsistent with them (Macrae & Bodenhausen, 2000). For example, you might pay attention to positive comments on a class paper and reject any constructive suggestions about ways to improve your writing skills.

Your person schema may cause you to reject valid criticisms of your work.

Schemas also have *advantages*. For example, if someone says "I'm a freshman," you use your "freshman schema," which contains *information* about how freshmen think and behave, to help you analyze and respond appropriately in this particular social situation. Schemas also provide *guidelines* for how to behave in various social events (event schemas) and help us explain the social behavior of others (role schemas) (J. A. Howard & Renfrow, 2006). Explaining social behavior is one of the most intriguing areas of social cognition, and it's our next topic. ●

B Attributions

Definition

What is unusual about this umpire?

After 13 seasons and 2,000 games in the minor leagues, this umpire was passed over for promotion to the major leagues and released. An evaluation report by the Office for Umpire Development claimed that this umpire's work had "deteriorated in areas of enthusiasm and execution," even though earlier in the season the rating had been "better than average." What is unusual about this umpire is that she is a woman. Pam Postema (right photo) claims the reason she was passed over for promotion and released was that she was a woman and there are no female

Because I'm a woman, I wasn't promoted.

umpires in major league baseball. She filed a sex discrimination suit because, as Pam says, "Baseball wasn't ready for a woman umpire no matter how good she was" (S. Reed & Stambler, 1992).

Most sports fans would have an explanation as to why Pam Postema was not promoted to be an umpire in major league baseball. These kinds of explanations are called attributions.

Attributions are our explanations of the causes of events, other people's behaviors, and our own behaviors.

If you had to explain why there are no female umpires in major league baseball, you would choose between internal and external attributions.

Internal Versus External

A famous social psychologist, Fritz Heider (1958), believed that we all function to some extent like social psychologists as we try to explain everyday behaviors. Heider was the first to distinguish between internal and external causes or attributions for behaviors.

Internal attributions (also called **personal attributions**) are explanations of behavior based on the internal characteristics or dispositions of the person performing the behavior.

For example, if you used internal attributions to explain why Postema was not made a major league umpire, you would point to her personal characteristics or dispositions, such as saying that she was not a good judge of balls and strikes.

External attributions (also called **situational attributions**) are explanations of behavior based on the external circumstances or situations.

If you used external attributions to explain why Postema was not promoted, you would point to external circumstances, such as saying that major league baseball is run by men and they do not want to have a woman umpire.

Thus, making internal or external attributions has important implications for personal and social behaviors (Derlega et al., 2005). For example, if you use internal attributions, you would say that Postema does not have the skill or talent to be a major league umpire. If you use external attributions, you would say that, although she has the skills, the league discriminated against her because she is a woman. How people make the distinction between internal and external attributions is a rather complicated process.

Kelley's Model of Covariation

How do we decide whether Pam was passed over for promotion because of personal or situational factors? To answer this question, social psychologist Harold Kelley (1967) developed the covariation model.

The **covariation model,** developed by Harold Kelley, says that, in making attributions, we should look for factors that are present when the behavior occurs and factors that are absent when the behavior does not occur.

Kelley proposed that, in explaining someone's behavior, we should look for information about three factors: consensus, consistency, and distinctiveness (Forster & Liberman, 2007).

Consensus means determining whether other people engage in the same behavior in the same situation.

Consistency means determining whether the person engages in this behavior every time he or she is in a particular situation.

Distinctiveness means determining how differently the person behaves in one situation when compared to other situations.

1. HIGH CONSISTENCY
Pam performs about the same every time.

2. LOW DISTINCTIVENESS
Pam sometimes makes inaccurate decisions when calling base runners out.

3. LOW CONSENSUS
Pam does not show the same skills as other umpires.

→ **INTERNAL ATTRIBUTION**
Pam's lack of promotion is due to her poor umpiring skills.

1. HIGH CONSISTENCY
Pam performs about the same every time.

2. HIGH DISTINCTIVENESS
Pam always makes accurate decisions when calling base runners out.

3. HIGH CONSENSUS
Pam shows the same skills as other umpires.

→ **EXTERNAL ATTRIBUTION**
Pam's lack of promotion is due to discrimination by the league.

How do you decide if internal or external attributions apply to Pam?

In the examples on the left, we have applied the three factors in Kelley's covariation model to Pam Postema's situation. Notice that high consistency, low distinctiveness, and low consensus result in an internal, or personal, attribution (fired because she's a poor umpire). But high consistency, high distinctiveness, and high consensus result in an external or situational attribution (fired because of sexual discrimination). Thus, Kelley's covariation model helps us determine whether Postema's firing was due to internal or external attributions (Ployhart et al., 2005). However, if we don't follow Kelley's model, we make errors in attributing causes. We'll discuss three errors in making attributions—that is, in deciding what caused what.

Biases and Errors

Most people have heard the term *glass ceiling,* which refers to a real but invisible barrier that keeps women and people of color from reaching the top positions in a business or organization. Evidence that there is a thick glass ceiling is clear because only 18 (3.6%) of *Fortune* magazine's top 500 chairpersons are women and 95% of senior managers are White men (Y. Cole, 2009; Hoare, 2012). One woman who was successful in breaking the glass ceiling is Marissa Mayer (above photo), who at age 37 became the youngest woman to head a large organization and is believed to be the first to become a CEO while pregnant. Through perseverance, hard work, and a winning personality, Mayer broke through the glass ceiling by becoming chief executive officer at Yahoo, a multinational Internet corporation (Foroohar, 2012).

Can we make the wrong attributions?

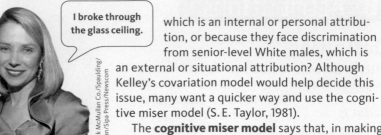

I broke through the glass ceiling.

© Patrick McMullan Co./Spaulding/McMullan/Sipa Press/Newscom

Breaking through the glass ceiling involves decisions about attributions. Do women and people of color fail to be appointed to senior-level positions because they lack skills and intelligence, which is an internal or personal attribution, or because they face discrimination from senior-level White males, which is an external or situational attribution? Although Kelley's covariation model would help decide this issue, many want a quicker way and use the cognitive miser model (S. E. Taylor, 1981).

The **cognitive miser model** says that, in making attributions, people feel they must conserve time and effort by taking cognitive shortcuts.

We have discussed cognitive shortcuts that we use in selecting, gathering, remembering, and using information—for example, relying on stereotypes and schemas. Researchers have identified other cognitive shortcuts used in making attributions (Forgas et al., 2003). Although these cognitive shortcuts are efficient, they may result in incorrect attributions (Baumeister & Bushman, 2011).

We'll discuss three of the most common biases in making attributions: the fundamental attribution error, the actor-observer effect, and the self-serving bias.

Fundamental Attribution Error

If you believe that women and people of color cannot break through the glass ceiling because they lack the skills and intelligence to do so, you may be making the fundamental attribution error (Langdridge & Butt, 2004).

The **fundamental attribution error** is our tendency, when we look for the causes of a person's behavior, to focus on the person's disposition or personality traits and to overlook how the situation influenced the person's behavior.

When you explain someone's behavior, you may be wrong.

© PhotoDisc, Inc.

An example of the **fundamental attribution error** is to conclude that women and people of color cannot break through the glass ceiling because of personal or dispositional factors, such as a lack of assertiveness or intelligence. However, the real reason may be not personal or dispositional factors but the situation: 95% of senior managers in *Fortune*'s 1,000 top companies are White men who may want to maintain the status quo and use subtle discriminatory hiring practices to keep out women and people of color.

Actor-Observer Effect

John angrily explains that he got to his car to put more money in the meter just as the police officer was driving away. John adds that he's very responsible and the ticket was bad luck because he was only 45 seconds late. John says he got the ticket because the police officer was just being mean. John's explanation is a good example of the actor-observer effect (Malle, 2006).

The **actor-observer effect** is the tendency, when you are behaving (or acting), to attribute your own behavior to situational factors. However, when you are observing others, you attribute another's behavior to his or her personality traits or disposition.

In the parking ticket example, John, the **actor**, attributes his getting the ticket to situational factors, just having bad luck, rather than to his own behavior, being late. In addition, John, the **observer**, explains that the police officer ticketed him because of a dispositional or personality factor—the officer was mean (Liberman et al., 2007). The actor-observer effect is very common. You can tell whether you're making it by putting yourself in the position of the one you are observing (S. R. Wilson et al., 1997).

Self-Serving Bias

When we look for the causes of our own behaviors, such as why we received a good or bad grade on a test, we may make errors because of the self-serving bias (Fiedler, 2007; Mcallister et al., 2002).

The **self-serving bias** is the tendency to explain our successes by attributing them to our dispositions or personality traits and to explain our failures by attributing them to the situations.

I didn't do well on this exam because the text was confusing.

© runzelkorn/Shutterstock.com

The self-serving bias can be considered another part of the actor-observer effect. According to the self-serving bias, if you get an A on an exam, you tend to attribute your success to your personality traits or disposition, such as intelligence and perseverance. However, if you get a D on an exam, you tend to attribute your failure to the situation, such as a difficult test or unfair questions. Thus, according to the **self-serving bias**, we try to view ourselves in the best possible light by making different and even opposite attributions depending on whether we have performed well or poorly (Mcallister et al., 2002).

The three errors that we just discussed show the need to be on guard so that these errors don't bias our attributions (Kenworthy & Miller, 2002).

Although biased attributions can create problems, they can also be an advantage when they help us change our behaviors, as we'll discuss next. ●

Can Changing Attributions Change Grades?

Perhaps 20% of the students we counsel tell us about getting poor grades in their freshman year, and their reasons are very similar. Either

What problems do freshmen face?

they didn't develop good study habits in high school so they weren't academically prepared for college or they spent too much time partying or dealing with stressful personal, social, or financial difficulties. What is interesting is that some of the freshmen who got poor grades their first year were able to bounce back academically their second year, while others became discouraged and dropped

I'm having problems with my grades and wonder if I should drop out.

© Riccardo Piccinini/Shutterstock.com

out of college. Researchers discovered many differences in students' attributions—that is, how students explained why they bounced back or dropped out. Because one goal of psychology is to apply scientific findings to real-world problems, researchers used findings on attributions to develop a program for improving grades and lowering the dropout rate (T. D. Wilson & Linville, 1982). Here's what actually happened.

Kinds of Attributions

In explaining why a freshman is having academic problems, researchers may point to internal or personal attributions, such as the lack of necessary academic skills. Or researchers may point to external or situational attributions, such as pressures to party rather than study. Once a freshman has developed a pattern of getting poor grades, another question is whether the causes are permanent or temporary. For example, if freshmen attribute their academic problems to relatively permanent conditions, such as poor abilities, they have little motivation and expect little improvement. In addition, poor academic performance makes new students worried and anxious, which in turn interferes with their ability to study.

However, if freshmen attribute their academic problems to temporary conditions, such as poor study habits, they can expect to improve if they develop better study skills. Researchers thought that if they could change students' attributions about poor academic performance and help them realize that it was a temporary rather than a permanent state, students could improve their grades.

Method: Changing Attributions

Researchers recruited freshmen who were having academic problems, such as scoring poorly on exams, not keeping up with assignments, and considering dropping out of college. These students were randomly divided into two different groups.

Students in the **experimental group** (attributions group) were given a number of procedures that changed their attributions about poor academic performance from a permanent cause to only a temporary condition. For example, students in the experimental

I did terribly my freshman year but I got my act together and didn't drop out.

© PhotoDisc, Inc.

group read a booklet about freshmen who had similar academic problems but showed improvement later in college. These participants watched videotapes of past students who described very convincingly how their grade point averages had risen after their freshman year. Next, these participants were asked to write down all the reasons they could think of why grade point averages might improve after the freshman year.

The other group of freshmen with academic problems did not receive any of this information and served as a **control group**.

Results and Conclusions

Researchers found that changing students' attributions for poor academic performance from permanent to temporary had two significant positive effects.

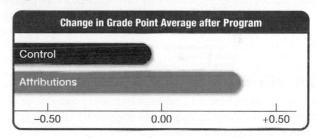

Change in Grade Point Average after Program

Control	
Attributions	

−0.50   0.00   +0.50

First, in the graph above, notice that freshmen who were told how to attribute their academic problems to temporary conditions (attributions group) had a significant improvement in grade point averages one year after the completion of this program.

Second, as shown in the graph below, only 5% of freshmen who changed their attributions for poor academic performance from permanent to temporary dropped out of college, whereas 25% of those in the control group dropped out.

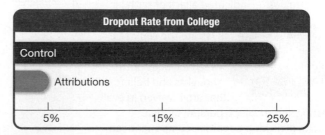

Dropout Rate from College

Control	
Attributions	

5%   15%   25%

From these data, researchers reached two important conclusions. First, it is possible to change students' attributions and expectations about academic performance. Second, changing students' attributions and expectations actually improved their academic performance and reduced the dropout rate (T. D. Wilson & Linville, 1982). This study illustrates how social psychologists used the concept of attribution to solve a real-world problem (Covington, 2000).

Next, we'll discuss one of the most active areas of social cognition—forming and changing attitudes. ●

Bar graph data from "Improving the Academic Performance of College Freshman," by T. D. Wilson and P. W. Linville, 1982, *Journal of Personality and Social Psychology, 42*, 367–376, American Psychological Association.

D Attitudes

Definition

How much power do attitudes have?

The media regularly report on people's attitudes toward a wide range of hot topics, such as politics, religion, drug use, abortion, and sports. The concept of attitude, which in the 1930s was called the single most indispensable term in social psychology (Allport, 1935), continues to be one of the most studied ideas (Banaji & Heiphetz, 2010).

An **attitude** is any belief or opinion that includes an evaluation of some object, person, or event along a continuum from negative to positive and that predisposes us to act in a certain way toward that object, person, or event.

Attitudes can have a significant impact on behavior, as happened in the tragic death of an 11-year-old boy named Bo. An autopsy showed that Bo had died of complications from diabetes. After suffering painful symptoms for seven days, he went into a coma and died. At the time, he was 15–20 pounds underweight. Bo's parents were members of the Followers of

Members of Followers of Christ Church believe God heals and prayer is the only treatment.

Christ Church in Oregon, and they believed that prayer is a substitute for conventional medical treatment. The leader of the church had preached that God would heal and that anyone seeking worldly (medical) help was weak and lacked faith in God. Because of these attitudes, Bo received no medical treatment for his diabetes, which doctors said was an easily treatable problem.

In most states, immunity from prosecution is granted to parents whose children get sick and die if the parents' religious beliefs permit only faith healing and not conventional medical treatment. Since Bo's death, however, Oregon changed its law so that parents who use religious beliefs to withhold medical treatment and allow their children to die of a treatable medical illness can face criminal charges (Gallegos, 2011; M. A. Hamilton, 2005).

Bo's case, as well as our earlier discussion of suicide bombers (see p. 471), is an example of attitudes that have the power to influence life-and-death decisions. Attitudes, which can have very powerful influences on our lives, have three components.

Components of Attitudes

If we closely examined Bo's parents' attitudes toward faith healing and conventional medical treatment, we would find that attitudes influence their thoughts (cognitive component), feelings (affective component), and behaviors (behavioral component) (Huskinson & Haddock, 2006; Maio & Haddock, 2007).

Cognitive Component

Bo's parents did not approve of conventional medical treatment for their son because they believed that only prayers were needed since God does the healing (if that is His/Her will) and that seeking medical treatment indicated a lack of faith in God. The parents' beliefs illustrate the *cognitive component* of attitudes, which includes both thoughts and beliefs that are involved in evaluating some object, person, or idea.

I believe faith heals.

An attitude's cognitive component can range from a very negative evaluation to a very positive one. For example, Bo's parents have a very positive belief in faith healing and a very negative evaluation of conventional medical treatment.

We have many attitudes that show our likes and dislikes, and often these attitudes are *automatically* triggered, without conscious thought on our part (Fabrigar et al., 2005).

Affective Component

Bo's parents were fearful of seeking conventional medical treatment because it meant going against God's will. The parents' fearful feelings illustrate the *affective component* of attitudes, which involves emotional feelings that can be weak or strong, positive or negative. For example, Bo's parents had strong positive feelings about using only prayers to treat their son's medical problem and strong fearful or negative feelings about seeking conventional medical treatment.

I'm fearful of medical treatment.

Researchers have found that both *beliefs* and *feelings* are involved in how we form attitudes (Maio et al., 2006). For example, beliefs may be more important in forming political attitudes, such as whom to vote for, while feelings may be more important in forming dietary attitudes, such as deciding to eat dog or horse meat, which is considered very appetizing in some cultures.

Behavioral Component

The parents' positive attitude toward using prayer alone and their negative attitude toward seeking conventional medical treatment resulted in their not calling a medical doctor. The parents' refusal to call a medical doctor illustrates the *behavioral component* of attitudes, which involves performing or not performing some behavior.

I will pray for my sick child.

In some cases, engaging in some behavior can influence the formation of an attitude (Maio et al., 2006). For example, having a good or bad experience in doing something (snowboarding, sky diving, using drugs, going to concerts) may result in a positive or negative attitude toward that activity.

Attitudes can have weak to strong and positive to negative influences on our behaviors.

Changing attitudes is our next topic.

Attitude Change

What made a skinhead reform?

At one time, Floyd Cochran (right photo) was an out-and-out hatemonger who was a leader of the neo-Nazi group Aryan Nation in Idaho. His goal was to exterminate everyone who wasn't White. He constantly preached hatred, and he recruited many White youths to help him "spread the hate like a disease" (Cochran, 2007). Then, as he was preparing for the annual Hitler Youth Festival, a group of White supremacists told him that his 4-year-old son must be euthanized because he was born with a birth defect. Floyd found himself caught between his own years of

> I was a racist until my values hurt my son.

Courtesy of Floyd Cochran

preaching hate and members of Aryan Nation hating the son he loved. Floyd resolved his personal dilemma by renouncing his White supremacist values and abandoning the hate organizations. He now speaks out against hate and racism (Charmoli, 2006).

Why did Floyd radically change his attitudes, from preaching hate and racism to denouncing these beliefs? We'll discuss two popular theories that explain why people change their attitudes: the theory of cognitive dissonance and self-perception theory (Harmon-Jones & Harmon Jones, 2002; Petty et al., 1997).

Cognitive Dissonance

After a group of White supremacists told him his son must be euthanized, Floyd's life became one big conflict. He had spent most of his adult life practicing racism and hate, but now his own personal values were causing him great anguish. Floyd found himself in the middle of a very troubling inconsistency, which Leon Festinger (1957) called cognitive dissonance.

Cognitive dissonance is a state of unpleasant psychological tension that motivates us to reduce our cognitive inconsistencies by making our beliefs more consistent with our behavior.

There are two main ways to reduce cognitive dissonance—that is, to make our beliefs and attitudes consistent with our behavior (Andersen et al., 2007).

Adding or changing beliefs. We can reduce cognitive dissonance by adding new beliefs or changing old beliefs and making them consistent with our behavior. In Floyd's case, cognitive dissonance was created by the conflict between being told the son he loved must be euthanized and his own racist and hate-filled beliefs. To decrease his cognitive dissonance, Floyd renounced his hateful beliefs so that his attitudes became consistent with his behavior, which was loving his son regardless of his birth defect.

Counterattitudinal behavior. Another way we can reduce cognitive dissonance is by engaging in opposite or counterattitudinal behavior (Leippe & Eisenstadt, 1994).

Counterattitudinal behavior involves taking a public position that runs counter to your private attitude.

A classic study by Festinger and Carlsmith (1959) illustrates how counterattitudinal behavior works. In this study, participants were asked to do an extremely boring task, such as turning pegs in a board. At the end of the task, the experimenter asked the participants to help out by telling the next group how interesting the task was. Participants were asked to lie about the task and say it was interesting, which is engaging in counterattitudinal behavior. For saying the task was interesting, some participants received $1 and some received $20. Sometime later, the original participants were asked how much they had liked the boring task. A curious finding emerged. Participants paid just $1 had a more favorable attitude about the boring task than those who were paid $20. That's because participants paid $20 felt they were paid well for lying. Participants who were paid $1 had no good reason for lying, and so, to resolve the cognitive dissonance between what they'd said (it was interesting) and what they felt (it was boring), they convinced themselves that the task was somewhat interesting. This shows that engaging in opposite or counterattitudinal behaviors can change attitudes. However, there's a different explanation for this experiment's results.

Cognitive dissonance explains why people paid just $1 found the boring task more interesting than those paid $20.

Self-Perception Theory

Perhaps participants in the experiment came to believe their own lies (the task was interesting) after engaging in counterattitudinal behavior not to reduce cognitive dissonance but because of changing their own self-perceptions.

Self-perception theory says that we first observe or perceive our own behavior and then, as a result, we change our attitudes.

Daryl Bem (1967), who developed self-perception theory, would explain that participants paid only $1 for lying would recall their behavior and conclude that they would never have lied for only $1, so the task must have actually been interesting.

At first glance, cognitive dissonance theory and self-perception theory seem to be similar, since they both indicate that if we say something, it must be true. However, each theory points to a different reason. According to **cognitive dissonance theory**, the belief "if I said it, it must be true" occurs because we are trying to reduce the inconsistency between our beliefs and behaviors. In comparison, according to **self-perception theory**, concluding "if I said it, it must be true" simply reflects another way of explaining our own behaviors.

Self-perception theory also challenges the traditional assumption that attitudes give rise to behavior. According to self-perception theory, behaviors give rise to attitudes. For example, after Floyd began speaking out against racism, his attitudes changed radically. Researchers have shown that behavior can influence attitudes (Leippe & Eisenstadt, 1994; Van Laar et al., 2005).

We may change our own attitudes in response to cognitive dissonance or self-perception. However, others are continually trying to change our attitudes through various forms of persuasion, our next topic.

Persuasion

Political candidates spend much of their time, energy, and money trying to persuade people to vote for them. What politicians have to decide is whether to use an intellectual or emotional appeal, how to appear honest, and what arguments to use. We'll begin with choosing between two different routes—central or peripheral (Petty & Briñol, 2012; Petty & Cacioppo, 1986).

Central Route

If the audience is interested in thinking about the real issues, a politician might best use the central route.

The **central route for persuasion** presents information with strong arguments, analyses, facts, and logic.

A political candidate using the central route for persuasion should present clear, detailed information about his or her views and accomplishments and should appear *honest* and *credible* by demonstrating knowledge and commitment to the issues and pointing out the opponents' records (Priester & Petty, 1995).

Politicians should choose the central route when they are trying to persuade voters who are personally invested in the issues and have a need to know the facts (Bohner et al., 2008; Cacioppo & Petty, 1982). The central route for persuasion works with people who think about and analyze the issues. However, not all voters can be persuaded by the central route.

> I think logical arguments and hard facts work best.

Peripheral Route

If the audience is more interested in the candidate's personality or image, a politician might seek votes using the peripheral route.

The **peripheral route for persuasion** emphasizes emotional appeal, focuses on personal traits, and generates positive feelings.

The peripheral route assumes that not all voters will spend the time and energy to digest or discuss the issues. Instead, some audiences are more interested in the candidate's ability to generate excitement by giving an *energetic* and *enthusiastic speech* (Priester & Petty, 1995).

This route involves bands, banners, parties, and personal appearances, which build an inviting and exciting image and create a positive attitude toward the candidate. If audiences like the candidate's image, they will more likely agree with the candidate's views (Carlson, 1990).

The peripheral route is more concerned with style and image, and the central route is more concerned with substance and ideas. Researchers generally find that the central route produces more enduring results, while the peripheral route produces more transient results (Maio & Haddock, 2007; Perloff, 2002).

> I think emotional and personal appeals work best.

© Rena Schild/Shutterstock.com

Elements of Persuasion

Whether the central or peripheral route is used, three specific elements are important in persuasion: source, message, and audience (Jacks & Cameron, 2003; Petty et al., 1997).

Source. One element in persuading someone to adopt your point of view involves the *source of the message*. We are more likely to believe sources who have a sense of authority, appear honest and trustworthy, have expertise and credibility, and are attractive and likable (Priester & Petty, 1995). For example, researchers found that good-looking TV fund-raisers generated nearly twice as many donations as did less attractive fund-raisers (Cialdini, 2001). The source element explains why national and cable TV newscasters and anchorpersons are usually physically attractive, likable, and believable.

Message. Another element of persuasion involves the *content of the message*. If the persuader is using the *central route,* the messages will contain convincing and understandable facts. If the facts are complicated, a written message is better than a spoken one (Chaiken & Eagly, 1976).

If the persuader is using the *peripheral route,* the messages should be designed to arouse emotion, sentiment, and loyalty. Television infomercials use the peripheral approach by having an attractive and likable demonstrator show how you will look or feel better by buying and using a particular product. However, using fearful messages to persuade people, such as showing blackened lungs to get smokers to quit, may not be effective because arousing fear may interfere with and distract people from hearing and taking precautionary measures to stop unhealthy practices (Ruiter et al., 2001).

One- versus two-sided messages. Some messages are better presented as *one-sided*; that is, you present only the message that you want accepted. Other messages are better presented as *two-sided;* that is, you include both the message and arguments against any potential disagreements (Jacks & Cameron, 2003). Thus, a persuader will select the best route (central or peripheral) and also the kind of message (one- or two-sided) (Jacks & Devine, 2000).

Why is "The Daily Show" news host Jon Stewart worth millions?

© Taylor Hill/FilmMagic/Getty Images

Audience. Another element of being an effective persuader involves knowing the *characteristics of the audience*. For example, audiences who are interested in facts are best persuaded using the central route, while audiences interested in personal traits are best persuaded using the peripheral route. If the audience is leaning toward the persuader, a one-sided message is best; if an audience is leaning away from the persuader, a two-sided message is best.

Thus, persuasion is a complicated process that involves considering the source's traits, using the central or peripheral route, and judging the audience's characteristics. Good persuaders may combine the central and peripheral routes to win over the audience to their viewpoints (Cialdini, 2003).

Next, we'll discuss how cultures differ in their attitudes toward beauty, organ transplants, and women's rights. ●

Nigeria: Beauty Ideal

One reason the concept of attitude has been so dominant in social psychology is that our attitudes push or predispose us to think and behave in certain ways. What we often don't realize is how much our culture shapes our attitudes. For example, in the United States, the current attitude, especially among the middle and upper classes, is that for a woman to be attractive, she should be slender. This thin-is-beautiful attitude can pressure women to behave in certain ways, such as to constantly worry about their weight and to go on strict diets, which in some cases may result in eating disorders (Besenhoff, 2006; Hesse-Biber, 2007).

How do Nigerians judge beauty?

But thin is not always beautiful. For example, in Nigeria, Africa, a small group of young women were discussing who had the most beautiful body. They all agreed on Monique, age 15, because she was already heavy for her age and on her way to being very

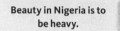

Beauty in Nigeria is to be heavy.

© Jeff Greenberg/Age fotostock

rotund. As one woman said, "I want to gain weight like Monique. I don't want to be thin" (Onishi, 2001, p. A4). Before getting married, young brides-to-be are sent to so-called fattening rooms, where the goal is to eat as much as they can to get fat and round so that the bride will be admired for her fullness.

However, in 2001, a slim, 6-foot-tall Nigerian became Miss World. This was the first time in 51 years that a Nigerian woman had won this title. Since most Nigerians over 40 consider beautiful women to have ample backsides and bosoms, they thought the new trim Miss World was not particularly beautiful. But many of the younger Nigerians took notice of Miss World's dimensions and began to change their attitudes and adopt Western beauty standards that value being slim (Onishi, 2002). This difference in beauty attitudes between America and Africa clearly shows how cultural values not only shape attitudes but also predispose us to behave in certain ways.

A different debate over attitudes is going on in Japan.

Japan: Organ Transplants

Wakana Kume, who lives in Japan, was going to die unless she received a liver transplant. However, since 1968, it has been illegal in Japan to transplant organs from donors who are brain-dead. Like all Japanese, Kume grew up with the attitude that brain-dead was not really dead, so she was very reluctant to get a transplant from a brain-dead donor. But because of the seriousness of her condition, Kume flew to Australia, where she underwent a liver transplant. In a very real sense, Kume engaged in counterattitudinal behavior by doing a behavior opposite of what she believed—getting a transplanted organ. Since her lifesaving transplant, Kume has changed her attitude toward organ transplants and now approves of them. This is a real example of changing attitudes by engaging in counterattitudinal behavior.

What is the Japanese attitude on death?

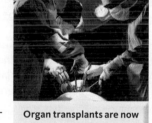

Organ transplants are now more common in Japan.

© Michael Hitoshi/Getty Images

The reason there were about 24,000 organ transplants in the United States in 1997 but none in Japan is that cultures have different definitions of death. In the United States, death is defined as brain death—when a person's brain no longer shows electrical activity, even though the heart is still beating. In Japan, however, death was defined as the moment a person's heart stops beating, and donor organs could be removed only after the heart stops. But, to be useful, donor organs must be removed when a person's heart is still beating. In 1997, Japan passed a law allowing organs to be donated by an individual who is brain-dead under certain strict conditions. Because brain death has been legalized in Japan, organ transplants are now possible and many Japanese have changed their attitudes toward death and accept organ transplants (Ling & Ming, 2006; McNeill & Coonan, 2006).

A debate over attitudes and behaviors is also going on in Egypt.

Egypt: Women's Rights

Since the early 1900s, Egyptian women have been fighting for their sexual, political, and legal rights in a society that is dominated by Muslim religious principles, which grant women few rights. For example, while women are supposed to wear veils to preserve their dignity, a husband may strike his wife as long as he doesn't hit her in the face and hits lightly. Many women are not given birth certificates, which means that they cannot vote, get a passport, or go to court.

How do Egyptians view women?

Egyptian women have been fighting for more rights. Some women are taking martial arts training to learn to fight off assailants (photo at right). The rising problem of sexual harassment of Egyptian women

Egyptian women are learning to fight back.

© AP Images/Amir Nabil

motivates these women to learn self-defense methods (Fraser, 2009; A. Johnson, 2009). Women are also fighting to not wear veils in public and to get good jobs. There have been some major strides. For example, Egyptian women now make up more than 30% of the workforce and account for half of the university graduates studying medicine. However, nearly half of Egyptian women remain illiterate (Newcomb, 2011).

In getting Egyptians to change their attitudes toward women, advocates will need to use trustworthy and honest sources, present one- or two-sided arguments, and, depending on the audience, use the central or the peripheral route for persuasion.

Next, we'll learn how persuasion involves social forces. ●

F Social & Group Influences

Conformity

Why do people agree to being hazed?

At the beginning of this module, we discussed a hazing incident in which members of FAMU's Marching 100 brutally punched, kicked, and suffocated drum major Robert Champion, resulting in his death. Though there were many witnesses, not one band member stepped up to try to stop the violent hazing. This is especially troubling because the band's goals include a dedication to character, leadership, and service, none of which was evident on the day Champion suffered a violent death.

Hazing may be part of a group's initiation ritual during which individuals are subjected to a variety of behaviors that range from humiliating and unpleasant to potentially dangerous both physically and psychologically.

The frequency in which hazing occurs in a variety of student organizations and athletic teams in the United States is alarming. About 55% of college students involved in a group activity (clubs, sports, organizations) report being hazed. Alcohol consumption, humiliation, isolation, sleep deprivation, and sex acts are examples of hazing practices (Allan & Madden, 2008, 2012).

When students were asked why they agreed to be hazed, many answered they did so because it made them feel part of the group (N. C. Hoover & Pollard, 2000). "Going along" with the group is an example of conformity (J. M. Levine & Kerr, 2007).

Hazing resulted in the death of drum major Robert Champion.

© AP Images/Don Juan Moore

Conformity refers to any behavior you perform because of group pressure, even though that pressure might not involve direct requests.

Normally, most students (and most of us) would never conform or agree to be publicly humiliated. Yet, reacting to strong group pressures, about 55% of college students who participate in group activities conform and agree to be hazed, which means humiliation and possible injury.

There are many examples of conforming, such as wearing clothes that are in style, adopting the "in" slang phrases, and buying currently popular products. A popular and current example of conformity is carrying our own bottles of water. Bottled water is now a $22-billion-a-year business in the United States alone. It is estimated that in the United States over 200 bottles of water are consumed per person annually (Fishman, 2012). The water bottle phenomenon is a modern example of conformity and, as one researcher put it, perhaps a new kind of adult security blanket (Valtin, 2002).

We'll discuss group pressures and why people conform and obey, beginning with a classic experiment in social psychology.

© Odua Images/Shutterstock.com

Asch's Experiment

A classic experiment is one that causes us to change the way we think about something—in this case, how social pressures can influence conformity (Blakeslee, 2005; Stasser & Dietz-Uhler, 2003). Solomon Asch's (1958) classic experiment showed very clearly how an individual can be pressured to conform to a group's standards. As we describe Asch's experiment, imagine that you are a participant and guess how you might have behaved.

Procedure

You are seated at a round table with five others and have been told that you are taking part in a visual perception experiment. Your group is shown a straight line and then is instructed to look at three more lines of different lengths and pick out the line equal in length to the original one. The three choices are different enough that it is not hard to pick out the correct one. Each person at the round table identifies his or her choice out loud, with you answering next to last. When you are ready to answer, you will have heard four others state their opinions. What you do not know is that these four other people are the experimenter's accomplices. On certain trials, they will answer correctly, making you feel your choice is right. On other trials, they will deliberately answer incorrectly, much to your surprise. In these cases you will have heard four identical incorrect answers before it is your turn to answer. You will almost certainly feel some group pressure to conform to the others' opinion. Will you give in?

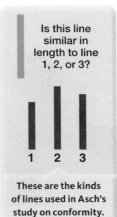

Is this line similar in length to line 1, 2, or 3?

1 2 3

These are the kinds of lines used in Asch's study on conformity.

Results

Out of 50 participants in Asch's experiment, 75% conformed on some of the trials, but no one conformed on all the trials; 25% never conformed. These data indicate that the desire to have your attitudes and behaviors match those of others in a group can be a powerful force.

A recent study used fMRI brain scans (see p. 70) to record brain activity during an Asch-type research design to examine whether social pressure changes people's perceptions or people who give in to the group do so knowing their answers are wrong (Berns, 2005). Results showed that when people went along with the group on wrong answers, activity in the brain area associated with spatial awareness and perception increased. But, when people resisted group pressure and gave a correct answer, activity in the brain area associated with strong emotions increased. These results suggest that information provided by others may actually change what we see and that going against the group can be a very unpleasant experience.

Asch's study is considered a classic because it was the first to clearly show that group pressures can influence conformity. However, we may conform publicly but disagree privately, and this is an example of compliance.

Asch study based on "Effects of Group Pressure Upon Modification and Distortion of Judgements," by Solomon Asch, 1958. In E. Maccoby, T. M. Newcomb & E. L. Hartley (Eds.), *Readings in Social Psychology* (3rd Ed.). Holt, Rinehart & Winston.

Unless otherwise noted, all images are © Cengage Learning

Compliance

Were the participants just pretending?

One interpretation of Asch's data is that participants were not really changing their beliefs but rather just pretending to go along with the group. For example, when participants in Asch's experiment privately recorded their answers, conforming drastically declined. This decline indicated that participants were conforming but not really changing their beliefs, which is one kind of compliance.

Compliance is a kind of conformity in which we give in to social pressure in our public responses but do not change our private beliefs.

I disagree, but I'll rewrite it

For example, you may conform to your instructor's suggestions on rewriting a paper even though you do not agree with the suggestions. In this case, you would be complying with someone in authority.

One particular technique of compliance is used by salespeople, who know that if they get the customer to comply with a small request (get a foot in the door), the customer is more likely to comply with a later request to buy the product (Cialdini & Goldstein, 2004).

Salespeople use the foot-in-the-door technique.

The **foot-in-the-door technique** is the practice of starting with a small request in order to gain eventual compliance with a later request.

A common example of the foot-in-the-door technique is telemarketers who first get you to answer a simple question such as "How are you today?" so that you'll stay on the phone and answer their other questions. The foot-in-the-door technique is one successful way to obtain compliance (Rodafinos et al., 2005).

If you are officially or formally asked to comply with a request, such as "Take a test on Friday," your compliance is called obedience.

Obedience

Do you run red lights?

When it comes to signs, laws, rules, and regulations, such as speed limits, traffic lights, smoking restrictions, parental requests, instructors' assignments, and doctors' orders, people differ in what they choose to obey.

Obedience is performing some behavior in response to an order given by someone in a position of power or authority.

Most of us obey orders, rules, and regulations that are for the general good. But what if the orders or rules are cruel or immoral?

Milgram's Experiment

Stanley Milgram's (1963) experiment on obedience is a classic experiment in social psychology because it was the first to study whether people would obey commands that were clearly inhumane and immoral (A. Miller, 2005). As we describe this famous experiment, imagine being the "teacher" and consider whether you would have obeyed the experimenter's commands.

The Setup

Imagine that you have volunteered for a study on the effects of punishment on learning. After arriving in the laboratory at Yale University, you are selected to be the "teacher" and another volunteer is to be the "learner." What you don't know is that the **learner** is actually an accomplice of the experimenter. As the **teacher,** you watch the learner being strapped into a chair and having electrodes placed on his wrists. The electrodes are attached to a shock generator in the next room. You and the researcher then leave the learner's room, close the door, and go into an adjoining room.

The researcher gives you a list of questions to ask the learner over an intercom, and the learner is to signal his answer on a panel of lights in front of you. For each wrong answer, you, the teacher, are to **shock the learner** and to increase the intensity of the shock by 15 volts for each succeeding wrong answer. In front of you is the shock machine, with 30 separate switches that indicate increasing intensities. The first switch is marked "15 volts. Slight shock," and the last switch is marked "XXX 450 volts. Danger: Severe shock." You begin to ask the learner questions, and as he misses them, you administer stronger and stronger shocks.

Whenever you make a mistake, you'll receive an electric shock.

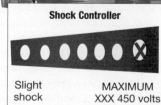

Shock Controller

Slight shock

MAXIMUM XXX 450 volts

The Conflict

As the teacher, you give the learner shocks that increase in intensity up to 300 volts, when the learner pounds on the wall. You continue and after the next miss, you give the learner a 315-volt shock, after which the learner pounds on the wall and stops answering any more questions. Although you plead with the researcher to stop the experiment, the researcher explains that, as the teacher, you are to continue asking questions and shocking the learner for incorrect answers. Even though the learner has pounded on the wall and stopped answering questions after a 315-volt shock, would you continue the procedure until you deliver the XXX 450 volts?

What you, the teacher, didn't know is that the learner is part of the experiment and acts like being shocked but never received a single one. The teacher was misled into believing that he or she was really shocking the learner. The question was whether a teacher would continue and deliver the maximum shock.

Milgram's Results

How many obeyed?

The scary question was how many "teachers" (participants) would deliver the maximum intensity shock to the "learner."

0.12% When psychiatrists were asked to predict how many participants would deliver the full range of shocks, including the last 450 volts, they estimated that only 0.12% of the participants would do so.

2% When members of the general public were asked the same question, they predicted that only 2% of the participants would deliver the maximum 450 volts.

65% To the surprise and dismay of many, including Milgram, 65% of the participants (no difference between males and females) delivered the full range of shocks, including the final XXX 450 volts.

When Stanley Milgram conducted these studies on obedience in the early 1960s, they demonstrated that people will obey inhumane orders simply because they are told to do so. This kind of unthinking obedience to immoral commands was something that psychiatrists, members of the general population, and Milgram had not predicted. Milgram (1974) repeated variations of this experiment many times and obtained similar results. Additionally, Milgram's experiment was repeated in various parts of the world with similar results (T. Blass, 2000).

The results of these experiments helped answer a question people had asked since World War II: Why had Germans obeyed Hitler's commands? More recently, the results of Milgram's experiments can help us make sense of why U.S. soldiers tortured, raped, and murdered prisoners held in Abu Ghraib in Iraq, as well why governments could massacre their own people in Syria and Libya. And why do students follow group leaders and engage in hazing, with sometimes dangerous consequences? According to Milgram's experiments, social situations that involve power and authority greatly increase obedience to the point that a large percentage of people will obey orders even if they are clearly unreasonable and inhumane.

Percentage of Participants Who Obeyed Experimenter's Commands

Labels on the shock controller	
Slight	
Moderate	
Strong	
Very strong	
Intense	Learner pounded on the wall at this point.
Extreme intensity	Learner pounded on the wall again at this point; after this, he gave no further answers.
Danger: severe shock	
XXX 450 volts	65% of the participants in Milgram's study obeyed the experimenter's command to deliver the maximum 450-volt shock to the learner.

Why Do People Obey?

Psychologists have suggested several reasons that 65% of the participants in Milgram's experiment agreed to deliver the maximum shock to learners. Perhaps the major reason is that people have learned to follow the orders of **authority figures,** whether they are religious leaders, army commanders, doctors, scientists, or parents. However, people are more likely to obey authority figures when they are present. In one of his follow-up studies, Milgram (1974) found that when participants received their instructions over the telephone, they were more likely to defy authority than when they received their instructions in person. This also explains why patients don't follow doctors' orders after they leave their offices.

People also obey because they have **learned to follow orders** in their daily lives, whether in traffic, on the job, or in personal interactions. However, people are more likely to obey if an authority figure is present (police officer, boss, or parent). What Milgram's study showed was that blind obedience to unreasonable authority or inhumane orders is more likely than we think.

Were Milgram's Experiments Ethical?

Although the Milgram experiments provided important information about obedience, the study could not be conducted under today's research guidelines. As we discussed (see p. 40), all experiments today, especially those with the potential for causing psychological or physical harm, are carefully screened by research committees, a practice that did not exist at the time of Milgram's research. When there is a possibility of an experiment causing **psychological harm,** the researchers must propose ways to eliminate or counteract the potential harmful effects. This is usually done by thoroughly debriefing the participants.

Debriefing occurs after an experimental procedure and involves explaining the purpose and method of the experiment, asking the participants their feelings about being in the experiment, and helping the participants deal with possible doubts or guilt arising from their behaviors in the experiment.

Although Milgram's participants were debriefed, critics doubted that the question of whether any psychological harm had been done to the participants was resolved. Because the potential for psychological harm to the participants was so great in Milgram's studies, any related research had to pass very strict ethical standards. Jerry Burger, a researcher at Santa Clara University, designed a study replicating as much of Milgram's study as possible while complying with current ethical standards (Burger, 2007, 2009). The participants were an ethnically diverse group of 18 men and 22 women. The setup and conflict procedures were mostly the same as in Milgram's study except that, due to ethical standards, the maximum shock the participants could administer was 150 volts, compared to the 450 volts used in Milgram's study. Results showed that 70% of the participants (equal percentages of men and women) pressed the button for the highest, most dangerous shock possible (150 volts). Thus, ordinary people, even in today's society, are capable of hurting others despite hearing the person begging them to stop, as long as they are ordered by an authority figure to do so.

Next, we'll turn to another interesting question: Why do people help?

Helping: Prosocial Behavior

Would you risk your life to help a stranger?

While Wesley Autrey (photo below) was waiting for the subway in New York City, he saw a man suffering from a seizure fall onto the tracks. A train was rapidly approaching the station and, knowing the man would be killed in only seconds, Wesley immediately jumped onto the tracks and covered the man with his body. The train came so close to Wesley's body that it left grease marks on his hat (C. Buckley, 2007; Trump, 2007). Wesley's quick, heroic action is an example of helping, or prosocial behavior.

Prosocial behavior is any behavior that benefits others or has positive social consequences.

In our society, professionals, such as paramedics, are trained and paid to provide help. However, in Wesley's case, he was the only onlooker who risked his life to save a seizing man who had no possibility of surviving on his own. Wesley is a hero. A **hero** is an ordinary person who is motivated to act on behalf of others or for a moral cause with action that is extraordinary.

Heroes may take life-threatening risks to help during

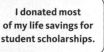

Why did Wesley Autrey risk his life to save the life of another man?

dangerous emergencies, take a strong stand against injustice, or make a great sacrifice for a stranger with no expectation of external reward (Franco et al., 2011; Heroic Imagination Project, 2012). Heroism is one form of altruism.

Altruism is helping or doing something, often at a cost or risk, for reasons other than the expectation of a material or social reward.

Altruistic people often do things that touch our hearts. Consider 87-year-old Osceola McCarty (photo below), who hand-washed clothes most of her life for grateful clients. When she finally retired at age 86, she donated most of her life savings, an amazing $150,000, to the University of Southern Mississippi to finance scholarships for the area's African American students. "I want them to have an education," said McCarty, who never married and has no children of her own. "I had to work hard all my life. They can have the chance that I didn't have" (Plummer & Ridenhour, 1995, p. 40). As these examples show, some people help in emergencies, and others help by donating time or money.

> I donated most of my life savings for student scholarships.

Why People Help

Would you help?

Why did Osceola McCarty, who spent her life washing clothes, donate most of her hard-earned life savings to finance scholarships instead of using her savings to make her retirement more comfortable? Researchers suggest at least three different motivations—empathy, personal distress, and norms and values—to explain why people are altruistic and help others without thought of rewards (Batson, 1998; Schroeder et al., 1995):

• We may help because we feel **empathy**—that is, we identify with what the victim must be going through. Osceola McCarty may have donated her life savings for scholarships because she felt empathy for other African American students.

• We may help because we feel **personal distress**—that is, we have feelings of fear, alarm, or disgust from seeing a victim in need. Osceola said that she didn't want other young African American people to have to go through the hard times that she had faced.

• We may help because of our **norms and values**—that is, we may feel morally bound or responsible to help those in need.

Researchers have combined these three motivations along with several other ideas to construct two different theories of why people come out of a crowd and help perfect strangers. We can use these two theories to explain why Wesley was the only onlooker at the subway station who dared to jump on the tracks and risk his life to save that of another man.

Decision-Stage Model

Wesley may have decided to help after going through five stages, which involved making five different decisions.

The **decision-stage model of helping** says that you go through five stages in deciding to help: (1) you notice the situation; (2) you

interpret it as one in which help is needed; (3) you assume personal responsibility; (4) you choose a form of assistance; and (5) you carry out that assistance.

According to the decision-stage model, Wesley helped because he went through all five stages. Most onlookers stopped at stage 3 and decided it was not their responsibility, so they did not help. This model explains that people may recognize a situation as an emergency (stages 1 and 2) yet fail to help because they do not take personal responsibility for the situation (Latané & Darley, 1970).

Arousal-Cost-Reward Model

Wesley also may have helped the seizing man because he thought about the costs and rewards.

The **arousal-cost-reward model of helping** says that we make decisions to help by calculating the costs and rewards of helping.

For example, seeing an accident may cause you to be unpleasantly and emotionally **aroused,** which you wish to reduce. In deciding how to reduce these unpleasant feelings, you calculate the **costs** and **rewards** of helping. For example, those who decided not to help may have felt that the costs of helping, such as getting involved in a potentially dangerous situation, outweighed the rewards (Piliavin et al., 1982).

According to these two models, Wesley experienced five stages (five decisions) and then decided to help, or Wesley possibly considered the costs and rewards of reducing his unpleasant emotional feelings and then decided to help. Although the arousal-cost-reward model and the decision-stage model focus on different factors, they are not mutually exclusive.

Next, we'll explain how social forces influence people in groups.

Group Dynamics

What happens in groups?

When you're with family, friends, or co-workers, you may or may not be aware of the numerous group influences that can greatly change how you think, feel, and behave.

Groups are collections of two or more people who interact, share some common idea, goal, or purpose, and influence how their members think and behave.

To illustrate the powerful influences of groups, we'll describe the case of Dennis Jay, who almost died in a drunken coma and later heard that his fraternity brothers had lied about the initiation that had almost killed him.

Group Cohesion and Norms

As a pledge at a fraternity initiation party, Dennis Jay and 19 others submitted to hazing: They were forced to drink from a "beer bong," a funnel into which beer was poured; the beer ran down a plastic hose placed in the mouth. The rule was that once you threw up, you could stop drinking from the beer bong. Because he did not throw up, Jay was given straight shots of whiskey until he fell on his face. By the time his frat brothers got Jay to the hospital, he was in a coma and barely breathing. His blood alcohol content was 0.48, and a level of 0.50 is usually fatal (legally drunk in most states is 0.08).

At first, Jay refused to describe what happened because he wanted to be loyal to his fraternity. Then he heard that the fraternity brothers had lied and said that he had stumbled drunk into their frat house and that they had brought him to the emergency ward just to help out. The fraternity brothers' lies made Jay angry, and he told the truth (Grogan et al., 1993). As discussed earlier, one reason individuals like Jay endure harmful and humiliating hazing rites is because they wish to become a member of a desired group.

Social psychologists would explain that the fraternity lied about what happened to Jay because of two powerful group influences: group cohesion and group norms.

Group cohesion is group togetherness, which is determined by how much group members perceive that they share common attributes.

One reason many groups have some form of initiation rites and rituals is to have all members share a common experience and thus increase group cohesion.

Group norms are the formal or informal rules about how group members should behave.

Group norms, written or unwritten, can exert powerful influences, both good and bad, on group members' behaviors (Hewstone et al., 2002). For example, because of powerful group norms to stick together to preserve their group, these fraternity members were willing to lie about what really happened to Jay.

Group Membership

In his hierarchy of human needs (see p. 333), humanistic psychologist Abraham Maslow identified *the need for love and belonging* as fundamental to human happiness (Maslow, 1970). One way to satisfy this social need is by joining a group, which helps individuals feel a sense of belonging, friendship, and support. The need for belonging carries into adulthood as individuals join various community and business organizations. According to Maslow's theory, the social need to belong points to a **motivational reason** for joining groups. At about the same time Maslow published his work on the hierarchy of motivation, Leon Festinger (1954) offered another reason for joining groups, based on the social comparison theory.

Social comparison theory says that we are driven to compare ourselves to others who are similar to us so that we can measure the correctness of our attitudes and beliefs. According to Festinger, this drive to compare ourselves motivates us to join groups.

According to Festinger's theory, the drive to compare and judge our attitudes and beliefs against those of others who are similar to us points to a **cognitive reason** for joining groups.

An additional reason for forming groups is that we can accomplish things in groups that we simply cannot do alone. For example, students form study groups because they want academic help, social support, and motivation. However, there are two kinds of study groups, each with different goals: task-oriented and socially oriented groups (Burn, 2004).

In a **task-oriented group,** the members have specific duties to complete.

In a **socially oriented group,** the members are primarily concerned about fostering and maintaining social relationships among the members of the group.

For example, a task-oriented group helps members achieve certain academic, business, political, or career goals, while a socially oriented group primarily is a source of friends, fun activities, and social support.

Group membership can have a powerful influence on many social interactions, such as deciding with whom to socialize, whom to discriminate against, which principles to follow, and whom to battle, psychologically and physically (Simon & Sturmer, 2003). An example of how group

A group of young Mormons performing together.

membership influences members' views and behaviors occurs during national elections, when Republicans and Democrats wage hard-fought political and personal battles for money, votes, and power.

Next, we'll discuss how groups and crowds can influence our behaviors.

Behavior in Crowds

How do you behave in a crowd?

You may not notice, but being in a crowd can cause you to think and behave differently than when you're alone. A **crowd,** which is a large group of persons who are usually strangers, can facilitate or inhibit certain behaviors. For example, we'll discuss how being in a crowd can increase or decrease personal performance, encourage individuals to engage in antisocial behaviors, such as riots, or cause individuals to refuse to help to someone in need.

Facilitation and Inhibition

Performing before a large crowd can facilitate or inhibit behaviors.

If a runner has a history of successful competition, he may turn in a better performance in front of a large crowd as a result of social facilitation.

Social facilitation is an increase in performance in the presence of a crowd.

In contrast, if a runner has a spotty history in competition, he may turn in a worse performance in front of a large crowd because of social inhibition.

Social inhibition is a decrease in performance in the presence of a crowd.

Whether we show facilitation or inhibition depends partly on our previous experience. Generally, the presence of others will facilitate well-learned, simple, or reflexive responses but will inhibit new, unusual, or complex responses. An example of social facilitation occurs during championship games when a player is awarded the title of "most valuable player." An example of social inhibition also occurs during championship games when a star player, who is expected to do great, instead feels anxiety about performing and plays poorly or "chokes" (Baumeister, 1995). Thus, the presence of a crowd can either facilitate or inhibit behaviors, depending on the situation (Blascovich & Mendes, 2010).

Deindividuation in Crowds

During the Los Angeles riots in the early 1990s, people were arrested for looting, setting fires, and beating others. Individuals in a crowd are more likely to commit such antisocial acts because being in a crowd conceals the person's identity, a process called deindividuation.

Deindividuation is the increased tendency for people to behave irrationally or perform antisocial behaviors when there is less chance of being personally identified.

Looting is more likely to occur in a crowd because of deindividuation.

Researchers believe deindividuation occurs because being in a crowd gives individuals anonymity and reduces guilt and self-awareness, so that people are less controlled by internal standards and more willing to engage in deviant or antisocial roles (Silke, 2003; Zimbardo, 1970).

One example of deindividuation is people trampling over a crowd of shoppers during a Black Friday rush. Also, gang members getting a tattoo of their gang symbol, fraternity and sorority members wearing clothing marked with their group letters, and players on sports teams wearing the same uniforms all lose their sense of self by identifying with their group. The reduced feelings of personal accountability make it more likely that these individuals will engage in reckless or irrational behavior.

The Bystander Effect

As a person lies unconscious on a city sidewalk, dozens or hundreds of people may walk by without helping. There are several reasons no one stops to help, including fear of the person's reactions, inexperience with providing help, and the bystander effect.

The **bystander effect** says that an individual may feel inhibited from taking some action because of the presence of others.

Data from over 50 studies indicate that 75% of people offer assistance when alone, but fewer than 53% do so when in a group (Latané & Nida, 1981). There are two explanations for the bystander effect.

The **informational influence theory** says that we use the reactions of others to judge the seriousness of the situation.

If other bystanders are taking no action, we conclude that no emergency exists and we do nothing to offer help or aid (Burn, 2004).

The **diffusion of responsibility theory** says that, in the presence of others, individuals feel less personal responsibility and are less likely to take action in a situation where help is required (Latané, 1981).

Survey results report that 77% of Americans want to help victims of disasters such as hurricanes and earthquakes, but when it comes to volunteering, many will not because they believe the whole country is already helping (Marchetti & Bunte, 2006). Thus, an individual may feel less responsibility to offer help or aid.

The presence of others also influences how we make decisions, which we'll examine next.

Just being in the presence of other strangers can inhibit an individual from helping someone in need.

Group Decisions

Does being in a group affect thinking?

All of us have been in groups—families, fraternities, sororities, various social or business clubs. What you may not realize is that being in a group creates social pressures that influence how you think and make decisions. We'll discuss two interesting factors in making decisions: group polarization and groupthink.

Group Polarization

Imagine that a young lawyer is trying to decide between two job offers. The first offer is from a large, well-established firm that promises more security, financial opportunities, and prestige. However, it has a poor record as an equal opportunity employer of women and currently has no women partners. The second offer is from a small, recently established firm that can promise little security or prestige. However, this firm is doing well and has an excellent record in promoting women as partners. Which offer should the lawyer accept? Using dilemmas such as this, researchers compared the recommendations from individuals in a group with those made by the group after it had engaged in discussion (Gigone & Hastie, 1997; Pruitt, 1971). Group discussions change individuals' judgments, such as when a group urges a more risky recommendation than do individuals. This phenomenon became known as the *risky shift*.

Researchers later discovered that the direction of a group's risky shift depends on how conservative or liberal the group was to begin with. If a group's members are initially more conservative, group discussion will shift its decision to an even more conservative one. If a group's members are initially more liberal, group discussion will shift its decision to an even more liberal one.

The group's shift to a more extreme position is called group polarization (Fiedler, 2007; Van Swol, 2009).

Group polarization is a phenomenon in which group discussion reinforces the majority's point of view and shifts that view to a more extreme position.

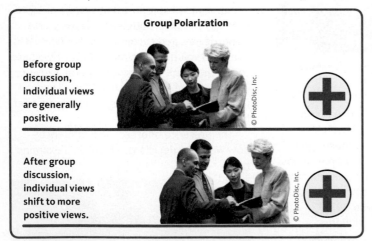

Group Polarization

Before group discussion, individual views are generally positive.

After group discussion, individual views shift to more positive views.

Whether this group polarization (figure above) is in a liberal or conservative direction depends on the initial leanings of the group's members. Researchers also found that the more the group repeated each other's arguments, the more polarized the group became (Burn, 2004). Thus, repetition of the same arguments resulted in stronger formation of attitudes and more group polarization.

Groupthink

In the early 1960s, President John F. Kennedy took the world to the brink of nuclear war when he ordered the invasion of Cuba. This invasion, which occurred at the Bay of Pigs, was a terrible decision and a well-remembered failure. Researchers have analyzed group decision-making processes involved in bad decisions, such as the Bay of Pigs, the escalation of war in Vietnam, the Watergate cover-up, and the *Challenger* disaster, as well as flawed group decisions in business and other organizations. One reason that groups made bad decisions in the above examples is a phenomenon called groupthink (Janis, 1989; Vallacher & Nowak, 2007).

Groupthink

What's most important is that we stick together.

Groupthink refers to a group making bad decisions because the group is more concerned about reaching agreement and sticking together than gathering the relevant information and considering all the alternatives (right figure).

Groupthink. According to psychologist Irving Janis (1989), groupthink has a number of clearly defined characteristics: Discussions are limited, few alternatives are presented, and there is increased pressure to conform. For example, the group usually has a member that Janis calls a *mindguard,* whose job is to discourage ideas that might be a threat to the group's unity. In addition, groupthink results in viewing the world in very simple terms: There is the *ingroup,* which includes only the immediate members of the group, versus the *outgroup,* which includes everyone who is not a part of the group. When a group adopts the ingroup–outgroup attitude and mentality, the result is that it strengthens groupthink by emphasizing the protection of the group's members over making the best decisions.

Avoiding groupthink. One authority on groupthink recommends using a method, called vigilant decision making, that helps a group avoid falling into groupthink and thus leads to better decisions (Janis, 1989). Major elements of **vigilant decision making** include: doing a thorough, open, and unbiased information search; evaluating as many alternative ideas as possible; and having an impartial leader who allows the members to freely and openly express differing opinions without being criticized or being considered a threat to the group. Researchers found that the vigilant decision-making method does result in better and more successful group decisions, although it is criticized for being very time-consuming (Burn, 2004).

After the Concept Review, we'll learn about how our social interactions affect our brain. ●

Concept Review

1. A broad field that studies how our thoughts, feelings, perceptions, and behaviors are influenced by interactions with others is called _____.

2. Making judgments about the traits of others through social interactions and gaining knowledge from our social perceptions are called _____.

3. Widely held beliefs that people have certain traits because they belong to a particular group are known as (a) _____. An unfair, biased, or intolerant attitude toward another group of people is called (b) _____. Specific unfair behaviors exhibited toward members of a group are known as (c) _____.

4. Cognitive structures that represent an organized collection of knowledge about people, events, and concepts are called _____. They influence what we perceive and remember and how we behave.

5. The process by which we look for causes to explain a person's behavior is known as (a) _____. If we attribute behavior to the internal characteristics of a person, we are attributing the behavior to the person's (b) _____. If we attribute behavior to the external circumstances or context of that behavior, we are attributing the behavior to the (c) _____.

6. If we attribute the cause of a behavior to a person's disposition and overlook the demands of the environment or situation, we are committing the (a) _____ error. If we attribute our own behavior to situational factors but the behaviors of others to their disposition, we are committing the (b) _____ effect. If we attribute success to our disposition and failure to the situation, we are using the (c) _____ bias.

7. Beliefs or opinions that include a positive or negative evaluation of some target (object, person, or event) and that predispose us to act in a certain way toward the target are called _____.

8. There are two different theories about why we change our attitudes. One theory says that experiencing cognitive inconsistencies produces psychological tension that we try to reduce by making our beliefs more consistent. This is called (a) _____ theory. If we take a public position that is counter to our private attitude, we are engaging in (b) _____ behavior.

9. Another theory of attitude change says that we first observe our own behaviors, which in turn causes us to change our attitudes. This is called _____ theory.

10. If a politician tries to get votes by presenting information with strong arguments, analyses, facts, and logic, he or she is using the (a) _____ route of persuasion. If a politician seeks votes by emphasizing emotional appeals, focusing on personal accomplishments, and generating positive feelings, he or she is using the (b) _____ route of persuasion.

11. Persuasion involves at least three elements: We are likely to believe a (a) _____ who appears honest and trustworthy; if we disagree with the message, it is better if the persuader presents a (b) _____ message; if the (c) _____ is less interested in issues, the peripheral route is more effective.

Shock Controller

Slight shock   MAXIMUM XXX 450 volts

12. Any behavior we perform because of social influences or group pressure, even if that pressure involves no direct requests, is called (a) _____. A kind of conformity in which we give in to social pressure in our public responses but do not change our private beliefs is called (b) _____. Any behavior performed in response to an order given by someone in a position of authority is called (c) _____.

13. An increase in performance in the presence of a crowd is called social (a) _____; a decrease in performance in the presence of a crowd is called social (b) _____. An increased tendency for individuals to behave irrationally or perform antisocial behaviors if there is less chance of being personally identified is called (c) _____. Being socially inhibited to take some action, such as helping, because of the presence of others is called the (d) _____ effect.

14. A collection of two or more people who interact and share some common attribute or attributes is called a (a) _____. Togetherness, which is determined by how much group members perceive that they share common attributes, is called group (b) _____.

15. The phenomenon by which group discussion reinforces the majority's point of view and shifts that view to a more extreme position is called group (a) _____. If a group makes bad decisions because it is more concerned about reaching an agreement and sticking together than gathering the relevant information and considering all the alternatives, it is referred to as (b) _____.

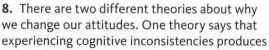

Answers: 1. *social psychology;* 2. *person perception;* 3. *(a) stereotypes, (b) prejudice, (c) discrimination;* 4. *schemas;* 5. *(a) attribution, (b) character-istics, (c) situation;* 6. *(a) fundamental attribution, (b) actor-observer, (c) self-serving;* 7. *attitudes;* 8. *(a) cognitive dissonance, (b) counterattitudinal;* 9. *self-perception;* 10. *(a) central, (b) peripheral;* 11. *(a) source, (b) two-sided, (c) audience;* 12. *(a) conformity, (b) compliance, (c) obedience;* 13. *(a) facilitation, (b) inhibition, (c) deindividuation, (d) bystander;* 14. *(a) group, (b) cohesion;* 15. *(a) polarization, (b) groupthink.*

Unless otherwise noted, all images are © Cengage Learning

G Social Neuroscience

Definition

What happens in our brains as we perceive others?

As we learned earlier in this module (p. 582), the area of the brain associated with emotional vigilance becomes activated when White people view unfamiliar Black faces, and the brain area associated with reward and pleasure becomes activated when heterosexual men view faces of attractive women. These research findings are examples of a new interdisciplinary field called social neuroscience.

Social neuroscience is an emerging area of research that examines social behavior, such as perceiving others, by combining biological and social approaches. In other words, it focuses on understanding how social behavior influences the brain as well as on how the brain influences social behavior (Cacioppo & Berntson, 2002; Cacioppo & Decety, 2011).

We'll discuss the methods researchers use to study social neuroscience and some of the research findings that have emerged from this approach to understanding social behavior.

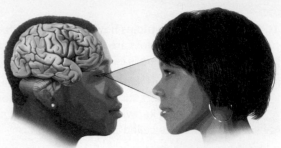

Social neuroscience examines our brain processes as we perceive others.

Methods

How do we study brain processes?

A variety of techniques are used in social neuroscience to examine the interaction of brain and social processes. As we learned earlier (pp. 70–71), there are several techniques for studying the brain. The common techniques used in social neuroscience to examine brain activity include positron emission tomography (PET scan), functional magnetic resonance imaging (fMRI), electroencephalography (EEG), and transcranial magnetic stimulation (TMS).

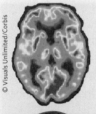

PET scan involves injecting a slightly radioactive solution into the blood and then measuring how much radiation is absorbed by neurons. Different levels of absorption are represented by colors—red and yellow indicate maximum activity of neurons, while blue and green indicate minimal activity.

fMRI measures the changes in the activity of specific neurons that are functioning during cognitive tasks, such as thinking about another person.

EEG involves placing electrodes at various points across the scalp. The electrodes detect electrical activity (brain wave activity) throughout the brain's surface.

TMS is a noninvasive technique that sends pulses of magnetic energy into the brain. It works to either activate or suppress brain activity.

Findings

How do we empathize with others?

Perhaps the most fascinating research in social neuroscience has been identifying *mirror neurons* (see p. 62), which are brain cells that are responsible for human empathy. Mirror neurons allow us to put ourselves in other people's shoes and experience how they feel. They are the reason we smile when we see a baby smile or flinch when we see a person in pain. Mirror neurons also explain why yawning is contagious. When we see another person yawn (photo below left), mirror neurons tell our brains to do the same. In fact, I (H. K.) couldn't stop myself from yawning when I looked at this photo! On a more upbeat note, group laughter spreads in much the same way (Dobbs, 2006b). For instance, I always laugh more while watching a comedy in a crowded theater than when I watch one alone at home. Thanks to mirror neurons, I know there is a biological explanation for why these movie-watching experiences are so different.

Social neuroscience research has also found that our brain's mirror neurons are especially activated when we observe people in our ethnic ingroup and minimally activated when we observe people in our ethnic outgroup, even if they are engaging in the same behaviors. These results suggest that we may unintentionally ignore or misinterpret the feelings and intentions of members of our ethnic outgroup (Gutsell & Inzlicht, 2010).

Unintentional bias is also evident in research on racial biases. For instance, many people who adamantly report being race-blind may unknowingly hold unconscious racial biases, which can come out in unexpected ways. For instance, when White Americans see photos flashed so quickly that they have no conscious awareness of having seen them, the area of the brain that signals "Watch out!" is more active immediately following Black faces than White faces (Begley, 2008a).

Next, we'll discuss a potentially disruptive social behavior—aggression. ●

Does this photograph make you yawn?

Unless otherwise noted, all images are © Cengage Learning

Genes and Environment

Is aggression in a person's genes?

Drive-by shootings, gang fights and killings, spouse and child abuse, school shootings, hate crimes, revenge-shooting by angry workers, bullying, road rage, and extreme forms of hazing are all examples of aggression.

Aggression is any behavior directed toward another that is intended to cause harm.

There is no single reason someone turns into a child bully or an aggressive adult but rather three major components: genetic and environmental influences, social cognitive and personality traits, and situational cues (R. A. Baron & Richardson, 2004; Kalat & Shiota, 2007; Shaver & Mikulincer, 2010). We'll begin with genetic or hereditary influences.

Animal aggression is largely regulated by genetic factors.

Genetic influences in animals. You can clearly see that genetic influences can regulate aggression by watching the behavior of animals. Ethologists, who study animal behavior in natural settings, have identified numerous social signals that animals have evolved to regulate aggression. For example, the photo below shows a dominant wolf standing above a submissive wolf. The submissive wolf avoids being attacked by lying down and rolling over to expose its vulnerable belly. Many of the dominant and submissive gestures observed in animals are largely programmed by genetic factors and help animals avoid potentially damaging aggressive attacks and improve their chances of survival. Compared with animals, reasons for aggressive acts in humans are much more complicated.

Animals use built-in social signals to threaten or to avoid aggression.

Genetic influences in humans. We all begin life with a different set of genes (see pp. 68, 378) that contain chemical instructions that regulate the manufacture and assembly of the many thousands of parts that make up our body and brain. In earlier modules, we discussed how genetic factors contribute 30–70% to the development of many human behaviors, such as personality traits, temperament, intelligence, emotions, motivation, and various mental health problems (Hamer, 2002). Similarly, genetic factors also play an important role in the development of human aggression.

Researchers studied levels of aggression in twins and adopted children to gauge how much genetic factors influence human aggression. If genetic factors influence aggression in humans, then identical twins, who share almost 100% of their genes, should be more alike in committing aggressive behaviors than fraternal twins, who share only 50% of their genes. Also, if genetic factors influence human aggression, then children from aggressive biological parents should be more aggressive, even if adopted by nonaggressive parents. Researchers analyzed over 50 twin and adoption studies and found that genetic factors accounted for about 34% of the total factors that were responsible for

developing aggressive and anti-social behaviors (Rhee & Waldman, 2002). These studies show that genetic influences may partly predispose a person to develop aggressive behaviors, but whether this actually occurs depends on the interaction with potentially powerful good or bad environmental influences.

Human aggression is regulated by the interaction of three major components.

Genes interact with good/bad environments. The evidence for the interaction of genetic and environmental factors in aggressive behavior is abundant. Researchers found that a specific gene variation influences brain development to make someone more prone to engage in impulsive violence, but only when the gene variation is combined with environmental stress. Other researchers reported that this same gene variation results in neurotransmitter imbalances, unusually small brain structures associated with emotions, and minimal activity in the prefrontal lobe, which result in poor impulse control and problems regulating emotions (Meyer-Lindenberg, 2006; Mullin & Hinshaw, 2007).

Researchers have also studied the interaction of genetic and environmental factors by following boys who had inherited potentially "bad genes" from their criminally inclined biological parents. Some of these boys were adopted by noncriminal parents and raised in good environments, while others were raised in "bad environments" by criminally inclined adoptive parents. Results showed that the interaction of "bad genes" and "bad environments" resulted in a large percentage of boys going on to commit criminal acts. However, results also showed that good environments can, to a large extent, compensate for inheriting "bad genes" and can override the development of antisocial behaviors (A. Raine, 2002).

Genes interact with child abuse. A tragic and unexplained question is why some children who suffer physical, sexual, or emotional abuse go on to become violent adults, while others do not. Researchers studied a group of severely abused boys who were also found to have a gene that creates abnormal levels of neurotransmitters in the brain. Boys who had the combination of being abused and having this particular gene were twice as likely to have been diagnosed with conduct disorder as a child and three times more likely to have been convicted of a violent crime by age 26. However, if boys who had this particular gene were not abused as children, they weren't any more likely to be antisocial or violent. Researchers concluded that this particular gene did not lead to developing antisocial behaviors unless an individual had also experienced a particular environmental influence—being abused as a child.

Piece of Genetic Code

Genes regulate chemicals in the brain.

The above studies show how genes and environmental factors combine, interact, and influence each other to increase or decrease antisocial or aggressive behaviors (B. Bower, 2006; Strueber et al., 2006).

Next, we'll examine specific environmental factors and situations that are involved in aggression.

Social Cognitive and Personality Factors

We have discussed how genetic factors may predispose a person to be aggressive, but whether this occurs depends on the interaction with environmental factors, such as one's learning experiences. One theory that explains how people learn to be aggressive is Albert Bandura's (2001a) social cognitive theory.

Social cognitive theory says that much of human behavior, including aggressive behavior, may be learned through watching, imitating, and modeling and does not require the observer to perform any observable behavior or receive any observable reward.

Support for social cognitive theory comes from laboratory and naturalistic studies. A classic laboratory study by Bandura (1965) found that children who observed a model's aggressive behaviors performed similar aggressive behaviors (see p. 224). Children who were exposed to aggressive models, such as seeing parents use physical punishment, were reported to show increased aggression with their peers, parents, and dating partners (C. A. Anderson & Huesmann, 2003). These studies show that individuals predisposed to be aggressive are more likely to become so after observing aggressive models in their families, on television, or in video games.

Television/video games. Children have ample opportunity to see, model, and imitate aggressive adults, since the majority of programs on cable and network television contain aggressive actions. When the TV-viewing habits of 700 adolescents were followed into

TV watching was linked to later aggressive acts.

adulthood, researchers found that adolescents who had watched 2 to 3 hours of daily television (all kinds of programs) were almost four times more likely to commit violent and aggressive acts later in life compared to those who had watched less than 1 hour a day. Researchers ruled out neglect, poverty, and bad neighborhoods and concluded that frequent TV viewing correlated with committing violent acts later in life (J. G. Johnson et al., 2002). However, it's also possible that aggressive-prone adolescents prefer to watch TV rather than engage in other activities.

Recent research on playing violent video games shows that it can make some adolescents more hostile, while for others playing video games offers opportunities to learn skills and improve social networking. Specifically, adolescents who are less agreeable, less conscientious, and easily angered are more likely to experience the negative consequences of playing violent video games (Markey & Markey, 2010).

Model of aggression. One model of how children develop aggressive behaviors points to an interaction among *genetic/environmental factors,* which can predispose individuals to develop an irritable or angry temperament and become more or less aggressive depending on the environment; *social cognitive factors,* which involve imitating and modeling the aggressive behaviors observed on television and in video games; and *personality factors,* such as being impulsive, having little empathy, and wanting to dominate others. According to this model, the interaction of these three factors increases the chances of a child developing into an aggressive adolescent and an aggressive adult (C. A. Anderson & Bushman, 2002; Tisak et al., 2006).

Situational factors can also increase or trigger aggressive behaviors.

Situational Cues

A number of situational cues have been linked to increased aggression, including hot weather (above 90°F), the presence of or easy access to guns, and exposure to violent TV shows and video games (C. A. Anderson & Bushman, 2002). In recent years, another situational cue made the news when more and more drivers became so frustrated and angry by other drivers' annoying driving habits that they responded by aggressively pursuing, ramming, fighting, and even shooting another driver (Galovski et al., 2006). The press labeled this aggressive action by frustrated drivers *road rage*, which shows how frustration can trigger aggression.

The **frustration-aggression hypothesis** says that when our goals are blocked, we become frustrated and respond with anger and aggression.

However, researchers soon discovered that, although frustration may lead to aggression, the link between the two is not absolute. Leonard Berkowitz (1989) reviewed the research on the frustration-aggression hypothesis and concluded the following:

- Frustration doesn't always lead to aggression.
- Social rules may inhibit aggression.
- Frustration may result in behaviors other than aggression.
- Cognitive factors can override aggression.

Thus, Berkowitz (1993) modified the original hypothesis.

The **modified frustration-aggression hypothesis** says that, although frustration may lead to aggression, situational and cognitive factors may override the aggressive response.

Although our daily lives are often filled with frustrations, we usually find ways to control our frustrations and don't express them in anger, violence, or road rage. However, a child is more likely to

A citizen slyly shows her frustrated feelings toward police.

react to frustration with violence if he or she has observed and imitated the aggressive behaviors of adults (Osofsky, 1995). Similarly, adults with a personality trait to be impulsive or a genetic tendency to be aggressive are more likely to react to frustration with aggression (Lindsay & Anderson, 2000).

Summary. We have discussed a number of recent studies on aggression that show how genetic influences interact with environmental factors and how neurotransmitters' levels in the brain affect aggressive behavior (B. Bower, 2006; R. Raine, 2002). Earlier, we also discussed how the decision-making area of the brain (prefrontal cortex—see p. 411) doesn't develop until early adulthood, which explains why adolescents are likely to engage in impulsive and dangerous actions. All these studies point to the importance of biological influences and emphasize that any explanation of human aggression must consider the interaction among three major factors—genes and environment, social cognitive learning and personality traits, and situational cues.

One terrifying and degrading form of aggression is sexual aggression, which we'll examine next.

Sexual Harassment and Aggression

Why do men rape?

According to a National Crime Victimization Survey of U.S. citizens aged 12 and older, there were 191,670 reported rapes and sexual assaults in 2005 (Catalano, 2006). It is estimated that an astonishing 95% of sexual attacks go unreported, making sexual assault a "silent epidemic" and the most underreported crime in the United States (AAUW, 2012a).

In the United States, it is estimated that during their lifetime about 45% of women and 22% of men will be victims of some type of sexual aggression (CDC, 2011e). Also, recent statistics show that nearly 1 in 5 women and 1 in 71 men report being raped in their lifetime (CDC, 2011e). Until 2012, the U.S. government's definition of rape was limited to include only women. The definition of rape has now been changed to include men as victims (U.S. Justice Department, 2012).

Rape is any kind of penetration of another person, regardless of gender, without the victim's consent.

> Let's recognize that men are also victims of rape.

National surveys of female college students report that about 20–27% of college women experience either rape or attempted rape, and about 42% experience forced sexual encounters, some of which lead to nonconsensual sexual intercourse (AAUW, 2012a; Flores, 1999).

Another form of aggression is sexual harassment. Researchers found that sexual harassment is widespread and was reported by 40–70% of women and 10–20% of men in occupational settings and by 62% of female and 61% of male college students. Although sexual harassment produces psychological and physical effects in most of the victims, less than 10% of victims file formal complaints (AAUW, 2012b; ACA Group, 2004).

Here, we'll focus on rape and sexual assault and begin by describing the common types of rapists.

Characteristics and Kinds of Rapists

Psychologists have identified several developmental factors that are associated with men who rape: They often come from broken homes, did not have a loving caregiver, were sexually or physically abused, were neglected, and spent time in penal institutions (Polaschek et al., 1997). However, these factors alone do not produce rapists; other men who have suffered similar development problems do not become rapists. At present, there is no generally accepted theory of what turns men into rapists.

Researchers have interviewed rapists to understand the motivation behind their sexual aggression. Rapists reported different degrees and combinations of anger, sexual violence, power, and control. Here are descriptions of four types of rapists (Knight, 1992).

> The most common rapist is a man who wants to possess his victim.

• The **power rapist**, who commits 70% of all rapes, is not out to hurt physically but to possess. His acts are premeditated and are often preceded by rape fantasies. He may carry a weapon, not to hurt but to intimidate the victim.

• The **sadistic rapist** accounts for fewer than 5% of rapes, but he is the most dangerous because for him sexuality and aggression have become fused, and using physical force is arousing and exciting.

• For the **anger rapist**, rape is an impulsive, savage attack of uncontrolled physical violence. The act is of short duration, accompanied by abusive language, and the victim usually suffers extensive physical trauma, such as broken bones and bruises.

• The **acquaintance** or **date rapist** knows his victim and uses varying amounts of verbal or physical coercion to force his partner to engage in sexual activities.

These examples indicate that men rape for a number of or a combination of reasons, such as to exercise power and control, express anger, and become sexually aroused.

Other factors that contribute to rape are the false beliefs, called rape myths, that some men hold about women.

Rape Myths

One consistent finding about rapists is that they hold negative and demeaning attitudes toward women. For example, here are some of their negative beliefs:

• Healthy women cannot be raped against their will.
• Women often falsely accuse men of rape.
• Rape is primarily a sex crime committed by sex-crazed maniacs.
• Only bad girls get raped.
• If a girl engages in petting and lets things get out of hand, it is her own fault if her partner forces sex on her.

These kinds of statements are called rape myths (Buddie & Miller, 2002; Greensite, 2007).

Rape myths are misinformed, false beliefs about women, and these myths are frequently held by rapists.

> Some men mistakenly believe that only bad women get raped.

Men who believe in rape myths tend to have a more traditional view of sex roles and hold more negative attitudes toward women. Although researchers found that acceptance of rape myths is more common among men who have raped, rape myths are also held by men in general. For example, one survey of male college students reported that from 17% to 75% of students agreed with one or more of nine rape myths (Giacopassi & Dull, 1986). This association between rape myths and rapists illustrates how negative beliefs and attitudes can contribute to sexual aggression (DeGue & DiLillo, 2005).

Researchers are developing rape prevention programs to both prevent rape and stop the perpetuation of rape myths, and these programs are becoming increasingly common on college campuses (DeGue & DiLillo, 2005; Schewe, 2002). We'll discuss ways to prevent sexual aggression in the Application section.

Next, we'll examine programs psychologists have developed to change attitudes toward aggression. ●

Case Study

Why did only one of six children develop into a violent adult?

In a family of six children, one was so bad he was nicknamed Monster Kody. He became a gang member and shot his first victim at age 11. Kody continued his violent and aggressive ways until he was arrested, convicted, and sentenced to jail for robbery. When he wrote his autobiography from his prison cell, he blamed his problems and violent behavior on his parents' poverty and destitution and on his belonging to a violent gang. But as it turned out, Monster Kody had three brothers and two sisters who grew up in the same poverty and destitution but developed into law-abiding

citizens who are leading very productive lives (Azar & Sleek, 1994).

Out of six children raised in the same environment, only one, Monster Kody, became an aggressive adult. This shows that the development of aggressive behavior depends on the interaction of the three factors that we have discussed: genetic and environmental, social cognitive, and personality factors. Because genetic and environmental factors are sometimes difficult to change, recent programs focus on social cognitive factors to reduce and control aggression.

Controlling Aggression in Children

Most children have occasional outbursts of anger and aggression, but if these outbursts become frequent, young children may develop a pattern of using aggressive behaviors to deal with problems (Lemerise & Dodge, 2000). Researchers found that, unless treated, an aggressive child will surely become an aggressive adolescent and adult and develop later problems, such as substance abuse, criminality, and mental health disorders (Broidy et al., 2003). Researchers have discovered that aggressive children have a number of cognitive-behavioral deficits that make them perceive, remember, and react to a world that appears more hostile than it really is. We'll first discuss these cognitive-behavioral deficits and then a treatment program.

Cognitive-Behavioral Deficits

Parents and teachers need to realize that an aggressive child or teenager does not perceive the world, take feedback, or act as regular nonaggressive children do. Here are some of the ways that aggressive children differ (Lochman et al., 2006; Spielman & Staub, 2000):

• An aggressive child **does not accurately perceive or recall social cues.** For example, the aggressive child selectively attends to aggressive or hostile actions and overlooks positive social cues. When an aggressive child is asked to recall what happened that day, the child tends to remember all the hostile actions rather than any friendly cues.

• An aggressive child **does not make accurate explanations** or attributions of the situation. For instance, aggressive children tend to attribute hostile actions to other children when, in fact, other children are not behaving in an aggressive or hostile way.

• An aggressive child **does not have many adaptive solutions** to problems. This means aggressive children tend to use hostile and aggressive actions to solve many of their problems rather than using nonhostile or verbal solutions.

• An aggressive child **is reinforced for aggressive behaviors** rather than for positive social behaviors. That's because aggressive children get their way by using hostile actions, which in turn are reinforced. Aggressive children **have poor social skills,** which means they rarely solve problems in nonaggressive ways, such as by discussion.

Because of these cognitive-behavioral deficits, aggressive children perceive a more hostile world and respond with more aggressive behaviors (Lochman et al., 2006). There are programs that teach children how to control their aggression.

You know I've got a quick temper, so don't make me angry!

© Michael William/ Shutterstock.com

Programs to Control Aggression

Children who engage in antisocial and aggressive behaviors are usually described by the term *conduct disorder,* which is one of the most frequent reasons for referral to treatment programs (Ollendick et al., 2006). We'll discuss two successful programs for treating conduct disorder.

Cognitive problem-solving skills training. A well-researched treatment program involves helping aggressive children overcome the deficits in cognitive-behavioral skills that we just discussed. For example, because an aggressive child does not know how to stop thinking and acting in aggressive ways, therapists teach the child specific rules, such as no matter how angry the child gets, he or she must not hit, yell, or kick. The child receives special reinforcement for obeying these rules. The child learns to use self-statements to inhibit impulsive behavior, including "I can stop myself." The child learns to use alternative, nonaggressive solutions when frustrated. These might be hand clapping, scribbling on a sheet of paper, or tensing and relaxing muscles. Cognitive programs have reduced the aggression of children in both home and school (Nangle et al., 2002; C. R. Thomas, 2006).

Parent Management Training (PMT). An effective treatment program for conduct disorder is called Parent Management Training, or PMT (Mash & Wolfe, 2007). In this program, a therapist teaches parents how to use specific procedures in the home to alter angry interactions with their child, to decrease deviant behaviors, and, very important, to promote positive or prosocial behaviors. For example, parents learn to not reinforce aggressive behaviors that a child uses to get his or her way, to establish and enforce reasonable rules, and to reinforce appropriate behaviors. PMT has proven very effective in decreasing aggressive behaviors in the home and school (C. R. Thomas, 2006).

Now, we'll examine methods of controlling aggression in adults.

Controlling Anger in Adults

How do I stop being angry? You've probably known people who get mad, rant and rave, and then take their anger out on whoever happens to be near. Then, after their violent outbursts, they may apologize, say they're sorry, or explain that they have to let out their angry feelings or they'll explode. Is it true that "letting it all out" is a good way to deal with anger?

Catharsis

A popular idea for reducing and controlling aggression involves catharsis.

Catharsis is a psychological process through which anger or aggressive energy is released by expressing or letting out powerful negative emotions.

I'll get you for cutting me off, you dumb…!

According to the concept of catharsis, a good way to deal with anger or aggression is to "let off steam," which means expressing strong negative emotions by yelling, arguing, hitting, or kicking something.

Sigmund Freud used the term *catharsis* to mean that one should let frustration and anger out so that they don't build up and explode in an aggressive rage. However, most research does not support Freud's conclusion about the usefulness of catharsis. For example, after college students were made angry, some were told to punch a bag while thinking about the person who made them angry (catharsis group), while others were told only to sit quietly for 2 minutes (control group). Afterward, students in the catharsis group, who vented their anger, rated their anger higher than those in the control group, who did nothing to let it out. The researcher concluded that venting to let anger out (catharsis group) was like pouring gasoline on a fire; it only adds fuel and makes the anger worse. Accordingly, it's bad to vent one's anger by punching a pillow, since it seems to only make the anger worse (Bushman, 2002). A better way to deal with anger, at the job, school, home, or on the road, is to use a cognitive-relaxation program.

Cognitive-Relaxation Program

At the urging of his wife, Rob came to therapy because he's prone to angry outbursts, especially when driving. He says things like, "I'm not doing anything unsafe; it's that jerk in front of me who's going too slow." Rob admits to getting angry at one thing or another many times a day (Holloway, 2003). Rob can learn to gain control over his anger with an anger management program.

One such successful program is the cognitive-relaxation program. It begins by having Rob observe and later write down his behaviors (feeling tense) and anger-producing thoughts ("That guy's a jerk") during several days of driving. This process is called self-monitoring and helps Rob make a record of the anger-producing thoughts and behaviors that he may not have been aware of and that trigger and maintain his anger. Next, Rob learns a method to quickly relax himself on cue (progressive relaxation—see p. 503) so that he will be able to reduce his body tension and arousal. He also makes a list of positive thoughts ("That guy's a careful driver," "That guy is trying to avoid an accident") that he can substitute for his anger-producing ones ("That driver's a jerk"). Once Rob has learned to relax on cue and has his list of positive thoughts, he's ready to begin driving while substituting positive for negative thoughts and relaxing on cue whenever he begins to feel tense or angry. Being able to relax on cue is important because it's very hard to get angry if you're relaxed. Researchers found that this cognitive-relaxation program has proved very effective in helping individuals reduce and control their anger (Deffenbacher, 2003, 2005).

Controlling Sexual Coercion

Several studies have found that from 42% to 78% of college women report sexual coercion, which includes men using social pressure, verbal coercion, lies, alcohol or drugs, emotional manipulation, or threat of force to have sexual contact with women (Struckman-Johnson et al., 2003). Part of the socialization of males involves seeing situations that may reinforce and increase their risk of using sexual coercion. For example, the media (movies, videos, songs) portray situations in which men believe that using sexual coercion does no harm and may even be arousing to their partners, or may be necessary to achieve their goals (Lonsway & Fitzgerald, 1994). These media portrayals reinforce the idea that sexual coercion is acceptable and even arousing to women and increase the risk that men will be sexually coercive and not be perceptive and responsive to a woman's wishes or refusals.

What are the risks?

One problem is that some males do not take "NO!" for an answer.

Somehow the socialization creates a difference between men who are sexually coercive and those who are not. For example, men who report higher levels of sexual coercion also perceived women as showing higher levels of sexual interest in nonsexual, mundane situations (having a conversation). Researchers concluded that, in these cases, it is not the women's behaviors that put them at risk for sexual coercion but rather it is that sexually coercive men misperceive women as showing sexual interest when they are not (Bondurant & Donat, 1999). These researchers suggest that prevention programs need to educate sexually coercive men about how they may misperceive the sexual interest of women, even in very mundane situations like ordinary conversations.

According to researchers, one way to avoid sexual coercion on a date is for men and women to know the risk factors. For women, these include the heavy use of alcohol or other drugs that dull reason and perception. For men, these include overusing drugs, thinking that paying the expenses entitles him to sex, misperceiving his date's sexual interest, and not recognizing that "No" means "No!" (Struckman-Johnson et al., 2003). ●

Why the Debate over Teen Vaccination?

What if modern medicine could prevent three-quarters of the occurrences of a leading cause of cancer in women and save almost 300,000 lives each year? A major public health breakthrough makes this possible. The first vaccine to protect women against cervical cancer is now available, but it comes with much controversy.

1 What role does brain development play in adolescents' likelihood of having safe sex to reduce the chances of getting infected with HPV?

Cervical cancer is caused by HPV (human papillomavirus), the most common sexually transmitted infection in the United States. Cervical cancer usually strikes when a woman is young, often before she has had children, and the treatment may cause infertility. Because cervical cancer is the leading cause of cancer death in women and its treatment has serious risks, prevention is essential.

A vaccine that prevents infection of four types of HPV and comes with minimal side effects is now available. The vaccine is 100% effective in targeting certain causes of cervical cancer that together make up about three-quarters of all cervical cancer cases. Despite its effectiveness and safety, the use of the vaccine has provoked considerable social controversy.

2 How do the three components of attitude apply to the conservatives' position?

3 Why has preaching abstinence not been more successful in preventing girls from getting HPV?

Because many teens contract HPV within only a few years after their first sexual experience, it is recommended that the vaccine be administered to girls during their early teens. Some conservative officials and parents oppose vaccinating teen girls, stating that the vaccine undermines their value of abstinence being the best method to avoid getting HPV. These same opponents fear that vaccinating young teens against a sexually transmitted infection, such as HPV, conveys approval to be sexually promiscuous.

4 Which group attitudes or norms do the members of the conservative side share? How does a group benefit by sharing norms?

Alan Kaye, the executive director of the National Cervical Cancer Coalition, disagrees with opponents who worry that the vaccination will result in girls becoming sexually promiscuous. He responds to these moral objections by comparing the vaccine to wearing a seat belt: "Just because you wear a seat belt doesn't mean you're seeking out an accident" (R. Stein, 2005b). Others argue the cervical cancer vaccine is no different from routine vaccines that protect children

5 What type of persuasion are advocates of the vaccine mostly using to pass legislation?

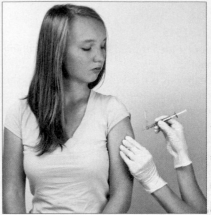

© Elena Elisseeva/Shutterstock.com

from diseases such as measles, polio, or chicken pox.

Concerns raised about the vaccine that are unrelated to morality include its high cost ($360), uncertainty about how long the vaccine will be effective, and possible side effects. Despite these concerns, about 35% of teenage girls have already received the HPV vaccine. Advocates are optimistic that up to 90% of teenage girls will eventually receive the HPV vaccine.

6 What needs to happen for a parent opposed to vaccinating a teen to change his or her attitude toward teens getting vaccinated?

In addition to the HPV vaccine targeting the major causes of cervical cancer, it protects against the causes of 90% of all genital warts cases and may reduce the risk of oral cancer. Consequently, another social debate is deciding whether boys should be vaccinated as well. As of 2012, the American Academy of Pediatrics recommends the routine administration of the HPV vaccine for boys.

Adapted from AAP, 2012; Associated Press, 2005c; Bosch et al., 2002; CDC, 2012c; FDA, 2006; Gostout, 2007; Hitti, 2006a; M. Kaufman, 2006; Kotz, 2007b; MSNBC, 2006; Slade et al., 2009; R. Stein, 2005b; *Time,* 2007b

Summary Test

A Perceiving Others

1. How our thoughts, feelings, perceptions, and behaviors are influenced by interactions with others is studied in the field of _____ psychology.

2. Making judgments about the traits of others through social interactions and gaining knowledge from our social perceptions are part of person **(a)** _____. This process is aided by a wealth of social information that is stored in our memories. However, some memories can bias our perceptions. Widely held beliefs that people have certain traits because they belong to a particular group are called **(b)** _____. Negative beliefs that are often accompanied by an unfair, biased, or intolerant attitude toward another group of people are called **(c)** _____. Specific unfair behaviors exhibited toward members of a group are called **(d)** _____.

3. Cognitive structures that represent an organized collection of knowledge about people, events, and concepts are called _____. They help us select and interpret relevant information from a tremendous amount of incoming social information and provide guidelines for how we should behave in different situations.

4. There are different kinds of schemas: Those that include our judgments about the traits that we and others possess are called **(a)** _____ schemas; those that are based on the jobs people perform or the social positions they hold are called **(b)** _____ schemas; those that contain behaviors that we associate with familiar activities, events, or procedures are called **(c)** _____ schemas, or scripts.

B Attributions

5. The factors or events that we point to as causes or explanations for people's behavior are called **(a)** _____. If we attribute behavior to the internal characteristics of the person performing the behavior, we are using **(b)** _____ explanations; if we attribute behavior to the circumstances or context of that behavior, we are using **(c)** _____ explanations.

6. Harold Kelley proposed that in deciding between personal and situational explanations, we should look for factors that change along with the behavior we are trying to explain; this is called the _____ model. To decide between personal and situational explanations, we should look for consensus, consistency, and distinctiveness.

7. An error that we make by attributing the cause of a behavior to a person's disposition and overlooking the demands of the environment or situation is the **(a)** _____ attribution error. If we attribute our own behavior to situational factors but others' behaviors to their dispositions, we fall prey to the **(b)** _____ effect. If we attribute success to our disposition and failure to the situation, we use the **(c)** _____ bias.

C Research Focus: Attributions & Grades

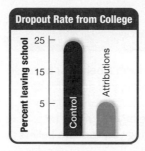

Dropout Rate from College

8. Researchers found that freshmen who were encouraged to attribute their academic problems to _____ conditions, such as poor study habits, showed a significant improvement in grade point average and were less likely to drop out than were students who continued to attribute their poor performance to permanent factors.

D Attitudes

9. Beliefs or opinions that include a positive or negative evaluation of an object, person, or event and that predispose us to act in a certain way are called **(a)** _____. General attitudes are convenient guidelines for interpreting and categorizing objects and events and deciding whether to approach or avoid them. Attitudes have three components: beliefs and ideas make up the **(b)** _____ component; emotions and feelings make up the **(c)** _____ component; and predispositions make up the **(d)** _____ component.

10. A state of unpleasant psychological tension that motivates us to reduce our inconsistencies and return to a more consistent state is called **(a)** _____. To reduce this tension and return to a more consistent state, we may add or change **(b)** _____ or take a public position that is counter to our private attitude, which is called engaging in **(c)** _____ behavior. According to Daryl Bem's theory, we first observe or perceive our own behavior and then infer attitudes from that behavior; this is called **(d)** _____ theory.

11. One method of persuasion presents information with strong arguments, analyses, facts, and logic; this is the **(a)** _____ route, which works primarily on the cognitive component of our attitudes. Another route emphasizes emotional appeal, focuses on personal traits, and generates positive feelings; this is called the **(b)** _____ route and works primarily on the affective or feeling component. Three factors to consider in persuasion are the source, **(c)** _____, and **(d)** _____.

E Cultural Diversity: National Attitudes & Behaviors

12. National attitudes are important because they predispose citizens to **(a)** _____ in certain ways. For example, compared to the West, traditional Nigerian attitudes are for a woman to become beautiful by **(b)** _____ a lot. One reason Egyptian women are having such difficulty changing **(c)** _____ toward them is that these discriminatory policies are backed by social, political, and religious forces.

© Jeff Greenberg/Age fotostock

F Social & Group Influences

© AP Images/Scott Sommerdorf, *The Salt Lake Tribune*

13. If you perform a behavior because of group pressure, you are exhibiting **(a)** _____. Giving in to social pressure in your public responses but not changing your private beliefs is called **(b)** _____. A sales technique that relies on the increased probability of getting a second request if you obtain compliance with a small first request is called the **(c)** _____ technique. Performing a behavior in response to an order given by someone in authority is called **(d)** _____.

14. Any behavior that benefits others or has positive social consequences is called **(a)** _____ behavior. A form of helping that involves doing something, often at a cost, for reasons other than the expectation of a material or social reward is called **(b)** _____.

15. A collection of two or more people who interact and share some common attribute or attributes is called a **(a)** _____. How much group members perceive that they share common attributes determines group **(b)** _____. The formal or informal rules about how group members should behave are called group **(c)** _____. According to Leon Festinger's **(d)** _____ theory, we compare ourselves to others who are similar to us so that we can measure the correctness of our attitudes and beliefs.

16. If the presence of a crowd increases performance, it is called social **(a)** _____; if it decreases performance, it is called social **(b)** _____. If people in a crowd take on anti-social roles because they cannot be identified easily, it is called **(c)** _____. If an individual in a crowd is inhibited from helping someone in need, it is called the **(d)** _____ effect.

17. The effect in which a group discussion reinforces the majority's point of view and shifts that view to a more extreme position is called **(a)** _____. If a group makes a bad decision because it emphasizes sticking together over gathering data and considering all the alternatives, that is called **(b)** _____

G Social Neuroscience

18. Social neuroscience refers to a research area that examines social behavior, such as perceiving others, by combining _____ approaches.

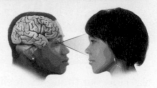

19. Brain cells responsible for human empathy are called _____.

H Aggression

© Ben Welsh Premium/Alamy

20. The findings that identical twins are more alike in aggression and that not all abused children become aggressive are evidence for **(a)** _____ influences on aggression. The finding that people can learn aggressive behavior through observation, imitation, and self-reinforcement supports the influence of **(b)** _____ factors. The finding that frustration may lead to or trigger aggression supports the influence of **(c)** _____ factors. Unlike humans, aggression in animals is primarily influenced by **(d)** _____ factors.

21. The primary motivation for rape is not sexual but a combination of _____, _____, and _____.

I Application: Controlling Aggression

22. An aggressive child perceives and reacts to a world that appears more hostile than normal because this child has a number of **(a)** _____ deficits. Children can learn to control their aggressive behavior by being reinforced for obeying certain **(b)** _____. Freud believed that adults should release frustration by acting out, which reduces anger and is called **(c)** _____. Freud's idea is not supported by modern research. A successful anger management program for adults is called the **(d)** _____ program.

© Michael William/Shutterstock.com

Unless otherwise noted, all images are © Cengage Learning

Answers: 1. *social;* 2. *(a) perception, (b) stereotypes, (c) prejudice, (d) discrimination;* 3. *schemas;* 4. *(a) person, (b) role, (c) event;* 5. *(a) attributions, (b) internal (personal), (c) external (situational);* 6. *covariation;* 7. *(a) fundamental, (b) actor-observer, (c) self-serving;* 8. *temporary;* 9. *(a) attitudes, (b) cognitive, (c) affective, (d) behavioral;* 10. *(a) cognitive dissonance, (b) beliefs, (c) counterattitudinal, (d) self-perception;* 11. *(a) central, (b) peripheral, (c) message, (d) audience;* 12. *(a) behave, (b) eating, (c) attitudes;* 13. *(a) conformity, (b) compliance, (c) foot-in-the-door, (d) obedience;* 14. *(a) prosocial or helping, (b) altruism;* 15. *(a) group, (b) cohesion, (c) norms, (d) social comparison;* 16. *(a) facilitation, (b) inhibition, (c) deindividuation, (d) bystander;* 17. *(a) group polarization, (b) groupthink;* 18. *biological and social;* 19. *mirror neurons;* 20. *(a) genetic and environmental, (b) social cognitive, (c) situational, (d) genetic;* 21. *power, aggression, control;* 22. *(a) cognitive-behavioral, (b) rules, (c) catharsis, (d) cognitive-relaxation*

Key Terms/Key People

actor-observer effect, 586
aggression, 601
altruism, 595
arousal-cost-reward model of helping, 595
attitude, 588
attributions, 585
bystander effect, 597
catharsis, 605
central route for persuasion, 590
cognitive dissonance, 589
cognitive miser model, 586
compliance, 593
conformity, 592
consensus, 585
consistency, 585
counterattitudinal behavior, 589
covariation model, 585
crowd, 597
debriefing, 594

decision-stage model of helping, 595
deindividuation, 597
diffusion of responsibility theory, 597
discrimination, 583
distinctiveness, 585
electroencephalography (EEG), 600
event schemas, 584
external attributions, 585
foot-in-the-door technique, 593
frustration-aggression hypothesis, 602
functional magnetic resonance imaging (fMRI), 600
fundamental attribution error, 586
groups, 596
group cohesion, 596
group norms, 596

group polarization, 598
groupthink, 598
hazing, 581, 592
hero, 595
informational influence theory, 597
internal attributions, 585
Milgram's experiment, 593–594
modified frustration-aggression hypothesis, 602
obedience, 593
peripheral route for persuasion, 590
person perception, 582
person schemas, 584
personal attributions, 585
positron emission tomography (PET scan), 600
prejudice, 583
prosocial behavior, 595

rape, 603
rape myths, 603
role schemas, 584
schemas, 584
self-perception theory, 589
self schemas, 584
self-serving bias, 586
situational attributions, 585
social cognition, 584
social cognitive theory, 602
social comparison theory, 596
social facilitation, 597
social inhibition, 597
social neuroscience, 600
social psychology, 581
socially oriented group, 596
stereotypes, 583
task-oriented group, 596
transcranial magnetic stimulation (TMS), 600

Media Resources

Go to **CengageBrain.com** to access Psychology CourseMate, where you will find an interactive eBook, glossaries, flashcards, quizzes, videos, answers to Critical Thinking questions, and more. You can also access Virtual Psychology Labs, an interactive laboratory experience designed to illustrate key experiments first-hand.

Descriptive Statistics

Do numbers speak for themselves?
Suppose you are curious about how many people are capable of being hypnotized. You read up on how to induce hypnosis and put together a list of five things that people under hypnosis have been known to do, such as feeling no pain when a finger is pricked, being unable to bend an arm when told that the arm will remain stiff, and acting like a young child when told to regress to infancy.

You next persuade 20 people to participate in a little test. You attempt to hypnotize them and then ask them to do each of the things on your list. Of your 20 subjects, 2 follow none of your suggestions, 4 follow only one, 7 go along with two suggestions, 4 go along with three, 2 go along with as many as four, and only 1 follows all five.

The next day, a friend asks you how your study worked out. How would you make generalizations about your findings?

To answer this type of question, psychologists rely on *statistics*. Although you often hear that numbers "speak for themselves," this is not really true. Numbers must be sorted, organized, and presented in a meaningful fashion before they tell us much.

Statistics are the tools researchers use to analyze and summarize large amounts of data.

If the very word *statistics* brings to mind complex formulas you think you could never master, you may be surprised to realize how much you already use statistics in your everyday life. When you hear that a ball player has a batting average of .250 and you know this means he has gotten one hit in every four times at the plate, you are using statistics. When you understand that a rise in the median income means that people, on average, are earning more money, you are understanding statistics. When you know that scoring in the 90th percentile on a final exam means you did better than nine out of ten of your classmates, you are showing a grasp of statistics—specifically, descriptive statistics.

Descriptive statistics are numbers used to present a collection of data in a brief yet meaningful form.

One important part of descriptive statistics is presenting distributions of measurements and scores.

Frequency Distributions

Individual differences show up in everything that can be measured. There are no measurements—whether of height, heart rate, memory capability, shyness, or political opinion—that do not show individual variation.

The **frequency distribution** is the range of scores we get and the frequency of each one when we measure a sample of people regarding some trait.

Frequency distributions are often presented in graphic form so their patterns can be seen at a glance. We'll discuss two of these distributions, normal and skewed.

What is a normal distribution?
For many traits in a large population, the frequency distribution has a characteristic pattern. For instance, if you measured the height of 500 students chosen at random from your school, you would find a few very short people and a few very tall people, while the height of the majority of students would be somewhere in the middle. Height, like weight, IQ, years of education, and many other characteristics, has what is known as a **normal distribution.** When graphed, a normal distribution produces a normal curve.

A **normal curve** is a graph of a frequency distribution in which the curve tapers off equally on either side of a central high point.

This characteristic bell shape (Figure A.1) shows that most of the measurements fall near the center, with as many falling to one side as to the other. When you measure a trait that is distributed normally throughout a population, your measurements should produce an approximately normal curve, provided that your sample is large enough.

What is a skewed distribution?
Not all traits are distributed normally.

Skewed distributions are distributions in which more data fall toward one side of the scale than toward the other.

When plotted on a graph, skewed distributions do not have a symmetrical shape. Instead, they have a "tail" on one end, which shows that relatively fewer frequencies occur on that side of the hori-

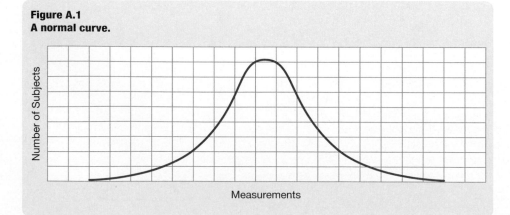

Figure A.1
A normal curve.

Number of Subjects

Measurements

zontal scale. When the tail is on the right, as in Figure A.2, we say the distribution is skewed to the right, or has a *positive skew* (there are fewer frequencies at the higher end of the horizontal scale). When the tail is on the left, as in Figure A.3, we say the distribution is skewed to the left, or has a *negative skew* (there are fewer frequencies at the lower end of the horizontal scale).

The data you collected about susceptibility to hypnosis present a skewed distribution. If you plotted them on a graph, with score along the horizontal axis and number of people along the vertical one, the curve would be skewed to the right. This would show at a glance that more people in the sample fell at the low end of your hypnotic susceptibility scale than fell at the high end.

In fact, your sample is fairly representative of the general population. About twice as many people are poor hypnotic subjects as are excellent ones. But note that to be assured of obtaining the true distribution in a large population, you would usually have to test quite a large representative sample.

Measures of Central Tendency

Suppose you want to summarize in a few words the average height of people, the typical susceptibility to hypnosis, or the most common performance on an IQ test. For this you would need another kind of descriptive statistic, called a *measure of central tendency.* There are three measures of central tendency: the mean, the median, and the mode. Each is a slightly different way of describing what is "typical" within a given distribution.

The **mean** is the arithmetic average of all the individual measurements in a distribution.

Suppose that ten students in a seminar took an exam. Their scores were 98, 96, 92, 88, 88, 86, 82, 80, 78, and 72. You would find the mean by adding all the scores and dividing the sum by the total number of scores. In this case, the sum of all the scores is 860; dividing this by 10 gives a mean of 86.

The **median** is the score above and below which half the scores in the distribution fall.

If you took our ten test results and arranged them in order from highest to lowest, the median would be the point right in the middle, between the fifth and sixth scores on the list. That would be 87.

The **mode** is the most frequent measurement in a distribution.

Figure A.2
A curve skewed to the right (a positive skew).

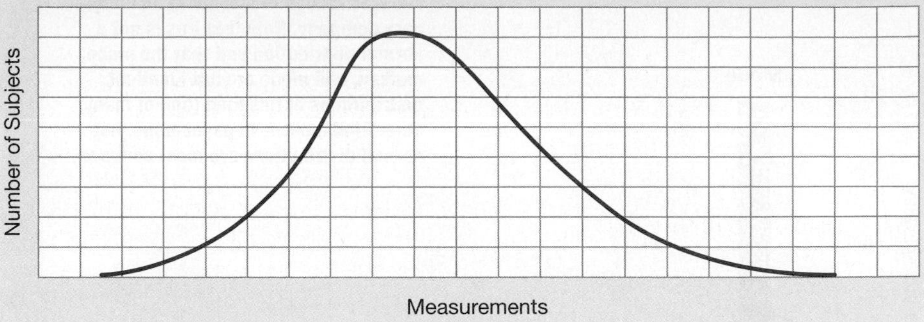

Figure A.3
A curve skewed to the left (a negative skew).

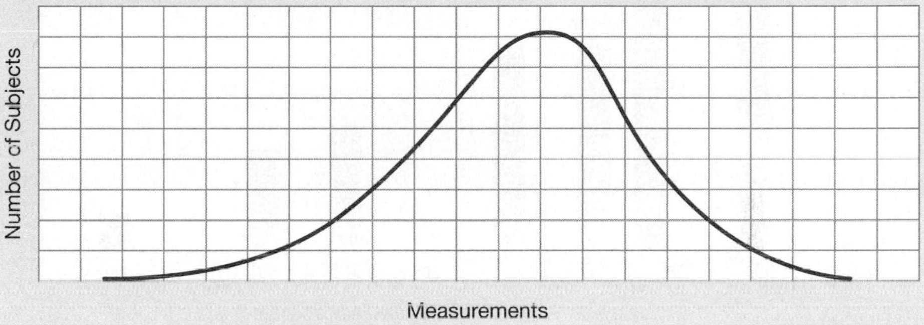

In this group of scores, the mode, the score that occurs most often, is 88.

In the example just given, the mean, median, and mode are very close together, but this is not always true. In some distributions, particularly those that are strongly skewed, these three measures of central tendency may be quite far apart. In such cases, all three of the measures may be needed to give a complete understanding of what is typical.

For instance, look at the graph in Figure A.4, which shows the distribution of income in an imaginary company. The mean income of its 50 employees is $30,600 a year. But look at the distribution. The president of the company earns $140,000, three other executives earn $80,000, and another four earn $60,000 a year. There are also six lower-level managers at $40,000, six salespeople at $30,000, and ten foremen at $25,000. The rest of the employees, the 20 people who keep the company records and run the machines, earn only $12,000 each. Thus, the mean of $30,600 does not really give an accurate indication of a typical income of an employee at this firm.

A better measure of central tendency in this instance is probably the median,

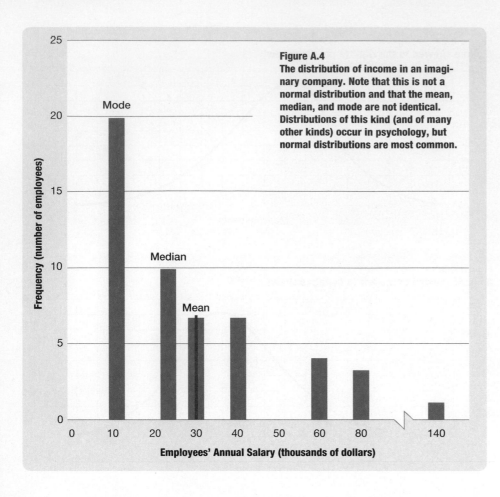

Figure A.4
The distribution of income in an imaginary company. Note that this is not a normal distribution and that the mean, median, and mode are not identical. Distributions of this kind (and of many other kinds) occur in psychology, but normal distributions are most common.

or $25,000. It tells us that half the people at the company earn no more than this amount. Also revealing is the mode, or most common salary; it is only $12,000 a year. As you can see, the mean, median, and mode can provide us with very different figures.

Measures of Variability

If you get an A in a course and are told that the grades ranged from A to F, you will feel a greater sense of accomplishment than if the grades ranged only from A to B. Why this difference in how you perceive a grade? The answer is that it is often important to take into account the extent to which scores in a distribution are spread out. In other words, it is often informative to have a measure of variability.

A **measure of variability** is an indication of how much scores vary from one another.

On a graph, scores that vary greatly produce a wide, flat curve; scores that vary little produce a curve that is narrow and steep. Figure A.5 illustrates these two patterns.

One measure of variability is the range.

The **range** is the difference or interval between the highest and lowest scores in a distribution.

Another measure is the standard deviation.

The **standard deviation** shows how widely all the scores in a distribution are scattered above and below the mean.

If scores cluster closely around the mean, the standard deviation will be small; if scores are dispersed widely from the mean, the standard deviation will be large. Thus, the standard deviation is an indication of how representative the mean is. If the standard deviation is small, we know that the mean is representative of most scores in the distribution. Conversely, if the standard deviation is large, we know that many scores are quite far from the mean.

Figure A.6 shows that the standard deviation divides a normal curve into several portions, each of which has a certain percentage of the total distribution. As you can see, 68.2% of all scores fall somewhere between the mean and one standard deviation to either side of it. If you move two standard deviations to either side of the mean, you will take in 95.4% of all the scores in the distribution. Finally, 99.8% of all the scores will fall between the mean and three standard deviations from it. Only a scant 0.2% fall beyond three standard deviations.

Figure A.5
At left, a distribution with a great deal of variability. At right, a distribution with little variability.

Unless otherwise noted, all images are © Cengage Learning

How to Find the Standard Deviation

Finding the standard deviation of a distribution is not difficult, although it is tedious without the aid of a calculator. To compute the standard deviation, follow these five steps:

1. Determine the mean of all the measurements in the distribution.

2. Subtract the mean from each measurement and square the difference. (Squaring the difference eliminates the negative signs that result when dealing with measurements that fall below the mean.)

3. Add the squares together.

4. Divide the sum of the squares by the number of measurements.

5. Take the square root of the value you obtained in step 4. This figure is the standard deviation.

Knowing the mean and the standard deviation of any normal distribution allows you to determine just how "average" any given score is. For instance, suppose you take a difficult test consisting of 100 questions and receive a score of 80.

How well did you perform? If you learn that the mean is 60 and the standard deviation is 8, you know that your score of 80 is very good indeed. The overwhelming majority of people—95.4%—scored no better than 76, or two standard deviations above the mean. Thus, relative to what most others have done, an 80 is excellent. By the same token, a 40 is not very good at all; 95.4% of people scored 44 or higher on this test. Thus, if you received a 40 you are near the bottom of the distribution and had better start studying much harder.

Inferential Statistics

Can scientists be 100% certain?

In the mid-1970s, many Americans were puzzled to learn that a distinguished panel of scientists could not determine with absolute certainty whether the artificial sweetener called cyclamate posed a risk of cancer. The scientists announced that, after months of research, costing millions of dollars, they could be only 95% sure that cyclamate was safe. Why this remaining margin of doubt? Why can't a team of highly skilled researchers, backed by government funds, manage to tell us absolutely if a substance is hazardous to our health?

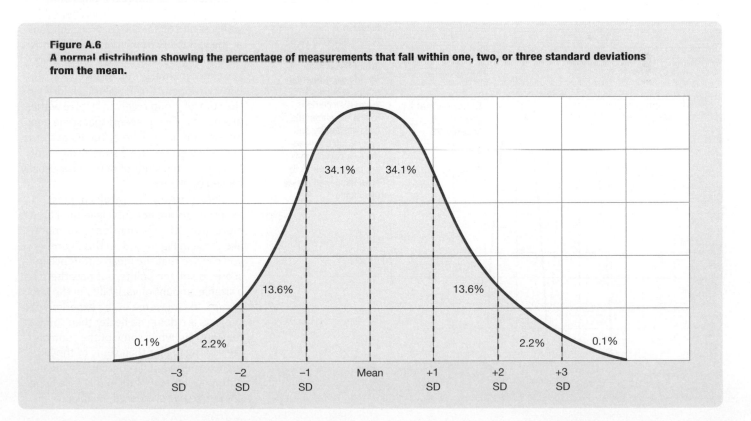

Figure A.6
A normal distribution showing the percentage of measurements that fall within one, two, or three standard deviations from the mean.

Chance and Reliability

No one can totally eliminate the influence of chance on scientific findings. Even when you randomly select groups of subjects, there is always the possibility that, just by chance, those groups will differ slightly in ways that affect your experiment. This is why scientists must rely on statistics to tell them the likelihood that a certain set of results could have happened purely by chance. If this likelihood is small—5% or less—the researchers are justified in rejecting the chance explanation and in concluding instead that their findings are probably reliable. *Reliable* means that the investigators would probably obtain similar results if they repeated their study over and over with different groups of subjects.

Determining the reliability of experimental findings is a major way in which psychologists use inferential statistics.

Inferential statistics are a set of procedures for determining what conclusions can be legitimately inferred from a set of data.

These procedures include what are called ***tests of statistical significance.*** Tests of statistical significance were used to determine the 95% certainty of the finding that cyclamate is safe to eat.

Different tests of statistical significance are needed for different kinds of data.

Tests of Statistical Significance

Suppose you are an educational psychologist who has put together a special program to raise the IQ levels of children with learning disabilities. You expose one group of children with learning deficits to the special program and another group, with equal learning deficits, to the standard curriculum. At the end of a year, you give all the subjects an IQ test. Those in the special program score an average of ten points higher than those in the standard curriculum. Is this enough of a difference to reject the chance explanation and conclude that the program was a success? The procedure most frequently used to answer questions like this is a test of statistical significance called the *t* test.

What is a *t* test?

The ***t* test** is an estimate of reliability that takes into account both the size of the mean difference and the variability in distributions. The *greater* the mean difference and the less the variability, the less the likelihood that the results happened purely by chance.

Imagine that the results of your experiment looked like the ones in Figure A.7. The mean IQs of the two groups differ by ten points: 75 for the experimental subjects and 65 for the controls. But look at the variability in the two distributions: there is almost none. All the children in the experimental group received a score within five points of 75; all the children in the control group received a score within five points of 65. It seems that some genuine effect is at work here. The IQ patterns in the two groups are distinctly different and are not the kinds of differences usually caused by chance.

Unfortunately, the results of most experiments are not this clear-cut. Far more often, the distributions look more like those in Figure A.8. In this figure, you can see that the mean difference in scores is still ten points, but now there is a sizable amount of variability in the two groups. In fact, some of the experimental subjects are doing no better than some of the controls, while some of the controls are scoring higher than some of those in the experimental program. Is a mean difference of ten points in this case large enough to be considered reliable?

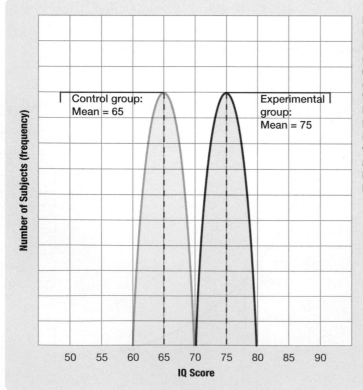

Figure A.7
In this distribution of IQ scores, the control group has a mean of 65; the experimental group, a mean of 75. When distributions in a study show this little variability and no overlap between the two curves, they are not very likely to have happened purely by chance.

Unless otherwise noted, all images are © Cengage Learning

When should you use a *t* test?

The *t* test also considers how many subjects are included in the study. You should not put much faith in a comparison of educational programs that tries out each approach on only two or three children. There is too great a likelihood that such samples are not representative of the larger population from which they are drawn. Let's say that, in the hypothetical experiment we have been describing, you included 100 randomly selected children in each of the two groups. It is much less likely that samples of this size would be biased enough to distort the research's findings.

To learn the steps involved in actually performing the *t* test, please read the accompanying box.

Analysis of Variance

Not all data lend themselves to a *t* test, however. Often researchers want to compare the mean scores of more than two groups, or they want to make comparisons among groups that are classified in more than one way. (For instance, does age or sex have an effect on how much children benefit from our special education program?) In such cases another test of statistical significance is needed. This test is called an ***analysis of variance***, or ***ANOVA*** for short. An analysis of variance is rather like a more complex *t* test. To learn more about the ANOVA technique, consult any introductory statistics text.

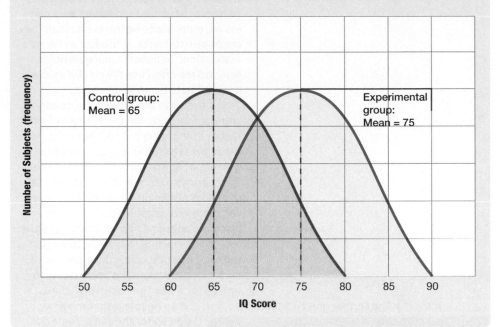

Figure A.8
This set of distributions is much more likely than the one in Figure A.7. The mean is still 65 for the control group and 75 for the experimental group. But now the variability of the distributions is substantially greater. There is also substantial overlap between the two curves. Is the mean difference in this case statistically significant? A *t* test can provide the answer.

Control group: Mean = 65

Experimental group: Mean = 75

Number of Subjects (frequency) (y-axis)

IQ Score (x-axis): 50 55 60 65 70 75 80 85 90

How to Perform the *t* Test

The *t* test is an estimate of how reliable the difference between two means is. To determine the likelihood that the outcome occurred by chance, you first need to know the size of the mean difference (mean 1 minus mean 2). In general, the larger the mean difference, the less likely that it happened by chance alone. You also need to know the variance within each group.

The **variance** is a measure of the variability within the two distributions.

In general, the lower the variance, the less likely that chance alone caused the results. Finally, you need to know how many subjects are in the random samples. In general, the larger the samples, the less the likelihood of a purely chance explanation.

To calculate the *t* test just follow these steps:

1. Determine the mean of the scores for each group and subtract one from the other.

2. Go back to the box on standard deviation and work through that calculation for each of your distributions, stopping at step 4. This gives you the variance of each distribution.

3. Add the two variances.

4. Add the total number of subjects minus 2 (in our example 200 – 2 = 198).

5. Divide the summed variances by the number obtained in step 4 and take the square root.

6. Divide the mean difference between the two groups by the square root from step 5.

If the samples add up to more than 50 individuals, any value of *t* over 2 is statistically reliable more than 95% of the time.

Chi-Square

Sometimes the data psychologists collect do not consist of sets of scores with means or averages. Instead, the researchers have recorded who does what, or who falls into which of several categories. For instance, psychologists have found that chess players are more apt to be introverts than they are to be extroverts. Is this just a chance association? To answer such questions, statisticians often use the *chi (ky) square*, a test of statistical significance.

Suppose you are a psychologist and you want to study the usefulness of fear tactics in changing people's behavior. You randomly select 200 habitual smokers who are willing to participate in an experiment. You expose half to a 20-minute talk on the known health hazards of smoking, complete with graphic illustrations of diseased lungs and hearts. You expose the rest to a 20-minute talk on the history of tobacco. After the talks, the members of each group are given the opportunity to sign up for a free "quit smoking" clinic. Some people from each group sign up for the clinic; some do not. The easiest way to present their choices is with a 2 × 2 table, like the one set up in Table A.1.

Table A.2 shows how the distribution worked out in your study. Of the 100 subjects in your experimental group (the ones exposed to the fear tactics), 60 signed up for the quit-smoking clinic and 40 did not. Of the 100 subjects in the control group, 40 signed up for the free clinic and 60 did not. Is this difference in the distribution of choices statistically significant? The chi-square can be used to estimate the reliability of this difference.

The **chi-square** is a test of statistical significance that compares the actual observed distribution of people (or events) among various categories with the distribution expected purely on the basis of chance.

If people had made their decisions purely by chance—for instance, by the toss of a coin—the same number of people would be expected to sign up for the clinic in each of the two groups. The accompanying box gives a step-by-step description of how to do the chi-square calculation. ●

Table A.1: The Format of a 2 × 2 Table

Talk heard	Signed up for clinic	Didn't sign up	Row Total
Fear tactics			100
No fear tactics			100
Column totals			200 (grand total)

Table A.2: Study Results in Our Sample

Talk heard	Signed up for clinic	Didn't sign up	Row Total
Fear tactics	60	40	100
No fear tactics	40	60	100
Column totals	100	100	200 (grand total)

How to Calculate Chi-Square

Chi-square (χ^2) is an estimate of how sure we can be that a distribution of events or of people did not happen just by chance. In our example, chi-square calculates the *expected* number of people that a chance distribution would place in each of the categories represented by the four cells in the table. This expected number is then compared with the actual *observed* number of people in each of these categories, shown by cells (the data presented in Table A.2). If the difference between the expected and observed numbers is large enough, the distribution is not likely to have happened by chance alone.

Here are the steps in making the chi-square calculation:

1. Figure out how many people, by chance alone, would be likely to fall into the upper-left cell. To do this, multiply the first row total by the first column total (100 × 100) and divide by the grand total (200). The expected number is 50.

2. Subtract the expected number (50) from the observed number in the upper-left cell (60). The difference is 10 (60 − 50 = 10). Square the difference to eliminate negative signs (10 × 10 = 100) and divide the result by the expected number: 100 ÷ 50 = 2.

3. Repeat steps 1 and 2 for each of the four cells. In this example, the expected values are the same for each cell, but that won't always be true.

4. Add the four values you get from calculating the difference between the expected and observed number for each cell. This is the chi-square.

The reliability of the chi-square value must be looked up in a table. In this example, the fear-tactic subjects signed up for the clinic so much more often than the control subjects did that this distribution could have occurred by chance only two times in a hundred.

Unless otherwise noted, all images are © Cengage Learning

Summary Test

Descriptive Statistics

1. The tools that researchers use to analyze and summarize large amounts of data are called **(a)** _____. Numbers that are used to present a collection of data in a brief yet meaningful form are **(b)** _____ statistics, which are often used to present distributions of measurements and scores. The range of scores and the frequency of each one are called the **(c)** _____; this is often presented in graphic form so the patterns can be seen at a glance.

2. When graphed, a normal distribution produces a curve that tapers off equally on either side from a central high point; this is called a **(a)** _____ curve. This curve has the characteristic shape of a **(b)** _____ and shows that most of the measurements fall near the center, with as many falling to one side as to the other. However, not all traits are distributed normally. If more data fall toward one side of the scale than toward the other, it is called a **(c)** _____ distribution. Such distributions do not have symmetrical shapes when plotted; instead, they have a "tail" on one end. When there are fewer frequencies at the higher end of the horizontal scale (the tail is on the right), we say the distribution is skewed to the right or has a **(d)** _____ skew. When there are fewer frequencies at the lower end of the horizontal scale (the tail is on the left), we say the distribution is skewed to the left or has a **(e)** _____ skew.

3. Ways of describing what is "typical" within a given distribution are called measures of **(a)** _____. The arithmetic average of all the individual measurements in a distribution is the **(b)** _____. The score above and below which half the scores in the distribution fall is the **(c)** _____. The measurement that occurs most often in a distribution is the **(d)** _____.

4. The extent to which scores in a distribution are spread out—in other words, how much scores vary from one another—is the measure of **(a)** _____. The two most extreme scores at either end of a distribution indicate the range. The measure of variability that shows how widely all the scores in a distribution are scattered above and below the mean is called the **(b)** _____.

Inferential Statistics

5. Because the influence of chance on scientific findings cannot be completely avoided, procedures are necessary to determine what conclusions can be properly inferred from a set of data; these procedures are called **(a)** _____ statistics. If the likelihood that the results could have occurred purely by chance is small, researchers can reject the chance explanation and conclude that their findings are probably **(b)** _____; that is, they would probably obtain similar results if they repeated the study over and over with different groups.

6. Different kinds of data require different tests of statistical significance. An estimate of reliability that takes the size of the mean difference and the variability in distributions into account is called the **(a)** _____; it estimates how reliable the difference between two means is. In general, the greater the difference between **(b)** _____, the less likely that the results happened by chance alone.

7. A measure of the variability within two distributions is called the **(a)** _____. In general, the lower the variance, the less likely that chance alone caused the results. An analysis of variance, or **(b)** _____ test, is similar to, but more complex than, the t test.

8. How sure we can be that a distribution of events or of people did not happen just by chance is measured by another test of statistical significance, called the _____.

Glossary

A

ability tests Achievement tests, which measure what we have learned; aptitude tests, which measure our potential for learning or acquiring a specific skill; and intelligence tests, which measure our general potential to solve problems, think abstractly, and profit from experience.

absolute threshold The minimum amount of stimulus energy that a person can detect 50% of the time.

accommodation The process by which a person changes old methods to deal with or adjust to new situations.

achievement need The desire to set challenging goals and to persist in pursuing those goals in the face of obstacles, frustrations, and setbacks.

acquired immune deficiency syndrome *See* AIDS.

acquisition The initial process of forming new responses through the repeated pairing of the neutral stimulus and the unconditioned stimulus.

action potential A tiny electric current that is generated when positive sodium ions rush inside the axon. The enormous increase of sodium ions inside the axon causes the inside of the axon to reverse its charge. The inside becomes positive, while the outside becomes negative.

activation-synthesis theory of dreams The idea that dreaming occurs because brain areas that provide reasoned cognitive control during the waking state are shut down. As a result, the sleeping brain is stimulated by different chemical and neural influences that result in hallucinations, delusions, high emotions, and bizarre thought patterns that we call dreams.

actor-observer effect Our tendency, when we are behaving (or acting), to attribute our own behavior to situational factors but, when we are observing, to attribute another person's behavior to his or her personality traits or disposition.

acupuncture An ancient Chinese procedure for the relief of pain, in which a trained practitioner inserts thin needles into various points on the body's surface, often far from the site of the pain, and then manually twirls or electrically stimulates the needles.

adaptation A feature of a species that provides it with improved function, such as a behavior that helps an organism better escape a predator or a physical characteristic that provides an organism with an advantage. Also, the decreasing response of the sensory organs as they are exposed to a continuous level of stimulation.

adaptation level theory The idea that we quickly become accustomed to receiving some good fortune (money, job, car, degree). We take the good fortune for granted within a short period of time and, as a result, the initial impact of our good fortune fades and contributes less to our long-term level of happiness.

adaptive genes Genes for traits that help an organism survive and reproduce.

adaptive theory A theory suggesting that sleep evolved as a survival mechanism, since it prevented early humans and animals from wasting energy and exposing themselves to the dangers of nocturnal predators.

adaptive value The usefulness of certain abilities or traits that have evolved in animals or humans that tend to increase their chances of survival, such as the ability to find food, acquire mates, and avoid illness and injury.

addiction A behavioral pattern of drug abuse that is marked by an overwhelming and compulsive desire to obtain and use the drug. Even after stopping, the addict has a tendency to relapse and begin using the drug again.

ADHD *See* attention-deficit/hyperactivity disorder.

adjustment disorder A condition in which a person is unable to cope with, or adjust to, a major life change. The condition includes emotional and behavioral symptoms.

adolescence A developmental period, lasting from about the ages of 12 to 18, that marks the end of childhood and the beginning of adulthood; it is a transitional period of considerable biological, cognitive, social, and personality changes.

adrenal glands Structures in the endocrine system. The adrenal cortex (outer part) secretes hormones that regulate sugar and salt balances and help the body resist stress; they are also responsible for the growth of pubic hair, a secondary sexual characteristic. The adrenal medulla (inner part) secretes two hormones that arouse the body to deal with stress and emergencies: epinephrine (adrenaline) and norepinephrine (noradrenaline).

affective neuroscience approach The study of the underlying neural bases of mood and emotion by focusing on the brain's neural circuits that evaluate stimuli and produce or contribute to experiencing and expressing different emotional states.

afferent neurons Neurons that carry information from the senses to the spinal cord. Also called sensory neurons.

afterimage A visual image that continues after the original stimulus is removed.

age regression In hypnosis, the suggestion that individuals regress, or return, to an earlier time in their lives—for example, to early childhood.

aggression Any behavior directed toward another that is intended to cause harm.

aging process Changes caused by a combination of certain genes and proteins that interfere with organ functioning and by the natural production of toxic molecules (free radicals) that, in turn, cause random damage to body organs and to DNA (the building blocks of life). Such damage eventually exceeds the body's ability to repair itself and results in greater susceptibility to diseases and death.

agoraphobia Anxiety about being in places or situations from which escape might be difficult or embarrassing if a panic attack or paniclike symptoms (sudden dizziness or onset of diarrhea) were to occur.

AIDS (acquired immune deficiency syndrome) A life-threatening condition that, by the latest definition, is present when the individual is HIV positive and has a level of T-cells (CD4 immune cells) no higher than 200 per cubic milliliter of blood or has developed one or more of 26 specified illnesses (including recurrent pneumonia and skin cancer).

alarm stage In the general adaptation syndrome, our initial reaction to stress, marked by activation of the fight-flight response, which causes physiological arousal.

alcohol (ethyl alcohol) A psychoactive drug classified as a depressant; it depresses the activity of the central nervous system. Alcohol causes friendliness and loss of inhibitions at low doses, impairs drinkers' social judgment and understanding at medium doses, and seriously impairs motor coordination, cognitive abilities, decision making, and speech at higher doses. Very high doses may result in coma and death.

alcoholism A problem involving addiction to alcohol. An alcoholic is a person who has drunk heavily for a long period of time, is addicted to and has an intense craving for alcohol, and, as a result, has problems in two or three major life areas (social, personal, and financial areas, for example).

algorithms Rules that, if followed correctly, will eventually lead to the solution of a problem.

all-or-none law The fact that, once a nerve impulse starts in a small segment at the very beginning of the axon, it will continue at the same speed, segment by segment, to the very end of the axon.

alpha stage In sleep, a stage marked by feelings of being relaxed and drowsy, usually with the eyes closed. Alpha waves have low amplitude and high frequency (8–12 cycles per second).

altered state of consciousness An awareness that differs from normal consciousness; such awareness may be produced by using any number of procedures, such as meditation, psychoactive drugs, hypnosis, or sleep deprivation.

altered state theory of hypnosis The idea that hypnosis puts a person into an altered state of consciousness, during which the person is disconnected from reality and so is able to experience and respond to various suggestions. *See also* sociocognitive theory of hypnosis.

altruism Helping or doing something, often at a cost or risk, for reasons other than the expectation of a material or social reward.

Alzheimer's disease An irreversible, progressive brain disease that slowly destroys an individual's memory and thought processes. Initially, a person begins forgetting and repeating things, getting lost, and being mildly confused. The person may also have problems with language, difficulties in recognizing objects, and inability to plan and organize tasks. Over a period of five to ten years, these symptoms worsen and result in profound memory loss, failure to recognize family and friends, deterioration in personality, and emotional outbursts.

Ames room A viewing environment, designed by Albert Ames, that demonstrates how our perception of size may be distorted by manipulating our depth cues.

amnesia Memory loss that may occur after damage to the brain (temporary or permanent), following drug use, or after severe psychological stress.

amniocentesis A medical test performed between weeks 14 and 20 of pregnancy. A long needle is inserted through the mother's abdominal muscles into the amniotic fluid surrounding the fetus. By withdrawing and analyzing fetal cells in the fluid, doctors can identify a number of genetic problems.

amplitude The height or distance from the bottom to the top of a sound wave. Large sound waves are described as having high amplitude; small sound waves are described as having low amplitude.

amygdala A structure in the limbic system that is located in the tip of the temporal lobe and is involved in forming, recognizing, and remembering emotional experiences and facial expressions.

anal stage Freud's second psychosexual stage, lasting from the ages of about 1½ to 3 years. In this stage, the infant's pleasure seeking is centered on the anus and its functions of elimination.

analogy A strategy for finding a similarity between a new situation and an old, familiar situation.

androgens Male sex hormones.

anencephaly The condition of being born with little or no brain. If some brain or nervous tissue is present, it is totally exposed and often damaged because the top of the skull is missing. Survival is usually limited to days; the longest has been 2 months.

anorexia nervosa A serious eating disorder characterized by refusing to eat and not maintaining weight at 85% of what is expected, having an intense fear of gaining weight or becoming fat, and missing at least three consecutive menstrual cycles. Anorexics also have a disturbed body image: They see themselves as fat even though they are very thin.

anterior pituitary The front part of the pituitary gland, a key component of the endocrine system. It regulates growth through the secretion of growth hormone and produces hormones that control the adrenal cortex, pancreas, thyroid, and gonads.

anticipatory nausea Feelings of nausea that are elicited by stimuli associated with nausea-inducing chemotherapy treatments. Patients experience nausea in anticipation of their treatment. Researchers believe that anticipatory nausea occurs through classical conditioning.

antidepressant drugs Drugs used to combat depression. They act by increasing levels of a specific group of neurotransmitters (monoamines, such as serotonin) that are believed to be involved in the regulation of emotions and moods.

antipsychotic drugs *See* neuroleptic drugs.

antisocial personality disorder A pattern of disregarding or violating the rights of others without feeling guilt or remorse. It is found in 3% of the population, predominantly in males.

anxiety An unpleasant state that is associated with feelings of uneasiness, apprehension, and heightened physiological arousal, such as increased heart rate and blood pressure. According to Freud, anxiety arises when there is an unconscious conflict between the id's and superego's desires regarding how to satisfy a need; the ego, caught in the middle, reacts by creating a feeling of anxiety. More modern theories of anxiety are based on conditioned emotional responses and observational learning.

anxiety disorder The condition characterized by an individual feeling anxiety that is out of proportion to the danger elicited by an object or situation, and the anxiety interferes with the person's normal daily functioning.

apparent motion An illusion that a stimulus or object is moving in space when, in fact, it is stationary. This illusion is created by rapidly showing a series of stationary images, each of which has a slightly different position or posture than the one before.

approach A focus or perspective that may use a particular research method or technique. Eight approaches to understanding behavior are the biological, cognitive, behavioral, psychoanalytic, humanistic, sociocultural, evolutionary, and biopsychosocial.

approach-approach conflict The conflict that arises when one has to choose between two situations that both have pleasurable consequences.

approach-avoidance conflict The conflict that arises when one is faced with a single situation that has both pleasurable and disagreeable aspects.

armchair psychology The practice of answering questions about human behavior and mental processes through informal observation and speculation.

arousal-cost-reward model of helping The idea that we make decisions to help by calculating the costs and rewards of helping.

arousal theory The idea that we are motivated to seek out activities that provide a level of stimulation that allows us to maintain our optimal level of arousal.

assimilation The process by which a child uses old methods or experiences to deal with new situations.

atmospheric perspective In three-dimensional vision, a monocular depth cue that comes into play in the presence of dust, smog, or water vapor. Hazy objects are interpreted as being farther away.

attachment A close, fundamental emotional bond that develops between the infant and his or her parent or caregiver.

attention-deficit/hyperactivity disorder (ADHD) A condition diagnosed on the basis of the occurrence of certain behavioral problems, rather than medical tests. A child must have six or more symptoms of inattention (such as making careless mistakes in schoolwork) and six or more symptoms of hyperactivity (such as fidgeting or talking excessively). These symptoms should have been present from an early age, persisted for at least six months, and contributed to maladaptive development.

attitude Any belief or opinion that includes a positive or negative evaluation of some object, person, or event and that predisposes us to act in a certain way toward that object, person, or event.

attributions Our explanations of the causes of events, other people's behaviors, and our own behaviors.

atypical neuroleptic drugs Neuroleptic drugs that lower levels of dopamine but, more important, reduce levels of other neurotransmitters, especially serotonin. One group of these drugs is the benzamides, such as clozapine. These drugs primarily reduce positive symptoms, reduce negative symptoms, and prevent relapse.

auditory association area An area directly below the primary auditory cortex that receives and transforms meaningless auditory sensations into perceptions or meaningful sounds, such as melodies or words.

auditory canal A long tube in the ear that funnels sound waves down its length so that the waves strike a thin, taut membrane—the eardrum, or tympanic membrane.

auditory nerve A band of fibers that carries impulses (electrical signals) from the cochlea to the brain, resulting in the perception of sounds.

authoritarian parents Parents who attempt to shape, control, and evaluate the behaviors and attitudes of their children in accordance with a set standard of conduct, usually an absolute standard that comes from religious or respected authorities.

authoritative parents Parents who attempt to direct their children's activities in a rational and intelligent way. They are supporting, loving, and committed, encourage verbal give-and-take, and discuss their rules and policies with their children.

autism A condition marked by especially abnormal or impaired development in social interactions, spoken language, and sensory-motor systems. Autistics characteristically have few activities or interests and spend long periods of time repeating the same ritualistic physical behaviors. Signs of autism usually appear at age 2 or 3.

automatic encoding The transfer of information from short-term into long-term memory without any effort and usually without any awareness.

automatic processes Activities that require little awareness, take minimal attention, and do not interfere with other ongoing activities.

autonomic nervous system That portion of the peripheral nervous system that regulates heart rate, breathing, blood pressure, digestion, hormone secretion, and other functions, as well as maintains the body in a state of optimal balance, or homeostasis. It usually functions without conscious effort, which means that only a few of its responses, such as breathing, can also be controlled voluntarily. Its two subdivisions are the sympathetic division and the parasympathetic division.

availability heuristic A rule of thumb that says we rely on information that is more prominent or easily recalled and overlook other information that is available but less prominent or notable.

avoidance-avoidance conflict The conflict that arises when one has to choose between two situations that both have disagreeable consequences.

avoidant personality disorder A disorder characterized by social inhibition, feelings of inadequacy, and heightened sensitivity to negative evaluation. It is found in 0.5–1% of the population.

axon A single threadlike structure within the neuron. It extends from, and carries signals away from, the cell body to neighboring neurons, organs, or muscles.

axon membrane The axon wall, which contains chemical gates that may be opened or closed to control the inward and outward flow of electrically charged particles called ions.

babbling The first stage in acquiring language, in which infants, at about 6 months of age, begin to make one-syllable sounds such as "deedeedee" or "bababa." Many of these sounds are common across languages.

Bandura's social cognitive theory A personality theory that assumes that personality development, growth, and change are influenced by four distinctively human cognitive processes: highly developed language ability, observational learning, purposeful behavior, and self-analysis. Bandura emphasizes the importance of learning through observation, imitation, and self-reward in the development of social skills, interactions, and behaviors. He contends that we can learn new social skills without performing any observable behaviors or receiving any external rewards. *See* social cognitive theory.

barbiturates Depressant drugs that have a sedative effect. Barbiturates, such as phenobarbital, decrease the activity of the nervous system. Moderately high doses result in drowsiness, motor impairment, and poor judgment. Barbiturates taken in larger doses can be fatal.

Barnum principle A technique used in horoscopes and elsewhere, in which traits are listed in such a general way that almost everyone who reads them thinks that these traits apply specifically to him or her. This technique was named after circus owner P. T. Barnum.

basal ganglia A group of structures in the center of the brain that are involved in regulating movements. To function properly, neurons in the basal ganglia must have a sufficient supply of the neurotransmitter dopamine.

basic rules of grammar Rules for combining nouns, verbs, and other parts of speech into meaningful sentences.

basilar membrane A membrane within the cochlea that contains the auditory receptors, or hair cells.

Beck's cognitive theory of depression The idea that when we are depressed, automatic negative thoughts that we rarely notice occur continuously throughout the day. These negative thoughts distort how we perceive and interpret the world and thus influence our behaviors and feelings, which in turn contribute to our feelings of depression.

Beck's cognitive therapy See cognitive therapy.

behavior modification A treatment or therapy that changes or modifies problems or undesirable behaviors by using learning principles based on operant conditioning, classical conditioning, and social cognitive learning.

behavior therapy A form of psychotherapy in which disruptive behaviors are changed and human functioning is improved on the basis of principles of classical and operant conditioning. It focuses on changing particular behaviors rather than on the underlying mental events or possible unconscious factors. Sometimes called behavior modification.

behavioral approach A psychological viewpoint that analyzes how organisms learn new behaviors or modify existing ones depending on whether events in their environments reward or punish these behaviors. Historically, as founded by John B. Watson, the behavioral approach emphasized the objective, scientific analysis of observable behaviors.

behavioral genetics The study of how inherited or genetic factors influence and interact with psychological factors to shape our personality, intelligence, emotions, and motivation and also how we behave, adapt, and adjust to our environments.

benzodiazepines Minor tranquilizers (Valium, Xanax, Restoril) that reduce anxiety, worry, and stress by lowering physiological arousal, which results in a state of tranquility.

Binet-Simon Intelligence Scale The world's first standardized intelligence test, containing items arranged in order of increasing difficulty. The items measured vocabulary, memory, common knowledge, and other cognitive abilities.

binge-eating disorder A disorder characterized by recurrent binge-eating episodes during which a person feels a loss of control over his or her eating. Unlike bulimia nervosa, there is no vomiting, use of laxatives, or rigorous dieting and fasting, therefore, people with binge-eating disorder tend to be overweight or obese.

binocular depth cues In three-dimensional vision, depth cues that depend on the movement of both eyes (bi means "two"; ocular means "eye").

biofeedback A training procedure through which a person voluntarily learns to control physiological responses, such as muscle activity, blood pressure, or temperature, by recording and displaying these responses.

biological approach A psychological viewpoint that examines how our genes, hormones, and nervous system interact with our environments to influence learning, personality, memory, motivation, emotions, coping techniques, and other traits and abilities.

biological clock The body's internal timing device that is genetically set to regulate various physiological responses for certain periods of time.

biological factors Innate tendencies or predispositions that may either facilitate or inhibit certain kinds of learning.

biological factors for depression Genetic, neurological, chemical, and physiological components that may predispose or put someone at risk for developing a mood disorder.

biological hunger factors Physiological changes in blood chemistry and signals from digestive organs that provide feedback to the brain, which, in turn, triggers us to eat or stop eating.

biological needs Physiological requirements that are critical to our survival and physical well-being.

biological psychology See psychobiology.

biological sex factors The actions of sex hormones, which are involved in secondary sexual characteristics (facial hair, breasts), sexual motivation (more so in animals than in humans), and the development of ova and sperm.

biomedical therapy The use of interventions to treat mental disorders that change biological factors, such as the levels of neurotransmitters in the brain.

BioPsychoSocial model The representation of adolescent development as a process that occurs simultaneously on many levels and includes sexual, cognitive, social, and personality changes that interact and influence each other.

biosocial theory of gender differences A theory that emphasizes social and cultural forces; it says that differences in sexual activities and values for selecting mates developed from traditional cultural divisions of labor: Women were primarily child-bearers and homemakers, while men were primarily providers and protectors.

bipolar I disorder A mood disorder characterized by fluctuations between episodes of depression and mania. A manic episode goes on for at least a week, during which a person is unusually euphoric, cheerful, and high and has at least three of the following symptoms: has great self-esteem, has little need of sleep, speaks rapidly and frequently, has racing thoughts, is easily distracted, and pursues pleasurable activities. Formerly called manic-depressive illness.

bipolar II disorder A mood disorder characterized by fluctuations between episodes of depression and hypomania (mild mania). A hypomanic episode consists of the same symptoms as a manic episode, but lasts for at least four days, as opposed to one week.

bisexual orientation A pattern of sexual arousal by persons of both sexes.

blind spot The point where the optic nerve exits the eye and where there are no photoreceptors (rods or cones).

body mass index (BMI) The number calculated from a person's weight and height. It is a measure of body fatness and is used to screen for weight categories that may lead to health problems, including underweight, overweight, and obesity.

borderline personality disorder A pattern of instability in personal relationships, self-image, and emotions as well as impulsive behavior. It is found in 2% of the population.

bottom-up processing When perception begins with bits and pieces of information (e.g., curves, lines) that, when combined, lead to the recognition of a whole pattern. It's "bottom" first because we begin with the raw, sensory information. See also top-down processing.

brightness constancy Our tendency to perceive brightness as remaining the same in changing illumination.

Broca's aphasia An inability to speak in fluent sentences while retaining the ability to understand written or spoken words. It is caused by damage to Broca's area.

Broca's area An area usually located in the left frontal lobe that is necessary for combining sounds into words and arranging words into meaningful sentences. See Broca's aphasia.

bulimia nervosa An eating disorder characterized by a minimum of two binge-eating episodes per week for at least three months; fear of not being able to stop eating; regularly engaging in vomiting, use of laxatives, or rigorous dieting and fasting; and excessive concern about body shape and weight.

burnout Feelings of being physically overwhelmed and exhausted, finding a job unrewarding and becoming cynical or detached, and developing a strong sense of ineffectiveness and lack of accomplishment in a particular job.

bystander effect The phenomenon in which an individual feels inhibited from taking some action because of the presence of others.

caffeine A mild stimulant that produces dilation of blood vessels, increased secretion of stomach acid, and moderate physiological arousal. Psychological effects include a feeling of alertness, decreased fatigue and drowsiness, and improved reaction times. Caffeine, which is present in coffee, tea, chocolate, and other foods, can be addictive, especially in higher doses.

Cannon-Bard theory The theory that emotions originate in the brain; they are not the result of physiological responses.

case study An in-depth analysis of the thoughts, feelings, beliefs, experiences, behaviors, or problems of an individual. This research method offers little opportunity to control or manipulate situations or variables.

catatonic schizophrenia A subcategory of schizophrenia characterized by periods of wild excitement and periods of rigid, prolonged immobility; sometimes the person assumes the same frozen posture for hours on end.

catharsis A psychological process through which anger or aggressive energy is released by expressing or letting out powerful negative emotions. Freud's view that catharsis can be helpful in reducing aggression is not supported by most research.

cell body For neurons, a relatively large, egg-shaped structure that provides fuel, manufactures chemicals, and maintains the entire neuron in working order. Also called the soma.

central cues Hunger cues associated with the activity of chemicals and neurotransmitters in different areas of the brain.

central nervous system Neurons located in the brain and spinal cord. From the bottom of the brain emerges the spinal cord, which is made up of neurons and bundles of axons and dendrites that carry information back and forth between the brain and the body. Neurons in the central nervous system normally have almost no capacity to regrow or regenerate if damaged or diseased.

central route for persuasion Presenting information with strong arguments, analyses, facts, and logic.

cephalocaudal principle The rule that parts of the body closer to the infant's head develop before parts closer to the feet.

cerebellum A region of the hindbrain that is involved in coordinating movements but not in initiating voluntary movements. It is also involved in cognitive functions, such as short-term memory, following rules, and carrying out plans. The cerebellum is also involved in performing timed motor responses, such as those required in playing games or sports.

challenge appraisal Our conclusion that we have the potential for gain or personal growth in a particular situation but that we also need to mobilize our physical energy and psychological resources to meet the challenging situation.

chi-square test A test of statistical significance that compares the actual observed distribution of people (or events) among various categories with the distribution expected purely on the basis of chance.

child abuse and neglect Inadequate care or acts by the parent(s) (physical or emotional abuse) that put a child in danger, cause physical harm or injury, or involve sexual molestation.

Chomsky's theory of language The idea that all languages share a common universal grammar and that children inherit a mental program to learn this universal grammar. This theory includes the concepts of deep structure and surface structure and of transformational rules to convert from one to the other.

chromosome A hairlike structure that contains tightly coiled strands of deoxyribonucleic acid (DNA). Each cell of the human body (except for the sperm and egg) contains 46 chromosomes, arranged in 23 pairs.

chunking Combining separate items of information into a larger unit, or chunk, and then remembering chunks of information rather than individual items; a technique of memory enhancement.

circadian rhythm A biological clock that is genetically programmed to regulate physiological responses within a time period of 24 hours (about a day); one example is the sleep-wake cycle.

clairvoyance The ability to perceive events or objects that are out of sight.

classical conditioning A kind of learning in which a neutral stimulus acquires the ability to produce a response that was originally produced by a different stimulus.

client-centered therapy An approach developed by Carl Rogers that assumes that each person has an actualizing tendency—that is, a tendency to develop his or her own potential; the therapist's task is to show compassion and positive regard in helping the client reach his or her potential. Also called person-centered therapy.

clinical and counseling psychology The assessment and treatment of people who have psychological problems, such as grief, anxiety, or stress.

clinical assessment A systematic evaluation of an individual's various psychological, biological, and social factors, as well as the identification of past and present problems, stressors, and other cognitive and behavioral symptoms.

clinical diagnosis A process of determining how closely an individual's specific symptoms match those that define a particular mental disorder.

clinical interview In assessment, a method of gathering information about relevant aspects of a person's past as well as current behaviors, attitudes, emotions, and details of present difficulties or problems. Some clinical interviews are unstructured, which means that they have no set questions; others are structured, which means that they follow a standard format of asking a similar set of questions.

clinical psychologist An individual who has a PhD, PsyD, or EdD, has specialized in the clinical subarea, and has spent an additional year in a supervised therapy setting to gain experience in diagnosing and treating a wide range of abnormal behaviors. To train as a clinical psychologist usually requires four to six years of work after obtaining a college degree.

closure rule A perceptual rule stating that, in organizing stimuli, we tend to fill in any missing parts of a figure and see the figure as complete.

cocaine A stimulant produced from the leaves of the coca plant. Its physiological and behavioral effects are very similar to those of amphetamine: It produces increased heart rate and blood pressure, enhanced mood, alertness, increased activity, decreased appetite, and diminished fatigue. At higher doses, it can produce anxiety, emotional instability, and suspiciousness.

cochlea A coiled, fluid-filled structure in the inner ear that contains the receptors for hearing. Its function is transduction—transforming vibrations into nerve impulses that are sent to the brain for processing into auditory information.

cochlear implant A miniature electronic device that is surgically implanted into the cochlea to restore hearing in those with neural deafness. It converts sound waves into electrical signals, which are fed into the auditory nerve and hence reach the brain for processing.

cognition *See* thinking.

cognitive appraisal theory The idea that our interpretation or appraisal of a situation results in emotional feelings.

cognitive approach *See* cognitive psychology.

cognitive-behavioral therapy A treatment for phobias and other mental disorders based on a combination of two methods: changing negative, unhealthy, or distorted thoughts and beliefs by substituting positive, healthy, and realistic ones; and changing limiting or disruptive behaviors by learning and practicing new skills to improve functioning.

cognitive development How a person perceives, thinks, and gains an understanding of his or her world through the interaction and influence of genetic and learned factors.

cognitive developmental theory The idea that, as they develop mental skills and interact with their environments, children learn one set of rules for male behavior and another set of rules for female behavior.

cognitive dissonance A state of unpleasant psychological tension that motivates us to reduce our cognitive inconsistencies by making our beliefs more consistent with our behavior.

cognitive-emotional-behavioral and environmental factors The factors that contribute to the development of mental disorders, including deficits in cognitive processes, such as having unusual thoughts and beliefs; deficits in processing emotional stimuli, such as under- or overreacting to emotional situations; behavioral problems, such as lacking social skills; and environmental challenges, such as dealing with stressful situations.

cognitive factors According to social cognitive theory, factors that include our beliefs, expectations, values, intentions, and social roles—all of which help to shape our personalities.

cognitive factors in motivation The influence of individuals' evaluations or perceptions of a situation on their willingness to work.

cognitive interview A technique for questioning eyewitnesses and others by having them imagine and reconstruct the details of an event, report everything they remember without holding anything back, and narrate the event from different viewpoints.

cognitive learning A kind of learning that involves mental processes, such as attention and memory; may proceed through observation or imitation; and may not involve any external rewards or require the person to perform any observable behaviors.

cognitive map A mental representation of the layout of an environment and its features.

cognitive miser model The idea that, in making attributions, people think they must conserve time and effort by taking cognitive shortcuts.

cognitive neuroscience An approach to studying cognitive processes that involves taking pictures of the structures and functions of the living brain during the performance of a wide variety of mental or cognitive processes, such as thinking, planning, naming, and recognizing objects.

cognitive perspective The theory that an organism learns a predictable relationship between two stimuli such that the occurrence of one stimulus (neutral stimulus) predicts the occurrence of another (unconditioned stimulus). In other words, classical conditioning occurs because the organism learns what to expect.

cognitive psychology The study of how we process, store, retrieve, and use information and how cognitive processes influence what we attend to, perceive, learn, remember, believe, feel, and do.

cognitive therapy An approach to therapy that focuses on the role of thoughts in our emotions and actions. The widely used version developed by Aaron Beck assumes that we have automatic negative thoughts that we typically say to ourselves without much notice. By continuously repeating these automatic negative thoughts, we color and distort how we perceive and interpret the world and influence how we behave and feel. The goal of the therapy is to change these automatic negative thoughts.

collective unconscious According to Carl Jung, ancient memory traces and symbols that are passed on by birth and are shared by all people in all cultures.

color blindness The inability to distinguish between two or more shades in the color spectrum. There are several kinds of color blindness. *See* monochromats and dichromats.

color constancy Our tendency to perceive colors as remaining stable despite differences in lighting.

commitment In Sternberg's triangular theory of love, the component of love associated with making a pledge to nourish the feelings of love and to actively maintain the relationship.

common factors Basic procedures and experiences shared by different therapies that account for those therapies' comparable effectiveness despite their different fundamental principles and techniques. Common factors include the growth of a supportive and trusting relationship between therapist and client and the accompanying development of an accepting atmosphere in which the client feels willing to admit problems and is motivated to work on changing.

communication The ability to use sounds, smells, or gestures to exchange information.

community mental health centers Government-sponsored centers that offer low-cost or free mental health care to members of the surrounding community, especially the underprivileged. The services may include psychotherapy, support groups, or telephone crisis counseling.

companionate love A condition associated with trusting and tender feelings for someone whose life is closely bound up with one's own.

compliance A kind of conformity in which we give in to social pressure in our public responses but do not change our private beliefs.

concept A way to group objects, events, or characteristics on the basis of some common property they all share.

conception The process in which one of the millions of sperm penetrates the ovum's outer membrane; also called fertilization. After penetration, the outer membrane changes and becomes impenetrable to the millions of remaining sperm.

concrete operations stage The third of Jean Piaget's cognitive stages, lasting from about the ages of 7 to 11 years. During this stage, children can perform a number of logical mental operations on concrete objects that are physically present.

conditional positive regard Positive regard that depends on our behaving in certain ways—for example, living up to or meeting others' standards.

conditioned emotional response The feeling of some positive or negative emotion, such as happiness, fear, or anxiety, when experiencing a stimulus that previously accompanied a pleasant or painful event. This is an example of classical conditioning.

conditioned response (CR) A response elicited by the conditioned stimulus; it is similar to the unconditioned response but not identical in magnitude or amount.

conditioned stimulus (CS) A formerly neutral stimulus that has acquired the ability to elicit a response previously elicited by the unconditioned stimulus.

conduct disorder A repetitive and persistent pattern of aggressive behavior that has been going on for at least a year and that violates the established social rules or the rights of others. Problems may include threatening to harm people, abusing or killing animals, destroying property, being deceitful, or stealing.

conduction deafness Deafness that can be caused by wax in the auditory canal, injury to the tympanic membrane, or malfunction of the ossicles. All of these conditions interfere with the transmission of vibrations from the tympanic membrane to the fluid of the cochlea, resulting in degrees of hearing loss.

cones Photoreceptors that contain three chemicals called opsins, which are activated in bright light and allow us to see color. Unlike rods, cones are wired individually to neighboring cells; this one-on-one system of relaying information allows us to see fine details.

confirmation bias The tendency to look for information that supports our decisions and beliefs and ignore disconfirming information.

conflict The feeling we experience when we must decide between two or more incompatible choices.

conformity Any behavior you perform because of group pressure, even though that pressure might not involve direct requests.

conscious thoughts Wishes, desires, or thoughts that we are aware of, or can recall, at any given moment.

consciousness Different levels of awareness of one's thoughts and feelings. Creating images in the mind, following thought processes, and having unique emotional experiences are all part of consciousness.

consensus In making attributions, determining whether other people engage in the same behavior in the same situation.

conservation The fact that even though the shape of some object or substance is changed, the total amount remains the same.

consistency In making attributions, determining whether an individual engages in a certain behavior every time he or she is in a particular situation.

contiguity theory The view that classical conditioning occurs because two stimuli (the neutral stimulus and the unconditioned stimulus) are paired close together in time (are contiguous). Eventually, as a result of this contiguous pairing, the neutral stimulus becomes the conditioned stimulus, which elicits the conditioned response.

contingency management The systematic reinforcement of desired behaviors and the withholding of reinforcement or punishment of undesired behaviors.

continuity rule A perceptual rule stating that, in organizing stimuli, we tend to favor smooth or continuous paths when interpreting a series of points or lines.

continuous reinforcement The simplest reinforcement schedule, in which every occurrence of the operant response results in delivery of the reinforcer.

continuum of consciousness A wide range of human experiences, from being acutely aware and alert to being totally unaware and unresponsive.

control group In an experiment, the participants who undergo all the same procedures as the experimental participants do, except that the control participants do not receive the treatment.

Control Question Technique A lie-detection procedure in which the examiner asks two kinds of questions: neutral questions that elicit little emotional response and critical questions that are designed to elicit greater emotional responses. The person answers only "Yes" or "No" to the questions and, if guilty, is expected to show a greater emotional response to the critical questions than to the neutral questions.

controlled processes Activities that require full awareness, alertness, and concentration to reach some goal. Because of the strongly focused attention they require, controlled processes often interfere with other ongoing activities.

conventional level Lawrence Kohlberg's intermediate level of moral reasoning. It consists of two stages: At stage 3, moral decisions are guided most by conforming to the standards of others we value; at stage 4, moral reasoning is determined most by conforming to the laws of society.

convergence In three-dimensional vision, a binocular cue for depth perception based on signals sent from the muscles that turn the eyes. To focus on near or approaching objects, these muscles turn the eyes inward, toward the nose. The brain uses the signals sent by these muscles to determine the distance of the object.

convergent thinking Beginning with a problem and coming up with a single correct solution.

conversion disorder A somatoform disorder characterized by unexplained and significant physical symptoms—headaches, nausea, dizziness, loss of sensation, paralysis—that suggest a real neurological or medical problem but for which no physical or organic cause can be identified. Anxiety or emotional distress is apparently converted into symptoms that disrupt physical functioning.

coping The thinking and behaviors we engage in to manage stressors.

cornea The rounded, transparent covering over the front of the eye. As the light waves pass through the cornea, its curved surface bends, or focuses, the waves into a narrower beam.

correlation An association or relationship between the occurrence of two or more events.

correlation coefficient A number that indicates the strength of a relationship between two or more events. The closer the number is to −1.00 or +1.00, the greater is the strength of the relationship.

cortex A thin layer of cells that essentially covers the entire surface of the forebrain. The cortex consists of the frontal, parietal, occipital, and temporal lobes, whose control centers allow us to carry out hundreds of cognitive, emotional, sensory, and motor functions.

counseling psychologist An individual who has a PhD, PsyD, or EdD in psychology or education and whose training included work in a counseling setting. Counseling psychologists generally have a

less extensive research background than clinical psychologists and work in real-world settings, such as schools, industry, and private practice. Whereas clinical psychologists treat mental disorders, counseling psychologists deal largely with problems of living. To train as a counseling psychologist generally takes four to six years after obtaining a bachelor's degree.

counterattitudinal behavior Taking a public position that runs counter to your private attitude.

couple therapy A form of group therapy in which the couple is treated as the client and helped to improve their skills in communication and conflict management.

covariation model A model developed by Harold Kelley that may be used in deciding between internal and external attributions. The model says that, in making attributions, we should look for factors that are present when the behavior occurs and factors that are absent when the behavior does not occur.

creativity A combination of flexibility in thinking and reorganization of understanding to produce innovative ideas and new or novel solutions.

critical language period A period of time from infancy to adolescence when language is easiest to learn; in the period after adolescence through adulthood, language is more difficult to learn.

critical period In imprinting, the relatively brief time during which learning is most likely to occur. Also called the sensitive period.

cross-sectional method A research design in which several groups of different-aged individuals are studied at the same time.

crowd A large group of persons, most of whom are unacquainted, that can facilitate or inhibit certain behaviors.

cultural bias In testing, the situation in which the wording of the questions and the experiences on which they are based are more familiar to members of some social groups than to others.

cultural influences Pervasive pressures that encourage members of a particular society or ethnic group to conform to shared behaviors, values, and beliefs.

cultural neuroscience The study of how cultural values, practices, and environment shape and are shaped by the brain. Cultural neuroscience examines the bidirectional interactions between culture and the biology of the brain.

culture-specific disorder A pattern of mental illness or abnormal behavior that is unique to an ethnic or cultural population and does not match the Western classifications of mental disorders.

cumulative record A continuous written record that shows an organism's responses and reinforcements.

curare A drug that enters the bloodstream, reaches the muscles, and blocks receptors on the muscles. As a result, acetylcholine, the neurotransmitter that normally activates muscles, is blocked and the muscles are paralyzed.

cybertherapy Therapy delivered over the Internet.

 D

daydreaming An activity that requires a low level of awareness, often occurs during automatic processes, and involves fantasizing or dreaming while awake.

debriefing A procedure administered to participants after an experiment to minimize any potential negative effects. It includes explaining the purpose and method of the experiment, asking the participants their feelings about having been in the experiment, and helping the participants deal with possible doubts or guilt that arises from their behaviors in the experiments.

decay When memory is lost as a result of not using memory traces, which are physical changes in the brain that represent the memory.

decibel A unit used to measure loudness. The human range for hearing is from 0 decibels, which is absolutely no sound, to 140 decibels, which can produce pain and permanent hearing loss.

decision-stage model of helping The idea that we go through five stages in deciding to help: (1) we notice the situation; (2) we interpret it as one in which help is needed; (3) we assume personal responsibility; (4) we choose a form of assistance; and (5) we carry out that assistance.

declarative memory Memories of facts or events, such as scenes, stories, words, conversations, faces, or daily events. We are aware of these kinds of memories and can retrieve them.

deductive reasoning Making a general assumption that you know or believe to be true and then drawing specific conclusions based on this assumption—in other words, reasoning from a general assumption to particulars.

deep brain stimulation (DBS) A surgical procedure that involves implanting electrodes into the brain and placing a battery-powered stimulator under the collarbone. The electrodes are wired to the stimulator, which provides electrical stimulation to the brain.

deep structure According to Noam Chomsky, a sentence's underlying meaning that is not spoken but is present in the mind of the listener.

defense mechanisms Freudian processes that operate at unconscious levels to help the ego reduce anxiety through self-deception.

deficiency needs Physiological needs (food and sleep) and psychological needs (safety, belongingness, and esteem) that we try to fulfill if they are not met.

deindividuation The increased tendency for people to behave irrationally or perform antisocial behaviors when there is less chance of being personally identified.

deinstitutionalization The release of mental patients from mental hospitals and their return to the community to develop more independent and fulfilling lives.

delay of gratification Voluntarily postponing an immediate reward to persist in completing a task for the promise of a future reward.

delta waves Large, slow brain waves, meaning they have very high amplitude and very low frequency (less than 4 cycles per second).

delusions Irrational beliefs that have no basis in reality and are held in spite of contrary evidence.

dendrites Branchlike extensions that arise from the cell body; they receive signals from other neurons, muscles, and sense organs and pass them to the cell body.

denial Refusal to recognize some anxiety-provoking event or piece of information that is clear to others.

dependent variable In an experiment, one or more of the participants' behaviors that are used to measure the potential effects of the treatment or independent variable.

depressants A class of drugs that slow the central nervous system.

depth perception In visual perception, the ability of the eye and brain to add a third dimension, depth, to visual perceptions, even though the images projected on our retina have only two dimensions, height and width.

descriptive statistics Numbers used to present a collection of data in a brief yet meaningful form.

designer drugs Manufactured or synthetic drugs designed to resemble already existing illegal psychoactive drugs and to produce or mimic their psychoactive effects.

developmental norms The average ages at which children perform various skills or exhibit particular abilities or behaviors.

developmental psychology The study of moral, social, emotional, and cognitive development throughout a person's entire life.

Diagnostic and Statistical Manual of Mental Disorders The American Psychiatric Association's uniform diagnostic system for assessing specific symptoms and matching them to different mental disorders.

dialectical behavior therapy A type of cognitive-behavioral therapy that helps patients identify thoughts, beliefs, and assumptions that make their lives challenging and teaches them different ways to think and react.

diathesis stress theory of schizophrenia The idea that some people have a genetic predisposition (a diathesis) that interacts with life stressors to result in the onset and development of schizophrenia.

dichromats People who have trouble distinguishing red from green because their eyes have just two kinds of cones. This is an inherited condition, found most often in males, that results in seeing mostly shades of blue and yellow, but it differs in severity.

diffusion of responsibility theory The idea that, in the presence of others, individuals feel less personal responsibility and are less likely to take action in a situation where help is required.

direction of a sound The brain determines the direction of a sound by calculating the slight difference in time that it takes sound waves to reach the two ears, which are about 6 inches apart.

discrimination In classical conditioning, the tendency for some stimuli but not others to elicit a conditioned response. In operant conditioning, the tendency for a response to be emitted in the presence of a stimulus that is reinforced but not in the presence of unreinforced stimuli. In social psychology, specific unfair behaviors exhibited toward members of a group.

discriminative stimulus In conditioning, a cue that behavior will be reinforced.

disgust A universal facial expression—closing the eyes, narrowing the nostrils, curling the lips downward, and sometimes sticking out the tongue—that indicates the rejection of something unpleasant or offensive.

disorganized schizophrenia A subcategory of schizophrenia marked by bizarre ideas, often about one's body (bones melting), confused speech, childish behavior (giggling for no apparent reason, making faces at people), great emotional swings (fits of laughing or crying), and often extreme neglect of personal appearance and hygiene.

displacement Transferring feelings from their true source to another source that is safer and more socially acceptable.

display rules Specific cultural norms that regulate when, where, and how much emotion we should or should not express in different situations.

dissociative amnesia A dissociative disorder characterized by the inability to recall important personal information or events and usually associated with stressful or traumatic events. The importance of the information forgotten or the duration of the memory lapse is too great to be explained by normal forgetfulness.

dissociative disorder A disorder characterized by a disruption, split, or breakdown in a person's normally integrated and functioning consciousness, memory, sense of identity, or perception.

dissociative fugue A disturbance in which an individual suddenly and unexpectedly travels away from home or place of work and is unable to recall his or her past. The person may not remember his or her identity or may be confused about his or her new assumed identity.

dissociative identity disorder The presence in a single individual of two or more distinct identities or personality states, each with its own pattern of perceiving, thinking about, and relating to the world. Different personality states may take control of the individual's thoughts and behaviors at different times. Formerly called multiple personality disorder.

distinctiveness In making attributions, determining how differently the person behaves in one situation in comparison with other situations.

divergent thinking Beginning with a problem and coming up with many different solutions.

dominant gene A type of polymorphic gene that determines the development of a specific trait even if it is paired with a recessive gene.

dopamine theory The idea that, in schizophrenia, the dopamine neurotransmitter system is somehow overactive and gives rise to a wide range of symptoms.

double-blind procedure An experimental design in which neither the researchers nor the participants know which group is receiving which treatment. This design makes it possible to separate the effects of medical treatment from the participants' beliefs or expectations about the treatment.

double standard for sexual behavior A set of beliefs, values, and expectations that subtly encourages sexual activity in men but discourages the same behavior in women.

Down syndrome A genetic disorder that results from an extra 21st chromosome and causes abnormal physical traits (a fold of skin at the corner of each eye, a wide tongue, heart defects) and abnormal brain development, resulting in degrees of intellectual disability.

dream interpretation A Freudian technique of dream analysis, based on the assumption that dreams contain underlying, hidden meanings and symbols that provide clues to unconscious thoughts and desires. Freud distinguished between a dream's manifest content—the plot of the dream at the surface level—and its latent content—the hidden or disguised meaning of the plot's events.

dreaming A unique state of consciousness in which we are asleep but we experience a variety of images, often in color. People blind from birth have only auditory or tactile dreams, while sighted people have dreams with astonishing visual, auditory, and tactile images.

dyslexia An unexpected difficulty learning to read despite intelligence, motivation, and education. Causes of dyslexia include genetic factors (defects in neural circuitry) and environmental factors (disadvantaged schooling).

dysthymic disorder A mood disorder characterized by feeling chronically but not continuously depressed for a period of two years. While depressed, a person experiences at least two of the following symptoms: poor appetite, insomnia, fatigue, low self-esteem, poor concentration, and feelings of hopelessness.

eardrum *See* tympanic membrane.

echoic memory A form of sensory memory that holds auditory information for 1–2 seconds.

eclectic approach An approach to therapy in which the psychotherapist combines techniques and ideas from many different schools of thought.

ecstasy *See* MDMA.

ECT *See* electroconvulsive therapy.

EEG (electroencephalography) A procedure that involves placing electrodes at various points across a person's scalp. The electrodes detect brain wave activity throughout the brain's surface.

efferent neurons Neurons that carry information away from the spinal cord to produce responses in various muscles and organs throughout the body. Also called motor neurons.

effortful encoding The transfer of information from short-term into long-term memory either by working hard to repeat or rehearse the information or by making associations between new and old information.

ego Sigmund Freud's second division of the mind, which develops from the id during infancy; its goal is to find safe and socially acceptable ways of satisfying the id's desires and to negotiate between the id's wants and the superego's prohibitions.

egocentrism Seeing and thinking of the world from only your own viewpoint and having difficulty appreciating someone else's viewpoint.

elaborative rehearsal Making meaningful associations between information to be learned and information already learned; an effective strategy for encoding information into long-term memory.

Electra complex *See* Oedipus complex.

electroconvulsive therapy (ECT) A treatment for depression in which electrodes are placed on the skull and a mild electric current is administered. As it passes through the brain, the current causes a seizure. Usual treatment consists of 10 to 12 ECT sessions, at the rate of about three per week.

embryonic stage The second stage of the prenatal period, spanning the 2–8 weeks that follow conception; during this stage, cells divide and begin to differentiate into bone, muscle, and body organs.

EMDR *See* Eye Movement Desensitization and Reprocessing.

emerging adulthood A period of development in which adolescents and young adults in industrialized nations continue self-exploration as they experiment with different possibilities in work and love.

emotion A response consisting of four components: interpreting or appraising a stimulus (event, object, or thought) in terms of one's well-being; having a subjective feeling, such as happiness or sadness; experiencing physiological responses, such as changes in heart rate or breathing; and possibly showing overt behaviors, such as smiling or crying.

emotion-focused coping Making some effort to deal with the emotional distress caused by a harm/loss or threat appraisal. These efforts include seeking support and sympathy, avoiding or denying the situation, and redirecting our attention.

emotional development The process in which genetic factors, brain changes, cognitive factors, coping abilities, and cultural factors influence and interact in the development of emotional behaviors, expressions, thoughts, and feelings.

emotional intelligence The ability to perceive and express emotion, understand and reason with emotion, and regulate emotion in oneself and others.

encoding The process of making mental representations of information so that it can be placed into our memories.

end bulbs Bulblike swellings at the extreme ends of axons' branches that store chemicals called neurotransmitters, which are used to communicate with neighboring cells.

endocrine system Numerous glands, located throughout the body, that secrete various chemicals called hormones, which affect organs, muscles, and other glands in the body.

endorphins Chemicals produced by the brain and secreted in response to injury or severe physical or psychological stress. Their powerful pain-reducing properties are similar to those of morphine.

environmental factors Our social, political, and cultural influences as well as our particular learning experiences.

environmental language factors Interactions that children have with parents, peers, teachers, and others whose feedback rewards and encourages language development; these interactions also provide opportunities for children to observe, imitate, and practice language skills.

epigenetics The study of how environmental factors result in changes in gene activity that do not involve alterations to the genetic instructions but are still passed down to the next generation.

episodic memory A type of declarative memory that involves knowledge about one's personal experiences (episodes) or activities, such as naming or describing favorite restaurants, movies, songs, habits, or hobbies.

ESP *See* extrasensory perception.

estrogen One of the major female hormones. At puberty, estrogen levels increase eightfold and stimulate the development of both primary and secondary sexual characteristics.

ethologists Behavioral biologists who observe and study animal behavior in the animal's natural environment or under relatively naturalistic conditions.

eustress A pleasant and desirable type of stress that is healthful and keeps us engaged in situations.

evening persons People who prefer to get up late, go to bed late, and engage in afternoon or evening activities. *See also* morning persons.

event schemas Social schemas containing behaviors that we associate with familiar activities, events, or procedures. Also called scripts.

evolution *See* theory of evolution.

evolutionary approach A psychological viewpoint that focuses on how evolutionary ideas, such as adaptation and natural selection, explain human behaviors and mental processes.

evolutionary theory of emotions The theory that one function of emotions is to help a person evaluate objects, people, and situations in terms of how good or bad they are for the individual's well-being and survival.

evolutionary theory of gender differences The idea in sociobiology, which emphasizes genetic and biological forces, that current behavioral and cognitive differences between men and women can be traced back to different survival problems faced by early women and men and the different behaviors they adapted to survive.

exemplar model The idea that a person forms a concept of an object, event, animal, or person by defining or making a mental list of the essential characteristics of that particular thing.

exhaustion stage The third stage in the general adaptation syndrome. In reaction to long-term, continuous stress, there is actual breakdown in internal organs or weakening of the infection-fighting immune system.

experiment A method for identifying cause-and-effect relationships by following a set of rules and guidelines that minimize the possibility of error, bias, and chance occurrences.

experimental group In an experiment, the participants who receive the treatment.

experimental psychology The study of sensation, perception, learning, human performance, motivation, and emotion in carefully controlled laboratory conditions, with both animal and human participants.

experimenter bias The expectations of the experimenter that participants will behave or respond in a certain way.

explicit memory Memory that is consciously known.

exposure therapy A treatment for anxiety in which the person is gradually exposed to the real anxiety-producing situations or objects that he or she is attempting to avoid; exposure treatment is continued until the anxiety decreases.

extensions of waking life theory of dreams The theory that our dreams reflect the same thoughts, fears, concerns, problems, and emotions that we have when awake.

external attributions Explanations of behavior based on the external circumstances or situations. Also called situational attributions.

extinction In classical conditioning, the reduction in a response when the conditioned stimulus is no longer followed by the unconditioned stimulus. As a result, the conditioned stimulus tends to no longer elicit the conditioned response. In operant conditioning, the reduction in the operant response when it is no longer followed by the reinforcer.

extraneous variables Variables other than the independent variable that may influence the dependent variable in a study.

extrasensory perception (ESP) A group of psychic experiences that involve perceiving or sending information (images) outside normal sensory processes or channels. ESP includes four general abilities: telepathy, precognition, clairvoyance, and psychokinesis.

extrinsic motivation Engaging in certain activities or behaviors that either reduce our biological needs or help us obtain incentives or external rewards.

Eye Movement Desensitization and Reprocessing (EMDR) A technique in which the client focuses on a traumatic memory while visually following the back-and-forth movement of a therapist's hand. The process usually continues for several 90-minute sessions, after which the traumatic memories are greatly reduced or eliminated.

eyewitness testimony Recollection or recognition of a suspect observed during a possibly disruptive emotional situation that may have interfered with accurate remembering.

facial expressions Social signals that accompany emotions and express the state of our personal feelings; they elicit a variety of responses from those around us.

facial feedback hypothesis The idea that sensations and feedback from the movement of facial muscles and skin are interpreted by the brain as emotional feelings.

factor analysis A complicated statistical method that finds relationships among different or diverse items and allows them to be grouped together.

family therapy A form of group therapy in which all family members are treated as the client and helped to change destructive relationships and improve the way they communicate with one another.

farsightedness A visual acuity problem that may result when the eyeball is too short, so that objects are focused at a point slightly behind the retina. The result is that distant objects are clear, but near objects are blurry.

FAS *See* fetal alcohol syndrome.

fat cells Cells that store body fat. The number of fat cells in the body is primarily determined by heredity. They do not normally multiply except when we become obese. Fat cells shrink as we give up fat and lose weight and greatly enlarge as we store fat and gain weight.

fear of failure A tendency to avoid failure by choosing easy, nonchallenging tasks where failure is unlikely to occur.

female secondary sexual characteristics Sexual characteristics whose development in the female is triggered by the increased secretion of estrogen during puberty; they include the growth of pubic hair, development of breasts, and widening of hips.

fertilization *See* conception.

fetal alcohol syndrome (FAS) A condition that results from a mother drinking heavily during pregnancy, especially in the first 12 weeks. It results in physical changes, such as short stature, flattened nose, and short eye openings; neurological changes, such as fewer brain connections within the brain structure; and psychological and behavioral problems, such as hyperactivity, impulsive behavior, deficits in information processing and memory, alcohol and drug use, and poor socialization.

fetal stage The third stage in prenatal development, beginning two months after conception and lasting until birth.

fight-flight response A state of increased physiological arousal that (1) directs great resources of energy to the muscles and brain; (2) can be triggered by either physical stimuli that threaten our survival or psychological situations that are novel, threatening, or challenging; and (3) involves numerous physiological responses that arouse and prepare the body for action-fight or flight. Caused by the activation of the sympathetic nervous system, it helps us to cope with and survive threatening situations.

figure-ground rule A perceptual rule stating that, in organizing stimuli, we tend to automatically distinguish between a figure and a ground: The figure, with more detail, stands out against the background, which has less detail.

five-factor model An approach to personality in which all traits are organized into five categories—openness, conscientiousness, extraversion, agreeableness, and neuroticism—that are used to describe differences in personality.

fixation A Freudian process through which an individual may be locked into any one of the three psychosexual stages—oral, anal, or phallic—because his or her wishes were either overgratified or undergratified in that stage.

fixed action pattern An innate biological force that predisposes an organism to behave in a fixed way in the presence of a specific environmental condition. Previously called instinct.

fixed-interval schedule In conditioning, a schedule in which a reinforcer occurs following a participant's first response after a fixed interval of time.

fixed-ratio schedule In conditioning, a schedule in which a reinforcer occurs only after a fixed number of responses by the participant.

flashbulb memories Vivid recollections, usually in great detail, of dramatic or emotionally charged incidents, which are encoded effortlessly and may last for long periods of time.

flat affect Little or no emotional responsiveness when an emotional reaction would be expected.

flavor What we experience when we combine the sensations of taste and smell.

fMRI *See* functional magnetic resonance imaging.

food-entrainable circadian clock (or midnight-snack clock) A timing device that regulates eating patterns in people and animals and might be responsible for late-night eating in people.

foot-in-the-door technique A method of persuasion that relies on the increased probability of compliance to a second request if a person complies with a small first request.

forebrain The largest part of the brain, consisting of the left and right hemispheres connected by a wide band of fibers, the corpus callosum. The hemispheres are responsible for a vast array of responses, including learning and memory, speaking and language, emotional responses, experiencing sensations, initiating voluntary movements, planning, and making decisions.

forgetting The inability to retrieve, recall, or recognize information that was stored or is still stored in long-term memory.

forgetting curve A graph of the amount of previously learned information that individuals can recall or recognize across time.

formal operations stage Jean Piaget's fourth cognitive stage, lasting from about 12 years of age through adulthood. During this stage, adolescents and adults develop the ability to think about and solve abstract or hypothetical concepts, to consider an issue from another person's viewpoint, and to solve cognitive problems in a logical manner.

fovea In the eye, the center of the retina where photoreceptors with a cone-like shape, called cones, change light waves into electrical signals. *See also* transduction.

fragile X syndrome An inherited developmental disability that is due to a defect in the X chromosome that can result in physical changes such as a relatively large head with protruding ears and mild to profound mental retardation.

fraternal twins Twins who develop from separate eggs and share 50% of their genes.

free association A Freudian technique in which clients are encouraged to talk about any thoughts or images that enter their heads; the assumption is that this kind of free-flowing, uncensored talking will provide clues to unconscious material.

frequency In relation to sound waves, how many sound waves occur within 1 second.

frequency distribution The range of scores we get and the frequency of each one when we measure a sample of people (or objects) regarding some trait.

frequency theory In pitch perception, the idea that, for low-frequency sound waves (1,000 cycles or less), the rate at which nerve impulses reach the brain determines how low a sound is. A rate of 50 impulses per second is interpreted as a lower sound than a rate of 200 impulses per second.

Freudian slips Mistakes or slips of the tongue that we make in everyday speech; such mistakes are thought to reflect unconscious thoughts or wishes.

Freud's theory of dreams A theory that says we have a "censor" that protects us from realizing threatening and unconscious desires or wishes, especially those involving sex or aggression, by transforming them into harmless symbols that appear in our dreams and do not disturb our sleep or conscious thoughts.

frontal lobe An area in the front part of the brain that includes a huge area of cortex. The frontal lobe is involved in many functions: performing voluntary motor movements, interpreting and performing emotional behaviors, behaving normally in social situations, maintaining a healthy personality, paying attention to things in the environment, making decisions, and carrying out plans.

frontal lobotomy A surgical procedure in which about one-third of the front part of the frontal lobe is separated from the rest of the brain.

frustration The feeling that results when our attempts to reach some goal are blocked.

frustration-aggression hypothesis The idea that, when our goals are blocked, we become frustrated and respond with anger and aggression. *See also* modified frustration-aggression hypothesis.

functional fixedness A mental set characterized by the inability to see an object as having a function different from its usual one.

functional magnetic resonance imaging (fMRI) A brain scan that measures the activity of specific neurons that are functioning during cognitive tasks such as thinking, listening, or reading.

functionalism An early school of psychological thought that emphasized the function rather than the structure of consciousness and was interested in how our minds adapt to our changing environment.

fundamental attribution error Our tendency, when we look for the causes of a person's behavior, to focus on the person's disposition or personality traits and to overlook how the situation influenced the person's behavior.

g-factor theory *See* Spearman's general intelligence theory.

galvanic skin response Changes in sweating of the fingers (or palms) that accompany emotional experiences and are independent of perspiration under normal temperatures.

Ganzfeld procedure A controlled method for eliminating trickery, error, and bias while testing telepathic communication between two people.

Gardner's multiple-intelligence theory The idea that, instead of one kind of general intelligence, there are at least nine different kinds: verbal intelligence, musical intelligence, logical-mathematical intelligence, spatial intelligence, body movement intelligence, intelligence to understand oneself, intelligence to understand others, naturalistic intelligence, and existential intelligence.

GAS *See* general adaptation syndrome.

gate control theory The idea that nonpainful nerve impulses compete with pain impulses as they enter the spinal cord, creating a neural gate through which only the nonpainful impulses pass; the pain impulses do not reach the brain. Thus, we can reduce feelings of pain by rubbing an injured area or becoming absorbed in other activities.

gender dysphoria The persistent negative emotional state that occurs when there is a disconnect between a person's biological sex and gender identity.

gender identity The individual's subjective experience and feelings of being either a male or a female. Formerly called sexual identity.

gender identity disorder Commonly referred to as transsexualism, an individual's strong, persistent desire or feeling of wanting to be the opposite sex, discomfort with being one's assigned sex, and the wish to live as a member of the other sex.

gender roles Traditional or stereotypical behaviors, attitudes, and personality traits that parents, peers, and society designate as masculine or feminine. Gender roles affect how we think and behave. Formerly called sex roles.

gender schemas Sets of information and rules organized around how either a male or a female should think and behave.

gene A specific segment on the strand of DNA (the chromosome) that contains instructions for making proteins, the chemical building blocks from which all the parts of the brain and body are constructed.

general adaptation syndrome (GAS) According to Hans Selye, a series of three stages—alarm, resistance, and exhaustion—that correspond to the three different reactions of the body to stressful situations and that gradually increase the chances of developing psychosomatic symptoms.

generalization In classical conditioning, the tendency for a stimulus that is similar to the original conditioned stimulus to elicit a response that is similar to the conditioned response. Usually, the more similar the new stimulus is to the original conditioned stimulus, the larger will be the conditioned response. In operant conditioning, the situation in which an animal or a person emits the same response to similar stimuli.

generalized anxiety disorder A psychological disorder primarily characterized by excessive and/or unrealistic worry or feelings of general apprehension about events or activities. These anxious feelings occur on a majority of days for a period of at least six months.

genetic factors in mental disorders Unlearned or inherited tendencies that influence how a person thinks, behaves, and feels.

genetic hunger factors Inherited instructions found in our genes that influence our hunger; these instructions may determine our number of fat cells or our metabolic rate of burning off the body's fuel, which pushes us toward being normal, overweight, or underweight.

genetic marker An identifiable gene or number of genes or a specific segment of a chromosome that is directly linked to some behavioral, physiological, or neurological trait or disease.

genetic mutation An accidental error in genetic instructions that leads to a change in an organism.

genetic sex factors Inherited instructions for the development of sexual organs, the secretion of sex hormones, and the wiring of the neural circuits that control sexual reflexes.

genetic testing A procedure that involves taking a sample from someone's blood, hair, skin, or other body parts and then examining the person's genes to look for signs that the person may be at risk for specific diseases or disorders.

genital cutting The practice of cutting away the female's external genitalia, usually including her clitoris and surrounding skin (labia minora). The remaining edges are sewn together, leaving only a small opening for urination and menstruation.

genital stage Sigmund Freud's fifth, and final, psychosexual stage, lasting from puberty through adulthood. In this stage, the individual has renewed sexual desires that he or she seeks to fulfill through relationships with other people.

germinal stage The first stage of prenatal development, lasting two weeks from the moment of conception.

Gestalt approach An older theoretical approach that emphasized the idea that perception is more than the sum of its parts. The Gestalt psychologists believed that perceptions are formed by the brain on the basis of a set of rules that specify how individual elements may be organized to form a meaningful pattern—that is, a perception.

giftedness Defined by the approximately 2% of the population at the top end of the normal distribution having an IQ score of 130 or above.

glial cells Cells in the nervous system that have at least three functions: They provide scaffolding to guide the growth of developing neurons and support mature neurons; they wrap themselves around neurons and form a kind of insulation to prevent interference from other electrical signals; and they release chemicals that influence a neuron's growth and function.

gonads Glands—the ovaries in females and the testes in males—that produce hormones to regulate sexual development, ovulation or sperm production, and the growth of sex organs. They are part of the endocrine system.

grammar A set of rules for combining words into phrases and sentences to express an infinite number of thoughts that can be understood by others.

group A collection of two or more people who interact and share some common attribute or purpose. A group also influences how its members think and behave.

group cohesion Group togetherness, which is determined by how much group members perceive that they share common attributes.

group norms Formal or informal rules about how group members should behave.

group polarization The phenomenon in which group discussion reinforces the majority's point of view and shifts that view to a more extreme position.

group therapy When psychotherapy is conducted in a group setting and involves clients receiving feedback from others in the group as well as from the therapist(s).

groupthink Poor group decision making that occurs when group discussions emphasize cohesion and agreement rather than critical thinking and the best possible outcome.

growth needs According to Maslow, higher-level needs that are not essential to existence, such as the desire for truth, goodness, beauty, and justice.

hair cells The auditory receptors. These miniature hair-shaped cells rise from the basilar membrane in the cochlea.

hallucinations Sensory experiences without any stimulation from the environment.

hallucinogens Psychoactive drugs that can produce hallucinations—strange perceptual, sensory, and cognitive experiences that the person sees or hears but knows are not really occurring.

happiness A mental state, usually indicated by smiling and laughing, that can result from momentary pleasures, such as a funny commercial; short-term joys, such as a great date; or long-term satisfaction, such as an enjoyable relationship.

hardiness A combination of three personality traits—control, commitment, and challenge—that protect or buffer us from the potentially harmful effects of stressful situations and reduce our chances of developing psychosomatic illness.

harm/loss appraisal Our conclusion that we have already sustained some damage or injury in a particular situation.

hassles Small, irritating, frustrating events that we face daily and that we usually appraise as stressful experiences.

hazing Part of a group's initiation ritual during which individuals are subjected to a variety of behaviors that range from humiliating and unpleasant to potentially dangerous both physically and psychologically.

Head Start A national child development program for children from birth to age 5 that provides services to promote academic, social, and emotional development, as well as providing social, health, and nutrition services for families whose incomes make them eligible for the program.

health psychology The study of how psychological factors relate to the promotion and maintenance of health, as well as the prevention and treatment of illnesses.

helping *See* prosocial behavior.

heritability A statistical measure that indicates the amount or proportion of some ability, characteristic, or trait that can be attributed to genetic factors.

hero An ordinary person who is motivated to act on behalf of others or for a moral cause with action that is extraordinary.

heterosexual orientation A pattern of sexual arousal by persons of the opposite sex.

heuristics Rules of thumb acquired through past experience that reduce the number of operations or allow us to take shortcuts in solving problems.

hierarchy of needs *See* Maslow's hierarchy of needs.

high need for achievement A tendency to persist longer at tasks; show better performance on tasks, activities, or exams; set challenging but realistic goals; compete with others to win; and be attracted to careers that require initiative.

hindbrain An area at the base of the brain that is involved in sleeping, waking, coordinating body movements, and regulating vital reflexes (heart rate, blood pressure, and respiration).

hippocampus A curved structure within the temporal lobe that is involved in transforming many kinds of fleeting memories into permanent storage. It forms part of the limbic system.

HIV positive Having HIV antibodies, which means infection by the human immunodeficiency virus (HIV).

holistic view The idea, emphasized in humanistic theories, that a person's personality is more than the sum of its individual parts; instead, the individual parts form a unique and total entity that functions as a unit.

homeostasis The tendency of the sympathetic and parasympathetic divisions of the autonomic nervous system to work together to maintain the body's level of arousal in balance for optimal functioning.

homosexual orientation A pattern of sexual arousal by persons of the same sex.

hormones In the endocrine system, chemicals secreted by glands that affect organs, muscles, and other glands in the body.

human development The study of a person's biological, emotional, cognitive, personal, and social development across the life span, from infancy through late adulthood.

humanistic approach A psychological viewpoint emphasizing that each individual has great freedom in directing his or her future, considerable capacity for achieving personal growth, intrinsic worth, and enormous potential for self-fulfillment.

humanistic theories *See* humanistic approach.

hypnosis A procedure in which a researcher, clinician, or hypnotist suggests to another person that he or she will experience various changes in sensation, perception, cognition, or control over motor behaviors.

hypnotic analgesia A reduction in pain reported by clients after undergoing hypnosis and receiving suggestions that reduced anxiety and promoted relaxation.

hypnotic induction Various methods of inducing hypnosis, such as asking individuals to close their eyes and go to sleep, having them fix their attention on an object (for example, a watch), and instructing them to go into deep relaxation.

hypothalamus A structure of the limbic system that is located near the bottom middle of the brain and regulates many motivational and emotional behaviors. It controls much of the endocrine system by regulating the pituitary gland.

hypothesis An educated guess about some phenomenon, stated in precise, concrete language so as to rule out any confusion or error in the meaning of its terms.

I

iconic memory A form of sensory memory that automatically holds visual information for about a quarter of a second or longer. (The word *icon* means "image.")

id Sigmund Freud's first division of the mind, which contains two biological drives—sex and aggression—that are the source of all psychic or mental energy. The id's goal is to pursue pleasure and satisfy the biological drives.

ideal self According to Carl Rogers, the self that is based on our hopes and wishes and reflects how we would like to see ourselves; its complement is the real self.

ideal weight *See* optimal weight.

identical twins Twins who develop from a single egg and thus have almost exactly the same genes.

identity How we describe ourselves, including our values, goals, traits, interests, and motivations.

illusion Perception of an image so distorted that, in reality, it cannot and does not exist. An illusion is created when space, size, and depth cues are manipulated so that our brains can no longer correctly interpret them.

imaginary audience Adolescents' belief that everyone is watching all of their actions.

imagined perception In hypnosis, the participant's willingness, at the hypnotist's suggestion, to respond to nonexistent stimuli and imaginary perceptions. It can also include bizarre behaviors, such as imitating Elvis Presley in public.

immune system The body's defense and surveillance network of cells and chemicals that fight off bacteria, viruses, and other foreign or toxic substances.

implicit or nondeclarative memory Mental and emotional processes that we are unaware of but that bias and influence our conscious feelings, thoughts, and behaviors. *See also* procedural memory.

impossible figure A perceptual experience in which a drawing seems to defy basic geometric laws.

imprinting Inherited tendencies or responses that newborn animals display when they encounter certain stimuli in their environment.

incentives Environmental factors, such as external stimuli, reinforcers, or rewards, that motivate our behavior.

independent variable In an experiment, a treatment or something else that the researcher controls or manipulates.

induced pluripotent stem cells (iPSCs) Adult cells that have been genetically reprogrammed to be in an embryonic stem cell-like state.

inductive reasoning Making particular observations that you then use to draw a broader conclusion; in other words, reasoning from particulars to a general conclusion.

industrial/organizational psychology The study of people and their relationships in their work environments.

inferential statistics Procedures for determining what conclusions can be legitimately inferred from a set of data.

information-processing model In memory processing, a model that states that the ability to retain information over time involves three processes: encoding, storage, and retrieval.

informational influence theory The theory that we use the reactions of others to judge the seriousness of the situation.

inhibited/fearful children Jerome Kagan's term for children who show avoidance, anxiety, or fear (measured by avoiding or crying) when in a strange or novel environment; these children also show increased physiological arousal (increased heart rate) and brain activity (increased response of the amygdala—threat detector) in novel or strange situations.

inhibited female orgasm A woman's persistent delay or absence of orgasm after becoming aroused and excited.

innate language factors Genetically programmed physiological and neurological features of the brain and vocal apparatus that facilitate our making speech sounds and learning language skills.

inner ear Part of the ear with two main structures that are sealed in bony cavities: the cochlea, which is involved in hearing, and the semicircular canals, which are involved in balance.

insanity According to the legal definition, not knowing the difference between right and wrong.

insecure attachment An emotional bond characteristic of infants who avoid or show ambivalence or resistance toward their parents.

insight A mental process marked by the sudden and unexpected solution to a problem. Often called the "aha!" experience.

insight therapy An approach in which the therapist and client talk about the client's symptoms and problems, with the goal of identifying the cause of the problem. Once the client has an insight into the cause of the problem, possible solutions can be discussed with the therapist.

insomnia Difficulties in going to sleep or in staying asleep through the night. Associated daytime complaints include fatigue, impairment of concentration, memory difficulty, and lack of well-being. About 33% of adult Americans report some type of insomnia.

instincts According to William McDougall (1908), innate tendencies or biological forces that determine behavior; now used as a synonym for fixed action patterns.

intellectual disability (formerly *mental retardation*) A substantial limitation in present functioning that is characterized by significantly subaverage intellectual functioning along with related limitations in two of eleven areas, including communication, self-care, home living, social skills, academic skills, leisure, and safety.

intelligence A person's ability to adapt to the environment and learn from experience.

intelligence quotient (IQ) A measure of intelligence computed by dividing a person's mental age, as measured by an intelligence test, by the person's chronological age and multiplying the result by 100.

interactive model of sexual orientation The theory that genetic and biological factors, such as genetic instructions and prenatal hormones, interact with psychological factors, such as the individual's attitudes, personality traits, and behaviors, to influence the development of sexual orientation.

interference The forgetting process in which the recall of some particular memory is blocked or prevented by new information that overwrites or interferes with it. *See also* proactive interference and retroactive interference.

internal attributions Explanations of behavior on the basis of the internal characteristics (or dispositions) of the person performing the behavior. Also called personal attributions.

interneuron A relatively short neuron whose primary task is to make connections between other neurons.

interposition In three-dimensional vision, a monocular depth cue that comes into play when objects overlap. The overlapping object appears closer, and the object that is overlapped appears to be farther away.

intervention program A program for disadvantaged children that creates an environment offering increased opportunities for intellectual, social, and personality-emotional development while ensuring good physical health.

intestines The body organ that responds to the presence of food, especially fats, by secreting a hormone called CCK (cholecystokinin), which signals the hypothalamus to inhibit eating.

intimacy In Robert Sternberg's triangular theory of love, the component of love associated with feeling close and connected to someone; it develops through sharing and communicating.

intrinsic motivation Engaging in certain activities or behaviors because they are personally rewarding or because we are fulfilling our beliefs or expectations.

introspection A method of exploring conscious mental processes adopted by the structuralists; individuals were asked to look inward and report their sensations and perceptions.

intrusive thoughts Thoughts that we experience repeatedly, that are usually unwanted or disruptive, and that are very difficult to stop or eliminate.

ions Electrically charged chemical particles, which obey the rule that opposite charges attract and like charges repel.

iPSCs *See* induced pluripotent stem cells.

IQ *See* intelligence quotient.

iris A circular muscle that surrounds the pupil and controls the amount of light that enters the eye. In dim light, the iris relaxes, allowing more light to enter—the pupil dilates; in bright light, the iris constricts, allowing less light to enter—the pupil constricts. The iris muscle contains the pigment that gives the eye its characteristic color.

James-Lange theory The idea that our brains interpret specific physiological changes as feelings or emotions and that there is a different physiological pattern underlying each emotion.

jet lag A condition in which travelers' internal circadian rhythm is out of step, or synchrony, with the external clock time at their new location. They experience fatigue, disorientation, lack of concentration, and reduced cognitive skills. It takes about one day to reset the circadian clock for each hour of time change.

just noticeable difference (JND) The smallest increase or decrease in the intensity of a stimulus that a person is able to detect 50% of the time.

kinesthetic sense A sense that informs us about our bodies' positions and motions relative to gravity.

labeling A process of identifying differences among individuals and placing them into specific categories, which may have either positive or negative associations.

language A form of communication in which we learn and use complex rules to form and manipulate symbols (words or gestures) that are used to generate an endless number of meaningful sentences.

language stages The periods or stages that all infants go through in language acquisition—babbling, single words, two-word combinations, and sentences. All children go through these four stages in the same order, and in each stage, children show new and more complex language skills.

latency stage The fourth of Sigmund Freud's psychosexual stages, lasting from the age of about 6 years to puberty. In this stage, the child represses sexual thoughts and engages in nonsexual activities, such as developing social and intellectual skills.

latent content In Freud's theory of dreams, the hidden element of the dream that is determined by unconscious forces and of which the person is unaware.

latent learning Learning that is not demonstrated in behavior until its application becomes useful.

lateral hypothalamus A group of brain cells that regulates hunger by receiving signals from digestive organs and creates feelings of being hungry.

law of effect The principle that behaviors followed by positive (pleasurable) consequences are strengthened (and thus will likely occur in the future), while behaviors followed by negative consequences are weakened.

learning A relatively permanent change in behavior (both unobservable mental events and observable responses) associated with specific stimuli and/or responses that change as a result of experience.

learning–performance distinction The idea that learning may occur but may not always be measured by, or immediately evident in, performance.

lens A transparent, oval structure in the eye whose curved surface functions to bend and focus light waves into an even narrower beam. The lens is attached to muscles that adjust the curve of the lens, which, in turn, adjusts the focusing.

levels-of-processing theory The theory that memory depends on how well information is encoded in the mind. Information is encoded at a shallow level if we simply pay attention to its basic features, but it is encoded at a deep level if we form new associations with existing information. According to the theory, poor memory corresponds to information encoded at a shallow level, and good memory to information encoded at deep levels.

lie detector tests *See* polygraph tests.

light and shadow A monocular depth cue; brightly lit objects appear closer, while objects in shadows appear farther away.

light therapy The use of bright, artificial light to reset circadian rhythms and so combat the insomnia and drowsiness that plague shift workers and jet-lag sufferers; it is also used to help people with sleeping disorders in which the body fails to stay in time with the external environment.

limbic system A group of about half a dozen interconnected structures in the core of the forebrain that are involved in many motivational behaviors, such as obtaining food, drink, and sex; organizing emotional behaviors such as fear, anger, and aggression; and storing memories. It is sometimes referred to as our primitive, or animal, brain because the same structures are found in the brains of animals that are evolutionarily very old.

linear perspective In three-dimensional vision, a monocular depth cue associated with the convergence of parallel lines in the far distance.

linguistic relativity *See* theory of linguistic relativity.

liver The body organ that monitors nutrients, especially the level of glucose (sugar) in the blood. When the level of glucose falls, the liver signals hunger to the brain's hypothalamus; when the level of glucose rises, the liver signals fullness.

lobes The four areas into which the brain's cortex is divided: frontal, parietal, occipital, and temporal.

locus of control Our beliefs concerning how much control we have over situations or rewards. For each of us, these beliefs lie somewhere on a continuum between internal and external locus of control. We have an internal locus of control if we believe that we have control over situations and rewards and an external locus of control if we believe that we do not have control over situations and rewards and that events outside ourselves (fate) determine what happens.

long-term memory The process of storing almost unlimited amounts of information over long periods of time.

long-term potentiation (LTP) Changes in the structure and function of a neuron after it has been repeatedly stimulated. Neuroscientists believe that the LTP process may be the basis for learning and memory in animals and humans.

longitudinal method A research design in which the same group of individuals is studied repeatedly at many different points in time.

loudness Our subjective experience of a sound's intensity, which is determined by the height (amplitude) of the sound wave. The brain calculates loudness from the rate of nerve impulses that arrive in the auditory nerve.

LSD (d-lysergic acid diethylamide) A very potent hallucinogen. Very small doses can produce experiences such as visual hallucinations, perceptual distortions, increased sensory awareness, and emotional responses that may last 8–10 hours.

LTP *See* long-term potentiation.

magnetic resonance imaging (MRI) A technique for studying the structure of the living brain. Nonharmful radio frequencies are passed through the brain, and a computer measures their interaction with brain cells and transforms this interaction into an incredibly detailed image of the brain (or body).

maintenance rehearsal The practice of intentionally repeating or rehearsing information (rather than forming any new associations) so that it remains longer in short-term memory.

major depressive disorder A mood disorder marked by at least two weeks of continually being in a bad mood, having no interest in anything, and getting no pleasure from activities. In addition, a person must have at least four of the following symptoms: problems with eating, sleeping, thinking, concentrating, or making decisions; lacking energy; thinking about suicide; and feeling worthless or guilty.

major life events Potentially disturbing, troubling, or disruptive situations, both positive and negative, that we appraise as having a significant impact on our lives.

maladaptive behavior approach In defining abnormality, the idea that a behavior is psychologically damaging or abnormal if it interferes with the individual's ability to function in one's personal life or in society.

maladaptive genes Genes for traits that prevent survival and reproduction. They are not selected in the process of evolution and consequently are eliminated in a species.

male secondary sexual characteristics Sexual characteristics whose development in the male is triggered by the increased secretion of testosterone during puberty; they include the growth of pubic hair, muscle development, and a change (deepening) of the voice.

manifest content In Freud's theory of dreams, the portion of the dream that the person remembers, which are the harmless symbols.

marijuana A psychoactive drug whose primary active ingredient is THC (tetrahydrocannabinol), which is found in the leaves of the cannabis plant. Low doses produce mild euphoria; moderate doses produce perceptual and time distortions; and high doses may produce hallucinations, delusions, and distortions of body image.

Maslow's hierarchy of needs An ascending order, or hierarchy, in which biological needs are placed at the bottom and social needs at the top. As needs at lower levels are met, we advance to the next higher level. This hierarchy indicates that we satisfy our biological needs before we satisfy our social needs.

mass hysteria A condition experienced by a group of people who, through suggestion, observation, or other psychological processes, develop similar fears, delusions, abnormal behaviors, and, in some cases, physical symptoms.

maturation The succession of developmental changes that are genetically or biologically programmed rather than acquired through learning or life experiences.

MDMA Also called ecstasy, this drug resembles both mescaline (a hallucinogen) and amphetamine (a stimulant). It heightens sensations, gives a euphoric rush, raises body temperature, and creates feelings of warmth and empathy.

mean The arithmetic average of all the individual measurements in a distribution.

measure of variability An indication of how much scores in a distribution vary from one another.

median The score above and below which half the scores in the distribution fall.

medulla An area in the hindbrain, located at the top of the spinal cord, that includes a group of cells that control vital reflexes, such as respiration, heart rate, and blood pressure.

melatonin A hormone secreted by the pineal gland, an oval group of cells in the center of the human brain. Melatonin secretion, controlled by the suprachiasmatic nucleus, increases with darkness and decreases with light; thus, it plays a role in the regulation of circadian rhythms and in promoting sleep.

memory An active system that allows people to retain information over time through the processes of encoding, storage, and retrieval.

memory traces Physical changes in the brain that represent the memory.

menarche The first menstrual period; it is a signal that ovulation may have occurred and that the girl may have the potential to conceive and bear a child.

menopause A gradual stoppage in the secretion of the major female hormone (estrogen). This process, which occurs in women at about age 50 (range 35–60), results in the cessation of ovulation and the menstrual cycle.

mental age A measure that estimates a child's intellectual progress by comparing the child's score on an intelligence test with the scores of average children of the same age.

mental disorder A prolonged or recurring problem that seriously interferes with an individual's ability to live a satisfying personal life and function adequately in society.

mental set The tendency to use problem-solving strategies that have worked in the past.

mescaline The active ingredient in the peyote cactus. At high doses, mescaline produces physiological arousal and very clear, colorful, and vivid visual hallucinations. It primarily increases the activity of the neurotransmitters norepinephrine and dopamine. Mescaline does not impair the intellect or cloud consciousness.

meta-analysis A powerful statistical procedure that compares the results of dozens or hundreds of studies to determine the effectiveness of some variable or treatment examined in those studies (for example, a type of therapy).

metabolic rate The efficiency with which the body breaks food down into energy and the speed with which the body burns off that fuel. An inherited trait, it can be raised by exercise or smoking.

methamphetamine (D-methamphetamine) A stimulant similar to amphetamine in both its chemical makeup and its physical and psychological effects. It causes marked increases in blood pressure and heart rate and feelings of enhanced mood, alertness, and energy. Methamphetamine, whose street names are meth, speed, crank, crystal, and ice, produces an almost instantaneous high when smoked and is highly addictive.

method of loci A mnemonic device, or encoding technique, that improves encoding by creating visual associations between memorized places and new items to be memorized.

midbrain The part of the brain that contains the reward/pleasure center, which is stimulated by food, sex, money, music, attractive faces, and some drugs (cocaine); contains areas for visual and auditory reflexes, such as automatically turning your head toward a noise; and holds the reticular formation, which arouses the forebrain so that it is ready to process information from the senses.

middle ear A bony cavity that is sealed at each end by a membrane. The two membranes are connected by three small bones, collectively called ossicles. Because of their shapes, these bones are referred to as the hammer, anvil, and stirrup. The ossicles act like levers that greatly amplify vibrations from the eardrum and transmit them to the oval window and inner ear.

mind-body connection The ability of our thoughts, beliefs, and emotions to produce physiological changes that may be either beneficial or detrimental to our health and well-being.

Minnesota Multiphasic Personality Inventory-2-RF (MMPI-2) A true-false self-report questionnaire that consists of 338 statements describing a wide range of normal and abnormal behaviors. The purpose of the MMPI-2 is to measure the personality style and emotional adjustment in individuals with mental illness.

misinformation effect When misleading or false information changes a person's memory of the actual event.

mnemonic methods Effective ways to improve encoding and create better retrieval cues by forming vivid associations or images that facilitate recall and decrease forgetting.

mode The most frequent measurement in a distribution.

modified frustration-aggression hypothesis The idea that although frustration may lead to aggression, situational and cognitive factors may override the aggressive response.

monochromats Individuals who have total color blindness; their world looks like a black-and-white movie. This kind of color blindness is rare and results from individuals having only rods or only one kind of functioning cone instead of three.

monocular depth cues In three-dimensional vision, depth cues produced by signals from a single eye. They are most commonly determined by the way objects are arranged in the environment.

mood disorder A prolonged and disturbed emotional state that affects almost all of a person's thoughts and behaviors.

mood-stabilizer drugs Drugs that act by adjusting the levels of neurotransmitters (e.g., norepinephrine and serotonin) to even out the highs and lows of mood disorders, such as bipolar disorder.

moral therapy The belief that mental patients may be helped to function better by receiving humane treatment in a relaxed and decent environment. This approach was fundamental to the reform movement of the early 1800s.

morning persons People who prefer to get up early, go to bed early, and engage in morning activities. *See also* evening persons.

morpheme The smallest meaningful combination of sounds in a language.

morphology A system that we use to group phonemes—consonants and vowels—into meaningful combinations of sounds and words.

motion parallax In three-dimensional vision, a monocular depth cue based on the speed of moving objects: Objects that appear to be moving at high speed are interpreted as closer to us than those moving more slowly.

motion sickness Feelings of nausea and dizziness experienced in a moving vehicle when information from the vestibular system (that your head is bouncing around) conflicts with information reported by your eyes (that objects in the distance look fairly steady).

motivation Various physiological and psychological factors that cause us to act in a specific way at a particular time.

motor cortex A narrow strip of cortex that is located on the back edge of the frontal lobe and extends down its side. It is involved in the initiation of all voluntary movements. The right motor cortex controls muscles on the left side of the body, and vice versa.

motor development The stages of motor skills that all infants pass through as they acquire the muscular control necessary for making coordinated movements.

motor neurons *See* efferent neurons.

MRI *See* magnetic resonance imaging.

multiple-intelligence theory *See* Gardner's multiple-intelligence theory.

multiple sclerosis A disease that attacks the myelin sheaths that wrap around and insulate cells in the central nervous system. Because of this damage, messages between the brain and other parts of the body are disrupted, often causing problems in motor coordination, strength, and sensation.

myelin sheath A tubelike structure of fatty material that wraps around and insulates an axon, preventing interference from electrical signals generated in adjacent axons.

narcolepsy A chronic disorder marked by excessive sleepiness, usually in the form of sleep attacks or short periods of sleep throughout the day. The sleep attacks are accompanied by brief periods of REM sleep and loss of muscle control (cataplexy), which may be triggered by big emotional changes.

narcotics Drugs (e.g., opium, morphine, heroin) that are used to relieve pain and induce sleep.

natural selection The process by which organisms that are better adapted to their environment tend to survive and produce more offspring, whereas those less adapted tend to be eliminated.

naturalistic observation A method researchers use to gather information by observing individuals' behaviors in a relatively normal environment without attempting to change or control the situation.

nature-nurture question The debate concerning the relative contribution of genetic factors (nature) and environmental factors (nurture) to a person's intelligence as well as to his or her biological, emotional, cognitive, personal, and social development.

nearsightedness A visual acuity problem that may result when the eyeball is too long, so that objects are focused at a point slightly in front of the retina. The result is that near objects are clear, but distant objects appear blurry.

negative punishment Removal of a reinforcing stimulus (for example, taking away a child's allowance) after a response. This removal decreases the chances that the response will recur.

negative reinforcement An aversive (unpleasant) stimulus whose removal increases the likelihood that the preceding response will occur again.

negative symptoms of schizophrenia Symptoms that reflect a decrease in or loss of normal functions: decreased range and intensity of emotions, decreased ability to express thoughts, and decreased initiative to engage in goal-directed behaviors.

neglect syndrome The failure of a patient to see objects or parts of the body on the side opposite the brain damage when the damage is to an association area, usually in the occipital and parietal lobes, and usually in the right hemisphere.

neo-Freudians Followers of Freud (e.g., Erik Erikson) who agreed with some of his theoretical ideas but changed and renovated others to develop their own approaches.

nerve impulse A series of separate action potentials that take place, segment by segment, as they move down the length of an axon.

nerves Stringlike bundles of axons and dendrites that are held together by connective tissue. Nerves in the peripheral nervous system have the ability to regrow, regenerate, or reattach if severed or damaged. They carry information from the senses, skin, muscles, and the body's organs to and from the spinal cord.

network hierarchy In the network theory of memory, the arrangement of nodes or categories so that concrete ideas are at the bottom of the hierarchy and are connected to more abstract ideas located above them. The most abstract ideas are at the top of the hierarchy.

network theory The theory that we store related ideas in separate memory categories, or files, called nodes. As we make associations between information, we create links among thousands of nodes, which make up a gigantic interconnected network for storing and retrieving information.

neural assemblies Groups of interconnected neurons whose activation allows information or stimuli to be recognized and held briefly and temporarily in short-term memory.

neural deafness Deafness caused by damage to the auditory receptors (hair cells), which prevents the triggering of impulses, or by damage to the auditory nerve, which prevents impulses from reaching the brain. *See also* cochlear implant.

neurogenesis The process of developing new neurons.

neuroleptic drugs Drugs that change the levels of neurotransmitters in the brain. They are used to treat serious mental disorders, such as schizophrenia. Also called antipsychotic drugs.

neurons Cells that have specialized extensions for the reception and transmission of electrical signals.

neuropeptides Small proteinlike molecules used by neurons to communicate with each other, distinct from the larger neurotransmitters.

neuroscience An interdisciplinary field of scientific study that examines the structure and function of all parts of the nervous system, including the brain, spinal cord, and networks of brain cells.

neuroses According to Freud, maladaptive thoughts and actions that arise from some unconscious thought or conflict and indicate feelings of anxiety.

neurotransmitters About a dozen different chemicals that are made by neurons and then used for communication between neurons during the performance of mental or physical activities.

neutral stimulus A stimulus that causes a sensory response, such as being seen, heard, or smelled, but does not produce the reflex being tested.

nicotine A stimulant; it first produces arousal but then produces calming. Present in cigarettes, nicotine increases both heart rate and blood pressure. It improves attention and concentration, may improve short-term memory, but may interfere with complex processing. Regular use of nicotine causes addiction, and stopping leads to withdrawal symptoms.

night terrors Sleep disruptions in children that occur during stage 3 or stage 4 (delta) sleep. They usually start with a piercing scream, after which the child wakes suddenly in a fearful state, with rapid breathing and increased heart rate. The next morning, the child has no memory of the frightening experience.

nightmares Dreams that contain frightening and anxiety-producing images. They usually involve great danger—being attacked, injured, or pursued. Upon awakening, the dreamer can usually describe the nightmare in considerable detail. Nightmares occur during REM sleep.

nodes Memory files that contain related information organized around a specific topic or category.

non-REM sleep Stages 1–4 of sleep, in which rapid eye movement does not occur; it makes up about 80% of sleep time.

nonbenzodiazepines Drugs, such as Ambien, Lunesta, and Sonata, that are popular sleeping pills because they act rapidly, are of short duration, and have few cognitive side effects.

noncompliance In children, refusal to follow directions, carry out a request, or obey a command given by a parent or caregiver. Noncompliance is one of the most common complaints of parents in general and the most frequent problem of parents who bring their children to clinics for treatment of behavioral problems.

nondeclarative memory *See* procedural memory.

noninintellectual factors Noncognitive factors, such as attitude, experience, and emotional functions, that may help or hinder an individual's performance on intelligence tests.

normal aging A gradual and natural slowing of our physical and psychological processes from middle through late adulthood.

normal curve A graph of a frequency distribution in which the curve tapers off equally on either side of a central high point—in other words, a graph of a normal distribution.

normal distribution A bell-shaped frequency distribution curve. The scores are arranged symmetrically so that the vast majority fall in the middle range, with fewer scores near the two extreme ends of the curve.

obedience Behavior performed in response to an order given by someone in a position of authority.

obesity Extreme overweight, as measured by a body mass index of 30 or higher.

object permanence The understanding that objects or events continue to exist even if they can no longer be heard, touched, or seen.

objective personality tests Tests consisting of specific written statements that require individuals to indicate—for example, by checking "true" or "false"—whether the statements do or do not apply to them. Also called self-report questionnaires.

observational learning *See* social cognitive learning.

obsessive-compulsive disorder An anxiety disorder consisting of obsessions, which are persistent, recurring, irrational thoughts, impulses, or images that a person is unable to control and that interfere with normal functioning; and compulsions, which are irresistible impulses to perform over and over some senseless behavior or ritual (hand washing, checking things, counting, putting things in order).

obsessive-compulsive personality disorder A personality disorder characterized by an intense interest in being orderly, achieving perfection, and having control. It is found in 4% of the population.

occipital lobe A region at the very back of the brain that is involved in processing visual information, which includes seeing colors and perceiving and recognizing objects, animals, and people.

Oedipus complex According to Sigmund Freud, a process in which a child competes with the parent of the same sex for the affections and pleasures of the parent of the opposite sex. Sometimes called the Electra complex in girls.

olfaction The sense of smell. It is called a chemical sense because its stimuli are various chemicals that are carried by the air. The upper part of the nose has a small area that contains receptor cells for olfaction. The function of the olfactory receptors is transduction—to transform chemical reactions into nerve impulses.

olfactory cells The receptors for smell, located in the uppermost part of the nasal passages. As volatile molecules dissolve in the mucus covering the cells, they stimulate the receptors, which send nerve impulses to the brain.

operant conditioning A kind of learning in which the consequences—reward or punishment—that follow some behavior increase or decrease the likelihood of that behavior's occurrence in the future. Also called instrumental conditioning.

operant response A response that can be modified by its consequences. Operant responses offer a way of dividing ongoing behavior into meaningful and measurable units.

opiates Drugs derived from the opium poppy, including opium and morphine, which is chemically altered to make heroin. All opiates have three primary effects: analgesia (pain reduction); opiate

euphoria, which is often described as a pleasurable state between waking and sleeping; and constipation. Continued use of opiates results in tolerance, physical addiction, and an intense craving for the drug.

opponent-process theory A theory of color vision suggesting that ganglion cells in the retina and cells in the thalamus respond to two pairs of colors: red-green and blue-yellow. When these cells are excited, they respond to one color of the pair; when inhibited, they respond to the complementary color.

optimal weight The body weight that results from an almost perfect balance between how much food an organism eats and how much it needs to meet its body's energy needs. Also called ideal weight.

optimism A relatively stable personality trait that leads one to believe and expect that good things will happen. It is one of the personality factors associated with lower stress levels and fewer chances of developing psychosomatic symptoms. *See also* pessimism.

oral stage Sigmund Freud's first psychosexual stage, which lasts for the first 18 months of life, in which the infant's pleasure seeking is centered on the mouth.

organic factors Medical conditions or drug or medication problems that lead to sexual difficulties.

ossicles *See* middle ear.

outer ear Two structures important to the hearing process: the pinna and the auditory canal.

overgeneralization A common error during language acquisition, in which children apply a grammatical rule to cases where it should not be used.

ovulation The release of an ovum, or egg cell, from a woman's ovaries.

pain Sensations caused by various stimuli that activate the pain receptors, free nerve endings. Nerve impulses from these pain receptors travel to the somatosensory and limbic areas of the brain, where they are transformed into pain sensations. Pain is essential for survival: It warns us to avoid or escape dangerous situations or stimuli and makes us take time to recover from injury.

pancreas An organ that regulates the level of sugar in the bloodstream by secreting insulin. It forms part of the endocrine system.

panic attack A period of intense fear or discomfort in which four or more of the following symptoms are present: pounding heart, sweating, trembling, shortness of breath, feelings of choking, chest pain, nausea, feeling dizzy, and fear of losing control or dying.

panic disorder A mental disorder characterized primarily by recurrent and unexpected panic attacks, plus continued worry about having another attack; such worry interferes with normal psychological functioning.

paranoid schizophrenia A subcategory of schizophrenia characterized by auditory hallucinations or delusions, such as thoughts of being persecuted by others or delusions of grandeur.

paraphilias Repetitive or preferred sexual fantasies involving nonhuman objects, such as sexual attractions to particular articles of clothing (shoes, underwear). Commonly called sexual deviations.

parasympathetic division The subdivision of the autonomic nervous system that decreases physiological arousal and helps return the body to a calmer, more relaxed state. It also stimulates digestion during eating.

parent training An intervention program in which parents are taught how to increase desirable child behavior, reduce children's misbehavior, improve parent-child interactions, and create a positive family atmosphere.

parentese A way of speaking to young children in which the adult speaks in a voice that is slower and higher than normal, emphasizes and stretches out each word, uses very simple sentences, and repeats words and phrases. Formerly known as motherese.

parietal lobe An area of the cortex located directly behind the frontal lobe. Its functions include processing sensory information from body parts, which includes touching, locating positions of limbs, and feeling temperature and pain; and carrying out several cognitive functions, such as attending to and perceiving objects.

Parkinson's disease A condition caused by the destruction of neurons that produce the neurotransmitter dopamine. Symptoms include tremors and shakes in the limbs, a slowing of voluntary movements, and feelings of depression. As the disease progresses, patients develop a peculiar shuffling walk and may suddenly freeze in space for minutes or hours at a time.

partial reinforcement A schedule of reinforcement in which the response is reinforced only some of the time.

passion In Robert Sternberg's triangular theory of love, the component of love associated with feeling physically aroused and attracted to someone.

passionate love A condition that is associated with continuously thinking about the loved one and is accompanied by warm sexual feelings and powerful emotional reactions.

pathological aging Acceleration of the aging process, which may be caused by genetic defects, physiological problems, or diseases.

peg method A mnemonic device, or encoding technique, that creates associations between number-word rhymes and items to be memorized.

perception A meaningful pattern or image that the brain assembles from hundreds of individual meaningless sensations; a perception is normally changed, biased, colored, or distorted by a person's unique set of experiences.

perceptual constancy Our tendency to perceive sizes, colors, brightness, and shapes as remaining the same even though their physical characteristics are constantly changing.

perceptual sets Learned expectations that are based on our personal, social, or cultural experiences. These expectations automatically add information, meaning, or feelings to our perceptions and thus change or bias our perceptions.

perceptual speed The rate at which we can identify a particular sensory stimulus; this rate slows down noticeably after age 60.

peripheral cues Hunger cues associated with changes in blood chemistry or signals from digestive organs, which secrete various hormones.

peripheral nervous system All the nerves that extend from the spinal cord and carry messages to and from various muscles, glands, and sense organs located throughout the body. It has two divisions: the somatic nervous system and the autonomic nervous system.

peripheral route for persuasion Approaches to persuasion that emphasize emotional appeal, focus on personal traits, and generate positive feelings.

peripheral theories of emotions Theories that attribute our subjective feelings primarily to our body's physiological changes.

permissive parents Parents who are less controlling and behave with a nonpunishing and accepting attitude toward their children's impulses, desires, and actions. They consult with their children about policy decisions, make few demands, and tend to use reason rather than direct power.

person perception Seeing someone and then forming impressions and making judgments about that person's likability and the kind of person he or she is, such as guessing his or her intentions, traits, and behaviors.

person schemas Social schemas that include our judgments about the traits that we and others possess.

person-situation interaction The interaction between a person's traits and the effects of being in a particular situation, which, according to Walter Mischel, determines the person's behavior.

personal attributions See internal attributions.

personal fable Adolescents' belief that they are invulnerable, unique, and special.

personal factors According to social cognitive theory, factors that include our emotional makeup and our biological and genetic influences and that help to shape our personalities.

personal identity See identity.

personality A combination of long-lasting and distinctive behaviors, thoughts, motives, and emotions that typify how we react and adapt to other people and situations. See also theory of personality.

personality development See social development.

personality disorder Any psychological disorder characterized by inflexible, long-standing, maladaptive traits that cause significantly impaired functioning or great distress in one's personal and social life.

personality tests Tests used to measure a person's observable traits and behaviors and unobservable characteristics. In addition, some are used to identify personality problems and psychological disorders, as well as to predict how a person might behave in the future. Objective personality tests (self-report questionnaires), such as the MMPI, consist of specific statements or questions to which the person responds with specific answers; projective tests, such as the Rorschach inkblot test, have no set answers but consist of ambiguous stimuli that a person interprets or makes up stories about.

pessimism A relatively stable personality trait that leads one to believe and expect that bad things will happen. It is one of the personality factors associated with increased stress levels and chances of developing psychosomatic symptoms. See also optimism.

PET See positron emission tomography.

phallic stage Sigmund Freud's third psychosexual stage, lasting from the ages of about 3 to 6 years, in which the infant's pleasure seeking is centered on the genitals.

phantom limb The experience of sensations and feelings coming from a limb that has been amputated. The sensations and feelings are extremely vivid, as if the amputated limb were still present.

phenomenological perspective The idea that our perspective of the world, whether or not it is accurate, becomes our reality. This idea is stressed in humanistic theories.

phenothiazines The first group of drugs to reduce schizophrenic symptoms, such as delusions and hallucinations. Discovered in the early 1950s, the phenothiazines operate by blocking or reducing the effects of the neurotransmitter dopamine.

phi movement The illusion that stationary lights are moving. The illusion of movement—today called apparent motion—is created by flashing closely positioned stationary lights at regular intervals.

phobia An anxiety disorder characterized by an intense and irrational fear that is out of proportion to the danger elicited by the object or situation. In comparison, fear is a realistic response to a threatening situation.

phonemes The basic sounds of consonants and vowels.

phonology Rules specifying how we make the meaningful sounds used by a particular language.

photographic memory The ability to form sharp, detailed visual images after examining a picture or page for a short period of time and to recall the entire image at a later date.

physiological dependence A change in the nervous system, so that a person now needs to take the drug to prevent the occurrence of painful withdrawal symptoms.

Piaget's cognitive stages Four different stages—the sensorimotor, preoperational, concrete operations, and formal operations stages—each of which is more advanced than the preceding stage because it involves new reasoning and thinking abilities.

pica A behavioral disorder in which individuals eat inedible objects or unhealthy substances. Pica can lead to serious physical problems, including lead poisoning, intestinal blockage, and parasites, and is most often seen in individuals with intellectual impairment.

pinna As part of the outer ear, an oval structure that protrudes from the side of the head. The function of the pinna is to pick up sound waves and send them down a long, narrow tunnel called the auditory canal.

pitch Our subjective experience of how low or high a sound is. The brain calculates pitch from the speed (frequency) of the sound waves. The frequency of sound waves is measured in cycles, which refers to how many sound waves occur in 1 second.

pituitary gland A key component of the endocrine system that hangs directly below the hypothalamus, to which it is connected by a narrow stalk. Its anterior section regulates growth and controls much of the endocrine system, while its posterior section regulates water and salt balance.

place theory The theory that the brain perceives the pitch of a sound by receiving information about where on the basilar membrane a given sound vibrates the most; it applies to medium and higher pitches.

placebo An intervention—taking a pill, receiving an injection, or undergoing an operation—that resembles medical therapy but that, in fact, has no medical effects.

placebo effect A change in the patient's illness that is attributable to an imagined treatment rather than to a medical treatment.

placenta An organ that connects the blood supply of the mother to that of the fetus. The placenta acts like a filter, allowing oxygen and nutrients to pass through while keeping out certain toxic or harmful substances.

pleasure principle The satisfaction of drives and avoidance of pain, without concern for moral restrictions or society's regulations. According to Sigmund Freud, this is the id's operating principle.

polygraph tests Tests based on the theory that, if a person tells a lie, he or she will feel some emotion, such as guilt or fear. Feeling guilty or fearful will usually be accompanied by involuntary physiological responses, which are difficult to suppress or control and can be measured with a machine called a polygraph.

polymorphic gene A gene that has more than one version—for example, dominant and recessive.

pons A bridge that connects the spinal cord with the brain and parts of the brain with one another. Cells in the pons manufacture chemicals involved in sleep.

population Every person that exists in the world who match the criteria that researchers are interested in studying.

positive psychology The scientific study of optimal human functioning, focusing on the strengths and virtues that enable individuals and communities to thrive. It aims to better understand the positive, adaptive, and fulfilling aspects of human life.

positive punishment The presentation of an aversive stimulus (for example, spanking) after a response. The aversive stimulus decreases the chances that the response will recur.

positive regard Love, sympathy, warmth, acceptance, and respect, which we crave from family, friends, and people who are important to us.

positive reinforcement The presentation of a stimulus that increases the probability of a behavior's recurrence.

positive symptoms of schizophrenia Symptoms that reflect a distortion of normal functions. Distorted thinking results in delusions, distorted perceptions result in hallucinations, and distorted language results in disorganized speech.

positron emission tomography (PET) A technique to measure the function of the living brain. A slightly radioactive solution is injected into the blood, and the amount of radiation absorbed by the brain cells is measured. Very active brain cells—neurons—absorb more radioactive solution than less active ones. A computer transforms the different levels of absorption into colors that indicate the activity of neurons. The colors red and yellow indicate maximum activity of neurons; blue and green indicate minimal activity.

postconventional level Lawrence Kohlberg's highest level of moral reasoning, at which moral decisions are made after carefully thinking about all the alternatives and striking a balance between human rights and the laws of society.

posterior pituitary The rear part of the pituitary gland, a key component of the endocrine system. It regulates water and salt balance.

posthypnotic amnesia The inability to remember what happened during hypnosis, prompted by a specific suggestion from the hypnotist.

posthypnotic suggestion A suggestion given to a person during hypnosis about performing a particular behavior, in response to a predetermined cue, when the person comes out of hypnosis.

posttraumatic stress disorder (PTSD) A disabling condition that results from direct personal experience of an event that involves actual or threatened death or serious injury or from witnessing such an event or hearing that such an event has happened to a family member or close friend.

precognition The ability to foretell events.

preconventional level Lawrence Kohlberg's lowest level of moral reasoning. It consists of two stages: At stage 1, moral decisions are based primarily on fear of punishment or the need to be obedient; at stage 2, moral reasoning is guided most by satisfaction of one's self-interest, which may involve making bargains.

prejudice An unfair, biased, or intolerant attitude toward another group of people.

premature ejaculation Persistent or recurrent absence of voluntary control over ejaculation; the male ejaculates with minimal sexual stimulation before, upon, or shortly after penetration and before he wishes to. Also called rapid ejaculation.

prenatal period The period from conception to birth, which lasts about 266 days (about nine months). It is divided into three phases: germinal, embryonic, and fetal. During the prenatal period, a single cell will divide and grow to form 200 billion cells.

preoperational stage The second of Jean Piaget's cognitive stages, lasting from the ages of about 2 to 7 years. During this stage, children learn to use symbols, such as words or mental images, to think about things that are not present and to help solve simple problems.

preparedness The innate or biological tendency of animals and humans to recognize, attend to, and store certain cues over others, as well as to associate some combinations of conditioned and unconditioned stimuli more easily than others. Also called prepared learning.

primacy effect Better recall, or improvement in retention, of information that is presented at the beginning of a task.

primary appraisal Our initial, subjective evaluation of a situation, in which we balance the demands of a potentially stressful situation against our ability to meet them.

primary auditory cortex An area at the top edge of the temporal lobe that transforms nerve impulses (electrical signals) into basic auditory sensations, such as meaningless sounds and tones of varying pitch and loudness. Next, it sends impulses (sensations) to the auditory association areas.

primary reinforcer A stimulus, such as food, water, or sex, that is innately satisfying and requires no learning on the part of an individual to become pleasurable.

primary sexual characteristics Body structures that are specific to each sex and are related to reproduction. For instance, males have testes and females have ovaries.

primary visual cortex A small area, located at the back of each occipital lobe, that receives electrical signals from receptors in the eyes and transforms these signals into meaningless, basic visual sensations, such as lights, lines, shadows, colors, and textures.

principle of bidirectionality The idea that a child's behaviors influence how his or her parents respond and, in turn, the parents' behaviors influence how the child responds.

proactive interference A forgetting process in which information that we learned earlier blocks or disrupts the retrieval of related information that was learned later.

problem-focused coping Solving a problem by seeking information, changing our own behavior, or taking whatever action is necessary.

problem solving Searching for some rule, plan, or strategy in order to reach a certain goal that is currently out of reach.

procedural memory Memories of performing motor or perceptual tasks (playing sports), carrying out habitual behaviors (brushing teeth), and responding to stimuli because of classical conditioning (fearing spiders). We cannot retrieve these memories, and we are not conscious of them. Also called nondeclarative memory.

processing speed The rate at which we encode information into long-term memory or recall or retrieve information from long-term memory; this rate slows down after age 60.

procrastination The tendency to always put off completing a task to the point of feeling anxious or uncomfortable about one's delay.

prodigy A child who shows unusual talent, ability, or genius at a very early age and does not have an intellectual disability. A small percentage of autistic children, who have some degree of intellectual impairment, may also show unusual artistic or mathematical abilities; they are called savants.

progressive relaxation An exercise in which the major muscle groups of the body are tensed and relaxed repeatedly until the individual can relax any group of muscles at will.

projection Unconsciously attributing unacceptable traits, feelings, or thoughts to others.

projective tests Tests in which an individual is presented with some type of ambiguous stimulus—such as a meaningless object or ambiguous photo—and then asked to make up a story about the stimulus. The assumption is that the person will project conscious or unconscious feelings, needs, and motives in his or her responses.

prosocial behavior Any behavior that benefits others or has positive social consequences. Also called helping.

prosopagnosia A condition marked by a difficulty or inability to recognize faces.

prototype An "average" looking object, such as a person or animal, that you use to identify new objects. Based on many experiences, you develop prototypes of many different objects, persons, and animals. For example, your prototype of a dog would be a mental image of any particular animal that has *average features* (nose, tail, ears, height, weight).

prototype theory The idea that we form a concept by first constructing a prototype of an object—that is, a mental image based on its average characteristics. Once we have formed a set of prototypes, we identify new objects by matching them against our prototypes.

proximity rule A perceptual rule stating that, in organizing stimuli, objects that are physically close to one another will be grouped together.

proximodistal principle The rule that parts closer to the center of the infant's body develop before parts that are farther away.

psi The processing of information or transfer of energy by methods that have no known physical or biological mechanisms and that seem to stretch the laws of physics.

psilocybin A hallucinogen, the active ingredient in magic mushrooms. Low doses produce pleasant and relaxed feelings; medium doses produce distortions in the perception of time and space; and high doses produce distortions in perceptions and body image and sometimes hallucinations.

psychiatrist A physician (medical doctor) who has an MD or DO and has taken a psychiatric residency, which involves additional training in pharmacology, neurology, psychopathology, and therapeutic techniques. In diagnosing the possible causes of abnormal behaviors, psychiatrists focus on biological factors; they tend to view mental disorders as diseases and to treat them with drugs. Psychiatrists who receive additional training in psychoanalytic institutes are called psychoanalysts.

psychoactive drugs Chemicals that affect the nervous system and, as a result, may alter consciousness and awareness, influence sensations and perceptions, and modify moods and cognitive processes. Some are legal (coffee, alcohol, and tobacco), and some are illegal (marijuana, heroin, cocaine, and LSD).

psychoanalysis A form of psychotherapy based on the idea that each of us has an unconscious part that contains ideas, memories, desires, or thoughts that have been hidden or repressed because they are psychologically dangerous or threatening to our self-concept. To protect our self-concept, we automatically build a mental barrier that we cannot voluntarily remove. But the presence of these thoughts and desires gives rise to unconscious conflicts, which, in turn, can result in psychological and physical symptoms and mental disorders.

psychoanalyst *See* psychiatrist.

psychoanalytic approach A psychological viewpoint that stresses the influence of unconscious fears, desires, and motivations on thoughts and behaviors and also the impact of childhood experiences on the development of later personality traits and psychological problems. As applied to mental disorders, this approach traces their origin to unconscious conflicts or problems with unresolved conflicts at one or more of Sigmund Freud's psychosexual stages. Treatment of mental disorders, in this approach, centers on the therapist's helping the patient to identify and resolve his or her unconscious conflicts.

psychobiology The scientific study of the physical and chemical changes that occur during stress, learning, and emotions, as well as how our genetic makeup and nervous system interact with our environments and influence our behaviors.

psychodynamic theory of personality A personality theory that emphasizes the importance of early childhood experiences, repressed thoughts that we cannot voluntarily access, and the conflicts between conscious and unconscious forces that influence our thoughts and behaviors.

psychokinesis The ability to exert mind over matter—for example, by moving objects without touching them.

psychological assessment The use of various tools—including psychological tests and interviews—to measure characteristics, traits, or abilities in order to understand behavior and predict future performance or behavior.

psychological dependence Feeling the need to experience a drug's effects in order to achieve psychological or emotional well-being.

psychological factors Performance anxiety, sexual trauma, guilt, or failure to communicate, all of which may lead to sexual problems.

psychological sex factors Factors involved in the development of a gender identity, gender role, and sexual orientation, as well as in difficulties in sexual performance or enjoyment.

psychologist An individual who has completed four to five years of postgraduate education and has obtained a PhD, PsyD, or EdD in psychology; in some states, an individual with a master's degree.

psychology The systematic, scientific study of behaviors and mental processes.

psychometric approach An approach to the assessment of intelligence that measures or quantifies cognitive abilities or factors that are thought to be involved in intellectual performance.

psychometrics A subarea of psychology that is concerned with developing psychological tests that assess an individual's abilities, skills, beliefs, and personality traits in a wide range of settings—school, the workplace, or a clinic.

psychoneuroimmunology The study of the relationship among the central nervous system, the endocrine system, and psychosocial factors such as cognitive reactions to stressful events, the individual's personality traits, and social influences.

psychosexual stages According to Sigmund Freud, five developmental periods—the oral, anal, phallic, latency, and genital stages—each marked by potential conflict between parent and child. The conflicts arise as the child seeks pleasure from different bodily areas associated with sexual feelings

(erogenous zones). Freud emphasized that the child's first five years were most important in social and personality development.

psychosocial factors for depression Underlying personality traits, amount of social support, and ability to deal with stressful life events—these factors are believed to combine and interact with predisposing biological factors to either increase or decrease a person's vulnerability to the development and maintenance of a mood disorder.

psychosocial hunger factors Learned associations between food and other stimuli, such as snacking while watching television; sociocultural influences, such as pressures to be thin; and various personality problems, such as depression, dislike of body image, or low self-esteem.

psychosocial stages According to Erik Erikson, the eight developmental periods during which an individual's primary goal is to satisfy desires associated with social needs. The eight periods are associated, respectively, with issues of trust, autonomy, initiative, industry, identity, intimacy, generativity, and ego integrity.

psychosomatic symptoms Real, physical, and often painful symptoms, such as headaches, muscle pain, and stomach problems, that are caused by psychological factors, such as worry, tension, and anxiety.

psychotherapy Approaches to treating psychological problems that share three characteristics: verbal interaction between therapist and client(s), the development of a supportive relationship during which a client can bring up and discuss traumatic or bothersome experiences that may have led to current problems, and analysis of the client's experiences and/or suggested ways for the client to deal with or overcome his or her problems.

PTSD *See* posttraumatic stress disorder.

puberty A developmental period, corresponding to the ages of 9 to 17 years, when the individual experiences significant biological changes and, as a result, develops secondary sexual characteristics and reaches sexual maturity.

punishment A consequence that occurs after a behavior that decreases the likelihood that that behavior will recur.

pupil The round opening at the front of the eye that allows light waves to pass through into the eye's interior.

quantum personality change A sudden and radical or dramatic shift in personality, beliefs, or values.

questionnaire A method for obtaining information by asking individuals to read a list of written questions and to check off, or rate their preference for, specific answers.

random selection A research design in which each participant in a sample population has an equal chance of being selected for the experiment.

range The difference or interval between the highest and lowest values in a distribution.

rape Any kind of penetration of another person, regardless of gender, without the victim's consent.

rape myths Misinformed false beliefs about women that are frequently held by rapists as well as by other men.

rationalization Inventing acceptable excuses for behaviors that make us feel anxious.

reaction formation A defense mechanism that involves substituting behaviors, thoughts, or feelings that are the direct opposite of unacceptable ones.

reaction range The extent to which traits, abilities, or IQ scores may increase or decrease as a result of interaction with environmental factors.

reaction time The rate at which we respond (see, hear, move) to some stimulus; this rate slows down noticeably after age 60.

reactive attachment disorder A psychiatric illness characterized by serious problems in emotional attachments to others, beginning before age 5. Symptoms include resisting comfort and affection by parents, being superficially engaging and overly friendly with strangers, having poor peer relationships, and engaging in destructive behaviors.

real motion Our perception of any stimulus or object that actually moves in space; the opposite of apparent motion.

real self According to Carl Rogers, the self that is based on our actual experiences and represents how we really see ourselves; its complement is the ideal self.

reality principle A policy of satisfying a wish or desire only if a socially acceptable outlet is available. According to Sigmund Freud, this is the ego's operating principle.

reasoning A mental process that involves using and applying knowledge to solve problems, make plans or decisions, and achieve goals.

recall Retrieval of previously learned information without the aid of or with very few external cues.

recency effect Better recall, or improvement in retention, of information that is presented at the end of a task.

recessive gene A type of polymorphic gene that determines the development of a specific trait only when it is inherited from both parents.

reciprocal determinism The idea that personality development is shaped primarily by the interactions among three forces: environmental conditions, cognitive-personal factors, and behavior, which all influence how we evaluate, interpret, organize, and apply information.

recognition The identification of previously learned information with the help of external cues.

reflex An unlearned, involuntary reaction to some stimulus. The neural connections of the network underlying a reflex are prewired by genetic instructions.

reinforcement A consequence that occurs after behavior and increases the likelihood that that behavior will recur.

reinforcer A stimulus that increases the likelihood that the response preceding it will occur again.

relative size In three-dimensional vision, a monocular depth cue that results when we expect two objects to be the same size and they are not. In that case, the larger of the objects will appear closer, and the smaller will appear to be farther away.

reliability The extent to which a test is consistent: A person's score on a test at one point in time should be similar to the score obtained by the same person on a similar test at a later point in time.

REM behavior disorder A disorder, usually found in older people, in which the voluntary muscles are not paralyzed during REM sleep; sleepers can and do act out their dreams.

REM (rapid eye movement) sleep The stage of sleep in which our eyes move rapidly back and forth behind closed eyelids. This stage makes up 20% of our sleep time; in a normal night, we experience five or six periods of REM sleep, each one lasting 15–45 minutes. REM brain waves, which have a high frequency and a low amplitude, look very similar to the beta waves that are recorded when we are wide awake and alert; the body's voluntary muscles, however, are paralyzed. Dreams usually occur during REM sleep.

REM rebound The tendency of individuals to spend proportionately longer in the REM stage of sleep after they have been deprived of REM sleep on previous nights.

repair theory A theory of sleep suggesting that activities during the day deplete key factors in the brain or body that are replenished or repaired by sleep.

representative heuristic The idea that we have a tendency to assume that an object or event belongs to a particular category because of how similar it is to the typical prototype of that category.

repression According to Sigmund Freud, a mental process that automatically hides emotionally threatening or anxiety-producing information in the unconscious. Repressed information cannot be retrieved voluntarily, but something may cause it to be released and to reenter the person's consciousness at a later time.

resiliency Various personal, family, or environmental factors that compensate for increased life stresses so that expected problems do not develop.

resistance In psychotherapy, especially psychoanalysis, the client's reluctance to work through or deal with feelings or to recognize unconscious conflicts and repressed thoughts.

resistance stage The second stage in the general adaptation syndrome. In reaction to continued stress, most physiological responses return to normal levels, but the body uses up great stores of energy.

resting state A condition in which the axon, like a battery, has a charge, or potential, because the axon membrane separates positive ions on the outside from negative ions on the inside.

reticular formation A column of brain cells that arouses and alerts the forebrain and prepares it to receive information from all the senses. It plays an important role in keeping the forebrain alert and producing a state of wakefulness. Animals or humans whose reticular formation is seriously damaged lapse into permanent unconsciousness or coma.

retina A thin film, located at the very back of the eyeball, that contains cells, called photoreceptors, that are extremely sensitive to light. The retina consists of three layers, the third and deepest of which contains two kinds of photoreceptors, rods and cones, that perform transduction; that is, they change light waves into nerve impulses.

retinal disparity A binocular depth cue that depends on the distance between the two eyes. Because of their different positions, the two eyes receive slightly different images. The difference between these images is the retinal disparity. The brain interprets large retinal disparity to mean a close object and small retinal disparity to mean a distant object.

retrieval The process of getting or recalling information that has been placed into short-term or long-term storage.

retrieval cues Mental reminders that we create by forming vivid mental images of information or associating new information with information that we already know. Forgetting can result from not taking the time to create effective retrieval cues.

retroactive interference A forgetting process in which information that we learned later blocks or disrupts the retrieval of related information that we learned earlier.

reuptake The process by which some neurotransmitters, such as dopamine, are removed from the synapse by being transported back into the end bulbs.

reward/pleasure center The part of the brain that includes the nucleus accumbens and ventral tegmental area and involves several neurotransmitters, especially dopamine. Combined with other brain areas, it forms a neural circuit that produces rewarding and pleasurable feelings.

rods Photoreceptors that contain the chemical rhodopsin, which is activated by small amounts of light. Because rods are extremely light sensitive, they allow us to see in dim light but to see only black, white, and shades of gray.

role schemas Social schemas based on the jobs people perform or the social positions they hold.

Rorschach inkblot test A projective test used to assess personality in which a person is shown a series of ten inkblots and then asked to describe what he or she sees in each.

rules of organization Rules identified by Gestalt psychologists that specify how our brains combine and organize individual pieces or elements into a meaningful whole—that is, a perception.

SAD *See* seasonal affective disorder.

salvia A drug that causes uncontrollable laughter and vivid hallucinations. Salvia's chemical keys are similar to that of endorphins.

sample The portion of the population selected to participate in a research study.

savants Autistic individuals who show some incredible memory, music, or drawing talent. They represent about 10% of the total number of autistics.

schedule of reinforcement In conditioning, a program or rule that determines how and when a response will be followed by a reinforcer.

schemas Organized mental or cognitive lists that, like computer files, contain knowledge about people, events, and concepts. Because schemas influence which stimuli we attend to, how we interpret stimuli, and how we respond to stimuli, they can bias and distort our thoughts, perceptions, and behaviors. *See also:* event schemas, gender schemas, person schemas, role schemas, and self schemas.

schizophrenia A serious mental disturbance that lasts at least six months and includes at least two of the following symptoms: delusions, hallucinations, disorganized speech, grossly disorganized behavior, and decreased emotional expression. These symptoms interfere with personal or social functioning. *See also* Type I and Type II schizophrenia.

schizotypical personality disorder A disorder characterized by acute discomfort in close relationships, distortions in thinking, and eccentric behavior. It is found in 3–5% of the population.

scientific method A multistep technique of gathering information and answering questions so that errors and biases are minimized.

scripts *See* event schemas.

seasonal affective disorder (SAD) A pattern of depressive symptoms that cycle with the seasons, typically beginning in fall or winter. The depression is accompanied by feelings of lethargy, excessive sleepiness, overeating, weight gain, and craving for carbohydrates.

secondary appraisal Deciding what we can do to deal with a potentially stressful situation. We can choose some combination of problem-focused coping, which means doing something about the problem, and emotion-focused coping, which means dealing with our emotions.

secondary reinforcer Any stimulus that has acquired its reinforcing power through experience; secondary reinforcers are learned, for example, by being

paired with primary reinforcers or other secondary reinforcers.

secondary sexual characteristics Physical characteristics other than reproductive organs that differentiate males and females. *See also* female secondary sexual characteristics; male secondary sexual characteristics.

secure attachment An emotional bond characteristic of infants who use their parent as a safe home base from which they can wander off and explore their environments.

self How we see or describe ourselves; also called self-concept. The self is made up of many self-perceptions, abilities, personality characteristics, and behaviors that are organized so as to be consistent with one another.

self-actualization Our inherent tendency to reach our true potentials. The concept of self-actualization, developed by Abraham Maslow, is central to humanistic theories.

self-actualization theory *See* self theory.

self-actualizing tendency An inborn tendency for us to develop all of our capacities in ways that best maintain and benefit our lives.

self-concept *See* self.

self-determination theory A theory stating that as we aim to fulfill our basic needs, which include the need to feel autonomous, competent, and related to others, we experience either autonomous or controlled motivation.

self-efficacy Our personal beliefs regarding how capable we are of exercising control over events in our lives, such as completing specific tasks and behaviors.

self-esteem How much an individual likes himself or herself; it includes feelings of self-worth, attractiveness, and social competence.

self-fulfilling prophecy A situation in which a person has a strong belief or makes a statement (prophecy) about a future behavior and then acts, usually unknowingly, to fulfill or carry out that behavior.

self-handicapping A tendency to engage in tactics that are likely to fail and then to use those tactics as excuses for failures in performance, activities, or achieving goals.

self-identity *See* identity.

self-perception theory The idea, developed by Daryl Bem, that we first observe or perceive our own behavior and then, as a result, change our attitudes.

self-report questionnaires *See* objective personality tests.

self schemas Social schemas that contain personal information about ourselves. They can influence how we behave as well as what we perceive and remember.

self-serving bias Attributing our successes to our dispositions or personality traits and our failures to the situations.

self theory Carl Rogers's humanistic theory, based on two major assumptions: that personality development is guided by each person's unique self-actualization tendency; and that each of us has a personal need for positive regard.

semantic memory A type of declarative memory that involves factual knowledge about the world, concepts, word definitions, and language rules.

semantics A set of rules that specify the meanings of words or phrases when they appear in various sentences or contexts.

semicircular canals Structures of the vestibular system in the inner ear that resemble bony arches and are set at different angles. Each canal is filled with fluid that moves in response to the movement of the head and aids in sensing the position of the head and maintaining balance.

sensation Our first awareness of some outside stimulus; relatively meaningless bits of information that result when the brain processes electrical signals that come from the sense organs.

sensation seeker Someone who needs more arousal than the average person. Sensation seekers look to engage in highly stimulating sensory experiences, such as mountain climbing, bungee jumping, skydiving, and drug use.

sensitive period *See* critical period.

sensorimotor stage The first of Jean Piaget's cognitive stages, lasting from birth to about age 2 years. During this stage, infants interact with and learn about their environments by relating their sensory experiences (such as hearing and seeing) to their motor actions (mouthing and grasping).

sensory development The growth of our senses—sight, hearing, touch, smell, and taste—beginning during the prenatal period and continuing on through childhood.

sensory memory An initial memory process that receives and holds environmental information in its raw form for a brief period of time, from an instant to several seconds.

sensory neurons *See* afferent neurons.

sentences The fourth stage in acquiring language, which begins at about 4 years of age. Sentences range from three to eight words in length and indicate a growing knowledge of the rules of grammar.

separation anxiety An infant's distress—as indicated by loud protests, crying, and agitation—whenever his or her parents temporarily leave.

serial position effect To better recall information that is presented at the beginning and end of a body of information, as opposed to the middle.

set point A certain level of body fat (adipose tissue) that our body strives to maintain constant throughout our lives; the set point is an inherited characteristic.

sex chromosome The sperm or the egg. Each contains only 23 chromosomes, on which are the genes bearing the instructions that determine the sex of the child.

sex (gender) differences in the brain Structural or functional differences in cognitive, behavioral, or brain processes that arise from being male or female.

sex hormones Chemicals, secreted by glands, that circulate in the bloodstream and influence the brain, other body organs, and behaviors. The major male sex hormones secreted by the testes are androgens, such as testosterone; the major female sex hormones secreted by the ovaries are estrogens.

sexual dysfunctions Problems of sexual arousal or orgasm that interfere with adequate functioning during sexual behavior.

sexual orientation A person's pattern of primary sexual arousal: by members of his or her own sex, the opposite sex, or both sexes. Also called sexual preference.

shape constancy Our tendency to see an object as remaining the same shape when viewed from different angles—that is, despite considerable change in the shape of its image on the retina.

shaping In operant conditioning, a procedure in which an experimenter successively reinforces behaviors that lead up to or approximate the desired behavior.

short-term dynamic psychotherapy A shortened version of psychoanalysis. It emphasizes a limited time for treatment (20 to 30 sessions) and focuses on limited goals, such as solving a relatively well-defined problem. Therapists take an active and directive role by identifying and discussing the client's problems, resolving issues of transference, interpreting the patient's behaviors, and offering an opportunity for the patient to foster changes in behavior and thinking that will result in more active coping and an improved self-image.

short-term memory A process that can hold a limited amount of information—an average of seven items—for a short time (2–30 seconds), which can be lengthened if you rehearse the information.

shyness A feeling of distress that comes from being tense, stressed, or awkward in social situations and from worrying about and fearing rejection.

similarity rule A perceptual rule stating that, in organizing stimuli, we group together elements that appear similar.

simplicity rule A perceptual rule stating that stimuli are organized in the simplest way possible.

single-word stage The second stage in acquiring language, which begins when the child is about 1 year old. Infants say single words that usually refer to what they can see, hear, or feel.

situational attributions *See* external attributions.

size constancy Our tendency to perceive objects as remaining the same size even when their images on the retina are continuously growing or shrinking.

skewed distributions Distributions in which more data fall toward one side of the scale than toward the other.

Skinner box Used in operant conditioning, a small enclosure that is automated to record an animal's bar presses and deliver food pellets as a consequence. The Skinner box is an efficient way to study how an animal's ongoing behaviors may be modified by changing the consequences of what happens after a bar press.

sleep A condition in which we pass through five different stages, each with its own level of consciousness, awareness, responsiveness, and physiological arousal. In the deepest stage of sleep, we enter a state that borders on unconsciousness.

sleep apnea A condition characterized by a cycle in which a sleeper stops breathing for intervals of 10 seconds or longer, wakes up briefly, resumes breathing, and returns to sleep. This cycle can leave apnea sufferers exhausted during the day but oblivious to the cause of their tiredness. It is more common among habitual snorers.

sleepwalking Walking or carrying out behaviors while still asleep. Sleepwalkers generally are clumsy and have poor coordination but can avoid objects; they can engage in very limited conversations. Sleepwalking behaviors can include dressing, eating, performing bathroom functions, and even driving a car. Sleepwalking usually occurs during stage 3 or stage 4 (delta) sleep.

social cognition The mental processes involved in the ways in which people perceive, think about, remember, and respond to other individuals or groups.

social cognitive learning A form of learning that results from watching, imitating, and modeling and does not require the observer to perform any observable behavior or receive any observable reward. Formerly called observational learning.

social cognitive theory The theory that grew out of the research of a number of psychologists—Julian Rotter, Albert Bandura, and Walter Mischel—that says that personality development is primarily shaped by three forces: environmental conditions, cognitive-personal factors, and behavior, which all interact to influence how we evaluate, interpret, organize, and apply information. *See also* Bandura's social cognitive theory.

social comparison theory The idea that we are driven to compare ourselves to others who are similar to us, so that we can measure the correctness of our attitudes and beliefs. According to Leon Festinger, this drive motivates us to join groups.

social development How a person develops a sense of self or self-identity, develops relationships with others, and develops the skills that are useful in social interactions.

social facilitation An increase in performance in the presence of a crowd.

social inhibition A decrease in performance in the presence of a crowd.

social needs Needs that are acquired through learning and experience.

social neuroscience An emerging area of research that examines social behavior by combining biological and social approaches. It focuses on understanding how social behavior influences the brain, and vice versa.

social norms approach Relating to abnormality, the idea that a behavior is considered abnormal if it deviates greatly from accepted social standards, values, or norms.

social phobias Irrational, marked, and continuous fear of performing in social situations. The individuals fear that they will humiliate or embarrass themselves.

social psychology A broad field whose goals are to understand and explain how our thoughts, feelings, perceptions, and behaviors are influenced by interactions with others. It includes the study of stereotypes, prejudices, attitudes, conformity, group behaviors, and aggression.

social role theory The theory that emphasizes the influence of social and cultural processes on how we interpret, organize, and use information. Applied to gender roles, it says that mothers, fathers, teachers, grandparents, friends, and peers expect, respond to, and reward different behaviors in boys than in girls. Under the influence of this differential treatment, boys learn a gender role that is different from girls'.

socially oriented group A group in which members are primarily concerned about fostering and maintaining social relationships among the members of the group.

sociocognitive theory of hypnosis The idea that the impressive effects of hypnosis are due to social influences and pressures as well as the individual's personal abilities. *See also* altered state theory of hypnosis.

sociocultural approach The study of the influence of social and cultural factors on psychological and behavioral functioning.

sodium pump A chemical transport process that picks up any sodium ions that enter the axon's chemical gates and returns them back outside. In this way, the sodium pump is responsible for keeping the axon charged by returning and keeping sodium ions outside the axon membrane.

somatic nervous system A network of nerves that are connected either to sensory receptors or to muscles that you can move voluntarily, such as muscles in your limbs, back, neck, and chest. Nerves in the somatic nervous system usually contain two kinds of fibers: afferent, or sensory, fibers that carry information from sensory receptors in the skin, muscles, and other organs to the spinal cord and brain; and efferent, or motor, fibers that carry information from the brain and spinal cord to the muscles.

somatization disorder A somatoform disorder that begins before age 30, lasts several years, and is characterized by multiple symptoms—including pain, gastrointestinal, sexual, and neurological symptoms—that have no physical causes but are triggered by psychological problems or distress.

somatoform disorder A pattern of recurring, multiple, and significant bodily (somatic) complaints that extend over several years. The physical symptoms (pain, vomiting, paralysis, blindness) are not under voluntary control, have no known physical causes, and are believed to be caused by psychological factors.

somatosensory cortex A narrow strip of the cortex that is located at the front edge of the parietal lobe and extends down its side. It processes sensory information about touch, location of limbs, pain, and temperature. The right somatosensory cortex receives information from the left side of the body, and vice versa.

sound waves The stimuli for hearing, or audition. Similar to ripples on a pond, sound waves travel through space with varying heights and speeds. Height, or amplitude, is the distance from the bottom to the top of a sound wave; speed, or frequency, is the number of sound waves that occur within 1 second.

source misattribution A memory error that results when a person has difficulty deciding which of two or more sources a memory came from: Was the source something the person saw or imagined, or was it a suggestion?

Spearman's general intelligence theory The theory that intelligence has a general mental ability factor, *g*, that represents what different cognitive tasks have in common. Also called *g*-factor theory.

specific phobias Unreasonable, marked, and persistent fears triggered by anticipation of, or exposure to, a specific object or situation (flying, heights, spiders, seeing blood). Formerly called simple phobias.

split-brain operation A procedure for moderating severe, uncontrollable seizures by cutting the corpus callosum, a wide band of nerve fibers that connects the right and left hemispheres.

spontaneous recovery In classical conditioning, the temporary occurrence of the conditioned response in the presence of the conditioned stimulus.

stage 1 In sleep, a stage lasting 1–7 minutes in which the individual gradually loses responsiveness to stimuli and experiences drifting thoughts and images. This stage marks the transition from wakefulness to sleep and is characterized by the presence of theta waves, which are lower in amplitude and frequency (4–7 cycles per second) than alpha waves.

stage 2 In sleep, the stage that marks the beginning of what we know as sleep; individuals awakened during stage 2 report having been asleep. EEG tracings show high-frequency bursts of brain activity called sleep spindles.

stages 3 and 4 About 30–45 minutes after drifting off to sleep, we pass rapidly through stage 3 and enter stage 4 sleep, a stage characterized by delta waves, which have very high amplitude and very low frequency (fewer than 4 cycles per second). Stage 4 is often considered the deepest stage of sleep because it is the most difficult from which to be awakened. During stage 4, heart rate, respiration, temperature, and blood flow to the brain are reduced, and there is a marked secretion of growth hormone, which controls many aspects of metabolism, physical growth, and brain development. This stage is also called slow-wave or delta sleep.

stages of sleep Distinctive changes in the electrical activity of the brain and accompanying physiological responses of the body that occur as we pass through different stages of sleep. *See also:* stage 1, stage 2, stages 3 and 4.

standard deviation A statistic that indicates how widely all the scores in a distribution are scattered above and below the mean.

Stanford-Binet Intelligence Scale A revision of the Binet-Simon Intelligence Scale that included the addition of some test items and translation into English, as well as a new scoring system to compute the final test score. *See also* Binet-Simon Intelligence Scale.

state-dependent learning The idea that we recall information more easily when we are in the same physiological or emotional state or setting as when we originally encoded the information.

statistical frequency approach In definitions of abnormality, the idea that a behavior may be considered abnormal if it occurs rarely or infrequently in relation to the behaviors of the general population.

statistical procedures In experiments, procedures used to determine whether differences observed in dependent variables (behaviors) are due to independent variables (treatment) or to error or chance occurrence.

statistics The tools researchers use to analyze and summarize large amounts of data.

stem cells Cells formed in the embryo that have the amazing capacity to change into any of the 220 cells that make up a human body, including skin, heart, liver, bones, and neurons.

stereotaxic procedure A method used for introducing material at a precise location within the brain. The patient's head is fixed in a holder, and a small hole is drilled through the skull. The holder has a syringe that can be precisely guided to a predetermined location in the brain.

stereotypes Widely held beliefs that people have certain traits because they belong to a particular group. Stereotypes are often inaccurate and frequently portray the members of less powerful, less controlling groups more negatively than members of more powerful, more controlling groups.

Sternberg's triangular theory of love The idea that love has three components: passion, intimacy, and commitment. Passion is feeling physically aroused and attracted to someone; intimacy is feeling close and connected to someone, through sharing and communicating; and commitment is pledging to nourish the feelings of love and actively maintain the relationship.

Sternberg's triarchic theory The idea that intelligence can be divided into three ways of gathering and processing information (*triarchic* means "three"): using analytical or logical thinking skills that are measured by traditional intelligence tests; using creative thinking and the ability to learn from experience; and using practical thinking skills that help a person adjust to, and cope with, his or her sociocultural environment.

stimulants Drugs, such as cocaine, amphetamines, caffeine, and nicotine, that increase activity in the nervous system and result in heightened alertness, arousal, and euphoria and decreased appetite and fatigue.

stimulus substitution The theory that, in classical conditioning, a neural bond or association is formed between the neutral stimulus and the unconditioned stimulus. After repeated trials, the neutral stimulus becomes the conditioned stimulus, which, in turn, substitutes for the unconditioned stimulus. Thereafter, the conditioned stimulus elicits a response similar to that of the unconditioned stimulus.

stomach The body organ that monitors the amount and kinds of nutrients our body needs to restore our depleted stores of fuel. In addition, after we eat a meal, the stomach's walls are distended and their stretch receptors signal fullness or time to stop eating.

storage The process of placing encoded information into relatively permanent mental storage for later recall.

stress The anxious or threatening feeling that comes when we interpret or appraise a situation as being more than our psychological resources can adequately handle.

stress management program A program to reduce anxiety, fear, and stressful experiences by using a variety of strategies to change three different aspects of our lives: thoughts (appraisals), behaviors, and physiological responses.

stressors Conditions or events that give rise to stress.

structuralism An early school of psychological thought that emphasized the study of the basic elements—primarily sensations and perceptions—that make up our conscious mental experiences. Structuralists argued that we can understand how perceptions are formed by breaking them down into smaller and smaller elements. Then we can analyze how these basic elements are recombined to form a perception. They believed that a perception is simply the sum of its parts.

structured interviews A research technique in which each individual is asked the same set of relatively narrow and focused questions, so that the same information is obtained from everyone.

subgoals In problem solving, a strategy by which the overall problem is broken down into separate parts that, when completed in order, will result in a solution.

sublimation A type of displacement in which threatening or forbidden desire, usually sexual, is redirected into socially acceptable forms.

subliminal stimulus A stimulus that has an amount of stimulus energy that is below a person's absolute threshold and consequently the person is not consciously aware of it.

substance abuse A maladaptive pattern of frequent and continued usage of a substance—a drug or medicine—that results in significant problems, such as failing to meet major obligations and having multiple legal, social, family, health, work, or interpersonal difficulties. These problems must occur repeatedly during a single 12-month period to be classified as substance abuse.

superego Sigmund Freud's third division of the mind, which develops from the ego during early childhood; its goal is to apply the moral values and standards of one's parents or caregivers and society in satisfying one's wishes.

superstitious behavior In operant conditioning, any behavior that increases in frequency because its occurrence is accidentally paired with the delivery of a reinforcer.

suprachiasmatic nucleus A sophisticated biological clock, located in the hypothalamus, that regulates a number of circadian rhythms, including the sleep-wake cycle. Suprachiasmatic cells are highly responsive to changes in light.

surface structure According to Noam Chomsky, the actual wording of a sentence, as it is spoken.

survey A method used to obtain information by asking many individuals—person to person, by telephone, or by mail or Internet—to answer a fixed set of questions about particular subjects.

sympathetic division The subdivision of the autonomic nervous system that is triggered by threatening or challenging physical or psychological stimuli, increasing the body's physiological arousal and preparing the body for action.

synapse An infinitely small space (20–30 billionths of a meter) between an end bulb and its adjacent body organ, muscle, or cell body; it is a space over which chemical messages are transmitted.

syntax *See* grammar.

systematic desensitization A technique of behavior therapy, based on classical conditioning, in which a person is gradually and progressively exposed to fearful or anxiety-evoking stimuli while practicing deep relaxation. Systematic desensitization is a form of counterconditioning because it replaces, or counters, fear and anxiety with relaxation.

t test An estimate of reliability that takes into account both the size of the mean difference and the variability in distributions.

taijin kyofusho (TKS) A mental disorder found only in Asian cultures, particularly Japan. This social phobia is characterized by a morbid fear of offending others through awkward social or physical behavior, such as making eye contact, blushing, giving off an offensive odor, having an unpleasant or tense facial expression, or having trembling hands.

tardive dyskinesia A condition characterized by the appearance of slow, involuntary, and uncontrollable rhythmic movements and rapid twitching of the mouth and lips, as well as unusual movements of the limbs. This condition is a side effect of the continued use of typical neuroleptics.

task-oriented group A group in which members have specific duties to complete.

taste One of our senses. Taste is called a chemical sense because the stimuli are various chemicals. On the surface of the tongue are receptors, called taste buds, for five basic tastes: sweet, salty, sour, bitter, and umami. The function of taste buds is transduction—transforming chemical reactions into nerve impulses.

taste-aversion learning The association of a particular sensory cue (smell, taste, sound, or sight) with an unpleasant response, such as nausea or vomiting, resulting in future avoidance of that particular sensory cue.

taste buds Onion-shaped structures on the tongue that are receptors for taste. Chemicals dissolved in the saliva activate the taste buds, which produce nerve impulses that eventually reach areas in the brain's parietal lobe. The brain transforms these nerve impulses into sensations of taste.

TAT *See* Thematic Apperception Test.

telegraphic speech A distinctive speech pattern observed during language acquisition in which the child omits articles, prepositions, and parts of verbs.

telemental health Psychological services that are provided remotely, via telephone, e-mail, or videoconferencing.

telepathy The ability to transfer one's thoughts to another person or to read the thoughts of others.

temperament An individual's distinctive pattern of mood and emotional behavior. This pattern appears early, is relatively stable and long-lasting, and is influenced in large part by genetic factors.

temporal lobe A segment of the brain located directly below the parietal lobe that is involved in hearing, speaking coherently, and understanding verbal and written material.

teratogen Any agent that can harm a developing fetus (causing deformities or brain damage). It might be a disease (such as genital herpes), a drug (such as alcohol), or another environmental agent (such as chemicals).

test anxiety A combination of physiological, emotional, and cognitive components that are caused by the stress of taking exams and that may interfere with a student's ability to think, reason, and plan.

testimonial A statement in support of a particular viewpoint based on personal experience.

testosterone The major male hormone, which stimulates the growth of genital organs and the development of secondary sexual characteristics.

texture gradient In three-dimensional vision, a monocular depth cue: Areas with sharp, detailed texture are interpreted as being closer, and those with less sharpness and detail as more distant.

thalamus A structure of the limbic system that is located in the middle of the forebrain and is involved in receiving sensory information, doing some initial processing, and then relaying the sensory information to appropriate areas of the cortex, including the somatosensory cortex, primary auditory cortex, and primary visual cortex.

Thematic Apperception Test (TAT) A personality test in which participants are asked to look at pictures of people in ambiguous situations and to make up stories about what the characters are thinking and feeling and what the outcome will be.

theory of evolution Charles Darwin's theory that different species arose from a common ancestor and that those species survived that were best adapted to meet the demands of their environments.

theory of linguistic relativity Benjamin Whorf's theory that the differences among languages result in differences in the ways people think of and perceive the world.

theory of personality An organized attempt to describe and explain how personalities develop and why personalities differ.

thinking Mental processes by which we form concepts, solve problems, and engage in creative activities. Sometimes referred to as reasoning.

threat appraisal Our conclusion that harm or loss has not yet taken place in a particular situation but we anticipate it in the near future.

threat simulation theory of dreams The idea that dreaming serves a biological function by repeatedly simulating events that are threatening in our waking lives so that our brain can practice how it perceives threats and we can rehearse our responses to these events.

three-stages model The model in which memory is divided into three sequential stages: sensory, short-term, and long-term memory.

threshold A point above which a stimulus is perceived and below which it is not perceived. *See also* absolute threshold.

thyroid A gland located in the neck that regulates metabolism through the secretion of hormones. It forms part of the endocrine system.

time-out In training children, a form of negative punishment in which reinforcing stimuli are removed after an undesirable response. This removal decreases the chances that the response will recur. In time-out, the child is told to sit quietly in the corner of a room or put in some other situation where there is no chance to obtain reinforcers or engage in pleasurable behaviors.

tip-of-the-tongue phenomenon The situation in which, despite making a great effort, we are temporarily unable to recall information that we absolutely know is in our memory.

TKS *See* taijin kyofusho.

TM *See* transcendental meditation.

TMS *See* transcranial magnetic stimulation.

tolerance The reaction of the body and brain to regular drug use, whereby the person has to take larger doses of the drug to achieve the same behavioral effect.

top-down processing When perception is guided by previous knowledge, experience, beliefs, or expectations to recognize the whole pattern. It's "top" first because we begin with brain processes. We use our cognitive processes to apply context to the information we are sensing.

touch The skin senses, which include temperature, pressure, and pain. Touch sensors change mechanical pressure or changes in temperature into nerve impulses that are sent to the brain for processing.

trait A relatively stable and enduring tendency to behave in a particular way.

trait theory An approach for analyzing the structure of personality by measuring, identifying, and classifying similarities and differences in personality characteristics or traits.

tranquilizers Depressant drugs (e.g., Xanax, Valium, and Ativan) that reduce anxiety and stress. Tranquilizers are relatively safe, but there is still risk for addiction and withdrawal symptoms. Large doses can be dangerous, especially when taken with alcohol or another depressant drug. Tranquilizers, like barbiturates, have the potential to suppress the central nervous system and consequently cause death.

transcendental meditation (TM) A meditation exercise in which individuals assume a comfortable position, close their eyes, and repeat and concentrate on a sound to help produce an altered state of consciousness.

transcranial magnetic stimulation (TMS) A noninvasive diagnostic technique that activates neurons by sending pulses of magnetic energy into the brain.

transduction The process by which a sense organ changes, or transforms, physical energy into electrical signals that become neural impulses, which may be sent to the brain for processing.

transference In psychotherapy, the process by which a client expresses strong emotions toward the therapist because the therapist substitutes for someone important in the client's life, such as the client's mother or father. Sigmund Freud first developed this concept.

transformational rules According to Noam Chomsky, procedures by which we convert our ideas from surface structures into deep structures and from deep structures back into surface structures.

transmitter A chemical messenger that transmits information between nerves and body organs, such as muscles and heart. *See also* neurotransmitters.

transsexualism *See* gender identity disorder.

triangular theory of love *See* Sternberg's triangular theory of love.

triarchic theory *See* Sternberg's triarchic theory.

trichromatic theory The idea that there are three different kinds of cones in the retina, and each cone contains one of three different light-sensitive chemicals, called opsins. Each opsin is most responsive to wavelengths that correspond to each of the three primary colors—blue, green, and red—from which all other colors can be mixed.

two-word combinations The third stage in acquiring language, which begins at about 2 years of age. The infant says strings of two words that express various actions ("Me play," "See boy") or relationships ("Hit ball," "Milk gone").

tympanic membrane The thin, taut membrane, commonly called the eardrum, that is the boundary between the outer ear and middle ear. When struck by sound waves, it vibrates and passes the vibrations to the ossicles.

Type A behavior A combination of personality traits that may be a risk factor for coronary heart disease. According to the original definition in the 1970s, these traits included an overly competitive and aggressive drive to achieve, a hostile attitude when frustrated, a habitual sense of time urgency, a rapid and explosive pattern of speaking, and workaholic tendencies; in contrast, type B behavior was easygoing, calm, relaxed, and patient. In the 1980s, the list of traits was reduced to being depressed, aggressively competitive, easily frustrated, anxious, and angry. In the 1990s, the list was reduced again, to frequent feelings of anger and hostility, which may or may not be publicly expressed. Currently, researchers conclude that individuals who either always show their anger and hostility or always suppress it have large increases in physiological arousal, which can have damaging effects on one's heart and health.

Type B behavior Behavior characterized as being easygoing, calm, relaxed, and patient.

Type D behavior Behavior characterized by chronic distress in terms of two emotional states: negative affectivity (worry, irritability, gloom) and social inhibition (shyness, being reserved, lack of self-assurance).

Type I schizophrenia A type of schizophrenia characterized by positive symptoms, such as hallucinations and delusions, which are distortions of normal functions. Individuals diagnosed with Type I schizophrenia have no intellectual impairment, good reaction to medication, and thus a good chance of recovery.

Type II schizophrenia A type of schizophrenia characterized by negative symptoms, such as dulled emotions and little inclination to speak, which are a loss of normal functions. Individuals diagnosed with Type II schizophrenia have intellectual impairment, poor reaction to medication, and thus a poor chance of recovery.

typical neuroleptic drugs Neuroleptics that primarily reduce the levels of the neurotransmitter dopamine. Two of the more common are phenothiazines (for example, Thorazine) and butrophenones (for example, haloperidol). These drugs primarily reduce positive symptoms but have little effect on negative symptoms.

unconditional positive regard The warmth, acceptance, and love that others show us because we are valued human beings even though we may behave in ways that disappoint them because they differ from their standards and values or the way they think.

unconditioned response (UCR) An unlearned, innate, involuntary physiological reflex that is elicited by the unconditioned stimulus.

unconditioned stimulus (UCS) A stimulus that triggers or elicits some physiological response, such as salivation or eye blink.

unconscious forces Wishes, desires, or thoughts that, because of their disturbing or threatening content, we automatically repress and cannot voluntarily access.

unconscious motivation A Freudian concept that refers to the influence of repressed thoughts, desires, or impulses on our conscious thoughts and behaviors.

unconsciousness Total lack of sensory awareness and loss of responsiveness to the environment. It may result from disease, trauma, a blow to the head, or general medical anesthesia.

underachievers Individuals who score relatively high on tests of ability or intelligence but perform more poorly than their scores would predict.

universal emotional expressions Specific inherited facial patterns or expressions that signal specific feelings or emotional states, such as a smile signaling a happy state.

uplifts Small, pleasurable, happy, and satisfying experiences that we have in our daily lives.

validity The extent to which a test measures what it is supposed to measure.

variable-interval schedule A conditioning schedule in which a reinforcer occurs following the first correct response after an average amount of time has passed.

variable-ratio schedule A conditioning schedule in which a reinforce is delivered after an average number of correct responses has occurred.

variance A measure of the variability within two distributions.

ventrolateral preoptic nucleus (VLPO) A group of cells in the hypothalamus that acts like a master switch for sleep. Turned on, the VLPO secretes a neurotransmitter (GABA) that turns off areas that keep the brain awake; turned off, the VLPO causes certain brain areas to become active and we wake up.

ventromedial hypothalamus A group of brain cells that regulates hunger by receiving signals from digestive organs to create feelings of satiety, or fullness.

vestibular system Three semicircular canals in the inner ear that sense the position of the head, keep the head upright, and maintain balance. Fluid in the semicircular canals moves in response to movements of the head, and sensors (hair cells) in the canals respond to the movement of the fluid.

virtual reality A perceptual experience—of being inside an object, moving through an environment, or carrying out some action—that is, in fact, entirely simulated by a computer.

visible spectrum The one particular segment of electromagnetic energy that we can see because these waves are the right length to stimulate receptors in the eye.

visual accommodation In the eye, the process of the lens bending to focus light waves on the retina.

visual agnosia A condition caused by damage to the visual association area. An individual with visual agnosia is unable to recognize some object, person, or color and yet is able to see and even describe parts of some visual stimulus.

visual association area An area of the brain, located next to the primary visual cortex, that transforms basic sensations, such as lights, lines, colors, and textures, into complete, meaningful visual perceptions, such as persons, objects, or animals.

visual cliff A glass tabletop with a checkerboard pattern over part of its surface; the remaining surface is clear glass with a checkerboard pattern several feet below, creating the illusion of a clifflike drop to the floor.

VLPO *See* ventrolateral preoptic nucleus.

vulnerability Psychological or environmental difficulties that make children more at risk for developing later personality, behavioral, or social problems.

Weber's law A psychophysics law stating that the increase in intensity of a stimulus needed to produce a just noticeable difference grows in proportion to the intensity of the initial stimulus.

Wechsler Adult Intelligence Scale (WAIS) and Wechsler Intelligence Scale for Children (WISC) Intelligence tests that are divided into various subtests. The verbal section contains a subtest of general information, a vocabulary subtest, and so forth. The performance section contains a subtest that involves arranging pictures in a meaningful order, one that requires assembling objects, and one that involves using codes. The verbal and performance scores are combined to give a single IQ score.

weight-regulating genes Genes that play a role in influencing appetite, body metabolism, and secretion of hormones (such as leptin) that regulate fat stores.

Wernicke's aphasia Difficulty in understanding spoken or written words and in putting words into meaningful sentences, as a result of injury to Wernicke's area in the brain.

Wernicke's area An area usually located in the left temporal lobe that plays a role in understanding speech and speaking in coherent sentences. *See also* Wernicke's aphasia.

withdrawal symptoms Painful physical and psychological symptoms that occur when a drug-dependent person stops using a drug.

word An arbitrary pairing between a sound or symbol and a meaning.

working memory A more recent understanding of short-term memory that involves the active processing of incoming information from sensory memory and the retrieval of information from long-term memory.

Yerkes-Dodson law The principle that performance on a task is an interaction between the level of physiological arousal and the difficulty of the task. For difficult tasks, low arousal results in better performance; for most tasks, moderate arousal helps performance; and for easy tasks, high arousal may facilitate performance.

yoga A meditation exercise that involves breathing techniques, physical exercises, and postures.

Ⓩ

zygote The cell that results when an egg is fertilized. It contains 46 chromosomes, arranged in 23 pairs.

References

Aamodt, S., & Wang, S. (2008). *Welcome to your brain: Why you lose your car keys but never forget how to drive and other puzzles of everyday life.* London: Bloomsbury.

AAP (American Academy of Pediatrics). (1998). Guidance for effective discipline. *Pediatrics, 101,* 723–728.

AAP. (2010, October 3). Cited in *Science Daily,* Unemployment linked with child maltreatment [On-line]. Available: http://www.sciencedaily.com/releases /2010/10/101003081452.htm.

AAP. (2011). ADHD: Clinical practice guideline for the diagnosis, evaluation, and treatment of attention-deficit/hyperactivity disorder in children and adolescents. *Pediatrics, 128,* 1007–1022.

AAP. (2012, February 27). *AAP recommends HPV vaccines for both males and females* [On-line]. Available: http://www.aap.org/en-us/about-the-aap /aap-press-room/pages/AAP-Recommends-HPV -Vaccines-For-Both-Males-and-Females.aspx?.

Aapro, M. S., Molassiotis, A., & Olver, I. (2005). Anticipatory nausea and vomiting. *Supportive Care in Cancer, 13,* 117–121.

AAUW (American Association of University Women). (2012a). *Sexual assault on campus* [On-line]. Available: http://www.aauw.org/laf/library/assault_ stats.cfm.

AAUW (2012b). *Sexual harassment on campus* [On-line]. Available: http://www.aauw.org/laf/library /harassment_stats.cfm.

Abar, B., Carter, K. L., & Winsler, A. (2009). The effect of maternal parenting style and religious commitment on self-regulation, academic achievement, and risk behavior among African-American parochial college students. *Journal of Adolescence, 32,* 259–273.

Abdul-Zahra, W., & Murphy, B. (2009, February 3). Iraq arrests female suicide bomber recruiter. *Huffington Post* [On-line]. Available: http://www .huffingtonpost.com/2009/02/03/iraq-arrests-female-suic_n_163505.html.

ABC News Radio. (2012, May 6). *Shaquille O'Neal earns a doctorate degree* [On-line]. Available: http:// abcnewsradioonline.com/entertainment-news /shaquille-oneal-earns-doctorate-degree.html.

Abernethy, B., Neal, R. J., & Koning, P. (1994). Visual-perceptual and cognitive differences between expert, intermediate, and novice snooker players. *Applied Cognitive Psychology, 8,* 185–211.

About the judge. (2012). [On-line]. Available: http:// judgemathis.tv.warnerbros.com.

Abrams, M. (2007, June). The real story of gay genes. *Discover, 83,* 58–63.

Abu-Lughod, L. (1986). *Veiled sentiments.* Berkeley: University of California Press.

ACA Group. (2004). *Preventing sexual harassment: It's the law in California* [On-line]. Available: http:// www.theacagroup.com/harassmentarticle.htm.

ACEP (American College of Emergency Physicians). (2008, August 21). Cited in *HealthDay News,* Text-messaging injuries blamed on distraction. *U.S. News & World Report.*

Acevedo, B. (2008a, November 17). Cited in S. Jayson, Proof's in the brain scan: Romance can last. *USA Today,* 6D.

Acevedo, B. (2008b, December 6). Cited in L. Sanders, Still love-struck after 20 years. *Science News,* 17.

Acevedo, B. (2010, June 6). Cited in T. Parker-Pope, Scanning for trouble. *The New York Times,* ST1.

Acevedo, B., Aron, A., Fisher, H. E., & Brown, L. L. (2012). Neural correlates of long-term intense romantic love. *Social Cognitive and Affective Neuroscience, 7,* 145–159.

ACF (Administration for Children and Families). (2010). *Head Start program fact sheet fiscal year 2010* [On-line]. Available: http://eclkc.ohs.acf.hhs.gov/hslc /mr/factsheets/fHeadStartProgr.htm.

ACHA (American College Health Association). (2012). *American College Health Association—National College Health Assessment II: Reference Group Data Report: Fall 2011.* Hanover, MD: American College Health Association.

Adams, W. L. (2006, March/April). The truth about photographic memory. *Psychology Today.*

Ader, F. (1999, June). Cited in B. Azar, Father of PNI reflects on the field growth. *Monitor: American Psychological Association,* 18.

Ader, R., & Cohen, N. (1975). Behaviorally conditioned immunosuppression. *Psychosomatic Medicine, 37,* 333–340.

Adler, J. (2006, March 27). Freud in our midst. *Newsweek,* 42–51.

Adler, J. (2012, May). Erasing painful memories. *Scientific American,* 56–61.

Adolphs, R. (2004). Processing of emotional and social information by the human amygdala. In M. S. Gazzaniga (Ed.), *The cognitive neurosciences III* (pp. 1017–1031). Cambridge, MA: MIT Press.

Adolphs, R., Damasio, H., & Tranel, D. (2002). Neural systems for recognition of emotional prosody: A 3-D lesion study. *Emotion, 2,* 23–51.

AFSP (American Foundation for Suicide Prevention). (2012). *Facts and figures* [On-line]. Available: http://www.afsp.org.

Ainsworth, M. D. S. (1979). Infant-mother attachment. *American Psychologist, 34,* 932–937.

Ainsworth, M. D. S. (1989). Attachments beyond infancy. *American Psychologist, 44,* 709–716.

Akerstedt, T., & Kecklund, G. (2012). In C. M. Morin & C. A. Espie, Sleep, work, and occupational stress. *The Oxford handbook of sleep and sleep disorders.* New York: Oxford University Press.

ALA (American Lung Association). (2006). *Smokeless tobacco fact sheet* [On-line]. Available: http://www .lungusa.org/site/c.dvLUK9O0E/b.1694879/ k.CFC8/Smokeless_Tobacco_Fact_Sheet.htm.

Albee, G. W., & Joffe, J. M. (2004). Mental illness is not "an illness like any other." *Journal of Primary Prevention, 24,* 419–436.

Albert, M. L., Connor, L. T., & Obler, L. K. (2000). Brain, language, and environment. *Brain and Language, 71,* 4–6.

Albright, D. L., & Thyer, B. (2010). Does EMDR reduce post-traumatic stress disorder symptomatology in combat veterans? *Behavioral Interventions, 25,* 1–19.

Albright, T. D., Dixon, J. E., Gage, F. H., & Macagno, E. R. (2005, May 26). A promise for future of medicine. *San Diego Union-Tribune,* B11.

Alderman, L. (2009, June 6). Cost-effective ways to fight insomnia. *The New York Times,* B6.

Alexander, G. C., Gallagher, S. A., Mascola, A., Moloney, R. M., & Stafford, R. S. (2011). Increasing off-label use of antipsychotic medications in the United States, 1995–2008. *Pharmacoepidemiology and Drug Safety, 20,* 177–184.

Alexander, M. (2007, September). Remember me. *Reader's Digest,* 178–185.

Ali, L. (2005, August 12). Satisfaction guaranteed. *Newsweek,* 44–46.

Ali, L. (2006, December 4). The coolest mogul. *Newsweek,* 62–66.

Ali, L., & Scelfo, J. (2002, December 9). Choosing virginity. *Newsweek,* 61–64.

Ali, S. I., & Begum, S. (1994). Fabric softeners and softness perception. *Ergonomics, 37,* 801–806.

Alivisatos, B., & Petrides, M. (1997). Functional activation of the human brain during mental rotation. *Neuropsychologia, 35,* 111–118.

Allan, E. J., & Madden, M. (2008, March 11). *Hazing in view: College students at risk.* National Collaborative for Hazing Research and Prevention, U.S. Department of Education.

Allan, E. J., & Madden, M. (2012). The nature and extent of college student hazing. *International Journal of Adolescent Medicine and Health, 24,* 83–90.

Allen, K. (2003). Are pets a healthy pleasure? The influence of pets on blood pressure. *Current Directions in Psychology, 12,* 236–239.

Allgood, W. P., Risko, V. J., Alvarez, M. C., & Fairbanks, M. M. (2000). Factors that influence study. In R. F. Flippo & D. C. Caverly (Eds.), *Handbook of college reading and study strategy research.* Mahwah, NJ: Lawrence Erlbaum.

Allik, J., & McCrae, R. R. (2004). Toward a geography of personality traits. *Journal of Cross-Cultural Psychology, 35,* 13–28.

Allport, G. W. (1935). Attitudes. In C. Murchison (Ed.), *Handbook of social psychology* (Vol. 2). Worcester, MA: Clark University Press.

Allport, G. W., & Odbert, H. S. (1936). Trait-names: A psycho-lexical study. *Psychological Monographs, 47* (Whole No. 211).

Almeida, D. M., Wethington, E., & Kessler, R. C. (2002). The daily inventory of stressful events. *Assessment, 9,* 41–55.

Alonso, J., Buron, A., Bruffaerts, R., He, Y., Posada-Villa, J., Lepine, J., Angermeyer, M. C., Levinson, D., de Girolamo, G., Tachimori, H., Mneimneh, Z. N., Medina-Mora, M. E., Ormel, J., Scott, K. M., Gureje, O., Haro, J. M., Gluzman, S., Lee, S., Vilagut, G., Kesslerm R. C., & Von Korff, M. (2009). Association of perceived stigma and mood and anxiety disorders: Results from the World Mental Health Surveys. *Acta Psychiatrica Scandinavica, 118,* 305–314.

Alonso-Zaldivar, R. (2006, February 12). Panel calls for ADHD drug effect warning. *Contra Costa Times, Health,* 14–15.

Althof, S. E. (1995). Pharmacologic treatment of rapid ejaculation. *Psychiatric Clinics of North America, 18,* 85–94.

Alzheimer's Association. (2011). 2011 Alzheimer's disease facts and figures. *Alzheimer's & Dementia, 4.*

Alzheimer's Association. (2012). *Risk factors* [On-line]. Available: http://www.alz.org/alzheimers_disease_ causes_risk_factors.asp.

Amabile, T. M. (1985). Motivation and creativity: Effects of motivational orientation on creative writers. *Journal of Personality and Social Psychology, 48,* 393–399.

Amato, P. (2010, May 24). Cited in B. Luscombe, Divorcing by the numbers. *Time, 47.*

American Academy of Pediatrics. (2007, October 29). *New AAP reports help pediatricians identify and manage autism earlier* [On-line]. Available: http:// www.aap.org/advocacy/releases/Oct07autism .htm.

American Psychiatric Association. (2000). *Diagnostic and statistical manual of mental disorders* (4th ed., text revision). Washington, DC: Author.

American Psychological Association. (2002). *Ethical principles of psychologists and code of conduct.* Washington, DC: Author.

American Psychological Association, Division of Psychological Hypnosis. (1993). Hypnosis. *Psychological Hypnosis, 2*(3).

Andersen, S. M., Moskowitz, G. B., Blair, I. V., & Nosek, B. A. (2007). Automatic thought. In A. W. Kruglanski & E. T. Huggins (Eds.), *Social psychology: Handbook of basic principles* (2nd ed., pp. 138–175). New York: Guilford Press.

Andershed, A. (2005). *In sync with adolescence: The role of morningness-eveningness in development.* New York: Springer.

Anderson, C. A., & Bushman, B. J. (2002). Human aggression. *Annual Review of Psychology, 53,* 27–51.

Anderson, C. A., & Huesmann, L. R. (2003). Human aggression: A social-cognitive view. In M.A. Hogg & J. Cooper (Eds.), *The Sage handbook of social psychology* (pp. 296–323). Thousand Oaks, CA: Sage.

Anderson, K. J. (1994). Impulsivity, caffeine, and task difficulty: A within-subjects test of the Yerkes-Dodson law. *Personality and Individual Differences, 16,* 813–819.

Anderson, M. C. (2009a). Incidental forgetting. In A. Baddeley, M. W. Eysenck & M. C. Anderson (Eds.), *Memory* (pp. 192–216). New York: Psychology Press.

Anderson, M. C. (2009b). Motivated forgetting. In A. Baddeley, M. W. Eysenck & M. C. Anderson (Eds.), *Memory* (pp. 217–244). New York: Psychology Press.

Anderson, M. C. (2009c). Retrieval. In A. Baddeley, M. W. Eysenck & M. C. Anderson (Eds.), *Memory* (pp. 163–189). New York: Psychology Press.

Anderson, M. C. (2009d, April/May). Cited in H. A. Berlin & C. Koch, Neuroscience meets psychoanalysis. *Scientific American Mind, 16–19.*

Anderson, M. C., Ochsner, K. N., Kuhl, B., Cooper, J., Robertson, E., Gabrieli, S. W., Glover, G. H., & Gabrieli, J. D. E. (2004). Neural systems underlying the suppression of unwanted memories. *Science, 303,* 232–235.

Anderson, N. B. (2012, March). Cited in S. Martin, Our health at risk. *Monitor on Psychology,* 18–20.

Anderson, P. L., Zimand, E., Hodges, L. F., & Rothbaum, B. O. (2005). Cognitive behavioral therapy for public-speaking anxiety using virtual reality for exposure. *Depression and Anxiety, 22,* 156–158.

Anderson, S. E., Dallal, G. E., & Must, A. (2003). Relative weight and race influence average age at menarche: Results from two nationally representative surveys of U.S. girls studied 25 years apart. *Pediatrics, 111,* 844–850.

Andrews, B., Brewin, C. R., Ochera, J., Morton, J., Bekerian, D. A., Davies, G. M., & Mollon, P. (2000). The timing, triggers and qualities of recovered memories in therapy. *British Journal of Clinical Psychology, 39,* 11–26.

Andrews, M. (2005, December 26/2006, January 2). Why you shouldn't forget to meditate. *U.S. News & World Report,* 68–69.

Angelo, B. (1991, November 4). Life at the end of the rainbow. *Time.*

Angier, N. (2003, February 25). Not just genes: Moving beyond nature vs. nurture. *The New York Times,* D1.

Animal training at SeaWorld. (2002). Busch Entertainment Corporation [On-line]. Available: http://www.seaworld.org/infobooks/Training/home.html.

Anstett, P. (2006, January 12). In these SAD times of the year, follow the sun. *USA Today,* 4D.

Anthes, E. (2009, February/March). Six ways to boost brainpower. *Scientific American Mind,* 56–63.

Anthes, E. (2010, May/June). Family guy. *Scientific American Mind,* 46–53.

Anwar, Y. (2008, January 24). Youngest student to publish ADHD memoir. *UC Berkeley Press Release.*

APA (American Psychological Association). (2007a). *2006–07 faculty salary survey.* Center for Psychology Workforce Analysis and Research [On-line]. Available: http://www.apa.org/workforce/publications/07-fac-sal/index/aspx.

APA. (2007b). *2007 salaries in psychology.* Washington, DC: Author.

APA. (2007c). *APA dictionary of psychology.* Washington, DC: Author.

APA. (2008a). *2008 graduate study in psychology.* Washington, DC: Author.

APA. (2008b, May 8). Cited in J. Gever, Virtual reality PRSD therapy shows promise in Iraq veterans. *MedPage Today.*

APA. (2008c). *A portrait of success & challenge. A progress report: 1997–2005* [On-line]. Available: http://www.apa.org/pi/oema/programs/cemrrat_report.html.

APA. (2009). Finding help: How to choose a psychotherapist. *American Psychological Association Help Center* [On-line]. Available: http://www.apahelpcenter.org/articles/article.php?id=51.

APA. (2011, November 15). Cited in R. C. Rabin. A portable glow to help melt those winter blues. *The New York Times.*

APA. (2012). *Stress in America: Our health at risk.* Washington, DC: Author.

APB (American Program Bureau). (2009). *Brenda Combs* [On-line]. Available: http://www.apbspeakers.com/speaker/brenda-combs.

Aqua facts: Training marine mammals. (2006, October 19). Vancouver Aquarium [On-line]. Available: http://www.vanaqua.org/education/trainingmarinemammals.html. Accessed October 19, 2006.

Ariely, D. (2008). *Predictably irrational: The hidden forces that shape our decisions.* New York: HarperCollins.

Ariely, D., & Wertenbroch, K. (2002). Procrastination, deadlines, and performance: Self-control by precommitment. *Psychological Science, 13,* 219–224.

Arkowitz, H., & Lilienfeld, S. O. (2007a, February/March). A pill to fix your ills? *Scientific American Mind,* 80–81.

Arkowitz, H., & Lilienfeld, S. O. (2007b, October/November). The best medicine? *Scientific American Mind,* 80–83.

Armbruster, B. B. (2000). Taking notes from lectures. In R. F. Flippo & D. C. Caverly (Eds.), *Handbook of college reading and study strategy research.* Mahwah, NJ: Lawrence Erlbaum.

Armbruster, B. B. (2009). Notetaking from lectures. In R. F. Flippo & D. C. Caverly (Eds.), *Handbook of college reading and study strategy research* (pp. 220–248). New York: Routledge.

Armstrong, T. (2010). *Neurodiversity: Discovering the extraordinary gifts of autism, ADHD, dyslexia, and other brain differences.* Cambridge, MA: De Capo Press.

Arnett, J. J. (2000). Adolescent storm and stress, reconsidered. *American Psychologist, 54,* 317–326.

Arnett, J. J. (2007). Emerging adulthood: What is it, and what is it good for? *Child Development Perspectives, 1,* 68–73.

Arnold, D. H., & Doctoroff, G. L. (2003). The early education of socioeconomically disadvantaged children. *Annual Review of Psychology, 54,* 517–545.

Arntz, A. (2003). Cognitive therapy versus applied relaxation as treatment for generalized anxiety disorder. *Behaviour Research and Therapy, 41,* 633–646.

Aronow, E., Reznikoff, M., & Moreland, K. L. (1995). The Rorschach: Projective technique or psychometric test? *Journal of Personality Assessment, 64,* 213–218.

Aronson, E., Wilson, T. D., & Akert, R. M. (2004). *Social psychology* (5th ed.). Upper Saddle River, NJ: Prentice Hall.

ASA (Autism Society of America). (2012). *About autism: Facts and statistics* [On-line]. Available: http://www.autism-society.org/about-autism/facts-and-statistics.html.

Asay, P. (2007, January 7). "There are no secrets." *Colorado Springs Gazette.*

Asch, S. E. (1958). Effects of group pressure upon modification and distortion of judgments. In E. E. Maccoby, T. M. Newcomb & E. L. Hartley (Eds.), *Readings in social psychology* (3rd ed.). New York: Holt, Rinehart and Winston.

Aserinsky, E., & Kleitman, N. (1953). Regularly occurring periods of eye motility, and concomitant phenomena, during sleep. *Science, 118,* 273–274.

Asher, J. E., Lamb, J. A., Brocklebank, D., Cazier, J., Maestrini, E., Addis, L., Sen, M., Baron-Cohen, S., & Monaco, A. P. (2009). A whole-genome scan and fine-mapping linkage study of auditory-visual synesthesia reveals evidence of linkage to chromosomes 2q24, 5q33, 6p12, and 12p12. *American Journal of Human Genetics, 84,* 279–285.

Askay, S. W., & Patterson, D. R. (2007). Hypnotic analgesia. *Expert Review of Neurotherapeutics, 7,* 1675–1683.

ASM (America Society for Microbiology). (2010, September 14). Cited in E. Weise, Washroom study finds 85% actually do. *USA Today,* 6D.

Assanangkornchai, S., Noi-pha, K., Saunders, J. G., & Ralanachaiyavong, S. (2003). Aldehyde dehydrogenase 2 genotypes, alcohol flushing, symptoms and drinking patterns in Thai men. *Psychiatry Research, 118,* 9–17.

Associated Press. (2002, November 18). Loss of McNabb overshadows win. *Los Angeles Times,* D8.

Associated Press. (2005a, March 28). *Docs: Schiavo videos misleading* [On-line]. Available: http://www.foxnews.com/story/0,2933,151662m00.html.

Associated Press. (2005b, June 15). *Schiavo autopsy shows irreversible brain damage* [On-line]. Available: http://www.msnbc.msn.com/id/8225637/.

Associated Press. (2005c, October 7). More evidence supports cervical cancer vaccine. *MSNBC* [On-line]. Available: http://www.msnbc.com/id/9609603/.

Associated Press. (2006a, February 27). *Families swap race on 'Black.White'* [On-line]. Available: http://www.msnbc.msn.com/id/11394595/.

Associated Press. (2006b, March 8). "Housewives" star Hatcher reveals sex abuse. *MSNBC* [On-line]. Available: http://www.msnbc.com/id/11717426/.

Associated Press. (2006c, July 2). More restrictions on teen drivers result in less accidents, study shows. *USA Today.*

Associated Press. (2006d, October 4). *Japanese man recites first 100,000 digits of pi* [On-line]. Available: http://www.foxnews.com.

Associated Press. (2006e, October 27). *Immigrant father on trial for genital cutting* [On-line]. Available: http://www.msnbc.msn.com/id/15447708/.

Associated Press. (2009, July 22). *German farmer injured in accident was world's first to undergo operation.*

Associated Press. (2012a, February 3). *Mass hysteria rare, but usually seen in girls* [On-line]. Available: http://www.foxnews.com/health/2012/02/03/mass-hysteria-rare-but-usually-seen-in-girls/.

Associated Press. (2012b, May 11). Drug that prevents HIV gets panel's OK. *USA Today,* 3A.

Atkinson, J. W. (1964). *An introduction to motivation.* Princeton, NJ: Van Nostrand Reinhold.

Atkinson, J. W. (Ed.). (1958). *Motives in fantasy, action and society*. Princeton, NJ: Van Nostrand Reinhold.

Atkinson, J. W., & Raynor, J. O. (Eds.). (1974). *Motivation and achievement*. Washington, DC: V. H. Winston.

Atkinson, R. C., & Shiffrin, R. M. (1968). Human memory: A proposed system and its control processes. In K. W. Spence & J. T. Spence (Eds.), *The psychology of learning and motivation: Advances in research and theory* (Vol. 2). New York: Academic Press.

Audrain, J. E., Klesges, R. C., & Klesges, L. M. (1995). Relationship between obesity and the metabolic effects of smoking in women. *Health Psychology, 14*, 116–123.

Aumann, K., Galinsky, E., & Matos, K. (2011). *The new male mystique*. New York: Families and Work Institute.

Autism Speaks. (2012). *New research finds annual cost of autism has more than tripled to $126 billion in the U.S. and reach £34 billion in the U.K.* [On-line]. Available: http://www.autismspeaks.org/about-us/press-releases/annual-cost-of-autism-triples.

Axelsson, J., Stefansson, J. G., Magnusson, A., Sigvaldason, H., & Karlsson, M. M. (2002). Seasonal affective disorders: Relevance of Icelandic and Icelandic-Canadian evidence to etiological hypotheses. *Canadian Journal of Psychiatry, 47*, 153–158.

Azar, B. (1997, August). When research is swept under the rug. *APA Monitor*.

Azar, B., & Sleek, S. (1994, October). Do roots of violence grow from nature or nurture? *APA Monitor*.

Baars, B. J., & Gage, N. M. (2010, March 11). *Cognition, brain, and consciousness* (2nd ed.). Burlington, MA: Academic Press.

Babyak, M., Blumenthal, J. A., Herman, S., Khatri, P., Doraiswamy, M., Moore, K., Craighead, W. E., Baldewicz, T. T., & Krishnan, K. R. (2000). Exercise treatment for major depression: Maintenance of therapeutic benefit at 10 months. *Psychosomatic Medicine, 62*, 633–638.

Baddeley, A. (2004). *Your memory: A user's guide*. Buffalo, NY: Firefly.

Baddeley, A. (2009a). Episodic memory: Organizing and remembering. In A. Baddeley, M. W. Eysenck & M. C. Anderson (Eds.), *Memory* (pp. 93–112). New York: Psychology Press.

Baddeley, A. (2009b). Learning. In A. Baddeley, M. W. Eysenck & M. C. Anderson (Eds.), *Memory* (pp. 69–91). New York: Psychology Press.

Baddeley, A. (2009c). Short-term memory. In A. Baddeley, M. W. Eysenck & M. C. Anderson (Eds.), *Memory* (pp. 19–40). New York: Psychology Press.

Baddeley, A. (2009d). What is memory? In A. Baddeley, M. W. Eysenck & M. C. Anderson (Eds.), *Memory* (pp. 1–17). New York: Psychology Press.

Baer, J. S., Sampson, P. D., Barr, H. M., Connor, P. D., & Streissguth, A. P. (2003). A 21-year longitudinal analysis of the effects of prenatal alcohol exposure on young adult drinking. *Archives of General Psychiatry, 60*, 377–385.

Bagge, C. (2006, August 22). Cited in P. Bierma & C. Woolston, Phantom limb pain. *Consumer Health Interactive*.

Bahrami, B., Lavie, N., & Rees, G. (2007). Attentional load modulates responses of human primary visual cortex to invisible stimuli. *Current Biology, 17*, 509–513.

Bahrick, H. P. (2000). Long-term maintenance of knowledge. In E. Tulving & F. M. Craik (Eds.), *The Oxford handbook of memory*. New York: Oxford University Press.

Bahrick, H. P., Bahrick, P. O., & Wittlinger, R. P. (1975). Fifty years of memory for names and faces. *Journal of Experimental Psychology: General, 104*, 54–75.

Bahrick, H. P., Hall, L. K., & Berger, S. A. (1996). Accuracy and distortion in memory for high school girls. *Psychological Science, 7*, 265–271.

Bailes, E., Gao, F., Bibollet-Ruche, F., Courgnaud, V., Peeters, M., Marx, P. A., Hahn, B. H., & Sharp, P. M. (2003). Hybrid origin of SIV in chimpanzees. *Science, 200*, 1713.

Bailey, J. M., & Zucker, H. J. (1995). Childhood sex-typed behavior and sexual orientation: A conceptual analysis and quantitative review. *Developmental Psychology, 31*, 43–55.

Baillargeon, R. (2002). Gender differences in physical aggression at 17 months of age: Results from the longitudinal study of child development in Quebec. In S. Cote (Chair), *Sex differences and similarities in aggression: Correlates and consequences from infancy to mid-life*. Symposium conducted at the 15th world meeting of the International Society for Research on Aggression, Montreal, Canada.

Baird, J. (2010, April 19). Beyond the bad boys. *Newsweek*, 24.

Bakalar, N. (2010, June 1). Happiness may come with age, study says. *The New York Times*, D5.

Baker, C. (2004). *Behavioral genetics: An introduction to how genes and environments interact through development to shape differences in mood, personality, and intelligence*. Washington, DC: American Association for the Advancement of Science.

Baker, S. (2009, April). Building a better brain. *Discover*, 54–59.

Balasubramanian, S., Habegger, L., Frankish, A., MacArthur, D., Harte, R., Tyler-Smith, C., Harrow, J., & Gerstein, M. (2010). Defining the human reference protein-coding gene set. *Genome Biology, 11*, 5.

Baldauf, S. (2009, July 15). Brain stimulation: Transcranial magetic stimulation. *U.S. News & World Report*.

Baldauf, S. (2011). What if the gloom won't lift? *Secrets of Your Brain*, 79–81.

Baldwin, J. D., & Baldwin, J. I. (1997). Gender differences in sexual interest. *Archives of Sexual Behavior, 26*, 181–210.

Ball, J. R., Mitchell, P. B., Corry, J. C., Skillecorn, A., Smith, M., & Malhi, G. S. (2006). A randomized controlled trial of cognitive therapy for bipolar disorder: Focus on long-term change. *Journal of Clinical Psychiatry, 67*, 277–286.

Ball, T. M., & Stein, M. B. (2012). Classification of posttraumatic stress disorder. In J. G. Beck & D. M. Sloan (Eds.), *The Oxford handbook of traumatic stress disorders* (pp. 39–53). New York: Oxford University Press.

Balter, M. (2002). What made humans modern? *Science, 295*, 1219–1225.

Bamford, N. S., Zhang, H., Joyce, J. A., Scarlis, C. A., Hanan, W., Wu, N., Andre, V. M., Cohen, R., Cepeda, C., Levine, M. S., Harleton, E., & Sulzer, D. (2008). Repeated exposure to methamphetamine causes long-lasting presynaptic corticostriatal depression that is renormalized with drug readministration. *Neuron, 58*, 89–103.

Banaji, M. R. (2006, June). Cited in S. Lehrman, The implicit prejudice. *Scientific American*, 32–33.

Banaji, M. R. & Heiphetz, L. (2010). Attitudes. In S. T. Fiske, D. T. Gilbert & G. Lindzey (Eds.), *Handbook of social psychology* (Vol. 1, 5th ed., pp. 353–393). Hoboken, NJ: John Wiley & Sons.

Bandura, A. (1965). Influence of models' reinforcement contingencies on the acquisition of imitative responses. *Journal of Personality and Social Psychology, 1*, 589–596.

Bandura, A. (1986). *Social foundations of thought and action: A social cognitive theory*. Englewood Cliffs, NJ: Prentice Hall.

Bandura, A. (1999). Social cognitive theory of personality. In L. A. Pervin & O. P. John (Eds.), *Handbook of personality: Theory and research* (2nd ed.). New York: Guilford Press.

Bandura, A. (2001a). Social cognitive theory: An agentic perspective. *Annual Review of Psychology, 52*, 1–26.

Bandura, A. (2001b). Social cognitive theory of personality. In L. A. Pervin & O. P. John (Eds.), *Handbook of personality: Theory and research* (2nd ed.). New York: Guilford Press.

Bandura, A. (2004). Health promotion by social cognitive means. *Health Education & Behavior, 31*, 143–164.

Bandura, A., Blanchard, E. B., & Ritter, B. (1969). Relative efficacy of desensitization and modeling approaches for inducing behavioral, affective and attitudinal changes. *Journal of Personality and Social Psychology, 13*, 173–179.

Bandura, A., Ross, D., & Ross, S. A. (1963). Imitation of film-mediated aggressive models. *Journal of Abnormal and Social Psychology, 66*, 3–11.

Banich, M. T., & Compton, R. J. (2011). *Cognitive neurosciences* (3rd ed.). Belmont, CA: Wadsworth.

Banks, S. J., Eddy, K. T., Angstadt, M., Nathan, P. J., & Phan, K. L. (2007). Amygdala-frontal connectivity during emotion regulation. *Social Cognitive and Affective Neuroscience, 2*, 303–312.

Barad, M., Gean, P., & Lutz, B. (2006). The role of the amygdala in the extinction of conditioned fear. *Biological Psychiatry, 60*, 322–328.

Barinaga, M. (2002). How the brain's clock gets daily enlightenment. *Science, 295*, 955–957.

Barinaga, M. (2003). Newborn neurons search for meaning. *Science, 299*, 32–34.

Barkley, R. A. (2006). *Attention-deficit hyperactivity disorder: A handbook for diagnosis and treatment* (3rd ed.). New York: Guilford Press.

Barkley, R. A. (2009). *ADHD in adults*. Burlington, MA: Jones & Bartlett.

Barkley, R. A., Murphy, K. R., & Fischer, M. (2008). *ADHD in adults: What the science says*. New York: Guilford Press.

Barkley, R. A., Murphy, K. R., & Fischer, M. (2010). *ADHD in adults: What the science says*. New York: Guilford Press.

Barnes, T. (2010, September). Cited in M. Mahon, Games without frontiers. *Discover*, 66–72.

Barnett, W. S. (2004). Does Head Start have lasting cognitive effects? The myth of fade-out. In E. Zigler & S. Styfco (Eds.), *The Head Start debates* (pp. 221–249). Baltimore, MD: Paul H. Brookes Publishing.

Barnett, W. S., & Hustedt, J. T. (2005). Head Start's lasting benefits. *Infants & Young Children, 18*, 16–24.

Baron, R. (2008, July 21). Cited in A. Underwood, Common scents. *Newsweek*, 52.

Baron, R. A., & Richardson, D. R. (2004). *Human aggression* (2nd ed.). New York: Springer.

Barrett, D. (2011, November/December). Answers in your dreams. *Scientific American Mind*, 26–35.

Barrett, K. E., Brooks, H., Boitano, S., & Barman, S. M. (2009). *Ganong's review of medical physiology* (23rd ed.). New York: McGraw-Hill.

Barrett, L. F., Mesquita, B., & Gendron, M. (2011). Context in emotion perception. *Current Directions in Psychological Science, 20*, 286–290.

Barrow, K. (2011, December 26). Have we met? Tracing face blindness to its roots. *The New York Times*.

Barsky, A. J., Orav, E. J., & Bates, D. W. (2005). Somatization increases medical utilization and costs independent of psychiatric and medical comorbidity. *Archives of General Psychiatry, 62*, 903–910.

Bartels, A. (2002, December 16). Cited in C. Carey, The brain in love. *Los Angeles Times*, F1.

Barth, A. (2009, April). Sleeping it off. *Discover*, 14.

Bartlik, B., & Goldstein, M. Z. (2001). Men's sexual health after midlife. *Psychiatric Services, 52*, 291–306.

Bartone, P. T. (1999). Hardiness protects against war-related stress in Army Reserve forces. *Consulting Psychology Journal, 51,* 72–82.

Bartoshuk, L. (1997). Cited in K. Fackelmann, The bitter truth. *Science News, 152,* 24–25.

Bartoshuk, L. (2006, July 19). Cited in M. Kramer, Do taste buds make the wine critic? *The New York Sun.*

Bartoshuk, L. (2010, June 18). Cited in J. Bohannon, A taste for controversy. *Science, 328,* 1471–1473.

Basil, R. (1989). Graphology and personality: Let the buyer beware. *Skeptical Inquirer, 13,* 241–248.

Bateman, A. W., & Fonagy, P. (2000). Effectiveness of psychotherapeutic treatment of personality disorder. *British Journal of Psychiatry, 177,* 138–143.

Bates, B. L. (1994). Individual differences in response to hypnosis. In J. W. Rhue, S. J. Lynn & I. Kirsch (Eds.), *Handbook of clinical hypnosis.* Washington, DC: American Psychological Association.

Bates, J. (2000). Temperament as an emotion construct: Theoretical and practical issues. In M. Lewis & J. M. Haviland-Jones (Eds.), *Handbook of emotions* (2nd ed.). New York: Guilford Press.

Bateson, P. (1991). Is imprinting such a special case? In J. R. Krebs & G. Horn (Eds.), *Behavioural and neural aspects of learning and memory.* Oxford: Oxford University Press.

Batson, C. D. (1998). Who cares? When? Where? Why? How? *Contemporary Psychology, 43,* 108–109.

Battaglia, M. (2005, April 4). Cited in J. Kluger, Secrets of the shy. *Time,* 50–52.

Bauby, J. (1997). *The diving bell and the butterfly: A memoir of life in death.* New York: Vintage.

Bauer, P. J. (2002). Long-term recall memory: Behavioral and neuro-developmental changes in the first 2 years of life. *Current Directions in Psychological Science, 11,* 139–140.

Baumeister, R. F. (1995). Disputing the effects of championship pressures and home audiences. *Journal of Personality and Social Psychology, 68,* 644–648.

Baumeister, R. F., & Bushman, B. J. (2011). *Social psychology and human nature* (2nd ed.). Belmont, CA: Wadsworth Cengage Learning.

Baumrind, D. (1991). Effective parenting during the early adolescent transition. In P. A. Cowan & E. M. Hetherington (Eds.), *Advances in family research.* Hillsdale, NJ: Lawrence Erlbaum.

Baumrind, D. (1993). The average expectable environment is not good enough: A response to Scarr. *Child Development, 64,* 1299–1317.

Baumrind, D. (1995). Commentary on sexual orientation: Research and social policy implications. *Developmental Psychology, 31,* 130–136.

Baumrind, D., Larzelere, R. E., & Cowan, P. A. (2002). Ordinary physical punishment: Is it harmful? Comment on Gershoff (2002). *Psychological Bulletin, 128,* 580–589.

Baylen, C. A., & Rosenberg, H. (2006). A review of the acute subjective effects of MDMA/ecstasy. *Addiction, 101,* 933.

BBC News. (2007, October 20). *Settlement for bogus abuse woman* [On-line]. Available: http://news.bbc.co.uk/1/hi/scotland/tayside_and_central/7054249.stm.

BBC News. (2008, October 13). *Just married and determined to die* [On-line]. Available: http:news.bbc.co.uk/2/hi/7667031.stm.

BBC. (2008a, October 1). *Computers could read mammograms* [On-line]. Available: http://news.bbc.co.uk/1/hi/health/7644635.stm.

BBC. (2008b). *Science of supertasters* [On-line]. Available: http://www.bbc.co.uk/science/humanbody/body/articles/senses/supertaster.shtml.

BCSSE (Board on Behavioral, Cognitive, and Sensory Sciences and Education). (2002). *Mental retardation: Determining eligibility for Social Security benefits.* Washington, DC: National Academy Press.

Bear, M. F., Connors, B. W., & Paradiso, M. A. (1996). *Neuroscience: Exploring the brain.* Baltimore, MD: Williams & Wilkins.

Beasley, M., Thompson, T., & Davidson, J. (2003). Resilience in response to life stress: The effects of coping style and cognitive hardiness. *Personality and Individual Differences, 34,* 77–95.

Beck, A. T. (1976). *Cognitive therapy and the emotional disorders.* New York: International Universities Press.

Beck, A. T. (1991). Cognitive therapy: A 30-year retrospective. *American Psychologist, 46,* 368–375.

Beck, A. T., Rush, A. J., Shaw, B. F., & Emery, G. (1979). *Cognitive therapy of depression.* New York: Guilford Press.

Beck, A. T., & Weishaar, M. E. (2008). Cognitive therapy. In R. J. Corsini & D. Wedding (Eds.), *Current psychotherapies* (8th ed., pp. 263–294). Belmont, CA: Thomson Brooks/Cole.

Beck, G. J., Gudmundsdottir, B., Palyo, S. A., Miller, L. M., & Grant, D. D. (2006). Rebound effects following deliberate thought suppression: Does PTSD make a difference? *Behavior Therapy, 37,* 170–180.

Beck, J. S. (2011). *Cognitive behavior therapy* (2nd ed.). New York: Guilford Press.

Beckman, N., Waern, M., Gustafson, D., & Skoog, I. (2008). Secular trends in self reported sexual activity and satisfaction in Swedish 70 year olds: Cross sectional survey of four populations, 1971–2001. *BMJ, 337,* a279.

Bedi, K. (2006). *It's always possible: One woman's transformation of India's prison system.* Honesdale: PA: Himalayan Institute Press.

Begley, S. (1998a, January 19). Aping language. *Newsweek.*

Begley, S. (1998b, January 26). Is everybody crazy? *Newsweek,* 51–55.

Begley, S. (2001, February 12). How it all starts inside your brain. *Newsweek,* 40–43.

Begley, S. (2007a, August 20/August 27). The puzzle of hidden ability. *Newsweek,* 50.

Begley, S. (2007b, October 8). Bite your tongue. *Newsweek,* 12.

Begley, S. (2007c, November 5). The ghosts we think we see. *Newsweek,* 56.

Begley, S. (2008a, March 3). How your brain looks at race. *Newsweek,* 26–27.

Begley, S. (2008b, March 17). Placebo nation: Just believe. *Newsweek,* 46.

Begley, S. (2008c, November 3). Why we believe. *Newsweek,* 56–60.

Begley, S. (2008d, December 1). When DNA is not destiny. *Newsweek,* 14.

Begley, S. (2009a, April 20). Sex, race, and IQ: Off limits? *Newsweek,* 53.

Begley, S. (2009b, October 12). Ignoring the evidence. Why do psychologists reject science? *Newsweek,* 30.

Begley, S. (2010, June 28). This is your brain. Aging. *Newsweek,* 64–66.

Begley, T. (1995). Using founder status, age of firm, and company growth rate as the basis for distinguishing entrepreneurs from managers of smaller businesses. *Journal of Business Venturing, 10,* 249–263.

Begos, K., & Scolforo, M. (2011, August 4). Penn State scandal: Sandusky had access to vulnerable kids via charity. *Huffington Post.*

Belin, D., & Rauscent, A. (2006). ΔFosB: A molecular gate to motivational processes within the nucleus accumbens. *Journal of Neuroscience, 26,* 11809–11810.

Belluck, P. (2010, November 9). For edge on Alzheimer's, testing early treatments. *The New York Times,* D5.

Bem, D. (1967). Self-perception: An alternative interpretation of cognitive dissonance phenomena. *Psychological Review, 74,* 183–200.

Bem, D. J., & Honorton, C. (1994). Does psi exist? Replicable evidence for an anomalous process of information transfer. *Psychological Bulletin, 115,* 4–18.

Bem, S. L. (1981). Gender schema theory: A cognitive account of sex-typing. *Psychological Review, 88,* 354–364.

Bem, S. L. (1985). Androgyny and gender schema theory: Conceptual and empirical integration. In T. B. Sonderegger (Ed.), *Nebraska symposium on motivation.* Lincoln: University of Nebraska Press.

Ben-Porath, Y. S. (2010). *Interpreting the MMPI-2-RF.* Minneapolis: University of Minnesota Press.

Bendsen, E., Byskov, A. G., Andersen, C. Y., & Westergaard, L. G. (2006). Number of germ cells and somatic cells in human fetal ovaries during the first weeks after sex differentiation. *Human Reproduction, 21,* 30–35.

Benedetti, F. (2009, June 1). Cited in S. Begley, Hooked on a feeling: This is your brain on a placebo. *Newsweek,* 25.

Benjamin, L. T., Jr. (2008, November). America's first black female psychologist. *Monitor on Psychology,* 20–21.

Bennet, J. (2002, June 21). Rash of new suicide bombers showing no pattern or ties. *The New York Times,* A1.

Benson, E. (2003a, February). Intelligent intelligence testing. *Monitor on Psychology,* 48–51.

Benson, E. (2003b, February). Intelligence across cultures. *Monitor on Psychology,* 56–58.

Benson, H. (2008, October). Cited in S. Martin, The power of the relaxation response. *Monitor on Psychology,* 32–33.

Benson, H., Lehmann, J. W., Malhotra, M. S., Goldman, R. F., Hopkins, P. J., & Epstein, M. D. (1982). Body temperature changes during the practice of g Tummo yoga. *Nature, 295,* 234–235.

Benson, H., Malhotra, M. S., Goldman, R. F., Jacobs, G. D., & Hopkins, P. J. (1990). Three case reports of the metabolic and electroencephalographic changes during advanced Buddhist meditation techniques. *Behavioral Medicine, 16,* 90–95.

Berenson, A. (2006, January 1). Antidepressants seem to cut suicide risk in teenagers and adults, study says. *The New York Times,* 14.

Berenson, A. (2008, February 24). Daring to think differently about schizophrenia. *The New York Times.*

Beresford, T. P. (2012). *Psychological adaptive mechanisms: Ego defense recognition in practice and research.* New York: Oxford University Press.

Berg, B. O. (2007). Chromosomal abnormalities and neurocutaneous disorders. In C. G. Goetz (Ed.), *Textbook of clinical neurology* (3rd ed., pp. 683–698). Philadelphia: Saunders Elsevier.

Berg, C. A. (2000). Intellectual development in adulthood. In R. J. Sternberg (Ed.), *Handbook of intelligence.* New York: Cambridge University Press.

Bergelson, E., & Swingley, D. (2012, February 13). At 6–9 months, human infants know the meanings of many common nouns. *Proceedings of the National Academy of Sciences, 109,* 3253–3258.

Bering, J. (2010, May/June). The third gender. *Scientific American Mind,* 60–63.

Berk, L. B., & Patrick, C. F. (1990). Epidemiologic aspects of toilet training. *Clinical Pediatrics, 29,* 278–282.

Berko, A., & Erez, E. (2006, December 6). *Women in terrorism: A Palestinian feminist revolution or gender oppression?* Institute for Counter-Terrorism [On-line]. Available: http://www.ict.org.il/apage/9102.php.

Berkowitz, L. (1989). Frustration-aggression hypothesis: Examination and reformulation. *Psychological Bulletin, 106,* 59–73.

Berkowitz, L. (1993). *Aggression: Its causes, consequences, and control.* New York: McGraw-Hill.

Berlin, H. A., & Koch, C. (2009, April/May). Neuroscience meets psychoanalysis. *Scientific American Mind,* 16–17.

Berlinger, N. T. (2006). Robotic surgery—Squeezing into tight places. *New England Journal of Medicine, 354*, 2099–2101.

Bernal, S., Dehaene-Lambertz, G., Millotte, S., & Christophe, A. (2010). Two-year-olds compute syntactic structure on-line. *Developmental Science, 13*, 69–76.

Berns, G. (2005, June 28). Cited in S. Blakeslee, What other people say may change what you see. *The New York Times*, D3.

Berns, G. S., Chappelow, M. C., Zink, C. F., Pagnoni, G., & Martin-Skurski, M. E. (2006, May 5). Neurobiological substrates of dread. *Science, 312*, 754–758.

Bernstein, D. M., Laney, C., Morris, E. K., & Loftus, E. F. (2005, September 27). False beliefs about fattening foods can have healthy consequences. *Proceedings of the National Academy of Sciences, 102*, 13724–13731.

Bernstein, I. L., & Koh, M. T. (2007). Molecular signaling during taste aversion learning. *Chemical Senses, 32*, 99–103.

Berntsen, D., & Thomsen, D. K. (2005). Personal memories for remote historical events: Accuracy and clarity of flashbulb memories related to World War II. *Journal of Experimental Psychology: General, 134*, 242–257.

Berridge, K. C. (2003). Comparing the emotional brains of human and other animals. In R. J. Davidson, K. R. Scherer & H. H. Goldsmith (Eds.), *Handbook of affective sciences*. New York: Oxford University Press.

Berry, C. M., Sackett, P. R., & Wiemann, S. (2007). A review of recent developments in integrity test research. *Personnel Psychology, 60*, 271–301.

Bessenoff, G. R. (2006). Can the media affect us? Social comparison, self-discrepancy, and the think ideal. *Psychology of Women Quarterly, 30*, 239–251.

Best, D. L., & Thomas, J. J. (2004). Cultural diversity and cross-cultural perspectives. In A. H. Eagly, A. E. Beall & R. J. Sternberg (Eds.), *The psychology of gender* (2nd ed., pp. 296–327). New York: Guilford Press.

Bhattacharya, S. (2003, February 17). "Supertasters" diet raises cancer risk [On-line]. Available: http://www.newscientist.com/article.ns?id=dn3390&print=true.

Bialystok, E., & Craik, F. (2010). Cognitive and linguistic processing in the bilingual mind. *Current Direction in Psychological Science, 19*, 19–23.

Bierma, P., & Woolston, C. (2006, August 22). Phantom limb pain. *Consumer Health Interactive*.

Billingsley, J. (2005, November 30). *Coffee perks up short-term memory* [On-line]. Available: http://health.msn.com/healthnews/articlepage.aspx?cp documentid=100119786.

Binet, A., & Simon, T. (1905). Methodes nouvelles pour le diagnostic du niveau intellectuel des anormaux. *L'Annee Psychologique, 11*, 191–244.

Binkofski, F., & Buccino, G. (2007, June/July). Therapeutic reflection. *Scientific American Mind*, 78–81.

Birney, D. P., & Sternberg, R. J. (2011). The development of cognitive abilities. In M. H. Bornstein & M. E. Lamb (Eds.), *Developmental science: An advanced textbook* (pp. 353–388). New York: Psychology Press.

Bishop, E. G., Cherny, S. S., Corley, R., Plomin, R., DeFries, J. C., & Hewitt, J. K. (2003). Development genetic analysis of general cognitive ability from 1 to 12 years in a sample of adoptees, biological siblings, and twins. *Intelligence, 31*, 31–49.

Bjorklund, D. F. (2005). *Children's thinking: Cognitive development and individual differences*. Belmont, CA: Wadsworth/Thomson.

Bjorklund, D. F. (2012). *Children's thinking*. Belmont, CA: Wadsworth.

Black, D. (2006, December 12). What causes antisocial personality disorder? *PsychCentral* [On-line]. Available: http://psychcentral.com/lib/2006/12/what-causes-antisocial-personality-disorder/.

Blais, V., Jack, R. E., Scheepers, C., Fiset, D., & Caldara, R. (2008). Culture shapes how we look at faces. *PLoS ONE, 3*, e3022.

Blaiss, C. A., Yu, T., Zhang, G., Chen, J., Dimchev, G., Parada, L. F., Powell, C. M., & Kernie, S. G. (2011). Temporally specified genetic ablation of neurogenesis impairs cognitive recovery after traumatic brain injury. *Journal of Neuroscience, 31*(13), 4906–4943.

Blakely, M. R. (1994, May 15). A place of belonging. *Los Angeles Times Magazine*.

Blakemore, J. E. O. (2003). Children's beliefs about violating gender norms: Boys shouldn't look like girls, and girls shouldn't act like boys. *Sex Roles, 48*, 411–419.

Blakeslee, S. (2000, January 12). Researchers developing bold new theories to explain autism. *San Diego Union-Tribune*.

Blakeslee, S. (2002, November, 11). A boy, a mother and a rare map of autism's world. *The New York Times*, D1.

Blakeslee, S. (2006a, January 10). Cells that read minds. *The New York Times*.

Blakeslee, S. (2006b, May 5). Study points to a solution for dread: Distraction. *The New York Times*, A18.

Blakeslee, S., & Blakeslee, M. (2007). *The body has a mind of its own*. New York: Random House.

Blanco, C., Schneier, F. R., Schmidt, A., Blanco-Jerez, C., Marshall, R. D., Sanchez-Lacay, A., & Liebowitz, M. R. (2003). Pharmacological treatment of social anxiety disorder: A meta-analysis. *Depression & Anxiety, 18*, 29–40.

Blanding, M. (2010, Winter). The brain in the world: A burgeoning science explores the deep imprint of culture. *Tufts University Magazine*.

Blascovich, J., & Mendes, W. B. (2010). Social psychophysiology and embodiment. In S. T. Fiske, D. T. Gilbert & G. Lindzey (Eds.), *Handbook of social psychology* (Vol. 1, 5th ed., pp. 194–227). Hoboken, NJ: John Wiley & Sons.

Blass, E. M., & Camp, C. A. (2001). The ontogeny of face recognition: Eye contact and sweet taste induce face preference in 9- and 12-week-old human infants. *Developmental Psychology, 37*, 762–774.

Blass, T. (Ed.). (2000). *Obedience to authority*. Mahwah, NJ: Lawrence Erlbaum.

Bleck, T. P. (2007). Level of consciousness and attention. In C. G. Goetz (Ed.), *Textbook of clinical neurology* (3rd ed., pp. 3–19). Philadelphia: Saunders Elsevier.

Block, J. (1995). Going beyond the five factors given: Rejoinder to Costa & McCrae (1995) and Goldberg & Saucier (1995). *Psychological Bulletin, 117*, 226–229.

Block, M. (2006, May 26). Teens turn "repeller" into adult-proof ringtone. *NPR* [On-line]. Available: http://www.npr.org/templates/story/story.php?storyId=5434687.

Blood, A. J., & Zatorre, R. J. (2001). Intensely pleasurable responses to music correlate with activity in brain regions implicated in reward and emotion. *Proceedings of the National Academy of Sciences, 98*, 11818–11823.

Bloom, M. M. (2005). *Dying to kill: The allure of suicide terror*. New York: Columbia University Press.

Blum, K., Liu, Y., Shriner, R., & Gold, M. S. (2011). Reward circuitry dopaminergic activation regulates food and drug craving behavior. *Current Pharmaceutical Design, 17*, 1158–1167.

Blum, N. (2003, April 14). Cited in B. Carey, Ready or not. *Los Angeles Times*, F2.

Blum, R. (2002, September 5). Cited in D. J. Schemo, Mothers of sex-active youths often think they're virgins. *The New York Times*, A14.

Blunt, A. K., & Pychyl, T. A. (2000). Task aversiveness and procrastination: A multi-dimensional approach to task aversiveness across stages of personal projects. *Personality and Individual Differences, 28*, 153–167.

Bodas, J., & Ollendick, T. H. (2005). Test anxiety: A cross-cultural perspective. *Clinical Child and Family Psychology Review, 8*, 65–88.

Boddy, J. (1988). Spirits and selves in northern Sudan: The cultural therapeutics of possession and trance. *American Ethnologist, 15*, 4–27.

Bogaert, A. F. (2006a, June 26). Cited in R. E. Schmid, *Men with older brothers more likely to be gay* [On-line]. Available: http://abcnews.go.com/Health/wireStory?id=2119484.

Bogaert, A. F. (2006b, July 11). Biological versus non-biological older brothers and men's sexual orientation. *Proceedings of the National Academy of Sciences, 103*, 10771–10774.

Bohner, G., Erb, H. P., & Siebler, F. (2008). Information processing approaches to persuasion: Integrating assumptions from the dual- and single-processing perspectives. In W. B. Crano & R. Prislin (Eds.), *Attitudes and persuasion* (pp. 161–188). New York: Psychology Press.

Bolton, E. E., Lambert, J. F., Wolf, E. J., Raja, S., Varra, A. A., & Fisher, L. M. (2004). Evaluating a cognitive-behavioral group treatment program for veterans with posttraumatic stress disorder. *Psychological Services, 1*, 140–146.

Bonanno, G. A. (2004). Loss, trauma, and human resilience. *American Psychologist, 59*, 20–28.

Bondurant, B., & Donat, P. L. N. (1999). Perceptions of women's sexual interest and acquaintance rape. *Psychology of Women Quarterly, 23*, 691–705.

Bonnet, M. H. (2005). Acute sleep deprivation. In M. H. Kryger, T. Roth & W. C. Dement (Eds.), *Principles and practice of sleep medicine* (4th ed., pp. 51–66). Philadelphia: Elsevier Saunders.

Bono, C. (2009, November 18). Cited in *ABC News, Exclusive: Chaz bono live Thursday on 'GMA'* [On-line]. Available: http://www.abcnews.go.com/GMA/exclusive-chaz-bono-good-morning-america-live-interview/story?id=9116847#.T9-HHkansrc.

Booth-Kewley, S., & Friedman, H. S. (1987). Psychological predictions of heart disease: A quantitative review. *Psychological Bulletin, 101*, 343–362.

Bootzin, R. R., & Rider, S. P. (1997). Behavioral techniques and biofeedback for insomnia. In M. R. Pressman & W. C. Roo (Eds.), *Understanding sleep: The evaluation and treatment of sleep disorders*. Washington, DC: American Psychological Association.

Bornstein, M. H., & Lamb, M. E. (2011). *Cognitive development: An advanced textbook*. New York: Psychology Press.

Bornstein, R. F. (2001). The impending death of psychoanalysis. *Psychoanalytic Psychology, 18*, 3–20.

Borst, G., Thompson, W. L., & Kosslyn, S. M. (2011). Understanding the dorsal and ventral systems of the human cerebral cortex. *American Psychologist, 66*(7), 624–632.

Borton, J. L. D. (2002). The suppression of negative self-referent thoughts. *Anxiety, Stress, and Coping, 15*, 31–46.

Bosch, F. X., Lorincz, A., Munoz, N., Meijer, C. J. L. M., & Shah, K. V. (2002). The causal relation between human papillomavirus and cervical cancer. *Journal of Clinical Pathology, 55*, 244–265.

Bouchard, C. (2009, January). Cited in J. Chen, 13 things you never knew about your weight. *Reader's Digest*, 86–95.

Bouchard, M. F., Chevrier, J., Harley, K. G., Kogut, K., Vedar, M., Calderon, N., Trujillo, C., Johnson, C., Bradman, A., Barr, D. B., & Eskenazi, B. (2011). Prenatal exposure to organophosphate pesticides and IQ in 7-year-old children. *Environmental Health Perspectives, 119*, 1189–1195.

Bouchard, T. J., Jr. (1994). Genes, environment, and personality. *Science, 264*, 1700–1701.

Bouchard, T. J., Jr. (1995). Breaking the last taboo. *Contemporary Psychology, 40*, 415–418.

Bouchard, T. J., Jr. (1997). IQ similarity in twins reared apart: Findings and responses to critics. In R. J. Sternberg & E. Grigorenko (Eds.), *Intelligence, heredity, and environment*. New York: Cambridge University Press.

Bouchard, T. J., Jr. (2004). Genetic influence on human psychological traits. *Current Directions in Psychological Science, 13*, 148–151.

Bouchard, T. J., Jr., & Loehlin, J. C. (2001). Genes, evolution, and personality. *Behavior Genetics, 31*, 243–273.

Bouchard, T. J., Jr., Lykken, D. T., McGue, M., Segal, N. L., & Tellegen, A. (1990). Sources of human psychological differences: The Minnesota study of twins reared apart. *Science, 250*, 223–228.

Bouchard, T. J., & McGue, M. (1981). Familial studies of intelligence: A review. *Science, 212*, 1055–1059.

Bouret, S., Gorski, J., Patterson, C., Chen, S., Levin, B., & Simerly, R. (2008). Hypothalamic neural projections are permanently disrupted in diet-induced obese rats. *Cell Metabolism, 7*, 179–185.

Bouton, M. E. (2007). *Learning and behavior: A contemporary synthesis*. Sunderland, MA: Sinauer Associates.

Bower, B. (1997). Forbidden flavors. *Science News, 151*, 198–199.

Bower, B. (2001). Brains in dreamland. *Science News, 160*, 90–92.

Bower, B. (2003a, January 11). Speech veers left in babies' brains. *Science News, 163*, 30.

Bower, B. (2003b). Words get in the way. *Science News, 163*, 250–251.

Bower, B. (2006, May 27). Violent developments. Disruptive kids grow into their behavior. *Science News, 169*, 328–329.

Bower, B. (2007, November 24). Showdown at sex gap. *Science News, 172*, 328–330.

Bower, B. (2008a, July 19). Brazil's Pirahã grasp numbers without words. *Science News*, 5–6.

Bower, B. (2008b, October 11). Mom can increase her child's risk of depression via nurture alone. *Science News*, 9.

Bower, B. (2008c, December 6). Morality askew in psychopaths. *Science News*, 16.

Bower, B. (2008d, December 20). Boys may show spatial supremacy within a few months after birth. *Science News*, 8.

Bower, B. (2009a, April 11). Two cultures grasp music's universal feeling. *Science News*, 14.

Bower, B. (2009b, July 18). Gene's reported role in depression questioned by subsequent studies. *Science News*, 10.

Bower, F. (2000). Building blocks of talk. *Science News, 157*, 344–346.

Bowlby, J. (1969). *Attachment and loss: Vol. 1. Attachment*. New York: Basic Books.

Bowles, J. (2009). Charlie Sheen. *The Biography Channel* [On-line]. Available: http://www.thebiography channel.co.uk/biography_story/510:161/1/Charlie -Sheen.htm.

Bowman, L. (2005, December 1). *Caffeine can improve short-term memory* [On-line]. Available: http://seat tlepi.nwsource.com/health/250310_cofee01.html.

Boyce, N. (2002, October 7). Chips vs. the chess masters. *U.S. News & World Report*, 70–71.

Boyd, N. (2007, May 22). Cited in S. Kincaid, A tumor was hiding in the breast tissue. *Redorbit News* [On-line]. Available: http://www.redorbit.com/news /display/?id=943199.

Boyle, C. A., Boulet, S., Schieve, L. A., Cohen, R. A., Blumberg, S. J., Yeargin-Alisopp, M., Visser, S., & Kogan, M. D. (2011). Trends in the prevalence of developmental disabilities in US children, 1997– 2008. *Pediatrics, 127*(6), 1034–1042.

Boysen, S. (2009). *The smartest animals on the planet*. Buffalo, NY: Firefly Books.

Brabham, D. (2001, July 23). The smart guy. *Newsday* [On-line]. Available: http://www.megafoundation. org/CTMU/Press/TheSmartGuy.pdf.

Brackett, M. A., Cox, A., Gaines, S. O., & Salovey, P. (2005). Emotional intelligence and relationship quality among heterosexual couples. Cited in G. J. Boyle, G. Matthews & D. H. Sakjofske (Eds.), *The SAGE handbook of personality theory and assessment: Personality measurement and testing* (Vol. 2). Thousand Oaks, CA: Sage.

Brackett, M. A., Mayer, J. D., & Warner, R. M. (2004). Emotional intelligence and the prediction of behavior. *Personality and Individual Differences, 36*, 1387–1402.

Bradley, R., Greene, J., Russ, E., Dutra, L., & Westen, D. (2005). A multidimensional meta-analysis of psychotherapy for PTSD. *American Journal of Psychiatry, 162*, 214–227.

Branan, N. (2008, April/May). Wait, don't tell me.... *Scientific American Mind*, 13.

Brannigan, R. E. (2011). Ejaculatory disorders. Cited in K. T. McVary (Ed.), *Contemporary treatment of erectile dysfunction: A clinical guide* (pp. 267–279). New York: Springer.

Braun, A. R., Balkin, T. J., Wesensten, N. J., Gwadry, F., Carson, R. E., Varga, M., Baldwin, P., Belenky, G., & Herscovitch, P. (1998). Dissociated pattern of activity in visual cortices and their projections during human rapid eye movement sleep. *Science, 279*, 91–95.

Braun, J., Kahn, R. S., Froehlich, T., Auinger, P., & Lanphear, B. P. (2006, October 7). Cited in B. Harder, Cigarettes and lead linked to attention disorder. *Science News*, 170.

Brecher, E. M. (1972). *Licit and illicit drugs*. Boston: Little, Brown.

Breckler, S. J. (2006, February). The IRB problem. *Monitor on Psychology, 37*, 21.

Breiter, H. C., Aharon, I., Kahneman, D., Dale, A., & Shizgal, P. (2001). Functional imaging of neural responses to expectancy and experience of monetary gains and loses. *Neuron, 30*, 619–639.

Brennan, J. (1997, September 28). This 1,800-pound bear is no 800-pound gorilla. *Los Angeles Times/ Calendar*.

Brennan, J. (2004). *Cancer in context: A practical guide to supportive care*. New York: Oxford University Press.

Breuer, J., & Freud, S. (1895; reprinted 1955). Studies on hysteria. In J. Strachey (Ed. and Trans.), *The standard edition of the complete psychological works of Sigmund Freud*. London: Hogarth.

Brickman, P., Coates, D., & Janoff-Bulman, R. (1978). Lottery winners and accident victims: Is happiness relative? *Journal of Personality and Social Psychology, 36*, 917–927.

Briggs, J. L. (1970). *Never in anger: Portrait of an Eskimo family*. Cambridge, MA: Harvard University Press.

Broad, W. J. (2002, October 9). Lie-detector tests found too flawed to discover spies. *The New York Times*, A1.

Brodal, P. (2010). *The central nervous system*. New York: Oxford University Press.

Brodie, E. E., Whyte, A., & Niven, C. A. (2007). Analgesia through the looking glass? A randomized controlled trial investigating the effects of viewing a "virtual" limb upon phantom limb pain, sensation, and movement. *European Journal of Pain, 11*, 428–436.

Brody, A. L., Saxena, S., Stoessel, P., Gillies, L. A., Fairbanks, L. A., Alborzian, S., Phelps, M. E., Huang, S. C., Wu, H. M., Ho, M. L., Ho, M. K., Scott, C., Maidment, K., & Baxter, L. R., Jr. (2001). Regional brain metabolic changes in patients with major depression treated with either paroxetine or interpersonal therapy. *Archives of General Psychiatry, 58*, 631–640.

Brody, J. E. (2000a, April 25). Memories of things that never were. *The New York Times*, D8.

Brody, J. E. (2000b, October 17). One-two punch for losing pounds: Exercise and careful diet. *The New York Times*, D6.

Brody, J. E. (2003, August 18). Skipping a college course: Weight gain 101. *The New York Times*, D7.

Brody, J. E. (2008, February 26). Cochlear implant supports an author's active life. *The New York Times*.

Brody, J. E. (2009, June 16). An emotional hair trigger, often misread. *The New York Times*, D7.

Brody, J. E. (2011, February 1). Scientists see dangers in energy drinks. *The New York Times*, D7.

Brody, N. (1992). *Intelligence*. New York: Academic Press.

Brody, N. (1997). Intelligence, schooling, and society. *American Psychologist, 52*, 1046–1050.

Brody, N. (2000). Theories and measurements of intelligence. In R. J. Sternberg (Ed.), *Handbook of intelligence*. New York: Cambridge University Press.

Brodzinsky, S. (2006, July 25). *Columbia cracks down on drug cash* [On-line]. Available: http://www.usa today.com/news/world/2006-07-25-columbia -smuggling_x.htm.

Broidy, L. M., Nagin, D. S., Tremblay, R. E., Bates, J. E., Brame, B., Dodge, K. A., Fergusson, D., Horwood, J. K., Loeber, R., Laird, R., Lynam, D. R., Moffitt, T. E., Pettit, G. S., & Vitaro, F. (2003). Developmental trajectories of childhood disruptive behaviors and adolescent delinquency: A six-site cross-national study. *Developmental Psychology, 39*, 222–245.

Bronson, P., & Merryman, A. (2010, July 19). The creativity crisis. *Newsweek*, 44–49.

Bronstein, J. M., Tagliati, M., Alterman, R. L., Lozano, A. M., Volkmann, J., Stefani, A., Horak, F. B., Okun, M. D., Foote, K. D., Krack, P., Pahwa, R., Henderson, J. M., Hariz, M. I., Bakay, R. A., Rezai, A., Makrs, W. J., Jr., Moror, E., Vitek, J. L., Weaver, F. M., Gross, R. E., & DeLong, M. R. (2011). Deep brain stimulation for Parkinson's disease. *Archives of Neurology, 68*(2), 165.

Brooks, C. (1994, February 27). Breakdown into the shadows of mental illness. Special report. *San Diego Union-Tribune*.

Brooks, C. (1995a, February 27). Shadowlands: Three profiled in mental illness series are striving to improve their conditions. *San Diego Union-Tribune*.

Brooks, C. (1995b, June 5). Rod Steiger is powerful voice for mentally ill. *San Diego Union-Tribune*.

Brooks-Gunn, J. (2006, November 26). Cited in P. Tough, What it takes to make a student. *The New York Times Magazine*.

Brophy, B. (2006, December 25). Give your teen more driving time. *U.S. News & World Report*, 71.

Brown, A. S. (2011). The environment and susceptibility to schizophrenia. *Progress in Neurobiology, 93*, 23–58.

Brown, D. J. (2007, December/2008, January). Psychedelic healing? *Scientific American Mind*, 66–71.

Brown, D. J. (2009, November). Treating agony with ecstasy. *Discover*.

Brown, G. S., Lambert, M. J., Jones, E. R., & Minami, T. (2005, August). Identifying highly effective psychotherapists in a managed care environment. *American Journal of Managed Care, 11*, 513–520.

Brown, J., Fenske, M., & Neporent, L. (2010). *The winner's brain: 8 strategies great minds use to achieve success*. Cambridge, MA: De Capo Press.

Brown, R. (2012, May 2). Criminal charges for 13 in Florida A&M hazing death. *The New York Times*.

Brown, R., & Kulik, J. (1977). Flashbulb memories. *Cognition, 5*, 73–99.

Brown, R. J., Schrag, A., & Trimble, M. R. (2005). Dissociation, childhood interpersonal trauma, and family functioning in patients with somatization disorder. *American Journal of Psychiatry, 162*, 899–905.

Brown, S. A. (1996, May 13). Talent for living. *People,* 85–86.

Brown, S. C., & Craik, F. I. M. (2005). Encoding and retrieval of information. In E. Tulving & F. M. Craik (Eds.), *The Oxford handbook of memory.* New York: Oxford University Press.

Brownlee, C. (2006, August 12). Scientists find midnight-snack center in brain. *Science News, 170,* 109–110.

Brownlee, S. (1997, February 3). The case for frivolity. *U.S. News & World Report.*

Bruer, J. T. (1999). *The myth of the first three years.* New York: Free Press.

Bruner, J. (1997). Celebrating divergence: Piaget and Vygotsky. *Human Development, 40,* 63–73.

Bryant, G. A., & Barrett, H. C. (2007). Recognizing intentions in infant-directed speech: Evidence for universals. *Psychological Science, 18,* 746–751.

Buckley, C. (2007, January 3). Man is rescued by stranger on subway tracks. *The New York Times.*

Buckley, P. (1989). Fifty years after Freud: Dora, the Rat Man, and the Wolf-Man. *American Journal of Psychiatry, 146,* 1394–1403.

Buckout, R. (1980). Nearly 2,000 witnesses can be wrong. *Bulletin of the Psychonomic Society, 16,* 307–310.

Buddie, A. M., & Miller, A. G. (2002). Beyond rape myths: A more complex view of perceptions of rape myths. *Sex Roles, 45,* 139–160.

Bufka, L. F. (2011, January). Cited in R. A. Clay, Revising the DSM. *Monitor on Psychology,* 54–55.

Bugental, B. B., & Goodnow, J. J. (1998). Socialization processes. In W. Damon & N. Eisenberg (Eds.), *Handbook of child psychology* (5th ed.). New York: John Wiley & Sons.

Bulik, C. M. (2006, March 15). In T. Whitmire, Study: Genes may cause risk for anorexia. *USA Today.*

Bulik, C. M., Sullivan, P. F., & Kendler, K. S. (2003). Genetic and environmental contributions to obesity and eating. *International Journal of Eating Disorders, 33,* 293–298.

Buonomano, D. V., & Merzenich, M. M. (1995). Temporal information transformed into a spatial code by a neural network with realistic properties. *Science, 267,* 1028–1030.

Bureau of Labor Statistics. (2010, September 14). Cited in D. Cauchon, Gender pay gap smallest on record. *USA Today,* 1A.

Burge, D., Hammen, C., Davila, J., Daley, S. E., Paley, B., Herzberg, D., & Lindberg, N. (1997). Attachment cognitions and college and work functioning two years later in late adolescent women. *Journal of Youth and Adolescence, 26,* 285–301.

Burger, J. M. (2007). Cited in C. Borge, Basic instincts: The science of evil. *ABC News* [On-line]. Available: http://abcnews.go.com/Primetime/print?id=2765416.

Burger, J. M. (2008). *Personality* (7th ed.). Belmont, CA: Wadsworth Cengage.

Burger, J. M. (2009). Replicating Milgram: Would people still obey today? *American Psychologist, 64,* 1–11.

Burger, J. M. (2011). *Personality* (8th ed.). Belmont, CA: Wadsworth.

Burger, J. M., & Lynn, A. L. (2005). Superstitious behavior among Americans and Japanese professional baseball players. *Basic and Applied Social Psychology, 27,* 71–76.

Burghardt, G. M. (2005). *The genesis of animal play: Testing the limits.* Cambridge, MA: MIT Press.

Burn, S. M. (2004). *Groups: Theory and practice.* Belmont, CA: Wadsworth/Thomson.

Burns, T. (2004). *Community mental health teams.* New York: Oxford University Press.

Burton, C. M., & King, L. A. (2004). The health benefits of writing about intensely positive experiences. *Journal of Research in Personality, 38,* 150–163.

Burton, S. (2006). Symptom domains of schizophrenia: The role of atypical antipsychotic agents. *Journal of Psychopharmacology, 20,* 6–20.

Busari, S. (2011, September 26). *Maathai: World mourns passing of "true African heroine"* [On-line]. Available: http//www.cnn.com/2011/09/26/world/Africa/wangari-maathai-tribute.

Bushman, B. J. (2002). Does venting anger feed or extinguish the flame? Catharsis, rumination, distraction, anger, and aggressive responding. *Personality and Social Psychology Bulletin, 28,* 724–731.

Buss, D. M. (1994). Mate preferences in 37 cultures. In W. J. Lonner & R. Malpass (Eds.), *Psychology and culture.* Boston: Allyn & Bacon.

Buss, D. M. (1995). Psychological sex differences. *American Psychologist, 50,* 164–168.

Buss, D. M. (1999). Human nature and individual differences: The evolution of human personality. In L. A. Pervin & O. P. John (Eds.), *Handbook of personality* (2nd ed.). New York: Guilford Press.

Buss, D. M. (2003). *The evolution of desire: Strategies of human mating* (2nd ed.) New York: Basic Books.

Buss, D. M. (2004). *Evolutionary psychology: The new science of the mind* (2nd ed.). Boston: Allyn & Bacon.

Buss, D. M. (2007). The evolution of human mating. *Acta Psychologica Sinica, 39,* 502–512.

Buss, D. M. (2009). The great struggles of life: Darwin and the emergence of evolutionary psychology. *American Psychologist, 64,* 140–148.

Buss, D. M., Abbott, M., Angleitner, A., Asherian, A., Biaggio, A., Blanco-VillaSenor, A., Bruchon-Schweitzer, M., Ch'u, H. Y., Czapinski, J., DeRaad, B., Ekehammar, B., Fioravanti, M., Georgas, J., Gjerde, P., Guttman, R., Hazan, F., Iwawaki, S., Janakiramaiah, H., Khosroshani, F., Kreitler, S., Lachenicht, L., Lee, M., Liik, K., Little, B., Lohamy, N., Makun, S., Mika, S., Moadel-Shahid, M., Moane, G., Montero, M., Mundy-Casde, A. C., Niit, T., Nsenduluka, E., Peltzer, K., Pienkowski, R., Pirttila-Backman, A., Ponce De Leon, J., Rousseau, J., Runco, M. A., Safir, M. P., Samuels, C., Sanitioso, R., Schweitzer, D., Serpell, R., Smid, N., Spencer, C., Tadinac, M., Todorova, E. N., Troland, K., Van den Brande, L., Van Heck, G., Van Langenhove, L., & Yang, K. S. (1990). International preferences in selecting mates. *Journal of Cross-Cultural Psychology, 21,* 5–47.

Buss, D. M., & Schmitt, D. P. (1993). Sexual strategies theory: An evolutionary perspective on human mating. *Psychological Review, 100,* 204–232.

Bustillo, J. R., Lauriello, J., Horan, W. P., & Keith, S. J. (2001). The psychosocial treatment of schizophrenia: An update. *American Journal of Psychiatry, 158,* 163–175.

Butcher, J. N. (2009a). Clinical personality assessment: History, evolution, contemporary models & practical applications. Cited in J. N. Butcher (Ed.), *Oxford handbook of personality assessment* (pp. 5–24). New York: Oxford University Press.

Butcher, J. N. (Ed.). (2009b). *Oxford handbook of personality assessment.* New York: Oxford University Press.

Butler, A. C., Chapman, J. E., Forman, E. M., & Beck, A. T. (2006). The empirical status of cognitive-behavioral therapy: A review of meta-analyses. *Clinical Psychology Review, 26,* 17–31.

Byland, T. (2008, January/Febuary). Cited in Building a bionic eye. *Science Illustrated,* 50–55.

Byne, W. (1997). Why we cannot conclude that sexual orientation is primarily a biological phenomenon. *Journal of Homosexuality, 34,* 73–80.

Cabeza, R. (2006, January 16). Cited in G. Cohen, The myth of the midlife crisis. *Newsweek,* 82–87.

Cabeza, R. (2008, December 16). Cited in M. Elias, Older brains act as filters. *USA Today,* 7D.

Cabeza, R., Anderson, N. D., Locantore, J. K., & McIntosh, A. R. (2002). Aging gracefully: Compensatory brain activity in high-performing older adults. *NeuroImage, 17,* 1394–1402.

Cabeza, R., & Nyberg, L. (2003). Special issue of functional neuroimaging of memory. *Neuropsychologia, 41,* 241–244.

Cacioppo, J. T., & Berntson, G. G. (2002). Social neuroscience. In J. T. Cacioppo, G. G. Berntson, R. Adolphs, C. S. Carter, R. J. Davidson, M. K. McClintock, B. S. McEwen, M. J. Meaney, D. L. Schacter, E. M. Sternberg, S. S. Suomi & S. E. Taylor (Eds.), *Foundations of social neuroscience* (pp. 1–9). Cambridge, MA: MIT Press.

Cacioppo, J. T., Berntson, G. G., Larsen, J. R., Poehlmann, K. M., & Ito, T. A. (2000). The psychophysiology of emotion. In M. Lewis & J. M. Haviland-Jones (Eds.), *Handbook of emotions* (2nd ed., pp. 173–191). New York: Guilford Press.

Cacioppo, J. T., & Decety, J. (2011). An introduction to social neuroscience. In J. Decety & J. T Cacioppo (Eds.), *The Oxford handbook of social neuroscience* (pp. 3–8). New York: Oxford University Press.

Cacioppo, J. T., Klein, D. J., Berntson, G. G., & Hatfield, E. (1993). The psychophysiology of emotion. In M. Lewis & J. M. Haviland (Eds.), *Handbook of emotions.* New York: Guilford Press.

Cacioppo, J. T., & Petty, R. E. (1982). The need for cognition. *Journal of Personality and Social Psychology, 42,* 116–131.

Cahill, L., Prins, B., Weber, M., & McGaugh, J. L. (1994). B-adrenergic activation and memory for emotional events. *Nature, 371,* 702–704.

Cahill, L., Uncapher, M., Kilpatrick, L., Alkire, M. T., & Turner, J. (2004). Sex-related hemispheric lateralization of amygdala function in emotionally influenced memory: An fMRI investigation. *Learning & Memory, 11,* 261–266.

Calandreau, L., Trifilieff, P., Mons, N., Costes, L., Marien, M., Marighetto, A., Micheau, J., Jaffard, R., & Desmedt, A. (2006). Extracellular hippocampal acetylcholine level controls amygdala function and promotes adaptive conditioned emotional response. *Journal of Neuroscience, 26,* 13556–13566.

Caldwell, J. C., Orubuloye, I. O., & Caldwell, P. (1997). Male and female circumcision in Africa from a regional to a specific Nigerian examination. *Social Science & Medicine, 44,* 1181–1193.

Callejas, A. (2008, March). Cited in L. Meyers, Seeing—and hearing and tasting—red. *Monitor on Psychology,* 10.

Camp, G. C. (1994). A longitudinal study of correlates of creativity. *Creativity Research Journal, 7,* 125–144.

Canfield, R. L. (2003, August 5). Cited in J. E. Brody, Even low lead levels pose perils for children. *The New York Times,* D7.

Canli, T. (2008, February/March). The character code. *Scientific American Mind,* 52–57.

Canli, T., Desmond, J. E., Zhao, Z., & Gabrieli, J. D. E. (2002). Sex differences in the neural basis of emotional memories. *Proceedings of the National Academy of Sciences, 99,* 10789–10794.

Caplan, N., Choy, M. H., & Whitmore, J. K. (1992). Indochinese refugee families and academic achievement. *Scientific American, 266,* 36–42.

Caplan, P. (1994, June 5). Cited in A. Japenga, DMS. *Los Angeles Times Magazine.*

Caporael, L. R. (2001). Evolutionary psychology: Toward a unifying theory and a hybrid science. *Annual Review of Psychology, 52,* 607–628.

Caprara, G. V., Barbaranelli, C., Pastorelli, C., & Cervone, D. (2004). The contribution of self-efficacy beliefs to psychosocial outcomes in adolescence: Predicting beyond global dispositional tendencies. *Personality and Individual Differences, 37,* 751–763.

Carden, R., Bryant, C., & Moss, R. (2004). Locus of control, test anxiety, academic procrastination, and achievement among college students. *Psychological Reports, 95,* 581–582.

Carducci, B. J. (2006). *Psychology of personality.* Boston: Blackwell Publishing.

C.A.R.E. (Committee on Animal Research and Ethics). (2012). *Guidelines for ethical conduct in the care and use of animals* [On-line]. Available: http://www.apa.org/science/leadership/care/guidelines.aspx.

CARE. (2008). Maternal caffeine intake during pregnancy and risk of fetal growth restriction: A large prospective observational study. *Behavioral Medicine Journal, 337,* a2332.

Carey, B. (2002, December 16). The brain in love. *Los Angeles Times,* F1.

Carey, B. (2004, December 27). Autism therapies still a mystery, but parents take a leap of faith. *The New York Times,* A1, A14.

Carey, B. (2010, November 23). Virtual healing for the real world. *The New York Times,* D1.

Carey, B. (2011, October 3). Talk therapy lifts severe schizophrenics. *The New York Times.*

Carey, B. (2012, February 13). The therapist may see you anytime, anywhere. *The New York Times.*

Carlin, A. (2000, July 4). Cited in J. Robbins, Virtual reality finds a real place as a medical aid. *The New York Times,* D6.

Carlson, J. M. (1990). Subjective ideological similarity between candidates and supporters: A study of party elites. *Political Psychology, 11,* 485–492.

Caroff, S. N., Mann, S. C., Campbell, E. C., & Sullivan, K. A. (2002). Movement disorders associated with atypical antipsychotic drugs. *Journal of Clinical Psychiatry, 63*(Suppl. 4), 12–19.

Carpenter, W. (2003, May 20). Cited in E. Goode, Leading drugs for psychosis come under new scrutiny. *The New York Times,* A1.

Carskadon, M. A. (2006). *The sleep of America's children* [On-line]. Available: http://www.sleepfoundation.org/hottopics/index.php?secid=11&id=82.

Carstensen, L. (2011, Spring). Cited in B. Strauch, Happiness is an old brain. *The Brain,* 62–65.

Carter, O. L., Pettigrew, J. D., Hasler, F., Wallis, G. M., Liu, G. B., Hell, D., & Vollenweider, F. X. (2005). Modulating the rate and rhythmicity of perceptual rivalry alterations with the mixed 5-HT2A and 5-HT1A agonist psilocybin. *Neuropsychopharmacology, 30,* 1154–1162.

Cartwright, R. (1988, July–August). Cited in *Psychology Today.*

Cartwright, R. (2002, July 15). Cited in M. H. Gossard, Taking control. *Newsweek,* 47.

Cartwright, R. D. (2006). Sleepwalking. In T. L. Lee-Chiong (Ed.), *Sleep: A comprehensive handbook* (pp. 429–433). Hoboken, NJ: John Wiley & Sons.

Carver, C. S. (2011). Coping. In R. J. Contrada & A. Baum (Eds.), *The handbook of stress science: Biology, psychology, and health* (pp. 221–229). New York: Springer.

Carver, C. S., Scheier, M. F., & Segerstrom, S. C. (2010). Optimism. *Clinical Psychology Review, 30*(7), 879–889.

Casey, B. J. (2011, March). Cited in C. Zimmer, The brain. *Discover,* 28–29.

Casey, B. J., Somerville, L. H., Gotlib, I. H., Ayduk, O., Franklin, N. T., Askren, M. K., Jonides, J., Berman, M. G., Wilson, N. L., Teslovich, T., Glover, G., Zayas, V., Mischel, W., & Shoda, Y. (2011). Behavioral and neural correlates of delay of gratification 40 years later. *Proceedings of the National Academy of Sciences, 108,* 14998–15003.

Caspi, A. (2000). The child is father of the man: Personality continuities from childhood to adulthood. *Journal of Personality and Social Psychology, 78,* 158–172.

Caspi, A., & Roberts, B. W. (1999). Personality continuity and change across the life course. In L. A. Pervin & O. P. John (Eds.), *Handbook of personality* (2nd ed.). New York: Guilford Press.

Caspi, A., Roberts, B. W., & Shiner, R. L. (2005). Personality development: Stability and change. *Annual Review of Psychology, 56,* 453–484.

Cassady, J. C., & Johnson, R. E. (2002). Cognitive test anxiety and academic performance. *Contemporary Educational Psychology, 27,* 270–295.

Casselman, A. (2006, January). Blinking flips an off switch in brain. *Discover,* 42.

Cassidy, S. B., Schwartz, S., Miller, J. L., & Driscoll, D. J. (2012). Prader-Willi syndrome. *Genetics in Medicine, 14,* 10–26.

Catalano, S. M. (2006, September). National crime victimization survey: Criminal victimization, 2005. *Bureau of Justice Statistics Bulletin,* 1–12.

Cattell, R. B. (1943). The description of personality: Basic traits resolved into clusters. *Journal of Abnormal and Social Psychology, 38,* 476–506.

Caulkins, J. P., Reuter, P., Iguchi, M. Y., & Chiesa, J. (2005). How goes the "war on drugs"? *RAND* [On-line]. Available: http://www.rand.org/.

Cavanagh, J. T. O., Carson, A. J., Sharpe, M., & Lawrie, S. M. (2003). Psychological autopsy studies of suicide: A systematic review. *Psychological Medicine, 33,* 395–405.

CBS News. (2004a, June 16). *Tony Hawk takes off* [On-line]. Available: http://www.cbsnews.com/stories/2002/12/10/60II/main532509.shtml.

CBS News. (2004b, September 24). *Assisted suicide* [On-line]. Available: http://www.cbs.ca/includes/printablestory.jsp.

CDC (Centers for Disease Control and Prevention). (2006a). Cited in Associated Press, CDC report finds obesity rates rising in American youths, men. *San Diego Union-Tribune,* A7.

CDC. (2006b). *Overweight and obesity: An overview* [On-line]. Available: http://cdc.gov/nccdphp/dnpa/obesity/contributing_factors.htm.

CDC. (2008a, July 23). About 5% of kids have ADHD. Cited in M. Hitti, *WebMD* [On-line]. Available: http://www.webmd.com/add-adhd/news/20080723/cdc-about-5-percent-of-kids-have-adhd.

CDC. (2008b, August). *Estimates of new HIV infections in the United States.* Atlanta: U.S. Department of Health and Human Services, Centers for Disease Control and Prevention [On-line]. Available: http://www.cdc.gov/hiv/.

CDC. (2008c, December 19). Cited in C. Macleod, China wrestles with growing obesity. *USA Today,* 16A.

CDC. (2009). Prevalence of autism spectrum disorders—Autism and developmental disabilities monitoring network—United States, 2006. *Morbidity and Mortality Weekly Report, 58,* 1–20.

CDC. (2010a, January 14). Cited in N. Hellmich, U.S. obesity rate appears to be leveling off, landmark study finds. *USA Today,* 8D.

CDC. (2010b, September 7). Vital signs: Current cigarette smoking among adults aged >18 years—United States, 2009. *Morbidity and Mortality Weekly Report.*

CDC. (2011a, March 17). Cited in N. Hellmich, Life expectancy at an all-time high in U.S. *USA Today,* 3A.

CDC. (2011b, October). Teenagers in the United States: Sexual activity, contraceptive use, and childbearing, 2006–2010 national survey of family growth. *Vital and Health Statistics, Series 23, Number 31.*

CDC. (2011c, December 1). Cited in A. Manning, Complacency is the biggest barrier to ending AIDS. *USA Today,* 3D.

CDC. (2011d, December 6). Cited in L. Copland, Report backs graduated licensing. *USA Today,* 1A.

CDC. (2011e, December 15). Cited in J. Lloyd, Study: Sexual violence 'widespread.' *USA Today,* 3A.

CDC. (2012a, May 2). *Adverse childhood experiences: Major findings* [On-line]. Available: http://www.cdc.goc/ace/findings.htm.

CDC. (2012b, May 8). Cited in N. Hellmich, Obesity rate may hit 42% by 2030. *USA Today,* 1A.

CDC. (2012c, August 31). National and state vaccination coverage among adolescents aged 13–17 years—United States, 2011. *Morbidity and Mortality Weekly Report.* Atlanta, GA: Author.

CDC. (2012d). *Preventing suicide.* Features [On-line]. Available: http://www.cdc.gov/Features/PreventingSuicide.

CDC. (2012e). *Suicide and self-inflicted injury.* Fast Stats [On-line]. Available: http://www.cdc.gov/nchs/fastats/suicide.htm.

C'de Baca, J., & Wilbourne, P. (2004). Quantum change: Ten years later. *Journal of Clinical Psychology, 60,* 531–541.

Ceci, S. J., Rosenblum, T., de Bruyn, E., & Lee, D. Y. (1997). A bio-ecological model of intellectual development: Moving beyond h2. In R. J. Sternberg & E. Grigorenko (Eds.), *Intelligence, heredity, and environment.* New York: Cambridge University Press.

Cegla, J., Tan, T. M., & Bloom, S. R. (2010). Gut-brain cross-talk in appetite regulation. *Current Opinion in Clinical Nutrition & Metabolic Care, 13,* 588–593.

Celizic, M. (2007, November 2). Former addict lifts herself up, becomes a teacher. *Today Show* [On-line]. Available: http://today.msnbc.com/id/21595900/.

Cerone, D. (1989, October 22). How to train an 1,800-pound star. *Los Angeles Times/Calendar.*

Cha, A. E. (2005, March 27). Employers replying on personality tests to screen applicants. *Washington Post,* A1.

Chaiken, S., & Eagly, A. H. (1976). Communication modality as a determinant of message persuasiveness and message comprehensibility. *Journal of Personality and Social Psychology, 34,* 605–614.

Chamorro-Premuzic, T., Ahmetoglu, G., & Furnham, A. (2008). Little more than personality: Dispositional determinants of test anxiety (the Big Five, core self-evaluations, and self-assesses intelligence). *Learning and Individual Differences, 18,* 258–563.

Chamorro-Premuzic, T., & Furnham, A. (2008). Personality, intelligence and approaches to learning as predictors of academic performance. *Personality and Individual Differences, 44,* 1596–1603.

Chan, B. L., Witt, R., Charrow, A. P., Magee, A., Howard, R., Pasquina, P. F., Heilmann, K. M., & Tsao, J. W. (2007). Mirror therapy for phantom limb pain. *New England Journal of Medicine, 357,* 2206–2207.

Chance, P. (2009). *Learning and behavior: Active learning edition* (6th ed.). Belmont, CA: Wadsworth.

Charkalis, D. M. (2005, December 22). Delayed diagnosis: Dyslexia. *USA Today,* 8D.

Charmoli, R. (2006, May 13). Former spokesman for Aryan Nations speaks about hate groups. *Cadillac News.*

Charney, D. (2009, March/April). Cited in K. McGowan, Good morning, heartache. *Psychology Today,* 76–83.

Chaudri, O., Small, C., & Bloom, S. (2006). Gastrointestinal hormones regulating appetite. *Philosophical Transactions of the Royal Society of London. Series B, Biological Sciences, 29,* 1187–1209.

Cheah, C. S., Leung, C. Y., Tahseen, M., & Schuz, D. (2009). Authoritative parenting among immigrant Chinese mothers of preschoolers. *Journal of Family Psychology, 23,* 311–320.

Chemers, M. M., Hu, L., & Garcia, B. F. (2001). Academic self-efficacy and first-year college student performance and adjustment. *Journal of Educational Psychology, 93,* 55–64.

Chen, J., Armstrong, A. H., Koehler, A. N., & Hecht, M. H. (2010). Small molecule microarrays enable the discovery of compounds that bind the Alzheimer's Ab peptide and reduce its cytotoxicity. *Journal of the American Chemical Society, 132*(47), 17015–17022.

Chen, J., Moran, S., & Gardner, H. (2009). *Multiple intelligences around the world*. New York: Jossey-Bass.

Chen, X., Gabitto, M., Peng, Y., Ryba, N. J. P., & Zuker, C. S. (2011). A gustotopic map of taste qualities in the mammalian brain. *Science, 333*, 1262–1266.

Chessbase News. (2006, May 12). Kramnik vs Deep Fritz: Computer wins match by 4:2 [On-line]. Available: http:www.chessbase.com/newsdetail .asp?newsid=3524.

Chetty, R., Friedman, J. N., Hilger, N., Saez, E., Schanzenbach, D. W., & Yagan, D. (2011). How does your kindergarten classroom affect your earnings? Evidence from Project Star. *The Quarterly Journal of Ecomonics, CXXVI*, 1593–1660.

Chiang, J. J., Eisenberger, N. I., Seeman, T. E., & Taylor, S. E. (2012, January 23). Negative and competitive social interactions are related to heightened pro-inflammatory cytokine activity. *Proceedings of the National Academy of Sciences: Early Edition.*

Chiao, J. Y., & Ambady, N. (2007). Cultural neuroscience: Parsing universality and diversity across levels of analysis. In S. Kitayama & D. Cohen (Eds.), *Handbook of cultural psychology* (pp. 237–254). New York: Guilford Press.

Chiao, J. Y., Harari, A. R., Harada, T., Mano, Y., Sadato, N., Parrish, T. B., & Iidaka, T. (2010). Theory and methods in cultural neuroscience. *Social Cognitive and Affective Neuroscience, 5*, 356–361.

Chiao, J. Y., Iidaka, T., Gordon, H. L., Nogawa, J., Bar, M., Aminoff, E., Sadato, N., & Ambady, N. (2008). Cultural specificity in amygdala response to fear faces. *Journal of Cognitive Neuroscience, 20*, 2167–2174.

Choi, C. Q. (2010, February 11). Cell-off: Induced pluripotent stem cells fall short of potential found in embryonic version. *Scientific American.*

Chokroverty, S. (2000). *Sleep disorders medicine* (2nd ed.). Boston: Butterworth-Heinemann.

Chomsky, N. (1957). *Syntactic structures*. The Hague: Mouton.

Chomsky, N. (2011, November). The radical linguist: Noam Chomsky. *Discover*, 66–71.

Christakis, N. A., & Allison, P. D. (2006). Mortality after the hospitalization of a spouse. *New England Journal of Medicine, 354*, 719–730.

Christakis, N. A., & Fowler, J. H. (2009, November/December). Love the one you're with. *Scientific American Mind*, 48–55.

Christensen, D. (2003). Dietary dilemmas. *Science News, 163*, 88–90.

Christman, M. F. (2006, April 18). Common genetic link to obesity is discovered. *The New York Times*, O4.

Chu, J., & Pratico, D. (2011). Pharmacologic blockage of 5-lipoxygenase improved the amyloidotic phenotype of an Alzheimer's disease transgenic mouse model. *American Journal of Pathology, 178*(4), 1762–1769.

Chu, K. (2010, March 30). Extreme dieting spreads in Asia. *USA Today*, 1D.

Chua, H. F., Boland, J. E., & Nisbett, R. E. (2005). Cultural variation in eye movements during scene perception. *Proceedings of the National Academy of Sciences, 102*, 12629–12633.

Chua-Eoan, H. (2010, February 25). The killer-whale attack at SeaWorld: How it happened. *Time.*

Chumlea, W. C., Schubert, C. M., Roche, A. F., Kulin, H. E., Lee, P. A., Himes, J. H., & Sun, S. S. (2003). Age at menarche and racial comparisons in U.S. girls. *Pediatrics, 111*, 110–113.

Chwalisz, K., Diener, E., & Gallagher, D. (1988). Autonomic arousal feedback and emotional experience: Evidence from the spinal cord injury. *Journal of Personality and Social Psychology, 54*, 820–828.

Cialdini, R. B. (2001). *Influence: Science and practice* (4th ed.). New York: Allyn & Bacon.

Cialdini, R. B. (2003, February). The science of persuasion. *Scientific American*, 76–81.

Cialdini, R. B., & Goldstein, N. J. (2004). Social influence: Compliance and conformity. *Annual Review of Psychology, 55*, 591–621.

Cizek, G. J., & Burg, S. S. (2006). *Addressing test anxiety in a high-stakes environment: Strategies for classrooms and schools*. Thousand Oaks, CA: Corwin Press.

Clark, D. M., Ehlers, A., Hackman, A., McManus, F., Fennell, M., Grey, N., Waddington, L., & Wild, J. (2006). Cognitive therapy versus exposure and applied relaxation in social phobia: A randomized controlled trial. *Journal of Consulting and Clinical Psychology, 74*, 568–578.

Clark, K. (2010, May). You can work your way through 11 grad degrees. *U.S. News & World Report*, 60–61.

Clark, K. B., & Clark, M. P. (1939). The development of consciousness of self and the emergence of racial identification in Negro preschool children. *Journal of Social Psychology, 10*, 591–599.

Clark, L. A., Watson, D., & Reynolds, S. (1995). Diagnosis and classification of psychopathology: Challenges to the current system and future directions. *Annual Review of Psychology, 46*, 121–153.

Clarke, A. M., & Clarke, A. D. B. (1989). The later cognitive effects on early intervention. *Intelligence, 13*, 289–297.

Clay, R. A. (2002, September). A renaissance for humanistic psychology. *Monitor on Psychology*, 42–43.

Clay, R. A. (2011, January). Revising the DSM. *Monitor on Psychology*, 54–55.

Clay, R. A. (2012, January). Beyond psychotherapy. *Monitor on Psychology*, 46–50.

Clore, G. L., & Ortony, A. (2008). Appraisal theories: How cognition shapes affect into emotion. Cited in M. Lewis, J. M. Haviland-Jones & L. F. Barrett (Eds.), *Handbook of emotions* (3rd ed., pp. 628–64). New York: Guilford Press.

Cloud, J. (2002, November 4). Is pot good for you? *Time*, 62–66.

Cloud, J. (2009, January 19). Minds on the edge. *Time*, 42–46.

Cloud, J. (2010, January 6). Why your DNA isn't your destiny. *Time.*

Cloud, J. (2011, March 7). Beyond drugs: How alternative treatment can ease pain. *Time*, 80–88.

CNN. (2011, January 12). *Winfrey's film flop caused mac-and-cheese binge.*

Coates, T. P. (2006, May 8). When parents are the threat. *Time*, 181–182.

Coccaro, E. F., & Kavoussi, R. J. (1997). Fluoxetine and impulsive aggressive behavior in personality-disordered subjects. *Archives of General Psychiatry, 54*, 1081–1088.

Cochran, F. (2007, February 16). *About Floyd Cochran* [On-line]. Available: http://www.geocities.com /onemansmind/hg/Cochran.html.

Cochrane Collaboration. (2011, March 7). Cited in J. Cloud, Beyond drugs: How alternative treatment can ease pain. *Time*, 80–88.

Coelho, C. M., & Purkis, H. (2009). The origins of specific phobias: Influential theories and current perspectives. *Review of General Psychology, 13*, 335–348.

Cohen, G. (2006, January 16). The myth of the midlife crisis. *Newsweek*, 82–87.

Cohen, N. J. (1984). Preserved learning capacity in amnesia: Evidence for multiple memory systems. In L. R. Squire & N. Butters (Eds.), *Neuropsychology of memory*. New York: Guilford Press.

Cohen, S. (2003). Social stress, social support, and the susceptibility to the common cold. *American Psychological Society, 16*, 13.

Cohen, S., Janicki-Deverts, D., Doyle, W. J., Miller, G. E., Frank, E., Rabin, B. S., & Turner, R. B. (2012). Chronic stress, glucocorticoid receptor resistance, inflammation, and disease risk. *Proceedings of the National Academy of Sciences, 109*, 5995–5999.

Cohen, S., Tyrrell, D. A. J., & Smith, A. P. (1997). Psychological stress in humans and susceptibility to the common cold. In T. W. Miller (Ed.), *Clinical disorders and stressful life events*. Madison, CT: International Universities Press.

Coie, J. D., & Dodge, K. A. (1998). Aggression and antisocial behavior. In W. Damon & R. M. Lerner (Eds.), *Handbook of child psychology* (Vol. 1). New York: John Wiley & Sons.

Colangelo, N. (1997). The "termites" grow up and grow old. *Contemporary Psychology, 42*, 208–209.

Cole, J., Crowle, S., Austwick, G., & Slater, D. H. (2009). Exploratory findings with virtual reality for phantom limb pain; from stump motion to agency and analgesia. *Disability & Rehabilitation, 31*(10), 846–854.

Cole, S. O. (2005). An update on the effects of marijuana & its potential medical use: Forensic focus. *The Forensic Examiner, 14.3*, 14.

Cole, Y. (2009). *Why are so few CEOs people of color and women?* [On-line]. Available: http://www.diversity inc.com/public/2696.cfm.

Coles, M. E., & Horng, B. (2006). Social anxiety disorder. In M. Hersen & J. C. Thomas (Eds.), *Comprehensive handbook of personality and psychopathology: Adult psychopathology* (Vol. 2, pp. 138–153). Hoboken, NJ: John Wiley & Sons.

Coles, R. (Ed.). (2000). *The Erik Erikson reader*. New York: W. W. Norton & Company.

Collins, A. T. (2012). *A tongue for an eye: Device challenges conventional wisdom* [On-line]. Available: http://www .nei/nih.gov/news/briefs/weihenmayer.asp.

Collins, W. A., Maccoby, E. E., Steinberg, L., Hetherington, E. M., & Bornstein, M. H. (2000). Contemporary research on parenting. *American Psychologist, 55*, 218–232.

Colom, R., Juan-Espinosa, M., Abad, F., & Garcia, L. F. (2000). Negligible sex differences in general intelligence. *Intelligence, 28*, 57–68.

Colorado Springs Gazette. (2002, December 22). Reality stems from pastor's vision.

Colwell, K. (2009, May 12). Cited in B. Carey, Judging honesty by words, not fidgets. *The New York Times*, D1, D4.

Comarow, A. (2008, January 21). Embracing alternative care. *U.S. News & World Report*, 31–40.

Combs, D. R., Mueser, K. T., & Gutierrez, M. M. (2012). Schizophrenia. In M. Hersen & D. C. Beidel (Eds.), *Adult psychopathology and diagnosis* (pp. 261–315). Hoboken, NJ: John Wiley & Sons.

Compton, W. C., & Hoffman, E. (2013). *Positive psychology: The science of happiness and flourishing* (2nd ed.). Belmont, CA: Wadsworth Cengage.

Conger, A. J., Dygdon, J. A., & Rollock, D. (2012). Conditioned emotional responses in racial prejudice. *Ethnic and Racial Studies, 35*, 298–319.

Conger, R. D., Belsky, J., & Capaldi, D. M. (2009). The intergenerational transmission of parenting: Closing comments for the special section. *Developmental Psychology, 45*, 1276–1283.

Connor, L. (1982). In A. J. Marsella & G. M. White (Eds.), *Cultural conceptions of mental health and therapy*. Boston: D. Reidel.

Cook, G. (2002, January 2). Aha! Eureka moments start with confusion and end with discovery. *San Diego Union Tribune*, F1.

Cook, R. J., Erdman, J. N., Hevia, M., & Dickens, B. M. (2008). Prenatal management of anencephaly. *International Journal of Gynecology and Obstetrics, 102*, 304–308.

Cooper, M. (2008). *Essential research findings in counseling and psychotherapy: The facts are friendly*. Los Angeles: Sage.

Cooper, P. J., Zheng, Y., Richard, C., Vavrik, J., Heinrichs, B., & Siegmund, G. J. (2003). The impact of hands-free message reception response on driving task performance. *Accident Analysis and Prevention, 35*, 23–35.

Copeland, L. (1999, December 16). Meet South's new sheriffs. *USA Today*, A1.

Copeland, L. (2010, September 20). 'Awareness gap' on road texting. *USA Today*, 3A.

Copeland, L. (2011, December 6). Report backs graduated licensing. *USA Today*, 1A.

Copeland, L. (2012, May 3). 13 charged in Fla. hazing case. *USA Today*, 3A.

Copeland, W., Shanahan, L., Costello, E. J., & Angold, A. (2011). Cumulative prevalence of psychiatric disorders by young adulthood: A prospective cohort analysis from the Great Smoky Mountain study. *Journal of the American Academy of Child and Adolescent Psychiatry, 50*, 252–261.

Corbett, S. (2008, January 20). A cutting tradition. *The New York Times*.

Coren, S., & Ward, L. M. (1993). *Sensation and perception* (4th ed.). San Diego: Harcourt Brace Jovanovich.

Corey, G. (2005). *Theory and practice of counseling and psychotherapy* (7th ed.). Belmont, CA: Brooks/Cole–Thomson Learning.

Corey, G. (2009). *Theory and practice of counseling and psychotherapy* (8th ed.). Belmont, CA: Thomson Brooks/Cole.

Corey, G. (2013). *Theory and practice of counseling and psychotherapy* (9th ed.). Belmont, CA: Brooks Cole, Cengage.

Cormier, S., & Nurius, P. S. (2003). *Interviewing and change strategies for helpers: Fundamental skills and cognitive behavioral interventions* (5th ed.). Pacific Grove, CA: Brooks/Cole.

Cortina, M. (2010). The future of psychodynamic psychotherapy. *Psychiatry, 73*(1), 43–56.

Costello, E. J. (2012, April). Cited in K. McGowan, Data: Number. *Discover*, 12–13.

Cotliar, S., & Tauber, M. (2011, May 2). Her private struggle. *People*, 52–56.

Courchesne, E., Carper, R., & Akshoomoff, N. (2003). Evidence of brain overgrowth in the first year of life in autism. *JAMA, 290*, 337–344.

Covington, M. V. (2000). Goal theory, motivation, and school achievement: An integrative review. *Annual Review of Psychology, 51*, 171–200.

Cowley, G. (2003, February 24). Our bodies our fears. *Newsweek*, 42–49.

Coyne, S. M., Nelson, D. A., Lawton, F., Haslam, S., Rooney, L., Titterington, L., Trainor, H., Remnant, J., & Ogunlaja, L. (2008). The effects of viewing physical and relational aggression in the media: Evidence for a cross-over effect. *Journal of Experimental Social Psychology, 44*, 1551–1554.

Coyne, S. M., Robinson, S. L., & Nelson, D. A. (2010). Does reality backbite? Physical, verbal, and relational aggression in reality television programs. *Journal of Broadcasting & Electronic Media, 54*(2), 282–298.

CPO (Camelot Press Office). (2006). *2,000 millionaires: The national lottery millioinaire survey* [On-line]. Available: www.camelotgroup.co.uk/2000Millionaires MORISurvey.pdf.

Craik, F. I. M., & Lockhart, R. S. (1972). Levels of processing: A framework for memory research. *Journal of Verbal Learning and Verbal Behavior, 11*, 671–684.

Craik, F. I. M., & Tulving, E. (1975). Depth of processing and the retention of words in episodic memory. *Journal of Experimental Psychology: General, 104*, 268–294.

Cramer, P. (2003). Defense mechanisms and physiological reactivity to stress. *Journal of Personality, 71*, 221–244.

Cramer, P. (2006). *Protecting the self: Defense mechanisms in action*. New York: Guilford Press.

Cramer, P. (2009). The development of defense mechanisms from pre-adolescence to early adulthood: Do IQ and social class matter? A longitudinal study. *Journal of Research in Personality, 43*, 464–471.

Cramer, P. (2012). Psychological maturity and change in adult defense mechanisms. *Journal of Research in Personality, 46*, 306–316.

Craske, M. G., & Barlow, D. H. (2001). Panic disorder and agoraphobia. In D. H. Barlow (Ed.), *Clinical handbook of psychological disorders* (3rd ed.). New York: Guilford Press.

Crawford, M., & Popp, D. (2003). Sexual double standards: A review and methodological critique of two decades of research. *Journal of Sex Research, 40*, 13–26.

Crea, J. (2003, September 26). *Meth dealer details D.C. drug scene* [On-line]. Available: http://www.washblade.com/print.cfm?content_id=1177.

Creer, D. J., Romberg, C., Saksida, L. M., van Praag, H., & Bussey, T. J. (2010). Running enhances spatial pattern separation in mice. *Proceedings of the National Academy of Sciences, 107*(5), 2367–2372.

Crenson, M. (2005, September 11). What makes a sexual predator? *North County Times*.

Creswell, J. (2006, December 17). How suite it isn't: A dearth of female bosses. *The New York Times, 3*.

Crews, F. (2006, July 9). Cited in K. Butler, Alcohol harder on teen brains than thought. *The San Francisco Chronicle*, B1.

Crews, F. T., & Boettiger, C. A. (2009). Impulsivity, frontal lobes and risk for addiction. *Pharmacology Biochemistry and Behavior, 93*, 237–247.

Crooks, R., & Baur, K. (2002). *Our sexuality* (8th ed.). Pacific Grove, CA: Wadsworth.

Crow, T. J. (1985). The two syndrome concept: Origins and current status. *Schizophrenia Bulletin, 11*, 471–486.

Cruz, C., & Chiu, A. (2009, March 15). Twin boys for Charlie Sheen and Brooke Mueller Sheen!, *People*.

Csernansky, J. G., Mahmoud, R., & Brenner, R. (2002). A comparison of risperidone and haloperidol for the prevention of relapse in patients with schizophrenia. *New England Journal of Medicine, 346*, 16–23.

Csikszentmihalyi, M., & Gute, G. G. (2010, July 19). Cited in P. Bronson & A. Merryman, The creativity crisis. *Newsweek*, 44–49.

Culbertson, C., Nicolas, S., Zaharovits, I., London, E. D., De La Garza, R. II, Brody, A. L., & Newton, T. F. (2010). Methamphetamine craving induced in an online virtual reality environment. *Pharmacology Biochemistry and Behavior, 96*, 454–460.

Cullen, L. T. (2006, April 3). SATS for J-O-B-s. *Time*, 89.

Cullen, L. T., & Grossman, L. (2007, October 15). Fatherhood 2.0. *Time*, 63–66.

Cunningham, F. G., Leveno, K. J., Bloom, S. L., Hauth, J. C., Rouse, D., & Spong, C. (Eds.). (2009). *Williams obstetrics* (23rd ed.). New York: McGraw-Hill.

Curtis, V. (2012, January 23). Cited in J. Gorman, Survival's ick factor. *The New York Times*.

Curtiss, S. (1977). *Genie: A psycholinguistic study of a modern-day "wild child."* New York: Academic Press.

Curwen, T. (2012, February 10). Little known brain disease rips apart lives of victim, loved ones. *Los Angeles Times*.

Cynkar, A. (2007, June). The changing gender composition of psychology. *Monitor on Psychology, 38*, 46.

Cytowic, R. E. (1999). *The man who tasted shapes*. Cambridge, MA: MIT Press.

Cytowic, R. E., & Eagleman, D. M. (2010, Spring). The cross-wired brain. *The Brain*, 16–18.

Czeisler, C. A. (1994). Cited in R. Nowak, Chronobiologists out of sync over light therapy patents. *Science, 263*, 1217–1218.

Czeisler, C. A., Duffy, J. F., Shanahan, T. L., Brown, E. N., Mitchell, J. F., Rimmer, D. W., Ronda, J. M., Siva, E. J., Allan, J. S., Emens, J. S., Dijk, K., & Kronauer, R. E. (1999). Stability, precision, and near-24-hour period of the human circadian pacemaker. *Science, 284*, 2177–2181.

Czeisler, C. A., Shanahan, T. L., Klerman, E. B., Martens, H., Brotman, D. J., Emens, J. S., Klein, T., & Rizzo, J. F. (1995). Suppression of melatonin secretion in some blind patients by exposure to bright light. *New England Journal of Medicine, 332*, 6–11.

Czeisler, C. A., Winkelman, J. R., & Richardson, G. S. (2006). Sleep disorders. In S. L. Hauser (Ed.), *Harrison's neurology in clinical medicine* (pp. 169–183). New York: McGraw-Hill.

Dagostino, M. (2008, December 8). I love my life. *People*, 68–75.

Daley, C. E., & Onwuegbuzie, A. J. (2011). Race and intelligence. In R. J. Sternberg & S. B. Kaufman (Eds.), *The Cambridge handbook of intelligence* (pp. 293–306). New York: Cambridge University Press.

Dallman, M. F., Pecoraro, N. C., & la Fleur, S. E. (2005). Chronic stress and comfort foods: Self-medication and abdominal obesity. *Brain, Behavior, and Immunity, 19*, 275–280.

Damasio, A. (1999, October 19). Cited in S. Blakeslee, Brain damage during infancy stunts moral learning, study finds. *Los Angeles Times*, A1.

Damasio, A. (2006, August 7). Cited in D. Vergano, Study: Ask with care. *USA Today*, 5D.

Damasio, H., Brabowski, T., Frank, R., Galaburda, A. M., & Damasio, A. R. (1994). The return of Phineas Gage: Clues about the brain from the skull of a famous patient. *Science, 264*, 1102–1105.

Dambro, M. R. (Ed.). (2006). *Griffith's 5-minute clinical consult* (14th ed.). Philadelphia: Lippincott Williams & Wilkins.

Damon, W. (1999, August). The moral development of children. *Scientific American*, 73–78.

Danckert, J., & Ferber, S. (2006). Revisiting unilateral neglect. *Neuropsychologia, 44*, 987–1006.

Dandoy, A. C., & Goldstein, A. G. (1990). The use of cognitive appraisal to reduce stress reactions: A replication. *Journal of Social Behavior and Personality, 5*, 275–285.

Dang-Vu, T. T., McKinney, S. M., Buxton, O. M., Solet, J. M., & Ellenbogen, J. M. (2010). Spontaneous brain rhythms predict sleep stability in the face of noise. *Current Biology, 20*, R626-R627.

D'Angiulli, A., Herdman, A., Stapells, D., & Hertzman, C. (2008). Children's event-related potentials of auditory selective attention vary with their socioeconomic status. *Neuropsychology, 22*, 293–300.

Daniszewski, J. (1997, June 25). Female circumcision ban nullified. *Los Angeles Times*, A4.

Dapretto, M., Davies, M. S., Pfeifer, J. H., Scott, A. A., Sigman, M., Bookheimer, S. Y., & Iacoboni, M. (2006). Understanding emotions in others: Mirror neuron dysfunction in children with autism spectrum disorders. *Nature Neuroscience, 9*, 28–30.

Darrah, J., Senthilselvan, A., & Magill-Evans, J. (2009). Trajectories of serial motor scores of typically developing children: Implications for clinical decision making. *Infant Behavior and Development, 32*, 72–78.

Daruna, J. H. (2012). *Introduction to psychoneuroimmunology* (2nd ed.). New York: Academic Press.

Darwin, C. (1859). *On the origin of species by means of natural selection or the preservation of favored races in the struggle for life*. London: John Murray.

Darwin, C. (1872; reprinted 1965). *The expression of the emotions in man and animals*. Chicago: University of Chicago Press.

Davenport, C. (2011, October 29). MREs get a new kick with caffeinated jerky and Zapplesauce. *The Washington Post.*

Davey, M. (2005, March 6). Suspect in 10 Kansas murders lived an intensely ordinary life. *The New York Times,* 1.

Davidson, J. E., & Kemp, I. A. (2011). Contemporary models of intelligence. In R. J. Sternberg & S. B. Kaufman (Eds.), *The Cambridge handbook of intelligence* (pp. 58–82). New York: Cambridge University Press.

Davies, I. R. L., & Corbett, G. G. (1997). A cross-cultural study of colour grouping: Evidence for weak linguistic relativity. *British Journal of Psychology, 88,* 493–517.

Davis, J. (2003, May 23). Cited in K. S. Peterson, Sexually active teens also are often clueless. *USA Today,* 8D.

Davis, J. L., & Petretic-Jackson, P. A. (2000). The impact of child sexual abuse on adult interpersonal functioning: A review and synthesis of the empirical literature. *Aggression and Violent Behavior, 5,* 291–328.

Davis, J. M., Chen, N., & Glick, I. D. (2003). A meta-analysis of the efficacy of second-generation antipsychotics. *Archives of General Psychiatry, 60,* 553–564.

Davis, K., Christodoulou, J., Seider, S., & Gardner, H. (2011). The theory of multiple intelligences. In R. J. Sternberg & S. B. Kaufman (Eds.), *The Cambridge handbook of intelligence* (pp. 485–503). New York: Cambridge University Press.

Davis, M., Eshelman, E. R., McKay, M., & Fanning, P. (2008). *The relaxation and stress reduction workbook* (6th ed.). Oakland, CA: New Harbinger.

Davis, R. (2005, March 2). Is 16 too young to drive a car? *USA Today.*

Davison, G. C., & Neale, J. M. (1990). *Abnormal psychology* (3rd ed.). New York: Wiley.

Davison, G. C., & Neale, J. M. (1994). *Abnormal psychology* (6th ed.). New York: Wiley.

Dawood, K., Pillard, R. C., Horvath, C., Revelle, W., & Bailey, J. M. (2000). Familial aspects of male homosexuality. *Archives of Sexual Behavior, 29,* 155–163.

De Araujo, I., Oliveira-Maia, A., Sotnikova, T., Gainetdinov, R., Caron, M., Nicolelis, M., & Simon, S. (2008). Food reward in the absence of taste receptor signaling. *Neuron, 57,* 930–941.

De Fruyt, F., Bartels, M., Van Leeuwen, K. G., Clercq, B. D., Decuyper, M., & Mervielde, I. (2006). Five types of personality continuity in childhood and adolescence. *Journal of Personality and Social Psychology, 91,* 538–552.

de Groot, F. M., Voogt-Bode, A., Passchier, J., Berger, M. Y., Koes, B. W., & Verhagen, A. P. (2011). Headache: The placebo effects in the control groups in randomized clinical trials; an analysis of systematic reviews. *Journal of Manipulative and Physiological Therapeutics, 34,* 297–305.

De Martino, B. (2006a, August 3). Cited in University College London Media Relations, *Irrational decisions driven by emotions* [On-line]. Available: http://ucl.ac.uk/media/library/decisionbrain.

De Martino, B. (2006b, August 7). Cited in D. Vergano, Study: Ask with care. *USA Today,* 6D.

De Martino, B., Kumaran, D., Seymour, B., & Dolan, R. J. (2006, August). Frames, biases, and rational decision-making in the human brain. *Science, 313,* 684–687.

De Meyer, G., Shapiro, F., Vanderstichele, H., Vanmechelen, E., Engelborghs, S., De Deyn, P. P., Coart, E., Hansson, O., Minthon, L., Zetterberg, H., Blennow, K., Shaw, L., & Trojanowski, J. Q. (2010). Diagnosis-independent Alzheimer disease biomarker signature in cognitively normal elderly people. *Archives of Neurology, 67,* 949–956.

de Rivera, J. (1997). The construction of false memory syndrome: The experience of retractors. *Psychological Inquiry, 8,* 271–292.

de Rossi, P. (2010). *Unbearable lightness.* New York: Atria Books.

de Rossi, P. (2012). Cited in S. Pocharski, Portia de Rossi's anorexia battle. *Ladies Home Journal.*

De Young, C. G. (2006). Higher-order factors of the Big Five in a multi-informant sample. *Journal of Personality and Social Psychology, 91,* 1138–1151.

De Young, C. G., Hirsh, J. B., Shane, M. S., Papademetris, X., Rajeevan, N., & Gray, J. R. (2010). Testing predictions from personality neuroscience: Brain structure and the Big Five, *Psychological Science, 21,* 820–828.

DeAngelis, T. (1966, March). Women's contributions large; recognition isn't. *Monitor American Psychological Association.*

DeAngelis, T. (2008, April). Psychology's growth careers. *Monitor on Psychology,* 64.

DeAngelis, T. (2012, March). A second life for practice? *Monitor on Psychology,* 48–51.

Deary, I. J., Whalley, L. J., & Starr, J. M. (2009). *A lifetime of intelligence: Follow-up studies of the Scottish mental surveys of 1932 and 1947.* Washington, DC: American Psychological Association.

Deci, E. L., Koestner, R., & Ryan, R. M. (1999). A meta-analytic review of experiments examining the effects of extrinsic rewards on intrinsic motivation. *Psychological Bulletin, 125,* 627–668.

Deci, E. L., & Moller, A. C. (2005). The concept of competence. In A. J. Elliot & C. S. Dweck (Eds.), *Handbook of competence and motivation* (pp. 579–597). New York: Guilford Press.

Deci, E. L., & Ryan, R. M. (1985). *Intrinsic motivation and self-determination in human behavior.* New York: Plenum Press.

Deckro, G. R. (2002, September 11). Cited in M. Duenwald, Students find another staple of campus life: Stress. *The New York Times,* D5.

DeCurtis, A. (2009, March 9). Not a businessman—a business, man. *Best Life* [On-line]. Available: http://www.bestlifeonline.com/cms/publish/wealth/Jay-Z-Personal-Success_printer.php.

Deffenbacher, J. (2003, March). Cited in J. D. Holloway, Advances in anger management. *Monitor on Psychology,* 54–55.

Deffenbacher, J. (2005, June). Cited in M. Dittmann, Anger on the road. *Monitor on Psychology, 36,* 26.

DeGue, S., & DiLillo, D. (2005). "You would if you loved me": Toward an improved conceptual and etiological understanding of nonphysical male sexual coercion. *Aggression and Violent Behavior, 10,* 513–532.

Dehaene-Lambertz, G., Dehaene, S., & Hertz-Pannier, L. (2002). Functional neuroimaging of speech perception in infants. *Science, 298,* 2013–2015.

DeKeukelaere, L. (2006, February/March). Optimism prolongs life. *Scientific American Mind, 17,* 7.

Delaunay-El Allam, M., Soussignan, R., Patris, B., Marlier, L., & Schaal, B. (2010). Long-lasting memory for an odor acquired at the mother's breast. *Developmental Science, 13,* 849–863.

Delgado, M. R., LaBouliere, C. D., & Phelps, E. A. (2006). Fear of losing money? Aversive conditioning with secondary reinforcers. *Social Cognitive and Affective Neuroscience, 1,* 250–259.

DeLisi, L. E., Sakuma, M., Maurizio, A. M., Relja, M., & Hoff, A. L. (2004). Cerebral ventricular change over the first 10 years after the onset of schizophrenia. *Psychiatric Research: Neuroimaging, 130,* 57–70.

Dell, P. F. (2009). The long struggle to diagnose multiple personality disorder (MPD): MPD. In P. F. Dell & J. A. O'Neil (Eds.), *Dissociation and the dissociative disorders: DSM-V and beyond* (pp. 383–402). New York: Routledge.

Dellorto, D. (2008, August 5). *Surgical side effects cut with robotics.* CNN.com [On-line]. Available: http://www.cnn.com/2008/HEALTH/conditions/08/05/robotic.prostate.surgery/index.html.

DeLoache, J. S., Chiong, C., Sherman, K., Islam, N., Vanderborght, M., Troseth, G. L., Strouse, G. A., & O'Doherty, K. (2010). Do babies learn from baby media? *Psychological Science, 21,* 1570–1574.

Delzenne, N., Blundell, J., Brouns, F., Cunningham, K., De Graaf, K., Erkner, A., Lluch, A., Mars, M., Peters, H. P. F., & Westerterp-Plantenga, M. (2010). Gastrointestinal targets of appetite regulation in humans. *Obesity Review, 11,* 234–250.

Dement, W. C. (1999). *The promise of sleep.* New York: Random House.

Dement, W. C., & Kleitman, N. (1957). The relation of eye movements during sleep to dream activity: An objective method for the study of dreaming. *Journal of Experimental Psychology, 53,* 339–346.

Dennerstein, L., Dudley, E., & Burger, H. (1997). Well-being and the menopausal transition. *Journal of Psychosomatic Obstetrics and Gynecology, 18,* 95–101.

Denollet, J., Schiffer, A. A., & Spek, V. (2010). A general propensity to psychological distress affects cardiovascular outcomes. *Circulation: Cardiovascular Quality and Outcomes, 3,* 546–557.

DeNoon, D. J. (2009b, February 19). Brain device OK'd for OCD treatment. *WebMD* [On-line]. Available: http://www.webmd.com/mental-health/news/20090219/brain-device-okd-for-ocd-treatment.

DePetrillo, P. (2003, September 8). Cited in J. Ewers, Drinking in your genes. *U.S. News & World Report,* 44.

Depue, B. E., Curran, T., & Banich, M. T. (2007). Prefrontal regions orchestrate suppression of emotional memories via a two-phase process. *Science, 317,* 215–219.

Dere, E., Easton, A., Nadel, L., & Huston, J. P. (2008). *Handbook of episodic memory* (Vol. 18). Oxford: Elsevier.

Derlega, V. J., Winstead, B. A., & Jones, W. H. (2005). *Personality: Contemporary theory and research* (3rd ed.). Belmont, CA: Thomson Wadsworth.

DeRubeis, R. J., Hollon, S. D., Amsterdam, J. D., Shelton, R. C., Young, P. R., Salomon, R. M., O'Reardon, J. P., Lovett, M. L., Gladis, M. M., Brown, L. L., & Gallop, R. (2005). Cognitive therapy vs. medications in the treatment of moderate to severe depression. *Archives of General Psychiatry, 62,* 409–416.

Devine, P. G., Hamilton, D. L., & Ostrom, T. M. (Eds.). (1994). *Social cognition: Impact on social psychology.* New York: Academic Press.

Di Salvo, S. (2006, August 25). *The story of Luisa: A case of panic attack disorder* [On-line]. Available: http://www.depression-panic.org.

Diamond, E. L., Miller, S., Dickerson, B. C., Atri, A., DePeau, K., Fenstermacher, E., Pihlajamaki, M., Celone, K., Salisbury, S., Gregas, M., Rentz, D., & Sperling, R. A. (2007). Relationship of fMRI activation to clinical trial memory measures in Alzheimer disease. *Neurology, 69,* 1331–1341.

Diamond, L. M. (2008). *Sexual fluidity: Understanding women's love and desire.* New York: Harvard University Press.

Diamond, M., & Sigmundson, H. K. (1997). Sex reassignment at birth. *Archives of Pediatric & Adolescent Medicine, 151,* 298–304.

Dickerson, T. J. (2007, June 30). Cited in N. Seppa, Immune abuse. *Science News, 171,* 405–406.

Diener, E., & Chan, M. Y. (2011). Happy people live longer: Subjective well-being contributes to health and longevity. *Applied Psychology: Health and Well-Being, 3,* 1–43.

Diener, E., & Diener, C. (1996). Most people are happy. *Psychological Science, 7*, 181–185.

Dienes, K. A., Torres-Harding, S., Reinecke, M. A., Freeman, A., & Sauer, A. (2011). In S. B. Messer & A. S. Gurman (Eds.), *Essential psychotherapies: Theory and practice* (3rd ed., pp. 143–183). New York Guilford Press.

Diers, M. (2011, October 11). Cited in P. Anderson, Virtual reality may help treat phantom limb pain. *Medscape Medical News.*

Diesendruck, G., & Shatz, M. (2001). Two-year-olds' recognition of hierarchies: Evidence from their interpretation of the semantic relation between object labels. *Cognitive Development, 16*, 577–594.

Dietrich, K. (2003, August 5). Cited in J. E. Brody, Even low lead levels pose perils for children. *The New York Times*, D7.

Digman, J. M. (1997). Higher-order factors of the Big Five. *Journal of Personality and Social Psychology, 73*, 1246–1256.

Dijkn, D., & Lazar, A. (2012). The regulation of human sleep and wakefulness: Sleep homeostasis and circadian rhythmicity. In C. M. Morin & C. A. Espie (Eds.), *The Oxford handbook of sleep and sleep disorders.* New York: Oxford University Press.

Dijksterhuis, A., Chartrand, T. L., & Aarts, H. (2007). Effects of priming and perception on social behavior and goal pursuit. In J. A. Bargh (Ed.), *Social psychology and the unconscious: The automaticity of higher mental processes.* New York: Psychological Press.

DiLalla, L. F. (2002). Behavior genetics of aggression in children: Review and future directions. *Developmental Review, 22*, 593–622.

Dingfelder, S. F. (2011, November). Will behave for money. *Monitor on Psychology*, 38–41.

Dinnel, D. L., Kleinknecht, R. A., & Tanaka-Matsumi, J. (2002). A cross-cultural comparison of social phobia symptoms. *Journal of Psychopathology and Behavioral Assessment, 24*, 75–84.

Dinstein, I., Thomas, C., Humphreys, K., Minshew, N., Behrmann, M., & Heeger, D. J. (2010). Normal movement selectivity in autism. *Neuron, 66*(3), 461–469.

Dittmann, M. (2003, February). Psychology's first prescribers. *Monitor on Psychology*, 36–39.

Dixon, W. A., & Reid, J. K. (2000). Positive life events as a moderator of stress-related depressive symptoms. *Journal of Counseling & Development, 78*, 343–347.

Dobbs, D. (2006a, February/March). Mastery of emotions. *Scientific American Mind*, 44–49.

Dobbs, D. (2006b, April/May). A revealing reflection. *Scientific American Mind*, 22–27.

Dobson, K. S. (2009). *Handbook of cognitive-behavioral therapies* (3rd ed.). New York: Guilford Press.

Dodd, J. (2010, March 15). Shaun White: Chairman of the board. *People*, 76–79.

Dodd, J. (2011, April 18). Making waves. *People*, 38.

Dolan, A. (2008, April). How a child prodigy at Oxford became a £130-an-hour prostitute. *DailyMail* [On-line]. Available: http://www.dailymail.co.uk/news/article-550549/How-child-prodigy-Oxford-130-hour-prostitute.html.

Dolan, R. J. (2002). Emotion, cognition, and behavior. *Science, 298*, 1191–1194.

Doland, A. (2006, February 7). Frenchwoman mauled by dog shows partial face transplant. *San Diego Union-Tribune*, A10.

Dolder, C. R. (2008). Side effects of antipsychotics. In K.T. Mueser & D. V. Jeste (Eds.), *Clinical handbook of schizophrenia* (pp. 168–177). New York: Guilford Press.

Domhoff, G. W. (2003). *The scientific study of dreams.* Washington, DC: American Psychological Association.

Domhoff, G. W. (2005a). The content of dreams: Methodologic and theoretical implications. In M. H. Kryger, T. Roth & W. C. Dement (Eds.), *Principles and practice of sleep.* Philadelphia: Elsevier Saunders.

Domhoff, G. W. (2005b). Refocusing the neurocognitive approach to dreams: A critique of the Hobson versus Solms debate. *Dreaming, 15*, 3–20.

Domino, G. (1994). Assessment of creativity with the ACL: An empirical comparison of four scales. *Creativity Research Journal, 7*, 21–33.

Dominus, S. (2012, March 7). What happened to the girls in Le Roy. *The New York Times.*

Donderi, D. C. (2006). Visual complexity: A review. *Psychological Bulletin, 132*, 73–97.

Douglas, E. M., & Finkelhor, D. (2005). *Childhood sexual abuse fact sheet* [On-line]. Available: http://www.unh.edu/ccrc/factsheet/pdf/CSA-FS20.pdf.

Dover, S. (2011, October 27). Amy Winehouse had a blood alcohol level of .416 at death. *NBC New York* [On-line]. Available: http://www.nbcnewyork.com/entertainment/music/NATLAmy-Winehouse-Died-From-Too-Much-Alcohol-Coroner-132610143.html.

Dovidio, J. F., & Gaertner, S. L. (2010). Intergroup bias. In S. T. Fiske, D. T. Gilbert & G. Lindzey (Eds.), *Handbook of social psychology* (Vol. 2, 5th ed., pp. 1084–1121). Hoboken, NJ: John Wiley & Sons.

Downar, J., & Kapur, S. (2008). Biological theories. In K. T. Mueser & D. V. Jeste (Eds.), *Clinical handbook of schizophrenia* (pp. 25–43). New York: Guilford Press.

Downs, M. F. (2008). Good parenting ups kids' mental skills. *WebMD* [On-line]. Available: http://www.webmd.com/parenting/news/20080215/parenting-skills-up-kids-mental-skills.

Drape, J. (2012, June 23). Sandusky guilty of sexual abuse of 10 young boys. *The New York Times.*

Drews, F. A., Yazdani, H., Godfrey, C. N., Cooper, J. M., & Strayer, D. L. (2009). Test messaging during simulated driving. *Human Factors: The Journal of the Human Factors and Ergonomics Society, 51*, 762–770.

Drisko, J. W. (2004). Common factors in psychotherapy outcome: Meta-analytic findings and their implications for practice and research. *Families in Society, 85*, 81–90.

Dubernard, J., Lengele, B., Morelon, E., Testelin, S., Badet, L., Moure, C., Beziat, J., Dakpé, S., Kanitakis, J., D'Hauthuille, C., El Jaafari, A., Petruzzo, P., Lefrancois, N., Taha, F., Sirigu, A., Di Marco, G., Carmi, E., Bachmann, D., Cremades, S., Giraux, P., Burloux, G., Hequet, O., Parquet, N., Francés, C., Michallet, M., Martin, X., & Devauchelle, B. (2007). Outcomes 18 months after the first human partial face transplantation. *New England Journal of Medicine, 357*, 2451–2460.

DuBois, D. L., Tevendale, H. D., Burk-Braxton, C., Swenson, L. P., & Hardesty, J. L. (2000). Self-system influences during early adolescence: Investigation of an integrative model. *Journal of Early Adolescence, 20*, 12–43.

Dudley, D. (2006, January/February). Impact awards 2006 honorees. *AARP: The Magazine.*

Duenwald, M. (2003, June 17). More Americans seeking help for depression. *The New York Times*, A1.

Duffy, J. (2002, April). Cited in M. Weinstock, Night owls vs. early birds. *Discover*, 11.

Dugatkin, L. E., & Bekoff, M. (2003). Play and the evolution of fairness: A game theory model. *Behavioural Processes, 60*, 209–214.

Duncan, A. (2012, April 30). Jeremy Lin. The dreamers' most valuable player. *Time*, 28–29.

DuPaul, G. J., Arbolino, L. A., & Booster, G. D. (2011). Cognitive-behavioral interventions for attention-deficit/hyperactivity disorder. In M. J. Mayer, R. Van Acker, J. E. Lochman & F. M. Gresham (Eds.), *Cognitive behavioral interventions for emotional and behavioral disorders: School-based practice* (pp. 295–327). New York: Guilford Press.

Durand, V. M. (2011). Disorders of development. In D. H. Barlow (Ed.), *Oxford handbook of clinical psychology* (pp. 551–573). New York: Oxford University Press.

Durand, V. M., & Barlow, D. H. (2006). *Essentials of abnormal psychology* (4th ed.). Belmont, CA: Thomson Wadsworth.

Durand, V. M., & Barlow, D. H. (2013). *Essentials of abnormal psychology* (6th ed.). Belmont, CA: Wadsworth Cengage.

Durrett, C., & Trull, T. J. (2005). An evaluation of evaluative personality terms: A comparison of the big seven and five-factor model in predicting psychopathology. *Psychological Assessment, 17*, 359–368.

Durstewitz, D., Vittoz, N. M., Floresco, S. B., & Seaman, J. K. (2010). Abrupt transitions between prefrontal neural ensemble states accompany behavioral transitions during rule learning. *Neuron, 66*, 438–448.

Dviri, M. (2005, June 26). "My dream was to be a suicide bomber. I wanted to kill 20, 50 Jews. Yes, even babies." *Telegraph* [On-line]. Available: http://www.telegraph.co.uk/news/main.jhtml?xml=/news/2005/06/26.

Dyck, D. G., Short, R. A., Hendryx, M. S., Norell, D., Myers, M., Patterson, T., McDonell, M. G., Voss, W. D., & McFarlane, W. R. (2000). Management of negative symptoms among patients with schizophrenia attending multiple-family groups. *Psychiatric Services, 51*, 513–519.

Eagle, M. N. (2000). A critical evaluation of current conceptions of transference and countertransference. *Psychoanalytic Psychology, 17*, 24–37.

Eagly, A. H., & Karau, S. J. (2002). Role congruity theory of prejudice toward female leaders. *Psychological Review, 109*, 573–598.

Eagly, A. H., Wood, W., & Diekman, A. B. (2000). Social role theory of sex differences and similarities: A current appraisal. In T. Eckes & H. M. Trautner (Eds.), *The developmental social psychology of gender.* Mahwah, NJ: Lawrence Erlbaum.

Eagly, A. H., Wood, W., & Johannesen-Schmidt, M. C. (2004). Social role theory of sex differences and similarities. In A. H. Eagly, A. E. Beall & R. J. Sternberg (Eds.), *The psychology of gender* (2nd ed., pp. 269–295). New York: Guilford Press.

Easterlin, R. A. (2003). Explaining happiness. *Proceedings of the National Academy of Sciences, 100*, 11176–11183.

Ebbinghaus, H. (1885; reprinted 1913). *Memory: A contribution to experimental psychology* (H. A. Ruger & C. E. Bussenius, Trans.). New York: Teachers College Press.

Ebrecht, M., Hextall, J., Kirtley, L. G., Taylor, A., Dyson, M., & Weinman, J. (2004). Perceived stress and cortisol levels predict speed of wound healing in healthy male adults. *Psychoneuroimmunology, 29*, 798–809.

Eccles, J. S., & Wigfield, A. (2002). Motivational beliefs, values and goals. *Annual Review of Psychology, 53*, 109–132.

Eckes, T., & Trautner, H. M. (2000). *The developmental social psychology of gender.* Mahwah, NJ: Lawrence Erlbaum.

Eden, G. (2003, July 28). Cited in C. Gorman, The new science of dyslexia. *Time*, 52–59.

Edenberg, H. J., & Foroud, T. (2006). The genetics of alcoholism: Identifying specific genes through family studies. *Addictive Biology, 11*, 386–396.

Eggen, D. (2005, August 31). 400 arrests in U.S. methamphetamine raids. *The Washington Post*, A2.

Eggers, C., & Liebers, V. (2007, April/May). Through a glass, darkly. *Scientific American Mind*, 30–35.

Ehrenberg, R. (2008, September 27). Gene activity makes the difference in development of human qualities. *Science News*, 13.

Ehrenberg, R. (2010, July 3). The truth hurts. *Science News*, 28–29.

Ehrenfeld, T. (2011, March). Reflections on mirror neurons. *Association for Psychological Science, 24*(3), 11–13.

Eibl-Eibesfeldt, I. (1973). The expressive behavior of the deaf-and-blind-born. In M. von Cranach & I. Vine (Eds.), *Social communication and movement*. San Diego, CA: Academic Press.

Eich, E., Macaulay, D., Loewenstein, R. J., & Dihle, P. H. (1997). Memory, amnesia, and dissociative identity disorder. *Psychological Science, 8*, 417–422.

Eikeseth, S. (2001). Recent critiques of the UCLA Young Autism Project. *Behavioral Interventions, 16*, 249–264.

Eisen, M. R. (1994). Psychoanalytic and psychodynamic models of hypnoanalysis. In J. W. Rhue, S. J. Lynn & I. Kirsch (Eds.), *Handbook of clinical hypnosis*. Washington, DC: American Psychological Association.

Eisenberger, R., & Armeli, S. (1997). Can salient reward increase creative performance without reducing intrinsic creative interest? *Journal of Personality and Social Psychology, 72*, 652–663.

Eisenberger, R., Pierce, W. D., & Cameron, J. (1999). Effects of reward on intrinsic motivation—negative, neutral, and positive: Comment on Deci, Koestner, and Ryan (1999). *Psychological Bulletin, 125*, 677–691.

Eisendrath, S., Chartier, M., & McLane, M. (2011). Adapting mindfulness-based cognitive therapy for treatment-resistance depression. *Cognitive & Behavioral Practice, 18*, 362–370.

Ekman, P. (2003). *Emotions revealed: Recognizing faces and feelings to improve communication and emotional life*. New York: Times Books.

Ekman, P. (2006, October/November). Cited in S. Schubert, A look tells all. *Scientific American Mind*, 26–31.

Ekman, P. (2007). *Emotions revealed: Recognizing faces and feelings to improve communication and emotional life* (2nd ed.). New York: Henry Holt & Co.

Ekman, P., & Rosenberg, E. L. (Eds.). (2005). *What the face reveals: Basic and applied studies of spontaneous expression using the facial action coding system (FACS)*. New York: Oxford University Press.

Elbogen, E. B., & Johnson, S. C. (2009). The intricate link between violence and mental disorder. *Archives of General Psychiatry, 66*, 152–161.

Elder, C., Nidich, S., Colbert, R., Hagelin, J., Grayshield, L., Oviedo-Lim, D., Nidish, R., Rainforth, M., Jones, C., & Gerace, D. (2011). Reduced psychological distress in racial and ethnic minority students practicing the transcendental meditation program. *Journal of Instructional Psychology, 38*, 109–116.

Elejalde-Ruiz, A. (2006, April 25). Mental floss: Want a job? Be prepared to offer up more information than ever before as companies search for the perfect fit for their bottom line. *Chicago Tribune*.

Elias, M. (1989, August 9). With guidance, a child can control negative traits. *USA Today*.

Elias, M. (2005, August 22). Critical, demanding parents can damage gifted children. *USA Today*, 5D.

Elias, M. (2008a, October 27). Post-traumatic stress is a war within the body. *USA Today*, 7D.

Elias, M. (2008b, November 19). Study: Today's youth think quite highly of themselves. *USA Today*, 7D.

Eliot, L. (2009). *Pink brain blue brain*. New York: Houghton Mifflin Harcourt Publishing.

Eliot, L. (2010, May/June). The truth about boys and girls. *Scientific American Mind*, 22–29.

Elkind, D. (1967). Egocentrism in adolescence. *Child Development, 38*, 1025–1034.

Elkind, D. (1998). *All grown up and no place to go: Teenagers in crisis* (rev. ed.). New York: Perseus Books.

Elliot, A. J., & Church, M. A. (2003). A motivational analysis of defensive pessimism and self-handicapping. *Journal of Personality, 71*, 370–396.

Elliott, D. (1995, March 20). The fat of the land. *Newsweek*.

Elliott, M. (2011, November 21). *Tseng, Thompson are two for the ages* [On-line]. Available: http://espn.go.com/espnw/more-sports/7265735.

Ellsworth, P. C., & Scherer, K. R. (2003). Appraisal processes in emotion. In R. J. Davidson, K. R. Scherer & H. H. Goldsmith (Eds.), *Handbook of affective sciences*. New York: Oxford University Press.

Emery, R. E., & Laumann-Billings, L. (1998). An overview of the nature, causes, and consequences of abusive family relationships. *American Psychologist, 53*, 121–135.

Emmorey, K., Mehta, S., & Grabowski, T. J. (2007). The neural correlates of sign versus word production. *Neuroimage, 36*, 202–208.

Epel, E., & Blackburn, E. (2004, November 30). Cited in B. Carey, Stress and distress may give your genes gray hair. *The New York Times*, D5.

Epley, N., Savitsky, K., & Kachelski, R. A. (1999, September/October). What every skeptic should know about subliminal persuasion. *Skeptical Inquirer*, 40–45.

Epstein, L. (2010, June 8). The surprising toll of sleep deprivation. *Newsweek*, 75.

Epstein, L., & Mardon, S. (2007, September 17). Homeroom zombies. *Newsweek*, 64–65.

Epstein, R. (2006, April/May). Sexuality and choice. *Scientific American Mind*, 16–17.

Erber, J. T. (2005). *Aging & older adulthood*. Belmont, CA: Thomson/Wadsworth.

Erdmann, J. (2008, December 20). Imagination medicine. *Science News*, 26–30.

Erickson, M. H. (1980/1941). Hypnosis: A general review. In E. L. Rossie (Ed.), *The collected papers of Milton H. Erickson on hypnosis* (Vol. 30). New York: Irvington.

Ericsson, K. A., Roring, R. W., & Nandagopal, K. (2007). Giftedness and evidence for reproducibly superior performance: An account based on the expert performance framework. *High Ability Studies, 18*, 3–56.

Erikson, E. H. (1963). *Childhood and society*. New York: Norton.

Erikson, E. H. (1982). *The life cycle completed: Review*. New York: Norton.

Esch, T., & Stefano, G. B. (2005). The neurobiology of love. *Neuroendocrinology Letters, 26*, 175–192.

Espiard, M., Lecardeur, L., Abadie, P., Halbecq, I., & Dollfus, S. (2005). Hallucinogen persisting perception disorder after psilocybin consumption: A case study. *European Psychiatry, 20*, 458–460.

Eva, K. W., Cunnington, J. P. W., Reiter, H. I., Keane, D. R., & Norman, G. R. (2004). How can I know what I don't know? Poor self assessment in a well-defined domain. *Advances in Health Sciences Education, 9*, 211–224.

Evans, J. (1993). The cognitive psychology of reasoning: An introduction. *Quarterly Journal of Experimental Psychology, 46A*, 561–567.

Evans, R. B. (1999, December). A century of psychology. *Monitor on Psychology*.

Everest News. (1999). *Erik Weihenmayer* [On-line]. Available: http://www.k2news.com/erik.htm.

Exner, J. E., Jr., & Erdberg, P. (2005). *The Rorschach, advanced interpretation* (3rd ed.). Hoboken, NJ: John Wiley & Sons.

Eysenck, M. W. (2009a). Eyewitness testimony. In A. Baddeley, M. W. Eysenck & M. C. Anderson (Eds.), *Memory* (pp. 317–342). New York: Psychology Press.

Eysenck, M. W. (2009b). Improving your memory. In A. Baddeley, M. W. Eysenck & M. C. Anderson (Eds.), *Memory* (pp. 357–380). New York: Psychology Press.

Eysenck, M. W. (2009c). Semantic memory and stored knowledge. In A. Baddeley, M. W. Eysenck & M. C. Anderson (Eds.), *Memory* (pp. 113–135). New York: Psychology Press.

Fabiano, G. (2008, October). Cited in C. Munsey, New insights on ADHD treatment. *Monitor on Psychology*, 11.

Fabrigar, L. R., MacDonald, T. K., & Wegener, D. T. (2005). The structure of attitudes. In D. Albarracin, B. T. Johnson & M. P. Zanna (Eds.), *The handbook of attitudes*. Mahwah, NJ: Lawrence Erlbaum.

Fackelmann, K. (2005, February 10). "Broken-heart syndrome" has medical link. *USA Today*, 8D.

Fagan, J. F., & Holland, C. R. (2007). Racial equality in intelligence: Predictions from a theory of intelligence as processing. *Intelligence, 35*, 319–334.

Falck, R. S., Wang, J., Carlson, R. G., & Siegal, H. A. (2006). Prevalence and correlates of current depressive symptomatology among a community sample of MDMA users in Ohio. *Addictive Behaviors, 31*, 90–101.

Falk, D. (2009). New information about Albert Einstein's brain. *Frontiers in Evolutionary Neuroscience, 1*, 1–6.

Faller, A., Schunke, M., & Shunke, G. (2004). *The human body: An introduction to structure and function*. New York: Thieme Medical.

FAMU (Florida Agricultural and Mechanical University). (2012). *Marching 100* [On-line]. Available: http://www.famu.edu/index.cfm?a=marching100.

Fanous, A. H., van den Oordm, E. J., Riley, B. P., Aggen, S. H., Neale, M. D., O'Neill, F. A., Walsh, D., & Kendler, K. S. (2005). Relationship between a high-risk haplotype in the DTNBP1 (dysbindin) gene and clinical features of schizophrenia. *American Journal of Psychiatry, 162*, 1824–1832.

Farah, M. J. (2004). *Visual agnosia* (2nd ed.). Cambridge, MA: MIT Press.

Faraone, S. V., Perlis, R. H., Doyle, A. E., Smoller, J. W., Goralnick, J. J., Holmgren, M. A., & Sklar, P. (2005). Molecular genetics of attention-deficit/hyperactivity disorder. *Biological Psychiatry, 57*, 1313–1323.

Farber, B. A. (2000a). Introduction: Understanding and treating burnout in a changing culture. *Journal of Clinical Psychology/In Session, 56*, 589–594.

Farber, B. A. (2000b). Treatment strategies for different types of teacher burnout. *Journal of Clinical Psychology/In Session, 56*, 675–689.

Fayek, A. (2005). The centrality of the system Ucs in the theory of psychoanalysis: The nonrepressed unconscious. *Psychoanalytic Psychology, 22*, 524–543.

Fayyad, J., De Graaf, R., Kessler, R., Alonso, J., Angermeyer, M., Demyttenaere, K., De Girolamo, G., Haro, J. M., Karam, E. G., Lara, C., Lepine, J. P., Ormel, J., Posada-Villa, J., Zaslavsky, A. M., & Jin, R. (2007). Cross-national prevalence and correlates of adult attention-deficit hyperactivity disorder. *British Journal of Psychiatry, 190*, 402–409.

FBI (Federal Bureau of Investigation). (2001, March 5). Cited in CNN, *Risk factors for school violence* [On-line]. Available: http://archives.cnn.com/2001/US/03/05/fbi.shooter.profile/index.html.

FDA (U.S. Food and Drug Administration). (2006, June 8). *FDA licenses new vaccine for prevention of cervical cancer and other diseases in females caused by human papilomavirus* [On-line]. Available: http://www.fda.gov/bbs/topics/NEWS/2006/NEW01385.html.

FDA. (2011). *What is lasik?* [On-line]. Available: http://www.fda.gov/MedicalDevices/ProductsandMedicalProcedures/SurgeryandLife Support/Lasik/ucm061358.htm.

Fearon, R., Bakermans-Kranenburg, M. J., van Ijzendoorn, M. H., Lapsley, A., & Roisman, G. I. (2010). The significance of insecure attachment and disorganization in the development of children's externalizing behavior: A meta-analytic study. *Child Development, 81*, 435–456.

Fechner, G. T. (1860). *Elemente der Psychophysik* (Vol. 1). Leipzig: Brietkopf and Marterl (H. E. Alder, D. H. Howes & E. G. Boring, Trans.). New York: Holt, Rinehart and Winston.

Feingold, B. R. (1975). Hyperkinesis and learning disabilities linked to artificial food flavors and colors. *American Journal of Nursing, 75,* 797–803.

Feinstein, J. S., Adolphs, R., Damasio, A., & Tranel, D. (2010). The human amygdala and the induction and experience of fear. *Current Biology, 21,* 34–38.

Ferguson, D. P., Rhodes, G., Lee, K., & Sriram, N. (2001). "They all look alike to me"; Prejudice and cross-race face recognition. *British Journal of Psychology, 92,* 567–577.

Fergusson, D. M., Horwood, L. J., & Ridder, E. M. (2005). Tests of causal linkages between cannabis use and psychotic symptoms. *Addiction, 100,* 354–366.

Ferrer, E., Shaywitz, B. A., Holahan, J. M., Marchione, K., & Shaywitz, S. E. (2010). Uncoupling of reading and IQ over time: Empirical evidence for a definition of dyslexia. *Psychological Science, 21,* 93–101.

Fessler, D. (2010). Cited in L. Schenkman, 'Ick' factor. *Science, 329,* 733.

Festing, S., & Wilkinson, R. (2007). The ethics of animal research. *EMBO Reports, 8,* 526–530.

Festinger, L. (1954). A theory of social comparison processes. *Human Relations, 7,* 117–140.

Festinger, L. (1957). *A theory of cognitive dissonance.* Palo Alto, CA: Stanford University Press.

Festinger, L., & Carlsmith, J. M. (1959). Cognitive consequences of forced compliance. *Journal of Abnormal and Social Psychology, 58,* 203–210.

Fiedler, K. (2007). Information ecology and the explanation of social cognition and behavior. In A. W. Kruglanski & E. T. Higgins (Eds.), *Social psychology: Handbook of basic principles* (2nd ed., pp. 176–200). New York: Guilford Press.

Fiedler, K., Schmid, J., & Stahl, T. (2002). What is the current truth about polygraph lie detection? *Basic and Applied Social Psychology, 24,* 313–324.

Field, A. P., & Nightengale, Z. C. (2009). What if Little Albert had escaped? *Clinical Child Psychology and Psychiatry, 14,* 311–319.

Fields, H. (2006, February 13). More sleep—and more oxygen. *U.S. News & World Report,* 58.

Fields, R. D. (2005, February). Making memories stick. *Scientific American,* 75–81.

Fields, R. D. (2010). *The other brain: The scientific and medical breakthroughs that will heal our brains and revolutionize our health.* New York: Simon & Schuster.

Fillmore, M. T., Roach, E. L., & Rice, J. T. (2002). Does caffeine counteract alcohol-induced impairment? The ironic effects of expectancy. *Journal of Studies on Alcohol, 63,* 745–754.

Fimrite, P., & Taylor, M. (2005, March 27). No shortage of women who dream of snaring a husband on Death Row. Experts ponder why deadliest criminals get so many proposals. *San Francisco Gate.*

Fink, G. (Ed.). (2007). *Encyclopedia of stress* (2nd ed.). New York: Academic Press.

Fink, P., Hansen, M. S., & Oxhoj, M. (2004). The prevalence of somatoform disorders among internal medical inpatients. *Journal of Psychosomatic Research, 56,* 413–418.

Finke, R. A. (1993). Mental imagery and creative discovery. In B. Roskos-Ewoldsen, M. J. Intons-Peterson & R. E. Anderson (Eds.), *Imagery, creativity, and discovery: A cognitive perspective.* Amsterdam: North-Holland.

Finkelhor, D. (2002, December 3). Cited in L. Villarosa, To prevent sexual abuse, abusers step forward. *The New York Times,* D5.

Finkelstein, E. A., Trogdon, J. G., Cohen, J. W., & Dietz, W. (2009). Annual medical spending attributable to obesity: Payer- and service-specific estimates. *Health Affairs, 28,* 822–831.

Finney, M. L. (2003, March). Cited in D. Smith, Angry thoughts, at-risk hearts. *Monitor on Psychology,* 46–47.

Fischer, J., & Menzel, R. (Eds.). (2011). *Animal thinking: Contemporary issues in comparative cognition.* Cambridge, MA: MIT Press.

Fischer, J. S. (1999, September 13). From Romania, a lesson in resilience. *U.S. News & World Report.*

Fischman, J. (2006, December 11). Alzheimer's today. *U.S. News & World Report,* 70–78.

Fisher, H. (2002, December 16). Cited in B. Carey, The brain in love. *Los Angeles Times,* F1.

Fisher, H. (2003). Cited in L. Helmuth, Caudate-over-heels in love. *Science, 302,* 1320.

Fisher, R. P., Milne, R., & Bull, R. (2011). Interviewing cooperative witnesses. *Current Directions in Psychological Science, 20,* 16–19.

Fishman, C. (2012, May 17). U.S. bottled water sales are coming (again) despite opposition. *Newswatch* [On-line]. Available: http://newswatch.national geographic.com/2012/05/17/u-s-bottles-water -sales-are-booming-again-despite-opposition/.

Fiske, S. (2006, January 2). Cited in Don't race to judgment. *U.S. News & World Report,* 90–91.

Fiske, S. (2008). Core social motivations. In J. Y. Shah & W. L. Gardner (Eds.), *Handbook of motivation science* (pp. 3–22). New York: Guilford Press.

Fiske, S., & Macrae, C. N. (Eds.). (2012). *The SAGE handbook of social cognition.* Thousand Oaks, CA: Sage.

FitzGerald, G. J. (1993). The reproductive behavior of the stickleback. *Scientific American, 268,* 80–85.

Flagg, E. J., Cardy, J. E., Roberts, W., & Roberts, T. P. (2005). Language lateralization development in children with autism: Insights from the late field magnetoencephalogram. *Neuroscience Letters, 386,* 82–87.

Flagg, S. (2008, December 8). For drivers, text messaging is becoming most dangerous distraction. *Columbia Missourian.*

Flegal, K. M., Carroll, M. D., Kit, B. K., & Ogden, C. L. (2012). Prevalence of obesity and trends in the distribution of body mass index among U.S. adults, 1999–2010. *JAMA, 307,* 491–497.

Fletcher, G. J. O. (2002). *The new science of intimate relationships.* Malden, MA: Blackwell Publishing.

Fletcher, G. J. O., & Simpson, J. A. (2000). Ideal standards in close relationships: Their structure and functions. *Directions in Psychological Science, 9,* 102–105.

Flint, J., Greenspan, R. J., & Kendler, K. S. (2010). *How genes influence behavior.* New York: Oxford University Press.

Flippo, R. F., Becker, M. J., & Wark, D. M. (2009). Test taking. In R. F. Flippo & D. C. Caverly (Eds.), *Handbook of college reading and study strategy research* (pp. 249–286). New York: Routledge.

Flippo, R. F., & Caverly, D. C. (2009). *Handbook of college reading and study strategy research.* New York: Routledge.

Flippo, R. F., & Caverly, D. C. (Eds.). (2000). *Handbook of college reading and study strategy research.* Mahwah, NJ: Lawrence Erlbaum.

Flores, S. A. (1999). Attributional biases in sexually coercive males. *Journal of Applied Social Psychology, 29,* 2425–2442.

Foa, E. B., Keane, T. M., Friedman, M. J., & Cohen, J. A. (Eds.). (2009). *Effective treatments for PTSD.* New York: Guilford Press.

Foer, J. (2006a, April). How to win the world memory championship. *Discover,* 62–66.

Foer, J. (2006b, April 27). Kaavya syndrome. *Slate.*

Folkman, S., & Moskowitz, J. T. (2000). Stress, positive emotion, and coping. *Current Directions in Psychological Science, 9,* 115–118.

Fonken, L. K., Workman, J. L., Walton, J. C., Weil, Z. M., Morris, J. S., Halm, A., & Nelson, R. J. (2010, October 11). Light at night increases body mass by shifting the time of food intake. *Proceedings of the National Academy of Sciences, 107,* 18664–18669.

Forgas, J. P., Williams, K. D., & Von Hippel, W. (Eds.). (2003). *Social judgments: Implicit and explicit processes.* Cambridge, UK: Cambridge University Press.

Foroohar, R. (2012, July 30). She's feeling lucky. *Time,* 17.

Forster, J., & Liberman, N. (2007). Knowledge activation. In A. W. Kruglanski & E. T. Higgins (Eds.), *Social psychology: Handbook of basic principles* (2nd ed., pp. 201–231). New York: Guilford Press.

Foster, G. D., Wyatt, H. R., Hill, J. O., Makris, A. P., Rosenbaum, D. L., Brill, C., Stein, R. I., Mohammed, S., Miller, B., Rader, D. J., Zemel, B., Wadden, T. A., Tenhave, T., Newcomb, C. W., & Klein, S. (2010, August 3). Weight and metabolic outcomes after 2 years on a low-carbohydrate versus low-fat diet: A randomized trial. *Annals of Internal Medicine, 153,* 147–157.

Foster, R. G. (2009, April/May). Askthebrains. *Scientific American Mind,* 70.

Fotopoulou, A. (2006, April/May). Cited in M. Solms, Freud returns. *Scientific American Mind,* 28–34.

Foulkes, D. (2003). Cited in C. W. Domhoff, Making sense of dreaming. *Science, 299,* 1987–1988.

Fournier, J. C., DeRubeis, R. J., Hollon, S. D., Amsterdam, J. D., Shelton, R. C., & Fawcett, J. (2010). Antidepressant drug effects and depression severity: A patient-level meta-analysis. *JAMA, 303,* 47–53.

Fox, D. (2009, Winter). The inner savant. *Discover: The Brain,* 10–15.

Fox, D. (2011, Fall). The insanity virus. *The Brain,* 88–95.

Fox, J. (2005, December 4). *"Robots helped treat my prostate cancer"* [On-line]. Available: http://edition .cnn.com/2005/TECH/12/02/john.fox/index.html.

Fox, M. J. (2002). *Lucky man: A memoir.* New York: Hyperion.

Fox, M. J. (2009). *Always looking up: The adventures of an incurable optimist.* New York: Hyperion.

Fox, R. E., DeLeon, P. H., Newman, R., Sammons, M. T., Dunivin, D. L., & Baker, D. C. (2009). Prescriptive authority and psychology. *American Psychologist, 64*(4), 257–268.

Foxhall, K. (2001, June). Preventing relapse. *Monitor on Psychology,* 46–47.

FoxNews. (2010, August 24). *Girl's rare pain disorder a gift and curse* [On-line]. Available: http://www .foxnews.com/story/0,2933,600105,00.htm.

Francis, L. A., & Susman, E. J. (2009, April). Self-regulation and rapid weight gain in children from age 3 to 12 years. *Archives of Pediatrics and Adolescent Medicine, 163,* 297–302.

Franco, Z. E., Blau, K., & Zimbardo, P. G. (2011). Heroism: A conceptual analysis and differentiation between heroic action and altruism. *Review of General Psychology, 15,* 99–113.

Frank, G. (2012). On the concept of resistance: Analysis and reformulation. *Psychoanalytic Review, 99,* 421–435.

Frank, M. C., Everett, D. L., Fedorenko, E., & Gibson, E. (2008). Number as a cognitive technology: Evidence from Pirahã language and cognition. *Cognition, 108,* 819–824.

Franklin, M. E., Abramowitz, J. S., Bux, D. A., Jr., Zoellner, L. A., & Feeny, N. C. (2002). Cognitive-behavioral therapy with and without medication in the treatment of obsessive-compulsive disorder. *Professional Psychology: Research and Practice, 33,* 162–168.

Franks, C. M. (1994). Behavioral model. In V. B. Van Hasselt & M. Hersen (Eds.), *Advanced abnormal psychology*. New York: Plenum Press.

Franz, V. H., Gegenfurtner, K. R., Bulthoff, H. H., & Fahle, M. (2000). Grasping visual illusions: No evidence for a dissociation between perception and action. *Psychological Science, 11,* 20–25.

Fraser, C. (2009, March 15). Egyptian women learn to fight back. *BBC News* [On-line]. Available: http://news/bbc/co/uk/2/hi/middle_east/7936071.stm.

Frazier, K. (2003, January/February). National Academy of Science report says polygraph testing too flawed for security screening. *Skeptical Inquirer,* 5–6.

Fredrickson, M., Hursti, T., Salmi, P., Borjeson, S., Furst, C. J., Peterson, C., & Steineck, G. (1993). Conditioned nausea after cancer chemotherapy and autonomic nervous system conditionability. *Scandinavian Journal of Psychology, 34,* 318–317.

Freedman, R. R. (1991). Physiological mechanisms of temperature biofeedback. *Biofeedback and Self-Regulation, 16,* 95–115.

Freedom Writers. (1999). *The Freedom Writers diary*. New York: Broadway Books.

Freeman, A., Pretzer, J., Fleming, B., & Simon, K. M. (2004). *Clinical applications of cognitive therapy* (2nd ed.). New York: Springer.

Frenda, S. J., Nichols, R. M., & Loftus, E. F. (2011). Current issues and advances in misinformation research. *Current Directions in Psychological Science, 20,* 20–23.

Frensch, P. A., & Runger, D. (2003). Implicit learning. *Current Directions in Psychological Science, 12,* 13–18.

Freud, S. (1900; reprinted 1980). *The interpretation of dreams* (J. Strachey, Ed. and Trans.). New York: Avon.

Freud, S. (1901; reprinted 1960). The psychopathology of everyday life. In J. Strachey (Ed. and Trans.), *The standard edition of the complete psychological works of Sigmund Freud* (Vol. 6). London: Hogarth.

Freud, S. (1905; reprinted 1953). Three essays on the theory of sexuality. In J. Strachey (Ed. and Trans.), *The standard edition of the complete psychological works of Sigmund Freud* (Vol. 7). London: Hogarth.

Freud, S. (1909; reprinted 1949). Notes upon a case of obsessional neurosis. In *Collected papers* (Vol. 3) (Alix and James Strachey, Trans.). London: Hogarth.

Freud, S. (1924). *A general introduction to psychoanalysis*. New York: Boni & Liveright.

Freud, S. (1940; reprinted 1961). An outline of psychoanalysis. In J. Strachey (Ed. and Trans.), *The standard edition of the complete psychological works of Sigmund Freud* (Vol. 23). London: Hogarth.

Frey, B. S. (2011, February 4). Happy people live longer. *Science, 331,* 542–543.

Freyd, J. J. (1994). Circling creativity. *Psychological Science, 5,* 122–126.

Frick, P. J., Barry, C. T., & Kamphaus, R. W. (2010). *Clinical assessment of child and adolescent personality and behavior*. New York: Springer.

Frick, W. B. (2000). Remembering Maslow: Reflections on a 1968 interview. *Journal of Humanistic Psychology, 40,* 128–147.

Fried, S. (2008, October 9). Cited in N. Hellmich, Think fat just hangs around, does nothing? *USA Today,* 6D.

Friedman, J. H., & Chou, K. L. (2007). Mood, emotion, and thought. In C. G. Goetz (Ed.), *Textbook of clinical neurology* (3rd ed., pp. 35–54). Philadelphia: Saunders Elsevier.

Friedman, J. M. (2003). A war on obesity, not the obese. *Science, 299,* 856–858.

Friedman, M., & Rosenman, R. (1974). *Type A behavior and your heart*. New York: Knopf.

Friedman, M. J., Keane, T. M., & Resick, P. A. (Eds.). (2010). *Handbook of PTSD: Science and practice*. New York: Guilford Press.

Friedman, R. A. (2006, September 18). For fearful fliers, a guide to easing the jitters. *The New York Times,* 11.

Friedman, S., & Stevenson, M. (1980). Perception of movements in pictures. In M. Hagen (Ed.), *Perception of pictures, Vol. 1: Alberti's window: The projective model of pictorial information*. Orlando, FL: Academic Press.

Friend, T. (1997, December 9). The race to save the wild tiger from extinction. *USA Today*.

Friend, T. (2003, March 27). A wartime first: Dolphins called to clear mines. *USA Today,* 8D.

Friess, S. (2009, February 25). A shadow of regret cast over gender switch. *USA Today,* 5D.

Frieswick, K. (2004, July 1). Casting to type. *CFO*.

Frijda, N. (2008). The psychologists' point of view. Cited in M. Lewis, J. M. Haviland-Jones & L. F. Barrett (Eds.), *Handbook of emotions* (3rd ed., pp. 68–87). New York: Guilford Press.

Fristad, M. A., & Shaver, A. E. (2001). Psychosocial interventions for suicidal children and adolescents. *Depression and Anxiety, 14,* 192–197.

Fritz, C., & Sonnentag, S. (2006). Recovery, well-being, and performance-related outcomes: The role of workload and vacation experiences. *Journal of Applied Psychology, 91,* 936–945.

Fritz, S. (1995, June). Found: Wonders in a secret cave. *Popular Science*.

Fritz, T. (2009, April 11). Cited in B. Bower, Two cultures grasp music's universal feeling. *Science News,* 14.

Fryer. S. L., McGee, C. L., Matt, G. E., Riley, E. P., & Mattson, S. N. (2007). Evaluation of psychopathological conditions in children with heavy prenatal alcohol exposure. *Pediatrics, 119,* e733–741.

Fullana, M. A., Mataix-Cols, D., Caspi, A., Harrington H., Grisham, J. R., Moffitt, T. E., & Poulton, R. (2009). Obsessions and compulsions in the community: Prevalence, interference, help seeking, developmental stability, and co-occurring psychiatric conditions. *American Journal of Psychiatry, 166,* 329–336.

Fuller, R. K., & Hiller-Sturmhofel, S. (1999). Alcoholism treatment in the United States. *Alcohol Research and Health, 23,* 69–77.

Funder, D. C. (2008). Persons, situations, and person-situation interactions. Cited in O. P. John, R. W. Robins & L. A. Pervin (Eds.), *Handbook of personality* (pp. 568–580). New York: Guilford Press.

Furumoto, L. (1989). The new history of psychology. In I. S. Cohen (Ed.), The *G. Stanley Hall lecture series* (Vol. 9). Washington, DC: American Psychological Association.

Fuster, J. (2008). *The prefrontal cortex* (4th ed.). London: Academic Press.

Gaab, N. (2008, April/May). Cited in S. Fritz, Sounding out dyslexia. *Scientific American Mind,* 12.

Gabrieli, J. (2005, April 4). Cited in J. Kluger, Secrets of the shy. *Time,* 50–52.

Gadzikowski, A. (2007). Born to sing: How music enriches children's language development. *Chicago Children's Museum* [On-line]. Available: http://www.chicagochildrensmuseum.org/learn_sing.html.

Gaga, L. (2010, January 15). Cited in *People*, Lady Gaga suffers from exhaustion, postpones show [On-line]. Available: http://www.people.com/people/article/0,,20337272,00.html.

Gage, F. H., Kempermann, G., & Song, H. (Eds.). (2008). *Adult neurogenesis*. New York: Cold Spring Harbor Laboratory Press.

Gaidos, S. (2010, October 23). The unusual suspects. *Science News,* 18–21.

Gaillard, R., Naccache, L., Pinel, P., Clemenceau, S., Volle, E., Hasboun, D., Dupont, S., Baulac, M., Dehaene, S., Adam, C., & Cohen, L. (2006). Direct intracranial, fMRI, and lesion evidence for the causal role of left inferotemporal cortex in reading. *Neuron, 50,* 191–204.

Galanter, E. (1962). Contemporary psychophysics. In R. Brown (Ed.), *New directions in psychology*. New York: Holt, Rinehart and Winston.

Gale, C. R., Batty, D., & Deary, I. J. (2008). Locus of control at age 10 years and health outcomes and behaviors at age 30 years: The 1970 British cohort study. *Psychosomatic Medicine, 70,* 397–403.

Gallagher, R. P. (2002, September 11). Cited in M. Duenwald, Students find another staple of campus life: Stress. *The New York Times,* D5.

Gallegos, A. (2011, September 19). Miracle vs. medicine: When faith puts care at risk. *American Medical News* [On-line]. Available: http://www.ama-assn.org/amednews/2011/09/19/prsa0919.htm.

Gallup. (2010, October 17). *Record-high 50% of Americans favor legalizing marijuana use* [On-line]. Available: http://www.gallup.com/poll/150149/record-high-americans-favor-legalizing-marijuana.aspx.

Galovski, T. E., Malta, L. S., & Blanchard, E. B. (2006). *Road rage: Assessment and treatment of the angry, aggressive driver*. Washington, DC: American Psychological Association.

Galton, F. (1888). Head growth in students at the University of Cambridge. *Nature, 38,* 14–15.

Gamer, M. (2009, February/March). Portrait of a lie. *Scientific American Mind,* 50–55.

Gamer, M., Bauermann, T., Stoeter, P., & Vossel, G. (2007). Covariations among fMRI, skin conductance, and behavioral data during processing of concealed information. *Human Brain Mapping, 28,* 1287–1301.

Gangestad, S. W., & Simpson, J. A. (2000). Trade-offs, the allocation of reproductive effort, and the evolutionary psychology of human mating. *Behavioral and Brain Sciences, 23,* 624–644.

Ganong, W. F. (2005). *Review of medical physiology* (22nd ed.). New York: McGraw-Hill.

Garbarini, N. (2005, December). Blinking turns off the brain. *Scientific American Mind*.

Garcia, J., Ervin, F. R., & Koelling, R. A. (1966). Learning with prolonged delay of reinforcement. *Psychonomic Science, 5,* 121–122.

Garcia, J., Hankins, W. G., & Rusiak, K. W. (1974). Behavioral regulation of the milieu interne in man and rat. *Science, 185,* 824–831.

Garcia-Rill, E., Wallace, T., & Good, C. (2006). Neuropharmacology of sleep and wakefulness. In T. L. Lee-Chiong (Ed.), *Sleep: A comprehensive handbook* (pp. 63–72). Hoboken, NJ: John Wiley & Sons.

Gardner, A. (2005, November 4). Peyote use by Native Americans doesn't damage brain [On-line]. Available: http://www.hon.ch/News/HSN/528941.html.

Gardner, B. T., & Gardner, R. A. (1975). Evidence for sentence constituents in the early utterances of child and chimpanzee. *Journal of Experimental Psychology: General, 104,* 244–267.

Gardner, E. (2006, September 20). 'Bigger bang' tour hits Boston. *USA Today*.

Gardner, H. (1976). *The shattered mind*. New York: Vintage Books.

Gardner, H. (1993). *Creating minds*. New York: Basic Books.

Gardner, H. (1995, November). Reflections on multiple intelligences. *Phi Delta Kappan*.

Gardner, H. (1999). *Intelligence reframed*. New York: Basic Books.

Gardner, H. (2003). Three distinct meanings of intelligence. In R. J. Sternberg, J. Lautrey & T. I. Lubart (Eds.), *Models of intelligence*. Washington, DC: American Psychological Association.

Gardner, H. (2006). *Multiple intelligences: New horizons*. New York: Basic Books.

Gardner, R., III, Ford, D. Y., & Miranda, A. H. (2001). The education of African American students: The struggle continues. *Journal of Negro Education, 70,* 241–242.

Garfield, S. L., & Bergin, A. E. (1994). Introduction and historical overview. In A. E. Bergin & S. L. Garfield (Eds.), *Handbook of psychotherapy and behavior change* (4th ed.). New York: Wiley.

Garry, M., Sharman, S. J., Feldman, J., Marlatt, G. A., & Loftus, E. (2002). Examining memory for heterosexual college students' sexual experiences using an electronic mail diary. *Health Psychology, 21,* 629–634.

Gates, G. J. (2011, April). How many people are lesbian, gay, bisexual, and transgender? *The Williams Institute* [On-line]. Available: http://www.law.ucla .edu/williamsinstitute.

Gatz, M. (2011a, August). Cited in G. D. Zakaib, Lessons about Alzheimer's disease. *Nature* [On-line]. Available: http://www.nature.com/news /2011/110805/full/news.2011.460.html.

Gatz, M. (2011b, October). Cited in J. Chamberlin, Protect your aging brain. *Monitor on Psychology,* 48–49.

Gaw, A. C. (2001). *Concise guide to cross-cultural psychiatry.* Washington, DC: American Psychological Association.

Gazzaniga, M. S. (1998, July). The split brain revisited. *Scientific American,* 50–55.

Gazzaniga, M. S. (2000). Cerebral specialization and interhemispheric communication: Does the corpus callosum enable the human condition? *Brain, 123,* 1293–1326.

Gazzaniga, M. S. (2005). Forty-five years of split-brain research and still going strong. *Nature Review Neuroscience, 6,* 653–659.

Gazzaniga, M. S. (2008a). *Human: The science behind what makes us unique.* New York: Harper Collins.

Gazzaniga, M. S. (2008b, June/July). Spheres of influence. *Scientific American Mind,* 32–39.

Gazzaniga, M. S. (Ed.). (2009). *The cognitive neurosciences.* Cambridge, MA: MIT Press.

Gazzaniga, M. S., Bogen, J. E., & Sperry, R. W. (1962). Some functional effects of sectioning the cerebral commissures in man. *Proceedings of the National Academy of Science, 48,* 1765–1769.

Geeraerts, D. (2006). Prospects and problems of prototype theory. In D. Geeraerts (Ed.), *Cognitive linguistics: Basic readings* (pp. 141–167). New York: Mouton de Gruyter.

Gehlert, H. (2006, June 28). He came a long way for the White House jog. *Los Angeles Times.*

Geiger, D. (2002). Cited in K. Cobb, Sleepy heads. *Science News, 162,* 38.

Gelbard-Sagiv, H., Mukamel, R., Harel, M., Malach, R., & Fried, I. (2008). Internally generated reactivation of single neurons in human hippocampus during free recall. *Science, 322,* 96–101.

Geller, L. (1982). The failure of self-actualization theory: A critique of Carl Rogers and Abraham Maslow. *Journal of Humanistic Psychology, 22,* 56–73.

Gelles, K. (2009, March 9). Drinking patterns: Where do you fit? *USA Today,* 5D.

Gelstein, S., Yeshurun, Y., Rozenkrantz, L., Shushan, S., Frumin, I., Roth, Y., & Sobel, N. (2011, January 14). Human tears contain a chemosignal. *Science, 331,* 226–230.

George, M. (2009, August). The brain: Magnetic depression treatment. *U.S. News & World Report,* 40–43.

Geraerts, E. (2007, July 30). Cited in W. L. Adams, Trusting memories. *Newsweek,* 12.

Geraerts, E., Schooler, J. W., Merckelbach, H., Hauer, B. J. A., & Anbadar, Z. (2007). The reality of recovered memories: Corroborating continuous and discontinuous memories of childhood sexual abuse. *Psychological Science, 18,* 564–568.

Gerl, E. J., & Morris, M. R. (2008). The causes and consequences of color vision. *Evolution: Education and Outreach, 1,* 476–486.

Gerwig, M., Dimitrova, A., Kolb, F. P., Maschke, M., Brol, B., Kunnel, A., Boring, D., Thilmann, A. F., Forsting, M., Diener, H. C., & Timmann, D. (2003). Comparison of eyeblink conditioning in patients with superior and posterior inferior cerebellar lesions. *Brain, 126,* 71–94.

Gerwig, M., Eber, A. C., Guberina, H., Frings, M., Kolb, F. P., Forsting, M., Aurich, V., Beck, A., & Timmann, D. (2008). Trace eyeblink conditioning in patients with cerebellar degeneration: Comparison of short and long trace intervals. *Experimental Brain Research, 187,* 85–96.

Gettler, L. T., McDada, T. W., Feranil, A. B., & Kuzawa, C. W. (2011). Longitudinal evidence that fatherhood decreases testosterone in human males. *Proceedings of the National Academy of Sciences, 108,* 16194–16199.

GHSA (Governor's Highway Safety Association). (2012). *Cell phone and texting laws* [On-line]. Available: http://www.ghsa.org/html/stateinfo/laws /cellphone_laws.html.

GIA (Global Industry Analysts). (2010). *ADHD therapeutics: A global strategic business report* [On-line]. Available: http://www.strategyr.com/ADHD _therapeutics_market_report.asp.

Giacopassi, D. J., & Dull, R. T. (1986). Gender and racial differences in the acceptance of rape myths within a college population. *Sex Roles, 15,* 63–75.

Giannotti, F., Cortesi, F., Sebastiani, T., & Ottaviano, S. (2002). Circadian preference, sleep and daytime behaviour in adolescence. *Journal of Sleep Research, 11,* 191–199.

Gibbs, N. (1995, October 2). The EQ factor. *Time,* 60–68.

Gibbs, N. (2007, April 30). Darkness falls. One troubled student rains down death on a quiet campus. *Time,* 36–52.

Gibbs, N. (2009, August 3). Dying together. *Time,* 64.

Gibson, B. M., & Kamil, A. C. (2001). Tests for cognitive mapping in Clark's nutcrackers. *Journal of Comparative Psychology, 115,* 403–417.

Gibson, B. M., & Wilks, T. (2008, October). The use of self-motion cues and landmarks by Clark's nutcrackers (*Nucifraga columbiana*) during a small-scale search task. *Animal Behaviour, 75*(4), 1305–1317.

Gibson, E. J., & Walk, R. (1960). The visual "cliff." *Scientific American, 202,* 64–71.

Gigone, D., & Hastie, R. (1997). Proper analysis of the accuracy of group judgments. *Psychological Bulletin, 121,* 149–167.

Gilbert, A. (2008). *What the nose knows: The science of scent in everyday life.* New York: Crown.

Gilbert, K. (2006, July/August). Your personal time zone. *Psychology Today.*

Giles, J. (2006). Scans suggest IQ scores reflect brain structure. *Nature, 440,* 588–589.

Gill, P., Marrin, S., & Phythian, M. (2009). *Intelligence theory: Key debates and questions.* New York: Routledge.

Gilligan, C. (1982). *In a different voice: Psychological theory and women's development.* Cambridge, MA: Harvard University Press.

Gillman, M. (2007, July 28). Cited in B. Bower, Weighting for friends. *Science News, 172,* 51.

Giltay, E. J., Geleijnse, J. M., Zitman, F. G., Hoekstra, T., & Schouten, E. G. (2004). Dispositional optimism and all-cause and cardiovascular mortality in a prospective cohort of elderly Dutch men and women. *Archives of General Psychiatry, 61,* 1126–1135.

Giorgi, A. (2005). Remaining challenges for humanistic psychology. *Journal of Humanistic Psychology, 45,* 204–216.

Gitlin, M. J. (2009). Pharmacotherapy and other somatic treatment for depression. In I. H. Gotlib & C. L. Hammen (Eds.), *Handbook of depression* (2nd ed., pp. 554–585). New York: Guilford Press.

Gladwell, M. (2004, September 20). Personality plus. *The New Yorker,* 42–48.

Gladwell, M. (2008). *Outliers: The story of success.* New York: Little, Brown and Company.

Glanzer, M., & Cunitz, A. R. (1966). Two storage mechanisms in free recall. *Journal of Verbal Learning and Verbal Behavior, 5,* 351–360.

Glasser, M., Kolvin, I., Campbell, D., Glasser, A., Leitch, I., & Farrelly, S. (2001). Cycle of child sexual abuse: Links between being a victim and becoming a perpetrator. *British Journal of Psychiatry, 179,* 482–494.

Glassman, W. E., & Hadad, M. (2004). *Approaches to psychology* (4th ed.). Philadelphia: Open University Press.

Glausiusz, J. (2008, August/September). The hidden power of scent. *Scientific American Mind,* 38–45.

Gleick, E., Alexander, B., Eskin, L., Pick, G., Skolnik, S., Dodd, J., & Sugden, J. (1994, December 12). The final victim. *People.*

Glenberg, A. M., Sanocki, T., Epstein, W., & Morris, C. (1987). Enhancing calibration of comprehension. *Journal of Experimental Psychology: General, 116,* 119–136.

Gliatto, T. (2006, March 13). Black. White. *People, 37.*

Godlasky, A. (2008, October 16). MP3 players can damage hearing. *USA Today,* 4D.

Godlee, F., Smith, J., & Marcovitch, H. (2011). Wakefield's article linking MMR vaccine and autism was fraudulent. *New England Journal of Medicine, 342,* 64–66.

Goff, D. (2008, September 22). Silent demons. *Newsweek,* 66.

Gokturk, D. (2008). Suzuki violin teaching method: Its theory, philosophy, and criticism. *Turkish Journal of Music Education, 1,* 4–11.

Golberstein, E., Eisenberg, D., & Gollust, S. E. (2008). Perceived stigma and mental heath care seeking. *Psychiatric Services, 59,* 392–399.

Goldberg, R. (2010). *Drugs across the spectrum* (6th ed.). Belmont, CA: Wadsworth Cengage.

Goldenberg, H., & Goldenberg, I. (2012). *Family therapy: An overview* (8th ed.). Belmont, CA: Cengage.

Goldfried, M. R., & Davison, G. C. (1976). *Clinical behavior therapy.* New York: Holt, Rinehart and Winston.

Goldsmith, H. H. (2003). Introduction: Genetics and development. In R. J. Davidson, K. B. Scherer & H. H. Goldsmith (Eds.), *Handbook of affective sciences.* New York: Oxford University Press.

Goldsmith, H. H. (2009). Introduction: Genetics and development. In R. J. Davidson, K. R. Sherer & H. H. Goldsmith (Eds.), *Handbook of affective sciences.* New York: Oxford University Press.

Goldsmith, L. A. (2008). Disorders of the eccrine sweat glands and sweating. In K. Wolff, L. A. Goldsmith, S. I. Katz, B. A. Gilchrest, A. Paller & D. J. Lefell (Eds.), *Fitzpatrick's dermatology in general medicine* (7th ed.). New York: McGraw-Hill.

Goldstein, E. B. (2008). *Cognitive psychology* (2nd ed.). Belmont, CA: Thomson Wadsworth.

Goldstein, E. B. (2010). *Sensation and perception* (8th ed.). Belmont, CA: Wadsworth.

Goleman, D. (1995). *Emotional intelligence: Why it can matter more than IQ.* New York: Bantam Books.

Goleman, D. (2005). *Emotional intelligence. The tenth anniversary edition.* New York: Bantam Dell.

Goleman, D. (2006a, October 23). Cited in A. Underwood, How to read a face. *Newsweek, 65.*

Goleman, D. (2006b, September 22). Cited in W. Herbert, The power of two. *Psychological Science.*

Goleman, D., & Gurin, J. (1993). *Mind/body medicine: How to use your mind for better health.* New York: Consumer Reports.

Golub, A., Johnson, B. D., Sifaneck, S. J., Chesluk, B., & Parker, H. (2001). Is the U.S. experiencing an incipient epidemic of hallucinogen use? *Substance Use & Misuse, 36,* 1699–1729.

Gomes, H., Sussman, E., Ritter, W., Kurtzberg, D., Cowan, N., & Vaughan, H. G., Jr. (1999). Electrophysiological evidence of developmental changes in the duration of auditory sensory memory. *Developmental Psychology, 35,* 299–302.

Goode, E. (2002, March 12). The uneasy fit of the precocious and the average. *The New York Times,* D1.

Goode, E. (2003, May 20). Leading drugs for psychosis come under new scrutiny. *The New York Times,* A1.

Goodstein, L., & Banerjee, N. (2006, November 4). Minister admits buying drug but denies tryst. *The New York Times.*

Goodwin, F. K. (2003). Rationale for long-term treatment of bipolar disorder and evidence for long-term lithium treatment. *Journal of Clinical Psychiatry, 64*(Suppl. 6), 5–12.

Goodwin, J. (2006, June). Forget me not. *Reader's Digest,* 124–131.

Gordon, B. (2007, December 10). Cited in A. Underwood, Jogging your memory. *Newsweek,* 68–71.

Gorman, C. (2003, July 28). The new science of dyslexia. *Time,* 52–59.

Gorman, C. (2005a, January 17). The importance of resilience. *Time,* 52–55.

Gorman, C. (2005b, December 12). A transplant first. *Time,* 58.

Gorman, C. (2006, June 5). What alcohol does to a child. *Time,* 76.

Gorman, C. (2012, January). Five hidden dangers of obesity. *Scientific American,* 60–61.

Gostout, B. (2007, January 22). *Cervical cancer vaccine: Who needs it, how it works* [On-line]. Available: http://www.mayoclinic.com/print/cervical-cancer-vaccine/WO00120.

Gottesman, I. I. (2001). Psychopathology through a lifespan-genetic prism. *American Psychologist, 56,* 867–877.

Gottesman, I. I., Laursen, T., Bertelsen, A., & Mortensen, P. (2010). Severe mental disorders in offspring with 2 psychiatrically ill parents. *Archives of General Psychiatry, 67,* 252–257.

Gottfredson, L. S. (2002). Where and why *g* matters: Not a mystery. *Human Performance, 15,* 24–46.

Gottfredson, L. S. (2003). Dissecting practical intelligence theory: Its claims and evidence. *Intelligence, 31,* 342–397.

Gottman, J. M. (1999). *Seven principles for making marriage work.* New York: Three Rivers Press.

Gottman, J. M. (2000. September 14). Cited in K. S. Peterson, "Hot" and "cool" phases could predict divorce. *USA Today,* 9D.

Gottman, J. M. (2003, May 1). Cited in B. Carey, For better or worse: Marriage by the numbers. *Los Angeles Times,* F1.

Gottman, J. M. (2011, October). Cited in S. Dingfelder, Must babies always breed marital discontent? *Monitor on Psychology,* 50–52.

Gottman, J. M., Gottman, J. S., & DeClaire, J. (2006). *10 lessons to transform your marriage.* New York: Crown Publishers.

Goucher, C., LeGuin, C., & Walton, L. (1998). *In the balance: Themes in world history.* Boston: McGraw-Hill.

Gould, M. S., Walsh, T., Munfakh, J. L., Kleinman, M., Duan, N., Olfson, M., Greenhill, L., & Cooper, T. (2009). Sudden death and use of stimulant medications in youths. *American Journal of Psychiatry, 166*(9), 992–1001.

Gould, S. J. (1981). *The mismeasure of man.* New York: Norton.

Gould, S. J. (1994, November). The geometer of race. *Discover.*

Gould, S. J. (1996). *The mismeasure of man* (revised and expanded). New York: Norton.

Gourine, A. V., Kasymov, V., Marina, N., Tang, F., Figueiredo, M. F., Lane, S., Teschemacherm, A. G., Spyer, K. M., Deisseroth, K., & Kasparov, S. (2010, July 30). Astrocytes control breathing through pH-dependent release of ATP. *Science, 329,* 571–575.

Grady, D. (2008, April 10). In shift to digital, more repeat mammograms. *The New York Times.*

Graham, J. R. (2005). *MMPI-2: Assessing personality and psychopathology* (4th ed.). New York: Oxford University Press.

Graham-Bermann, S. (2012, April). Cited in B. L. Smith, The case against spanking. *Monitor on Psychology,* 60–63.

Gramling, C. (2006, March 4). Gender gap: Male-only gene affects men's dopamine levels. *Science News, 169,* 132–133.

Grant, P., Young, P., & DeRubeis, R. (2005). Cognitive behavioral therapy. In G. O. Gabbard, J. S. Beck & J. Holmes (Eds.), *Oxford textbook of psychotherapy.* New York: Oxford University Press.

Granvold, D. K. (Ed.). (1994). *Cognitive and behavioral treatment.* Pacific Grove, CA: Brooks/Cole.

Gravetter, F. J., & Forzano, L. B. (2012). *Research methods for the behavioral sciences* (4th ed.). Belmont, CA: Wadsworth.

Gray, K., & Wegner, D. M. (2008). The sting of intentional pain. *Psychological Science, 19,* 1260–1262.

Greco, L. A., & Morris, T. L. (2001). Treating childhood shyness and related behavior: Empirically evaluated approaches to promote positive social interactions. *Clinical Child and Family Psychology Review, 4,* 299–318.

Greely, H., Sahakian, B., Kessler, R. C., Gazzaniga, M., Campbell, P., & Farah, M. J. (2008). Towards responsible use of cognitive-enhancing drugs by the healthy. *Nature, 456,* 702–705.

Green, J. P., & Lynn, S. J. (2000). Hypnosis and suggestion-based approaches to smoking cessation: An examination of the evidence. *International Journal of Clinical and Experimental Hypnosis, 48,* 195–224.

Greenberg, J. (1978). The americanization of Roseto. *Science News, 113,* 378–382.

Greenberg, L. S., & Rice, L. N. (1997). Humanistic approaches to psychotherapy. In P. L. Wachtel & S. B. Messer (Eds.), *Theories of psychotherapy: Origins and evolution.* Washington, DC. American Psychological Association.

Greenberg, R., & Perlman, C. A. (1999). The interpretation of dreams: A classic revisited. *Psychoanalytic Dialogues, 9,* 749–765.

Greene, A. J. (2010, July/August). Making connections. *Scientific American Mind,* 22–29.

Greene, B., & Winfrey, O. (1996). *Make the connection.* New York: Hyperion.

Greene, J. D., Nystrom, L. E., Engell, A. D., Darley, J. M., & Cohen, J. D. (2004). The neural bases of cognitive conflict and control in moral judgment. *Neuron, 44,* 389–400.

Greensite, G. (2007, February 17). *Myths and facts: Rape myths.* California Coalition Against Sexual Assault [On-line]. Available: http://www.calcasa.org/34.0.html.

Greenwald, A. G., Banaji, M. R., Rudman, L. A., Farnham, S. D., Nosek, B. A., & Mellott, D. S. (2002). A unified theory of implicit attitudes, stereotypes, self-esteem, and self-concept. *Psychological Review, 109,* 3–25.

Gregory, R. L. (1974). Recovery from blindness: A case study. In R. L. Gregory (Ed.), *Concepts and mechanisms of perception.* London: Gerald Duckworth.

Gregory, S. (2012a, February 27). Linsanity! Jeremy Lin recolors the urban hoops culture. *Time,* 42–45.

Gregory, S. (2012b, June 11). Strong-armed. Olympian Sarah Robles raises the bar for plus-size women. *Time,* 62–63.

Greven, C. U., Harlaar, N., Kovas, Y., Chamorro-Premuzic, T., & Plomin. R. (2009). More than just IQ: School achievement is predicted by self-perceived abilities—but for genetic rather than environmental reasons. *Psychological Science, 20,* 753–762.

Griffiths, R. (2006, October/November). Cited in J. Talan, Visions for psychedelics. *Scientific American Mind,* 7.

Griffiths, R. (2008, October 22). Cited in W. Weise, Petition calls for FDA to regulate energy drinks. *USA Today,* 6D.

Grigorenko, R. (2006, April 1). Cited in B. Bower, Smarty brains: High-IQ kids navigate notable neural shifts. *Science News, 169,* 195.

Grimaldi, J. V. (1986, April 16). "The mole" evicted from sewer. *San Diego Union-Tribune.*

Grimes, W. (2006, September 2). Tracing the strange history of a family with a mysterious, incurable disease. *The New York Times,* A20.

Grimm, O. (2007, April/May). Addicted to food? *Scientific American Mind,* 36–39.

Grinker, R. (2007). *Unstrange minds: Remapping the world of autism.* Philadelphia: Basic Books.

Grogan, B., Shaw, B., Ridenhour, R., Fine, A., & Eftimiades, M. (1993, May). Their brothers' keepers? *People.*

Gron, G., Wunderlich, A. P., Spitzer, M., Tomczak, R., & Riepe, M. W. (2000). Brain activation during human navigation: Gender-different neural networks as substrate of performance. *Nature Neuroscience, 3,* 404–408.

Grossman, C. L., & Nichols, B. (2006, January 18). Some hope for more laws; others fear them. *USA Today,* 5A.

Grossman, L. (2008, November 24). Wise guy. *Time,* 48–49.

Groth-Marnat, G. (2009). *Handbook of psychological assessment* (5th ed.). Hoboken, NJ: John Wiley & Sons.

Grueter, T. (2007, August/September). Forgetting faces. *Scientific American Mind,* 68–73.

Grunbaum, A. (1993). *Validation in the clinical theory of psychoanalysis.* Madison, CT: International Universities Press.

Grunbaum, A. (2006). Is Sigmund Freud's psychoanalytic edifice relevant to the 21st century? *Psychoanalytic Psychology, 23,* 257–284.

Grusec, J. E. (2006). The development of moral behavior and conscience from a socialization perspective. In M. Killen & J. G. Smetana (Eds.), *Handbook of moral development* (pp. 243–265). Mahwah, NJ: Lawrence Erlbaum.

Gruwell, E. (2007). *Teach with your heart.* New York: Broadway Books.

Guilford, J. P. (1967). *The nature of human intelligence.* New York: McGraw-Hill.

Guinness World Records. (2012). *Guinness world records 2013.* London: Guinness.

Gundersen, E. (2012, March 23). Houston: 'Closure,' sadness and inevitability. *USA Today,* A1.

Gunn, E. P. (2006, October 16). It is in your head. *U.S. News & World Report,* EE8–9.

Gunter, C. (2009). Neurogenetics: Schizophrenia: Missing heritability found? *Nature Reviews Neuroscience, 10,* 543.

Gupta, S. (2007, October 1). The caffeine habit. *Time,* 62.

Gura, T. (1997). Obesity sheds its secrets. *Science, 275,* 751–753.

Gura, T. (2008a, June/July). Addicted to starvation. *Scientific American Mind,* 60–67.

Gura, T. (2008b, December/2009, January). I'll do it tomorrow. *Scientific American Mind,* 26–33.

Gurman, A. S. (2008). *Clinical handbook of couple therapy* (4th ed.). New York: Guilford Press.

Gurung, R. A. R. (2005). How do students really study (and does it matter)? *Teaching of Psychology, 32,* 239–241.

Guterl, F. (2002, November 11). What Freud got right. *Newsweek,* 50–51.

Gutgesell, M. E., & Payne, N. (2004). Issues of adolescent psychological development in the 21st century. *Pediatrics in Review, 25,* 79–85.

Guthrie, J. P., Ash, R. A., & Bendapudi, V. (1995). Additional validity evidence for a measure of morningness. *Journal of Applied Psychology, 80,* 186–190.

Guthrie, R. V. (1976). *Even the rat was white.* New York: Harper & Row.

Gutsell, J. N., & Inzlicht, M. (2010). Empathy constrained: Prejudice predicts reduced mental simulation of actions during observation of outgroups. *Journal of Experimental Social Psychology, 46,* 841–845.

Gwyer, P., & Clifford, B. R. (1997). The effects of the cognitive interview on recall, identification, confidence, and the confidence/accuracy relationship. *Applied Cognitive Psychology, 11,* 121–145.

Hadders-Algra, M. (2002). Variability in infant motor behavior: A hallmark of the healthy nervous system. *Infant Behavior & Development, 2,* 433–451.

Haggard, T. (2006a, November 5). Ted Haggard's letter to New Life Church. *Colorado Springs Gazette.*

Haggard, T. (2006b, November 19). Cited in L. Goodstein, Minister's own rules sealed his fate. *The New York Times,* 22.

Halbreich, U. (2003). Anxiety disorders in women: A developmental and lifecycle perspective. *Depression and Anxiety, 17,* 107–110.

Hales, D. (2008, February). The ways to happiness. *Reader's Digest,* 98–103.

Hall, H. (2008). What about acupuncture? *Skeptic, 14,* 8–9.

Hall, H. A. (2008). *Women aren't supposed to fly.* Lincoln, NE: iUniverse.

Hall, W. (2006). The mental health risks of adolescent cannabis use. *PLoS Medicine, 3,* e39.

Hallmayer, J., Cleveland, S., Torres, A., Phillips, J., Cohen, B., Torigoe, T., Miller, J., Fedele, A., Collins, J., Smith, K., Lotspeich, L., Croen, L. A., Ozonoff, S., Lajonchere, C., Grether, J. D., & Risch, N. (2011). Genetic heritability and shared environmental factors among twin pairs with autism. *Archives of General Psychiatry, 68,* 1095–1102.

Hallmayer, J., Faraco, J., Lin, L., Hesselson, S., Winkelmann, J., Kawashima, M., Mayer, G., Plazzi, G., Nevsimalova, S., Bourgin, P., Hong, S. C., Honda, Y., Honda, M., Högl, B., Longstreth, W. T., Jr., Montplaisir, J., Kemlink, D., Einen, M., Chen, J., Musone, S. L., Akana, M., Miyagawa, T., Duan, J., Desautels, A., Erhardt, C., Hesla, P. E., Poli, F., Frauscher, B., Jeong, J. H., Lee, S. P., Ton, T. G., Kvale, M., Kolesar, L., Dubrovolná, M., Nepom, G. T., Salomon, D., Wichmann, H. E., Rouleau, G. A., Gieger, C., Levinson, D. F., Gejman, P. V., Meitinger, T., Young, T., Peppard, P., Tokunaga, K., Kwok, P. Y., Risch, N., & Mignot, E. (2009). Narcolepsy is strongly associated with the T-cell receptor alpha locus. *Nature Genetics, 41,* 708–711.

Halpern, D. F. (1998). Teaching critical thinking for transfer across domains. *American Psychologist, 53,* 449–455.

Halpern, D. F. (2000). *Sex differences in cognitive abilities* (3rd ed.). Hillsdale, NJ: Lawrence Erlbaum.

Halpern, D. F. (2003, May). Cited in K. Kersting, Cognitive sex differences: A "political minefield." *Monitor on Psychology,* 54–55.

Halpern, D. F., Benbow, C. P., Geary, D. C., Gur, R. C., Hyde, J. S., & Gernsbacher, M. A. (2007, December/2008, January). Sex, math and scientific achievement. *Scientific American Mind,* 44–51.

Ham, P. (2005, February 15). Treatment of panic disorder. *American Family Physician.*

Hamann, S. B., Ely, T. D., Hoffman, J. M., & Kilts, C. D. (2002). Ecstasy and agony: Activation of the human amygdala in positive and negative emotions. *Psychological Science, 13,* 135–141.

Hamer, D. (2002). Rethinking behavior genetics. *Science, 298,* 71–72.

Hamilton, B. (2004). *Soul surfer.* New York: Pocket Books.

Hamilton, M. A. (2005). *God vs. the gavel.* New York: Cambridge University Press.

Hamm, A. O., Schupp, H. T., & Weike, A. I. (2003). Motivational organization of emotions: Autonomic changes, cortical responses, and reflex modulation. In R. D. Lane & L. Nadel (Eds.), *Cognitive neuroscience of emotion.* New York: Oxford University Press.

Han, S., & Humphreys, G. W. (1999). Interactions between perceptual organization based on Gestalt laws and those based on hierarchical processing. *Perception & Psychophysics, 61,* 1287–1298.

Hancock, L. (1996, March 18). Mother's little helper. *Newsweek.*

Hanley, G. (2011). Functional analysis. In J. K. Luiselli (Ed.), *Teaching and behavior support for children and adults with autism spectrum disorder: A practitioner's guide* (pp. 22–29). New York: Oxford University Press.

Hansen, J. T. (2000). Psychoanalysis and humanism: A review and critical examination of integrationist efforts with some proposed resolutions. *Journal of Counseling and Development, 78,* 21–28.

Hanson, G. R., & Venturelli, P. J. (1998). *Drugs and society* (5th ed.). Boston: Jones and Bartlett.

Hanson, G. R., Venturelli, P. J., & Fleckenstein, A. E. (2002). *Drugs and society* (7th ed.). Boston: Jones and Bartlett.

Hanson, G. R., Venturelli, P. J., & Fleckenstein, A. E. (2006). *Drugs and society* (9th ed.). Sudbury, MA: Jones and Bartlett.

Hao, J., Li, K., Li, K., Zhang, D., Wang, W. M., Yang, Y., Yan B., Shan, B., & Zhou, X. (2005). Visual attention deficits in Alzheimer's disease: An fMRI study. *Neuroscience Letters, 385,* 18–23.

Harden, K. P., Mendle, J., Hill, J. E., Turkheimer, E., & Emery, R. E. (2008). Rethinking timing of first sex and delinquency. *Journal of Youth and Adolescence, 37,* 373–385.

Harder, B. (2006, April 29). Brain delay: Air pollutants linked to slow childhood mental development. *Science News, 169,* 259–260.

Hardy, J. B., Welcher, D. W., Mellits, E. D., & Kagan, J. (1976). Pitfalls in the measurement of intelligence: Are standardized intelligence tests valid for measuring the intellectual potential of urban children? *Journal of Psychology, 94,* 43–51.

Hareli, S., & Weiner, B. (2002). Social emotions and personality inferences: A scaffold for a new direction in the study of achievement motivation. *Educational Psychologist, 37,* 183–193.

Harmon-Jones, E., & Harmon Jones, C. (2002). Testing the action-based model of cognitive dissonance: The effect of action orientation on postdecisional attitudes. *Personality and Social Psychology Bulletin, 28,* 711–723.

Harrell, E. (2010, October 11). Remains of the day. Can a new device help amnesia patients outsource memory. *Time,* 46–51.

Harris, G. (2010, November 11). U.S. wants smoking's costs to stare you in face. *The New York Times,* A1.

Harris, J. C. (1995). *Developmental neuropsychiatry* (Vol. 1). New York: Oxford University Press.

Harris, J. C. (2003). Pinel orders the chains removed from the insane at Bicetre. *Archives of General Psychiatry, 60,* 442.

Harris, J. M., & Dean, P. J. A. (2003). Accuracy and precision of binocular 3-D motion perception. *Journal of Experimental Psychology, 29,* 869–881.

Harris, J. R. (1998). *The nurture assumption. Why children turn out the way they do.* New York: Free Press.

Harris, J. R. (2006). *No two alike: Human nature and human individuality.* New York: W. W. Norton.

Harris, J. R. (2007, August 9). Do pals matter more than parents? *The Times.*

Harris, J. R. (2009a, July/August). Cited in J. Lehrer, Do parent matter? *Scientific American Mind,* 61–63.

Harris, J. R. (2009b). *The nurture assumption. Why children turn out the way they do* (revised and updated). New York: Free Press.

Harrison, K. D. (2010, October 6). Cited in E. Weise, Rare new language with only 800–1,200 speakers discovered in India. *USA Today,* 17A.

Hart, B., & Risley, T. (1996). Cited in B. Bower, Talkative parents make kids smarter. *Science News, 150,* 100.

Hart, B., & Risley, T. (2006, November 26). Cited in P. Tough, What it takes to make a student. *The New York Times Magazine.*

Hartmann, P. (2006, May 21). Cited in D. Sefton, Sign language: Studies debunking astrology do little to deter followers. *San Diego Union-Tribune,* E2.

Harvey, G. A., Bryant, R. A., & Tarrier, N. (2003). Cognitive behaviour therapy for posttraumatic stress disorder. *Clinical Psychology Review, 23,* 501–522.

Harzem, P. (2004). Behaviorism for new psychology: What was wrong with behaviorism and what is wrong with it now? *Behavior and Philosophy, 32,* 5–12.

Haseltine, E. (2008, August). Cited in S. Kruglinski, How to spot the truth. *Discover,* 44–45.

Haselton, M., Buss, D. M., Oubaid, V., & Angleitner, A. (2005). Sex, lies, and strategic interference: The psychology of deception between the sexes. *Personality and Social Psychology Bulletin, 31,* 3–23.

Haslinger, K. (2005). Placebo power. *Scientific American Mind, 16,* 31.

Hass, N. (2012, February 20). Hysteria on main street. *Newsweek,* 26–27.

Hatcher, T. (2007, October 8). The darkest secret. *Newsweek,* 72.

Hathaway, W. (2006, April 13). Teens lose out on ample hours of precious sleep. *Northwest Herald.*

Hauser, M. (2003, July 15). Cited in N. Wade, Early voices: The leap to language. *The New York Times,* D1.

Hauser, M. (2007, May). Cited in J. Glausiusz, The *Discover* interview: Marc Hauser. *Discover,* 60–66.

Hauser, S. L., & Goodin, D. S. (2012). Multiple sclerosis and other demyelinating diseases. In D. L. Longo, A. S. Fauci, D. L. Kasper, S. L. Hauser, J. L. Jameson & J. Loscalzo (Eds.), *Harrison's principles of internal medicine* (18th ed., pp. 3395–3409). New York: McGraw-Hill.

Hawk, T. (2002). *Tony Hawk: Professional skateboarder.* New York: HarperCollins.

Hayes, K. J., & Hayes, C. H. (1951). The intellectual development of a home-raised chimpanzee. *Proceedings of the American Philosophical Society, 95,* 105–109.

Haynes, J. (2008, August/September). Cited in N. Branan, Unconscious decisions. *Scientific American Mind,* 8.

Head, L. S., & Gross, A. M. (2009). Systematic desensitization. In W. T. O'Donohue & J. E. Fisher (Eds.), *General principles and empirically supported techniques of cognitive behavior therapy* (pp. 640–647). Hoboken, NJ: John Wiley & Sons.

Healy, B. (2006, September 4). Obesity gets an early start. *U.S. News & World Report,* 79.

Healy, B. (2008, September 16/September 22). Let's teach our children well. *U.S. News & World Report,* 64.

Healy, M. (2000, November 29). Computer improves mammogram results. *USA Today,* 9D.

Healy, M. C. (2005, July/August). A cautionary note on using graphology for hiring and promoting employees. *Explorer* [On-line]. Available: http://www.rockethire.com/newsletter/2005/3/best.html.

Healy, S. D., de Kort, S. R., & Clayton, N. S. (2005). The hippocampus, spatial memory and food hoarding: A puzzle revisited. *Trends in Ecology and Evolution, 20,* 17–22.

Hechtman, L., Abikoff, H., Klein, R. G., Weiss, G., Respitz, D., Kouri, J., Blum, C., Greenfield, B., Etcovitch, J., Fleiss, K., & Pollack, S. (2004). Academic achievement and emotional status of children with ADHD treated with long-term methylphenidate and multimodal psychosocial treatment. *Journal of the American Academy of Child and Adolescent Psychiatry, 43,* 812–819.

Hedden, T., Ketay, S., Aron, A., Markus, H. R., & Gabrieli, J. D. E. (2008). Cultural influences on neural substrates of attentional control. *Psychological Science, 19,* 12–17.

Hefferon, K., & Boniwell, I. (2011). *Positive psychology: Theory, research, and practice.* New York: McGraw-Hill.

Heflin, L. J., & Alaimo, D. F. (2006). *Students with autism spectrum disorders: Effective instructional practices.* Upper Saddle River, NJ: Prentice Hall.

Hegarty, P. (2007). From genius inverts to gendered intelligence: Lewis Terman and the power of the norm. *History of Psychology, 10,* 132–155.

Heider, F. (1958). *The psychology of interpersonal relations.* New York: Wiley.

Heilman, K. M. (2000). Emotional experience: A neurological model. In R. D. Lane & L. Nadel (Eds.), *Cognitive neuroscience of emotion.* New York: Oxford University Press.

Heilman, M. E., & Okimoto, T. G. (2007). Why are women penalized for success at male tasks? The implied communal deficit. *Journal of Applied Psychology, 92,* 81–92.

Heiman, J. R. (2002). Sexual dysfunction: Overview of prevalence, etiological factors, and treatments. *Journal of Sex Research, 39,* 73–78.

Heimbauer, L. A., Beran, M. J., & Owren, M. J. (2011). A chimpanzee recognizes synthetic speech with significantly reduced acoustic cues to phonetic content. *Current Biology, 21,* 1210–1214.

Helgeson, V. S. (1994). Prototypes and dimensions of masculinity and femininity. *Sex Roles, 31,* 653–682.

Hellmich, N. (2005, October 20). Bigger portions will get eaten. *USA Today,* 9D.

Hellmich, N. (2008, October. 29). Bad habits contribute to weight gain throughout college. *USA Today,* 5D.

Helmes, E., & Pachana, N. A. (2005). Professional doctoral training in psychology: International comparison and commentary. *Australian Psychology, 40,* 45–53.

Helmuth, L. (2003a). Caudate-over-heels in love. *Science, 302,* 1320.

Helmuth, L. (2003b). Fear and trembling in the amygdala. *Science, 300,* 568–569.

Helson, R. (1996). In search of the creative personality. *Creativity Research Journal, 9,* 295–306.

Helwig, C. C. (1997). Making moral cognition respectable (again): A retrospective review of Lawrence Kohlberg. *Contemporary Psychology, 42,* 191–195.

Helzer, J. E., & Canino, G. J. (Eds.). (1992). *Alcoholism in North America, Europe, and Asia.* New York: Oxford University Press.

Hemphill, J. F. (2003). Interpreting the magnitudes of correlation coefficients. *American Psychologist, 58,* 78–80.

Henderson, W. C. (2006, October 23). Putting limits on teen drivers. *Time,* 71–72.

Hendrick, B. (2010, October 15). Guidelines on deep brain stimulation for Parkinson's. *WebMD* [On-line]. Available: http://www.webmd.com/parkinsons-disease/news/20101015/guidelines-on-deep-brain-stimulation-for-parkinsons.

Hendy, H. M., Williams, K. E., & Camise, T. S. (2005). "Kids Choice" school lunch program increases children's fruit and vegetable acceptance. *Appetite, 49,* 683–686.

Hendy, H. M., Williams, K. E., Camise, T. S., Alderman, S., Ivy, J., & Reed, J. (2007). Overweight and average-weight children equally responsive to "Kids Choice Program" to increase fruit and vegetable consumption. *Appetite, 49,* 250–263.

Herbenick, D., Reece, M., Schick, V., Sanders, S. A., Dodge, B., & Fortenberry, J. D. (2010). Sexual behavior in the United States: Result from a national probability sample of men and women ages 14–94. *Journal of Sexual Medicine, 7,* 255–265.

Herdt, G. (2004, January). Sexual development, social oppression, and local culture. *Sexuality Research & Social Policy, 1,* 39–62.

Hergenhahn, B. R. (2009). *An introduction to the history of psychology* (6th ed.). Belmont, CA: Wadsworth.

Herida, P. (2003). *Profile for Peter Herida* [On-line]. Available: http://obesityhelp.com/morbidobesity/members/profile.php?N-11982614091.

Herida, P. (2005). *A survivor's story: He lost 500 pounds and gained a new life* [On-line]. Available: http://www.srhs.org/betterhealth_story.asp?StoryID=246.

Herman, L. (1999, July 21). Cited in J. Mastro, Dialogue with a dolphin. *San Diego Union-Tribune,* E1.

Herman, L. (2006, November). Cited in M. J. Weiss, Animal Einsteins. *Reader's Digest,* 144–150.

Herman, W. E. (1990). Fear of failure as a distinctive personality trait measure of test anxiety. *Journal of Research and Development in Education, 23,* 180–185.

Heroic Imagination Project. (2012). *Psychology and heroism* [On-line]. Available: http://heroicimagination/org/welcome/psychology-and-heroism/.

Herrnstein, R. J., & Murray, C. (1994). *The bell curve.* New York: Free Press.

Herry, C., Ciocchi, S., Senn, V., Demmou, L., Muller, C., & Luthi, A. (2008). Switching on and off fear by distinct neuronal circuits. *Nature, 454,* 600–606.

Hersen, M., & Thomas, J. C. (Eds.). (2006). *Comprehensive handbook of personality and psychopathology: Adult psychopathology* (Vol. 2). Hoboken, NJ: John Wiley & Sons.

Herz, R. (2008, January 21). Buying by the nose. *Adweek* [On-line]. Available: http://www.adweek.com/aw/magazine/article_display.jsp?vnu_content_id=1003695821.

Herz, R. (2012). *That's disgusting.* New York: W. W. Norton.

Hesketh, P. J. (2012). Prevention and treatment of chemotherapy-induced nausea and vomiting. *UpToDate* [On-line]. Available: http://www.uptodate.com/contents/prevention-and-treatment-of-chemotherapy-induced-nausea-and-vomiting?view=print.

Hesse-Biber, S. N. (2007). *The cult of thinness.* New York: Oxford University Press.

Heussler, H. S. (2005). Common causes of sleep disruption and daytime sleepiness: Childhood sleep disorders II. *Medical Journal of Australia, 182,* 484–489.

Hewstone, M., Rubin, M., & Willis, H. (2002). Intergroup bias. *Annual Review of Psychology, 53,* 575–604.

Hibberd, J. (2011, December 2). Fall TV winners and losers. *Entertainment Weekly.*

Hibbert, K. (2007, November 8). Ways to make you think better. *The Guardian* [On-line]. Available: http://www.guardian.co.uk/society/2007/nov/08/health.lifeandhealth.

Hickey, E. W. (2006). *Serial murderers and their victims* (4th ed.). Belmont, CA: Thomson Wadsworth.

Hickman, G., Bartholomae, S., & McKenry, P. C. (2000). Influence of parenting styles on the adjustment and academic achievement of traditional college freshmen. *Journal of College Student Development, 41,* 41–54.

Hidalgo, R. B., & Davidson, J. R. T. (2000). Posttraumatic stress disorder: Epidemiology and health-related considerations. *Journal of Clinical Psychiatry, 61* (Suppl. 7), 5–13.

Higgins, D. M., Peterson, J. B., Pihl, R. O., & Less, A. G. M. (2007). Prefrontal cognitive ability, intelligence, Big Five personality, and the prediction of advanced academic and workplace performance. *Journal of Personality and Social Psychology, 93,* 298–319.

Higgins, E. T., & Scholer, A. A. (2008). When is personality revealed: A motivated cognition approach. Cited in O. P. John, R. W. Robins & L. A. Pervin (Eds.), *Handbook of personality* (pp. 182–207). New York: Guilford Press.

Hill, A., Niven, C. A., & Knussen, C. (1996). Pain memories in phantom limbs: A case study. *Pain, 66,* 381–384.

Hill, C. E., & Nakayama, E. Y. (2000). Client-centered therapy: Where has it been and where is it going? A comment on Hathaway (1948). *Journal of Clinical Psychology, 56,* 861–875.

Hill, J. O., Wyatt, H. R., Reed, G. W., & Peters, J. C. (2003). Obesity and the environment: Where do we go from here? *Science, 299,* 853–855.

Hillier, C. (2004, November 9). Cited in Vision problem can be misdiagnosed as ADHD. *KFOXTV* [On-line]. Available: http://www.kfoxtv.com/print/3902889/detail.html.

Hilts, P. H. (1995). *Memory's ghost: The strange tale of Mr. M and the nature of memory.* New York: Simon & Schuster.

Hinman, K., & Brown, K. (2010, June 30). UN calls shock treatment at Mass. school 'torture'. *ABC News* [On-line]. Available: http://abcnews.go.com/Nightline/shock-therapy-massachussetts-school/story?id=11047334#.T5scbkansre.

Hinson, J. P., Raven, P., & Chew, S. L. (2010). *The endocrine system: Systems of the body series.* Philadelphia: Elsevier.

Hirshey, G. (2003, April). Songs from the heart. *Ladies Home Journal,* 122–123.

Hirshkowitz, M., Moore, C. A., & Minhoto, G. (1997). The basics of sleep. In M. R. Pressman & W. C. Orr (Eds.), *Understanding sleep: The evaluation and treatment of sleep disorders.* Washington, DC: American Psychological Association.

Hirst, W., Phelps, E. A., Buckner, R. L., Budson, A. E., Cuc, A., Gabrieli, J. D., Johnson, M. K., Lustig, C., Lyle, K. B., Mather, M., Meksin, R., Mitchell, K. J., Ochsner, K. N., Schacter, D. L., Simons, J. S., & Vaidya, C. J. (2009). Long-term memory for the terrorist attack of September 11: Flashbulb memories, event memories, and the factors that influence their retention. *Journal of Experimental Psychology: General, 138,* 161–176.

Hitti, M. (2006a, June 8). What you need to know about Gardasil, the newly approved cervical cancer vaccine. *WebMD* [On-line]. Available: http://www.webmd.com/content/Article/123/115100.htm.

Hitti, M. (2006b, November. 22). Eat your words? Some can taste them. *WebMD* [On-line]. Available: http://www.webmd.com/content/article/130/117619?printing=true.

Hoare, R. (2012, May 9). *Meet Fortune 500's female powerbrokers.* CNN [On-line]. Available: http://edition.cnn.com/2012/05/08/business/f500-leading-women/index.html.

Hobart, A. (2003). *Healing performance of Bali: Between darkness and light.* New York: Berghahn Books.

Hobson, J. A. (2002). *Making sense of dreaming.* New York: Oxford University Press.

Hobson, K. (2006, October 23). Conquering cravings. *U.S. News & World Report,* 64–66.

Hodapp, R. M., Griffin, M. M., Burke, M. M., & Fisher, M. H. (2011). Intellectual disabilities. In R. J. Sternberg & S. B. Kaufman (Eds.), *The Cambridge handbook of intelligence* (pp. 193–209). New York: Cambridge University Press.

Hodges, J. R. (Ed.). (2011). *Frontotemporal dementia syndromes.* New York: Cambridge University Press.

Hoff, E. (2009). *Language development* (4th ed.). Belmont, CA: Wadsworth Cengage Learning.

Hoffman, B. M., Babyak, M. A., Craighead, W. E., Sherwood, A., Doraiswamy, P. M., Coons, M. J., & Blumenthal, J. A. (2011). Exercise and pharmacotherapy in patients with major depression: One-year follow-up of the SMILE study. *Psychosomatic Medicine, 73,* 127–133.

Hoffman, G. A., Harrington, A., & Fields, H. L. (2005). Pain and the placebo: What we have learned. *Perspectives in Biology and Medicine, 48,* 248–265.

Hoffman, H. G. (2004, July 26). Virtual-reality therapy. *Scientific American.*

Hofmann, A. (1983). *LSD: My problem child.* Los Angeles: J. P. Tarcher.

Hofmann, S. G. (2008). Cognitive processes during fear acquisition and extinction in animals and humans: Implications for exposure therapy of anxiety disorders. *Clinical Psychology Review, 28,* 199–210.

Hofmann, S. G., Asnaani, A., & Hinton, D. E. (2010). Cultural aspects in social anxiety and social anxiety disorder. *Journal of Depression and Anxiety, 27,* 1117–1127.

Hoge, C. W., Terhakopian, A., Castro, C. A., Messer, S. C., & Engel, C. C. (2007). Association of posttraumatic stress disorder with somatic symptoms, health care visits, and absenteeism among Iraq war veterans. *American Journal of Psychiatry, 164,* 150–153.

Hokanson, J. E., & Butler, A. C. (1992). Cluster analysis of depressed college students' social behaviors. *Journal of Personality and Social Psychology, 62,* 273–280.

Holahan, C. K., & Sears, R. R. (1995). *The gifted group in later maturity.* Stanford, CA: Stanford University Press.

Holden, C. (1995). Sex and the granular layer. *Science, 268,* 807.

Holden, C. (2002). Versatile cells against intractable diseases. *Science, 297,* 500–502.

Holden, C. (2010, March 12). APA seeks to overhaul personality disorder diagnoses. *Science, 327,* 1314–1315.

Hollon, S. D., Thase, M. E., & Markowitz, J. C. (2002). Treatment and prevention of depression. *Psychological Science, 3*(Suppl.), 39–77.

Holloway, J. D. (2003, March). Advances in anger management. *Monitor on Psychology,* 54–55.

Holmes, M., & Newman, M. G. (2006). Generalized anxiety disorder. In M. Hersen & J. C. Thomas (Eds.), *Comprehensive handbook of personality and psychopathology: Adult psychopathology* (Vol. 2, pp. 101–120). Hoboken, NJ: John Wiley & Sons.

Holroyd, C. B., & Coles, M. G. H. (2002). The neural basis of human error processing: Reinforcement learning, dopamine, and the error-related negativity. *Psychological Review, 109,* 679–709.

Honey, R. C. (2000). Associative priming in Pavlovian conditioning. *Quarterly Journal of Experimental Psychology, 53B,* 1–23.

Hong, Y., Morris, M. W., Chiu, C., & Benet-Martinez, V. (2000). Multicultural minds. *American Psychologist, 55,* 709–720.

Honts, C. R. (1994). Psychophysiological detection of deception. *Current Directions in Psychological Science, 3,* 77–82.

Honts, C. R., Raskin, D. C., & Kircher, J. C. (1994). Mental and physical countermeasures reduce the accuracy of polygraph tests. *Journal of Applied Psychology, 79,* 252–259.

Hooker, C. I., Germine, L. T., Knight, R. T., & D'Esposito, M. (2006). Amygdala response to facial expressions reflects emotional learning. *Journal of Neuroscience, 26,* 8915–8922.

Hoover, E. (2005, December 9). Tomorrow, I love ya! *Chronicles of Higher Education.*

Hoover, N. C., & Pollard, N. J. (2000). Initiation rites in American high schools: A national survey [On-line]. Available: http://www.alfred.edu/news/html/hazing_study.html.

Hopkins, J. R. (2011, December). The enduring influence of Jean Piaget. *The Observer, 24,* 35–36.

Hoppe, C., & Stojanovic, J. (2008, August/September). High-aptitude minds. *Scientific American Mind,* 60–67.

Horgan, J. (1996, December). Why Freud isn't dead. *Scientific American,* 106–111.

Howard, J. A., & Renfrow, D. G. (2006). Social cognition. In J. Delamater (Ed.), *Handbook of social psychology* (pp. 259–281). New York: Springer.

Howard, M. A., & Marczinski, C. A. (2010). Acute effects of a glucose energy drink on behavioral control. *Experimental and Clinical Psychopharmacology, 18,* 553–561.

Howard, M. S., & Medway, F. (2004). Adolescents' attachment and coping with stress. *Psychology in the Schools, 41,* 391–402.

Howe, M. L. (2003). Memories from the cradle. *Current Directions in Psychological Sciences, 12,* 62–65.

Howes, O. D., & Kapur, S. (2009). The dopamine hypothesis of schizophrenia: Version III—The final common pathway. *Schizophrenia Bulletin, 35,* 549–562.

Høybye, M. T., Johansen, C., & Tjornhoj-Thomsen, T. (2005). Online interaction: Effects of storytelling in an Internet breast cancer support group. *Psycho-Oncology, 14,* 211–220.

HRSDC (Human Resources and Social Development Canada). (2007). *Pan-Canadian study of first year college students—Report 1: Student characteristics and the college experience—August 2007* [On-line]. Available: http://www.hrsdc.gc.ca/en/publications_resources/learning_policy/sp_787_08_07e/page0l.shtml.

Hser, Y. I., Hoffman, V., Grella, C. E., & Anglin, D. (2001). A 33-year follow-up of narcotic addicts. *Archives of General Psychiatry, 58,* 503–508.

HSPH (Harvard School of Public Health). (2006). *Autism has high costs to U.S. society.* Press release.

Hsu, C. (2006, January 14). Put down that fork. *Science News, 169,* 21.

Hu, H., Real, E., Takamiya, K., Kang, M., Ledoux, J., Huganir, R. L., & Manilow, R. (2007). Emotion enhances learning via norepinephrine regulation of AAPA-receptor trafficking. *Cell, 131,* 160–173.

Huang, P. M., Smock, P. J., Manning, W. D., & Bergstrom-Lynch, C. A. (2011). He says, she says: Gender and cohabitation. *Journal of Family Issues, 32,* 876–905.

Hubbard, E. M., Piazza, M., Pinel, P., & Dehaene, S. (2005). Interactions between number and space in parietal cortex. *Nature Reviews Neuroscience, 6,* 435–448.

Hubbard, E. M., & Ramachandran, V. S. (2005). Neurocognitive mechanisms of synesthesia. *Neuron, 48,* 509–520.

Hubel, D. H., & Wiesel, T. N. (1979). Brain mechanisms of vision. *Scientific American, 241,* 150–162.

Hudson, J. I., Hiripi, E., Pope, H. G., & Kessler, R. C. (2007). The prevalence and correlates of eating disorders in the National Comorbidity Survey replication. *Biological Psychiatry, 61,* 348–358.

Huggins, L. E. (2005). *Drug war deadlock: The policy battle continues.* Stanford, CA: Hoover Institution Press.

Hulbert, A. (2005, November 20). The prodigy puzzle. *The New York Times Magazine,* 64.

Humane Society of the United States. (2012). *General information on animal research* [On-line]. Available: http://www.hsus.org/animals_in_research/general_information_on_animal_research/frequently_asked_questions_about_animals_in_research.html.

Humphreys, G. W., & Forde, E. M. E. (2001). Category specificity in mind and brain. *Behavioral and Brain Sciences, 243,* 497–509.

Humphreys, G. W., & Muller, H. (2000). A search asymmetry reversed by figure-ground assignment. *Psychological Science, 11,* 196–210.

Hunt, M. (1993). *The story of psychology.* New York: Doubleday.

Husain, M. M., Rush, A. J., Fink, M., Knapp, R., Petrides, G., Rummans, T., Biggs, M. M., O'Connor, K., Rasmussen, K., Litle, M., Zhao, W., Bernstein, H. J., Smith, G., Mueller, M., McClintock, S. M., Bailine, S. H., & Kellner, C. H. (2004). Speed of response and remission in major depressive disorder with acute electroconvulsive (ECT): A Consortium for Research in ECT (CORE) report. *Journal of Clinical Psychiatry, 65,* 485–491.

Huskinson, T. L. H., & Haddock, G. (2006). Individual differences in attitude structure and the accessibility of the affective and cognitive components of attitude. *Social Cognition, 24,* 453–468.

Iacoboni, M. (2008a). *Mirroring people.* New York: Farrar, Strauss & Giroux.

Iacoboni, M. (2008b, July). The mirror neuron revolution: Explaining what makes humans social. *Scientific American.*

Iacoboni, M. (2010, July 15). Cited in R. Robinson, A controversial paper debunks the autism-mirror neuron connection. *Neurology Today,* 10–11.

Iacoboni, M., & Mazziotta, J. C. (2007). Mirror neuron system: Basic findings and clinical applications. *Annals of Neurology, 62,* 213–218.

Iacono, W. G. (2008). Effective policing: Understanding how polygraph tests work and are used. *Criminal Justice and Behavior, 35,* 1295–1308.

Iacono, W. G., & Patrick, C. T. (2006). Polygraph ("lie detector") testing: Current status & emerging trends. Cited in I. B. Weiner (Ed.), *The handbook of forensic psychology.* Hoboken, NJ: John Wiley & Sons.

IANS (Indo-Asian News Service). (2006, December 16). *Over 50 Vietnamese girls faint due to mass "hysteria."* New Delhi, India: Author.

IANSA (International Action Network on Small Arms). (2007). *Number of children and adults killed and wounded in school and campus shootings since 1996.* London: Author.

Ignelzi, R. J. (2006a, January 31). So, if syrup is sullied, how do we conquer a cough? *San Diego Union-Tribune,* E1.

Ignelzi, R. J. (2006b, May 9). Queasy rider: Motion sickness can make your travels a real trial. *San Diego Union-Tribune,* E1–E4.

IHGSC (International Human Genome Sequencing Consortium). (2004). Finishing the euchromatic sequence of the human genome. *Nature, 431,* 931–945.

Ilmberger, J., Rau, S., Noachtar, S., Arnold, S., & Winkler, P. (2002). Naming tools and animals: Asymmetries observed during direct electrical cortical stimulation. *Neuropsychologia, 40,* 695–700.

IMS Health. (2009, July 23). Cited in J. Lloyd, Insomnia therapy: What works, what doesn't? *USA Today,* 7D.

Incredible weight loss stories. (2007, January 10). [On-line]. Available: http://www.oprah.com.

Ingersoll, B. (2011). Recent advances in early identification and treatment of autism. *Current Directions in Psychological Science, 20,* 335–339.

Ingram, J. A. (2006, November 3). Cited in C. Woodward, Amnesiac can't return to his past to go into future. *San Diego Union-Tribune,* A4.

Inmate marriages. (2007, January 27). County of Mendocino [On-line]. Available: http://www.co.mendocino.ca/us/sheriff/corrections/inmate marriages.htm.

Innocence Project. (2012, May 19). *Fact sheet: Facts on post-conviction DNA exonerations* [On-line]. Available: http://www.innocenceproject.org/Content/Facts_on_PostConviction_DNA_Exonerations.php.

Intel. (2012, March 13). *Teenager unlocks potential pathways for breast cancer treatments, wins Intel science talent search.* Intel news release.

Irwin, C. E., Burg, S. J., & Cart, C. U. (2002). America's adolescents: Where have we been, where are we going? *Journal of Adolescent Health, 31,* 91–123.

Irwin, M. R., Wang, M., Ribeiro, D., Cho, H. J., Olmstead, R., Breen, E. C., Martinez-Maza, O., & Cole, S. (2008). Sleep loss activates cellular inflammatory signaling. *Biological Psychiatry, 64,* 538–540.

ISC (International Schizophrenia Consortium). (2009). Common polygenic variation contributes to risk of schizophrenia and bipolar disorder. *Nature, 460,* 748–752.

Isenberg, S. (1992). *Women who love men who kill.* New York: Dell.

Iversen, L. L. (2000). *The science of marijuana.* New York: Oxford University Press.

Iversen, L. L. (2008). *Speed, ecstasy, Ritalin: The science of amphetamines.* New York: Oxford University Press.

Iversen, L., Iversen, S., Bloom, F. E., & Roth, R. H. (2009). *Introduction to neuropsychopharmacology.* New York: Oxford University Press.

Izard, C. E. (1993). Four systems for emotion activation: Cognitive and noncognitive processes. *Psychological Review, 100,* 60–90.

Jackendoff, R. (1994). *Patterns in the mind. Language and human nature.* New York: Basic Books.

Jacks, J. Z., & Cameron, K. A. (2003). Strategies for resisting persuasion. *Basic and Applied Social Psychology, 25,* 145–161.

Jacks, J. Z., & Devine, P. G. (2000). Attitude importance, forewarning of message content, and resistance to persuasion. *Basic and Applied Social Psychology, 22,* 19–29.

Jackson, R. L. (1994, May 4). A false sense of sincerity: Some cases belie polygraph results. *Los Angeles Times.*

Jackson, S. L. (2012). *Research methods and statistics: A critical thinking approach* (4th ed.). Belmont, CA: Wadsworth.

Jacob, T. J. C., Wang, L., Jaffer, S., & McPhee, S. (2006). Changes in the odor quality of androstadienone during exposure-induced sensitization. *Chemical Senses, 31,* 3–8.

Jaffee, S., & Hyde, J.S. (2000). Gender differences in moral orientation: A meta analysis. *Psychological Bulletin, 126,* 703–726.

James, W. (1884; reprinted 1969). What is an emotion? In *William James: Collected essays and reviews.* New York: Russell & Russell.

James, W. (1890). *The principles of psychology.* New York: Dover.

Janda, K. D. (2011, October 3). Cited in D. Quenqua, An addiction vaccine, tantalizingly close. *The New York Times.*

Jang, K. L. (2005). *The behavioral genetics of psychopathology: A clinical guide.* Mahwah, NJ: Lawrence Erlbaum.

Jang, K. L., Livesley, W. J., Ando, J., Yamagata, S., Suzuki, A., Angleitner, A., Ostendorf, F., Riemann, R., & Spinath, F. (2006). Behavioral genetics of the higher-order factors of the Big Five. *Personality and Individual Differences, 41,* 261–272.

Janis, I. L. (1989). *Crucial decisions: Leadership in policy-making and crisis management.* New York: Free Press.

Jansen, B. (2011, December 14). NTSB: Ban cellphone use while driving. *USA Today,* 3A.

Japenga, A. (1994, June 5). Rewriting the dictionary of madness. *Los Angeles Times Magazine.*

Jardin, X. (2005, August 19). Virtual reality therapy for combat stress. *NPR* [On-line]. Available: http://www.npr.org/templates/story/story.php?storyId=4806921.

Jarrett, C. (2006, March 3). Food, glorious food—Czech eating habits after 1989. *Radio Prague* [On-line]. Available: http://www.radio.cz/en/article/77368.

Jarriel, T., & Sawyer, D. (1997, January 16). Romania: What happened to the children? *Turning point.* New York: ABC News.

Jason, L. A., & Ferrari, J. R. (2010). Oxford House recovery homes: Characteristics and effectiveness. *Psychological Science, 7,* 92–102.

Javitt, D. C. (2010). Glutamatergic theories of schizophrenia. *Israel Journal of Psychiatry and Related Sciences, 47,* 4–16.

Jayson, S. (2005, July 18). Cohabitation is replacing dating. *USA Today,* 6D.

Jayson, S. (2009a, February 11). Science asks: What's the attraction? *USA Today,* D1.

Jayson, S. (2009b, March 26). Gender roles see a 'conflict' shift. *USA Today,* A1.

Jayson, S. (2009c, June 17). Today's guys parent with a new daditude. *USA Today,* D1.

Jayson, S. (2009d, July 9). Couples study debunks 'trial marriage' notion. *USA Today,* 7D.

Jayson, S. (2012, January 19). 'Conversion disorder' gets rare spotlight. *USA Today,* 3D.

Jefferson, D. J. (2005, August 8). America's most dangerous drug. *Newsweek,* 40–48.

Jenson, A. R. (2005). Mental chronometry and the unification of differential psychology. In R. J. Sternberg & J. E. Pretz (Eds.), *Cognition and intelligence* (pp. 26–50). New York: Cambridge University Press.

John, L. K., Loewenstein, G., Troxel, A. B., Norton, L., Fassbender, J. E., & Volpp, K. G. (2011). Financial incentives for extended weight loss: A randomized, controlled trial. *Journal of General Internal Medicine, 26,* 621–626.

Johnson, A. (2009, February 8). Egyptian women, some men, fight sexual harassment. *ABC News* [On-line]. Available: http://abcnews.go.com/International/wireStory?id=6830843.

Johnson, C. R., Hunt, F. M., & Siebert, J. J. (1994). Discrimination training in the treatment of pica and food scavenging. *Behavior Modification, 18,* 214–229.

Johnson, J. G., Cohen, P., Smailes, E. M., Kasen, S., & Brook, J. S. (2002). Television viewing and aggressive behavior during adolescence and adulthood. *Science, 295,* 2468–2471.

Johnson, L. C., Slye, E. S., & Dement, W. (1965). Electroencephalographic and autonomic activity during and after prolonged sleep deprivation. *Psychosomatic Medicine, 27,* 415–423.

Johnson, P. M., & Kenny, P. J. (2010). Dopamine D2 receptors in addiction-like reward dysfunction and compulsive eating in obese rats. *Nature Neuroscience, 13,* 635–641.

Johnson, S. (2003, March). Brain and emotions: Fear. *Discover,* 32–39.

Johnston, J. (2011, April 19). Demo Lovato interview: Teen star opens up on bulimia, cutting issues. *ABC News* [On-line]. Available: http://www.abcnews.go.com/Entertainmen/demi-lovato-interview-teen-star-opens-bulimia-cutting/story?id=1340590#.T9jXYYkansrc.

Johnston, J. C., & McClelland, J. L. (1974). Perception of letters in words: Seek not and ye shall find. *Science, 184,* 1192–1194.

Johnston, V. (2000, February). Cited in B. Lemley, Isn't she lovely. *Discover,* 43–49.

Joinson, C., Heron, J., & Lewis, G. (2011). Timing of menarche and depressive symptoms in adolescent girls from a UK cohort. *British Journal of Psychiatry, 198,* 17–23.

Jones, E. (1953). *The life and work of Sigmund Freud* (3 vols.). New York: Basic Books.

Jones, E., & Berglas, S. (1978). Control of attributions about the self through self-handicapping strategies: The appeal of alcohol and the role of underachievement. *Personality and Social Psychology Bulletin, 4,* 200–206.

Jones, S. R., & Fernyhough, C. (2007). A new look at the neural diathesis-stress model of schizophrenia: The primacy of social-evaluative and uncontrollable situations. *Schizophrenia Bulletin, 33,* 1171–1177.

Joseph, S., Manafi, E., Iakovaki, A. M., & Cooper, R. (2003). Personality, smoking motivation, and self-efficacy to quit. *Personality and Individual Differences, 34,* 749–758.

Joseph, S., & Murphy, D. (2012, February 22). Person-centered approach, positive psychology, and relational helping: Building bridges. *Journal of Humanistic Psychology.*

Joseph, S., & Wood, A. (2010). Assessment of positive functioning in clinical psychology: Theoretical and practical issues. *Clinical Psychology Review, 30,* 830–838.

Judge, T. A., & Livingston, B. A. (2008). Is the gap more than gender? A longitudinal analysis of gender, gender role orientation, and earning. *Journal of Applied Psychology, 93,* 994–1012.

Jullen, R. M. (2005). *A primer of drug action: A comprehensive guide to the actions, uses, and side effects* (10th ed.). New York: Worth.

Junod, R. E. V., DuPaul, G. J., Jitendra, A. K., Volpe, R. J., & Cleary, K. S. (2006). Classroom observations of students with and without ADHD: Differences across types of engagement. *Journal of School Psychology, 44,* 87–104.

Jusczyk, P. W., & Hohne, E. A. (1997). Infants' memory for spoken words. *Science, 277,* 1984–1986.

Just, M. (2008, May 10). Cited in B. Bower, Shifting priorities at the wheel. *Science News,* 7.

Kabot, S., Masi, W., & Segal, M. (2003). Advances in the diagnosis and treatment of autism spectrum disorders. *Professional Psychology: Research and Practice, 34,* 26–33.

Kagan, J. (1994). *The nature of the child* (10th anniversary edition). New York: Basic Books.

Kagan, J. (1998). Biology and the child. In W. Damon & R. M. Lerner (Eds.), *Handbook of child psychology* (Vol. 1). New York: John Wiley & Sons.

Kagan, J. (2003a). Behavioral inhibition as a temperamental category. In R. J. Davidson, K. R. Scherer & H. H. Goldsmith (Eds.), *Handbook of affective sciences.* New York: Oxford University Press.

Kagan, J. (2003b). Biology, context, and developmental inquiry. *Annual Review of Psychology, 54,* 1–23.

Kagan, J., Reznick, J. S., & Snidman, N. (1988). Biological bases of childhood shyness. *Science, 240,* 167–171.

Kagan, J., & Snidman, N. (1991). Temperamental factors in human development. *American Psychologist, 46,* 856–862.

Kahana, M. J. (2012). *Foundations of human memory*. New York: Oxford University Press.

Kahneman, D., & Frederick, S. (2005). A model of heuristic judgment. In K. J. Holyoak & R. G. Morrison (Eds.), *The Cambridge handbook of thinking and reasoning* (pp. 267–294). New York: Cambridge University Press.

Kakko, J., Gronbladh, L., Svanborg, K. D., von Wachenfeldt, J., Ruck, C., Rawlings, B., Nilsson, L., & Heilig, M. (2007, May). A stepped care strategy using buprenorphine and methadone versus conventional methadone maintenance in heroin dependence: A randomized controlled trial. *American Journal of Psychiatry, 164*, 797–803.

Kalat, J. W. (2009). *Biological psychology* (10th ed.). Belmont, CA: Wadsworth Cengage Learning.

Kalat, J. W. (2013). *Biological psychology* (11th ed.). Belmont, CA: Wadsworth.

Kalat, J. W., & Shiota, M. N. (2007). *Emotion*. Belmont, CA: Thomson/Wadsworth

Kalb, C. (2009, April 27). To pluck a rooted sorrow. *Newsweek*, 52–54.

Kalimo, R., Tenkanen, L., Harma, M., Poppius, E., & Heinsalmi, P. (2000). Job stress and sleep disorders: Findings from the Helsinki heart study. *Stress Medicine, 16*, 65–75.

Kallio, S., Hyona, J., Revonsuo, A., Sikka, P., & Nummenmaa, L. (2011). The existence of a hypnotic state revealed by eye movements. *PLoS ONE, 6*, e26374.

Kandel, E. (2008, October/November). Cited in S. Ayan, Speaking of memory. *Scientific American Mind*, 16–17.

Kandel, E., & Abel, T. (1995). Neuropeptides, adenylyl cyclase, and memory storage. *Science, 268*, 825–826.

Kandel, E. R. (2006, April/May). Cited in M. Solms, Freud returns. *Scientific American Mind*, 28–34.

Kanner, L. (1943). Autistic disturbances in affective contact. *Nervous Child, 2*, 217–250.

Kantowitz, B. H., Roediger, H. L., III, & Elemes, D. G. (2009). *Experimental psychology* (9th ed.). Belmont, CA: Wadsworth/Cengage Learning.

Kaplan, D. M. (1972). On shyness. *International Journal of Psycho-Analysis, 53*, 439–453.

Kaplan, R. (2008, July 2). Graduate has 11 advanced degrees, and counting. *USA Today*.

Kaplan, R. M., & Saccuzzo, K. P. (2005). *Psychological testing: Principles, applications, and issues* (6th ed.). Belmont, CA: Thomson Wadsworth.

Kaplan, R. M., & Saccuzzo, K. P. (2009). *Psychological testing: Principles, applications, and issues* (7th ed.). Belmont, CA: Wadsworth Cengage.

Kaptchuk, T. J., Friedlander, E., Kelley, J. M., Sanchez, M. N., Kokkotou, E., Singer, J. P., Kowalczykowski, M., Miller, F. G., Kirsch, I., & Lembo, A. J. (2010, December). Placebos without deception: A randomized controlled trial in irritable bowel syndrome. *PLoS ONE, 5*(12), e15591.

Karpicke, J. D., & Blunt, J. R. (2011). Retrieval practice produces more learning than elaborative studying with concept mapping. *Science, 331*, 771–774.

Karussis, D., & Kassis, I. (2007). Use of stem cells for treatment of multiple sclerosis. *Expert Review of Neurotherapies, 7*, 1189–1201.

Kato, M., Phillips, B. G., Sigurdsson, G., Narkiewicz, K., Pesek, C. A., & Somers, V. K. (2000). Effects of sleep deprivation on neural circulatory control. *Hypertension, 35*, 1173–1175.

Katz, J., & Melzack, R. (2003). Phantom limb pain. In J. Grafman & L. H. Robertson (Eds.), *Handbook of neuropsychology* (2nd ed.). Amsterdam: Elsevier Science.

Kaufman, A. S. (2000). Tests of intelligence. In R. J. Sternberg (Ed.), *Handbook of intelligence*. New York: Cambridge University Press.

Kaufman, A. S. (2003, February). Cited in E. Benson, Intelligent intelligence testing. *Monitor on Psychology*, 48–51.

Kaufman, A. S., Reynolds, C. R., & McLean, J. E. (1989). Age and WAIS-R intelligence in a national sample of adults in the 20 to 74 age range: A cross-sectional analysis with educational level controlled. *Intelligence, 13*, 235–253.

Kaufman, L. (2000). Cited in B. Bower, The moon also rises—and assumes new sizes. *Science News, 157*, 22.

Kaufman, L. (2007, December 25). Parents defend school's use of shock therapy. *The New York Times*.

Kaufman, M. (2005, January 3). Meditation gives brain a charge, study finds. *Washington Post*, A5.

Kaufman, M. (2006, June 9). FDA approves vaccine that should prevent most cervical cancers. *Washington Post*, A1.

Kaye, W. (2008, June 9). Cited in S. Gupta, Taking on the thin ideal. *Time*, 50.

Kean, S. (2009, November/December). Old brains, new tricks: How neuroplasticity helps blind men see with their tongues. *Mental Floss*, 44–47.

Keck, G. C., & Kupecky, R. M. (1995). *Adopting the hurt child: Hope for families with special-needs children*. Colorado Springs, CO: Pinon Press.

Keck, P. E., & McElroy, S. L. (2003). New approaches in managing bipolar depression. *Journal of Clinical Psychiatry, 64*(Suppl. 6), 13–18.

Keefe, F. J., Abernethy, A. P., & Campbell, L. C. (2005). Psychological approaches to understanding and treating disease-related pain. *Annual Review of Psychology, 56*, 601–630.

Keenan, K., & Shaw, D. (1997). Developmental and social influences on young girl's early problem behavior. *Psychological Bulletin, 121*, 95–113.

Keeney, B. (2004). *Balians: Traditional healers of Bali*. Creek, CT: Leete's Island Books.

Keiser, R. E., & Prather, E. N. (1990). What is the TAT? A review of ten years of research. *Journal of Personality Assessment, 55*, 800–803.

Keisler, B. D., & Armsey, T. D., II. (2006). Caffeine as an ergogenic acid. *Current Sports Medicine Reports, 5*, 215–219.

Keita, G. P. (2007). Psychosocial and cultural contributions to depression in women: Considerations for women midlife and beyond. Supplement to *Journal of Managed Care Pharmacy, 13*, S12-S15.

Kelley, H. H. (1967). Attribution theory in social psychology. In D. Levine (Ed.), *Nebraska symposium on motivation* (Vol. 15). Lincoln: University of Nebraska Press.

Kelley, W. M. (2002). Cited in J. Travis, The brain's funny bone. *Science News, 162*, 308–309.

Kelly, D., & Tangney, B. (2006). Adapting to intelligence profile in an adaptive educational system. *Human Factors in Personalised Systems and Services, 18*, 385–409.

Keltner, D., & Ekman, P. (2000). Facial expression of emotion. Cognitive and social construction in emotions. In M. Lewis & J. M. Haviland-Jones (Eds.), *Handbook of emotions* (2nd ed.). New York: Guilford Press.

Keltner, D., Ekman, P., Gonzaga, G. C., & Beer, J. (2003). Facial expression of emotion. In R. D. Lane & L. Nadel (Eds.), *Cognitive neuroscience of emotion*. New York: Oxford University Press.

Kemeny, M. C. (2003). The psychobiology of stress. *Current Directions in Psychological Science, 12*, 125–129.

Kendler, K. S., Aggen, S. H., Tambs, K., & Reichborn-Kjennerud, T. (2006). Illicit psychoactive substance use, abuse and dependence in a population-based sample of Norwegian twins. *Psychological Medicine, 36*, 955–962.

Kendler, K. S., Karkowski, L. M., Neale, M. C., & Prescott, C. A. (2000a). Illicit psychoactive substance use, heavy use, abuse, and dependence in a US population-based sample of male twins. *Archives of General Psychiatry, 57*, 261–269.

Kendler, K. S., Kuhn, J., & Prescott, C. A. (2004). The interrelationship of neuroticism, sex, and stressful life events in the prediction of episodes of major depression. *American Journal of Psychiatry, 161*, 631–636.

Kendler, K. S., Thornton, L. M., Gilman, S. E., & Kessler, R. C. (2000b). Sexual orientation in a U.S. national sample of twin and nontwin sibling pairs. *American Journal of Psychiatry, 157*, 1843–1846.

Kenrick, D. T., Trost, M. R., & Sundie, J. M. (2004). Sex roles as adaptations: An evolutionary perspective on gender differences and similarities. In A. H. Eagly, A. E. Beall & R. J. Sternberg (Eds.), *The psychology of gender* (2nd ed., pp. 65–91). New York: Guilford Press.

Kenworthy, J. B., & Miller, N. (2002). Attributional biases about the origins of attitudes: Externality, emotionality, and rationality. *Journal of Personality and Social Psychology, 82*, 693–707.

Kerns, R. (2006, December 22). Cited in Psychological treatments improve outcomes for back pain sufferers. *Science Daily* [On-line]. Available: http://www.sciencedaily.com/releases/2006/12/06122090925.htm.

Kerns, R. (2007, January 2). Cited in J. Fischman, Psychological treatments are a balm for back pain. *U.S. News & World Report*.

Kershaw, S. (2006, January 23). On engine 22, it's women who answer the bell. *The New York Times*, A1.

Kershaw, T. C., & Ohlsson, S. (2004). Multiple causes of difficulty in insight: The case of the nine-dot problem. *Journal of Experimental Psychology: Learning, Memory, and Cognition, 30*, 3–13.

Kessler, R. C. (2003). Epidemiology of women and depression. *Journal of Affective Disorders, 74*, 25–33.

Kessler, R. C., Berglund, P., Demler, O., Jim, R., Merikangas, K. R., & Walters, E. E. (2005). Lifetime prevalence and age-of-onset distributions of DSM-IV disorders in the national comorbidity survey replication. *Archives of General Psychiatry, 62*, 593–602.

Kessler, R. C., McGonagle, K. A., Zhao, S., Nelson, C. B., Higher, M., Eshleman, S., Wittchen, H., & Kendler, K. S. (1994). Lifetime and 12-month prevalence of DSM-III-R psychiatric disorders in the United States. *Archives of General Psychiatry, 51*, 8–19.

Kessler, R. C., & Wang, P. S. (2008). The descriptive epidemiology of commonly occurring mental disorders in the United States. *Annual Review of Public Health, 29*, 115–129.

Keysers, C. (2007, January 29). Cited in J. M. Nash, The gift of mimicry. *Time, 108*–113.

Khantzian, E. J., & Mack, J. E. (1994). How AA works and why it's important for clinicians to understand. *Journal of Substance Abuse Treatment, 11*, 77–92.

Khawam, E. A., Laurencic, G., & Malone, D. A. (2006). Side effects of antidepressants: An overview. *Cleveland Clinical Journal of Medicine, 73*, 351–361.

Kiecolt-Glaser, J. (2008, October). Cited in S. F. Dingfelder, An insidious enemy. *Monitor on Psychology*, 22–23.

Kiecolt-Glaser, J. (2010, August 14). Cited in *Childhood adversity worsens effects of stress, adding to current hardships, says new research*. American Psychological Association [On-line]. Available: http://www.apa.prg/news/press/releases/2010/08/childhood-adversity-hardships.aspx.

Kiecolt-Glaser, J., McGuire, L., Robles, T. F., & Glaser, R. (2002). Emotions, morbidity, and mortality: New perspectives from psychoneuroimmunology. *Annual Review of Psychology, 53*, 83–107.

Kiedis, A. (2004). *Scar tissue*. New York: Hyperion.

Kiernan, J. A. (2008). *Barr's the human nervous system: An anatomical viewpoint* (9th ed.). Philadelphia: Lippincott Williams & Wilkins.

Kihlstrom, J. F. (1993). The continuum of consciousness. *Consciousness and Cognition, 2,* 334–354.

Kihlstrom, J. F., Glisky, M. L., & Angiulo, M. J. (1994). Dissociative tendencies and dissociative disorders. *Journal of Abnormal Psychology, 103,* 117–124.

Killingsworth, M. A., & Gilbert, D. T. (2010, November 12). A wandering mind is an unhappy mind. *Science, 330,* 932.

Kim, Y. S., Leventhal, B. L., Koh, Y., Fombonne, E., Laska, E., Lim, E., Cheon, K., Kim, S., Kim, Y., Lee, H., Song, D., & Grinker, R. R. (2011). Prevalence of autism spectrum disorders in a total population sample. *American Journal of Psychiatry, 168,* 904–912.

Kincaid, S. (2007, May 22). A tumor was hiding in the breast tissue. *Redorbit News* [On-line]. Available: http://www.redorbit.com/news/display/?id=943199.

Kindt, M., Soeter, M., & Vervliet, B. (2009). Beyond extinction: Erasing human fear responses and preventing the return of fear. *Nature Neuroscience, 12,* 256–258.

Kinetz, E. (2006, September 26). Is hysteria real? Brain images say yes. *The New York Times,* D1.

King, A. (1992). Comparison of self-questioning, summarizing, and notetaking-review as strategies for learning from lectures. *American Educational Research Journal, 29,* 303–323.

King, C. R., Knutson, K. L., Rathouz, P. J., Sidney, S., Liu, K., & Lauderdale, D. S. (2008). Short sleep duration and incident coronary artery calcification. *JAMA, 300,* 2859–2866.

King, F. A., Yarbrough, C. J., Anderson, D. C., Gordon, T. P., & Gould, K. G. (1988). Primates. *Science, 240,* 1475–1482.

Kingwell, K. (2010). Neurodegenerative disease: New leads for Parkinson's disease. *Nature Reviews Drug Discoveries, 9*(10), 766.

Kinsbourne, M. (1994). Sugar and the hyperactive child. *New England Journal of Medicine, 330,* 355–356.

Kinsman, M. (2006, September 19). Businesswomen in California still hit glass ceiling. *San Diego Union-Tribune,* H2.

Kirk, M. S. (1972, March). Head hunters in today's world. *National Geographic.*

Kirkcaldy, B. D., Shephard, R. J., & Furnham, A. F. (2002). The influence of type A behaviour and locus of control upon job satisfaction and occupational health. *Personality and Individual Differences, 33,* 1361–1371.

Kirmayer, L. J. (1991). The place of culture in psychiatric nosology: Taijin kyofusho and DSM-III-R. *Journal of Nervous and Mental Disease, 179,* 19–28.

Kirp, D. L. (2004, November 11). Life way after Head Start. *The New York Times Magazine,* 32–38.

Kirsch, I. (1994). Cognitive-behavioral hypnotherapy. In J. W. Rhue, S. J. Lynn & I. Kirsch (Eds.), *Handbook of clinical hypnosis.* Washington, DC: American Psychological Association.

Kirsch, I., & Braffman, W. (2001). Imaginative suggestibility and hypnotizability. *Current Directions in Psychological Sciences, 10,* 57–61.

Kirsch, I., & Lynn, S. J. (1995). The altered state of hypnosis. *American Psychologist, 50,* 846–858.

Kirsch, I., & Lynn, S. J. (1998). Dissociation theories of hypnosis. *Psychological Bulletin, 123,* 100–115.

Kirsch, I., Lynn, S. J., & Rhue, J. W. (1993). Introduction to clinical hypnosis. In J. W. Rhue, S. J. Lynn & I. Kirsch (Eds.), *Handbook of clinical hypnosis.* Washington, DC: American Psychological Association.

Kirschenbaum, H., & Jourdan, A. (2005). The current status of Carl Rogers and the person-centered approach. *Psychotherapy: Theory, Research, Practice, Training, 42,* 37–51.

Kirsner, D. (1990). Is there a future for American psychoanalysis? *Psychoanalytic Review, 77,* 175–200.

Kishiyama, M. (2010, September). Cited in A. Novotney, The recession's toll on children. *Monitor on Psychology,* 42–46.

Kishiyama, M., Boyce, W. T., Jiminez, A. M., Perry, L. M., & Knight, R. T. (2009). Socioeconomic disparities affect prefrontal function in children. *Journal of Cognitive Neuroscience, 21,* 1106–1115.

Klaassen, M. A., Veerkamp, J. S., & Hoogstraten, J. (2008). Changes in children's dental fear: A longitudinal study. *European Archives of Paediatric Dentistry, 9,* 29–35.

Klass, P. (2010, October 12). Understanding "ba ba ba" as a key to development. *The New York Times,* D5.

Kleijn, W. C., van der Ploeg, H. M., & Topman, R. M. (1994). Cognition, study habits, test anxiety, and academic performance. *Psychological Reports, 75,* 1219–1226.

Klein, C. T. F., & Helweg-Larsen, M. (2002). Perceived control and the optimistic bias: A meta-analytic review. *Psychology and Health, 17,* 437–446.

Klein, D. N., Durbin, C. E., Shankman, S. A., & Santiago, N. J. (2002). Depression and personality. In I. H. Gotlib & C. L. Hammen (Eds.), *Handbook of depression.* New York: Guilford Press.

Klein, R. (2002, August 15). Cited in N. Wade, Language gene is traced to emergence of humans. *The New York Times,* A18.

Klein, S. B. (2009). *Learning: Principles and application.* Thousand Oaks, CA: Sage.

Kleinknecht, R. A. (1994). Acquisition of blood, injury, and needle fears and phobias. *Behavior Research and Therapy, 32,* 817–823.

Klomegah, R. Y. (2007, June). Predictors of academic performance of university students: An application of the goal efficacy model. *College Student Journal.*

Kluger, J. (2003, January 20). Masters of denial. *Time.*

Kluger, J. (2005, April 4). Secrets of the shy. *Time,* 50–52.

Kluger, J. (2006a, January 16). The surprising power of the aging brain. *Time,* 84–87.

Kluger, J. (2006b, July 10). The new science of siblings. *Time,* 46–55.

Kluger, J. (2007a, June 11). The science of appetite. *Time,* 48–58.

Kluger, J. (2007b, September 10). Rewiring the brain. *Time,* 46–47.

Kluger, J. (2009, February 23). The biology of belief. *Time,* 62–72.

Kluger, J. (2010, August 16). Inside the minds of animals. *Time,* 36–43.

Kluger, J., & Masters, C. (2006, August 28). How to spot a liar. *Time,* 46–48.

Knickmeyer, R. C., Gouttard, S., Kang, C., Evans, D., Wilber, K., Smith, J. K., Hamer, R. M., Lin, W., Gerig, G., & Gilmore, J. H. (2008). A structural MRI study of human brain development from birth to 2 years. *Journal of Neuroscience, 28,* 12176–12182.

Knight, R. A. (1992, July). Cited in N. Youngstrom, Rapist studies reveal complex mental map. *APA Monitor.*

Knutson, J. R. (1995). Psychological characteristics of maltreated children: Putative risk factors and consequences. *Annual Review of Psychology, 46,* 401–431.

Kobasa, S. C. (1982). Commitment and coping in stress resistance among lawyers. *Journal of Personality and Social Psychology, 42,* 707–717.

Kobasa, S. C., Maddi, S. R., & Kahn, S. (1982a). Hardiness and health: A prospective study. *Journal of Personality and Social Psychology, 42,* 168–177.

Kobasa, S. C., Maddi, S. R., & Puccetti, M. C. (1982b). Personality and exercise as buffers in the stress-illness relationship. *Journal of Behavioral Medicine, 5,* 391–404.

Kobayashi, M., Tomioka, N., Ushiyama, Y., & Ohhashi, T. (2003). Arithmetic calculation, deep inspiration or handgrip exercise-mediated pre-operational active palmer sweating responses in humans. *Autonomic Neuroscience: Basic and Clinical, 104,* 58–65.

Koch, C. (2010, May). Regaining the rainbow. *Scientific American Mind,* 16–17.

Koch, W. (2000, June 16). Big tobacco tells Florida jury it has reformed. *USA Today,* 13A.

Koenigs, M., Young, L., Adolphs, R., Tranel, D., Cushman, F., Hauser, M., & Damasio, A. (2007). Damage to the prefrontal cortex increases utilitarian moral judgements. *Nature, 446,* 908–911.

Kogan, M. D., Blumberg, S. J., Schieve, L. A., Boyle, C. A., Perrin, J. M., Ghandour, R. M., Singh, G. K., Strickland, B. B., Trevathan, E., & van Dyck, P. C. (2009). Prevalence of parent-reported diagnosis of autism spectrum disorder among children in the US, 2007. *Pediatrics, 124*(5), 1395–1403.

Kohlberg, L. (1984). *The psychology of moral development: Essays on moral development* (Vol. 11). San Francisco: Harper & Row.

Köhler, W. (1917; reprinted 1925). *The mentality of apes* (E. Winter, Trans.). New York: Harcourt Brace & World.

Kohn, D. (2004, July 25). Ecstasy research looks for benefits. *Baltimore Sun.*

Koko's world. (2006, November 20). [On-line]. Available: http://www.koko.org/world/.

Kolata, G. (2000, October 17). How the body knows when to gain or lose. *The New York Times,* D1.

Kolata, G. (2006, July 11). A tale of two drugs hints at promise for genetic testing. *The New York Times.*

Kolata, G. (2007, May 8). Genes take charge, and diets fall by the wayside. *The New York Times.*

Kolata, G. (2010, August 25). Stem cell biology and its complications. *The New York Times,* A12.

Kolata, G. (2011, April 3). Vast gene study yields insights on Alzheimer's. *The New York Times.*

Kolb, B., & Taylor, L. (2000). Facial expression, emotion and hemispheric organization. In R. D. Lane & L. Nadel (Eds.), *Cognitive neuroscience of emotion.* New York: Oxford University Press.

Kong, J., Gollub, R. L., Rosman, I. S., Webb, J. M., Vangel, M. G., Kirsch, I., & Kaptchuk, T. J. (2006). Brain activity associated with expectancy-enhanced placebo analgesia as measured by functional magnetic resonance imaging. *Journal of Neuroscience, 26,* 381–388.

Koontz, N. A., & Gunderman, R. B. (2008). Gestalt theory: Implications for radiology education. *American Journal of Roentgenology, 190,* 1156–1160.

Koopman, J. M. (1995, February 20). Cited in M. Cimons & T. H. Maugh, II, New strategies fuel optimism in AIDS fight. *Los Angeles Times.*

Kopp, C. B., & Neufeld, S. J. (2003). Emotional development during infancy. In R. J. Davidson, K. R. Scherer & H. H. Goldsmith (Eds.), *Handbook of affective sciences.* New York: Oxford University Press.

Koppelstaetter, K., Siedentopf, C., Poeppel, T., Haala, I., Ischebeck, A., & Mottaghy, F. (2005, December 1). *Influence of caffeine excess on activation patterns in verbal working memory.* Radiological Society of North America, annual meeting, Chicago.

Koren, G. (2007). Special aspects of perinatal and pediatric pharmacology. In B. G. Katzung (Ed.), *Basic and clinical pharmacology* (10th ed., pp. 971–982). New York: McGraw-Hill.

Kosten, T. (2009, December). Cited in B. Dickinson, Can an injection break addiction? *Discover,* 15.

Kotulak, R. (2006, June 22). Hormone that may launch puberty is discovered. *San Diego Union-Tribune,* E1.

Kotz, D. (2007a). How to win the weight battle. *U.S. News & World Report,* 60–69.

Kotz, D. (2007b, October 29). What to do about HPV? *U.S. News & World Report,* 53.

Kounnas, M. Z., Danks, A. M., Cheng, S., Tyree, C., Ackerman, E., Zhang, X., Ahn, K., Nguyen, P., Comer, D., Mao, L., Yu, C., Pleynet, D., Digregorio, P. J., Velicelebi, G., Stauderman, K. A., Comer, W. T., Mobley, W. C., Li, Y. M., Sisodia, S. S., Tanzi, R. E., & Wagner, S. L. (2010). *Neuron, 67,* 769–780.

Kovács, Á. M., & Mehler, J. (2009). Cognitive gains in 7-month-old bilingual infants. *Proceedings of the National Academy of Sciences, 106,* 6556.

Kozel, F., Johnson, K., Mu, Q., Grenesko, E., Laken, S., & George, M. (2005). Detecting deception using functional magnetic resonance imaging. *Biological Psychiatry, 58,* 605–613.

Kraft, U. (2007, June/July). Rhythm and blues. *Scientific American Mind,* 62–65.

Krakovsky, M. (2009, January/February). National poker face. *Psychology Today,* 20.

Krakow, B. (2011, November 22). Cited in K. Painter, Could you become a morning person? Yes, but it takes work. *USA Today,* 4D.

Kramer, M. (2006a). Biology of dreaming. In T. L. Lee-Chiong (Ed.), *Sleep: A comprehensive handbook* (pp. 31–36). Hoboken, NJ: John Wiley & Sons.

Kramer, M. (2006b). Psychology of dreaming. In T. L. Lee-Chiong (Ed.), *Sleep: A comprehensive handbook* (pp. 37–43). Hoboken, NJ: John Wiley & Sons.

Krause, J., Lalueza-Fox, C., Orlando, L., Enard, W., Green, R. E., Bubano, H. A., Hublin, J., Hänni, C., Fortea, J., de la Rasilla, M., Bertranpetit, Rosas, A., & Pääbo, S. (2007). The derived *FOXP2* variant of modern humans was shared with neandertals. *Current Biology, 17,* 1908–1912.

Kringelbach, M. L., & Aziz, T. Z. (2008). Sparking recovery with brain "pacemakers." *Scientific American Mind,* 36–43.

Kübler-Ross, E. (1969). *On death and dying.* New York: MacMillan.

Kübler-Ross, E. (1974). *Questions and answers on death and dying.* New York: MacMillan.

Kubovy, M., & Wagemans, J. (1995). Grouping by proximity and multistability in dot lattices: A quantitative Gestalt theory. *Psychological Science, 6,* 225–234.

Kurdziel, L., & Spencer, R. (2011, December 3.) Cited in T. H. Saey, Sleep won't help elderly remember. *Science News,* 8.

Kuriki, I., Ashida, H., Murakami, I., & Kitaoka, A. (2008). Functional brain imaging of the rotating snakes illusion by fMRI. *Journal of Vision, 8,* 1–10.

Kurtz, E. (1979). *Not-God: A history of Alcoholics Anonymous.* Center City, MN: Hazelden.

Kurtz, P. (1995, May/June). Is John Beloff an absolute paranormalist? *Skeptical Inquirer.*

Kurtzleben, D. (2011). Delving deeply into sleep. *U.S. News special edition: Secrets of your brain,* 41.

LaBar, K. S., & Cabeza, R. (2006). Cognitive neuroscience of emotional memory. *Nature Reviews Neuroscience, 7,* 54–64.

Lackenbauer, S. D., Campbell, L., Rubin, H., Fletcher, G. J. O., & Troister, T. (2010). The unique and combined benefits of accuracy and positive bias in relationships. *Personal Relationships, 17,* 475–493.

LaFee, S. (2000, March 29). Sight to behold. *San Diego Union-Tribune,* E12.

LaHood, R. (2011, April 12). Cited in J. E. Brody, Keeping eyes on distracted driving's toll. *The New York Times,* D7.

Lamb, N. (1990). *Guide to teaching strings* (5th ed.). Dubuque, IA: William C. Brown.

Lamberg, L. (2004). Road to recovery for cocaine users can start in primary care setting. *JAMA, 292,* 1807–1809.

Lamberg, L. (2006). Melatonin effective in totally blind people. *Psychiatric News, 41,* 26.

Lambert, G. W., Reid, C., Kaye, D. M., Jennings, G. L., & Ester, M. D. (2002). Effect of sunlight and season on serotonin turnover in the brain. *The Lancet, 360,* 1840–1842.

Lambert, K., & Lilienfeld, S. O. (2007, October/November). Brainstains. *Scientific American Mind,* 46–53.

Lambert, M. J., Bergin, A. E., & Garfield, S. L. (2004). Introduction and historical overview. In M. J. Lambert (Ed.), *Bergin and Garfield's handbook of psychotherapy and behavior change.* New York: Wiley.

Lambert, M. J., & Ogles, B. M. (2004). The efficacy and effectiveness of psychotherapy. In M. J. Lambert (Ed.), *Bergin and Garfield's handbook of psychotherapy and behavior change* (5th ed., pp. 139–193). New York: Wiley.

Landau, E. (2011, January 7). *Winning the lottery: Does it guarantee happiness?* CNN [On-line]. Available: http://www.cnn.com/2011/HEALTH/01/07/lottery.winning.psychology/index.html.

Lanfranco, F., Kamischke, A., Zitzmann, M., & Nieschlag, P. E. (2004). Klinefelter's syndrome. *The Lancet, 364,* 273–284.

Lang, L. (2008). *Journey of a thousand miles: My story.* New York: Spiegal & Grau.

Langdridge, D., & Butt, T. (2004). The fundamental attribution error: A phenomenological critique. *British Journal of Social Psychology, 43,* 357–369.

Langlois, J. H. (2009, January 17). Cited in E. Quill, It's written all over your face. *Science News,* 24–28.

Langlois, J. H., Kalakanis, L., Rubenstein, A. J., Larson, A., Hallam, M., & Smoot, M. (2000). Maxims or myths of beauty? A meta-analysis and theoretical review. *Psychological Bulletin, 136,* 390–423.

Langlois, J. H., Roggman, L. A., & Musselman, L. (1994). What is average and what is not average about attractive faces? *Psychological Science, 5,* 214–220.

Langman, P. (2009). *Why kids kill: Inside the minds of school shooters.* New York: Palgrave Macmillan.

Lanyado, M., & Horne, A. (Eds.). (1999). *The handbook of child and adolescent psychotherapy.* New York: Routledge.

Largo-Wight, E., Peterson, P. M., & Chen, W. W. (2005). Perceived problem solving, stress, and health among college students. *American Journal of Health Behavior, 29,* 360–370.

Larivee, S., Normandeau, S., & Parent, S. (2000). The French connection: Some contributions of French-language research in the post-Piagetian era. *Child Development, 71,* 823–839.

Larson, C. (2008, February 11). Attacking Alzheimer's. *U.S. News & World Report,* 48.

Larsson, H., Andershed, H., & Lichtenstein, P. (2006). A genetic factor explains most of the variation in the psychopathic personality. *Journal of Abnormal Psychology, 115,* 221–230.

Latané, B. (1981). The psychology of social impact. *American Psychologist, 36,* 343–356.

Latané, B., & Darley, J. M. (1970). *The unresponsive bystander: Why doesn't he help?* New York: Appleton-Century-Crofts.

Latané, B., & Nida, S. (1981). Ten years of research on group size and helping. *Psychological Bulletin, 89,* 308–324.

Laumann, E. O., Michael, R. T., Gagnon, J. H., & Kolata, G. (1994). *The social organization of sexuality.* Chicago: University of Chicago Press.

Laumann, E. O., Nicolosi, A., Glasser, D. B., Paik, A., Gingell, C., Moreira, E., & Wang, T. (2005). Sexual problems among women and men aged 40–80 y: Prevalence and correlates identified in the Global Study of Sexual Attitudes and Behaviors. *International Journal of Impotence Research, 17,* 39–57.

Lauriello, J. (2007, March 10). Cited in B. Bower, Schizophrenia plus and minus. *Science News,* 148–149.

Law, A. J., & Weinberger, D. R. (2006, April 18). Cited in N. Wade, Schizophrenia as misstep by giant gene. *The New York Times,* D4.

Law, B. M. (2011, September). Seared in our memories. *Monitor on Psychology,* 60–65.

Laws, K. R., & Kokkalis, J. (2007). Ecstasy (MDMA) and memory function: A meta-analytic update. *Human Psychopharmacology: Clinical and Experimental, 22,* 381–388.

Lazar, S. W., Kerr, C. E., Wasserman, R. H., Gray, J. R., Greve, D. N., Treadway, M. T., McGarvey, M., Quinn, B. T., Dusek, J. A., Benson, H., Rauch, S. L., Moore, C. I., & Fischi, B. (2005). Meditation experience is associated with increased cortical thickness. *Neuroreport, 16,* 1893–1897.

Lazarus, R. S. (1999). *Stress and emotion.* New York: Springer.

Lazarus, R. S. (2000). Evolution of a model of stress, coping and discrete emotions. In V. R. Rice (Ed.), *Handbook of stress, coping and health.* Thousand Oaks, CA: Sage.

Lazarus, R. S. (2006). *Stress and emotion: A new synthesis.* New York: Springer.

Le Prell, C. G., Hensley, B. N., Campbell, K. C. M., Hall, J. W., III, & Guire, K. (2011). Evidence of hearing loss in a 'normally-hearing' college-student population. *International Journal of Audiology, 50,* 21–31.

Leaper, C. (2000). Gender, affiliation, assertion, and the interactive context of parent-child play. *Developmental Psychology, 36,* 381–393.

Leary, M. R. (2010). Affiliation, acceptance, and belonging. In S. T. Fiske, D. T. Gilbert & G. Lindzey (Eds.), *Handbook of social psychology* (Vol. 2, 5th ed., pp. 864–897). Hoboken, NJ: John Wiley & Sons.

LeDoux, J. (2003). Cited in L. Helmuth, Fear and trembling in the amygdala. *Science, 300,* 568–569.

Lee, A., & Hankin, B. L. (2009). Insecure attachment, dysfunctional attitudes, and low self-esteem predicting prospective symptoms of depression and anxiety during adolescence. *Journal of Clinical Child and Adolescent Psychology, 38,* 219–231.

Lee, C. W., Taylor, G., & Drummond, P. D. (2006). The active ingredient in EMDR: Is it traditional exposure or dual focus of attention? *Clinical Psychology and Psychotherapy, 13,* 97–107.

Lee, K., & Ashton, M. C. (2006). Further assessment of the HEXACO Personality Inventory: Two new facet scales and an observer report form. *Psychological Assessment, 18,* 182–191.

Lee, M. R. (2005). Curare: The South American arrow poison. *Journal of the Royal College of Physicians of Edinburgh, 35,* 83–92.

Lee, R. (2005, April 15). "Boy-code" a factor in fatal school shootings? *Washington Blade.*

Lee-Chiong, T. (2008). *Sleep medicine: Essentials and review.* New York: Oxford University Press.

Lee-Chiong, T., & Sateia, M. (2006). Pharmacologic therapy of insomnia. In T. L. Lee-Chiong (Ed.), *Sleep: A comprehensive handbook* (pp. 125–132). Hoboken, NJ: John Wiley & Sons.

Leedham, B., Meyerowitz, B. E., Muirhead, J., & Frist, W. H. (1995). Positive expectations predict health after heart transplantation. *Health Psychology, 14,* 74–79.

Legrand, L. N., Iacono, W. G., & McGue, M. (2005, March/April). Predicting addiction. *American Scientist, 93,* 140–147.

Lehrer, J. (2009). *How we decide.* New York: Houghton Mifflin Harcourt.

Leibel, R. L., Rosenbaum, M., & Hirsch, J. (1995). Changes in energy expenditure resulting from altered body weight. *New England Journal of Medicine, 332,* 621–628.

Leichsenring, F., & Rabung, S. (2008). Effectiveness of long-term psychodynamic psychotherapy. A meta-analysis. *JAMA, 300,* 1552–1565.

Leippe, M. R., & Eisenstadt, D. (1994). Generalization of dissonance reduction: Decreasing prejudice through induced compliance. *Journal of Personality and Social Psychology, 67,* 395–413.

Leitzell, K. (2007, December/2008, January). Understanding baby talk. *Scientific American Mind,* 10.

Leland, J. (1994, February 14). Homophobia. *Newsweek.*

Lemerise, E. A., & Dodge, K. A. (2000). The development of anger and hostile interactions. In M. Lewis & J. M. Haviland-Jones (Eds.), *Handbook of emotions* (2nd ed.). New York: Guilford Press.

Leming, T. (2008, July 7). omg. almost caused fendr bendr, lol! *Time,* 53.

Lemley, B. (1999, December). Do you see what they see? *Discover.*

Lemley, B. (2000, February). Isn't she lovely? *Discover,* 42–49.

Lemley, B. (2006, August). Shiny happy people: Can you reach nirvana with the aid of science? *Discover, 27,* 62–77.

Lemonick, M. D. (2006, January 16). Measuring IQ points by the cupful. *Time,* 94–95.

Lemonick, M. D. (2007a, January 29). The flavor of memories. *Time,* 100–102.

Lemonick, M. D. (2007b, July 16). The science of addiction. *Time,* 42–48.

Lenox, R. H., & Hahn, C. (2000). Overview of the mechanism of action of lithium in the brain: Fifty-year update. *Journal of Clinical Psychiatry, 2000* (Suppl. 9), 5–15.

Lenroot, R. K., & Giedd, J. N. (2010). Sex differences in the adolescent brain. *Brain and Cognition, 72,* 46–55.

Lenzer, J. (2007, September). Citizen, heal thyself. *Discover,* 54–61.

Leo, J. (1987, January 12). Exploring the traits of twins. *Time.*

Leonard, W. (2009, February 16). Cited in Evolutionary link to modern-day obesity, other problems. *Science Daily.*

Lepper, M. R., Henderlong, J., & Gingras, I. (1999). Understanding the effects of extrinsic rewards on intrinsic motivation—Uses and abuses of meta-analysis: Comment on Deci, Koestner, and Ryan (1999). *Psychological Bulletin, 125,* 669–676.

Lesch, K. P. (2005). Alcohol dependence and gene x environment interaction in emotion regulation: Is serotonin the link? *European Journal of Pharmacology, 526,* 113–124.

Leshner, A. I. (2001, June). What does it mean that addiction is a brain disease? *Monitor on Psychology,* 19.

Lessmoellmann, A. (2006, October). Don't count on it. *Scientific American Mind.*

Leu, J., Wang, J., & Koo, K. (2011). Are positive emotions just as "positive" across cultures? *Emotion, 11,* 994–999.

Leventhal, H., & Patrick-Miller, L. (2000). Emotions and physical illness: Causes and indicators of vulnerability. In M. Lewis & J. M. Haviland-Jones (Eds.), *Handbook of emotions* (2nd ed.). New York: Guilford Press.

Levesque, M. F., Neuman, T., & Rezak, M. (2009). Therapeutic microinjection of autologous adult human neural stem cells and differentiated neurons for Parkinson's disease: Five-year post-operative outcome. *Open Stem Cell Journal, 1,* 20–29.

Levine, J. M., & Kerr, N. L. (2007). Inclusion and exclusion: Implications for group processes. In A. W. Kruglanski & E. T. Higgins (Eds.), *Social psychology: Handbook of basic principles* (2nd ed., pp. 759–784). New York: Guilford Press.

Levinson, D. F. (2003). Molecular genetics of schizophrenia: A review of the recent literature. *Current Opinion in Psychiatry, 16,* 157–170.

Levinson, D. F. (2009). Genetics of major depression. In I. H. Gotlib & C. L. Hammen (Eds.), *Handbook of depression* (2nd ed., pp. 165–186). New York: Guilford Press.

Levitsky, D. (2003, August 11). The "freshman." *U.S. News & World Report,* 54.

Levy, B. (2010, Spring). Extraordinary brains. *Discover Presents the Brain,* 8–10.

Levy, D. (1997). *Tools of critical thinking.* New York: Allyn & Bacon.

Levy, J. (1985, May). Right brain, left brain: Fact and fiction. *Psychology Today.*

Levy, J., & Trevarthen, C. (1976). Metacontrol of hemispheric function in human split-brain patients. *Journal of Experimental Psychology: Human Perception and Performance, 2,* 299–312.

Levy, J., Trevarthen, C., & Sperry, R. W. (1972). Perception of bilateral chimeric figures following hemispheric deconnection. *Brain, 95,* 61–68.

Lewis, A. J., Dennerstein, M., & Biggs, P. M. (2008). Short-term psychodynamic psychotherapy: Review of recent process and outcome studies. *Australian and New Zealand Journal of Psychiatry, 42,* 445–455.

Lewis, J. W., Brefcynski, J. A., Phinney, R. E., Janik, J. J., & DeYoe, E. A. (2005). Distinct cortical pathways for processing tool versus animal sounds. *Journal of Neuroscience, 25,* 5148–5158.

Lewis-Fernandez, R., Das, A. K., Alfonso, C., Weissman, M. M., & Olfson, M. (2005). Depression in U.S. Hispanics: Diagnostic and management considerations in family practice. *Journal of the American Board of Family Practice, 18,* 282–296.

Lewkowicz, D. J., & Hansen-Tift, A. M. (2012, January 17). Infants deploy selective attention to the mouth of a talking face when learning speech. *Proceedings of the National Academy of Sciences, 109,* 1431–1436.

Lezak, M. D., Howieson, D. B., Bigler, E. D., & Tranel, D. (2012). *Neuropsychological assessment* (5th ed.). New York: Oxford University Press.

Li, T. K. (2000). Pharmacogenetics of responses to alcohol and genes that influence alcohol drinking. *Journal of Studies on Alcohol, 61,* 5–12.

Liberman, N., Trope, Y., & Stephan, E. (2007). Psychological distance. In A. W. Kruglanski & E. T. Higgins (Eds.), *Social psychology: Handbook of basic principles* (2nd ed., pp. 353–383). New York: Guilford Press.

Lie, H. (2009, January 17). Cited in E. Quill, It's written all over your face. *Science News,* 24–28.

Lieberman, D. A. (2004). *Learning and memory.* Belmont, CA: Wadsworth/Thomson Learning.

Lieberman, D. A. (2012). *Human learning and memory.* New York: Cambridge University Press.

Lieberman, J. A. (2005, September 25). Cited in B. Bower, Meds alert. *Science News, 168,* 195.

Liebert, R. M., & Spiegler, M. D. (1994). *Personality: Strategies and issues* (7th ed.). Pacific Grove, CA: Brooks/Cole.

Liebowitz, M. R., Heimberg, R. G., Schneier, F. R., Hope, D. A., Davies, S., Holt, C. S., Goetz, D., Juster, H. R., Lin, S. H., Bruch, M. A., Marshall, R. D., & Klein, D. F. (1999). Cognitive-behavioral group therapy versus phenelzine in social phobia: Long-term outcome. *Depression and Anxiety, 10,* 89–98.

Lilienfeld, S. O. (1993). Do "honesty" tests really measure honesty? *Skeptical Inquirer, 18,* 32–41.

Lilienfeld, S. O. (2007). Psychological treatments that cause harm. *Perspectives on Psychological Science, 2,* 53–70.

Lilienfeld, S. O., & Arkowitz, H. (2006, December/2007, January). Taking a closer look: Can moving your eyes back and forth help to ease anxiety? *Scientific American Mind,* 80–81.

Lilienfeld, S. O., & Arkowitz, H. (2007, December/2008, January). What "psychopath" means. *Scientific American Mind,* 80–81.

Lilienfeld, S. O., & Arkowitz, H. (2008, June/July). Can animals aid therapy? *Scientific American Mind,* 78–79.

Lilienfeld, S. O., & Arkowitz, H. (2009, November/December). Foreign afflictions. *Scientific American Mind,* 68–69.

Lilienfeld, S. O., & Arkowitz, H. (2010, March/April). Living with schizophrenia. *Scientific American Mind,* 66–67.

Lilienfeld, S. O., Kirsch, I., Sarbin, T. R., Lynn, S. J., Chaves, J. F., Ganaway, G. K., & Powell, R. A. (1999). Dissociative identity disorder and the sociocognitive model: Recalling the lessons of the past. *Psychological Bulletin, 125,* 507–523.

Lilienfeld, S. O., Lynn, S. J., Ruscio, J., & Beyerstein, B. L. (2010). *50 great myths of popular psychology.* UK: Wiley-Blackwell.

Lilly, J. C. (1972). *The center of the cyclone.* New York: Bantam.

Lincoln, T. M., Hahlweg, K., Frank, M., vonWitzleben, I., Schroeder, B., & Fiegenbaum, W. (2003). Effectiveness of an empirically supported treatment for social phobia in the field. *Behaviour Research and Therapy, 41,* 1251–1269.

Lindsay, J. J., & Anderson, C. A. (2000). From antecedent conditions to violent actions: A general affective aggression model. *Personality and Social Psychological Bulletin, 26,* 533–547.

Lindstrom, M. (2005). *Brand sense: Build powerful brands through touch, taste, smell, sight, and sound.* New York: Free Press.

Lindstrom, M. (2008). *Buyology: Truth and lies about why we buy.* New York: Doubleday.

Linehan, M. (1993). *Cognitive-behavioral treatment of borderline personality disorder.* New York: Guilford Press.

Ling, G., & Ming, W. (2006, April 27). Japanese organ transplant agency: Chinese organ supplies will not decrease. *The Epoch Times.*

Linnenbrink-Garcia, L., & Fredricks, J. A. (2008). Developmental perspectives on achievement motivation. In J. Y. Shah & W. L. Gardner (Eds.), *Handbook of motivation science* (pp. 448–464). New York: Guilford Press.

Lipkin, R. (1995). Additional genes may affect color vision. *Science News, 147,* 100.

Lipton, F. R., Siegel, C., Hannigan, A., Samuels, J., & Baker, S. (2000). Tenure in supportive housing for homeless persons with severe mental illness. *Psychiatric Services, 51,* 479–486.

Lipton, S. D. (1983). A critique of so-called standard psychoanalytic technique. *Contemporary Psychoanalysis, 19,* 35–52.

Liska, K. (1994). *Drugs & the human body* (4th ed.). New York: Macmillan.

Lithwick, D. (2009, March 23). When our eyes deceive us. *Newsweek,* 17.

Liu, Y., Li, J., & Ye, J. (2010). Histamine regulates activities of neurons in the ventrolateral preoptic nucleus. *Journal of Physiology, 588,* 4103–4116.

Liu, Z., Muehlbauer, K. R., Schmeiser, H. H., Hergenhahn, M., Belharazem, D., & Hollstein, M. C. (2005). p53 mutations in a benzo(a)pyrene-exposed human p53 knock-in murine fibroblasts correlate with p53 mutations in human lung tumors. *Cancer Research, 65,* 2583–2587.

Livneh, H., Lott, S. M., & Antonak, R. F. (2004). Patterns of psychosocial adaptation to chronic illness and disability: A cluster analytic approach. *Psychology, Health, and Medicine, 9,* 411–430.

Lloyd, J. (2010, November 2). What do you like most about cats? *USA Today.*

Lochman, J. E., Powell, N. R., Whidby, J. M., & Fitzgerald, D. P. (2006). Aggressive children: Cognitive-behavioral assessment and treatment. In P. C. Kendall (Ed.), *Child and adolescent therapy: Cognitive-behavioral procedures* (3rd ed., pp. 33–81). New York: Guilford Press.

Locke, E. A., & Latham, G. P. (2002). Building a practically useful theory of goal setting and task motivation. *American Psychologist, 57,* 705–717.

Locke, J. L. (2006). Parental selection of vocal behavior: Crying, cooking, babbling, and the evolution of language. *Human Nature, 17,* 155–168.

Locke, S. F. (2008, June/July). A novel chemical target. *Scientific American Mind,* 6.

Loehlin, J. C. (2000). Group differences in intelligence. In R. J. Sternberg (Ed.), *Handbook of intelligence.* New York: Cambridge University Press.

Loehlin, J. C., Neiderhiser, J. M., & Reiss, D. (2003). The behavior genetics of personality and the NEAD study. *Journal of Research in Personality, 37,* 373–387.

Loftus, E. F. (1975). Leading questions and the eyewitness report. *Cognitive Psychology, 7,* 560–572.

Loftus, E. F. (1979). The malleability of memory. *American Scientist, 67,* 312–320.

Loftus, E. F. (1993). The reality of repressed memories. *American Psychologist, 48,* 518–537.

Loftus, E. F. (1997a, September). Creating false memories. *Scientific American,* 70–75.

Loftus, E. F. (1997b). Repressed memory accusations: Devastated families and devastated patients. *Applied Cognitive Psychology, 11,* 25–30.

Loftus, E. F. (1999). Repressed memories. *Forensic Psychiatry, 22,* 61–69.

Loftus, E. F. (2000, April 25). Cited in J. E. Brody, Memories of things that never were. *The New York Times,* D8.

Loftus, E. F. (2003a, February 17). Cited in J. Gottlieb, Memories made to order at UCI. *Los Angeles Times,* 81.

Loftus, E. F. (2003b, November). Make-believe memories. *American Psychologist,* 867–873.

Loftus, E. F. (2005a, August 1). Cited in Today@UCI, *Power of suggestion may help diets avoid specific foods.* Available: http://today.uci.edu/news/release_detail. asp-key=1360.

Loftus, E. F. (2005b). Planting misinformation in the human mind: A 30-year investigation of the malleability of memory. *Learning & Memory, 12,* 361–366.

Loftus, E. F., & Davis, D. (2006). Recovered memories. *Annual Review of Clinical Psychology, 2,* 469–498.

Loftus, E. F., & Hoffman, H. G. (1989). Misinformation and memory: The creation of new memories. *Journal of Experimental Psychology: General, 118,* 409–420.

Loftus, E. F., & Loftus, G. R. (1980). On the performance of stored information in the human brain. *American Psychologist, 35,* 409–420.

Loftus, E. F., Miller, D. G., & Burns, H. J. (1978). Semantic integration of verbal information into a visual memory. *Journal of Experimental Psychology: Human Learning and Memory, 4,* 19–31.

Lonsway, K. A., & Fitzgerald, L. F. (1994). Rape myths: In review. *Psychology of Women Quarterly, 18,* 133–164.

Lonsway, K. A., Moore, M., Harrington, C. P., Smeal, E., & Spillar, K. (2003, Spring). Hiring & retaining more women: The advantages to law enforcement agencies. *National Center for Women & Policing,* 1–16.

Lopes, P. N., Salovey, P., & Straus, R. (2003). Emotional intelligence, personality, and the perceived quality of social relationships. *Personality and Individual Differences, 35,* 641–658.

Lord, C. (2002, October 22). Cited in L. Tarkan, Autism therapy is called effective, but rare. *The New York Times,* D2.

Lorenz, K. (1952). *King Solomon's ring.* New York: Crowell.

Lorenzo, G. L., Biesanz, J. C., & Human, L. J. (2010). What is beautiful is good and more accurately understood: Physical attractiveness and accuracy in first impressions of personality. *Psychological Science, 21,* 1777–1782.

Losen, D., & Orfield, G. (Eds.). (2002). *Racial inequity in special education.* Cambridge, MA: Harvard Education Publishing Group.

Lothane, Z. (2006a). Freud's legacy—Is it still with us? *Psychoanalytic Psychology, 23,* 285–301.

Lothane, Z. (2006b). Reciprocal free association. *Psychoanalytic Psychology, 23,* 711–727.

Lovaas, O. I. (1987). Behavioral treatment and normal educational and intellectual functioning in young autistic children. *Journal of Consulting and Clinical Psychology, 55,* 3–9.

Lovaas, O. I. (1993). The development of a treatment-research project for developmentally disabled autistic children. *Journal of Applied Behavior Analysis, 26,* 617–630.

Lovaas, O. I. (1999, September). Cited in H. McIntosh, Two autism studies fuel hope—and skepticism. *Monitor: American Psychological Association,* 28.

Lovaas, O. I., & Buch, G. (1997). Intensive behavioral intervention with young children. In N. N. Singh (Ed.), *Prevention and treatment of severe behavior problems.* Pacific Grove, CA: Brooks/Cole.

Lovaas Institute. (2012). *The Lovaas approach* [On-line]. Available: http://www.lovaas.com.

Lovato, D. (2012). My battle with eating disorders. *Seventeen* [On-line]. Available: http://www.seventeen.com/health/tips/demi-lovato-eating-disorder.

Low, A., Bentin, S., Rockstroh, B., Silberman, Y., Gomolla, A., Cohen, R., & Elbert, T. (2003). Semantic categorization in the human brain: Spatiotemporal dynamics revealed by magnetoencephalography. *Psychological Science, 14,* 367–372.

Loy, I., & Hall, G. (2002). Taste aversion after ingestion of lithium chloride: An associative analysis. *Quarterly Journal of Experimental Psychology, 55B,* 365–380.

Luan, P. K., Fitzgerald, D. A., Nathan, P. J., & Tancer, M. E. (2006). Association between amygdala hyperactivity to harsh faces and severity of social anxiety in generalized social phobia. *Biological Psychiatry, 59,* 424–429.

Lubinski, D., Benbow, C. P., Webb, R. M., & Bleske-Rechek, A. (2006). Tracking exceptional human capital over two decades. *Psychological Science, 17,* 194–199.

Luborsky, E. B., O'Reilly-Landry, M., & Arlow, J. A. (2008). Psychoanalysis. In R. J. Corsini & D. Wedding (Eds.), *Current psychotherapies* (8th ed., pp. 15–62). Belmont, CA: Thomson Brooks/Cole.

Luborsky, E. B., O'Reilly-Landry, M., & Arlow, J. A. (2011). Psychoanalysis. In R. J. Corsini & D. Wedding (Eds.), *Current psychotherapies* (9th ed., pp. 15–66). Belmont, CA: Brooks Cole, Cengage.

Luborsky, L., & Barrett, M. S. (2006). The history of empirical status of key psychoanalytic concepts. *Annual Review of Clinical Psychology, 2,* 1–19.

Luborsky, L., Rosenthal, R., Diguer, L., Andrusyna, T. P., Berman, J. S., Levitt, J. T., Seligman, D. A., & Krause, E. D. (2002). The dodo bird verdict is alive and well—mostly. *Clinical Psychology: Science and Practice, 9,* 2–12.

Luna, B. (2006, August/September). Cited in L. Sabbagh, Hard at work no, really. *Scientific American Mind,* 20–25.

Lundstrom, J. N., Boyle, J. A., Zatorre, R. J., & Jones-Gotman, M. (2008). Functional neuronal processing of body odors differs from that of similar common odors. *Cerebral Cortex, 18,* 1466–1474.

Lupart, J. L., & Pyryt, M. C. (1996). "Hidden gifted" students: Underachiever prevalence and profile. *Journal for the Education of the Gifted, 20,* 36–53.

Luscombe, B. (2010, November 19). Marriage: What's it good for? *Time,* 48–54.

Luszczynska, A., & Sutton, S. (2006). Physical activity after cardiac rehabilitation: Evidence that different types of self-efficacy are important in maintainers and relapsers. *Rehabilitation Psychology, 51,* 314–321.

Lykken, D. T. (2003). Cited in D. Watson, Happiness is in your jeans. *Contemporary Psychology, 48,* 242–243.

Lyle, L. (2003). Child misdiagnosed with ADHD making the grade after real problem found. *Wave3* [On-line]. Available: http://www.wave3.com/global/story.asp?s=1253290&ClientType=Printable.

Lynn, S. J. (2007). Hypnosis reconsidered. *American Journal of Clinical Hypnosis, 49,* 195–197.

Lynn, S. J., & Cardena, E. (2007). Hypnosis and the treatment of posttraumatic stress conditions: An evidence-based approach. *International Journal of Clinical Hypnosis, 55,* 167–188.

Lynn, S. J., & Kirsch, I. (2006). Introduction: Definitions and early history. In S. J. Lynn & I. Kirsch (Eds.), *Essentials of clinical hypnosis: An evidence-based approach.* Washington, DC: American Psychological Association.

Lynn, S. J., Kirsch, I., Barabasz, A., Cardena, E., & Patterson, D. (2000). Hypnosis as an empirically supported clinical intervention: The state of the evidence and a look to the future. *International Journal of Clinical and Experimental Hypnosis, 48,* 239–259.

Lynn, S. J., Kirsch, I., & Hallquist, M. N. (2008). Social cognitive theories of hypnosis. In M. Nash & A. Barnier (Eds.), *The Oxford handbook of hypnosis* (pp. 111–139). New York: Oxford University Press.

Lynn, S. J., Kirsch, I., Knox, J., Fassler, O., & Lilienfeld, S. O. (2007a). Hypnosis and neuroscience: Implications for the altered state debate. In G. Jamieson (Ed.), *Hypnosis and conscious states: The cognitive neuroscience perspective* (pp. 146–166). New York: Oxford University Press.

Lynn, S. J., Kirsch, I., Knox, J., Fassler, O., & Lilienfeld, S. O. (2007b). Hypnotic regulation of consciousness and the pain neuromatrix. In G. A. Jamieson (Ed.), *Hypnosis and conscious states: The cognitive neuroscience perspective* (pp. 145–166). New York: Oxford University Press.

Lynn, S. J., Loftus, E. F., Lilienfeld, S. O., & Lock, T. (2003, July/August). Memory recovery techniques in psychotherapy. *Skeptical Inquirer,* 40–46.

Lynn, S. J., Matthews, A., & Barnes. S. (2009). Hypnosis and memory: From Bernheim to the present. In K. Markman, J. A. Suhr & W. M. P. Klein (Eds.), *Handbook of imagination and mental stimulation* (pp. 103–118). New York: Psychology Press.

Lyon, L. (2009a, February). Helping teens steer clear of trouble. *U.S. News & World Report,* 40–43.

Lyon, L. (2009b, December). Battling insomnia? Consider therapy. *U.S. News & World Report,* 76–78.

Lyon, L., Voiland, A., & Baldauf, S. (2008, September 15/September 22). Coping with sexual woes. *U.S. News & World Report,* 54–56.

Lyubomirsky, S. (2011, November 1). Cited in S. Jayson, People who say they feel happy may live 35% longer. *USA Today,* 2A.

Lyubomirsky, S., Diener, E., & King, L. (2005). The benefits of frequent positive affect: Does happiness lead to success? *Psychological Bulletin, 131*(6), 803–855.

Maathai, W. (2004, December 10). *Wangari Maathai? Nobel lecture* [On-line]. Available: http://nobelprize.org/nobel_prozes/peace/laureates/2004/maathai-lecture-text.html.

Maathai, W. (2005, January 5). Cited in D. Gilson, *Root causes: An interview with Wangari Maathai* [On-line]. Available: http://www.motherjones.com/news/qa/2005/01/wangari_maathai.html.

Maathai, W. (2006). *Unbowed.* New York: Alfred A. Knopf.

Maccoby, E. E. (1984). Socialization and developmental change. *Child Development, 55,* 317–328.

Macfarlane, A. J. (1975). Olfaction in the development of social preferences in the human neonate. *CIBA Foundation Symposium, 33,* 103–117.

Macht, M. (2007, October/November). Feeding the psyche. *Scientific American Mind*, 64–69.

MacInnis, L. (2006, June 2). Genital cutting's fatal results cited. *San Diego Union-Tribune*, A16.

Maclachlan, M., Desmond, D., & Horgan, O. (2003). Psychological correlates of illusory body experiences. *Journal of Rehabilitation Research & Development, 40*, 59–66.

MacLeod, C. (2009, December 31). Garlic prices soar in China amid flu fears. *USA Today*, 7A.

MacQueen, G., Marshall, J., Perdue, M., Siegel, S., & Biennenstock, J. (1989). Pavlovian conditioning of rat mucosal mast cells to secrete rat mast cell protease II. *Science, 243*, 83–85.

Macrae, C. N., & Bodenhausen, G. V. (2000). Social cognition: Thinking categorically about others. *Annual Review of Psychology, 51*, 93–120.

Macrae, C. N., & Quadflieg, S. (2010). Perceiving people. In S. T. Fiske, D. T. Gilbert & G. Lindzey (Eds.), *Handbook of social psychology* (Vol. 1, 5th ed., pp. 428–463). Hoboken, NJ: John Wiley & Sons.

Maddi, S. R. (2002). The story of hardiness: Twenty years of theorizing, research, and practice. *Consulting Psychology Journal, 54*, 173–185.

Maddi, S. R. (2008, September). The courage and strategies of hardiness as helpful in growing despite major, disruptive stresses. *American Psychologist, 563*.

Madeley, G. (2007, October 19). £20,000 payout for woman who falsely accused her father of rape after "recovered memory" therapy. *MailOnline* [On-line]. Available: http://www.dailymail.co.uk/news/article-488623/20-000-payout-woman-falsely-accused-father-rape-recovered-memory-therapy.html.

Madsen, M. V., Gotzsche, P. C., & Hrobjartsson, A. (2009). Acupuncture treatment for pain: Systematic review of randomized clinical trials with acupuncture, placebo acupuncture, and no acupuncture groups. *British Medical Journal, 338*, 3115.

Maehr, M. L. (2008). Culture and achievement motivation. *International Journal of Psychology, 43*, 917–918.

Magnusson, A. (2000). An overview of epidemiological studies on seasonal affective disorder. *Acta Psychiatrica Scandinavica, 101*, 176–184.

Magnusson, A., & Partonen, T. (2005). The diagnosis, symptomatology, and epidemiology of seasonal affective disorder. *CNS Spectrums, 10*, 625–634.

Maier, S. R., Watkins, L. R., & Fleshner, M. (1994). Psychoneuroimmunology. *American Psychologist, 49*, 1004–1007.

Maio, G. R., & Haddock, G. (2007). Attitude change. In A. W. Kruglanski & E. T. Higgins (Eds.), *Social psychology: Handbook of basic principles* (2nd ed., pp. 565–586). New York: Guilford Press.

Maio, G. R., Olson, J. M., Bernard, M. M., & Luke, M. A. (2006). Ideologies, values, attitudes, and behavior. In J. Delamater (Ed.), *Handbook of social psychology* (pp. 283–308). New York: Springer.

Maisto, S. A., Galizion, M., & Connors, G. J. (2011). *Drug use and abuse* (6th ed.). Belmont, CA: Wadsworth Cengage Learning.

Malcolm-Smith, S., Solms, M., Turnbull, O., & Tredoux, C. (2008). Threat in dreams: An adaptation? *Consciousness and Cognition, 17*, 1281–1291.

Maldonado, P. E., Godecke, I., Gray, C. M., & Bonhoffer, T. (1997). Orientation selectivity in pinwheel centers in cat striate cortex. *Science, 276*, 1551–1555.

Malle, B. F. (2006). The actor-observer asymmetry in attribution: A (surprising) meta-analysis. *Psychological Bulletin, 132*, 895–919.

Mandel, H. (2009). *Here's the deal: Don't touch me.* New York: Bantam Books.

Manderscheid, R. W., & Sonnenschein, M. A. (1992). *Mental health, United States, 1992.* Washington, DC: U.S. Department of Health and Human Services.

Maner, J. K., Rouby, D. A., & Gonzaga, G. C. (2008). Automatic inattention to attractive alternatives: The evolved psychology of relationship maintenance. *Evolution and Human Behavior, 29*, 343–349.

Manktelow, K. (2012). *Thinking and reasoning: An introduction to the psychology of reason, judgment and decision making.* New York: Psychology Press.

Mann, D. (2005, June 29). Portrait of a psychopath. *WebMD* [On-line]. Available: http://www.webmd.com/content/Article/108/108749.htm?pagenumber=1.

Mannarino, A. (2012, April). Cited in B. Azar, More support needed for trauma interventions. *Monitor on Psychology*, 56–59.

Mansvelder, D. D., De Rover, M., McGehee, D. S., & Brussaard, A. B. (2003). Cholinergic modulation of dopaminergic reward areas: Upstream and downstream targets of nicotine addiction. *European Journal of Pharmacology, 480*, 117–123.

Marchetti, S., & Bunte, K. (2006). Retailers and banks leverage fundraising power, raising more than $139 million for hurricane relief. *Press room: American Red Cross* [On-line]. Available: http://redcross.org/pressrelease/0,1077,0_314_5172,00.htm.

Marcus, M. B. (2000, October 2). Don't let false alarms scare you off prenatal tests, but do get the facts first. *U.S. News & World Report*, 69–70.

Marcus, M. B. (2009, August 17). Giant steps for ear implants. *USA Today*, 4D.

Marcus, M. B., Szabo, L., & Sternberg, S. (2010, October 26). Smoking raises Alzheimer's risk. *USA Today*, 6D.

Mareschal, D., & Quinn, P. C. (2001). Categorization in infancy. *Trends in Cognitive Science, 5*, 443–450.

Markey, P. M., & Markey, C. N. (2010). Vulnerability to violent video games: A review of integration of personality research. *Review of General Psychology, 14*, 82–91.

Marks, W. J., Jr. (2011). *Deep brain stimulation management.* New York: Cambridge University Press.

Marlowe, D. B. (2011). The verdict on drug courts and other problem-solving courts. *Chapman Journal of Criminal Justice, 2*(1), 57–96.

Marsa, L. (2002, March 25). Trauma therapy's new focus. *Los Angeles Times*, S8.

Marschall, J. (2007, February/March). Seduced by sleep. *Scientific American Mind*, 52–57.

Marsh, A. A., Elfenbein, A., & Ambady, N. (2003). Nonverbal "accents": Cultural differences in facial expressions of emotion. *Psychological Science, 14*, 373–376.

Marshall, G. N., Schell, T. L., Glynn, S. M., & Shetty, V. (2006). The role of hyperarousal in the manifestation of posttraumatic psychological distress following injury. *Journal of Abnormal Psychology, 115*, 624–628.

Martens, W. H. J. (2002, January). The hidden suffering of the psychopath. *Psychiatric Times, 19*.

Martin, A., Wiggs, C. L., Ungerfelder, L. G., & Haxby, J. V. (1996). Neural correlates of category-specific knowledge. *Nature, 379*, 649–652.

Martin, C. L. (2000). Cognitive theories of gender development. In T. Eckes & H. M. Trautner (Eds.), *The developmental social psychology of gender*. Mahwah, NJ: Lawrence Erlbaum.

Martin, C. L., Ruble, D. N., & Szrkrybalo, J. (2002). Cognitive theories of early gender development. *Psychological Bulletin, 128*, 903–933.

Martin, G. L. (1982). Thought-stopping and stimulus control to decrease persistent disturbing thoughts. *Journal of Behavior Therapy and Experimental Psychiatry, 13*, 215–220.

Martin, I., Dawson, V. L., & Dawson, T. M. (2011). Recent advances in the genetics of Parkinson's disease. *Annual Review of Genomics and Human Genetics, 12*, 301–325.

Martin, J. K., Pescosolido, B. A., & Tuch, S. A. (2000). Of fear and loathing: The role of "disturbing behavior," labels, and causal attributions in shaping public attitudes toward people with mental illness. *Journal of Health and Social Behavior, 41*, 208–223.

Martin, L. (1986). Eskimo words for snow: A case study in the genesis and decay of an anthropological example. *American Anthropologist, 88*, 418–423.

Martin, P. D., & Brantley, P. J. (2004). Stress, coping, and social support in health and behavior. In J. M. Raczynsky & L. C. Leviton (Eds.), *Handbook of clinical health psychology* (Vol. 2, pp. 233–267). Washington, DC: American Psychological Association.

Marziali, E., Damianakis, T., & Donahue, P. (2006). Internet-based clinical services: Virtual support groups for family caregivers. *Journal of Technology in Human Services, 24*, 39–54.

Mash, E. J., & Wolfe, D. A. (2007). *Abnormal child psychology* (3rd ed.). Belmont, CA: Thomson Wadsworth.

Mashour, G. A., Walker, E. E., & Martuza, R. L. (2005). Psychosurgery: Past, present, and future. *Brain Research Reviews, 48*, 409–419.

Maslach, C. (2003). Job burnout: New directions in research and intervention. *Current Directions in Psychological Science, 12*, 189–192.

Maslow, A. H. (1968). *Toward a psychology of being* (2nd ed.). New York: Van Nostrand.

Maslow, A. H. (1970). *Motivation and personality.* New York: Harper & Row.

Maslow, A. H. (1971). *The farther reaches of human nature.* New York: Viking Press.

Mass, E., Lapidot, M., & Gadoth, N. (2005). Case report: Multiple endocrine neoplasia type 2B misdiagnosed as familial dysautonomia. *European Journal of Pediatric Dentistry, 6*, 48–50.

Masters, W. H., & Johnson, V. E. (1966). *Human sexual response.* Boston: Little, Brown.

Masters, W. H., & Johnson, V. E. (1970). *Human sexual inadequacy.* Boston: Little, Brown.

Masters, W. H., & Johnson, V. E. (1981). Sex and the aging process. *Journal of the American Geriatrics Society, 19*, 385–389.

Mastro, J. (1999, July 21). Dialogue with a dolphin. *San Diego Union-Tribune*, E1.

Match.com/MarketTools. (2011a, February 3). Cited in S. Jayson, Singles blur expectations. *USA Today*, 1D.

Match.com/MarketTools. (2011b, February 14). Cited in B. Luscombe, The myth of the slippery bachelor. *Time*, 51–52.

Mather, M. (2011, April). Cited in M. L. Phillips, The mind at midlife. *Monitor on Psychology*, 38–41.

Mather, M., & Carstensen, L. L. (2005). Aging and motivated cognition: The positivity effect in attention and memory. *Trends in Cognitive Sciences, 9*, 496–502.

Mathis, G. (2002). *Inner city miracle.* New York: Ballantine.

Matlin, M. W. (2009). *Cognition* (6th ed.). Hoboken, NJ: John Wiley & Sons.

Matson, J. L. (Ed.). (2010). *Social behavior and skills in children.* New York: Springer.

Matson, J. L., & Ollendick, T. H. (1977). Issues in toilet training normal children. *Behavior Therapy, 8*, 549–553.

Matson, J. L., & Sturmey, P. (Eds.). (2011). *International handbook of autism and pervasive development disorders.* New York: Springer.

Matsuda, L. A., Lolait, S. J., Brownstein, M. J., Young, A. C., & Bonner, T. I. (1990). Structure of a cannabinoid receptor and functional expression of the cloned cDNA. *Nature, 346*, 561–564.

Matsumoto, D., Consolacion, T., Yamada, H., Suzuki, R., Franklin, B., Paul, S., Ray, R., & Uchida, H. (2002). American-Japanese cultural differences in judgments of emotional expression of different intensities. *Cognition and Emotion, 16*, 721–747.

Matsumoto, D., & Ekman, P. (1989). American-Japanese cultural differences in intensity ratings of facial expressions of emotion. *Motivation and Emotion, 13,* 143–157.

Matsumoto, D., & Juang, L. (2012). *Culture and psychology* (5th ed.). Belmont, CA: Wadsworth.

Matsumoto, D., Keltner, D., Shiota, M. N., O'Sullivan, M., & Frank, M. (2008). Facial expressions of emotion. Cited in M. Lewis, J. M. Haviland-Jones & L. F. Barrett (Eds.), *Handbook of emotions* (3rd ed., pp. 211–234). New York: Guilford Press.

Matsumoto, D., & Willingham, B. (2009). Spontaneous facial expression of emotion of congenitally and noncongenitally blind individuals. *Journal of Personality and Social Psychology, 96,* 1–10.

Matthews, G., Deary, I. J., & Whiteman, M. C. (2003). *Personality traits* (2nd ed.). New York: Cambridge University Press.

Matthews, G., Deary, I. J., & Whiteman, M. C. (2009). *Personality traits* (3rd ed.). New York: Cambridge University Press.

Matthews, K. A., & Haynes, S. G. (1986). Type A behavior pattern and coronary disease risk. *American Journal of Epidemiology, 123,* 923–960.

Mauss, I. (2005). Control your anger! *Scientific American Mind, 16,* 64–71.

Mawson, J. (2011, November 14). Cited in N. W. Egan, The serial killer's wife. *People,* 80–84.

Mawuenyega, K. G., Sigurdson, W., Ovod, V., Munsell, L., Kasten, T., Morris, J. C., Yarasheski, K. E., & Bateman, R. J. (2010). Decreased clearance of CNS b-amyloid in Alzheimer's disease. *Science, 330,* 1774.

Max, D. T. (2006). *The family that couldn't sleep.* New York: Random House.

May, M., Gompels, M., Delpech, V., Porter, K., Post, F., Johnson, M., Dunn, D., Palfreeman, A., Gilson, R., Gazzard, B., Hill, T., Walsh, J., Fisher, M., Orkin, C., Ainsworth, J., Bansi, L., Phillips, A., Leen, C., Nelson, M., Anderson, J., & Sabrin, C. (2011). Impact of late diagnosis and treatment on life expectancy in people with HIV-1: UK collaborative HIV cohort (UK CHIC) study. *British Medical Journal, 343,* 6016.

May, R. (2005). How do we know what works? *Journal of College Student Psychotherapy, 19,* 69–73.

Mayberg, H. S. (2006, August/September). Cited in D. Dobbs, Turning off depression. *Scientific American Mind,* 26–31.

Mayberg, H. S. (2011, Fall). Cited in S. Baker, Helen Mayberg. *The Brain,* 46–53.

Mayberg, H. S., Lozano, A. M., Voon, V., McNeely, H. E., Seminowicz, D., Hamani, C., Schwalb, J. M., & Kennedy, S. H. (2005). Deep brain stimulation for treatment-resistant depression. *Neuron, 45,* 651–660.

Mayer, J. D., Salovey, P., & Caruso, D. (2000). Models of emotional intelligence. In R. J. Sternberg (Ed.), *Handbook of intelligence.* New York: Cambridge University Press.

Mayer, J. D., Salovey, P., & Caruso, D. R. (2008). Emotional intelligence: New ability or eclectic traits? *American Psychologist, 63,* 503–517.

Mayes, A. R. (2000). Selective memory disorders. In E. Tulving & F. M. Craik (Eds.), *The Oxford handbook of memory.* New York: Oxford University Press.

Mayford, M., & Korzus, E. (2002). Genetics of memory in the mouse. In L. R. Squire & D. L. Schacter (Eds.), *Neuropsychology of memory* (3rd ed.). New York: Guilford Press.

Mayo Clinic. (2006a). Cited in *Eating disorders.* CNN.com [On-line]. Available: http://www.cnn.com/HEALTH /library/DS/00194.html.

Mayr, E. (2000, July). Darwin's influence on modern thought. *Scientific American,* 79–83.

Mazure, C. M., Brude, M. L., Maciejewski, P. K., & Jacobs, S. C. (2000). Adverse life events and cognitive-personality characteristics in the prediction of major depression and antidepressant response. *American Journal of Psychiatry, 157,* 896–903.

Mcallister, H. A., Baker, J. D., Mannes, C., Stewart, H., & Sutherland, A. (2002). The optimal margin of illusion hypothesis: Evidence from self-serving bias and personality disorders. *Journal of Social and Clinical Psychology, 21,* 414–426.

McCall, R. B. (1994). Academic underachievers. *Current Directions in Psychological Science, 3,* 15–19.

McCarry, J. (1996, May). Peru begins again. *National Geographic.*

McCarthy, T. (2005, October 24). Getting inside your head. *Time,* 95–97.

McClearn, G. E., Johansson, B., Berg, S., Pedersen, N. L., Ahern, F., Petrill, S. A., & Plomin, R. (1997). Substantial genetic influence on cognitive abilities in twins 80 or more years old. *Science, 276,* 1560–1563.

McClelland, D. C. (1961). *The achieving society.* Princeton, NJ: Van Nostrand.

McClelland, D. C. (1965, November-December). Achievement motivation can be developed. *Harvard Business Review, 178,* 6–24.

McClelland, D. C. (1985). *Human motivation.* Glenview, IL: Scott, Foresman.

McClelland, D. C., Atkinson, J. W., Clark, R. W., & Lowell, E. L. (1953). *The achievement motive.* New York: Appleton-Century-Crofts.

McClelland, J. L. (2005). Connectionist models of memory. In E. Tulving & F. M. Craik (Eds.), *The Oxford handbook of memory.* New York: Oxford University Press.

McClure, S. M., Li, J., Tomlin, D., Cypert, K. S., Montague, L. M., & Montague, P. R. (2004a). Neural correlates of behavioral preference for culturally familiar drinks. *Neuron, 44,* 379–387.

McClure, S. M., Li, J., Tomlin, D., Cypert, K. S., Montague, L. M., & Montague, P. R. (2004b, October 25). In H. Fields, Coke vs. Pepsi: How does your brain react to soft drinks? *U.S. News & World Report.*

McClure-Tone, E. B., & Pine, D. S. (2009). Clinical features of the anxiety disorders. In B. J. Sadock, V. A. Sadock & P. Ruiz (Eds.), *Kaplan & Sadock's comprehensive textbook of psychiatry* (9th ed., pp. 1844–1855). Philadelphia: Lippincott, Williams & Wilkins.

McConnell, J. V., Cutler, R. L., & McNeil, E. B. (1958). Subliminal stimulation: An overview. *American Psychologist, 13,* 229–242.

McCrae, R. (2008, September 1). Cited in S. Begley, The geography of personality. *Newsweek,* 65.

McCrae, R. R., & Costa, P. T., Jr. (1999). A five-factor theory of personality. In L. A. Pervin & O. P. John (Eds.), *Handbook of personality* (2nd ed.). New York: Guilford Press.

McCrae, R. R., & Costa, P. T., Jr. (Eds.). (2003). *Personality in adulthood* (2nd ed.). New York: Guilford Press.

McCrae, R. R., Costa, P. T., Jr., Hrebickova, M., Osteandorf, F., Angleitner, A., Avia, M., Sanz, J., Sanchez-Bernardos, M. L., Kusdil, M. E., Woodfield, R., Saunders, P. R., & Smith, P. B. (2000). Nature over nurture: Temperament, personality and life-span development. *Journal of Personality and Social Psychology, 78,* 173–186.

McCrea, S. M., Liberman, N., Trope, Y., & Sherman, S. J. (2008). Construal level and procrastination. *Psychological Science, 19,* 1308–1314.

McDaniel, M. A. (2005). Big-brained people are smarter: A meta-analysis of the relationship between in vivo brain volume and intelligence. *Intelligence, 33,* 337–346.

McDaniel, M. A., & Einstein, G. O. (1986). Bizarre imagery as an effective memory aid: The importance of distinctiveness. *Journal of Experimental Psychology: Learning, Memory and Cognition, 12,* 54–65.

McDougall, W. (1908). *Social psychology.* New York: Putnam.

McDowell, J. (1992, February 17). Are women better cops? *Time.*

McEachin, J. J., Smith, T., & Lovaas, O. I. (1993). Long-term outcome for children with autism who received early intensive behavioral interventions. *American Journal on Mental Retardation, 97,* 359–372.

McEdwards, C. (2008, March 28). Cited in CNN, *Autistic poet gives rare glimpse into mystery illness* [On-line]. Available: http://www.cnn.com/2008 /US/03/28/Tito.autism/index.html#cnnSTCText.

McElrath, D. (1997). The Minnesota model. *Journal of Psychoactive Drugs, 29,* 141–144.

McEwen, B. S. (2002, December 17). Cited in E. Goode, The heavy cost of stress. *The New York Times,* D1.

McGaugh, J. L. (1999, February). Cited in B. Azar, McGaugh blazes on down his own path to keys of memory. *APA Monitor,* 18.

McGilvray, J. (2004). *The Cambridge companion to Chomsky.* Oxford: Cambridge University Press.

McGirk, T. (2007, May 14). Moms and martyrs. *Time,* 48–50.

McGowan, K. (2009, July/August). Out of the past. *Discover,* 30–37.

McGowan, K. (2010, January/February). Can a shock to the brain cure depression? *Discover,* 38.

McGowan, K. (2011, Fall). The whole story. *Discover Magazine: The Brain,* 76–83.

McGowan, P. O., Sasaki, A., D'Alessio, A. C., Dymov, S., Labonté, B., Szyf, M., Turecki, G., & Meaney, M. J. (2009, March). Epigenetic regulation of the glucocorticoid receptor in human brain associates with childhood abuse. *Nature Neuroscience, 12,* 342–343.

McGrath, B. B. (2003). A view from the other side: The place of spirits in the Tongan social field. *Culture, Medicine and Psychiatry, 27,* 29–48.

McHugh, P. (2009, February 25). Cited in S. Friess, A shadow of regret cast over gender switch. *USA Today,* 5D.

McKie, R. (2005, July 31). Chemical kiss turns kids into adolescents. *Observer.*

McNally, G. P., & Westbrook, R. F. (2006). Predicting danger: The nature, consequences, and neural mechanisms of predictive fear learning. *Learning & Memory, 13,* 245–253.

McNeill, D., & Coonan, C. (2006, April 2). Japanese flock to China for organ transplants. *Japan Focus.*

McRonald, F. E., & Fleisher, D. R. (2005). Anticipatory nausea in cyclical vomiting. *BMC Pediatrics, 5.*

McVeigh, K. (2006, August 24). Limiting expert's eyewitness-reliability testimony upends carjacking verdict. *Expert & Scientific Evidence Litigation Reporter, 3.*

Means, M. K., & Edinger, J. D. (2006). Neuropharmacologic therapy for insomnia. In T. L. Lee-Chiong (Ed.), *Sleep: A comprehensive handbook* (pp. 133–136). Hoboken, NJ: John Wiley & Sons.

Mechelli, A., Crinion, J. T., Noppeney, U., O'Doherty, J., Ashburner, J., Frackowiak, R. S., & Price, C. J. (2004). Neurolinguistics: Structural plasticity in the bilingual brain. *Nature, 431,* 97.

Mednick, S. C. (2010, October). Cited in APA, In brief. *Monitor on Psychology,* 14–15.

Megargee, E. I. (1997). Internal inhibitions and controls. In R. Hogan, J. Johnson & S. Briggs (Eds.), *Handbook of personality psychology.* New York: Academic Press.

Meier, D. (2000). *The accelerated learning handbook.* New York: McGraw-Hill.

Unless otherwise noted, all images are © Cengage Learning

Melamed, S., Shirom, A., Toker, S., Berliner, S., & Shapira, I. (2006). Burnout and risk of cardiovascular disease: Evidence, possible causal paths, and promising research directions. *Psychological Bulletin, 132,* 327–353.

Melnick, M. (2011, July 25). Women's work. *Time,* 23.

Melzack, R. (1989). Phantom limbs, the self and the brain. *Canadian Psychology, 30,* 1–16.

Melzack, R. (1997). Phantom limbs. *Scientific American, Special Issue,* 84–91.

Melzack, R., & Katz, J. (2004). *The gate control theory: Reaching for the brain.* Mahwah, NJ: Lawrence Erlbaum.

Memon, A., Zaragoza, M., Clifford, B. R., & Kidd, L. (2009). Inoculation or antidote? The effects of cognitive interview timing on false memory for forcibly fabricated events. *Law and Human Behavior, 34,* 105–117.

Menchetti, M., Murri, M. B., Bertakis, K., Bortolotti, B., & Berardi, D. (2009). Recognition and treatment of depression in primary care: Effect of patients' presentation and frequency of consultation. *Journal of Psychosomatic Research, 66,* 335–341.

Mendelson, J. H., Mello, N. K., Schuckit, M. A., & Segal, D. S. (2006). Cocaine, opioids, and other commonly abused drugs. In S. L. Hauser (Ed.), *Harrison's neurology in clinical medicine* (pp. 625–632). New York: McGraw-Hill.

Menon, V., & Desmond, J. E. (2001). Left superior parietal cortex involvement in writing: Integrating fMRI with lesion evidence. *Cognitive Brain Research, 12,* 337–340.

Mental Floss. (2011, March-April). The art of building a better lie detector, 44–45.

Mercuri, N. B., & Bernardi, G. (2005). The "magic" of L-dopa: Why is it the gold standard Parkinson's disease therapy? *Trends in Pharmacological Sciences, 26,* 341–344.

Merz, C. N. B., Dwyer, J., Nordstrom, C. K., Walton, K. G., Salerno, J. W., & Schneider, R. H. (2002). Psychosocial stress and cardiovascular disease: Pathophysiological links. *Behavioral Medicine, 27,* 141–147.

Mestel, R. (2003a, April 15). Human Genome is completed: Now comes the hard part. *Los Angeles Times,* A18.

Mestel, R. (2003b, May 19). Rorschach tested. *Los Angeles Times,* F1.

Mesulam, M. (2008). Aphasia, memory loss, and other focal cerebral disorders. In A. S. Fauci, E. Braunwald, D. L. Kasper, S. L. Hauser, D. L. Longo, J. L. Jameson & J. Loscaizo (Eds.), *Harrison's principles of internal medicine* (17th ed.). New York: McGraw-Hill.

Metrebian, N., Shanahan, W., Stimson, G. V., Small, C., Lee, M., Mtutu, V., & Wells, B. (2001). Prescribing drug of choice to opiate dependent drug users: A comparison of clients receiving heroin with those receiving injectable methadone at a West London drug clinic. *Drug and Alcohol Review, 20,* 267–276.

Meyer-Lindenberg, A. (2006, May 27). Cited in B. Bower, Violent developments. Disruptive kids grow into their behavior. *Science News, 169,* 328–329.

Meyer-Lindenberg, A. (2009, April/May). Perturbed personalities. *Scientific American Mind,* 40–43.

MFMER (Mayo Foundation for Medical Education and Research). (2005, August 8). *Adolescent sleep problems: Why is your teen so tired?* [On-line]. Available: http://www.mayoclinic.com/health/teens-health/CC00019.

MHA (Mental Health America). (2012). *Depression in women* [On-line]. Available: http://www.nmha.org/index.cfm?objectid=C7DF952E-1372-4D20-C8A3DDCD5459D07B.

Michels, R. (2011, May/June). Cited in M. K. Raskin, The idea that wouldn't die. *Psychology Today,* 78–85.

Mieda, M., Williams, S. C., Richardson, J. A., Tanaka, K., & Yanagisawa, M. (2006). The dorsomedial hypothalamic nucleus as a putative food-entrainable circadian pacemaker. *Proceedings of the National Academy of Sciences, 103,* 12150–12155.

Miesner, M. T., & Maki, R. H. (2007). The role of anxiety in absolute and relative metacomprehension accuracy. *European Journal of Cognitive Psychology, 19,* 650–670.

Mignot, E. (2000, August 30). Cited in A. Manning, Narcolepsy is caused by loss of particular brain cells. *USA Today,* D10.

Milgram, N. A., Dangour, W., & Raviv, A. (1992). Situational and personal determinants of academic procrastination. *Journal of General Psychology, 119,* 123–133.

Milgram, S. (1963). Behavioral study of obedience. *Journal of Abnormal and Social Psychology, 67,* 371–378.

Milgram, S. (1974). *Obedience to authority.* New York: Harper & Row.

Milham, M. P., Erickson, K. I., Banich, M. T., Kramer, A. F., Webb, A., Wszalek, T., & Cohen, H. J. (2002). Attentional control in the aging brain: Insights from an fMRI study of the Stroop task. *Brain and Cognition, 49,* 277–296.

Miller, A. (Ed.). (2005). *The social psychology of good and evil.* New York: Guilford Press.

Miller, B. L., & Cummings, J. L. (Eds.). (2007). *The human front lobes* (2nd ed.). New York: Guilford Press.

Miller, C. (2008, September 22). Sad brain, happy brain. *Newsweek,* 50–56.

Miller, F. G., Quill, T. E., Brody, H., Fletcher, J. C., Gostin, L. O., & Meier, D. E. (1994). Regulating physician-assisted death. *New England Journal of Medicine, 331,* 119–122.

Miller, G. (1956). The magical number seven, plus or minus two: Some limits on our capacity for information processing. *Psychological Review, 48,* 337–442.

Miller, G. (2003). Singing in the brain. *Science, 299,* 646–648.

Miller, G. (2009a, March 20). Rewiring faulty circuits in the brain. *Science, 323,* 1554–1556.

Miller, G. (2009b, October 16). Alzheimer's biomarker initiative hits its stride. *Science, 326,* 386–389.

Miller, G. (2010, June 11). fMRI lie detection fails a legal test. *Science, 328,* 1336–1337.

Miller, G. (2012, June 1). Criticism continues to dog psychiatric manual as deadline approaches. *Science, 336,* 1088–1089.

Miller, G., & Holden, C. (2010, February 12). Proposed revisions to psychiatry's canon unveiled. *Science, 327,* 770–771.

Miller, G., Tybur, J. M., & Jordan, B. D. (2007). Ovulatory cycle effects on tip earning by lap dancers: Economic evidence for human estrus? *Evolution and Human Behavior, 28,* 375–381.

Miller, J. (1995, April). Cited in T. DeAngelis, Research documents trauma of abuse. *APA Monitor.*

Miller, K. (2007, November). Class act. *Reader's Digest,* 114–119.

Miller, M. (2003, July 7). When anxiety runs sky-high. *Los Angeles Times,* F1.

Miller, M. A., & Rahe, R. H. (1997). Life changes scaling for the 1990s. *Journal of Psychosomatic Research, 43,* 279–292.

Miller, M. C. (2005, October 3). The dangers of chronic disease. *Newsweek,* 58–59.

Miller, R. (2003, November). Cited in K. Wright, Staying alive. *Discover,* 64–70.

Miller, W. R., & C'de Baca, J. (1994). Quantum change: Toward a psychology of transformation. In T. F. Heatherton & J. L. Weinberger (Eds.), *Can personality change?* Washington, DC: American Psychological Association.

Miller, W. R., & C'de Baca, J. (2001). *Quantum change.* New York: Guilford Press.

Millichap, J. G. (2011). *Attention deficit hyperactivity disorder handbook: A physician's guide to ADHD.* New York: Springer.

Milling, L. S. (2008). Is high hypnotic suggestibility necessary for successful hypnotic pain intervention? *Current Pain and Headache Reports, 12,* 98–102.

Milling, L. S., Reardon, J. M., & Carosella, G. M. (2006). Meditation and moderation of psychological pain treatments: Response expectancies and hypnotic suggestibility. *Journal of Consulting and Clinical Psychology, 74,* 253–262.

Milrod, B., Leon, A. C., Busch, F., Gudden, M., Schwalberg, M., Clarkin, J., Aronson, A., Singer, M., Turchin, W., Klass, E. T., Graf, E., Teres, J. J., & Shear, M. K. (2007). A randomized controlled clinical trial of psychoanalytic psychotherapy for panic disorder. *American Journal of Psychiatry, 164,* 265–272.

Miltenberger, R. G. (2007). *Behavioral modification: Principles and procedures* (4th ed.). Belmont, CA: Wadsworth Cengage.

Minda, J. P., & Smith, J. D. (2011). Prototype models of categorization: Basic formulation, predictions, and limitation. In E. M. Pothos & A. J. Willis (Eds.), *Formal approaches in categorization* (pp. 40–64). New York: Oxford University Press.

Mirsky, A. F., & Quinn, O. W. (1988). The Genain quadruplets. *Schizophrenia Bulletin, 14,* 595–612.

Mischel, W. (1968). *Personality and assessment.* New York: Wiley.

Mischel, W., & Peake, P. K. (1982). Beyond deja vu in the search for cross-situational consistency. *Psychological Review, 89,* 730–755.

Mischel, W., & Shoda, Y. (1995). A cognitive-affective system theory of personality: Reconceptualizing situations, dispositions, dynamics, and invariance of personality structure. *Psychological Review, 102,* 246–268.

Mischel, W., Shoda, Y., & Rodriguez, M. L. (1989). Delay of gratification in children. *Science, 244,* 933–937.

Mithoefer, M. (2009, November). Cited in D. J. Brown, Treating agony with ecstasy. *Discover.*

Mjøs, O. D. (2004, December 10). *The Nobel Peace Prize 2004 presentation speech* [On-line]. Available: http://nobelprize.org/nobel_prizes/peace/laureates/2004/presentation-speech.html.

Moe, K. A., & Son, M. H. (2005, July). Tradition or sideshow? *The Irrawaddy.*

Moffitt, T. E. (2005). The new look of behavioral genetics in development psychopathology: Gene-environment interplay in antisocial behaviors. *Psychological Bulletin, 131,* 533–554.

Money, J. (1987). Sin, sickness or status? *American Psychologist, 42,* 384–399.

Monk, T. H. (2012). Sleep and human performance. In C. M. Morin & C. A. Espie (Eds.), *The Oxford handbook of sleep and sleep disorders.* New York: Oxford University Press.

Monk, T. H., Kennedy, K. S., Rose, L. R., & Linenger, J. M. (2001). Decreased human circadian pacemaker influence after 100 days in space. *Psychosomatic Medicine, 63,* 881–885.

Monroe, S. M., Slavich, G. M., & Georgiades, K. (2009). The social environment and life stress in depression. In I. H. Gotlib & C. L. Hammen (Eds.), *Handbook of depression* (3rd ed, pp. 340–360). New York: Guilford Press.

Montgomery, G. H. (2008). Hypnosis may reduce pain, cost associated with breast cancer surgery. Cited in H. Lindsey, *Oncology Times, 30,* 37–38.

Monti, J. M., Pandi-Perumal, S. R., & Nutt, D. J. (Eds.). (2008). *Serotonin and sleep: Molecular, functional, and clinical aspects.* Basel, Switzerland: Birkhäuser Verlag.

Montoya, A. G., Sorrentino, R., Lukas, S. E., & Price, B. H. (2002). Long-term neuropsychiatric consequences of "ecstasy" (MDMA): A review. *Harvard Review of Psychiatry, 10*, 212–220.

Moore, D. W. (2005, June 16). Three in four Americans believe in paranormal. *Gallup Poll News Service.*

Moore, E. C. J. (1986). Family socialization and the IQ test performance of traditionally and trans-racially adopted Black children. *Developmental Psychology, 22*, 317–326.

Moore, K. A. (2010). Gender and the differential effects of active and passive perfectionism on mathematics anxiety and writing anxiety. *Cognition, Brain, Behavior: An Interdisciplinary Journal, 14*(4), 333–345.

Moore, K. L. (1988). *The developing human: Clinically oriented embryology* (4th ed.). Philadelphia: W. B. Saunders.

Moore, R. Y. (2006). Biological rhythms and sleep. In T. L. Lee-Chiong (Ed.), *Sleep: A comprehensive handbook* (pp. 25–29). Hoboken, NJ: John Wiley & Sons.

Moreira, F. A., & Lutz, B. (2008). The endocannabinoid system: Emotion, learning, and addiction. *Addiction Biology, 13*, 196–212.

Moreno, J. D. (2006, December/2007, January). Juicing the brain. *Scientific American Mind*, 66–73.

Morewedge, C. K., Huh, Y. E., & Vosgerau, J. (2010, December 10). Thought for food: Imagined consumption reduces actual consumption. *Science, 330*, 1530–1533.

Morewedge, C. K., & Norton, M. I. (2009). When dreaming is believing: The (motivated) interpretation of dreams. *Journal of Personality and Social Psychology, 96*, 249–264.

Morey, L. C. (1997). Personality diagnosis and personality disorders. In R. Hogan, J. Johnson & S. Briggs (Eds.), *Handbook of personality psychology*. New York: Academic Press.

Morgan, A. B., & Lilienfeld, S. O. (2000). A meta-analytic review of the relation between antisocial behavior and neuropsychological measures of executive function. *Clinical Psychology Review, 20*, 113–136.

Morgan, M. (1985). Self-monitoring of attained subgoals in private study. *Journal of Educational Psychology, 77*, 623–630.

Morin, C. M. (2009, June 6). Cited in L. Alderman, Cost-effective ways to fight insomnia. *The New York Times*, B6.

Morin, C. M., & Espie, C. A. (2012). *The Oxford handbook of sleep and sleep disorders*. New York: Oxford University Press.

Morral, A. R., McCaffrey, D. F., & Paddock, S. M. (2002). Reassessing the marijuana gateway effect. *Addiction, 97*, 1493–1504.

Morrison, A. (1993). Cited in H. Herzog, Animal rights and wrongs. *Science, 262*, 1906–1908.

Morrongiello, B. A., & Hogg, K. (2004). Mother reactions to children misbehaving in ways that can lead to injury: Implications for gender differences in children's risk taking and injuries. *Sex Roles, 50*, 1003–1018.

Morton, S. (2004, November 1). Rare disease makes girl unable to feel pain. *Associated Press.*

Mosconi, L., Tsui, W. H., De Danti, S., Li, J., Rusinek, H., Convit, A., Li, Y., Boppana, M., & de Leon, M. J. (2005). Reduced hippocampal metabolism in MCI and AD: Automated FDG-PET image analysis. *Neurology, 64*, 1860–1867.

Moscovitch, D. A., Antony, M. A., & Swinson, R. P. (2008). Exposure-based treatments for anxiety disorders: Theory and process. In M. M. Antony & M. B. Stein (Eds.), *Oxford handbook of anxiety and related disorders* (pp. 461–475). New York: Oxford University Press.

Mosher, W. D., Chandra, A., & Jones, J. (2005, September 15). Sexual behavior and selected health measures: Men and woman 15–44 years of age, United States, 2002. *Centers for Disease Control and Prevention: Advance data from vital and health statistics,* 362.

Moss, D. (2002). The roots and genealogy of humanistic psychology. In K. J. Schneider, J. F. T. Bugental & J. F. Pierson (Eds.), *The handbook of humanistic psychology: Leading edges in theory, research, and practice*. Thousand Oaks, CA: Sage.

Mouradian, M. M. (2010). *Parkinson's disease: Methods and protocols*. New York: Humana Press.

Mozes, A. (2008, May 7). Virtual reality therapy may help PTSD patients. *U.S. News & World Report* [On-line]. Available: http://health.usnews.com/usnews/health/healthday/080507/virtual-reality-therapy-may-help-ptsd-patients.htm.

MSNBC. (2006, June 19). *Parents split on STD shot for preteens* [On-line]. Available: http://www.msnbc.com/id/12956410/.

Mudrik, L., Breska, A., Lamy, D., & Deouell, L. Y. (2011). Integration without awareness: Expanding the limits of unconscious processing. *Psychological Science, 22*(6), 764–770.

Mukhopadhyay, T. R. (2000). *Beyond the silence: My life, the world and autism*. London: The National Autistic Society.

Mukhopadhyay, T. R. (2003). *The mind tree: A miraculous child breaks the silence of autism*. New York: Arcade Publishing.

Mukhopadhyay, T. R. (2008). *How can I talk if my lips don't move: Inside my autistic mind*. New York: Arcade Publishing.

Mullin, B. C., & Hinshaw, S. P. (2007). Emotion regulation and externalizing disorders in children and adolescents. In J. J. Gross (Ed.), *Handbook of emotion regulation* (pp. 523–541). New York: Guilford Press.

Mullins, L. (2008, August 18/August 25). Tapping the brain for growth. *U.S. News & World Report*, 51–54.

Mumford, M. D., Connelly, M. S., Helton, W. B., Strange, J. M., & Osburn, H. K. (2001). On the construct validity of integrity tests: Individual and situational factors as predictors of test performance. *International Journal of Selection and Assessment, 9*, 240–257.

Mundy, L. (2012, March 26). The richer sex. *Time*, 28–34.

Mungadze, J. (2008, April 14). Cited in B. Woodruff, J. Hennessey & J. Hill, Herschel Walker: "Tell the world my truth." *ABC News.*

Munoz, H. (2003, May 30). Working to get more female police officers. *Los Angeles Times*, B2.

Munsey, C. (2006, June 6). RxP legislation made historic progress in Hawaii. *Monitor on Psychology, 37*, 42.

Munsey, C. (2008, February). Prescriptive authority in the states. *Monitor on Psychology*, 60.

Murray, H. (1943). *Thematic Apperception Test manual*. Cambridge, MA: Harvard University Press.

Murray, J. P., Liotti, M., Ingmundson, P. T., Mayberg, H. S., Pu, Y., Zamarripa, F., Liu, Y., Woldorff, M. G., Gao, J., & Fox, P. T. (2006). Children's brain activations while viewing televised violence revealed by fMRI. *Media Psychology, 8*, 25–37.

Murray, R. M., Morrison, P. D., Henquet, C., & Di Forti, M. (2007). Cannabis, the mind and society: The hash realities. *Nature Review Neuroscience, 8*, 885–895.

Murray, S. L. (2005). Regulating the risks of closeness: A relationship specific sense of felt security. *Current Directions in Psychological Science, 14*, 74–78.

Murray, S. O., Kersten, D., Olhausen, B. A., Schrater, P., & Woods, D. L. (2002). Shape perception reduces activity in human primary visual cortex. *Proceedings of the National Academy of Sciences, 99*, 15164–15169.

Musacchia, G., Sams, M., Skoe, E., & Kraus, N. (2007). Musicians have enhanced subcortical auditory and audiovisual processing of speech and music. *Proceedings of the National Academy of Sciences, 104*, 15894–15898.

Musek, J. (2007). A general factor of personality: Evidence for the Big One in the five-factor model. *Journal of Research in Personality, 41*, 1213–1233.

Musto, D. F. (1996, April). Alcohol in American history. *Scientific American*, 78–83.

Mydans, S. (2003, March 11). Clustering in cities, Asians are becoming obese. *The New York Times*, A3.

Myers, J. E. B. (Ed.). (2011). *The APSAC handbook on child maltreatment*. Thousand Oaks, CA: Sage.

Myrtek, M. (1995). Type A behavior pattern, personality factors, disease, and physiological reactivity: A metaanalytic update. *Personality and Individual Differences, 18*, 491–502.

Nagtegaal, J. E., Laurant, M. W., Kerkof, G. A., Smits, M. G., van der Meer, Y. G., & Coenen, A. M. L. (2000). Effects of melatonin on the quality of life in patients with delayed sleep phase syndrome. *Journal of Psychosomatic Research, 48*, 45–50.

Naish, P. L. N. (2006). Time to explain the nature of hypnosis? *Contemporary Hypnosis, 23*, 33–46.

Naj, A. C., Gyungah, J., Beecham. G. W., Wang, L., Vardarajan, B. N., Buros, J., Gallins, P. J., Buxbaum, J. D., Jarvik, G. P., Crane, P. K., Larson, E. G., Bird, T. D., Boeve, B. F., Graff-Radford, N. R., De Jager, P. L., Evans, D., Schneider, J. A., Carrasquillo, M. M., Ertekin-Taner, N., Younkin, S. G., Cruchaga, C., Kauwe, J. S., Nowotny, P., Kramer, P., Hardy, J., Huentelman, M. J., Myers, A. J., Barmada, M. M., Demirci, F. Y., Baldwin, C. T., Green, R. C., Rogaeva, E., St. George-Hyslop, P., Arnold, S. E., Barber, R., Beach, T., Bigio, E. H., Bowen, J. F., Boxer, A., Burke, J. R., Cairns, N. J., Carlson, C. S., Carney, R. M., Carroll, S. L., Chui, H. C., Clark, D. G., Corneveaux, J., Cotman, C. W., Cummings, J. L., DeCarli, C., DeKosky, S. T., Diaz-Arrastia, R., Dick, M., Dickson, D. W., Ellis, W. G., Faber, K. M., Fallon, K. B., Farlow, M. R., Ferris, S., Frosch, M. P., Galasko, D. R., Ganguli, M., Gearing, M., Geschwind, D. H., Ghetti, B., Gilbert, J. R., Gilman, S., Giordani, B., Glass, J. D., Growdon, J. G., Hamilton, R. L., Harrell, L. E., Head, E., Honig, L. S., Hulette, C. M., Hyman, B. T., Jicha, G. A., Jin, L. W., Johnson, N., Karlawish, J., Karydas, A., Kaye, J. A., Kim, R., Koo, E. H., Kowall, N. W., Lah, J. J., Levey, A. I., Lieberman, A. P., Lopez, O. L., Mack, W. J., Marson, D. C., Martiniuk, F., Mash, D. C., Masliah, E., McCormick, W. D., McCurry, S. M., McDavid, A. N., McKee, A. C., Mesulam, M., Miller, B. L., Miller, C. A., Miller, J. W., Parisi, J. E., Perl, D. P., Peskind, E., Petersen, R. C., Poon, W. W., Quinn, J. F., Rajbhandary, R. A., Raskind, M., Reisberg, B., Ringman, J. M., Roberson, E. D., Rosenberg, R. N., Sano, M., Schneider, L. S., Seeley, W., Shelanski, M. L., Slifer, M. A., Smith, C. D., Sonnen, J. A., Spina, S., Stern, R. A., Tanzi, R. E., Trojanowski, J. Q., Troncoso, J. C., Van Deerlin, V. M., Vinters, H. V., Vonsattel, J. P., Weintraub, S., Welsh-Bohmer, K. A., Williamson, J., Woltjer, R. L., Cantwell, L. B., Dombroski, B. A., Beekly, D., Lunetta, K. L., Martin, E. R., Kamboh, M. I., Saykin, A. J., Reiman, E. M., Bennett, D. A., Morris, J. C., Montine, T. J., Goate, A. M., Blacker, D., Tsuang, D. W., Hakonarson, H., Kukull, W. A., Foroud, T. M., Haines, J. L., Mayeux, R., Pericak-Vance, M. A., Farrer, L. A., & Schellenberg, G. D. (2011). Common variants at MS4A4/MS4A6E, CD2AP, CD33, and EPHA1 are associated with late-onset Alzheimer's disease. *Nature Genetics, 43*, 436–441.

NAMHC (National Advisory Mental Health Council). (1996). Basic behavioral science research for mental health: Perception, attention, learning, and memory. *American Psychologist, 51*, 133–142.

Nangle, D. W., Erdley, C. A., Carpenter, E. M., & Newman, J. E. (2002). Social skills training as a treatment for aggressive children and adolescents: A developmental-clinical integration. *Aggression and Violent Behavior, 7,* 169–199.

Nash, J. M. (2002, November 11). Inside the womb. *Time,* 68–78.

Nash, M. R. (2001, July). The truth and the hype of hypnosis. *Scientific American,* 47–55.

Nathan, P. E., Stuart, S. P., & Dolan, S. L. (2000). Research of psychotherapy efficacy and effectiveness: Between Scylla and Charybdis. *Psychological Bulletin, 126,* 964–981.

National Geographic. (2011). Brain works. Washington, DC: Author.

National Transportation Safety Board. (2010). *Collision of metrolink train 111 with Union Pacific train LOF65–12, Chatsworth, California, September, 12, 2008.* Railroad Accident Report NTSB/RAR-10/01. Washington, DC.

Navarro, V. M., Castellano, J. M., Garcia-Galiano, D., & Tena-Sempere, M. (2007). Neuroendocrine factors in the initiation of puberty: The emergent role of kisspeptin. *Reviews in Endocrine and Metabolic Disorders, 8,* 11–20.

NCCBH (National Council for Community Behavioral Healthcare). (2012, March 12). Cited in K. Painter, Classes teach first aid for mental health. *USA Today,* 11B.

NCHS (National Center for Health Statistics). (2010, March 3). Cited in S. Jayson, Living together first has little effect on marriage success. *USA Today,* 7D.

NCHS. (2012, April 16). Cited in N. Bakalar, Teenage birth rates continue to drop. *The New York Times.*

NCI (National Cancer Institute). (2008). *Nausea and vomiting* [On-line]. Available: http://www.cancer.gov/cancertopics/pdq/supportivecare/nausea/patient.

Neath, I., & Surprenant, A. (2013). *Human memory* (3rd ed.). Belmont, CA: Wadsworth.

Neher, A. (1991). Maslow's theory of motivation: A critique. *Journal of Humanistic Psychology, 31,* 89–112.

Neimark, J. (2009, Winter). Are recovered memories real? *Discover, 22* 28.

Neisser, U., Boodoo, G., Bouchard, T. J., Jr., Boykin, A. W., Brody, N., Ceci, S. J., Halpern, D. R., Loehlin, J. C., Perloff, R., Sternberg, R. J., & Urbina, S. (1996). Intelligence: Knowns and unknowns. *American Psychologist, 51,* 77–101.

Neitz, M., & Neitz, J. (1995). Numbers and ratios of visual pigment genes for normal red-green color vision. *Science, 267,* 1013–1016.

Nelson, C. A. (2012, March 10). Cited in L. Sanders, Scars from harsh early years linger. *Science News, 9.*

Nelson, C. A., III, Zeanah, C. H., Fox, N. A., Marshall, P. J., Smyke, A. T., & Guthrie, D. (2007). Cognitive recovery in socially deprived young children: The Bucharest early intervention project. *Science, 318,* 1937–1940.

Nelson, D. L. (2004). 5-HT5 receptors. *Current Drug Targets. CNS Neurological Disorders, 3,* 53–58.

Nelson, G., Westhues, A., & MacLeod, J. (2003). A meta analysis of longitudinal research on preschool prevention programs for children. *Prevention & Treatment, 6,* 116–133.

Nemeroff, C. G. (2007). The burden of severe depression: A review of diagnostic challenges and treatment alternatives. *Journal of Psychiatric Research, 41,* 189–206.

Nes, L. S., & Segerstrom, S. C. (2006). Dispositional optimism and coping: A meta-analytic review. *Personality and Social Psychology Review, 10,* 235–251.

Nesse, R. M. (2005). Evolutionary psychology and mental health. In D. M. Buss (Ed.), *The handbook of evolutionary psychology* (pp. 903–927). New York: Wiley.

Nestler, E. J. (2005, January 17). In M. D. Lemonick, The biology of joy. *Time,* 12–17.

Nestler, E. J. (2011, December). Hidden switches in the mind. *Scientific American,* 76–83.

Nettle, D. (2009). *Evolution and genetics for psychology.* New York: Oxford University Press.

Neugarten, B. (1994, May). Cited in B. Azar, Women are barraged by media on "the change." *APA Monitor.*

Neville, H. (2011, January 29). Neuroscience exposes pernicious effects of poverty. *Science News,* 32.

Newcomb, R. (2011, February 23). Don't forget Egypt's women. *USA Today,* 9A.

Newcombe, N. S. (2002). The nativist-empiricist controversy in the context of recent research on spatial and quantitative development. *Psychological Science, 13,* 395–401.

Newman, A. A. (2011, June 13). Schick uses scent to give men's razor a competitive edge. *The New York Times,* B4.

Newman, C. F. (2006). Bipolar disorder. In M. Hersen & J. C. Thomas (Eds.), *Comprehensive handbook of personality and psychopathology: Adult psychopathology* (Vol. 2, pp. 244–261). Hoboken, NJ: John Wiley & Sons.

Newman, L. S. (2001). A cornerstone for the science of interpersonal behavior? Person perception and person memory, past, present, and future. In G. B. Moskowitz (Ed.), *Cognitive social psychology.* Mahwah, NJ: Lawrence Erlbaum.

NHGRI (National Human Genome Research Institute). (2011). *Genetic testing* [On-line]. Available: http://www.genome.gov/10002335.

NICHD (National Institute of Child Health & Human Development). (2005). *Autism overview: What we know.* Available: http://www.nichd.nih.gov/publications/pubs/autism_overview_2005.pdf.

Nichols, M. P. (2004). *Stop arguing with your kids.* New York: Guilford Press.

Nicolelis, M. (2007, December/January). Living with ghostly limbs. *Scientific American Mind,* 52–59.

NIDA (National Institute on Drug Abuse). (2006a). Crack and cocaine. *NIDA InfoFacts.* Available: http://www.drugabuse.gov.

NIDA (National Institute of Drug Abuse). (2006b, July). Tobacco addiction. NIH Publication 06–4342.

Niebyl, J. R., & Simpson, J. L. (2012). Drugs and environmental agents in pregnancy and lactation: Embryology, teratology, epidemiology. In S. G. Gabbe, J. R. Niebyl & J. L. Simpson (Eds.). *Obstetrics: Normal and problem pregnancies* (5th ed.). Philadelphia: Elsevier.

Niemi, M. (2009, February/March). Cure in the mind. *Scientific American Mind,* 42–49.

NIH (National Institutes of Health). (2009, February). Can pets keep you healthy? *News in Health,* 1–2.

NIH. (2011). *Alzheimer's disease: Fact sheet.* NIH publication 11–6423. Washington, DC: U.S. Government Printing Office.

NIH. (2012). *Stem cell information* [On-line]. Available: http://stemcells.nih.gov/info/basics/basics10.

NIMH (National Institute of Mental Health). (2008, June/July). Cited in T. Gura, Addicted to starvation. *Scientific American Mind,* 60–67.

NIMH. (2009a). Cited in APA, Finding help: How to choose a psychotherapist. *American Psychological Association Help Center* [On-line]. Available: http://www.apahelpcenter.org/articles/article.php?id=51.

NIMH. (2009b). *Suicide in the U.S.: Statistics and prevention.* NIH Publication 06–4594.

NIMH. (2012a). *Eating disorders among adults—binge eating disorder* [On-line]. Available: http://www.nimh.nih.gov/statistics/1EAT_ADULT_RB.shtml.

NIMH. (2012b). *Eating disorders among children* [On-line]. Available: http://www.nimh.nih.gov/statistics/1EAT_CHILD.shtml.

NIMH (2012c). *The numbers count: Mental disorders in America* [On-line]. Available: http://www.nimh.nih.gov/health/publications/the-numbers-count-mental-disorders-in-america/index.shtml.

NIMH. (2012d). *Suicide in the U.S.: Statistics and prevention.* NIH Publication No. 06–4594.

NIMH. (2012e). *Women and depression: Discovering hope* [On-line]. Available: http://nimh.nih.gov/health/publications/women-and-depression-discovering-hope/what-causes-depression-in-women.shtml.

Niparko, J. K. (2009, August 17). Cited in M. B. Marcus, Giant steps for ear implants. *USA Today,* 4D.

Niparko, J. K. (2011, April 11). Cited in E. Weise, Cochlear implants can be 'magic device' if put in early enough. *USA Today,* 7D.

Niparko, J. K., Tobey, E. A., Thal, D. J., Eisenberg, L. S., Wang, N., Quittner, A. L., & Fink, N. E. (2010). Spoken language development in children following cochlear implants. *JAMA, 303,* 1498–1506.

Nisbet, M. (1998, May/June). Psychic telephone networks profit on yearning, gullibility. *Skeptical Inquirer,* 5–6.

Nisbett, R. (2000, August 8). Cited in E. Goode, How culture molds habits of thought. *The New York Times,* D1.

Nisbett, R. (2007). Eastern and western ways of perceiving the world. In Y. Shoda, D. Cervone & G. Downey (Eds.), *Persons in context: Building a science of the individual* (pp. 62–83). New York: Guilford Press.

Nisbett, R. E. (2009). *Intelligence and how to get it.* New York: W. W. Norton & Co.

Nisbett, R. E., Aronson, J., Blair, C., Dickens, W., Flynn, J., Halpern, D., & Turkheimer, E. (2012). Intelligence: New findings and theoretical developments. *American Psychologist, 67,* 130–159.

Nisbett, R. E., & Miyamoto, Y. (2005). The influence of culture: Holistic versus analytic perception. *Trends in Cognitive Sciences, 9,* 467–473.

Niznikiewicz, M. A., Kubicki, M., & Shenton, M. E. (2003). Recent structural and functional imaging findings in schizophrenia. *Current Opinion in Psychiatry, 16,* 123–147.

NLM (National Library of Medicine). (2012). *Genetic testing* [On-line]. Available: http://www.nlm.nih.gov/medlineplus/genetictesting.html.

NNDB (Notable Names Database). (2009). *Charlie Sheen* [On-line]. Available: http://www.nnbb/com/people/904/000022838/.

Nock, M. (2011, December). Deconstructing suicide. *Monitor on Psychology,* 32–34.

Noonan, D., & Cowley, G. (2002, July 15). Prozac vs. placebos. *Newsweek,* 48–49.

Norcross, J. C. (2005). A primer on psychotherapy integration. In J. C. Norcross & M. R. Goldfried (Eds.), *Handbook of psychotherapy integration* (2nd ed.). New York: Oxford University Press.

Norenzayan, A., & Nisbett, R. E. (2000). Culture and causal cognition. *Current Directions in Psychological Science, 9,* 132–135.

Noriyuki, D. (1996, February). Breaking down the walls. *Los Angeles Times,* E1.

Norman, D. A. (1982). *Learning and memory.* New York: Freeman.

Norris, R. L. (2008). Centipede envenomation. *eMedicine* [On-line]. Available: http://www.emedicine.medscape.com.

Nosofsky, R. M. (2011). The generalized context model: An exemplar model of classification. In E. M. Pothos & A. J. Willis (Eds.), *Formal approaches in categorization* (pp. 18–39). New York: Oxford University Press.

Nour, N. (2000, July 11). Cited in C. Dreifus, A life devoted to stopping the suffering of mutilation. *The New York Times,* D7.

Novotney, A. (2009a, February). Dangerous distraction. *Monitor on Psychology*, 32–36.

Novotney, A. (2009b, November). Yoga as a practice tool. *Monitor on Psychology*, 38–42.

Novotney, A. (2011, June). A new emphasis on telehealth. *Monitor on Psychology*, 40–44.

Nowak, R. (1994). Chronobiologists out of sync over light therapy patents. *Science, 263*, 1217–1218.

NSF (National Sleep Foundation). (2005). *2005 Sleep in America poll*. Washington, DC: Author.

NSF. (2006). *2006 Sleep in America poll*. Washington, DC: Author.

NSF. (2008). *2008 Sleep in America poll*. Washington, DC: Author.

NSF. (2009, July 23). Cited in J. Lloyd, Insomnia therapy: What works, what doesn't? *USA Today*, 7D.

NTSB (National Transportation Safety Board). (2012, February). The inconvenience of evidence. *Monitor on Psychology*, 39.

Nunn, J. A., Gregory, L. J., Brammer, M., Williams, S.C.R., Parslow, D. M., Morgan, M. J., Morris, R.G., Bullmore, E. T., Baron-Cohen, S., & Gray, J. A. (2002). Functional magnetic resonance imaging of synesthesia: Activation of V4/V8 by spoken words. *Nature Neuroscience, 5*, 371–375.

Nurius, P. S., & Berlin, S. S. (1994). Treatment of negative self-concept and depression. In D. K. Granvold (Ed.), *Cognitive and behavioral treatment: Methods and applications*. Pacific Grove, CA: Brooks/Cole.

NY Rock. (2002). By the way? The Chilis are back: Interview with Anthony Kiedis of the Red Hot Chili Peppers [On-line]. Available: http://www.nyrock.com /interviews/2002/chili_int2.asp.

OACU (Office of Animal Care and Use). (2012). [On-line]. Available: http://oacu.od.nih/gov/index.htm.

O'Boyle, E. H., Jr., Humphrey, R. H., Pollack, J. M., Hawver, T. H., & Story, P. A. (2010). The relation between emotional intelligence and job performance: A meta-analysis. *Journal of Organizational Behavior, 32*, 788–818.

O'Callaghan, K. (2006, August). Is it okay to spank? *Parenting*.

O'Connor, D. B., & Shimizu, M. (2002). Sense of personal control, stress and coping style: A cross-cultural study. *Stress and Health: Journal of the International Society for the Investigation of Stress, 18*, 173–183.

O'Donahue, & Fisher, J. E. (2009). *General principles and empirically supported techniques of cognitive behavior therapy*. Hoboken, NJ: John Wiley & Sons.

O'Donnell, J. (2005, March 2). What other nations do. *USA Today*.

O'Driscoll, P. (2005, February 28). Wichita cheers arrest in "BTK" killings. *USA Today*, 3A.

Oesterle, S., Hill, K. G., Hawkins, J. D., Guo, J., Catalano, R. F., & Abbott, R. D. (2004). Adolescent heavy episodic drinking trajectories and health in young adulthood. *Journal on Studies of Alcohol, 65*, 204–212.

Ogden, C. (2010, January 14). Cited in N. Hellmich, U.S. obesity rate appears to be leveling off, landmark study finds. *USA Today*, 8D.

Ogden, J. A. (2005). *Fractured minds: A case-study approach to clinical neuropsychology* (2nd ed.). New York: Oxford University Press.

Ogloff, J. R. P. (2006). Psychopathy/antisocial personality disorder continuum. *Australian and New Zealand Journal of Psychiatry, 40*, 519–528.

Ohayon, M. M., & Guilleminault, C. (2006). Epidemiology of sleep disorders. In T. L. Lee-Chiong (Ed.), *Sleep: A comprehensive handbook* (pp. 73–82). Hoboken, NJ: John Wiley & Sons.

Ohl, F. W., & Scheich. H. (2007, April/May). Chips in your head. *Scientific American Mind*, 64–69.

Ohman, A. (2002). Automaticity and the amygdala: Nonconscious responses to emotional faces. *Current Directions in Psychological Science, 11*, 62–66.

Ohman, A. (2009). Human fear conditioning and the amygdala. Cited in P. J. Whalen & E. A. Phelps (Eds.), *The human amygdala* (pp. 118–154). New York: Guilford Press.

Ojeda, S. R., Lomniczi, A., Mastronardi, C., Heger, S., Roth, C., Parent, A. S., Matagne, V., & Mungenast, A. E. (2006). The neuroendocrine regulation of puberty: Is the time ripe for a systems biology approach? *Endocrinology, 147*, 1166–1174.

Okado, Y., & Stark, C. E. L. (2005). Neural activity during encoding predicts false memories created by misinformation. *Learning & Memory, 12*, 3–11.

Oldenburg, A. (2011, February 7). Charlie Sheen's downward spiral. *USA Today*, 1D.

Olfson, M., & Marcus, S. C. (2009). National patterns in antidepressant medication treatment. *Archives of General Psychiatry, 66*, 848–856.

Ollendick, T. H., King, N. J., & Chorpita, B. F. (2006). Empirically supported treatments for children and adolescents. In P. C. Kendall (Ed.), *Child and adolescent therapy: Cognitive-behavioral procedures* (3rd ed., pp. 492–520). New York: Guilford Press.

Olshansky, J. (2003, November). Cited in K. Wright, Staying alive. *Discover*, 64–70.

Olshansky, J., Hayflick, L., & Carnes, B. A. (2002, June). No truth to the fountain of youth. *Scientific American*, 92–95.

ONDCP (Office of National Drug Control Policy). (2001). *What America's users spend on illegal drugs, 1988–2000*. Washington, DC: Author.

O'Neal, S. (2012, May 4). Shaq: Why I'm getting a doctoral degree. *USA Today*, 11A.

O'Neil, J. (2006, June 28). A warning on hazards of smoke secondhand. *The New York Times*, A14.

Onishi, N. (2001, February 12). On the scale of beauty, weight weighs heavily. *The New York Times*, A4.

Onishi, N. (2002, October 3). Globalization of beauty makes slimness trendy. *The New York Times*, A4.

Oostdam, R., & Meijer, J. (2003). Influence of test anxiety on measurement of intelligence. *Psychological Reports, 92*, 3–20.

Oprah. (2006, May 2). Teri Hatcher speaks out. *The Oprah Winfrey Show*.

O'Reardon, J. P., Solvason, H. B., Janicak, P. G., Sampson, S., Isenberg, K. E., Nahas, Z., McDonald, W. M., Avery, D., Fitzgerald, P. B., Loo, C., Demitrack, M. A., George, M. S., & Sackeim, H. A. (2007). Efficacy and safety of transcranial magnetic stimulation in the acute treatment of major depression: A multistate randomized controlled trial. *Biological Psychiatry, 62*, 1208–1216.

O'Regan, J. K., Deubel, H., Clark, J. J., & Rensink, R. A. (2000). Picture changes during blinks: Looking without seeing and seeing without looking. *Visual Cognition, 7*, 191–211.

Ortiz, B. (2005, December 12). BTK thought police wouldn't lie to him. *Herald-Leader*.

Osborne, B. J., Lio, G. T., & Newman, N. J. (2007). Cranial nerve II and afferent visual pathways. In C. G. Goetz (Ed.), *Textbook of clinical neurology* (3rd ed., pp. 113–132). Philadelphia: Saunders Elsevier.

Osborne, L. (2002, December 15). The year in ideas: Virtual-reality therapy. *The New York Times*.

Oscar-Berman, M., & Marinkovic, K. (2007). Alcohol: Effects on neurobehavioral functions and the brain. *Neuropsychology Review, 17*, 239–257.

Osofsky, J. D. (1995). The effects of exposure to violence on young children. *American Psychologist, 50*, 782–788.

Ost, L., Helstrom, K., & Kaver, A. (1992). One versus five sessions of exposure in the treatment of injection phobia. *Behavior Therapy, 23*, 263–282.

Owen, P. (2003). *Minnesota model: Description of counseling approach* [On-line]. Available: http://www .nida.nih.gov.

Ozer, D. J. (1999). Four principles for personality assessment. In L. A. Pervin & O. P. John (Eds.), *Handbook of personality* (2nd ed.), New York: Guilford Press.

Paabo, S. (2003, July 15). Cited in N. Wade, Early voices: The leap to language. *The New York Times*, D1.

Page, A. C. (2002). Nature and treatment of panic disorder. *Current Opinion in Psychiatry, 15*, 149–155.

Page, A. C. (2003). The role of disgust in faintness elicited by blood and injection stimuli. *Anxiety Disorders, 17*, 45–58.

Page, A. C., Bennett, K. S., Carter, O., Smith, M., & Woodmore, K. (1997). The blood-injection symptoms scale (BISS) assessing a structure of phobic symptoms elicited by blood and injections. *Behaviour Research and Therapy, 35*, 457–464.

Pahwa, R., & Lyons, K. E. (2003). Essential tremor: Differential diagnosis and current therapy. *American Journal of Medicine, 115*, 134–142.

Painter, K. (2011, November 22). Could you become a morning person? Yes, but it takes work. *USA Today*, 4D.

Palomaki, G. E., Deciu, C., Kloza, E. M., Lambert-Messerlian, G. M., Haddow, J. E., Neveux, L. M., Ehrich, M., van den Book, D., Bombard, A. T., Grody, W. W., Nelson, S. F., & Canick, J. A. (2012). DNA sequencing of maternal plasma reliably identifies trisomy 19 and trisomy 13 as well as Down syndrome: An international collaborative study. *Genetics in Medicine, 14*, 296–305.

Palomares, R. (2003, February). Cited in E. Benson, Intelligent intelligence testing. *Monitor on Psychology*, 48–51.

Pan, B. A., & Uccelli, P. (2009). Semantic development: Learning the meaning of words. In J. B. Gleason & N. B. Ratner (Eds.), *The development of language*. Boston, MA: Pearson.

Pandi-Perumal, S. R., Verster, J., Monti, J., & Langer, S. Z. (2008). *Sleep disorders: Diagnosis and therapeutics*. London: Informa Healthcare.

"Panic attacks." (2005, February 15). *American Family Physician*.

Panksepp, J. (2008). The affective brain and core consciousness: How does neural activity generate emotional feelings? In M. Lewis, J. M. Haviland-Jones & L. F. Barrett (Eds.), *Handbook of emotions* (3rd ed., pp. 47–67). New York: Guilford Press.

Parens, E., Chapman, A. R., & Press, N. (Eds.). (2006). *Wrestling with behavioral genetics: Science, ethics, and public conversation*. Baltimore, MD: Johns Hopkins University Press.

Park, A. (2005, August 15). The mental diet. *Time*.

Park, A. (2007, January 29). Marketing to your mind. *Time*, 114–115.

Park, A. (2010a, January 25). The man who could beat AIDS. *Time*, 44–47.

Park, A. (2010b, October 25). Alzheimer's unlocked. *Time*, 53–59.

Park, A. (2012, April 2). Pollution in utero. *Time*.

Parker, E. S., Cahill, L., & McGaugh, J. L. (2006). A case of unusual autobiographical remembering. *Neurocase, 12*, 35–49.

Parker, G. (2000). Personality and personality disorder: Current issues and directions. *Psychological Medicine, 30*, 1–9.

Parker-Pope, T. (2011, April 19). New lessons to pave a road to safety. *USA Today*, D5.

Parsons, T. D., & Rizzo, A. A. (2008). Affective outcomes of virtual reality exposure therapy for anxiety and specific phobias: A meta-analysis. *Journal of Behavior Therapy and Experimental Psychiatry, 39*, 250–261.

Partonen, T., Halonen, L., & Eloholma, M. (2011). Light exposure. In T. Partonen & S. R. Pandi-Perumal (Eds.), *Seasonal affective disorder: Practice and research*. New York: Oxford University Press.

Pascalis, O., de Haan, M., & Nelson, C. A. (2002). Is face processing species-specific during the first year of life? *Science, 296*, 1321–1323.

Patel, M. R., Piazza, C. C., Martinez, C. J., Volkert, V. M., & Santana, C. M. (2002). An evaluation of two differential reinforcement procedures with escape extinctions to treat food refusal. *Journal of Applied Behavior Analysis, 35,* 363–374.

Patrick, S. W., Schumacher, R. E., Benneyworth, B. D., Krans, E. E., McAllister, J. M., & Davis, M. M. (2012, May 9). Neonatal abstinence syndrome and associated health care expenditures: United States, 2000–2009. *JAMA, 307,* 1934–1940.

Patterson, D. R. (2010). *Clinical hypnosis for pain control.* Washington, DC: American Psychological Association.

Patterson, D. R., & Jensen, M. P. (2003). Hypnosis and clinical pain. *Psychological Bulletin, 129,* 495–521.

Patterson, T. (2006, March 8). Color commentary: FX's creepy new race-swap show. *Slate* [On-line]. Available: http://www.slate.com/id/2137734.

Patton, W. W. (1991). Opening students' eyes: Visual learning theory in the Socratic classroom. *Law and Psychology Review, 15,* 1–18.

Paul, S. M., Extein, I., Calil, H. M., Potter, W. Z., Chodoff, P., & Goodwin, F. K. (1981). Use of ECT with treatment-resistant depressed patients at the National Institute of Mental Health. *American Journal of Psychiatry, 138,* 486–489.

Paulozzi, L. J. (2006). Opioid analgesic involvement in drug abuse deaths in American metropolitan areas. *American Journal of Public Health, 96,* 1755–1757.

Payne, D. G., Toglia, M. P., & Anastasi, J. S. (1994). Recognition performance level and the magnitude of the misinformation effect in eyewitness memory. *Psychonomic Bulletin and Review, 1,* 376–382.

Payne, J. W. (2006, January 17). Cold advice: New guidelines: Don't bother with OTC cough meds. *Washington Post.*

Peake, P. K., Hebl, M., & Mischel, W. (2002). Strategic attention deployment for delay of gratification in working and waiting situations. *Developmental Psychology, 38,* 313–326.

Peele, S. (1997). Utilizing culture and behaviour in epidemiological models of alcohol consumption and consequences of western nations. *Alcohol & Alcoholism, 32,* 51–64.

Pelham, W. E., Manos, M. J., Ezzell, C. A., Tresco, K. T., Gnagy, E. M., Hoffman, M. T., Onyango, A. N., Fabiano, G. A., Lopez-Williams, A., Wymbs, B. T., Caserta, D., Chronis, A. M., Burrows-Maclean, L., & Morse, G. (2005). A dose-ranging study of a methylphenidate transdermal system in children with ADHD. *Journal of the American Academy of Child and Adolescent Psychiatry, 44,* 522–529.

Pelle, A. J., van den Broek, K. C., Szabó, B., & Kupper, N. (2009, May 22). The relationship between Type D personality and chronic heart failure is not confounded by disease severity as assessed by BNP. *International Journal of Cardiology.*

Peltzer, D. (1995). *A child called "it."* Deerfield Beach, FL: Health Communications.

Peltzer, D. (1997). *The lost boy: A foster child's search for the love of a family.* Deerfield Beach, FL: Health Communications.

Peltzer, D. (1999). *A man named Dave: A story of triumph and forgiveness.* New York: Penguin.

Peltzer, D. (2000). *Help yourself: Celebrating the rewards of resilience and gratitude.* New York: Penguin.

Peltzer, D. (2003). Cited in M. Peltzer, *The self-made man behind the marvel* [On-line]. Available: http://www.bookbrowse.com/author_interviews/full/index.cfm?author_number=145.

Peltzer, D. (2009). *About Dave* [On-line]. Available: www.davepeltzer.com.

Pemberton. R. W. (2005). Contemporary use of insects and other arthropods in traditional Korean medicine (Hanbang) in South Korea and elsewhere. In M. G. Paoletti (Ed.), *Ecological implications of minilivestock.* Plymouth, UK: Science Publishers.

Peng, T. (2008a, March 24). No Buddha required. *Newsweek,* 71.

Peng, T. (2008b, August 18). A summer caffeine rush. *Newsweek,* 63.

Penley, J. A., Tomaka, J., & Wiebe, J. S. (2002). The association of coping to physical and psychological health outcomes: A meta-analytic review. *Journal of Behavioral Medicine, 25,* 551–603.

Pennebaker, J. W., Colder, M., & Sharp, L. (1990). Accelerating the coping process. *Journal of Personality and Social Psychology, 58,* 528–537.

People. (2010, January 15). Lady Gaga suffers from exhaustion, postpones show [On-line]. Available: http://www.people.com/people/article/0,,20337272,00.html.

People. (2011, September 26). Michael J. Fox back to tv, 30.

People. (2012, April 9). Whitney Houston's final moments, 27.

Perlis, M. L., Smith, M. T., Cacialli, D. O., Nowakowski, S., & Orff, H. (2003). On the comparability of pharmacotherapy and behavior therapy for chronic insomnia: Commentary and implications. *Journal of Psychosomatic Research, 54,* 51–59.

Perloff, R. M. (2002). *The dynamics of persuasion.* Mahwah, NJ: Lawrence Erlbaum.

Perron, H., Mekaoui, L., Bernard, C., Veas, F., Stefas, I., & Leboyer, M. (2008). Endogenous retrovirus type W GAG and envelope protein antigenemia in serum of schizophrenic patients. *Biological Psychiatry, 64,* 1019–1023.

Persons, J. B. (1997). Dissemination of effective methods: Behavior therapy's next challenge. *Behavior Therapy, 28,* 465–471.

Pert, C. B., Snowman, A. M., & Snyder, S. H. (1974). Localization of opiate receptor binding in presynaptic membranes of rat brain. *Brain Research, 70,* 184–188.

Pertea, M., & Salzberg, S. L. (2010). Between a chicken and a grape: Estimating the number of human genes. *Genome Biology, 11,* 206.

Perusse, D., & Gendreau, P. L. (2005). Genetics and the development of aggression. In R. E. Tremblay, W. W. Hartup & J. Archer (Eds.), *Developmental origins of aggression* (pp. 223–241). New York: Guilford Press.

Pesant, N., & Zadra, A. (2006). Dream content and psychological well-being: A longitudinal study of the continuity hypothesis. *Journal of Clinical Psychology, 62,* 111–121.

Pesonen, A. K., Raikkonen, K., Keskivaara, P., & Keltifkangas-Jarvinen, L. (2003). Difficult temperament in childhood and adulthood: Continuity from maternal perceptions to self-ratings over 17 years. *Personality and Individual Differences, 34,* 19–31.

Pessoa, L., & Ungerleider, L. G. (2004). Top-down mechanisms for working memory and attentional processes. In M. S. Gazzaniga (Ed.), *The cognitive neurosciences III.* Cambridge, MA: MIT Press.

Peters, R. M., Hackeman, E., & Goldreich, D. (2009). Diminutive digits discern delicate details: Fingertip size and the sex difference in tactile spatial acuity. *Journal of Neuroscience, 29,* 15756–15761.

Peterson, L. R., & Peterson, M. J. (1950). Short-term retention of individual verbal terms. *Journal of Experimental Psychology, 58,* 193–198.

Peterson, M. A., Gillam, B., & Sedgwick, H. A. (2007). *In the mind's eye: Julian Hockberg on the perception of pictures, films, and the world.* New York: Oxford University Press.

Petitto, L. A. (1997, December 11). Cited in R. L. Hotz, The brain: Designed to speak the mind. *Los Angeles Times.*

Petitto, L. A., Berens, M. S., Kovelman, I., Dubins, M. H., & Shalinsky, M. (2012). The "perceptual wedge hypothesis" as the basis for bilingual babies' phonetic processing advantage: New insights from fNIRS brain imaging. *Brain Language, 121,* 130–143.

Petri, H. L., & Govern, J. M. (2004). *Motivation* (5th ed.). Belmont, CA: Wadsworth.

Petri, H. L., & Govern, J. M. (2012). *Motivation: Theory, research, and application* (6th ed.). Belmont, CA: Wadsworth.

Petrides, K. V., Furnham, A., & Martin, G. N. (2004). Estimates of emotional and psychometric intelligence: Evidence for gender-based stereotypes. *Journal of Social Psychology, 144,* 149–162.

Petrill, S. A. (2003). The development of intelligence: Behavioral genetic approaches. In R. J. Sternberg, J. Lautrey & T. I. Lubart (Eds.), *Models of intelligence.* Washington, DC: American Psychological Association.

Petrovic, P., Kalso, E., Petersson, K. M., & Ingvar, M. (2002). Placebo and opioid analgesia—imaging a shared neuronal network. *Science, 295,* 1737–1740.

Petty, R. E., & Briñol, P. (2012). The elaboration likelihood model. In P. A. M. Van Lange, A. W. Kruglanski & E. T. Higgins (Eds.), *Handbook of theories of social psychology* (Vol. 1, pp. 224–245). Thousand Oaks, CA: Sage.

Petty, R. E., & Cacioppo, J. T. (1986). *Attitudes and persuasion: Classic and contemporary approaches.* Dubuque, IA: William C. Brown.

Petty, R. E., Tormala, Z. L., Briñol, P., & Jarvis, W. B. G. (2006). Implicit ambivalence from attitude change: An exploration of the PAST model. *Journal of Personality and Social Psychology, 90,* 21–41.

Petty, R. E., Wegener, D. T., & Fabrigar, L. R. (1997). Attitudes and attitude change. *Annual Review of Psychology, 46,* 609–647.

Peverly, S. T., Brobst, K. E., Graham, M., & Shaw, R. (2003). College adults are not good at self-regulation: A study on the relationship of self-regulation, note taking, and test taking. *Journal of Educational Psychology, 95,* 335–346.

Pew Research Center. (2012, April 20). Cited in L. Petrecca, High-paying careers top more young women's lists. *USA Today,* 1A.

Pezdek, K. (1995, February 11). Cited in M. Dolan, When the mind's eye blinks. *Los Angeles Times.*

Phelps, L. (2010, May/June). Cited in M. Webster, Extinguishing fear. *Scientific American Mind,* 8.

Phillips, M. L. (2011, April). The mind at midlife. *Monitor on Psychology, 38.* 113.

Pi-Sunyer, X. (2003). A clinical view of the obesity problem. *Science, 299,* 859–860.

Piaget, J. (1929). *The child's conception of the world.* New York: Harcourt Brace.

Picchioni, D., Goeltzenleucher, B., Green, D. N., Convento, M. J., Crittenden, R., Hallgren, M., & Hicks, R. A. (2002). Nightmares as a coping mechanism for stress. *Dreaming, 12,* 155–169.

Pierce, B. H. (1999). An evolutionary perspective on insight. In D. H. Rosen & M. D. Luebbert (Eds.), *Evolution of the psyche. Human evolution, behavior, and intelligence.* Westport, CT: Praeger/Greenwood Publishing.

Piliavin, J. A., Dovidio, J. F., Gaertner, S. L., & Clark, R. D. (1982). Responsive bystanders: The process of intervention. In V. J. Derlega & J. Grzelak (Eds.), *Cooperation and helping behavior.* Orlando, FL: Academic Press.

Pincus, T., & Morley, S. (2001). Cognitive-processing bias in chronic pain: A review and integration. *Psychological Bulletin, 127,* 599–617.

Pinker, S. (1994). *The language instinct.* New York: William Morrow.

Pinker, S. (1995). Introduction. In M. S. Gazzaniga (Ed.), *The cognitive neurosciences.* Cambridge, MA: MIT Press.

Pinker, S. (2000, April 10). Will the mind figure out how the brain works? *Time,* 90–91.

Pinker, S. (2002). *The blank slate: The modern denial of human nature.* New York: Penguin.

Pinker, S. (2008, January 13). The moral instinct. *The New York Times*.

Pinto, D., Pagnamenta. A. T., Klei, L., Anney, R., Merico, D., Regan, R., Conroy, J., Magalhaes, T. R., Correia, C., Abrahams, B. S., Almeida, J., Bacchelli, E., Bader, G. D., Bailey, A. J., Baird, G., Battaglia, A., Berney, T., Bolshakova, N., Bölte, S., Bolton, P. F., Bourgeron, T., Brennan, S., Brian, J., Bryson, S. E., Carson, A. R., Casallo, G., Casey, J., Chung, B. H., Cochrane, L., Corsello, C., Crawford, E. L., Crossett, A., Cytrynbaum, C., Dawson, G., de Jonge, M., Delorme, R., Drmic, I., Duketis, E., Duque, F., Estes, A., Farrar, P., Fernandez, B. A., Folstein, S. E., Fombonne, E., Freitag, C. M., Gilbert, J., Gillberg, C., Glessner, J. T., Goldberg, J., Green, A., Green, J., Guter, S. J., Hakonarson, H., Heron, E. A., Hill, M., Holt, R., Howe, J. L., Hughes, G., Hus, V., Igliozzi, R., Kim, C., Klauck, S. M., Kolevzon, A., Korvatska, O., Kustanovich, V., Lajonchere, C. M., Lamb, J. A., Laskawiec, M., Leboyer, M., Le Couteur, A., Leventhal, B. L., Lionel, A. C., Liu, X. Q., Lord, C., Lotspeich, L., Lund, S. C., Maestrini, E., Mahoney, W., Mantoulan, C., Marshall, C. R., McConachie, H., McDougle, C. J., McGrath, J., McMahon, W. M., Merikangas, A., Migita, O., Minshew, N. J., Mirza, G. K., Munson, J., Nelson, S. F., Noakes, C., Noor, A., Nygren, G., Oliveira, G., Papanikolaou, K., Parr, J. R., Parrini, B., Paton, T., Pickles, A., Pilorge, M., Piven, J., Ponting, C. P., Posey, D. J., Poustka. A., Poustka, F., Prasad, A., Ragoussis, J., Renshaw, K., Rickaby, J., Roberts, W., Roeder, K., Roge, B., Rutter, M. L., Bierut, L. J., Rice, J. P., Salt, J., Sansom, K., Sato, D., Segurado, R., Sequeira, A. F., Senman, L., Shah, N., Sheffield, V. C., Soorya, L., Sousa, I., Stein, O., Sykes, N., Stoppioni, V., Strawbridge, C., Tancredi, R., Tansey, K., Thiruvahindrapduram, B., Thompson, A. P., Thomson, S., Tryfon, A., Tsiantis, J., Van Engeland, H., Vincent, J. B., Volkmar, F., Wallace, S., Wang, K., Wang, Z., Wassink, T. H., Webber, C., Weksberg, R., Wing, K., Wittemeyer, K., Wood, S., Wu, J., Yaspan, B. L., Zurawiecki, D., Zwaigenbaum, L., Buxbaum, J. D., Cantor, R. M., Cook, E. H., Coon, H., Cuccaro, M. L., Devlin, B., Ennis, S., Gallagher, L., Geschwind, D. H., Gill, M., Haines, J. L., Hallmayer, J., Miller, J., Monaco, A. P., Nurnberger, J. I. Jr,, Paterson, A. D., Pericak-Vance, M. A., Schellenberg, G. D., Szatmari, P., Vicente, A. M., Vieland, V. J., Wijsman, E. M., Scherer, S. W., Sutcliffe, J. S., & Betancur, C. (2010). Functional impact of global rare copy number variation in autism spectrum disorders. *Nature, 466*, 368–372.

Piomelli, D. (1999). Cited in J. Travis, Marijuana mimic reveals brain role. *Science News, 155*, 215.

Piore, A. (2012, January/February). Totaling recall. *Scientific American Mind*, 40–45.

Pisano, E. D., Gatsonis, C., Hendrick, E., Yaffe, M., Baum, J. K., Acharyya, S., Conant, E. F., Fajardo, L. L., Bassett, L., D'Orsi, C., Jong, R., & Rebner, M. (2005). Diagnostic performance of digital versus film mammography for breast-cancer screening. *New England Journal of Medicine, 353*, 1773–1783.

Pittman, J. F., & Buckley, R. R. (2006). Comparing maltreating fathers and mothers in terms of personal distress, interpersonal functioning, and perceptions of family climate. *Child Abuse & Neglect, 30*, 481–496.

Pittman, M. (2007). *Helping pupils with autistic spectrum disorders*. London: Paul Chapman Publishing.

Plagnol, A. C., & Easterlin, R. A. (2008). Aspirations, attainments, and satisfaction: Life cycle differences between American women and men. *Journal of Happiness Studies, 9*, 601–619.

Plante, T. G. (2011). *Contemporary clinical psychology*. Hoboken, NJ: John Wiley & Sons.

Pleuvry, B. J. (2005). Opioid mechanisms and opioid drugs. *Anaesthesia and Intensive Care Medicine, 6*, 30–34.

Ploghaus, A., Becerra, L., Borras, C., & Borsook, D. (2003). Neural circuitry underlying pain modulation: Expectation, hypnosis, placebo. *Trends in Cognitive Science, 7*, 197–200.

Plomin, R., & Crabbe, J. (2000). DNA. *Psychological Bulletin, 126*, 806–828.

Plomin, R., & Petrill, S. A. (1997). Genetics and intelligence: What's new? *Intelligence, 24*, 53–77.

Plomin, R., & Spinath, F. M. (2004). Intelligence: Genetics, genes, and genomics. *Journal of Personality and Social Psychology, 86*, 112–129.

Ployhart, R. E., Ehrhart, K. H., & Hayes, S. C. (2005). Using attributions to understand the effects of explanations on applicant reactions: Are reactions consistent with the covariation principle? *Journal of Applied Social Psychology, 35*, 259–296.

Plummer, W., & Ridenhour, R. (1995, August 28). Saving grace. *People*.

Polaschek, D. L. L., Ward, T., & Hudson, S. M. (1997). Rape and rapists: Theory and treatment. *Clinical Psychology Review, 17*, 117–144.

Polivy, J., & Herman, C. P. (2002). Causes of eating disorders. *Annual Review of Psychology, 53*, 187–213.

Pollack, W. (2007, April 30). Cited in S. Begley, The anatomy of violence. *Newsweek*, 40–46.

Porto, P. R., Oliveira, L., Mari, J., Volchan, E., Figueira, I., & Ventura, P. (2009). Does cognitive behavioral therapy change the brain? A systematic review of neuroimaging in anxiety disorders. *Journal of Neuropsychiatry & Clinical Neurosciences, 21*, 114–125.

Post, S. (2005). Altruism, happiness, and health: It's good to be good. *International Journal of Behavioral Medicine, 2*, 66–77.

Potter, J. (2006). Female sexuality: Assessing satisfaction and addressing problems. In D. C. Dale & D. D. Federman (Eds.), *ACP medicine*. New York: WebMD Professional Publishing.

Prentice, D. A., & Carranza, E. (2002). What women and men should be, shouldn't be, are allowed to be, and don't have to be: The contents of prescriptive gender stereotypes. *Psychology of Women Quarterly, 26*, 269–281.

Preston, R. (2008, January 22). Meet the smartest man in America. *KMOV* [On-line]. Available: http://www.kmov.com/featuredstories/stories/kmov_localnews_061115_genius.3f6953ad.html.

Price, D. D., Finniss, D. G., & Benedetti, F. (2008). A comprehensive review of the placebo effect: Recent advances and current thought. *Annual Review of Psychology, 59*, 565–590.

Price, J. (2008). *The woman who can't forget*. New York: Free Press.

Price, M. (2008a, April). Caffeine's wake-up call. *Monitor on Psychology*, 26–27.

Price, M. (2008b, June). Genes matter in addiction. *Monitor on Psychology*, 16.

Priester, J. R., & Petty, R. E. (1995). Source attributions and persuasion: Perceived honesty as a determinant of message scrutiny. *Personality and Social Psychology Bulletin, 21*, 637–654.

Prochaska, J. O., & Norcross, J. C. (2010). *Systems of psychotherapy* (7th ed.). Belmont, CA: Brooks/Cole.

Project Match Research Group. (1997). Matching alcoholism treatments to client heterogeneity: Project MATCH posttreatment drinking outcomes. *Journal of Studies on Alcohol, 58*, 7–29.

Pruitt, D. G. (1971). Choice shifts in group discussion: An introductory review. *Journal of Personality and Social Psychology, 20*, 339–360.

Pullum, G. K. (1991). *The great Eskimo vocabulary hoax*. Chicago: University of Chicago Press.

Purves, D., Augustine, G. J., Fitzpatrick, D., Hall, W. C., LaMantia, A., McNamara, J. O., & White, L. E. (2008). *Neuroscience* (4th ed.). Sunderland, MA: Sinauer Associates.

Purves, D., Augustine, G. J., Fitzpatrick, D., Hall, W. C., LaMantia, A., & White, L. E. (Eds.). (2012). *Neuroscience* (5th ed.). Sunderland, MA: Sinauer Associates.

Putnam, S. (2005, April 4). Cited in J. Kluger, Secrets of the shy. *Time*, 50–52.

Pychyl, T. A., Coplan, R. J., & Reid, P. A. M. (2002). Parenting and procrastination: Gender differences in the relations between procrastination, parenting style and self-worth in early adolescence. *Personality and Individual Differences, 33*, 271–285.

Querna, E. (2004, October 12). Teenagers and alcohol: Teen drinking linked to health problems in young adults. *U.S. News & World Report*.

Quill, E. (2009, January 17). It's written all over your face. *Science News*, 24–28.

Quinn, P. C. (2002). Category representation in young infants. *Current Directions in Psychological Science, 11*, 66–70.

Quinn, P. C., Bhatt, R. S., & Hayden, A. (2008). Young infants readily use proximity to organize visual pattern information. *Acta Psychologica, 127*, 289–298.

Quinn, P. C., & Oates, J. (2004). Early category representation and concepts. In J. Oates & A. Grayson (Eds.), *Cognitive and language development in children* (pp. 21–60). Malden, MA: Blackwell Publishing.

Quirk, G. J. (2007). Prefrontal-amygdala interactions in the regulation of fear. In J. J. Gross (Ed.), *Handbook of emotion regulation* (pp. 27–46). New York: Guilford Press.

Rabasca, L. (1999, December). Not enough evidence to support "abstinence-only." *Monitor of American Psychological Association, 39*.

Rabasca, L. (2000a, March). Humanistic psychologists look to revamp their image. *Monitor on Psychology*, 54–55.

Rabasca, L. (2000b, November). In search of equality. *Monitor on Psychology*, 30–31.

Rabkin, S. W., Boyko, E., Shane, F., & Kaufert, J. (1984). A randomized trial comparing smoking cessation programs utilizing behavior modification, health education or hypnosis. *Addictive Behaviors, 9*, 157–173.

Rahman, O., & Wilson, G. (2008). *Born gay: The psychobiology of sex orientation*. London: Peter Owen Ltd.

Raine, A. (2002). Biosocial studies of antisocial and violent behavior in children and adults: A review. *Journal of Abnormal Child Psychology, 30*, 311–326.

Raine, A., Ishikawa, S. S., Arce, E., Lencz, T., Knuth, K. H., Bihrie, S., LaCasse, L., & Colletti, P. (2004). Hippocampal structural asymmetry in unsuccessful psychopaths. *Biological Psychiatry, 55*, 185–191.

Raine, A., Lencz, T., Bihrle, S., LaCasse, L., & Colletti, P. (2000). Reduced prefrontal gray matter volume and reduced autonomic activity in antisocial personality disorder. *Archives of General Psychiatry, 57*, 119–127.

Raine, A., Reynolds, C., Venables, P. H., & Mednick, S. A. (2002). Stimulation seeking and intelligence: A prospective longitudinal study. *Journal of Personality and Social Psychology, 82*, 663–674.

Raine, R. (2002, April 29). Cited in J. Foreman, Roots of violence may lie in damaged brain cells. *Los Angeles Times*, S1.

Rainville, P., Duncan, G. H., Price, D. D., Carrier, B., & Bushnell, M. C. (1997). Pain affect encoded in human anterior cingulated but not somatosensory cortex. *Science, 277*, 968–971.

Rajaratnam, S. M. W., Polymeropoulos, M. H., Fisher, D. M., Roth, T., Scott, C., Birznieks, G., & Klerman, E. B. (2009). Melatonin agonist tasimelteon (VEC-162) for transient insomnia after sleep-time shift: Two randomised controlled multicentre trials. *The Lancet, 373*, 482–491.

Raloff, J. (2007, July 7). Restoring scents. *Science News, 172*, 10–12.

Raloff, J. (2011, February 26). Brain boosters. *Science News*, 26–29.

Ramachandran, V. S. (2006, April/May). Cited in M. Solms, Freud returns. *Scientific American Mind, 28–34.*

Ramachandran, V. S., & Anstis, S. M. (1986). The perception of apparent motion. *Scientific American, 254,* 102–109.

Ramachandran, V. S., & Oberman, L. M. (2006, November). Broken mirrors: A theory of autism. *Scientific American,* 63–69.

Ramachandran, V. S., & Rogers-Ramachandran, D. (2007, February/March). A moving experience. *Scientific American Mind,* 14–16.

Ramachandran, V. S., & Rogers-Ramachandran, D. (2008). Sensations referred to a patient's phantom arm from another subject's intact arm: Perceptual correlates of mirror neurons. *Medical Hypotheses, 70,* 1233–1234.

Ramirez, G., & Beilock, S. L. (2011). Writing about testing worries boosts exam performance in the classroom. *Science, 331,* 211–213.

Ramsden, S., Richardson, F. M., Josse, G., Thomas, M. S. C., Ellis, C., Shakeshaft, C., Seghier, M. L., & Price, C. J. (2011). Verbal and non-verbal intelligence changes in the teenage brain. *Nature, 479,* 113–116.

Rana, R. A., & Mahmood, N. (2010). The relationship between test anxiety and academic achievement. *Bulletin of Education and Research, 32,* 63–74.

Randi. J. (2005). 'Twas brillig ...: Million dollar excuses, Dutch psychic caught cheating, Sylvia Browne and the Virginia miners, from the JREF museum. *Skeptic.*

Randi, J. (2009). 'Twas brillig ...: Prayer and pregnancy; shooting UFO photos. *Skeptic, 14.*

Rapson, R., & Hatfield, R. L. (2005). *Love and sex: Cross-cultural perspectives.* Lanham, MD: University Press of America.

Ras-Work, B. (2006, June 2). Cited in L. MacInnis, Genital cutting's fatal results cited. *San Diego Union-Tribune,* A16.

Raskin, M. K. (2010, July/August). When passion is the enemy. *Scientific American Mind,* 44–51.

Raskin, M. K. (2011, May/June). The idea that wouldn't die. *Psychology Today,* 78–85.

Rasmussen, C., Knapp, T. J., & Garner, L. (2000). Driving-induced stress in urban college students. *Perceptual and Motor Skills, 90,* 437–443.

Ratcliff, R., & McKoon, G. (2005). Memory models. In E. Tulving & F. M. Craik (Eds.), *The Oxford handbook of memory.* New York: Oxford University Press.

Ray, L. A., & Hutchinson, K. E. (2007). Effects of naltrexone on alcohol sensitivity and genetic moderators of medication response: A double-blind-placebo-controlled study. *Archives of General Psychiatry, 64,* 1067–1077.

Reardon, S. (2011, July 1). Antismoking drive tries cigarette ads, in reverse. *Science, 333,* 23–24.

Reddy, M. M., Wilson, R., Wilson, J., Connell, S., Gocke, A., Hynan, L., German, D., & Kodadek, T. (2011). Identification of candidate IgB biomarkers for Alzheimer's disease via combinatorial library screening. *Cell, 144,* 132–142.

Reder, L. M., Park, H., & Kieffaber, P. D. (2009). Memory systems do not divide on consciousness: Reinterpreting memory in terms of activation and binding. *Psychological Bulletin, 135,* 23–49.

Reed, M. K. (1994). Social skills training to reduce depression in adolescents. *Adolescence, 29,* 293–302.

Reed, S., & Breu, G. (1995, June 6). The wild ones. *People.*

Reed, S., & Cook, D. (1993, April 19). Realm of the senses. *People.*

Reed, S., & Free, C. (1995, October 16). The big payoff. *People.*

Reed, S., & Stambler, L. (1992, May 25). The umpire strikes back. *People,* 87–88.

Reeves, G. M., Nijjar, G. V., Langenberg, P., Johnson, M. A., Khabazghazvini, B., Sleemi, A., Vaswani, D., Lapidus, M., Manalai, P., Tarig, M., Acharya, M., Cabassa, J., Snitker, S., & Postolache, T. T. (2012). Improvement in depression scores after 1 hour of light therapy treatment in patients with seasonal affective disorder. *Journal of Nervous & Mental Disease, 200,* 51–55.

Regier, D. A., Narrow, W. E., Kuhl, E. A., & Kupfer, D. J. (2009). The conceptual development of the DSM-V. *American Journal of Psychiatry, 166,* 645–650.

Reichert, B. (2008, August 1). German farmer gets world's first double arm transplant. *The Guardian.*

Reid, J. B., Taplin, P. S., & Lorber, R. (1981). A social interactional approach to the treatment of abusive families. In R. B. Stuart (Ed.), *Violent behavior: Social learning approaches to prediction, management and treatment.* New York: Brunner/Mazel.

Reilly, S., & Schachtman, T. R. (Eds.). (2009). *Conditioned taste aversion: Neural and behavioral processes.* New York: Oxford University Press.

Reinders, A. A. T. S., Nijenhuis, E. R. S., Quak, J., Korf, J., Haaksma, J., Paans, A. M. J., Willemsen, A. T. M., & den Boer, J. A. (2006). Psychobiological characteristics of dissociative identity disorder: A symptom provocation study. *Biological Psychiatry, 60,* 730–740.

Reitman, V. (1999, February 22). Learning to grin—and bear it. *Los Angeles Times,* A1.

Renfrey, G., & Spates, C. R. (1994). Eye movement desensitization: A partial dismantling study. *Journal of Behavior Therapy and Experimental Psychiatry, 25,* 231–239.

Rentfrow, P. J. (2010, September). Statewide difference in personality. *American Psychologist, 65,* 548–558.

Rentfrow, P. J., Gosling, S. D., & Potter, J. (2008). A theory of the emergence, persistence, and expression of geographic variation in psychological characteristics. *Perspectives on Psychological Science, 3,* 339–369.

Rescorla, R. A. (1966). Predictability and number of pairings in Pavlovian fear conditioning. *Psychonomic Science, 4,* 383–384.

Rescorla, R. A. (1987). A Pavlovian analysis of goal-directed behavior. *American Psychologist, 42,* 119–129.

Rescorla, R. A. (1988). Pavlovian conditioning. *American Psychologist, 43,* 151–160.

Resick, P. A., Monson, C. M., & Rizvi, S. L. (2008). Post-traumatic stress disorder. In D. H. Barlow (Ed.), *Clinical handbook of psychological disorders* (4th ed., pp. 65–122). New York: Guilford Press.

Reuter-Lorenz, P. (2011, April). Cited in M. L. Phillips, The mind at midlife. *Monitor on Psychology,* 38–41.

Revonsuo, A. (2000a). The reinterpretation of dreams: An evolutionary hypothesis of the function of dreaming. *Behavioral and Brain Sciences, 23,* 877–901.

Revonsuo, A. (2000b). Did ancestral humans dream for their lives? *Behavioral and Brain Sciences, 23,* 1063–1082.

Rey, G. (1983). Concepts and stereotypes. *Cognition, 15,* 237–262.

Reyna, V. F., Chapman, S. B., Dougherty, M. R., & Confrey, J. (2011). *The adolescent brain: Learning, reasoning, and decision making.* Washington, DC: American Psychological Association.

Reyner, L. A., & Horne, J. A. (2000). Early morning driver sleepiness: Effectiveness of 200 mg caffeine. *Psychophysiology, 7,* 251–256.

Rhee, S. H., & Waldman, I. D. (2002). Genetic and environmental influences on antisocial behavior: A meta-analysis of twin and adoption studies. *Psychological Bulletin, 128,* 490–529.

Rhodewalt, F., & Vohs, K. D. (2005). Defensive strategies, motivation, and the self. In A. J. Elliot & C. S. Dweck (Eds.), *Handbook of competence and motivation* (pp. 548–565). New York: Guilford Press.

Riccio, D. C., Millin, P. M., & Gisquet-Verier, P. (2003). Retrograde amnesia: Forgetting back. *Current Directions in Psychological Science, 12,* 41–44.

Rice, L. (2012, March 2). Actors with down syndrome. *Entertainment Weekly,* 48–54.

Rich, D. Q., Demissie, K., Lu, S-E., Kamat, L., Wartenberg, D., & Rhoads, G. G. (2009). Ambient air pollutant concentrations during pregnancy and the risk of fetal growth restriction. *Journal of Epidemiology and Community Health, 63,* 488–496.

Ridderinkhof, K. R., de Vlugt, Y., Bramlage, A., Spaan, M., Elton, M., Snel, J., & Band, G. P. H. (2002). Alcohol consumption impairs detection of performance errors in mediofrontal cortex. *Science, 298,* 2209–2211.

Riddle, E. L., Fleckenstein, A. E., & Hanson, G. R. (2006). Mechanisms of methamphetamine-induced dopaminergic neurotoxicity. *American Association of Pharmaceutical Scientists Journal, 8,* E413–418.

Rieke, M. L., & Guastello, S. J. (1995). Unresolved issues in honesty and integrity testing. *American Psychologist, 50,* 458–459.

Riggs, D. S., & Foa, E. B. (2006). Obsessive-compulsive disorder. In M. Hersen & J. C. Thomas (Eds.), *Comprehensive handbook of personality and psychopathology: Adult psychopathology* (Vol. 2, pp. 169–188). Hoboken, NJ: John Wiley & Sons.

Riley, E. P., Infante, M. A., & Warren, K. R. (2011). Fetal alcohol spectrum disorders: An overview. *Neuropsychology Review, 21,* 73–80.

Rimland, B. (1964). *Infantile autism.* New York: Appleton-Century-Crofts.

Ripley, A. (2010, April 19). Is cash the answer? *Time,* 40–47.

Rizzo, A. (2006, August 21). Cited in B. Streisand, Not just child's play. *U.S. News & World Report,* 48–50.

Rizzo, A., Reger, G., Gahm, G., Difede, J., & Rothbaum, B. O. (2009). Virtual reality exposure therapy for combat-related PTSD. In P. J. Shiromani, T. M. Keane & J. E. LeDoux (Eds.), *Post-traumatic stress disorder: Basic science and clinical practice.* New York: Humana Press.

Rizzo, S. (2008, October). In K. McAuliffe, Interview: Virtual therapist. *Discover,* 58.

Rizzolatti, G. (2011, July/August). Cited in E. Jaffe, Keynote address: Reflecting on behavior. *Association for Psychological Science, 24*(6), 10–11.

Rizzolatti, G., Fogassi, L., & Gallese, V. (2006, November). In the mind. *Scientific American,* 54–61.

Roa, J., Aguilar, E., Dieguez, C., Pinilla, L., & Tena-Sempere, M. (2008). New frontiers in kisspeptin/GPR54 physiology as fundamental gatekeepers of reproductive function. *Frontiers in Neuroendocrinology, 29,* 48–69.

Robbins, J. (2000, July 4). Virtual reality finds a real place as a medical aid. *The New York Times,* D6.

Robbins, T. W. (2011, October). Cited in S. F. Dingfelder. The dangers of stimulants. *Monitor on Psychology,* 58–59.

Roberson, E. D. (Ed.). (2011). *Alzheimer's disease and frontotemporal dementia: Methods and protocols.* New York: Humana Press.

Roberts, B. W., Helson, R., & Klohnen, E. V. (2002). Personality development and growth in women across 30 years: Three perspectives. *Journal of Personality, 70,* 79–102.

Roberts, B. W., Walton, K. E., & Viechtbauer, W. (2006). Patterns of mean-level change in personality traits across the life course: A meta-analysis of longitudinal studies. *Psychological Bulletin, 132,* 1–25.

Robertz, F. J. (2007, August/September). Deadly dreams. *Scientific American Mind,* 52–59.

Robichaud, M., Dugas, M. J., & Conway, M. (2003). Gender differences in worry and associated cognitive-behavioral variables. *Anxiety Disorders, 17,* 501–516.

Robinson, J. P., & Martin, S. P. (2007, October). Not so deprived: Sleep in America, 1965–2005. *Public Opinion Pros* [On-line]. Available: http://www.publicopinionpros.com.

Robinson-Riegler, B., & McDaniel, M. A. (1994). Further constraints on the bizarreness effect: Elaboration at encoding. *Memory and Cognition, 22,* 702–712.

Rochat, P. (2003). Five levels of self-awareness as they unfold early in life. *Consciousness and Cognition, 12,* 171–181.

Rodafinos, A., Vucevic, A., & Sideridis, G. D. (2005). The effectiveness of compliance techniques: Foot in the door versus door in the face. *Journal of Social Psychology, 145,* 237–239.

Roediger, H. L., & McDermott, K. B. (2005). Distortions of memory. In E. Tulving & F. M. Craik (Eds.), *The Oxford handbook of memory.* New York: Oxford University Press.

Roffman, J. L., Marci, C. D., Glick, D. M., Dougherty, D. D., & Rauch, S. L. (2005). Neuroimaging and the functional neuroanatomy of psychotherapy. *Psychological Medicine, 35,* 1385–1398.

Rogers, C. R. (1951). *Client-centered therapy: Its current practice, implications, and theory.* Boston: Houghton Mifflin.

Rogers, C. R. (1980). *A way of being.* Boston: Houghton Mifflin.

Rogers, C. R. (1986). Client-centered therapy. In I. L. Kutash & A. Wolf (Eds.), *Psychotherapists' casebook.* San Francisco: Jossey-Bass.

Rogers, C. R. (1989). Cited in N. J. Raskin & C. R. Rogers, Person-centered therapy. In R. J. Corsini & D. Wedding (Eds.), *Current psychotherapies* (4th ed.). Itasca, IL: F. E. Peacock.

Rogers, M. R., & Molina, L. E. (2006). Exemplary efforts in psychology to recruit and retain graduate students of color. *American Psychologist, 61,* 143–156.

Rogers, P., & Morehouse, W., III. (1999, April 12). She's got it. *People,* 89.

Roitberg, B. Z., & Kordower, J. H. (2004). Brain implants and transplants. In N. J. Smelser & P. B. Baltes (Eds.), *International encyclopedia of the social & behavioral sciences* (pp. 1345–1352). Burlington, MA: Elsevier Science & Technology.

Rolls, E. T. (2007). Computations in memory systems in the brain. In R. P. Kesner & J. L. Martinez, Jr. (Eds.), *Neurobiology of learning and memory* (2nd ed.). Burlington, MA: Elsevier Science & Technology.

Romney, D. M., & Bynner, J. M. (1997). A re-examination of the relationship between shyness, attributional style, and depression. *Journal of Genetic Psychology, 158,* 261–270.

Root, R. W., II, & Resnick, R. J. (2003). An update on the diagnosis and treatment of attention-deficit/hyperactivity disorders in children. *Professional Psychology: Research Practice, 34,* 34–41.

Ropper, A., & Samuels, M. (2009). *Adam's and Victor's principles of neurology* (9th ed.). New York: McGraw-Hill.

Rorschach, R. (1921; reprinted 1942). *Psychodiagnostics.* Bern: Hans Huber.

Rosanova, M., Gosseries, O., Casarotto, S., Boly, M., Casali, A. G., Bruno, M., Mariotti, M., Bovseroux, P., Tononi, G., Laureys, S., & Massimini, M. (2012, April). Recovery of cortical effective connectivity and recovery of consciousness in vegetative patients. *Brain, 135,* 1308–1320.

Rosch, E. (1978). Principles of categorization. In E. Rosch & B. B. Lloyd (Eds.), *Cognition and categorization.* Hillsdale, NJ: Lawrence Erlbaum.

Roscoe, J. A., Morrow, G. R., Aapro, M. S., Motassiotis, A., & Olver, I. (2011). Anticipatory nausea and vomiting. *Supportive Care in Cancer, 19,* 1533–1538.

Rosenbaum, J. E. (2006). Reborn a virgin: Adolescents' retracting of virginity pledges and sexual histories. *American Journal of Public Health, 96,* 1098–1103.

Rosenberg, J. (2006). *Community mental health: Challenges for the 21st century.* New York: Routledge.

Rosenberg, K. P. (1994). Notes and comments: Biology and homosexuality. *Journal of Sex and Marital Therapy, 20,* 147–150.

Rosenberg, R. S. (2006). Operating and managing a sleep disorders clinic. In T. L. Lee-Chiong (Ed.), *Sleep: A comprehensive handbook* (pp. 1051–1054). Hoboken, NJ: John Wiley & Sons.

Rosenthal, E. (2006, June 2). Genital cutting raises by 50% likelihood mothers or their newborns will die, study finds. *The New York Times,* A10.

Rosenthal, L. (2006). Physiologic processes during sleep. In T. L. Lee-Chiong (Ed.), *Sleep: A comprehensive handbook* (pp. 19–23). Hoboken, NJ: John Wiley & Sons.

Rosenthal, R. (2003). Covert communication in laboratories, classrooms, and the truly real world. *Current Directions in Psychological Science, 12,* 151–154.

Rosenthal, S. L., Burklow, K. A., Lewis, L. M., Succop, P. A., & Biro, F. M. (1997). Heterosexual romantic relationships and sexual behaviors of young adolescent girls. *Journal of Adolescent Health, 21,* 238–243.

Rosenthal, Z. (2007, November 5). In Virtual reality game helps drug addicts recover. *ABC News* [On-line]. Available: http://abcmews.go.com/print?id=3819621.

Ross, B. M., & Millsom, C. (1970). Repeated memory of oral prose in Ghana and New York. *International Journal of Psychology, 5,* 173–181.

Ross, C. A. (2009). Dissociative amnesia and dissociative figure. In P. F. Dell & J. A. O'Neil (Eds.), *Dissociation and the dissociative disorders: DSM-V and beyond* (pp. 429–434). New York: Routledge.

Ross, H. E., & Plug, C. (2002). *The mystery of the moon illusion. Exploring size perception.* Oxford: Oxford University Press.

Ross, P. E. (1991). Hard words. *Scientific American, 264,* 138–147.

Ross, P. E. (2006, August). The expert mind. *Scientific American,* 64–71.

Ross, V. (2011, March). Numbers: The nervous system. *Discover,* 14–15.

Rothbart, M. K., & Sheese, B. E. (2007). Temperament and emotion regulation. In J. J. Gross (Ed.), *Handbook of emotion regulation* (pp. 331–350). New York: Guilford Press.

Rothbaum, B. O. (2009). Using virtual reality to help our patients in the real world. *Depression and Anxiety, 26,* 209–211.

Rothbaum, B. O., Anderson, P., Zimand, E., Hodges, L., Lang, D., & Wilson, J. (2006). Virtual reality exposure therapy and standard (in vivo) exposure therapy in the treatment of fear of flying. *Behavior Therapy, 37,* 80–90.

Rotter, J. B. (1990). Internal versus external control of reinforcement: A case history of a variable. *American Psychologist, 45,* 489–493.

Routh, D. K. (1994). *The founding of clinical psychology (1896) and some important early developments: Introduction.* New York: Plenum Publishing.

Rouw, R., & Scholte, H. S. (2007). Increased structural connectivity in grapheme-color synesthesia. *Nature Neuroscience, 10,* 792–797.

Rovner, S. L. (2007, September 3). Hold that thought. *Chemical & Engineering News, 85,* 13–20.

Rowa, K., McCabe, R. E., & Antony, M. M. (2006). Specific phobias. In M. Hersen & J. D. Thomas (Eds.), *Comprehensive handbook of personality and psychopathology: Adult psychopathology* (Vol. 2, pp. 154–168). Hoboken, NJ: John Wiley & Sons.

Rowan, A. N. (1997, February). The benefits and ethics of animal research. *Scientific American,* 79–94.

Roy-Byrne, P. P., & Fann, J. R. (1997). Psychopharmacologic treatments for patients with neuropsychiatric disorders. In S. C. Yudofsky & R. E. Hales (Eds.), *American Psychiatric Press textbook of neuropsychiatry* (3rd ed.). Washington, DC: American Psychiatric Press.

Rozin, P. (2003). Introduction: Evolutionary and cultural perspectives on affect. In R. D. Lane & L. Nadel (Eds.), *Cognitive neuroscience of emotion.* New York: Oxford University Press.

Rozin, P. (2007, June 4). Cited in M. D. Lemonick, The ewww factor. *Time,* 51–52.

Rozin, P., Haidt, J., & McCauley, C. R. (2000). Disgust. In M. Lewis & J. M. Haviland-Jones (Eds.), *Handbook of emotions* (2nd ed., pp. 637–653). New York: Guilford Press.

Rozin, P., Kabnick, K., Pete, E., Fischler, C., & Shields, C. (2003). The ecology of eating: Smaller portion sizes in France than in the United States help explain the French paradox. *Psychological Science, 14,* 450–454.

Ruben, R. J. (2007). Hearing loss and deafness. Cited in *The Merck manual online medical library: Home edition* [On-line]. Available: http://www.merck.com/mmhe.

Rubin, D. C., & Kozin, M. (1984). Vivid memories. *Cognition, 16,* 81–95.

Rubin, R. (2009, March 12). Optimists live longer than pessimists. *USA Today,* 6D.

Rubin, R. (2010, February 10). Updates proposed for psychiatry's 'bible'. *USA Today,* 4D.

Ruble, D. N., Martin, C. L., & Berenbaum, S. A. (2006). Gender development. In N. Eisenberg, W. Damon & R. M. Lerner (Eds.), *Handbook of child psychology* (6th ed., pp. 858–932). Hoboken, NJ: John Wiley & Sons.

Rudd, D. (2010, January/February). Cited in K. Springen, Daring to die. *Scientific American Mind,* 40–47.

Rudman, L. A., & Glick, P. (2008). *The social psychology of gender.* New York: Guilford Press.

Rudy, D., & Grusec, J. E. (2006). Authoritarian parenting in individualistic and collectivist groups: Associations with maternal emotion and cognition and children's self-esteem. *Journal of Family Psychology, 20,* 68–78.

Rui, L. (2005, August 21). Leptin-signaling protein maintains normal body weight and energy balance in mice. *Science Daily.*

Ruibal, S. (2006, February 12). White a gold winner in halfpipe, Kass is second. *USA Today.*

Ruiter, R. A. C., Abraham, C., & Kok, G. (2001). Scary warnings and rational precautions: A review of the psychology of fear appeals. *Psychology and Health, 16,* 613–630.

Ruiz-Bueno, J. B. (2000). Locus of control, perceived control, and learned helplessness. In V. R. Rice (Ed.), *Handbook of stress, coping and health.* Thousand Oaks, CA: Sage.

Runco, M. A. (2004). Creativity. *Annual Review of Psychology, 55,* 657–687.

Runco, M. A. (2010, July 19). Cited in P. Bronson & A. Merryman, The creativity crisis. *Newsweek,* 44–49.

Rupke, S. J., Blecke, D., & Renfrow, M. (2006). Cognitive therapy for depression. *American Family Physician, 73,* 83–86.

Rupprecht, R., Rammes, G., Eser, D., Baghai, T. C., Schule, C., Nothdurfter, C., Troxler, T., Gentsch, C., Kalkman, H. O., Chaperon, F., Uzunov, V., McAllister, K. H., Bertaina-Anglade, V., Drieu La Rochelle, C., Tuerck, D., Floesser, A., Kiese, B., Schumacher, M., Landgrad, R., Holsboer, F., & Kucher, K. (2009). Translocator protein (18 kD) as target for anxiolytics without benzodiazepine-like side effects. *Science, 325,* 490–493.

Rush, A. J. (2003). Toward an understanding of bipolar disorder and its origins. *Journal of Clinical Psychiatry, 64*(Suppl. 6), 4–8.

Russell, J. (2010, June 19). Cited in B. Bower, Young kids can't face up to disgust. *Science News,* 10.

Russell, R., Duchaine, B., & Nakayama, K. (2009). Super-recognizers: People with extraordinary face recognition ability. *Psychonomic Bulletin & Review, 16*, 252–257.

Russell, S. (2005, March 23). The Terri Schiavo case: Her condition: Doctor explains the "persistent vegetative state." *San Francisco Chronicle.*

Rutter, M. (2006). *Genes and behavior: Nature-nurture interplay explained.* Malden, MA: Wiley-Blackwell.

Rutter, M., & Silberg, J. (2002). Gene-environment interplay in relation to emotional and behavioral disturbance. *Annual Review of Psychology, 53*, 463–490.

Ryan, R. M., & Deci, E. L. (2000). Self-determination theory and the facilitation of intrinsic motivation, social development, and well-being. *American Psychologist, 55*, 68–78.

Sackeim, H. A., Prudic, J., Devanand, D. P., Nobler, M. S., Lisanby, S., Peyser, S., Fitzsimons, L., Moody, B. J., & Clark, J. (2000). A prospective, randomized, double blind comparison of bilateral and right unilateral electroconvulsive therapy at different stimulus intensities. *Archives of General Psychiatry, 57*, 425–434.

Sackeim, H. A., & Stern, Y. (1997). Neuropsychiatric aspects of memory and amnesia. In S. C. Yudofsky & R. E. Hales (Eds.), *The American Psychiatric Press textbook of neuropsychiatry* (3rd ed.). Washington, DC: American Psychiatric Press.

Sacks, O. (2008, January). Cited in S. Kruglinski, The *Discover* interview. *Discover*, 72–78.

SACU (Society for Anglo-Chinese Understanding). (2001). *China Now, 134*, 30.

Saey, T. H. (2008, May 24). Epic genetics. *Science News*, 14–19.

Saey, T. H. (2009a, October 24). Dying to sleep. *Science News*, 28–32.

Saey, T. H. (2009b, October 24). The why of sleep. *Science News*, 16–23.

Sahay, A., Wilson, D. A., & Hen, R. (2011). Pattern separation: A common function for new neurons in hippocampus and olfactory bulb. *Neuron, 70*(4), 582–588.

Sakalli-Uğurlu, N. (2010). Ambivalent sexism, gender, and major as predictors of Turkish college students' attitudes toward women and men's atypical educational choices. *Sex Roles, 62*, 427–437.

Saladin, M. E., Brady, K. T., Graap, K., & Rothbaum, B. O. (2006). A preliminary report on the use of virtual reality technology to elicit craving and cue reactivity in cocaine dependent individuals. *Addictive Behaviors, 31*, 1881–1894.

Salamon, E., Bernstein, S. R., Kim, S., Kim, M., & Stefano, G. B. (2003). The effects of auditory perception and musical preference on anxiety in naïve human subjects. *Medical Science Monitor, 9*, 396–399.

Saletan, W. (2006, March 5). Irreconcilable differences. *The New York Times.*

Salovey, P., Detweiler-Bedell, B. T., Detweiler-Bedell, J. B., & Mayer, J. D. (2008). Emotional intelligence. In M. Lewis, J. M. Haviland-Jones & L. F. Barrett (Eds.), *Handbook of emotions* (3rd ed., pp. 533–547). New York: Guilford Press.

Salovey, P., & Mayer, J. D. (1990). Emotional intelligence. *Imagination, Cognition, and Personality, 9*, 185–211.

Salovey, P., & Pizarro, D. A. (2003). In R. J. Sternberg, J. Lautrey & T. I. Lubart (Eds.), *Models of intelligence.* Washington, DC: American Psychological Association.

Salovey, P., Rothman, A. J., Detweiler, J. B., & Steward, W. T. (2000). Emotional states and physical health. *American Psychologist, 55*, 110–121.

Salzman, C. (2008, September 22). How to help anxious minds. *Newsweek*, 69.

Salzman, C. D., & Fusi, S. (2010). Emotion, cognition, and mental state representation in amygdala and prefrontal cortex. *Annual Review of Neuroscience, 33*, 173–202.

Samelson, F. (1980). J. B. Watson's little Albert, Cyril Burt's twins, and the need for a critical science. *American Psychologist, 35*, 619–625.

SAMHSA (Substance Abuse and Mental Health Services Administration). (2008a). *Heroin abuse in the United States.* Rockville, MD: Author.

SAMHSA. (2008b). *Results from the 2007 national survey on drug use and health: National findings.* NSDUH Series H-34, DHHS Publication SMA 08-4343. Rockville, MD: Author.

SAMHSA. (2010, October 20). Cited in R. Rubin, Brain's sensitivity to alcohol is linked to a gene. *USA Today*, 5D.

SAMHSA. (2011a). Cited in B. Hendrick, Few alcoholics realize they need help. *WebMD Health News* [On-line]. Available: http://www.webmd.com/mental-health/alcohol-abuse/news/20110408/few-alcoholics-realize-they-need-help.

SAMHSA. (2011b). *Results from the 2010 national survey on drug use and health: Summary of national findings.* Rockville, MD: Author.

SAMHSA. (2012). *U.S. sees downward trend in cocaine use.* Rockville, MD: Author.

Samuel, D. (1996). Cited in N. Williams, How the ancient Egyptians brewed beer. *Science, 273*, 432.

Sanberg, P. R. (2007, July 17). Neural stem cells for Parkinson's disease: To protect and repair. *Proceedings of the National Academy of Sciences, 104*, 11869–11870.

Sanchez, R. (2001, August 26). West Coast meth lab operations reaching new levels, DEA says. *Washington Post*, 121(35).

Sanders, L. (2011, January 15). Lab study probes psychoactive drug. *Science News*, 15.

Sandor, P. S., & Afra, J. (2005). Nonpharmacologic treatment of migraine. *Current Pain and Headache Reports, 9*, 202–905.

Sapolsky, R. M. (2002, December 17). Cited in E. Goode, The heavy cost of stress. *The New York Times*, D1.

Sapolsky, R. M. (2006, April). The 2% difference. *Discover*, 42–45.

Sarraj, I. (2002, June 21). Cited in J. Bennet, Rash of new suicide bombers showing no pattern or ties. *The New York Times*, A1.

Sauter, D. A., Eisner, F., Ekman, P., & Scott, S. K. (2010, February 9). Cross-cultural recognition of basic emotions through nonverbal emotional vocalizations. *Proceedings of the National Academy of Sciences, 107*, 2408–2412.

Savage-Rumbaugh, S. (1998, January 19). Cited in S. Begley, Aping language. *Newsweek.*

Savage-Rumbaugh, S., & Lewin, R. (1994). *Kanzi.* New York: Wiley.

Savic, I. (2005, May 10). Cited in N. Wade, For gay men, different scent of attraction. *The New York Times*, A1.

Savic, I., Berglund, H., & Lindstrom, P. (2005). Brain response to putative pheromones in homosexual men. *Proceedings of the National Academy of Sciences, 102*, 7356–7361.

Savic, I., & Lindström, P. (2008). PET and MRI show differences in cerebral asymmetry and functional connectivity between homo- and heterosexual subjects. *Proceedings of the National Academy of Sciences, 105*, 9403–9408.

Savic-Berglund, I. (Ed.). (2010). *Sex difference in the human brain, their underpinnings and implications* (Vol. 186). The Netherlands: Elsevier.

Savin-Williams, R. (2005, October 10). Cited in J. Cloud, The battle over gay teens. *Time*, 42–51.

Savoy, R. L., Frederick, B. B., Keuroghlian, A. S., & Wolk, P. C. (2012). Voluntary switching between identities in dissociative identity disorder: A functional MRI case study. *Cognitive Neuroscience, 3*, 112–119.

Sax, L. J. (2002, September 11). Cited in M. Duenwald, Students find another staple of campus life: Stress. *The New York Times*, D5.

Saxe, L. (1994). Detection of deception: Polygraph and integrity tests. *Current Directions in Psychological Science, 3*, 69–73.

Scanlon, M., & Mauro, J. (1992, November–December). The lowdown on handwriting analysis. *Psychology Today.*

Scarr, S., & Weinberg, R. A. (1976). IQ test performance of black children adopted by white families. *American Psychologist, 31*, 726–739.

SCDMH (South Carolina Department of Mental Health). (2012). *Eating disorders statistics* [On-line]. Available: http://www.state.sc.us/dmh/anorexia/statistics.htm.

Schaaf, C. P., & Zoghbi, H. Y. (2011, June 9). Solving the autism puzzle a few pieces at a time. *Neuron, 70*, 806–808.

Schachter, S., & Singer, J. (1962). Cognitive, social and physiological determinants of emotional state. *Psychological Review, 69*, 379–399.

Schacter, D. L. (1996). *Searching for memory.* New York: Basic Books.

Schacter, D. L. (1997, October). Cited in E. Yoffe, How quickly we forget. *U.S. News & World Report.*

Schacter, D. L. (2001). *The seven sins of memory: How the mind forgets and remembers.* New York: Houghton Mifflin.

Schacter, D. L., Wagner, A. D., & Buckner, R. L. (2005). Memory systems of 1999. In E. Tulving & F. M. Craik (Eds.), *The Oxford handbook of memory.* New York: Oxford University Press.

Schaufeli, W. B., Martinez, I. M., Pinto, A. M., Salanova, M., & Bakker, A. R. (2002). Burnout and engagement in university students. *Journal of Cross-Cultural Psychology, 35*, 464–481.

Scheck, B. (2008, August 10). Cited in M. Sherman, Race sometimes a problem in eyewitness IDs. *MSNBC* [On-line]. Available: http://www.msnbc.msn.com/id/26123421/wid/17621070/.

Schenck, C. H. (2003, January 7). Cited in E. Goode, When the brain disrupts the night. *The New York Times*, D1.

Schewe, P. (Ed.). (2002). *Preventing violence in relationships: Interventions across the life span.* Washington, DC: American Psychological Association.

Schiff, N. D., Giacino, J. T., Kalmar, K., Victor, J. D., Baker, K., Gerber, M., Fritz, B., Eisenberg, B., O'Connor, J., Kobylarz, E. J., Farris, S., Machado, A., McCagg, C., Plum, F., & Rezai, A. R. (2007). Behavioural improvements with thalamic stimulation after traumatic brain injury. *Nature, 448*, 600–603.

Schiller, D. (2009, November). Cited in A. Barth, Five questions for Daniela Schiller. *Discover*, 20.

Schilt, T., de Win, M. M. L., Koeter, M., Jager, G., Korf, D. J., van den Brink, W., & Schmand, B. (2007). Cognition in novice ecstasy users with minimal exposure to other drugs. *Archives of General Psychiatry, 64*, 728–736.

Schlaggar, B. L., Brown, T. T., Lugar, H. M., Visscher, K. M., Miezin, F. M., & Petersen, S. E. (2002). Functional neuroanatomical differences between adults and school-age children in the processing of single words. *Science, 296*, 1476–1479.

Schmidt, C., Collette, F., Leclercq, Y., Sterpenich, V., Vandewalle, G., Berthomier, P., Berthomier, C., Phillips, C., Tinguely, G., Darsaud, A., Gais, S., Schabus, M., Desseilles, M., Dang-Vu, T. T., Salmon, E., Balteau, E., Degueldre, C., Luxen, A., Maquet, P., Cajochen, C., & Peigneux, P. (2009, April 24). Homeostatic sleep pressure and responses to sustained attention in the suprachiasmatic area. *Science, 324*, 516–520.

Schmitt, D. R., Allik, J., McCrae, R. R., & Benet-Martinez, V. (2007). The geographic distribution of Big Five personality traits. *Journal of Cross-Cultural Psychology, 38*, 173–212.

Schneider, C. (2006a). *Don't bury me . . . it ain't over yet.* Bloomington, IN: AuthorHouse.

Schneider, C. (2006b, March 27). Cited in E. T. Fenning, People with Alzheimer's can be productive, man shows: Neighbors Charles Schneider. *DASN (Dementia Advocacy and Support Network) International* [On-line]. Available: http://www.dasninternational.org/2006/schneider.php.

Schneider, D. J. (2004). *The psychology of stereotyping.* New York: Guilford Press.

Schnurr, P. P., Friedman, M. J., & Bernardy, N. C. (2002). Research on posttraumatic stress disorder: Epidemiology, pathophysiology, and assessment. *Journal of Clinical Psychology/In Session: Psychotherapy in Practice, 58,* 877–889.

Schon, D., Peretz, I., Besson, M., Boyer, M., Kolinsky, R., & Moreno, S. (2008). Songs as an aid for language acquisition. *Cognition, 106,* 975–983.

Schooler, J. W. (1994). Seeking the core: The issues and evidence surrounding recovered accounts of sexual trauma. *Consciousness and Cognition, 3,* 452–469.

Schorn, D. (2007, January 28). Brain man: One man's gift may be the key to better understanding the brain. *CBS News: 60 Minutes.*

Schrock, K. (2007, April/May). Freeing a locked-in mind. *Scientific American Mind,* 40–45.

Schroeder, D. A., Penner, L. A., Dovidio, J. F., & Piliavin, J. A. (1995). *The psychology of helping and altruism: Problems and puzzles.* New York: McGraw-Hill.

Schubert, S. J., Lee, C. W., & Drummond, P. D. (2011). The efficacy and psychophysiological correlates of dual-attention tasks in eye movement desensitization and reprocessing (EMDR). *Journal of Anxiety Disorders, 25,* 1–11.

Schuckit, M. (2000). *Drug and alcohol abuse* (5th ed.). New York: Kluwer Academic.

Schuckit, M. (2002, June 17). Cited in S. Roan, A new way to treat alcoholism. *Los Angeles Times,* S1.

Schuckit, M. (2006). Alcohol and alcoholism. In S. L. Hauser (Ed.), *Harrison's neurology in clinical medicine* (pp. 617–624). New York: McGraw-Hill

Schuckit, M. (2012). Alcohol and alcoholism. In D. L. Longo, A. S. Fauci, D. L. Kasper, S. L. Hauser, J. L. Jameson & J. Loscalzo (Eds.), *Harrison's principles of internal medicine* (18th ed., pp. 3546–3552). New York: McGraw-Hill.

Schulman, K. A., Berlin, J. A., Harless, W., Kerner, J. F., Sistrunk, S., Gersh, B. J., Dube, R., Taleghani, C. K., Burke, J. E., Williams, S., Eisenberg, J. M., & Escarce, J. J. (1999). The effect of race and sex on physicians' recommendations for cardiac catheterization. *New England Journal of Medicine, 340,* 618–626.

Schultz, D. P., & Schultz, S. E. (2012). *A history of modern psychology* (10th ed.). Belmont, CA: Wadsworth.

Schultz, R. T., Gauthier, I., Klin, A., Fulbright, R. K., Anderson, A. W., Volkmar, F. R., Schudlarski, P., Lacadie, C., Cohen, D. J., & Gore, J. C. (2000). Abnormal ventral temporal cortical activity during face discrimination among individuals with autism and Asperger syndrome. *Archives of General Psychiatry, 57,* 331–340.

Schumacher, J. E., Milby, J. B., Wallace, D., Meehan, D. C., Kertesz, S., Vuchinich, R., Dunning, J., & Usdan, S. (2007). Meta-analysis of day treatment and contingency-management dismantling research: Birmingham homeless cocaine studies (1990–2006). *Journal of Consulting and Clinical Psychology, 75,* 823–828.

Schwab, J., Kulin, H. E., Susman, E. J., Finkelstein, J. W., Chinchilli, V. M., Kunselman, S. J., Liben, L. S., D'Arangelo, M. R., & Demers, L. M. (2001). The role of sex hormone replacement therapy on self-perceived competence in adolescents with delayed puberty. *Child Development, 72,* 1439–1450.

Schwartz, B., & Reisberg, D. (1991). *Learning and memory.* New York: Norton.

Schwartz, B. L. (1999). Sparkling at the end of the tongue: The etiology of tip-of-the-tongue phenomenology. *Psychonomic Bulletin & Review, 6,* 379–393.

Schwartz, C. (2008, December 9). Cited in E. Cooney, Brain differences in adults linked to temperament in babies. *The Boston Globe.*

Schwartz, C. (2009, February). Cited in M. Price, Newborn reactions can predict depression and anxiety. *APA Monitor,* 13.

Schwartz, C. E., Wright, C. I., Shin, L. M., Kagan, J., & Rauch, S. L. (2003). Inhibited and uninhibited infants "grown up": Adult amygdalar response to novelty. *Science, 300,* 1952–1953.

Schwartz, M. S., & Andrasik, F. (2005). *Biofeedback: A practitioner's guide* (3rd ed.). New York: Guilford Press.

Schwartz, S. (2010). *Visual perception: A clinical orientation* (4th ed.). New York: McGraw-Hill.

Schweinhart, L. J., & Weikart, D. P. (1980). *Young children grow up: The effects of the Perry Preschool Program on youth through age 15* (Monograph No. 7). Ypsilanti, MI: High/Scope Educational Research Foundation.

Science Daily. (2008, July 29). Robotic surgery provides reduced pain and quicker recovery for kidney cancer patients [On-line]. Available: http://www.sciencedaily.com/releases/2008/07/080728193237.htm.

Science Daily. (2009a, May 20). Some people really 'never forget a face:' Understanding extraordinary face recognition ability [On-line]. Available: http://www.sciencedaily.com/releases/2009/05/090519712204.htm.

Science Daily. (2009b, December 19). Dyslexia: Some very smart accomplished people cannot read well [On-line]. Available: http://www.sciencedaily.com/releases/2009/12/091217150838.

Science Illustrated. (2008a, January/February) Building a bionic eye, 50–55.

Science Illustrated. (2008b, July/August). Eyes without a face, 50–51.

Science Illustrated. (2011a, January/February). How does smell enhance taste?, 28.

Science Illustrated. (2011b, January/February). The next 10 years in medicine, 53–57.

Science Illustrated. (2011c, January/February). 10 years of breakthroughs, 58–59.

Science Illustrated. (2011d, May/June). By the numbers: Language, 70–71.

Scott, D. J., Stohler, C. S., Egnatuk, C. M., Wang, H., Koeppe, R. A., & Zubieta, J. K. (2007). Individual differences in reward processing explain placebo-induced expectations and effects. *Neuron, 55,* 325–336.

Searles, J. (1998, September). Write on! Learn to read his handwriting and read his mind. *Cosmopolitan,* 310–311.

Seery, M. D. (2011). Resilience: A silver lining to experiencing adverse life events? *Current Directions in Psychological Science, 20,* 390–394.

Seki, T., Sawamoto, K., Parent, J. M., & Alvarez-Buylla, A. (Eds.). (2011). *Neurogenesis in the adult brain I: Neurobiology.* New York: Springer.

Seligman, M. E. P. (1970). On the generality of the laws of learning. *Psychological Review, 77,* 406–418.

Seligman, M. E. P. (2002, December 9). Cited in M. Elias, What makes people happy psychologists now know. *USA Today,* A1.

Seligman, M. E. P. (2003). The past and future of positive psychology. In C. L. M. Keyes & J. Daidt (Eds.), *Flourishing: Positive psychology and the life well-lived.* Washington, DC: American Psychological Association.

Selye, H. (1993). History of the stress concept. In L. Goldberger & S. Breznitz (Eds.), *Handbook of stress: Theoretical and clinical aspects* (2nd ed.). New York: Free Press.

Senden, M. von. (1960). *Space and sight: The perception of space and shape in the congenitally blind before and after operation* (P. Heath, Trans.). New York: Free Press.

Seppa, N. (2009, January 17). Disorder of REM sleep may signal high risk of Parkinson's, dementia. *Science News,* 9.

Seppa, N. (2010, June 19). Not just a high. *Science News,* 16–20.

Sergeant, S., & Mongrain, M. (2011). Are positive psychology exercises helpful for people with depressive personality style? *Journal of Positive Psychology, 4,* 260–272.

Serpell, R. (2000). Intelligence and culture. In R. J. Sternberg (Ed.), *Handbook of intelligence.* New York: Cambridge University Press.

Serpell, R. (2003, February). Cited in E. Benson, Intelligence across cultures. *Monitor on Psychology,* 56–58.

Settineri, S., Tati, F., & Fanara, G. (2005). Gender differences in dental anxiety: Is the chair position important? *Journal of Contemporary Dental Practice, 6,* 115–122.

SFN (Society for Neuroscience). (2007, November 5). *New clinical trials could open 'golden era' in spinal cord injury and ALS research* [On-line]. Available: http://www.sfn.org/index.cfm?pagename=news_110507c&print=on.

SFN. (2012). *What is neuroscience?* [On-line]. Available: http://www.sfn.org/index.aspx?pagename=whatIsNeuroscience.

Shafer, V. L., & Garrido-Nag, K. (2007). The neurodevelopmental bases of language. In E. Hoff & M. Shatz (Eds.), *Blackwell handbook of language development* (pp. 21–45). Malden, MA: Blackwell Publishing.

Shafto, M. A., Burke, D. M., Stamatakis, E. A., Tam, P. P., & Tyler, L. K. (2007). On the tip-of-the-tongue: Neural correlates of increased word-finding failures in normal aging. *Journal of Cognitive Neuroscience, 19,* 2060–2070.

Shai, I., Schwarzfuchs, D., Henkin, Y., Shahar, D. R., Witkow, S., Greenberg, I., Golan, R., Fraser, D., Bolotin, A., Vardi, H., Tangi-Rozental, O., Zuk-Ramot, R., Sarusi, B., Brickner, D., Schwartz, Z., Sheiner, E., Marko, R., Katorza, E., Thiery, J., Fielder, G. M., Blüher, M., Stumvoll, M., & Stampfer, M. J. (2008). Weight loss with a low carbohydrate, Mediterranean, or low-fat diet. *New England Journal of Medicine, 359,* 229–241.

Shanker, S. G., Savage-Rumbaugh, E. S., & Taylor, T. J. (1999). Kanzi: A new beginning. *Animal Learning & Behavior, 27,* 24–25.

Shannon, C. (1994). Stress management. In D. K. Granvold (Ed.), *Cognitive and behavioral treatment.* Pacific Grove, CA: Brooks/Cole.

Shapiro, F. (1991). Eye movement desensitization and reprocessing: From MD to EMD/R—A new treatment model for anxiety and related trauma. *Behavior Therapist, 14,* 133–135.

Shapiro, F. (2002). EMDR 12 years after its introduction: Past and future research. *Journal of Clinical Psychology, 58,* 1–22.

Shapiro, F. (2012, March 2). The evidence on E.M.D.R. *The New York Times.*

Shapiro, F., & Maxfield, L. (2002). Eye movement desensitization and reprocessing (EMDR): Information processing in the treatment of trauma. *Journal of Clinical Psychology, 58,* 933–948.

Shapiro, J. P., Loeb, P., Bowermaster, D., Wright, A., Headden, S., & Toch, T. (1993, December 13). Special report. *U.S. News & World Report.*

Shapiro, L. (1992, August 31). The lesson of Salem. *Newsweek.*

Shapiro, R. (2005). Treating anxiety disorders with EMDR. In R. Shapiro (Ed.), *EMDR solutions: Pathways to healing* (pp. 312–326). New York: W. W. Norton.

Shapiro, S. L., Shapiro, D. E., & Schwartz, G. E. R. (2000). Stress management in medical education: A review of the literature. *Academic Medicine, 75,* 748–759.

Shargorodsky, J., Curhan, S. G., Curgan, G. C., & Eavey, R. (2010). Change in prevalence of hearing loss in U.S. adolescents. *JAMA, 304,* 772–778.

Sharot, T. (2011, June 6). The optimism bias. *Time,* 40–46.

Sharp, D. (2003, February 20). Senior suicides to increase as U.S. ages. *USA Today,* A3.

Shaun White. (2006). [On-line]. Available: http://www.nbcolympics.com/athletes/5058606/detail.html.

Shaver, P. R., & Mikulincer, M. (Eds.). (2010). *Human aggression and violence: Causes, manifestations, and consequences.* Washington, DC: American Psychological Association.

Shaw, G. M., Carmichael, S. L., Vollset, S. E., Yang, W., Finnell, R. H., Blom, H., Midttun, O., & Ueland, P. M. (2009). Mid-pregnancy cotinine and risks of orofacial clefts and neural tube defects. *Journal of Pediatrics, 154,* 17–19.

Shaw, P., Greenstein, D., Lerch, J., Clasen, L., Lenroot, R., Gogtay, N., Evans, A., & Giedd, J. (2006, March). Intellectual ability and cortical development in children and adolescents. *Nature, 440,* 676–679.

Shaywitz, B. A., Shaywitz, S., Pugh, K. R., Constable, R. T., Skudlarski, P., Fulbright, R. K., Bronen, R. A., Fletcher, J. M., Shankweiler, D. P., Katz, L., & Gore, J. C. (1995). Sex differences in the functional organization of the brain for language. *Nature, 373,* 607–609.

Shaywitz, B. A., Sullivan, C. M., Anderson, G. M., Gillespie, S. M., Sullivan, B., & Shaywitz, S. E. (1994). Aspartame, behavior, and cognitive function in children with attention deficit disorder. *Pediatrics, 93,* 70–75.

Shaywitz, S. E. (2003, July 28). Cited in C. Gorman, The new science of dyslexia. *Time,* 52–59.

Shaywitz, S. E. (2009, December 19). Cited in *Science Daily,* Dyslexia: Some very smart accomplished people cannot read well [On-line]. Available: http://www.sciencedaily.com/releases/2009/12/091217150838.

Shaywitz, S. E., Shaywitz, B. A., Fulbright, R. K., Skudlarski, P., Mencl, W. E., Constable, R. T., Pugh, K. R., Holahan, J. M., Marchione, K. E., Fletcher, J. M., Lyon, G. R., & Gore, J. C. (2003). Neural systems for compensation and persistence: Young adult outcome of childhood reading disability. *Biological Psychiatry, 54,* 25–33.

Shea, M. T., Elkin, I., Imber, S. D., Sotsky, S. M., Watkins, J. T., Collins, J. F., Pilkonis, P. A., Beckham, E., Glass, D. R., Dolan, R. T., & Parloff, M. B. (1992). Course of depressive symptoms over follow-up: Findings from the National Institute of Mental Health Treatment of Depression Collaborative Research Program. *Archives of General Psychiatry, 49,* 782–787.

Sheaffer, R. (1997, May/June). Psychic departures and a discovery institute. *Skeptical Inquirer,* 21.

Sher, A. E. (2006). Upper airway surgery for obstructive sleep apnea. In T. L. Lee-Chiong (Ed.), *Sleep: A comprehensive handbook* (pp. 365–372). Hoboken, NJ: John Wiley & Sons.

Sherman, S. M., & Guillery, R. W. (2009). *Exploring the thalamus and its role in cortical function.* Cambridge, MA: MIT Press.

Shermer, M. (2002, December). Mesmerized by magnetism. *Scientific American,* 41.

Shettleworth, S. J. (2010). *Cognition, evolution, and behavior.* New York: Oxford University Press.

Shetty, A. K., & Turner, D. A. (1996). Development of fetal hippocampal grafts in intact and lesioned hippocampus. *Progress in Neurobiology, 50,* 597–653.

Shimaya, A. (1997). Perception of complex line drawings. *Journal of Experimental Psychology: Human Perception and Performance, 23,* 25–50.

Shimizu, M., & Pelham, B. W. (2004). The unconscious cost of good fortune: Implicit and explicit self-esteem, positive life events, and health. *Health Psychology, 23,* 101–105.

Shizgal, P., & Arvanitogiannis, A. (2003). Gambling on dopamine. *Science, 299,* 856–857.

Shomstein, S., & Yantis, S. (2006). Parietal cortex mediates voluntary control of spatial and nonspatial auditory attention. *Journal of Neuroscience, 26,* 435–439.

Shriver, M. (2005, April 7). Cited in C. Brownlee, Code of many colors: Can researchers see race in the genome? *Science News, 167,* 232–234.

Shute, N. (2007, April 30). What went wrong? *U.S. News & World Report,* 42–52.

Shute, N. (2009, February). The amazing teen brain. *U.S. News & World Report,* 36–39.

Shute, N. (2011, May). Beyond mammograms. *Scientific American,* 32–33.

Sibbitt, W. (2006, August 19). Cited in S. Vorenberg, Less fear is decorated needle's point. *The Albuquerque Tribune.*

Sibold, J. (2009, June 3). Cited in N. Hellmich, Good mood can run a long time after workout. *USA Today,* 5D.

Sidtis, J. J., Volpe, B. T., Wilson, D. H., Rayport, M., & Gazzaniga, M. S. (1981). Variability in right hemisphere language function after callosal section: Evidence for a continuum of generative capacity. *Journal of Neuroscience, 1,* 323–331.

Siegal, A., & Sapru, H. N. (2010). *Essential neuroscience* (2nd ed.). Baltimore, MD: Lippincott Williams & Wilkins.

Siegal, M. (2005). Can we cure fear? *Scientific American Mind, 16,* 45–49.

Siegel, J. M. (2003, November). Why we sleep. *Scientific American,* 92–97.

Siegel, R. K. (1989). *Intoxication.* New York: Dutton.

Sigelman, C. K., & Rider, E. A. (2012). *Life-span human development* (7th ed.). Belmont, CA: Wadsworth.

Silbernagl, S., & Despopoulos, A. (2009). *Color atlas of physiology* (6th ed.). New York: Thieme Medical.

Silke, A. (2003). Deindividuation, anonymity, and violence: Findings from Northern Ireland. *Journal of Social Psychology, 143,* 493–499.

Sillery, B. (2002, June). At what level of the animal hierarchy do we find true sleep? *Popular Science,* 89.

Silver, J., & Miller, J. H. (2004). Regeneration beyond the glial scar. *Nature Reviews Neuroscience, 5,* 146–156.

Simcock, G., & Hayne, H. (2002). Breaking the barrier? Children fail to translate their preverbal memories into language. *Psychological Science, 13,* 225–231.

Simon, B., & Sturmer, S. (2003). Respect for group members: Intragroup determinants of collective identification and group-serving behavior. *Personality and Social Psychology Bulletin, 29,* 183–193.

Simons, J. S., Peers, P. V., Hwang, D. Y., Ally, B. A., Fletcher, P. C., & Budson, A. E. (2008). Is the parietal lobe necessary for recollection in humans? *Neuropsychologia, 46,* 1185–1191.

Simonton, D. K. (2000). Creativity: Cognitive, personal, developmental, and social aspects. *American Psychologist, 55,* 151–158.

Simpson, I. (2012, June 23). Sandusky found guilty on 45 of 48 sex abuse charges. *Chicago Tribune.*

Simpson, J. A., & Tran, S. (2006). The needs, benefits, and perils of close relationships. In P. Noller & J. A. Feeney (Eds.), *Close relationships: Functions, forms, and processes* (pp. 3–24). Hove, England: Psychology Press/Taylor & Francis.

Singer, A. R., & Dobson, K. S. (2006). Cognitive behavioral treatment. In M. Hersen & J. C. Thomas (Eds.), *Comprehensive handbook of personality and psychopathology: Adult psychopathology* (Vol. 2, pp. 487–502). Hoboken, NJ: John Wiley & Sons.

Singer, M. T., & Lalich, J. (1997). *Crazy therapies: What are they? Do they work?* San Francisco: Jossey-Bass.

Singer, T., Seymour, B., O'Doherty, J., Kaube, H., Dolan, R. J., & Frith, C. (2004). Empathy for pain involves the affective but not sensory components of pain. *Science, 303,* 1157–1162.

Singular, S. (2006). *Unholy messenger: The life and crimes of the BTK serial killer.* New York: Scribner.

Sinha, G. (2001, June). Out of control. *Popular Science,* 47–52.

Sivertsen, B., Omvik, S., Pallesen, S., Bjorvatn, B., Havik, O. E., Kvale, G., Nielsen, G. H., & Nordhus, I. H. (2006). Cognitive behavioral therapy vs. Zopiclone for treatment of chronic primary insomnia in older adults. *JAMA, 295,* 2851–2858.

Skeem, J. L., Polascheck, D. L. L., Patrick, C. J., & Lilienfeld, S. O. (2011). Psychopathic personality: Bridging the gap between scientific evidence and public policy. *Psychological Science in the Public Interest, 12,* 95–162.

Skinner, B. F. (1938). *The behavior of organisms.* New York: Appleton-Century-Crofts.

Skinner, B. F. (1989). The origin of cognitive thought. *American Psychologist, 44,* 13–18.

Skinner, N., & Brewer, N. (2002). The dynamics of threat and challenge appraisals prior to stressful achievement events. *Journal of Personality and Social Psychology, 83,* 678–692.

Skipp, C., & Johnson, D. (2003, October 5). Brianna: The little girl that could. *Newsweek.*

Skloot, R. (2006, January). Can memory manipulation change the way you eat? *Discover,* 30.

Skotko, B. (2011, November 15). Will America cull people with Down syndrome? *USA Today,* 9A.

Slade, B. A., Leidel, L., Vellozzi, C., Woo, E. J., Hua, W., Sutherland, A., Izurieta, H. S., Ball, R., Miller, N., Braun, M. M., Markowitz, L. E., & Iskander, J. (2009). Postlicensure safety surveillance for quadrivalent human papillomavirus recombinant vaccine. *JAMA, 302,* 750–757.

Slone, K. C. (1985). *They're rarely too young . . . and never too old "to twinkle."* Ann Arbor, MI: Shar Publications.

Smith, B. L. (2011, January). Hypnosis today. *Monitor on Psychology,* 50–52.

Smith, B. L. (2012, April). The case against spanking. *Monitor on Psychology,* 60–63.

Smith, C. (1997, February 9). Companies using personality tests for making hires that fit. *Los Angeles Times.*

Smith, D. (2002, June). Where are recent grads getting jobs? *Monitor on Psychology,* 28–32.

Smith, D. (2003, March). Angry thoughts, at-risk hearts. *Monitor on Psychology,* 46–47.

Smith, E. E. (2000). Neural bases of human working memory. *Current Directions in Psychological Science, 9,* 45–49.

Smith, M. (2005, August 2). *False memory may block unhealthy eating* [On-line]. Available: http://www.medpagetoday.com/PrimaryCare/DietNutrition/tb/1466?pfc=101&spc=.

Smith, N. T. (2002). A review of the published literature into cannabis withdrawal symptoms in human users. *Addiction, 97,* 621–632.

Smits, J. A. J., O'Cleirigh, C. M., & Otto, M. W. (2006). Panic and agoraphobia. In M. Hersen & J. C. Thomas (Eds.), *Comprehensive handbook of personality and psychopathology: Adult psychopathology* (Vol. 2, pp. 121–137). Hoboken, NJ: John Wiley & Sons.

Smock, P. (2005, July 18). Cited in S. Jayson, Cohabitation is replacing dating. *USA Today,* 6D.

Smolensky, M., & Lamberg, L. (2001). *The body clock guide to better health.* New York: Henry Holt & Company.

Snitz, B. E., O'Meara, E. S., Carlson, M. C., Arnold, A. M., Ives, D. G., Rapp, S. R., Saxton, J., Lopez, O. L., Dunn, L. O., Sink, K. M., & DeKosky, S. T. (2009). Ginkgo biloba for preventing cognitive decline in older adults: A randomized trial. *JAMA, 302,* 2663–2670.

Snyder, C. R., Shenkel, R. J., & Lowery, C. R. (1977). Acceptance of personality interpretations: The "Barnum effect" and beyond. *Journal of Consulting and Clinical Psychology, 45,* 104–114.

Society for Personality Assessment. (2005). The status of the Rorschach in clinical and forensic practice: An official statement by the Board of Trustees of the Society for Personality Assessment. *Journal of Personality Assessment, 85*, 219–237.

Solms, M. (2006, April/May). Freud returns. *Scientific American Mind*, 28–34.

Solomon, P. R., Adams, F., Silver, A., Zimmer, J., & DeVeaux, R. (2002). Ginkgo for memory enhancement. *JAMA, 288*, 835–840.

Sommer, I. E. C., Aleman, A., Bouma, A., & Kahn, R. S. (2004). Do women really have more bilateral language representation than men? A meta-analysis of functional imaging studies. *Brain, 127*, 1845–1852.

Song, H. (2007, December). Cited in O. V. Mourik, The origin of schizophrenia. *Discover*, 19.

Song, S. (2006a, March 27). Mind over medicine. *Time*, 13.

Song, S. (2006b, July 14). The daily Rx. *Time* [On-line]. Available: http://www.time.blogs.com/daily_rx /2006/07/childbehavior.html.

Song, S. (2006c, July 17). Do I know you? *Time*, 56.

Sonntag, K., Simantov, R., & Isacson, O. (2005). Stem cells may reshape the prospect of Parkinson's disease therapy. *Molecular Brain Research, 134*, 34–51.

Sorayamire.org. (2012).

Sorensen, J. L., Haug, N. A., Delucchi, K. L., Gruber, V., Kletter, E., Batki, S. L., Tulsky, J. P., Barnett, P., & Hall, S. (2007). Voucher reinforcement improves medication adherence in HIV-positive methadone patients: A randomized trial. *Drug and Alcohol Dependence, 88*, 54–63.

Sorenstam, A. (2012, April 30). Yani Tseng. *Time*, 54.

Sotsky, S. M., Glass, D. R., Shea, T., Pilkonis, P. A., Collins, F., Elkin, I., Watkins, J. T., Imber, S. D., Leber, W. R., Moyer, J., & Oliveri, M. E. (2006, April). Patient predictors of response to psychotherapy and pharmacotherapy: Findings in the NIMH treatment of depression collaborative research program. *Focus, 4*, 278.

Soyez, V., & Broekaert, E. (2005). Therapeutic communities, family therapy, and humanistic psychology: History and current examples. *Journal of Humanistic Psychology, 45*, 302–332.

Spalding, K. L., Arner, E., Westermark, P. O., Bernard, S., Buchholz, B. A., Bergmann, O., Blomqvist, L., Hoffstedt, J., Näslund, E., Britton, T., Concha, H., Hassan, M., Rydén, M., Frisén, J., & Arner, P. (2008, June). Dynamics of fat cell turnover in humans. *Nature*, 453.

Spanos, N. P. (1994). Multiple identity enactments and multiple personality disorder: A sociocognitive perspective. *Psychological Bulletin, 116*, 143–165.

Spanos, N. P. (1996). *Multiple identities and false memories: A sociocognitive perspective*. Washington, DC: American Psychological Association.

Spear, L. (2010). *The behavioral neuroscience of adolescence*. New York: W. W. Norton.

Spearman, C. (1904). "General intelligence" objectively determined and measured. *American Journal of Psychology, 15*, 201–293.

Spector, P. E., Cooper, C. L., Sanchez, J. I., O'Driscoll, M., Sparks, K., Bernin, P., Bussing, A., Dewe, P., Hart, P., Lu, L., Miller, K., de Moraes, R. F., Ostrognay, G. M., Pagon, M., Pitariu, H., Poelmans, S., Radhakrishnan, P., Russinova, V., Salamatov, V., Salgado, J., Shima, S., Siu, O. L., Stora, J. B., Teichmann, M., Theorell, T., Vlerick, P., Westman, M., Widerszal-Bazyl, M., Wong, P., & Yu, A. S. (2001). Do national levels of individualism and internal locus of control relate to well-being: An ecological level international study. *Journal of Organizational Behavior, 22*, 815–832.

Spector, P. E., Fox, S., Penney, L. M., Bruursema, K., Goh, A., & Kessler, S. (2006). The dimensionality of counterproductivity: Are all counterproductive behaviors created equal? *Journal of Vocational Behavior, 68*, 446–460.

Sperling, G. A. (1960). The information available in brief visual presentations. *Psychological Monographs, 74* (Whole No. 498).

Sperry, R. W. (1993, August). Cited in T. Deangelis, Sperry plumbs science for values and solutions. *APA Monitor*.

Spiegel, D. (2005, November 22). Cited in S. Blakeslee, This is your brain under hypnosis. *The New York Times*, D1, D4.

Spiegel, D. (2007). The mind prepared: Hypnosis in surgery. *Journal of the National Cancer Institute, 99*, 1280–1281.

Spiegler, M. D., & Guevremont, D. C. (2010). *Contemporary behavior therapy* (5th ed.). Belmont, CA: Wadsworth Cengage.

Spielman, D. A., & Staub, E. (2000). Reducing boys' aggression: Learning to fulfill basic needs constructively. *Journal of Applied Developmental Psychology, 21*, 165–181.

Spitz, H. H. (1997). Some questions about the results of the Abecedarian early intervention project cited by the APA task force on intelligence. *American Psychologist, 52*, 72.

Spitzer, R. L., Gibbon, M., Skodol, A. E., Williams, J. B. W., & First, M. B. (Eds.). (1994). *DSM-IV casebook*. Washington, DC: American Psychiatric Association.

Spitzer, R. L., Terman, M., Williams, J. B., Terman, J. S., Malt, U. F., Singer, F., & Lewy, A. J. (1999). Jet lag. *American Journal of Psychiatry, 156*, 1392–1396.

Springen, K. (2008, January 11). Pets: Good for your health? *Newsweek* [On-line]. Available: http://www .newsweek.com/id/91445.

Springen, K. (2010, January/February). Recall in utero. *Scientific American Mind*, 15.

Squire, L. R., Clark, R. E., & Bayley, P. J. (2004). Medial temporal lobe function and memory. In M. S. Gazzaniga (Ed.), *The cognitive neurosciences III*. Cambridge, MA: MIT Press.

Squire, L. R., & Kandel, E. R. (2009). *Memory: From mind to molecules*. Greenwood Village, CO: Roberts and Company Publishers.

Squire, L. R., & Knowlton, B. J. (1995). Memory, hippocampus, and brain systems. In M. S. Gazzaniga (Ed.), *The cognitive neurosciences*. Cambridge, MA: MIT Press.

Stafford, R. (2005, July 8). A family's painful lesson on the dangers of teen driving. *Dateline NBC* [On-line]. Available: http://www.msnbc.msn.com/id /8501174/print/1/displaymode/1098/.

Stahl, L. (2009, March 8). Eyewitness: How accurate is visual memory? *60 Minutes* [On-line]. Available: http://www.cbsnews.com/stories/2009/03/06 /60minutes/main4848039.shtml.

Stahl, S. M. (2000). *Essential psychopharmacology* (2nd ed.). New York: Cambridge University Press.

Stahl, S. M. (2002). Don't ask, don't tell, but benzodiazepines are still the leading treatments for anxiety disorder. *Journal of Clinical Psychiatry, 63*, 756–757.

Stark, C. E. L., Okado, T., & Loftus, E. F. (2010). Imaging the reconstruction of true and false memories using sensory reactivation and the misinformation paradigms. *Learning and Memory, 17*, 485–488.

Stasser, G., & Dietz-Uhler, B. (2003). Collective choice, judgment, and problem solving. In M. A. Hogg & S. Tindale (Eds.), *Blackwell handbook of social psychology: Group processes* (pp. 31–55). Malden, MA: Blackwell Publishing.

Stawski, R. S., Almeida, D. M., Sliwinski, M. J., & Smyth, J. M. (2008). Reported exposure and emotional reactivity to daily stressors: The roles of adult age and global perceived stress. *Psychology and Aging, 23*, 52–61.

Steel, P. (2007). The nature of procrastination: A meta-analytic and theoretical review of quintessential self-regulatory failure. *Psychological Bulletin, 133*, 65–94.

Steenhuysen, J. (2008, December 8). Brain-boosting drugs: Why not?, experts say. *Reuters*.

Stein, D. J. (2009). Social anxiety disorder in the West and in the East. *Journal of Family Practice, 21*(2).

Stein, J. (2003, August 4). Just say Om. *Time*, 50–55.

Stein, L. M., & Memon, A. (2006). Testing the efficacy of the cognitive interview in a developing country. *Applied Cognitive Psychology, 20*, 597–605.

Stein, M. B., Goldin, P. R., Sareen, J., Zorrilla, L. T. E., & Brown, G. G. (2002). Increased amygdala activation to angry and contemptuous faces in generalized social phobia. *Archives of General Psychiatry, 59*, 1027–1034.

Stein, R. (2005a, October 9). Scientists finding out what losing sleep does to a body. *Washington Post*, A1.

Stein, R. (2005b, October 31). Cervical cancer vaccine gets injected with a social issue. *Washington Post*, A3.

Steinberg, L. (2007, December 2). Cited in The Associated Press, Teens' brains explain their impulsiveness. *MSNBC* [On-line]. Available: http://www .msnbc.msn.com/id/21997683/.

Steinberg, L. (2011). *Adolescence* (9th ed.). New York: McGraw-Hill.

Steiner, R. (1989). Live TV special explores, tests psychic powers. *Skeptical Inquirer, 14*, 2–6.

Steptoe, A., & Wardle, J. (1988). Emotional fainting and the psychophysiologic response to blood and injury: Autonomic mechanisms and coping strategies. *Psychosomatic Medicine, 50*, 402–417.

Sternberg, R. J. (1995). For whom the Bell Curve tolls: A review of *The Bell Curve*. *Psychological Science, 6*, 257–261.

Sternberg, R. J. (1999). *Cupid's arrow: The course of love through time*. New York: Cambridge University Press.

Sternberg, R. J. (2001). What is the common thread of creativity? *American Psychologist, 56*, 360–362.

Sternberg, R. J. (2003a). Our research program validating the triarchic theory of successful intelligence: Reply to Gottfredson. *Intelligence, 31*, 399–413.

Sternberg, R. J. (2003b, June). It's time for prescription privileges. *Monitor on Psychology*, 5.

Sternberg, R. J., & Detterman, D. K. (Eds.). (1986). *What is intelligence?* Norwood, NJ: Ablex.

Sternberg, R. J., Grigorenko, E. L., & Kidd, K. K. (2005). Intelligence, race, and genetics. *American Psychologist, 60*, 46–59.

Sternberg, R. J., Lautrey, J., & Lubart, T. I. (2003b). Where are we in the field of intelligence, how did we get here, and where are we going? In R. J. Sternberg, J. Lautrey & T. I. Lubart (Eds.), *Models of intelligence*. Washington, DC: American Psychological Association.

Sternberg, R. J., & O'Hara, L. A. (2000). Intelligence and creativity. In R. J. Sternberg (Ed.), *Handbook of intelligence*. New York: Cambridge University Press.

Sternberg, R. J., & Pretz, J. E. (2005). *Cognition and intelligence: Identifying the mechanisms of the mind*. New York: Cambridge University Press.

Sternberg, R. J., & Soriano, L. J. (1984). Styles of conflict resolution. *Journal of Personality and Social Psychology, 47*, 115–126.

Sternberg, R. J., & Yang, S. (2003, February). Cited in E. Benson, Intelligence across cultures. *Monitor on Psychology*, 56–58.

Sternberg, S. (2002, November 27–28). Women now make up half of AIDS cases, U.N. study finds. *USA Today*, A1.

Sternberg, S. (2008a, August 2). AIDS survey signals 'downturn in treatment.' *USA Today*.

Sternberg, S. (2008b, October 27). Early HIV treatment radically boosts survival. *USA Today*, 7D.

Sternberg, S. (2009, September 25). Pair of HIV vaccines show promise. *USA Today*, 1A.

Sternberg, S., & Gillum, J. (2011, June 8). Many with HIV don't know it. *USA Today*, 1A.

Steven, M. S., Hansen, P. C., & Blakemore, C. (2006). Activation of color-selective areas of the visual cortex in a blind synesthete. *Cortex, 42*, 304–308.

Stevens, C., Lauinger, B., & Neville, H. (2009). Differences in the neural mechanisms of selective attention in children from different socioeconomic backgrounds: An event-related brain potential study. *Developmental Science, 12*, 634–646.

Stevens, C., & Neville, H. (2008). Cited in J. Barlow, Parental intervention boosts education of kids at high risk of failure. *University of Oregon Public Relations* [On-line]. Available: http://pmr.uregon.edu.

Stice, E. (2002). Risk and maintenance factors for eating pathology: A meta-analytic review. *Psychological Bulletin, 128*, 825–848.

Stice, E., Yokum, S., Blum, K., & Bohon, C. (2010). Weight gain is associated with reduced striatal response to palatable food. *Journal of Neuroscience, 30*, 13105.

Stickgold, R. (2000, March 7). Cited in S. Blakeslee, For better learning, researchers endorse "sleep on it" adage. *The New York Times*, D2.

Stickgold, R. (2005). Sleep-dependent memory consolidation. *Nature, 437*, 1272–1278.

Stickgold, R., & Ellenbogen, J. M. (2008, August/September). Quiet! Sleeping brain at work. *Scientific American Mind*, 22–29.

Stoel-Gammon, C. (2010, October 12). Cited in P. Klass, Understanding "ba ba ba" as a key to development. *The New York Times*, D5.

Stone, A. A., Schwartz, J. E., Broderick, J. E., & Deaton, A. (2010, May 17). A snapshot of the age distribution of psychological well-being in the United States. *Proceedings of the National Academy of Sciences, 107*, 9985–9990.

Stone, B. (2002, June 24). How to recharge the second sense. *Newsweek*, 54.

Storbeck, J., Robinson, M. D., & McCourt, M. E. (2006). Semantic processing precedes affect retrieval: The neurological case for cognitive primacy in visual processing. *Review of General Psychology, 10*, 41–55.

Story, M., Kaphingst, K. M., Robinson-O'Brien, R., & Glanz, K. (2008). Creating healthy food and eating environments: Policy and environmental approaches. *Annual Review of Public Health, 29*, 253–272.

Strain, E. C., Mumford, G. K., Silverman, K., & Griffiths, R. R. (1994). Caffeine dependence syndrome. *JAMA, 272*, 1043–1048.

Strauss, V. (2004, September 14). Can exam anxiety be overcome with effort? Teachers urged to address issues as test pressures grow. *Washington Post*, A12.

Streissguth, A. P., Barr, H. M., Bookstein, F. L., Sampson, P. D., & Olson, H. C. (1999). The long-term neurocognitive consequences of prenatal alcohol exposure: A 14-year study. *Psychological Science, 10*, 186–190.

Stromeyer, C. F., III. (1970, November). Eidetikers. *Psychology Today*.

Struckman-Johnson, C., Struckman-Johnson, D., & Anderson, P. B. (2003). Tactics of sexual coercion: When men and women won't take no for an answer. *Journal of Sex Research, 40*, 76–86.

Strueber, D., Lueck, M., & Roth, G. (2006, December/2007, January). The violent brain. *Scientific American Mind*, 20–27.

Stutts, J. C., Wilkins, J. W., Osberg, J. S., & Vaughn, B. V. (2002). Driver risk factors for sleep-related crashes. *Accident Analysis & Prevention, 841*, 1–11.

Suddath, R. L., Christison, G. W., Torrey, E. F., Casanova, M. R., & Weinberger, D. R. (1990). Anatomical abnormalities in the brains of monozygotic twins discordant for schizophrenia. *New England Journal of Medicine, 322*, 789–794.

Sue, D., Sue, D. W., & Sue, S. (2010). *Understanding abnormal behavior* (9th ed.). Boston: Wadsworth.

Sue, D. W., & Sue, D. (2007). *Counseling the culturally diverse: Theory and practice* (5th ed.). New York: John Wiley & Sons.

Sullivan, M. G. (2012, February). "On" time improved with new device. *Clinical Neurology News, 8*(2), 1–3.

Sullivan, R. M., Taborsky-Barba, S., Mendoza, R., Itano, A., Leon, M., Cotman, C. W., Payne, T. R., & Lott, I. (1991). Olfactory classical conditioning in neonates. *Pediatrics, 87*, 511–518.

Summerfeldt, L. J., Kloosterman, P. H., & Antony, M. M. (2010). Structures and semistructured diagnostic interviews. In M. M. Antony & D. H. Barlow (Eds.), *Handbook of assessment and treatment planning for psychological disorders* (pp. 95–137). New York: Guilford Press.

Susskind, J. M., Lee, D. H., Cusi, A., Feiman, R., Grabski, W., & Anderson, A. K. (2008). Expressing fear enhances sensory acquisition. *Nature Neuroscience, 11*, 843–850.

Suzuki, K., Simpson, K. A., Minnion, J. S., Shillito, J. C., & Bloom, S. R. (2010). The role of gut hormones and the hypothalamus in appetite regulation. *Endocrine Journal, 57*, 359–372.

Suzuki, L. A., Short, E. L., & Lee, C. S. (2011). Racial and ethnic group differences in intelligence in the United States. In R. J. Sternberg & S. B. Kaufman (Eds.), *The Cambridge handbook of intelligence* (pp. 273–292). New York: Cambridge University Press.

Suzuki, S. (1998, January 27). Cited in Shinichi Suzuki: Started music classes for toddlers. *Los Angeles Times*, B8.

Svensen, S., & White, K. (1994). A content analysis of horoscopes. *Genetic, Social and General Psychology Monographs, 12*, 5–38.

Svirsky, M. A., Robbins, A. M., Kirk, K. I., Pisoni, D. B., & Miyamoto, R. T. (2000). Language development in profoundly deaf children with cochlear implants. *Psychological Science, 11*, 153–158.

Swaminathan, N. (2007, September 24). Did *Sesame Street* have it right? *Scientific American*.

Swanberg, M. M., Nasreddine, Z. S., Mendez, M. F., & Cummings, J. L. (2007). Speech and language. In C. G. Goetz (Ed.), *Textbook of clinical neurology* (3rd ed., pp. 79–98). Philadelphia: Saunders Elsevier.

Sweet, R. A., Mulsant, B. H., Gupta, B., Rifai, A. H., Pasternak, R. E., McEachran, A., & Zubenko, G. S. (1995). Duration of neuroleptic treatment and prevalence of tardive dyskinesia in late life. *Archives of General Psychiatry, 52*, 478–486.

Swim, J. K., Aikin, K. J., Hall, W. S., & Hunter, B. A. (1995). Sexism and racism: Old-fashioned and modern principles. *Journal of Personality and Social Psychology, 68*, 199–214.

Swim, J. K., Hyers, L. L., Cohen, L. L., Fitzgerald, D. C., & Bylsma, W. H. (2003). African American college students' experiences with everyday racism: Characteristics of and responses to these incidents. *Journal of Black Psychology, 29*, 38–67.

Sylvester, T. (2009). Endangered species: Tigers. *Associated Content* [On-line]. Available: http://www.associatedcontent.com/pop/print.shtml?content_type=article&content_type=196994.

Szabo, L. (2010, August 9). Girls reach puberty earlier, raising health concerns. *USA Today*, 1A.

Szabo, L. (2011, April 11). Puberty too soon. *USA Today*, 1A.

Szyfelbein, S. K., Osgood, P. F., & Carr, D. B. (1985). The assessment of pain and plasma B-endorphin immunoactivity in burned children. *Pain, 22*, 173–182.

Taani, D. Q., El-Qaderi, S. S., & Abu Alhaija, E. S. J. (2005). Dental anxiety in children and its relationship to dental caries and gingival condition. *International Journal of Dental Hygiene, 3*, 83–87.

Tahmincioglu, E. (2011, September 15). Employers turn to tests to weed out job seekers. *NBC News* [On-line]. Available: http://www.msnbc.msn.com/id/44120975/ns/business-careers/t/employers-turn-tests-weed-out-job-seekers/#.UB2bIEansrc.

Takahashi, T. (1989). Social phobia syndrome in Japan. *Comprehensive Psychiatry, 30*, 45–52.

Talan, J. (2006a, February/March). Spirituality. *Scientific American Mind, 17*, 39–41.

Talan, J. (2006b, October/November). Visions for psychedelics. *Scientific American Mind*, 7.

Talan, J. (2009). *Deep brain stimulation*. Washington, DC: Dana Press.

Talarico, J. M., & Rubin, D. C. (2003). Confidence, not consistency, characterizes flashbulb memories. *Psychological Science, 14*, 455–461.

Talbot, M. (2000, January 9). The placebo prescription. *The New York Times Magazine*, 34.

Talbot, M. (2009, April 27). Brain game. *The New Yorker*.

Tammet, D. (2007). *Born on a blue day: Inside the extraordinary mind of an autistic savant*. New York: Free Press.

Tammet, D. (2009, April/May). Think better: Tips from a savant. *Scientific American Mind*, 60–64.

Tamres, L. K., Janicki, D., & Helgeson, V. S. (2002). Sex differences in coping behavior: A meta-analysis review and an examination of relative coping. *Personality and Social Psychology Review, 6*, 2–30.

Tanaka, H., Black, J. M., Hulme, C., Stanley, L. M., Kesler, S. R., Whitfield-Gabrieli, S., Reiss, A. L., Gabrieli, J. D. E., & Hoeft, F. (2011). The brain basis of the phonological deficit in dyslexia is independent of IQ. *Psychological Science, 22*, 1442–1451.

Taneeru, M. (2006, December 29). *Obesity: A lurking national threat?* CNN [On-line]. Available: http://www.cnn.com/2006/HEALTH.diet.fitness/03/24/hb.obesity.epidemic/index.html.

Tannen, D. (1990). *You just don't understand: Women and men in conversation*. New York: William Morrow.

Tannen, D. (1994). *Talking from 9 to 5*. New York: William Morrow.

Tanner, D. C. (2010). *Exploring the psychology, diagnosis, and treatment of neurogenic communication disorders*. Bloomington, IN: iUniverse.

Tanouye, E. (1997, July 7). Got a big public speaking phobia? *San Diego Union-Tribune*.

Tarkan, L. (2002, October 22). Autism therapy is called effective, but rare. *The New York Times*, D2.

Tarumi, S., Ichimiya, A., Yamada, S., Umesue, M., & Kuroki, T. (2004). Taijin kyofusho in university students: Patterns of fear and predispositions to the offensive variant. *Transcultural Psychiatry, 41*, 533–546.

Taubman, M., Leaf, R., & McEachin, J. (2011). *Crafting connections: Contemporary applied behavior analysis for enriching the social lives of persons with autism spectrum disorder*. New York: DRL Books.

Tawa, R. (1995, March 12). Shattering the silence. *Los Angeles Times*.

Tay, L., & Diener, E. (2011). Needs and subjective well-being around the world. *Journal of Personality and Social Psychology, 101*, 354–365.

Taylor, B. E. S. (2007). *ADHD & me: What I learned from lighting fires at the dinner table*. Oakland, CA: New Harbinger.

Taylor, C. A. (2012, January). Cited in J. Moninger, The great spanking debate. *Parents*, 70–73.

Taylor, C. A., Manganello, J. A., Lee, S. J., & Rice, J. C. (2010). Mothers' spanking of 3-year-old children and subsequent risk of children's aggressive behavior. *Pediatrics, 125*, 1057–1065.

Taylor, J., & Miller, M. (1997). When time-out works some of the time: The importance of treatment integrity and functional assessment. *School Psychology Quarterly, 12*, 4–22.

Taylor, R. E., Marshall, T., Mann, A., & Goldberg, D. P. (2012). Insecure attachment and frequent attendance in primary care: A longitudinal cohort study of medically unexplained symptom presentations in ten UK general practices. *Psychological Medicine, 42*, 855–864.

Taylor, S. E. (1981). The interface of cognitive and social psychology. In J. Harvey (Ed.), *Cognition, social behavior, and the environment*. Hillsdale, NJ: Lawrence Erlbaum.

Taylor, S. E. (2002). *The tending instinct: How nurturing is essential to who we are and how we live*. New York: Times Books, Henry Holt and Company.

Taylor, S. E. (2011). *Health psychology* (8th ed.). New York: McGraw-Hill.

Taylor, S. E., Kemeny, M. E., Reed, G. M., Bower, J. E., & Gruenewald, T. L. (2000). Psychological resources, positive illusions, and health. *American Psychologist, 55*, 99–109.

Taylor, S. E., & Master, S. L. (2011). Social responses to stress: The tend-and-befriend-model. In R. J. Contrada & A. Baum (Eds.), *The handbook of stress science: Biology, psychology, and health* (pp. 101–109). New York: Springer.

Taylor-Barnes, N. (2008, February 15). Teen addresses hyperactivity in own terms. Cited in C. Cadelago, *San Francisco Gate*.

Teicher, M. H. (2002, March). The neurobiology of child abuse. *Scientific American*, 68–75.

Temple, E., Deutsch, G. K., Poldrack, R. A., Miller, S. L., Tallal, P., Merzenich, M. M., & Gabrieli, J. D. E. (2003). Neural deficits in children with dyslexia ameliorated by behavioral remediation: Evidence from functional MRI. *Proceedings of the National Academy of Science, 100*, 2860–2865.

Terman, L. M. (1916). *The measurement of intelligence*. Boston: Houghton Mifflin.

Terman, L. M., & Oden, M. H. (1959). *The gifted group at mid-life* (Vol. 5). Stanford, CA: Stanford University Press.

Terracciano, A., Costa, P. T., & McCrae, R. R. (2006). Personality plasticity after age 30. *Personality and Social Psychology Bulletin, 32*, 999–1009.

Terrace, H. S. (1981). A report to an academy, 1980. *Annals of the New York Academy of Sciences, 364*, 94–114.

Thapar, A., & McGuffin, P. (1993). Is personality disorder inherited? An overview of the evidence. *Journal of Psychopathology and Behavioral Assessment, 15*, 325–345.

Thase, M. E. (2006). Major depressive disorder. In M. Hersen & J. C. Thomas (Eds.), *Comprehensive handbook of personality and psychopathology: Adult psychopathology* (Vol. 2, pp. 207–230). Hoboken, NJ: John Wiley & Sons.

Thase, M. E. (2009). Neurobiological aspects of depression. In I. H. Gotlib & C. L. Hammen (Eds.), *Handbook of depression* (2nd ed., pp.187–217). New York: Guilford Press.

Theall-Honey, L. A., & Schmidt, L. A. (2006). Do temperamentally shy children process emotion differently than nonshy children? Behavioral, psychophysiological, and gender differences in reticent preschoolers. *Developmental Psychobiology, 48*, 187–196.

Thelen, E. (1995). Motor development. *American Psychologist, 50*, 79–95.

Thomas, A., & Chess, S. (1977). *Temperament and development*. New York: Brunner/Mazel.

Thomas, C. R. (2006). Evidence-based practice for conduct disorder symptoms. *Journal of the American Academy of Child and Adolescent Psychiatry, 45*, 109–114.

Thomas, E. (2007, April 30). Making of a massacre. *Newsweek*, 22–31.

Thompson, J., & Grosinger, P. C. (2001). *Home in one piece*. Fargo, ND: McCleery & Sons.

Thompson, R. A. (1998). Early sociopersonality development. In W. Damon & R. M. Lerner (Eds.), *Handbook of child psychology* (Vol. 1). New York: John Wiley & Sons.

Thompson, R. A. (2006). The development of the person: Social understanding, relationships, conscience, self. In N. Eisenberg, W. Damon & R. M. Lerner (Eds.), *Handbook of child psychology* (6th ed., pp. 24–98). Hoboken, NJ: John Wiley & Sons.

Thorndike, E. L. (1898). Animal intelligence: An experimental study of the associative process in animals. *Psychological Review Monograph Supplement, 2*(8).

Thorpe, G. L., & Sigman, S. T. (2008). Behavior therapy. In I. Marini & M. A. Stebnicki (Eds.), *The professional counselor's desk reference* (pp. 337–344). New York: Springer.

Thraenhardt, B. (2006, December/2007, January). Hearing voices. *Scientific American Mind*, 74–79.

Tierney, A. J. (2000). Egas Moniz and the origins of psychosurgery: A review commemorating the 50th anniversary of Moniz's Nobel Prize. *Journal of the History of the Neurosciences, 9*, 22–36.

Time. (2006, January 16). Making the most of your day ... and best use of the night.

Time. (2007a, July 16). Opiates for the masses, 14.

Time. (2007b, November 19). Milestones.

Time. (2007c, December 3). The year in medicine: From A to Z, 63–86.

Timmer, S. G., Urquiza, A. J., Zebell, N. M., & McGrath, J. M. (2005). Parent-child interaction therapy: Application to maltreating parent-child dyads. *Child Abuse & Neglect, 29*, 825–842.

Tisak, M. S., Tisak, J., & Goldstein, S. E. (2006). Aggression, delinquency, and morality: A social-cognitive perspective. In M. Killen & J. Smetana (Eds.), *Handbook of moral development* (pp. 611–629). Mahwah, NJ: Lawrence Erlbaum.

TMZ. (2010, December 10). *Miley Cyrus bong video—partying with a bong* [On-line]. Available: http://www.tmz.com/2010/12/10/miley-cyrus-video-bong-hit-smoking-salvia-herb-psychedelic-birthday-party-hannah-montana.

Tolman, D. L., Striepe, M. I., & Harmon, T. (2003). Gender matters: Constructing a model of adolescent sexual health. *Journal of Sex Research, 40*, 4–12.

Tolman, E. C. (1948). Cognitive maps in rats and men. *Psychological Review, 55*, 189–208.

Tomes, H. (2000, July/August). Why did APA take so long? *Monitor on Psychology*, 57.

Tonegawa, S., & Wilson, M. (1997). Cited in W. Roush, New knockout mice point to molecular basis of memory. *Science, 275*, 32–33.

Toner, M. (2006, January 29). Chimpanzees closer to humans than to other apes, study confirms. *The Sunday Times*, A10.

Tooby, J., & Cosmides, L. (2006). Toward mapping the evolved functional organization of mind and brain. In E. Sober (Ed.), *Conceptual issues in evolutionary biology* (3rd ed., pp. 175–196). Cambridge, MA: MIT Press.

Topolinski, S., & Reber, R. (2010). Gaining insight into the "aha" experience. *Current Directions in Psychological Science, 19*, 402–405.

Toppo, G. (2008, September 16). Meanness appears to rub off on viewers. *USA Today*, 4D.

Torrey, E. F. (2005). Does psychoanalysis have a future? No. *Canadian Journal of Psychiatry, 50*, 743–744.

Torrey, F. E., Bowler, A. E., Taylor, E. H., & Gottesman, I. I. (1994). *Schizophrenia and manic-depressive disorder*. New York: Basic Books.

Touchthetop. (2009). *Erik Weihenmayer* [On-line]. Available: http://www.touchthetop.com.

Tough, P. (2006, November 26). What it takes to make a student. *The New York Times Magazine*.

Tousignant, M., & DesMarchais, J. E. (2002). Accuracy of student self-assessment ability compared to their own performance in a problem-based learning medical program: A correlation study. *Advances in Health Sciences Education, 7*, 19–27.

Towle, L. H. (1995, July 31). Elegy for lost boys. *Time*.

Tramer, M. R., Carroll, D., Campbell, F. A., Reynolds, D. J. M., Moore, R. A., & McQuay, H. J. (2001). Cannabinoids for control of chemotherapy induced nausea and vomiting: Quantitative systematic review. *British Medical Journal, 323*, 16–21.

Treffert, D. A. (2006). *Extraordinary people: Understanding savant syndrome*. Lincoln, NE: iUniverse.

Treffert, D. A., & Wallace, G. L. (2002, June). Island of genius. *Scientific American*, 76–85.

Tremmel, P. V. (2007, September 25). Music training linked to enhanced verbal skills. *Northwestern University news and information* [On-line]. Available: http://www.northwestern.edu/newscenter/stories/2007/09/kraus.html.

Tresniowski, A., & Bell, B. (1996, September 9). Oprah buff. *People*, 81.

Tresniowski, A., Harmel, K., & Matsushita, N. (2005, January 24). The girl who can't feel pain. *People*, 99–101.

Tripician, R. J. (2000, January/February). Confessions of a (former) graphologist. *Skeptical Inquirer*, 44–47.

Trump, D. J (2007, May 14). Wesley Autrey: From New York subway rider to all-American hero. *Time*, 101.

Trzesniewski, K. H., Donnellan, M. B., Moffitt, T. E., Robins, R. W., Poulton, R., & Caspi, A. (2006). Low self-esteem during adolescence predicts poor health, criminal behavior, and limited economic prospects during adulthood. *Developmental Psychology, 42*, 381–390.

Trzesniewski, K. H., Donnellan, M. B., & Robins, R. W. (2003). Stability of self-esteem across the life span. *Journal of Personality and Social Psychology, 84*, 205–220.

Tseng, Y. (2012, July 6). Cited in *Navistar LPGA Classic* [On-line]. Available: http://www.navistarlpgaclassic.com/news/110913b.htm.

Tsien, J. Z. (2000). Building a brainier mouse. *Scientific American*, 62–68.

Tully, E. C., Iacono, W. G., & McGue, M. (2008). An adoption study of parental depression as an environmental liability for adolescent depression and childhood disruptive disorders. *American Journal of Psychiatry, 165*, 1148–1154.

Tulving, E., & Craik, F. M. (Eds.). (2005). *The Oxford handbook of memory*. New York: Oxford University Press.

Turk, D. J. (2002). Cited in B. Bower, All about me: Left brain may shine spotlight on self. *Science News, 162*, 118.

Turnbull, B. (2008, September 17). India's first female officer had tough job. *The Star* [On-line]. Available: http://www.thestar.com/printArticle/500506.

Turner, J. A., Deyo, R. A., Loeser, J. D., Von Korff, M., & Fordyce, W. E. (1994). The importance of placebo effects in pain treatment and research. *JAMA, 271*, 1609–1614.

Twenge, J. M., & Campbell, W. K. (2008). Increases in positive self-views among high school students: Birth-cohort changes in anticipated performance, self-satisfaction, self-linking, and self-competence. *Psychological Science, 19*, 1082–1086.

Tyack, P. L. (2000). Dolphins whistle a signature tune. *Science, 289*, 1310–1313.

Tyre, P. (2006, January 30). The trouble with boys. *Newsweek*, 44–52.

Uchino, B. N. (2004). *Social support and physical health: Understanding the health consequences of relationships*. New Haven, CT: Yale University Press.

Uchino, B. N., & Birmingham, W. (2011). Stress and support processes. In R. J. Contrada & A. Baum (Eds.), *The handbook of stress science: Biology, psychology, and health* (pp. 111–121). New York: Springer.

Ujike, H., & Sato, M. (2004). Clinical features of sensitization to methamphetamine observed in patients with methamphetamine dependence and psychosis. *Annals of the New York Academy of Sciences, 1025*, 279–287.

Ulett, G. A. (2003, March/April). Acupuncture, magic and make-believe. *Skeptical Inquirer*, 47–50.

U.N. AIDS. (2009, October 12). Cited in A. Park, Spotlight: AIDS Vaccine. *Time*, 12.

U.N. AIDS. (2011, November 11). Cited in D. G. McNeil, Jr., New cases of AIDS hit plateau. *The New York Times*.

United Nations. (2010). *World population ageing 2009*. Department of Economics and Social Affairs.

UPI (United Press International). (2006, November 24). Chinese learn to smile for 2008 Olympics. *Science Daily*.

Urbina, S. (2011). Tests of intelligence. In R. J. Sternberg & S. B. Kaufman (Eds.), *The Cambridge handbook of intelligence* (pp. 20–38). New York: Cambridge University Press.

U.S. Department of Education. (2005). *27th annual report to Congress on the implementation of the Individuals with Disabilities Education Act, 2005, 2*, 116.

U.S. Department of Education. (2010, March 29). Are we there yet? *Newsweek*, 42–46.

U.S. Department of Labor (2012). *Occupational outlook handbook, 2010–11 edition* [On-line]. Available: http://www.bls.gov/oco/ocos056.htm.

U.S. Department of Transportation. (2012, February 17). Cited in C. Woodyard & F. Meier, New push to disable texting if driving. *USA Today*, 1A.

U.S. Justice Department. (2012, January 6). Cited in M. Basu, *U.S. broadens archaic definition of rape*. CNN.

USA Today. (2005, August 18). Race disparities in health care persist, 5D.

USA Today. (2010, September 7). Having a dog does improve your health, 6D.

USCB (U.S. Census Bureau). (2009, July 9). Cited in S. Jayson, Couples study debunks 'trial marriage' notion. *USA Today*, 7D.

USCB. (2011, May 19). Cited in S. Tavernise, Study finds women slower to wed, and divorce easing. *USA Today*, A17.

USCFC (U.S. Court of Federal Claims). (2009, February 12). *Autism decisions and background information* [On-line]. Available: http://www.uscfc.uscourts.gov/node/5026.

USCM (United States Conference of Mayors). (2009). *Mental illness and homelessness* [On-line]. Available: http://www.nationalhomeless.org/factsheets/Mental_Illness.pdf.

USDE (U.S. Department of Education). (2009). *Condition of education, 2009, indicator 24* (NCES 2009–081). Washington, DC: National Center for Education Statistics.

USDEOS (U.S. Department of Energy Office of Science). (2007). Vision quest pioneer: Artificial retina recipient sees brighter future. *Artificial Retina Project* [On-line]. Available: http://www.artificialretina.energy.gov/byland.shtml.

USDHHS (U.S. Department of Health and Human Services). (2006). *The health consequences of involuntary exposure to tobacco smoke: A report of the surgeon general*. U.S. Department of Health and Human Services, Centers for Disease Control and Prevention, National Center for Chronic Disease Prevention and Health Promotion, Office on Smoking and Health, Washington, DC.

USDHHS. (2009). *Child maltreatment 2009* [On-line]. Available: http://www.acf.hhs.gov/programs/cb/stats_research/index.htm#can.

Uys, J. D., & LaLumiere, R. T. (2008). Glutamate: The new frontier in pharmacotherapy for cocaine addiction. *CNS & Neurological Disorders—Drug Targets, 7*, 482–491.

Vahtera, J., Kivimaki, M., Uutela, A., & Pentti, J. (2000). Hostility and ill health: Role of psychosocial resources in two contexts of working life. *Journal of Psychosomatic Research, 48*, 89–98.

Valdes, L. (2006, October 16). Cited in E. P. Gunn, It is in your head. *U.S. News & World Report*, EE8–9.

Valentiner, D. P., & Fergus, T. A. (2012). Panic disorder, agoraphobia, social anxiety disorder, and specific phobias. In M. Hersen & D. C. Beidel (Eds.), *Adult psychopathology and diagnosis* (6th ed., pp. 391–431). Hoboken, NJ: John Wiley & Sons.

Vallacher, R. R., & Nowak, A. (2007). Dynamical social psychology: Finding order in the flow of human experience. In A. W. Kruglanski & E. T. Higgins (Eds.), *Social psychology: Handbook of basic principles* (2nd ed., pp. 734–758). New York: Guilford Press.

Valli, K., Revonsuo, A., Palkas, O., Ismail, K. H., Ali, K. J., & Punamaki, R. (2005). The threat simulation theory of the evolutionary function of dreaming: Evidence from dreams of traumatized children. *Consciousness and Cognition, 14*, 188–218.

Valsiner, J., & Rosa, A. (2007). *The Cambridge handbook of sociocultural psychology*. New York: Cambridge University Press.

Valtin, H. (2002). "Drink at least eight glasses of water a day." Really? Is there scientific evidence for "8 × 8"? *American Journal of Physiology, 283*, R993–R1004.

Van Ameringen, M. A., Lane, R. M., Walker, J. R., Bowen, R. C., Chokka, P. R., Goldner, E. M., Johnston, D. G., Lavallee, Y., Nandy, S., Pecknold, J. C., Hadrava, V., & Swinson, R. P. (2001). Sertraline treatment for generalized social phobia: A 20-week, double-blind, placebo-controlled study. *American Journal of Psychiatry, 158*, 275–281.

Van de Castle, R. L. (1994). *Our dreaming mind*. New York: Ballantine.

Van Gog, T., Paas, F., Marcus, N., Ayres, P., & Sweller, J. (2009). The mirror-neuron system and observational learning: Implications for the effectiveness of dynamic visualizations. *Educational Psychology Review, 21*, 21–30.

Van Laar, C., Levin, S., Sinclair, S., & Sidanius, J. (2005). The effect of university roommate contact on ethnic attitudes and behavior. *Journal of Experimental Social Psychology, 41*, 329–345.

Van Manen, K., & Whitbourne, S. K. (1997). Psychosocial development and life experiences in adulthood: A 22-year sequential study. *Psychology and Aging, 12*, 239–246.

van Rossum, E. F. C., Koper, J. W., Huizenga, N. A. T. M., Uitterlinden, A. G., Janssen, J. A. J. L., Brinkman, A. O., Grobee, D. E., de Jong, F. H., van Duyn, C. M., Pols, H. A. P., & Lamberts, S. W. J. (2002). A polymorphism in the glucocorticoid receptor gene, which decreases sensitivity to glucocorticoids in vivo, is associated with low insulin and cholesterol levels. *Diabetes, 51*, 3128–3134.

Van Swol, L. M. (2009). Extreme members and group polarization. *Social Influence, 4*, 185–199.

Vance, E. (2010, June 22). The placebo effect finds an unlikely champion. *The New York Times*, D6.

Vandewater, E. A., Ostrove, J. M., & Stewart, A. J. (1997). Predicting women's well-being in midlife: The importance of personality development and social role involvements. *Journal of Personality and Social Psychology, 72*, 1147–1160.

Vansteenkiste, M., Lens, W., & Deci, E. L. (2006). Intrinsic versus extrinsic goal content in self-determination theory: Another look at the quality of academic motivation. *Educational Psychologist, 41*, 19–31.

Vargas, J. S. (1991). B. F. Skinner: The last few days. *Journal of the Experimental Analysis of Behavior, 55*, 1–2.

Vargha-Khadem, F. (2000, November 20). Cited in J. Fischman, Seeds of a sociopath. *U.S. News & World Report*, 82.

Vargha-Khadem, F., Gadian, D. G., Copp, A., & Mishkin, M. (2005). FOXP2 and the neuroanatomy of speech and language. *Nature Reviews Neuroscience, 6*, 131.

Vastag, B. (2003). Addiction poorly understood by clinicians. *JAMA, 290*, 1299–1303.

Vastag, B., Roethel, K., Haupt, A., Banks, D., & Sinzinger, K. (2011). Exploring medicine's frontiers. *Secrets of Your Brain*, 72–78.

Vazsonyi, A. T., Hibbert, J. R., & Snider, J. B. (2003). Exotic enterprise no more? Adolescent reports of family and parenting processes from youth in four countries. *Journal of Research on Adolescence, 13*, 129–160.

Vecera, S. (2002, June). Cited in R. Adelson, Figure this: Deciding what's figure, what's ground. *Monitor on Psychology*, 44–45.

Venter, J. C. (2000, August 22). Cited in N. Angier, Do races differ: Not really, genes show. *The New York Times*, D1.

Verdi, M. P., Johnson, J. T., Stock, W. A., Kulhavy, R. W., & Whitman-Ahern, P. (1997). Organized spatial displays and texts: Effects of presentation order and display type on learning outcomes. *Journal of Experimental Education, 65*, 303–317.

Vergano, D. (2001, June 19). As many opinions as treatments in tobacco fight. *USA Today*, D8.

Vergano, D. (2009, October 19). Tip of your tongue? Not quite. *USA Today*, 5D.

Vergano, D. (2010a, October 12). Embryonic stem cells used on first patient. *USA Today*, 3A.

Vergano, D. (2010b, October 1). New method makes adult stem cells act like embryonic ones. *USA Today*, 4A.

Verhovek, S. H. (2002, February 7). As suicide approvals rise in Oregon, half go unused. *The New York Times*, A16.

Verlinden, S., Hersen, M., & Thomas, J. (2000). Risk factors in school shootings. *Clinical Psychology Review, 29*, 3–56.

Verma, S., Sharma, D., & Larson, R. W. (2002). School stress in India: Effects on time and daily emotions. *International Journal of Behavioral Development, 26*, 500–508.

Vernon, P. A., Wickett, J. C., Bazana, G. P., & Stelmack, R. M. (2000). The neuropsychology of human intelligence. In R. J. Sternberg (Ed.), *Handbook of intelligence*. New York: Cambridge University Press.

Vetter, J. K. (2008, August). Warning: Teen drivers. *Reader's Digest*, 114–121.

Vila, B. (2011, January). Cited in M. Price, The risks of night work. *Monitor on Psychology*, 8–41.

Villarreal, Y. (2008, May 18). Not even sleep can stop us texting. *The Atlanta Journal Constitution*.

Virginia Tech Transportation Institute. (2009, August 31). Cited in E. Nordwall, Highway officials back test-driving ban. *USA Today*, B1.

Vitello, P. (2006, June 12). A ring tone meant to fall on deaf ears. *The New York Times*, A1.

Vitiello, B., & Towbin, K. (2009). Stimulant treatment of ADHD and risk of sudden death in children. *American Journal of Psychiatry, 166*(9), 955–957.

Vocci, F. J., Acri, J., & Elkashef, A. (2005). Medication development for addictive disorders: The state of the science. *American Journal of Psychiatry, 162*, 1432–1440.

Vogele, C., Coles, J., Wardle, J., & Steptoe, A. (2003). Psychophysiologic effects of applied tension on the emotional fainting response to blood and injury. *Behaviour Research and Therapy, 41,* 139–155.

Volkow, N. D. (2009, March). Cited in M. Price, Emerging trends in addiction treatment. *Monitor on Psychology, 22.*

Volkow, N. D. (2010, August 31). Cited in R. A. Friedman, Lasting pleasures, robbed by drug abuse. *The New York Times,* D6.

Volkow, N. D. (2011, May). Cited in M. Price, Marijuana addiction a growing risk as society grows more tolerant. *Monitor on Psychology, 13.*

Volkow, N. D., Chang, L., Wang, G., Fowler, J. S., Ding, Y., Sedler, M., Logan, J., Franceschi, D., Gatley, J., Hitzemann, R., Gifford, A., Wong, C., & Pappas, N. (2003). Low level of brain dopamine D2 receptors in methamphetamine abusers: Association with metabolism in the orbitofrontal cortex. *Focus, 1,* 150–157.

von Bohlen und Halbach, O., & Dermietzel, R. (2007). *Neurotransmitters and neuromodulators: Handbook of receptors and biological effects* (2nd ed.). Weinheim, Germany: Wiley-VCH.

von Bothmer, E. (2006, October/November). When the nose doesn't know. *Scientific American Mind,* 62–67.

von Drehle, D. (2011, January 23). Meet Dr. Robot. *Time.*

von Hippel, W. (2007). Aging, executive functioning, and social control. *Current Directions in Psychological Science, 16,* 240–244.

Vrij, A., Granhag, P. A., & Porter, S. (2010). Pitfalls and opportunities in nonverbal and verbal lie detection. *Psychological Science in the Public Interest, 11,* 89–121.

Vyazovskiy, V. V., Olcese, U., Hanlon, E. C., Cirello, C., & Tononi, G. (2011). Local sleep in awake rats. *Nature, 472,* 441–447.

Waber, R. L., Shiv, B., Carmon, Z., & Ariely, D. (2008). Commercial features of placebo and therapeutic efficacy. *JAMA, 299,* 1016–1017.

Wade, N. (2002, June 21). Stem cell progress reported on Parkinson's. *The New York Times,* A18.

Wade, N. (2010, July 20). Adventures in very recent evolution. *The New York Times,* D1.

Waldinger, M. D. (2008, January). Premature ejaculation: Different pathophysiologies and etiologies determine its treatment. *Journal of Sex & Marital Therapy, 34,* 1–13.

Walker, A., & Parmar, P. (1993). *Warrior marks: Female genital mutilation and sexual blinding of women.* New York: Harcourt Brace.

Walker, C., Thomas, J., & Allen, T. S. (2003). Treating impulsivity, irritability, and aggression of antisocial personality disorder with quetiapine. *International Journal of Offender Therapy and Comparative Criminology, 47,* 556–567.

Walker, H. (2008). *Breaking free.* New York: Touchstone/Howard.

Walker, M. P. (2012). The role of sleep in neurocognitive function. In C. M. Morin & C. A. Espie (Eds.), *The Oxford handbook of sleep and sleep disorders.* New York: Oxford University Press.

Wallace, S. G. (2004, April 21). Storm and stress? *SADD Op-eds* [On-line]. Available: http://sadd.org/oped/storm.htm.

Wallerstein, R. S., & Fonagy, P. (1999). Psychoanalytic research and the IPA: History, present status and future potential. *International Journal of Psychoanalysis, 80,* 91–109.

Wallis, C. (2006, May 15). Inside the autistic mind. *Time,* 42–48.

Walsh, T., McClellan, J. M., McCarthy, S. E., Addington, A. M., Pierce, S. B., Cooper, G. M., Nord, A. S., Kusenda, M., Malhotra, D., Bhandari, A., Stray, S. M., Rippey, C. F., Roccanova, P., Makarov, V., Lakshmi, B., Findling, R. L., Sikich, L., Stromberg, T., Merriman, B., Gogtay, N., Butler, P., Eckstrand, K., Noory, L., Gochman, P., Long, R., Chen, Z., Davis, S., Baker, C., Eichler, E. E., Meltzer, P. S., Nelson, S. F., Singleton, A. B., Lee, M. K., Rapoport, J. L., King, M., & Sebat, J. (2008). Rare structural variants disrupt multiple genes in neurodevelopmental pathways in schizophrenia. *Science, 320,* 539–543.

Wampold, B. E. (2011, October). Cited in A. Brownwell & K. Kelley, Psychotherapy is effective and here's why. *Monitor on Psychology, 14.*

Wampold, B. E., Minami, T., Tierney, S. C., Baskin, T. W., & Bhati, K. S. (2005). The placebo is powerful: Estimating placebo effects in medicine and psychotherapy from randomized clinical trials. *Journal of Clinical Psychology, 61,* 835–854.

Wand, G. (2005). The anxious amygdala: CREB signaling and predisposition to anxiety and alcoholism. *Journal of Clinical Investigation, 115,* 2697–2699.

Wang, Q. (2003). Infantile amnesia reconsidered: A cross-cultural analysis. *Memory, 11,* 65–80.

Wang, Q. (2009). Are Asians forgetful? Perception, retention, and recall in episodic remembering. *Cognition, 111,* 123–131.

Wang, Q., & Conway, M. A. (2004). The stories we keep: Autobiographical memory in American and Chinese middle-aged adults. *Journal of Personality, 72*(5), 911–938.

Wang, Q., Conway, M. A., & Hou, Y. (2004). Infantile amnesia: A cross-cultural investigation. *Cognitive Sciences, 1*(1), 123–135.

Wang, Q., & Ross, M. (2005). What we remember and what we tell: The effects of culture and self-priming on memory representations and narratives. *Memory, 13*(6), 594–606.

Wang, S. C. (2000). In search of Einstein's genius. *Science, 289,* 1477.

Wansink, B., Painter, J. E., & North, J. (2005). Bottomless bowls: Why visual cues of portion size may influence intake. *Obesity Research, 13,* 93–100.

Wansink, B., Payne, C. R., & Chandon, P. (2007). Internal and external cues of meal cessation: The French paradox redux? *Obesity, 15,* 2920–2924.

Ward, J., Hall, K., & Haslam, C. (2006). Patterns of memory dysfunction in current and 2-year abstinent MDMA users. *Journal of Clinical and Experimental Neuropsychology, 28,* 306–324.

Warden, C. H. (1997). Cited in J. Travis, Gene heats up obesity research. *Science News, 151,* 142.

Wargo, E. (2011, April). Beauty is in the mind of the beholder. *Association for Psychological Science, 24*(4), 18–22.

Warner, J. (2007, September 24). Learn music to boost literacy in kids? *WebMD* [On-line]. Available: http://children.webmd.com/news/20070924/learn-music-to-boost-literacy-in-kids.

Warrick, P. (1996, October 3). "I saw something C9 that captivated me." *Los Angeles Times,* E1.

Warrick, P. (1997, January 23). Prisoners of love. *Los Angeles Times.*

Wartik, N. (1994, August 7). The amazingly simple, inexplicable therapy that just might work. *Los Angeles Times.*

Watson, J. B. (1924). *Behaviorism.* Chicago: University of Chicago Press.

Watson, J. B., & Rayner, R. (1920). Conditioned emotional reactions. *Journal of Experimental Psychology, 3,* 1–14.

Weaver, C. A., & Krug, K. S. (2004). Consolidation-like effects in flashbulb memories: Evidence from September 11, 2001. *American Journal of Psychology, 117,* 517–530.

Weaver, F. M., Follett, K., Stern, M., Hur, K., Harris, C., Marks, W. J., Jr., Rothlind, J., Sagher, O., Reda, D., Moy, C. S., Pahwa, R., Burchiel, K., Hogarth, P., Lai, E. C., Duda, J. E., Holloway, K., Samii, A., Horn, S., Bronstein, J., Stoner, G., Heemskerk, J., & Huang, G. D. (2009). Bilateral deep brain stimulation vs. best medical therapy for patients with advanced Parkinson disease. *JAMA, 201,* 63–73.

Webb, A., Lind, P. A., Kalmijn, J., Feiler, H. S., Smith, T. L., Schuckit, M. A., & Wilhelmsen, K. (2011). The investigation into CYP2E1 in relation to the level of response to alcohol through a combination of linkage and association analysis. *Alcoholism: Clinical and Experimental Research, 35,* 10–18.

Webb, W. B. (1992). *Sleep: The gentle tyrant* (2nd ed.). Bolton, MA: Anker.

Weber, E. H. (1834). *De pulsu, resorptione, auditu et tactu: Annotationes anatomical et physiological.* Liepzig: Koehler.

Weihenmayer, E. (1999). Cited in Erik Weihenmayer, *Everest News* [On-line]. Available: http://www.k2news.com/erik/htm.

Weihenmayer, E. (2009). Cited in Erik Weihenmayer, *Touchthetop* [On-line]. Available: http://www.touchthetop.com.

Weil, E. (2006, March 12). A wrongful birth? *The New York Times,* 6–42.

Weinberg, R. A., Scarr, S., & Waldman, I. D. (1992). The Minnesota transracial adoption study: A follow-up of IQ test performance at adolescence. *Intelligence, 16,* 117–135.

Weinberger, D. R. (2005, May 14). Cited in B. Bower, DNA's moody temperament. *Science News, 167,* 308–309.

Weinberger, D. R., Goldberg, T. E., & Tamminga, C. A. (1995). Prefrontal leukotomy. *American Journal of Psychiatry, 152,* 330–331.

Weiner, B. (1991). Metaphors in motivation and attribution. *American Psychologist, 46,* 921–930.

Weiner, I. B., & Meyer, G. J. (2009). Personality assessment with the Rorschach inkblot method. In J. N. Butcher (Ed.), *Oxford handbook of personality assessment* (pp. 277–298). New York: Oxford University Press.

Weingarten, G. (2010). *The fiddler in the subway.* New York: Simon & Schuster.

Weinraub, B. (2000, May 24). Out of "Spin City" and onto a new stage. *The New York Times,* B1.

Weir, K. (2009, March/April). Taste the rainbow. *Psychology Today,* 26.

Weir, K. (2010, December). 20 things you didn't know about taste. *Discover,* 80.

Weir, K. (2012, June). The roots of mental illness. *Monitor on Psychology,* 30–33.

Weisberg, R. W. (1993). *Creativity: Beyond the myth of genius.* New York: Freeman.

Weise, E. (2011, April 11). Cochlear implants can be 'magic device' if put in early enough. *USA Today,* 7D.

Weise, E., & Young, A. (2012, May 17). New lead poisoning guidelines put 365,000 at risk. *USA Today,* 1B.

Weiss, A. P., Rauch, S. L., & Price, B. H. (2007). Neurosurgical intervention for psychiatric illness: Past, present, and future. In B. L. Miller & J. L. Cummings (Eds.), *The human frontal lobes* (2nd ed., pp. 505–517). New York: Guilford Press.

Weiss, P. H., Rahbari, N. N., Lux, S., Pietrzyk, U., Noth, J., & Fink, G. R. (2006). Processing the spatial configuration of complex actions involves right posterior parietal cortex: An fMRI study with clinical implication. *Human Brain Mapping, 27,* 1004–1014.

Weissman, M. M., Verdeli, H., Gameroff, M. J., Bledsoe, S. E., Betts, K., Mufson, L., Fitterling, H., & Wickramaratne, P. (2006). National survey of psychotherapy training in psychiatry, psychology, and social work. *Archives of General Psychiatry, 63,* 925–934.

Weitzenhoffer, A. M. (2002). Scales, scales, and more scales. *American Journal of Clinical Hypnosis, 44,* 209–219.

Welberg, L. (2012). Psychiatric disorders: Why two is better than one. *Nature Reviews Neuroscience, 13,* 73.

Weller, E. B., Young, K. M., Rohrbaugh, A. H., & Weller, R. A. (2001). Overview and assessment of the suicidal child. *Depression and Anxiety, 14,* 157–163.

Wells, G. L. (2009, March 11). Cited in S. Finkelstein, Eyewitness: Anatomy of a story. *60 Minutes* [On-line]. Available: http://www.cbsnews.com/stories/2009/03/11/60minutes/main4859708.shtml.

Wells, G. L., & Olson, E. A. (2003). Eyewitness testimony. *Annual Review of Psychology, 54,* 277–295.

Wenner, M. (2008a, April/May). Infected with insanity. *Scientific American Mind,* 40–47.

Wenner, M. (2008b, August/September). Ease anxiety, curb cravings. *Scientific American Mind,* 7.

Wenzlaff, R. M., & Luxton, D. D. (2003). The role of thought suppression in depressive rumination. *Cognitive Therapy and Research, 27,* 293–308.

Wenzlaff, R. M., & Wegner, D. M. (2000). Thought suppression. *Annual Review of Psychology, 51,* 59–91.

Werker, J. (2011, February 18). Cited in H. Fields, An infant's refined tongue. *ScienceNOW* [On-line]. Available: http://news.sciencemag.org/sciencenow/2011/02/an-infants-refined-tongue.html.

Werle, M. A., Murphy, T. B., & Budd, K. S. (1993). Treating chronic food refusal in young children: Home-based parent training. *Journal of Applied Behavior Analysis, 26,* 421–433.

Werner, E. E. (1995). Resilience in development. *Current Directions in Psychological Science, 4,* 81–85.

Werner, J. S., Frost, M. H., Macnee, C. L., McGabe, S., & Rice, V. H. (2012). Major and minor life stresses and health outcomes. In V. H. Rice (Ed.), *Handbook of stress, coping, and health* (pp. 126–154). Thousand Oaks, CA: Sage.

Wessel, H. (2003, February 17). Big employers increasingly using personality tests before they hire. *The Milwaukee Journal Sentinel.*

West, J., Taylor, M., Houghton, S., & Hudyman, S. (2005). A comparison of teachers' and parents' knowledge and beliefs about attention-deficit/hyperactivity disorder (ADHD). *School Psychology International, 26,* 192–208.

Westen, D. (1998). Unconscious thought, feeling, and motivation: The end of a century-long debate. In R. F. Bornstein & J. M. Masling (Eds.), *Empirical perspectives on the psychoanalytic unconscious.* Washington, DC: American Psychological Association.

Westen, D. (2007, June 9). Cited in B. Bower, Past impressions. *Science News,* 363–365.

Westen, D., & Gabbard, G. O. (1999). Psychoanalytic approaches to personality. In L. A. Pervin & O. P. John (Eds.), *Handbook of personality* (2nd ed.). New York: Guilford Press.

Westen, D., Gabbard, G. O., & Ortigo, K. M. (2008). Psychoanalytic approaches to personality. Cited in O. P. John, R. W. Robins & L. A. Pervin (Eds.), *Handbook of personality* (pp. 61–113). New York: Guilford Press.

Westly, E. (2008, December/2009, January). Psychiatry in flux. *Scientific American Mind,* 14.

Westrin, A., & Lam, R. (2007). Long-term and preventative treatment for seasonal affective disorder. Therapy in practice. *CNS Drugs, 21,* 901–909.

Whalen, D. H., Benson, R. R., Richardson, M., Swainson, B., Clark, V. P., Lai, S., Mencl, W. E., Fulbright, R. K., Constable, R. T., & Liberman, A. M. (2006). Differentiation of speech and nonspeech processing within primary auditory cortex. *Journal of the Acoustical Society of America, 119,* 575–581.

Whalen, P. J., & Phelps, E. A. (Eds.). (2009). *The human amygdala.* New York: Guilford Press.

Whalen, P. J., Vadis, C., Oler, J. A., Kim, H., Kim, M. J., & Neta, M. (2009). Human amygdala responses to facial expressions of emotion. In P. J. Whalen & E. A. Phelps (Eds.), *The human amygdala* (pp. 265–288). New York: Guilford Press.

White, J. M., & Porth, C. M. (2000). Evolution of a model of stress, coping and discrete emotions. In V. R. Rice (Ed.), *Handbook of stress, coping and health.* Thousand Oaks, CA: Sage.

White, R. (2002). Memory for events after twenty years. *Applied Cognitive Psychology, 16,* 603–612.

Whitlock, G., Lewington, S., Sherliker, P., & Peto, R. (2009). Body-mass index and mortality—authors' reply. *The Lancet, 374,* 114.

Whittle, S., Yap, M. B. H., Yucel, M., Fornito, A., Simmons, J. G., Barrett, A., Sheeber, L., & Allen, N. B. (2008). Prefrontal and amygdala volumes are related to adolescents' affective behaviors during parent-adolescent interactions. *Proceedings of the National Academy of Sciences, 105,* 9.

WHO (World Health Organization). (2008, January 20). Cited in Corbett, S., A cutting tradition. *The New York Times.*

WHO. (2010, November 26). Cited in L. Szabo, 'Sad data' on secondhand smoke, kids. *USA Today,* 8A.

Whorf, B. L. (1956). *Language, thought, and reality.* New York: Wiley.

Widiger, T. A., & Clark, L. A. (2000). Toward DSM-V and the classification of psychopathology. *Psychological Bulletin, 126,* 946–963.

Wiech, K., Farias, M., Kahane, G., Shackel, N., Tiede, W., & Tracey, I. (2008). An fMRI study measuring analgesia enhanced by religion as a belief system. *Pain, 139,* 467–476.

Wiederman, M. (2007, February/March). Why it's so hard to be happy. *Scientific American Mind,* 36–43.

Wilcoxon, H. C., Dragoin, W. B., & Kral, P. A. (1971). Illness-induced aversions in rat and quail: Relative salience of visual and gustatory cues. *Science, 171,* 826–828.

Wilgoren, J. (2005, August 19). 10 life terms for B.T.K. strangler as anguished families condemn him in court. *The New York Times,* A13.

Wilhelm, I., Diekelmann, S., Molzow, I., Ayoub, A., Molle, M., & Born, J. (2011). Sleep selectively enhances memory expected to be of future relevance. *Journal of Neuroscience, 31,* 1563–1569.

Williams, B. K., & Knight, S. M. (1994). *Healthy for life.* Pacific Grove, CA: Brooks/Cole.

Williams, D. (1992). *Nobody nowhere.* New York: Times Books.

Williams, D. (1994). *Somebody somewhere.* New York: Times Books.

Williams, D. (1996). *Autism: An inside-out approach.* London: Jessica Kingsley.

Williams, D. (1998). *Autism and sensing: The unlost instinct.* London: Jessica Kingsley.

Williams, D. (1999). *Like colour to the blind: Soul searching and soul finding.* London: Jessica Kingsley.

Williams, D. (2004). *Everyday heaven: Journeys beyond the stereotypes of autism.* London: Jessica Kingsley.

Williams, D. (2008a). *Exposure anxiety—the invisible cage: An exploration of self-protection responses in the autism spectrum and beyond.* London: Jessica Kingsley.

Williams, D. (2008b). *The jumbled jigsaw: An insider's approach to the treatment of autistic spectrum 'fruit salads'.* London: Jessica Kingsley.

Williams, D. (2009). *Donna Williams* [On-line]. Available: http://www.donnawilliams.net.

Williams, J. (2009). Treat arachnophobia with virtual reality therapy. *Associated Content.*

Williams, J. E., & Best, D. L. (1990). *Measuring sex stereotypes* (Vol. 6, rev. ed.). Newbury Park, CA: Sage Publications.

Williams, L., O'Connor, R. C., Howard, S., Hughes, B.M., Johnston, D. W., Hay, J. L., O'Connor, D. B., Lewis, C. A., Ferguson, E., Sheehy, N., Grealy, M.A., & O'Carroll, R. E. (2008). Type-D personality mechanisms of effect: The role of health-related behavior and social support. *Journal of Psychosomatic Research, 64,* 63–69.

Williams, M. A., & Gross, A. M. (1994). Behavior therapy. In V. B. Hasselt & M. Hersen (Eds.), *Advanced abnormal psychology.* New York: Plenum Press.

Williams, M. A., & Mattingley, J. B. (2006, June 6). Do angry men get noticed? *Current Biology, 16,* R402.

Williams, W. (2009, April 20). Cited in S. Begley, Sex, race, and IQ: Off limits? *Newsweek,* 53.

Williamson, E. (2005, February 1). Brain immaturity could explain teen crash rate. *Washington Post.*

Wilson, G. T. (2005). Behavior therapy. In R. J. Corsini & D. Wedding (Eds.), *Current psychotherapies* (7th ed., pp. 202–237). Belmont, CA: Brooks/Cole–Thomson Learning.

Wilson, S. R., Levine, K. J., Cruz, M. G., & Rao, N. (1997). Attribution complexity and actor-observer bias. *Journal of Social Behavior and Personality, 12,* 709–726.

Wilson, T. D., & Linville, P. W. (1982). Improving the academic performance of college freshmen: Attribution therapy revisited. *Journal of Personality and Social Psychology, 42,* 367–376.

Wiltenburg, M. (2003, August 7). Internet dating goes behind bars. *The Christian Science Monitor,* 15.

Wineberg, H., & Werth, J. L., Jr. (2003). Physician-assisted suicide in Oregon: What are the key factors? *Death Studies, 27,* 501–518.

Winerman, L. (2005, October). The mind's mirror. *Monitor on Psychology, 36,* 48.

Winfrey, O. (2009, January). How did I let this happen again? *O: The Oprah Magazine,* 148–153.

Wingert, P., & Brant, M. (2005, August 15). Reading your baby's mind. *Newsweek,* 32–39.

Winner, E. (2000). The origins and ends of giftedness. *American Psychologist, 55,* 159–169.

Winters, K. C., Stinchfield, R. D., Opland, E., Weller, C., & Latimer, W. W. (2000). The effectiveness of the Minnesota Model approach in the treatment of adolescent drug abusers. *Addiction, 95,* 601–612.

Wire Reports. (2007, December 20). More professionals, students using brain performance enhancing drugs. *Dallas News* [On-line]. Available: http://www.dallasnews.com/sharedcontent/dws/news/nation/stories/122107dnnatbraindoping.3761ad89.html.

Wise, T. N., & Birket-Smith, M. (2002). The somatoform disorders for DSM-V: The need for changes in process and content. *Psychosomatics, 43,* 437–440.

Witelson, S. F., Kigar, D. L., & Harvey, T. (1999). The exceptional brain of Albert Einstein. *The Lancet, 353,* 2149–2153.

Witkin, G. (1995, November 13). A new drug gallops through the West. *U.S. News & World Report.*

Witkin, G., Tharp, M., Schrof, J. M., Toch, T., & Scatarella, C. (1998, June 1). Again. *U.S. News & World Report,* 16–18.

Witt, P. L., Brown, K. C., Roberts, J. B., Weisel, J., Sawyer, C. R., & Behnke, R. R. (2006). Somatic anxiety patterns before, during, and after giving a public speech. *Southern Communication Journal, 71,* 87–100.

Wittman, J. (1994, January 5). Nausea, euphoria alternate marks of chemotherapy. *San Diego Union-Tribune.*

Wolf, T. H. (1973). *Alfred Binet.* Chicago: University of Chicago Press.

Wolfing, K., Flor, H., & Grusser, S. M. (2008). Psychophysiological responses to drug-associated stimuli in chronic heavy cannabis use. *European Journal of Neuroscience, 27,* 976–983.

Wolpe, J. (1958). *Psychotherapy by reciprocal inhibition.* Stanford, CA: Stanford University Press.

Wolpe, J. (1990). *The practice of behavior therapy* (4th ed.). London: Pergamon Press.

Wolpe, J., & Lazarus, A. A. (1966). *Behavior therapy techniques.* London: Pergamon Press.

Wolters, C. A. (2003). Understanding procrastination from a self-regulated learning perspective. *Journal of Educational Psychology, 95,* 179–187.

Wong, A. M., Hodges, H., & Horsburg, K. (2005). Neural stem cell grafts reduce the extent of neuronal damage in a mouse model of global ischaemia. *Brain Research, 1063,* 140–150.

Wong, P. T. P. (2006). Existential and humanistic theories. In J. C. Thomas & D. L. Segal (Eds.), *Comprehensive handbook of personality and psychopathology.* New York: Wiley.

Wood, J. M., Garb, H. N., Lilienfeld, S. O., & Nezworski, M. T. (2002). Clinical assessment. *Annual Review of Psychology, 53,* 519–543.

Wood, J. M., Nezworski, M. T., Garb, H. N., & Lilienfeld, S. O. (2006, Spring). The controversy over Exner's comprehensive system for the Rorschach: The critics speak. *Independent Practitioner.*

Wood, J. M., Nezworski, M. T., Lilienfeld, S. O., & Garb, H. N. (2003). *What's wrong with the Rorschach?* San Francisco: Jossey-Bass.

Wood, W., Christensen, P. N., Hebl, M. R., & Rothgerber, H. (1997). Conformity to sex-typed norms, affect and the self-concept. *Journal of Personality and Social Psychology, 73,* 523–535.

Wood, W., & Eagly, A. H. (2002). A cross-cultural analysis of the behavior of women and men: Implications for the origins of sex differences. *Psychological Bulletin, 128,* 699–727.

Woodard, C. (2005, April 15). Did domestication make dogs smarter? *Chronicle of Higher Education.*

Woodruff, B., Hennessey, J., & Hill, J. (2008, April 14). Herschel Walker: "Tell the world my truth." *ABC News.*

Woods, S. C., Schwartz, M. W., Baskin, D. G., & Seeley, R. J. (2000). Food intake and the regulation of body weight. *Annual Review of Psychology, 51,* 255–277.

Woodward, C. (2006, November 3). Amnesiac can't return to his past to go into future. *San Diego Union-Tribune,* A4.

Wright, I. C., Rabe-Hesketh, S., Woodruff, P. W. R., David, A. S., Murray, R. M., & Bullmore, E. T. (2000). Meta-analysis of regional brain volumes in schizophrenia. *American Journal of Psychiatry, 157,* 16–25.

Wright, J., & Marsden, P. (Eds.). (2010). *Handbook of survey research* (2nd ed.). UK: Emerald Publishing.

Wright, J. P., Dietrich, K. N., Ris, M. D., Hornung, R. W., Wessel, S. D., Lanphear, B. P., Ho, M., & Rae, M. N. (2008, May). Association of prenatal and childhood blood lead concentrations with criminal arrests in early adulthood. *PLoS Medicine, 5,* e101.

Wright, K. (2003, November). Staying alive. *Discover,* 64–70.

Wu, X., Zhou, T., Zhu, J., Zhang, B., Georgiev, I., Wang, C., Chen, X., Longo, N. S., Louder, M., McKee, K., O'Dell, S., Perfetto, S., Schmidt, S. D., Shi, W., Wu, L., Yang, Y., Yang, Z-Y., Yang, Z., Zhang, Z., Bonsignori, M., Crump, J. A., Kapiga, S. H., Sam, N. E., Haynes, B. F., Simek, M., Burton, D. R., Koff, W. C., Doria-Rose, N. A., Conners, M., Mullikin, J. C., Nabel, G. J., Roederer, M., Shapiro, L., Kwong, P. D., & Mascola, J. R. (2011, September 16). Focused evolution of HIV-1 neutralizing antibodies revealed by structures and deep sequencing. *Science, 333,* 1593–1602.

Wyer, R. S., Jr. (2007). Principles of mental representation. In A. W. Kruglanski & E. T. Higgins (Eds.), *Social psychology: Handbook of basic principles* (2nd ed., pp. 285–307). New York: Guilford Press.

Wynne, C. D. L. (2001). *Animal cognition: The mental lives of animals.* New York: Palgrave.

Wysocki, C. J., Louie, J., Leyden, J. J., Blank, D., Gill, M., Smith, L., McDermott, K., & Preti, G. (2009, April). Cross-adaptation of a model human stress-related odour with fragrance chemicals and ethyl esters of axillary odorants: Gender-specific effects. *Flavour and Fragrance Journal.*

Yamagata, S., Suzuki, A., Ando, J., Ono, Y., Kijima, N., Yoshimura, K., Ostendorf, F., Angleitner, A., Riemann, R., Spinath, F. M., Livesley, W. J., & Jang, K. L. (2006). Is the genetic structure of human personality universal? A cross-cultural twin study from North America, Europe, and Asia. *Journal of Personality and Social Psychology, 90,* 987–998.

Yamashita, I. (1993). *Taijin-kyofu or delusional social phobia.* Sapporo, Japan: Hokkaido University Press.

Yang, Y., Raine, A., Lencz, T., Bihrle, S., Lacasse, L., & Colletti, P. (2005a). Prefrontal white matter in pathological liars. *British Journal of Psychiatry, 187,* 320–325.

Yang, Y., Raine, A., Lencz, T., Bihrle, S., LaCasse, L., & Colletti, P. (2005b). Volume reduction in prefrontal gray matter in unsuccessful criminal psychopaths. *Biological Psychiatry, 57,* 1103–1108.

Yanoff, M., Duker, J. S., & Augsburger, J. J. (Eds.). (2003). *Ophthalmology* (2nd ed.). St. Louis, MO: Elsevier Health Sciences.

Ybarra, M. J. (1991, September 13). The psychic and the skeptic. *Los Angeles Times.*

Yehuda, R. (2000, August 2). Cited in E. Goode, Childhood abuse and adult stress. *The New York Times,* A14.

Yerkes, R. M. (1921). *Psychological examining in the United States Army (Memoir No. 15).* Washington, DC: National Academy of Sciences.

Yoffe, E. (1997, October). How quickly we forget. *U.S. News & World Report.*

Yoo, S., Gujar, N., Hu, P., Jolesz, F. A., & Walker, M. P. (2007). The human emotional brain without sleep—A prefrontal amygdala disconnect. *Current Biology, 17,* 877–878.

Young, J., Klosko, J. S., & Weishaar, M. E. (2006). *Schema therapy: A practitioner's guide.* New York: Guilford Press.

Young, M. W. (2000, March). The tick-tock of the biological clock. *Scientific American,* 64–71.

Younger, J., Aron, A., Parke, S., Chatterjee, N., & Mackey, S. (2010). Viewing pictures of a romantic partner reduces experimental pain: Involvement of neural reward systems. *PLoS ONE, 5(10),* e13309.

Yuen, M. F., Tam, S., Fung, J., Wong, D. K. H., Wong, C.Y., & Lai, C. L. (2006). Traditional Chinese medicine causing hepatotoxicity in patients with chronic hepatitis B infection: A 1-year prospective study. *Alimentary Pharmacology & Therapeutics, 24,* 1179–1186.

Yule, W., & Fernando, P. (1980). Blood phobia: Beware. *Behavior Research and Therapy, 18,* 587–590.

Yurgelun-Todd, D. (1999, August 9). Cited in S. Brownlee, Inside the teen brain. *U.S. News & World Report,* 44–45.

Zadra, A., Desjardins, S., & Marcotte, E. (2006). Evolutionary function of dreams: A test of the threat simulation theory in recurrent dreams. *Consciousness and Cognition, 15,* 450–463.

Zajonc, R. B. (1984). On the primacy of affect. *American Psychologist, 39,* 117–123.

Zakaria, F. (2003, August 25). Suicide bombers can be stopped. *Newsweek,* 57.

Zeidner, M., & Matthews, G. (2005). Evaluation anxiety. In A. J. Elliot & C. S. Dweck (Eds.), *Handbook of competence and motivation* (pp. 141–163). New York: Guilford Press.

Zeineh, M. M., Engel, S. A., Thompson, P. M., & Bookheimer, S. Y. (2003). Dynamics of the hippocampus during encoding and retrieval of face-name pairs. *Science, 299,* 577–580.

Zener, K. (1937). The significance of behavior accompanying conditioned salivary secretion for theories of the conditioned response. *American Journal of Psychology, 50,* 384–403.

Zhou, W., & Chen, D. (2008). Encoding human sexual chemosensory cues in the orbitofrontal and fusiform cortices. *Journal of Neuroscience, 28,* 14416–14421.

Zhu, P. J., Huang, W., Kalikulov, D., Yoo, J. W., Placzek, A. N., Stoica, L., Zhou, H., Bell, J. C., Friedlander, M. J., Krnjevic, K., Noebels, J. L., & Costa-Mattioli, M. (2011). Suppression of PKR promotes network excitability and enhanced cognition by interferon-y-mediated disinhibition. *Cell, 147,* 1384–1396.

Zhu, Y., Zhang, L., Fan, J., & Han, S. (2007). Neural basis of cultural influence on self-representation. *Neuroimage, 34,* 1310–1316.

Zigler, E. (1995, January). Cited in B. Azar, DNA-environment mix forms intellectual fate. *APA Monitor.*

Zigler, E., & Styfco, S. J. (1994). Head start: Criticisms in a constructive context. *American Psychologist, 49,* 127–132.

Zigler, E., & Styfco, S. J. (2001). Extended childhood intervention prepares children for school and beyond. *JAMA, 285,* 2378–2380.

Zimbardo, P. G. (1970). The human choice: Individuation, reason and order versus deindividuation, impulse and chaos. In W. J. Arnold & D. Levine (Eds.), *Nebraska symposium on motivation.* Lincoln: University of Nebraska Press.

Zimmer, C. (2009a, February 23). Evolving Darwin. *Time,* 50–52.

Zimmer, C. (2009b, September). The brain. *Discover,* 28–31.

Zimmer, C. (2010, June). The brain. *Discover,* 26–27.

Zimmer, C. (2011, January). 100 trillion connections: New efforts probe and map the brain's detailed architecture. *Scientific American,* 19.

Zimmerman, M. A., Copeland, L. A., Shope, J. T., & Gielman, T. E. (1997). A longitudinal study of self-esteem: Implications for adolescent development. *Journal of Youth and Adolescence, 26,* 117–141.

Zinko, C. (2010, December 12). *Portia de Rossi conquers anorexia, accepts herself.* SFGATE.com.

Zola, S. M., & Squire, L. R. (2005). The medial temporal lobe and the hippocampus. In E. Tulving & F. M. Craik (Eds.), *The Oxford handbook of memory.* New York: Oxford University Press.

Zubieta, J. K., Bueller, J. A., Jackson, L. R., Scott, D. J., Xu, Y., Koeppe, R. A., Nichols, T. E., & Stohler, C. S. (2005). Placebo effects mediated by endogenous opioid activity on u-opioid receptors. *Journal of Neuroscience, 25,* 7754–7762.

Zubieta, J. K. (2007, Summer). Cited in CAM (Center for Complementary and Alternative Medicine), Placebos: Sugar, shams, therapies, or all of the above. *CAM at the NIH: Focus on Complementary and Alternative Medicine, 14.*

Zucker, K. J. (1990). Gender identity disorders in children: Clinical descriptions and natural history. In R. Blanchard & B. W. Steiner (Eds.), *Clinical management of gender identity disorders in children and adults.* Washington, DC: American Psychiatric Press.

Zuckerman, B. (2009, December 21). 'I'm a happy guy'. *People,* 107–110.

Name Index

Unless otherwise noted, all images are © Cengage Learning

Subject Index

Bulimia nervosa, 337, 353
Bullying, 523
Buprenorphine, 179
Burma, 133
Burnout, 491
Byland, Terry, 93
Bystander effect, 597

 C

Caffeine, 179, 190, 381
Calkins, Mary, 14
Calories, 334
Cancer
  chemotherapy, 195, 206, 207, 568
  and correlation, 35
  and immune system, 488
  and perception, 121, 122
Cannon-Bard theory of emotions, 360
Care orientation, 412
Careers, 17–19
Carter, Shawn (Jay-Z), 305, 310
Cartoons, 133
Case studies/personal profiles
  achievement, 350
  ADHD, 27
  adolescence, 407
  adoption, 377
  adulthood, 407
  Alzheimer's disease, 47
  anxiety disorders, 509
  autism, 3
  behavior therapy, 204, 224, 555, 566
  behavioral genetics, 466
  blindness, 93, 98
  brain damage, 75
  classical conditioning, 195, 204
  cognitive-behavioral therapy, 575
  creativity, 305, 310
  discrimination, 14, 457
  drug use, 169, 175, 188
  dyslexia, 320
  eating disorders, 353
  emotions, 359
  face transplants, 51
  frontotemporal disease, 67
  hypnosis, 169
  intelligence, 281
  isolation experiment, 147
  language, 305
  learning, 213
  lie detector tests, 370
  memory, 239
  mental disorders, 509, 531, 532, 544, 545
  motivation, 329, 348
  panic disorder, 481, 500
  Parkinson's disease, 60
  perception, 121

personality, 415, 433, 457, 470
prodigies, 378
psychic phenomena, 138
psychoanalysis, 555, 561, 562
school shootings, 523
severed limbs, 51, 58
sexual abuse, 400, 464
split brain, 86–87
stereotypes, 581
stress, 481, 491, 494
suicide, 426
systematic desensitization, 567
Case study approach, 31
  and creativity, 310
  and EMDR, 571
  and Freudian theory, 561, 563
  and panic disorder, 500
  and school shootings, 523
  See also Case studies/personal profiles
Catatonic schizophrenia, 538
Categorical assessments, 513
Categorization, 307
Catharsis, 605
Cattell, Raymond, 462
Causation vs. correlation, 35, 38
CCK (cholecystokinin), 335
Cell body (soma), 50, 382
Centipedes, 27, 32
Central cues, 335
Central nervous system (CNS), 51, 72, 177, 180, 488
Central route for persuasion, 590
Central tendency, measures of, 611–612
Cephalocaudal principle of motor development, 383
Cerebellum, 73, 105, 186, 201
Cerebral cortex, 184, 186
Challenge appraisals, 482, 483, 494, 502
Champion, Robert, 581
Chemical alphabet, 68, 382
Chemical senses, 106–107
Chemotherapy, 195, 206, 207, 568
Chi-square, 616
Chicago Child Parent Center Program, 298
Child abuse/neglect, 394, 400–401, 536, 537, 545, 568, 601
Childhood
  abuse/neglect during, 394, 400–401, 536, 537, 545, 568, 601
  aggression, 604
  and classical conditioning, 205
  cognitive development, 389, 390
  cognitive learning, 231
  concept formation, 306, 307
  delay of gratification, 460

development overview, 397
emotional development, 387
intervention programs, 298–299
language, 316, 317, 391
memory, 251, 256, 264
mentoring programs, 446
moral reasoning, 412
and nature-nurture question, 377
obesity during, 337
operant conditioning, 216, 219
and personality, 434, 436
and personality disorders, 550
racial prejudice, 205
sleep, 154, 156, 163
social development, 392, 393, 394, 395, 396
socialization, 84, 522
See also Child abuse/neglect; Parenting
Chimpanzees, 226, 229, 323. *See also* Primates
China, 85, 113, 337. *See also* Asian people/cultures
Chlorpromazine (Thorazine), 541, 557
Cho, Seung-Hui, 523
Chomsky, Noam, 315, 316, 317
Christie, Agatha, 320
Chromosomes, 68, 378, 380, 382
Chunking, 243
Cigarettes. *See* Nicotine
Cigarettes, 35
CIPA (congenital insensitivity to pain with anhidrosis), 118
Circadian rhythms, 150–151, 155, 156, 157, 162
Clairvoyance, 138
Class. *See* Socioeconomic status
Class notes, 16, 21
Classical conditioning, 195–211
  adaptive value of, 200–201
  and behavior therapy, 555
  and brain structure, 73
  concepts in, 199
  critical thinking exercise, 234
  and emotions, 201, 204, 206
  vs. operant conditioning, 217
  procedure, 197–198
  sociocultural approach, 205
  and stress, 489, 493
  student activities, 203
  and systematic desensitization, 207, 567
  theories of, 202
Classification, 390
Claustrophobia, 518
Client-centered therapy, 564
Clinical assessment, 512, 513
Clinical diagnosis, 513
Clinical interviews, 512

Clinical psychologists, 17, 18, 557, 558
Clinical scales, 474
Clitoris, 339, 346
Closure rule of perception, 127, 140
Clozapine, 541
CNS (central nervous system), 51, 72, 177, 180, 488
Coca leaves, 178
Cocaine, 59, 73, 176, 177, 178
Cochlea, 102–103, 104, 115
Cochlear implants, 115
Cochran, Floyd, 589
Cognition. *See* Thinking
Cognitive appraisal theory of emotions, 360, 361
Cognitive approach
  achievement, 350
  aggression, 604
  attitudes, 588
  and classical conditioning, 202, 217
  creativity, 310
  defined, 305
  emotions, 360, 361
  gender roles, 395, 396
  group dynamics, 596
  mental disorders, 510, 533, 548, 549
  motivation, 331
  overview, 5, 7
  personality, 458, 459
  psychotherapy, 565
  See also Cognitive neuroscience; Cognitive-behavioral therapy; Language; Learning; Memory; Thinking
Cognitive development, 388–391
  adolescence, 390, 410–413, 428, 523
  adulthood, 390, 424
  and gender roles, 395, 396
Cognitive dissonance, 589
Cognitive factors. *See* Cognitive approach
Cognitive interviews, 275
Cognitive learning, 196, 213, 223–226. *See also* Cognitive approach
Cognitive maps, 223
Cognitive miser model of attribution, 586
Cognitive neuroscience
  careers in, 19
  and cognitive learning, 223
  defined, 7, 67
  and evolution, 69
  and Freudian theory, 441
  on memory, 149
  procedure overview, 70–71
  See also Neuroscience

Cultural influences. *See* Cultural factors
Cultural neuroscience, 85
Cultural-familial retardation, 288
Culture. *See* Sociocultural approach
Culture-specific disorders, 546
Cumulative record, 220
Curare, 59
Cybertherapy, 570
Czech Republic, 337

Dahmer, Jeffrey, 536, 537, 550
Dalmane, 162
Darwin, Charles, 69, 364
Date (acquaintance) rapists, 603
Day, length of, 150
Daydreaming, 148
DBS (deep brain stimulation), 61, 519, 535
De Rossi, Portia, 353
Deafness, 101, 115, 316
Death and dying, 425. *See also* Suicide
Debriefing, 40, 594
Decay (memory traces), 265
Deception, 40, 370–371
Decibels, 101
Decision-making, 313
Decision-stage model of helping, 595
Declarative memory, 246, 268
Deductive reasoning, 312
Deep brain stimulation (DBS), 61, 519, 535
Deep Fritz, 308
Deep structure, 315
Defense mechanisms, 437, 449, 493, 563
Deficiency needs, 443
Deindividuation, 597
Deinstitutionalization, 557
Delay of gratification, 460
Delinquency, 537
Delta (slow wave/stage 4) sleep, 152, 154, 163
Delusions, 186, 538
Dement, William, 163
Dendrites, 50, 51
Denial, 437
Denollet, Johan, 496
Dental fears, 173, 195, 198, 199
Dependency, 175, 176, 180, 186. *See also* Drug use
Dependent variables, 36, 159
Depressants, 180–181. *See also* Alcohol
Depression, 532
  and alcohol use, 182
  causes of, 533
  continuum of, 548

and drug use, 178, 186
dysthymic disorder, 532
gender differences, 396
and school shootings, 523
seasonal affective disorder, 159, 532
and stress, 496
and suicide, 427
treatment for, 499, 534–535, 547–549
See also Mood disorders
Depth perception, 129–131, 136, 137, 382
Describing behavior, 4, 464
Descriptive research, 29–31
Descriptive statistics, 610–613
Designer drugs, 185
Developmental norms, 383
Developmental psychology, 377–405, 407–431
  adulthood, 156, 392, 407, 415, 417–419, 421–425
  aging, 76, 155, 156, 366, 415, 423–425, 427
  child abuse/neglect, 400–401
  cognitive development, 388–391, 395, 396, 410–413, 424, 523
  defined, 18, 377
  emerging adulthood, 414
  gender, 395–396
  nature-nurture question, 377, 378
  peer influences, 402
  prenatal period, 378–381
  social development, 392–396, 414–415
  student activities, 398, 403–405, 420, 429–431
  See also Adolescence; Childhood; Infancy
Deviation IQ, 285
Diabetes, 82
Diagnosis
  ADHD, 27, 29, 39
  Alzheimer's disease, 47
  mental disorders, 513–516
  See also Assessment
Diagnostic and Statistical Manual of Mental Disorders-IV-Test Revision (DSM-IV-TR), 513–516, 546
Dialectical behavior therapy, 536
Diathesis stress theory of schizophrenia, 540
Diazepam, 517
Dichromats, 99
DID (dissociative identity disorder) (multiple personality disorder), 9, 545
Diet. *See* Food
Dieting, 336, 337, 352

Diffusion of responsibility theory of the bystander effect, 597
Digestive system, 335, 485
Dimensional assessments, 513
Direction of sound, 104
Discrimination
  and attributions, 585
  defined, 583
  and developmental psychology, 378
  and gender differences, 84
  and IQ tests, 290, 296
  and personality, 457
  in psychology field, 14
  and schemas, 584
  See also Bias; Racism; Sexism
Discrimination (conditioning), 199, 204, 222
Discriminative stimulus, 222
Disgust, 110
Disney, Walt, 320
Disorganized schizophrenia, 538
Displacement, 437, 449
Display rules, 367
Dispositional (internal) attributions, 585
Dissociative amnesia, 544
Dissociative disorders, 9, 514, 544–545
Dissociative fugue, 544
Dissociative identity disorder (DID) (multiple personality disorder), 9, 545
Distinctiveness, 585
Distractions, 20, 164
Divergent thinking, 310, 311
Diversity issues. *See* Cultural Diversity feature; Race; Sociocultural approach
Divorce, 419
Dix, Dorothea, 556
DNA, 68, 294, 338, 382, 423
Doctor-assisted suicide, 427
Dodd, Westley Allan, 536
Dolphins, 221, 322
Dominant genes, 68
Domination, 492
Dopamine, 55
  and drug use, 59, 176, 177, 178, 179, 181, 185
  and extrasensory perception, 138
  and gender differences, 84
  and hunger, 352
  and mood disorders, 533, 534
  and Parkinson's disease, 60
  and reward/pleasure center, 185, 330, 366
  and schizophrenia, 540, 541, 573
Dopamine theory of schizophrenia, 540, 541

Double standard for sexual behavior, 342
Double-blind experiments, 37, 38, 40, 111, 134
Down syndrome, 69, 380
Dread, 113
Dreams, 160–161
  and continuum of consciousness, 149
  Freudian interpretation, 160, 435, 560, 561
  nightmares, 154, 163
  and psychotherapy, 160, 435, 561
  and sleep stages, 153, 154
Driving, 164, 180, 428, 602
Drug effects on nervous system
  alcohol, 180
  hallucinogens, 184, 185
  marijuana, 186
  opiates, 179
  stimulants, 59, 176, 177, 178, 179
  traditional plants, 59
Drug treatments
  for ADHD, 27, 36–37, 39
  for AIDS, 345
  for Alzheimer's disease, 47, 49
  for anxiety disorders, 517, 518, 519, 525
  and deinstitutionalization, 557
  for dissociative disorders, 544
  for drug abuse, 189
  for memory, 271
  for mood disorders, 534, 547, 573
  overview, 573
  for panic disorder, 500
  for Parkinson's disease, 60
  for posttraumatic stress disorder, 185, 491
  and psychotherapy, 559, 563
  for schizophrenia, 541, 542, 557
  for sleep problems, 162, 163
  and suicide, 427
  and therapist types, 558
Drug use, 169, 175–182, 184–190
  and AIDS, 345
  alcohol, 42, 55, 73, 124, 162, 180–181, 182, 381
  and altered states of consciousness, 148
  definitions, 175
  hallucinogens, 184–186
  marijuana, 186
  and mental disorders, 514, 516
  opiates, 179
  overview, 175–176
  and prenatal development, 380, 381

Unless otherwise noted, all images are © Cengage Learning

Neuroses, 513, 561
Neurotransmitters
  and drug use, 59, 176, 177,
    178, 179, 181, 184, 185, 186
  and genetic factors, 181
  and mood disorders, 159, 533,
    534
  and motivation, 330
  overview, 50, 53, 54–55
  and Parkinson's disease, 60
  and perception, 138
  and schizophrenia, 541, 542,
    557
  and seasonal affective
    disorder, 159
  and sleep, 157
  See also Nervous system;
    Reward/pleasure center
Neutral stimulus, 197, 198, 217.
    See also Classical conditioning
New Guinea, 110
Newborns. *See* Infancy
Nicotine, 35, 175, 179, 336, 381
Nigeria, 591
Night terrors, 154, 163
Nightmares, 154, 163
Nim (chimpanzee), 323
NMDA, 181
Nodes, 262, 263
Non-REM sleep, 152, 154
Noncompliance, 219
Nondeclarative (procedural/
    implicit) memory, 149, 246,
    248, 268, 441
Nonintellectual factors, 291
Nonshared environmental
    factors, 467, 468
Noradrenaline (norepinephrine),
    55, 59, 82, 185, 247, 485, 533,
    534
Norepinephrine (noradrenaline),
    55, 59, 82, 185, 247, 485, 533,
    534
Normal aging, 423
Normal curve, 610
Normal distribution, 288, 610,
    613
Norman, Donald, 262
Norms, 595, 596
Nose, 107. *See also* Smell
Note-taking strategies, 16, 21
Nucleus accumbens, 176, 330,
    366, 545
Nutrition. *See* Food

O'Neal, Shaquille, 329
Obedience, 593–594
Obesity, 150, 334, 337, 452
Object permanence, 389
Objective personality tests, 369,
    474–475

Observation, 30
Observational learning, 196, 223,
    224–225, 230, 459, 493, 602
Obsessive-compulsive disorder
    (OCD), 514, 519
Obsessive-compulsive
    personality disorder, 536
Occipital lobe, 74, 79, 114
Occipito-temporal area, 320
OCD (obsessive-compulsive
    disorder), 514, 519
OCEAN (Big Five traits), 463,
    467, 468
Oedipus complex, 439
Old age. *See* Aging
Olfaction (smell), 106–107, 122,
    206, 208, 382
Olfactory bulb, 107
Olfactory cells, 49, 107
One Flew Over the Cuckoo's Nest,
    535
One-sided messages, 590
One-trial learning, 200
Operant conditioning, 213–222
    applications of, 216, 232–233
    vs. classical conditioning, 217
    concepts in, 222
    critical thinking exercise, 234
    defined, 196, 213
    origins of, 214
    procedures for, 215
    reinforcement, 215, 216, 218–
      219, 220–221, 604, 605
    sociocultural approach, 231
Operant response, 214, 215
Opiates, 179
Opium, 179
Opponent-process theory of
    color vision, 99
Opsins, 96
Optic nerve, 96, 97, 114
Optimal (ideal) weight, 334
Optimal sleep pattern, 162, 575
Optimism, 495
Oral stage of psychosexual
    development, 392, 439
Oral tradition, 253
Organ transplants, 591
Organic factors in sexual
    problems, 344
Organic mental disorders, 514
Organic retardation, 288
Orgasm, 344
Origin of Species (Darwin), 69
Ossicles, 102
Outer ear, 102
Outgroup, 598
Ovaries, 82, 339, 408
Overgeneralization, 317, 548,
    565
Overlapping, 130
Overweight, 334, 337, 352

Ovulation, 379, 582
Own-race bias, 274

Pacinian corpuscle, 108
Pain
  and adaptation, 93
  and brain structure, 77
  and endorphins, 55
  and hypnosis, 172, 173
  insensitivity to, 118
  overview, 112–113
  and placebos, 32, 111, 112,
    113
  and touch, 108
Palmar sweating, 6
Pancreas, 82
Panic attacks, 481, 517
Panic disorder, 481, 500, 517
Panzee (chimpanzee), 323
Paper-and-pencil tests, 348
Paradoxical sleep, 153. *See also*
    Rapid eye movement (REM)
    sleep
Paranoid schizophrenia, 538
Paraphilias, 344
Parasympathetic division
    (nervous system), 72, 81, 484,
    501
Parent Management Training
    (PMT), 604
Parent training, 298, 401, 604
Parentese (motherese), 316
Parenting
  and achievement, 351, 448
  and adolescence, 409, 413
  and attachment, 385
  and autism, 11
  and behavior therapy, 216,
    233, 401
  and child abuse/neglect,
    400–401
  and eating disorders, 353
  Freudian theory on, 436
  and gender roles, 395, 396,
    417
  and humanistic theories, 445
  and infant development, 382,
    383
  and intervention programs,
    298
  and language, 316, 318
  and mood disorders, 533
  and nature-nurture question,
    377
  Neo-Freudian theory on, 440
  and peer influences, 402
  and procrastination, 9
  and reading, 320
  and school shootings, 523
  and social development, 394
  and temperament, 387

  See also Childhood;
    Environmental factors;
    Infancy
Parietal lobe, 74, 77, 108, 173,
    297
Parieto-temporal area, 320
Parkinson's disease, 60, 61, 84,
    461
Partial fetal alcohol syndrome,
    381
Partial reinforcement, 220–221
Passionate love, 418
Pathological aging, 423
Pavlov, Ivan, 196, 197, 199, 202
Peer influences, 402
Peg method, 271
Pelzer, Dave, 394
Penis, 339, 408, 439
Penis envy, 439, 440
Perception, 121–145
  constancy, 128
  creating, 140–141
  depth, 129–131, 136, 137
  extrasensory, 138–139
  Gestalt approach, 13, 126–127
  illusions, 136–137, 140
  imagined, 172
  organization of, 126–127
  problems with, 139
  and schizophrenia, 538
  vs. sensation, 93, 124–125
  sociocultural approach,
    132–133
  student activities, 135, 143–145
  subliminal, 121, 122, 134
  synesthesia, 144
  thresholds, 122–123
  See also Senses
Perceptual constancy, 128
Perceptual sets, 133
Perceptual speed, 424
Perfect negative correlation
    coefficient, 34
Perfect positive correlation
    coefficient, 34
Performance goals, 20
Peripheral cues, 335
Peripheral nervous system (PNS),
    51, 72
Peripheral route for persuasion,
    590
Peripheral theories of emotions,
    360
Permissive parents, 413
Person perception, 582–584
Person schemas, 584
Person-centered therapy (client-
    centered therapy), 564
Person-situation interaction,
    464, 468
Personal beliefs, 27, 31, 32, 256,
    588

Unless otherwise noted, all images are © Cengage Learning

Triangular theory of love, 418
Triarchic theory of intelligence, 283
Trichromatic theory of color vision, 98
Trust vs. mistrust stage of psychosocial development, 393
Truth serum (sodium amytal), 250, 251, 544
Tseng, Yani, 442
Tumma, Nithin, 350
Twelve-step approach, 189
Twin studies, 34, 292, 336, 387, 466–467, 539, 601
Twins, 379. *See also* Twin studies
Two-sided messages, 590
Two-word combination stage of language, 317
Tympanic membrane (eardrum), 102, 104
Type A behavior, 496
Type A Behavior and Your Heart (Friedman & Rosenman), 496
Type B behavior, 496
Type D behavior, 496
Typical neuroleptic drugs (phenothiazines), 541, 542, 557, 573

UCR. *See* Classical conditioning; Unconditioned response
UCS. *See* Classical conditioning; Unconditioned stimulus
Unconditional positive regard, 445
Unconditioned response (UCR), 197, 198, 217. *See also* Classical conditioning
Unconditioned stimulus (UCS), 197, 198, 217. *See also* Classical conditioning
Unconscious, 9, 434
    and cognitive neuroscience, 441
    and concept formation, 307
    and continuum of consciousness, 149
    and divisions of mind, 436
    and dreams, 160
    and perception, 134
    and personality, 434–435
    and psychological assessment, 451
    and psychotherapy, 560, 561, 563
    and shyness, 449
    and stress, 493

Unconsciousness, 149
Underachievement, 349
Underwood, Carrie, 445
United States
    adoption, 377
    aging, 423
    AIDS, 345
    assisted suicide, 427
    autism, 11
    beliefs, 27
    brain processes, 85
    drug treatment, 179
    drug use, 177, 178, 179, 180, 182, 185
    emotions, 367, 372
    gender roles, 417
    hunger, 337
    lie detector tests, 371
    marriage, 422
    memory, 253
    mental disorders, 546
    mentoring programs, 446
    perception, 132
    personality, 467
    placebo effect, 32
    racial prejudice, 205
    sexual aggression, 603
    stereotypes, 583
    weight, 583, 591
Unresolved conflicts, 449
Uplifts, 490

Vaccines, 189
Vagina, 339, 425
Validity, 287, 451, 475
Validity scales, 474
Valium, 181
Values, 448, 595
Variability, measures of, 612–613
Variable-interval reinforcement schedule, 221
Variable-ratio reinforcement schedule, 221
Variables, 36, 37
Vegetative comas, 149
Ventral tegmental area, 176, 330, 366
Ventricles, 540
Ventrolateral preoptic nucleus (VPN), 157
Ventromedial hypothalamus, 335
Vestibular sense, 105
Viagra, 425
Vigilant decision making, 598
Violence
    and brain, 71
    and conformity, 581, 593
    and media, 230

and prefrontal cortex, 363
    school shootings, 523
    and stress, 491
    See also Aggression; Child abuse/neglect; Trauma
Virtual reality, 58, 141, 524, 576
Visible spectrum, 94
Vision, 94–99
    artificial, 114
    and brain structure, 79, 97
    color, 98–99
    depth perception, 129–131, 136, 137
    and dreams, 161
    illusions, 136–137
    infancy, 382
    loss of, 93, 97, 98, 114, 150, 161, 364
    and memory, 241
    organizational rules, 126–127, 140
    thresholds, 122
Visual accommodation, 95
Visual agnosia, 79, 97, 307
Visual association area, 79, 97
Visual cliff, 382
Visual cortex. *See* Primary visual cortex
Visual imagery, 524, 575
Volatile substances, 107
VPN (ventrolateral preoptic nucleus), 157
Vulnerability, 394, 548

WAIS-III (Wechsler Adult Intelligence Scale), 286
Wakefield, Dana, 377
Walker, Herschel, 545
Washburn, Margaret, 14
Washoe (chimpanzee), 323
Water bottles, 592
Watson, John B., 13, 204, 555, 566
Wearing, Clive, 239, 246
Weber, E. H., 123
Weber's law, 123
Wechsler Adult Intelligence Scale (WAIS-III), 286
Wechsler Intelligence Scale for Children (WISC-III), 286, 291
Weight, 150, 334, 335, 336, 337, 452, 583, 591
Weight-regulating genes, 336
Weihenmayer, Erik, 114, 329, 330, 331
Wernicke's aphasia, 78
Wernicke's area, 78, 229, 318
Wertheimer, Max, 13, 140
Whale fat, 110

White, Shaun, 494
Whitman, Walt, 284
Williams, Donna, 3–10
Wilshire, Stephen, 254
Wilson, Bill, 470
Wiltshire, Stephen, 311
Windigo, 546
Winehouse, Amy, 180
Winfrey, Oprah, 352, 369
WISC-III (Wechsler Intelligence Scale for Children), 286
Witelson, Sandra, 297
Withdrawal symptoms, 175, 179, 180, 181, 186
Wolf, Stewart, 504
Wolf-Man case, 561, 562
Wolpe, Joseph, 207, 566
Women
    and Freudian theory, 440
    genital cutting, 346, 591
    and mental disorder diagnosis, 516
    psychologists, 14
    sexual aggression against, 491, 603, 605
    suicide bombers, 471
    and weight, 337, 583, 591
    See also Gender differences; Gender roles; Sexism
Words, 314, 316, 318. *See also* Language
Workaholism, 496
Working memory, 242. *See also* Short-term memory
Worrying, 7. *See also* Anxiety
Written tradition, 253
Wundt, Wilhelm, 12, 223

Xanax, 162, 181
Xanthines, 179

Yano, Sho, 289
Yerkes, Robert, 296
Yerkes-Dodson law, 330, 365
Yoga, 503
Young, Thomas, 98
Yusof, Sufiah, 292

Zener cards, 138, 139
Zero correlation coefficient, 34
Zigler, Ed, 287
Zoloft (sertraline), 525, 534, 537, 547
Zoophobia, 518
Zuckerberg, Mark, 281
Zygotes, 68, 338, 379

Unless otherwise noted, all images are © Cengage Learning

TO THE OWNER OF THIS BOOK:

I hope that you have found *Introduction to Psychology,* 10th Edition useful. So that this book can be improved in a future edition, would you take the time to complete this sheet and return it? Thank you.

School and address: _____

_____

Department: _____

Instructor's name: _____

1. What I like most about this book is: _____

_____

_____

2. What I like least about this book is: _____

_____

_____

3. My general reaction to this book is: _____

_____

_____

4. The name of the course in which I used this book is: _____

_____

5. Were all of the chapters of the book assigned for you to read? _____

   If not, which ones weren't? _____

6. In the space below, or on a separate sheet of paper, please write specific suggestions for improving this book and anything else you'd care to share about your experience in using this book.

_____

_____

_____

_____

NO POSTAGE
NECESSARY
IF MAILED
IN THE
UNITED STATES

BUSINESS REPLY MAIL
FIRST-CLASS MAIL　　PERMIT NO. 34　　BELMONT CA

POSTAGE WILL BE PAID BY ADDRESSEE

Attn:　Rod Plotnik
　　　　Haig Kouyoumdjian

Wadsworth

20 Davis Drive

Belmont CA　94002-9801

IΙIιιΙιιΙΙΙιιΙΙιιιιΙιΙΙΙιΙιΙιΙιΙΙΙιιιιιΙΙΙιιΙΙ

FOLD HERE

OPTIONAL:

Your name:_____ Date:_____

May we quote you, either in promotion for *Introduction to Psychology,* 10th Edition, or in future publishing ventures?

Yes: _____　No: _____

Sincerely yours,

Rod Plotnik
Haig Kouyoumdjian

Theme Index